A Comparative Anthology of
CHILDREN'S LITERATURE

A Comparative Anthology of
CHILDREN'S LITERATURE

MARY ANN NELSON

Eastern Washington State College
Cheney, Washington

HOLT, RINEHART AND WINSTON, INC.
New York   Chicago   San Francisco   Atlanta
Dallas   Montreal   Toronto

Cover Design by Colin Chow

Text Design by Margaret Tsao and Colin Chow

Copyright © 1972 by Mary Ann Nelson
All rights reserved
Library of Congress Catalog Card Number: 74-177980
ISBN: 0–03–083379–5
Printed in the United States of America
2 3 4 5   061   9 8 7 6 5 4 3 2 1

This anthology, having grown from a desire to foster
within my students a sense of the joy of reading,
is dedicated to all who love both children and literature.

Preface

The study of children's books is fun. Faint, half-remembered memories from childhood gain substance in the re-reading of childhood favorites, and new worlds are discovered in previously unread books. Each year my students are surprised at how involved they become in novels like *Johnny Tremain, The Gammage Cup,* and *Mary Jane*. They chuckle over *Millions of Cats* and laugh out loud at the ending of *Yertle the Turtle*. The language and philosophy of *John J. Plenty and Fiddler Dan* charm and intrigue college readers just as they do fifth and sixth graders. It is fortunate that there is so much pleasure in reading these books because adults who hope to influence children's reading need to enjoy the literature honestly and obviously. Such pleasure brings deserved respect to the field of children's literature.

But the librarian, teacher, or parent who wishes to encourage children to read needs to be able to distinguish between mediocrity and excellence. Reading books that have been described as "well-written" or even reading anthologies of "good" juvenile fiction and poetry does not give most students, teachers, or librarians confidence in their ability to evaluate undesignated books and poems. Therefore, they tend to rely solely on lists of "approved" books. But lists, no matter how distinguished and time-saving, can never substitute for the judgment of an adult who knows the interests of a specific child and understands how to choose a book that will increase his pleasure and trust in reading. Such judgment can come only from wide reading of children's fiction, folklore, and poetry and from a thorough understanding of the criteria of excellence for each genre. A comparative approach to the study of children's literature is the most effective method of developing literary evaluation skills.

Three types of comparison have been employed in this anthology. First, there is an emphasis on critical comparison. In folklore, fiction, nonfiction, and poetry, excerpts from poorly written examples of literature have been included and discussed so that the reader can contrast them with the many well-written selections. In fiction, the student finds that comparing plot developments, characterizations, and appropriateness of styles and themes leads to a greater understanding of the elements of fiction. Comparing well-developed plot structures and characterizations with those of less successfully composed books, the reader learns what lifts a story or character portrayal above the ordinary. In poetry, comparing verses with unoriginal imagery or awkward rhyme patterns to poems with evocative images and rhymes adds to the reader's understanding of poetic quality. Such a comparative approach permits inductive discoveries and allows the student to develop and trust his own critical judgment.

A second comparative approach provides historical perspective about the development of children's literature and many of its enduring trends. Every section has examples of works significant in the history of children's literature. An excerpt from a chapbook is compared with a folktale still told in Appalachia. Pages from Newbery's *A Little, Pretty Pocket-Book* are reproduced so that the woodblock illustrations and moralistic writing can be contrasted with modern book illustrations and stories. An excerpt from the first children's novel, *Little Goody Two-Shoes*, is included to show how this genre began and how far it has progressed. Modern literature about minority groups and foreign cultures is contrasted with excerpts from Victorian literature and writings from the early decades of this century—works that not only condoned but fostered prejudice. Historical comparison is central to a thorough study of children's literature. Without it, many trends, such as didacticism (which is playing an increasingly important role in modern children's books), cannot be completely understood. True understanding of contemporary children's literature is possible only through a familiarity with its past.

A third comparative approach used in this anthology is the cross-cultural. Through literature, we see how different cultures have felt about children and their books. The folktale chapter has been carefully organized to facilitate cross-cultural comparisons. Instead of being grouped by countries of origin, stories have been arranged by types: wonder tales, tales of trickery, animal tales, drolls, and cumulative tales. This grouping reveals how similar themes and motifs have been used by different cultures.

A Comparative Anthology of Children's Literature has been developed as a text for children's literature courses offered by English or education departments and schools of library science. It also can be used effectively as a guide or reference book for experienced teachers and librarians who wish to develop further methods and criteria for evaluating the quality and effectiveness of children's literature.

Children need to be familiar with the best literature available to them. Many of the attitudes, concepts, and values that will guide their adult lives are formed by their childhood reading. Through the insights provided by well-written prose and poetry, they can learn much of the human condition and potential.

Mary Ann Nelson

Cheney, Washington
October 1971

Contents

Contents

Contents

A Comparative Anthology of
CHILDREN'S
LITERATURE

YESTERDAY AND TODAY

To appreciate fully the diversity and wealth of children's contemporary literature, it is helpful to understand its history. Fiction, poetry, and pictures produced specifically for children are relatively recent developments. In our culture they have been in existence for a little over three hundred years. Books intended to amuse rather than to instruct are even more recent; their history goes back little more than one hundred years.

The first part of this anthology is a discussion of the history and development of children's fiction, poetry, and illustrated books. This past is interesting in its own right, but is also significant because trends from former centuries, some good and some bad, are still to be found in contemporary books. For example, the didacticism of Puritan literature unfortunately has its counterpart in some novels and poetry written in the last decade. By understanding the past of children's literature, the adult interested in the genre can develop a greater understanding of contemporary books and evaluate them more knowledgeably.

This brief overview also can give a historical perspective for the selections from eighteenth- and nineteenth-century children's literature that are to be found within almost every chapter of this anthology. They will further illustrate the points discussed in this section.

The following history of books and illustrations for children is concerned not only with past centuries but also with the trends and developments of the present period. The last ten years have revealed many dramatic changes in children's literature, not only in the treatment of traditional subjects but also in the widening of topics considered suitable for children's reading. In the late 1960s sociologists and anthropologists began to write that the world of the young is essentially different from that in which their parents grew up. Today's youth are living with television coverage of world events, the threat of nuclear destruction, almost continual warfare on some parts of the globe, moon walks and exploration into outer space. These children are not and cannot be as sheltered as were their parents.

These pressures have created a demand for more "honest" fiction, which in turn has created a new type of realism in juvenile literature. Some of it is well written, but most of it is mediocre. This new development cannot be ignored; it will not just go away, as some adults hope. But the adult in a position to influence children's reading needs to know how such books have developed and needs to recognize the valid and reject the specious.

The aim of the following chapter is to provide a helpful overview of the history of children's literature to this day. Not only the following section but the entire anthology is written to help in the development of individual critical standards for children's books.

Chapter 1

A History of Children's Literature

Children
in

the
Wood.

With clay-cold lips the babes they kissed.

He bargained with two ruffians strong.

Away the little babes were sent.

To fight they go right suddenly.

Then hand in hand they took their way.

Till death did end their grief.

Illustration from *Children in the Wood*, an old chapbook.

The twentieth-century view that children need and deserve amusement is remarkably new in the history of adult–child relationships. Until the middle of the nineteenth century, literature was used primarily to instruct and improve children, never simply to entertain them. Before recreational books could be written adults had to develop a new attitude toward children and reading, to acknowledge that reading for pleasure was at least as important as reading for instruction.

In the history of the English peoples, the earliest children's books were developed as texts for the Anglo-Saxon church schools of medieval England. These textbooks, in question and answer form, were written in Latin, the language of the church, by Bishop Aldhelm (656?–709), The Venerable Bede (673–735), Alcuin (735?–804), and other less well remembered men. But with the ninth-century Danish invasions a sense of nationalism developed. Alfred the Great and, in the tenth century, Alfric the Grammarian encouraged the use of Anglo-Saxon rather than Latin as the language of texts and teaching.

During all these centuries, the only stories available for entertainment were oral—the folk ballads, tales, and legends that were enjoyed by adults and children alike. Since many of these must have come from the pre-Christian Anglo-Saxon tradition, it is likely they were disapproved of by the clergy and had no recognition by the church schools.

In feudal England education became more widespread; still only instructional books were available to children. These were the Latin grammars and books, often written in verse, that instructed boys and girls in the behavior and morals proper for their social position. Some titles were *How the Good Wijf Taugte Hir Dougtir*, *The Boke of Curtasye*, *Lesson of Wysedome for All Manner Children*, *The Babees Book*, and *The Schoole of Virtue*.

With the advent of printing in the last half of the fifteenth century, more books became available for literate adults. It is assumed that children who could read chose from their parents' books those that appealed to them just as they had appropriated many oral, adult folktales. Caxton, England's first printer, translated Aesop's fables from the French and published them in 1484. A very popular book, it seems probable that entire families read and enjoyed it. In 1485 Caxton printed Malory's *Morte d'Arthur*, another adult book children must have liked. Other books published for adults by Caxton that were enjoyed by literate children of the fifteenth century were *The Recuyell of the Historyes of Troye*, *The Boke of Histories of Jason*, and *The Historye of Reynart the Foxe*.

CHAPBOOKS

In the seventeenth century, especially after 1641, chapbooks began to be published. In contrast to Caxton's books which were large and printed on heavy paper, these were small booklets, 4 by 2½ inches, of sixteen, thirty-two, or sixty-four pages folded or stitched together. They were carried to all parts of England by traveling peddlers called chapmen. These cheap books, which sold for a farthing or a few pence, were the only written literature available to the poor masses.

Chapbooks were produced on many subjects— religious, romantic, humorous, legendary, historical, biographical, criminal, diabolical, supernatural, superstitious, and so forth. The stories seldom were original; rather they were rewritings of old legends and tales condensed to emphasize vigorous action and adventure. Today chapbooks are condemned as ribald, obscene, and coarse, but that judgment ignores the fact that each age is embarrassed by different things. Many words and situations now found offensive were acceptable or amusing to the common people in the seventeenth and eighteenth centuries. It is unwise to evaluate past literature out of its cultural context and to judge it only by modern standards, because this leads to serious misinterpretations of these works.

While early chapbooks were intended for adults, many of them also interested children. Later chapbooks written specifically for children began to appear and were the first English books written to entertain as well as instruct children. They included *The Tragical Death of an Apple Pie, The Butterfly's Ball, Jack Jingle,* and *Cock Robin.* One chapbook printed in 1563 was written to teach children to read: *A Boke in Englyssh Metre, of the great Marchante Man called Dives Pragmaticus, very preaty for Children to reade . . .* A chapbook probably enjoyed by both children and adults, *The History of Jack and the Giants,* reprinted on pages 15–17, reveals the vitality of chapbooks and illustrates that some of them told good stories which can still be enjoyed.

THE PURITAN MORAL TALES

Even though there were some "good, godly" chapbooks, many educated Englishmen and all Puritans condemned the form. In opposition to chapbooks, moral tales were developed and dominated English children's literature for seventy years.

Religion was central to the Puritans, who interpreted every aspect of life through religious belief. They used literature to strengthen their children's resistance against sin and to reinforce the Puritan social, economic, and religious ideals. These stories now seem morbid and terrifying with their emphasis on martyrdom and death. A typical example of their approach is found in James Janeway's famous book, entitled *A Token for Children: An exact account of the conversion, holy and exemplary lives, and joyful deaths of several young children* (1671). The Puritans sincerely believed children were more vulnerable than adults. These deeply religious adults earnestly wished to preserve their children from, as Janeway said, "falling into everlasting Fire."

John Bunyan, a Puritan who went to jail for his beliefs and the author of one of England's greatest books, *Pilgrim's Progress,* denounced chapbooks. Like many other Puritan writers he wanted to create a new type of literature for children that would replace such secular works. He wrote *A Book for Boys and Girls: or, Country Rhymes for children* (1686), later retitled *Divine Emblems for Youth.* In addition to verse "emblems" about animals and the country similar to "Upon the Bee" that follows, this book contained the Ten Commandments, the Creed, the Lord's Prayer, an ABC, lessons in reading and arithmetic, and a spelling list composed of Christian names.

Upon the Bee
The Bee goes out, and Honey home doth bring;
   And some who seek that Honey
     find a Sting..
Now would'st thou have the Honey, and be free
From stinging; in the first place kill the bee.
Comparison
This Bee an Emblem truly is of Sin,
Whose Sweet unto a many, Death had been.
Now would'st have sweet from Sin,
   and yet not die.
Do thou it in the first place mortify.

Many books were written in imitation of Janeway's book about pious, if short-lived, children and of Bunyan's moral lessons in verse. It is now difficult for most people to sympathize with and understand the dogmatic Puritan fervor, but it was sincere. Their stories and verses for children were meant to be enjoyable substitutes for the often bawdy and secular chapbooks. While it now seems improbable, there is no evidence that these moralistic books were disdained by Puritan children who, as part of the culture that created these didactic sermons, must have accepted the religious and moral code expressed within them.

Even though the Puritans' didactic use of fiction and verse was instrumental in the development of children's literature, it is important to remember that not all Englishmen were Puritans and that chapbooks survived the Puritan era as a popular form of English literature.

FAIRY TALES

In France at this time, the late seventeenth century, a new movement developed that had a lasting influence on English children's literature. Fairy tales became extremely popular among the French nobility and their followers. Many adults wrote original tales or polished and elaborated authentic oral folktales to be read aloud in literary salons. "The White Cat" by Countess d'Aulnoy and "Beauty and the Beast" are two that still remain popular.

The most enduring French tales, however, were written by Pierre Perrault d'Armancour.[1] His *Histories ou Contes du temps passé; avec des Moralitez* was printed in 1698 at Paris. It contained eight tales: *La belle au bois dormant*, "The Sleeping Beauty"; *Le petit chaperon rouge*, "Red Riding Hood"; *La Barbe Bleüe*, "Blue Beard"; *Le maître Chat, ou le Chat Botté*, "Puss in Boots"; *Les Fees*, "Toads and Diamonds"; *Cendrillon, ou la petite Pantoufle de Verre*, "Cinderella, or the Glass Slipper"; *Riquet à la Houppe*, "Rique with the Tuft"; *Le Petit Poucet*, "Hop o' My Thumb." Perrault's style in retelling these tales, which he ascribes to his nurse, is much simpler than most French literary fairy tales. For that reason his stories were especially enjoyed by children as well as adults. It is not known exactly when Perrault's tales were translated into English, but individual stories quickly were printed in chapbooks and became very popular with many English children and adults.

The appearance of the *Arabian Nights* reinforced a growing interest in fantasy. Galland, a French diplomat, translated twelve volumes of eastern tales into French between 1704 and 1717. These tales achieved great popularity throughout Europe and were immediately translated into English and individual tales, especially the Aladdin and Sinbad adventures, were quickly revised into chapbook form.

The Puritans and other English religious groups spoke out strongly against such secular and frivolous literature, and for the next hundred and fifty years fairy tales were under attack by English moralists. Even in the nineteenth century they were considered by some as too fantastic and frivolous to be appropriate for children.[2]

THE ADVENT OF THE NOVEL

English children's literature underwent a significant change in the early eighteenth century. In 1719 Daniel Defoe's *The Life and Strange Surprising Adventures of Robinson Crusoe, of York, Mariner* was published for adults. Four months after its first publication an unauthorized abridged edition was printed for children. *Gulliver's Travels* by Swift was published in 1726 and again children adopted an adult book. Both *Robinson Crusoe* and *Gulliver's Travels* were quickly put into chapbooks for children. As novels for adults flourished, it was inevitable that children would be given similar books.

Many novel-reading parents were quite likely to be willing to buy secular works for their children. Thus a ready market for a new type of children's books existed in the first half of the eighteenth century, the growing, literate middle class being less insistent than the Puritans about religious instruction.

EARLY CHILDREN'S PUBLISHERS

John Newbery has been credited as being the first publisher to print books for children's entertainment. However, many children's chapbooks were solely for amusement, and these as well as the children's abridgment of *Robinson Crusoe* predate Newbery's publications.

Percy Muir, in *English Children's Books*, reveals that Thomas Boreman published a number of books for children before Newbery, several of which were for entertainment. In 1736 Boreman printed *A Description of a Great Variety of Animals, and Vegetables . . . especially for the*

---

[1] His father, Charles Perrault, is often given credit for these tales even though the Privilege was granted "au sieur P. Darmancour." Percy Muir gives ample evidence in favor of Pierre Perrault's authorship in *English Children's Books*.

[2] There has always been an attitude and vision of the world that rejects all forms of fantasy. Literature and recreation, it is felt, can be justified only if they "improve" children.

A Little Pretty
POCKET-BOOK,
Intended for the
INSTRUCTION and AMUSEMENT
OF
LITTLE MASTER *TOMMY*,
AND
PRETTY MISS *POLLY*.
With Two Letters from
JACK the GIANT-KILLER;
AS ALSO
A BALL and PINCUSHION;
The Use of which will infallibly make *Tommy*
a good Boy, and *Polly* a good Girl.

To which is added,
A LITTLE SONG-BOOK,
BEING
A *New Attempt* to teach Children the Use of
the *English Alphabet*, by Way of Diversion.
LONDON:
Printed for J. NEWBERY, at the *Bible and Sun*
in St. *Paul's Church-Yard*. 1767,
[Price Six-pence bound.]

The great A Play.

CHUCK-FARTHING.

AS you value your Pence,
At the *Hole* take your Aim;
Chuck all safely in,
And you'll win the Game.

MORAL.
Chuck-Farthing, like Trade,
Requires great Care;
The more you observe,
The better you'll fare.

B 3   *Flying*

Excerpts from A *Little Pretty Pocket-Book*, published by John Newbery, 1744, continue through page 13.

Entertainment of Youth. He began publishing a nine-volume set of histories of famous London buildings in 1740 and in 1742 printed *The History of Cajanus, the Swedish Giant.* Muir believes several eighteenth-century printers simultaneously decided to publish books for children, using chapbooks as a model. Newbery is now the most famous of these printers because he was evidently the most successful and not because he was the first.

Like Boreman, most of Newbery's juvenile books were instructional. The advertisement for his first children's book, A *Little Pretty Pocket-Book* published June 18, 1744, however, is significant for the inclusion of the word amusement.[3]

> This Day is publish'd According to
> Act of Parliament (Neatly bound
> and gilt)
> A LITTLE PRETTY POCKET-BOOK, intended for the
> Instruction and Amusement of little Master

[3] Excerpts from A *Little Pretty Pocket-Book* can be found on pages 9 through 13.

Tommy and pretty Miss Polly; with an agreeable Letter to each from *Jack the Giant-Killer*; as also a Ball and Pincushion, the Use of which will infallibly make Tommy a good Boy and Polly a good girl.

To the Whole is prefix'd, A Lecture on Education, humbly address'd to all Parents, Guardians, Governesses, etc.; wherein Rules are laid down for making their Children strong, hardy, healthy, virtuous, wise, and happy . . .

Printed for J. Newbery, at the *Bible and Crown*, near Devereux Court, without Temple Bar. Price of the Book alone 6d., with Ball or Pincushion 8d.

The shift from stern morality to amusing instruction was not simply the idea of Newbery or the other publishers. Rather it grew from John Locke's beliefs, expressed in the 1690s, that a child could "be cozen'd into a Knowledge of the Letters" through games and "some easy pleasant Book, suited to his Capacity . . . wherein the Entertainment that he finds might draw him on, and reward his Pains in Reading."

The little e Play.

KING I AM.

AMBITION here fires every Heart,
    And all assume the Monarch's Part;
For a few Minutes, though in Play,
Each rules with arbitrary Sway.

RULE of LIFE.

Descend into thyself, to find
The Imperfections of thy Mind.

PIG-

(69)

FABLE IV.

MERCURY *and the* WOODMAN.

A Woodman, at Work,
    Dropp'd his Ax in a Pond,
And in Sorrow and Tears,
    His Disaster bemoan'd.
Merc'ry brings one all Gold,
    And cries, Friend, is this thine?
No Sir, (says the Woodman)
    Mine was not so fine.
Then he shew'd him the right,
    Ah! that's mine by my Troth:
Thou art honest, says *Merc'ry,*
    So, Friend, take them both.
        E 3   To

In April of 1765 Newbery published a remarkable book, *The Renowned History of Little Goody Two Shoes, Otherwise Called Mrs. Margery Two Shoes.* This was the first novel written for children; previous books had been miscellaneous collections rather than unified stories. The authorship of *Little Goody Two Shoes* is unknown, for there were no "children's authors"; publishers hired hacks who wrote books to order. However, some of these hacks were excellent writers, and among the men Newbery employed were Oliver Goldsmith and Dr. Samuel Johnson. While *Little Goody Two Shoes* has been ascribed to Goldsmith, this has never been proved, but the novel has a charm that suggests its author was above the ordinary.

Little Goody Two Shoes has been condemned by twentieth-century readers for its stereotyped characters and its moralistic tone. It is unfair, however, to impose current standards on the first book of a new genre. The plot is strong enough to hold the reader's interest; Mrs. Margery's progress from poverty to wealth is both amusing and, at times, moving. Considering the harshly didactic books that preceded and followed it, *Little Goody*

Two Shoes is remarkable. It was, understandably, extremely popular when it first appeared and had many imitators such as *Primrose Prettyface, Goody Goosecap,* and *Sally Spellwell.*

While Newbery was neither the original nor the only children's publisher, he was the first to make juvenile books an important part of his trade. Newbery took pains with his books, which were of good quality and proved children's literature could be profitable. By 1780 many publishers began to print juvenile fiction. One printer, John Marshal, seems to have published little else; between 1780 and 1790 he advertised seventy separate titles for children.

ROUSSEAU

When children's books became profitable some writers began to specialize in juvenile fiction. Many of these writers for children were influenced by Rousseau, a leader in the Age of Enlightenment which emphasized reason. It was claimed that man was not, as the Puritans held, innately sinful; he could accomplish anything. The simple, natural, and the unspoiled became idealized, and

(70)

To Master Tommy, *or Miss* Polly.

BY this you may see, my Dear, that *Honesty is the best Policy*; had Mercury found the Woodman a Rogue, he would not have given him any Thing; but as he was an honest Man, he not only gave him his own Ax, but a golden one also. Consider, my Dear, 'tis a fine Thing *to have a Golden Ax*, and at the same Time the Love and Esteem of all the World beside, and that you will certainly have if you are strictly honest.

I am

Your affectionate Friend,

JACK *the* Giant-killer.

S I R,

(71)

S I R,

THere was in my Country a little Boy, who learned his Book to that surprising Degree, that his Master could scarce teach him fast enough, for he had his Lesson almost as soon as it was pointed out to him; which raised the Attention of every Body; and as he was also very dutiful to his Parents and obliging to his Playmates, every Body loved him. His Learning and Behaviour purchased him the Esteem of the greatest People, and raised him from a mean State of Life to a Coach and Six, in which he rides to this Day. Learning is a most excellent Thing, and is easily acquired too, when little Boys set themselves earnestly about it. I know several Masters at this Time, who all bid fair for the same Honour the above Gentleman enjoys.   *I am, Sir, &c.*

universal brotherhood became an increasingly important, if little practiced, concept.

In *Émile* Rousseau set forth his educational theories. The child, Émile, was free to develop and learn through his own interests rather than through formal schooling. He was not encompassed by restrictions, not forced to conform. He learned "naturally" with no pressure from adults. Rousseau's theories of education should have freed children's literature from didacticism. Instead his followers seized on the idea that the child's spontaneous interests should be used for educational purposes; juvenile books became a new tool for didactic teaching of facts.[4]

THE MORAL TALE

Between 1780 and 1820 the moral tale dominated children's literature. These stories, which ranged from the heavily didactic to the gently moralistic, were written to help children

develop reasoning ability and moral judgment so they could always choose the correct action. The tales often contained only personified moralistic abstractions based on a rigid sense of the ideal.

Maria Edgeworth, although an English follower of Rousseau, showed a more humane attitude toward children and human error than did her predecessor Thomas Day; where Day is insistent she is gentle. Day's characters in *Sandford and Merton* are stereotypes of Rousseauian theories, but Miss Edgeworth's characters are more believably human. Rosamond, the heroine of "The Purple Jar" (1801), *hopes* she will choose more wisely next time. She is not all good or all bad as most children in books were at that time. Miss Edgeworth's stories were more interesting than most, yet she sincerely believed in Rousseau's theories of education and always had a moral purpose behind her writings.

POETRY

Ann and Jane Taylor also combined moralistic instruction with enjoyment. Their verses were first published in *Original Poems for*

[4] For more information on how Rousseau's theories were applied to English literature for children, see the introduction to "Tommy Decides to Study Arithmetic" in Chapter 7, Domestic Action.

(72)

MADAM,

I Know of a little Lady, no bigger than
your pretty Mifs, who has behaved fo well
that every Body is in Love with her. She is
extremely dutiful to her Parents and Go-
vernefs, kind to her School-fellows, and obliging to every body.   Then fhe learns her
Book to Admiration, works well with her
Needle, and is fo modeft, fo willing to do as
fhe is bid, and fo engaging in Company,
that my Lady *Meanwell* has made her a
Prefent of a fine Gold Watch, and declares
that fhe fhall ride in her own Coach. 'Tis
this Learning, Madam, and good Behaviour, that brings us the Efteem of the whole
World.   *I am, Madam, yours, &c.*

---

(87)

S E L E C T

P R O V E R B S

For the U S E of

C H I L D R E N.

A Fool's Bolt is foon fhot.
A good Beginning, a good Ending.
A Fool and his Money are foon parted.
After Dinner fit a while,
After Supper walk a Mile.
After a Storm cometh a Calm.

F 4   **As**

Infant Minds (two volumes) (1804–1805), *Rhymes for the Nursery* (1806), and *Hymes for Infant Minds* (1810). "Twinkle, Twinkle, Little Star" is Jane's most famous poem. The sisters' verse had a freshness and charm lacking in most children's literature of that period, and many other writers soon began to imitate them; often, however, with heavy-handed didacticism.

Original Poems for Infant Minds, in which there were also poems by authors other than the Taylors, was an innovation in children's literature. Before these two volumes there had been few books of poetry for children. In 1715 Isaac Watts had written, in reaction to Puritan harshness, some gentle, moral poems for children, *Divine Songs Attempted in Easy Language for the Use of Children*. As the title indicates, he tried to use the language of children in these poems. There were no imitators. Between Watts and the Taylor sisters, ninety years later, the only other poets for children, except a few hacks who produced rough verses, were John Marchant and William Blake. Blake is now recognized as a great poet, but until this century his poetry for children, *Songs of Innocence* (1789), was as ignored as the poetry of the

mediocre Mr. Marchant. Blake was a mystic and his children's poetry is now read primarily by adults.

In the 1780s and 1790s many people believed poetry was inappropriate for children. Some suggested that poetry's meter, rhyme, and form were too difficult or unnatural for children to read. The same kind of attitude forbade sweets and spices from children's diets as being unwholesome. It was not until the Taylors' first book of gently moralistic poetry gained parental approval that many English children were permitted to read poems.

Even though the Taylor sisters revealed that a new approach to children's literature was coming, there were still remnants of sterner beliefs. *The History of the Fairchild Family, or the Children's Manual, being a collection of Stories calculated to show the importance and effects of a religious education* by Mrs. Sherwood was published in 1818 and reprinted throughout the nineteenth century. The author upheld the Puritan beliefs about life and the inherent sinfulness of children. Mrs. Trimmer, an influential woman in the early nineteenth century, believed England was in dan-

(89)

Nothing's fo certain as Death.
Neceffity has no Law.
New Lords, new Laws.
None fo proud as an enrich'd Beggar,
Pride will have a Fall.
Proffer'd Service ftinks.
Set a Knave to catch a Knave.
Two Heads are better than one.
Too much Familiarity breeds Contempt.
They who are bound muft obey.
Time and Tide ftay for no Man.
Tell Truth and fhame the Devil.
The beft may mend.
Truth may be blam'd, but can't be fham'd.
The new Broom fweeps clean.
The Eye is bigger than the Belly.
The Weakeft goes to the Wall.
When the Fox preaches beware of the
   Geefe.
                                   Wifdom

ger from French ideas because of the influx of both Rousseauian theories and the French fairy tales. She established *The Guardian*, a magazine to protect "young and innocent" children from the dangers of "infantine and juvenile literature."

NEW TRENDS

Although they reigned over the first half of the nineteenth century, time was against the Trimmers and the Sherwoods. By mid-century education was available for most English and American children. Adults were beginning to accept the idea that children had a right to personal desires, that they needed not only education but also entertainment. While there were still many didactic stories, especially religious tracts, recreational literature was creeping in. In spite of Mrs. Trimmers' opposition, fairy tales were more widely read, and the publication of the Grimm brothers' folktales in England in the 1820s gave impetus to the growing acceptance of fantasy for children.

In 1846 one of the miracles in children's literature occurred with the publication of Edward

Lear's first book of poetry. It was indeed *A Book of Nonsense* and children loved it. In 1865 Lewis Carroll's *Alice in Wonderland* appeared and the course of children's literature was changed. Before *Alice*, juvenile fiction had been very inexpensive, but Carroll's novel not only commanded a good price but sold many copies to the increasing number of literate children. It revealed that juvenile fiction could be quite profitable. More importantly, by proving nondidactic stories were wanted, *Alice in Wonderland* established a trend toward interesting novels. After the *Alice* books more varied types of fiction were written for children.

Didacticism did not disappear entirely, however, and morals were still taught through literature, as Kingsley's *The Water Babies* shows. This book, which was published in 1863, two years before *Alice*, is patronizing and heavily didactic; yet its plot was strong enough to hold many nineteenth-century children's interest. Saccharine novels were still being written, especially for girls, in the last decades of the century, but in contrast to them, in 1868 an American author, Louisa May Alcott, created a family of believable girls. Although the ideas of goodness, selflessness, and proper behavior run through *Little Women*, the characters are exceptionally well developed.

A trend toward realistic adventure stories for boys began in the mid-nineteenth century. The 1840s saw the rise of dime novels, cheap books published for ten- to sixteen-year-old boys in which the emphasis was on thrilling action with stereotyped plots and characters. This type of literature was very popular with boys although most educated parents opposed it. Captain Frederick Marryat and Robert Ballantyne were two of the most famous authors of boy's adventure stories at this time. Popular Marryat books were *Mr. Midshipman Easy, Masterman Ready*; Ballantine wrote *The Young Fur-Trader*.

In America Mark Twain's *Adventures of Tom Sawyer* was published in 1876. The book's plot was strong, nondidactic, believable; the characters were neither idealized nor types. Stevenson's *Treasure Island* appeared in 1883 and, although serialized for boys, this adventure story won adult approval. These two books, with *Alice in Wonderland* and *Little Women*, were the beginnings of children's nondidactic novels.

CONTEMPORARY
TRENDS

Didacticism, however, has continued even into the twentieth century. Many of today's adults were brought up with Munro Leaf's "amusing" Fun books: *Manners Can Be Fun, Grammar Can Be Fun, Safety Can Be Fun.* These books and the attitude they express toward children are very like the books and attitudes of the seventeenth and eighteenth centuries. So too is Gelett Burgess's *New Goops and How To Know Them,* read by many of the parents of today's children. The 1963 Newbery Award winner, *A Wrinkle in Time,* is a thinly disguised moralistic treatise. Such books make it impossible to believe complacently that children's literature has escaped from the overly moralistic influences. Many adults enjoy writing and buying books that will overtly teach and improve "youth," yet themes must be handled with subtlety to be accepted by today's child, who expects to be entertained by literature.

Twentieth-century children's literature reflects its past. Books, such as *What Do You Say, Dear?* and *An Anteater Named Arthur,* are still used to teach and amuse. Stereotypes are still present in, for example, the *Henry Huggins* and *Homer Price* books. In many novels characters and plot are sometimes still little more than sugarcoating to make facts more interesting. Some historical fiction is of this type: Gray's *Adam of the Road* is more a tour of thirteenth-century England than a unified novel. The boy's search for his dog is only a slender thread to hold together the picture of a past age.

It is probably true that the preceding weaknesses will always be found, but equally true is the fact that there is today a wider selection of well-written recreational literature for children than at any other time. Fantasy is acceptable to most adults, realistic fiction deals with many aspects of life, and many excellent writers now specialize in children's literature.

Contrary to the prevailing opinion that children's fiction has not changed significantly since the shift to realism and more rounded characterization in the late nineteenth century, children's literature is currently evolving toward greater honesty and a less idealized view of childhood. Controversial topics, such as drugs, infidelity,

unfit parents, and antisocial behavior, are now being explored. While there is a great difference between the characterization of Goody Two Shoes and the March sisters, so too the visions and understandings of childhood and the parent–child relationship in *Henry Huggins* and *Homer Price* are quite different from those in *Where the Wild Things Are, Harriet the Spy, Mary Jane, The Winners,* and *Skinny.* Some contemporary novels show that not all parents are loving, not all children's problems are easily solved, the world is not always equitable—even to the hero or heroine in a book—and not all situations can be happily resolved.

Unfortunately, many of the authors writing books that deal with such contemporary topics strive too hard for relevance, and seem more interested in being modern than in creating well-written works that strive to develop understandings and perspectives. Sensationalism is too often mistaken for honesty. However, a growing number of thoughtful authors are finding they now are free to write more realistically about the relationships, situations, and problems of modern life. They are writing serious books that have relevance but do not substitute sensationalism for perceptive insights about contemporary society.

Today children know turmoil, fear, and insecurity—personal and global. To exclude such emotions and their causes from juvenile literature and to continue many of the former rules of publishing, which eliminated such things as sibling rivalry, parental–child disharmony, and unsolvable problems, is to present a false image of life—one that will seem unbelievable to many young readers. This, of course, does not mean all children's books must deal with contemporary, controversial problems to be valid. But it is significant that an increasing number of contemporary juvenile novels do have a new type of realism.

Although some critics deplore this realism, it is generally a healthy trend. True, children need the reassurance that there is order in life and kindness in man, but young people must not be led into the false belief that effort and merit are always rewarded. Some of their books are now revealing many problems of life more pointedly than before, and one of the most interesting aspects of contemporary children's literature will be to see how realism develops in the next decade.

THE HISTORY OF JACK AND THE GIANTS

Anonymous

The following selection is excerpted from a seventeenth-century chapbook printed by J. Eddowes. The only changes are that the modern letter s is used and only four of the chapters are here reprinted.

That chapbooks had a liveliness and a charm that can please even twentieth-century readers is apparent from this short passage. Jack's discussion with the Parson may seem inappropriate for children, but chapbooks were seldom for any specific age group; children and adults enjoyed them together, each laughing at what he enjoyed. The chapbooks were rather like today's family television shows that have some humor for adults which is missed by the child viewer.

See page 6 for more information about the role of chapbooks in the history of English children's literature. Notice, too, the similarities between Chapter V and the Appalachian folktale "Jack in the Giants' Newground" in Chapter 8, Tales of Trickery. Both narratives must once have had a common source.

CHAP. I.

Of his Birth and Parentage; and how he discoursed with a Country Vicar, when he was but seven Years old.

In the Reign of King *Arthur*, near the Lands-End of *England*, namely, the County of *Cornwall*, there lived a wealthy Farmer, who had one only Son, commonly known by the Name of JACK THE GIANT-KILLER: He was brisk, and of a lively ready Wit, so that whatever he could not perform by Force and Strength, he compleated by ingenious Wit and Policy, never was any Person heard of that could worst him, nay, the very Learned many times he baffled, by his cunning and sharp ready Inventions. For Instance, when he was no more than 7 Years of Age, his Father, the Farmer, sent him into the Field to look after the Oxen, which were then feeding in a pleasant Pasture; a Country Vicar, by chance one Day coming a-cross the Fields, called to Jack, and asked him several Questions; in particular, *How many Commandments are there? Jack* told him *There were Nine.* The Parson replied, *There are Ten. Nay,*

quoth *Jack, Mr. Parson, you are out it's true there were Ten, but you broke one with your Maid* Margery. The Parson replied, *Thou art an arch Wag,* Jack. Well, Mr. *Parson,* quoth *Jack,* You have asked me one Question, and I have answered it, I beseech you let me ask you another. *Who made these Oxen?* the Parson replied, *God made them, Child*: Now you are out again, quoth *Jack*; for God made them Bulls but my Father and his Man *Hobson* made Oxen of them. These were the witty Answers of *Jack*. The Parson finding himself out-witted trudged away, leaving *Jack* in a Fit of Laughter.

CHAP. II.

How a Giant inhabited the Mount of Cornwall, *and of the great Spoils he made in the Neighbouring Lands.*

In those Days the Mount of *Cornwall* was kept by a huge and monstrous Giant, eighteen Foot in Height, and about three Yards in compass, of a fierce and grim Countenance, the Terror of all the neighbouring Towns and Villages; his Habitation was a Cave in the midst of all the Mount. Never would he suffer any living Creature to inhabit near him: His Feeding was upon other Men's Cattle, which often became his Prey; for whensoever he wanted Food, he would wade over the main Land, where he would furnish himself with whatsoever he found; for the People at his Approach would forsake their Habitations, then would he seize upon their Cows and Oxen, of which he would make nothing to carry over on his Back half a Dozen at a Time; and as for their Sheep and Hogs, he would tie them round his Waste like Bandaliers. This he for many Years had practised, so that great Part of the County of *Cornwall* was much impoverished by him.

But one Day *Jack* coming to the Town-Hall when the Magistrates were sitting in Consultation about this Giant, he asked them *What reward they would give to any Person that should destroy him?* They replied, *he should have all the Giant's Treasure in recompence.* Quoth *Jack*, then I myself will undertake the Work.

CHAP. III.

How Jack *slew this Monster, and from that was called* Jack *the* Giant-Killer.

Jack having undertaken the Task, he furnishes himself with a Horn, Shovel and Pick-ax, and over to the Mount he goes in the beginning of a dark Winter Evening, where he fell to work, and before Morning had digged a Pit two and twenty Feet deep, and almost as broad, covering the same over with long Sticks and Straw; then strowing a little of the Mould upon it, it appeared like the plain Ground; this done, *Jack* places himself on the contrary Side of the Pit, just about the dawning of the Day, when putting his Horn to his Mouth, he blew the same *Tan-tive, Tan-tive,* which unexpected Noise roused the Giant, who came running towards *Jack,* saying: *You incorrigible Villain, are you come here to disturb my Rest, you shall pay dearly for this; Satisfaction I will have, and it shall be this, I will have you whole, and broil you for my Breakfast.* Which Words were no sooner out of his *Mouth,* but he tumbled headlong into the Pit, whose heavy fall made the very Foundation of the Mount to shake. *O Giant, quoth* Jack, where are you now; *in faith you are gotten into* Lob's Pound, *where I will*

plague you for your threatening Words: What do you think now of broiling me for your Breakfast will no other Diet serve you but poor Jack? Thus having tantalized the Giant for a while, he took him such a considerable Blow upon the Crown of his Head with his Pick-ax, that he tumbled down, and with a dreadful Groan died; this done, Jack threw the Earth in upon him, and so buried him. And then going and searching his Cave, he found much Treasure. Now when the Magistrates which employed him, heard the Work was over, they sent for him, declaring, that he should henceforth be called, *Jack the Giant-Killer,* and in Honour thereto; presented him with a Sword, together with an embroidered Belt, on which these Words were wrought in Letters of Gold.

> *Here's the right valiant* Cornish *Man,*
> *Who slew the Giant* Cormilan.

*   *   *

CHAP. V.

How Jack *travelled into* Flintshire; *and what happened.*

Jack having but little Money, thought it prudent to make the best of his Way by Travelling hard, and at length losing his Road was belated, and could not get a Place of Entertainment, till coming to a Valley placed between two Hills, he found a large House in that lonesome Place, and by reason of his present Necessity, he took Courage to knock at the Gate, where to his Amazement, there came forth a monstrous Giant with two Heads, yet he did not seem to be so fiery as the others had been, for he was a *Welsh* Giant, and what he did was by private and secret Malice, under the false Shew of Friendship; for *Jack* telling his Condition he bid him Welcome, shewing him a Room with a Bed in it, where he might take his Night's Repose, whereupon *Jack* undresses, and as the Giant was walking away to another Apartment, *Jack* heard him mutter these Words to himself.

> *Tho' here you lodge with me this Night,*
> *You shall not see the Morning Light,*
> *My Club shall dash your Brains out quite.*

Say'st thou so, quoth *Jack,* that's like one of your *Welsh Tricks,* yet I hope to be cunning enough for you; then getting out of his Bed and feeling about in the dark, he found a thick Billet, which he laid in the Bed in his stead, and laid himself in a dark Corner of the Room, when in the dead of the Night came the *Welsh* Giant, with his Club, and struck several heavy Blows upon his Bed, where *Jack* had laid the Billet, and then returned to his Chamber, supposing he had broken all the Bones in his Skin.

The next Morning *Jack* came to give him Thanks for his Lodging. Quoth the Giant, How have you rested? did you not feel something in the Night? No, nothing, quoth *Jack*, but a Rat, which gave me three or four Slaps with her Tail.

Soon after the Giant arose, and went to his Breakfast with a Bowl of Hasty-Pudding, con-

taining four Gallons, giving *Jack* the like Quantity, who being loth to let the Giant know he could not eat with him, got a large Leathern Bag putting it artificially under his loose Coat, into which he secretly conveyed the Pudding, telling the Giant he would shew him a Trick; then taking a large Knife rips open the Bag, which the Giant supposed to be his Belly, and out came the Hasty-Pudding, which the Giant seeing cried out, *Cotsplut, hur can do that Trick hurself*; then taking a sharp Knife he rips open his own Belly from the Bottom to the Top, and out drops his Tripes and Trolly-bubs, so that hur fell down dead. Thus *Jack* outwitted the *Welsh* Giant, and proceeded forward on his Journey.

Related Reading

Arbuthnot, May Hill. *Children and Books,* 3d ed. Glenview, Ill.: Scott, Foresman, 1964. Chapter 3 presents an overview of the history of children's literature.

Avery, Gillian, *In the Window-Seat.* Ilustrated by Susan Einzig. New York: Van Nostrand, 1965. A collection of stories from the nineteenth century that will be of interest to the student of children's literature and to some children who may enjoy the old-fashioned tales.

Barchilon, Jacques and Henry Pettit, eds. *The Authentic Mother Goose, Fairy Tales and Nursery Rhymes.* Chicago: Alan Swallow, 1960. Facsimiles of the 1729 English translation of Perrault's fairy tales and the complete *Mother Goose's Melody* as well as a discussion of the history of Perrault's tales.

Comenius, Johann Amos. *The Orbis Pictus of John Amos Comenius.* Syracuse, N.Y.: C. W. Bardeen, 1887. See the introduction to Chapter 13, for a discussion of this book.

Darton, F. J. Harvey. *Children's Books in England: Five Centuries of Social Life.* Cambridge, England: Cambridge University Press, 1932. The history of children's literature is discussed in detail with an emphasis on the effects of social attitudes on writings for young people.

de Vries, Leonard, compiler. *Flowers of Delight.* Illustrated with woodcuts and engravings from old

children's books. New York: Pantheon, 1965. For the student of children's literature. A selection of early writing for children from 1765 to 1830 taken from the Osborne Collection of Early Children's Books in the Toronto Public Library.

————. *Little Wide Awake.* Illustrated with woodcuts and engravings from old children's books. Cleveland: World, 1967. Selections "from Victorian Children's Books and Periodicals in the collection of Anne and Fernand G. Renier." Although the editor's lack of order in arranging the works is frustrating, the individual selections are fascinating.

Dodgson, Charles Lutwidge. *Alice's Adventures under Ground.* (Xerox) Ann Arbor, Mich.: University Microfilms, 1964.

————. *Alice's Adventures under Ground.* New York: Dover, 1965. Two facsimile reproductions of Carroll's hand-printed book with thirty-seven drawings by the author.

Folmsbee, Beulah. *A Little History of the Horn Book.* Boston: Horn Book, 1942. The background and methods of making hornbooks are explained in this small volume the size of the original horn books.

Gignilliat, George W., Jr. *The Author of Sanford and Merton: A Life of Thomas Day, Esq.* New York: Columbia University Press, 1932.

Gillespie, Margaret C. *Literature for Children: His-*

tory and Trends. Dubuque, Iowa: Wm. C. Brown, 1970. A paperback history of children's literature with helpful information.

Huck, Charlotte S., and Doris Young Kuhn. *Children's Literature in the Elementary School*, 2d ed. New York: Holt, Rinehart and Winston, 1968. Excellent discussion of the history of children's literature.

Jordan, Alice M. *From Rollo to Tom Sawyer*. Boston: Horn Book, 1948. Biographical sketches of many authors of children's books in the last half of the nineteenth century.

Kiefer, Monica. *American Children through Their Books 1700–1835*. Philadelphia: University of Philadelphia Press, 1948. A valuable study of American literature for children, with social and educational influences carefully explored.

Laski, Marghanita. *Mrs. Ewing, Mrs. Molesworth and Mrs. Hodgson Burnett*. New York: Oxford University Press, 1951. Biographies and analyses of three important nineteenth-century authors for children.

Meigs, Cornelia, *et al*. A *Critical History of Children's Literature*. New York: Macmillan, 1953. A helpful review of children's literature from its beginnings to the middle of the twentieth century.

Muir, Percy. *English Children's Books 1600 to 1900*, 2d ed. New York: Praeger, 1969. One of the best and most complete discussions of the history of children's literature.

Newbery, John, publisher. A *Little Pretty Pocket-Book*. New York: Harcourt, 1966. A facsimile of one of the earliest books published (1744) for "amusement" as well as instruction. It contains many woodcuts, a letter from Jack the Giant-Killer, verses for the alphabet, maxims, information on how to raise children, etc. Also included in the reproduction is a historical introduction about Newbery's time and his role in the development of children's literature.

Newbery, John. *The Original Mother Goose's Melody*, as first issued by John Newbery, of London, about A.D., 1760. Reproduced in facsimile from the edition as reprinted by Isaiah Thomas of Worcester, Mass., about A.D., 1785, with introductory notes by William H. Whitmore. Albany: Joel Munsell's Sons, 1889. Detroit: Gale Research Company, Singing Tree Press. n.d.

Robinson, Evelyn Rose, ed. *Readings about Children's Literature*. New York: McKay, 1966. A collection of articles, most of which first appeared in professional journals, about children's reading interests; will be of interest to teachers, students of children's literature, librarians, and parents.

Sloane, William. *Children's Books in England and America in the Seventeenth Century*. New York: Kings Crown, 1955. Interesting account of literature available to seventeenth-century children.

Smith, Dora V. *Fifty Years of Children's Books 1910–1960: Trends, Backgrounds, Influences*. Champaign, Ill.: National Council of Teachers of English, 1963. A brief but enjoyable survey of twentieth-century children's books.

Smith, James Steel. A *Critical Approach to Children's Literature*. New York: McGraw-Hill, 1967. One chapter presents an interesting short history of children's literature.

Thwaite, M. F. *From Primer to Pleasure: An Introduction to the History of Children's Books in England from the Invention of Printing to 1900*. London: Library Association, 1963. An interesting survey of children's literature. Of particular interest is the chapter that explains the influence American books had on English writing for children.

Townsend, John Rowe. *Written for Children*. New York: Lothrop, 1967. A well-written, interesting "outline of English children's literature" by a reviewer of children's books for *The Manchester Guardian* and an author of young people's books. Although only English books are discussed, it is still of interest to students of children's literature.

Tuer, Andrew W. compiler. *Stories from Old-Fashioned Children's Books*. Adorned with 250 amusing cuts. First published in England by The Leadenhall Press, 1899–1900. Detroit: Singing Tree Press, 1968. An excellent collection of early English writings and illustrations for children. A delightful and essential book for those interested in the history of children's literature.

Chapter 2

Illustrations
in Children's
Literature

From *Under the Window*, written and illustrated by Kate Greenaway. Published by George Routledge & Sons, Ltd., 1879.

For most young children a book with illustrations is more attractive than one without them. Some children even choose their books by the pictures. Recognizing this, each year publishers produce an increasing number of picture books. Since they are usually the child's first experience with literature, picture books have long been a significant part of children's literary experience. As youngsters develop reading skills they still enjoy illustrations in their novels and informational books.

Pictures can not only add to the reader's enjoyment, but by clarifying or extending the textual meaning add to the reader's understanding of the situation or information presented. Early writers of children's books were aware of the effectiveness of pictures and included them in their works.

EARLY DEVELOPMENTS

The first European illustrated book for children was *Orbis Sensualuim Pictus* written by John Amos Comenius, a bishop of the Moravian church. Instead of having his book printed in Hungary, Comenius traveled to Nuremberg so the illustrated plates could be engraved, a process that took three years. Each page of *Orbis Pictus* contains a Latin text, a literal translation, and a picture designed not only to illustrate the lesson, but also to make it more interesting.

Soon after its publication in 1657, *Orbis Pictus* was translated into English by Charles Hoole under the title of "John Amos Comenius' *Visible World* or, a Nomenclature, and Pictures of all the Chief Things that are in the World, and of Mens Employments therein; In above 150 Copper Cuts."

The Clouds.   VIII.   Nubes.

A *Vapour*, 1. ascendeth from the *Water*.
From it a *Cloud*, 2. is made, and a *white Mist*, 3. near the Earth.
Rain, 4. and a small *Shower* distilleth out of a *Cloud*, drop by drop.
Which being frozen, is *Hail*, 5. half frozen is *Snow*, 6. being warm is *Mel-dew*.
In a rainy Cloud, set over against the Sun the *Rainbow*, 7. appeareth.
A *drop* falling into the water maketh a *Bubble*, 8. many *Bubbles* make froth, 9.
Frozen Water is called *Ice*, 10.
Dew congealed, is called a *white Frost*.
Thunder is made of a brimstone-like *vapour*, which breaking out of a Cloud, with *Lightning*, 11. thundereth and striketh with lightning.

Vapor, 1. ascendit ex *Aquâ*.
Inde *Nubes*, 2. fit, et *Nebula*, 3. prope terram.
Pluvia, 4. et *Imber*, stillat e *Nube*, guttatim.
Quæ gelata, *Grando*, 5. semigelata, *Nix*, 6. calefacta, *Rubigo* est.
In nube pluviosâ, oppositâ soli *Iris*, 7. apparet.

Gutta incidens in aquam, facit *Bullam*, 8. multæ *Bullæ* faciunt spumam, 9.
Aqua congelata *Glacies*, 10.
Ros congelatus, dicitur *Pruina*.
Tonitru fit ex *Vapore* sulphureo, quod erumpens è Nube cum *Fulgure*, 11. tonat & fulminat.

From *Orbis Sensualuim Pictus* by John Amos Comenius, published in 1657.

Chapbooks, also published in the seventeenth century, included tiny woodcuts. The early pictures were used first only as decoration, but as chapbooks became more and more popular the simple cuts were used to illustrate the text. However, each printer had a limited supply and one picture of a man on horseback could be found representing a king, a soldier, or a farmer in different booklets. While these woodcuts look crude in comparison to modern illustrations, many of them have a dramatic and well-balanced design. They certainly must have added to the delight felt by the children and adults who read chapbooks.

Some of the Puritan admonitory literature for children, which developed partly in opposition to the chapbooks, included illustrations. The *New England Primer* had an illustrated alphabet in addition to its religious instruction. Each letter was introduced by a rhymed couplet or triplet and a small woodcut.

By the mid-eighteenth century, battledores had developed from the horn books—small, paddle-

An early chapbook woodcut of Jack the Giant Killer, from *Illustrators of Children's Books, 1744–1945* by Bertha E. Mahony et al., 1958. Courtesy of The Horn Book, Inc.

shaped pieces of board which held lesson sheets covered with thin slices of transparent horn. Printed on these lesson sheets were a cross, the alphabet, syllables, the Lord's Prayer, and "In the name of the Father, Son, and Holy Ghost." Battledores, in contrast, were secular cardboard lesson sheets. They included the alphabet, numerals, simple reading lessons, and small illustrations.

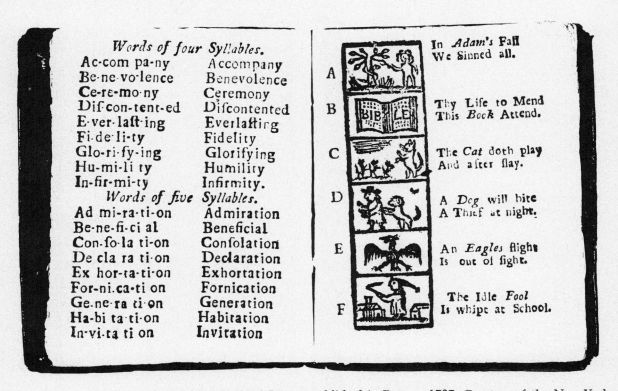

From the *New England Primer*, published in Boston, 1727. Courtesy of the New York Public Library, Rare Book Division.

Reproduction of a colonial horn book. Courtesy American Antiquarian Society.

John Newbery, one of England's first producers of children's books, published *A Little Pretty Pocket-Book* in 1744. It included "plentiful cuts" that today might be judged rather rough and crude. (See pages 9–13 for pages from this book.) But even if these illustrations were of little higher quality than the chapbook pictures, they were designed specifically for this book. The same was true for *Little Goody Two Shoes*, the first novel written for children, also published by Newbery.

Just as the authors who wrote the early children's books were anonymous, so too were the early illustrators. Not until Thomas Bewick, the first artist of merit to illustrate children's literature, made the craft respectable did other talented people sign their illustrations. Bewick became a master of wood engraving, in which the picture is carved on the end of the wood against its grain, achieving a finer line and greater control than is possible in woodcutting. In addition to Newbery's *A Pretty Book of Pictures for Little Masters and Misses: or, Tommy Trip's History of Beasts and Birds,* Bewick illustrated a number of other children's books.

Pictures were a part of most children's literature in the late eighteenth and early nineteenth centuries, but none of the artists equaled Bewick's talent. In 1846 Edward Lear's *A Book of Nonsense* was published, making Lear one of the first artist-authors for children. His line drawings for each verse are far more amusing than are any of the more recent illustrations that have since been attempted.

THE BEGINNINGS OF EXPERIMENTATION

However, except for such occasional well-designed books as Lear's, the quality of English and American pictures for children was unexceptional. In 1865 Edmund Evans, an English printer who believed color picture books of excellent quality could be inexpensively produced with the new invention of photography, began work with Frederick Warne, the only publisher willing to try the new approach, and Walter Crane, a young artist. These three men experimented with color and design in the production of "toy books" a

A wood engraving by Thomas Bewick from *History of Quadrupeds*, in *Illustrators of Children's Books, 1744–1945* by Bertha E. Mahony et al., 1958. Courtesy of The Horn Book, Inc.

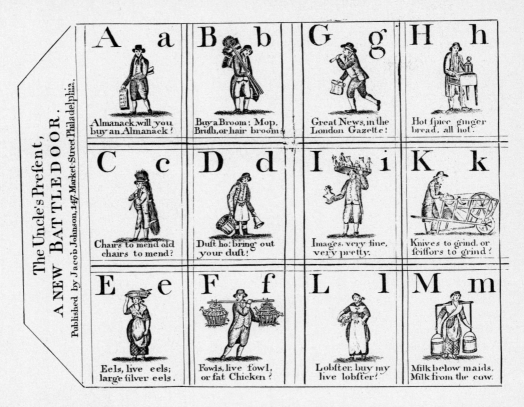

Reproduction of cardboard battledore. Courtesy American Antiquarian Society.

term used for children's small books popular at the time. Crane is also important in the history of children's literature because he was one of the first artists to be interested in the design of the entire page, the balance between text and picture.

Randolph Caldecott and Kate Greenaway, two other significant artists important in the development of children's illustrated books, also worked with Edmund Evans. Caldecott's pictures have few lines; little that is unnecessary is included, but they are filled with action and excitement. Kate Greenaway envied the life Caldecott could give a scene. Her pictures are far more static for she drew quaintly dressed, decorous children in formal English gardens. For *Under the Window* and *Marigold Garden* she wrote slight verses to accompany her pictures. While Greenaway's drawings lacked Caldecott's vitality, her work was not only very popular in England and America but also highly respected by art critics. Examples of Caldecott's and Greenaway's work can be found on color plates following page 22.

Two other important English illustrators in the nineteenth century were George Cruikshank and John Tenniel. Cruikshank's work shows both fine talent and great humor. His illustrations for fairy

There was an old person in black,
A Grasshopper jumped on his back;
When it chirped in his ear, He was smitten with fear,
That helpless old person in black.

From *A Book of Nonsense* by Edward Lear, published in 1846.

Wanda Gág's black and white picture book has already become an American classic. The repetition of curved lines in the clouds, hills, trees, and road echoes the feeling of warmth and security developed by the text. Illustrations and words are balanced to create well-designed pages. Reprinted by permission of Coward-McCann, Inc. from *Millions of Cats* by Wanda Gág. Copyright © 1928, 1956 by Wanda Gág.

"If we only had a cat!" sighed the very old woman.
"A cat?" asked the very old man.
"Yes, a sweet little fluffy cat," said the very old woman.
"I will get you a cat, my dear," said the very old man.

tales and Mrs. Ewing's *Brownies and Other Tales* (1870) are especially good because he was able to give each character a unique and recognizable personality. John Tenniel's most important illustrations for children were for *Alice's Adventures in Wonderland* and *Through the Looking-glass and What Alice Found There*. The relationship between text and pictures is exceptionally good. No one who first read the Alice books with Tenniel's illustrations can accept any other concept of Alice or the many fantastic creatures that seem as much a vision of Tenniel's mind as of Dodgson's, (Lewis Carroll).

AMERICAN DEVELOPMENTS

America's Howard Pyle deserves to stand with the leading nineteenth-century English illustrators. His work, beginning in 1877, had a great influence on American children's literature. Before Pyle, the American artistic tradition was sentimental and "elegant," and technical excellence

"Pig and Pepper" from *Alice's Adventures in Wonderland* by Lewis Carroll, illustrated by John Tenniel, published in 1865.

"Robin Shooteth His Last Shaft" from *The Merry Adventures of Robin Hood* by Howard Pyle, published in 1883 by Charles Scribners' Sons.

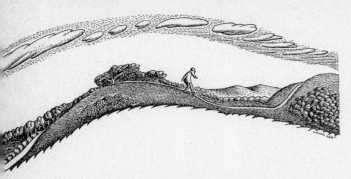

And he set out over the hills to look for one. He climbed over the sunny hills. He trudged through the cool valleys. He walked a long, long time and at last he came to a hill which was quite covered with cats.

bordering on photographic realism was considered "artistic." The results were lifeless, stilted, saccharine pictures. Pyle's style was vigorous and bold. His drawings showed a heroic romance of knighthood and his stories were filled with adventure. They must have delighted children accustomed to the sentimental. No one has more powerfully revealed the life and personalities of Robin Hood and his band than Howard Pyle.

His influence on American children's literature extended into the twentieth century, not simply because his last books were published in the first decade of this century, but because he had great influence on younger American illustrators. From 1894 until 1900 Pyle taught two weekly classes for the Drexel Institute of Arts and Sciences in Philadelphia. In 1900 he built a studio adjoining his own where he worked daily with selected advanced students such as N. C. Wyeth, Maxfield Parrish, Elizabeth Shippen Green, Frank Schoonover, and Jessie Willcox Smith, artists who significantly contributed to twentieth-century American children's literature.

In the 1920s and 1930s, book illustrations became increasing important and creative. Many artists had come to America to escape the troubles in Europe. The d'Aulaires from Switzerland, the Petershams from Hungary, Boris Artzybasheff from Russia, Kate Sereday from Hungary, and Fritz Eichenberg from Germany are the most well known, and all have enriched the illustrated books available for American children.

Picture books became more varied during these years because new technological developments in printing made possible better and less expensive reproduction of illustrations done in a variety of media. A greater realism and new freshness developed in children's books with fewer attempts to give the readers only what was "good" for them. It was during this period that Wanda Gág's *Millions of Cats*, considered by many to be America's first great picture book, was published. World War II interrupted these developments, but since the war's end the number of picture and illustrated books published in America has mushroomed.

TYPES OF PICTURE BOOKS

Some books for very young children have no text, the story being told entirely by the illustrations. *What Whiskers Did* by Ruth Carroll shows what happens to a rabbit-chasing dog when he is pursued by a bigger dog. Without words *The Magic Stick* by Kjell Ringi lets the reader become a weight lifter, or a general, and play many other active roles.

Other picture books use only a few words to extend the illustrations. Brian Wildsmith's *Birds* is one such book; under each picture is a phrase. Alphabet books often have only a few words. The best of these books for the very young use objects familiar to children as illustrations for each letter. Such words as "gnat" and "knight" are not only meaningless to most three- and four-year-olds, but their initial sound does not match the first letters. Wanda Gág's *ABC Bunny* and Roger Duvoisin's *A for the Ark* are more complex than many alphabet books because they have slender narrative threads to give continuity. Thomas Mathiesen's *ABC, An Alphabet Book* has complete sentences. Both Edward Lear, in his *Lear Alphabet: ABC*, and Phyllis McGinley, in her *All around the Town*, illustrated by Helen Stone, wrote verses to accompany each letter and its picture.

There is no more enjoyable introduction to poetry and art than a beautifully illustrated collection of Mother Goose. Many editions are available. Kate Greenaway's *Mother Goose, or Old Nursery Rhymes* was published in 1881, but its quaint illustrations still have charm. Tasha

Tudor's *Mother Goose* also has a quiet softness. A bolder style of illustration, but still with period costumes, is found in Blanche Fisher Wright's *The Real Mother Goose*. In contrast to these books, Feodor Rojankovsky's characters wear modern dress in *The Tall Book of Mother Goose*. Brian Wildsmith's *Mother Goose* is illustrated with vivid watercolors. Other editions too lovely not to mention are *Lavender's Blue*, edited by Kathleen Lines and illustrated by Harold Jones, and *Mother Goose and Nursery Rhymes* by Phillip Reed, an exceptional example of a well-designed book. Two large collections are *The Book of Nursery and Mother Goose Rhymes* by Marguerite de Angeli, with over two hundred pictures, and *The Mother Goose Treasury* by Raymond Briggs, which has four hundred rhymes and illustrations.

There are, of course, many more Mother Goose collections, and each year new ones appear. The following are some points to be considered in selecting a Mother Goose edition:

Are the illustrations original and fresh or do they seem imitative?

Do they extend and complement the verses or are they used merely to decorate the pages?

Does the arrangement of verses and pictures add to the book's beauty or are they too crowded together to be enjoyed and "read" by young children?

Which type of illustrations, modern or traditional, do you prefer?

How extensive a collection do you wish?

In a true picture book, as the term is commonly used, neither the words nor the illustrations are separable since both are needed for the full story to be understood. Because these books are meant to be read aloud, the vocabulary is not controlled. While the parent, teacher, or librarian

Beth and Joe Krush's use of spidery lines appropriately suggests the fragility of the Borrower's life. This scene reinforces the author's use of detail to create believability. From *The Borrowers* by Mary Norton, illustrated by Beth and Joe Krush. Copyright, 1952, 1953, by Mary Norton. Reprinted by permission of Harcourt Brace Jovanovich, Inc.

reads the text, the children follow the story through the pictures. Children pay close attention to details and are disappointed when the picture disagrees in number, size, shape, or color with the word descriptions. But the pictures do more than accurately represent the text, they help develop the story's mood, reveal characterization, and can even portray action without words. Maurice Sendak does this in *Where the Wild Things Are.* (See color insert following page 22.) When Max reaches the land of the "wild things," Sendak stops the text for several pages of a "wild rumpus." These illustrations take the longest for three- and four-year-old boys to "read." They look, touch, and discuss each monster. This is the type of child participation that is important in the development of a child's love of reading. It can be encouraged by giving the child the time he wants to study the pictures, by listening to his running commentary as he "reads" them, and by asking him questions about what he sees. One three-year-old considered very carefully before he decided that Max was his favorite "monster." Sendak's pictures not only carry the action but also qualify the idea of "monster." His muted grayish blues, greens, and pinks create soft, roly-poly, fantastic creatures that look almost cuddly. In these ways, then, illustrations can extend the text and reveal the story's mood as well as its action.

As Mother Goose is the young child's first introduction to poetry, picture books are his introduction to fiction, and so the quality of writing is as important as the illustrations. While the book may be too brief to allow for character development, personality can be revealed. *Millions of Cats* by Wanda Gág proves that even simple, short books can be written in an excellent style. Yet excellent pictures may accompany and support a poorly written text. This imbalance can prevent the book from being as valuable an addition to children's literature as it could have been. Unfortunately the Caldecott Committee is less concerned with the text than with the quality of the illustrations in the selection of their annual award for the best American picture book.

Most picture books are for young children but there are some for older students. Barbara Cooney's *Chanticleer and the Fox* is one excellent example. Her text is long and complete enough to stand alone but, as every reader would agree, is

Mary Shepard's sketch reveals Mary Poppin's stiffness and vanity, yet also shows Jane and Michael's trust and affection. Both *Mary Poppins* and *The Borrowers* are excellently illustrated books. They show how black and white sketches add to the reader's understanding of scene and character development. From *Mary Poppins* by P. L. Travers, illustrated by Mary Shepard. Copyright 1934, 1962, by P. L. Travers. Reprinted by permission of Harcourt Brace Jovanovich, Inc.

enriched by her excellent pictures. (See color insert following page 22.) However, relatively few picture books are published for children who can read alone and who thus are less dependent on pictures for meaning.

While illustrations play a less important role in books for independent readers, they can still be used effectively to extend and clarify the text. In *Rabbit Hill*, Robert Lawson's pictures of Father Rabbit in a rocking chair stroking his whiskers and of Uncle Analdas taking his first bath in years give this fantasy a greater sense of reality. Beth and Joe Krush's line drawings in *The Borrowers* not only picture the Borrower's world but give the reader a more vivid understanding of Pod, Homily, and Arrietty's size by showing them in relation to pencils, spools of thread, and potatoes.

There are picture books in every category of

Maurice Sendak's sophisticated engravings suit the tone of his picture book for older children. A *New Yorker* book reviewer suggested in 1967 that Sendak has too much talent to illustrate children's books, an idea with shocking overtones. He is one of the best modern artists for children. Illustration from *Higglety Pigglety Pop! or There Must Be More to Life* by Maurice Sendak. Copyright © 1967 by Maurice Sendak. Reprinted with permission of Harper & Row, Publishers.

fiction and nonfiction. Some deal with minority literature, others show life in a foreign country. In this anthology no separate section has been devoted to picture books. It is impossible to reprint them in their entirety, and so the texts have been placed with selections from books for older children that deal with similar topics. While the entire texts of the picture books may be printed, they do not represent the entire book. Only by reading the pictures as well as the words can the adult or child experience the complete story.

VARIETY IN STYLE AND TECHNIQUE

Not only are the subjects and types of picture books varied, but so too are the art styles. As Marcia Brown explains in her article "Distinction in Picture Books" from *Illustrators of Children's Books, 1946–1956*, no one style is most appropriate for children. Realistic pictures are not inherently "better" than impressionistic or abstract illustrations. Drawings done by children

reveal both a delight in abstract form as well as an attempt to picture the world realistically. It is important to realize that art for children is not removed from art for adults, for children's artists are influenced by the pictures they have studied, and hints of Van Gogh, Cézanne, Picasso, Roualt, and Chagall can be found in children's books.

There is also variety in the amount of intensity of color found in children's books. Some inexpensive, mass-produced books rely on bold colors to attract buyers. While children do enjoy color, many excellent books have used it quietly. *Where the Wild Things Are*, Marcia Brown's *Once a Mouse* and *Cinderella*, and Robert McCloskey's *Time of Wonder* are only four examples of subtly colored books that have delighted many children. And the importance of color can be overestimated, for many black and white drawings have been popular and quite effective. Wanda Gág's *Millions of Cats* and Howard Pyle's many illustrations prove the evocative ability of line. The continued popularity of Robert McCloskey's brown-toned *Make Way for Ducklings* and his blue and white

One Morning in Maine show that children accept monochromatic pictures. It is not the amount of color used that is important in children's books, but the ability of the colors to accent and complement the story's mood and plot.

Modern artists use a great variety of techniques. Woodcuts, so important in early printing, are still effective. Marcia Brown used the wood's grain to add texture in *Once a Mouse*, her literary version of an Indian fable. Stone lithography was used by McCloskey for *Make Way for Ducklings*. The pictures were drawn on stone with a greased pencil, and the exposed stone was then treated with ink repellent so that when printed the ink would adhere only to the grease. The stone's grain was used for added texture. Both of these techniques are quite old. Additional advances in photographic methods of printing have given the artists a wider selection of media. With new photographic methods combined with offset lithography, originals done in collage, watercolor, crayon, oil, pastel, tempera, and gouache can be accurately and economically mass produced.

The relatively new advances in printing have been accompanied by a proliferation of children's picture books. Some of these books have been quickly and cheaply produced. Yet each year care-

Beatrix Potter's small books are as beloved by young children today as they were when first published. *The Tale of Peter Rabbit* is one of the most popular classics for small children. Miss Potter's pictures reveal with quiet charm her love of animals and the country. From *The Tale of Peter Rabbit*, written and illustrated by Beatrix Potter. Published by Frederick Warne & Co., Ltd., 1903.

Robert McCloskey brought ducklings into his home so he could sketch their stages of development. That careful preparation shows in this scene which has so much life and reality. This picture also is an exceptional example of pictorial unity. From *Make Way for Ducklings* by Robert McCloskey. Copyright 1941, copyright © renewed 1969 by Robert McCloskey. Reprinted by permission of The Viking Press, Inc.

Garth Williams' sketches perfectly illustrates Laura Ingalls Wilder's stories of pioneer childhood. The many pictures reveal the family solidarity and love so important in these books. It is interesting to compare the bold illustrations of the early books with the finer, more restrained line drawings of the later novels. Williams adjusted his style to Mrs. Wilder's increasingly mature language in each succeeding book. Illustration by Garth Williams from *The Little House in the Big Woods* by Laura Ingalls Wilder. Copyright 1953, as to pictures, by Garth Williams. Reprinted with permission of Harper & Row, Publishers.

ful, artistically written and illustrated books appear for sale. These can provide the experiences that will help mold children's growing aesthetic taste. Good pictures in early books may not develop adult art lovers, but they will help each child become more aware of the beauty around him. The artist's selection and arrangement of detail, color, line, and form all can attune the child's eye to those elements in his own world.

The pictures that can bring such insight go beyond skill. They have life, vitality, and originality. They do not show one-sided, still forms and shapes lying flat on the paper nor are they simply colorful decorations to catch and momentarily hold the eye. The illustrations that a child returns to again and again are those with enough in them to invite and permit the reader's imaginative involvement.

Related Reading

Books for Adults

Aesop. *Aesop: Five Centuries of Illustrated Fables.* Selected by John J. McKendry. New York: Metropolitan Museum of Art, 1964. The illustrations are from the Museum's collections of prints. Scholars and children will both enjoy this beautiful book. Provides an overview of book illustrations from 1476 to 1963.

Arbuthnot, May Hill. *Children and Books,* 3d ed. Glenview, Ill.: Scott, Foresman, 1964. Chapter 4 discusses the history of illustrations in children's books.

Cianciolo, Patricia. *Illustrations in Children's Books.* Dubuque, Iowa: William C. Brown, 1970. An interesting discussion of quality, style, and media in children's illustrated books.

Colby, Jean Poindexter. *Writing, Illustrating and Editing Children's Books.* New York: Hastings, 1967. An editor's insights on children's literature. An interesting discussion of illustrated books.

Foster, Joanna. *Pages, Pictures, and Print.* New York: Harcourt, 1958. Explains the stages in publishing and printing a book.

Greenaway, Kate. *The Kate Greenaway Treasury.* Edited by Edward Ernest, assisted by Patricia Tracy Lowe. Introduction by Ruth Hill Viguers. Cleveland, Ohio: World, 1967. A collection of Kate Greenaway's writings and illustrations.

Huck, Charlotte S., and Doris Young Kuhn. *Children's Literature in the Elementary School,* 2d ed. New York: Holt, Rinehart and Winston, 1968. Excellent discussion of picture books and illustrated books. Helpful in developing evaluation skill.

Hudson, Derek. *Arthur Rackham: His Life and Work.* New York: Scribner, 1961. A biography of an important nineteenth-century illustrator.

Hürlimann, Bettina. *Picture-Book World.* Translated and edited by Brian W. Alderson with a bio-bibliographical supplement by Elizabeth Waldmann. Cleveland: World, 1968. A broad discussion of the developments in picture books in twenty-four countries since World War II. Most of the book is a collection of illustrations with brief comments.

James, Philip B. *English Book Illustrations: 1800–1900.* Baltimore, Md.: Penguin Books, 1947. Helpful for the many examples of early illustrations beginning with the Bewicks and Blake.

Kingman, Lee, ed. *Newbery and Caldecott Medal Books: 1956–1965.* Boston: Horn Book, 1965. Biographies and acceptance speeches by the winners of the two American awards for excellence in children's literature.

Kingman, Lee, Joanna Foster, and Ruth Giles Lontoft, eds. *Illustrators of Children's Books 1957–1966.* Boston: Horn Book, 1968. Excellent articles by Adrienne Adams, Marcia Brown, Rumer Godden, and Grace Hogarth accompany information about the development of illustration in contemporary children's literature. As in the two earlier books of this series, also included are helpful biographies of artists and artist and author bibliographies.

Klemin, Diana. *The Art of Art for Children's Books.* New York: Potter, 1966. Examples of sixty-four contemporary artists' work with brief notes on each.

Miller, Bertha Mahony, *et al.*, compilers. *Illustrators of Children's Books: 1744–1945*. Boston: Horn Book, 1947 (reprinted in 1961).
————. *Illustrators of Children's Books: 1946–1956*. Boston: Horn Book, 1958. Excellent reference books: many fine essays by experts and helpful biographies of illustrators.
Miller, Bertha Mahony, and Elinor W. Field, eds. *Caldecott Medal Books: 1938–1957*. Boston: Horn Book, 1957. Biographies and acceptance speeches of each winner of the Caldecott Award.
Muir, Percy. *English Children's Books 1600 to 1900*. London: Batsford, 1954. An excellent discussion of children's literature with a very helpful chapter on illustrations in early books.

Pitz, Henry C. *Illustrating Children's Books: History—Technique—Production*. New York: Watson Guptill, 1963. English, European, and American illustrated books are discussed. Information about the technical aspects of illustrating is also given. A thoughtful survey of children's literature from the viewpoint of the illustrator.
Smith, James Steel. *A Critical Approach to Children's Literature*. New York: McGraw-Hill, 1967. One chapter deals with illustrated books.
Smith, Lillian H. *The Unreluctant Years; A Critical Approach to Children's Literature*. Chicago: American Library Association, 1953. An excellent discussion of children's books with a fine chapter on picture books.

Selected Bibliography for Children

PICTURE BOOKS

Alexander, Lloyd. *Coll and His White Pig*. Illustrated by Evaline Ness. New York: Holt, Rinehart and Winston, 1965. An introduction to the land of Prydain for children too young for Alexander's stories about that country. Coll rescues Hen Wen from the Lord of the Land of Death. (Grades 1–3)
Bontemps, Arna. *Lonesome Boy*. Illustrated by Feliks Topolski. Boston: Houghton Mifflin, 1955. A mood story about a young New Orleans Negro boy and his love for his trumpet and jazz. (Grade 5–up)
Brooke, L. Leslie, author-illustrator. *Johnny Crow's Garden*. New York: Warne, 1903, first published. A charmingly illustrated picture book that still delights children. Other books in the series are: *Johnny Crow's New Garden*, 1935, 1963; *Johnny Crow's Party*, 1907, first published. (Preschool–grade 2)
Brown, Marcia, author-illustrator. *Felice*. New York: Scribner, 1958. A well-written, lushly illustrated story of a homeless cat in Venice. (Grades K–2)
————. *Tamarindo*. New York: Scribner, 1960. The adventures of four Italian boys who set out to recover a lost donkey and lose their clothes to goats. (Grades K–2)
Brown, Margaret Wise. *The Dead Bird*. Illustrated by Remy Charlip. New York: Scott, 1958. A simple picture book about a group of children who while playing find a dead bird which they bury. Soon they are playing again. (Preschool–grade 1)
Bulla, Clyde Robert. *The Moon Singer*. Illustrated by Trina Schart Hyman. New York: Crowell, 1969. A sensitively written and beautifully illustrated story about a young boy who is at first scorned and then honored for his singing. Perhaps Bulla's best book. An illustration from this picture book is found in the color plates. Older children will have even more enjoyment than younger readers. (Grades 3–6)
Burton, Virginia Lee, author-illustrator. *The Little House*. Boston: Houghton Mifflin, 1942. As the years pass, the town reaches toward the little farm house in the country. Eventually it is surrounded by the busy city. After even more years someone moves the house into the country and it is among the hills and farms once more. Awarded the 1943 Caldecott Medal. (Grades K–2)
————, author-illustrator. *Mike Mulligan and His Steam Shovel*. Boston: Houghton Mifflin, 1939. Mary Ann, Mike's steam shovel, faces obsolescence; only when they succeed in one last challenge can they settle down. (Grades K–2)
Carlson, Natalie Savage. *A Brother for the Orphelines*. Illustrated by Garth Williams. New York: Harper & Row, 1959. A popular series of books about a group of contented French orphans who do not want to be adopted. (Grades K–3)
————. *The Happy Orphelines*. Illustrated by Garth Williams. New York: Harper & Row, 1957. (Grades K–3)
————. *The Orphelines in the Enchanted Castle*. Illustrated by Adriana Saviozzi. New York: Harper & Row, 1964. (Grades K–3)
————. *A Pet for the Orphelines*. Illustrated by Fermin Rocker. New York: Harper & Row, 1962. (Grades K–3)
Caudill, Rebecca. *A Pocketful of Cricket*. Illustrated

by Evaline Ness. New York: Holt, Rinehart and Winston, 1964. A discussion of and an excerpt from this picture book can be found in Chapter 7, Domestic Fiction. (Grades K–2)

Dennis, Wesley, author-illustrator. *Flip*. New York: Viking, 1941. A horse story for the youngest readers. (Grades K–1)

————. *Flip and the Cows*. New York: Viking, 1942. A sequel to *Flip*. (Grades K–1)

De Regniers, Beatrice Schenk. *May I Bring a Friend?* Illustrated by Beni Montressor. New York: Atheneum, 1964. An amusing story of the antics of unusual "friends" brought to visit the king and queen. (Grades K–2)

Duvoisin, Roger, author-illustrator. *Petunia*. New York: Knopf, 1950. An amusing picture book about a goose. Some of the other animal fantasies by Duvoisin are: *Lonely Veronica*, 1963; *Veronica*, 1961; *Veronica's Smile*, 1964. (Preschool–grade 2)

Economakis, Olga. *Oasis of the Stars*. Illustrated by Blair Lent. New York: Coward-McCann, Inc., 1965. A picture book about the life of a nomadic desert family. The stylized illustrations add to the story. (Grades K–2)

Edmonds, Walter D. *The Matchlock Gun*. Illustrated by Paul Lantz. New York: Dodd, Mead, 1941. An excellent historical fiction picture book. Awarded the 1942 Newbery Medal. A discussion of and an excerpt from this novel can be found in Chapter 10, Historical Fiction. (Grades 2–4)

Estes, Eleanor. *The Hundred Dresses*. Illustrated by Louis Slobodkin. New York: Harcourt, 1944. A moving story of a little girl who always wore the same dress but, when teased and taunted by her classmates, claimed to have one hundred others at home. (Grades 2–4)

Ets, Marie Hall, author-illustrator. *Gilberto and the Wind*. New York: Viking, 1963. A picture story about a young boy's relationship with the wind. (Grades K–1)

————. *Mr. Penny's Race Horse*. New York: Viking, 1956. An amusing picture story of how Mr. Penny's animals conspire to help him win prizes at the fair. (Grades 1–3)

Fatio, Louise. *The Happy Lion*. Illustrated by Roger Duvoisin. New York: McGraw-Hill, 1954. A picture book about a lion in a French zoo who decides to visit all his friends among the townspeople. Other books in the series are: *The Happy Lion and the Bear*, 1964; *The Happy Lion in Africa*, 1955; *The Happy Lion Roars*, 1957; *The Happy Lion's Quest*, 1961; *The Three Happy Lions*, 1959. (Grades 1–3)

Francoise, pseud. (Francoises Seignobosc), author-illustrator. *Jeanne-Marie* Series. New York: Scribner. *The Big Rain*, 1961. A picture storybook about a French farm family caught in a flood. Other books about the same girl are: *Jeanne-Marie at the Fair*, 1959; *Jeanne-Marie Counts Her Sheep*, 1957; *Jeanne-Marie in Gay Paris*, 1956; *Noel for Jeanne-Marie*, 1953; *Springtime for Jeanne-Marie*, 1955; *What Time Is It, Jeanne-Marie?* 1963. (Preschool–grade 2)

Gág, Wanda, author-illustrator. *Millions of Cats*. New York: Coward-McCann, Inc., 1928. A discussion of this book and its entire text can be found in Chapter 11, Fantasy. A picture from it is reproduced on pages 24–25. (Preschool–grade 4)

Gramatky, Hardie, author-illustrator. *Little Toot*. New York: Putnam, 1939. A picture book about a small tugboat who proves his worth by rescuing an ocean liner. (Grades K–2)

Hader, Berta and Elmer, authors–illustrators. *The Big Snow*. New York: Macmillan, 1948. A plotless picture book about a little old man and woman who put out food for the animals and birds all winter. Awarded the 1949 Caldecott Medal. (Grades K–3)

Handforth, Thomas, author-illustrator. *Mei Li*. New York: Doubleday, 1938. A picture book about a little Chinese girl who goes to the fair. Awarded the 1939 Caldecott Medal. (Grades 1–3)

Johnson, Crockett, author-illustrator. *Harold and the Purple Crayon*. New York: Harper & Row, 1955. Imaginative picture book. Harold's crayon can draw him into and out of anything. Other books in the series are: *Harold's Circus*, 1959; *Harold's Fairy Tale*, 1956; *Harold's Trip to the Sky*, 1957. (Preschool–grade 2)

Keats, Ezra Jack, author-illustrator. *Goggles!* New York: Macmillan, 1969. Peter finds a pair of motorcycle goggles and has to flee a gang of boys who want to take them away from him. (Grades K–2)

————. *Jennie's Hat*. New York. Harper & Row, 1966. With the birds' help, Jennie's plain hat is transformed into the most elaborately beautiful hat of all. A charming picture book. (Grades K–2)

————. *John Henry: An American Legend*. New York: Pantheon, 1965. Powerfully illustrated picture book, one that reflects the power of the John Henry legend. Good introduction to American hero tales for younger children; will also be enjoyed by older elementary graders. (Grades K–3)

————. *Peter's Chair*. New York: Harper & Row, 1967. Peter's jealousy of his baby sister who was sleeping in his crib and was going to use his highchair shows Peter's adjustment to sharing. While not as successful as *The Snowy Day*, it is still a charming book. (Grades K–3)

————. *The Snowy Day*. New York: Viking, 1962. An excellent picture-book story about a young Negro boy's enjoyment of a beautiful snowy day. Awarded the 1963 Caldecott Award. (Preschool–Grade 1)

————. *Whistle for Willie*. New York: Viking, 1964. A picture book about a little boy who wanted to whistle like the bigger boys. (Preschool–grade 1)

Kipling, Rudyard. *The Elephant's Child*. Illustrated by Feodor Rojankovsky. New York: Garden City Books, 1942. (Grades 3–6)

————. *How the Camel Got His Hump*. Illustrated by Feodor Rojankovsky. New York: Garden City Books, 1942. (Grades 3–6)

————. *How the Leopard Got His Spots*. Illustrated by Feodor Rojankovsky. New York: Garden City Books, 1942. Picture-book treatment of three of Kipling's most popular titles. (Grades 3–6)

————. *Just-So Stories*. Illustrated by Nicolas. New York: Doubleday, 1902, 1952. Ever-popular tales. (Grades 3–6)

Langstaff, John, reteller. *Frog Went A-Courtin'*. Illustrated by Feodor Rojankovsky. New York: Harcourt, 1955. Picture-book treatment of a nonsensical old Scottish ballad. Awarded the 1956 Caldecott Medal. (Grades K–2)

Lawson, Robert, author-illustrator. *Rabbit Hill*. New York: Viking, 1945. With a new family moving into the Big House, all the wild animals were anxious about their attitudes toward gardening and animals. A fine fantasy with good characterization. (Grades 3–6)

————. *Robbut, A Tale of Tails*. New York: Viking, 1948. An amusing story about a rabbit discontented with his tail. The moral does not spoil the reader's enjoyment. (Grades 1–4)

————. *The Tough Winter*. New York: Viking, 1954. A sequel to *Rabbit Hill*. (Grades 3–6)

Leaf, Munro. *The Story of Ferdinand*. Illustrated by Robert Lawson. New York: Viking, 1936. The amusing story of a peace-loving bull who did not want to hurt bullfighters. (Grades K–3)

Lindgren, Astrid. *Springtime in Noisy Village*. Illustrated by Ilon Wikland. New York: Viking, 1965. A picture-book story about the everyday adventures of seven Swedish country children. (Grades K–3)

Lindgren, Astrid, adapter. *The Tomten and the Fox*. From a poem by Karl-Erik Forsslund. Illustrated by Harald Wiberg. New York: Coward-McCann, Inc., 1961. The Tomten is a protector of Swedish farms. The peace of Christmas night and a snow covered farm are shown in this exceptionally beautiful picture book. (Grades 1–4)

Lionni, Leo, author-illustrator. *Inch by Inch*. New York: Obolensky, 1959. A simple picture book about an inchworm who cleverly avoids being eaten by the birds. (Preschool–grade 1) Also of interest:

————. *Little Blue and Little Yellow*. New York: Obolensky, 1959. (Grades K–2)

————. *Swimmy*. New York: Pantheon, 1963. These last two picture books have overtones of subtle social commentary. (Grades K–1)

Lobel, Anita, author-illustrator. *The Troll Music*. New York: Harper & Row, 1966. A picture book about a group of bewitched musicians whose music sounds like animal noises. They attempt to placate the troll whose spell has them in its power. (Grades K–3)

McCloskey, Robert, author-illustrator. *Blueberries for Sal*. New York: Viking, 1948. An amusing picture storybook about a little girl and a baby bear who follow each other's mothers while picking berries. (Preschool–grade 2)

————. *Burt Dow, Deep-Water Man*. New York: Viking, 1963. A delightful fantasy about the encounter of a seaman and his leaky boat with a school of whales. (Grades 1–3)

————. *Lentil*. New York: Viking, 1940. An amusing picture-book story of a young boy who saves the day. (Grades 1–3)

————. *Make Way for Ducklings*. New York: Viking, 1941. An interesting picture book about a pair of ducks who hatch their eggs in a Boston park. Awarded the 1942 Caldecott Medal. (Grades K–3)

————. *One Morning in Maine*. New York: Viking, 1952. A sequel to *Blueberries for Sal*, three years later. (Preschool–grade 2)

————. *Time of Wonder*. New York: Viking, 1957. A beautiful picture book about the beauties of nature and the pleasures of spending summer on a Maine Island. Awarded the 1958 Caldecott Medal. (Grades 2–5)

MacDonald, Golden, pseud. (Margaret Wise Brown.) *The Little Island*. Illustrated by Leonard Weisgard. New York: Doubleday, 1946. Illustrated with lovely painting which, together with the text, builds an appreciation of beauty and nature. (Preschool–grade 2)

Matsuno, Masako. *A Pair of Red Clogs*. Illustrated by Kazue Mizamura. Cleveland: World Publishing, 1960. A poignant picture story about a young girl in Japan. (Grades K–2)

Miles, Miska. *The Fox and the Fire*. Illustrated by John Schoenherr. Boston: Little, Brown, 1966.

Powerful, realistic picture book about a fox caught in a forest fire. (Grades K–3)

Ness, Evaline, author-illustrator. *Sam, Bangs & Moonshine*. New York: Holt, Rinehart and Winston, 1966. Sam (Samantha, a motherless girl) liked to talk "moonshine"—her mother was not dead, she was a mermaid, her cat Bangs talked to her, her pets included a baby kangaroo and a lion (both imaginary). This imagining worried her father, but it was not until it almost caused her friend's death that Sam learned the seriousness of "moonshine." An interesting book, but one whose message implies that imagination is not only dangerous, but bad. Awarded the 1967 Caldecott Medal. (Preschool–grade 3)

Newberry, Clare Turlay, author-illustrator. *April's Kittens*. New York: Harper & Row, 1940.

————. *Mittens*. New York: Harper & Row, 1936. Picture storybooks about children and the cats they love. (Preschool–grade 2)

Oleson, Claire. *For Pepita—An Orange Tree*. Illustrated by Margot Tomes. Garden City, New York: Doubleday, 1967. A picture book about a young Spanish girl who wants an orange tree for her seventh birthday. (Grades 1–3)

Payne, Emmy. *Katy No-Pocket*. Illustrated by H. A. Rey. Boston: Houghton Mifflin, 1944. An amusing picture book about a kangaroo who had no pocket in which to carry her son. (Grades K–2)

Potter, Beatrix, author-illustrator. *The Tailor of Gloucester*. New York: Warne, n.d. A Christmas story. (Preschool–grade 2)

————. *The Tale of Benjamin Bunny*. New York: Warne, 1904, first published. A sequel to *Peter Rabbit*. (Preschool–grade 2)

————. *The Tale of Jemima Puddle-Duck*. New York: Warne, 1908, first published. A humorous story of a duck who is determined to hatch her eggs. (Preschool–grade 2)

————. *The Tale of Mrs. Tittlemouse*. New York: Warne, 1910, first published. An amusing story about a very tidy woodmouse. (Preschool–grade 2)

————. *The Tale of Peter Rabbit*. New York: Warne, 1903, first published. Still a classic young children love. The entire text and discussion of this book can be found in Chapter 11, Fantasy. (Preschool–grade 2)

————. *The Tale of Squirrel Nutkin*. New York: Warne, 1903, originally published. Nutkin asks many riddles of Mr. Brown. (Preschool–grade 2)

————. *The Tale of Tom Kitten*. New York: Warne, 1907, first published. Three kittens undo their mother's meticulous grooming of them. (Preschool–grade 2)

————. *The Tale of Two Bad Mice*. New York: Warne, 1904, first published. A story of two mischievous mice. (Preschool–grade 2)

Rand, Ann and Paul. *I Know a Lot of Things*. Illustrated by Paul Rand. New York: Harcourt, 1956. A book to help young children notice the beauty of nature. Stylized illustrations make an effective picture book for the very young. (Preschool–grade 1)

Raskin, Ellen. *Nothing Ever Happens on My Block*. New York: Atheneum, 1967. An amusing picture book in which a bored boy complains about how dull his neighborhood is, while behind him a house burns, robbers sneak past, etc. (Grades K–2)

Sendak, Maurice, author-illustrator. *Higglety, Pigglety, Pop! Or There Must Be More to Life*. New York: Harper & Row, 1967. A humorous picture book, beautifully illustrated with engravings that will delight older children and adults. Adapted from an old nursery rhyme. (Grade 4–up)

————. *The Nutshell Library*. New York: Harper & Row, 1962. Four amusing picture books popular with young children: *Alligator All Around; Pierre; One Was Johnny; Chicken Soup with Rice*. (Preschool–grade 2)

————. *Where the Wild Things Are*. New York: Harper & Row, 1963. A naughty little boy is sent superless to bed. In his room he sails away to where the "wild things" live, where he is made king of all wild things. An excellent picture book, especially enjoyed by boys. Awarded the 1964 Caldecott Medal. (Preschool–grade 2)

Seuss, Dr., pseud. (Theodore Seuss Geisel), author-illustrator. *And To Think That I Saw It on Mulberry Street*. New York: Vanguard, 1937. A nonsense story told in verse. A small boy's imagination transforms a plain horse and wagon into an elaborate parade. (Grades K–3)

————. *The 500 Hats of Bartholomew Cubbins*. New York: Vanguard, 1938. A young peasant boy removes his hat as the king rides by only to find he still has a hat on his head. Again and again he removes his hats, each time angering the king more and more. (Grades 1–3) Other deservedly popular books by Dr. Seuss are:

————. *Horton Hatches an Egg*. New York: Random House, 1940. (Grades 1–3)

————. *Yertle the Turtle, and other Stories*. New York: Random House, 1958. A discussion of this story and its entire text can be found in Chapter 11, Fantasy. (Grade 1–up)

Tresselt, Alvin. *Hi, Mr. Robin*. Illustrated by Roger Duvoisin. New York: Lothrop, 1950. A little boy longs for spring. Duvoisin writes and illustrates simple picture books filled with love of natural beauty. Others by the same author are: *Hide and Seek Fog*, 1965; *Sun Up*, 1949; *Wake Up, City!*, 1957; *Wake Up, Farm!*, 1955; *White Snow, Bright Snow*, 1947 (Awarded the 1948 Caldecott Medal). (Preschool–grade 1)

————. *Rain Drop Splash*. Illustrated by Leonard Weisgard. New York: Lothrop, 1946. (Preschool–grade 2)

————. *A Thousand Lights and Fireflies*. Illustrated by John Moodle. New York: Parents Institute, 1965. (Preschool–grade 2)

Turkle, Brinton, author-illustrator. *Thy Friend, Obadiah*. New York: Viking, 1969. A picture book about a young boy's annoyance at the seagull who followed him everywhere. In time he learns to like its friendship. Awarded the 1969 Children's Spring Festival Award. (Grades K–3)

Uldry, Janice May. *The Moon Jumpers*. Illustrated by Maurice Sendak. New York: Harper & Row, 1959. A dreamy picture book about four children who dance and play in the moonlight before bed. (Grades K–3)

Waber, Bernard, author-illustrator. *An Anteater Named Arthur*. Boston: Houghton Mifflin, 1967. Arthur, an anteater, is very like many little boys: stubborn, loving, forgetful, lovable, funny, finicky. His story is told with amused affection by his mother. A book that comments on children's behavior in a humorous, nondidactic way. (Grades K–3) Other books by the same author are: *Lyle, Lyle, Crocodile*, 1965; *Rich Cat, Poor Cat*, 1963; *You Look Ridiculous, Said the Rhinoceros to the Hippopotamus*, 1966. Humorous picture books about animals who act and talk like people. (Grades K–2)

Ward, Lynd, author-illustrator. *The Biggest Bear*. Boston: Houghton Mifflin, 1952. A young boy raises a bear cub that grows and grows. A humorous picture book. (Grades K–3)

————. *Nic of the Woods*. Boston: Houghton Mifflin, 1965. The picture-book adventures of a boy and his dog who spend summer vacation in the woods. (Grades 1–3)

Yashima, Taro, pseud. (Jun Iwamatsu), author-illustrator. *Crow Boy*. New York: Viking, 1955. A moving picture story about a country boy who is "different" and attends a Japanese school. (Grades 2–4)

————, author-illustrator. *Umbrella*. New York: Viking, 1958. The picture story of a Japanese-American preschool girl who longs to use her new umbrella. (Preschool–grade 2)

Yashima, Taro and Mitsu, authors-illustrators. *Plenty To Watch*. New York: Viking, 1954. Simple picture-book presentation of Japanese everyday life as it was when the authors were young. (Grades K–3)

Zemach, Harve. *The Judge: An Untrue Tale*. Illustrated by Margot Zemach. New York: Farrar, 1969. An original verse story written in the style of a cumulative folktale. Amusing; will delight both elementary children and adults. (Grades K–3)

Zemach, Margot, adapter-illustrator. *Mommy, Buy Me a China Doll*. Chicago: Follett, 1966. A picture book adaptation of an Ozark children's song. A little girl begs for a china doll that her parents cannot afford. Humorous situations occur as she tries to find an object for trade. (Preschool–grade 3)

Zion, Gene. *Do You Know What I'll Do?* Illustrated by Garth Williams. New York: Harper & Row, 1958. A simple picture book about the seasons. (Preschool–grade 1)

————. *Over and Over*. Illustrated by Garth Williams. New York: Harper & Row, 1951. Picture story treatment of a progression through the year, highlighting the holidays. (Preschool–grade 1)

————. *The Sky Was Blue*. Illustrated by Garth Williams. New York: Harper & Row, 1963. A young girl looks through the photograph albums and learns about life in the past. A picture book. (Grades K–2)

Zolotow, Charlotte. *Mr. Rabbit and the Lovely Present*. Illustrated by Maurice Sendak. New York: Harper & Row, 1962. With Mr. Rabbit's help, a little girl searches for the perfect gift for her mother. An entertaining picture book. (Preschool–grade 2)

A list of individual folktales in picture book form can be found in the bibliography for Chapter 6, Folktales.

The young boy's vulnerability as well as the stolidity and annoyance
of the miller and his wife are vividly portrayed in this picture from
The Moon Singer, a sensitive, poetic literary folktale fantasy. From
The Moon Singer, text by Clyde Robert Bulla; copyright © 1969
by Clyde Robert Bulla; illustrations by Trina Shart Hyman; copyright © 1969 by Trina Shart Hyman. Thomas Y. Crowell, Inc.,
publishers.

Suddenly the wind whips the water
into sharp, choppy waves.
It tears off the sharp tops and slashes them
into ribbons of smoky spray.
And the rain comes slamming down.
The wind comes in stronger and stronger gusts.
A branch snaps from a tree.
A gull flies over, flying backward,
hoping for a chance to drop
into the lee of the island.
Out in the channel a tardy fishing boat
wallows in the waves, seeking the shelter
of Bucks Harbor.

Robert McCloskey chose watercolor to illustrate his mood story about a Maine island summer. Most of the pictures show the calm beauty of nature, but McCloskey is able to portray the force of a hurricane through powerful swatches of color. From *Time of Wonder* by Robert McCloskey. Copyright © 1957 by Robert McCloskey. Reprinted by permission of The Viking Press, Inc.

Randolph Caldecott's ability to picture action dramatically was envied by Kate Greenaway, his contemporary and friend. This scene is embossed on the Caldecott Medal given annually to the best American picture book. From *John Gilpin, Picture Book Number 1*, published 1879, illustrated by Randolph Caldecott. Reproduced by permission of Frederick Warne & Co., Ltd.

Ezra Jack Keats used collage to show Peter in the bath. The highly stylized illustrations effectively create a picture book for preschool children. Each picture carries the plot forward in a beauty of design that heightens the story's mood. From *The Snowy Day* by Ezra Jack Keats. Copyright © 1962 by Ezra Jack Keats. All rights reserved. Reprinted by permission of The Viking Press, Inc.

And he thought and thought and thought about them.

Hansel put his arm around his little sister. On and on they wandered, and the farther they went, the deeper they lost themselves in the thick black forest.

Kate Greenaway's figures are much more static than Caldecott's but they have as much quiet charm for today's viewer as they did in the nineteenth century. From *Little Ann and Other Poems* by Ann and Jane Taylor, illustrated by Kate Greenaway. Published by George Routledge & Sons, Ltd., 1882.

Left: In contrast to illustrators who achieve a variety of styles by choosing the most suitable technique and medium for each work, some illustrators are content to perfect one style. Their work is easily recognizable but can become a cliché. In *Nibble Nibble Mousekin*, Joan Walsh Anglund reveals her ability to use line and color powerfully, quite unlike the sentimental pictures in her many small books. But even in *Nibble Nibble Mousekin* she draws the noseless, mouthless, chinless, puffy-cheeked children that have become her trademark. They seem out of place amidst so much detail. Her small books, which are about but not really appropriate for children, are all drawn in the same style which in time loses its appeal. From *Nibble Nibble Mousekin* © 1962 by Joan Walsh Anglund. Reproduced by permission of Harcourt Brace Jovanovitch, Inc.

Right: From *Spring Is a New Beginning* © 1963 by Joan Walsh Anglund. Reproduced by permission of Harcourt Brace Jovanovitch, Inc.

Marcia Brown is one of the most versatile illustrators of children's books. She carefully and artistically chooses a style and medium appropriate to the mood of each story. The boldness and dramatic power of wood block prints suit this Indian fable. The picture shows an excellent use of line and design to build tension. The tiger's stripes echo and merge with the tall grass, and the wise man, no longer meditating, must watch the angry tiger. Illustration (Copyright © 1961 Marcia Brown) from *Once a Mouse*, by Marcia Brown, is reproduced with the permission of Charles Scribner's Sons.

The tiger felt offended and humiliated. He forgot all the good he had received from the old man.

"No one shall tell me that I was once a mouse. I will kill him!"

When it was first published, Maurice Sendak's *Where the Wild Things Are* shocked some adults who felt the topic of monsters was inappropriate for children. Sendak's use of soft colors as well as the monsters' paunchy bodies and long hair mute the terror of their claws and teeth. Adults may worry about the subject but young children, especially boys, relish Max's adventures as "king of all wild things." Illustration and text from *Where the Wild Things Are* by Maurice Sendak. Copyright © 1963 by Maurice Sendak. Reprinted by permission of Harper & Row, Publishers.

Bold pen line and watercolor are used to illustrate a story about friendship. This action picture brings the story to a dramatic climax. Illustration (Copyright © 1967 Marcia Brown) from *The Neighbors* by Marcia Brown is reproduced with the permission of Charles Scribner's Sons.

The fox jumped out, the fur flew about, and the fox ran off into the forest with his tail between his legs and never came back.

Now this fine rooster had seven hens, all colored exceedingly like him. The hen with the prettiest throat was called fair Demoiselle Partlet. She was polite, discreet, debonair, and companionable, and she had conducted herself so well since the time

that she was seven days old that, truly, she held the heart of Chanticleer all tightly locked. It was a great joy to hear them sing in sweet harmony when the bright sun began to rise. For in those days, so I'm told, beasts and birds could talk and sing.

Marcia Brown's pen line and crayon pictures complement the theme of beauty and kindness rewarded. Illustration (Copyright © 1954 Marcia Brown) from *Cinderella* is reproduced with the permission of Charles Scribner's Sons.

Typical of the mass produced "supermarket" books for children, this illustration is in sharp contrast to Marcia Brown's artistic interpretation of the Cinderella story. Such cake decoration art cannot give children the pleasure that original picture books can. From *Walt Disney's Cinderella*, adapted by Campbell Grant. Illustrated by the Walt Disney Studio. Copyright © 1950 Walt Disney Productions. Published by Golden Press, Inc.

Part II
FOLK LITERATURE

Nonliterate people have always depended on oral folk literature (myths, tales, legends, fables, ballads, hero tales, proverbs, maxims) for entertainment and information. And since much of the world's population is illiterate, among them this oral tradition is still alive and important. Not only does folk literature provide entertainment for these people similar to that provided by books, movies, and television for literate Europeans and Americans, but folklore is also used to explain and support the nonliterate culture's moral and social codes by holding certain types of behavior up to ridicule or praise. In addition it can give status to rituals, religious beliefs, and historical traditions by endowing them with a noble past, one often associated with or coming from the gods.

Except in the American Negro and Indian cultures, folklore no longer has an important role in the life of western man. In most of America and Europe, folk literature is seldom part of the oral tradition; rather, it is preserved in books which are primarily read by and to children.

THE IMPORTANCE
OF FOLKLORE

Yet adults as well as children can gain great understanding and pleasure from reading folklore. Not only are there many references to mythology and folktales in classical literature, these are also present in everyday speech. We say someone has a "Midas touch," is an "ugly duckling," or a "wolf in sheep's clothing." "Open Sesame" is still a fairly common expression. More important than understanding such allusions, however, is the value recognized by W. H. Auden, who in a review of an edition of Grimm's *Fairy Tales* in the November 12, 1944, *New York Times*, stated that these narratives are second only in importance to the Bible in carrying on the western tradition and so should be read by adults for their cultural significance.

Folklore offers not just a glimpse of former beliefs and universal values, but also retains the necessary continuity with the past. Histories and folklore are similar in that both attempt to find order and pattern in a chaotic world. But history is supposed to be objective and so deals primarily with outward life. Folklore, on the other hand, deals not simply with what has occurred, but with the universal, emotional truths of human nature: that the weak are abused but hope to succeed, that the clever dupe the gullible, that greed for power or gold is dangerous. These are not objective records of what has happened, but the psychological motivations that underlie man's nature and his history; therefore, folklore can provide adults with a needed insight of man, his hopes and fears, his dreams and his on-going attempts to understand himself and his world.

Mythology that embodies former beliefs should not be patronized. It is not, as it has been considered, savage man's ignorant imaginings that have been proved false and childish by scientific advancements. The makers of myths understood man as an integral part of nature. The prevalence of anthropomorphism demonstrates that they believed man was not alone in having a "spirit"; trees, animals, mountains, and the elements were all related to man and were considered to be like him in many ways. Western civilization long ago turned away from this attitude and by adopting scientific reason separated man from his environment. An increasing value was placed on man's control and manipulation of other forms of life. The technological advances made possible by such an outlook have taken western man to the moon. But his water and air are polluted, his earth abused. Perhaps the tales and myths that reveal the old relationships of mutual dependence can help reunite modern civilization and nature.

There are other values present in folklore. Many show virtue rewarded, cruelty punished. Through identifying with the underling, readers may learn to feel compassion for the abused. These narratives also offer comfort in today's confusing world, just as they have done for thousands of years. The development of the imagination is another important value of folktales. What a barren world it would be if there were no sense of wonder.

Children may read these narratives only for the sense of wonder, but adults can and should read them for their insights. They record not just the past but the forever.

Folklore has been relegated to the nursery only recently. It originally was developed by adults for adults and deals with adult concerns. For that reason many folk narratives include topics that seem incomprehensible to or inappropriate for children. Violence, hatred, jealousy, sex, infidelity, and mutilation are a part of many narratives. The inclusion of these elements has caused some adults to question the propriety of giving folk literature to children. Collections for children, however, do not emphasize these elements. Joseph Jacobs rewrote his English and Celtic tales to exclude those elements he felt were inappropriate for children. The European stories that do show violence and mutilation do not dwell upon them; they are mentioned briefly with no sense of immediacy, quite unlike some movies and television programs that prolong and emphasize brutality and terror.

Children enjoy the swiftness of action, excitement, and sense of wonder in folk literature. The simplified conflict between good and evil with the usual triumph of good satisfies their developing moral sense.

THE ORIGIN OF FOLKLORE

The serious study of folklore began in the mid-nineteenth century as an outgrowth of language study. The Grimm brothers, believing authentic folk narratives contain remnants of old forms of language, seriously collected and studied many German tales. As their language theories developed and their studies became known, more philologists turned to folklore. Soon it was discovered that folktales from many European countries were quite similar. In addition, many traditional European tales and fables were found in the early Buddhist collections from India. Soon the search for the origin of folk literature and an explanation of these similarities assumed increasing importance and attracted many scholars.

Monogenesis

Two general theories were developed to explain multiple existence of folktales. The first, *monogenesis*, or one origin, suggested that each tale, myth, or fable, had one original source from which all other variants were derived. The Grimm brothers theorized that a prehistoric group, which they called the Aryans and which present-day linguists call the Indo-Europeans, developed the originals for all the traditional tales known in Europe, India, and much of the Near East. As these people separated and migrated in many directions, they carried with them their folklore. Nineteenth-century philologists also postulated that as the original language changed and developed into many different languages, the narratives became confusing and had to be revised somewhat to make sense to new generations.

Other comparative philologists of the nineteenth century discovered a linguistic relationship between the names of some gods: e.g., Greek *Zeus*, Latin *Jupiter*, Sanskirt *Dyauspitar*, Old High German *Zui*, and old Norse *Try*. The common root of all these names means "shine." From this a theory developed that the Indo-European religion centered around a sun god and that all folktales and myths are, as Max Muller, a nineteenth-century philologist-folklorist claimed, degenerated solar myths. Traditional tales were thus considered allegories. "Little Red Ridinghood" was interpreted as an allegory about night devouring day and day escaping each morning. The tales and myths concerning imprisoned maidens rescued by heroes were also felt to show the sun's escape from night or spring's rescue from winter's hold.

This solar-myth-allegory theory developed from early language study that has, in many cases, been found to be inaccurate. It is not a presently accepted theory, although the relationship between some myths and folktales cannot be denied. The story of the Greek myth "Cupid and Psyche" is widespread in the folklore of Europe. Its similarities to the Norse tale "East o' the Sun and West o' the Moon" are obvious, as are those to "Beauty and the Beast." In some African and North American Indian cultures the relationship between myths and tales is very close; the same narrative may be told as a myth or as an entertaining story.

Another monogenic theory claimed that India was the source of all folk literature. Since early Indian collections of stories and religious writings were found to contain a number of traditional European tales and fables, this theory gained support. However, further study has revealed that many myths and tales obviously have no Oriental origins. India has contributed more than her share of folk narratives, but it is not known if the Indians created all of the tales or if India acted as a storehouse of folklore, collecting and recording from many other cultures.

Diffusion

Monogenesis theories explain multiple existence through diffusion. Travelers, traders, and soldiers, it is assumed, helped in the gradual transmission of folklore. Such a process would, of course, take much time because stories are transmitted only when a tale is heard by a storyteller, who in turn repeats it to another group. The teller must move on to more groups or pass it on to another storyteller if the tale is to continue its progress. Cultural, religious, and language differences also inhibit a narrative's diffusion. However, famines, migrations, and wars hasten the intermingling of various groups, and diffusion is traceable in the folklore of American Indians and in the Asian and African areas where European trade and colonialization were common in the eighteenth and nineteenth centuries. Diffusion, in part, is a logical explanation for the worldwide existence of some plots ("Cupid and Psyche"), themes (love overcoming sleep), and motifs, the smallest narrative elements that have independent life and occur in tales from widely scattered groups (unlikely heroes and heroines such as Boots and Cinderella).

Polygenesis

Another approach to folklore is based on the theory of *polygenesis*, many origins. Each narrative, it is theorized, could have been created independently by several or many cultures. One such approach is based on psychology. All men are said to be alike, to have the same hopes, fears, drives, and instincts. Jung claimed myths reveal a great deal about the preconscious psyche and show man's frustrations and attempts to escape from society's repressions. Certainly the many narratives that show abused, scorned heroes and heroines suddenly gaining wealth and status can be interpreted as the daydreams of the lowly or the dissatisfied, but the psychological approach goes much farther and interprets all folklore as psychological allegories. "Sleeping Beauty" is thus interpreted as a young girl's awakening to womanhood. Her pricked finger symbolizes menstruation and her long sleep the passions that lie dormant until a man's touch arouses her. While the psychological approach can provide useful insights into some tales, it can also be carried to extremes.

Another polygenesis theory is built on the assumption that every society passes through the same stages from savagery to civilization. Just as all groups have independently developed fire, weapons, homes, and family units, so too they have independently originated the same plot elements, motifs, themes, myths, and tales. Sir James Frazer, who had, as modern anthropologists point out, no actual experience with any culture other than his own, stated that all cultures develop the same rituals, myths, songs, and stories. Anthropological studies have shown, however, that this is an overstatement. More and more differences among cultures are being discovered and the old generalizations about "primitive man" are being reexamined.

There have been many theories and doubtless more will be developed to explain how some tales such as "Cupid and Psyche" and "Cinderella" have traveled so far. Over five hundred "Cinderella" stories have been found in Europe alone, and the tale is also told in Africa, Asia, and by the American Indians. There are versions of the

"Tom Thumb" story in England, France, Germany, Africa, Japan, and among some American Indian tribes. A worldwide narrative is told about swans who become girls when they lay aside their swan coats to bathe. A young man discovers them and takes one swan coat which he hides and refuses to return to the swan-girl unless she marries him. The story then continues in several different ways. It is told throughout Europe, Asia, Africa, Oceania, and by almost all of the North American Indian tribes.

Some themes appear to be universal. Almost every culture has a story in which love defeats sleep, kindness is rewarded, and selfishness, greed, and rudeness are punished. Most cultures have tales about clever tricksters and how wit wins honor or riches.

No one theory can account for the origin and development of all folk literature. However, for the modern reader and teller of folklore, multiple existence is a delight, not a puzzle. It is interesting to see how peoples in far distant parts of the world tell and enjoy similar oral and written folk literature. Also fascinating and revealing are the ways in which similar plots and themes have been adapted by each culture.

The following narratives have been selected to facilitate crosscultural comparisons. Cinderella tales from African, European, and North American Indian groups show not only the universality of this plot but also how different groups have used it to express and reinforce their social values. So too, tales from many areas that deal with clever tricksters have been grouped together. Myths from three sources important to the North American culture were chosen to reveal how these peoples explored and explained their relationship to each other, their deities, and nature.

Language excellence is an essential ingredient of all writing, but is especially important in this genre which was traditionally passed on through the oral tradition. Since the best storytellers were and are masters of language, it is essential that written tales reflect their original beauty. Too many poor retellings are on the market today. Several examples of mediocre writing are included in the following collection to permit stylistic comparisons.

Folklore has a great deal to offer both children and adults. It is hoped that this crosscultural selection will reveal how universal the tradition is and how much joy and insight it has for modern society.

Chapter 3

Mythology

From *Mythology* by Edith Hamilton. Illustration by Steele Savage. Copyright 1942 by Edith Hamilton. Reprinted by permission of Little, Brown and Company.

Greek Mythology

Myths are commonly thought to be primitive imaginings by simple people. Whatever the form of Greek mythology when told by rustic peasants, the myths that have survived to the present reveal a sophisticated and complex view of life, man, and his deities. The stories and language of these myths were polished for centuries before being recorded in the *Iliad* sometime after 1000 B.C.

A knowledge of Greek mythology is essential to an understanding of western culture and literature. There are allusions to Greek mythology not only in the "classics" but also in contemporary literature, both profound and popular. If these allusions are not understood, much of the mean-

ing and depth of literature are lost. Even newspapers, magazine articles, and television programs use mythological references. Because Greek mythology has long been central in western civilization it should be familiar to everyone. Fortunately these myths have many interesting stories so reading them is pleasurable for both children and adults.

Not all Greek myths are appropriate for children, especially those dealing with the gods' love affairs. Some of the allegorical myths are concerned with ideas too mature for young readers. But many myths are appropriate for children, and there are a number of collections rewritten for

From *Iliad of Homer* engraved from the compositions of John Flaxman. Longman, Hurst, Rees, & Orme, 1805. Reprinted in *Illustrations of Children's Books, 1744–1945* by Bertha E. Mahony et al., 1958. Courtesy of The Horn Book, Inc.

the young. Unfortunately not all books of mythology are well written, so care must be taken when selecting versions for children. Some retellings are so simplified as to be inaccurate. Such books do not transmit the Greek culture, they only mislead the reader. Another weakness is the use of imaginative embroideries that distort the original tone or significance of the myths. Style is another aspect that must be carefully evaluated. Some books have rough, choppy sentences and stilted dialogue that lose the excitement and beauty present in Greek myths. To illustrate these weaknesses a selection about Prometheus from *Adventures of the Greek Heroes* by Mollie McLean and Anne Wiseman is included in the following group of myths. A more accurate and well-written version of the Prometheus story by Olivia E. Coolidge is also included for comparison.

PRONUNCIATION GUIDE

Greek		*Roman*
Amphitryon	ăm-phĭ′-trў-ōn	
Aphrodite	ăf′ rŏ · dĭ′ · tĕ	Venus
Apollo, Phoebus	à · pŏl′ō, fē′bŭs	
Athena, Pallas	à · thē′ nà, păl′ às	Minerva
Artemis	är′ tê · mĭs	Diana
Atlas	ăt′ lăs	
Cerberus	sûr′ bĕr · ŭs	
Charon	kā′ rŏn	
Cyclops (sing.),	sī′klŏps,	
Cyclopes (plural)	sī-klō′pēz	
Daedalus	dĕd′à-lus; dē′dà-lus	
Demeter	dê · mē′ tĕr	Ceres sē′ rēz
Dionysus	dĭ′ ô · nĭ′ sŭs	Bacchus băk′ ŭs
Echo	ĕk′ ō	
Epimethus	ĕp′ ĭ · mē′ thus	
Eros	ē′ rŏs	Cupid
Eurydice	ū-rĭd′ĭ-sē	
Hades or Pluto		Dis (dĭs)
Hera	hē′ rà; hẽr′ă	Juno
Heracles	hĕr′ a · klēz	Hercules
Hermes	hĕr′ mēs	Mercury
Icarus	ĭk′ à · rŭs	
Iphicles	ĭph′ĭ clēs	
Iris	ī′rĭs	
Ixion	ĭx ī′ ŏn	
Maenads	mē′ năds	
Menelaus	mĕn ê lā′-ŭs	
Metanira	mĕt-ăn-nē′rà	
Olympus	ô · lĭm′ pŭs	
Orpheus	ôr′ fê · ŭs	
Persephone	pẽr-sĕf′ ô-nê	Proserpina pro · sûr′ pĭ · nà
Perseus	pûr′ sūs	
Phaethon	fā′ĕ-thŏn	
Polyphemus	pŏl-y-fē′mŭs	
Poseidon	pō · sī′ dŏn	Neptune
Prometheus	prô · mē′ thūs	
Procrustes	prô-krŭs′tēs	
Psyche	sī′kê	
Sisyphus	sĭs′ĭ-fŭs	
Telemachus	tē lĕm′ à kŭs	
Theseus	thē′sūs, thē′sê-ŭs	
Titan	tī′tn	

THE CREATION OF MAN

Olivia E. Coolidge

*There are many versions of the Greek creation myth; some even say Prome-
theus shaped men from clay and water and that Athena breathed life into
them. However all narratives agree that Prometheus so loved mortals that
he defied Zeus' anger for them.*

*Prometheus, wisest of all Titans, the pre-Olympic gods, instructed men in
astronomy, architecture, mathematics, medicine, metallurgy, navigation, and
other skills. He also tricked Zeus into choosing the worst part of sacrificed
animals, their bones and fat, leaving the edible portions to man.*

*Not one to accept defiance, Zeus became jealous of man's growing knowl-
edge and power. When Prometheus stole fire from the gods, Zeus, forgetful
of past help in the war between the Titans and the Olympians, had him
chained to a rock.*

*Prometheus' foresight had warned him of Zeus' revenge, yet this did not
stop the Titan. Such courage became a part of the Greek heroic ideal. His
foreknowledge adds so much depth to the myth it is unfortunate that it is
often excluded from retellings for children.*

The Greeks have several stories about how man came to be. One declares that he was created in the age of Kronos, or Saturn, who ruled before Zeus. At that time, the legend says, there was no sorrow, toil, sickness, or age. Men lived their lives in plenty and died as though they went to sleep. They tilled no ground, built no cities, killed no living thing, and among them war was unknown. The earth brought forth strawberries, cherries, and ears of wheat for them. Even on the bramble bushes grew berries good to eat. Milk and sweet nectar flowed in rivers for men to drink, and honey dripped from hollow trees. Men lived in caves and thickets, needing little shelter, for the season was always spring.

Another legend declares that Zeus conceived of animals first and he entrusted their creation to Prometheus and Epimetheus, his brother. First,

Epimetheus undertook to order all things, but he was a heedless person and soon got into trouble. Finally he was forced to appeal to Prometheus.

"What have you done?" asked Prometheus.

"Down on the earth," answered his brother, "there is a green, grassy clearing, ringed by tall oak trees and shaded by steep slopes from all but the midday sun. There I sat and the animals came to me, while I gave to each the gifts which should be his from this time forward. Air I gave to the birds, seas to the fishes, land to four-footed creatures and the creeping insects, and to some, like the moles, I gave burrows beneath the earth."

"That was well done," answered Prometheus. "What else did you do?"

"Strength," said Epimetheus, "I gave to lions and tigers, and the fierce animals of the woods. Size I gave to others like the great whales of the sea. The deer I made swift and timid, and the insects I made tiny that they might escape from sight. I gave warm fur to the great bears and the little squirrels, keen eyes and sharp talons to the birds of prey, tusks to the elephant, hide to the wild boar, sweet songs and bright feathers to the birds. To each I gave some special excellence, that whether large or small, kind or terrible, each might live in his own place, find food, escape enemies, and enjoy the wide world which is his to inhabit."

"All this is very good," said his brother, Prometheus. "You have done well. Wherein lies your trouble?"

"Because I did not think it out beforehand," said the heedless brother sadly, "I did not count how many animals there were to be before I started giving. Now when I have given all, there comes one last animal for whom I have neither skill nor shape, nor any place to dwell in. Everything has been given already."

"What is this animal," said Prometheus, "who has been forgotten?"

"His name," said Epimetheus, "is Man."

Thus it was that the future of man was left to Prometheus, who was forced to make man different from all other creatures. Therefore he gave him the shape of the gods themselves and the privilege of walking upright as they do. He gave him no special home, but made him ruler over the whole earth, and over the sea and air. Finally, he gave him no special strength or swiftness, but stole a spark from heaven and lighted a heavenly fire within his mind which should teach him to understand, to count, to speak, to remember. Man learned from it how to build cities, tame animals, raise crops, build boats, and do all the things that animals cannot. Prometheus also kindled fire on earth that man might smelt metals and make tools. In fact, from this heavenly fire of Prometheus all man's greatness comes.

Before this time fire was a divine thing and belonged only to the gods. It was one of their greatest treasures, and Zeus would never have given Prometheus permission to use it in the creation of man. Therefore when Prometheus stole it, Zeus was furious indeed. He chained Prometheus to a great, lofty rock, where the sun scorched him by day and the cruel frost tortured him by night. Not content with that, he sent an eagle to tear him, so that, though he could not die, he lived in agony. For many centuries Prometheus hung in torment, but he was wiser than Zeus, and by reason of a secret he had, he forced Zeus in later ages to set him free. By then, also, Zeus had learned that there is more in ruling than power and cruelty. Thus, the two at last were friends.

HERCULES AND PROMETHEUS

Mollie McLean
Anne Wiseman

Prometheus was a Titan, one of the pre-Olympian gods. When Zeus and his brothers and sisters challenged the Titans, Prometheus counseled compromise because, with his ability to see into the future, he knew the Olympians would be victorious. Zeus banished most of the Titans but allowed Prometheus and his brother Epimetheus their freedom because they had not fought against the Olympians.

In the following story Prometheus is said to be a mortal with no understanding of the consequences of stealing fire. This departure from the original Greek conception is unnecessary and destroys the significance and nobility of the Prometheus myth, which is as concerned with the relationship between the gods and men as it is with the origin of fire.

First of all the heroes that the poets told about was strong Hercules. He was the son of Zeus, who was king of the Greek gods. One of the stories told about Hercules was that when he was a little child two giant snakes had tried to kill him. Most babies would have been afraid, but Hercules was not. He held the snakes away from him and, with his two small hands, killed them.

As Hercules grew older, he became more and more powerful. He could do things which no other man could do. He could have used his power to hurt others, but he was kind and good. He went about the world helping people who were not as strong as he.

The first man Hercules helped was Prometheus. This is the way the story was told.

There were many Greek gods. Zeus, their king, was the most powerful of all. At one time, he called all the gods and goddesses to a meeting at his palace on Mount Olympus. They came as fast as they could because they heard that Zeus was angry. When he came before them, he had a fierce look on his face.

"I am not pleased with the kingdom of Man," roared Zeus. "Men forget their gods, and use their time looking for riches."

The gods and goddesses were angry when they heard this. They had given Man many gifts and did not want the people of the world to forget them.

"What shall we do to make Man more thankful for the things he has been given?" asked Diana, goddess of the moon.

"We shall take away one of the gifts he uses the most," answered Zeus.

The gods and goddesses began to think of the gifts they had given the world.

"We could take back my gift," said beautiful Diana. "Without my light the people would find the nights very black."

"The moon is very pretty, but men do not use it much," said Neptune, god of the sea. "They would not miss your gift as they would mine. Were the sea to dry up, men would be very unhappy."

"You are right," said Apollo, god of the sun,

"but think of what the world would be like without my gift. There would be no daylight. Trees and flowers would not grow. The world would be cold. No one could live without the sun."

"Apollo forgets one thing," said Zeus. "I do not want to kill the people of the world. I only wish to teach them a lesson. If we took the sun from Man, he would soon die."

"There is one thing we can take away from Man which he will miss very much," said Vulcan. "Let us take away my gift, fire. Without it, he will be unhappy, but he will not die."

"Good!" roared Zeus. "It shall be as you have said, Vulcan. From this day on, there will be no fire for men."

As he said this, the warm day became cold and black. A strong wind shook the trees. All the fires on earth began to go out. Soon only one was left. This, Zeus put in a hollow tube which he carried back to Mount Olympus.

"Now," said Zeus fiercely. "I shall keep this hollow tube with me always. Man will never have fire again."

After Zeus took fire away, the world was sad. When the sun went down, there was no light. Men could not find their way. Many people were lost in the black night. There was no fire to warm the people. They would try to sleep and forget how cold they were. There was no cooking. Men would bring home animals which they had killed, only to find they must eat them as they were. They remembered the feasts they had had before.

Now fierce monsters who once had been afraid of the fire carried off sheep, chickens, and cows. Sometimes they even took a little child.

Year by year, the people of the world became more unhappy. Over and over again they asked Zeus to give them back the gift of fire. They said they would not forget the gods again. They said that they would thank the gods every day for the many gifts they had been given.

The gods and goddesses did not think Zeus should keep fire from Man for so long a time. They wanted people to be happy again. They asked Zeus to give fire back to the world.

Zeus roared, "I am the king of the gods. I took fire from Man and I will give it back when I wish."

The gods and goddesses could not make Zeus

forget his anger. But they did not like to look down on a world so cold and black.

When the people of the world found that Zeus would not forget, they called a meeting. They met in an underground cave where the farseeing eyes of Zeus could not find them. They said how unhappy they were without fire. They said that they had done everything they could to please Zeus but that he would not give fire back to them.

"We must find a way to take fire back from Zeus," said one man.

"Yes," said another. "We cannot live without it any longer."

"Who would be so brave as to try to take something from the king of the gods?" asked a girl.

The people looked at one another. Their faces were sad. Every man wanted to help the world, but none was brave enough.

All at once a man stood up in the crowd.

"I will steal the fire from Zeus," he said.

Everyone at the meeting looked at him.

Then a man asked, "Who are you?"

All the people shouted, "Yes, tell us your name!"

"I am Prometheus," he said.

"I have heard of you," one man said, "and I know you are brave. But how will you take fire from Zeus? The king of the gods can see all the world from where he sits. You could not steal it, for he would see you."

Prometheus gave a laugh and said, "He can see nothing when he sleeps! I shall steal it at night."

The people looked at one another. They had not known there was so brave a man in all the world.

"When will you go?" they asked.

"I shall go now," said Prometheus. He put on his sword and walked out into the black night.

As Prometheus came near Mount Olympus, he heard the gods and goddesses laughing and singing. He saw the bright palace of Zeus where all had come to eat and drink. He heard fierce Zeus telling the story of how he had taken fire from Man. He saw the king of the gods laugh as he held over his head the hollow tube in which he had put the fire. As Zeus laughed, the walls of the palace shook, but Prometheus was not afraid.

For a long time Prometheus watched the bright windows of the palace. At last, one by one, the lights went out as the gods and goddesses went home. All was dark. Prometheus knew his time had come. Quietly, he opened the golden door of the palace. Without a sound he walked to the room where the king of the gods was sleeping. He saw the hollow tube in which Zeus had put the fire. He picked it up. Just then, powerful Zeus turned over. Prometheus jumped back and, still holding the hollow tube, put his hand on his sword. He stood quietly watching. Soon Zeus was sleeping soundly again. Prometheus ran from the palace, the hollow tube in his hand. When he reached the earth, he gave fire to everyone. The night which had been black was bright, and once again the world was happy.

In the morning Zeus found that the hollow tube was gone. His anger was so great that even Mount Olympus shook. He sent his messenger, Mercury, to earth to find out who had taken the fire. Mercury came back and said, "A man named Prometheus came in the night and took the fire back to earth."

"Who is this Prometheus that steals from the gods?" roared Zeus. "Bring him here at once!"

Mercury went back to earth as fast as he could. Soon Prometheus was standing before the king of the gods. Zeus looked hard at him. "Did you think you could steal from me, little man?" he said. As he spoke, the ground shook and the sky grew black. "I will teach you not to steal from the king of the gods," he roared.

"I am not afraid," said Prometheus. "I would steal from you again to help Man. It was not right to keep fire from him so long."

"You will never steal from anyone again," shouted Zeus. He pulled Prometheus to the window of the palace. From there they could see the whole world.

"Look down, little man," he said. "Do you see that far-off rock that overlooks the angry sea? That will be your home until the world ends."

The king of the gods went to another room in the palace and came back carrying an ugly black vulture.

"This bird will be your guard. He will watch you day and night." Zeus turned to Mercury and said, "Take this man to the place I have shown you. Chain him to the rock so he cannot move. Let the vulture fly around him." Turning to Prometheus he said, "Now, little man, we will see how brave you are." He gave a cruel laugh and left the room.

Mercury took Prometheus to the far-off place. He chained him to the rock. Leaving the vulture to guard him, he went back to Olympus.

For many years Prometheus stayed chained to the rock. In the day, the hot sun beat down on him. At night, the cold rain fell on him. All he could hear was the roaring of the wind and sea. All he could see was the ugly black bird flying around him. No one came near him. The people of the world wanted to help, but they were afraid of the anger of Zeus.

Prometheus did not like being chained to the rock, but he was happy that he had taken the fire from Zeus. He knew he had helped the people of the world. Also he had a secret which he had not told Zeus. He knew that one day a great hero would come to save him. He did not know the name of the hero or when he would come. All he knew was that one day he would be saved by a strong and powerful man. Prometheus looked for the hero every day.

One morning Prometheus saw a white sail far out on the angry sea. As it came nearer, he saw a powerful man jump from the boat and swim to the rock.

"Are you the hero who has come to save me?" shouted Prometheus.

"I am Hercules," the man shouted back. "I have come to save you because you helped the people of the world."

As Hercules came out of the water, Prometheus could see he was more powerful than other men. He was very tall, and his arms were strong. In his hands he carried a great sword. With one jump he landed on the rock.

"Watch out for the vulture which guards me," shouted Prometheus. "He will try to kill you."

"Let him try," laughed the hero as the vulture flew at him. With his giant sword he cut off the head of the ugly bird.

Hercules turned to Prometheus. With his powerful hands, he pulled the chain from the rock.

"How can I thank you, strong Hercules, for saving me?" asked Prometheus.

"Do not thank me," said Hercules. "You gave the gift of fire back to Man. It is my wish to help people who have been kind and good. Come now, let us go back to the world." The two heroes swam to the boat and sailed home over the angry sea.

The people of the world were happy to see Prometheus again. They thanked Hercules for helping the man who had taken fire from Zeus. They asked Hercules to stay with them. He said he would like to stay but that he must go to a far-off land where there was a king he must help. He said goodbye and sailed away.

DEMETER

Edith Hamilton

While most of the Greek gods were capricious and at times cruel in their relationships to mortals, Demeter, the goddess of corn, was helpful. Since Greek women cared for the fields, plowed, planted, and harvested the grain while their husbands fought and hunted, it was natural that a goddess rather than a god should be the divinity of the harvest.

Every five years a great harvest festival was held. The ceremonies of these sacred days were very secret and are still unknown. Cicero reported that, "Nothing is higher than these mysteries. They have sweetened our charac-

ters and softened our customs; they have made us pass from the condition of savages to true humanity. They have not only shown us the way to live joyfully, but they have taught us how to die with a better hope."

All Olympian gods were untouched by sorrow except Demeter and Dionysus, god of the vine; as the two deities of plant life saw their grasses and vines die they grieved. Demeter was the sorrowing mother, her daughter Persephone the transient rebirth of spring and summer, the life that carried with it knowledge of its own death. Both represented the ever-present duality of joy and sorrow in human life.

The Demeter story is very old; its first literary record is an early Homeric hymn from the eighth or early seventh century B.C., *but its roots are even more ancient. This is revealed by the personification of seasonal change which comes from an I–Thou relationship between man and nature, the heart of prescientific-man's philosophy. It is in contrast to modern man's I-It relationship with the world around him.*

Demeter had an only daughter, Persephone (in Latin, Proserpine), the maiden of the spring. She lost her and in her terrible grief she withheld her gifts from the earth, which turned into a frozen desert. The green and flowering land was icebound and lifeless because Persephone had disappeared.

The lord of the dark Underworld, the king of the multitudinous dead, carried her off when, enticed by the wondrous bloom of the narcissus, she strayed too far from her companions. In his chariot drawn by coal-black steeds he rose up through a chasm in the earth, and grasping the maiden by the wrist set her beside him. He bore her away, weeping, down to the Underworld. The high hills echoed her cry and the depths of the sea, and her mother heard it. She sped like a bird over sea and land seeking her daughter. But no one would tell her the truth, "no man nor god, nor any sure messenger from the birds." Nine days Demeter wandered, and all that time she would not taste of ambrosia or put sweet nectar to her lips. At last she came to the Sun and he told her all the story: Persephone was down in the world beneath the earth, among the shadowy dead.

Then a still greater grief entered Demeter's heart. She left Olympus; she dwelt on earth, but so disguised that none knew her, and, indeed, the gods are not easily discerned by mortal men. In her desolate wanderings she came to Eleusis and

sat by the wayside near a wall. She seemed an aged woman, such as in great houses care for the children or guard the storerooms. Four lovely maidens, sisters, coming to draw water from the well, saw her and asked her pityingly what she did there. She answered that she had fled from pirates who had meant to sell her as a slave, and that she knew no one in this strange land to go to for help. They told her that any house in the town would welcome her, but that they would like best to bring her to their own if she would wait there while they went to ask their mother. The goddess bent her head in assent, and the girls, filling their shining pitchers with water, hurried home. Their mother, Metaneira, bade them return at once and invite the stranger to come, and speeding back they found the glorious goddess still sitting there, deeply veiled and covered to her slender feet by her dark robe. She followed them, and as she crossed the threshold to the hall where the mother sat holding her young son, a divine radiance filled the doorway and awe fell upon Metaneira.

She bade Demeter be seated and herself offered her honey-sweet wine, but the goddess would not taste it. She asked instead for barley-water flavored with mint, the cooling draft of the reaper at harvest time and also the sacred cup given the worshipers at Eleusis. Thus refreshed, she took the child and held him to her fragrant bosom and his mother's heart was glad. So Demeter nursed Demophoon, the son that Metaneira had borne to wise Celeus. And the child grew like a young god, for daily Demeter anointed him with ambrosia and at night she would place him in the red heart of the fire. Her purpose was to give him immortal youth.

Something, however, made the mother uneasy, so that one night she kept watch and screamed in terror when she saw the child laid in the fire. The goddess was angered; she seized the boy and cast him on the ground. She had meant to set him free from old age and from death, but that was not to be. Still, he had lain upon her knees and slept in her arms and therefore he should have honor throughout his life.

Then she showed herself the goddess manifest. Beauty breathed about her and a lovely fragrance; light shone from her so that the great house was filled with brightness. She was Demeter, she told the awestruck women. They must build her a great temple near the town and so win back the favor of her heart.

Thus she left them, and Metaneira fell speechless to the earth and all there trembled with fear. In the morning they told Celeus what had happened and he called the people together and revealed to them the command of the goddess. They worked willingly to build her a temple, and when it was finished Demeter came to it and sat there—apart from the gods in Olympus, alone, wasting away with longing for her daughter.

That year was most dreadful and cruel for mankind over all the earth. Nothing grew; no seed sprang up; in vain the oxen drew the plowshare through the furrows. It seemed the whole race of man would die of famine. At last Zeus saw that he must take the matter in hand. He sent the gods to Demeter, one after another, to try to turn her from her anger, but she listened to none of them. Never would she let the earth bear fruit until she had seen her daughter. Then Zeus realized that his brother must give way. He told Hermes to go down to the Underworld and to bid the lord of it let his bride go back to Demeter.

Hermes found the two sitting side by side, Persephone shrinking away, reluctant because she longed for her mother. At Hermes' words she sprang up joyfully, eager to go. Her husband knew that he must obey the word of Zeus and send her up to earth away from him, but he prayed her as she left him to have kind thoughts of him and not be so sorrowful that she was the wife of one who was great among the immortals. And he made her eat a pomegranate seed, knowing in his heart that if she did so she must return to him.

He got ready his golden car and Hermes took the reins and drove the black horses straight to the temple where Demeter was. She ran out to meet her daughter as swiftly as a Maenad runs down the mountain-side. Persephone sprang into her arms and was held fast there. All day they talked of what had happened to them both, and Demeter grieved when she heard of the pomegranate seed, fearing that she could not keep her daughter with her.

Then Zeus sent another messenger to her, a great personage, none other than his revered mother Rhea, the oldest of the gods. Swiftly she hastened down from the heights of Olympus to the barren, leafless earth, and standing at the door of the temple she spoke to Demeter.

Come, my daughter, for Zeus, far-seeing, loud-
     thundering, bids you.
Come once again to the halls of the gods where
     you shall have honor,
Where you will have your desire, your daughter,
     to comfort your sorrow
As each year is accomplished and bitter winter is
     ended.
For a third part only the kingdom of darkness
     shall hold her.
For the rest you will keep her, you and the happy
     immortals.
Peace now. Give men life which comes alone
     from your giving.

Demeter did not refuse, poor comfort though it was that she must lose Persephone for four months every year and see her young loveliness go down to the world of the dead. But she was kind; the "Good Goddess," men always called her. She was sorry for the desolation she had brought about. She made the fields once more rich with abundant fruit and the whole world bright with flowers and green leaves. Also she went to the princes of Eleusis who had built her temple and she chose one, Triptolemus, to be her ambassador to men, instructing them how to sow the corn. She taught him and Celeus and the others her sacred rites, "mysteries which no one may utter, for deep awe checks the tongue. Blessed is he who has seen them; his lot will be good in the world to come."

Queen of fragrant Eleusis,

Giver of earth's good gifts,
Give me your grace, O Demeter,
You, too, Persephone, fairest,
Maiden all lovely, I offer
Song for your favor.

CUPID AND PSYCHE

Edith Hamilton

In her introduction to "Cupid and Psyche" Edith Hamilton writes, "This story is told only by Apuleuis, a Latin writer of the second century A.D. The Latin names of the gods are therefore used. It is a prettily told tale, after the manner of Ovid. The writer is entertained by what he writes; he believes none of it."
The allegorical nature of this myth about the union of love and the soul is clear. So too are the similarities between "Cupid and Psyche," "Beauty and the Beast,", and "East o' the Sun and West o' the Moon," (see Chapter 6, Wonder Tales, for both). The original folk source may have been the same for all three narratives.

There was once a king who had three daughters, all lovely maidens, but the youngest, Psyche, excelled her sisters so greatly that beside them she seemed a very goddess consorting with mere mortals. The fame of her surpassing beauty spread over the earth, and everywhere men journeyed to gaze upon her with wonder and adoration and to do her homage as though she were in truth one of the immortals. They would even say that Venus herself could not equal this mortal. As they thronged in ever-growing numbers to worship her loveliness no one any more gave a thought to Venus herself. Her temples were neglected; her altars foul with cold ashes; her favorite towns deserted and falling in ruins. All the honors once hers were now given to a mere girl destined some day to die.

It may well be believed that the goddess would not put up with this treatment. As always when she was in trouble she turned for help to her son, that beautiful winged youth whom some call

Cupid and others Love, against whose arrows there is no defense, neither in heaven nor on the earth. She told him her wrongs and as always he was ready to do her bidding. "Use your power," she said, "and make the hussy fall madly in love with the vilest and most despicable creature there is in the whole world." And so no doubt he would have done, if Venus had not first shown him Psyche, never thinking in her jealous rage what such beauty might do even to the God of Love himself. As he looked upon her it was as if he had shot one of his arrows into his own heart. He said nothing to his mother, indeed he had no power to utter a word, and Venus left him with the happy confidence that he would swiftly bring about Psyche's ruin.

What happened, however, was not what she counted on. Psyche did not fall in love with a horrible wretch, she did not fall in love at all. Still more strange, no one fell in love with her. Men were content to look and wonder and worship—and then pass on to marry someone else. Both her sisters, inexpressibly inferior to her, were splendidly married, each to a king. Psyche, the all-beautiful, sat sad and solitary, only admired, never loved. It seemed that no man wanted her.

This was, of course, most disturbing to her parents. Her father finally traveled to an oracle of Apollo to ask his advice on how to get her a good husband. The god answered him, but his words were terrible. Cupid had told him the whole story and had begged for his help. Accordingly Apollo said that Psyche, dressed in deepest mourning, must be set on the summit of a rocky hill and left alone, and that there her destined husband, a fearful winged serpent, stronger than the gods themselves, would come to her and make her his wife.

The misery of all when Psyche's father brought back this lamentable news can be imagined. They dressed the maiden as though for her death and carried her to the hill with greater sorrowing than if it had been to her tomb. But Psyche herself kept her courage. "You should have wept for me before," she told them, "because of the beauty that has drawn down upon me the jealousy of Heaven. Now go, knowing that I am glad the end has come." They went in despairing grief, leaving the lovely helpless creature to meet her doom alone, and they shut themselves in their palace to mourn all their days for her.

On the high hilltop in the darkness Psyche sat, waiting for she knew not what terror. There, as she wept and trembled, a soft breath of air came through the stillness to her, the gentle breathing of Zephyr, sweetest and mildest of winds. She felt it lift her up. She was floating away from the rocky hill and down until she lay upon a grassy meadow soft as a bed and fragrant with flowers. It was so peaceful there, all her trouble left her and she slept. She woke beside a bright river; and on its bank was a mansion stately and beautiful as though built for a god, with pillars of gold and walls of silver and floors inlaid with precious stones. No sound was to be heard; the place seemed deserted and Psyche drew near, awestruck at the sight of such splendor. As she hesitated on the threshold, voices sounded in her ear. She could see no one, but the words they spoke came clearly to her. The house was for her, they told her. She must enter without fear and bathe and refresh herself. Then a banquet table would be

spread for her. "We are your servants," the voices said, "ready to do whatever you desire."

The bath was the most delightful, the food the most delicious, she had ever enjoyed. While she dined, sweet music breathed around her: a great choir seemed to sing to a harp, but she could only hear, not see, them. Throughout the day, except for the strange companionship of the voices, she was alone, but in some inexplicable way she felt sure that with the coming of the night her husband would be with her. And so it happened. When she felt him beside her and heard his voice softly murmuring in her ear, all her fears left her. She knew without seeing him that here was no monster or shape of terror, but the lover and husband she had longed and waited for.

This half-and-half companionship could not fully content her; still she was happy and time passed swiftly. One night, however, her dear though unseen husband spoke gravely to her and warned her that danger in the shape of her two sisters was approaching. "They are coming to the hill where you disappeared, to weep for you," he said; "but you must not let them see you or you will bring great sorrow upon me and ruin to yourself." She promised him she would not, but all the next day she passed in weeping, thinking of her sisters and herself unable to comfort them. She was still in tears when her husband came and even his caresses could not check them. At last he yielded sorrowfully to her great desire. "Do what you will," he said, "but you are seeking your own destruction." Then he warned her solemnly not to be persuaded by anyone to try to see him, on pain of being separated from him forever. Psyche cried out that she would never do so. She would die a hundred times over rather than live without him. "But give me this joy," she said: "to see my sisters." Sadly he promised her that it should be so.

The next morning the two came, brought down from the mountain by Zephyr. Happy and excited, Psyche was waiting for them. It was long before the three could speak to each other; their joy was too great to be expressed except by tears and embraces. But when at last they entered the palace and the elder sisters saw its surpassing treasures; when they sat at the rich banquet and heard the marvelous music, bitter envy took possession of them and a devouring curiosity as to who was the lord of all this magnificence and their sister's husband. But Psyche kept faith; she told them only that he was a young man, away now on a hunting expedition. Then filling their hands with gold and jewels, she had Zephyr bear them back to the hill. They went willingly enough, but their hearts were on fire with jealousy. All their own wealth and good fortune seemed to them as nothing compared with Psyche's, and their envious anger so worked in them that they came finally to plotting how to ruin her.

That very night Psyche's husband warned her once more. She would not listen when he begged her not to let them come again. She never could see him, she reminded him. Was she also to be forbidden to see all others, even her sisters so dear to her? He yielded as before, and very soon the two wicked women arrived, with their plot carefully worked out.

Already, because of Psyche's stumbling and contradictory answers when they asked her what her husband looked like, they had become convinced that she had never set eyes on him and did not really know what he was. They did not tell her this, but they reproached her for hiding her terrible state from them, her own sisters. They had learned, they said, and knew for a fact, that her husband was not a man, but the fearful serpent Apollo's oracle had declared he would be. He was kind now, no doubt, but he would certainly turn upon her some night and devour her.

Psyche, aghast, felt terror flooding her heart instead of love. She had wondered so often why he would never let her see him. There must be some dreadful reason. What did she really know about him? If he was not horrible to look at, then he was cruel to forbid her ever to behold him. In extreme misery, faltering and stammering, she gave her sisters to understand that she could not deny what they said, because she had been with him only in the dark. "There must be something very wrong," she sobbed, "for him so to shun the light of day." And she begged them to advise her.

They had their advice all prepared beforehand. That night she must hide a sharp knife and a lamp near her bed. When her husband was fast asleep she must leave the bed, light the lamp, and get the knife. She must steel herself to plunge it swiftly into the body of the frightful being the light would certainly show her. "We will be near," they said, "and carry you away with us when he is dead."

Then they left her torn by doubt and distracted what to do. She loved him, he was her dear husband. No; he was a horrible serpent and she loathed him. She would kill him—She would not. She must have certainty—She did not want certainty. So all day long her thoughts fought with each other. When evening came, however, she had given the struggle up. One thing she was determined to do: she would see him.

When at last he lay sleeping quietly, she summoned all her courage and lit the lamp. She tiptoed to the bed and holding the light high above her she gazed at what lay there. Oh, the relief and the rapture that filled her heart. No monster was revealed, but the sweetest and fairest of all creatures, at whose sight the very lamp seemed to shine brighter. In her first shame at her folly and lack of faith, Psyche fell on her knees and would have plunged the knife into her own breast if it had not fallen from her trembling hands. But those same unsteady hands that saved her betrayed her, too, for as she hung over him, ravished at the sight of him and unable to deny herself the bliss of filling her eyes with his beauty, some hot oil fell from the lamp upon his shoulder. He started awake: he saw the light and knew her faithlessness, and without a word he fled from her.

She rushed out after him into the night. She could not see him, but she heard his voice speaking to her. He told her who he was, and sadly bade her farewell. "Love cannot live where there is no trust," he said, and flew away. "The God of Love!" she thought. "He was my husband, and I, wretch that I am, could not keep faith with him. Is he gone from me forever? . . . At any rate," she told herself with rising courage, "I can spend the rest of my life searching for him. If he has no more love left for me, at least I can show him how much I love him." And she started on her journey. She had no idea where to go; she knew only that she would never give up looking for him.

He meanwhile had gone to his mother's chamber to have his wound cared for, but when Venus heard his story and learned that it was Psyche whom he had chosen, she left him angrily alone in his pain, and went forth to find the girl of whom he had made her still more jealous. Venus was determined to show Psyche what it meant to draw down the displeasure of a goddess.

Poor Psyche in her despairing wanderings was trying to win the gods over to her side. She offered ardent prayers to them perpetually, but not one of them would do anything to make Venus their enemy. At last she perceived that there was no hope for her, either in heaven or on earth, and she took a desperate resolve. She would go straight to Venus; she would offer herself humbly to her as her servant, and try to soften her anger. "And who knows," she thought, "if he himself is not there in his mother's house." So she set forth to find the goddess who was looking everywhere for her.

When she came into Venus' presence the goddess laughed aloud and asked her scornfully if she was seeking a husband since the one she had had would have nothing to do with her because he had almost died of the burning wound she had given him. "But really," she said, "you are so plain and ill-favored a girl that you will never be able to get you a lover except by the most diligent and painful service. I will therefore show my good will to you by training you in such ways." With that she took a great quantity of the smallest of the seeds, wheat and poppy and millet and so on, and mixed them all together in a heap. "By nightfall these must all be sorted," she said. "See to it for your own sake." And with that she departed.

Psyche, left alone, sat still and stared at the heap. Her mind was all in a maze because of the cruelty of the command; and, indeed, it was of no use to start a task so manifestly impossible. But at this direful moment she who had awakened no compassion in mortals or immortals was pitied by the tiniest creatures of the field, the little ants, the swift-runners. They cried to each other, "Come, have mercy on this poor maid and help her diligently." At once they came, waves of them, one after another, and they labored separating and dividing, until what had been a confused mass lay all ordered, every seed with its kind. This was what Venus found when she came back, and very angry she was to see it. "Your work is by

no means over," she said. Then she gave Psyche a crust of bread and bade her sleep on the ground while she herself went off to her soft, fragrant couch. Surely if she could keep the girl at hard labor and half starve her, too, that hateful beauty of hers would soon be lost. Until then she must see that her son was securely guarded in his chamber where he was still suffering from his wound. Venus was pleased at the way matters were shaping.

The next morning she devised another task for Psyche, this time a dangerous one. "Down there near the riverbank," she said, "where the bushes grow thick, are sheep with fleeces of gold. Go fetch me some of their shining wool." When the worn girl reached the gently flowing stream, a great longing seized her to throw herself into it and end all her pain and despair. But as she was bending over the water she heard a little voice from near her feet, and looking down saw that it came from a green reed. She must not drown herself, it said. Things were not as bad as that. The sheep were indeed very fierce, but if Psyche would wait until they came out of the bushes toward evening to rest beside the river, she could go into the thicket and find plenty of the golden wool hanging on the sharp briars.

So spoke the kind and gentle reed, and Psyche, following the directions, was able to carry back to her cruel mistress a quantity of the shining fleece. Venus received it with an evil smile. "Someone helped you," she said sharply. "Never did you do this by yourself. However, I will give you an opportunity to prove that you really have the stout heart and the singular prudence you make such a show of. Do you see that black water which falls from the hill yonder? It is the source of the terrible river which is called hateful, the river Styx. You are to fill this flask from it." That was the worst task yet, as Psyche saw when she approached the waterfall. Only a winged creature could reach it, so steep and slimy were the rocks on all sides, and so fearful the onrush of the descending waters. But by this time it must be evident to all the readers of this story (as, perhaps, deep in her heart it had become evident to Psyche herself) that although each of her trials seemed impossibly hard, an excellent way out would always be provided for her. This time her savior was an eagle, who poised on his great wings beside her, seized the flask from her with his beak and brought it back to her full of the black water.

But Venus kept on. One cannot but accuse her of some stupidity. The only effect of all that had happened was to make her try again. She gave Psyche a box which she was to carry to the underworld and ask Proserpine to fill with some of her beauty. She was to tell her that Venus really needed it, she was so worn-out from nursing her sick son. Obediently as always Psyche went forth to look for the road to Hades. She found her guide in a tower she passed. It gave her careful directions how to get to Proserpine's palace, first through a great hole in the earth, then down to the river of death, where she must give the ferryman, Charon, a penny to take her across. From there the road led straight to the palace. Cerberus, the three-headed dog, guarded the doors, but if she gave him a cake he would be friendly and let her pass.

All happened, of course, as the tower had foretold. Proserpine was willing to do Venus a service, and Psyche, greatly encouraged, bore back the box, returning far more quickly than she had gone down.

Her next trial she brought upon herself through her curiosity and, still more, her vanity. She felt that she must see what that beauty-charm in the box was; and, perhaps, use a little of it herself. She knew quite as well as Venus did that her looks were not improved by what she had gone through, and always in her mind was the thought that she might suddenly meet Cupid. If only she could make herself more lovely for him! She was unable to resist the temptation; she opened the box. To her sharp disappointment she saw nothing there; it seemed empty. Immediately, however, a deadly languor took possession of her and she fell into a heavy sleep.

At this juncture the God of Love himself stepped forward. Cupid was healed of his wound by now and longing for Psyche. It is a difficult matter to keep Love imprisoned. Venus had locked the door, but there were the windows. All Cupid had to do was to fly out and start looking for his wife. She was lying almost beside the palace, and he found her at once. In a moment he had wiped the sleep from her eyes and put it back into the box. Then waking her with just a prick from one of his arrows, and scolding her a little for her curiosity, he bade her take Proserpine's box to his mother and he assured her that all thereafter would be well.

While the joyful Psyche hastened on her errand, the god flew up to Olympus. He wanted to make certain that Venus would give them no more trouble, so he went straight to Jupiter himself. The Father of Gods and Men consented at once to all that Cupid asked—"Even though," he said, "you have done me great harm in the past —seriously injured my good name and my dignity by making me change myself into a bull and a swan and so on . . . However, I cannot refuse you."

Then he called a full assembly of the gods, and announced to all, including Venus, that Cupid and Psyche were formally married, and that he proposed to bestow immortality upon the bride. Mercury brought Psyche into the palace of the gods, and Jupiter himself gave her the ambrosia to taste which made her immortal. This, of course, completely changed the situation. Venus could not object to a goddess for her daughter-in-law; the alliance had become eminently suitable. No doubt she reflected also that Psyche, living up in heaven with a husband and children to care for, could not be much on the earth to turn men's heads and interfere with her own worship.

So all came to a most happy end. Love and the Soul (for that is what Psyche means) had sought and, after sore trials, found each other; and that union could never be broken.

ORPHEUS

Padraic Colum

*Because Apollo's lyre music was so beautiful that even the gods forgot every-
thing as they listened to him, it is understandable that Padraic Colum would
suggest he was Orpheus' father. Yet both Edith Hamilton and Robert Graves
agree that Orpheus' mother was one of the Muses and his father a Thracian
prince.*

*Apollo gave Orpheus a lyre and the Muses taught him to play; only the
gods could surpass his skill. As he played, animals, trees, rocks, and even rivers
followed him. When he entered Tartarus to find his wife, he moved stern
Pluto to cry iron tears.*

Many were the minstrels who, in the early days of the world, went amongst men, telling them stories of the Gods, of their wars and their births, and of the beginning of things. Of all these minstrels none was so famous as Orpheus; none could tell truer things about the Gods; he himself was half divine, and there were some who said that he was in truth Apollo's son.

But a great grief came to Orpheus, a grief that stopped his singing and his playing upon the lyre. His young wife, Eurydike, was taken from him. One day, walking in the garden, she was bitten on the heel by a serpent; straightway she went down to the World of the Dead.

Then everything in this world was dark and bitter for the minstrel of the Gods; sleep would not come to him, and for him food had no taste. Then Orpheus said, "I will do that which no mortal has ever done before; I will do that which even the Immortals might shrink from doing; I will go down into the World of the Dead, and I will bring back to the living and to the light my bride, Eurydike."

Then Orpheus went on his way to the cavern which goes down, down to the World of the Dead—the Cavern Tainaron. The trees showed him the way. As he went on, Orpheus played upon his lyre and sang; the trees heard his song and were moved by his grief, and with their arms and their heads they showed him the way to the deep, deep cavern named Tainaron.

Down, down, down by a winding path Orpheus went. He came at last to the great gate that opens upon the World of the Dead. And the silent guards who keep watch there for the Rulers of the Dead were astonished when they saw a living being coming towards them, and they would not let Orpheus approach the gate.

The minstrel took the lyre in his hands and played upon it. As he played, the silent watchers gathered around him, leaving the gate unguarded. As he played the Rulers of the Dead came forth, Hades and Persephone, and listened to the words of the living man.

"The cause of my coming through the dark and fearful ways," sang Orpheus, "is to strive to gain a fairer fate for Eurydike, my bride. All that is above must come down to you at last, O Rulers of the most lasting World. But before her time has Eurydike been brought here. I have desired strength to endure her loss, but I cannot endure it. And I have come before you, Hades and Persephone, brought here by love."

When Orpheus said the name of love, Persephone, the queen of the dead, bowed her young head, and bearded Hades, the king, bowed his head also. Persephone remembered how Demeter, her mother, had sought her all through the world, and she remembered the touch of her mother's tears upon her face. And Hades remembered how his love for Persephone had led him to carry her away from the valley where she had been gathering flowers. He and Persephone stood aside, and Orpheus went through the gate and came amongst the dead.

Still upon his lyre he played. Tantalos—who for his crime had been condemned to stand up to his neck in water and yet never be able to assuage his thirst—Tantalos heard, and for a while did not strive to put his lips toward the water that ever flowed away from him; Sisyphos—who had been condemned to roll up a hill a stone that ever rolled back—Sisyphos heard the music that Orpheus played, and for a while he sat still upon his stone. Ixion, bound to a wheel, stopped its turning for a while; the vultures abandoned their torment of Tityos; the daughters of Danaos ceased to fill their jars; even those dread ones, the Erinyes, who bring to the dead the memories of all their crimes and all their faults, had their cheeks wet with tears.

In the throng of the newly-come dead Orpheus saw Eurydike. She looked upon her husband, but she had not the power to come near him. But slowly she came when Hades, the king, called her. Then with joy Orpheus took her hands.

It would be granted them—no mortal ever gained such privilege before—to leave, both together, the World of the Dead, and to abide for another space in the World of the Living. One condition there would be—that on their way up neither Orpheus nor Eurydike should look back.

They went through the gate and came out amongst the watchers that are around the portals. These showed them the path that went up to the World of the Living. That way they went, Orpheus and Eurydike, he going before her.

Up and through the darkened ways they went, Orpheus knowing that Eurydike was behind him, but never looking back upon her. As he went his heart was filled with things to tell her—how the trees were blossoming in the garden she had left; how the water was sparkling in the fountain; how the doors of the house stood open; how they, sitting together, would watch the sunlight on the laurel bushes. All these things were in his heart to tell her who came behind him, silent and unseen.

And now they were nearing the place where the cavern opened on the world of the living. Orpheus looked up toward the light from the sky. Out of the opening of the cavern he went; he saw a white-winged bird fly by. He turned around and cried, "O Eurydike, look upon the world I have won you back to!"

He turned to say this to her. He saw her with her long dark hair and pale face. He held out his arms to clasp her. But in that instant she slipped back into the gloom of the cavern. And all he heard spoken was a single word, "Farewell!" Long, long had it taken Eurydike to climb so far, but in the moment of his turning around she had fallen back to her place amongst the dead. For Orpheus had looked back.

Back through the cavern Orpheus went again. Again he came before the watchers of the gate. But now he was not looked at nor listened to; hopeless, he had to return to the World of the Living.

The birds were his friends now, and the trees and the stones. The birds flew around him and mourned with him; the trees and stones often followed him, moved by the music of his lyre. But a savage band slew Orpheus and threw his severed head and his lyre into the River Hebrus. It is said by the poets that while they floated in mid-stream the lyre gave out some mournful notes, and the head of Orpheus answered the notes with song.

And now that he was no longer to be counted with the living, Orpheus went down to the World of the Dead, going down straightway. The silent watchers let him pass; he went amongst the dead, and he saw his Eurydike in the throng. Again they were together, Orpheus and Eurydike, and them the Erinyes could not torment with memories of crimes and faults.

ICARUS AND DAEDALUS

Josephine Preston Peabody

Daedalus was not so innocent as Mrs. Peabody suggests in her revision of this myth. According to Apollodorus, a first-century B.C. Greek source, Daedalus incurred Minos' wrath by showing Ariadne, Minos' daughter, how Theseus could escape from the Labyrinth. Several sources claim Daedalus helped Minos' wife satisfy her lust for her husband's white bull. It is understandable that the second reason for his imprisonment is not included in children's versions of this tale.

Icarus' foolish behavior in flying too close to the sun, in the contrast to his father's careful behavior, introduces a fable-like element into the myth. A pourquoi motif is also hinted at by the explanation of the island's name.

Sir Arthur Evans has theorized that Minos' palace at Cnossus, a complex arrangement of rooms that could confuse a stranger, was the historical basis for the maze. Another theory is that it was the maze-like mosaic pattern in the pavement which was followed in ritual dances.

Among all those mortals who grew so wise that they learned the secrets of the gods, none was more cunning than Daedalus.

He once built, for King Minos of Crete, a wonderful Labyrinth of winding ways so cunningly tangled up and twisted around that, once inside, you could never find your way out again without a magic clue. But the king's favor veered with the wind, and one day he had his master architect imprisoned in a tower. Daedalus managed to escape from his cell; but it seemed impossible to leave the island, since every ship that came or went was well guarded by order of the king.

At length, watching the sea-gulls in the air— the only creatures that were sure of liberty—he thought of a plan for himself and his young son Icarus, who was captive with him.

Little by little, he gathered a store of feathers great and small. He fastened these together with thread, molded them in with wax, and so fashioned two great wings like those of a bird. When

they were done, Daedalus fitted them to his own shoulders, and after one or two efforts, he found that by waving his arms he could winnow the air and cleave it, as a swimmer does the sea. He held himself aloft, wavered this way and that with the wind, and at last, like a great fledgling, he learned to fly.

Without delay, he fell to work on a pair of wings for the boy Icarus, and taught him carefully how to use them, bidding him beware of rash adventures among the stars. "Remember," said the father, "never to fly very low or very high, for the fogs about the earth would weigh you down, but the blaze of the sun will surely melt your feathers apart if you go too near."

For Icarus, these cautions went in at one ear and out by the other. Who could remember to be careful when he was to fly for the first time? Are birds careful? Not they! And not an idea remained in the boy's head but the one joy of escape.

The day came, and the fair wind that was to set them free. The father bird put on his wings, and, while the light urged them to be gone, he waited to see that all was well with Icarus, for the

"Icarus and Daedalus" from *Old Greek Folk Stories Told Anew* by Josephine Preston Peabody. Published by Houghton Mifflin, 1897.

two could not fly hand in hand. Up they rose, the boy after his father. The hateful ground of Crete sank beneath them; and the country folk, who caught a glimpse of them when they were high above the tree-tops, took it for a vision of the gods—Apollo, perhaps, with Cupid after him.

At first there was a terror in the joy. The wide vacancy of the air dazed them—a glance downward made their brains reel. But when a great wind filled their wings, and Icarus felt himself sustained, like a halcyonbird in the hollow of a wave, like a child uplifted by his mother, he forgot everything in the world but joy. He forgot Crete and the other islands that he had passed over: he saw but vaguely that winged thing in the distance before him that was his father Daedalus. He longed for one draft of flight to quench the thirst of his captivity: he stretched out his arms to the sky and made toward the highest heavens.

Alas for him! Warmer and warmer grew the air. Those arms, that had seemed to uphold him, relaxed. His wings wavered, drooped. He fluttered his young hands vainly—he was falling—and in that terror he remembered. The heat of the sun had melted the wax from his wings; the feathers were falling, one by one, like snowflakes; and there was none to help.

He fell like a leaf tossed down by the wind, down, down, with one cry that overtook Daedalus far away. When he returned, and sought high and low for the poor boy, he saw nothing but the bird-like feathers afloat on the water, and he knew that Icarus was drowned.

The nearest island he named Icaria, in memory of the child; but he, in heavy grief, went to the temple of Apollo in Sicily, and there hung up his wings as an offering. Never again did he attempt to fly.

PHÄETHON

Edith Hamilton

This myth illustrates the Greek attitude toward hubris, *similar to the Christian sin of pride. Phäethon, presuming to place himself on the same level as his father, Helios the sun god, must be punished. Not only does "Phaethon" reinforce the ancient Greek's moral code, it also includes* pourquoi *elements by indirectly giving prescientific explanations of the sunrise and sunset and, perhaps, of a great drought.*

The palace of the Sun was a radiant place. It shone with gold and gleamed with ivory and sparkled with jewels. Everything without and within flashed and glowed and glittered. It was always high noon there. Shadowy twilight never dimmed the brightness. Darkness and night were unknown. Few among mortals could have long endured that unchanging brilliancy of light, but few had ever found their way thither.

Nevertheless, one day a youth, mortal on his mother's side, dared to approach. Often he had to

pause and clear his dazzled eyes, but the errand which had brought him was so urgent that his purpose held fast and he pressed on, up to the palace, through the burnished doors, and into the throne-room where surrounded by a blinding, blazing splendor the Sun-god sat. There the lad was forced to halt. He could bear no more.

Nothing escapes the eyes of the Sun. He saw the boy instantly and he looked at him very kindly. "What brought you here?" he asked. "I have come," the other answered boldly, "to find out if you are my father or not. My mother said you were, but the boys at school laugh when I tell them I am your son. They will not believe me. I told my mother and she said I had better go and ask you." Smiling, the Sun took off his crown of burning light so that the lad could look at him without distress. "Come here, Phäethon," he said. "You are my son. Clymene told you the truth. I expect you will not doubt my word too? But I will give you a proof. Ask anything you want of me and you shall have it. I call the Styx to be witness to my promise, the river of the oath of the gods."

No doubt Phaëthon had often watched the Sun riding through the heavens and had told himself with a feeling, half awe, half excitement, "It is my father up there." And then he would wonder what it would be like to be in that chariot, guiding the steeds along that dizzy course, giving light to the world. Now at his father's words this wild dream had become possible. Instantly he cried, "I choose to take your place, Father. That is the only thing I want. Just for a day, a single day, let me have your car to drive."

The Sun realized his own folly. Why had he taken that fatal oath and bound himself to give in to anything that happened to enter a boy's rash young head? "Dear lad," he said, "this is the only thing I would have refused you. I know I cannot refuse. I have sworn by the Styx. I must yield if you persist. But I do not believe you will. Listen while I tell you what this is you want. You are Clymene's son as well as mine. You are mortal and no mortal could drive my chariot. Indeed, no god except myself can do that. The ruler of the gods cannot. Consider the road. It rises up from the sea so steeply that the horses can hardly climb it, fresh though they are in the early morning. In midheaven it is so high that even I do not like to look down. Worst of all is the descent, so precipitous that the Sea-gods waiting to receive me wonder how I can avoid falling headlong. To guide the horses, too, is a perpetual struggle. Their fiery spirits grow hotter as they climb and they scarcely suffer my control. What would they do with you?

"Are you fancying that there are all sorts of wonders up there, cities of the gods full of beautiful things? Nothing of the kind. You will have to pass beasts, fierce beasts of prey, and they are all that you will see. The Bull, the Lion, the Scorpion, the great Crab, each will try to harm you. Be persuaded. Look around you. See all the goods the rich world holds. Choose from them your heart's desire and it shall be yours. If what you want is to be proved my son, my fears for you are proof enough that I am your father."

But none of all this wise talk meant anything to the boy. A glorious prospect opened before him. He saw himself proudly standing in that wondrous car, his hands triumphantly guiding those steeds which Jove himself could not master. He did not give a thought to the dangers his father detailed. He felt not a quiver of fear, not a doubt of his own powers. At last the Sun gave up trying to dissuade him. It was hopeless, as he saw. Besides, there was no time. The moment for starting was at hand. Already the gates of the east glowed purple, and Dawn had opened her courts full of rosy light. The stars were leaving the sky; even the lingering morning star was dim.

There was need for haste, but all was ready. The seasons, the gatekeepers of Olympus, stood waiting to fling the doors wide. The horses had been bridled and yoked to the car. Proudly and joyously Phaëthon mounted it and they were off. He had made his choice. Whatever came of it he could not change now. Not that he wanted to in that first exhilarating rush through the air, so swift that the East Wind was outstripped and left far behind. The horses' flying feet went through the low-banked clouds near the ocean as through a thin sea mist and then up and up in the clear air, climbing the height of heaven. For a few ecstatic moments Phaëthon felt himself the Lord of the Sky. But suddenly there was a change. The chariot was swinging wildly to and fro; the pace was faster; he had lost control. Not he, but the horses were directing the course. That light weight in the car, those feeble hands clutching the reins, had told them their own driver was not there. They were the masters then. No one else could command them. They left the road and rushed where they chose, up, down, to the right, to the left. They nearly wrecked the chariot against the Scorpion; they brought up short and almost ran into the Crab. By this time the poor charioteer was half fainting with terror, and he let the reins fall.

That was the signal for still more mad and reckless running. The horses soared up to the very top of the sky and then, plunging headlong down, they set the world on fire. The highest mountains were the first to burn, Ida and Helicon, where the Muses dwell, Parnassus, and heaven-piercing Olympus. Down their slopes the flame ran to the low-lying valleys and the dark forest lands, until all things everywhere were ablaze. The springs turned into steam; the rivers shrank. It is said that it was then the Nile fled and hid his head, which still is hidden.

In the car Phaëthon, hardly keeping his place there, was wrapped in thick smoke and heat as if from a fiery furnace. He wanted nothing except to have this torment and terror ended. He would have welcomed death. Mother Earth, too, could bear no more. She uttered a great cry which reached up to the gods. Looking down from Olympus they saw that they must act quickly if the world was to be saved. Jove seized his thunderbolt and hurled it at the rash, repentant driver. It struck him dead, shattered the chariot, and made the maddened horses rush down into the sea.

Phaëthon all on fire fell from the car through the air to the earth. The mysterious river Eridanus, which no mortal eyes have ever seen, received him and put out the flames and cooled the body. The naiads, in pity for him, so bold and so young to die, buried him and carved upon the tomb:—

Here Phäethon lies who drove the Sun-god's car.
Greatly he failed, but he had greatly dared.

His sisters, the Heliades, the daughters of Helios, the Sun, came to his grave to mourn for him. There they were turned into poplar trees, on the bank of the Eridanus,

Where sorrowing they weep into the stream
    forever.
And each tear as it falls shines in the water
A glistening drop of amber.

Norse Mythology

In the early thirteenth century, Snorri Sturluson, an Icelandic scholar, poet, politican, and historian, collected many Norse myths and legends into the *Prose Edda* as a poets' reference book of pre-Christian Norse customs, values, and beliefs. Even though most Germanic groups had forgotten this heritage, Christianity reached Iceland late and Snorri was able to find numerous sources for his *Edda*. Today, this *Prose Edda* and an earlier verse collection called the *Poetic Edda*, in which, Edith Hamilton says, there is material for an epic as great as the *Iliad*, are the primary sources for knowledge of Norse mythology.

A people's mythology, their early attempts to understand life, reflects the natural environment, the physical world in which they lived. The Vikings knew frost, ice, and snow in their often cloud-covered world. Their land demanded great effort to farm and the seas were usually unfriendly. Norsemen felt life was made of contests in which man faced overwhelming odds, and that the only victory came from fighting even certain defeat; laughing in the face of death is shown in the stories they told about their gods.

These deities, the Aesir, were engaged in a ceaseless struggle with the giants, the Jotuns, who were the enemies not only of the gods but of order itself. While the gods knew this contest was doomed to end in their defeat, they continued to resist the forces of chaos. To gain the additional wisdom necessary to save something from the inevitable destruction of the world, Odin, the All-Father, sacrificed one eye at Mimir's Well. The struggle between the forces of order and chaos entered even into the gods' dwelling place through the mischief and trouble caused by Loki, a giant who lived in Asgard.

Finding English versions of Norse myths for children that are true to the spirit of the original conception is difficult. The language of the *Eddas* is compressed, simple, and lacks the extended metaphors found in Greek mythology. When retold in English, Norse myths should not assume the characteristics of the Greek stories with their gentle beauty of nature, because the Norse world

From *Thunder of the Gods* by Dorothy Hosford. Illustrated by Claire and George Louden. Copyright 1952 by Dorothy Hosford. Reproduced by permission of Holt, Rinehart and Winston, Inc.

view and their conception of the deities as revealed in *Eddas* are quite different from that in Greek mythology. Retellings of Norse myths should always reflect the undercurrent of doom, the knowledge of the Wyrd of the gods.

Abbie Farwell Brown's retelling of "Balder and the Mistletoe" is included in the following selection of Norse myths as an example of poor retelling. Her emotional tone detracts from the tragedy and significance of Balder's death; the dialogue is not only inappropriate for the tone of the myth but is not god-like. Dorothy Hosford's version of the same story is also included for comparison. Her terse style is truer to the original and is better able to reflect the drama central to Norse mythology.

PRONUNCIATION OF PROPER NAMES

Aegir	ĕ′ gir	Jotunheim	yō′ tŏŏn häm
Aesir	â′sĭr	Loki	lō′ kē
Asgard	äs′ gärd	Midgard	mĭd′ gärd
Audhumla	oud′ hōōm lä	Mimir	mē′ mir
Balder	bäl′ der	Modgud	mōōd′ gŏŏd
Bergelmir	bĕr′ gĕl mir	Muspellheim	mōŏs′ pĕl häm
Bifrost	bēf′ rŏst	Nanna	nän′ nä
Borr	bŏŏr	Niflheim	nĭfl′ häm
Buri	bōō′ ri	Odin	ō′ din
Draupnir	droup′ nir	Ratatosk	rä′ tä tosk
Favnir	Fȧv′ nēr	Skinfax	shĭn′ fäk
Frey	frā	Sleipnir	slāp′ nir
Freyja	frā′ yä	Thjazi	thyät′ sē
Frigg	frĭg	Thor	thor
Gjol	yōl	Urd	ōord
Heimdal	häm′ däl	Vafthrudgen	väf′ thrōō dgĕn
Hela	hĕl′ ä	Valhalla	văl′ hăl a
Hermod	hĕr′ mōd	Valkyrie	văl′ kĭr ĭ
Hod	hōd	Vanir	vä′ nir
Hoenir	hē′ nir	Ve	vā
Hyrrokin	hĕr′ ro kin	Vili	vē′ lē
Iduna	ē′ dōōn a	Yggdrasil	ĭg′ drä sil
Jotun	yō′ tŏŏn	Ymir	ē′ mir

The preceding vowels are pronounced as in : hāte, fäther, hē, bĕt, hĭt, bōld, hŏt, fŏŏt, sōōn, sūre.

THE WORLD OF THE GODS

Dorothy Hosford

While the Greek gods were immortal and their home, Mt. Olympus, impregnable, the Norse gods knew they and their home, Asgard, would eventually be destroyed. Because Asgard was shadowed by destruction it was a solemn place; because the Norse gods knew they would die their lives were unlike those of the Greek deities.

Long ago, in the early days of the world, the gods of the Norsemen lived in a beautiful city called Asgard. It stood on a high plain, on top of a lofty mountain, in the very center of the universe. Its towers and battlements shone among the clouds. Odin, the strong and wise father of the gods, had built this shining city and here he ruled over gods and men. Odin was called All-Father because he was the lord and ruler of all. His wife was named Frigg. She was queen among the goddesses.

Many great palaces and halls rose in Asgard. One belonged to Odin. In this hall Odin had a high seat from which he could look out over the whole world. He looked across the highest mountains and into deep valleys and beyond the distant seas, and saw all that took place among men. He watched men plowing their fields and building their houses and fighting their wars.

Odin could look even beyond the realm of men to the dark edges of the world where the giants or Jotuns lived. Their land, which was called Jotunheim, was dark and gloomy, with great mountains and strange valleys. The Frost-Giants and Hill-Giants fought an unceasing war against the gods. The gods wished men well and strove to make life fair and good. But the giants loved evil and destruction. They wished to bring disaster to the whole world of gods and men.

A race of very small creatures also lived in the world, in caves deep beneath the mountains. They were called dwarfs. They were skillful craftsmen and could make every kind of remarkable thing. But they were not always friendly to the gods or to men. There was also a race of lesser deities, called the Vanir, who helped the gods. The winds and the sea and the rain were in their keeping.

Odin looked out from his high seat over all this world and those who lived in it. He had two ravens named Hugin and Munin, which in our language would be Thought and Memory. Each day they flew out over the earth and returned at nightfall to perch on his shoulders and tell what they had seen. In this way Odin gained much knowledge. And often Odin left Asgard and went himself among men.

Thor, the mighty god of thunder, was the son of Odin. He was tall and broad and of great strength. He had a red beard and a hasty temper. When Thor was angered he was terrible in his wrath and all feared him. But he was blunt and honest in his ways and for the most part good-natured and kindly. He waged a constant war against the giants and they knew to their sorrow his prowess as a fighter.

Thor owned a chariot drawn by two goats. When he rode forth the hills trembled, the lightning flashed, and the thunder rolled across the sky. Thor's goats had a remarkable virtue. They could always provide food, no matter into what waste and distant lands his journeys took him. Thor would cook the goats for his supper. He carefully saved the skins and the bones, and in the morning the goats were made whole again. Thor's most priceless possession was his hammer. When he hurled it at a foe, the hammer would always return to his hand. It served him well in his battles against the giants. Many adventures might have turned out differently had it not been for Thor's hammer. He wore iron gauntlets when he hurled it. Thor also possessed a belt of strength. When it was buckled on, the god's strength was doubled. With these possessions and his own great might and courage, Thor overcame all who withstood him—though that is not to say that he had always an easy victory.

Many gods and goddesses lived in Asgard. There was only one among them who did not desire to bring beauty and healing to the world, and to make the ways of men pleasant and prosperous. This was Loki. He came from the race of the giants, though he now lived among the gods and was the foster-brother of Odin. He was pleasing to look upon and beguiling in his ways. But in his heart he loved evil and malice, and the gods learned to their sorrow how little they could trust him.

Also there lived in Asgard a mighty army of heroes. Odin chose the bravest from all who had died on the field of battle. He sent the Valkyries, beautiful maidens mounted on swift steeds, to bear the fallen warriors from the world of men to Asgard. There they remained with the gods. It was the favorite pastime of the heroes to fight battles among themselves each day. Though they might be wounded in the fighting, they were always strong and sound when night came and eager to enjoy the feasts which Odin gave in their honor.

The feasts were held in the great banquet hall called Valhalla. This hall had five hundred and forty portals and through each of these eight hundred warriors could march abreast. The roof of Valhalla rose so high that one could not easily make out the top of it. It was laid with golden shields and glittered in the sunlight. Outside of Valhalla stood the shining grove of Glaser. The leaves of its trees were red gold.

Odin sat on his high seat at the head of the feasts, with his ravens on his shoulders and two wolves at his feet. He wore a blue-gray mantle, the color of sky and clouds, and wings of gold shone on his helmet. Odin drank only wine, which was both food and drink to him. The heroes drank ale and mead which was served to them by the Valkyries. There was never lack of food or drink in Valhalla, no matter how great the company.

So the days passed in Asgard, in adventure and battle, feasting and merriment. Wondrous tales are told of this ancient time, of Odin's journeys and Thor's battles with the giants, of all that happened among the gods. Yet there had been a time in the world when neither Asgard nor the gods were in existence, and there was yet to come a time when all should end.

IN THE BEGINNING

Dorothy Hosford

Almost all cultures attempt to explain the origin of life, the deities, and the world. The following myth not only shows the Norse vision of creation but also creates order out of chaos. The tension between the forces of chaos and the forces of order are ever present in Norse mythology. As the gods nourish their root of the tree of the universe, the serpent Nidhogg gnaws away at another root. While the gods help the race of men, the giants work for their destruction.

The city of Asgard did not always shine forth in heaven, with its glittering roofs and towers rising above the clouds and the gods walking its broad roads.

There was a time when there was nothing; neither sea nor land nor sky. No cool waves washed the sandy shores; no grass grew anywhere. Nor had the sun and the moon and the stars yet found their places. All was a great void, a wide abyss. On one side of the abyss was a region of fire and heat called Muspellheim. On the other side was a region of icy frosts and mists called Niflheim. The breath of heat met the frost so that it melted and dripped. Life was quickened from the drops and slowly became a man's form. That man was called Ymir, and from him came all the races of the giants. There also sprang from the melting frost the cow called Audhumla, whose milk nourished the giant Ymir.

The cow licked the blocks of ice, which were salty. The first day that she licked the ice, there came forth from the blocks a man's hair. The second day a man's head came forth, and the third day the whole man was there. He was called Buri and he was great and mighty. He had a son who was called Borr. And Borr, in turn, was the father of Odin and Vili and Ve. These three brothers were good and fair to look upon and worthy of honor. From them was born the whole race of the gods.

From the beginning the giants, sons of Ymir,

were the enemies of the gods. They loved to do harm. When the giants were many in number, the three gods put Ymir to death. He was so tremendous in size that the river of blood which flowed from his wounds drowned all the other giants, save one called Bergelmir. He fled, with his wife, in a boat. Thus the gods did not succeed in destroying their enemies, for Bergelmir became the father of a new race of giants.

Odin and his brothers took the body of Ymir and from it they made the earth. First they made the land from his flesh. Then they made the sea from his blood and laid it in a ring about the land. From his bones they fashioned mountains. The gods made the dome of heaven from Ymir's skull and set it up over the earth. Under each corner they placed a dwarf, and the names of these were East, West, North, and South. They made clouds from Ymir's brain. Then the gods took glowing embers and sparks from the fiery region of Muspellheim and made light for the heavens, a sun and a moon and stars.

As yet there were no men in the world. One day as the gods walked along the seashore they took up two trees and formed human beings from them.

"I will give them life and spirit," said Odin.

"I will give them knowledge and understanding," said Vili.

"I will give them bodily shape," said Ve, "and the power to see and hear and speak."

The gods named the man Ask and the woman Embla. From them was all mankind created.

The giants continued without ceasing to disturb the gods at their labors, and they soon began to harry the race of men. To protect men the gods built a great fortress encircling the midmost region of the world. They made it from the eyebrows of Ymir. This fortress and all that it contained was given the name of Midgard. It was the domain of man. Beyond its borders, where the sea joined the edge of the world, lay Jotunheim, the land of the giants.

In the very center of the universe, in the highest part, the gods built the city of Asgard. Here the gods and their kindred dwelt. Many tales and wonders are told of it. The way to Asgard lay across the bridge Bifrost, which we call the rainbow. It was made with cunning and great magic, and its colors shone brightly in the sky. The god Heimdal guarded the bridge. He needed less sleep than a bird and by day or night could see for a hundred leagues. Heimdal could hear the growing of the grass upon the ground and of wool upon the backs of sheep. He was a fit watchman for the gods.

A mighty ash tree rose above Asgard, whose branches spread abroad over the whole world. It was called Yggdrasil, the tree of the universe. The tree had three great roots. One root was in the realm of the gods, the second was among the Frost-Giants, and the third in the depths of Niflheim. Beside the root in Niflheim was a fearfull well, deep and dark, and in its depths lay the dreadful serpent Nidhogg. The serpent gnawed continually at the root of the tree, threatening to destroy it.

The tree flourished in spite of the serpent because it was watered daily with the water from Urd's Well. This well lay beside the root of the tree in the realm of the gods. Its waters were so pure that all things which came into it were made as white as the film which lies within an eggshell. Three of the Norns, those sisters who determined the fate of gods and men, lived beside the root. Each day they took water from Urd's Well and sprinkled it over the tree Yggdrasil so that its limbs would not wither or rot.

Two swans also lived beside Urd's Well. In the branches of the tree lived many animals: a wise eagle, four stags, and the little squirrel named Ratatosk. He ran up and down the tree bearing news between the eagle and the serpent.

It was beside Urd's Well that the gods held their assemblies and gathered together to pass judgment. They crossed over by way of the bridge Bifrost. Only Thor did not trouble to use the bridge. In his impatient way he waded the streams with his long strides and arrived before the others.

Another well lay beside the root in the country of the giants. It belonged to the giant Mimir. Wisdom and knowledge were contained in the waters of this well, and Mimir guarded it closely. One day Odin decided to seek out Mimir and ask a drink from his well. Odin set out from Asgard and traveled the long journey to Jotunheim and Mimir's Well.

"O Mimir," asked Odin, "I would gain wisdom from the waters that lie in your well. Will you give me leave to drink of it?"

"How greatly," asked Mimir, "do you desire this wisdom? The price is dear."

"What do you ask?" said Odin.

"If you will leave one of your eyes with me you shall drink of the well," said Mimir. "That is the only price."

And because Odin so greatly desired to be wise he gave his eye in exchange for a drink from Mimir's Well. Henceforth he had but one eye to view the outward world, but his wisdom taught him to see deep into the hearts of men.

ODIN GOES TO MIMIR'S WELL

Padraic Colum

Odin was a sky god, as was Zeus, yet unlike his Greek counterpart, Odin was solemn because he took seriously his role as protector of the human race. Zeus punished Prometheus for giving men fire. Odin suffered great pain to gain knowledge that would enrich the lives of men—the knowledge of magic runes that gave protection and skaldic mead which made the drinker a poet. In this story Odin willingly exchanges an eye for the understanding that, while it would not prevent the gods' doom, would save the human race from the Wyrd of the Gods. Odin is here more than the god of battle; he assumes the mantle of savior.

And so Odin, no longer riding on Sleipner, his eight-legged steed; no longer wearing his golden armour and his eagle-helmet, and without even his spear in his hand, travelled through Midgard, the World of Men, and made his way towards Jötunheim, the Realm of the Giants.

No longer was he called Odin All-Father, but Vegtam the Wanderer. He wore a cloak of dark blue and he carried a traveller's staff in his hands. And now, as he went towards Mimir's Well, which was near to Jötunheim, he came upon a Giant riding on a great Stag.

Odin seemed a man to men and a giant to giants. He went beside the Giant on the great Stag and the two talked together. "Who art thou, O brother?" Odin asked the Giant.

"I am Vafthrudner, the wisest of the Giants," said the one who was riding on the Stag. Odin knew him then. Vafthrudner was indeed the wisest of the Giants, and many went to strive to gain wisdom from him. But those who went to him had to answer the riddles Vafthrudner asked, and if they failed to answer the Giant took their heads off.

"I am Vegtam the Wanderer," Odin said, "and I know who thou art, O Vafthrudner. I would strive to learn something from thee."

The Giant laughed, showing his teeth. "Ho, ho," he said, "I am ready for a game with thee. Dost thou know the stakes? My head to thee if I cannot answer any question thou wilt ask. And if thou canst not answer any question that I may ask, then thy head goes to me. Ho, ho, ho. And now let us begin."

"I am ready," Odin said.

"Then tell me," said Vafthruder, "tell me the name of the river that divides Asgard from Jötunheim?"

"Ifling is the name of that river," said Odin. "Ifling that is dead cold, yet never frozen."

"Thou hast answered rightly, O Wanderer," said the Giant. "But thou hast still to answer other questions. What are the names of the horses that Day and Night drive across the sky?"

"Skinfaxe and Hrimfaxe," Odin answered. Vafthrudner was startled to hear one say the names that were known only to the Gods and to the wisest of the Giants. There was only one question now that he might ask before it came to the stranger's turn to ask him questions.

"Tell me," said Vafthrudner, "what is the name of the plain on which the last battle will be fought?"

"The Plain of Vigard," said Odin, "the plain that is a hundred miles long and a hundred miles across."

It was now Odin's turn to ask Vafthrudner questions. "What will be the last words that Odin will whisper into the ear of Baldur, his dear son?" he asked.

Very startled was the Giant Vafthrudner at that question. He sprang to the ground and looked at the stranger keenly.

"Only Odin knows what his last words to Baldur will be," he said, "and only Odin would have asked that question. Thou art Odin, O Wanderer, and thy question I cannot answer."

"Then," said Odin, "if thou wouldst keep thy head, answer me this: what price will Mimir ask for a draught from the Well of Wisdom that he guards?"

"He will ask thy right eye as a price, O Odin," said Vafthrudner.

"Will he ask no less a price than that?" said Odin.

"He will ask no less a price. Many have come to him for a draught from the Well of Wisdom, but no one yet has given the price Mimir asks. I have answered thy question, O Odin. Now give up thy claim to my head and let me go on my way."

"I give up my claim to thy head," said Odin. Then Vafthrudner, the wisest of the Giants, went on his way, riding on his great Stag.

It was a terrible price that Mimir would ask for a draught from the Well of Wisdom, and very troubled was Odin All-Father when it was revealed to him. His right eye! For all time to be

without the sight of his right eye! Almost he would have turned back to Asgard, giving up his quest for wisdom.

He went on, turning neither to Asgard nor to Mimir's Well. And when he went towards the South he saw Muspelheim, where stood Surtur with the Flaming Sword, a terrible figure, who would one day join the Giants in their war against the Gods. And when he turned North he heard the roaring of the cauldron Hvergelmer as it poured itself out of Niflheim, the place of darkness and dread. And Odin knew that the world must not be left between Surtur, who would destroy it with fire, and Niflheim, that would gather it back to Darkness and Nothingness. He, the eldest of the Gods, would have to win the wisdom that would help to save the world.

And so, with his face stern in front of his loss and pain, Odin All-Father turned and went towards Mimir's Well. It was under the great root of Yggdrasill—the root that grew out of Jötunheim. And there sat Mimir, the Guardian of the Well of Wisdom, with his deep eyes bent upon the deep water. And Mimir, who had drunk every day from the Well of Wisdom, knew who it was that stood before him.

"Hail, Odin, Eldest of the Gods," he said.

Then Odin made reverence to Mimir, the wisest of the world's beings. "I would drink from your well, Mimir," he said.

"There is a price to be paid. All who have come here to drink have shrunk from paying that price. Will you, Eldest of the Gods, pay it?"

"I will not shrink from the price that has to be paid, Mimir," said Odin All-Father.

"Then drink," said Mimir. He filled up a great horn with water from the well and gave it to Odin.

Odin took the horn in both his hands and drank and drank. And as he drank all the future became clear to him. He saw all the sorrows and troubles that would fall upon Men and Gods. But he saw, too, why the sorrows and troubles had to fall, and he saw how they might be borne so that Gods and Men, by being noble in the days of sorrow and trouble, would leave in the world a force that one day, a day that was far off indeed, would destroy the evil that brought terror and sorrow and despair into the world.

Then when he had drunk out of the great horn

that Mimir had given him, he put his hand to his face and he plucked out his right eye. Terrible was the pain that Odin All-Father endured. But he made no groan nor moan. He bowed his head and put his cloak before his face, as Mimir took the eye and let it sink deep, deep into the water of the Well of Wisdom. And there the Eye of Odin stayed, shining up through the water, a sign to all who came to that place of the price that the Father of the Gods had paid for his wisdom.

THE APPLES OF IDUNA

Dorothy Hosford

Loki, who plays an important part in most of the well-known Norse myths, is a puzzling figure. Although a thief, a liar, and a deceiver, he is the companion and friend of the gods. In the early tales his nature is ambivalent: he is neither entirely evil nor entirely good. In this story, Loki is forced to steal Iduna's apples and is the one to undo his wrong by rescuing her.

That Iduna's apples are necessary to the deities, (without them they will age and die) emphasizes the vulnerability of the Norse gods. The symbol of apples of the gods is very old in Scandinavian and in Irish mythology.

Odin often traveled forth from Asgard to take part in the affairs of men and to see what was going on in all the wide expanses of the world. One day he set out on such a journey, taking Loki and Hoenir with him. They wandered a long way over mountains and waste land and at length they grew hungry. But food was hard to find in that lonely country.

They had walked many miles when they saw a herd of oxen grazing in a valley.

"There is food for us at last," said Hoenir.

They went down into the valley and it was not long before they had one of the oxen roasting on a fire. While their meal cooked they stretched out on the ground to rest. When they thought the meat had cooked long enough they took it off the fire. But it was not yet ready. So they put it back over the embers and waited.

"I can wait no longer," cried Loki at last. "I am starving. Surely the meat is ready."

The gods scattered the fire once more and pulled forth the ox, but it seemed as though it had not even begun to cook. It was certainly not fit for eating.

This was a strange thing and not even Odin knew the meaning of it. As they wondered among themselves, they heard a voice speak from the great oak tree above them.

"It is because of me," said the voice, "that there is no virtue in your fire and your meat will not cook."

They looked up into the branches of the tree and there sat a huge eagle.

"If you are willing to give me a share of the ox, then it will cook in the fire," said the eagle.

There was little the gods could do but agree to this. The eagle let himself float down from the tree and alighted by the fire. In no time at all the ox was roasted. At once the eagle took to himself the two hindquarters and the two forequarters as well.

This greediness angered Loki. He snatched up a great pole, brandished it with all his strength, and struck the eagle with it. The eagle plunged violently at the blow and whirled into the air. One end of the pole stuck fast to the eagle's back and Loki's hands stuck fast to the other end. No matter how he tried he could not free them. Swooping and turning, the eagle dragged Loki after him in his flight, flying just low enough that Loki's feet and legs knocked against stones and rock heaps and trees. Loki thought his arms would be torn from his shoulders. He cried out for mercy.

"Put me down! Put me down!" begged Loki. "Free me and you shall have the whole ox for your own."

"I do not want the ox," cried the eagle. "I want only one thing—Iduna and her apples. Deliver them into my power and I will set you free."

Iduna was the beautiful and beloved wife of the god Bragi. She guarded the most precious possession of the gods, the apples of youth. Unless they might eat of them the gods would grow old and feeble like mortal men. They kept the gods ever young. Iduna and her apples were priceless beyond words.

"Iduna and her apples! Such a thing cannot be done," shouted Loki.

"Then I will fly all day," screamed the eagle. "I will knock you against the rocks until you die." And he dragged Loki through rough tree branches and against the sides of mountains and over the rocky earth. Loki could endure it no longer.

"I will do as you ask," he cried. "I will bring Iduna to you, and her apples as well."

"Give me your oath," said the eagle. Loki gave his oath. A time was set when Loki should put Iduna in the eagle's power.

The eagle straightway made Loki free and flew off into the sky. A much-bruised Loki returned to his companions and all three set off on their homeward journey. But Odin and Hoenir did not know the promise which Loki had made.

Loki pondered how he could keep his word to the eagle, whom he now knew to be the giant Thjazi in disguise. When the appointed day came Loki approached Iduna.

"Iduna," he said, speaking gently, "yesterday I found a tree on which grow wondrous apples. It is in the wood to the north of Asgard. They are like your apples in color and shape. Surely they must have the same properties. Should we not gather them and bring them to Asgard?"

"There are no apples anywhere," said Iduna, "like to my apples."

"These are," said Loki. "They are very like. Come and look for yourself. If you bring your apples we can put them side by side and you will see."

So Iduna went with Loki to the wood, taking her apples with her. While they were in the wood the giant Thjazi swooped down in his eagle's plumage and carried Iduna and her apples off to his abode.

The gods soon missed Iduna. And they knew her apples were gone, for the signs of old age began to show among them. They grew bent and stiff and stooped.

Odin called a hasty council of the gods. They asked each other what they knew of Iduna.

"Where was she last seen?" asked Odin.

Heimdal had seen her walking out of Asgard with Loki. That was the last that was known of her.

Odin sent Thor to seize Loki and to bring him to the council. When Loki was brought the gods threatened him with tortures and death unless he told what he knew of Iduna. Loki grew frightened and admitted that Iduna had been carried off to Jotunheim.

"I will go in search of her," he cried, "if Freyja will lend me her falcon wings."

Freyja was more than willing. When Loki had put on the feather dress he flew to the north in the direction of Jotunheim.

He flew for a long time before he came to the home of Thjazi, the giant. Then he circled slowly overhead and saw Iduna walking below. She carried in her arms her golden casket of apples. Thjazi was nowhere to be seen, for he had rowed out to sea to fish. Loki quickly alighted on the ground beside Iduna.

"Hasten, Iduna," he cried, "I will rescue you." And he changed Iduna into the shape of a nut and flew off with her in his claws.

Loki had no sooner gone than Thjazi arrived home. At once he missed Iduna and her precious apples. Putting on his eagle's plumage, he flew into the air. Far off in the distance he saw the falcon flying. Instantly he took after him. The eagle's wings beat powerfully, making a deep rushing sound like a great wind. Thjazi drew nearer and nearer to Loki. Loki flew with all his might, but the eagle was bearing down upon the falcon just as the towers of Asgard came into view. With a last burst of strength Loki hastened toward the shining battlements.

The gods were on watch for Loki's return. They saw the falcon bearing the nut between his claws, with the eagle in close pursuit. Quickly they built a great pile of wood shavings just outside the wall of Asgard. As Loki came near he swooped down low over the shavings. Thjazi swooped down too, hoping to seize the falcon

before he reached the safety of Asgard. Just as the eagle came close to the pile the gods set fire to the shavings. Instantly the fire blazed up, but Thjazi could not stop himself. He plunged into the flames and the feathers of his wings took fire. Then he could fly no more and the gods slew him where he was.

There was great rejoicing within the walls of Asgard to have Iduna safe once more. And the gods grew young and bright again.

THE DEATH OF BALDER

Dorothy Hosford

In this version, taken from Snorri's Prose Edda, Loki is the direct cause of Balder's death, while in the earlier sources there is little evidence of his treachery. Snorri emphasized the evil side to Loki's nature. Scholars explain the development of Loki from a mischievous trickster to an evildoer as reflecting the influence of Christianity and its tradition of the devil on Norse mythology. Snorri's sources and his own Christian background would likely have been touched by this.

Balder was the fairest and most beloved of all the gods. He was wise in judgment, gracious in speech, and all his deeds were pure and good. Wherever Balder went there was joy and warmth and gladness. He was beloved by gods and men, and so beautiful that the whitest flower which grew on the hillside was named "Balder's Brow."

It came about that Balder dreamed great and perilous dreams touching his life. Night after night they troubled his sleep. When Balder spoke of these dreams to the other gods they were filled with foreboding. They knew some danger threatened him and all the gods took counsel together as to how they might save Balder. They came to this decision: they would ask safety for Balder from every kind of danger.

Frigg, who was the mother of Balder, went to

all things in the world to ask their help. Fire and water, stones, earth, and trees, iron and metal of all kinds, birds, beasts, and even serpents promised they would not harm Balder.

When the gods knew that Balder was safe they made up a game which they took delight in playing. Balder would stand in a circle of the gods and they would strike at him or hurl stones or cast missiles of one kind or another. But Balder stood unhurt in the midst of it all. And this seemed to the gods a wondrous thing, full of awe.

Loki alone was not pleased that Balder took no hurt. His evil, crafty mind began to plot against Balder the Good. Loki made himself appear like an old woman and in this likeness he went to the dwelling of Balder's mother. He greeted Frigg and she asked him if he knew what the gods were doing at their assembly.

"The gods have a new game. Balder stands before them and they hurl weapons of every kind at him," answered Loki, speaking with the voice of an old woman. "It is a strange thing that nothing harms him."

"Nothing will harm Balder, neither weapons nor rocks nor trees," said Frigg. "I have taken oaths of them all."

"Have all things taken oaths to spare Balder?" asked the old woman.

"All things save one," said Frigg. "A small tree-spout grows west of Valhalla. It is called Mistletoe. I thought it too young a thing to be bound by an oath."

Immediately the old woman went away. Loki changed himself into his own shape and went west of Valhalla. He tore up the Mistletoe by the roots and carried it to where the gods were assembled.

Hod, the brother of Balder, took no part in the game because he was blind. He stood outside the ring of men.

Loki spoke to him. "Why do you not shoot at Balder?"

"I cannot see where Balder stands, nor have I any weapons," answered Hod.

Then Loki said: "You should do as the others do and show Balder honor. I will show you where he stands. Shoot at him with this wand."

Hod took the Mistletoe wand and shot at Balder, and Loki guided his hand.

The shaft flew through Balder and he fell dead to the earth. This was the greatest mischance that had ever befallen gods and men.

When Balder fell to the earth the gods could not speak a word for grief and anguish, nor could they move to lift him where he lay. Each looked at the other and they were all of one mind whose evil hand had done this deed. Yet they could take no revenge for they stood on hallowed ground.

When they tried to speak the tears came and the gods wept bitterly for the loss of Balder. They had no words with which to name their sorrow. Of them all Odin grieved most, for he understood best how great was the loss which had come to the gods.

The mother of Balder was the first to speak. "If any among you," said Frigg, "would win all my love and favor, let him ride the road to Hela's realm and seek Balder among the dead. Let him offer Hela a ransom if she will but let Balder come home to Asgard."

Hermod the Bold undertook the perilous journey. The great eight-footed horse of Odin, named Sleipnir, was brought forth. Hermod mounted and sped at once upon his way.

The gods took the body of Balder and brought it down to the sea, where Balder's ship was drawn up upon the shore. The gods wished to launch the ship and build Balder's funeral pyre upon it, but they could not move it from its place.

Then Odin sent for the giantess Hyrrokin, famed for her strength. She thrust the boat into the waters with such might that fire burst from the rollers beneath it and the earth trembled.

When the funeral pyre had been built, the body of Balder was borne to the ship. When his wife, Nanna, saw it her heart broke with grief and she died. The gods, with sorrow, laid her body beside Balder. The fire was kindled. Thor stood near. With a sad heart he lifted his hammer above the blaze and hallowed the flames.

People of many races came to the burning. First of all was Odin. His two ravens flew above him and Frigg was by his side. The Valkyries were also with him. Frey rode in his chariot drawn by his boar called Gold-Mane and Freyja drove her cats. Then came the other gods and goddesses. Many from the lands of the Frost-Giants and the Hill-Giants were there also. All grieved for Balder.

Odin laid upon the fire his ring which was called Draupnir, from which every ninth night dropped eight gold rings like to itself. The flames from the funeral ship rose on high, shining in the air and on the waters. The hearts of the gods were heavy with grief as they watched the burning.

Meanwhile Hermod was on his way to Hela. He rode nine nights through valleys so dark and deep that he could see nothing. At length he came to the river Gjoll. He rode on to the bridge which is paved with glittering gold and guarded by the maiden Modgud. She asked Hermod his name and from what country and people he came.

"Only yesterday," she said, "five companies of dead men crossed this bridge. But today it thunders as much under you riding alone. Nor have you the pallor of death. Why come you this way?"

"I have been sent to seek Balder among the

dead," Hermod answered. "Has Balder passed this road?"

The maiden answered that Balder had crossed the bridge. "The way lies downward and to the north," she said.

Hermod rode on until he came to the wall of Hela's realm. He got down from his horse and made the girths of the saddle tight. Then he mounted again and pricked the horse with his spurs. In one great leap Sleipnir cleared the gates.

Hermod rode to the great hall where the dead were gathered. He dismounted and went inside. There he saw Balder sitting in the place of honor. Hermod stayed through the night. When morning came he begged Hela that Balder might ride home with him.

"The gods are desolate without him," said Hermod. "Every being in the world longs for his return."

Hela answered that it should be put to a test whether Balder were so greatly beloved.

"If all things in the world, living and dead, weep for him," said Hela, "he shall go back to Asgard and the gods. But if there is one thing which bears him no love and will not weep, Balder must remain with me."

When Hermod rose to leave, Balder went with him out of the hall. Balder gave the ring Draupnir to Hermod and asked that he take it to Odin for a remembrance. Nanna, Balder's wife, sent Frigg a linen smock and other gifts.

Hermod rode back and came to Asgard. He told all that he had seen and heard. Then the gods sent messengers all over the world to ask all things to weep for Balder, that he might return to them. All wept for Balder: men, and all living things; the earth and stones and trees, and every kind of metal. In the early morning you can still see their tears when the dew lies upon the grass.

As the messengers came home, their work well done, they found an old woman sitting by a cave. They asked her, as they had asked all others, to weep tears that Balder might come forth from the place of the dead. But she answered:

"I will weep no tears for Balder. I loved him not. Let Hela keep what she holds. Let her keep what she holds."

And because one out of all the world would not weep for the god, Balder must stay where he was. Gods and men knew that this again was Loki's evil work. This time he must pay the price for all that he had done. The gods revenged themselves on Loki. But Balder remained with Hela, and the earth was never again as fair to gods or men.

BALDER AND THE MISTLETOE

Abbie Farwell Brown

This version of Balder's death has an emotional tone inappropriate to the tragedy it reveals. It is included in this comparative anthology only as an example of the poorly told Norse myths.

Please see the introduction to Norse Mythology for a discussion of style and the previous selection for a well-told version of Balder's death.

Now at this time Balder the beautiful had a strange dream. He dreamed that a cloud came before the sun, and all Asgard was dark. He waited for the cloud to drift away, and for the

"Balder and the Mistletoe" from *In the Days of the Giants* by Abbie Farwell Brown. Published by Houghton Mifflin, 1902.

sun to smile again. But no; the sun was gone forever, he thought; and Balder awoke feeling very sad. The next night Balder had another dream. This time he dreamed that it was still dark as before; the flowers were withered and the gods were growing old; even Idun's magic apples could not make them young again. And all were weeping and wringing their hands as though some dreadful thing had happened. Balder awoke feeling strangely frightened, yet he said no word to Nanna his wife, for he did not want to trouble her.

When it came night again Balder slept and dreamed a third dream, a still more terrible one than the other two had been. He thought that in the dark, lonely world there was nothing but a sad voice, which cried, "The sun is gone! The spring is gone! Joy is gone! For Balder the beautiful is dead, dead, dead!"

This time Balder awoke with a cry, and Nanna asked him what was the matter. So he had to tell her of his dream, and he was sadly frightened; for in those days dreams were often sent to folk as messages, and what the gods dreamed usually came true. Nanna ran sobbing to Queen Frigg, who was Balder's mother, and told her all the dreadful dream, asking what could be done to prevent it from coming true.

Now Balder was Queen Frigg's dearest son. Thor was older and stronger, and more famous for his great deeds; but Frigg loved far better gold-haired Balder. And indeed he was the best-loved of all the Aesir; for he was gentle, fair and wise, and wherever he went folk grew happy and light-hearted at the very sight of him, just as we do when we first catch a glimpse of spring peeping over the hilltop into Winterland. So when Frigg heard of Balder's woeful dream, she was frightened almost out of her wits.

"He must not die! He shall not die!" she cried. "He is so dear to all the world, how could there be anything which would hurt him?"

And then a wonderful thought came to Frigg. "I will travel over the world and make all things promise not to injure my boy," she said. "Nothing shall pass my notice. I will get the word of everything."

So first she went to the gods themselves, gathered on Ida Plain for their morning exercise; and telling them of Balder's dream, she begged them to give the promise. Oh, what a shout arose when they heard her words!

"Hurt Balder!—our Balder! Not for the world, we promise! The dream is wrong—there is nothing so cruel as to wish harm to Balder the beautiful!" they cried. But deep in their hearts they felt a secret fear which would linger until they should hear that all things had given their promise. What if harm were indeed to come to Balder! The thought was too dreadful.

Then Frigg went to see all the beasts who live in field or forest or rocky den. Willingly they gave their promise never to harm hair of gentle Balder. "For he is ever kind to us," they said, "and we love him as if he were one of ourselves. Not with claws or teeth or hoofs or horns will any beast hurt Balder."

Next Frigg spoke to the birds and fishes, reptiles and insects. And all—even the venomous serpents—cried that Balder was their friend, and that they would never do aught to hurt his dear body. "Not with beak or talon, bite or sting or poison fang, will one of us hurt Balder," they promised. . . .

*   *   *

Oh, the sad thing that befell! Straight through the air flew the little arrow, straight as magic and Loki's arm could direct it. Straight to Balder's heart it sped, piercing through jerkin and shirt and all, to give its bitter message of "Loki's love," as he had said. And that was the end of sunshine and spring and joy in Asgard, for the dream had come true, and Balder the beautiful was dead.

When the Aesir saw what had happened, there was a great shout of fear and horror, and they rushed upon Höd, who had thrown the fatal arrow.

"What is it? What have I done?" asked the poor blind brother, trembling at the tumult which had followed his shot.

"You have slain Balder!" cried the Aesir. "Wretched Höd, how could you do it?"

"It was the old woman—the evil old woman, who stood at my elbow and gave me a little twig to throw," gasped Höd. "She must be a witch."

Then the Aesir scattered over Ida Plain to look for the old woman who had done the evil deed; but she had mysteriously disappeared.

"It must be Loki," said wise Heimdal. "It is Loki's last and vilest trick."

"Oh, my Balder, my beautiful Balder!" wailed Queen Frigg, throwing herself on the body of her son. "If I had only made the mistletoe give me the promise, you would have been saved. It was I who told Loki of the mistletoe—so it is I who have killed you. Oh, my son, my son!" . . .

*   *   *

American Indian Mythology

While American Indian folklore has a long history, it is more than a reflection of past beliefs and forgotten traditions—unlike European folklore. Anthropologists have found that many Indian groups have preserved and are still preserving elements of their native culture and religion through ancient folk narratives.

The Spanish military missionaries of the seventeenth and eighteenth centuries were extremely firm in their zeal to Christianize the Indians of the Southwest. Entire tribes were baptized en masse and Indian names were changed to European ones. The alternatives to Christianity were fleeing from the whites or death. All this drove the Indian religion underground, into the kivas. While the most significant myths were taught in secrecy, only the "little stories," the *pourquoi* tales, were told openly. This is why the most well-known and most collected stories are these explanatory tales.

There is no standard folklore tradition shared by all American Indian groups. Each culture, and even individual tribes, developed their own myths. While a number of motifs appear to be common throughout the continent, their use and arrangement within narratives varies significantly from tribe to tribe. Similarly, many groups have quite different narratives dealing with the same

From *The Earth Is on a Fish's Back* by Natalia Belting. Illustrated by Esta Nesbitt. Copyright © 1965 by Natalia Belting. Reproduced by permission of Holt, Rinehart and Winston, Inc.

ideas: the origin of the earth, the first people, the beginnings of culture, as well as tales about a Culture Hero and his exploits.

Although some Indian narratives seem quite similar to European tales, there is no way to be certain how many of these were developed independently. Diffusion can account for a number of them. More than two hundred European folk tales are known to have entered the Indian tradition through early French and Spanish trading and intermarriage with the Indians. "Little Burnt Face," an allegory about the transformation of the scorched earth after the rains, and "Poor Turkey Girl" have been shown by folklorists to be adaptations of the European "Cinderella" story. Because "Little Burnt Face" is an allegory, it is included in the following selection, while "Poor Turkey Girl," which lacks the mythic overtones, is included in the folktale section.

As the above distinction shows, it is not always easy to classify Indian folk narratives because they are not clearly divided into tales and myths. A story may be told primarily for entertainment one time and at another may be used as part of a religious ceremony. This often confuses the outsider but not the member of the culture. Since Indian myths and tales are not sharply distinguished, English retellings are published as legends, myths, tales, or traditions. Whatever they are called, children enjoy hearing and reading them.

HOW THE WORLD WAS MADE / Cheyenne

Alice Marriott
Carol K. Rachlin

The following myth is unusually complex in its detailed explanation of the origin of all life. Most tribes have only fragmentary myths about the establishment of the world and the creation of animals and people.

The motif of the turtle holding the earth on her back is common among the Northeast Woodlands peoples, and its inclusion in this Cheyenne tale reveals that they retained their mythology even after they left the Great Lakes region in the mid-seventeenth century. Horses made it possible for them to abandon their former agricultural life for buffalo hunting.

In the beginning there was nothing, and Maheo, the All Spirit, lived in the void. He looked around him, but there was nothing to see. He listened, but there was nothing to hear. There was only Maheo, alone in nothingness.

Because of the greatness of his Power, Maheo was not lonesome. His being was a Universe. But as he moved through the endless time of nothing-

ness, it seemed to Maheo that his Power should be put to use. What good is Power, Maheo asked himself, if it is not used to make a world and people to live in it?

With his Power, Maheo created a great water, like a lake, but salty. Out of this salty water, Maheo knew he could bring all life that ever was to be. The lake itself was life, if Maheo so commanded it. In the darkness of nothingness, Maheo could feel the coolness of the water and taste on his lips the tang of the salt.

"There should be water beings," Maheo told

his Power. And so it was. First the fish, swimming in the deep water, and then the mussels and snails and crawfish, lying on the sand and mud Maheo had formed so his lake should have a bottom.

Let us also create something that lives on the water, Maheo thought to his Power.

And so it was. For now there were snow geese, and mallards and teal and coots and terns and loons living and swimming about on the water's surface. Maheo could hear the splashing of their feet and the flapping of their wings in the darkness.

I should like to see the things that have been created, Maheo decided.

And, again, so it was. Light began to grow and spread, first white and bleached in the east, then golden and strong till it filled the middle of the sky and extended all around the horizon. Maheo watched the light, and he saw the birds and fishes, and the shell fish lying on the bottom of the lake as the light showed them to him.

Then the snow goose paddled over to where she thought Maheo was, in the space above the lake. "I do not see You, but I know that You exist," the goose began. "I do not know where You are, but I know You must be everywhere. Listen to me, Maheo. This is good water that You have made, on which we live. But birds are not like fish. Sometimes we get tired swimming. Sometimes we would like to get out of the water."

"Then fly," said Maheo, and he waved his arms, and all the water birds flew, skittering along the surface of the lake until they had speed enough to rise in the air. The skies were darkened with them.

"How beautiful their wings are in the light," Maheo said to his Power, as the birds wheeled and turned, and became living patterns against the sky.

The loon was the first to drop back to the surface of the lake. "Maheo," he said, looking around, for he knew that Maheo was all about him, "You have made us sky and light to fly in, and You have made us water to swim in. It sounds ungrateful to want something else, yet still we do. When we are tired of swimming and tired of flying, we should like a dry solid place where

we could walk and rest. Give us a place to build our nests, please, Maheo."

"So be it," answered Maheo, "but to make such a place I must have your help, all of you. By myself, I have made four things: the water, the light, the sky, and the peoples of the water. Now I must have help if I am to create more, for my Power will only let me make four things by myself."

"Tell us how we can help You," said all the water peoples. "We are ready to do what You say."

Maheo stretched out his hand and beckoned. "Let the biggest and the swiftest try to find land first," he said, and the snow goose came to him.

"I am ready to try," the snow goose said, and she drove herself along the water until the white wake behind her grew and grew to a sharp white point that drove her up into the air as the feathers drive an arrow. She flew high into the sky, until she was only a dark spot against the clearness of the light. Then the goose turned, and down she plunged, faster than any arrow, and dived into the water. She pierced the surface with her beak as if it were the point of a spear.

The snow goose was gone a long time. Maheo counted to four four hundred times before she rose to the surface of the water and lay there floating, her beak half open as she gasped for air.

"What have you brought us?" Maheo asked her, and the snow goose sighed sadly, and answered, "Nothing. I brought nothing back."

Then the loon tried, and after him, the mallard. Each in turn rose until he was a speck against the light, and turned and dived with the speed of a flashing arrow into the water. And each in turn rose wearily, and wearily answered, "Nothing," when Maheo asked him what he had brought.

At last there came the little coot, paddling across the surface of the water very quietly, dipping his head sometimes to catch a tiny fish, and shaking the water beads from his scalp lock whenever he rose.

"Maheo," the little coot said softly, "when I put my head beneath the water, it seems to me that I see something there, far below. Perhaps I can swim down to it—I don't know. I can't fly or dive like my sister and brothers. All I can do is swim, but I will swim down the best I know how, and go as deep as I can. May I try, please, Maheo?"

"Little brother," said Maheo, "no man can do more than his best, and I have asked for the help of all the water peoples. Certainly you shall try. Perhaps swimming will be better than diving, after all. Try, little brother, and see what you can do."

"Hah-ho!" the little coot said. "Thank you, Maheo," and he put his head under the water and swam down and down and down and down, until he was out of sight.

The coot was gone a long, long, long, long time. Then Maheo and the other birds could see a little dark spot beneath the water's surface, slowly rising toward them. It seemed as if they would never see the coot himself, but at last the spot began to have a shape. Still it rose and rose, and at last Maheo and the water peoples could surely see who it was. The little coot was swimming up from the bottom of the salty lake.

When the cot reached the surface, he stretched his closed beak upward into the light, but he did not open it.

"Give me what you have brought," Maheo said, and the coot let his beak fall open, so a little ball of mud could fall from his tongue into Maheo's hand, for when Maheo wanted to, he could become like a man.

"Go, little brother," Maheo said. "Thank you, and may what you have brought always protect you."

And so it was and so it is, for the coot's flesh still tastes of mud, and neither man nor animal will eat a coot unless there is nothing else to eat.

Maheo rolled the ball of mud between the palms of his hands, and it began to grow larger, until there was almost too much mud for Maheo to hold. He looked around for a place to put the mud, but there was nothing but water or air anywhere around him.

"Come and help me again, water peoples," Maheo called. "I must put this mud somewhere. One of you must let me place it on his back."

All the fish and all the other water creatures came swimming to Maheo, and he tried to find the right one to carry the mud. The mussels and

snails and crawfish were too small, although they all had solid backs, and they lived too deep in the water for the mud to rest on them. The fish were too narrow, and their back fins stuck up through the mud and cut it to pieces. Finally only one water person was left.

"Grandmother Turtle," Maheo asked, "do you think that you can help me?"

"I'm very old and very slow, but I will try," the turtle answered. She swam over to Maheo, and he piled the mud on her rounded back, until he had made a hill. Under Maheo's hands the hill grew and spread and flattened out, until the Grandmother Turtle was hidden from sight.

"So be it," Maheo said once again. "Let the earth be known as our Grandmother, and let the Grandmother who carries the earth be the only being who is at home beneath the water, or within the earth, or above the ground; the only one who can go anywhere by swimming or by walking as she chooses."

And so it was, and so it is. Grandmother Turtle and all her descendants must walk very slowly, for they carry the whole weight of the whole world and all its peoples on their backs.

Now there was earth as well as water, but the earth was barren. And Maheo said to his Power, "Our Grandmother Earth is like a woman; she should be fruitful. Let her begin to bear life. Help me, my Power."

When Maheo said that, trees and grass sprang up to become the Grandmother's hair. The flowers became her bright ornaments, and the fruits and the seeds were the gifts that the earth offered back to Maheo. The birds came to rest on her hands when they were tired, and the fish came close to her sides. Maheo looked at the Earth Woman and he thought she was very beautiful; the most beautiful thing he had made so far.

She should not be alone, Maheo thought. Let me give her something of myself, so she will know that I am near her and that I love her.

Maheo reached into his right side, and pulled out a rib bone. He breathed on the bone, and laid it softly on the bosom of the Earth Woman. The bone moved and stirred, stood upright and walked. The first man had come to be.

"He is alone with the Grandmother Earth as I once was alone with the void," said Maheo. "It is not good for anyone to be alone." So Maheo fashioned a human woman from his left rib, and set her with the man. Then there were two persons on the Grandmother Earth, her children and Maheo's. They were happy together, and Maheo was happy as he watched them.

After a year, in the springtime, the first child was born. As the years passed, there were other children. They went their ways, and founded many tribes.

From time to time, after that, Maheo realized that his people walking on the earth had certain needs. At those times, Maheo, with the help of his Power, created animals to feed and care for the people. He gave them deer for clothing and food, porcupines to make their ornaments, the swift antelopes on the open plains, and the prairie dogs that burrowed in the earth.

At last Maheo thought to his Power, Why, one animal can take the place of all the others put together, and then he made the buffalo.

Maheo is still with us. He is everywhere, watching all his people, and all the creation he has made. Maheo is all good and all life; he is the creator, the guardian, and the teacher. We are all here because of Maheo.

As told to Alice Marriott and Carol K. Rachlin by Mary Little Bear Inkanish, Cheyenne, 1960.

HOW THE WORLD WAS MADE /Modoc

Alice Marriott
Carol K. Rachlin

In contrast to the previous Cheyenne tale, the following Modoc myth is much simpler. It is an example of the short origin tales that explain local geographical features. The motifs of the world being covered by a primeval water and the Culture Hero-Creator sending various animals to the bottom to bring up mud are common in all areas of North America except the Southwest.

An interesting feature of the Modoc myth is the teller's belief that Kumokums will return. Such a statement reveals a contemporary endurance of the traditional heritage.

Kumokums was the one that made the world and everything that is in it. This is how he did it.

Kumokums sat down beside Tule Lake, on its east shore. He was not afraid, but he was interested, because there was nothing anywhere but Tule Lake.

That's a lot of water, Kumokums said to himself. I wonder how it would look if it had some land around it?

So he reached down, down, down, down, down, five times, to the bottom of Tule Lake, and the fifth time he reached, Kumokums drew up a handful of mud. He piled it up in front of him, like a hill, and patted it with the palm of his hand.

As Kumokums patted the mud, it began to spread beneath his hand, out and around him, until Tule Lake was completely surrounded by earth, and Kumokums was left sitting on a little island of mud in the middle of the water.

"Well!" said Kumokums. "I didn't know it would do that."

So he drew back some of the earth on the west

and the north, to make the mountains. He cut grooves in the mountain sides with his fingernail, so the rivers could flow down to the lakes. That is why you should bury your fingernail parings, or throw them back into the water, so they will return to Kumokums.

Kumokums drew trees and plants out of the earth, and he put birds in the air, fish in the water, and animals on the land. He had shaped and decorated the world as a woman shapes and decorates a basket.

Then Kumokuns was tired. He had done everything he could think of to do, and winter was about to begin.

I will do what the bear does, Kumokums thought. I will make myself a hole where I will be safe, and sleep the winter through.

Kumokums dugs himself a hole under the bottom of Tule Lake, with the hill where he had created the world to mark the spot. By now the

hill had dried out and turned to solid rock, as it is today.

Just at the last moment, as he was about to go underground, Kumokums thought, I might want to look out sometime and see what is going on, without bothering to move around. So he scratched and scratched with his fingernail until he had made a hole in the rock, near its top, that was big enough to see through. It is still there, and people can climb the rock and look out through the hole, all around the country, for Tule Lake dried up and became planted land many years ago.

But some day Kumokums will surely wake up, and when he looks out and sees how this world has changed, perhaps he will bring the water back to the floor of Tule Lake, and things will again be as they were when Kumokums first made them.

As told to Alice Marriott by Evangeline Schonchin. Translated by Mary Chiloquin, Modocs.

THE ORIGIN OF FIRE / Nez Percé

Ella E. Clark

Fire is so important that its acquisition is one of the most popular motifs in American Indian folklore. Some tales, as in the next narrative, have animals as the main characters while other stories deal with people's need for fire. Such an interchange is common in all folklore, European as well as Indian.

Long ago the Nimipu had no fire. They could see fire in the sky sometimes, but it belonged to the Great Power. He kept it in great black bags in the sky. When the bags bumped into each other, there was a crashing, tearing sound, and through the hole that was made fire sparkled.

People longed to get it. They ate fish and meat raw as the animals do. They ate roots and berries raw as the bears do. The women grieved when they saw their little ones shivering and blue with cold. The medicine men beat on their drums in

their efforts to bring fire down from the sky, but no fire came.

At last a boy just beyond the age for the sacred vigil said that he would get the fire. People laughed at him. The medicine men angrily complained, "Do you think that you can do what we are not able to do?"

But the boy went on and made his plans. The first time that he saw the black fire bags drifting in the sky, he got ready. First he bathed, brushing himself with fir branches until he was entirely clean and was fragrant with the smell of fir. He looked very handsome.

With the inside bark of cedar he wrapped an

arrowhead and placed it beside his best and largest bow. On the ground he placed a beautiful white shell that he often wore around his neck. Then he asked his guardian spirit to help him reach the cloud with his arrow.

All the people stood watching. The medicine men said among themselves, "Let us have him killed, lest he make the Great Power angry."

But the people said, "Let him alone. Perhaps he can bring the fire down. If he does not, then we can kill him."

The boy waited until he saw that the largest fire bag was over his head, growling and rumbling. Then he raised his bow and shot the arrow straight upward. Suddenly, all the people heard a tremendous crash, and they saw a flash of fire in the sky. Then the burning arrow, like a falling star, came hurtling down among them. It struck the boy's white shell and there made a small flame.

Shouting with joy, the people rushed forward. They lighted sticks and dry bark and hurried to their tipis to start fires with them. Children and old people ran around, laughing and singing.

When the excitement had died down, people asked about the boy. But he was nowhere to be seen. On the ground lay his shell, burned so that it showed the fire colors. Near it lay the boy's bow. People tried to shoot with it, but not even the strongest man and best with bow and arrow could bend it.

The boy was never seen again. But his abalone shell is still beautiful, still touched with the colors of flame. And the fire he brought from the black bag is still in the center of each tipi, the blessing of every home.

HOW THE ANIMALS SECURED FIRE

Catherine Chandler

Coyote appears as a Culture Hero in this tale by using his cleverness to help the world. He is a familiar figure to many California, Southwest, Plateau, and Plains Indians. Yet he has other sides to his nature; he is a clever if malicious trickster in some tales and a stupid buffoon in others. The three roles can all exist in any series of adventures. Since not all of these tales are suitable for children, separate incidents such as the following are collected independently.

A long, long time ago all the fire on the earth was owned by two old women. They kept it in a little mat house and would not let a spark escape. The animal people were shivering with cold and were sick from their raw food, so they journeyed two moons to the little mat house and begged the old women to give them a firebrand.

But the old women only muttered, "No, no," and crouched closer to their fire.

Then the animals begged earnestly: "Oh, lend us a brand just for a few minutes. Our teeth are chattering and our stomachs refuse the uncooked meat. We pray you, Old Women, lend us a firebrand."

Then the animals piled all their treasures together—shells from the seashore, cones from the mountains, bows from the oak tree, and arrows from the volcanic region. They carried them to the old women's door. "Old Women," they cried, "here are all our treasures. Take them and give us one burning fagot."

Still the old women muttered, "No, no," and covered their fire with their stooping bodies.

"How the Animals Secured Fire" from *In the Reign of the Coyote* by Catherine Chandler. Published by Ginn and Company, 1905.

The animals went shivering home. They found Coyote and besought him to think of some way to get them fire.

Coyote thought and thought. Then he said, "It will be a hard struggle to get it safe to our own country. Summon every animal and then station yourselves along the route to the old women's house, each one a half sun's distance from the other. The strongest and swiftest must stand nearest the little mat house. Let each one be ready to run swiftly in his turn with the firebrand. Bear will hide himself outside the old women's home. I will go in. When I signal to him, he will make a rush and frighten them."

Coyote went to the little mat house and knocked at the door. The old women opened it. "Good morning," said Coyote in his politest voice. "May I come in and warm my feet? They are very cold."

The old women muttered, "Yes, yes."

When Coyote's toes were all flexible again, he coughed. Bear rushed in with a growl and dashed toward the old women. As they tried to protect themselves, Coyote snatched a blazing brand and fled.

But the old women were swift of foot, and as Coyote ran on with lolling tongue and panting breath, they sped after him. Just as he was beginning to slacken his pace, he reached Panther.

Panther seized the brand and bounded onward. The old women followed close. As Panther began to get weary, he arrived at Elk's station. Elk speeded like the wind, but still the old women followed close behind. Then Fox carried the stolen fire on a space, and so on in turn the animals kept up their fight, with the old women always close behind.

At last the firebrand had been carried from one animal to another across the cold country until bushytailed Squirrel was reached, and he was the next-to-the-last animal. As he seized the brand, the old women made a dash at him. He was so frightened that he almost dropped it, and in catching it firmly again, his tail caught fire. He curled his tail over his back, and it burned a black place between his shoulders. Down to this very day the squirrel has a black spot between his shoulders.

When Squirrel could run no more, he tossed the brand to the last animal in the line. This was poor little Squatty Frog. He never was much of a runner, but he did his best, hopping frantically along. The rough stones cut all his tail away; yet he managed to reach the bank of the river, on the other side of which lay the animals' country. Here the old women overtook him and tried to snatch both the brand and poor Frog. The brand had dwindled down to a tiny spark during this long race, so Frog just swallowed it and dived into the river. He swam under water to the other side and there spat out the fire on pieces of wood.

Poor Frog! He suffered in the struggle. Never since that day has his tail grown again. Then, too, the brand burned away one of his vocal cords, so that he no longer rivals the birds as he once did. That is why he dislikes fire and even to this day keeps far away from it.

From that time fire has dwelt in wood, and by rubbing two twigs together the animals can always get enough to make themselves comfortable.

WHY THE SUN IS BRIGHTER THAN THE MOON
Lilloet — British Columbia

Natalia Belting

Many tales have been told about the sun's supremacy over the moon. This simple anecdote is interesting in its combination of gentle humor and the pourquoi *explanation of the sun's brightness.*

Once the sun was pale, as pale as the moon.

The sun saw a boy fishing. The boy wore a garment of feathers, and the feathers were bright. The sun said to himself, "If I had such a garment, I would be more splendid than the moon."

The sun came down to the boy. "Give me your feather robe," he said. "And I will give you my goatskin blanket for it."

The boy looked at the plain goatskin blanket. He looked at the feather cloak. "My grandmother made this for me," he said. "I cannot give it to you."

"But you can say that the sun gave this blanket to you. Is there anyone else who has a blanket from the sun?"

"My grandmother was long in making this robe," the boy said. "And longer in getting the feathers for it."

"Your grandmother can look into the sky every day and see her feather robe if you give it to me."

"Not even the chief of our village has such a feather cloak," the boy said.

"Does the sun visit the chief and bargain with him?"

"The blanket is only a goatskin blanket," the boy said.

"It is a magic blanket," the sun said. "See the fringe at the ends of it."

"The blanket is gray. It is not like my feather cloak."

"But it is a magic blanket," the sun said. "See. It is better than your fishing line. If you put the ends of the fringe into the water, you will catch a fish on each tassel. You cannot do that with your feather cloak."

The sun took the feather garment from the boy's shoulders.

"I am not sure my grandmother will like it," the boy said. "She made the feather cloak for me."

"Your grandmother will be the chief woman of the village. She will say, 'I have made a feather cloak for the sun,' and she will be proud," the sun said.

"I do not know whether she will or not," the boy said. "But if I take home a basket of fish for her, perhaps she will not punish me."

The sun is still wearing the feather cloak. That is why the sun is brighter than the moon.

LITTLE BURNT-FACE / Micmac

Frances Jenkins Olcott

The Cinderella story entered American Indian folklore through contact with European traders and through intermarriage. "Little Burnt-Face" was adapted to the Micmac culture so thoroughly that it became an allegory of seasonal change. The abused child represents the scorched earth, her cruel sisters the burning sun, the Great Chief the life-giving rains. The pourquoi elements and abstract quality of "Little Burnt-Face" provide interesting comparisons with "Poor Turkey Girl," in Chapter 6, Wonder Tales, another Indian Cinderella story, and with the simpler Indian myths of this section.

Once upon a time, in a large Indian village on the border of a lake, there lived an old man who was a widower. He had three daughters. The eldest was jealous, cruel, and ugly; the second was vain; but the youngest of all was very gentle and lovely.

Now, when the father was out hunting in the forest, the eldest daughter used to beat the youngest girl, and burn her face with hot coals; yes, and even scar her pretty body. So the people called her "Little Burnt-Face."

When the father came home from hunting he would ask why she was so scarred, and the eldest would answer quickly: "She is a good-for-nothing! She was forbidden to go near the fire, and she disobeyed and fell in." Then the father would scold Little Burnt-Face and she would creep away crying to bed.

By the lake, at the end of the village, there was a beautiful wigwam. And in that wigwam lived a Great Chief and his sister. The Great Chief was invisible; no one had ever seen him but his sister. He brought her many deer and supplied her with good things to eat from the forest and lake, and with the finest blankets and garments. And when visitors came all they ever saw of the Chief were his moccasins; for when he took them off they became visible, and his sister hung them up.

Now, one Spring, his sister made known that her brother, the Great Chief, would marry any girl who could see him.

Then all the girls from the village—except Little Burnt-Face and her sisters—and all the girls for miles around hastened to the wigwam, and walked along the shore of the lake with his sister.

And his sister asked the girls, "Do you see my brother?"

And some of them said, "No"; but most of them answered, "Yes."

Then his sister asked, "Of what is his shoulder-strap made?"

And the girls said, "Of a strip of rawhide."

"And with what does he draw his sled?" asked his sister.

And they replied, "With a green withe."

Then she knew that they had not seen him at all, and said quietly, "Let us go to the wigwam."

So to the wigwam they went, and when they entered, his sister told them not to take the seat next the door, for that was where her brother sat.

Then they helped his sister to cook the supper, for they were very curious to see the Great Chief eat. When all was ready, the food disappeared, and the brother took off his moccasins, and his sister hung them up. But they never saw the Chief, though many of them stayed all night.

One day Little Burnt-Face's two sisters put on their finest blankets and brightest strings of beads, and plaited their hair beautifully, and slipped embroidered moccasins on their feet. Then they started out to see the Great Chief.

As soon as they were gone, Little Burnt-Face made herself a dress of white birch-bark, and a cap and leggings of the same. She threw off her ragged garments, and dressed herself in her birch-bark clothes. She put her father's moccasins on her bare feet; and the moccasins were so big that they came up to her knees. Then she, too, started out to visit the beautiful wigwam at the end of the village.

Poor Little Burnt-Face! She was a sorry sight! For her hair was singed off, and her little face was as full of burns and scars as a sieve is full of holes; and she shuffled along in her birch-bark clothes and big moccasins. And as she passed through the village the boys and girls hissed, yelled, and hooted.

And when she reached the lake, her sisters saw her coming, and they tried to shame her, and told her to go home. But the Great Chief's sister received her kindly, and bade her stay, for she saw how sweet and gentle Little Burnt-Face really was.

Then as evening was coming on, the Great Chief's sister took all three girls walking beside the lake, and the sky grew dark, and they knew the Great Chief had come.

And his sister asked the two elder girls, "Do you see my brother?"

And they said, "Yes."

"Of what is his shoulder-strap made?" asked his sister.

"Of a strip of rawhide," they replied.

"And with what does he draw his sled?" asked she.

And they said, "With a green withe."

Then his sister turned to Little Burnt-Face and asked, "Do you see him?"

"I do! I do!" said Little Burnt-Face with awe. "And he is wonderful!"

"And of what is his sled-string made?" asked his sister gently.

"It is a beautiful Rainbow!" cried Little Burnt-Face.

"But, my sister," said the other, "of what is his bow-string made?"

"His bow-string," replied Little Burnt-Face, "is the Milky Way!"

Then the Great Chief's sister smiled with delight, and taking Little Burnt-Face by the hand, she said, "You have surely seen him."

She led the little girl to the wigwam, and bathed her with dew until the burns and scars all disappeared from her body and face. Her skin became soft and lovely again. Her hair grew long and dark like the Blackbird's wing. Her eyes were like stars. Then his sister brought from her treasures a wedding-garment, and she dressed Little Burnt-Face in it. And she was most beautiful to behold.

After all this was done, his sister led the little girl to the seat next the door, saying, "This is the Bride's seat," and made her sit down.

And then the Great Chief, no longer invisible, entered, terrible and beautiful. And when he saw Little Burnt-Face, he smiled and said gently, "So we have found each other!"

And she answered, "Yes."

Then Little Burnt-Face was married to the Great Chief, and the wedding-feast lasted for days, and to it came all the people of the village. As for the two bad sisters, they went back to their wigwam in disgrace, weeping with shame.

A Literary Myth

When any oral tale is written down it becomes, in the strictest sense, a literary folk tale because few writers can resist polishing the oral version or at least adapting the oral idiom to the conventions of writing. Even the Grimm brothers, before publishing their *Marchen*, rewrote the tales they had so accurately recorded for philological studies. Today, exact transcriptions of oral narratives are found only in scholarly folklore books and journals, not in collections for the casual reader.

Some of the tales in other sections of this book began as literary inventions. Madame d'Aulnoy's "The White Cat" and Perrault's eight tales all entered the English tradition, at least, from printed sources. Stories from the *Arabian Nights* were introduced into the European oral repertory through Galland's translation. The Greek and Norse myths now are known only from literary sources. However, at some time these stories, in a less polished form, were a part of the oral tradition. Many of these re-entered the oral folk tradition after story tellers had read them, for there has been a complex interrelationship between the oral and literary traditions.

Recognizing the literary quality of all printed folk tales and the influence of literature on the oral tradition, there are still many narratives that can be defined as literary works. Such stories use the structure and conventions of traditional tales but are the original product of a literate artist's mind.

Very few literary myths are successful; too often they are patronizing. The pattern may be imitated but the spirit of belief and reality are missing. Rudyard Kipling was successful, however, in the following *pourquoi* myth about how man came to domesticate the dog, the horse, and the cow. The cat? Well, the cat still walks by himself.

THE CAT THAT WALKED BY HIMSELF

Rudyard Kipling

Hear and attend and listen; for this befell and behappened and became and was, O my Best Beloved, when the Tame animals were wild. The Dog was wild, and the Horse was wild, and the Cow was wild, and the Sheep was wild, and the Pig was wild—as wild as wild could be—and they walked in the Wet Wild Woods by their wild lones. But the wildest of all the wild animals was the Cat. He walked by himself, and all places were alike to him.

Of course the Man was wild too. He was

"The Cat That Walked by Himself" from *Just So Stories* by Rudyard Kipling. Reprinted by permission of Mrs. George Bambridge and Doubleday & Company, Inc., and of the Macmillan Company, Inc. and the Macmillan Company of Canada.

dreadfully wild. He didn't even begin to be tame till he met the Woman, and she told him that she did not like living in his wild ways. She picked out a nice dry Cave, instead of a heap of wet leaves, to lie down in; and she strewed clean sand on the floor; and she lit a nice fire of wood at the back of the Cave; and she hung a dried wild-horse skin, tail-down, across the opening of the Cave; and she said, 'Wipe your feet, dear, when you come in, and now we'll keep house.'

That night, Best Beloved, they ate wild sheep roasted on the hot stones, and flavoured with wild garlic and wild pepper; and wild duck stuffed with wild rice and wild fenugreek and wild coriander; and marrow-bones of wild oxen; and wild cherries, and wild grenadillas. Then the Man went to sleep in front of the fire ever so happy; but the Woman sat up, combing her hair. She took the bone of the shoulder of mutton—the big fat blade-bone—and she looked at the wonderful marks on it, and she threw more wood on the fire, and she made a Magic. She made the First Singing Magic in the world.

Out in the Wet Wild Woods all the wild animals gathered together where they could see the light of the fire a long way off, and they wondered what it meant.

Then Wild Horse stamped with his wild foot and said, 'O my Friends and O my Enemies, why have the Man and the Woman made that great light in that great Cave, and what harm will it do us?'

Wild Dog lifted up his wild nose and smelled the smell of roast mutton, and said, 'I will go up and see and look, and say; for I think it is good. Cat, come with me.'

'Nenni!' said the Cat. 'I am the Cat who walks by himself, and all places are alike to me. I will not come.'

'Then we can never be friends again,' said Wild Dog, and he trotted off to the Cave. But when he had gone a little way the Cat said to himself, 'All places are alike to me. Why should I not go too and see and look and come away at my own liking.' So he slipped after Wild Dog softly, very softly, and hid himself where he could hear everything.

When Wild Dog reached the mouth of the Cave he lifted up the dried horse-skin with his nose and sniffed the beautiful smell of the roast mutton, and the Woman, looking at the bladebone, heard him, and laughed, and said, "Here comes the first. Wild Thing out of the Wild Woods, what do you want?'

Wild Dog said, 'O my Enemy and Wife of my Enemy, what is this that smells so good in the Wild Woods?'

Then the Woman picked up a roasted mutton-bone and threw it to Wild Dog, and said, 'Wild Thing out of the Wild Woods, taste and try.' Wild Dog gnawed the bone, and it was more delicious than anything he had ever tasted, and he said, 'O my Enemy and Wife of my Enemy, give me another.'

The Woman said, 'Wild Thing out of the Wild Woods, help my Man to hunt through the day and guard this Cave at night, and I will give you as many roast bones as you need.'

'Ah!' said the Cat, listening. 'That is a very wise Woman, but she is not so wise as I am.'

Wild Dog crawled into the Cave and laid his head on the Woman's lap, and said, 'O my Friend and Wife of my Friend, I will help your Man to hunt through the day, and at night I will guard your Cave.'

'Ah!' said the Cat, listening. 'That is a very foolish Dog.' And he went back through the Wet Wild Woods waving his wild tail, and walking by his wild lone. But he never told anybody.

When the Man waked up he said, 'What is Wild Dog doing here?' And the Woman said, 'His name is not Wild Dog any more, but the First Friend, because he will be our friend for always and always and always. Take him with you when you go hunting.'

Next night the Woman cut great green armfuls of fresh grass from the water-meadows, and dried it before the fire, so that it smelt like new-mown hay, and she sat at the mouth of the Cave and plaited a halter out of horse-hide, and she looked at the shoulder of mutton-bone—at the big broad blade-bone—and she made a Magic. She made the Second Singing Magic in the world.

Out in the Wild Woods all the wild animals wondered what had happened to Wild Dog, and at last Wild Horse stamped with his foot and said, 'I will go and see and say why Wild Dog has not returned. Cat, come with me.'

'Nenni!' said the Cat. 'I am the Cat who walks

by himself, and all places are alike to me. I will not come.' But all the same he followed Wild Horse softly, very softly, and hid himself where he could hear everything.

When the woman heard Wild Horse tripping and stumbling on his long mane, she laughed and said, "Here comes the second. Wild Thing out of the Wild Woods what do you want?'

Wild Horse said, 'O my Enemy and Wife of my Enemy, where is Wild Dog?'

The Woman laughed, and picked up the blade-bone and looked at it, and said, 'Wild Thing out of the Wild Woods, you did not come here for Wild Dog, but for the sake of this good grass.'

And Wild Horse, tripping and stumbling on his long mane, said, 'That is true; give it me to eat.'

The Woman said, 'Wild Thing out of the Wild Woods, bend your wild head and wear what I give you, and you shall eat the wonderful grass three times a day.'

'Ah,' said the Cat, listening, 'this is a clever Woman, but she is not so clever as I am.'

Wild Horse bent his wild head, and the Woman slipped the plaited hide halter over it, and Wild Horse breathed on the Woman's feet and said, 'O my Mistress, and Wife of my Master, I will be your servant for the sake of the wonderful grass.'

'Ah,' said the Cat, listening, 'that is a very foolish Horse.' And he went back through the Wet Wild Woods, waving his wild tail and walking by his wild lone. But he never told anybody.

When the Man and the Dog came back from hunting, the Man said, 'What is Wild Horse doing here?' And the Woman said, 'His name is not Wild Horse any more, but the First Servant, because he will carry us from place to place for always and always and always. Ride on his back when you go hunting.'

Next day, holding her wild head high that her wild horns should not catch in the wild trees, Wild Cow came up to the Cave, and the Cat followed, and hid himself just the same as before; and everything happened just the same as before; and the Cat said the same things as before, and when Wild Cow had promised to give her milk to the Woman every day in exchange for the wonderful grass, the Cat went back through the Wet Wild Woods waving his wild tail and walking by his wild lone, just the same as before. But he never told anybody. And when the Man and the Horse and the Dog came home from hunting and asked the same questions same as before, the Woman said, 'Her name is not Wild Cow any more, but the Giver of Good Food. She will give us the warm white milk for always and always and always, and I will take care of her while you and the First Friend and the First Servant go hunting.'

Next day the Cat waited to see if any other Wild thing would go up to the Cave, but no one moved in the Wet Wild Woods, so the Cat walked there by himself; and he saw the Woman milking the Cow, and he saw the light of the fire in the Cave, and he smelt the smell of the warm white milk.

Cat said, 'O my Enemy and Wife of my Enemy, where did Wild Cow go?'

The Woman laughed and said, 'Wild Thing out of the Wild Woods, go back to the Woods again, for I have braided up my hair, and I have put away the magic blade-bone, and we have no more need of either friends or servants in our Cave.'

Cat said, 'I am not a friend, and I am not a servant. I am the Cat who walks by himself, and I wish to come into your cave.'

Woman said, 'Then why did you not come with First Friend on the first night?'

Cat grew very angry and said, 'Has Wild Dog told tales of me?'

Then the Woman laughed and said, 'You are the Cat who walks by himself, and all places are alike to you. You are neither a friend nor a servant. You have said it yourself. Go away and walk by yourself in all places alike.'

Then Cat pretended to be sorry and said, 'Must I never come into the Cave? Must I never sit by the warm fire? Must I never drink the warm white milk? You are very wise and very beautiful. You should not be cruel even to a Cat.'

Woman said, 'I knew I was wise, but I did not know I was beautiful. So I will make a bargain with you. If ever I say one word in your praise you may come into the Cave.'

'And if you say two words in my praise?' said the Cat.

'I never shall,' said the Woman, 'but if I say two words in your praise, you may sit by the fire in the Cave.

'And if you say three words?' said the Cat.

'I never shall,' said the Woman, 'but if I say three words in your praise, you may drink the warm white milk three times a day for always and always and always.'

Then the Cat arched his back and said, 'Now let the Curtain at the mouth of the Cave, and the Fire at the back of the Cave, and the Milk-pots that stand beside the Fire, remember what my Enemy and the Wife of my Enemy has said.' And he went away through the Wet Wild Woods waving his wild tail and walking by his wild lone.

That night when the Man and the Horse and the Dog came home from hunting, the Woman did not tell them of the bargain that she had made with the Cat, because she was afraid that they might not like it.

Cat went far and far away and hid himself in the Wet Wild Woods by his wild lone for a long time till the Woman forgot all about him. Only the Bat—the little upside-down Bat—that hung inside the Cave, knew where Cat hid; and every evening Bat would fly to Cat with news of what was happening.

One evening Bat said, 'There is a Baby in the Cave. He is new and pink and fat and small, and the Woman is very fond of him.'

'Ah,' said the Cat, listening, 'but what is the Baby fond of?'

'He is fond of things that are soft and tickle,' said the Bat. 'He is fond of warm things to hold in his arms when he goes to sleep. He is fond of being played with. He is fond of all those things.'

'Ah,' said the Cat, listening, 'then my time has come.'

Next night Cat walked through the Wet Wild Woods and hid very near the Cave till morning-time, and Man and Dog and Horse went hunting. The Woman was busy cooking that morning, and the Baby cried and interrupted. So she carried him outside the Cave and gave him a handful of pebbles to play with. But still the Baby cried.

Then the Cat put out his paddy paw and pat-ted the Baby on the cheek, and it cooed; and the Cat rubbed against its fat knees and tickled it under its fat chin with his tail. And the Baby laughed; and the Woman heard him and smiled.

Then the Bat—the little upside-down Bat—that hung in the mouth of the Cave said, 'O my Hostess and Wife of my Host and Mother of my Host's Son, a Wild Thing from the Wild Woods is most beautifully playing with your Baby.'

'A blessing on that Wild Thing whoever he may be,' said the Woman, straightening her back, 'for I was a busy woman this morning and he has done me a service.'

That very minute and second, Best Beloved, the dried horse-skin Curtain that was stretched tail-down at the mouth of the Cave fell down—woosh!—because it remembered the bargain she had made with the Cat, and when the Woman went to pick it up—lo and behold!—the Cat was sitting quite comfy inside the Cave.

'O my Enemy and Wife of my Enemy and Mother of my Enemy,' said the Cat, 'it is I: for you have spoken a word in my praise, and now I can sit within the Cave for always and always and always. But still I am the Cat who walks by himself, and all places are alike to me.'

The Woman was very angry, and shut her lips tight and took up her spinning-wheel and began to spin.

But the Baby cried because the Cat had gone away, and the Woman could not hush it, for it struggled and kicked and grew black in the face.

'O my Enemy and Wife of my Enemy and Mother of my Enemy,' said the Cat, 'take a strand of the wire that you are spinning and tie it to your spinning-whorl and drag it along the floor, and I will show you a magic that shall make your Baby laugh as loudly as he is now crying.'

'I will do so,' said the Woman, 'because I am at my wits' end; but I will not thank you for it.'

She tied the thread to the little clay spindle-whorl and drew it across the floor, and the Cat ran after it and patted it with his paws and rolled head over heels, and tossed it backward over his shoulder and chased it between his hind-legs and pretended to lose it, and pounced down upon it again, till the Baby laughed as loudly as it had been crying, and scrambled after the Cat and frolicked all over the Cave till it grew tired and settled down to sleep with the Cat in its arms.

'Now,' said the Cat, 'I will sing the Baby a song that shall keep him asleep for an hour.' And he began to purr, loud and low, low and loud, till the Baby fell fast asleep. The Woman smiled as she looked down upon the two of them and said, 'That was wonderfully done. No question but you are very clever, O Cat.'

That very minute and second, Best Beloved, the smoke of the fire at the back of the Cave came down in clouds from the roof—*puff!*—because it remembered the bargain she had made with the Cat, and when it had cleared away—lo and behold!—the Cat was sitting quite comfy close to the fire.

'O my Enemy and Wife of my Enemy and Mother of My Enemy,' said the Cat, 'it is I, for you have spoken a second word in my praise, and now I can sit by the warm fire at the back of the Cave for always and always and always. But still I am the Cat who walks by himself, and all places are alike to me.'

Then the Woman was very very angry, and let down her hair and put more wood on the fire and brought out the broad blade-bone of the shoulder of mutton and began to make a Magic that should prevent her from saying a third word in praise of the Cat. It was not a Singing Magic, Best Beloved, it was a Still Magic; and by and by the Cave grew so still that a little wee-wee mouse crept out of a corner and ran across the floor.

'O my Enemy and Wife of my Enemy and Mother of my Enemy,' said the Cat, 'is that little mouse part of your magic?'

'Ouh! Chee! No indeed!' said the Woman, and she dropped the blade-bone and jumped upon the footstool in front of the fire and braided up her hair very quick for fear that the mouse should run up it.

'Ah,' said the Cat, watching, 'then the mouse will do me no harm if I eat it?'

'No,' said the Woman, braiding up her hair, 'eat it quickly and I will ever be grateful to you.'

Cat made one jump and caught the little mouse, and the Woman said, 'A hundred thanks. Even the First Friend is not quick enough to catch little mice as you have done. You must be very wise.'

That very moment and second, O Best Beloved, the Milk-pot that stood by the fire cracked in two pieces—*ffft*—because it remembered the bargain she had made with the Cat, and when the Woman jumped down from the footstool—lo and behold!—the Cat was lapping up the warm white milk that lay in one of the broken pieces.

'O my Enemy and Wife of my Enemy and Mother of my Enemy,' said the Cat, 'it is I; for you have spoken three words in my praise, and now I can drink the warm white milk three times a day for always and always and always. But *still* I am the Cat who walks by himself, and all places are alike to me.'

Then the Woman laughed and set the Cat a bowl of the warm white milk and said, 'O Cat, you are as clever as a man, but remember that your bargain was not made with the Man or the Dog, and I do not know what they will do when they come home.'

'What is that to me?' said the Cat. 'If I have my place in the Cave by the fire and my warm white milk three times a day I do not care what the Man or the Dog can do.'

That evening when the Man and the Dog came into the Cave, the Woman told them all the story of the bargain while the Cat sat by the fire and smiled. Then the Man said, 'Yes, but he has not made a bargain with *me* or with all proper Men after me.' Then he took off his two leather boots and he took up his little stone axe (that makes three) and he fetched a piece of wood and a hatchet (that is five altogether), and he set them out in a row and he said, 'Now we will make *our* bargain. If you do not catch mice when you are in the Cave for always and always and always, I will throw these five things at you whenever I see you, and so shall all proper Men do after me.'

'Ah,' said the Woman, listening, 'this is a very clever Cat, but he is not so clever as my Man.'

The Cat counted the five things (and they looked very knobby) and the said, 'I will catch mice when I am in the Cave for always and always and always; but *still* I am the Cat who walks by himself, and all places are alike to me.'

'Not when I am near,' said the Man. 'If you had not said that last I would have put all these things away for always and always and always; but I am now going to throw my two boots and my little stone axe (that makes three) at you whenever I meet you. And so shall all proper Men do after me!"

Then the Dog said, 'Wait a minute. He has not made a bargain with *me* or with all proper Dogs after me.' And he showed his teeth and said, 'If you are not kind to the Baby while I am in the Cave for always and always and always, I will hunt you till I catch you, and when I catch you I will bite you. And so shall all proper Dogs do after me.'

'Ah,' said the Woman, listening, 'this is a very clever Cat, but he is not so clever as the Dog.'

Cat counted the Dog's teeth (and they looked very pointed) and he said, 'I will be kind to the Baby while I am in the Cave, as long as he does not pull my tail too hard, for always and always and always. But *still* I am the Cat that walks by himself, and all places are alike to me.'

'Not when I am near,' said the Dog. 'If you had not said that last I would have shut my mouth for always and always and always; but now I am going to hunt you up a tree whenever I meet you. And so shall all proper Dogs do after me.'

Then the Man threw his two boots and his little stone axe (that makes three) at the Cat, and the Cat ran out of the Cave and the Dog chased him up a tree; and from that day to this, Best Beloved, three proper Men out of five will always throw things at a Cat whenever they meet him, and all proper Dogs will chase him up a tree. But the Cat keeps his side of the bargain too. He will kill mice and he will be kind to Babies when he is in the house, just as long as they do not pull his tail too hard. But when he has done that, and between times, and when the moon gets up and night comes, he is the Cat that walks by himself, and all places are alike to him. Then he goes out to the Wet Wild Woods or up the Wet Wild Trees or on the Wet Wild Roofs, waving his wild tail and walking by his wild lone.

Related Reading

References for Adults

Arbuthnot, May Hill. *Children and Books*, 3d ed. Glenview, Illinois: Scott, Foresman, 1964. Chapter 10 discusses theories of folklore origin. Chapter, 11 examines myths, epics, and fables.

Clarke, Kenneth and Mary. *Introducing Folklore.* New York: Holt, Rinehart and Winston, 1963. Interesting introduction to folklore for the general reader and beginning student. One section deals with mythology.

Colum, Padraic. *Myths of the World.* Illustrated by Boris Artzybasheff. New York: Grosset & Dunlap, 1930. Many unfamiliar myths from the ancient world.

Davidson, H. R. Ellis. *Gods and Myths of Northern Europe.* Baltimore: Penguin, 1964. A scholarly discussion of Norse mythology for the teacher or librarian who wishes background information on the development of ancient Norse beliefs and literature.

Frazer, Sir James George. *The Golden Bough: A Study in Magic and Religion.* One-volume abridged ed. New York: Macmillan, 1951. Interesting study of folklore. Abridgment of a twelve-volume series.

Graves, Robert. *The Greek Myths*, vols 1 and 2. Baltimore: Penguin, 1955. Excellent discussions of Greek mythology. The development of individual myths traced at length.

Huck, Charlotte S., and Doris Young Kuhn. *Children's Literature in the Elementary School.* 2d ed. New York: Holt, Rinehart and Winston, 1968. Chapter 4 presents interesting information on mythology, folktales, fables, and epics.

Leach, Maria, editor. *Funk & Wagnalls Standard Dictionary of General Folklore, Mythology and Legend.* Two vols. New York: Funk & Wagnalls, 1949–1950. Valuable reference work.

Marriott, Alice, and Carol K. Rachlin. *American Indian Mythology*. New York: Crowell, 1968. A collection of traditional and modern Indian legends and myths, many of which can be read to upper elementary school children. Excellent introductions for each tale give background information and illustrate the anthropological approach to folklore. (Grade 6 and up)

Ohrman, Richard, editor. *The Making of Myth*. New York: Putnam, 1962. Essays from the anthropologist's, psychologist's, and folklorist's points of view.

Zimmerman, J. E. *Dictionary of Classical Mythology*. New York: Harper & Row, 1964. One of the most useful reference books for those interested in mythology.

Collections for Children

d'Aulaire, Ingri, and Edgar Parin, authors-illustrators. *Book of Greek Myths*. New York: Doubleday, 1962. Picture book treatment for children in the middle and upper elementary grades. (Grades 3–6)

Belting, Natalia. *The Long-Tailed Bear and Other Indian Legends*. Illustrated by Louis Cary. Indianapolis: Bobbs-Merrill, 1961. Pourquoi myths about animals. (Grades 2–4)

————. *The Sun Is a Golden Earring*. Illustrated by Bernarda Bryson. New York: Holt, Rinehart and Winston, 1962. Folk sayings from many peoples. Poetic metaphors no child should miss. (Grade 3 and up)

————. *Calendar Moon*. Illustrated by Bernarda Bryson. New York: Holt, Rinehart and Winston, 1964. Poetic folk sayings about the months of the year from many cultures. (Grade 3 and up)

————. *The Earth Is on a Fish's Back: Tales of Beginnings*. Illustrated by Esta Nesbitt. New York: Holt, Rinehart and Winston, 1965. Pourquoi stories, most from North American Indian tribes but a few from other continents. (Grades 4–6)

————. *The Stars Are Silver Reindeer*. Illustrated by Esta Nesbitt. New York: Holt, Rinehart and Winston, 1966. Poetic folk sayings from many cultures about the stars. (Grade 3 and up)

Benson, Sally. *Stories of the Gods and Heroes*. Illustrated by Steele Savage. New York: Dial, 1940. Interesting retellings of Greek myths. (Grades 5–8)

Bulfinch, Thomas. *A Book of Myths*. Illustrated by Helen Sewell. New York: Macmillan, 1942. Excellent book for good junior high school readers.

————. *The Age of Fable*. New York: New American Library, 1962. Excellent source book for adults and mature children. First published in 1855.

Colum, Padraic. *The Children of Odin*. Illustrated by Willy Pogany. New York: Macmillan, 1920, 1962. Norse hero tales and myths woven into one unified narrative. Ends with Sigurd's death. (Grades 5–7)

————. *Legends of Hawaii*. Illustrated by Don Forrer. New Haven, Conn.: Yale University Press, 1937. Well written retellings of Polynesian myths. (Grades 5–9)

Coolidge, Olivia E. *Greek Myths*. Illustrated by Edouard Sandoz. Boston: Houghton Mifflin, 1949. Enjoyable retellings of the most familiar Greek myths. (Grades 4–9)

Green, Roger Lancelyn. *A Book of Myths*. Illustrated by Joan Kiddell-Monroe. New York: Dutton, 1965. Six familiar Greek myths, three Scandinavian, three Babylonian, two Egyptian, and one each from the Cretan, Roman, Hittite, Phoenician, Phrygian, and Persian mythologies make this collection valuable for those children who especially enjoy mythology. (Grades 4–9)

Hamilton, Edith. *Mythology*. Illustrated by Steele Savage. Boston: Little, Brown, 1942. An excellent source book for the adult and the capable young reader. Retellings of many Greek myths. A few myths from other cultures also included. The background information especially helpful. (Grades 7 and up)

Hosford, Dorothy G. *Thunder of the Gods*. Illustrated by Claire and George Louden. New York: Holt, Rinehart and Winston, 1952. The style is easier to read than Colum's in *Children of Odin*. Excellent retelling of the Norse myths; true to the spirit of the original narratives. (Grades 4–7)

Leach, Maria. *How the People Sang the Mountain Up*. Illustrated by Glen Rounds. New York: Viking, 1967. Pourquoi stories from many countries. (Grades 4–6)

Sellew, Catharine. *Adventures with the Gods*. Illustrated by George and Doris Hauman. Boston: Little, Brown, 1945. Simplified retellings of the most familiar Greek myths. (Grades 4–6)

Thompson, Vivian. *Hawaiian Myths of Earth, Sea, and Sky*. Illustrated by Leonard Weisgard. New York: Holiday, 1966. *Pourquoi* myths in which the god Kane creates the sky, the world, and its inhabitants. (Grades 4–6)

Chapter 4
Hero Tales

From *The Merry Adventures of Robin Hood* by Howard Pyle, published in 1883 by Charles Scribner's Sons.

Almost every culture has developed a series of narratives around the activities of its cultural heroes. Exaggeration is important in most of these tales. Superhuman strength or cleverness is attributed to the central figure, who often must struggle against overwhelming odds. These culture heroes embody the virtues admired by their group and the weaknesses forgiven by it. Hercules' courage, strength, and endurance were admired by the Greeks even though he acted rashly and at times lacked wisdom. His fits of madness were blamed on Hera's hatred. Theseus, not Hercules, was the Athenian culture hero because he combined wisdom with courage and strength. Robin Hood's thievery was forgiven because he stole from the oppressor. He was generous, robust, open, fair, and honest in his own way.

Because America had a continent to conquer, the first American heroes were wilderness men. Mike Fink represented the strength, stubborness, and independence the wilderness demanded and Americans admired. As the nation became industrialized its heroes changed. John Henry and Paul Bunyan characterized the superhuman ideal of the American worker. Paul Bunyan is probably the most widely known American folk hero. Although there is some dispute about the origin of this cycle of tales, whether it was developed by the folk or was the result of literary invention, it is now a part of oral folk tradition. While America did not invent the tall tale, it is the form of most of her hero tales.

The folk hero of American Negro slaves was not a giant who overcame great forces by strength. Their hero was Brer Rabbit. He was small, defenseless, and made mistakes, but his clever wit helped him fool the larger, predatory animals. Joel Chandler Harris, unaware both of the literary value and the allegorical nature of some of the Brer Rabbit tales, called them "old darkey's poor little stories . . . fantasies as uncouth as the original man ever conceived of." This was a serious misconception. The Negro narratives were not only influenced by European tales (e.g., "Heyo the House") but also had a long history in Africa. As all groups have done, the slaves adapted folk narratives to their culture and life. It is interesting to compare "The Wonderful Tarbaby" with a version of its African source, "The Rubber Man."[1] In the African folktale Spider is the antagonist and is not allowed to escape his deserved punishment. In the American version Brer Rabbit is the protagonist; the reader not only wants him to escape but enjoys the clever way he tricks his captors.

Many, but not all, hero tales came from the epic tradition. Epics, long narrative poems centering around the actions of a single hero, have given the western world several of its greatest hero stories: e.g., those of the Greek heroes, Beowulf, and others. But the King Arthur cycle, as it was part of folklore before Malory's literary treatment, must have developed from legends. The stories about Robin Hood have been transmitted through ballads. The Scandinavian cycle about Sigurd began as sagas sung by Viking skalds and entered the literary tradition through the Icelandic *Younger, Prose Edda*. The American hero tales about Paul Bunyan, Pecos Bill, and so on began, many folklorists claim, as literary tall tales that later to some extent entered the oral tradi-

---

[1] See Chapter 6, Tales of Trickery. This tale appeared first in the *Jataka Tales* and shows that some African folklore had the same source as many traditional European tales.

tion. Brer Rabbit stories developed through the adaptation of African and European tales by American Negroes to fit the conditions of slavery. The antecedents of hero tales are varied; to classify them as epics as many books do is an oversimplification that inaccurately combines epics and non-epics under one classification. This also excludes some hero tales from consideration.

Regardless of the origin, size, or cleverness, the culture hero is a composite of all that a society admires and idealizes. All people seem to need heroes who are larger than life in size or spirit.

PRONUNCIATION GUIDE

Aegeus	ē′ jōōs, ē′ jē-ŭs	Lugh	lōōH
Ainli	ĕn′ lĭ	Menelaus	mĕn′ ĕ-lā′ ŭs
Beowulf	bā′ ô-wōōlf	Odysseus	ŏ-dĭs′ ūs, ŏ-dĭs′ ē-ŭs
Conor Mac Nessa	kŏn′ awr măk-nĕs′ să	Priam	prī′ ăm
Cuchulain	koo Hōōl′ ĭn	Procrustes	prŏ-krŭs′ tēz
Dectera	dĕk′ tĕ-ră	Regin	rā′ yĭn
Emain Macha	ĕv′ ăn mah′ Hă	Sidhe	shee
Fafnir	fäv′ nĭr	Sigurd	zē′ gōort
Fianna	fee′ ăn-nă	Theseus	thē′ sŭs, thē′ sê-sŭs
Hrothgar	hrōth′ gär	Usna	ōōsh′ nă
Laegh	layH	Uther	y′ ōother

H has the ch sound of the Scottish *loch* or the German *ich* sound.

ODYSSEUS / Greece

Padraic Colum

Padraic Colum's retelling of Odysseus' life is an excellent introduction to the Aeneid, *a primary source for the story of the fall of Troy, and the* Odyssey, *the only source for information about Odysseus' wanderings after the Trojan War.*

In the following passage Odysseus recounts some of his adventures and hardships. Children especially enjoy Odysseus' clever escape from the Cyclops. The play on the words Noman *and* no man *are typical of this Greek hero who survived by his wit rather than his strength. Menelaus once called Odysseus a "master of devices"; others called him crafty, cunning, wily.*

In addition to being entrapped by the Cyclops, Odysseus and his men were held captive for a year by Circe, a beautiful enchantress. Only after ten years of wandering did Odysseus return home and then it was in the manner foretold by the Cyclops' curse. Odysseus' wit, however, rescued his son and wife from angry seekers after the kingdom.

Demodocus took down the lyre and sang. His song told how one part of the Greeks sailed away

"The Story of Odysseus" from *Children's Homer* by Padraic Colum. Reprinted with permission of The Macmillan Company. Copyright 1918 by The Macmillan Company, renewed 1944 by Padraic Colum.

in their ships and how others with Odysseus to lead them were now in the center of Priam's City all hidden in the great Wooden Horse which the Trojans themselves had dragged across their broken wall. So the Wooden Horse stood, and the people gathered around and talked of what should be done with so wonderful a thing—whether to break open its timbers, or drag it to a steep hill and hurl it down on the rocks, or leave it there as an offering to the gods. As an offering to the gods it was left at last. Then the minstrel sang how Odysseus and his comrades poured forth from the hollow of the horse and took the City.

As the minstrel sang, the heart of Odysseus melted within him and tears fell down his cheeks. None of the company saw him weeping except Alcinous the King. But the King cried out to the company saying, "Let the minstrel cease, for there is one amongst us to whom his song is not pleasing. Ever since it began the stranger here has wept with tears flowing down his cheeks."

The minstrel ceased, and all the company looked in surprise at Odysseus, who sat with his head bowed and his mantle wrapped around his head. Why did he weep? each man asked. No one had asked of him his name, for each thought it was more noble to serve a stranger without knowing his name.

Said the King, speaking again, "In a brother's place stands the stranger and the suppliant, and as a brother art thou to us, O unknown guest. But wilt thou not be brotherly to us? Tell us by what name they call thee in thine own land. Tell us, too, of thy land and thy city. And tell us, too, where thou wert borne on thy wanderings, and to what lands and peoples thou camest. And as a brother tell us why thou dost weep and mourn in spirit over the tale of the going forth of the Greeks to the war of Troy. Didst thou have a kinsman who fell before Priam's City—a daughter's husband, or a wife's father, or someone nearer by blood? Or didst thou have a loving friend who fell there—one with an understanding heart who wast to thee as a brother?"

Such questions the King asked, and Odysseus taking the mantle from around his head turned round to the company.

IV

Then Odysseus spoke before the company and said, "O Alcinous, famous King, it is good to listen to a minstrel such as Demodocus is. And as for me, I know of no greater delight than when men feast together with open hearts, when tables are plentifully spread, when wine-bearers pour out

good wine into cups, and when a minstrel sings to them noble songs. This seems to me to be happiness indeed. But thou has asked me to speak of my wanderings and my toils. Ah, where can I begin that tale? For the gods have given me more woes than a man can speak of!

"But first of all I will declare to you my name and my country. I am Odysseus, son of Laertes, and my land is Ithaka, an island around which many islands lie. Ithaka is a rugged isle, but a good nurse of hardy men, and I, for one, have found that there is no place fairer than a man's own land. But now I will tell thee, King, and tell the Princes and Captains and Councillors of the Phaeacians, the tale of my wanderings.

"The wind bore my ships from the coast of Troy, and with our white sails hoisted we came to the cape that is called Malea. Now if we had been able to double this cape we should soon have come to our own country, all unhurt. But the north wind came and swept us from our course and drove us wandering past Cythera.

"Then for nine days we were borne onward by terrible winds, and away from all known lands. On the tenth day we came to a strange country. Many of my men landed there. The people of that land were harmless and friendly, but the land itself was most dangerous. For there grew there the honey-sweet fruit of the lotus that makes all men forgetful of their past and neglectful of their future. And those of my men who ate the lotus that the dwellers of that land offered them became forgetful of their country and of the way before them. They wanted to abide forever in the land of the lotus. They wept when they thought of all the toils before them and of all they had endured. I led them back to the ships, and I had to place them beneath the benches and leave them in bonds. And I commanded those who ate of the lotus to go at once aboard the ships. Then, when I had got all my men upon the ships, we made haste to sail away.

"Later we came to the land of the Cyclopes, a giant people. There is a waste island outside the harbor of their land, and on it there is a well of bright water that has poplars growing round it. We came to that empty island, and we beached our ships and took down our sails.

"As soon as the dawn came we went through

the empty island, starting the wild goats that were there in flocks, and shooting them with our arrows. We killed so many wild goats there that we had nine for each ship. Afterwards we looked across to the land of the Cyclopes, and we heard the sound of voices and saw the smoke of fires and heard the bleating of flocks of sheep and goats.

"I called my companions together and I said, 'It would be well for some of us to go to that other island. With my own ship and with the company that is on it I shall go there. The rest of you abide here. I will find out what manner of men live there, and whether they will treat us kindly and give us gifts that are due to strangers —gifts of provisions for our voyage.'

"We embarked and we came to the land. There was a cave near the sea, and round the cave there were mighty flocks of sheep and goats. I took twelve men with me and I left the rest to guard the ship. We went into the cave and found no man there. There were baskets filled with cheeses and vessels of whey, and pails and bowls of milk. My men wanted me to take some of the cheeses and drive off some of the lambs and kids and come away. But this I would not do, for I would rather he who owned the stores would give us of his own free will the offerings that were due to strangers.

"While we were in the cave, he whose dwelling it was, returned to it. He carried on his shoulder a great pile of wood for his fire. Never in our lives did we see a creature so frightful as this Cyclops was. He was a giant in size, and, what made him terrible to behold, he had but one eye, and that single eye was in his forehead. He cast down on the ground the pile of wood that he carried, making such a din that we fled in terror into the corners and recesses of the cave. Next he drove his flocks into the cave and began to milk his ewes and goats. And when he had the flocks within, he took up a stone that not all our strengths could move and set it as a door to the mouth of the cave.

"The Cyclops kindled his fire, and when it blazed up he saw us in the corners and recesses. He spoke to us. We knew not what he said, but our hearts were shaken with terror at the sound of his deep voice.

"I spoke to him saying that we were Agamem-non's men on our way home from the taking of Priam's City, and I begged him to deal with us kindly, for the sake of Zeus who is ever in the company of strangers and suppliants. But he answered me saying, 'We Cyclops pay no heed to Zeus, nor to any of thy gods. In our strength and our power we deem that we are mightier than they. I will not spare thee, neither will I give thee aught for the sake of Zeus, but only as my own spirit bids me. And first I would have thee tell me how you came to our land.'

"I knew it would be better not to let the Cyclops know that my ship and my companions were at the harbor of the island. Therefore I spoke to him guilefully, telling him that my ship had been broken on the rocks, and that I and the men with me were the only ones who had escaped utter doom.

"I begged again that he would deal with us as just men deal with strangers and suppliants, but he, without saying a word, laid hands upon two of my men, and swinging them by the legs, dashed their brains out on the earth. He cut them to pieces and ate them before our very eyes. We wept and we prayed to Zeus as we witnessed a deed so terrible.

"Next the Cyclops stretched himself amongst his sheep and went to sleep beside the fire. Then I debated whether I should take my sharp sword in my hand, and feeling where his heart was, stab him there. But second thoughts held me back from doing this. I might be able to kill him as he slept, but not even with my companions could I roll away the great stone that closed the mouth of the cave.

"Dawn came, and the Cyclops awakened, kindled his fire and milked his flocks. Then he seized two others of my men and made ready for his midday meal. And now he rolled away the great stone and drove his flocks out of the cave.

"I had pondered on a way of escape, and I had thought of something that might be done to baffle the Cyclops. I had with me a great skin of sweet wine, and I thought that if I could make him drunken with wine I and my companions might be able for him. But there were other preparations to be made first. On the floor of the cave there was a great beam of olive wood which the Cyclops had cut to make a club when the wood should be seasoned. It was yet green. I and my companions went and cut off a fathom's length of the wood, and sharpened it to a point and took it to the fire and hardened it in the glow. Then I hid the beam in a recess of the cave.

"The Cyclops came back in the evening, and opening up the cave drove in his flocks. Then he closed the cave again with the stone and went and milked his ewes and his goats. Again he seized two of my companions. I went to the terrible creature with a bowl of wine in my hands. He took it and drank it and cried out, 'Give me another bowl of this, and tell me thy name that I may give thee gifts for bringing this honey-tasting drink.'

"Again I spoke to him guilefully and said, 'Noman is my name. Noman my father and my mother call me.' "

" 'Give me more of the drink Noman,' he shouted. 'And the gift that I shall give to thee is that I shall make thee the last of thy fellows to be eaten.'

"I gave him wine again, and when he had taken the third bowl he sank backwards with his face upturned, and sleep came upon him. Then I, with four companions, took that beam of olive wood, now made into a hard and pointed stake, and thrust it into the ashes of the fire. When the pointed end began to glow we drew it out of the flame. Then I and my companions laid hold on the great stake and, dashing at the Cyclops, thrust it into his eye. He raised a terrible cry that made the rocks ring and we dashed away into the recesses of the cave.

"His cries brought other Cyclopes to the mouth of the cave, and they, naming him as Polyphemus, called out and asked him what ailed him to cry. 'Noman,' he shrieked out, 'Noman is slaying me by guile.' They answered him saying, 'If no man is slaying thee, there is nothing we can do for thee, Polyphemus. What ails thee has been sent to thee by the gods.' Saying this, they went away from the mouth of the cave without attempting to move away the stone.

"Polyphemus then, groaning with pain, rolled away the stone and sat before the mouth of the cave with his hands outstretched, thinking that he would catch us as we dashed out. I showed my companions how we might pass by him. I laid hands on certain rams of the flock and I lashed three of them together with supple rods. Then on

the middle ram I put a man of my company. Thus every three rams carried a man. As soon as the dawn had come the rams hastened out to the pasture, and, as they passed, Polyphemus laid hands on the first and the third of each three that went by. They passed out and Polyphemus did not guess that a ram that he did not touch carried out a man.

"For myself, I took a ram that was the strongest and fleeciest of the whole flock and I placed myself under him, clinging to the wool of his belly. As this ram, the best of all his flock, went by, Polyphemus, laying his hands upon him, said, 'Would that you, the best of my flock were endowed with speech, so that you might tell me where Noman who has blinded me, has hidden himself.' The ram went by him, and when he had gone a little way from the cave I loosed myself from him and went and set my companions free.

"We gathered together many of Polyphemus' sheep and we drove them down to our ship. The men we had left behind would have wept when they heard what had happened to six of their companions. But I bade them take on board the sheep we had brought and pull the ship away from that land. Then when he had drawn a certain distance from the shore I could not forbear to shout my taunts into the cave of Polyphemus. 'Cyclops,' I cried, 'you thought that you had the company of a fool and a weakling to eat. But you have been worsted by me, and your evil deeds have been punished.'

So I shouted, and Polyphemus came to the mouth of the cave with great anger in his heart. He took up rocks and cast them at the ship and they fell before the prow. The men bent to the oars and pulled the ship away or it would have been broken by the rocks he cast. And when we were further away I shouted to him:

" 'Cyclops, if any man should ask who it was set his mark upon you, say that he was Odysseus, the son of Laertes.'

"Then I heard Polyphemus cry out, 'I call upon Poseidon, the god of the sea, whose son I am, to avenge me upon you, Odysseus. I call upon Poseidon to grant that you, Odysseus, may never come to your home, or if the gods have ordained your return, that you come to it after much toil and suffering, in an evil plight and in a stranger's ship, to find sorrow in your home.'

"So Polyphemus prayed, and, to my evil fortune, Poseidon heard his prayer. But we went on in our ship rejoicing at our escape. We came to the waste island where my other ships were. All the company rejoiced to see us, although they had to mourn for their six companions slain by Polyphemus. We divided amongst the ships the sheep we had taken from Polyphemus' flock and we sacrificed to the gods. At the dawn of the next day we raised the sails on each ship and we sailed away."

* * *

"So Circe spoke to me, and having told me such things she took her way up the island. Then I went to the ship and roused my men. Speedily they went aboard, and, having taken their seats upon the benches, struck the water with their oars. Then the sails were hoisted and a breeze came and we sailed away from the Isle of Circe, the Enchantress.

"I told my companions what Circe had told me about the Sirens in their field of flowers. I took a great piece of wax and broke it and kneaded it until it was soft. Then I covered the ears of my men, and they bound me upright to the mast of the ship. The wind dropped and the sea became calm as though a god had stilled the waters. My company took their oars and pulled away. When the ship was within a man's shout from land we had come near the Sirens espied us and raised their song.

"'Come hither, come hither, O Odysseus,' the Sirens sang, 'stay thy bark and listen to our song. None hath ever gone this way in his ship until he had heard from our own lips the voice sweet as a honeycomb, and hath joy of it, and gone on his way a wiser man. We know all things—all the travail the Greeks had in the war of Troy, and we know all that hereafter shall be upon the earth. Odysseus, Odysseus, come to our field of flowers, and hear the song that we shall sing to thee.'

"My heart was mad to listen to the Sirens. I nodded my head to the company commanding them to unloose me, but they bound me the tighter, and bent to their oars and rowed on. When we had gone past the place of the Sirens the men took the wax from off their ears and loosed me from the mast.

"But no sooner had we passed the Island than I saw smoke arising and heard the roaring of the sea. My company threw down their oars in terror. I went amongst them to hearten them, and I made them remember how, by my device, we had escaped from the Cave of the Cyclops. I told them nothing of the monster Scylla, lest the fear of her should break their hearts. And now we began to drive through that narrow strait. On one side was Scylla and on the other Charybdis. Fear gripped the men when they saw Charybdis gulping down the sea. But as we drove by, the monster Scylla seized six of my company—the hardiest of the men who were with me. As they were lifted up in the mouths of her six heads they called to me in their agony. But I could do nothing to aid them. They were carried up to be devoured in the monster's den. Of all the sights I have seen on the ways of the water, that sight was the most pitiful.

"Having passed the rocks of Scylla and Charybdis we came to the Island of Thrinacia. While we were yet on the ship I heard the lowing of the Cattle of the Sun. I spoke to my company and told them that we should drive past that Island and not venture to go upon it.

"The hearts of my men were broken within them at that sentence, and Eurylochus answered me, speaking sadly.

"'It is easy for thee, O Odysseus, to speak like that, for thou art never weary, and thou hast strength beyond measure. But is thy heart, too, of iron that thou wilt not suffer thy companions to set foot upon shore where they may rest themselves from the sea and prepare their supper at their ease?'

"So Eurylochus spoke and the rest of the company joined in what he said. Their force was greater than mine. Then said I, 'Swear to me a mighty oath, one and all of you, that if we go upon this Island none of you will slay the cattle out of any herd.'

"They swore the oath that I gave them. We brought our ship to a harbor, and landed near a spring of fresh water, and the men got their supper ready. Having eaten their supper they fell to weeping for they thought upon their comrades that Scylla had devoured. Then they slept.

"The dawn came, but we found that we could not take our ship out of the harbor, for the North

Wind and the East Wind blew a hurricane. So we stayed upon the Island and the days and the weeks went by. When the corn we had brought in the ship was all eaten the men went through the island fishing and hunting. Little they got to stay their hunger.

"One day while I slept, Eurylochus gave the men a most evil counsel. 'Every death,' he said, 'is hateful to man, but death by hunger is by far the worst. Rather than die of hunger let us drive off the best cattle from the herds of the Sun. Then, if the gods would wreck us on the sea for the deed, let them do it. I would rather perish on the waves than die in the pangs of hunger.'

"So he spoke, and the rest of the men approved of what he said. They slaughtered them and roasted their flesh. It was then that I awakened from my sleep. As I came down to the ship the smell of the roasting flesh came to me. Then I knew that a terrible deed had been committed and that a dreadful thing would befall all of us.

"For six days my company feasted on the best of the cattle. On the seventh day the winds ceased to blow. Then we went to the ship and set up the mast and the sails and fared out again on the deep.

"But, having left that island, no other land appeared, and only sky and sea were to be seen. A cloud stayed always above our ship and beneath that cloud the sea was darkened. The West Wind came in a rush, and the mast broke, and, in breaking, struck off the head of the pilot, and he fell straight down into the sea. A thunderbolt struck the ship and the men were swept from the deck. Never a man of my company did I see again.

"The West Wind ceased to blow but the South Wind came and it drove the ship back on its course. It rushed toward the terrible rocks of Scylla and Charybdis. All night long I was borne on, and, at the rising of the sun, I found myself near Charybdis. My ship was sucked down. But I caught the branches of the fig tree that grew out of the rock and hung to it like a bat. There I stayed until the timbers of my ship were cast up again by Charybdis. I dropped down on them. Sitting on the boards I rowed with my hands and passed the rock of Scylla without the monster seeing me.

"Then for nine days I was borne along by the waves, and on the tenth day I came to Ogygia where the nymph Calypso dwells. She took me to her dwelling and treated me kindly. But why tell the remainder of my toils? To thee, O King, and to thy noble wife I told how I came from Calpyso's Island, and I am not one to repeat a plain-told tale."

HERACLES / Greece

Olivia E. Coolidge

The Greek hero Heracles was stronger than all other men of his day, so strong he could not be defeated except by the gods or by magic. His confidence in his strength was so great he even was willing to fight Apollo. Yet Heracles' mind was not the equal of his body. Once when the sun was too hot he threatened to shoot it. While he was exceptionally good natured, he was easily angered and in violent rages often murdered innocent people, after which he suffered great remorse. Much of his life was spent expiating these terrible deeds.

In retelling Heracles' life Olivia Coolidge wisely does not gloss over his weakness. To make him a paragon would be to distort his humanity, for one of the most important of the Greek heroes' characteristics is their roundedness. Miss Coolidge, however, does simplify Heracles' parentage. Zeus was his true father and from this developed Hera's hatred; but the gods' amorous adventures are not considered appropriate in versions for children.

The first story about Heracles tells of his strength when he was less than a year old. One night his mother, Alcmena, fed him, bathed him as usual, and then put him to bed for the night with his twin brother, Iphicles, in a cradle made of a great bronze shield which their father, Amphitryon, had won in battle. She kissed the little boys lying close together, and rocked them gently for a time until they fell asleep. Presently she crept away, and not long after, the whole house lay silent and dark.

Now Zeus was the protector of Heracles, but his wife, Hera, had other favorites and was jealous. This night she sent two dark snakes silently coiling past the pillars of the house door, sliding across the floor towards the shield. Just as they reared their dark heads and coiled themselves up to strike, Zeus lit up the whole room with brightness, and at the warning the children awoke. When Iphicles saw the swaying heads peering at him over the rim of the shield, he screamed aloud in fright and kicked aside the blanket over him, trying to pull himself over to the other side. Not so Heracles; he grasped the snakes by the neck in his fat baby hands and clutched with all his might.

In another moment all the house was in an uproar. The angry snakes whipped back and forward. They wound their coils about the baby's arms and tried to squeeze. But Heracles only gripped tighter and choked them till they could not hold on any more. In the next room, Alcmena leaped from the bed, seeing it bright as daylight in the house and hearing the sounds of struggle and Iphicles screaming.

"Quick!" she gasped to her husband. "Quick! Get your sword!"

Amphitryon jumped up half awake and fumbled for the weapon that hung on a peg beside his bed. At that moment the bright light vanished. They could hear no more struggle. Only the sound of Iphicles' crying went lustily on and on.

"Lights! Lights!" Amphitryon shouted to his household. "Bring torches, unbolt the doors!"

People flocked into the room, Amphitryon first with his drawn sword in his hand, Alcmena close behind him, and the servants crowding with torches through the door. There in the cradle lay Iphicles, hushed now but white with fear. Beside him lay Heracles chuckling to himself as he held out his arms to his father, while in the two tiny fists lay the dead bodies of the snakes, choked to death by the strength of his grip.

Alcmena picked up Iphicles and comforted him, but Amphitryon merely tucked the blanket in again over Heracles and let him go back to sleep. From that time on both parents knew that their child would be a mighty hero.

The youth of Heracles was spent in Thebes, where famous men taught him the skills that a hero should know. He learned poetry and music, but cared far more for sports, in which he excelled. He rode and ran, threw the javelin and wielded the spear. Above all he was famous as an archer and a wrestler and for his incredible strength. Indeed, even in his early youth he is said to have killed a man by accident, striking him too hard when he was in one of his rages. Yet he performed such services in war for Thebes that his fellow citizens soon forgave him, and the king gave him his own daughter to wife. Heracles was very happy with her for a while, but at last, the story says, in a fit of madness he killed both his wife and his three little sons, not knowing what he did.

None of the legends explain very well this terrible action of Heracles. Some say he went mad from rage at an injury done him and for a moment could not tell friend from foe. Others say this madness was sent on him by his old enemy, Hera. However it was, when he came to his senses Heracles most bitterly repented. Even though he had not known what he was doing, for a long

"The Youth of Heracles" and "The First Two Labors" from *Greek Myths.* Copyright 1949 by Olivia E. Coolidge. Reprinted by permission of the publisher, Houghton Mifflin Company.

while he hid his face from other people and would not even speak to them. At last he asked the gods what he should do to pay for this terrible sin, and was told to bind himself for eight years as servant to King Eurystheus and to perform ten tasks for him.

This was a very hard punishment for Heracles. He was a proud man, and besides King Eurystheus was a weakling and a coward who was jealous of the great hero and proceeded to give him the hardest tasks he could find. Also he objected to two of the tasks Heracles performed because the hero had had help in one and had earned a profit from another. Eventually, therefore, instead of doing him ten services, Heracles had to do twelve. These twelve are generally called the Twelve Labors of Heracles and are the most famous things he did. Several of them involved killing dangerous monsters, while for some of the others Heracles had to take long journeys on which he did many brave deeds for the people into whose lands he came. Thus there are numerous stories about the services of Heracles to men, and of the glory and profit he won for himself; the twelve labors are merely the ones that we know best.

THE FIRST TWO LABORS

The first of the twelve tasks given to Heracles was the killing of the Nemean Lion. This great beast had his lair near the sacred grove of Zeus at Nemea whence he ravaged the nearby countryside. Heracles took the great bow that none but he could bend, and made himself a mighty club from the trunk of an olive tree which he tore up by the roots. With these weapons he went up the valley toward the rocky cleft where the beast was supposed to live. It was noon as Heracles passed through Nemea, finding no track of the monster and hearing no sound of roaring. Though it was midday, the whole place seemed deserted. No man was busy plowing, and the cattle strayed in the fields untended while the inhabitants shut themselves up safe indoors. It was better to lose a cow or a sheep than one's own life, and from this beast not even the bravest man was safe.

Heracles passed through the silent valley and began to climb the wooded hill as the sun sank low. Presently he heard a rustling in the undergrowth. He made towards it, and as he came out onto a wide clearing, he saw the lion. The lion was not in a warlike mood; it had killed and eaten already and was now going home to sleep. It was an enormous monster, and its great, hairy face was dark with blood and streaked with dust. It padded up the hill, head low, making for its den.

Heracles crouched down behind a group of bushes fitting an arrow to the string. With all his strength he let fly, and his aim was true. The arrow struck the lion full in the side, but to the hero's amazement it simply bounded off and fell on the grass. Then Heracles knew that it was no ordinary lion. Nevertheless before the enraged beast could turn upon him, he shot again. Again he hit, and again the arrow bounded off and was lost. Before he could shoot a third time, the lion was on him with a mighty spring. Heracles met him in mid air. In his left hand he held his folded cloak hastily flung over his arm to break the force of the blow, but with the right he raised his club and struck the lion full on the forehead with such fearful force that the club broke clear in half and he was left defenseless.

The lion dropped to the ground dazed. Were it not for the bush of hair that protected his head, even his huge skull might have been cracked. As it was, he still stood on his four feet but blinded and staggering, shaking his great head slowly to and fro. Then with a quick spring, Heracles was on his back and his arms were about the lion's throat. In vain did the beast rear up and rend the air with his claws then drop back and scrape great furrows in the ground. In vain did he dash himsel from side to side. The man still clung, and the mighty arms gripped ever more tightly round his throat. He opened his mouth to roar, but no sound came forth. He reared up again and this time was held there helpless while his useless forepaws beat the air. At last his struggles grew fainter until finally he went limp. Heracles had strangled him by main strength.

Heracles was immensely proud of his first achievement. He skinned the lion—no easy task to cut off that iron hide—and went back to Eurystheus with the thing slung about him as a cloak. The two forepaws fastened it about his neck, and if he wanted, he could draw up the lion's head over his own. He came swaggering into the presence of Eurystheus, and that coward king, who had hoped to get rid of Heracles and feared that the hero knew it, was so terrified at the fierce lion's head and the great man who carried it that he turned white and trembled before the eyes of all his court. He quickly left the hall before Heracles could come near him, and the bold hero shouted with laughter, while the attendants whispered among themselves.

*　　*　　*

HERCULES/Greece

Mollie McLean
Anne Wiseman

The following excerpt reveals how oversimplification can distort a retelling of a traditional tale. Hercules' ignorance of the reason for his servitude to Eurystheus is false to the original and unfortunate in this revision because it adds an unnecessary confusion. While in a blind rage, Hercules had murdered his wife and children. For this crime the gods had decreed he must serve Eurystheus. Compare this brief version with the much more accurate and interesting retelling by Olivia E. Coolidge.

After sailing for seven days and seven nights, Hercules came to the land of a powerful king named Eurystheus. The people of the country had heard of Hercules. They crowded about him and asked why he had come.

"I wish to see the king," said Hercules.

"We will take you to him," the people said.

When they came to the palace, the king came out to meet Hercules. He was a small man with a wrinkled face and a black beard. His eyes were cruel.

"Well, strong Hercules, you have come at last," said Eurystheus. "I have many things to say to you. Come with me into my palace."

Inside the palace it was cold and dark. Hercules turned to the king and said, "Why have you sent for me?"

The king gave a cruel laugh and said, "The gods have put you in my power, strong Hercules. You will have to do just as I tell you. I am going to make you work very hard."

"Why have the gods done this to me?" asked Hercules with surprise.

"That is not for you to ask," shouted the king. "You must do as you are told."

The earth shook and the sky grew black. Hercules knew that what the king said was true.

Sadly he said, "I shall do as you wish."

For many long years Hercules worked for King Eurystheus.

*　　*　　*

THESEUS/Greece

Olivia E. Coolidge

Theseus was the hero of the Athenians, a people who placed more value on intelligence and ideas than did the other people of Greece. Heracles, hero of most Greeks, was too dense and emotional to please the Athenians. Both men were brave, but Theseus was also compassionate and highly intelligent. The lives and personalities of these two heroes make an interesting contrast.

THE YOUTH OF THESEUS

Two Greek heroes, Heracles and Theseus, had many adventures, not just one, and were famous for their characters as much as for their achievements. Heracles was the outstanding example of physical strength and fitness. Theseus was the wise, just ruler. Each of them therefore stood for something which the Greeks greatly admired. These are the best of the many stories about them.

Theseus was brought up by his mother, Aethra, in her father's palace in the little kingdom of Troezen. It was a quiet, pleasant household where the boy learned to associate kindness and justice with the office of a king. Aethra saw to it that he was educated in running, jumping, wrestling, throwing the discus and javelin, boxing, swordplay, and all the skills of a prince. He was taught also to love poetry and music. Wandering minstrels came to the palace singing of the great deeds of old. At the same time they brought news of the world as it was then, of greater kingdoms less pleasantly ruled than Troezen, of lawlessness, robbery, injustice, and of the heroes of Theseus' own time who fought against these evils. Aethra encouraged her son to listen, for she said he was a great prince and must take thought for these things. Yet when the boy asked her of his father, she would tell him nothing. She always answered that he must be patient until the time came for him to learn the truth.

The years went by and the boy became a youth fired with ambition to be worthy of a great destiny. At last he went to his mother one birthday and said to her, "Mother, I am now a man. Tell me about my father, for I am old enough to seek him out and to take my place in the world."

Aethra looked at her son thoughtfully, taking in the brown arms, the steady blue eyes, the upright carriage, and the slender, athletic form that had not yet come to its full strength. "Perhaps it is time," she said at last. "Come with me and we will see."

Mother and son walked together up a pleasant hill towards a little grove of trees. As they went, the quiet voice of Aethra spoke of the daily tasks of the household, just as though this were an ordinary day and she had nothing to tell her son. When they came to the summit, she showed him a great, grey stone lying flat on its side half buried in the clinging grass.

"Lift up that stone for me if you can," she said quietly.

Theseus bent down to the stone and strained at it with all his strength. First he tried it from one side and then from the other. Finally he stood up and wiped his brow for a moment while he had a look at it. Then he dug a little of the earth away with his fingers to get a better grip and tore at it till it seemed as though his back would break, but it was no good. He might just as well have tried to lift a mountain for all the success he had.

"Never mind, my son," said the gentle Aethra. "Next year we will try again." She walked back towards the palace with her arm in her son's, talking calmly of other things.

Next year when his birthday came, Theseus went up once more with his mother to lift the mighty stone. This time he stirred it a little from its bed, and had it not been sunk so deeply in the earth, he might have raised it.

"Never mind, my son," said Aethra once more. "We can wait another year."

This was his second failure, and Theseus determined that the third time, come what would, he must lift that stone. All day long he was out-of-doors, running, wrestling, exercising, even helping his grandfather's servants harvest the grain, carrying the heavy baskets of grapes to the winepress, and doing whatever hard work he could find. Therefore, when they walked up the hill again, mother and son were silent, for they knew the great day was come and each felt glad and sorry for the parting that lay ahead.

They looked down from the hilltop still in silence at the harbor, the quiet town, the few miles of pasture and plowland, and the uplands of scrub and heather which made up the little kingdom of Troezen. Far off to the north lay purple lines of rocky hills, pathless, and dangerous, but near at hand it was early summer and everything was green. Theseus and his mother stood there for a moment, listening to the distant baaing of goats and the calls of children, while the birds sang in the branches above them, bees hummed in the grass, and the warm sunlight fell across the stone. Then Theseus strode quickly across to it, got his fingers beneath, and with a mighty heave raised it first knee high, then to his shoulder, and with a final gasp rolled it clear over onto its back in triumph. Beneath the stone, kept safe in a little hollow that had been scooped out for them many years before, lay a pair of sandals and a sword.

Theseus gathered up the treasures and turned back to his mother. "The time is come," he said to her. "Now tell me who is the father who left these things for me."

"He is Aegeus, king of Athens," Aethra answered him.

"Aegeus, king of Athens" cried Theseus in exultaton. "Aegeus, the lover of justce, the protector of the weak!"

"He said good-bye to me on this hilltop," said Aethra. "He rolled aside the stone himself and hid the sword and sandals beneath. Then he told me that if our child should prove a daughter, I was to keep her and bring her up and marry her well. If we had a son, I was to take him to this stone when he was grown a man and bid him roll it away. If he could not, I should keep him with me; but if he were strong enough, I should send him to Athens with the sandals and the sword that he might claim his inheritance."

"His inheritance," repeated Theseus softly. He slung the sword about him and with the sandals in his hand turned to his mother. "Let us go," said he.

"Yes, we will go," answered Aethra, "and tomorrow we will fit out a ship for you that you may travel like a prince."

"No, not by sea," said Theseus. "I shall travel by land, and alone."

"Alone and by land!" said Aethra quickly. "No, that can never be. By land the route is almost pathless. It is savage and lawless; robbers and strange monsters haunt it. No man travels by land, at least not alone."

"That is how I shall go," said Theseus firmly. "Is not Athens the city of justice, the refuge of the weak? I will destroy these robbers and monsters who rule the land. Thus when I come to my father, my fame will come with me and he will know that I am a worthy son."

Aethra begged her son to be reasonable, and her old father added his prayers, but it was no use. The next day Theseus put on the sandals, took his sword, kissed his mother, and walked quietly out of the palace toward the hills.

Athens is many days' journey to the north of Troezen, and, as Aethra had said, the way is perilous. Theseus was at home in the open, and he had a friendly word for the people in town or cottage wherever he came. Yet the hills were wild and lawless, so that he never knew whether a stranger was a peaceful shepherd or hunter or whether he was one of the fierce robbers who held the whole countryside in terror. One day a curious looking man stepped out of the wood onto the path in front of him in a lonely stretch of the road. At first sight he seemed quite dangerous. He was immensely shaggy with matted hair and beard. His shoulders were enormous, and he carried a huge club bound with iron. Yet from the waist down he was tiny, with little, crooked legs, and he came shuffling along the path calling out in a high, nasal voice to the noble young stranger to have pity on a poor cripple and give him money. Theseus let him come near, thinking him harmless, but when he was within arm's length he reared up and struck a blow with the massive club which would have dashed Theseus' brains out if he had not been young and quick. As it was, the youth jumped aside just in time, and, as the man swayed for a moment overbalanced by the force of his own stroke, he snatched out his father's sword and stabbed the robber to the heart. He put back the sword in its sheath, took up the great club as a trophy of his first fight, and walked on. At the next village there was great excitement when people saw him carrying it. They crowded round to thank him and to tell him that the robber was named the Club Bearer and had terrorized innocent travelers for many years.

Theseus' next adventure was with a robber called Sinis, or the Pine Bender, because he bent down to earth the tops of two pine trees and tied his prisoners between them. Then he let go, and the trees sprang upright again with a terrific force, tearing the poor wretches apart. Sinis rushed at Theseus with a mighty weapon made from the trunk of a pine tree, but strong as he was, Theseus was stronger, and the iron-bound club was superior to the pine. The Pine Bender was vanquished and came to the miserable end he had often prepared for others.

Theseus traveled on, and now his fame spread before him far and wide until people came down to the way to meet him, both to speak with a great hero and to beg him to deliver them from trouble. In this way Theseus was persuaded to kill the great wild boar of Crommyon which was laying waste the countryside. Then he came upon the dreadful Sciron, who sat by the road where it passed over a steep cliff by the sea and forced all passers-by to wash his feet. As the trembling victim was busy with his task, Sciron kicked out and tumbled him backwards over the cliff onto the rocks below. Theseus gave him, too, a dose of his own medicine and passed on to another place where he killed a great wrestler by dashing him to the ground.

By now even in the remotest parts, people would come to greet Theseus and thank him for rescuing them. Therefore he was not surprised when one evening a man stepped out onto the road in a lonely spot and offered him shelter for the night. He was a queer man, though; he was very tall and thin with a pale face and pale eyes that never stood still for a second. He shuffled his feet and cracked his fingers. Everything about him was jerky except his voice, which was smooth as oil. "You do my poor home honor," he kept on saying. "So great a hero! So poor a shelter! Yet perhaps you are wise. Many great and noble men have spent the night with me." He laughed, not very loud but on and on, as though at a joke of which he was never weary.

"Where is your house?" said Theseus shortly, for he saw no point in laughing and he did not like the man. "Perhaps it is too far. I must be on my road at dawn."

"Ah no," said the strange man quickly. "It is not far. Just over the hill. In ten minutes, in five minutes if the noble hero is willing, we shall be at the door. Just five minutes from the highway! Think how easy. Yet of all the noble strangers who have rested in my bed, not one has roused himself to be on the roadway in the dawning. So sound a sleep! And dreamless! It is a noble bed!" He laughed again and jerked a hand onto Theseus' arm above the elbow as if to guide him. The grip was surprisingly strong. The youth suffered himself to be hurried up a rocky path, for he thought he knew the man now from stories that he had heard, and was anxious to see what he would do.

At last they came in sight of a mean hovel roughly piled together in the midst of the rocks. "Come in, come in," said the stranger quickly, pulling a little harder at his arm. "Come and rest. Did I tell you I have a bed for you? You are very tall, yet my bed will fit you. Oh yes, it will fit!"

Theseus pulled his arm free and turned on the man in the doorway. "I have heard of you," he said quietly. "Your bed is a hard plank and narrow, and it needs no blankets. Yet all men exactly fit it, so they say, and when they are laid upon it, they sleep very soundly in death. Is not your name Procrustes?"

Procrustes turned upon him and grasped his arm again. "Better men than you," he cried, "have fitted my dreadful bed. For if a man be too short when he is laid thereon, I stretch him till he fits it. But if he be too long, I shorten him with the knife. Now you shall lie, my young hero, where so many better men have lain before. You are tall for my bed at present, but it will fit you yet."

With that he threw his arms about Theseus and made as though to lift him. But the hero burst the grip with a mighty heave and seized him by the waist. Then he lifted him to his shoulder and bore him struggling through the dark doorway. Accordingly as night fell, Theseus set forth once more upon his road in the dark, leaving Procrustes stretched upon the terrible bed which had fitted all other men and now at last fitted him.

SIGURD/Norse

Dorothy Hosford

Sigurd is the most famous of all Norse heroes; he is the main character of the Volsungasaga *and its German counterpart, the* Nibelungenlied, *in which he is called Siegfried. Wagner's operas have given this narrative wide exposure.*

Although the following excerpt shows Sigurd's success, the Ring of Gain which he takes from Fafnir's treasure brings with it a curse that leads to Sigurd's death.

The death of young heroes is one of the most common themes of early Germanic and Scandinavian literature. The lives of these people were insecure: famine, war, and destruction were always near. And so their heroes also lived precarious lives. The object of gods, heroes, and common men, as reflected in their literature, was not to live long but to meet danger unflinchingly.

Of the race of the sons of Odin were born many brave heroes who performed mighty deeds. One was Sigurd, whose feats of valor are chronicled in song and story.

Now when the moon was full and the month of May had begun, Sigurd returned again to Regin, the king of the dwarfs. Regin stood by his smithy and the light of the fire showed him dim-eyed and weary.

He spake to Sigurd: "Hail, son of the Volsungs! I have toiled as thou hast desired, and lo, there is the fateful blade."

Then Sigurd saw it lying on the gray ashes.

"Sigurd the Volsung" from *Songs of the Volsungs*; adapted by Dorothy G. Hosford from *Sigurd the Volsung* by William Morris; illustrated by Frank Dobias. Published by The Macmillan Company, 1932.

The hilt was ruddy and shining, the edges pale and fine, and a gleam like the flame of lightning ran down to the very point of it and burned through the runes that were scored on its sides. No sound did Sigurd utter as he stooped down for his sword. The blade leapt white over his head, then blazed like fire as he played it hither and thither, till he brought it down on the anvil with a fierce and mighty stroke. Then Sigurd cried aloud in his glory and held out the sword full length, as one who would show it to the world, for the edges were dulled no whit, but the anvil was cleft in twain.

Then turned the Volsung to Regin and said: "Now shall I work thy will. My father hath made me mighty, but I shall give thee the gold and the craft thou desirest. Thou hast taught me many things a prince should know. Thou hast failed me in nought, and the sword is a wondrous thing."

No word for a while spake Regin, and he looked down as a man that pondereth deeply. Then he spake, and his voice was no more weary: "This sword, this Wrath of thine, hath cleft what is hard and heavy. It shall shear the light and soft. Come forth to the night and prove it."

So the twain went forth to the river, and the stream was swift and full, and the moon shone white upon it. Then Regin cast on the water a lock of fine-spun wool and held the sword in the water's edge. The wool spun round on the eddy, but when it met the blade's edge it was sheared in twain.

Then Regin spake: "It is good, this sword that I have wrought. And now thy works beginneth, Thy Wrath is alive and awake and the tale of thy deeds is begun."

Then the sword, which ever since has been called the Wrath of Sigurd, was laid in a golden sheath and the peace-strings were knit about it.

On the morrow after Sigurd had received his Wrath, he mounted Greyfell and rode toward the dwelling of Gripir. He had promised Gripir that he would return thence when he had won his sword and was ready for the road that lay before him. So with the Wrath girded to his side, he wended his way across the wild heaths to the foot of the mountains. His heart rejoiced that he had won his sword, and now should do the deeds of a man, yea, even the deeds of a Volsung.

When Sigurd reached his dwelling, Gripir greeted him with great friendliness, and they had talk together. Sigurd asked of him how his life should go, because Gripir in his exceeding wisdom knew what things were to come, and what was fated to men. Gripir told Sigurd what his life should be, and the fate thereof, even as it afterwards came to pass. Gripir gave Sigurd his blessing and Sigurd departed. As the sun set and the evening came on, he returned to the dwelling of the kings.

On the day following, Sigurd the Volsung went forth again and by his side fared Regin, the master smith. They left the dwelling of the kings and rode throughout the day, till in the evening they had left the plain behind and the hills were about them. They wended their way higher and higher, nor rested till it was midnight. When they awakened in the early dawn, far away they could see valleys and meadows, but before them rose the sheer wall of the mountains.

Then spake Regin: "We have come to the gate of the mountains. Behind thee there is youth and rest, and many a pleasure. And mayhap I could find rest and a peaceful end to my years. We have come to the gate of the mountains. Thinkest thou we should fare further?"

"Yea! What else?" answered Sigurd. "What of the tale thou hast told me? Didst thou not tell me your brother Fafnir had stolen a great treasure of gold that was rightfully thine, and that he had changed himself into a dragon to guard it? Did I not pledge its return to thee? Was it not for that the Wrath was forged? Or was thy tale but lies and mockeries?"

"It was truth, it was truth," said Regin, "and more I might have told thee had I heart and space to remember."

But Regin hung his head as he spake these words, and there was fear in his face. Then he spake again: "At times I dream that thou hadst neither father nor mother; that I alone have wrought thee, a bright and glorious thing, to work my will. Then my hope riseth and I behold the world molded to my desires. But then I awake and remember that thou art the son of Sigmund, who was the great king of the Volsungs, and the mighty sword I forged is in thy hand. Ah, if only the world might turn backward to the days when the dwarfs were in power!"

But Sigurd heeded not the words of Regin, nor answered him. He leapt on the back of Greyfell, and the sun rose and the heavens glowed above him like the bowl of Baldur's cup. He cried to Greyfell and rode swift for the pass in the mountains, and Regin followed after.

All day long they fared through the mountains, and the way was steep and treacherous. And when the moon rose up and the stars were shining, they slept on the ground. In the cold dawn they wakened, and Sigurd was fair and strong as he drew the girths of Greyfell's saddle. But Regin seemed old and like a ghost, and his words were full of foreboding. But Sigurd was merry of heart, and no fear of Regin's could turn him from the deed he had sworn to do. So for another day they rode through the desolate mountains and slept again beneath the naked heavens. Again with the first light they arose, and on this morning Sigurd donned his war gear.

Then Regin asked of him: "What is thine hope this morning, O Sigurd, that thou arrayest thyself in war gear?"

"Who needeth hope," said Sigurd, "when the heart of the Volsungs turns to the Glittering Heath and the house of the dragon? I shall slay the foe of the gods, as thou didst bid me, and then with the gold and its curse shalt thou be left alone."

"O child," said the king of the dwarfs, "when the last day comes and 'tis the end even of the gods, shalt thou praise thy hope and still praise the gods that made this world?"

"Thou art a foe of the gods!" said Sigurd. "Thou wouldst hide the evil thing, and the curse that is greater than thou, lest death should overtake thee. It is me, it is me thou fearest, if indeed I know thy thought!"

And Sigurd sprang aloft to the saddle as he spake these words, and the Wrath burned in its sheath by his side. The sun rose and the gray pass in the mountains was filled with living light, and Regin turned from the glory with eyes that were blinded and dazed. But Sigurd, seated on Greyfell, gleamed in the light.

Then Sigurd spake in a great voice: "O Regin, in truth, I have hearkened not nor heeded thy words of fear and of foreboding. Thou hast told thy tale and thy longing and to that I hearkened well. The deed shall be done tomorrow. Thou shalt have the measureless gold; with the blood of thy brother thou shalt sate thy hunger, and this deed shall be mine and thine. But take heed for what followeth after! Let us each do after his kind! And for me, I shall do the deeds of men; to them shall I give my life, and to the gods my glory to keep."

Then Sigurd shook the bridle reins of Greyfell and rode forth from the mountain pass and took his way to the westward. And Regin rode after him. And now Regin forgot his fears and thought only of the gold that should be his. They journeyed on and on, between high mountain walls, past dark fathomless lakes that held no fish, nor any sign of life. They kept riding to the westward, and the mountains grew huge and their peaks reached to the very heavens. They rode through the noontide, and the sun grew low; not even

then did they tarry though the world was dark about them. On and on they rode, each man alone, through the night. And though the stars and the moon grew pale, no change came over the darkness, and no streak of dawn lit the sky.

In the blackness Sigurd felt for the walls of the pass, but though he rode first to one side and then the other, he found no wall before him. But lo, at last there came a glimmer in the sky, and the light grew, and a faint dawn came to the world. Sigurd strained his eyes, and all about him he saw a deserted land, barren and changeless as far as his eye could reach. Then his heart leapt up within him, for he knew that his journey was over, and here before him lay the Glittering Heath. He drew bridle and leapt down from Greyfell, and the Wrath burned in its sheath by his side; and on foot he wended his way through the gray light to meet the foe of the gods.

Sigurd saw nought of Regin, nor did he take any heed of him. He strode across the desert heath and Greyfell paced behind him. As he wended his way in the silence, a gray thing glimmered before him and became a mighty man, one-eyed and seeming ancient, and clad in cloud-gray raiment. A friendly man and glorious, and his face was smiling glad as he spake to Sigurd in a voice deep as the wind of winter: "Hail, Sigurd! Give me thy greeting ere thou wendest thy ways alone!"

And Sigurd answered: "Hail! I greet thee, my friend and my fathers' friend."

"And whither," said the elder, "goest thou?"

"To the house of the serpent, the greedy king of the gold," said Sigurd.

"And wilt thou smite him, O Sigurd?" quoth the ancient gray-clad one.

"Yea, I shall smite," said the Volsung, "unless the gods be against me."

"And how," said the elder, "shalt thou smite, so that thou thyself be not devoured?"

"I have this sword," said Sigurd, "and the sword shall find a way."

"Be learned of me," said the Wise One, "for I was the first of thy folk."

And Sigurd answered: "I shall obey thy bidding, and for thee I shall do the deed."

Then spake the Wise One: "Thus shalt thou do. Thou shalt come to a path, a road in this desert place that is smooth and deep and hollow.

The rains have not made it, but it is Fafnir's track whereby he wends his way to the ancient pool when he is athirst. When thou reachest it, remember the greatness of thy father, and bare thy sword, and dig a pit in that highway. Lie thou in it, O Sigurd, and appear as dead for a time. When the great worm passeth over thee, then shalt thou thrust him through."

Sigurd said: "I shall obey thy bidding, and for thee shall I do the deed. For I love thee, thou friend of my fathers."

So spake the son of Sigmund, but lo, no man was near. So Sigurd went on his way till he came to the path of Fafnir, and it was a mighty track. Sigurd drew forth his Wrath and dug the pit as he had been told, and lay therein. Now the dragon came on his way, and afar off Sigurd could hear him roaring as he dragged himself over the earth. And the roaring grew as he came nearer, and he snorted forth venom. Sigurd trembled not nor was afraid, but lay waiting. Then the dark rolled over Sigurd and the blackness covered him. He gathered his strength and, with a mighty upward thrust, drove his sword through the heart of the serpent. Then he leapt from the pit and the rushing river of blood.

There lay Fafnir wounded with the death stroke, and the folds of the serpent lay huddled on the plain. And forth from the face of the terror came the sound of speech: "Child, who art thou that hast smitten me? And whence is thy birth?"

"I am Sigurd the Volsung, the son of Sigmund the King."

Said Fafnir: "What matter hath taught thee of death? Hast thou not heard how all men feared me?"

"I desired the deed, and the bright sword learned the way."

And Fafnir answered: "Thou hast done it, thou child of Sigmund, but the gold and the red rings shall bring thee evil."

"But I shall cast them abroad," quoth Sigurd, "so that all men may gather them."

"Woe, woe!" cried Fafnir. "In the days that are past the hoarded gold was mine. I overcame and was mighty, till I met thine hand, O Sigurd."

As Sigurd leaned on his sword, a dreadful cry went by on the wind, and Fafnir died. Then all sank into silence and Sigurd stood alone on the desert by the pool of Fafnir's blood and before him lay the serpent, gray and dead.

So Sigurd stood, and now was Greyfell beside him, and Regin came afoot over the desert. When Regin stood before Sigurd, he stared at him and at the Wrath yet bloody and unsheathed, and at the serpent lying dead at the feet of Sigurd.

Then Regin lay on the ground and drank the blood of the serpent where it lay in a pool. And he cried: "Now shall I be free from the yoke that binds my soul to a withered body. Now shall I have again the wisdom and might of the dwarfs of old."

Regin turned and saw how Sigurd wiped the blood from his sword, and how above him a flock of mountain eagles screamed in the sky. And Regin's mood grew dark and he came to Sigurd and spake: "Child, thou hast slain my brother."

"Yea," answered Sigurd, "the deed is mine and thine. But now our ways shall go asunder."

But Regin darkened before him and grew exceeding grim: "Thou hast slain my brother, and wherewith wilt thou atone?"

"Stand up, O Master," cried Sigurd, "and take the wealth I have won for thee, ere we go our ways. I have toiled and thou hast desired, and the treasure is surely near. Thou hast the wisdom to find it."

But Regin cried again to Sigurd: "Thou hast slain my brother."

Then Regin crept to the coils of the dragon and drew a sword and cut the heart from Fafnir. Overhead the flock of wild eagles circled about. Then Regin spake to Sigurd: "Wilt thou be free of this slaying? Then build thou a fire and roast the heart for me, that I may eat it and live."

Then Regin lay on the ground and slept, but his sword lay bare by his side with his hand on the hilt. He seemed a fearful thing as he lay and dreamed of the power that would be his.

Sigurd took the dragon's heart. He found waste wood on the heath, and he built a hearth of stones and kindled a fire, and he sat before it and sang as he roasted the heart. The eagles flew low about him, but he little heeded their cries.

After the heart had roasted for a space, Sigurd reached his hand to see if the cooking were enough. But the blood and fat seethed forth and scalded Sigurd's finger, and he put it quick in his mouth to quench the smart. And thus he tasted the flesh of the serpent and the blood of Fafnir's heart. Then there came a change upon him, for he knew the speech of fowl, and grew as wise in the ways of the beast kind as were the dwarfs of old.

Sigurd knitted his brows and hearkened and began to understand the cries of the eagles that circled above. Anger rose in his heart, for he saw the net of evil and death that Regin sought to draw about him. For the eagles cried out a warning to Sigurd that Regin would wake from his sleep all-powerful and cunning with the ancient craft of the dwarf kind and that he would destroy Sigurd. This, from the beginning, had he planned, said the eagles.

With the eagles crying about him, Sigurd rose swiftly and the Wrath gleamed in his hand. Regin lay in sleep, but his eyes glared wide-open and his hand was on his sword. His lips smiled as he slept, for he dreamt that Sigurd was no more and that he at last was master of the world. But Sigurd saw the evil in Regin's heart and cried aloud in his anger: "Thou wouldst betray me and keep me here for my destruction, that my death might serve thy need. It is for this thou feared me and my sword. Lo, then, here is the sword and the stroke!"

Then the Wrath of Sigurd flashed thin and white and the head of Regin was severed from his body. And there in that desert place lay Regin, lifeless by the side of his brother, Fafnir, the serpent. But Sigurd cried in triumph: "The blind heart of the dwarf kind shall not rule the world. Dead are the foes of the gods!"

Then Sigurd himself ate of the heart of Fafnir and grew exceeding wise in the ancient wisdom of the dwarf kind. Then he leapt on the back of Greyfell and went in search of the treasure.

Sigurd followed the track of Fafnir, and still the eagles flew above him, until at length he reached the dwelling of the serpent. It was built of unwrought iron, and it went high to the heavens and reached deep into the earth; and there was nought within it save the heaped-up piles of gold.

Sigurd entered and beheld the treasure. There were coins of ancient cities and war gear and spoils from the battlefield; there was rich ore from the depth of the earth where none but the dwarfs had mined; and tawny gold from the sands of rivers no man had discovered. And in the midst of all these riches glittered a war coat of gold, the like of which there was not anywhere in the heavens or the earth. Sigurd beheld, moreover, the Ring of Gain, which Loki had so coveted.

Then laughed the son of Sigmund and set the ring on his hand and donned the war coat of gold. Then he labored to bring forth the treasure. He toiled and loaded Greyfell, though it seemed more than one horse could carry. And as Sigurd went about the work, the eagles sang triumphantly above him.

When the steed was fully laden it was well on in the night, and the stars shone. Then Sigurd took Greyfell's reins and turned toward the wall of the mountains, for he thought that the way out of the Glittering Heath lay there. But Greyfell would move not a whit for aught that Sigurd might do.

Sigurd pondered a space, till he knew the will of Greyfell; and then, clad all in his war gear, he leapt into the saddle. With a proud and mirthful toss of his head Greyfell sprang unguided over the desert plain. Light and swift he went and breasted the wall of the mountains and climbed the summit. And the Glittering Heath, that dread place where the serpent had so long held sway, was left behind.

BEOWULF/Anglo-Saxon England

Dorothy Hosford

Beowulf, *a unique example of the Old English, Anglo-Saxon epic tradition, is considered by many to be the greatest surviving epic of the Germanic peoples. Although written in England, probably during the first half of the eighth cenuty, it deals with the Danish and Swedish forebears of the Anglo-Saxons. One event in the poem happened in 520, only seventy years after the first Germanic invasion of England.*

Beowulf has a mixture of Christian and Norse values. While there are references to God, although none to Christ, the Norse sense of doom and fate is strong. Courage and the warrior's heroic life are central to the epic. Beowulf expresses the pre-Christian code in his answer to Hrothgar's sorrow over Aeschere's death. He gives no Christian comfort, rather counsels revenge.

The following excerpt begins after Beowulf and his men have come from Geat, an island off the Swedish coast, to destroy the monster that has been devouring Hrothgar's men.

Beowulf, in the hall, took off his corselet of iron and the helmet from his head. He gave them and his richly carved sword to his henchman and bade him guard them. Before he sought his bed, Beowulf, valiant hero of the Geats, spoke these proud words:

"I count myself as great in battle, in deeds of war, as Grendel. Not with the sword shall I give him over to the sleep of death, though I have that power. He has no skill with weapons. Therefore we both shall spurn the sword this night. If he seek me here I shall meet him unarmed. Let the Almighty Father award the mastery as He sees fit."

Beowulf laid him down on his bed and his warriors, weary, stretched themselves to rest. Not one of them thought that he would ever go forth alive from that place or return again to his home and the folk from whom he came. They remembered how many warriors Grendel had seized in that hall of the Danes. But they sank to slumber, worn with their journeying; all save one. Beowulf,

wakeful, ready, waited fiercely through the night the oncoming battle.

Then from the moorland, from the misty crags, Grendel came. Mighty in his wrath, he made ready to seize upon the warriors gathered in the mead-hall. Under the clouds he strode until the great hall, brave with gold, came into sight. Many times he had sought out the home of Hrothgar, but never before had such hardy warriors awaited him. Straight to the hall came the evil one. The door, though fastened with bands forged in the fire, gave way when his fists struck it and he burst into the hall fierce in his rage. He strode across the shining floor. Flashes, like flame, came from his eyes. He spied the hero-band sleeping together. And he laughed in his heart and thought that before morning he would rend the life from each of them and have his fill of feasting. But it was fated that never, after that night, should he feed again on the race of men.

Beowulf, strong in his might, watched his foe eagerly to see how he would set about the onslaught. Nor did the monster pause. Straightway he seized a sleeping warrior and destroyed him, devouring his blood and body. Then he stepped forward again and grasped the hero Beowulf where he lay on his bed. The fiend reached for him with his claw, but Beowulf clutched Grendel's arm and threw his weight against it. At once that monster knew that never in this world, on any of the ways of the earth, had he met with so mighty a hand-grip. He was afraid and trembled in his heart, but he could not escape. He would fain have fled to his fastness, to that den of devils. This was not as it had been in other raids upon the hall.

Then the hardy Beowulf remembered his battleboast. Up he sprang and laid fast hold upon his foe. Grendel's fingers cracked in that iron grip, but the fiend strove fiercely to wrench himself free. He longed to escape to the fens, yet he knew his power was caught in the strength of this grim one. Din filled the hall. Panic fell upon the Danes, upon all who heard the uproar. Maddened were the strugglers; the house resounded with their clashing. It was a wonder that the hall held firm, that it did not fall to earth with the rage of their battle. Strong iron bands, without and within, held it fast, though many a gold-decked mead bench crashed to the floor. The wise Danes had built their house to withstand all onslaughts, save the creeping embrace of fire.

The turmoil grew. Suddenly a strange outcry rose through the night. The Danes quaked with terror as they heard the monster's wail of pain and defeat. Caught in Beowulf's fierce grip, Grendel cried aloud in anguish. Beowulf would not suffer that murderous one to live.

Now many of Beowulf's warriors drew their weapons to aid their lord. They did not know, as they came close to Grendel, striking at him from every side with their swords, that no blade fashioned on earth could do him harm. He had laid his spell on every weapon and none could hurt him. But the evil one, who had wrought murder many a time in days past, found that his strength now failed him. The bold kinsman of Hygelac held him fast. As they struggled the monster took a fearful hurt; a great wound showed on his shoulder, his sinews cracked and the bones broke. Now was the victory given to Beowulf, and Grendel, sick unto death, fled to his den in the dark moor. He knew that his wound was mortal—that the end of his days had come, the last of his life on earth.

By this bloody battle the Danes had at last won peace. Beowulf, strong in arm and brave of heart, had brought safety to Hrothgar's hall. The Geat had made good his battle-boast to the Danes, and the sorrow they had long endured was ended now. It was proof of this, when Beowulf laid down in the hall the limb, the whole arm and shoulder of Grendel, which he had torn from him in the struggle.

HOW THE DANES REJOICE OVER BEOWULF'S VICTORY

In the morning, as men tell the tale, many warriors from far and near gathered round the hall. The people came over many roads to view this strange token of the battle, Grendel's claw. None of those who followed the bloody track of the monster to his den in the moors was sorry for Grendel's ending. There the waters of the mere seethed with blood where Grendel had laid down his life in the dark waves.

Joyfully the clansmen rode back from the dread place, many warriors and youths as well, on their gray horses. As they rode they sang of Beowulf's glory. Nowhere under the sky, from the south to the north, from sea to sea, was there one like him. None was more valiant, no warrior more worthy to rule than he. And in so saying they did no dishonor to the kindly Hrothgar, for a good king was he.

From time to time, when the road was fair, they set their steeds at a gallop and raced. As they rode along, a thane whose mind was filled with tales of old and who knew how to weave words into song, began to tell the story of Beowulf's battle and likened him to Sigmund, the mighty hero of the Volsungs.

Again they raced when the tale was over, their swift steeds measuring the yellow roads. And so, as the sun mounted ever higher in the sky, they came again to Heorot. Here were gathered many to witness Beowulf's triumph. The king himself, the wise and virtuous Hrothgar, came with a stately company from the queen's bower; and the queen, with her train of women, walked beside him the path to the great hall.

Hrothgar stood by the steps of the hall and looked at the steep roof, shining with gold. He looked at Grendel's paw nailed above the doorway and spoke these words:

"For the sight I see thanks be given to the Almighty Father. Long have I borne evil from Grendel, but God still works wonder on wonder. It was not long ago that I thought never to have help in my trouble, while this fairest of houses stood battle-stained and bloody. It was a sorrow to all of us who could not guard this hall from foes and demons. Now this hero, by his own might, has done a work that none of us could do by craft or wisdom. Well can the woman who bore this son say, if she lives still among men, that she was blessed in her child. Now will I love you, Beowulf, best of men, as mine own son. You shall never lack for gifts that are in my power to bestow. Often I have showered riches and rewards on those less worthy, weaker in battle. You have done such deeds that your fame shall endure through all the ages. May God reward you with good as He has done in the past."

Beowulf answered: "Most willingly have we fought this work of war, this battle, and dared the strength of the foe. I would that you, yourself, had seen the downfall of the monster. I had hoped swiftly to bind him to his death here, but he broke away. God willed not that I should hinder him from his flight. But he has left behind for a token his arm and shoulder. Now he lives no longer, the loathsome fiend, but must suffer such doom as the Almighty Father shall mete out to him."

Unferth, who had taunted Beowulf's battle-prowess, was more silent now that he, with the other earls, viewed that hand on the high roof. The nails of the claw were like steel. It was clear that no blade, however keen, could have severed that arm.

Now there was hurry and running to and fro in Heorot to cleanse the feasting hall and bedeck it. The walls were hung with golden hangings beautiful to see, and all was made fair and bright. The dwelling had suffered sorely in that mighty struggle, though it was braced with iron bands. The door-hinges were torn away and the walls battered; the roof alone remained whole.

When the hall was ready and the banquet prepared, Hrothgar himself came to the feast. His liegemen and friends gathered round him and the hall of Heorot was filled with rejoicing. Then Hrothgar gave gifts to Beowulf, as he had prom-

ised,—a gold-embroidered battle-flag, a breast-plate and helmet, and a splendid sword. Eight steeds, their bridles carved with gold, were led indoors to the hall; and on one of them was a saddle set with shining jewels, that had been part of Hrothgar's war-gear. These the lord Hrothgar gave also to Beowulf, in such wise giving him reward for his good deeds. To each of the earls who had come over the sea with Beowulf he gave precious swords handed down from old. And Hrothgar ordered that payment he made in gold for the Geatish warrior slain by Grendel.

Then song and music rose in the great hall, and the gleeman touched his harp and sang an ancient tale of battle, of the feud of the Danes and the Frisians.

When the lay was finished the noise of revel rose again along the benches. The wine-bearers brought wine in carven vessels. Wealtheow came forth, gold-crowned, making her way to where the king and Hrothulf, her nephew, sat. She gave them greeting. Then she turned to the place where her sons Hrethric and Hrothmund were seated, with Beowulf between them. To Beowulf she gave the wine-cup to drink and made him greeting and brought gifts,—two arm-jewels, a coat of ringed mail, and the fairest collar that was ever heard tell of on earth.

Wealtheow spoke: "May these gifts bring you pleasure, beloved Beowulf. You have done such deeds that men both far and near shall forever honor you, as far as the sea washes his windy walls. Many your riches be great and your way in life prosper."

Wealtheow went to her place and the proud feast went on. The men drank their wine and thought little of Fate, whose shadow already crept upon them. When night came and Hrothgar went to his rest, many earls kept watch of the hall as they had often done before. They cleared away the long tables and spread out their beds on the benches and floor. One whose doom was fixed lay down with the others. At their heads the earls set their shields of war and on the bench over each atheling were his battle helmet, his corselet of rings, and his mighty spear. It was their custom to be so prepared for battle, at home or abroad, ready against whatever evil might threaten their liege lord. Good clansmen they were. And so they went to their rest.

HOW THE MOTHER
OF GRENDEL
AVENGES HIS DEATH

The warriors slept. But one paid dearly for his rest that night, even as had happened full often when Grendel ruled the hall before Beowulf destroyed him. For an avenger survived that fiend. Now his mother, grim and evil, came forth to avenge her son. To Heorot she came, where the Danes lay sleeping in the hall. The old sorrows of the earls returned when the mother of Grendel burst upon them. The Danes seized their shields and their hard-edged swords when they saw that terror. The monster was in haste. She would be off to save her life when she saw she was discovered, but she seized fast one of the athelings as she fled to the moor. And the man she bore off was of all Hrothgar's heroes the most dearly beloved, a warrior of great renown. Beowulf was not there, for another house had been prepared for him after the feast and the giving of gifts. Uproar filled Heorot. Grendel's hand, the trophy nailed on high for all to see, his mother bore with her. Great was the sorrow of the Danes, doomed once more to give up the lives of their loved ones. Then was the good kind Hrothgar sick at heart when he knew that his thane, his best beloved, was dead.

In haste Beowulf was brought to the king's bower. As daylight broke the mighty warrior, together with his earls, went forth to where the king awaited him. The hero strode across the floor and gave greeting to the wise old ruler of his people, asking, as was courteous, if the night had passed in peace.

"Speak not of peace or joy," answered Hrothgar. "Sorrow has returned to the Danes. Aeschere is dead, my counselor and friend, the comrade who stood shoulder to shoulder with me in battle. Would that every earl were as true a hero as Aeschere was. But here in Heorot has a hand slain him, a prowling fiend. I know not what road she has taken, bearing him with her. She has avenged your deed, that you did kill Grendel in your pitiless grip, he who so long harried and ravished my people. Now comes a second one, his mother, to avenge her kin, and lays low him whom we all loved. This is of all sorrows the hardest to bear. Gone is he who was ever ready and worthy to serve.

"I have heard the people of my land say, they who live in those parts, that they have seen a pair such as these stalking the haunts of men, making the moors their own. One seemed, so far as my folk could fairly judge, in form a woman; the other of man's shape, but greater in size than any human. In days long past the folk of the land named him Grendel. Theirs is a country uninhabited by man, hidden among the perilous fens and windy moors, where the mountain streams pour underground through dark rocky caverns to a dark sea. It is not far from here, measured in miles, that the mere lies. Frost-covered trees hang over it; a deep forest shadows it. By night is a marvel strange to see: fire glows on the waves. No one of the sons of men has dared to search those depths. Even the hunted stag, trailed by the dogs, though he seek this wood, will give up his life on the brink rather than plunge his head in those waters. It is an evil place. When the wind stirs up foul weather there is a great churning of waves till the air grows thick and the heavens weep.

"Now again we turn to you for help, Beowulf. This land you know not, this place of fear, where you may find the evil one. Seek it if you dare. I shall reward you with gifts and treasure and twisted gold, as I did before, if you win your way back."

"Grieve not," spoke Beowulf. "It befits us better to avenge our friends than to mourn them. Each of us must come to the end of his days in the world; so let us win glory, if we can, before death takes us. Rise, O King. We shall ride and seek the trail of the mother of Grendel. No harbor shall hide her, I promise, let her flee where she will; nor any field or forested mountain, not even the floor of the sea itself. Be you patient and endure your woes today."

The king rose to his feet and thanked the Almighty Father for Beowulf's brave words.

A horse was saddled for Hrothgar and the king rode forth. His warriors accompanied him on foot. The footprints of Grendel's mother led along the woodland and over the plain, where she had passed across the murky moor bearing the bravest and best beloved of Hrothgar's thanes.

The band of armed men, with Hrothgar and

Beowulf at their head, went along the stony way, through narrow passes and over steep cliffs and jutting headlands. Suddenly they came upon the dark forest overhanging the hoary rocks. The waves below were dyed with blood. Great was the sorrow of the Danes, sad were the earls, when they found the head of Aeschere lying on the sea-cliff. The waters surged, hot with blood and gore, as the men gazed upon them.

A thane blew on his horn and the song of battle rang out. The band sat down and watched on the waters strange sea-dragons. Nickers and other sea-snakes and monsters who bring destruction on the sea-road lay along the rocky ledges. These started away, wrathful and swollen with fury, when they heard the blast of the war-horn. Beowulf sent a deadly shaft from his bow into one sea-serpent and they hemmed it in with spears and dragged it up on the headland. The warriors viewed the fearsome thing.

Then Beowulf girt on his armor. He was not in any way afraid for his life. His broad breastplate, cunningly woven by hand to protect his body from the thrusts of battle, must withstand the waters. The white helmet guarding his head, wound with chains and adorned with gold, it too must make trial of the flood. Not the least of Beowulf's helps was the mighty sword, Hrunting by name, which Hrothgar's spokesman gave to him. It was one of the best of ancient treasures. Its edge was iron, hardened with blood and poison; never had it betrayed in battle the hand of the hero who bore it. Unferth, who offered the gift for the king, was the man who, drunken with wine, had taunted Beowulf and questioned his deeds of strength. But now he remembered that not, now when he dared not himself risk his life beneath the waves, and so must give up the sword and the chance for glory to a warrior stronger than he.

When Beowulf was arrayed for the strife, he spoke: "O Hrothgar, son of Healfdene, now that I go on this quest, remember what once was said: If I should lose my life for your sake you would still be as a father to me though I were gone. Be then a guardian to my thanes, these comrades of mine, if the strife takes me. And the goodly gifts that you have given me, send to Hygelac. Then will the king of the Geats know when he sees that treasure that I found a friend gracious and

kind and had joy of him while I could. And let Unferth, honored earl, have this wondrous sword of mine, this precious treasure of olden time with its hard-biting edge."

The lord of the Geats waited no answer to his words but boldly hastened to the waters and the flood closed over him.

HOW BEOWULF
SEEKS OUT
GRENDEL'S MOTHER
IN HER LAIR
BENEATH THE SEA

A whole hour of the day passed before Beowulf touched the floor of the sea. Then that fiend who for a hundred winters had held unmolested her domain in the flood knew that some creature from above, some man, had dared invade her realm. She seized the warrior, laying hold upon him with terrible claws, yet his strong body was unhurt and his breastplate stood firm as she strove to rend his war-gear. Then this sea-wolf, Grendel's mother, bore the warrior in her grasp to her lair. Other monsters of the sea beset him as she bore him through the waves. He struggled vainly to wield his sword against them, but they swarmed on him and tore at his mail.

Suddenly Beowulf found that he was in some strange hall, of what kind he knew not, whose strong roof held out the quick flood so that the waters could not enter. He saw firelight, the flash of a blaze that shone brightly. Then the warrior looked full on that she-wolf of the deep, that monstrous water-witch. He swung his sword with a mighty stroke, giving it all his strength. The blade sang out its fierce war-song. But he found that his battle-blade would not bite, nor harm her in any way. The hard edge failed him, though it had gone through many an encounter in the past and cloven many a helmet. Now for the first time it failed in battle.

Beowulf in no wise lost courage, but remembered his proud deeds and stood firm. In wrath he flung away the sword, strong and steel-edged, bright with jewels, so that it lay upon the earth. He trusted in his own strength, in the might of his hand grip. Thus must a man do if he would win fame in battle; he cares nought for his life.

Then the lord of the Geats—he shrank not from the combat—seized Grendel's mother by the shoulders. So fiercely he flung her, in his great wrath, that she fell to the ground. She rose swiftly and grappled with him, clutching with her sharp claws. Worn with struggle, Beowulf, mightiest of warriors, stumbled and fell to earth. The monster hurled herself on the stranger in her hall and drew her dagger to avenge her son. Then had the son of Ecgtheow, bravest of the Geats, gone to his death had not his breast-mail, his stout battle-coat, withstood the blade. Quickly he gained his feet, unharmed by the blow.

Then Beowulf caught sight of an old sword of the giants hanging on the wall, a weapon unmatched and prized by ancient warriors, save that it was heavier than most men could wield. The giants had wrought it and made its edge ready and keen. Beowulf, bold and grim with battle, seized it by the chain hilt. Reckless of his life, he brandished the sword and smote his enemy with such wrath that the hard edge gripped her neck and the bones broke. The blade pierced her flesh and she sank lifeless to the floor.

Beowulf was proud of his deed as he looked on the sword dripping with the monster's blood. The fire flamed up and it grew light within that cavern as when the sun shines forth brightly in the sky. Beowulf looked about the hall. In a corner he saw the body of Grendel lying lifeless on its bed; thus had the battle at Heorot left him. The warrior went toward that wall with his weapon raised high, wrathful and intent of purpose. He would now pay Grendel back for the many raids he had waged on the Danish folk. And with a savage sword-stroke Beowulf cut off Grendel's head.

The companions who waited with Hrothgar, watching the flood, saw the waters grow turbid and blood-stained. The men spoke together of the hero Beowulf. They deemed he would not return again, proud of conquest. Many thought because of the blood mingled with the waters that the sea-wolf had slain him. It was evening. The noble Danes left the headland; homeward went Hrothgar with his men. But the Geats sat on, sick of heart, and stared at the waters. They wished, though without hope, that they might see their lord once more.

In the cave under the sea a marvelous thing took place. The sword that Beowulf held began to drop away, to melt like the icicles when the bonds of the frost are loosed. The blade burned to nothing, so hot was the blood, so poisonous the sea-witch who had perished there.

Beowulf left the hall. The lord of the Geats took no precious things away with him, though he saw many. He carried only Grendel's head and the jeweled hilt of the sword.

Soon Beowulf was swimming upward through the flood. The churning waters were cleansed now, that waste of waves where the demon had yielded up her life. The strong-hearted one came swimming to the shore, proud of his spoil, of the mighty burden he bore with him. Then his band of thanes rose to greet him and they thanked God that once more they saw him safe and sound. Quickly they loosed his helmet and war-gear. The mere, that had been stained with the blood of slaughter, grew still.

Then the band went forth along the footpaths. Merry of heart they tramped the roadway. It was a heavy task even for those men of great strength to carry Grendel's head from that cliff by the sea. It took four to bear it on a spear. Presently the fourteen Geats, fearless foemen, reached the hall of Heorot. Their chieftain, mighty hero, strode in their midst.

CUCHULAIN/Ireland

Rosemary Sutcliff

Many cultures tell of heroes who willingly choose glory and an early death: Achilles, Siegfried, and Cuchulain are all of this tradition. But Cuchulain is more than a mortal hero. Because he is the son of Lugh, the Irish sun god,

Cuchulain is also a solar hero. When at peace he is small, even Conor ques-
tions his size; when angry or in the battle-fury he grows in size; when fully
aroused, it is said no one could look him in the face. Only witchcraft is strong
enough to overthrow him and give him the early death he accepted as the
price of leadership.

DECTERA'S GIFT

This is the story of Cuchulain, the Champion of Ulster, the greatest of all the Heroes of the Red Branch. Listen, now.

In the great days long past, there was a King of Ulster whose name was Ross the Red, and Maga his Queen was a woman of the Sidhe, the Lordly Ones, whose home is in Tir-Nan-Og, the Land of Youth. And Fiachtna the Giant was their son, and Fiachtna's son was Conor Mac Nessa, and both of them after Ross were to be Kings of Ulster in their turn. But the time came when Maga was no longer content with Ross the Red, and since no one can hold the Lordly People against their will, they parted, and she became the wife of Cathbad, who, though he had not then a grey hair in his beard, was the wisest of all the Druids in the land. And Ross the Red took a second wife, and the name of that one was Roy —a mortal maiden, this time, for he had had his fill of the Lordly Kind—and the son she bore him was Fergus Mac Roy.

And Cathbad and Maga had three daughters, Dectera, Elva and Finchoom. And Finchoom's son was Conall of the Victories; and Elva's three sons by her husband Usna were Naisi, Ainle and Ardan, and Dectera's son was no other than Cuchulain himself.

And these are the names and kindreds that you must remember, for these, with their comrades and henchmen and the sons who came after them were the Heroes of the Red Branch, because they were all of them sprung from Ross the Red, or linked with him through his first Queen.

One Midsummer Eve when Conor had not long been King, Dectera his kinswoman went down with her fifty maidens to wash their clothes in the stream that ran below the Royal Dun, at Emain Macha. And when the shadows grew long at evening, and still they had not come carrying their new-washed linen back up the hill, search was made for them beside the ford and under the ancient hazel trees. But not so much as a golden hair of them was to be found.

For many days Conor and his warriors searched through the length and breadth of Ulster, and far south into Ireland beyond, but all to no avail. 'They have heard the music of the Silver Branch and gone into the Hollow Hills, into Tir-Nan-Og,' said Cathbad the Druid. 'Dectera has gone to her mother's kind, and taken the others with her like a flock of birds behind their leader.'

Three years went by, and it was as though Dectera and her maidens had never been; and then on another Midsummer's Eve, a flock of small bright birds descended on the barley fields about Emain Macha and the little stone-walled plots where the half wild fruit trees grew, and began to destroy the ripening fruit. Word of this was brought to Conor Mac Nessa and it seemed to him that there was sport to be had, as well as the saving of the crops. And so with a band of his household warriors—with Fergus Mac Roy and young Laery the Triumphant and Bricrieu of the Bitter Tongue and others—he took his pouch filled with sling stones, and set out. But try as they would, they could not hit one of the small bright birds among the apple boughs, and the birds for their part only flew a little way and began to feed again. And when the warriors followed them with fresh pebbles in their slings, they fluttered a little farther—and the fluttering of them was like laughter—and so drew the hunters on and on, until at dusk when they could no longer see to sling the polished stones, the King and his companions found themselves near to the fairy mound at Brugh-Na-Boyna.

'It is too far to be going back to Emain Macha

tonight,' said Conor. 'It is past cowstalling time, and they will have closed the gates and set free the ban dogs and we shall rouse the whole Dun and bring the women squealing round our ears. We can make a fire and 'twill not harm us to sleep one night fasting.' And so they made a fire of dry thorn branches and lay down about it, wrapped in their cloaks with their feet to the warmth, while one of their number sat up to keep the blaze going, though indeed 'twas little there was to fear from the wolves at Midsummer.

But Fergus Mac Roy was restless and could not sleep, so that at last he said to himself, 'Ach, the moonlight is in my feet that I cannot be still,' and he drew his legs under him and went off along the banks of the river towards the fairy mound. As he drew towards it, he saw that a little mist lay low about the hillock, snail-silver in the light of the full summer moon; and then it seemed to him that the mist flowered from silver into gold, and that the light came no longer from the moon but from within the mist itself, as though there were a hundred torches blazing at the heart of it. And as he came to a halt, thinking maybe the thing was best not meddled with, a great burst of light opened upon him, and he saw that the gates of the fairy hill stood wide. Indeed it was no hill at all, but a King's hall greater and more glorious even than the Hall of the High Kings of Ireland at Tara itself; and he moved towards it as though his feet were drawn by the suck of a tide. There were half-seen shapes about him, and half-heard music in his ears more sweet than any harping in any King's hall of the world of men; and on the shining threshold a man stepped out to meet him, golden and fiercely beautiful, so that it seemed the light shone from himself and not from any torches at all, as one would not need torches with the sun blazing in a clear sky. And Fergus knew that even among the Lordly People only one could shine with such a flame, and that was Lugh of the Long Spear, the Sun Lord himself; and he shielded his eyes under his arm. But when he looked at the woman who had come also to stand in the gateway, his eyes grew cool again, for she was like the shadow behind the sun, as graceful and finedrawn as the shadow of a wild cherry tree.

And looking at her, Fergus saw that she was the lost Princess Dectera.

'You are welcome, Fergus Mac Roy,' said Lugh the Sun Lord, 'most gladly welcome, tonight of all the nights there are.'

And Dectera said to him 'You are welcome as the rain in a dry summer on the orchards of Emain Macha, for my heart has looked of late for one of my own kin to come to me.'

'Not only I, but Conor himself and others of the Red Branch are close at hand, for a flock of birds led us on this way until we were too far from Emain Macha to return this night, and so we made a fire to sleep by, and there they sleep in their cloaks. Give me leave now to go back and rouse them and bring them here, for they will weep for gladness to see Dectera again.'

Dectera smiled as though at a secret when he spoke of the birds that had led them. But she shook her head. 'You have seen me and you know that it is well with me and I am happy. Go back to the camp now, and sleep with the rest.'

And then it seemed to Fergus that the mist returned, and he found that he was running back towards the camp. He saw the gleam of the watch fire and ran towards it, between the sleeping warriors who startled awake at his coming, until he was beside Conor the King, who had risen to his elbow, flinging back the cloak from his dark head. 'Is there a wolfpack on your heels then, my Uncle?' he demanded, dashing the sleep from his eyes.

And dropping beside him, Fergus told his story, and he was gasping for breath, for he had been running hard. Before all was told, the young King was on his feet, and the rest of the warriors pressing about him, and he chose out several of the men and bade them go swiftly to the fairy hill, and bring Dectera back to him with all honour.

And when the warriors were gone, running silently as they would be on the hunting trail, the rest cast more thorn branches on the fire and sat down on their haunches to wait. In a while and a while the warriors returned, but Dectera was not with them. 'Ach, you need not tell it. There was nothing there but the hillock in the moonlight, and it with a wisp of ground-mist about its loins,' Fergus said disgustedly, pulling up tufts of grass and throwing them in the river.

'All was as you saw it,' said Laery the Triumphant, and then to the King he said, 'My Lord, we have seen the Lady Dectera, and Himself who is with her. But she bade us to say to you that she is sick, and beg you to forgive her and wait a while; and she bade us say that when the sickness passes from her, she will come, and bring with her a gift for Ulster.'

Conor's dark brows drew together, for he was not a patient man, but there was no other thing to be done. And so they waited, gathered about the fire, and from waiting they fell at last, every one of them, into sleep, as though the harp of the Dagda had laid its spell on them.

In the first green light of dawn, with the ringed plover calling, the warriors awoke, and stared with startled eyes at the thing they found in the midst of them. For there, wrapped in a piece of golden silk within a dappled fawn skin, and mewing for all the world like the ringed plover, lay a new-born man child!

The Princess Dectera had come and gone again, leaving behind her her promised gift for Ulster.

Fergus Mac Roy carried the babe in the crook of his shield arm back to Emain Macha, and they gave him to Dectera's youngest sister Finchoom, who had a child of her own a few months old. And Finchoom nursed the two together. They called him Setenta on his naming-day, and the Plain of Murthemney that runs from Dūn Deal-gan southward into Meath was given to him for his inheritance. But it was little enough that Setenta cared for that, sprawling with Conall and the hound puppies about the threshold of the King's Hall.

When they were seven summers old, and be-sides being cousins and foster brothers, were grown to be the closest and staunchest of friends, Setenta and Conall went to the Boys' House, where the sons of the princes and chieftains of Ulster learned the lessons that would make them warriors when the time came. And there, Setenta found the second of the three friends who were to be dearest to him through all his life. And this was Laeg, son of a Leinster noble killed in a cattle raid, who had been set in Conor's house-hold for a hostage when he was yet too young to know the meaning of what had befallen him, and had long since forgotten that he was anything but Ulster-born among his own kind. He was a year older than Setenta, a tall boy, red-haired, and freckled as a foxglove; and such a way with horses he had that even at eight years old he had but to whisper in the ear of an angry stallion for the beast to grow gentle as a filly foal.

One day when Setenta was nearing the end of his time in the Boys' House, King Conor and his nobles were bidden to a great feast at the Dūn of a certain Cullen who was the greatest swordsmith in all Ulster, and young Setenta was to go with them—for was it not time, said Conor, that the boy learned the ways of courtesy as well as the ways of war? But he forgot the time of day and when the hour came for setting out, he was in the middle of a game of hurley with his compan-ions, and standing, hurley stick in hand at the King's chariot wheel, he expained, 'If I come now, we shall lose the game.'

Conor smiled in the black of his beard. He was a stern man easily moved to anger, but he was fond of this small dark fighting cock of a cousin and allowed him freedoms that he would not have allowed to any other of the Boys' Band. 'What's to be done, then?'

'Let my Lord the King ride on,' Setenta said, 'and when the game is over and we have won, I will follow.'

So the King laughed and rode on with his nobles, and Setenta went back to his companions.

At dusk, Conor and his warriors reached the Rath of Cullen, and the master smith made them warmly and richly welcome, and brought them into his house-place and feasted them on fresh boar meat and badger's flesh roasted with wild honey, and fine imported Greek wine in splendid bronze and silver cups of his own forging. Mean-while his people, not knowing of Setenta's coming, or else forgetting about it, dragged the night-time barricade of thorn bushes into the gateway, and let loose Cullen's huge hound, who guarded his master's house so well and mightily that Cullen, who loved him, was wont to boast that with his dog loose in the forecourt he feared nothing less than the attack of a full war host.

In the midst of the feasting, with the harp music leaping to the firelit rafters, there rose an appalling uproar in the night outside, a baying and yelling that brought every man to his feet and snatching up his weapons. 'Here is your war host, by the sound of it!' Conor said, and ran for the doorway, the lord of the house beside him and the warriors pounding at their heels. Men with torches were running towards the outer gates, where the yelling and snarling had sunk suddenly and horribly silent. And in the ragged glare of the torches, Conor and his warriors saw that the gate pillar was splashed with blood, and the thorn bushes had been thrust aside from the gateway, and in the opening, with the moon-watered darkness of the night behind him, stood Setenta, breathing like a runner after a race, and looking down at the body of the great speckled wolfhound that lay dead at his feet.

'What has happened here? Conor demanded.

The boy looked up at their coming, and said, 'He would have killed me, so I killed him.'

And Cullen said harshly, 'How was it done?'

And Setenta looked at his hands as though he were seeing them for the first time. 'I caught him by the throat as he sprang at me, and dashed his life out against the gate pillar.'

'Ach now, that was a deed that few among full-grown warriors could perform.' Conor beat his fist against his thigh in approval, and there was a roar of praise and laughter from the men about him.

Only Cullen the Swordsmith stood silent, staring down at the body of the great hound; and all the lines on his face were cut heavy with grief as with one of his own sword blades. And as they looked at him, a silence fell on the rest, so that they heard the night wind and the spluttering of the torches. Setenta broke the stillness, looking slowly up into the man's face. 'Give me a whelp of the same breed, Cullen the Swordsmith, and I will train him to be all to you that this one was. And meanwhile, let you lend me a shield and a spear, and I will be your guard-dog and keep your house as well as ever hound could do.'

Cullen shook his head, and set a hand kindly enough on the boy's thin shoulder. 'It is a fine offer, but I can still train my own hounds. Go you back to your own training, for it is in my heart that when the time comes, you will be the guard-hound of all Ulster.'

'And meanwhile,' said Fergus Mac Roy proudly, for he had never forgotten that it was himself had carried Setenta back to Emain Macha in the crook of his shield arm on the day

that he was born, 'let us call him Cuchulain, the Hound of Cullen, in remembrance of his first battle and the offer he made afterwards!'

And so they caught the boy up and carried him into the fire-lit hall, shouting his new name after him: 'Cuchulain! Cuchulain!'

And Cuchulain he remained, until the day that he went beyond the sunset.

A DAY FOR TAKING VALOUR

A short while after the slaying of Cullen's hound, the time came for first Laeg and then Conall to Take Valour, which is to say, to take the weapons of manhood upon them, and bid farewell to the Boys' House. And Cuchulain was left behind to serve out the last months of his training.

But 'twas few enough Cuchulain served of those remaining months, for one soft autumn day with the colours of the world all rich and dark as though the bloom of bilberries were on them, he came up from spear practice, and passed close by the thicket of ancient hazels that dropped their nuts into the water above the ford of the stream. And under the hazel trees, Cathbad sat with some of the Boys' Band about him, propounding to them the laws of their people—for it was his task to teach them such things, together with star wisdom and the art of cutting the Ogham word signs on willow rods. The lesson was over, but as Cuchulain came splashing through the ford, there was laughter and a dappling of eager voices, for the boys, who were all of them near their time for becoming men, were trying to coax him into foretelling to them what days would be most fortunate for Taking Valour, for Cathbad was wise in other things than law and writing.

'I am tired. I have told enough,' Cathbad said.

'Of law, yes,' the others chorused, 'but this is another thing.' And one of them, Cormac Coilinglass, the second son of the King, leaned forward with his arms across his knees and grinned at him. 'If you give us a day under good stars for our starting out, shall we not be like to do you the more credit among men, master dear?'

Cathbad smiled into his long beard that was

still streaked with gold, though the hair of his head was white as a swan's wing; but under his white brows was a frown. 'Children, children you are, seeking to make the old man prance for you like a juggler with apples and silver cups. This much I will do, and no more. I will tell you what fortune lies upon this day, waiting for any boy who Takes Valour on it,' and he smoothed a space on the bare earth before him, and shook red and white sand upon it from two thorns at his girdle, and began with his long forefinger to trace in the sand the strange curved lines of divination, while Cuchulain his grandson checked and stood watching with his hand on the trunk of the nearest hazel tree. Cathbad was scarcely aware of him, as he stooped frowning over the patterns in the sand, for he never put forth the least part of his power without giving to it his whole self, as though the fate of all Ireland hung upon what he did. He drew more lines and studied them, frowning still, while the boys crowded closer, half of them breathing down his neck, then he brushed all smooth again, and looked up, slowly, pressing his hands across his eyes, as though he would brush away the things that he had seen. 'The boy who takes up the spear and shield of manhood on this day will become the greatest and most renowned of all the warriors of Ireland, men will follow at his call to the world's end, and his enemies will shudder at the thunder of his chariot wheels, and the harpers shall sing of him while green Ireland yet rises above the sea; but his flowering-time shall be brief as that of the white bellbine, opening in the morning and drooping before night. For he shall not live to count one grey hair at his temples . . . I can see no more.'

Cuchulain turned away from the hazel thicket where the nuts fell splashing into the water above the ford, and set himself to the steep heathery slope that was crowned by the turf and timber ramparts and the great gate of Emain Macha. Once within the gates, he went in search of Conor the King, and found him just back from the hunting, sitting at east on the bench before the Great Hall, with his legs stretched out before him, and his favourite hounds at his knee.

Cuchulain went and stood before him, and Conor, who was at peace with the world after his day's hunting, looked up and said, 'Well now, and what will you be wanting, standing there so big and fierce, with your shadow darkening the sun?'

'My Lord the King, I come to claim the weapons of my manhood today. I have learned all that the Boys' House teaches, and now I would be a man among men.'

'Your time is not yet for close on another half year,' Conor said, startled.

'That I know, but there is nothing I shall gain by the longer waiting.'

Conor looked at him long under his brows, and shook his head, and indeed, slight and dark as Cuchulain was, and small for his age, he seemed very far as yet from being a man. 'Nothing save maybe a wind-puff of strength and a thumbnail or so of height.'

The boy flushed. 'Size is not all that makes a warrior, and as for strength—give me your hunting spears, my lord and kinsman.'

So Conor gave him the two great wolf spears that were still red like rust on the blade, and Cuchulain took them lightly and broke them across his knee as though they had been dry hazel sticks, and tossed the pieces aside. 'You must give me better spears than these,' he said, and it was as though deep within him a spark kindled and spread into a small fierce flame.

Conor beckoned his armour-bearer, and bade him bring war spears; but when they were brought, Cuchulain took them and whirled them above his head, and broke them almost as easily as he had done the wolf spears, and tossed the jagged pieces away. By now there was a crowd begun to gather, and Cuchulain stood in the midst of them, waiting for someone to bring him better weapons. They brought him more spears, and then swords, and each he treated as he had done the first, and flung contemptuously away. They brought chariots into the forecourt, and he smashed them as easily as he had smashed the spears, by stamping his feet through the interlaced floor straps and twisting the ash frame of the bow between his hands, until all the forecourt lay littered with wreckage as though a battle had been fought there. And at last Conor the King burst into a harsh roar of laughter and beat his hands upon his knees and shouted, 'Enough! In the name of the High Gods, enough, or we shall have not a spear nor a war chariot left whole in Emain Macha! Bring the boy my own weapons, my spears and sword that were forged for me by Goban himself, and harness him my own chariot, for 'tis in my mind that those are beyond even his breaking!'

So the King's armour-bearer brought out Conor's own angry battle spears headed with black iron and decked with collars of blue-green heron hackles, and his sword whose blade gave off fire at every blow like shooting stars on a frosty night; and the charioteer brought the King's chariot, with polished bronze collars to the wheel hubs and its wicker sides covered with red and white oxhides, and in the yoke of it the King's own speckled stallions that scorned any hand on their reins save that of Conor himself or his driver.

And Cuchulain took the spears and sword and strove to break them across his knee, and could not, though he strained until the muscles stood out on his neck like knotted cords. 'These weapons I cannot break,' he said at last.

So Cuchulain sprang up beside the charioteer, and the horses felt the stranger behind them and began to plunge and rear so that their own driver could do nothing with them and it seemed that they and not Cuchulain would crash their heels through the chariot floor. Then Cuchulain laughed, and the fire in him blazed up like the smoky flames of a wind-blown torch, and he caught the reins from the hands of the King's charioteer and fought the team as a man might fight with a hurricane. For a while the watchers could see little but the cloud of red dust, hear nothing but the trampling and neighing of the horses flinging their plunging circles about the forecourt, and the screech and thunder of the wracked chariot wheels—until at last Cuchulain reined the panting beasts back on their haunches close before the King, and the uproar fell away, and there above them in the unharmed chariot stood Cuchulain alone, for the charioteer had been flung clear in the struggle, looking down at them out of his dark face with a smile that was both triumphant and a little sad, as though he were saying to his own heart that all good things passed too soon, and the horses standing with heaving flanks in their traces, and the last red dust sinking, eddying down about the wheels.

'Assuredly you are a warrior, and there is no place for you in the Boys' House any more,' the King said.

And Cuchulain sprang down over the chariot bow to the horses' heads, and standing between them with his shoulders leaned against the yoke, he set an arm over the neck of each horse. 'Then if I am a warrior and have my war chariot, let the King also give me a charioteer. No man can well fight his chariot and drive at the same time—not even Cuchulain.'

'Choose for yourself,' said Conor Mac Nessa. 'That is the right of every warrior.'

Cuchulain looked about him, and saw among the crowding warriors the red head and long freckled face of Laeg who had been with him in the Boys' House only a few months before. And he cared nothing for the fact that Laeg was older than himself and a noble's son and should be no man's charioteer, but called out 'Laeg! Hai! Laeg! There is none that can handle a horse like you. Let you come and drive for me, that we may be together when the war horns sound!'

And as for Laeg, he flushed like a girl under his freckles, and a light sprang into his eyes that made his whole face kindle, and he strode out from the rest to Cuchulain's side. 'Let any other man try for the place that is mine, Hound Cub!' and he bent his head before young Cuchulain as though he and not Conor Mac Nessa were the King.

FINN MAC COOL/The Gaelic-Speaking Peoples

Rosemary Sutcliff

Although most of his adventures are set in Ireland, the Finn cycle belongs to Scotland, Ireland, and the Isle of Man—to the Gaelic-speaking peoples. That these narratives developed after the Cuchulain cycle is revealed by their lack of mythic remnants. Finn MacCool is a mortal, no descendant of the gods, yet he is the embodiment of the Gaelic ideal: wise, courageous, daring, and honorable.

Rosemary Sutcliff's style has faint hints of the Gaelic rhythms. Her repetitive use of "And" is an effective stylistic device to suggest an oral presentation.

THE BIRTH AND BOYHOOD OF FINN

In the proud and far back days, though not so far back nor yet so proud as the days of the Red Branch Heroes, there rose another mighty brotherhood in Erin, and they were called the Fianna. They were a war-host whose task was to hold the shores of Erin safe from invaders, and they were a peace-host, for it was their task also to keep down raids and harryings and blood feuds between the five lesser kingdoms into which Erin was divided. Ulster, Munster, Connact, Leinster and Mide had each their own companies of the Fianna under their own Fian Chiefs; but one Captain was over them all. And each and every man must take his oath of loyalty, not to his own king, nor to his own Fian Chief alone, but to the Captain and to the High King of Erin himself, sitting in his high hall at Tara with his right foot upon the Stone of Destiny.

The Fianna came to their most full and valiant flowering and to their greatest power in the time when the hero Finn Mac Cool was their Captain, and Cormac Mac Art, the grandson of Conn the Hundred-Fighter, was High King of Erin.

But the story has its beginning back in the days of Finn's father Cool Mac Trenmor, lord of the Clan Bascna of Leinster, who was Captain before him, and of Aed Mac Morna, Lord of the Clan Morna and Chief of the Connacht Fianna, who sought the Captaincy for himself.

At Cnucha, near where Dublin stands today, a great and bloody battle was fought between Clan Bascna and Clan Morna, as two bulls battle for the lordship of the herd. And one of Cool's household warriors wounded Aed in the eye, so

sorely that he went by the name of Goll, which means one-eyed, ever after. But this Aed, who was now Goll Mac Morna, dealt Cool Mac Trenmor a still fiercer blow that cost him not the sight of an eye, but life itself, and he took from Cool's best a certain bag of blue-and crimson-dyed crane-skin that was the Treasure Bag of Fianna. And with the death of Cool and the loss of the Treasure Bag, the battle went against Clan Bascna, and there was a great slaughter, and those that were left of the Leinster Fianna, including Crimnal, the brother of Cool, as well as the Munster men who had stood with them, were driven into exile in the Connacht hills. And there was blood feud between Clan Bascna and Clan Morna from that day, which was to bring black sorrow upon Erin in the end.

News of the battle and of Cool's death was brought to his young wife, Murna of the White Neck, and she near her time to bear his child. And Murna, knowing that her lord's enemies would not allow any child of his to live after him if they would help it, fled, taking two of her most trusted women with her, into the wild fastnesses of Slieve Bloom. And there, like a hind lying up among the fern in the whitethorn month when the fawns are brought into the world, she bore a man-child, and not daring to keep him with her for fear of the hunters on her trail, she called him Demna, and gave him to the two women, bidding them bring him up in the hidden glens of Slieve Bloom, until he was of an age to fight for his rightful place as Cool's son. Then, sadly, she went her way alone, and no more is known of her save that at last, after many wanderings, she found shelter with a chieftain of Kerry.

In the hidden glens of Slieve Bloom, Demna grew from a babe into a child and from a child into a boy; and the women trained him in all the ways of the wild, so that by the time he was a youth, he was such a hunter that he could bring a flying bird out of the sky with one cast of a sling-stone, and run down the deer on his naked feet without even a hound to help him; and he knew the ways of wolf and otter, badger and fox and falcon as a good hound-master knows the ways of his own dogs. As he grew older he began to range far and wide from the turf bothie that was all the home he knew, and so one day he came to the hall of a great chieftain, before which some boys of his own age were playing hurley. The game looked to him good, and he asked if he might join in; and they gave him a hurley stick and told him the rules. And so soon as he got into the way of it, he could play better than any of them, even taking the ball from their best and swiftest player.

The next day he played with them again, and though they divided the teams so that a fourth of all their number were set to play against him, he won the game. The day after, it was half their number, and the day after that, their whole number played against him, but he won those games too. That evening in the hall, the boys told the chieftain of the strange boy who had joined them and beaten their whole double team at hurley.

'And what is he like, this boy,' asked the chieftain, 'and what is his name?'

'We do not know his name,' said the leader among the boys, 'but he is tall and strong, and the hair of him as bright as barley when it whitens in the sun at harvest time.'

'If he is as fair as that, then there's only one name for him,' said the chieftain, 'and that is Finn.'

And Finn, which means fair, he became, from that day forward.

The chieftain talked of the strange boy to a friend who passed that way on the hunting trail and lodged under his roof for the night, and the friend spoke of him to another, and so as time went by, rumours of his skill and daring spread like ripples on a pool when a stone is tossed into the water, until they came to the ears of Goll Mac Morna. And it seemed to Goll that if Cool had a son, he would be just such a one as this Finn . . . Murna of the White Neck had been heavy with child when she fled to the wilds; what if the child had been safely born and was a son? The boy would be fourteen by now, just coming to manhood. Goll Mac Morna smelled danger. He mustered the Connacht Fianna, and bade

them to hunt the boy down—they were great hunters as well as great warriors, the Fianna—and bring him back, living or dead.

But one of Finn's two foster-mothers was a Wise Woman, and she saw in a pool of black bog-water in the cupped palms of her hands how the Fianna of Connacht were hunting the hills for him. And she told the other woman, and together they spoke to Finn.

'The hunt is out for you, fosterling. Goll Mac Morna has heard more of you than is for your own good, and his men are questing through the woods to kill you, for you and not Goll are by rights the Captain of the Fianna of Erin. Therefore the time has come for you to leave this glen.'

Then Finn took the spear which they gave him, and his sling and his warmest cloak, and set out on his wanderings.

To and fro and up and down the length and breadth of Erin he wandered, taking service with now this king or chieftain and now that, and so getting his weapon-skill and his warrior training, against the day when he should stand out into the open and fight for his rightful place in the world. He began to gather to him a band of young men of much his own kind, fierce and gay and daring; and when he felt that the time was come, he led them into Connacht to seek out any of his father's old followers who might yet be living in the hills.

The day after they crossed the Connacht border, they came upon a woman bowed altogether with grief, and keening over the body of a young man outstretched on the stained and trampled grass.

Finn stopped when he saw her, and asked, 'What ill thing has happened here?'

She looked up at him, and her grief was so terrible that the tears falling from her eyes were great drops of blood. 'Here is my son Glonda, my only son, dead! Slain by Lia of Luachair and his followers. If you are a warrior as you seem, go now and avenge his death, since I have no other man to avenge it.'

So Finn went after this Lia of Luachair, and found him, and slew him in single combat, the followers of both standing by. And when Lia lay dead, Finn saw that a strange-seeming bag of crane-skin dyed blue and crimson was fastened to his belt. He knelt and untied the beltthong, and opened the bag. Inside was a spearhead of fine dark blue iron, and a war-cap inlaid with silver, a shield with bronze studs around the rim, and a gold-clasped boar's-hide belt. Finn had no knowledge as to why the man should be carrying these things, but they looked worth the keeping, so he put them back in the bag, and tied the thong to his own belt, and he and his companions went on their way.

Beyond the Shannon, in the shadowed depths of the Connacht forests, he came upon a clearing in the woods, and in the clearing a cluster of branch-woven bothies; and as he looked, out from the low door-holes, one after another came old men, gaunt as wolves in a famine winter, bent and white-haired and half clad in animal skins and rags of old once-brilliant cloth. But each man carried in his hand an ancient sword or spear, for it seemed to them that the strange-comers could only be young warriors of the Clan Morna who had discovered their refuge at last; and they chose to meet their deaths fighting, rather than go down tamely without a blow. And something about their bearing and the way they handled their weapons even now, told Finn that they were the men he had come to seek, and he could have howled like a dead man's dog, thinking of the tall and splendid warriors that they had been on the morning that they stood out to fight at Cnucha.

Then he swallowed the grief in him and cried out to them with joy, 'You are the Clan Bascna! Which of you is Crimnal the brother of Cool?'

Then one of the old men stepped forward, sword in hand—and he not yet knowing whether or not he faced Clan Morna—and said fearlessly, 'I am Crimnal the brother of Cool.'

Finn looked in his old tired eyes, and said, 'I am Finn, the son of Cool,' and he knelt and laid the crane-skin bag at the old man's feet for a gift, since he had nothing else to give.

Crimnal looked at the bag, and cried out in a great voice to come from such a thin and bent old body, 'The Treasure Bag of the Fianna! Brothers, the time of our waiting is over!'

He opened the bag, and one by one drew out the things that it contained, the old men and the young men standing round to watch. And it seemed to Finn that the eyes of the old men grew

brighter and their backs straighter and the grip of their weapon hands stronger with each object that appeared; the spearhead and the war cap, the shield and the boar's-hide belt.

'Goll Mac Morna took this from your father's body after the slaying; and for eighteen years it has been lost to us. Now it returns again to Clan Bascna and with it will return also the lordship of the Fianna. Go you and take your father's place for it is yours, Finn Mac Cool.'

'Keep the Treasure Bag for me, then,' said Finn. 'My comrades I leave with you, to guard both it and you until I send you word to bring it out to me.'

And again he went his way, alone as at the first time.

But he knew that there was yet one more thing he had to learn before he was fitted to take his father's place; and he went to study poetry and the tales in which lay the ancient wisdom and history of his people with a certain Druid by the name of Finegas, who lived on the banks of the River Boyne.

Seven years Finegas had lived beside the Boyne, and all that while he had been striving by every means that he could think of to catch Fintan the Salmon of Knowledge, who lived in a dark pool of the river, where a great hazel tree bent its branches and dropped nuts of knowledge into the water. Fintan ate the nuts as they fell, and their power passed into him, and whoever ate of Fintan would possess the wisdom of all the ages. In seven years, a man—and he a Druid— may think of many ways to catch a salmon, but Fintan the Salmon of Knowledge had escaped them all, until Finn came treading lightly through the woods to be the old man's pupil.

Soon after that, Finegas caught the Salmon quite easily, as though it had simply been waiting its own chosen time to be caught.

Finegas gave the Salmon to Finn to cook for him. 'And look that you eat nothing of the creature, not the smallest mouthful, yourself, but bring it to me as soon as it is ready, for it's wearing I've been for the taste of it, this seven long years past.'

Then he sat him down in the doorway of his bothie, and waited. And a long wait it seemed to him. At last Finn brought the Salmon, steaming on a long dish of polished maple wood. But as he set it down, Finegas looked into his face, and saw there was a change in it, and that it was no longer the face of a boy. And he asked, 'Have you eaten any of the Salmon in spite of my words to you?'

And Finn shook his head. 'I have not. But when I turned it on the spit I scorched my thumb, and I sucked it to ease the smart. Was there any harm in that, my master?'

Finegas sighed a deep and heavy sigh, and pushed the dish away. 'Take the rest of the Salmon and eat it, for already in the hot juice on your thumb, you have had all the knowledge and power that was in it. And in you, and not in me as I had hoped, the prophecy is fulfilled. And when you have eaten, go from here, for there is nothing more that I can teach you.'

From that day forward, whenever Finn wished to know how some future thing would turn out, or the meaning of some mystery, or to gain tidings of events happening at a distance, he had only to put his scorched thumb between his teeth and the knowledge would come to him as though it were the Second Sight.

And another power came to him also at that time, so that he could save the life of any sick or wounded man, no matter how near to death, by giving him a drink of water from his cupped hands.

HOW FINN WON HIS FATHER'S PLACE

Now, when he left his Druid master beside the Boyne, Finn knew that the time was fully come for him to be claiming his father's place, and he set out for Tara of the High Kings.

It was Samhein, the time of the great autumn feast, and as he drew nearer, his road, and the four other roads that met at Tara, became more and more densely thronged with chiefs and warriors, on horseback or in chariots decorated with bronze and walrus ivory, with their women in gowns of green and saffron and crimson and heather-dark plaid and the golden apples swinging from the ends of their braided hair, and their tall feather-heeled hounds running alongside. For at Samhein all the kings and chiefs of Erin came together, and all men were free to sit at table in the High King's hall if they could find room—and so long as they left their weapons outside.

So up the Royal Hill and in through the gate, and across the broad forecourt went Finn, amid the incoming throng, and sat himself down with the King's household warriors, ate badger's meat baked with salt and honey, and drank the yellow mead from a silver-bound oxhorn, and watched the High King and the tall scarred man close beside him, who he knew from his lack of an eye must be Goll Mac Morna, and waited for the King to notice that there was a stranger among his warriors.

And presently the High King did notice him, and sent one of his court officials to bid him come and stand before the High Table.

'What is your name? And why do you come and seat yourself unannounced among my household warriors?' demanded the King.

And Finn flung up his pale bright head and gave him back stare for stare. 'I am Finn the son of Cool who was once Captain of all the Fianna of Erin, Cormac High King, and I am come to carry my spear in your service as he did; but for me, I will carry it in the ranks of your household warriors, and not with the Fianna.' This he said because he knew that to join the Fianna he would have to swear faith to Goll Mac Morna, and he was no light faithbreaker.

'If you are the son of Cool, then you may be proud of your birth,' said the King. 'You father was a mighty hero, and his spear I trusted as I would trust my own and as I will trust yours.'

Then Finn swore faith to Cormac the High King; and Cormac gave him a place among his household warriors, and the feasting went on as it had done before, and the King's harper beat upon his curved harp while the mead horns passed from hand to hand, and the great hounds fought over the bones among the rushes on the floor.

But little by little the drink began to pass more slowly, the laughter grew fitful and the harp-song fell away, and men began to half glance into each other's eyes and break off the glance quickly, as though afraid of what they might see.

And indeed they had good reason.

Every Samhein for the past twenty years, Tara had been weirdly and terribly visited. Fiend or Fairy, no one knew what the strange-comer was, only that his name was Aillen of the Flaming

Breath, and that every Samhein at midnight he came upon them from the Fairy hill close by, and burned the royal dun over their heads. No use for any warrior, however valiant, to try to withstand him, for he carried a silver harp, and as he came he drew from its strings the sweetest and most drowsy music that ever breathed upon the ears of men, and all who heard it drifted into a deep enchanted sleep. So each Samhein it was the same; he came upon Tara with no one left awake to withstand him, and he breathed where he would with a licking breath of fire until thatch and timber blackened and scorched and twisted, and kindled into leaping flame. So every year Tara must be rebuilt, and every year again—and yet again.

When the sounds of feasting had died quite away, and an uneasy hush with little stirrings and little eddies in it held the King's hall, Cormac rose in his High Place, and offered a mighty reward in gold and horses and women slaves to any warrior who could prevail against Aillen of the Flaming Breath, and keep the thatch on Tara till the next day's dawn. He had made the same offer, and his father before him, twenty Samhein nights, and after the first few times, no man, not the boldest of his warriors, had come forward in answer, for they knew that neither courage nor skill nor strength would avail them against the wicked silvery music. So Cormac made the offer, and waited, without hope.

And then Finn rose in his place, and stood to face the troubled King. 'Cormac Mac Art, High King of Erin, I will forgo the gold and the horses and the women slaves, but if I prevail against this horror of the night, and keep the thatch on Tara till tomorrow's dawn, will you swear before all these in your hall to give me my rightful heritage?'

'It is a bold man, I'm thinking, who seeks to bargain with the High King,' said Cormac. 'What heritage is that?'

'The Captaincy of the Fianna of Erin.'

'I have given you the place that you asked for among my own warriors,' said Cormac, 'and is that not good enough for you?'

'Not if I keep the thatch on Tara,' said Finn.

Then a murmur ran round the hall, and men looked at each other and at Goll Mac Morna,

who sat looking straight before him with his one bright Falcon's eye.

'I swear,' said the King, 'and let all those gathered here, the kings and chiefs of Erin, warriors of my household and of all the Fianna, witness to my swearing. If you overcome Aillen of the Flaming Breath, you will have earned the Captaincy in your own right, and in your own right, as well as by heritage, you shall hold it.'

So Finn left the King's hall, and took up his spear that he had laid by when he entered, and went up to the rampart walk that crested the encircling turf wall. He did not know at all how he should succeed when so many had failed before him, but his faith was in his destiny, and he did not doubt that he would prevail. And while he paced to and fro, waiting and watching, and listening more than all, one of the older warriors came after him, carrying a spear with its head laced into a leather sheath.

'Long ago your father saved my life,' said the man, 'and now is the time to be repaying my debt. Take the spear, to aid you in your fight.'

'I have a good spear of my own,' Finn said.

But the other shook his head. 'Not such a spear as this, that must be kept hooded like a hawk lest it run wild and drink blood of its own accord. It was forged by Lein, the Smith of the Gods, and he beat into it the fire of the sun and the potency of the moon. When you hear the first breath of the fairy music, lay the blade to your forehead, and the fierceness and the bloodlust in it will drive away all sleep from you. Take it.'

And Finn hooded the spear again, but left the thongs loose. And carrying it, he returned to his pacing up and down, looking always out over the plains of Mide, white under the moon, and listening, listening until the silence in his own ears sounded loud as the hushing of the sea in a shell.

And then it came, the faintest gossamer shimmer of distant harp-music. Nearer and clearer, even as he checked to listen, clearer and nearer; the fairy music lapped like the first gentle wavelets of sleep about him. It was the light summer wind through the moorland grasses of Slieve Bloom, it was the murmur of bees among the sun-warmed bell heather; it was all the lullabies that ever his foster mothers had sung to him when he was too young to remember . . .

Finn tore himself free of the enchantment that was weaving itself around him, and with fingers that seemed weak and numb, dragged the leather hood from the spear and pressed the blade to his forehead. Instantly he heard the voice of the spear more clearly than the voice of Aillen's harp; an angry hornet note that drove all sleep away from him. His head cleared, and looking out once more towards the Fairy hill, he saw a thing like a mist-wraith floating towards him along the ground. Nearer and nearer, taking shape and substance as it came, until Finn was looking at the pale airy shape of Aillen of the Flaming Breath, so near and clear now that he could even catch the silver ripple of the harpstrings on which the thing played with long white fingers as he came. Now Aillen had reached the stockade which crowned the turf walls, and a long tongue of greenish flame shot from his mouth and lapped at the timbers.

Finn tore off his mantle of saffron-dyed ram skins, and with one sweep of it, beat the flame into the ground.

With his flame beaten out, Aillen gave a terrible wailing cry, and turned over and back, streaming through himself like a wave flung back by a rocky shore, and fled away towards the Fairy hill. But Finn, with the hornet-shouting of the spear loud and urgent in his ears, leapt the stockade and was after him, as swift as he.

The doorway of the Fairy hill stood open, letting out a green twilight, and as Aillen fled wailing towards it, Finn made one mighty cast with the spear, and the spear flew on its way rejoicing, and passed through the creature's body and out at the other side. And there on the threshold of the Fairy hill—or where the threshold had been, for now the door was gone, and only the frost-crisped grass and brambles gleaned faintly under the moon—Aillen of the Flaming Breath lay dead, like a heap of thistledown and touchwood and the fungus that grows on the north side of trees, tangled together into somewhat the shape of a man.

Then Finn cut off the head and set it on the point of his spear and carried it back to Tara and set it up on the walls for all to see.

When morning came, and Tara still stood as it had stood last night, all men knew that Finn must have prevailed against Aillen of the Flaming Breath, and led by the High King they went out to the ramparts; and there they found Finn leaning wearily on the stockade and waiting for their coming, and nothing to show for the happenings of the night but the scorch marks on his saffron cloak which he had wrapped close about himself against the dawn chill, and the strange and ghastly head upreared on his spear point against the morning sky.

'I have kept the thatch on Tara,' Finn said.

Then Cormac Mac Art set his arm across the young man's shoulders, and turned with him to face the mighty gathering in the forecourt below. 'Chiefs and kings and warriors, last night ye bore witness when I swore in the mead hall that if this Finn son of Cool should prevail against Aillen of the Flaming Breath, I would set him in his father's place as Captain of the Fianna of Erin. Last night it was in my mind that it was small chance he had, where so many had failed before. But he has prevailed; he has slain the fire fiend and saved Tara, and therefore I give him to you of the Fianna for your Captain, according to my word and yours. Any of you that will not serve under him, let you leave Erin, freely and without disgrace; there are other war bands and kings' bodyguards overseas in other lands.' He turned to the tall one-eyed man who stood out before the rest. 'That is for you also, Goll Mac Morna, for you who have been the Fian Captain these eighteen years past. Will you strike hands with Finn Mac Cool, and lead the Connacht Fianna under him? Or will you cross the sea and carry your sword into the service of another king?'

'I will strike hands with Finn the son of Cool my old enemy,' said Goll Mac Morna, though the words stuck a little in his throat, and he and Finn spat in their palms and struck hands like two men sealing a bargain.

No man went out from the High King's forecourt to carry his sword overseas, and the feud between Clan Morna and Clan Bascna, though it was not healed, was skinned over and remained so for many years to come.

So Finn Mac Cool became Captain of the Fianna of Erin, as his father had been before him.

KING ARTHUR/England

Mary MacLeod

A sixth-century British chieftain, the leader of the fight against the Saxons who invaded England after the Roman withdrawal, is the historical figure around which the Arthurian legend has developed. The leader of such a dramatic struggle would naturally become the center of legends and folktales. Many stories about earlier heroes were ascribed to him, as were those of later heroes during the centuries following his death. Geoffrey of Monmouth discusses Arthur's parentage and career in his twelfth-century Latin History of the Kings of Britain. French versions and German versions were developed in the same century, the French adding the courtly romance theme to what had once been martial adventure.

Thus, through the centuries Arthur changed from a warrior chieftain to the quintessence of medieval chivalry and romance. Sir Thomas Malory used both the folk sources and the French tradition for his Morte d'Arthur (1469), which not only unified the Arthurian tales but also changed their focus from adventure stories to a cycle dealing with man's highest ideals, the search for the Christ-like life.

HOW ARTHUR BECAME KING

When Uther Pendragon, King of England, died, the country for a long while stood in great danger, for every lord that was mighty gathered his forces, and many wished to be King. For King Uther's own son, Prince Arthur, who should have succeeded him, was but a child, and Merlin, the mighty magician, had hidden him away.

Now a strange thing had happened at Arthur's birth, and this was how it was.

Some time before, Merlin had done Uther a great service, on condition that the King should grant him whatever he wished for. This thé King swore a solemn oath to do. Then Merlin made him promise that when his child was born it should be delivered to Merlin to bring up as he

chose, for this would be to the child's own great advantage. The King had given his promise so he was obliged to agree. Then Merlin said he knew a very true and faithful man, one of King Uther's lords, by name Sir Ector, who had large possessions in many parts of England and Wales, and that the child should be given to him to bring up.

On the night the baby was born, while it was still unchristened, King Uther commanded two knights and two ladies to take it, wrapped in a cloth of gold, and deliver it to a poor man whom they would find waiting at the postern gate of the Castle. This poor man was Merlin in disguise, although they did not know it. So the child was delivered unto Merlin and he carried him to Sir Ector, and made a holy man christen him, and named him Arthur; and Sir Ector's wife cherished him as her own child.

Within two years King Uther fell sick of a great malady, and for three days and three nights he was speechless. All the Barons were in much sorrow, and asked Merlin what was best to be done.

"How Arthur Became King" from *King Arthur and His Noble Knights* by Mary MacLeod. Published by Blue Ribbon Books, 1902.

"There is no remedy," said Merlin, "God will have His Will. But look ye all, Barons, come before King Uther tomorrow, and God will make him speak."

So the next day Merlin and all the Barons came before the King, and Merlin said aloud to King Uther:

"Sir, after your days shall your son Arthur be King of this realm and all that belongs to it?"

Then Uther Pendragon turned to him and said in hearing of them all:

"I give my son Arthur God's blessing and mine, and bid him pray for my soul, and righteously and honorably claim the Crown, on forfeiture of my blessing."

And with that, King Uther died.

But Arthur was still only a baby, not two years old, and Merlin knew it would be no use yet to proclaim him King. For there were many powerful nobles in England in those days, who were all trying to get the kingdom for themselves, and perhaps they would kill the little Prince. So there was much strife and debate in the land for a long time.

When several years had passed, Merlin went to the Archbishop of Canterbury and counseled him to send for all the lords of the realm, and all the gentlemen of arms, that they should come to London at Christmas, and for this cause—that a miracle would show who should be rightly King of the realm. So all the lords and gentlemen made themselves ready, and came to London, and long before dawn on Christmas Day they were all gathered in the great church of St. Paul's to pray.

When the first service was over, there was seen in the churchyard a large stone, four-square, like marble, and in the midst of it was an anvil of steel, a foot high. In this was stuck by the point a beautiful sword, with naked blade, and there were letters written in gold about the sword, which said thus:

"Whoso pulleth this sword out of this stone and anvil is rightly King of all England."

Then the people marveled, and told it to the Archbishop.

"I command," said the Archbishop, "that you keep within the church, and pray unto God still and that no man touch the sword till the service is over."

So when the prayers in church were over, all the lords went to behold the stone and sword; and when they read the writing some of them— such as wished to be King—tried to pull the sword out of the anvil. But not one could make it stir.

"The man is not here that shall achieve the sword," said the Archbishop, "but doubt not God will make him known. But let us provide ten knights, men of good fame, to keep guard over the sword."

So it was ordained, and proclamation was made that everyone who wished might try to win the sword. And upon New Year's Day the Barons arranged to have a great tournament, in which all knights who would joust or tourney might take a part. This was ordained to keep together the Lords and Commons, for the Archbishop trusted that it would be made known who should win the sword.

On New Year's Day, after church, the Barons rode to the field, some to joust, and some to tourney, and so it happened that Sir Ector, who had large estates near London, came also to the tournament; and with him rode Sir Kay, his son, with young Arthur, his foster brother.

As they rode, Sir Kay found he had lost his sword, for he had left it at his father's lodging, so he begged young Arthur to go and fetch it for him.

"That will I gladly," said Arthur, and he rode fast away.

But when he came to the house, he found no one at home to give him the sword, for everyone had gone to see the jousting. Then Arthur was angry and said to himself:

"I will ride to the churchyard, and take the sword with me that sticketh in the stone, for my brother, Sir Kay, shall not be without a sword this day."

When he came to the churchyard he alighted, and tied his horse to the stile, and went to the tent. But he found there no knights, who should have been guarding the sword, for they were all away at the joust. Seizing the sword by the handle he lightly and fiercely pulled it out of the stone, then took his horse and rode his way, till he came to Sir Kay his brother to whom he delivered the sword.

As soon as Sir Kay saw it, he knew well it was

the sword of the Stone, so he rode to his father Sir Ector, and said:

"Sir, lo, here is the sword of the Stone, wherefore I must be King of this land."

When Sir Ector saw the sword he turned back, and came to the church, and there they all three alighted and went into the church, and he made his son swear truly how he got the sword.

"By my brother Arthur," said Sir Kay, "for he brought it to me."

"How did you get this sword?" said Sir Ector to Arthur.

And the boy told him.

"Now," said Sir Ector, "I understand you must be King of this land."

"Wherefore I?" said Arthur; "and for what cause?"

"Sir," said Ector, "because God will have it so; for never man could draw out this sword but he that shall rightly be King. Now let me see whether you can put the sword there as it was, and pull it out again."

"There is no difficulty," said Arthur, and he put it back into the stone.

Then Sir Ector tried to pull out the sword, and failed; and Sir Kay also pulled with all his might, but it would not move.

"Now you shall try," said Sir Ector to Arthur.

"I will, well," said Arthur, and pulled the sword out easily.

At this Sir Ector and Sir Kay knelt down on the ground before him.

"Alas," said Arthur, "mine own dear father and brother, why do you kneel to me?"

"Nay, nay, my lord Arthur, it is not so; I was never your father, nor of your blood; but I know well you are of higher blood than I thought you were."

Then Sir Ector told him all, how he had taken him to bring up, and by whose command; and how he had received him from Merlin. And when he understood that Ector was not his father, Arthur was deeply grieved.

"Will you be my good gracious lord, when you are King?" asked the knight.

"If not, I should be to blame," said Arthur, "for you are the man in the world to whom I am the most beholden, and my good lady and mother your wife, who has fostered and kept me as well as her own children. And if ever it be God's will that I be King, as you say, you shall desire of me what I shall do, and I shall not fail you; God forbid I should fail you."

"Sir," said Sir Ector, "I will ask no more of you but they you will make my son, your foster brother Sir Kay, seneschal of all your lands."

"That shall be done," said Arthur, "and by my faith, never man but he shall have that office while he and I live."

Then they went to the Archbishop and told him how the sword was achieved, and by whom.

On Twelfth Day all the Barons came to the Stone in the churchyard, so that any who wished might try to win the sword. But not one of them all could take it out, except Arthur. Many of them therefore were very angry, and said it was a great shame to them and to the country to be governed by a boy not of high blood, for as yet none of them knew that he was the son of King Pendragon. So they agreed to delay the decision till Candlemas, which is the second day of February.

But when Candlemas came, and Arthur once more was the only one who could pull out the sword, they put it off till Easter; and when Easter came, and Arthur again prevailed in presence of them all, they put it off till the Feast of Pentecost.

Then by Merlin's advice the Archbishop summoned some of the best knights that were to be got—such knights as in his own day King Uther Pendragon had best loved and trusted most—and these were appointed to attend young Arthur, and never to leave him night or day till the Feast of Pentecost.

When the great day came, all manner of men once more made the attempt, and once more not one of them all could prevail but Arthur. Before all the Lords and Commons there assembled he pulled out the sword, whereupon all the Commons cried out at once:

"We will have Arthur for our King! We will put him no more in delay, for we all see that it is God's will that he shall be our King, and he who holdeth against it, we will slay him."

And therewith they knelt down all at once, both rich and poor, and besought pardon of Arthur, because they had delayed him so long.

And Arthur forgave them, and took the sword in both his hands, and offered it on the altar where the Archbishop was, and so he was made knight by the best man there.

After that, he was crowned at once, and there he swore to his Lords and Commons to be a true King, and to govern with true justice from thenceforth all the days of his life.

ROBIN HOOD/England

Howard Pyle

Robin Hood and King Arthur are the two Culture Heroes of England. Arthur appealed to the nobility and to those who dreamed of the courtly life; Robin was the ideal for the peasantry who longed for security, justice, and freedom. Robin Hood is brave and intelligent, although he is more a man of action than of thought; he is strong, although others are stronger than he, as is seen in the following story; he has a sense of humor that makes him pleasant even when tumbled into a river; he is compassionate to those in distress. His robbing the rich to help the poor and his free life in Sherwood Forest still appeal to contemporary romantic readers.

There is disagreement as to whether Robin Hood really was a medieval outlaw. Some scholars suggest the tales are based around a pre-Christian mythological figure who gave fertility to herds and land. Perhaps, like the Arthurian cycle, historical facts and half-forgotten mythology joined in the ballads about Robin Hood. Many of these ballads were printed in chapbooks in the eighteenth century.

The following adventure comes from Howard Pyle's The Merry Adventures of Robin Hood of Great Renown in Nottinghamshire, *first published in 1883. The rhythmic language is exceptionally suitable to these stories, but the use of archaic words makes this valuable book more appropriate for older children.*

ROBIN HOOD AND LITTLE JOHN

Up rose Robin Hood one merry morn when all the birds were singing blithely among the leaves, and up rose all his merry men, each fellow washing his head and hands in the cold brown brook that leaped laughing from stone to stone. Then said Robin: "For fourteen days have we seen no sport, so now I will go abroad to seek

adventures forthwith. But tarry ye, my merry men all, here in the greenwood; only see that ye mind well my call. Three blasts upon the bugle horn I will blow in my hour of need; then come quickly, for I shall want your aid."

So saying, he strode away through the leafy forest glades until he had come to the verge of Sherwood. There he wandered for a long time, through highway and byway, through dingly dell and forest skirts. Now he met a fair buxom lass in a shady lane, and each gave the other a merry word and passed their way; now he saw a fair lady upon an ambling pad, to whom he doffed his cap,

"Robin Hood and Little John" from *The Merry Adventures of Robin Hood* by Howard Pyle. Published by Charles Scribner's Sons, 1883.

and who bowed sedately in return to the fair youth; now he saw a fat monk on a pannier-laden ass; now a gallant knight, with spear and shield and armor that flashed brightly in the sunlight; now a page clad in crimson; and now a stout burgher from good Nottingham Town, pacing along with serious footsteps; all these sights he saw, but adventure found he none. At last he took a road by the forest skirts; a bypath that dipped toward a broad, pebbly stream spanned by a narrow bridge made of a log of wood. As he drew nigh this bridge, he saw a tall stranger coming from the other side. Thereupon Robin quickened his pace, as did the stranger likewise; each thinking to cross first.

"Now stand thou back," quoth Robin, "and let the better man cross first."

"Nay," answered the stranger, "then stand back thine own self, for the better man, I wot, am I."

"That will we presently see," quoth Robin; "and meanwhile stand thou where thou art, or else, by the bright brow of Saint Ælfrida, I will show thee right good Nottingham play with a clothyard shaft betwixt thy ribs."

"Now," quoth the stranger, "I will tan thy hide till it be as many colors as a beggar's cloak, if thou darest so much as touch a string of that same bow that thou holdest in thy hands."

"Thou pratest like an ass," said Robin, "for I could send this shaft clean through thy proud heart before a curtal friar could say grace over a roast goose at Michaelmastide."

"And thou pratest like a coward," answered the stranger, "for thou standest there with a good yew bow to shoot at my heart, while I have nought in my hand but a plain blackthorn staff wherein to meet thee."

"Now," quoth Robin, "by the faith of my heart, never have I had a coward's name in all my life before. I will lay by my trusty bow and eke my arrows, and if thou darest abide my coming, I will go and cut a cudgel to test thy manhood withal."

"Ay, marry, that will I abide thy coming, and joyously, too," quoth the stranger; whereupon he leaned sturdily upon his staff to await Robin.

Then Robin Hood stepped quickly to the coverside and cut a good staff of round oak, straight, without flaw, and six feet in length, and came

back trimming away the tender stems from it, while the stranger waited for him, leaning upon his staff, and whistling as he gazed roundabout. Robin observed him furtively as he trimmed his staff, measuring him from top to toe from out the corner of his eye, and thought that he had never seen a lustier or a stouter man. Tall was Robin, but taller was the stranger by a head and a neck, for he was seven feet in height. Broad was Robin across the shoulders, but broader was the stranger by twice the breadth of a palm, while he measured at least an ell around the waist.

"Nevertheless," said Robin to himself, "I will baste thy hide right merrily, my good fellow"; then, aloud, "Lo, here is my good staff, lusty and tough. Now wait my coming, and thou darest, and meet me, an thou fearest not; then we will fight until one or the other of us tumble into the stream by dint of blows."

"Marry, that meeteth my whole heart!" cried the stranger, twirling his staff above his head, betwixt his fingers and thumb, until it whistled again.

Never did the Knights of Arthur's Round Table meet a stouter fight than did these two. In a moment Robin stepped quickly upon the bridge where the stranger stood; first he made a feint, and then delivered a blow at the stranger's head that, had it met its mark, would have tumbled him speedily into the water; but the stranger turned the blow right deftly, and in return gave one as stout, which Robin also turned as the stranger had done. So they stood, each in his place, neither moving a finger's breadth back, for one good hour, and many blows were given and received by each in that time, till here and there were sore bones and bumps, yet neither thought of crying "Enough!" or seemed likely to fall from off the bridge. Now and then they stopped to rest, and each thought that he never had seen in all his life before such a hand at quarter-staff. At last Robin gave the stranger a blow upon the ribs that made his jacket smoke like a damp straw thatch in the sun. So shrewd was the stroke that the stranger came within a hair's breadth of falling off the bridge; but he regained himself right quickly, and, by a dexterous blow, gave Robin a crack on the crown that caused the blood to flow. Then Robin grew mad with anger, and smote with all his might at the other; but the stranger warded the blow, and once again thwacked Robin, and this time so fairly that he fell heels over head into the water, as the queen pin falls in a game of bowls.

"And where art thou now, good lad?" shouted the stranger, roaring with laughter.

"Oh, in the flood and floating adown with the tide," cried Robin; nor could he forbear laughing himself at his sorry plight. Then, gaining his feet, he waded to the bank, the little fish speeding hither and thither, all frightened at his splashing.

"Give me thy hand," cried he, when he had reached the bank. "I must needs own thou art a brave and a sturdy soul, and, withal, a good stout stroke with the cudgels. By this and by that, my head hummeth like to a hive of bees on a hot June day."

Then he clapped his horn to his lips, and winded a blast that went echoing sweetly down the forest paths. "Ay, marry," quoth he again, "thou are a tall lad, and eke a brave one, for ne'er, I trow, is there a man betwixt here and Canterbury Town could do the like to me that thou hast done."

"And thou," quoth the stranger, laughing, "takest thy cudgeling like a brave heart and a stout yeoman."

But now the distant twigs and branches rustled with the coming of men, and suddenly a score or two of good stout yeomen, all clad in Lincoln green, burst from out the covert, with merry Will Stutely at their head.

"Good master," cried Will, "how is this? Truly thou art all wet from head to foot, and that to the very skin."

"Why, marry," answered jolly Robin, "yon stout fellow hath tumbled me neck and crop into the water, and hath given me a drubbing beside."

"Then shall he not go without a ducking and eke a drubbing himself!" cried Will Stutely. "Have at him, lads!"

Then Will and a score of yeomen leaped upon the stranger, but though they sprang quickly they found him ready and felt him strike right and left with his stout staff, so that, though he went down with press of numbers, some of them rubbed cracked crowns before he was overcome.

"Nay, forbear!" cried Robin, laughing until his sore sides ached again; "he is a right good man and true, and no harm shall befall him. Now hark ye, good youth, wilt thou stay with me and be one of my band? Three suits of Lincoln green shalt thou have each year, beside forty marks in fee, and share with us whatsoever good shall befall us. Thou shalt eat sweet venison and quaff the stoutest ale, and mine own good right-hand man shalt thou be, for never did I see such a cudgel-player in all my life before. Speak! wilt thou be one of my good merry men?"

"That know I not," quoth the stranger, surlily, for he was angry at being so tumbled about. "If ye handle yew bow and apple shaft no better than ye do oaken cudgel, I wot ye are not fit to be called yeomen in my country; but if there be any men here that can shoot a better shaft than I, then will I bethink me of joining with you."

"Now, by my faith," said Robin, "thou art a right saucy varlet, sirrah; yet I will stoop to thee as I never stooped to man before. Good Stutely, cut thou a fair white piece of bark four fingers in breadth, and set it fourscore yards distant on yonder oak. Now, stranger, hit that fairly with a gray goose shaft and call thyself an archer."

"Ay, marry, that will I," answered he. "Give me a good stout bow and a fair broad arrow, and if I hit it not, strip me and beat me blue with bow-strings."

Then he chose the stoutest bow amongst them all, next to Robin's own, and a straight gray goose shaft, well-feathered and smooth, and stepping to the mark—while all the band, sitting or lying upon the greensward, watched to see him shoot —he drew the arrow to his cheek and loosed the shaft right deftly, sending it so straight down the path that it clove the mark in the very center. "Aha!" cried he, "mend thou that if thou canst"; while even the yeomen clapped their hands at so fair a shot.

"That is a keen shot, indeed," quoth Robin; "mend it I cannot, but mar it I may, perhaps."

Then taking up his own good stout bow and notching an arrow with care, he shot with his very greatest skill. Straight flew the arrow, and so true that it lit fairly upon the stranger's shaft and split it into splinters. Then all the yeomen leaped to their feet and shouted for joy that their master had shot so well.

"Now, by the lusty yew bow of good Saint

Withold," cried the stranger, "that is a shot indeed, and never saw I the like in all my life before! Now truly will I be thy man henceforth and for aye. Good Adam Bell was a fair shot, but never shot he so!"

"Then have I gained a right good man this day," quoth jolly Robin. "What name goes thou by, good fellow?"

"Men call me John Little whence I came," answered the stranger.

Then Will Stutely, who loved a good jest, spoke up. "Nay, fair little stranger," said he, "I like not they name and fain would I have it otherwise. Little art thou, indeed, and small of bone and sinew; therefore shalt thou be christened Little John, and I will be thy godfather."

Then Robin Hood and all his band laughed aloud until the stranger began to grow angry.

"An thou make a jest of me," quoth he to Will Stutely, "thou wilt have sore bones and little pay, and that in short season."

"Nay, good friend," said Robin Hood, "bottle thine anger, for the name fitteth thee well. Little John shalt thou be called henceforth, and Little John shall it be. So come, my merry men, and we will go and prepare a christening feast for this fair infant."

So turning their backs upon the stream, they plunged into the forest once more, through which they traced their steps till they reached the spot where they dwelt in the depths of the woodland. There had they built huts of bark and branches of trees, and made couches of sweet rushes spread over with skins of fallow deer. Here stood a great oak tree with branches spreading broadly around, beneath which was a seat of green moss where Robin Hood was wont to sit at feast and at merry-making with his stout men about him. Here they found the rest of the band, some of whom had come in with a brace of fat does. Then they all built great fires and after a time roasted the does and broached a barrel of humming ale. Then when the feast was ready, they all sat down, but Robin Hood placed Little John at his right

hand, for he was henceforth to be the second in the band.

Then, when the feast was done, Will Stutely spoke up. "It is now time, I ween, to christen our bonny babe, is is not so, merry boys?" and "Aye! Aye!" cried all, laughing till the woods echoed with their mirth.

"Then seven sponsors shall we have," quoth Will Stutely; and hunting among all the band he chose the seven stoutest men of them all.

"Now, by Saint Dunstan," cried Little John, springing to his feet, "more than one of you shall rue it an you lay finger upon me."

But without a word they all ran upon him at once, seizing him by his legs and arms and holding him tightly in spite of his struggles, and they bore him forth while all stood around to see the sport. Then one came forward who had been chosen to play the priest because he had a bald crown, and in his hand he carried a brimming pot of ale. "Now who bringeth this babe?" asked he right soberly.

"That do I," answered Will Stutely.

"And what name callest thou him?"

"Little John call I him."

"Now Little John," quoth the mock priest, "thou hast not lived heretofore, but only got thee along through the world, but henceforth thou wilt live indeed. When thou livedst not, thou wast called John Little, but now that thou dost live indeed, Little John shalt thou be called, so christen I thee." And at these last words he emptied the pot of ale upon Little John's head.

Then all shouted with laughter as they saw the good brown ale stream over Little John's beard and trickle from his nose and chin, while his eyes blinked with the smart of it. At first he was of a mind to be angry, but he found he could not because the others were so merry; so he, too, laughed with the rest. Then Robin took this sweet, pretty babe, clothed him all anew from top to toe in Lincoln green, and gave him a good stout bow, and so made him a member of the merry band.

MIKE FINK/United States

Adrien Stoutenburg

No one knows if historical figures lie behind the stories about Odysseus, King Arthur, Robin Hood or other Culture Heroes, but in tales told about Mike Fink an interplay between fact and fantasy can be seen. This riverman's character intrigued his countrymen in the middle of the nineteenth century. They elaborated on his deeds in broadly humorous anecdotes.

Born in 1770, Mike Fink became an Indian scout and had the reputation of being the best shot in Philadelphia. After the country became too settled, he turned to the river and later was a trapper in the Rockies. In the stories that developed around him, Mike epitomized the tough, independent fighter of the frontier. The following semifictional history of his life excludes the bully aspect of his nature and emphasizes his boasting. The title is especially appropriate, for "roarer" means boaster.

An interesting cross-cultural comparison can be made between the European Culture Heroes and those of America, who have no mythic or godlike overtones. The American frontiersmen left behind the heroes of their homelands and in their place told stories of men like themselves, only larger, tougher, even more courageous.

MIKE FINK, RIVER ROARER

The Mississippi and the Missouri rivers are usually pretty quiet these days. It was a lot different when Mike Fink was whooping up and down them in his keelboat. But then, Mike was about the noisiest thing next to thunder that this country has ever heard.

Mike was born to be a riverman, although he didn't know it until he was old enough to find out. Until then he spent his time in the woods around Pittsburgh, where he was born, shooting at wolves, bobcats, mosquitoes, or anything else that could be shot at. He wasn't especially big, but he was as tough as a bale of barbed wire and as touchy as dynamite.

Even the wild Indians took a different path when they saw young Mike coming. He could flip a tomahawk through the air and hit a fly, even if the fly was in a hurry. With his rifle, called Bang-All, he could straighten out the curl in a pig's tail from fifty feet away.

Mike was as good at bragging as he was at shooting and fighting. "I can shoot faster than greased lightning going through a slippery thundercloud!" Mike boasted when he was still only ten years old. "I can shoot all the scales off a leaping trout with one bullet."

People who didn't know Mike too well laughed.

"I'll prove it!" Mike said. He jumped into the air, clapped his heels together, yelled "Cock-a-doodle-doo!" and loaded his long flintlock rifle at the same time. "Hold on to your hats and beards while I find something worth shooting at," he said.

"Farmer Neal's having a big shooting contest next Sunday," a townsman told him. "If you can shoot as well as you claim, you'll win a nice hunk of fresh beef. But you'll have to pay a quarter for each shot you try."

Mike went off and sharpened up his shooting eye by practicing on the wolves skulking around the woods near his family's log cabin. The wolves were low-slung, shifty fellows, hunting for a farmer's fat duck or even a skinny chicken. The government paid money for wolfskins, because wolves were a nuisance to the settlers. Mike banged and boomed at the wolves until he had about fifty skins. He took the skins to town and got enough money to enter the shooting match.

On Sunday, Mike dressed up in his best buckskin, stuck a wild-turkey feather in his cap, and marched off to Farmer Neal's place. The silver trimmings on his rifle stock were polished like glass.

At the shooting contest, the field was crowded with people. The men trying for the prize were soldiers and hunters, Indian scouts and boatmen, all of them the best shots in the country. They grinned and winked at seeing young Mike there, and one said:

"You'd better let me lift you up so you can see the target, sonny."

"I can jump higher than a Plymouth Rock rooster and yell louder," Mike said. He gave a loud crow, jumped, waved his heels, and fired at a passing bee. The bee flipped over, closed its eyes, and landed at Mike's feet. But in a second, the bee sat up and buzzed.

"You didn't kill that bee, young fellow," a man said.

"Didn't plan to," Mike said and held up the bee. "I just snipped off his stinger so he won't bother me when I'm aiming at the target."

Everyone was silent after that, though each really believed Mike had been merely lucky. When his turn came, Mike stepped up to the firing line and got set to take his first shot. The target was a round, white piece of paper tacked to a board on a distant oak tree. At the very center of the paper was a small circle called the bull's-eye.

No one had hit the center of the white circle yet. Mike pulled the trigger. Bang-All banged, and the bullet zipped straight through the bull's-eye.

People whistled in surprise, but one man said, "I'll bet you can't do that again, sonny."

Mike blew the smoke from the muzzle of Bang-All. "I paid for five shots," he said, "and I'll drive every bullet right on top of the other, even with a blindfold on. For I can out-shoot, out-thunder, and out-lick any man, mountain lion, or war-whooping redskin this side of the Alleghenies, and the other side too!"

"Move the target farther back!" somebody yelled.

The target was moved so far off that some of the older people in the crowd started hunting for spyglasses in order to see it. Mike whipped his second bullet through the heart of the target. He sent his third bullet whamming in on top of the one before. When he had hit the bull's-eye five times, the rest of the marksmen decided they might as well go home and take up knitting.

Mike went home, too, lugging five quarters of beef with him. The Fink family had enough chops and roasts for a whole winter, even though Mike could eat a dozen steaks all by himself for breakfast.

At other shooting contests after that, the rival sharpshooters would give Mike a quarter of beef beforehand if he would promise not to take part. So Mike had to be satisfied with roaming in the woods, scouting for Indians. He wanted to join George Washington's army and fight the English in the American Revolution, but he was still a little too young to be a soldier.

With plenty of free meat, plus hominy and dried cornmeal and buckets of molasses, Mike grew stronger than ever, though he never grew overly tall. When he was seventeen, he started hanging around the river docks in Pittsburgh, watching the boats. There were barges and keelboats, flatboats and Indian canoes, and a few ships left over from the Revolutionary Navy. Some craft carried cargoes of flour, cloth, lumber, and nails. Some carried people and livestock from one town to another, for there were not many roads through the wilderness then.

Mike leaned on his six-foot-long rifle and dreamed about becoming a boatman. He watched the water churn against the sides of the river craft, sparkling like soapsuds. Best of all, he liked watching the men who ran the boats. Most of them were as powerful and as full of brag and fight as he was. A few wore red feathers in their hats. A red feather meant that the person wearing it was the roughest, toughest, hardest-to-beat riverman around.

"I aim to get me a red feather," Mike decided. "I aim to get me all the red feathers there are, from here to the Rockies, and on the other side, too!"

Mike told his folks good-by, polished up Bang-All until it glittered like a hive of bees, and walked up to the first keelboat captain he found in Pittsburgh.

"What can you do?" the captain asked Mike.

"There's just about nothing I can't do," said Mike, "except possibly drink up the Pacific Ocean in one swallow. Otherwise, I can out-roar a mother hurricane and all her family, knock down a thunderbolt with my breath, spit the Sahara Desert into a flood, and in my spare time, haul up so many whales, the Atlantic will sink a hundred feet. I can also do a few other things that I can't even think of right at the moment."

"I'll try you out," said the captain, and he wrote Mike's name down on the crew list.

Mike bought himself a proper keelboatman's outfit—a red shirt, blue jacket, linsey-woolsey pants, moccasins, a fur cap, and a wide belt from which he hung a knife. He strutted on board and looked around until he saw a big-nosed man with a red feather stuck in his cap. Mike swaggered over to the man, doubled up his fists, and roared:

"Whoop, hi-ho, and cock-a-doodle-do! I'm the original Pittsburgh screamer, weaned on shark's milk, raised in a crib with rattlesnakes, mad scorpions, and hungry bumblebees. I'm second cousin to a hurricane, first cousin to a seven-day blizzard, and brother to an earthquake! I'm so all-fired ferocious and ornery, it scares even me to think about it! And I'm so chock-full of fight and fury, I have to lick somebody or my muscles will bust like cannon balls!"

The big-nosed boatman, whose name was Carpenter, puffed up his chest and roared right back at Mike, "Whoop and holler! I'm a man-eating panther, with teeth like buzz saws and eyes sharp enough to bore holes through midnight. My mother was a tiger, and my father was a rhinoc-

eros. I can crack an elephant's bones in one hand, break five grizzly bears' backs with the other, and blow down a forest with one breath. I'm so rough I don't dare scratch myself for fear my skin will come off!"

There was nothing to do but fight to prove who was the better man. The rest of the keelboatmen watched and trembled. The boat itself trembled as Mike and Carpenter wrestled and writhed, struck and staggered, panted and puffed. They fought for two hours, sweating so hard that a crew of men had to bail the boat out to keep everyone from drowning. Finally, Mike gave a whoop loud enough to tear a hole through the boat deck, leaped, drove his feet into Carpenter's belly, and knocked Carpenter flat as a pancake turner.

Carpenter lay still. He said, "Whoop," but his voice was so weak that a ladybug sitting right on his chin couldn't hear it. When he gained enough strength, he stood up and gave Mike the red feather from his hat.

"Mike Fink," he said, "you're the best fighter on the Ohio, the Mississippi, the Missouri, and any other river in the U.S. of A."

"I don't want to brag," Mike said, "but I guess I am." He put the feather in his cap and shook Carpenter's hand.

The two felt so friendly that they promised they would die for each other, if they absolutely had to.

In between fighting and friendship-making, which amounted to the same thing, Mike learned how to be a regular keelboatman. He learned how to ram a long pole down to the bottom of the river and push the boat upstream against the current. He learned to watch out for sandbars or snags that could stop the boat. He could see a dead tree floating in the water almost before it died and dropped there.

Mike became the best keelboatman anywhere. Up and down the rivers he went, from Pittsburgh to St. Louis and to New Orleans. He could load up a boat with cargo in less time than it took the other boatmen to drink a cup of hard cider, and usually they drank so fast, they swallowed before they even got the cider to their mouths. Mike himself could drink so fast that he only swallowed in between two-gallon sips.

By the time Mike had been on the river

awhile, he had so many red feathers in his cap that he threw most of them away, for fear people would think he was a bonfire.

There were lazy times on the river, too, when Mike and his friend Carpenter would stretch out on the deck and watch the sun go by, or fish for catfish, or sit on shore at night studying a campfire.

On one of those lazy days, Mike felt the need for a little extra target practice. He took a tin cup full of cider, handed it to Carpenter, and said, "Pace off about sixty yards and set that cup on your head. I'll shoot it off."

Carpenter looked a bit nervous, but he did as he was told. Mike aimed Bang-All and fired. The bullet whistled through the cup's brim, not spilling a drop. Carpenter took his turn with the same trick. He hit the cup on Mike's head, but he spilled the cider.

From then on, Mike and Carpenter would show off their trick to all the other boatmen. One time, before Mike could fire at the cup on Carpenter's head, there was a blast from another rifle in the woods nearby. The cup flew into the air.

Mike spun around so fast the ground smoked. "Who did that?" he roared.

"My name's Talbot," a man said, stepping out of the woods. He was a red-headed fellow with muscles bunched up as thick as thunderclouds.

"Whoop, holler, and hailstones!" Mike yelled, jumping into the air and banging his heels together. "My name's cholera, pestilence, and sudden death! I'm the original meat-grinder, man-mauler, muscle-ripper, and the meanest, cruelest, blood-thirstiest creation that ever drew breath!"

Talbot took a deep breath and shouted back, "Whoop! I'm the man who invented fighting. I've got fists so big they make mountains look like bumps. I've got a hide like an alligator and a heart as black as a buzzard in a coal mine! I'm so mean, I hate not being able to kill a man more than once!"

They leaped at each other. They hissed and hollered. They slammed, rolled, and punched. The ground shook, and the trees shook until all the leaves fell off. At last, after several hours, Mike swung his fist up from the ground. His knuckles banged Talbot's chin so hard that Talbot flew up and hit his head on a tree branch.

When he sailed down to earth again, his head was considerably flatter, and all the fight had gone out of him.

Talbot and Mike shook hands, and when the men went back onto the keelboat, Talbot went along. He, Carpenter, and Mike all swore they would die for each other, if they absolutely had to.

With three mighty men like that fighting for each other and whooping up and down the rivers, it seemed there was no one they couldn't lick. But there was. The man who had them licked wasn't even very good with his fists, and he didn't whoop and holler at all. His name was Robert Fulton, and all he did to become the new ruler of the river was invent the steamboat.

Mike hated steamboats even more than he hated to sit still. Every time he saw one coming, its big side-wheels churning the water, he shook his fists at the sky. But the streamboats kept on coming, getting bigger and faster, pushing the keelboats out of the way, and winning every race.

Mike still worked on the keelboats, but it wasn't like the old days. He wasn't the real boss of the river anymore. And Pittsburgh, St. Louis, and New Orleans were growing too civilized for his liking.

That's how Mike happened to become a mountain man. Talbot and Carpenter did, too. In St. Louis one day, they signed up with a fur-trapping party to go up the Missouri River, farther west than almost anyone but Lewis and Clark had been before. They went in two keelboats loaded down with traps, guns, and supplies.

The Missouri was muddier than the underside of a mud turtle. It was so full of snags, the men useds axes more than they used oars. The wild animals and Indians swarmed around the river banks in such numbers that Mike's rifle barrel grew so hot from shooting, it nearly melted.

"Come on, mountains!" Mike would roar, beating his chest. "Come on, you beaver and buffalo and grizzlies! I'm the original mountain-beater and grizzly-tamer, and I can out-trap, out-skin, and out-trade any man west or east of the sun!"

Mike turned out to be almost as good a trapper as he had been a riverman. That first winter, near the mouth of the Yellowstone River, he brought in so many furs that half the beaver population was left running around naked.

Mike was mighty happy and proud those days, and it seemed he could beat the Rockies down with his fists the way he claimed he could. But then he and his friend Carpenter had a quarrel. They whooped and hollered at each other and almost had a fist fight before they remembered that they were supposed to be friends. They made up and shook hands, but Mike didn't seem quite so hearty about it as usual.

Spring came to Fort Henry, the main camp. The men felt like celebrating, so they tuned up their banjos and blew the frost out of their harmonicas.

"Let's give them a show," Mike said to Carpenter. "We'll show them what real shooting's like." He handed Carpenter a cup of cider for Carpenter to place on his head.

Carpenter walked off sixty yards, put the cup on his head, and faced Mike. Some people say Carpenter trembled and didn't trust Mike, because of the quarrel. Others say he was as calm as a fence post on a windless day.

Mike brought Bang-All up against his cheek and squinted. For the first time in his life he had trouble holding the barrel steady. And the sunlight, glancing along the muzzle, made him blink. He shook himself, squeezed the trigger, and fired.

Carpenter gave a surprised look and fell, a bullet hole gleaming in the middle of his forehead.

"You've killed him dead!" a man yelled at Mike.

Mike stared, and then he ran over to Carpenter. He bent down, silent.

"It was an accident," Mike said at last. He ran back and picked up Bang-All. He broke the rifle over his knee. He roared with grief. He swore at the bullet and the powder horn, and at the mountains and himself. "It was an accident!" he cried. "I aimed for the cup."

A trapper jeered, "I guess you must be getting old, Mike Fink. I guess maybe you're not the best sharpshooter around!"

Mike turned red in the face, but he didn't say anything.

Another trapper called out, "Hey, Mike, I though you never missed a shot yet. Just big talk, huh?"

Mike turned purple.

Talbot stepped forward. His eyes were both sharp and sad. "What made you miss, Mike?"

Mike felt a shrill "Whoop!" gather in his throat, as it had every time before when he knew he could out-shoot any man east or west.

"I didn't miss!" he roared at Talbot. "I aimed right for Carpenter's forehead. I'm the greatest sharpshooter that ever drew a bead . . ."

He never finished, because Talbot lifted his own rifle and shot Mike through the heart, not spilling a drop of blood.

Mike slumped to the ground. He had only enough breath left to puff his chest up one final time.

"Whoop!" he roared. "Cock-a-doodle-do! I'm the original Pittsburgh screamer, roarer, and thunderer! I can out-shoot, out-fight, and out-yell anybody anywhere at any time!" He took a final, small breath, and the words came out so faintly that it was almost a whisper. "And I was the best keelboatman that ever lived."

Mike was bragging still, there at the end. But those last words, as everybody knows, were the honest truth.

PAUL BUNYAN/United States

Glen Rounds

In 1914 the Red River Lumber Company published a book of stories about Paul Bunyan. The writer-illustrator W. B. Laughead claimed he invented many of the characters but would never clarify his source for the tales. While

James Stevens states in the preface to his book, Paul Bunyan, *that the original Paul Bunyan was a French-Canadian logger of the first half of the nineteenth century, other experts question the folk source. They believe he was first a literary invention of the timber industry and entered the oral tradition late. (See "Paul Bunyan—Myth or Hoax?" in* Minnesota History, *Volume XXI, March, 1940.)*

The anecdotes about Paul's prowess achieved such popularity that many older regional heroes were forgotten and their exploits ascribed to him. Tony Beaver, the lumber-jack hero of West Virginia, and Tebold Teboldson, a hero of the plains, were patterned after Paul Bunyan.

These tall tales rely almost solely on impossible exaggeration for their humor: Paul was so quick he could blow out a candle and get into bed on the opposite side of the room before it was dark. Such an overstatement delights older children but confuses most elementary school students, who try to find a logical explanation instead of enjoying the joke.

Regardless of the controversy over their development, the Paul Bunyan tales are now a part of our culture. He represents the gigantic effort and daring necessary to industrialize America.

THE WHISTLING RIVER

It seems that some years before the winter of the Blue Snow (which every old logger remembers because of a heavy fall of bright blue snow which melted to ink, giving folks the idea of writing stories like these, so they tell) Ol' Paul was logging on what was then known as the Whistling River. It got its name from the fact that every morning, right on the dot, at nineteen minutes after five, and every night at ten minutes past six, it r'ared up to a height of two hundred and seventy-three feet and let loose a whistle that could be heard for a distance of six hundred and three miles in any direction.

Of course, if one man listening by himself can hear that far, it seems reasonable to suppose that two men listening together can hear it just twice as far. They tell me that even as far away as Alaska, most every camp had from two to four whistle-listeners (as many as were needed to hear the whistle without straining), who got two bits a listen and did nothing but listen for the right time, especially quitting time.

However, it seems that the river was famous for more than its whistling, for it was known as

the orneriest river that ever ran between two banks. It seemed to take a fiendish delight in tying whole rafts of good saw logs into more plain and fancy knots than forty-three old sailors even knew the names of. It was an old "side winder" for fair. Even so, it is unlikely that Ol' Paul would ever have bothered with it, if it had left his beard alone.

It happened this way. It seems that Ol' Paul is sitting on a low hill one afternoon, combing his great curly beard with a pine tree, while he plans his winter operations. All of a sudden like, and without a word of warning, the river h'ists itself up on its hind legs and squirts about four thousand five hundred and nineteen gallons of river water straight in the center of Ol' Paul's whiskers.

Naturally Paul's considerably startled, but says nothing, figuring that if he pays it no mind, it'll go 'way and leave him be. But no sooner does he get settled back with his thinking and combing again, than the durn river squirts some more! This time, along with the water, it throws in for good measure a batch of mud turtles, thirteen large carp, a couple of drowned muskrat, and half a raft of last year's saw logs. By this time Ol' Paul is pretty mad, and he jumps up and lets loose a yell that causes a landslide out near Pike's Peak, and startles a barber in Missouri so he cuts half the hair off the minister's toupee, causing somewhat of a stir thereabouts. Paul stomps around waving his arms for a spell, and allows:

"By the Gee-Jumpin' John Henry and the Great Horn Spoon, I'll tame that river or bust a gallus tryin'."

He goes over to another hill and sits down to think out a way to tame a river, forgetting his winter operations entirely. He sits there for three days and forty-seven hours without moving, thinking at top speed all the while, and finally comes to the conclusion that the best thing to do is to take out the kinks. But he knows that taking the kinks out of a river as tricky as this one is apt to be quite a chore, so he keeps on sitting there while he figures out ways and means. Of course, he could dig a new channel and run the river through that, but that was never Paul's way. He liked to figure out new ways of doing things, even if they were harder.

Meanwhile he's gotten a mite hungry, so he hollers down to camp for Sourdough Sam to bring him up a little popcorn, of which he is very fond. So Sam hitches up a four-horse team while his helpers are popping the corn, and soon arrives at Paul's feet with a wagon load.

Paul eats popcorn and thinks. The faster he thinks the faster he eats, and the faster he eats the faster he thinks, until finally his hands are moving so fast that nothing shows but a blur, and they make a wind that is uprooting trees all around him. His chewing sounds like a couple hundred coffee grinders all going at once. In practically no time at all the ground for three miles and a quarter in every direction is covered to a depth of eighteen inches with popcorn scraps, and several thousand small birds and animals, seeing the ground all white and the air filled with what looks like snowflakes, conclude that a blizzard is upon them and immediately freeze to death, furnishing the men with pot pies for some days.

But to get back to Ol' Paul's problem. Just before the popcorn is all gone, he decides that the only practical solution is to hitch Babe, the Mighty Blue Ox, to the river and let him yank it straight.

Babe was so strong that he could pull mighty near anything that could be hitched to. His exact size, as I said before, is not known, for although it is said that he stood ninety-three hands high, it's not known whether that meant ordinary logger's hands, or hands the size of Paul's which, of course, would be something else again.

However, they tell of an eagle that had been in the habit of roosting on the tip of Babe's right horn, suddenly decided to fly to the other. Columbus Day, it was, when he started. He flew steadily, so they say, night and day, fair weather and foul, until his wing feathers were worn down to pinfeathers and a new set grew to replace them. In all, he seems to have worn out seventeen sets of feathers on the trip, and from reaching up to brush the sweat out of his eyes so much, had worn all the feathers off the top of his head, becoming completely bald, as are all of his descendants to this day. Finally the courageous bird won though, reaching the brass ball on the tip of the left horn on the seventeenth of March. He waved a wing weakly at the cheering lumberjacks and 'lowed as how he'd of made it sooner but for the head winds.

But the problem is how to hitch Babe to the river, as it's a well-known fact that an ordinary log chain and skid hook will not hold water. So after a light lunch of three sides of barbecued beef, half a wagon load of potatoes, carrots and a few other odds and ends, Ol' Paul goes down to the blacksmith shop and gets Ole, the Big Swede, to help him look through the big instruction book that came with the woods and tells him how to do most everything under the sun. But though Paul reads the book through from front to back twice while Ole reads it from back to front, and they both read it once from bottom to top, they find nary a word about how to hook onto a river. However, they do find an old almanac stuck between the pages and get so busy reading up on the weather for the coming year, and a lot of fancy ailments of one kind and another that it's supper time before they know it, and the problem's still unsolved. So Paul decides that the only practical thing to do is to invent a rigging of some kind himself.

At any rate he has to do something, as every time he hears the river whistle, it makes him so mad he's fit to be tied, which interferes with his work more than something. No one can do their best under such conditions.

Being as how this was sort of a special problem, he thought it out in a special way. Paul was like that. As he always thought best when he walked, he had the men survey a circle about thirty miles in diameter to walk around. This was so that if he was quite a while thinking it out he wouldn't be finding himself way down in Australia when he'd finished.

When everything is ready, he sets his old fur cap tight on his head, clasps his hands behind him, and starts walking and thinking. He thinks and walks. The faster he walks the faster he thinks. He makes a complete circle every half hour. By morning he's worn a path that is knee-deep even on him, and he has to call the men to herd the stock away and keep them from falling in and getting crippled. Three days later he thinks it out, but he's worn himself down so deep that it takes a day and a half to get a ladder built that will reach down that far. When he does get out, he doesn't even wait for breakfast, but whistles for Babe and tears right out across the hills to the north.

The men have no idea what he intends to do, but they know from experience that it'll be good, so they cheer till their throats are so sore they have to stay around the mess hall drinking Paul's private barrel of cough syrup till supper time. And after that they go to bed and sleep very soundly.

Paul and the Ox travel plenty fast, covering twenty-four townships at a stride, and the wind from their passing raises a dust that doesn't even begin to settle for some months. There are those who claim that the present dust storms are nothing more or less than that same dust just beginning to get back to earth—but that's a matter of opinion. About noon, as they near the North Pole, they begin to see blizzard tracks, and in a short time are in the very heart of their summer feeding grounds. Taking a sack from his shoulder, Paul digs out materials for a box trap, which he sets near a well-traveled blizzard trail, and baits with fresh icicles from the top of the North Pole. Then he goes away to eat his lunch, but not until he's carefully brushed out his tracks—a trick he later taught the Indians.

After lunch he amuses himself for a while by throwing huge chunks of ice into the water for Babe to retrieve, but he soon has to whistle the great beast out, as every time he jumps into the water he causes such a splash that a tidal wave

threatens Galveston, Texas, which at that time was inhabited by nobody in particular. Some of the ice he threw in is still floating around the ocean, causing plenty of excitement for the iceberg patrol.

About two o'clock he goes back to his blizzard trap and discovers that he has caught seven half-grown blizzards and one grizzled old nor'wester, which is raising considerable fuss and bids fair to trample the young ones before he can get them out. But he finally manages to get a pair of half-grown ones in his sack and turns the others loose.

About midnight he gets back to camp, and hollers at Ole, the Big Swede:

"Build me the biggest log chain that's ever been built, while I stake out these dadblasted blizzards! We're goin' to warp it to 'er proper, come mornin'."

Then he goes down to the foot of the river and pickets one of the blizzards to a tree on the bank, then crosses and ties the other directly opposite. Right away the river begins to freeze. In ten minutes the slush ice reaches nearly from bank to bank, and the blizzards are not yet really warmed to their work, either. Paul watches for a few minutes, and then goes back to camp to warm up, feeling mighty well satisfied with the way things are working out.

In the morning the river has a tough time r'aring up for what it maybe knows to be its last whistle, for its foot is frozen solid for more than seventeen miles. The blizzards have really done the business.

By the time breakfast is over, the great chain's ready and Babe all harnessed. Paul quick-like wraps one end of the chain seventy-two times around the foot of the river, and hitches Babe to the other. Warning the men to stand clear, he shouts at the Ox to pull. But though the great beast strains till his tongue hangs out, pulling the chain out into a solid bar some seven and a half miles long, and sinks knee-deep in the solid rock, the river stubbornly refuses to budge, hanging onto its kinks like a snake in a gopher hole. Seeing this, Ol' Paul grabs the chain and, letting loose a holler that blows the tarpaper off the shacks in the Nebraska sandhills, he and the Ox together give a mighty yank that jerks the river loose from end to end, and start hauling it out across the prairie so fast that it smokes.

After a time Paul comes back and sights along the river, which now is as straight as a gun barrel. But he doesn't have long to admire his work, for he soon finds he has another problem on his hands. You see, it's this way. A straight river is naturally much shorter than a crooked one, and now all the miles and miles of extra river that used to be in the kinks are running wild out on the prairie. This galls the farmers in those parts more than a little. So it looks like Paul had better figure something out, and mighty soon at that, for already he can see clouds of dust the prairie folks are raising as they come at top speed to claim damages.

After three minutes of extra deep thought he sends a crew to camp to bring his big cross-cut saw and a lot of baling wire. He saws the river into nine-mile lengths and the men roll it up like linoleum and tie it with the wire. Some say he used these later when he logged off the desert, rolling out as many lengths as he needed to float his logs. But that's another story.

But his troubles with the Whistling River were not all over. It seems that being straightened sort of took the gimp out of the river, and from that day on it refused to whistle even a bird call. And as Paul had gotten into the habit of depending on the whistle to wake up the men in the morning, things were a mite upset.

First, he hired an official getter-upper who rode through the camp on a horse, and beat a triangle. But the camp was so big that it took three hours and seventy-odd minutes to make the trip. Naturally some of the men were called too early and some too late. It's hard to say what might have happened if Squeaky Swanson hadn't showed up about that time. His speaking voice was a thin squeak, but when he hollered he could be heard clear out to Kansas on a still day. So every morning he stood outside the cookshack and hollered the blankets off every bunk in camp. Naturally the men didn't stay in bed long after the blankets were off them, what with the cold wind and all, so Squeaky was a great success and for years did nothing but holler in the mornings.

BRER RABBIT/American Negro Slave

Joel Chandler Harris

Behind the Negro's early animal stories lie allegories of slavery and antagonism. Many of these tales came from Africa, but with a changed social position the Negroes altered their point of view. This can be seen by comparing the African tale "The Rubber Man," Chapter 6, Tales of Trickery, in which Spider is the lazy one, the cheat who deserves to be punished, with "The Wonderful Tar-Baby," in which the spider has been changed into Brer Rabbit, the trickster-hero, the clever one whose wit wins him the audience's admiration.

The slaves' Culture Hero was not a strong, openly independent, and defiant figure like Mike Fink. He was one whose keen wit compensated for his weakness and dependance and allowed him to laugh at his superiors. This can be clearly seen in the second paragraph of "Heyo, House!"

Although much about the slaves' attitudes toward themselves and whites is obvious in these stories (and all tales about Culture Heroes reveal similar insights about the people who tell them), the Brer Rabbit tales are filled with fun and should be enjoyed by all North American children. As the following two selections reveal, the dialect is difficult for many children to read. For this reason and because many Negroes are sensitive to the use of dialect, saying it has often been used to suggest ignorance, it is hoped some writer will "translate" these stories and yet keep them true to their origin.

HEYO, HOUSE!

"I don't think Brother Lion had much sense," remarked the little boy after awhile.

"Yit he had some," responded Uncle Remus. "He bleedz ter had some, but he ain't got much ez Brer Rabbit. Dem what got strenk ain't got so mighty much sense. You take niggers—dey er lots stronger dan what white folks is. I ain't so strong myse'f," remarked the old man, with a sly touch of vanity that was lost on the little boy, "but de common run er niggers is lots stronger dan white folks. Yit I done tuck notice in my time dat what white folks calls sense don't turn out ter be sense eve'y day en Sunday too. I ain't never see de patter-roller what kin keep up wid me. He may go hoss-back, he may go foot-back, it don't make no diffunce ter me. Dey never is kotch me yit, en when dey does, I'll let you know.

"Dat de way wid Brer Rabbit," Uncle Remus went on, after a pause. "De few times what he been outdone he mighty willin' fer ter let um talk 'bout it, ef it'll do um any good. Dem what outdo 'im got de right ter brag, en he ain't make no deniance un it.

"Atter he done make way wid ole Brer Lion, all de yuther creeturs say he sholy is a mighty man, en dey treat 'im good. Dis make 'im feel so proud dat he bleedz ter show it, en so he strut 'roun' like a boy when he git his fust pa'r er boots.

" 'Bout dat time, Brer Wolf tuck a notion dat ef Brer Rabbit kin outdo ole Brer Lion, he can't outdo him. So he pick his chance one day whiles ole Miss Rabbit en de little Rabs is out pickin' sallid fer dinner. He went in de house, he did, en wait fer Brer Rabbit ter come home. Brer Rabbit had his hours, en dis wuz one un um, en 'twan't long 'fo' here he come. He got a mighty quick eye, mon, en he tuck notice dat ev'ything mighty still. When he got little nigher, he tuck notice

dat de front door wuz on de crack, en dis make 'im feel funny, kaze he know dat when his ole 'oman en de chillun out, dey allers pulls de door shet en ketch de latch. So he went up a little nigher, en he step thin ez a batter-cake. He peep here, en he peep dar, yit he ain't see nothin'. He lissen in de chimbley cornder, en he lissen und' de winder, yit he ain't hear nothin'.

"Den he sorter wipe his mustach en study. He 'low ter hisse'f, 'De pot rack know what gwine on up de chimbley, de rafters know who's in de loft, de bed-cord know who und' de bed. I ain't no pot-rack, I ain't no rafter, en I ain't no bed-cord, but, please gracious! I'm gwine ter fin' who's in dat house, en I ain't gwine in dar nudder. Dey mo' ways ter fin' out who fell in de mill-pond widout fallin' in yo'se'f.'

"Some folks," Uncle Remus went on, "would 'a' rushed in dar, en ef dey had, dey wouldn't 'a' rushed out no mo', kaze dey wouldn't 'a' been nothin' 'tall lef' un um but a little scrap er hide en a han'ful er ha'r.

"Brer Rabbit got better sense dan dat. All he ax anybody is ter des gi' 'im han'-roomance, en dem what kin ketch 'im is mo' dan welly-come ter take 'im. Dat 'zackly de kinder man what Brer Rabbit is. He went off a little ways fum de house en clum a 'simmon stump en got up dar en 'gun ter holler.

"He 'low, 'Heyo, house!'

"De house ain't make no answer, en Brer Wolf, in dar behime de door, open his eyes wide. He ain't know what ter make er dat kinder doin's.

"Brer Rabbit holler, 'Heyo, house! Whyn't you heyo?'

"House ain't make no answer, en Brer Wolf in dar behime de door sorter move roun' like he gittin' restless in de min'.

"Brer Rabbit out dar on de 'simmon stump holler mo' louder dan befo', 'Heyo, house! Heyo!'

"House stan' still, en Brer Wolf in dar behime de door 'gun ter feel col' chills streakin' up and

"Heyo, House!" and "The Wonderful Tar-Baby" from *Uncle Remus and His Friends* by Joel Chandler Harris. Published by Appleton-Century-Crofts.

down his back. In all his born days he ain't never hear no gwines on like dat. He peep thoo de crack er de door, but he can't see nothin'.

"Brer Rabbit holler louder, 'Heyo, house! Ain't you gwine ter heyo? Is you done los' what little manners you had?'

"Brer Wolf move 'bout wuss'n befo'. He feel des like some un done hit 'im on de funny-bone.

"Brer Rabbit holler hard ez he kin, but still he ain't git no answer, en den he 'low, 'Sholy sump'n nudder is de matter wid dat house, kaze all de times befo' dis, it been holler'n back at me, Heyo, yo'se'f!'

"Den Brer Rabbit wait little bit, en bimeby he holler one mo' time, 'Heyo, house!'

"Ole Brer Wolf try ter talk like he speck a house 'ud talk, en he holler back, 'Heyo, yo'se'f!'

"Brer Rabbit wunk at hisse'f. He 'low, 'Heyo, house! Whyn't you talk hoarse like you got a bad col?'

"Den Brer Wolf holler back, hoarse ez he kin, 'Heyo, yo'se'f!'

"Dis make Brer rabbit laugh twel a little mo' en he'd a drapt off'n dat ar 'simmon stump en hurt hisse'f.

"He 'low, 'Eh-eh, Brer Wolf! dat ain't nigh gwine ter do. You'll hatter stan' out in de rain a mighty long time 'fo' you kin talk hoarse ez dat house!'

"I let you know," continued Uncle Remus, laying his hand gently on the little boy's shoulder, "I let you know, Brer Wolf come a-slinkin' out, en made a break fer home. Atter dat, Brer Rabbit live a long time wid'out any er de yuther creeturs a-pesterin' un 'im!"

THE WONDERFUL TAR-BABY

"One day atter Brer Rabbit fool 'im wid dat calamus root, Brer Fox went ter wuk en got 'im some tar, en mix it wid some turkentime, en fix up a contrapshun wat he call a Tar-Baby, en he tuck dish yer Tar-Baby en he sot 'er in de big road, en den he lay off in de bushes fer to see wat de news wuz gwineter be. En he didn't hatter wait long, nudder, kaze bimeby here come Brer Rabbit pacin' down de road—lippity-clippity, clippity-lippity—dez ez sassy ez a jay-bird. Brer Fox, he lay low. Brer Rabbit come prancin' long twel he spy de Tar-Baby, en den he fotch up on his behime legs like he wuz 'stonished. De Tar-Baby, she sot dar, she did, en Brer Fox, he lay low.

" 'Mawnin'!' sez Brer Rabbit, sezee—'nice wedder dis mawnin',' sezee.

"Tar-Baby ain't sayin' nothin', en Brer Fox, he lay low.

" 'How duz yo' sym'tums seem ter segashuate?' sez Brer Rabbit, sezee.

"Brer Fox, he wink his eye slow, en lay low, en de Tar-Baby, she ain't sayin' nothin'.

" 'How you come on, den? Is you deaf?' sez Brer Rabbit, sezee. 'Kaze if you is, I kin holler louder,' sezee.

"Tar-Baby stay still, en Brer Fox, he lay low.

" 'Youer stuck up, dat's w'at you is,' says Brer Rabbit, sezee, 'en I'm grineter kyore you, dat's w'at I'm a gwineter do,' sezee.

"Brer Fox, he sorter chuckle in his stummuck, he did, but Tar-Baby ain't sayin' nothin'.

" 'I'm gwineter larn you howter talk ter 'specttubble fokes ef hit's de las' ack,' sez Brer Rabbit, sezee. 'If you don't take off dat hat en tell me howdy, I'm gwineter bus' you wide open,' sezee.

"Tar-Baby stay still, en Brer Fox, he lay low.

"Brer Rabbit keep on axin' 'im, en de Tar-Baby she keep on sayin' nothin', twel present'y Brer Rabbit draw back wid his fis', he did, en blip he tuck 'er side er de head. Right dar's whar he broke his merlasses jug. His fis' stuck, en he can't pull loose. De tar hilt 'im. But Tar-Baby, she stay still, en Brer Fox, he lay low.

" 'Ef you don't lemme loose, I'll knock you agin,' sez Brer Rabbit, sezee, en wid dat he fotch 'er a wipe wid de udder han', en dat stuck. Tar-Baby, she ain't sayin' nothin', en Brer Fox, he lay low.

" 'Tu'n me loose, fo' I kick de natal stuffin' outten you,' sez Brer Rabbit, sezee, but de Tar-Baby, she ain't sayin' nothin'. She des hilt on, en den Brer Rabbit lose de use er his feet in de same way. Brer Fox, he lay low. Den Brer Rabbit squall out dat ef de Tar-Baby don't tu'n 'im loose he butt 'er crank-sided. En den he butten, en his head got stuck. Den Brer Fox, he sa'ntered fort', lookin' des ez innercent ez one er yo' mammy's mockin'-birds.

" 'Howdy, Brer Rabbit,' sez Brer Fox, sezee. 'You look sorter stuck up dis mawnin',' sezee, en den he rolled on de groun', en laughed en laughed twel he couldn't laugh no mo'. 'I speck you'll take dinner wid me dis time, Brer Rabbit. I done laid in some calamus root, en I ain't gwineter take no skuse,' sez Brer Fox, sezee.

.   .   .

" 'You been runnin' roun' here sassin' atter me amighty long time, but I speck you done come ter de een 'er de row. You bin cuttin' up yo' capers en bouncin' 'roun' in dis neighberhood ontwel you come ter b'leeve yo'se'f de boss er de whole gang. En den youer allers some'rs whar you got no bizness,' sez Brer Fox, sezee. 'Who ax you fer ter come en strike up a 'quaintance wid dish yer Tar-Baby? En who stuck you up dar whar you iz? Nobody in de roun' worril. You des tuck en jam yo'se'f on dat Tar-Baby widout waitin' fer enny invite,' sez Brer Fox, sezee, 'en dar you is' en dar you'll stay twel I fixes up a bresh-pile and fires her up, kaze I'm gwineter bobby-cue you dis day, sho,' sez Brer Fox, sezee.

"Den Brer Rabbit talk mighty 'umble.

" 'I don't keer w'at you do wid me, Brer Fox,' sezee, 'so you don't fling me in dat brier-patch. Roas' me, Brer Fox,' sezee, 'but don't fling me in dat brier-patch,' sezee.

" 'Hit's so much trouble fer ter kindle a fier,' sez Brer Fox, sezee, 'dat I speck I'll hatter hang you,' sezee.

" 'Hang me des ez high as you please, Brer Fox,' sez Brer Rabbit, sezee, 'but do fer de Lord's sake don't fling me in dat brier-patch,' sezee.

" 'I ain't got no string,' sez Brer Fox, sezee, 'en now I speck I'll hatter drown you,' sezee.

" 'Drown me dez ez deep ez you please, Brer Fox,' sez Brer Rabbit, sezee, 'but do don't fling me in dat brier-patch,' sezee.

" 'Dey ain't no water nigh,' sez Brer Fox, sezee, 'en now I speck I'll hatter skin you,' sezee.

" 'Skin me, Brer Fox,' sez Brer Rabbit, sezee, 'snatch out my eyeballs, t'ar out my years by de roots, en cut off my legs,' sezee, 'but do please, Brer Fox, don't fling me in dat brier-patch,' sezee.

"Co'se Brer Fox wanter hurt Brer Rabbit bad ez he kin, so he cotch 'im by de behime legs en slung 'im right in de middle er de brier-patch. Dar wuz a considerbul flutter whar Brer Rabbit struck de bushes, en Brer Fox sorter hang 'roun' fer ter see w'at wuz grineter happen. Bimeby he hear somebody call 'im, en way up de hill he see Brer Rabbit settin' cross-legged on a chinkapin log koamin' de pitch outen his har wid a chip. Den Brer Fox know dat he bin swoop off mighty bad. Brer Rabbit wuz bleedzed fer ter fling back some er his sass, en he holler out:

" 'Bred en bawn in a brier-patch, Brer Fox— bred en bawn in a brier-patch!' en wid dat he ski out des ez lively ez a cricket in de embers."

JOHN HENRY/United States

Walter Blair

In contrast to the Norse tales, most American narratives about Culture Heroes are optimistic and exuberant. Yet with industrialization came a new relationship for the working man and his job. Paul Bunyan, although his stories are of recent origin, is a hero of an earlier day. John Henry's life tells of the painful adjustment to machines. When machines began to prove superior to men, tragedy entered the tales of American Culture Heroes, white as well as black (Joe Magarac, Casey Jones, and John Henry).

At Big Bend Tunnel, West Virginia, in 1870 a real John Henry had a contest with a steam-drill and died. A folk ballad, a blues song, and a work song, as well as a few tales, all developed around this man who challenged the hated machine. As his legend moved west it spoke to the fears of other occupational groups who chose him as their hero and transformed him into a railroader, a cotton picker, and so on. As the modern world goes through another technological revolution, John Henry's tragedy may speak to new generations caught in the insecurity of change.

JOHN HENRY AND THE MACHINE IN WEST VIRGINIA

From his birth, it was clear that John Henry's life would be out of the ordinary. The day before, there was a rainbow, and a coal black preacher rode by the Henry cabin on a gray mule. The night was black, with a round red moon and no stars. Near by a cock crowed, a hound bayed, and somewhere in the forest panthers screamed. A great black cloud came from the southwest to cover the moon, and rain and forked lightning darted out of the cloud. And the thunder made a hammer of itself that pounded the earth till the trees quivered.

Then John Henry was born.

And the cloud went away, the moon shone white and bright, the stars came out, and the nightbirds started their singing. But in the moonlight a coal black preacher rode by the cabin again, and he was riding on a gray mule.

First thing John Henry knew, someone was saying, "He weigh thirty-three pound!" Next thing he knew, someone else was saying, "My, my, see them great big shoulders!"

"Course I weigh thirty-three pounds," says John Henry. "Course I got big shoulders. And I got me a voice that's deep and strong. And I got me a cravin' in my soul. What's more, I's hungry."

"My, my," John Henry's pappy said. "John Henry's talkin' already. What you aim to eat, son? Want a little old milk, son?"

"Milk's for babies," John Henry answered him back, "and already I's a natural boy, and soon I'll be a natural man. And I's hollow as an old dry well, sure as you born. So bring me seven hawg jowls and three kettle full of black-eyed peas.

"John Henry and the Machine in West Virginia" reprinted by permission of Coward-McCann, Inc., from *Tall Tale America* by Walter Blair, illustrated by Glen Rounds. Copyright © 1944 by Walter Blair.

Bring me seven ham bones and three pot full of giant cabbage sloshed around in gravy. Bring me a bait of turnip greens that's higher than my woolly head, and a like amount of ash cake to soak in the pot-likker."

"Lawd, Lawd," says John Henry's mammy. "Sound like we got a bragful son on our weary hands. Pappy, maybe if we start right now and learn him his eyes is bigger than his stomach, it'll start him on a good life."

So, with the help of the neighbors, they got all those mountains of food together. And there wasn't room for all the food in the fireplace room, so they had to set it forth on seven tables in the yard.

When John Henry's pappy looked at all that food, he grinned from ear to ear. Then he went to that newborn son of his, and he said, "It's all there, son, set forth on seven tables. If you can eat it, it's steamin' in the moonlight."

John Henry walked to the tables, and he started to eat. The food began to fly, and everybody that watched him grinned to see the way he prized his food. Of course, they expected that he'd stop after the first or second table.

But soon every table was clean as a hound dog's tooth, and John Henry was untying his napkin from around his neck.

"My, my," his pappy said. "He done et up all that food."

"Course I did," says John Henry. "I told you I was hungry."

"We thought you was just a bragful son," his mammy said.

"No," John Henry told her. "I's not bragful and I's not humble. I's a natural boy, and what I says, I means. And now I's goin' to sleep for nine hours."

Nine hours after he went to sleep—nine hours on the dot—John Henry woke up. "I got me a cravin' in my soul, and I's hungry," he said. "Bring me thirteen possums with sweet taters piled treetop high around them. Bring me three gallons of hominy grits to put gravy onto. Bring me ninety-nine slices of fried razorback ham and the red gravy. And bring me thirty-three buttermilk biscuits and tree-sweetnin' for them, for to finish off with."

Knowing by now, that the boy meant business, they brought what he asked and served it forth on nine tables. He ate it, easy as could be, untied his napkin from around his neck, and went back to bed.

And it went like that for quite a few month, while John Henry grew and grew. By good luck, that was back in the slave days before the war, so Ole Massa had to furnish all that food.

But John Henry grew fast, and his strength grew likewise.

He wasn't many weeks old when he got hold of a piece of steel and his pappy's five-pound hammer when the family was at meeting one fine Sunday morning.

When the family was a good peice from the cabin—"Lawd, Lawd," says John Henry's mammy. "Hear that hammer ringin'. It sounds like the meetin'-house bells when they's tollin' for a buryin.'"

When the family came to the house, they found John Henry had gone out with that peice of steel and that hammer. He'd found every big stone he could find, and he'd used the steel and the five-pound hammer to break the big stones. He was working away on the biggest stone of the lot now, hammering the steel and singing in time:

> If I die (WHAM!)
> A railroad man, (WHAM!)
> Go bury me (WHAM!)
> Under the sand, (WHAM!)
> With a pick and shovel (WHAM!)
> At my head and feet, (WHAM!)
> And a twenty-pound hammer (WHAM!)
> In my hand. (WHAM!)

With the last wham the rock broke in two, just as clean as if it'd been sawed, and John Henry stood up, grinning, his white teeth shining in his dark face.

"Hello, folkses," says he. "Look like I's found what I want to do—swing a hammer and make the steel ring like a bell. Never been so happy in all my born days, and I's seven weeks old come

Thursday. Seem like when I swings this old hammer, I don't have a cravin' in my soul—don't have a cravin' any more."

"My, my," his pappy said. "Look like our son was goin' to be a steel-drivin' man."

. . . John Henry was the best steel-driving man in the world. He could sink a hole down or he could sink it sideways, in soft rock or hard—it made no difference. When he worked with two twenty-pound hammers, one in each hand, it sounded as if the Big Bend Tunnel was caving in, the ring of the steel was so loud.

And John Henry and his sweet Polly Ann were as happy as singing birds, for their roaming days were over, and they felt they'd found a home.

Everything was going fine until a man came along and tried to peddle his steam drill to Captain Tommy. This man had pictures of the steam drill in a book, and he had a wagging tongue in his head. "This steam drill of mine," he said, "will out-drill any twenty men. It doesn't have to rest or eat either, so it'll save you lots of money."

"Hm, maybe," Captain Tommy said, "*maybe*. But I've got one steel-driving man here that's the finest in the world, and I'm mighty fond of big John Henry. So I'll tell you what I think we might do. We might have a race between the steam drill and this man of mine. If the steam drill wins, I'll buy it. But if John Henry wins, you give me the steam drill and five hundred dollars."

"I heard about John Henry, all right, and I know he's good," the man said. "But I know a man is nothing but a man. So I'll have that race, the way you say."

"Fine," says Captain Tommy, "except for one thing: I've got to ask John Henry, but I know pretty well what he'll say." So he went to John Henry, and asked him if he'd race that drill for a favor and a hundred dollars to boot.

John Henry said, "Course I'll race it, and course I'll beat it. For I's a natural-born steel-drivin' man that can beat any nine men or any of the traps that ever drove steel. I don't want any old machine to take my place at the happiest work I's ever found. So before I let that steam drill beat me, I'll die with my hammer in my hand."

The day of the race, country folks and all the steel-driving gangs in the whole section came to see whether John Henry meant what he said. The race was to be outside the mouth of the tunnel —out there by the blacksmith shops where the steels were sharpened and the hammers were fixed—a place where everybody could see. The steam drill, with a boiler about twenty feet long to make the steam, was on the right-hand corner, and the spot where John Henry was to drive was on the left. The crowd was sprinkled all around the edges of the quarry.

At the time the race was to start, the blacksmiths had sharpened piles of drills, the steam drill had its steam up, and the carriers were ready with pads on their shoulders to carry the sharpened steels from the shop and the dull ones back to be sharpened. When there was one minute to go, the steam drill whistled, and John Henry lifted one of his twenty-pound hammers. Then Captain Tommy dropped his hat, and the race started.

Says John Henry to Li'l Bill, the shaker, "Boy you'd better pray. Cause if I miss this piece of steel, tomorrow be your buryin' day, sure as you born."

Then the steam drill was chugging, and John Henry was swinging and singing-singing "Oh, My Hammer," "Water Boy, Where Is you Hidin'," "If I Die a Railroad Man," and other hammer songs he could keep time to. The steel rang like silver, the carrier trotted to and fro the blacksmith shops, and the crowd watched with all its might and main.

It wasn't long after the start that John Henry took the lead. The steam-drill salesman wasn't worried though—or if he was his talk didn't show it. "That man's a mighty man," he said. "But when he hits the hard rock, he'll weaken." Then when John Henry hit the hard rock, and kept driving fast as ever, the salesman said, "He can't keep it up."

John Henry did keep it up though, swinging those two hammers and driving down the steel, stopping only once an hour, maybe, to take a drink of water from the dipper Polly Ann had carried in her slender little hands. Six hours— seven hours—eight hours of that nine-hour race he made his hammer ring like gold. And though Li'l Bill got plumb played out and a new shaker

had to take his place, all through the eighth hour John Henry was going strong as ever, with the rhythm in every muscle and joint helping him wham the steel.

It wasn't until the ninth hour that John Henry showed any signs of getting tired. Then, when Captain Tommy came up to ask him how things were going, he answered him back, "This rock is so hard and this steel is so tough, I feel my muscles givin' way. But," he went on to say, "before I let that machine beat me, I'll die with my hammer in my hand."

After that, the crowd that was watching could see signs that John Henry was a weary man— very, very tired and weary.

And John Henry wasn't singing any more. All you could hear was the ring of the hammer on the steel and the shug-chug of the steam drill.

When Captain Tommy, at the end of the ninth hour, looked at his watch and yelled, "The race is over," and when the drills stopped going down, everything was as still as a graveyard. Captain Tommy was looking at the holes. Then, when Captain Tommy said, "John Henry won— three holes ahead of the steam drill," everybody cheered, everybody, that is, excepting the salesman and the steam drill crew—and John Henry.

When the crowd looked at John Henry, they saw the great man was lying on the ground, and his loving Polly Ann was holding his head. John Henry was moaning, and he sort of mumbled, "Before I let that steam drill beat me, I'll die with my hammer in my hand." (Sure enough, he had *two* hammers in his big black hands.)

Then he said, "Give me a cool drink of water 'fore I die."

Polly Ann was crying when she gave him the water.

Then John Henry kissed his hammer and he kissed his loving Polly Ann. She had to stoop down so he could kiss her. Then he lay very still, and Polly Ann cried harder than ever—sounded mighty loud in that quiet quarry.

Just at that minute, there was the sound of hoofs, and a coal black preacher came riding up on a gray mule. "You got troubles, sister?" he said to Polly Ann. "Can I help you?"

"Only way you can help," she answered him back, "is to read the buryin' service for my lovin'

John Henry. Cause his home ain't here no more."

So the coal black preacher read the burying services. They buried John Henry on a hillside—

with a hammer on each hand, a rod of steel across his breast, and a pick and shovel at his head and feet. And a great black cloud came out of the southwest to cover the copper sun.

Related Reading

France

Baldwin, James. *The Story of Roland*. Illustrated by Peter Hurd. New York: Scribner, 1930. A retelling of the eleventh century French epic. (Grades 6–9)

Sherwood, Merriam. *The Song of Roland*. Illustrated by Edith Emerson. New York: McKay, 1938. An excellent translation. (Grade 5–up)

Great Britain

Hieatt, Constance, reteller. *Sir Gawain and the Green Knight*. Illustrated by Walter Lorraine. New York: Crowell, 1967. The testing of Gawain, King Arthur's nephew, is well told in this brief narrative by a medieval specialist. (Grades 2–5)

Hosford, Dorothy G. *By His Own Might; The Battles of Beowulf*. Illustrated by Laszlo Matulay. New York: Holt, Rinehart and Winston, 1947. One of the best prose versions. (Grades 5–7)

Lanier, Sidney. *The Boy's King Arthur*. Illustrated by N. C. Wyeth. New York: Scribner, 1880. A retelling of Malory's *History of King Arthur and His Knights of the Round Table*. The many archaic words make this version difficult for children to read. (Grades 5–9)

MacLeod, Mary. *King Arthur, Stories from Sir Thomas Malory's Morte d'Arthur*. Illustrated by Herschel Levit. New York: Macmillan, 1963. Easier to read than Lanier's and Pyle's retellings. (Grades 5–8)

Picard, Barbara Leonie. *Tales of the British People*. Illustrated by Eric Fraser. New York: Criterion, 1961. Tales about Beowulf, Maxen, Wledig, Hereward the Wake, Sir Bevis of Hampton, William of Cloudslee, and Gawain. (Grades 5–7)

————. *Hero Tales from the British Isles*. Illustrated by Gay Galsworthy. London: Edward Ward, 1963. Well told tales about English, Welsh, Irish, and Scottish heroes. (Grade 5–up)

————. *Celtic Tales: Legends of Tall Warriors & Old Enchantments*. Illustrated by John G. Galsworthy. New York: Criterion, 1965, 1964. Fine collection of hero tales from Britain. (Grades 5–8)

Pyle, Howard. *The Story of King Arthur and His Knights*. New York: Scribner, 1933, 1903. Three fine books about one of the most popular of all heroes. (Grades 7–9)

————. *The Merry Adventures of Robin Hood*. New York: Scribner, 1946, 1883. (Grades 7–9)

————. *Some Merry Adventures of Robin Hood*. New York: Scribner, 1954. A shorter version of the 1883 book. (Grades 5–7)

Robinson, Mabel L. *King Arthur and His Knights*. Illustrated by Douglas Gorsline. New York: Random House, 1953. Easily read in contemporary language. (Grades 7–9)

Serraillier, Ian. *Beowulf the Warrior*. Illustrated by Severin. New York: Walck, 1961. A dramatic verse retelling for older children and adults. (Grade 6–up)

Sutcliff, Rosemary. *Beowulf*. Illustrated by Charles Keeping. New York: Dutton, 1962. Excellent prose version. (Grade 5–up)

————. *The Hound of Ulster*. Illustrated by Victor Ambrus. New York: Dutton, 1963. Dramatic retelling in a continuous narrative of the legends about the Irish culture here Cuchulain. (Grade 5–up)

Young, Ella. *The Wonder Smith and His Son; A Tale from the Golden Childhood of the World*. Illustrated by Boris Artzybasheff. New York: Longmans, 1927. Narratives of the Gubbaun Saor from Irish mythology. (Grades 5–7)

Greece

Church, Alfred J. *The Iliad and the Odyssey of Homer*. Illustrated by Eugene Karlin. Afterword by Clifton Fadiman. New York: Macmillan, 1964. Combination of the author's *The Iliad for Boys and Girls*, 1907, and *The Odyssey for Boys and Girls*, 1906. Retellings of the Trojan War and Odysseus's wanderings. (Grades 5–8)

Colum, Padraic. *The Children's Homer: The Adventures of Odysseus and the Tale of Troy*. Illustrated by Willy Pogany. New York: Crowell-Collier and Macmillan, 1962a. Well-written and beautifully illustrated retelling of the *Odyssey*.

————. *The Golden Fleece and the Heroes who Lived Before Achilles*. Illustrated by Willy Pogany. New York: Crowell-Collier and Macmillan, 1962b. Also well written and illustrated. (Grades 5–9)

Lang, Andrew. *The Adventures of Odysseus*. Illustrated by Joan Kiddell-Monroe. New York: Dutton, 1962. A reissue of the 1907 *Tales of Greece and Troy* with new illustrations. Still interesting to junior high school readers. (Grades 7–9)

Picard, Barbara Leonie. *The Iliad of Homer*. Illustrated by Joan Kiddell-Monroe. New York: Walck, 1960a.

————. *The Odyssey of Homer*. Illustrated by Joan Kiddell-Monroe. New York: Walck, 1960b. Excellent retellings of the Greek epics. (Grades 6–9)

Serraillier, Ian. *The Gorgon's Head: The Story of Perseus*. Illustrated by William Stobbs. New York: Scholastic, 1961.

————. *The Way of Danger: The Story of Theseus*. Illustrated by William Stobbs. New York: Walck, 1963. Well written narratives. (Grades 4–7)

The Orient

Gaer, Joseph. *The Adventures of Rama*. Illustrated by Randy Monk. Boston: Little, Brown, 1954. The life of Prince Rama, the human form of the Indian god Vishnu, is dramatically told in this version. (Grades 6–9)

Mukerji, Dhan Gopal. *Rama, the Hero of India*. Illustrated by Edgar Parin d'Aulaire. New York: Dutton, 1930. Another interesting retelling of this culture hero of India. (Grades 6–9)

Seeger, Elizabeth. *The Ramayana*. Adapted from the English translation of Hari Prasad Shastri. Illustrated by Gordon Laite. New York: W. R. Scott, 1969. The life of Rama, one of the incarnations of Vishnu the Hindu god, is presented in dramatic detail. (Grade 5 and up)

Scandinavia

Coolidge, Olivia. *Legends of the North*. Illustrated by Edouard Sandoz. Boston: Houghton Mifflin,

1951. A collection of Norse sagas, legends, hero-tales and myths. (Grades 4–8)

Deutsch, Babette. *Heroes of the Kalevala*. Illustrated by Fritz Eichenberg. New York: Messner, 1940. Well written version; true to the spirit of the original Finnish epic cycle. (Grades 6–9)

Hosford, Dorothy G. *Sons of the Volsungs*. Illustrated by Frank Dobias. New York: Holt, Rinehart and Winston, 1949. An excellent prose adaptation of William Morris' *The Story of Sigurd the Volsung and the Fall of the Niblungs*. (Grades 5–8)

United States

Felton, Harold W. *John Henry and His Hammer*. Illustrated by Aldren A. Watson. New York: Knopf, 1950. Rhythmic retelling of one of America's most powerful hero tales. Ends with the completion of the tunnel after John Henry's death. (Grades 5–7)

Harris, Joel Chandler. *Uncle Remus: His Songs and Sayings*, rev. ed. Illustrations by A. B. Frost. Frontispiece by Edward C. Caswell. New York: Appleton, 1921. Thirty-four legends, nine verses, twenty-one sayings, and some proverbs. Dialect unaltered. (Grades 5–7)

————. *Brer Rabbit; Stories from Uncle Remus*. Adapted by Margaret Wise Brown. The A. B. Frost illustrations redrawn by Victor Dowling. New York: Harper & Row, 1941. Dialect modified for easier reading. (Grades 3–7)

————. *The Complete Tales of Uncle Remus*. Compiled by Richard Chase. Illustrated by Arthur Frost and others. Boston: Houghton Mifflin, 1955. No changes in dialect or plot. A glossary helps provide definitions. (Grades 5–7)

Keats, Ezra Jack, author-illustrator. *John Henry: An American Legend*. New York: Pantheon, 1965. Powerfully illustrated picture book; one that reflects the power of the John Henry Legend. Good introduction to American hero tales for younger children; will also be enjoyed by older elementary graders. (Grades K–3)

Leekley, Thomas B. *The World of Manabozho: Tales of the Chippewa Indians*. New York: Vanguard, 1965. Retellings of the tales about Manabozho, the miracle worker. Background information about Indian mythology. (Grades 4–6)

McCormick, Dell J. adapter-illustrator. *Paul Bunyan Swings His Axe*. Caldwell, Idaho: Caxton, 1936.

————. *Tall Timber Tales; More Paul Bunyan Stories*. Illustrated by Lorna Lively. Caldwell, Idaho: Caxton, 1939. Short retellings for children of the Paul Bunyan tall tales. (Grades 5–8)

Malcolmson, Anne, and Dell J. McCormick. *Mister Stormalong*. Illustrated by Joshua Tolford. Boston: Houghton Mifflin, 1952. Tall tales about the adventures of Alfred Bulltop Stormalong, the American seaman's equivalent of the logger's Paul Bunyan. (Grades 4–6)

Rounds, Glen. *Ol' Pauly, the Mighty Logger*. New York: Holiday, 1936, 1949. Lively retellings of the Paul Bunyan tales. Will be enjoyed by older children. (Grades 5–9)

Shapiro, Irwin. *Heroes in American Folklore*. Illustrated by Donald McKay and James Daugherty. New York: Messner, 1962. Tales about Casey Jones, Stormalong, John Henry, and Joe Magarac. (Grades 4–7)

Shay, Frank. *Here's Audacity. American Legendary Heroes*. New York: Macauley, 1930. Enjoyable, swiftly paced narratives about American heroes; in each story many tales have been combined and compressed. Old Stormalong, Kwasind, Casey Jones, Pecos Bill, Paul Bunyan, and John Henry are some of the subjects. (Grades 5–9)

Other

Almedingen, E. M. *The Knights of the Golden Table*. Illustrated by Charles Keeping. Philadelphia: Lippincott, 1964a. Knights protect Kiev from evil and danger, their courage constantly tested in always exciting adventures. The Kiev Cycle should be better known; this is an excellent introduction. (Grades 4–7)

————. *The Treasure of Siegfried*. Illustrated by Charles Keeping. Philadelphia: Lippincott, 1964b. Retelling of the German epic. (Grades 7–9)

Brown, Marcia. *Backbone of the King, the Story of Pakaa and His Son Ku*. New York: Scribner, 1966. A striking picture book retelling of a Hawaiian legend. The unfamiliar words and chants make this a difficult book for children to read. Should be read aloud to younger students and introduced to those capable of reading it independently. (Grades 2–5)

Reid, Dorothy M. *Tales of Nanabozho*. New York: Walck, 1963. Stories about the Indian miracle worker, the manitou; a Canadian prizewinner. (Grades 4–6)

White, Ann Terry. *The Golden Treasury of Myths and Legends*. Illustrated by Alice and Martin Provensen. New York: Golden Press, 1959. Myths from many lands. (Grades 4–6)

From *The Baby's Own Aesop*, illustrated by Walter Crane. Published by George Routledge & Sons, Ltd., 1887.

Fables are written to teach ethical truths in an entertaining form. Although a few have human or inanimate objects as their subjects, usually animals are ascribed human characteristics, virtues, and vices. Because the animals symbolize human behavior, their true "animal" natures are usually ignored.

Aesop is often given credit for first creating the fable form. But it is doubtful that Aesop, who is said to have lived in the sixth century B.C., actually existed. Since many of the fables he is supposed to have written were recorded earlier than the sixth century in Egypt and India, scholars have felt a more likely place of origin for the fable form was India.

The *Jataka* (or birth) *Tales* form a part of very old Buddhist religious literature. These animal tales deal with the Buddha's cycle of reincarnations and show the noble examples he set while in animal form. Some scholars, however, believe the animal stories are older than the Buddhist structure which was later added to existing folklore.

The Panchatantra, also very old, is another Indian collection of moralistic animal tales that was used as a textbook for the conduct of life. *The Panchatantra* means "the five books," which indicates its general structure. Each book has a framing narrative with many inserted stories told by the characters of the beginning tale. Today this stylistic device is usually eliminated in versions for children. So, too, are the epigrammatic verses from sacred or authoritative writings used by the characters to support their opinions. These elements, however, are important if the differences in tone and mood between the Aesopic and Indian fables are to be seen. For that reason the following selection of fables includes the framing story and its sequel from Book IV of *The Panchatantra*.

In the sixth century A.D. *The Panchatantra* was translated into Persian under the title of *The Tales of Bidpai* or "tales of a wise man." As separate narratives the same fables have been collected under both titles.

Although most of the Aesopic fables originally came from these Indian sources, they are quite different from the eastern animal tales. Indian narratives have much more detail than the Aesopic fables, use a greater richness of language, have more depth of characterization, and revolve around more involved plots. While Aesopic fables are brief, unembellished narratives whose sole purpose is didactic through a stated or implied moral, Indian fables are more subtle and seem closer to the folktale form.

The following collection of fables begins with fables from *The Panchatantra* and *The Tales of Bidpai*, for historical perspective, for comparison with the Aesopic fables that follow, and for enjoyment. In addition to the well-known Aesopic fables, less familiar fables from Africa, Asia, and Russia are included, plus one narrative from an American Indian tribe, to illustrate how many cultures and periods of history have used this genre and to permit cross-cultural comparisons.

Examples of the work of three famous writers who used the fable form with special effectiveness are also included. La Fontaine (1621–1695) rewrote older fables, Aesop's and others, in sophisticated, polished poetry. These were published in France in 1688 and gave new status to the genre. Ivan Krylov (about 1769–1844) was a Russian imitator of La Fontaine's work. Krylov's fables were so well adapted to the Russian philosophy that many proverbs were taken from his work. Leo Tolstoy (1828–1910) a Russian noble interested in social reform and one of the world's greatest novelists, wrote a number of fables for students of his estate school.

Fables are an on-going literary tradition. Many reworkings of traditional fables as well as original fables have been written in this century. John Ciardi in *Fiddler Dan and John J. Plenty* has reinterpreted "The Ant and the Grasshopper" to show the role and significance of the artist in society and nature.

Although fables, or any other types of didactic literature, are unlikely to influence children's behavior dramatically, those ten years and older enjoy reading and even writing fables. They should have the opportunity to read not only Aesopic fables but also the Indian ones which they may enjoy more. Even first graders will enjoy Marcia Brown's *Once A Mouse*, and older children should not miss her *Chanticleer and the Fox* and Ciardi's *John J. Plenty and Fiddler Dan.*

THE PANCHATANTRA / India

BOOK IV: LOSS OF GAINS

Here, then, begins Book IV, called "Loss of Gains." The first verse runs:

> Blind folly always has to pay
> For giving property away
> Because of blandishments and guile—
> The monkey tricked the crocodile.

"How was that?" asked the princes. And Vishnusharman told the story of

The Monkey and the Crocodile
On the shore of the sea was a great rose-apple tree that was never without fruit. In it lived a monkey named Red-Face.

Now one day a crocodile named Ugly-Mug crawled out of the ocean under the tree and burrowed in the soft sand. Then Red-Face said: "You are my guest, sir. Pray eat these rose-apples which I throw you. You will find them like nectar. You know the proverb:

> A fool or scholar let him be,
> Pleasant or hideous to see,
> A guest, when offerings are given,
> Is useful as a bridge to heaven.

"The Monkey and the Crocodile" and "Handsome and Theodore" reprinted by permission of University of Chicago Press from *The Panchatantra*. Translated from the Sanskrit by Arthur W. Ryder. Copyright 1956 by the publisher.

> Ask not his home or education,
> His family or reputation,
> But offer thanks and sacrifice:
> For so prescribes the lawbook wise.

And again:

> By honoring the guests who come
> Wayworn from some far-distant home
> To share the sacrifice, you go
> The noblest way that mortals know.

And once again:

> If guests unhonored leave your door,
> And sadly sighing come no more,
> Your fathers and the gods above
> Turn from you and forget their love."

Thus he spoke and offered rose-apples. And the crocodile ate them and enjoyed a long and pleasant conversation with the monkey before returning to his home. So the monkey and the crocodile rested each day in the shade of the rose-apple tree. They spent the time in cheerful conversation on various subjects, and were happy.

Now the crocodile went home and gave his wife the rose-apples which he had not eaten. And one day she asked him: "My dear husband, where do you get such fruits? They are like nectar."

"My dear," he said, "I have an awfully good

friend, a monkey named Red-Face. He gives me
these fruits in the most courteous manner."

Then she said: "If anyone eats such nectar
fruit every day, his heart must be turned to
nectar. So, if you value your wife, give me his
heart, and I will eat it. Then I shall never grow
old or sick, but will be a delightful companion for
you."

But he objected: "In the first place, my dear,
he is our adopted brother. Secondly, he gives us
fruit. I cannot kill him. Please do not insist. Besides, there is a proverb:

> To give us birth, we need a mother;
> For second birth we need another:
> And friendship's brothers seem by far
> More dear than natural brothers are."

But she said: "You have never refused me before. So I am sure it is a she-monkey. You love
her and spend the whole day with her. That is
why you will not give me what I want. And when
you meet me at night, your sighs are hot as a
flame of fire. And when you hold me and kiss me,
you do not hug me tight. I know some other
woman has stolen into your heart."

Then the crocodile was quite dejected, and
said to his wife:

> When I am at your feet
> And at your service, sweet,
> Why do you look at me
> With peevish jealousy?

But her face swam in tears when she heard
him, and she said:

> "You love her, you deceiver;
> Your wishes never leave her;
> Her pretty shamming steals upon your heart.
>   My rivalry is vain, sir;
>   And so I pray abstain, sir,
> From service that is only tricky art.

"Besides, if you do not love her, why not kill
her when I ask you? And if it is really a he-mon-
key, why should you love him? Enough! Unless I
eat his heart, I shall starve myself to death in
your house."

Now when he saw how determined she was, he
was distracted with anxiety, and said: "Ah, the
proverb is right:

> Remember that a single grab
> Suffices for a fish or crab,
> For fool or woman; and 'tis so
> For sot, cement, or indigo.

"Oh, what shall I do? How can I kill him?"
With these thoughts in mind, he visited the
monkey.

Now the monkey had missed his friend, and
when he saw him afflicted, he said: "My friend,
why have you not been here this long time? Why
don't you speak cheerfully, and repeat something
witty?"

The crocodile replied: "My friend and brother,
my wife scolded me today. She said: 'You ungrateful wretch! Do not show me your face. You
are living daily at a friend's expense, and make
him no return. You do not even show him the
door of your house. You cannot possibly make
amends for this. There is a saying:

> The Brahman-murderer or thief,
> Drunkard or liar, finds relief;
> While for ingratitude alone
> No expiation will atone.

"'I regard this monkey as my brother-in-law.
So bring him home, and we will make some return for his kindness. If you refuse, I will see you
later in heaven.' Now I could not come to you
until she had finished her scolding. And this long
time passed while I was quarreling with her about
you. So please come home with me. Your brother's wife has set up an awning. She has fixed her
clothes and gems and rubies and all that, to pay
you a fitting welcome. She has hung holiday garlands on the doorposts. And she is waiting
impatiently."

"My friend and brother," said the monkey,
"your lady is very kind. It is quite according to
the proverb:

> Six things are done by friends:
>   To take, and give again;
> To listen, and to talk;
>   To dine, to entertain.

"But we monkeys live in trees, and your home
is in the water. How can I go there? Rather bring
your lady here, brother, that I may bow down
and receive her blessing."

The crocodile said: "My friend, our home is

on a lovely sand-bank under the water. So climb on my back and travel comfortably with nothing to fear."

When the monkey heard this, he was delighted and said: "If that is possible, my friend, then hasten. Why delay? Here I am on your back."

But as he sat there and saw the crocodile swimming in the bottomless ocean, the monkey was terribly frightened and said: "Go slow, brother. My whole body is drenched by the great waves."

And the crocodile thought when he heard this: "If he fell from my back, he could not move an inch, the water is so deep. He is in my power. So I will tell him my purpose, and then he can pray to his favorite god."

And he said: "Sir, I have deceived you and brought you to your death, because my wife bade me do it. So pray to your favorite god."

"Brother," said the monkey, "what harm have I done her or you? Why have you planned to kill me?"

"Well," replied the crocodile, "those nectar fruits tasted so sweet that she began to long to eat your heart. That is why I have done this."

Then the quick-witted monkey said: "If that is the case, sir, why didn't you tell me on shore? For then I might have brought with me another heart, very sweet indeed, which I keep in a hole in the rose-apple tree. As it is, I am forlorn in this heart, at being taken to her in vain, without my sweet heart."

When he heard this, the crocodile was delighted and said: "If you feel so, my friend, give me that other heart. And my cross wife will eat it and give up starving herself. Now I will take you back to the rose-apple tree."

So he turned back and swam toward the rose-apple tree, while the monkey murmured a hundred prayers to every kind of a god. And when at last he came to shore, he hopped and jumped farther and farther, climbed up the rose-apple tree, and thought: "Hurrah! My life is saved. Surely, the saying is a good one:

> We dare not trust a rogue; nor must
> We trust in those deserving trust:
> For danger follows, and we fall
> Destroyed and ruined, roots and all.

So today is my rebirthday."

The crocodile said: "My friend and brother, give me the heart, so that my wife may eat it and give up starving herself."

Then the monkey laughed, and scolded him, saying: "You fool! You traitor! How can anyone have two hearts? Go home, and never come back under the rose-apple tree. You know the proverb:

> Whoever trusts a faithless friend
> And twice in him believes,
> Lays hold on death as certainly
> As when a mule conceives."

Now the crocodile was embarrassed when he heard this, and he thought: "Oh, why was I such a fool as to tell him my plan? If I can possibly win his confidence again, I will do it." So he said: "My friend, she has no need of a heart. What I said was just a joke to test your sentiments. Please come to our house as a guest. Your brother's wife is most eager for you."

The monkey said: "Rascal! Go away this moment. I will not come. For

> The hungry man at nothing sticks;
> The poor man has his heartless tricks.
> Tell Handsome, miss, that Theodore
> Will see him in the well no more."

"How was that?" asked the crocodile. And the monkey told the story of

Handsome and Theodore

There was once a frog-king in a well, and his name was Theodore. One day when tormented by his relatives, he climbed from bucket to bucket up the water-wheel, and finally emerged. Then he thought: "How can I pay those relatives back? For the proverb says:

> While one brings comfort in distress,
> Another jeers at pain;
> By paying both as they deserve,
> A man is born again."

With this in mind, he saw a black snake named Handsome crawling out of his hole. And on seeing him, he thought once more: "I will invite that black snake into the well, and clean out all my relatives. For the saying goes:

A sliver draws a sliver out;
  Just so the wise employ
Grim foes to slaughter foes; and thus
  Turn danger into joy."

Having come to this conclusion, he went to the mouth of the hole and called: "Come out! Come out, Handsome! Come out!" But when the snake heard this, he thought: "Whoever he may be that is calling me, he does not belong to my race. That is no snake's voice. And I have no alliance with anyone else in the living world. So I will just stay here until I am sure who he may be. For the proverb says:

Until you have full information
Of prowess, character, and station,
To no man let your trust be given—
Such is the current saw in heaven.

Perhaps it is some conjurer or druggist who is calling me in order to put me in a cage. Or a man who bears a grudge and summons me in the interest of his friend."

So he said: "Who are you?" The other said: "I am a frog-king named Theodore, and I have come to make friends with you."

When the snake heard this, he said: "Why, it is incredible. Does grass make friends with fire? You know the proverb:

You do not, even in a dream,
  Approach the kind of foe
Who kills at sight. What can you mean?
  Why should you babble so?"

But Theodore said: "You are quite right, sir. You are my born enemy. And yet I come to you because I have been insulted. You know well:

When all your property is gone
  And life itself at stake—
To save that life and property
  You grovel to a snake."

The snake said: "Well, who insulted you?" And the frog answered: "My relatives." "But where is your home?" asked the snake. "In a pond? or a well? or a cistern? or a tank?" "My home is in a well," said the frog. "But," said the snake, "I can't get in. And if I could, there is no

place for me to lie while killing your relatives. Begone. Besides, you know:

Eat only what will swallow
And gratify the hollow
Within with good digestion—
Put not your health in question."

But Theodore replied: "No, sir. Come with me. I will show you an easy way into the well. And inside there is a very attractive hole at water-level. There you can lie, and you will find it child's play to finish my relatives."

Then the snake reflected: "Yes, I am old. Now and then, with great effort, I catch one mouse. And often I don't. Yes, yes. The proverb is right:

When strength is ebbing, dying,
  When friends are gone, and wife,
The prudent should be trying
  A carpet-slippery life."

After these reflections, he said: "Well, Theodore, if you really mean it, lead the way. We will go together." "Friend Handsome," said Theodore, "I will take you there by an easy way and show you the resting-place. But you must spare my family. You must not eat any except those I point out."

"My dear fellow," said the snake, "you and I are now friends. Have no fear. I will do nothing but what you wish."

Then he came out of his hole, hugged the frog, and started off with him. So they came to the edge of the well, and the snake went in with the frog by way of the buckets on the water-wheel. Then Theodore settled the black snake in the hole and showed him the relatives. And he ate them all one after another. And lacking relatives, he made up to a few of the friends, and ate them, too, with much circumspection.

Then the snake said: "My dear fellow, I have disposed of your enemies. Please give me something to eat, for you brought me here."

"But, my dear fellow," said Theodore, "you have done what a friend should do. Pray return by way of the buckets."

"Friend Theodore," said Handsome, "you make a serious mistake. How can I go home? My hole was my fortress, and it is surely occupied by strangers. Here I stay, and you must give me a frog at a time, even from your own family. If not, I will eat every one."

At this, Theodore was disturbed in spirit, and reflected: "Oh, what was I about when I brought him here? And if I deny him now, he will eat every one. Yes, the proverb is right:

> Whoever fraternizes with
> Too vigorous a foe,
> Is eating poison, and will soon
> Perceive it to be so.

"So I will give him one a day, even if it must be a friend. For they say:

> Calm with a prudent, pretty bribe
> A foe who may desire
> To seize your all. So calm the sea
> Its fierce subaqueous fire.

And again:

> 'Tis wise, when all is threatened,
> To give a half, and guard
> The other half to win one's ends;
> For total loss is hard.

And yet again:

> No prudent soul would lose
> Much good for little use;
> Prudence implies much gain
> Acquired with little pain."

So he made up his mind, and assigned a frog a day. And the snake ate this one and another, too, behind the frog-king's back. Ah, it is too true:

> As muddied garments dirty
> All that you sit upon,
> So, when one virtue tumbles,
> The rest are quickly gone.

Now one day, while eating frogs, he ate a frog named Theodosius, the son of Theodore. And Theodore, seeing him do it, wailed with piercing shrillness. But his wife said:

> "Why so shrill? You were still
> While you worked your cruel will.
> Hope has fled with your dead;
> Who will save your hapless head?

So think out a plan of escape this very day, or else a scheme to kill him."

Now in course of time the frogs were finished one and all; only Theodore remained. And then Handsome said: "My dear Theodore, I am hungry and all the frogs are finished. Please give me something to eat, for you brought me here."

Theodore said: "My friend, feel no anxiety on that head while I am alive. If you permit me to leave, I will persuade the frogs in other wells, and bring them all here."

The snake said: "Well, I can't eat you, for you are like a brother. Now if you do as you say, you will be like a father."

So the frog planned his escape, and left the well, while Handsome waited there, impatient for his return. But after a long time Handsome said to a lizard that lived in another hole in the same well: "My dear madam, do me a small favor, since Theodore is an old friend of yours. Please go and find him in some pool or other, and take him a message from me. Tell him to return quickly, alone if need be, if no other frogs will come. I cannot live here without him. And tell him that if I hurt him, he may have all the merit I have acquired in a lifetime."

So the lizard did as she was bid, quickly hunted Theodore out, and said: "My dear sir, your friend Handsome is waiting, waiting for your return. Please hurry back. And furthermore, in case of his doing you any harm, he pledges you the merit acquired in a lifetime. So drop all anxious thoughts, and come home." But Theodore said:

> The hungry man at nothing sticks;
> The poor man has his heartless tricks.
> Tell Handsome, miss, that Theodore
> Will see him in the well no more.

And so he sent her back.

"So then, you rascally water-beast! Like Theodore, I will never, never enter your house."

When he heard this, the crocodile said: "My good friend, you are quite wrong. I beg of you to come to my house, and so wipe out my sin of ingratitude. Otherwise, I shall starve myself to death on your doorstep."

"You fool!" said the monkey, "shall I go there

like Flop-Ear, in full sight of the danger, and let myself be killed?"

"But who was Flop-Ear?" asked the crocodile. "And how did he perish in full sight of the dan-ger? Please tell me." So the monkey told the story of
Flop-Ear and Dusty

*   *   *

BIDPAI / Persia

THE TORTOISE AND THE DUCKS

There was a Tortoise that lived for many years in a pond with some Ducks, her old companions, in full contentment and much happiness. But at length there happened so dry a season that there was at last no water in the pond. The Ducks, upon finding themselves forced to move to some other place, went to the Tortoise to take their leave of him. The Tortoise blamed them for leaving him at this time and begged them to carry him along with them. The Ducks replied,—

"We are grieved to leave you in this condition; but we are compelled to go. As to what you propose to take you with us, we have a long journey to make, and you can never follow us, because you cannot fly. On this condition, however, it is possible for us to save you if you can only be enough your own friend to follow our advice and keep a strict and perfect silence. If you will promise us not to speak a word by the way, we will carry you. But we shall meet with some that will talk to us, and then it is ten to one you will be talking. If you are, remember that we now tell you beforehand, it will be your destruction."

"No," answered the Tortoise, "fear me not. I will do whatever you ask."

Things being thus settled, the Ducks ordered the Tortoise to take a little stick and hold it by the middle fast in his mouth; and then exhorting him to keep steady, they took the stick by each end and so raised him up. Thus they carried him along in triumph; but it was not long before they flew over a village and the inhabitants, wondering at the novelty of the sight, fell a shouting with all their might. The Tortoise grew impatient and, at length, not being able to keep silent any longer was going to wish the people's mouths sewed up for making such a clamor. As soon as he opened his mouth to speak, he let go the stick, and so fell to the ground and killed himself.

"The Tortoise and the Ducks" from *Fables of Pilpay*, translated by Thomas D. Scott. Published by E. Lumley, 1852.

THE TIGER, THE BRAHMAN, AND THE JACKAL/India

Once upon a time a tiger was caught in a trap. He tried in vain to get out through the bars, and rolled and bit with rage and grief when he failed.

"The Tiger, the Brahman, and the Jackal" from *Tales of the Punjab* by Flora Annie Steel. Reprinted by permission of Macmillan, London and Basingstroke.

By chance a poor Brahman came by. "Let me out of this cage, O pious one!" cried the tiger.

"Nay, my friend," replied the Brahman mildly, "you would probably eat me if I did."

"Not at all!" swore the tiger with many oaths; "on the contrary, I should be for ever grateful, and serve you as a slave!"

Now when the tiger sobbed and sighed and wept and swore, the pious Brahman's heart softened, and at last he consented to open the door of the cage. Out popped the tiger, and, seizing the poor man, cried, "What a fool you are! What is to prevent my eating you now, for after being cooped up so long I am just terribly hungry!"

In vain the Brahman pleaded for his life; the most he could gain was a promise to abide by the decision of the first three things he chose to question as to the justice of the tiger's action.

So the Brahman first asked a *pipal* tree what it thought of the matter, but the *pipal* tree replied coldly, "What have you to complain about? Don't I give shade and shelter to every one who passes by, and don't they in return tear down my branches to feed their cattle? Don't whimper—be a man!"

Then the Brahman, sad at heart, went farther afield till he saw a buffalo turning a well-wheel; but he fared no better from it, for it answered, "You are a fool to expect gratitude! Look at me! While I gave milk they fed me on cotton-seed and oil-cake, but now I am dry they yoke me here, and give me refuse as fodder!"

The Brahman, still more sad, asked the road to give him its opinion.

"My dear sir," said the road, "how foolish you are to expect anything else! Here am I, useful to everybody, yet all, rich and poor, great and small, trample on me as they go past, giving me nothing but the ashes of their pipes and the husks of their grain!"

On this the Brahman turned back sorrowfully, and on the way he met a jackal, who called out, "Why, what's the matter, Mr. Brahman? You look as miserable as a fish out of water!"

Then the Brahman told him all that had occurred. "How very confusing!" said the jackal, when the recital was ended; "would you mind telling me over again? for everything seems so mixed up!"

The Brahman told it all over again, but the jackal shook his head in a distracted sort of way, and still could not understand.

"It's very odd," said he sadly, "but it all seems to go in at one ear and out at the other! I will go to the place where it all happened, and then perhaps I shall be able to give a judgment."

So they returned to the cage, by which the tiger was waiting for the Brahman, and sharpening his teeth and claws.

"You've been away a long time!" growled the savage beast, "but now let us begin our dinner."

"*Our* dinner!" thought the wretched Brahman, as his knees knocked together with fright; "what a remarkably delicate way of putting it!"

"Give me five minutes, my lord!" he pleaded, "in order that I may explain matters to the jackal here, who is somewhat slow in his wits."

The tiger consented, and the Brahman began the whole story over again, not missing a single detail, and spinning as long a yarn as possible.

"Oh, my poor brain! oh, my poor brain!" cried the jackal, wringing his paws. "Let me see! how did it all begin? You were in the cage, and the tiger came walking by—"

"Pooh!" interrupted the tiger, "what a fool you are! *I* was in the cage."

"Of course!" cried the jackal, pretending to tremble with fright; "yes! I was in the cage—no, I wasn't—dear! dear! where are my wits? Let me see—the tiger was in the Brahman, and the cage came walking by—no, that's not it either! Well, don't mind me, but begin your dinner, for I shall never understand!"

"Yes, you shall!" returned the tiger, in a rage at the jackal's stupidity; "I'll *make* you understand! Look here—I am the tiger——"

"Yes, my lord!"

"And that is the Brahman——"

"Yes, my lord!"

"And that is the cage——"

"Yes, my lord!"

"And I was in the cage—do you understand?"

"Yes—no—Please, my lord—"

"Well?" cried the tiger, impatiently.

"Please, my lord!—how did you get in?"

"How!—why, in the usual way, of course!"

"Oh dear me!—my head is beginning to whirl again! Please don't be angry, my lord, but what is the usual way?"

At this the tiger lost patience, and, jumping into the cage, cried, "This way! Now do you understand how it was?"

"Perfectly!" grinned the jackal, as he dexterously shut the door; "and if you will permit me to say so, I think matters will remain as they were!"

AESOP'S FABLES

THE FOX AND THE GRAPES

A fox, feeling very hungry, made his way to a vineyard near by, where he knew he would find a plentiful supply of grapes.

The season had been a good one, and he licked his lips when he saw the huge bunches hanging from the vine.

His joy was short-lived, however, for, try as he would, the grapes were just out of his reach.

At last, tired by his vain efforts, he turned away in disgust, remarking: "Anyone who wants them may have them for me. They are too green and sour for my palate; I would not touch them even if they were given to me."

It is a mean nature which affects to dislike that which it is unable to obtain.

THE DOG AND THE SHADOW

A dog had stolen a piece of meat out of a butcher's shop, and was crossing a river on his way home when he saw his own reflection in the stream below. Thinking that it was another dog, with a larger piece of meat in his mouth, he made up his mind to get that also; but in snapping at the shadow he dropped the meat he was carrying, and so lost all.

He who grasps at the shadow may lose the substance.

THE CROW AND THE PITCHER

A crow was almost dying of thirst when he spied a pitcher at no great distance. When he came up to it, however, he found that it was nearly empty; the little water in it was so low that, try as he might, he was unable to reach it. Thereupon he tried to break the pitcher, then to overturn it, but his strength was not sufficient to do one or the other.

At last, seeing a number of small pebbles close by, he took these and dropped them, one by one, into the pitcher until the water rose to the brim and he was able to quench his thirst.

Necessity is the mother of invention.

THE FOX AND THE CROW

A crow snatched a piece of cheese from a window and flew with it to a tree, intent on enjoying her prize. A fox spied her with the dainty morsel and stood beneath the branch on which she sat.

"O crow," he said, "what beautiful wings you have, and what bright eyes! What a graceful neck is yours, and the plumage of your breast is like an eagle's! Surely your voice must equal your beauty. Pray sing to me and let me hear for myself." The crow, pleased with the flattery, opened her mouth to give a loud caw—and down fell the cheese!

The fox snapped up the dainty morsel and remarked, as he walked away: "Whatever I have said of her beauty, I will make no remarks concerning her brains!"

Beware of flatterers.

THE ANT AND THE GRASSHOPPER

On a cold and frosty day an ant which had laid up some corn in the summer-time was bringing it out to dry.

A grasshopper, half dead with hunger, begged the ant to give him a morsel to preserve his life.

"What were you doing," asked the ant, "all through last summer?"

"Oh," said the grasshopper, "I was not idle. I sang all day long."

The ant laughed and, collecting her grain, said, "Since you could sing all the summer, you may dance all the winter."

We should never lose a good opportunity.

THE LION AND THE MOUSE

A lion was sleeping in his lair when a mouse, not knowing where he was going, ran over the nose of the mighty beast and awakened him.

The lion put his paw upon the frightened little creature and was about to make an end of him, when the mouse, in a pitiful voice, said, "Spare me, I pray you, for I had lost my way and was so scared that I did not know what I was doing. Do not stain your honourable paws with so tiny a creature as me."

The fright of his little captive put the lion into a good humour and he generously let him go.

Now it happened soon after that the lion, while hunting in the woods, fell into a trap set for him, and finding himself entangled beyond hope of escape, he set up a roar that filled the forest with its echo.

The mouse, recognizing the voice of his former captor, ran to the spot and, without wasting a moment, set to work to nibble the knot in the cord that held the lion.

His teeth were sharp, and so it was not long before the noble beast was once more at liberty, wiser by the knowledge that the most lowly creature may have it in his power to return a kindness.

An act of kindness is a good investment.

THE TOWN MOUSE AND THE COUNTRY MOUSE

Once upon a time a country mouse who had a friend in town invited him, for the sake of old times, to pay him a visit in the country.

The invitation being accepted in due course, the country mouse, though plain and rough in his habits of living, opened his heart in honour of an old friend. There was not a carefully stored up morsel that he did not bring forth out of his larder—peas and barley, cheese-parings and nuts —hoping by quantity to make up what he feared was wanting in quality.

The town mouse, who was used to more dainty fare, at first picked a bit here and a bit there, while the host sat nibbling a blade of barley straw.

At length he exclaimed, "How is it, my good friend, that you can endure the dullness of this life? You are living like a toad in a hole. You can't really prefer these lonely rocks and woods to streets filled with shops and carriages and men! Believe me, you are wasting your time here. We must make the most of life while it lasts. A mouse, you know, does not live for ever. So come with me, and I'll show you life and the town."

These fine words were too much for the simple country mouse, and he agreed to go with his friend to town.

It was late in the evening when the two crept into the city, and midnight ere they reached the great house where the town mouse lived. Here were couches of crimson velvet, carvings in ivory, everything, in short, that told of wealth and ease. On the table were the remains of a splendid meal, and it was now the turn of the town mouse to play the host; he ran to and fro to supply his friend's wants, pressed dish upon dish and dainty upon dainty, and, as though he were waiting on a king, tasted every course before placing it before his rustic cousin.

The country mouse, for his part, tried to appear quite at home, and blessed the good fortune that had brought such a change in his way of life; when, in the midst of his enjoyment, as he was wondering how he could have been content with the poor fare he was used to at home, on a sudden the door opened and a party of ladies and gentlemen, returning from the theatre, entered the room.

The two friends jumped from the table in the greatest fright and hid themselves in the first corner they could reach. When the room was quiet again they ventured to creep out, but the barking of dogs drove them back in still greater terror than before. At length, when all the household was asleep, the country mouse stole out from his hiding-place, and, bidding his host good-bye, whispered in his ear, "My good friend, this fine mode of living may do for those who like it; but give me barley bread in peace and security before the daintiest feast where Fear and Care lie in wait."

A humble life with peace and quiet is better than a splendid one with danger and risk.

THE HARE AND THE TORTOISE

A hare met a tortoise one day and made fun of him for the slow and clumsy way in which he walked.

The tortoise laughed and said, "I will run a race with you any time that you choose."

"Very well," replied the hare, "we will start at once."

The tortoise immediately set off in his slow and steady way without waiting a moment or looking back. The hare, on the other hand, treated the matter as a joke and decided to take a little nap before starting, for she thought that it would be an easy matter to overtake her rival.

The tortoise plodded on, and meanwhile the hare overslept herself, with the result that she arrived at the winning-post only to see that the tortoise had got in before her.

Slow and steady wins the race.

THE FOX AND THE STORK

A fox one day invited a stork to dinner and amused himself, at the expense of his guest, by providing nothing for the entertainment but some thin soup in a shallow dish.

This the fox lapped up very quickly, while the stork, unable to gain a mouthful with her long, narrow bill, was as hungry at the end of the dinner as when she began.

The fox expressed his regret at seeing her eat so sparingly, and feared that the dish was not seasoned to her liking.

The stork said little, but begged that the fox would do her the honour of returning the visit on the following day, which invitation Reynard readily accepted.

The fox kept the appointment, and, having greeted his hostess, turned his attention to the dinner placed before them.

To his dismay Reynard saw that the repast was served in a narrow-necked vessel, and, while the stork was able to thrust in her long bill and take her fill, he was obliged to content himself with licking the outside of the jar.

Unable to satisfy his hunger, he retired with as good grace as he could, knowing that he could hardly find fault with his hostess, for she had only paid him back in his own coin.

Those who love practical jokes must be prepared to laugh when one is made at their expense.

THE WIND AND THE SUN

Once upon a time when everything could talk, the Wind and the Sun fell into an argument as to which was the stronger. Finally they decided to put the matter to a test; they would see which one could make a certain man, who was walking along the road, throw off his cape. The Wind tried first. He blew and he blew and he blew. The harder and colder he blew, the tighter the traveler wrapped his cape about him. The Wind finally gave up and told the Sun to try. The Sun began to smile and as it grew warmer and warmer, the traveler was comfortable once more. But the Sun shone brighter and brighter until the man grew so hot, the sweat poured out on his face, he became weary, and seating himself on a stone, he quickly threw his cape to the ground.

Gentleness accomplished what force could not.

THE PIGEON-HAWK AND THE TORTOISE/American Indian

The Pigeon-Hawk challenged the Tortoise to a race: but the Tortoise declined it unless the Hawk would consent to run several days' journey. The Hawk very quickly consented, and they immediately set out. The Tortoise knew that if he was to obtain the victory it must be by great diligence; so he went down into the earth and, taking a straight line, stopped for nothing. The

Hawk, on the contrary, knowing that he could easily beat his competitor, kept carelessly flying this way and that way in the air, stopping to visit one friend and then another, till so much time had been lost that when he came in sight of the winning point, the Tortoise had just come up out of the earth and gained the prize.

TORTOISE AND THE BABOON/Africa—the Nyanja

Kathleen Arnott

One evening when the tortoise was crawling slowly home, he met the baboon on his path.

'Hello, old fellow,' said the baboon heartily. 'Have you found much to eat today?'

'No,' replied Tortoise sadly. 'Very little indeed.'

The baboon danced up and down, chortling with laughter at an idea which had just come to him.

'Follow me, poor old Tortoise,' he exclaimed, 'and when you reach my home I will have supper all ready for you.'

'Thank you. Thank you,' said the grateful Tortoise, as the baboon turned round and bounced gaily along the path that led to his home.

Tortoise followed as fast as he could, which was very slow indeed, especially when he went uphill. Once or twice he stopped to rest, when the ground became so bumpy that he got disheartened, but holding in his mind the picture of a wonderful feast, he plodded on.

At last he reached the place in the bush that the baboon called his home. There he was, leaping about and grinning to himself, and as soon as he caught sight of Tortoise he exclaimed:

'Bless my tail! What a long time you have taken to get here. I declare it must be tomorrow already!'

'I'm so sorry,' said Tortoise, puffing a little after his long journey. 'But I'm sure you have had plenty of time to get the supper ready, so do not grumble at me.'

'O yes, indeed!' replied the baboon, rubbing

his hands together. 'Supper's all ready. All you have to do is to climb up and get it. Look!' he said, pointing to the top of a tree. 'Three pots of millet-beer, brewed especially for you.'

The poor tortoise looked up at the pots which the baboon had wedged in the branches high above his head. He knew he could never reach them, and the baboon knew that too.

'Bring one down for me, there's a good friend,' begged Tortoise, but the baboon climbed the tree in the twinkling of an eye and shouted down to him:

'O no! Anybody who wants supper with me must climb up to get it.'

So poor Tortoise could only begin his long homeward journey with a very empty stomach, cursing at his inability to climb trees. But as he went he worked out a splendid plan for getting his own back on the unkind baboon.

A few days later the baboon had an invitation to eat with Tortoise. He was very surprised, but knowing how slow and good-natured the tortoise was, the baboon said to himself:

'O well! The fellow evidently saw the joke and bears me no malice. I'll go along and see what I can get out of him.'

At the appointed time the baboon set out along the track that led to Tortoise's home. Now it was the dry season, when many bush fires occur which leave the ground scorched and black. Just beyond the river the baboon found a wide stretch of burnt and blackened grass, over which he bounded towards Tortoise, who stood waiting beside a cooking pot from which issued the most savoury of smells.

'Ah, it's my friend the baboon!' said Tortoise. 'I'm very pleased to see you. But did your mother

"Tortoise and the Baboon" from *African Myths and Legends*, © 1962 Kathleen Arnott. Used by permission of Henry Z. Walck, Inc., publisher, and Oxford University Press.

never teach you that you must wash your hands before meals? Just look at them! They're as black as soot.'

The baboon looked at his hands, which were indeed very black from crossing the burnt patch of ground.

'Now run back to the river and wash,' said Tortoise, 'and when you are clean I will give you some supper.'

The baboon scampered across the black earth and washed himself in the river, but when he came to return to Tortoise he found he had to cross the burnt ground again and so arrived as dirty as before.

'That will never do! I told you that you could only eat with me if you were clean. Go back and

wash again! And you had better be quick about it because I have started my supper already,' said Tortoise, with his mouth full of food.

The poor baboon went back to the river time and again, but try as he would he got his hands and feet black each time he returned, and Tortoise refused to give him any of the delicious food that was fast disappearing. As Tortoise swallowed the last morsel, the baboon realized he had been tricked and with a cry of rage he crossed the burnt ground for the last time and ran all the way home.

'That will teach you a lesson, my friend,' said the Tortoise, smiling, as, well-fed and contented, he withdrew into his shell for a long night's sleep.

THE FROG'S SADDLE HORSE / Angola

Once upon a time the Elephant and the Frog went courting the same girl, and at last she promised to marry the Elephant. One day the Frog said to her,

"That Elephant is nothing but my saddle horse."

When the Elephant came to call that night the girl said to him: "You are nothing but the Frog's saddle horse!"

When he heard this the Elephant went off at once and found the Frog, and asked him:

"Did you tell the girl that I am nothing but your saddle horse?"

"Oh, no indeed," said the Frog, "I never told her that!"

Thereupon they both started back together to see the girl. On the way the Frog said:

"Grandpa Elephant, I am too tired to walk any further. Let me climb up on your back."

"Certainly," said the Elephant, "Climb up, my grandson." So the Frog climbed up on the Elephant's back. Presently he said:

"Grandpa Elephant, I am afraid that I am going to fall off. Let me take some little cords and fasten them to your tusks, to hold on by."

"Certainly, my grandson," said the Elephant; and he stood still while the Frog did as he had asked. Presently the Frog spoke again:

"Grandpa Elephant, please stop and let me pick a green branch so that I can keep the flies off of you."

"Certainly, my grandson," said the Elephant, and he stood quite still while the Frog broke off the branch. Pretty soon they drew near to the house where the girl lived. And when she saw them coming, the Elephant plodding patiently along with the little Frog perched on his broad back, holding the cords in one hand, and waving the green branch she came to meet them, calling out,

"Mr. Elephant, you certainly are nothing but the Frog's saddle horse!"

THE BOAR AND THE CHAMELEON / Madagascar

A boar hunting for food, met a Chameleon at the foot of a tree.

"Hello!" said the Boar, "you act as though you were half dead, dragging yourself along in that lazy way!"

"Don't be so proud of your strength, brother Boar," retorted the Chameleon, "I am a match for you any day!"

"Hold your tongue, you wretched little beast!" rejoined the Boar angrily. "If you think so well of yourself, will you run a race with me?"

"Of course I will," agreed the Chameleon readily. "Do you see that little hill over there? Let that be the goal."

"All right," said the Boar, and at once started to run. But the tricky little Chameleon caught hold of the Boar's tail. When the hill was reached, the Boar said, "Well, Chameleon, where are you now?"

"Here I am," said the Chameleon, who had been quick to let go of the Boar's tail and drop to the earth.

"Well, you run faster than I thought you could," said the Boar. "Let's try again. This time I won't let myself be beaten!" So they ran again and the Chameleon repeated his trick and for the second time reached the goal at the same time as his enemy.

"Haha! Haha! Where are you this time, little brother?" called the Boar gleefully.

"Here I am, big brother!" shouted back the tricky little Chameleon. And so the Boar, puzzled and ashamed, had to admit that the Chameleon had won the race.

"The Boar and the Chameleon" from *An Argosy of Fables*, edited by Frederick Taber Cooper. Copyright © 1921 by Frederick A. Stokes Company, New York. Reprinted by permission of Platt & Munk, publishers.

THE JACKAL WHO TRIED TO COPY THE LION/Asia

Once there was a lion who, not unjustly, considered himself to be king of the other animals, because he was so powerful and strong. He lived in a lair in the middle of a thick forest, and every morning he stepped out of his lair, looked all around him, and three times gave a dreadful roar. Then he walked majestically forth to find his prey, kill it and eat until he was full. When he had finished his meal he turned and walked back into the forest.

Every day a small timid jackal crept behind the King of the Beasts, followed him, and sat at a respectful distance behind him, waiting hungrily and greedily until the lion left his meal and returned into the forest. The jackal then pounced on the remains of the royal meal and gobbled it up. One day the lion left over so much of his kill that the jackal ate until he was almost about to burst, and could barely manage to swallow the last bite.

With a stomach full of meat the jackal felt very brave. "*Who* does this lion in the forest think he *is*? Is he as strong and as clever as *I* am? Indeed not! From now on I will rule this forest. Every morning I shall step out of my cave, look all round me and give three terrible roars. Then I shall sally majestically forth to find and devour my prey!"

With these thoughts he ambled to his den and went to sleep. The next morning he stepped outside, looked all round and tried to give three

"The Jackal Who Tried To Copy the Lion" from *The Big Book of Animal Fables*, edited by Margaret Green, 1965. By permission of Dobson Books Ltd., London.

terrible roars. But however wide he opened his mouth, all that came out was the miserable howl of a jackal, which made none of the animals tremble.

So, if the jackal did not want to go hungry, all he could do was continue humbly to follow the King of the Animals, wait till he had eaten his fill and then finish up the remains of the meal.

THE BITTERN AND THE MUSSEL / China

Once on the bank of the River Yi a Mussel was basking in the sunshine. All at once a Bittern, happening to pass by, discovered the Mussel and pecked at it. The Mussel snapped its shell together and nipped the bird's beak; but no matter how tightly the Mussel nipped, the bird would not withdraw his beak. Presently the Bittern said:

"The Bittern and the Mussel" from *An Argosy of Fables*, edited by Frederick Taber Cooper. Copyright © 1921 by Frederick A. Stokes Company, New York. Reprinted by permission of Platt & Munk, publishers.

"If you don't open your shell to-day, if you don't open your shell to-morrow, there will be a dead Mussel."

The shell-fish said in reply:

"If you don't take your beak out to-day, if you don't take your beak out to-morrow, there will be a dead Bittern."

But as neither could make up its mind to loose its hold upon the other, a fisherman, who happened to come that way, seized the pair of them and carried them off for his dinner.

Literary Fables

THE BAT AND THE TWO WEASELS/France

La Fontaine

A BAT in his blind flight,
   Rushed headlong into an old Weasel's hole,
Who hated Mice with all his heart and soul,
And straight made at him, furious at the sight.
"What! Have you dared to show your hateful
    face
   Inside my house—
One of your mischievious, accursed race?
As sure as I'm a Weasel, you're a Mouse!"
"Spare me," said the trembling refugee.
   "That really is not my vocation;
Some wretched slanderer, I plainly see,
   Has wronged me in your estimation.
A Mouse?—Oh, dear, no! What? With wings,
    like me
   I am a Bird, I say,

Long live the feathered race, that skims the air!"
   Such reasoning sounded fair;
Proof positive, it seemed, was there,
   And the Bat went his way.
Some two days afterwards the stupid creature
Into a second Weasel's lodgings flew,
Who was at feud with all the feathered crew:
Again, by reason of his doubtful feature,
He found himself in peril of his life:
   Rising to meet him, the Weasel's long-nosed
    Wife
Thought him a Bird, and was prepared to eat him.
Again he made his piteous protest heard:
   "Oh, Madam, you're mistaken! I a Bird!
   Why, you can't see!
What makes a Bird? Feathers, not fur, like me!
No—I'm a Mouse: Long live the Mice and Rats!
   And Jove confound all Cats!"
   So by his two-fold plea
The Trimmer kept his life and liberty.

CHANTICLEER AND THE FOX/England and the United States

Barbara Cooney

Once upon a time a poor widow, getting on in years, lived in a small cottage beside a grove which stood in a little valley. This widow, about whom I shall tell you my tale, had patiently led a very simple life since the day her husband died. By careful management she was able to take care of herself and her two daughters.

She had only three large sows, three cows, and also a sheep called Molly.

Her bedroom was very sooty, as was her kitchen in which she ate many a scanty meal. She was never sick from overeating. Her table was usually set with only white and black—milk and dark bread, of which there was no shortage—and sometimes there was broiled bacon and an egg or two, for she was, as it were, a kind of dairywoman.

She had a yard, fenced all around with sticks, in which she had a rooster named Chanticleer. For crowing there was not his equal in all the land. His voice was merrier than the merry organ that plays in church, and his crowing from his resting place was more trustworthy than a clock. His comb was redder than fine coral and turreted like a castle wall, his bill was black and shone like jet, and his legs and toes were like azure. His nails were whiter than the lily, and his feathers were like burnished gold.

Now this fine rooster had seven hens, all colored exceedingly like him. The hen with the prettiest throat was called fair Demoiselle Partlet. She was polite, discreet, debonair, and companionable, and she had conducted herself so well since the time that she was seven days old that, truly, she held the heart of Chanticleer all tightly locked. It was a great joy to hear them sing in sweet harmony when the bright sun began to rise. For in those days, so I'm told, beasts and birds could talk and sing.

And so it happened, one day at dawn, as Chanticleer sat on his perch surrounded by the hens, that he began to groan in his throat like a man troubled by his dreams. When Partlet heard him moaning this way she was frightened and said: "Dear heart, what ails you that you groan in such a manner?"

And he answered saying: "Madam, I dreamed just now that I was in much danger. I dreamed that I was roaming up and down within our yard, when I saw a beast like a hound which tried to grab my body and would have killed me. His color was between yellow and red, and his tail and both ears were tipped with black, different from the rest of his fur. His snout was small and his two eyes glowed. I almost died of fear at the sight of him; doubtless that's what caused my groaning."

"Go on!" she said. "Shame on you, you know I cannot love a coward, by my faith! Haven't you a man's heart and haven't you a beard? Be merry, husband. Do not fear dreams."

"Thank you, Madam Partlet," he said, "for your learned advice. I do say that when I see the beauty of your face all scarlet red about the eyes, my fears die away."

And with these words he flew down from the rafter, along with all the hens, for it was day. With a clucking he called them all to some grain which he found lying about the yard. He was as regal as a prince in his palace and was no longer afraid. He looked like a lion as he roamed up and down on his toes; he barely set foot to the earth.

Chanticleer, walking in all his pride, with his seven wives beside him, cast up his eyes at the bright sun. He crowed with a happy voice, "Listen how the happy birds sing, and how fresh flowers grow; my heart is full of gaiety and joy.

But suddenly a sorrowful event overtook him.

A fox, tipped with black, and full of sly wickedness, had lived in the grove three years. That same night he burst through the hedges into the yard where fair Chanticleer and his wives were in the habit of going. And this fox lay quietly in a bed of herbs until almost noon of that day.

Partlet, with all her sisters nearby, lay merrily bathing in the sand, with her back to the sun, and the lordly Chanticleer sang more joyfully than the mermaid in the sea.

Now it happened that, as he cast his eye upon a butterfly among the herbs, Chanticleer became aware of the fox lying low. He had no desire to crow then, but at once cried, "Cok! Cok!" and started up like a man frightened in his heart.

And he would have fled at once, if the fox had not said: "My dear sir, alas, where are you going? Are you afraid of me, your father's friend? The reason I came was only to listen to you sing. For, truly, you have as merry a voice as any angel in heaven. My lord your father—God bless his soul —and also your courteous mother did me the great honor of visiting my house. Except for you I have never heard anyone who could sing as your father did in the morning. In order to make his voice stronger, he would close both his eyes. And he would stand on his tiptoes and stretch forth his long slender neck. Now sing, sir, for holy charity; let's see whether you can sing as well as your father."

Chanticleer began to beat his wings. He stood high on his toes and stretched his neck, closed his eyes and crowed loudly. At once the fox jumped up, grabbed Chanticleer by the throat, and carried him toward the woods.

Alas, that Chanticleer flew down from the rafters! Alas, that his wife took no heed of dreams! And all this trouble came on a Friday.

Such a cry was never made as was made by all the hens in the yard when they saw Chanticleer captured. The poor widow and her two daughters heard the woeful cries of the hens and at once ran out of doors. They saw the fox going toward the grove, carrying away the rooster. "Help! Help! Woe is me! Look, a fox!" they screamed, and ran after him.

The cows, the sheep, and even the hogs, so frightened were they by the shouting, ran after him, too. They ran so hard they thought their hearts would burst.

The neighbors' ducks quacked as if they were to be killed; and their geese, from fear, flew over the trees; the noise was so terrible that the bees swarmed from their hive. It seemed that heaven would fall.

Now, good people, I beg you all to listen. This rooster in the fox's mouth spoke to the fox in spite of his fear, saying, "Sir, if I were you, so help me God, I would say, 'Turn back, you proud peasants! I have reached the edge of the wood now; the rooster shall stay here. In spite of you I will eat him, in faith, and not be long about it.'"

"In faith," the fox answered, "it shall be done." As soon as he spoke the words, the rooster nimbly broke away from his mouth and flew at once high into a tree.

When the fox saw that the rooster was gone, he said, "Alas! Oh, Chanticleer, alas! I have done you a bad turn. I frightened you when I grabbed you and took you out of the yard. But, sir, I did it without evil intention. Come down and I shall tell you what I meant."

"Nay, then," said Chanticleer. "Never again shall you with your flattery get me to sing with my eyes closed. For he who closes his eyes when he should watch, God let him never prosper."

"No," said the fox, "but God bring misfortune to him who is so careless about his self-control as to prattle when he should hold his peace."

"See," said the widow as the fox slunk into the grove, "that is the result of trusting in flattery."

And she marched with her flock back to the yard in the little valley.

FABLES FROM RUSSIA

THE MOUSE WHO LIVED UNDER THE GRANARY

Leo Tolstoy

There was once a mouse who lived under a granary. And in the floor of the granary there was a little hole through which the grain sifted.

Thus the mouse lived well. He wanted to show off before his friends, so he gnawed at the hole until it was larger, and then invited the other mice to be his guests. "Come to my place," he said to them, "and I'll treat everyone. There'll be food for all."

When his guests arrived he led them to the hole, only to find that it was no longer there.

The large hole had attracted the peasant's notice, and he had stopped it up.

MISUSE OF A NAME

Ivan Krylov

A donkey met a pig in tears by the roadside. "Why are you crying?" asked the donkey, wishing to help.

"The Mouse Who Lived under the Granary" from *Leo Tolstoy's Fables and Fairy Tales*, translated by Ann Dunnigan. Copyright © 1962 by Ann Dunnigan. Reprinted by arrangement with The New American Library, Inc., New York.

"Misuse of a Name" from *The Big Book of Animal Fables*, edited by Margaret Green. By permission of Dobson Books Ltd., London.

"How can I do anything else," replied the pig. "When human beings swear, they keep on using my name. They always insult each other in my name! If somebody has done something bad, they say he's a swine; if somebody has deceived an- other, they say he's a swine; if there's any dirt or untidiness, they say, how perfectly swinish!"

The donkey gave the matter a great deal of thought and then he said sympathetically, "Yes, it really *is* swinish!"

THE LITTLE GIRL AND THE WOLF

James Thurber

One afternoon a big wolf waited in a dark forest for a little girl to come along carrying a basket of food to her grandmother. Finally a little girl did come along and she was carrying a basket of food. "Are you carrying that basket to your grandmother?" asked the wolf. The little girl said yes, she was. So the wolf asked her where her grandmother lived and the little girl told him and he disappeared into the wood.

When the little girl opened the door of her grandmother's house she saw that there was some- body in bed with a nightcap and nightgown on. She had approached no nearer than twenty-five feet from the bed when she saw that it was not her grandmother but the wolf, for even in a nightcap a wolf does not look any more like your grandmother than the Metro-Goldwyn lion looks like Calvin Coolidge. So the little girl took an automatic out of her basket and shot the wolf dead.

Moral: It is not so easy to fool little girls nowadays as it used to be.

THE SCOTTY WHO KNEW TOO MUCH

James Thurber

Several summers ago there was a Scotty who went to the country for a visit. He decided that all the farm dogs were cowards, because they were afraid of a certain animal that had a white stripe down its back. "You are a pussy-cat and I can lick you," the Scotty said to the farm dog who lived in the house where the Scotty was visiting. "I can lick the little animal with the white stripe, too. Show him to me." "Don't you want to ask any questions about him?" said the farm dog. "Naw," said the Scotty. "*You* ask the questions."

So the farm dog took the Scotty into the woods and showed him the white-striped animal and the Scotty closed in on him, growling and slashing. It was all over in a moment and Scotty lay on his back. When he came to, the farm dog said, "What happened?" "He threw vitriol," said the Scotty, "but he never laid a glove on me."

A few days later the farm dog told the Scotty there was another animal all the farm dogs were afraid of. "Lead me to him," said the Scotty. "I can lick anything that doesn't wear horseshoes." "Don't you want to ask questions about him?"

"The Little Girl and the Wolf" and "The Scotty Who Knew Too Much," from *Fables of Our Time*, published by Harper & Row, New York. Copyright © 1940 James Thurber. Copyright © 1968 Helen Thurber. Originally printed in *The New Yorker*.

said the farm dog. "Naw," said the Scotty. "Just show me where he hangs out." So the farm dog led him to a place in the woods and pointed out the little animal when he came along. "A clown," said the Scotty, "a pushover," and he closed in, leading with his left and exhibiting some mighty fancy footwork. In less than a second the Scotty was flat on his back, and when he woke up the farm dog was pulling quills out of him. "What happened?" said the farm dog. "He pulled a knife on me," said the Scotty, "but at least I have learned how you fight out here in the country, and now I am going to beat *you* up." So he closed in on the farm dog, holding his nose with one front paw to ward off the vitriol and covering his eyes with the other front paw to keep out the knives. The Scotty couldn't see his opponent and he couldn't smell his opponent and he was so badly beaten that he had to be taken back to the city and put in a nursing home.

Moral: It is better to ask some of the questions than to know all the answers.

Related Reading

Aesop. *Aesop: Five Centuries of Illustrated Fables.* Selected by John J. McKendry. New York: Metropolitan Museum, 1964. The illustrations are from the museum's collection of prints. Both scholars and children will enjoy this beautiful book. Provides an overview of book illustrations from 1476 to 1963. (Grades 4–6)

Artzybasheff, Boris, editor-illustrator. *Aesop's Fables.* New York: Viking, 1933. Beautiful edition based on the Coxall edition of 1722 and the James edition of 1848. (Grade 5–up)

Brown, Marcia. *Once a Mouse.* New York: Scribner, 1961. An excellent picture book treatment of a fable from *The Hitopadesa,* an old collection of Indian fables. Awarded the 1962 Caldecott Medal. (Grades K–4)

Ciardi, John. *John J. Plenty and Fiddler Dan.* Illustrated by Madeleine Gekiere. Philadelphia: Lippincott, 1963. A remarkable reworking of the ant and grasshopper fable with echoes of the Orpheus myth and a poet's insight on the role of the artist in society. (Grade 4–up)

Cooney, Barbara. *Chanticleer and the Fox.* Adapted from Geoffrey Chaucer. New York: Crowell, 1958. A beautifully illustrated adaptation of the "Nun's Priest's Tale" from the *Canterbury Tales.* Perhaps the best American picture book. Awarded the 1959 Caldecott Medal. (Grade 4–up)

Gaer, Joseph. *The Fables of India.* Illustrated by Randy Monk. Boston: Little, Brown, 1955. Fables from *The Panchatantra, The Hitopadesa,* and *The Jatakas.* Interesting supplement to the more familiar fables of Aesop. (Grades 5–7)

Galdone, Paul, reteller-illustrator. *The Monkey and the Crocodile, A Jataka Tale from India.* New York: Seabury, 1969. A brief picture book adaptation of the first fable in this chapter. (Grades K–2)

Jacobs, Joseph, editor. *The Fables of Aesop.* Illustrated by David Levine. Afterword by Clifton Fadiman. New York: Macmillan, 1964. Introduction by Jacobs traces the history of the Aesopic fables. Originally published in 1894. (Grades 4–6)

La Fontaine. *The North Wind and the Sun.* Illustrated by Brian Wildsmith. New York: F. Watts, 1963. A simplified retelling, strikingly illustrated. (Grades K–3)

Reeves, James, reteller. *Fables from Aesop.* Illustrated by Maurice Wilson. New York: Walck, 1962. An interesting retelling of fifty-one fables. The dialogue will interest youngsters. (Grades 4–6)

Ryder, Arthur W., translator. *The Panchatantra.* Chicago: University of Chicago Press, 1956. The best source for these Indian fables. Many can be read aloud to older elementary children and some junior high schoolers will be interested in reading the book. See the first fable in this chapter for an excerpt.

Chapter 6
Folktales

Illustration by George Cruikshank for *Hop-o'-My-Thumb and the Seven-League Boots*. Bogue, 1854. Reprinted in *Illustrations of Children's Books, 1744–1945* by Bertha E. Mahony et al., 1958. Courtesy of The Horn Book, Inc.

While universal superstitions, fears, ideals, and social codes can be found in folktales, they have always been primarily used for entertainment. The Cinderella tales certainly advocate kindness, but the morality is integrated within and second to the rise from poverty to riches, quite unlike fables, in which the moral position is usually paramount.

Folktales may be simple or may be complex, brief anecdotes or sustained action, depending upon the number and variety of motifs. A motif is the smallest part of a tale that can exist independently; it may appear in several variants of the same tale or be combined with other motifs to form an entirely different narrative. Stith Thompson in *The Folktale* identifies three types of motifs. The first consists of the actors in tales, some of whom are relatively standard characters, found again and again in folktales from all parts of the world. They may be people: the abused child, the youngest of three children, the handsome prince, the wicked stepmother, the *dümmling*, the clever trickster. Some are animals: the sly fox, in the European tradition; the dumb fox in the Brer Rabbit cycle; any talking beasts that actively participate in the story. Supernatural beings may also be motifs: the fairy godmother, wicked or stupid ogres, dwarfs, trolls, witches, enchanted people. In addition to these standard characters, there are numerous miscellaneous motifs that regularly occur in folktales, enchanted places and magical objects, for example. The third type of motif consists of single plot incidents: the quest upon which many folktale heroes and heroines must go; the possession of extraordinary powers, such as superhuman speed, strength, or eyesight; rescue from a harsh life.

Simple Tales, short anecdotes or jests, have only one of these plot incidents, commonly called narrative motifs. "The Hunters and the Antelope" is little more than a statement of the men's possession of extraordinary powers. In contrast, "The Seven Simeons," a much longer narrative, recounts the adventures of seven brothers who also have superhuman abilities. Because of its length and more involved plot, "The Seven Simeons" is classified as a Complex Tale. Such stories have a series of narrative motifs which develop around a conflict that must be overcome.

The distinction between Simple and Complex Tales is not always easily made, because some stories have very simple plot structures but complicated stylistic patterns. Many cumulative tales are of this intermediate type. "The Three Billy Goats Gruff" is little more than three goats trying to cross a bridge, but the repetition adds complexity to this short tale.

Both Simple and Complex Tales can operate within the real world or the world of magic. Both can deal with animals, people, and supernatural beings.

Most folktales begin quickly, with little introduction, delineation of characters, or location of scene. While the action takes place in a "small hut," "a palace," "a forest," or "a far distant land," in European folktales there is no further attempt to describe the scene. Action moves rapidly, usually along a straight plot line, with no detours.

Eastern folktales, however, after brief introductions, have a less direct line of action. Their plots often include several episodes, in which one problem or situation leads into another, which in turn leads into a third. These tales employ more embroidery and elaboration of both action and language. When rewritten for English-reading children they usually are simplified and made to follow the European structure.

In both European and Oriental tales the plot centers on an interaction between contrasting forces and characters: the kind and the rude, the clever and the stupid, the greedy and the generous, for example. Not only are the good and bad characters easily recognizable, their actions are always consistent. They are flat types rather than round characters, because they represent one-sided, universal facets of human nature. The virtuous and the clever are rewarded while the wicked and the stupid are usually punished and, as symbols for human weaknesses rather than real characters, their punishment satisfies the reader. There is, on the other hand, great empathy felt by the reader toward heroes and heroines who overcome great odds or plan daring deeds; they succeed as the reader himself would like to succeed.

The folktales reprinted here are not arranged by country but by the following types: Wonder Tales, Tales of Trickery, Animal Tales, Drolls, and Cumulative Tales. While there can never be any firm classifications of folklore and some narratives can be placed in more than one category, this arrangement permits a comparison of how different cultures have worked with similar themes, motifs, plots, and character types. For a few tales several versions are given to illustrate how the same story has been adapted or independently developed by various groups; for example, seven variants of "Cinderella" are included in this collection. In many anthologies only one or, at most, two versions are printed with a note that there are several hundred other similar tales. It is hoped that a careful reading of a few variants made easily available will provide insights into the theories of multiple existence and the origins of folk literature as well as help develop familiarity with individual tales.

Wonder Tales

Wonder tales, in which virtue is rewarded and evil punished, are one of the most common and most popular types of folklore. The stories vary from brief incidents involving only one motif, such as "Who Was Most Skillful?", to the complex narratives of "Cinderella" and "Beauty and the Beast." These tales begin in the real world, where suffering, injustice, and hunger all exist and where the lowly are scorned and the successful are usually proud. And yet improbable, wonderful things happen—princes marry cinder-girls, bears become handsome kings, fairy godmothers bring happiness and prosperity. Magic is an almost universal motif in these tales. The hero often has supernatural adversaries; witches, ogres, and giants abound; magical powers and superhuman strength are common. Enchantments and transformations are natural occurrences in this type of story, often called the fairy tale. Explanations are seldom given for the magical or the supernatural. In folktales they are as accepted as rain is in the every-day world—a natural phenomenon that can bring help or cause trouble.

Wonder tales reveal an idealized vision of life in which virtue always is rewarded while evil always is punished. The characters are not real people but types representative of human strengths and weaknesses. They move in a never-never land that is at once terrifying in the power of evil and reassuring in its ultimate defeat. While such a world has never existed outside of the imagination, its ephemeral existence has colored man's aspirations and dreams and brought comfort not only to the child who suffers and triumphs with Cinderella but also to the child-who-once-was in us all.

CINDERELLA TALES

Cinderella stories are told over much of the world; there are more than five hundred European versions and at least one hundred non-

Illustration from *The Moon Singer*, text by Clyde Robert Bulla; copyright © 1969 by Clyde Robert Bulla; illustrations by Trina Shart Hyman; copyright © 1969 by Trina Shart Hyman. Thomas Y. Crowell Company, Inc., publishers.

European variants recorded. The following thirteen tales are part of this cycle and have been chosen to permit comparisons of how different cultures have treated the same theme and motifs.

Included in this selection are stories about young men, because the Cinderella cycle is not limited to heroines. In these tales the hero or heroine is usually the abused or scorned youngest child. The girls are beautiful and kind, and the boys, though they may seem lazy and dull, are brave and clever—or at least not as stupid as their families believe. These lowly protagonists must overcome great obstacles to reach happiness.

Often they must perform impossible tasks, as in "The Twelve Months" where Marushka is sent first to find violets, then strawberries, and then apples in the middle of winter. But because the Cinderella heroine, and the hero, too, is polite and kind, such tasks are performed with supernatural help.

These tales show the rewards of virtue: the good are helped while the proud are defeated. Marushka's haughty stepsister finds no apples but freezes to death because she could not be polite to the Twelve Months. Such is the justice of wonder tales.

CINDERELLA / France

Andrew Lang

Perrault insured that "Cinderella" would never be lost when he included it in his Histories du Temps Passé; avec les Moralitez (1697). *The following beautiful version by Andrew Lang is perhaps the most familiar of all the many retellings of this best-loved wonder tale. Compare Lang's polished style and excellent use of detail with the poorly-written next tale.*

Once there was a gentleman who married, for his second wife, the proudest and most haughty woman that was ever seen. She had, by a former husband, two daughters of her own humor, who were, indeed, exactly like her in all things. He had likewise a young daughter but of unparalleled goodness and sweetness of temper, which she took from her mother, who was the best creature in the world.

No sooner were the ceremonies of the wedding over but the mother began to show herself in her true colors. She could not bear the good qualities of this pretty girl, and all the less because they made her own daughters appear the more odious. She employed her in the meanest work of the house: scouring the dishes and tables and scrubbing madam's room, also those of her daughters. The girl slept in a sorry garret, upon a wretched

"Cinderella," from *The Blue Fairy Book*. Edited by Andrew Lang. Originally published in 1889.

straw bed, while her sisters lay in fine rooms, with floors all inlaid, upon beds of the very newest fashion, and where they had looking glasses so large they might see themselves at full length from head to foot.

The poor girl bore all patiently and dared not tell her father who would have rattled her off, for his wife governed him entirely. When she had done her work, she used to go into the chimney corner and sit down among cinder and ashes, which caused her to be called Cinderwench. But the younger, who was not so rude and uncivil as the elder, called her Cinderella. However, Cinderella, notwithstanding her mean apparel, was a hundred times handsomer than her sisters, though they were always dressed very richly.

It happened that the king's son gave a ball and invited all persons of fashion to it. The two sisters were also invited, for they cut a very grand figure among the quality. They were delighted at this invitation and wonderfully busy in choosing such gowns, petticoats and headdresses as might become them. This was a new trouble to Cinderella, for it was she who ironed her sisters' linen and plaited their ruffles, while they talked all day long of nothing but how they should be dressed.

"For my part," said the elder, "I will wear my red-velvet suit with French trimming."

"And I," said the younger, "shall have my usual petticoat. But then, to make amends for that, I will put on my gold-flowered manteau, and my diamond stomacher, which is far from being the most ordinary one in the world."

They sent for the best tirewoman they could get to make up their headdresses and adjust their double pinners, and they had their red brushes and patches from Mademoiselle de la Poche.

Cinderella was likewise consulted in all these matters, for she had excellent notions, and advised them always for the best and offered her services to dress their hair, which they were very willing she should do. As she was doing this, they said to her:

"Cinderella, would you not like to go to the ball?"

"Alas," she said, "you only jeer at me. It is not for such as I to go thither."

"You are in the right of it," replied they. "It would certainly make people laugh to see a cinderwench at a palace ball."

Anyone but Cinderella would have dressed their heads awry, but she was very good and dressed them perfectly. They were almost two days without eating, so much were they transported with joy. They broke above a dozen of laces in trying to be laced up close, that they might have a fine slender shape, and they were continually at their looking glass. At last the happy day came. They went to court, and Cinderella followed them with her eyes as long as she could, and when she had lost sight of them, she fell a-crying.

Her godmother, who saw her all in tears, asked her what was the matter.

"I wish I could—I wish I could—" She was not able to speak the rest, being interrupted by her tears and sobbing.

This godmother of hers, who was a fairy, said

to her, "You wish to go to the ball. Is it not so?"

"Yes," cried Cinderella, with a great sigh.

"Well," said her godmother, "be a good girl, and I will contrive that you shall go." Then she said to her, "Run into the garden and bring me a pumpkin."

Cinderella went immediately to gather the finest one and brought it to her godmother, not being able to imagine how this pumpkin could make her go to the ball. Her godmother scooped out all the inside of it, leaving nothing but the rind; which done, she struck it with her wand, and the pumpkin was instantly turned into a fine coach, gilded all over with gold.

She then went to look in to her mousetrap, where she found six mice, all alive. She told Cinderella to lift up the little trap door, when, giving each mouse, as it went out, a little tap with her wand, the mouse was at that moment turned into a fine horse. Altogether they made a very fine set of six horses of a beautiful mouse-colored gray.

Being at a loss for a coachman, Cinderella said, "I will go and see if there is a rat in the rat-trap—we may make a coachman of him."

"You are in the right," replied her godmother. "Go and look."

Cinderella brought the trap to her, and in it there were three huge rats. The fairy made choice of the one which had the largest beard, and having touched him with her wand, he was turned into a fat, jolly coachman, who had the smartest whiskers eyes ever beheld. After that, she said to her:

"Go ahead into the garden, and you will find six lizards behind the watering pot; bring them to me."

Cinderella had no sooner done so that her godmother turned them into six footmen, who skipped up immediately behind the coach, with their liveries all covered with gold and silver. They clung as close behind each other as if they had done nothing else their whole lives. The fairy then said to Cinderella:

"Well, you see here an equipage fit to take you to the ball. Are you not pleased with it?"

"Oh, yes," cried Cinderella, "but must I go thither as I am, in these old rags?"

Her godmother just touched her with her wand, and at the same instant her clothes were turned into cloth of gold and silver, all beset with jewels. This done, she gave her a pair of glass slippers, the prettiest in the whole world. Being thus decked out, Cinderella climbed into her coach, but her godmother, above all things, commanded her not to stay till after midnight, telling her, at the same time, that if she stayed one moment longer, the coach would be a pumpkin again, her horses mice, her coachman a rat, her footmen lizards, and her clothes would become just as they were before.

Cinderella promised her godmother she would not fail to leave the ball before midnight. And then away she drove, scarce able to contain herself for joy. The king's son, who was told that a great princess, whom nobody knew, had come, ran out to receive her. He gave her his hand as she alighted from the coach and led her into the hall, among all the company. There was immediately a profound silence. They left off dancing, and the violins ceased to play, so attentive was everyone to contemplate the singular beauties of the unknown newcomer. Nothing was then heard but the confused noise of:

"Ha! How handsome she is! Ha! How handsome she is!"

The king himself, old as he was, could not help watching her and telling the queen softly that it was a long time since he had seen so beautiful and lovely a creature. All the ladies were busied in considering her clothes and headdress, that they might have some made next day after the same pattern, provided they could meet with such fine materials and find able hands to make them.

The king's son conducted her to the most honorable seat, and afterward took her out to dance with him, and she danced so gracefully that all more and more admired her. A fine collation was served, whereof the young prince ate not a morsel, so intently was he busied in gazing on Cinderella.

She sat down by her sisters, showing them a thousand civilities, giving them part of the oranges and citrons with which the prince had presented her, which very much surprised them, for they did not know her. While Cinderella was thus amusing her sisters, she heard the clock strike eleven and three-quarters, whereupon she immediately made a curtsy to the company and hastened away as fast as she could.

Reaching home, she ran to seek out her godmother and, after having thanked her, said she could not but heartily wish she might go the next day to the ball, because the king's son had asked her. As she was eagerly telling her godmother whatever had passed at the ball, her two sisters knocked at the door, which Cinderella ran and opened.

"How long you have stayed!" cried she, rubbing her eyes and stretching herself as if she had been just waked out of her sleep. She had not, however, had any inclination to sleep since they went from home.

"If you had been at the ball," said one of her sisters, "you would not have been tired with it. There came thither the finest princess, the most beautiful ever seen with mortal eyes; she showed us a thousand civilities and gave us oranges and citrons."

Cinderella seemed very indifferent in the matter but asked them the name of that princess. They told her they did not know it and that the king's son would give all the world to know who she was. At this Cinderella, smiling, replied:

"She must, then, be very beautiful indeed. How happy you have been! Could not I see her? Ah, dear Miss Charlotte, do lend me your yellow clothes which you wear every day."

"Ay, to be sure," cried Miss Charlotte, "lend my clothes to a dirty cinderwench! I should be a fool."

Cinderella, indeed, expected such an answer and was very glad of the refusal, for she would have been sadly put to it if her sister had done what she asked for jestingly.

The next day the two sisters were at the ball, and so was Cinderella, but dressed more magnificently than before. The king's son was always by her and never ceased his compliments and kind speeches to her. All this was so far from being tiresome that she quite forgot what her godmother had commanded her. At last, she counted the clock striking twelve when she took it to be no more than eleven. She then rose up and fled, as nimble as a deer. The prince followed but could not overtake her. She left behind one of her glass slippers which the prince took up most carefully. Cinderella reached home, quite out of breath, and in her old clothes, having nothing left of all her finery but one of the little slippers, fellow to the one she had dropped.

The guards at the palace gate were asked if they had not seen a princess go out. They had seen nobody but a young girl, very meanly dressed, and who had more the air of a poor country wench than a gentlewoman.

When the two sisters returned from the ball Cinderella asked them if they had been well diverted, and if the fine lady had been there. They told her, yes, but that she hurried away immediately when it struck twelve and with so much haste that she dropped one of her little glass slippers, the prettiest in the world. The king's son had taken it up. He had done nothing but look at her all the time at the ball, and most certainly he was very much in love with the beautiful girl who owned the glass slipper.

What they said was very true, for a few days afterward the king's son caused it to be proclaimed, by sound of trumpet, that he would marry her whose foot this slipper fit. They whom he employed began to try it upon the princesses, then the duchesses, and all the court, but in vain. It was brought to the two sisters, who each did all she possibly could to thrust her foot into the slipper. But they could not effect it. Cinderella, who saw all this, and knew her slipper, said to them, laughing:

"Let me see if it will not fit me."

Her sisters burst out laughing and began to banter her. The gentleman who was sent to try the slipper looked earnestly at Cinderella and, finding her very handsome, said it was but just she should try, and that he had orders to let everyone make trial.

He obliged Cinderella to sit down, and putting the slipper to her foot, he found it went on easily and fitted her as if it had been made of wax. The astonishment of her two sisters was great, but still greater when Cinderella pulled out of her pocket the other slipper and put it on her foot. Thereupon, in came her godmother who, having touched Cinderella's clothes with her wand, made them richer and more magnificent than any she had worn before.

And now her two sisters found her to be that fine, beautiful lady they had seen at the ball. They threw themselves at her feet to beg pardon for all the ill-treatment they had made her undergo. Cinderella raised them up and, as she embraced them, cried that she forgave them with all her heart and desired them always to love her.

She was conducted to the young prince. He thought her more charming than ever and, a few days after, married her. Cinderella, who was no less good than beautiful, gave her two sisters lodgings in the palace, and that very same day matched them with two great lords of the court.

CINDERELLA

Evelyn Andreas

The following version is included as an example of the poorly revised, inexpensive books of fairy tales sold in drugstores and supermarkets. Many parents purchase these books unaware of their lack of style. All of the grace and charm have been removed in these uninspired potboilers. Read aloud from Andrew Lang's "Cinderella" and then from this one and compare the rhythms. Notice, too, the superficiality of this version, which has been stripped of detail. All of the "fey" quality so necessary to wonder tales is lost.

This is not to say that only expensive books are well written, for the Little Golden Book "Cinderella," which sells for less than fifty cents, has a well-

written text although the pictures are rather like Walt Disney cartoons. Many excellent retellings from the last century have never been surpassed and, as many are now within the public domain and can therefore be reproduced, there is no need to use inferior versions.

Once there was a girl who was as good as she was beautiful. She lived with her stepmother and two stepsisters who were ugly and cruel. They made her do all the hard work, scrubbing and cleaning and tending the fire. At night she sat in the chimney corner to rest. Her ragged clothes were always covered with cinder and ashes and so she was called Cinder-wench, or Cinderella.

One day the king's son announced that he was going to have a ball. The stepmother and the stepsisters were invited and they bought fine clothes for themselves. But they told Cinderella that she could not go to the ball. Cinderella worked harder than ever to help her stepmother and sisters dress for the ball. But in spite of their fine clothes and feathers, they could not hide their ugliness.

When they left for the ball, Cinderella was so unhappy that she began to cry. Suddenly a fairy godmother appeared. "My child," she said, "you, too, shall go to the ball." She touched Cinderella with her wand and the rags fell away. Cinderella was dressed in a beautiful ball gown, with jewels in her hair, and she wore a lovely pair of glass slippers on her feet.

Then the fairy godmother waved her wand and made a fine carriage out of a pumpkin. She made eight horses out of mice to drive the carriage. She made a coachman out of a rat and six footmen out of lizards. When she had finished her magic work, Cinderella was as splendid as any princess.

"But you must be home by midnight!" said the

"Cinderella," from *Fairy Tales Retold* by Evelyn Andreas. Copyright 1954 by Grosset & Dunlap, Inc., the publisher.

fairy godmother. "The magic will end at twelve o'clock and after that you will be all in rags again."

Cinderella was the most beautiful girl at the ball. Everyone talked about her and wondered who she was. Even her stepmother and stepsisters did not recognize her. The king's son danced with her all night and fell in love with her. Cinderella was so happy that she forgot about the time.

Suddenly the clock struck the first notes of twelve. Cinderella knew that she must hurry away from the palace. But even before she got back to her chimney corner, everything had disappeared and she was again dressed all in rags.

In her haste, Cinderella had lost one of her pretty glass slippers on the palace steps. The slippers were so dainty and small that no one but Cinderella could wear them. The king's son found the slipper. He thought, "Now I shall be able to find the lovely girl who ran away so quickly." He sent his messengers to find the girl whose foot fitted the slipper.

All the fine ladies of the court tried on the slipper. But it did not fit any of them. Then Cinderella's stepmother and sisters tried the slipper on. But it did not fit them either. At last one of the messengers saw Cinderella hiding in her corner. He asked her to try on the slipper.

The slipper fitted Cinderella perfectly! Then Cinderella pulled the other slipper out of her pocket and put it on. Now everyone knew that the lovely girl at the ball had been the young Cinder-wench.

Cinderella was taken to the palace where she married the king's son. And they lived happily every after.

ASHPUTTEL / Germany

The Grimm brothers

For those who grew up with Grimms' fairy tales, no variant of the Cinderella story can surpass "Ashputtel." Not only are the tree and the birds lovely substitutions for the French fairy godmother, but the sisters' self-inflicted wounds satisfy the child's belief that the cruel should be cruelly punished. Versions that end with Cinderella forgiving her sisters and marrying them to dukes somehow are less satisfying to a youngster's sense of justice.

The wife of a rich man fell sick. When she felt that her end drew near, she called her only daughter to her bedside, and said, "Always be a good girl, and I will look down from heaven and watch over you."

Soon afterwards she shut her eyes and died and was buried in the garden. The little girl went every day to her grave and wept and was always good and kind to all about her. The snow spread a beautiful white covering over the grave; but by the time the sun had melted it away again, her father had married another wife.

This new wife had two daughters of her own that she brought home with her. They were fair in face but foul at heart, and it was now a sorry time for the poor little girl.

"What does the good-for-nothing thing want in the parlor?" the sisters said. "They who would eat bread should first earn it. Away with the kitchen maid!" Then they took away her fine clothes, and gave her an old gray frock to put on, and laughed at her, and turned her into the kitchen.

There she was forced to do hard work; to rise early before daylight, to bring the water, to make the fire, to cook, and to wash. Besides that, the sisters tormented her in all sorts of ways and laughed at her. In the evening when she was tired, she had no bed to lie on, but was made to lie by the hearth among the ashes. Then as she was of course always dusty and dirty, they called her Ashputtel.

"Ashputtel," from Edgar Taylor, *Grimms' Popular Stories*, 1856, 1902, 1904.

It happened once that the father was going to the fair, and asked his wife's daughters what he should bring them.

"Fine clothes," said the first.

"Pearls and diamonds," cried the second.

"Now, child," said he to his own daughter, "what will you have?"

"The first sprig, dear father, that rubs against your hat on your way home," said she.

He bought for the two first the fine clothes and pearls and diamonds they had asked for. On his way home as he rode through a grove of small trees, a sprig of hazel brushed against him and almost pushed off his hat. He broke it off and brought it to his daughter. She took it and went to her mother's grave and planted it there and cried so much that it was watered with her tears; and there it grew and became a fine tree. Three times every day she went to it and wept; and soon a little bird came and built its nest in the tree, and talked with her, and watched over her, and brought her whatever she wished for.

Now it happened that the king of the land held a feast which was to last three days, and out of those who came to it his son was to choose a bride. Ashputtel's two sisters were asked to come. They called her and said, "Now comb our hair, brush our shoes, and tie our sashes for us, for we are going to dance at the king's feast."

Ashputtel did as she was told, but when all was done she could not help crying, for she thought to herself, she would have liked to go to the dance too. At last she begged her stepmother very hard to let her go.

"You! Ashputtel?" she said. "You who have nothing to wear, no clothes at all, and who cannot even dance—you want to go to the ball?"

To get rid of her, she said at last, "I will throw this basin full of peas into the ash heap, and if you have picked them all out in two hours' time you shall go to the feast." Then she threw the peas into the ashes, but the little maiden ran out at the back door into the garden and cried out:

> "Hither, hither, through the sky,
> Turtledoves and linnets fly!
> Blackbird, thrush, and chaffinch gay,
> Hither, hither, haste away!
> One and all, come help me quick,
> Haste ye, haste ye, pick, pick, pick!"

First came two white doves flying, and next came two turtledoves, and after them, all the little birds under heaven came chirping and fluttering, and flew down into the ashes. The little doves stooped their heads down and set to work, pick, pick, pick. Then the others began to pick, pick, pick. They picked out all the good grain and put it in a dish, and left the ashes. At the end of one hour the work was done, and all the birds flew away.

Ashputtel brought the dish to her mother, overjoyed at the thought that now she could go to the wedding. But her mother said, "No, no! You have no clothes and cannot dance. You shall not go."

When Ashputtel begged very hard to go, she said, "If you can in one hour's time pick two of those dishes of peas out of the ashes, you shall go." Thus she thought she should at last get rid of her. So she shook two dishes of peas into the ashes; but the little maiden went out into the garden at the back of the house and cried out as before:

> "Hither, hither, through the sky,
> Turtledoves and linnets fly!
> Blackbird, thrush, and chaffinch gay,
> Hither, hither, haste away!
> One and all, come help me quick,
> Haste ye, haste ye, pick, pick, pick!"

First came two white doves, and next came the turtledoves, and after them, all the little birds under heaven came chirping and hopping about, and flew down into the ashes. The little doves put their heads down and set to work, pick, pick, pick. Then the others began to pick, pick, pick. They picked out all the good grain and put it into the dishes, and left the ashes. Before half an hour's time, all was done, and away they flew.

Ashputtel took the dishes to her mother, rejoicing to think that she could now go to the ball. But her mother said, "It is all of no use. You cannot go, you have no clothes, and cannot dance, and you would only put us to shame!" Off she went with her two daughters to the feast.

Now when all were gone, and nobody left at home, Ashputtel went sorrowfully and sat down under the hazel tree and cried out:

> "Shake, shake, hazel tree,
> Gold and silver over me!"

Her friend the bird flew out of the tree and brought a gold and silver dress for her, and slippers of spangled silk. She put them on and followed her sisters to the feast. But they did not know her, and thought it must be some strange princess, she looked so fine and beautiful in her rich clothes. They never once thought of Ashputtel, but took it for granted that she was safe at home in the ashes.

The king's son soon came up to her, and took her by the hand and danced with her and no one else. He never left her, and when anyone else came to ask her to dance, he said, "This lady is dancing with me."

They danced till a late hour of the night. When she wanted to go home, the king's son said, "I shall go and take you to your home." He wanted to see where the beautiful maid lived, but she slipped away from him unawares and ran off towards home. The prince followed her, but she jumped up into the pigeon house and shut the door.

The prince waited till her father came home and told him that the unknown maiden who had been at the feast had hid herself in the pigeon house. But when they had broken open the door, they found no one within; and as they came back into the house, Ashputtel lay, as she always did, in her dirty frock by the ashes, and her dim little lamp burned in the chimney. She had run as quickly as she could through the pigeon house and on to the hazel tree. She had taken off her beautiful clothes and laid them beneath the tree, that the bird might carry them away. Then she lay down in the ashes in her little gray frock.

The next day when the feast was again held, and her father, mother, and sisters were gone, Ashputtel went to the hazel tree and said:

> "Shake, shake, hazel tree,
> Gold and silver over me!"

The bird came and brought a still finer dress than the one she had worn the day before. When she came in it to the ball, everyone wondered at her beauty. The king's son, who was waiting for her, took her by the hand, and danced with her; and when anyone asked her to dance, he said as before, "This lady is dancing with me."

When it grew late, she wanted to go home. The king's son followed her as before, that he might see into what house she went; but she sprang away from him and ran into the garden behind her father's house. In this garden stood a fine large pear tree full of ripe fruit and Ashputtel, not knowing where to hide herself, jumped up into it without being seen.

The king's son could not find out where she had gone, but he waited till her father came home, and said to him, "The unknown lady who danced with me has slipped away, and I think she must have sprung into the pear tree."

The father thought to himself, "Can it be Ashputtel?" So he ordered an ax to be brought and they cut down the tree, but found no one in it. When they came back into the kitchen, there lay Ashputtel in the ashes as usual; for she had slipped down on the other side of the tree, and carried her beautiful clothes back to the bird at the hazel tree, and then put on her little gray frock.

The third day, when her father and mother and sisters were gone, she went again into the garden and said:

> "Shake, shake, hazel tree,
> Gold and silver over me!"

Her kind friend the bird brought a dress still finer than the former ones, and slippers which were all of gold. When she came to the feast no one knew what to say for wonder at her beauty. The king's son danced with her alone, and when anyone else asked her to dance, he said, "This lady is my partner."

When it grew late, she wanted to go home. The king's son went with her, and said to himself, "I will not lose her this time." But before they left the palace, she managed to slip away from him, though in such a hurry that she dropped her left golden slipper upon the stairs.

The prince took the shoe and the next day went to the king his father and said, "I will take for my wife the lady that this golden slipper fits." Both the sisters were overjoyed to hear this; for they had beautiful feet, and had no doubt that they could wear the golden slipper.

The eldest sister went first into the room where the slipper was and wanted to try it on, and the mother stood by. But her great toe could not get into it for the shoe was altogether much too small for her. The mother gave her a knife, and said, "Never mind, cut it off! When you are queen, you will not care about toes. You will not go about on foot."

So the silly girl cut her great toe off, and squeezed the shoe on, and went to the king's son. Then he took her for his bride, and set her beside him on his horse and rode away with her.

On their way to the palace, they had to pass by the hazel tree that Ashputtel had planted. There sat a little dove on the branch singing:

> "Back again! Back again! Look to the shoe!
> The shoe is too small and not made for
>   you!
> Prince! Prince! Look again for thy bride,
> For she's not the true one that sits by thy
>   side."

The prince got down and looked at her foot and saw by the blood that streamed from it what a trick she had played on him. So he turned his horse round and brought the false bride back to her home, and said, "This is not the right bride. Let the other sister try to put on the slipper."

The other sister went into the room and got her foot into the shoe, all but the heel, which was too large. But her mother squeezed it in till the blood came and took her to the king's son. He set her as his bride by his side on the horse, and rode away with her.

When they came to the hazel tree, the little dove sat there still and sang:

"Back again! Back again! Look to the shoe!
The shoe is too small and not made for
you!
Prince! Prince! Look again for thy bride,
For she's not the true one that sits by thy
side."

The prince looked down and saw that the blood streamed so from the shoe that her white stocking was quite red. So he turned his horse and brought her back again also. "This is not the true bride," said he to the father. "Have you no other daughters?"

"No," said the father, "there is only little dirty Ashputtel here, the child of my first wife. I am sure she cannot be the bride."

However, the prince told him to send her to him. But the mother said, "No, no, she is much too dirty. She will not dare to show herself." But the prince would have her come.

First Ashputtel washed her face and hands, and then went in and curtsied to the prince. He gave her the golden slipper. She took her clumsy shoe off her left foot and put on the golden slipper. It fitted her as if it had been made for her! The prince came near and looked into her face. He knew her, and said, "This is the right bride." But the mother and both the sisters were frightened and turned pale with anger as he took Ashputtel on his horse and rode away with her. When they came to the hazel tree, the white dove sang:

"Home! Home! Look at the shoe!
Princess! The shoe was made for you!
Prince! Prince! Take home thy bride,
For she is the true one that sits by thy side!"

When the dove had finished its song, it came flying and perched upon Ashputtel's right shoulder. Then the white dove went with her to live in the palace.

TATTERCOATS / Ireland

Joseph Jacobs

In this variant the prince loves Cinderella even when she is dirty and tattered. Before the king and his nobles he declares his love. Here is a romance that surpasses any of the tales in which princes fall in love with beautifully dressed strangers. Also there is the herdboy who plays "low sweet notes" and who adds a mystical quality not found in the other Cinderella stories.

In a great Palace by the sea there once dwelt a very rich old lord, who had neither wife nor children living, only one little granddaughter, whose face he had never seen in all her life. He hated her bitterly, because at her birth his favourite daughter died; and when the old nurse brought him the baby, he swore that it might live or die as it liked, but he would never look on its face as long as it lived.

"Tattercoats," from *More English Fairy Tales* by Joseph Jacobs.

So he turned his back, and sat by his window looking out over the sea, and weeping great tears for his lost daughter, till his white hair and beard grew down over his shoulders and twined round his chair and crept into the chinks of the floor, and his tears, dropping on to the window-ledge, wore a channel through the stone, and ran away in a little river to the great sea. And, meanwhile, his granddaughter grew up with no one to care for her, or clothe her; only the old nurse, when no one was by, would sometimes give her a dish of scraps from the kitchen, or a torn petticoat from the rag-bag; while the other servants of the Palace would drive her from the house with blows and mocking words, calling her "Tattercoats," and pointing at her bare feet and shoulders, till she ran away crying, to hide among the bushes.

And so she grew up, with little to eat or wear, spending her days in the fields and lanes, with only the gooseherd for a companion, who would play to her so merrily on his little pipe, when she was hungry, or cold, or tired, that she forgot all her troubles, and fell to dancing, with his flock of noisy geese for partners.

But, one day, people told each other that the King was travelling through the land, and in the town near by was to give a great ball to all the lords and ladies of the country, when the Prince, his only son, was to choose a wife.

One of the royal invitations was brought to the Palace by the sea, and the servants carried it up to the old lord who still sat by his window, wrapped in his long white hair and weeping into the little river that was fed by his tears.

But when he heard the King's command, he dried his eyes and bade them bring shears to cut him loose, for his hair had bound him a fast prisoner and he could not move. And then he sent them for rich clothes, and jewels, which he put on; and he ordered them to saddle the white horse, with gold and silk, that he might ride to meet the King.

Meanwhile Tattercoats had heard of the great doings in the town, and she sat by the kitchen-door weeping because she could not go to see them. And when the old nurse heard her crying she went to the Lord of the Palace, and begged him to take his granddaughter with him to the King's ball.

But he only frowned and told her to be silent, while the servants laughed and said: "Tattercoats is happy in her rags, playing with the gooseherd, let her be—it is all she is fit for."

A second, and then a third time, the old nurse begged him to let the girl go with him, but she was answered only by black looks and fierce words, till she was driven from the room by the jeering servants, with blows and mocking words.

Weeping over her ill-success, the old nurse went to look for Tattercoats; but the girl had been turned from the door by the cook, and had run away to tell her friend the gooseherd how unhappy she was because she could not go to the King's ball.

But when the gooseheard had listened to her story, he bade her cheer up, and proposed that they should go together into the town to see the King, and all the fine things; and when she looked sorrowfully down at her rags and bare feet, he played a note or two upon his pipe, so gay and merry, that she forgot all about her tears and her troubles, and before she well knew, the herdboy had taken her by the hand, and she, and he, and the geese before them, were dancing down the road towards the town.

Before they had gone very far, a handsome young man, splendidly dressed, rode up and stopped to ask the way to the castle where the King was staying; and when he found that they too were going thither, he got off his horse and walked beside them along the road.

The herdboy pulled out his pipe and played a low sweet tune, and the stranger looked again and again at Tattercoats' lovely face till he fell deeply in love with her, and begged her to marry him.

But she only laughed, and shook her golden head.

"You would be finely put to shame if you had a goosegirl for your wife!" said she; "go and ask one of the great ladies you will see to-night at the King's ball, and do not flout poor Tattercoats."

But the more she refused him the sweeter the pipe played, and the deeper the young man fell in love; till at last he begged her, as a proof of his sincerity, to come that night at twelve to the King's ball, just as she was, with the herdboy and his geese, and in her torn petticoat and bare feet, and he would dance with her before the King and the lords and ladies, and present her to them all, as his dear and honoured bride.

So when night came, and the hall in the castle was full of light and music, and the lords and ladies were dancing before the King, just as the clock struck twelve, Tattercoats and the herdboy, followed by his flock of noisy geese, entered at the great doors, and walked straight up the ball-room, while on either side the ladies whispered, the lords laughed, and the King seated at the far end stared in amazement.

But as they came in front of the throne, Tattercoats' lover rose from beside the King, and came to meet her. Taking her by the hand, he kissed her thrice before them all, and turned to the King.

"Father!" he said, for it was the Prince himself, "I have made my choice, and here is my bride, the loveliest girl in all the land, and the sweetest as well!"

Before he had finished speaking, the herdboy put his pipe to his lips and played a few low notes that sounded like a bird singing far off in the woods; and as he played, Tattercoats' rags were changed to shining robes sewn with glittering jewels, a golden crown lay upon her golden hair, and the flock of geese behind her became a crowd of dainty pages, bearing her long train.

And as the King rose to greet her as his daughter, the trumpets sounded loudly in honour of the new Princess, and the people outside in the street said to each other:

"Ah! now the Prince has chosen for his wife the loveliest girl in all the land!"

But the gooseherd was never seen again, and no one knew what became of him; while the old lord went home once more to his Palace by the sea, for he could not stay at Court, when he had sworn never to look on his granddaughter's face.

So there he still sits by his window, if you could only see him, as you some day may, weeping more bitterly than ever, as he looks out over the sea.

THE POOR TURKEY GIRL / American Indian—Zuni

Frank H. Cushing

Spanish traders and settlers brought their traditional tales to the American Southwest and many of them were adapted by the Indians. In this tale the Cinderella figure herds turkeys, a motif that appears in some European versions. It is interesting to note the modifications made by the Zuni who, as Stith Thompson reports in The Folktale, *adapted it to their own environment. Compare the ending of this tale to the other versions of the Cinderella cycle. Another interesting comparison can be made with "Little Burnt Face" in Chapter 3, Indian Mythology.*

Once long, long ago, in Matsaki the Salt City, there lived many rich Indians who owned large flocks of Turkeys. The poor people of the town herded them on the mesas, or on the plains around Thunder Mountain, at the foot of which Matsaki stood.

Now, at this time, on the border of the town was a little tumble-down hut in which there lived alone a very poor girl. Her clothes were patched and ragged; and though she had a winning face

and bright eyes, she was shameful to behold because her hair was uncombed and her face dirty. She herded Turkeys for a living, in return for which she received a little food, and now and then an old garment.

But she had a kind heart, and was lonely, so she was good to her Turkeys as she drove them to and from the plains each day. The birds loved her very much, and would come at her call, or go wherever she wished.

One day this poor girl was driving her Turkeys past Old Zuñi, and as she went along she heard a man, who was standing upon a housetop, invite all the people of Zuñi and the other towns to come to a great dance that was to take place in four days.

Now this poor girl had never been allowed to join in, or even to watch, the dances, and she longed to see this one. She sighed, and said to her Turkeys—for she often talked to them—"Alas! How could a girl, so ugly and ill-clad as I am watch, much less join in, the great dance!" Then she drove her Turkeys to the plain, and when night came, returned them to their cage on the edge of the town.

So every day, for three days, this poor girl drove her Turkeys out in the morning, and saw the people busy cleaning and mending their garments, cooking all sorts of good things, and making ready for the festival. And she heard them laughing and talking about the great dance. And as she went along with her Turkeys, she talked to them, and told them how sad she was. Of course she did not think they understood a word.

They did understand, however, for on the fourth day, when all the people of Matsaki, had gone to Old Zuñi, and the poor girl was herding her Turkeys on the plain, a big Gobbler strutted up to her. He made a fan of his tail, and skirts of his wings, and, blushing with pride and puffing with importance, he stretched his neck, and said:—

"O Maiden Mother, we know what your thoughts are, and truly pity you. We wish that, like the other people of Matsaki, you might enjoy the great dance. Last night, after you had placed us safely and comfortably in our cage, we said to ourselves, 'Our maiden mother is just as worthy to enjoy the dance as any maiden of Matsaki or Zuñi.'

"So now, listen, Maiden Mother," continued the old Gobbler. "Would you like to go to the dance, and be merry with the best of your people? If you will drive us home early this afternoon, when the dance is most gay and the people are most happy, we will make you so handsome and dress you so prettily that no one will know you. And the young men will wonder whence you came, and lay hold of your hand in the dance."

At first the poor girl was very much surprised to hear the Gobbler speak, then it seemed so natural that her Turkeys should talk to her as she did to them, that she sat down on a little mound, and said: "My beloved Turkeys, how glad I am

that we may speak together! But why should you promise me things that you know I cannot have?"

"Trust us," said the old Gobbler, "and when we begin to call, and gobble, gobble, and turn toward our home in Matsaki, do you follow us; and we will show you what we can do for you. Only let me tell you one thing. If you remain true and kind of heart, no one knows what happiness and good fortune may come to you. But if you forget us, your friends, and do not return to us before sunset, then we will think, 'Behold, our maiden mother deserves all her poverty and hard life, for when good fortune came she forgot her friends and was ungrateful.' "

"Never fear my Turkeys!" cried the girl, "never fear! Whatever you tell me to do I will do! I will be as obedient as you have always been to me!"

The noon hour was scarcely passed, when the Turkeys of their own accord turned homeward, gobbling as they went. And the girl followed them, light of heart. They knew their cage, and immediately ran into it. When they had all entered, the old Gobbler called to the girl, "Come into our house!"

So they went in, and he said, "Maiden Mother, sit down, and give us one by one your garments, and we will see what we can do with them."

The girl obediently drew off her ragged mantle, and cast it on the floor in front of the gobbler. He seized it in his beak, and spread it out. Then he picked and picked at it, and trod upon it. Lowering his wings, he began to strut back and forth upon it. Next, taking it up in his beak, he puffed and puffed, and laid it down at the feet of the girl—a beautiful white embroidered mantle.

Another Gobbler came forward, and the girl gave him one of her garments, which in the same manner, he made very fine. And then another and another Gobbler did the same, until each garment was made into as new and beautiful a thing as that worn by any maiden of Matsaki.

Before the girl put these on, the Turkeys circled about her, singing and brushing her with their wings, until she was clean, and her skin as smooth and bright as that of the loveliest maiden of Matsaki. Her hair was soft and waving, her cheeks full and dimpled, and her eyes dancing with smiles.

Then an old Turkey Gobbler came forward, and said: "O Maiden Mother, all you lack now is some rich ornaments. Wait a minute!"

Spreading his wings, he trod round and round, throwing his head back, and laying his wattled beard upon his neck. By and by he began to cough, and he produced in his beak a beautiful necklace. And one by one the other Gobblers did the same thing and coughed up earrings, and all the ornaments befitting a well-clad maiden and laid them at the feet of the poor Turkey girl.

With these beautiful things, she decorated herself, and thanking the Turkeys over and over, she started to go to the great dance. But the Turkeys called out: "O Maiden Mother, leave open the wicket gate, for who knows whether you will remember your Turkeys when your fortunes are changed! Perhaps you will be ashamed of being the maiden mother of Turkeys. But we love you, and would bring you good fortune! Therefore remember our words, and do not stay too late."

"I will surely remember you, my Turkeys," answered the girl, and she opened the wicket, and sped hastily away toward Old Zuñi.

When she arrived there, the people looked at her, and she heard murmurs of astonishment at her beauty and the richness of her dress. The people were asking one another, "Who is this lovely maiden?"

The Chiefs of the dance, all gorgeous in their attire, hastily came to her, and invited her to join the youths and maidens in the dance. With a blush and a smile and a toss of her hair over her eyes, the girl stepped into the circle, and the finest youths among the dancers sought to lay hold of her hand.

Her heart became merry, her feet light, and she danced and danced until the Sun began to go down. Then alas! in her happiness she thought of her Turkeys, and said to herself: "Why should I go away from this delightful place, to my flock of gobbling Turkeys? I will stay a little longer, and just before the Sun sets, I will run back to them. Then these people will not know who I am, and I shall have the joy of hearing them talk day after day, wondering who the girl was, who joined their dance."

So the time sped on, and soon the Sun set, and the dance was well-nigh over. Then the girl, breaking away, ran out of the town, and being swift of foot, she sped up the river-path before any one could follow the course she took.

As for the Turkeys, when they saw that it grew late, they began to wonder and wonder that their maiden mother did not return to them. And when the Sun had set, the old Gobbler mournfully said: "Alas! It is as we might have known! She has forgotten us! So she is not worthy of better things than those she has been used to. Let us go to the mountains, and endure captivity no longer, since our maiden mother is not so good and true as we once thought her."

So, calling, calling to one another, and gobbling, in a loud voice, they trooped out of their cage, and ran through the cañon, and around Thunder Mountain, and up the valley.

All breathless the girl arrived at the wicket, and looked in. And, lo, not a Turkey was there! She ran and she ran along their trail. And when she reached the valley, they were far ahead, and she could hear them calling, calling to one another, and gobbling, gobbling loudly. She redoubled her speed, and as she drew nearer, she heard them singing sadly:

"Oh, our maiden mother,
Whom we love so well,
To the dance went today!

"Therefore, as she lingers,
To the cañon mesa,
We'll all run away!"

Hearing this, the girl called to her Turkeys, called and called in vain! They quickened their steps, and spreading their wings to help themselves along, ran on till they came to the base of the cañon mesa. Then, singing once more their sad song, they spread their wings, and fluttered away over the plain above.

As for the girl, she looked down at her garments, and, lo, they were changed again to rags and patches and dirt! And she was the same poor Turkey girl that she had been before.

Weary and weeping, and very much ashamed, she returned to Matsaki.

A CHINESE CINDERELLA / West China

L. C. Hume

In Chinese literature a Cinderella story has been traced back to the ninth century A.D., and the following selection is a translation of a Chinese variant. Although the style of this translation is unexecptional and cannot compare with the styles of Andrew Lang and Joseph Jacobs, it is interesting to see a familiar story colored by a different tradition.

In the dim past, before the Ts'in and Han dynasties, there was a chieftain named Wu, who lived in a mountain cave. The people of the countryside called him "Cave Chief Wu."

Now Cave Chief Wu had two wives and a beautiful daughter named Shih Chieh. When this daughter was ten years old, her mother died, and she and her father became close friends. Shih Chieh was not only beautiful; she was clever, as well, and always happy. But one day her father died, and after that the stepmother became so jealous of Shih Chieh's beauty that she sought every possible way to mistreat her. She made the girl cut wood in dangerous places and draw water from deep wells, hoping that some day she would meet with an accident.

One day when Shih Chieh was out in her garden, she caught a beautiful little fish with red fins and golden eyes. It was so tiny that she kept it in a basin in her room. Every day she changed the water in the basin, but at last the fish grew so big that she had no bowl large enough to hold it.

Shih Chieh waited until her cruel stepmother had gone away one day, then she took the fish out and slipped it into the pond in the garden. Everyday after that, she crept secretly into the garden to feed the fish scraps of food. So Shih Chieh and the beautiful fish became great friends and when she came to the pond each morning,

the fish would swim to the edge of the pool, lift its head from the water, and rest it on the bank as on a pillow.

The cruel stepmother somehow heard about the beautiful fish with red fins and golden eyes, and she went often to the garden to try to see it for herself; but the fish would never show itself for anyone but Shih Chieh. The stepmother became very frustrated and angry and secretly determined to kill the fish. One day she said to Shih Chieh: "Aren't you tired today? It is a bright day, so let me wash your coat for you. Go draw water from the neighbor's well. When you return with it, I will wash your coat."

As soon as Shih Chieh had left with her pail, the stepmother hurriedly put on the daughter's clothes and, hiding a sharp sword in her sleeve, she went to the pond and called to the fish. The fish, thinking it was his mistress, raised his head out of the water. Instantly the cruel stepmother drew the sword from her sleeve and killed the fish. She carried it home, cooked it and ate its delicious meat, then buried the bones under a mound in the field.

The next day Shih Chieh came out to the garden as usual and scattered crumbs on the pool, but the lovely fish with red fins and golden eyes did not come to greet her. Sitting on the bank, she wept piteously. Suddenly a man with tousled hair, and dressed in rough clothing, came down from heaven and comforted her.

"Do not weep, my child. Your mother has killed your fish and hidden its bones under a mound in the field."

Then he leaned close to her and whispered: "I will tell you a great secret. If you will pray to those bones, every wish you have will be granted.

As Shih Chieh turned to thank this stranger, he disappeared from view.

Shih Chieh did exactly as the strange visitor had told her. Each day she prayed to the bones of the fish and, just as she had been promised, gold, pearls, and beautiful dresses came to her as soon as she had wished for them.

Now, as it happened, the seventh day of the seventh moon was the day of the Cave Festival. The stepmother took her own daughter, who was not nearly so beautiful as Shih Chieh, and went off to the festival, leaving Shih Chieh behind to tend the house.

"Mind you watch the fruit in the courtyard while we are gone," she called out sharply to Shih Chieh as they went out the gate.

But as soon as they were out of sight, Shih Chieh raced to the mound in the field and asked her fish's bones a beautiful gown and slippers to wear to the festival. At once she found herself clad in a delectable gown of azure blue and wearing a pair of shining golden slippers. She might have been a fairy queen tripping down the road, so beautiful was she as she followed her mother and sister to the festival.

As she entered the court and joined the dances, everyone turned to look at her, for among all the guests there was no one so lovely as Shih Chieh.

"Why, this girl looks exactly like Shih Chieh," whispered her stepsister. The stepmother scowled in anger. When Shih Chieh saw that they had recognized her, she hurried away from the ball and made haste back to her house. But, in her rush, she dropped one of her golden slippers. The merrymaking was at its height, and no one noticed the Cave Man as he stooped and picked up the shining golden slipper after she had dropped it.

When the stepmother returned home, she found Shih Chieh fast asleep, and she decided that she could not have been at the festival, after all.

The Cave Man's home was on an island on which was the kingdom of T'o Huan, whose military power was the strongest among all the thirty islands in the region. The Cave people sold the golden slipper Shih Chieh had dropped at the festival to the king of T'o Huan.

The king thought that he had never seen anything in his life so lovely as that golden slipper. He was sure that the person who had worn the slipper must be as lovely. The slipper was as light as a moonbeam and it made no sound, even when treading upon stone. So the king sent his heralds to all parts of his realm to ask all the women to try the slipper on. But no one was found who could wear it. Then he commanded the heralds to search every house far and wide to find the mate to the slipper. At last the emissaries returned with the news that another slipper, identical in design, had been found in Shih Chieh's house.

The king of T'o Huan was so excited at this news that he decided to go himself to find the maiden who could wear the slipper.

Shih Chieh hid when she heard that the king was coming, but, when he demanded to see her, she appeared dressed in the same gown of azure blue that she had worn at the festival, and wearing one golden slipper. She looked as beautiful as a goddess, and, when she slipped her slender foot into the lost sandal, it fitted perfectly, and the king bore her away to his kingdom to be his wife. Her stepmother was beside herself with rage and her stepsister wept for a week in annoyance. Before she left, Shih Chieh visited the garden to collect the fish's bones and bring them away with her to her new home.

During the first year of their new life, the king discovered the secret of the fish bones and greedily asked for such an endless number of jewels and jade pieces that the next year his requests went unanswered. Then the king buried the fish bones on the sea coast, together with one hundred bushels of pearls, enclosing them all in a golden parapet.

Several years later the king went back to this spot to unearth the pearls in order to distribute them among his soldiers, who had threatened to rebel. To his dismay, he found that pearls and bones had all been washed away in the tide.

THE GIRL WITH THE ROSE-RED SLIPPERS / Egypt

Roger Lancelyn Green

Several groups of folktales written on papyri have been preserved from ancient Egypt, some of which are animal stories similar to Aesopic fables. Most of the tales, however, are not well organized and, Stith Thompson suggests, perhaps the priest-authors did not clearly understand the narratives. The stories do, however, reveal that folklore somewhat like our own existed over 5000 years ago in Egypt.

In the last days of ancient Egypt, not many years before the country was conquered by the Persians, she was ruled by a Pharaoh called Amasis. So as to strengthen his country against the threat of invasion by Cyrus of Persia, who was conquering all the known world, he welcomed as many Greeks as wished to trade with or settle in Egypt, and gave them a city called Naucratis to be entirely their own.

In Naucratis, not far from the mouth of the Nile that flows into the sea at Canopus, there lived a wealthy Greek merchant called Charaxos. His true home was in the island of Lesbos, and the famous poetess Sappho was his sister; but he had spent most of his life trading with Egypt, and in his old age he settled at Naucratis.

One day when he was walking in the market place he saw a great crowd gathered around the place where the slaves were sold. Out of curiosity he pushed his way into their midst, and found that everyone was looking at a beautiful girl who had just been set up on the stone rostrum to be sold.

She was obviously a Greek with white skin and cheeks like blushing roses, and Charaxos caught his breath—for he had never seen anyone so lovely.

Consequently, when the bidding began, Charaxos determined to buy her and, being one of the wealthiest merchants in all Naucratis, he did so without much difficulty.

When he had bought the girl, he discovered that her name was Rhodopis and that she had been carried away by pirates from her home in the north of Greece when she was a child. They had sold her to a rich man who employed many slaves on the island of Samos, and she had grown up there, one of her fellow slaves being an ugly little man called Aesop who was always kind to her and told her the most entrancing stories and fables about animals and birds and human beings.

But when she was grown up, her master wished to make some money out of so beautiful a girl and had sent her to rich Naucratis to be sold.

Charaxos listened to her tale and pitied her deeply. Indeed very soon he became quite besotted with her. He gave her a lovely house to live in, with a garden in the middle of it, and slave girls to attend on her. He heaped her with presents of jewels and beautiful clothes, and spoiled her as if she had been his own daughter.

One day a strange thing happened as Rhodopis was bathing in the marble-edged pool in her secret garden. The slave girls were holding her clothes and guarding her jeweled girdle and her rose-red slippers of which she was particularly proud, while she lazed in the cool water—for a summer's day even in the north of Egypt grows very hot about noon.

Suddenly when all seemed quiet and peaceful, an eagle came swooping down out of the clear blue sky—down, straight down as if to attack the little group by the pool. The slave girls dropped everything they were holding and fled shrieking to hide among the trees and flowers of the garden; and Rhodopis rose from the water and stood with her back against the marble fountain at one end of it, gazing with wide startled eyes.

But the eagle paid no attention to any of them. Instead, it swooped right down and picked up one of her rose-red slippers in its talons. Then it soared up into the air again on its great wings and, still carrying the slipper, flew away to the south over the valley of the Nile.

Rhodopis wept at the loss of her rose-red slipper, feeling sure that she would never see it again, and sorry also to have lost anything that Charaxos had given to her.

But the eagle seemed to have been sent by the gods—perhaps by Horus himself whose sacred bird he was. For he flew straight up the Nile to Memphis and then swooped down toward the palace.

At that hour Pharaoh Amasis sat in the great courtyard doing justice to his people and hearing any complaints that they wished to bring.

Down over the courtyard swooped the eagle and dropped the rose-red slipper of Rhodopis into Pharaoh's lap.

The people cried out in surprise when they saw this, and Amasis too was much taken aback. But, as he took up the little rose-red slipper and admired the delicate workmanship and the tiny size of it, he felt that the girl for whose foot it was made must indeed be one of the loveliest in the world.

Indeed Amasis the Pharaoh was so moved by what had happened that he issued a decree:

"Let my messengers go forth through all the cities of the Delta and, if need be, into Upper Egypt to the very borders of my kingdom. Let them take with them this rose-red slipper which

the divine bird of Horus has brought to me, and let them declare that her from whose foot this slipper came shall be the bride of Pharaoh!"

Then the messengers prostrated themselves crying, "Life, health, strength be to Pharaoh! Pharaoh has spoken and his command shall be obeyed!"

So they set forth from Memphis and went by way of Heliopolis and Tanis and Canopus until they came to Naucratis. Here they heard of the rich merchant Charaxos and how he had bought the beautiful Greek girl in the slave market, and how he was lavishing all his wealth upon her as if she had been a princess put in his care by the gods. So they went to the great house beside the Nile and found Rhodopis in the quiet garden by the pool.

When they showed her the rose-red slipper she cried out in surprise that it was hers. She held out her foot so that they could see how well it fitted her; and she bade one of the slave girls fetch the pair to it which she had kept carefully in memory of her strange adventure with the eagle.

Then the messengers knew that this was the girl whom Pharaoh had sent them to find, and they knelt before her and said, "The good god Pharaoh Amasis—life, health, strength be to him! —bids you come with all speed to his palace at Memphis. There you shall be treated with all honor and given a high place in his Royal House of Women: for he believes that Horus the son of Isis and Osiris sent that eagle to bring the rose-red slipper and cause him to search for you."

Such a command could not be disobeyed. Rhodopis bade farewell to Charaxos, who was torn between joy at her good fortune and sorrow at his loss, and set out for Memphis.

And when Amasis saw her beauty, he was sure that the gods had sent her to him. He did not merely take her into his Royal House of Women, he made her his Queen and the Royal Lady of Egypt. And they lived happily together for the rest of their lives and died a year before the coming of Cambyses the Persian.

THE TWELVE MONTHS / Czechoslovakia

Parker Fillmore

Cinderella motifs included in this tale are the beautiful girl abused by a cruel stepmother and stepsister, kindness and goodness rewarded, cruelty and rudeness punished. An unusual variation is that Marushka instead of finding a prince marries a farmer. But, true to the wonder tale pattern, they do live happily ever after.

There was once a woman who had two girls. One was her own daughter, the other a stepchild. Holena, her own daughter, she loved dearly, but she couldn't bear even the sight of Marushka, the stepchild. This was because Marushka was so much prettier than Holena. Marushka, the dear child, didn't know how pretty she was, and so she never understood why, whenever she stood beside Holena, the stepmother frowned so crossly.

Mother and daughter made Marushka do all the housework alone. She had to cook and wash and sew and spin and take care of the garden and look after the cow. Holena, on the contrary, spent all her time decking herself out and sitting around like a grand lady.

Marushka never complained. She did all she was told to do and bore patiently their everlasting fault-finding. In spite of all the hard work she did, she grew prettier from day to day, and in spite of her lazy life, Holena grew uglier.

"This will never do," the stepmother thought to herself. "Soon the boys will come courting, and once they see how pretty Marushka is, they'll pay no attention at all to my Holena. We had just better do all we can to get rid of that Marushka as soon as possible."

So they both nagged Marushka all day long. They made her work harder, they beat her, they didn't give her enough to eat, they did everything they could think of to make her ugly and nasty.

But all to no avail. Marushka was so good and sweet that, in spite of all their harsh treatment, she kept on growing prettier.

One day in the middle of January Holena took the notion that nothing would do but she must have a bunch of fragrant violets to put in her bodice.

"Marushka!" she ordered sharply. "I want some violets. Go out to the forest and get me some."

"Good heavens, my dear sister!" cried poor Marushka. "What can you be thinking of? Whoever heard of violets growing under the snow in January?"

"What, you lazy little slattern!" Holena shouted. "You dare to argue with me! You go this minute and if you come back without violets, I'll kill you!"

The stepmother sided with Holena and, taking Marushka roughly by the shoulder, she pushed her out of the house and slammed the door.

The poor child climbed slowly up the mountain-side, weeping bitterly. All around the snow lay deep with no track of man or beast in any direction. Marushka wandered on and on, weak with hunger and shaking with cold.

"Dear God in heaven," she prayed, "take me to yourself away from all this suffering."

Suddenly ahead of her she saw a glowing light. She struggled toward it and found at last that it came from a great fire that was burning on the top of the mountain. Around the fire there were twelve stones, one of them much bigger and higher than the rest. Twelve men were seated on the stones. Three of them were very old and white; three were not so old; three were middle-aged; and three were beautiful youths. They did not talk. They sat silent gazing at the fire. They were the Twelve Months.

For a moment Marushka was frightened and hesitated. Then she stepped forward and said, politely:

"Kind sirs, may I warm myself at your fire? I am shaking with cold."

Great January nodded his head and Marushka reached her stiff fingers toward the flames.

"This is no place for you, my child," Great January said. "Why are you here?"

"I'm hunting for violets," Marushka answered.

"Violets? This is no time to look for violets with snow on the ground!"

"I know that, sir, but my sister, Holena, says I must bring her violets from the forest or she'll kill me, and my mother says so, too. Please, sir, won't you tell me where I can find some?"

Great January slowly stood up and walked over to the youngest Month. He handed him a long staff and said:

"Here, March, you take the high seat."

So March took the high seat and began waving the staff over the fire. The fire blazed up and instantly the snow all about began to melt. The trees burst into bud; the grass revived; the little pink buds of the daisies appeared; and, lo, it was spring!

While Marushka looked, violets began to peep out from among the leaves, and soon it was as if a great blue quilt had been spread on the ground.

"Now, Marushka," March cried, "there are your violets! Pick them quickly!"

Marushka was overjoyed. She stooped down and gathered a great bunch. Then she thanked the Months politely, bade them good day, and hurried away.

Just imagine Holena and the stepmother's surprise when they saw Marushka coming home through the snow with her hands full of violets. They opened the door and instantly the fragrance of the flowers filled the cottage.

"Where did you get them?" Holena demanded rudely.

"High up in the mountain," Marushka said.

"The ground up there is covered with them."

Holena snatched the violets and fastened them in her waist. She kept smelling them herself all afternoon and she let her mother smell them, but she never once said to Marushka:

"Dear sister, won't you take a smell?"

The next day, as she was sitting idle in the chimney corner, she took the notion that she must have some strawberries to eat. So she called Marushka and said:

"Here you, Marushka, go out to the forest and get me some strawberries."

"Good heavens, my dear sister," Marushka said, "where can I find strawberries this time of year? Whoever heard of strawberries growing under the snow?"

"What, you lazy little slattern!" Holena shouted. "You dare to argue with me! You go this minute, and if you come back without strawberries, I'll kill you!"

Again the stepmother sided with Holena and, taking Marushka roughly by the shoulder, she pushed her out of the house and slammed the door.

Again the poor child climbed slowly up the mountain-side, weeping bitterly. All around the snow lay deep with no track of man or beast in any direction. Marushka wandered on and on, weak with hunger and shaking with cold. At last she saw ahead of her the glow of the same fire that she had seen the day before. With happy heart she hastened to it. The Twelve Months were seated as before with Great January on the high seat.

Marushka bowed politely and said:

"Kind sirs, may I warm myself at your fire? I am shaking with cold."

Great January nodded and Marushka reached her stiff fingers toward the flames.

"But Marushka," Great January said, "why are you here again? What are you hunting now?"

"I'm hunting for strawberries," Marushka answered.

"Strawberries? But, Marushka, my child, it is winter and strawberries do not grow in the snow."

Marushka shook her head sadly.

"I know that, sir, but my sister, Holena, says I must bring her strawberries from the forest or she will kill me, and my mother says so, too. Please, sir, won't you tell me where I can find some?"

Great January slowly stood up and walked over to the Month who sat opposite him. He handed him the long staff and said:

"Here, June, you take the high seat."

So June took the high seat and began waving the staff over the fire. The flames blazed high, and with the heat the snow all about melted instantly. The earth grew green; the trees decked themselves in leaves; the birds began to sing; flowers bloomed and, lo, it was summer! Presently little starry white blossoms covered the ground under the beech trees. Soon these turned to fruit, first green, then pink, then red, and, with a gasp of delight, Marushka saw that they were ripe strawberries.

"Now, Marushka," June cried, "there are your strawberries! Pick them quickly!"

Marushka picked an apronful of berries. Then she thanked the Months politely, bade them good-bye, and hurried home.

Just imagine again Holena and the stepmother's surprise as they saw Marushka coming through the snow with an apronful of strawberries!

They opened the door and instantly the fragrance of the berries filled the house.

"Where did you get them?" Holena demanded rudely.

"High up in the mountain," Marushka answered, "under the beech trees."

Holena took the strawberries and gobbled and gobbled and gobbled. Then the stepmother ate all she wanted. But it never occured to either of them to say:

"Here, Marushka, you take one."

The next day, when Holena was sitting idle, as usual, in the chimney corner, the notion took her that she must have some red apples. So she called Marushka and said:

"Here you, Marushka, go out to the forest and get me some red apples."

"But, my dear sister," Marushka gasped, "where can I find red apples in winter?"

"What, you lazy little slattern, you dare to argue with me! You go this minute, and if you come back without red apples, I'll kill you!"

For the third time the stepmother sided with Holena and, taking Marushka roughly by the shoulder, pushed her out of the house and slammed the door.

So again the poor child went out to the forest. All around the snow lay deep with no track of man or beast in any direction. This time Marushka hurried straight to the mountain-top. She found the Months still seated about their fire with Great January still on the high stone.

Marushka bowed politely and said:

"Kind sirs, may I warm myself at your fire? I am shaking with cold."

Great January nodded, and Marushka reached her stiff fingers toward the flames.

"Why are you here again, Marushka?" Great January asked. "What are you looking for now?"

"Red apples," Marushka answered. "My sister, Holena, says I must bring her some red apples from the forest or she will kill me, and my mother says so, too. Please sir, won't you tell me where I can find some?"

Great January slowly stood up and walked over to one of the older Months. He handed him the long staff and said:

"Here, September, you take the high seat."

So September took the high seat and began waving the staff over the fire. The fire burned and glowed. Instantly the snow disappeared. The fields about looked brown and yellow and dry. From the trees the leaves dropped one by one and a cool breeze scattered them over the stubble. There were not many flowers, old wild asters on the hillside, and meadow saffron in the valleys, and under the beeches ferns and ivy. Presently Marushka spied an apple tree weighted down with ripe fruit.

"There, Marushka," September called, "there are your apples. Gather them quickly."

Marushka reached up and picked one apple. Then she picked another.

"That's enough, Marushka!" September shouted. "Don't pick any more!"

Marushka obeyed at once. Then she thanked the Months politely, bade them good-bye, and hurried home.

Holena and her stepmother were more surprised than ever to see Marushka coming through the snow with red apples in her hands. They let her in and grabbed the apples from her.

"Where did you get them?" Holena demanded.

"High up on the mountain," Marushka answered. "There are plenty of them growing there."

"Plenty of them! And you only brought us two!" Holena cried angrily. "Or did you pick more and eat them yourself on the way home?"

"No, no, my dear sister," Marushka said. "I haven't eaten any, truly I haven't. They shouted to me not to pick any more."

"I wish the lightning had struck you dead!" Holena sneered. "I've a good mind to beat you!"

After a time the greedy Holena left off her scolding to eat one of the apples. It had so delicious a flavor that she declared she had never in all her life tasted anything so good. Her mother said the same. When they had finished both apples, they began to wish for more.

"Mother," Holena said, "go get me my fur cloak. I'm going up the mountain myself. No use sending that lazy little slattern again, for she would only eat up all the apples on the way home. I'll find that tree and when I pick the apples, I'd like to see anybody stop me!"

The mother begged Holena not to go out in such weather, but Holena was headstrong and would go. She threw her fur cloak over her shoulders and put a shawl on her head and off she went up the mountain-side.

All around the snow lay deep with no track of man or beast in any direction. Holena wandered on and on determined to find those wonderful apples. At last she saw a light in the distance and when she reached it she found it was the great fire about which the Twelve Months were seated.

At first she was frightened, but, soon growing bold, she elbowed her way through the circle of men and without so much as saying, "By your leave," she put out her hands to the fire. She hadn't even the courtesy to say: "Good-day."

Great January frowned.

"Who are you?" he asked in a deep voice. "And what do you want?"

Holena looked at him rudely.

"You old fool, what business is it of yours who I am or what I want!"

She tossed her head airily and walked off into the forest.

The frown deepened on Great January's brow. Slowly he stood up and waved the staff over his head. The fire died down. Then the sky grew dark; an icy wind blew over the mountain; and the snow began to fall so thickly that it looked as if someone in the sky were emptying a huge feather bed.

Holena could not see a step before her. She struggled on and on. Now she ran into a tree, now she fell into a snowdrift. In spite of her warm cloak her limbs began to weaken and grow numb. The snow kept on falling, the icy wind kept on blowing.

Did Holena at last begin to feel sorry that she had been so wicked and cruel to Marushka? No, she did not. Instead, the colder she grew, the more bitterly she reviled Marushka in her heart, the more bitterly she reviled even the good God Himself.

Meanwhile, at home her mother waited for her and waited. She stood at the window as long as she could, then she opened the door and tried to peer through the storm. She waited and waited, but no Holena came.

"Oh dear, oh dear, what can be keeping her?" she thought to herself. "Does she like those apples so much that she can't leave them, or what is it? I think I'll have to go out myself and find her."

So the stepmother put her fur cloak about her shoulders, threw a shawl over her head, and started out.

She called: "Holena! Holena!" but no one answered.

She struggled on and on up the mountainside. All around the snow lay deep with no track of man or beast in any direction.

"Holena! Holena!"

Still no answer.

The snow fell fast. The icy wind moaned on.

At home Marushka prepared the dinner and looked after the cow. Still neither Holena nor the stepmother returned.

"What can they be doing all this time?" Marushka thought.

She ate her dinner alone and then sat down to work at the distaff.

The spindle filled and daylight faded, and still no sign of Holena and her mother.

"Dear God in heaven, what can be keeping them!" Marushka cried anxiously. She peered out the window to see if they were coming.

The storm had spent itself. The wind had died down. The fields gleamed white in the snow, and up in the sky the frosty stars were twinkling brightly. But not a living creature was in sight. Marushka knelt down and prayed for her sister and mother.

The next morning she prepared breakfast for them.

"They'll be very cold and hungry," she said to herself.

She waited for them, but they didn't come. She cooked dinner for them, but still they didn't come. In fact they never came, for they both froze to death on the mountain.

So our good little Marushka inherited the cottage and the garden and the cow. After a time she married a farmer. He made her a good husband and they lived together very happily.

THE SNAKE CHIEF / Africa—the Xhosa

Kathleen Arnott

Even in Africa tales are told in which well-mannered girls achieve great position and happiness while proud, rude girls are destroyed. Notice that again the younger daughter is the heroine. It is an almost universal motif in folklore—the heroes and heroines are the youngest in a family. Sometimes sympathy is aroused for them because they are abused but, as in this tale, often the only reason for their prominence is that they are the youngest.

"The Snake Chief" is similar to both the European Cinderella cycle and to "Beauty and the Beast." By not showing fear and by being willing to marry him, Mpunzanyana breaks the enchantment that had transformed the handsome man into a snake with five heads.

There were once two sisters who lived in a village beside a river. When they were old enough to be married, their father looked around for suitors, but alas, none came, so he decided he must visit other villages and let it be known that he had two daughters ready to be wed.

One day, he took his small canoe and crossed the big river. Then he walked along a path until he came to a village. It appeared to be a happy place and the people greeted him kindly.

'Welcome!' they cried. 'What news have you brought?'

'I have no news of importance,' he replied. 'Have you?'

'Our chief is looking for a wife,' the people replied, 'otherwise nothing we can think of is worth repeating.'

Now the man had found out what he wanted to know, and he told the people that he would send a wife for the chief the next day.

He re-crossed the river and went to his house, smiling contentedly. When his daughters came back from their work in the fields he called them and said:

'At last I have found a man who is worthy to be the husband of one of my daughters. The chief in the village across the water is looking for a wife. Which of you shall I send?'

"The Snake Chief," from *African Myths and Legends.* © 1962 Kathleen Arnott. Used by permission of Henry Z. Walck, Inc., publisher.

The elder daughter said quickly: 'I shall go, of course, since I am the elder.'

'Very well,' replied the man. 'I shall call all my friends and bid the drummers lead you to your husband's home.'

'Indeed you will not,' said the girl haughtily. 'When I go to the home of my husband, I shall go alone.'

Now in that part of Africa it was unheard of for a bride to go to her wedding without a host of friends and relations all singing and dancing for joy. So the father was astonished when his daughter said she would go alone, even though he knew she had been proud and headstrong from childhood.

'But, my daughter,' he pleaded, 'no woman ever goes alone to her marriage. It is not the custom.'

'Then I shall start a new custom,' said the girl. 'Unless I go alone, I shall not go at all.'

At last the father, realizing that no amount of persuasion would induce the girl to change her mind, agreed to her going alone, and early the next morning she set out. He took her across the river and pointed out the way, then returned home unhappily.

The girl began her journey without looking back and after a little while she met a mouse on the path. It stood up on its hind-legs, and rubbing its two front paws together, asked politely:

'Would you like me to show you the way to the chief's village?'

The girl scarcely stopped walking and almost trod on the mouse as she replied:

'Get out of my sight! I want no help from you.'

Then she continued on her way while the mouse screeched after her:

'Bad luck to you!'

A little further on the girl met a frog, sitting on a stone at the side of the path.

'Would you like me to show you the way?' he croaked.

'Don't you speak to me!' answered the girl, tipping the frog off the stone with her foot. 'I am going to be a chief's wife and am far too important to have anything to do with a mere frog.'

'Bad luck to you then,' croaked the frog, as he picked himself up from where he had fallen and jumped off into the bush.

Soon after this the girl began to feel tired and she sat down under a tree to rest. In the distance she could hear goats bleating and presently a herd of them passed by, driven by a little boy.

'Greetings, sister,' he said politely. 'Are you going on a long journey?'

'What busines is that of yours?' demanded the girl.

'I thought you might be carrying food with you,' replied the boy, 'and I hoped you might give me something to eat for I am so hungry.'

'I have no food,' said the girl, 'and even if I had I should not dream of giving any to you.'

The boy looked disappointed and hurried after his goats, turning back to say over his shoulder:

'Bad luck to you then.'

Presently the girl got to her feet and continued her journey. Suddenly she found herself face to face with a very old woman.

'Greetings, my daughter,' she said to the girl. 'Let me give you some advice.'

'You will come to some trees which will laugh at you, but do not laugh back at them.

'You will find a bag of thick, curdled milk, but do not on any account drink it.

'You will meet a man who carries his head under his arm, but you must not drink water if he offers you any.'

'Be quiet, you ugly old thing!' exclaimed the girl, pushing the old woman aside. 'If I want any advice from you, I'll ask for it.'

'You will have bad luck if you don't listen to me,' quavered the old woman, but the girl took no notice and went on her way.

Sure enough she soon came to a clump of trees which began to laugh loudly as she approached them.

'Stop laughing at me,' she commanded, and when they did not, she laughed noisily at them in return as she passed them by.

A little further on, she saw a bag made from a whole goat-skin, lying at her feet. On picking it up, she discovered it was full of curdled milk and since this was something she was particularly fond of, she drank it with relish, exclaiming:

'How lucky I found this! I was getting so thirsty with such a long journey.'

Then she threw the bag into the bush and continued on her way. As she walked through a shady grove, she was a little taken aback at the strange sight of a man coming towards her, carrying his head under one arm. The eyes in the head looked at her and the mouth spoke:

'Would you like some water to drink, my daughter?' it said, and the hand that was not carrying the head held out a calabash of water to the girl.

She was not really thirsty but decided to taste the water and see whether it was sweet, so she took a sip, found it delicious and drank the whole calabash full. Then she continued, without a word of thanks to the strange creature.

As she turned the next bend in the path, she saw in the distance the village she was seeking and knew that her journey was almost over. She had to cross a small stream and found a girl bending there, filling her water-pot.

She was about to pass on when the village girl greeted her and asked:

'Where are you going, pray?'

With scarcely a glance at her questioner she replied:

'I am going to that village to marry a chief. You have no right to speak to me, for I am older than you and far more important.'

Now the younger girl was the chief's sister, but she did not boast about this. She merely said:

'Let me give you some advice. Do not enter the village from this side. It is unlucky to do so. Go right round past those tall trees and enter it on the far side.'

The girl took no notice at all but just walked on to the nearest entrance with her head in the air. When she arrived, the women crowded round her to find out who she was and what she wanted.

'I have come to marry your chief,' she explained. 'Get away, and let me rest.'

'How can you be a bride if you come alone?' they asked. 'Where is the bridal procession, and are there no drummers with you?'

The girl did not answer, but she sat down in the shade of a hut to rest her aching legs.

Presently some of the older women came over to her.

'If you are to be the wife of our chief,' they said, 'then you must prepare his supper, as all good wives do.'

The girl realized that this was true, so she asked:

'And from where shall I get the millet to cook my husband's supper?'

They gave her some millet and told her to grind it, showing her where the grinding-stones were, but unlike most women, she only ground the corn for a very short time, so that the flour was coarse and gritty. Then she made some bread, and when the other women saw it, they went away together and laughed at her incompetence.

As the sun set, a mighty wind blew up. The roof of the hut shook and shivered and the girl crouched against the mud walls in fear. But worse was to come. A huge snake with five heads suddenly appeared, and coiling itself up at the door of the hut, told her to bring it the supper she had cooked.

'Did you not know that I am the chief?' asked the snake, as it began to eat the bread. Then it uttered a fearful scream, spat the food from its mouth and hissed:

'This supper is so badly cooked, I refuse to have you for a wife! So I shall slay you!' and with a mighty blow from his tail, he killed her.

When the news of her death at last reached her father, he still had not found a husband for his younger daughter, whose name was Mpunzanyana.

'Let *me* go to this chief,' she begged him. 'I am sure I could please him if I tried.'

Rather reluctantly the father called together all his relations and friends and asked them to make up a bridal procession for his second daughter. They were all delighted and went away to put on their best clothes, while the father summoned the musicians and drummers who were to lead the way.

They set off early in the morning, and crossing the big river, they sang joyfully as they went. They began the long journey along the same little path that the eldest daughter had taken not so long ago, and presently they met a mouse.

'Shall I tell you how to get there?' it asked of Mpunzanyana, as she stopped to avoid treading on it.

'Thank you very much,' she replied, and listened courteously as the tiny animal told them which path to take.

On they went until they came to a deep valley and found a very old woman sitting beside a tree. The ugly old creature rose shakily to her feet to stand before the girl. Then she said:

'When you come to a place where two paths meet, you must take the little one, not the big one as that is unlucky.'

'Thank you for telling me, grannie,' Mpunzanyana answered. 'I will do as you say and take the little path.'

They journeyed on and on, meeting no one for some time, until suddenly a coney stood on the path in front of them all. Stretching up its head, it looked at the girl and said:

'You are nearly there! But let me give you some advice. Soon you will meet a young girl carrying water from the stream. Mind you speak politely to her.

'When you get to the village they will give you millet to grind for the chief's supper. Make sure you do it properly.

'And finally, when you see your husband, do not be afraid. I beg you, have no fear, or at least, do not show it.'

'Thank you for your advice, little coney,' said the girl. 'I will try to remember it all and do as you say.'

Sure enough, as they turned the last bend in the path, they caught sight of the village, and coming up from the stream they overtook a young girl carrying a pot of water on her head. It was the chief's sister, and she asked:

'Where are you bound for?'

'We are going to this village where I hope to be the chief's bride,' answered Mpunzanyana.

'Let me lead you to the chief's hut,' said the younger girl, 'and do not be afraid when you see him.'

Mpunzanyana followed the girl, and the bridal party followed Mpunzanyana, so that all the people came out of their huts to see what the joyful noise was about. They welcomed the vistors politely and gave them food to eat. Then the chief's mother brought millet to Mpunzanyana and said:

'If you are to be the wife of our chief, then you must prepare his supper, as all good wives do.'

So the girl set to work and ground the millet as finely as she could, then made it into light, delicious bread.

As the sun set, a strong wind arose which shook the house and when Mpunzanyana heard the people saying: 'Here comes our chief,' she began to tremble. Then she remembered what she had been told and even when one of the poles which supported the roof fell to the ground, she did not run outside in a panic but stood quietly waiting for her husband to come home.

She almost cried out when she saw the huge snake, but when it asked her for food, she gave it the bread she had cooked and it ate it with obvious enjoyment.

'This bread is delicious,' said the snake. 'Will you be my wife?'

For one moment, Mpunzanyana was struck dumb, but she smiled bravely when she thought of all the advice she had had, and replied:

'Yes, O chief, I will marry you.'

At her words, the shining snake-skin fell from the chief and he rose up, a tall, handsome man.

'By your brave words, you have broken the spell,' he explained.

That night a feast was begun in the chief's village which lasted for twenty days. Oxen were slaughtered, beer was brewed and all the time the sound of music and drumming made the people's hearts glad.

So Mpunzanyana became the wife of a rich and splendid chief, and in course of time they had many sons, while the village prospered under her husband's wise rule.

BOOTS AND HIS BROTHERS / Scandinavia

Peter Christen Asbjörnsen

As in the Cinderella tales that have heroines, these male Cinderella stories are about abused or scorned children. Boots, again the youngest of three sons, is considered a fool by his brothers, yet his behavior about the ax, shovel, and the walnut prove he is not stupid. But why should he be the one to find such magical objects? Because he is the youngest. In some more complex variants, Boots' brothers steal the magical objects and he must recover them.

Once upon a time there was a man who had three sons, Peter, Paul, and John. John was Boots, of course, because he was the youngest.

I can't say the man had anything more than these three sons, for he hadn't one penny to rub against another. So he told his sons over and over again they must go out into the world and try to earn their bread, for there at home there was nothing to be looked for but starving to death.

Now, a short way from the man's cottage was the King's palace, and you must know, just against the King's windows a great oak had sprung up, which was so stout and big that it took away all the light from the palace. The King had said he would give many, many dollars to the man who could fell the oak, but no one was man enough for that, for as soon as ever one chip of the oak's trunk flew off, two grew in its stead.

A well, too, the King would have dug, which was to hold water for the whole year; for all his neighbors had wells, but he hadn't any, and that he thought a shame. So the King said he would give any one who could dig him a well that would hold water for a whole year round, both money and goods. But no one could do it, for the King's palace was high, high up on a hill, and they hadn't dug a few inches before they came upon solid rock.

"Boots and His Brothers," from *Popular Tales from the Norse* by Peter Christen Asbjörnsen, translated by G. W. Dasent. Published by G. P. Putnam's Sons, 1908.

But as the King had set his heart on having these two things done, he had it given out far and wide, in all parts of his kingdom, that he who could fell the big oak in the king's courtyard and dig a well that would hold water the whole year round should have the Princess and half the kingdom.

Well! As you can easily guess, there was many a man who came to try his luck. But all their hacking and hewing, and all their digging and delving did them no good. The oak got bigger and stouter at every stroke, and the rock didn't get softer either.

One day the three brothers thought they'd set off to try too, and their father hadn't a word against it. Even if they didn't get the Princess and half the kingdom, they might get a place somewhere with a good master; and that was all he wanted. When the brothers said they thought of going to the palace, their father agreed at once. So the three brothers started out.

They hadn't gone far before they came to a fir wood, and up along one side of it rose a steep hillside. As the brothers went along, they heard something hewing and hacking away up on the hill among the trees.

"I wonder now what it is that is hewing away up wonder," said Boots.

"You're always so clever with your wonderings," said his brothers both at once. "What wonder is it, pray, that a woodcutter should stand and hack on a hillside?"

"Still, I'd like to see what it is, after all," said Boots; and up he went.

"Oh, if you're such a child, 'twill do you good to go and take a lesson," bawled out his brothers after him.

But Boots didn't care for what they said. He climbed the steep hillside toward the noise, and when he reached the place, what do you think he saw? Why, an ax that stood there hacking and hewing, all of itself, at the trunk of a fir.

"Good day," said Boots. "So you stand here all alone and hew, do you?"

"Yes; here I've stood and hewed and hacked a long, long time, waiting for you," said the ax.

"Well, here I am at last," said Boots.

He took the ax, pulled it off its handle, and stuffed both head and handle into his wallet.

When he got down again to his brothers, they began to jeer and laugh at him.

"And now, what funny thing was it you saw up yonder on the hillside?" they said.

"Oh, it was only an ax we heard," said Boots.

When they had gone a bit farther, they came under a steep spur of rock; and up above the rock they heard something digging and shoveling.

"I wonder now," said Boots, "what it is digging and shoveling up yonder at the top of the rock."

"Oh, you're always so clever with your wonderings," said his brothers again. "As if you'd never heard a woodpecker hacking and pecking at a hollow tree!"

"Well, well," said Boots, "I think it would be a piece of fun just to see what it really is."

So off he set to climb the rock, while the others laughed and made game of him. But he didn't care a bit for that. Up he climbed, and when he got near the top, what do you think he saw? Why, a spade that stood there digging and delving.

"Good day," said Boots. "So you stand here all alone and dig and delve?"

"Yes, that's what I do," said the spade. "And that's what I've done this many a long day, waiting for you."

"Well, here I am," said Boots.

He took the spade and knocked it off its handle and put them into his wallet. Then he went down again to his brothers.

"Well, what was it, so rare and strange," said Peter and Paul, "that you saw up there at the top of the rock?"

"Oh," said Boots, "nothing more than a spade; that was what we heard."

So they went on again a good bit, till they came to a brook. They were thirsty, all three after their long walk, and they lay down beside the brook to have a drink.

"I wonder now," said Boots, "where all this water comes from."

"I wonder if you're right in your head," said Peter and Paul, in one breath. "If you're not mad already, you'll go mad very soon, with your wonderings. Where the brook comes from, indeed! Have you never heard how water rises from a spring in the earth?"

"Yes, but still I've a great fancy to see where this brook comes from," said Boots.

Up alongside the brook he went. In spite of all that his brothers bawled after him, nothing could stop him.

On he went. As he went up and up, the brook got smaller and smaller; and at last, a little way farther on, what do you think he saw? Why, a great walnut, and out of that the water trickled.

"Good day," said Boots. "So you lie here and trickle and run all alone?"

"Yes, I do," said the walnut. "And here have I trickled and run this many a long day, waiting for you."

"Well, here I am," said Boots.

He took up a lump of moss and plugged up the hole, that the water mightn't run out. Then he put the walnut into his wallet and ran down to his brothers.

"Well, now," said Peter and Paul, "have you found out where the water comes from? A rare sight it must have been!"

"Oh, after all, it was only a hole it ran out of," said Boots. And so the others laughed and made game of him again, but Boots didn't mind that a bit.

"After all, I had the fun of seeing it," said he.

When they had gone a bit farther, they came to the King's palace. Everyone in the kingdom had heard how a man might win the Princess and half the realm, if he could only fell the big oak and dig the King's well. Many had come to try their luck, so many that the oak was now twice as stout and big as it had been at first. Two chips grew for every one they hewed out with their axes.

Peter and Paul did not let themselves be scared by that; they were quite sure they could fell the oak. Peter, as he was the eldest, was to try his hand first. But it went with him as with all the rest who had hewn at the oak; for every chip he cut out, two grew in its place.

Now Paul was to try his luck, but he fared just the same. When he had hewn two or three strokes, they began to see the oak grow and so the King's men seized him and made him stop.

Now Boots was to try.

"You might as well save yourself the bother," said the King, for he was angry with him because of his brothers.

"Well, I'd just like to try," said Boots, and so he got leave. Then he took his ax out of his walet and fitted it to its handle.

"Hew away!" said he to his ax.

Away it hewed, making the chips fly, so that it wasn't long before down came the oak.

When that was done, Boots pulled out his spade and fitted it to its handle.

"Dig away!" said he to his spade.

The spade began to dig and delve till the earth and rock flew out in splinters, and soon he had the well dug.

When he had got it as big and deep as he chose, Boots took out his walnut and laid it in one corner of the well. He pulled out the plug of moss.

"Trickle and run!" said Boots.

The nut trickled and ran, till the water gushed out of the hole in a stream. In a short time the well was brimful.

Now Boots had felled the oak which shaded the King's palace and dug a well in the palace yard; so he got the Princess and half the kingdom, as the king had said.

Then Peter and Paul had to say, "Well, after all, Boots wasn't so much out of his mind when he took to wondering."

THE WATER OF LIFE / Germany

The Grimm brothers

This popular story is told throughout Europe, western and southern Asia, Indonesia, and central Africa. Three brothers are sent on a quest; the youngest brother, because of a kindness to animals or an old man or woman, is successful; rescues his brothers who betray him; and must prove his merit again. Quests are as common in folktales as are jealous brothers and broken promises.

There was once a king who was so ill that it was thought impossible his life could be saved. He had three sons, and they were all in great distress on his account, and they went into the castle gardens and wept at the thought that he must die. An old man came up to them and asked the cause of their grief. They told him that their father was dying, and nothing could save him.

"The Water of Life," from *Grimms' Fairy Tales*, translated by Mrs. E. V. Lucas, Lucy Crane, and Marian Edwards. Published by Grossett and Dunlap, 1945.

The old man said, "There is only one remedy which I know. It is the Water of Life. If he drinks of it he will recover, but it is very difficult to find."

The eldest son said, "I will soon find it." And he went to the sick man to ask permission to go in search of the Water of Life, as that was the only thing to cure him.

"No," said the King. "The danger is too great. I would rather die." But he persisted so long that at last the King gave his permission.

The Prince thought, "If I bring this water I

shall be the favorite, and I shall inherit the kingdom."

So he set off, and when he had ridden some distance he came upon a dwarf standing in the road, who cried, "Whither away so fast?"

"Stupid little fellow," said the Prince proudly, "what busines is it of yours?" And he rode on.

The little man was very angry and made an evil vow.

Soon afterwards, the Prince came to a gorge in the mountains, and the farther he rode the narrower it became, till he could go no farther. His horse could neither go forward nor turn round for him to dismount. So there he sat, jammed in.

The sick King waited a long time for him, but he never came back. Then the second son said, "Father, let me go and find the Water of Life." He was thinking, "If my brother is dead I shall have the kingdom."

The King at first refused to let him go but at last he gave his consent. So the Prince started on the same road as his brother and met the same dwarf, who stopped him and asked where he was going in such a hurry.

"Little snippet, what does it matter to you?" he said, and rode away without looking back.

But the dwarf cast a spell over him, and he, too, got into a narrow gorge like his brother, where he could neither go backwards nor forwards. That is what happens to the haughty.

As the second son also stayed away, the youngest one offered to go and fetch the Water of Life, and at last the King was obliged to let him go.

When he also met the dwarf, and the dwarf asked him where he was hurrying to, he stopped and said, "I am searching for the Water of Life, because my father is dying."

"Do you know where it is to be found?"

"No," said the Prince.

"As you have spoken pleasantly to me, and not been haughty like your false brothers, I will help you and tell you how to find the Water of Life. It flows from a fountain in the courtyard of an enchanted castle. But you will never get in unless I give you an iron rod and two loaves of bread. With the rod strike three times on the iron gate of the castle and it will spring open. Inside you will find two lions with wide-open jaws, but if you throw a loaf to each they will be quiet. Then you must make haste to fetch the Water of Life be-

fore it strikes twelve, or the gates of the castle will close and you will be shut in."

The Prince thanked him, took the rod and the loaves, and set off. When he reached the castle all was just as the dwarf had said. At the third knock the gate flew open, and when he had pacified the lions with the loaves, he walked into the castle. In the great hall he found several enchanted princes, and he took the rings from their fingers. He also took a sword and a loaf which were lying by them.

On passing into the next room he found a beautiful maiden, who rejoiced at his coming. She embraced him and said that he had saved her, and should have the whole of her kingdom, and if he would come back in a year she would marry him. She also told him where to find the fountain with the enchanted water, but she said he must make haste to get out of the castle before the clock struck twelve.

Then he went on and came to a room where there was a beautiful bed freshly made, and as he was very tired he thought he would take a little rest. So he lay down and fell asleep. When he woke it was striking a quarter to twelve. He sprang up in a fright, and ran to the fountain and took some of the water in a cup which was lying near, and then hurried away. The clock struck just as he reached the iron gate, and it banged so quickly that it took off a bit of his heel.

He rejoiced at having got some of the Water of Life, and hastened on his homeward journey. He again passed the dwarf, who said when he saw the sword and the loaf, "Those things will be of much service to you. You will be able to strike down whole armies with the sword, and the loaf will never come to an end."

The Prince did not want to go home without his brothers and he said, "Good dwarf, can you not tell me where my brothers are? They went in search of the Water of Life before I did, but they never came back."

"They are both stuck fast in a narrow mountain gorge. I cast a spell over them because of their pride."

Then the Prince begged so hard that they might be released that at last the dwarf yielded. But he warned him against them and said, "Beware of them! They have bad hearts."

He was delighted to see his brothers when they came back, and told them all that had happened to him: how he had found the Water of Life and brought a gobletful with him; how he had released a beautiful princess, who would wait a year for him and then marry him, and he would then become a great prince.

Then they rode away together and came to a land where famine and war were raging. The King thought he would be utterly ruined, so great was the destitution.

The Prince went to him and gave him the loaf, and with it he fed and satisfied his whole kingdom. The Prince also gave him his sword, and he smote the whole army of his enemies with it, and then he was able to live in peace and quiet. Then the Prince took back his sword and his loaf, and the three brothers rode on.

But later they had to pass through two more countries where war and famine were raging, and each time the Prince gave his sword and his loaf to the King and in this way he saved three kingdoms.

After that they took a ship and crossed the sea. During the passage the two elder brothers said to each other, "Our youngest brother found the Water of Life, and we did not. So our father will give him the kingdom which we ought to have, and he will take away our fortune from us."

This thought made them very vindictive and they made up their minds to get rid of him. They waited till he was asleep, and then they emptied the Water of Life from his goblet and took it themselves, and filled up his cup with salt sea water.

As soon as they got home the youngest Prince took his goblet to the King so that he might drink of the water which was to make him well. But after drinking only a few drops of the sea water he became more ill than ever. As he was bewailing himself, his two elder sons came to him and accused the youngest of trying to poison him, and said that they had the real Water of Life, and gave him some. No sooner had he drunk it than he felt better, and he soon became as strong and well as he had been in his youth.

Then the two went to the youngest brother and mocked him, saying, "It was you who found the Water of Life. You had all the trouble, while we have the reward. You should have been wiser and kept your eyes open. We stole it from you while you were asleep on the ship. When the end of the year comes, one of us will go and bring away the beautiful Princess. But don't dare to betray us. Our father will certainly not believe you, and if you say a single word you will surely lose your life. Your one and only chance is to keep silence."

The old King was very angry with his youngest son, thinking that he had tried to take his life. So he had the court assembled to give judgment upon him, and it was decided that he must be secretly got out of the way.

One day when the Prince was going out hunting, thinking no evil, the King's huntsman was ordered to go with him. Seeing the huntsman look sad, the Prince said to him, "My good huntsman, what is the matter with you?"

The huntsman answered, "I can't bear to tell you, and yet I must."

The Prince said, "Say it out. Whatever it is I will forgive you."

"Alas!" said the huntsman, "I am to shoot you dead. It is the King's command."

The Prince was horror-stricken and said, "Dear huntsman, do not kill me. Give me my life. Let me have your dress, and you shall have my royal robes."

The huntsman said, "I will gladly do so. I could never have shot you." So they changed clothes and the huntsman went home, but the Prince wandered away into the forest.

After a time three wagonloads of gold and precious stones came to the King for his youngest son. They were sent by the kings who had been saved by the Prince's sword and his miraculous loaf, and who now wished to show their gratitude.

Then the old King thought, "What if my son really was innocent?" And he said to his people, "If only he were still alive! How sorry I am that I ordered him to be killed."

"He is still alive," said the huntsman. "I could not find it in my heart to carry out your commands." And he told the King what had taken place.

A load fell from the King's heart on hearing the good news, and he sent out a proclamation to all parts of his kingdom that his son was to come home, where he would be received with great favor.

In the meantime, the Princess had caused a road to be made of pure shining gold leading to her castle, and told her people that whoever came riding straight along it would be the true bridegroom, and they were to admit him. But anyone who came either on one side of the road or the other would not be the right one, and he was not to be let in.

When the year had almost passed, the eldest Prince thought that he would hurry to the Princess, and by giving himself out as her deliverer would gain a wife and a kingdom as well. So he rode away, and when he saw the beautiful golden road he thought it would be a thousand pities to ride upon it, so he turned aside and rode to the right of it. But when he reached the gate the people told him that he was not the true bridegroom, and he had to go away.

Soon after the second Prince came, and when he saw the golden road he thought it would be a thousand pities for his horse to tread upon it, so

he turned aside and rode up on the left of it. But when he reached the gate he was also told that he was not the true bridegroom, and like his brother was turned away.

When the year had quite come to an end, the third Prince came out of the wood to ride to his beloved, and through her to forget all his past sorrows. So on he went, thinking only of her and wishing to be with her, and he never even saw the golden road. His horse cantered right along the middle of it, and when he reached the gate it was flung open and the Princess received him joyfully, and called him her deliverer and the lord of her kingdom. Their marriage was celebrated without delay and with much rejoicing. When it was over, she told him that his father had called him back and forgiven him. So he went to him and told him everything: how his brothers had deceived him, and how they had forced him to keep silence. The old King wanted to punish them, but they had taken a ship and sailed away over the sea, and they never came back as long as they lived.

THE PRINCESS ON THE GLASS HILL / Scandinavia

Peter Christen Asbjörnsen

Boots is an unlikely hero who has done nothing "but sit in the ashes and toast" himself, but there is more bravery and wisdom in Boots than anyone suspects—for the simple reason that he is the youngest of three sons and therefore the hero.

Three horses come in three successive years and each time Boots repeats the same refrain, "Ho, ho! it's you, is it, that comes here eating up our hay? I'll soon put a spoke in your wheel, I'll soon stop that." Things often occur in threes in wonder tales—three children, three wishes, three horses, three guesses.

An interesting comparision of motifs can be made between "Boots and His Brothers" and this more complex tale and also between "The Princess on the Glass Hill" and "Cinderella."

Once on a time there was a man who had a meadow, which lay high up on the hillside, and in the meadow was a barn, which he had built to

keep his hay in. Now, I must tell you there hadn't been much in the barn for the last year or two, for every Saint John's night, when the grass stood greenest and deepest, the meadow was eaten down to the very ground the next morning, just as if a whole drove of sheep had been there

"The Princess on the Glass Hill," from Peter Christen Asbjörnsen, *Popular Tales from the Norse,* translated by G. W. Dasent. Published by G. P. Putnam's Sons, 1908.

feeding on it over night. This happened once, and it happened twice; so that at last the man grew weary of losing his crop of hay, and said to his sons—for he had three of them, and the youngest was named Boots, of course—that now one of them must just go and sleep in the barn in the outlying field when Saint John's night came, for it was too good a joke that his grass should be eaten, root and blade, this year, as it had been the last two years. So whichever of them went he must keep a sharp lookout; that was what their father said.

Well, the eldest son was ready to go and watch the meadow; trust him for looking after the grass! It shouldn't be his fault if man or beast, or the fiend himself, got a blade of grass. So, when evening came, he set off to the barn and lay down to sleep; but a little later on in the night there came such a clatter, and such an earthquake, that walls and roof shook, and groaned, and creaked; then up jumped the lad and took to his heels as fast as ever he could; nor dared he once look round till he reached home; and as for the hay, why, it was eaten up this year just as it had been twice before.

The next Saint John's night, the man said again it would never do to lose all the grass in the outlying field year after year in this way, so one of the sons must trudge off to watch it, and watch it well, too. Well, the next oldest son was ready to try his luck. So off he went and lay down to sleep in the barn as his brother had done before him; but as night came on, there came a rumbling and quaking of the earth, worse even than on the last Saint John's night. When the lad heard it, he got frightened, and took to his heels as though he were running a race.

Next year the turn came to Boots; but when he made ready to go, the other two began to laugh, and make game of him, saying:

"You're just the man to watch the hay, that you are; you who have done nothing all your life but sit in the ashes and toast yourself by the fire."

Boots did not care a pin for their chattering, and stumped away, as evening drew on, up the hillside to the outlying field. There he went inside the barn and lay down; but in about an hour's time the barn began to groan and creak, so that it was dreadful to hear.

"Well," said Boots to himself; "if it isn't any worse than this I can stand it well enough."

A little while after there came another creak and an earthquake, so that the litter in the barn flew about the lad's ears.

"Oh," said Boots to himself; "if it isn't any worse than this, I daresay I can stand it out."

But just then came a third rumbling, and a third earthquake, so that the lad thought walls and roof were coming down on his head; but it passed off, and all was still as death about him.

"It'll come again, I'll be bound," thought Boots; but no, it did not come again; still it was and still it stayed; but after he had lain a little while he heard a noise as if a horse were standing just outside the barndoor, and cropping the grass. He stole to the door and peeped through a chink; and there stood a horse feeding away. So big and fat and grand a horse, Boots had never set eyes on; by his side on the grass lay a saddle and bridle, and a full set of armor for a knight, all of brass, so bright that the light gleamed from it.

"Ho, ho!" thought the lad; "it's you, is it, that eats up our hay? I'll soon put a spoke in your wheel; just see if I don't."

So he lost no time, but took the steel out of his tinder-box and threw it over the horse; then it had no power to stir from the spot and became so tame that the lad could do what he liked with it. He got on its back and rode off with it to a place which no one knew of, and there he put up the horse. When he got home his brothers laughed and asked how he fared.

"You didn't lie long in the barn, even if you had the heart to go as far as the field."

"Well," said Boots, "all I can say is, I lay in the barn till the sun rose, and neither saw nor heard anything; I can't think what there was in the barn to make you both so afraid."

"A pretty story!" said his brothers; "but we'll soon see how you watched the meadow." So they set off, but when they reached it, there stood the grass as deep and thick as it had been the night before.

Well, the next Saint John's night it was the same story over again; neither of the elder brothers dared to go out to the outlying field to watch the crop; but Boots, he had the heart to go, and everything happened just as it had happened the year before. First a clatter and an earthquake, then a greater clatter and another earthquake, and so on a third time; only this year the earthquakes were far worse than the year before. Then all at once, everything was as still as death, and the lad heard how something was cropping the grass outside the barn-door, so he stole to the door and peeped through a chink; and what do you think he saw? Why, another horse standing right up against the wall, and chewing and champing with might and main. It was far finer and fatter than that one which came the year before; and it had a saddle on its back and a bridle on its neck and a full suit of mail for a knight lay by its side, all of silver, and as grand as you would wish to see.

"Ho, ho!" said Boots to himself; "it's you that gobbles up our hay, is it? I'll soon put a spoke in your wheel"; and with that he took the steel out of his tinder-box and threw it over the horse's crest, which stood still as a lamb. Well, the lad rode this horse, too, to the hiding place where he kept the other one; and after that he went home.

"I suppose you'll tell us," said one of the brothers, "there's a fine crop this year, too, in the hayfield."

"Well, so there is," said Boots; and off ran the others to see, and there stood the grass thick and deep, as it was the year before; but they didn't give Boots softer words for all that.

Now, when the third Saint John's eve came, the two elder still hadn't the heart to lie out in the barn and watch the grass, for they had got so scared the night they lay there before, that they couldn't get over the fright; but Boots, he dared to go; and, to make a long story short, the very same thing happened this time as had happened twice before. Three earthquakes came, one after the other, each worse than the one which went before; and when the last came, the lad danced about with the shock from one barn wall to the other; and after that, all at once, it was as still as death. Now when he had lain a little while he heard something tugging away at the grass outside the barn; so he stole again to the door-chink and peeped out, and there stood a horse close outside —far, far bigger and fatter than the two he had taken before.

"Ho, ho!" said the lad to himself; "it's you, is it, that comes here eating up our hay? I'll soon put a spoke in your wheel, I'll soon stop that." So he caught up his steel and threw it over the horse's neck, and in a trice it stood as if it were nailed to the ground, and Boots could do as he pleased with it. Then he rode off with it to the hiding place where he kept the other two, and then went home. When he got there his two brothers made game of him as they had done before, saying they could see he had watched the grass well, for he looked for all the world as if he were walking in his sleep, and many other spiteful things they said; but Boots gave no heed to them, only asking them to go and see for themselves; and when they went, there stood the grass as fine and deep this time as it had been twice before.

Now, you must know that the king of the country where Boots lived had a daughter, whom he would give only to the man who could ride up over the hill of glass, for there was a high, high hill, all of glass, as smooth and slippery as ice, close by the king's palace. Upon the tip-top of the hill, the king's daughter was to sit, with three golden apples in her lap, and the man who could ride up and carry off the three golden apples was to have half of the kingdom and the princess for his wife. This the king had stuck up on all the church doors in his realm, and had given it out in many other kingdoms besides. Now, this princess was so lovely that all who set eyes on her fell over head and ears in love with her whether they would or not. So I needn't tell you how all the princes and knights who heard of her were eager to win her, as a wife, and half of the kingdom besides; and how they came riding from all parts of the world on high prancing horses, and clad in the grandest clothes, for there wasn't one of them who hadn't made up his mind that he, and he alone, was to win the princess.

When the day of trial came, which the king had fixed, there was such a crowd of princes and knights under the glass hill, that it made one's head to whirl to look at them; and everyone in the country who could even crawl along was off to the hill, for they were all eager to see the man who was to win the princess.

The two elder brothers set off with the rest; but as for Boots, they said outright he shouldn't go with them, for if they were seen with such a dirty changeling, all begrimed with smut from cleaning their shoes and sifting cinders in the dusthole, they said folk would make game of them.

"Very well," said Boots; "it's all one to me. I can go alone, and stand or fall by myself."

Now when the two brothers came to the hill of glass, the knights and princes were all hard at it, riding their horses till they were all in a foam; but it was no good, by my troth; for as soon as ever the horses set foot on the hill, down they slipped, and there wasn't one who could get a yard or two up; and no wonder, for the hill was as smooth as a sheet of glass and as steep as a housewall. But all were eager to have the princess and half the kingdom. So they rode and slipped, and slipped and rode, and still it was the same story over again. At last their horses were so weary that they could scarce lift a leg, and in such a sweat that the lather dripped from them, and so the knights had to give up trying any more. The king was just thinking that he would proclaim a new trial for the next day, to see if they would have better luck, when all at once a knight came riding up on so brave a steed that no one had ever seen the like of it in his born days, and the knight had mail of brass, and the horse, a brass bit in its mouth, so bright that the sunbeams shone from it. Then all the others called out to him that he might just as well spare himself the trouble of riding up the hill, for it would lead to no good; but he gave no heed to them, and put his horse at the hill, and up it went like nothing for a good way, about a third of the height; and when he had got so far, he turned his horse and rode down again. So lovely a knight the princess thought she had never seen; and while he was riding she sat and thought to herself—"Would to heaven he might only come up, and down the other side."

And when she saw him turning back, she threw down one of the golden apples after him, and it rolled down into his shoe. But when he got to the bottom of the hill he rode off so fast that no one could tell what had become of him. That evening all the knights and princes were to go before the king, that he who had ridden so far up the hill might show the apple the princess had thrown; but there was no one who had anything to show. One after the other they all came, but not a man of them could show the apple.

At evening, the brothers of Boots came home

too, and had a long story to tell about the riding up the hill.

"First of all," they said, "there was not one of the whole lot who could get so much as a stride up; but at last came one who had a suit of brass mail, and a brass bridle and saddle, all so bright that the sun shone from them a mile off. He was a chap to ride, just! He rode a third of the way up the hill of glass and he could easily have ridden the whole way up, if he chose; but he turned round and rode down thinking, maybe, that was enough for once."

"Oh! I should so like to have seen him, that I should," said Boots, who sat by the fireside, and stuck his feet into the cinders as was his wont.

"Oh!" said his brothers, "you would, would you? You look fit to keep company with such high lords, nasty beast that you are, sitting there amongst the ashes."

Next day the brothers were all for setting off again; and Boots begged them this time, too, to let him go with them and see the riding; but no, they wouldn't have him at any price, he was too ugly and nasty, they said.

"Well, well," said Boots; "if I go at all, I must go by myself. I'm not afraid."

So when the brothers got to the hill of glass, all the princes and knights began to ride again, and you may fancy they had taken care to shoe their horses sharp; but it was no good—they rode and slipped, and slipped and rode, just as they had done the day before, and there was not one who could get as far as a yard up the hill. And when they had worn out their horses, so that they could not stir a leg, they were all forced to give it up as a bad job. The king thought he might as well proclaim that the riding should take place the next day for the last time, just to give them one chance more; but all at once it came across his mind that he might as well wait a little longer to see if the knight in the brass mail would come this day too. Well, they saw nothing of him; but all at once came one riding on a steed far, far braver and finer than that on which the knight of brass had ridden, and he had silver mail, and a silver saddle and bridle, all so bright that the sunbeams gleamed and glanced from far away. Then the others shouted out to him again, saying he might as well hold hard and not try to ride up the hill, for all his trouble would be thrown away;

but the knight paid no attention to them, and rode straight at the hill and right up it, till he had gone two thirds of the way, and then he wheeled his horse round and rode down again. To tell the truth, the princess liked him still better than the knight in brass, and she sat and wished he might only be able to come right to the top, and down the other side; but when she saw him turning back, she threw the second apple after him, and it rolled into his shoe. But as soon as ever he had come down the hill of glass, he rode off so fast that no one knew what became of him.

At evening when all were to go before the king and the princess, that he who had the golden apple might show it, in they went, one after the other; but there was no one who had any golden apple to show. The two brothers, as they had done on the former day, went home and told how things had gone, and how all had ridden at the hill and none got up.

"But, last of all," they said, "came one in a silver suit, and his horse had a silver bridle and a silver saddle. He was just a chap to ride; and he got two-thirds up the hill, and then turned back. He was a fine fellow and no mistake; and the princess threw the second gold apple to him."

"Oh!" said Boots, "I should so like to have seen him too, that I should."

"A pretty story," they said. "Perhaps you think his coat of mail was as bright as the ashes you are always poking about and sifting, you nasty, dirty beast."

The third day everything happened as it had happened the two days before. Boots begged to go and see the sight, but the two wouldn't hear of his going with them. When they got to the hill there was no one who could get so much as a yard up it; and now all waited for the knight in silver mail, but they neither saw nor heard of him. At last came one riding on a steed, so brave that no one had ever seen his match; and the knight had a suit of golden mail, and a golden saddle, and bridle, so wondrous bright that the sunbeams gleamed from them a mile off. The other knights and princes could not find time to call out to him not to try his luck, for they were amazed to see how grand he was. He rode at the hill, and tore up it like nothing, so that the princess hadn't even time to wish that he might get up the whole way. As soon as ever he reached the top, he took the third golden apple from the princess's lap, and then turned his horse and rode down again. As soon as he got down, he rode off at full speed, and out of sight in no time.

Now, when the brothers got home at evening, you may fancy what long stories they told, how the riding had gone off that day; and amongst other things, they had a deal to say about the knight in golden mail.

"He was just a chap to ride!" they said; "so grand a knight isn't to be found in the whole world."

"Oh!" said Boots, "I should so like to have seen him, that I should."

"Ah!" said his brothers, "his mail shone a deal brighter than the glowing coals which you are always poking and digging at; nasty, dirty beast that you are."

Next day all the knights and princes were to pass before the king and the princess—it was too late to do so the night before, I suppose—that he who had the golden apple might bring it forth; but one came after another, first the princes and then the knights, and still no one could show the gold apple.

"Well," said the king, "someone must have it, for it was something that we all saw with our own eyes, how a man came and rode up and bore it off."

He commanded that everyone who was in the kingdom should come up to the palace and see if he could show the apple. Well, they all came, one after another, but no one had the golden apple, and after a long time the two brothers of Boots came. They were the last of all, so the king asked them if there was no one else in the kingdom who hadn't come.

"Oh, yes," said they. "We have a brother, but he never carried off the golden apple. He hasn't stirred out of the dusthole on any of the three days."

"Never mind that," said the king; "he may as well come up to the palace like the rest."

So Boots had to go up to the palace.

"How, now," said the king; "have you got the golden apple? Speak out!"

"Yes, I have," said Boots; "here is the first, and here is the second, and here is the third one, too"; and with that he pulled all three golden apples out of his pocket, and at the same time threw off his sooty rags, and stood before them in his gleaming golden mail.

"Yes!" said the king; "you shall have my daughter and half my kingdom, for you well deserve both her and it."

So they got ready for the wedding, and Boots got the princess for his wife, and there was great merry-making at the bridal-feast, you may fancy, for they could all be merry though they couldn't ride up the hill of glass; and all I can say is, that if they haven't left off their merry-making yet, why, they're still at it.

THE SON OF THE BAKER OF BARRA / Scotland

Sorche Nic Leodhas

Ian Beg is not the brightest of heroes, but he is a "goodhearted, biddable lad" who is generous to three cake-loving old gray cailleachs. The king's daughter falls in love with Ian, and he begins his quest to find an empty castle for her. It is an unsuccessful quest until he meets the three cailleachs again. While this is not a part of the Cinderella cycle, it is a charming, little-known wonder tale.

Once a baker of Barra had a son and one son only, and the son's name was Ian Beg. There was nothing amiss with the lad at all, except that he was so goodhearted that he'd give the coat off his back to anyone who wanted it, and follow it with his shirt if that was asked for too.

One day the baker of Barra made a very fine cake and told his son to take it up to the castle so that the king's daughter could have it for her supper.

"That I'll do, and gladly," said Ian Beg. "Give me the cake, then, and let me be on my way." So the baker laid the cake in a clean white cloth, and gave it into his son's hands.

It was a fair way to go to the castle, but the lad walked along briskly, carrying the cake by the corners of the cloth gathered into his hand. The road ran along by the burn, and then it ran along through the glen, and then it took a turn into a wood that stood in the way. There under the trees Ian Beg met three old gray cailleachs, and he gave them *"Fáilte"* and bade them leave him

go by. But the three old women stood in his way and would not let him pass.

"Fáilte, Ian, son of the baker of Barra," they said. "What is it that you have in the napkin, that you carry it with such care?"

"'Tis a cake my father made for the daughter of the king," Ian answered proudly. "And 'tis myself that is taking it to her, that she may have it for her supper the night."

"For the king's daughter, do you say!" said the first old gray cailleach.

"Such a cake would be a wonder to see!" the second one said.

"Could you not open the napkin a wee bit and let us just have the smidgen of a look at it?" the third one begged.

Well, a bit of a look could do no harm, so Ian opened the napkin and showed them the cake. When he thought they had admired it long enough, he got ready to gather up the cloth about it so that he could be on his way again. But the three old cailleachs would not let him.

"Not more than two or three times in my life have I tasted such a cake," said the first one.

"Not more than once in my life have I done the same," sighed the second one.

And then the third one said, "Och, I have ne'er once, in all the days of my life, put so much as a crumb of such a cake in my mouth!"

Then, as if the thought struck them all at the one time, they cried out, "Och, Ian Beg, *mo graidh*, will ye not let us have a wee crumb to taste of the cake?"

Well, Ian being so goodhearted, although he wanted to say no, he could not do it. So he held the cake up on his hand, and told them they might each pinch off a wee crumb of it, but to make sure to take it where it wouldn't show.

And so they did. They savored the wee bit of a crumb with delight and Ian, pleased with their pleasure, forgot where his duty lay.

"Och, now, have a wee bit more," he pressed them kindly. "'Twill ne'er be missed!" And to encourage them, he took a taste of the cake himself. Then one crumb followed another, and all of a sudden Ian Beg discovered the cloth was empty except for a few last crumbs. Among them all they'd finished the cake.

"Och, ochone," Ian Beg lamented. "Now the king's daughter will have no cake for her supper, and my father will flay the skin off my back when I go home."

"Och, nay, Ian Beg!" the first old cailleach told him. "Do you think so poorly of us to think we'd let you go home to face your father's wrath, and the three of us doing naught to save you?"

Then she took the cloth from his hand and folded it carefully to keep the crumbs inside. The three old creatures passed it from one to another until it came back to the hands of the first one again. She put it into the hands of Ian Beg. "Carry the napkin home to your father," she bade him. "Tell him to shake it out over the table and I'll warrant he'll be leaving the skin of your back alone. That will pay you for what I had of the cake. As for my sisters, they will pay for their share some time when you're needing it more than now." And, as Ian Beg started off home, she called after him, "Tell your father to bake another cake for you to take to the king's daughter in the morn."

Ian Beg, being a biddable lad, did as he was told. When he got home his father asked him, "Were they liking the cake at the castle?" for he was eager to keep the castle trade.

"They were not!" said Ian Beg. "And how would they be liking it, the way they never got it?" he asked.

"Ne'er got it?" said the baker. "And why did they not?"

"Och, on the road through the wood I met three old gray cailleachs who begged so prettily for a taste of the cake that I let them have it." said Ian Beg. "And then they ate it all up."

"You let them have it!" roared the baker, reaching for his great wooden paddle that he put the loaves into the oven with. "Och, I'll be letting you have a bit of something too, my fine lad!"

"Not so fast," cried Ian Beg, skipping nimbly out of the way of the paddle. "Here's the cloth the cake was in, and they bade me tell you to shake the cloth out over the table, and you'd be willing to leave me be."

The baker grumbled, but he set the batter paddle aside. Taking the cloth in his hands he went over to the table, where he unfolded it and shook it out above the table top.

"Och! Crumbs!" he said, looking at them with disgust. "Losh! Have we not crumbs enough in our bakehouse now?" But before he had finished speaking every crumb had turned into a shining golden coin. "Look ye now, lad!" the baker cried joyfully. "Well paid am I for the cake, and no mistake. And a very good thing it was for you to let the old ones have the cake, for I'm thinking that they belong to the People of Peace, the fairy folk, themselves."

"I'd not be knowing about that," said Ian Beg. "They looked to me like any old cailleachs you might be meeting. But they said to tell you to bake another cake for me to take to the king's daughter in the morn."

As Ian Beg said, so it was done, and the next day Ian went off again with a cake for the king's daughter happed in a fresh white cloth which he carried with the four corners of it gathered into his hand. He went along by the burn, and then he went along through the glen, and into the wood and out of it again. This day he did not see the three old gray cailleachs at all, but when he came out of the wood and took the high road, he saw a great sluagh of gentlefolk all on their way to the castle like himself. Some rode by on horseback and some rolled by in carriages, but he was the only one with naught but his own legs to carry him there. So he strode along in the dust of their passing, and soon he found himself trudging along behind them all. When he got to the castle he asked the man who guarded the door what was the occasion that had brought so many of the gentry there that day.

"'Tis the birthday of the daughter of the king," said the man. "And now that she is of an age to wed, she has given out the word that she will have for a husband the man who brings her the gift she likes the best."

"'Tis nothing to me," said Ian Beg. "I am not in the running, for all I've brought is the cake that my father, the baker of Barra, made this morn for the supper of the daughter of the king."

So the man passed Ian Beg through the door, and Ian went into the castle hall with his cake.

The king sat in his chair of state at a long table, which was placed at one end of the hall. Beside him sat his daughter, ready to choose the gift that she preferred above all the rest. One by one, the gentlemen came up to the table and set their gifts upon it for her to see. Some of the gentles were very young, and some were very old, and the others were somewhere in between, but the lot of them all had the same proud and haughty look that showed they thought very well of themselves.

The richness of their gifts was beyond imagination, and soon the top of the table glimmered and glittered and shone with the gold and the silks and the precious stones that covered it from end to end. The king's daughter sat and looked down at the brave show with as little interest as if all these rich things were no more than pebbles and shells and driftwood, such as a bairn might find along the shore.

When the last gift had been laid on the table, and the suitors had drawn off to the side to wait until the choice was made, Ian Beg walked up, and pushing some of the gifts aside to make room for it, he set his cake down on the table in front of the daughter of the king.

"'Tis no gift at all that I'm bringing you," he told her. "Naught but a cake that my father, the baker of Barra, made for your supper this night."

The king's daughter looked at the cake and then she looked at the lad who had brought it.

Her eyes began to smile but as yet her lips did not. "*Moran taing*! Thank you!" she said gravely. "Thank you, son of the baker of Barra, for the cake. It will come in handy, this being my birthday, and us without a crumb of cake in the house before you came."

Her eyes saw more than the cake, although that was well worth seeing. What she saw, forbye, was that the lad was tall and well-built, a big, handsome, yellow-haired laddie, and under the dust that had gathered upon him, stirred up by the wheels of the carriages and by the horses' feet, his face was bonnie and good-humored, and she could tell that he was honest, too. But she asked him to stand to the side, for the moment, while she settled in her mind which of the gifts on the table she'd choose.

She looked the gifts over again, and then she looked at the suitors, and the more she saw of the latter the less she liked them. Slowly she rose from her chair beside the king, her father. The time had come for her to make her decision known. And so she did.

In a clear voice she said, "Jewels galore I have and more I need not. Silks I have in abundance —so many that I shall never wear them all. I am no longer a bairn so I have no use for your golden toys and trinkets. The gift I like best is the cake that was brought to me by the son of the baker of Barra, and he's the one I shall wed!"

Ian Beg thought that his ears belied him, but the king's daughter looked at him, and her lips were smiling now, as well as her eyes.

"Will you have me then, son of the baker of Barra?" she asked him.

Ian's heart leaped within him, for joy, and he answered. "Och, I don't mind if I do!"

Then there was a great to-do in the castle when the suitors understood that the king's daughter had passed them and their gifts by for a dusty baker's lad and a cake. They all seized their gifts in a great huff and went home. So there was the cake, sitting alone upon the table, with the king and his daughter behind it, and Ian Beg before.

"Well, my dear," said the king to his daughter, "I have naught to say against the baker of Barra. A very good baker he is, to be sure. And his son, no doubt, is a very fine lad. And this cake well may be, and probably is, the very best of cakes.

But after all, a cake is a cake, and a husband is a husband. A cake is soon eaten and forgotten, and other cakes take its place. But a husband you must keep until the end of your days. Why not let the son of the baker of Barra go home to his father who will bake you a cake every day if you like?"

"Nay!" said his daughter. "My choice is made. I'll bide by it, come what may."

Och, this will not do at all! the king thought to himself. The world would ne'er stop laughing, should I let my daughter wed with a baker's son. He knew he'd never be able to argue his daughter out of it, for she was terribly set in her mind, and what she said she'd do, she intended to do. He sat looking at the pair of them, then he suddenly had what seemed to him a very good thought.

"Och, well," said the king to his daughter, "if you're of a mind to have the lad for a husband, I'll have naught to say against it. But you being my daughter, and my lone bairn, you'll understand I have your welfare at heart. No home have you e'er had in your life but in a castle, with all that was in it exactly as a king's daughter should have it. I have my doubts that you could be happy otherwise. You may wed the son of the baker of Barra with my blessing when he can give you a castle as good as this one, with everything in it the way you've always had it, forbye. Now I've had my say, and 'tis all I'll say."

The king's daughter looked sadly at Ian Beg, but Ian Beg gave her a great smile. "A man can but try," he told her. "Will you wait for me till I come back again?" he asked.

"Aye!" replied the king's daughter. "I'll wait."

Then Ian Beg went home and told his father what the king had said.

"Now, bake me some bannocks to eat on the road, and give me your blessing," said Ian Beg. "And I'll be off. The world will be my pillow and the sky will be my coverlet, and I'll find a castle for the king's daughter to live in or I'll not come back at all."

Ian Beg's father gave him a bundle of bannocks and his blessing and wished him Godspeed, and off Ian went on his journey. But though he traveled the length of the land, up and down and back and forth for many a weary mile, and saw many a strange sight upon the way, he could not find a castle for himself. At last he came to the end of the world, and there was no place farther for him to go, for there was nothing before him but the great empty green sea with the gray sky beyond it.

"*Truagh mo charadh*! How heavy my sorrow!" said Ian Beg, and he stood and stared hopelessly at the sea. Then his eye caught a glimpse of a house that stood beyond on the shore, and as the night was drawing in and he was weary, he thought he would go there and ask for shelter until the day's dawn. So up to the house he went, and the door was open, so he went in. There were three seated there at a table, and he saw in the blink of an eye that it was the three old gray cailleachs whom he had met in the wood. They looked up at him as he came in and cried out a greeting.

"Fáilte! Welcome, Ian Beg," said the first one.

"Mile fáilte! A thousand welcomes!" the second one said.

"Ceud mile fáilte! A hundred thousand welcomes!" and the third. "Now that you're here, you must have a bite to eat with us."

So Ian Beg drew up a stool and sat down to the table. Then the old women discovered that he ate little, but sat leaning his head upon his hand, so they asked him how he came to be so sad. Soon they had coaxed all of Ian's troubles out of him, and himself was telling them everything that had happened to him since he last saw them in the wood.

"I've been up and down and back and forth through all the weary world, and there's not a castle that has not an owner to it already," Ian said.

"Och, I'd not say that," said the first old cailleach.

"'Tis not impossible to find a castle," the second one said.

"'Tis not, to be sure," said the third one. "Only you must choose the proper place to look."

"I'll give you a wee bit of something to help you," said the second old gray cailleach, and she took out of her sleeve a small black iron box. The three old women passed it about among them from one to another until it came into the hands of the second one again.

"I've not forgotten your kindness in sharing the cake with us," said she, as she put the wee box in his hands. "This will pay for what I had of it, but be careful to keep it always with you, for it is a box that can do you good or harm!"

Ian Beg thanked her, and took the box and dropped it into his pouch, but indeed, he could not see how such a wee box could help him, so he soon forgot about it. But telling the old sisters about his troubles so relieved him that he felt as if a great load of grief had slipped off his back, and he slept very well that night.

In the morning they woke Ian Beg early and started him off upon his way home, bidding him to be of good heart for he'd be finding his castle very soon. So back he went through the world, up hill and down and over moor and mountain, and on the third day he came to a burn in flood and the water was too deep for crossing, so he sat down to rest a bit and cool his feet in the stream before seeking a better place to get across. While he was sitting there a hunger came on him, for all that day he had not passed so much as a shepherd's bothan where he could beg a bite to eat. As he felt around in his sporran to find if a bit of bannock remained there, his fingers came upon the box that the second gray sister had given him, so he took it out. Och, what was the good of a wee iron box, and what would be in it, forbye?

So he opened the box.

Out jumped three spry lads, crying out "*Easgadh*! Easgadh! Ready! Ready, Master Baker's Son!" and bowing low before Ian Beg, they asked politely, "What will you have us do for you?"

When Ian Beg got over his surprise, he told them to bring him food at once. Soon they brought him his dinner on a great silver tray, and waited upon him while he ate. When he had finished he told them that he needed nothing more, so into the box they popped. Ian shut the lid down upon them and put the box into his pouch again. "Och," said he, "if these creatures can bring me a dinner so easily, happen they can help me to a castle, too." Then off he went on his journey again, lighthearted and fast-footed, and within a few days, reached home.

The baker of Barra was happy to have his son back again. As for the castle, the baker was of the opinion that Ian was well enough off without it,

and as for the king's daughter, who ever heard of one of those who wedded a baker's son?

Ian said naught one way or the other to all his father told him. He said not a word about the wee iron box either, but ate his supper and went early to bed.

While the moon was yet high and the night dark and still, Ian rose from his bed and got into his clothes. Out of the house he went, and down the road, along by the burn and through the glen, until he came to the wood. There he took out the wee box and opened it, and at once the three spry lads leaped out, crying "Easgadh! Easgadh! Master Son of the Baker! What will you have us do for you?"

"Build me a fine castle here, with the wood to be a park about it, and the castle to be bigger than the king's own and better. Make everything in it finer than anything in the king's house, and put a great stable behind it, and in the stable a gold coach with four white horses to draw it for me to go to the king's castle in, in the morn. And look to it that there be plenty of servants, both indoors and out, that the king's daughter and myself may be well served."

Long before cock's crow that morn all was done, exactly as Ian had commanded. The three spry lads were back in their box, and the box safely in Ian's pouch again.

When the sun was high in the sky that morn, Ian Beg dressed in his best and rode up to the king's castle in his gold coach drawn by four white horses with gold plumes on their heads. There was a fine coachman to drive the horses, with four footmen behind, and a postilion riding before. The king looked out the window and wondered who this grand laird was that came riding so fine. His daughter came and looked over his shoulder, and then she laughed aloud.

"Och, what way would your eyes be telling you 'tis a laird at all?" she asked. "Is it not plain to be seen that 'tis Ian Beg, come back to make me his bride?"

The king was terribly vexed. "Och, well," he grumbled, "happen the lad has got hold of a coach and four horses, but that does not mean he'll be having the castle, too."

"Aye, but he will!" the king's daughter said.

After the king saw Ian's castle, he could say no more against the wedding of his daughter to the baker's son. Had not the lad got a castle even bigger and better than his own? So the wedding was set for a week come Sunday, and the king's daughter hurried off to see to her wedding gown, while Ian Beg took his gold coach back to his castle and left it there. Then he walked home to his father's house and there wasn't a man in Barra that day could match him for happiness.

He was late getting to bed that night, because he had so much to tell his father, and it took time to make the baker understand that his baking days were over, and that he should sell his bakehouse and live at ease for the rest of his days. It wasn't until he was getting ready for bed that Ian discovered that his wee iron box was not in his pouch.

"Och, woe!" he said, yawning. "I've laid it down somewhere up at the castle, no doubt. Well, I'm too tired to go fetch it now. I'll rise early and go for it, in the morn." Half asleep, he tumbled into bed.

When the king came home from having a look at Ian Beg's castle, he sat and chewed his fingers with rage. There was some trick or other about the way Ian Beg's castle had appeared, but what it was he couldn't think. At least, he decided, he could go see the spae-wife and see what she could tell him. She had the name for having all sorts of uncanny wisdom, and folk called her a witch. Maybe she could tell him what to do.

So down the stairs he stomped, and out the back door of the castle and kept on going until he came to the spae-wife's cottage at the end of the hen run. The spae-wife cast her spells for him and then she said. "It has all been done with the help of a magic box that the People of Peace have given the baker's son. As long as he carried it with him there was nothing you could do about it, but by mischance he has mislaid it this night. You will find it where it has slipped down behind the cushions of his gold coach. My advice to you is to take your daughter at once to the castle, and when you have found the box tell those who come out of it when you open it to take the castle, yourself, and your daughter to some distant place where the son of the baker will not be able to find you."

"Well and good," said the king. "But where would such a place be?"

"The Island of the Kingdom of the Rats would be the best place," the spae-wife said. "I doubt he'll e'er have heard tell of it. You should be safe there."

The king did as the spae-wife told him. He went back to his castle and roused his daughter from her bed, and made her go to Ian's castle with him that very night. Long before Ian Beg woke in the morning the three spry lads from the wee black iron box had obeyed the king's command and carried the king and the king's daughter and the castle of Ian Beg to the Island of the Kingdom of the Rats far away over the sea, and set them all down there.

When Ian Beg went up the road to his castle in the morning his heart was blithe and gay, but when he got to the wood, it sank like a weight of lead. There was no sign of a castle among the trees, and all that was left was the bare empty space where it had stood.

Ian rushed up to the king's castle to tell the king's daughter that his castle was gone, but neither the king nor his daughter were at home, the servants said. All that they could say was that the king had taken his daughter and gone away with her in the night, and where he had taken her they would not be able to say, for they had not been told. So Ian Beg went back to the wood and sat down by the road, not knowing what else to do. While he was sitting there, along the road the three old cailleachs came, and stopped before him.

"Och, Ian Beg, *mo graidh*! What is the trouble now?" they said.

Ian Beg looked up at them and answered. "Och, my castle is gone, and the king's daughter, and my wee black box as well."

"You should have kept the wee box with you," said the second old cailleach. "We knew by our spells that it was gone. 'Tis why we came."

"The king got hold of the box and used it to carry the castle and his daughter away," her sisters said.

"How could I be knowing he'd do the like? I'd not have thought it of a king!" said Ian Beg. "Och, well, 'tis my own fault for being careless. The castle's gone and the lass is gone, and without the box I cannot get them back again, so there's naught I can do about it. I'll go back to my father and help him in the bakehouse."

"Och, do not talk so daft!" said the third old

cailleach. "You must go after them and bring the lot of them home."

"What luck would I have at that," asked Ian Beg, "and me not even knowing where they've gone?"

"That we can tell you," said the old cailleachs. "It's over the sea to the Island of the Kingdom of the Rats the castle and the king and his daughter have gone."

"In that case it might as well be behind the world's end for all that I can do," said Ian Beg.

"You're forgetting one thing," the third old cailleach told him. "Am I not here to help you, and me still beholden to you for my share of your cake?" So she took Ian Beg by the hand and pulled him up to his feet, and led him away until they came to the shore of the sea.

"You'll be needing a ship," she said. And looking about her, she picked up a piece of driftwood that lay nearby on the sands. She tossed it out upon the waves and at once it became a fine ship.

"Now you'll be needing a captain to chart your course and steer your ship," she said. She looked about her again and saw a great black cat on the shore catching a fish for his supper, so she picked him up and threw him upon the deck of the ship.

"You shall be captain," she told the cat, "and sail the ship."

So the cat sat up straight in the captain's place, waiting the word to go.

"Now heed me well, Ian Beg," said the third old gray cailleach. "When you get to the Island of the Kingdom of the Rats, do not set foot from the ship, but send the cat to get the box and bring it to you. And when you have it safe in your hands again, you will know what to do."

Then Ian Beg thanked her for her help, and bade her farewell, and joined the cat on the ship. The cat sailed the ship well, and in good time they came to the place in the sea where the Island of the Kingdom of the Rats lay, and there Ian Beg saw his castle rising up high and proud a short piece up from the shore. The cat brought the ship up to a wharf of stones and anchored it, and Ian was just about to step off the ship, when he remembered what the old cailleach had said. So he told the cat to go up to the castle and find his wee black iron box and bring it back to him.

The cat jumped out of the ship, and the first thing he saw was a huge rat sitting at the end of the wharf, fishing with its tail for a line. The cat, being hungry, pounced on the rat and held him down, intending to have him for his supper.

"Nay!" said the rat, trembling with fear from his whiskers to the tip of his tail. "Pray do not eat me! Spare my life and I will help you. I know this kingdom better than you will ever know it, and if there is anything I can get for you I will gladly do so."

The cat held the rat down while he thought the offer over. At last he said, "It's a wee black iron box I'm wanting, and from what I hear it's somewhere in that castle up there. Have you see it anywhere about?"

"That I have!" cried the rat. "As I came by the castle not long ago, such a box lay on one of the window sills near the road. Let me go and I'll fetch it for you."

So the cat released the rat and away he ran. Soon the rat came back with the box and gave it to the cat, who carried it to Ian Beg. Ian Beg opened the box and out jumped the three spry lads crying, "Easgadh! Easgadh! Ready! Ready! What will you have us do for you?" And Ian Beg wasted no time in telling them what to do.

"Carry my castle back to the place in the wood where it belongs, with the king's daughter and the king in it, too," he told them. "And let one of you make sure to beat the king well, all the way back, for making you bring my castle here."

So the three spry lads jumped off the ship and the cat jumped on, and the cat sailed the ship back home.

When they got back to Barra, Ian Beg got off the ship and started out to walk back to the wood in which he had built his castle. The cat got off the ship, too, and went to catch a fish for his supper, and what became of the ship nobody knows. Ian walked up the road along by the burn, and through the glen, and came at last to the wood, and there was his castle, standing tall and proud among the trees again.

In front of the castle were the three old cailleachs and the three spry lads, and the king, who was looking a bit battered and dazed from the beating he'd got for taking the castle away. And, best of all, there was the king's daughter herself, running to meet him and to welcome him home.

So the king's daughter married the son of the baker of Barra, and a very grand wedding it was. The king kept his promise and gave the young couple his blessing. He could not do less, for he knew that his son-in-law had in his pouch the wee black iron box that had the three spry lads within it, and the king had no wish to make their acquaintance again.

The wedding lasted for a week and a month and a day, and the guests came from far and near. There were so many guests at the wedding that both the king's castle and Ian Beg's were filled with folk. And who came to the wedding but the three old cailleachs, and they sat at the table with Ian Beg, who showed them every kind attention he could. There was music and dancing and feasting from morn till morn, and, for those who wanted to hear them, there were tellers of tales and those with their wallets full of such stories as you ne'er heard before. It was from one of them that I got this story that I've just told you about the son of the baker of Barra who married the king's daughter, and the two of them lived happily in Ian Beg's castle, all the rest of their days.

THE ADVENTURES OF HASSAN OF BALSORA

From The Arabian Nights

The stories in The Arabian Nights *differ greatly from European folktales. The most striking difference is that of length. The Oriental narratives are far more complex, and each incident is treated in as much detail as an entire western story. Many of the eastern tales are fifty pages long, even when they have been shortened for children.*

The following selection is the first half of a tale from The Arabian Nights; *the second half is equally long. This excerpt is included for comparative purposes. Notice the greater complexity of plot, the more detailed descriptions, the cultural differences reflected by Hassan's behavior, and the reliance on Allah.*

Hassan's capture of his wife is a very old plot motif. (See page 42 for more information.) After a few years he loses her and their two sons, and sets off on a dangerous quest to recover them. By supernatural help and after facing great danger, each crisis told in detail, Hassan rescues his family. A long journey home brings them riches and safety.

Although the eastern narratives are five and even ten times longer than the European tales, they have so much suspense and wonder that the reader never becomes bored. They create a world of magic that enchants not only the characters who live within it, but also those who read about it.

THE FIRE WORSHIPER

There was in ancient times a merchant residing in Balsora, who had two sons and great wealth. And it happened that when the merchant died, his two sons divided the wealth between them equally, and each took his portion and opened a shop. One was a dealer in copper wares and the other was a goldsmith. The name of the young goldsmith was Hassan.

Now, while Hassan the goldsmith was sitting in his shop one day, a Persian walked along the market street and approaching the shop spoke to him, saying: "O my son, thou art a comely young man. I have not a son and I know a wonderful art, numbers of people have asked me to teach it to them and I would not. But my soul inclineth to thee, so that I would teach thee, and drive poverty from thy door, then thou shalt not need any more to labor with the hammer and the charcoal and the fire." "O my master," answered Hassan, "when wilt thou teach me this wonderful art?" The Persian answered: "To-morrow I will come to thee and will make for thee, of copper, pure gold, in thy presence."

Upon this Hassan rejoiced and bade farewell to the Persian, and went to his mother. He entered, and saluted her, and ate with her, and told her all that had happened. But his mother said: "O my son, beware of listening to Persians for they are great deceivers, who know the art of alchemy and trick people, and take their wealth, and despoil them." But Hassan replied: "O my mother, we are poor people, we have nothing to covet that any one should trick us. The Persian who came to me is a dignified sheikh and a virtuous man, and Allah hath inclined him towards me." Thereupon his mother kept silence in her anger.

When the morning came Hassan rose, took the keys, and opened the shop, and soon the Persian approached him. Hassan rose and desired to kiss his hand but the Persian refused and would not permit his doing that. "O Hassan," he said, "prepare the crucible and place the bellows." He did as the Persian ordered him, and lighted the charcoal, after which the Persian said: "O my son, hast thou any copper?" And Hassan brought forth from a press a broken copper plate. Then the Persian ordered him to take the shears and to cut the plate into small pieces, and he did as he told him. Hassan cut it into small pieces, and threw it into the crucible, and blew upon it with the bellows until it became liquid. The Persian put his hand to his turban and took forth a folded paper. He opened it and sprinkled some of its contents into the crucible and the copper in the crucible became a lump of gold.

When Hassan beheld this he was overcome by joy. He took the lump and turned it over, and he took the file and filed it, and saw it to be of pure gold of the very best quality. Then he bent over the hand of the Persian to kiss it, and the Persian

said to him: "Take this lump to the market and sell it, and take its price quickly without speaking." So Hassan went down to the market and gave the lump to the broker, who took it and rubbed it on the touchstone and found it to be of pure gold, and he bought it for fifteen thousand pieces of silver. And Hassan went home and related to his mother all that he had done, and she kept silence in her anger.

Now on the next day, as Hassan was sitting in his shop, he looked and, lo, the Persian approached and entered. "O my son," he said, "dost thou desire to make gold this day? If so, let us repair to thy house and I will teach thee there." So Hassan arose, closed his shop and went with the Persian. He entered his house, and found his mother and informed her that the Persian stood at the door. So she put in order a chamber, and spread the carpets and cushions, and departed to a neighbor's house.

Then Hassan taking the Persian by the hand, drew him into the chamber, and placed food and drink before him, saying: "Eat, O my master, that the bond of bread and salt may be established between us. May Allah, whose name be exalted, execute vengeance upon him who is unfaithful to the bond of bread and salt!" "Thou hast spoken the truth, O my son," answered the Persian, "who knoweth the true value of the bond of bread and salt?" and he ate with Hassan until they were satisfied. The Persian then took forth secretly a packet from his turban, unfolded it and wrapped its contents in a piece of sweetmeat. "O Hassan," said he, "thou art now my son, and hast become dearer to me than my soul or my wealth, and I have a daughter to whom I will marry thee," and he handed him the piece of sweetmeat. Hassan took it, kissed his hand, and put the sweetmeat into his mouth, not knowing what was secretly decreed to befall him. He swallowed the piece and immediately lost his senses and his head sank down to his feet. When the Persian saw Hassan in this state he rejoiced exceedingly. Rising to his feet he said to him: "Thou has fallen into the snare, O young wretch! O dog of the Arabs! For many years have I been searching for thee until I have now gotten thee, O Hassan!"

He then tied Hassan's hands behind his back, and bound his feet to his hands. After which he took a chest, emptied it of the things that were in it, put Hassan into it, and locked it. He emptied also another chest and put into it all the wealth that was in Hassan's house. Then he went forth, running to the market, and brought a porter, who carried off the two chests to the river bank, where was waiting a ship. That vessel was fitted for the Persian, and her master was expecting him, so when her crew saw the Persian, they came and carried the two chests, and put them on board the ship. The master then cried out to the sailors: "Pull up the anchor, and loose the sails!" And the ship proceeded with a fair wind.—Such was the case with the Persian and Hassan.

But as to the mother of Hassan, when she came to the house, and beheld no one in it, nor found the chests nor the wealth, she knew her son was lost and that Fate had overtaken him. She slapped her face, and rent her garments, and cried out, and wailed. And she ceased not to weep during the hours of the night and the day, and she built in the midst of the house a tomb, on which she inscribed the name of Hassan, with the date of his loss. She quitted not the tomb, but sat by it night and day.

Now to return to Hassan and the Persian. The Persian was a Magian, a wicked, vile alchemist. The name of that accursed wretch was Bahram the Magian. He used every year to take a Mohammetan youth, and to slaughter him over a hidden treasure. And having now treacherously stolen Hassan the goldsmith he proceeded with him that day and night.

At sunrise the next morning, Bahram the Magian ordered his black slaves to bring to him the chest in which was Hassan. They brought the chest and opened it and took him forth. The Magian then poured some vinegar into his nostrils, and blew a powder into his nose, whereupon Hassan sneezed and, opening his eyes, looked right and left, and found himself on shipboard in the middle of the sea, with the Persian sitting by him. He knew then that the cursed one had done it, and that he had fallen into the calamity against which his mother had cautioned him. So Hassan pronounced the words: "There is no strength nor power but in Allah, the High, the Great! Verily unto Allah we belong, and verily unto him we return! O Allah, act graciously with me and make me to endure with patience thine

affliction. O Lord of all creatures!" Then looking towards the Persian he spoke to him with soft words, and said to him: "O my father, what are these deeds? Where is the respect for the bond of bread and salt, and the oath thou swearest to me?" "O dog," answered the Persian, "doth such a one as myself know any obligation imposed by bread and salt? I have slain a thousand youths like thee, save one youth, and thou shalt complete the thousand."

Then Bahram the Magian rose and ordered Hassan's bonds to be loosed, saying: "By the fire and the light and the shade and the heat I did not imagine that thou wouldest fall so easily into my net! But the fire strengthened me against thee, and aided me to seize thee, and now I will make thee a sacrifice to it!" Hassan replied: "Thou hast been unfaithful to the bond of bread and salt!" Upon this the Magian raised his hand, and gave him a blow, and he fell and bit the deck with his teeth, and fainted, the tears running down his cheeks.

The Magian then ordered his slaves to light for him a fire, saying: "This is the fire that emitteth light and sparks, and it is what I worship. If thou wilt worship it as I do, I will give thee half my wealth and marry thee to my daughter." But Hassan cried out: "Woe to thee! Thou art surely an infidel Magian, and worshipest the fire instead of Allah, the Almighty King, the Creator of the night and the day!" Thereupon the accursed Magian was enraged, and arose and prostrated himself to the fire, and ordered his slaves to throw Hassan down upon his face. So they threw him down and the Magian proceeded to beat him with a whip of plaited thongs. Then he ordered the slaves to bring Hassan food and drink, and they brought it, but he could not eat or drink. The Magian proceeded to torture him night and day during the voyage.

And they pursued their voyage over the sea for the period of three months, during which time the Magian continued to torture Hassan. At the end of the three months Allah, whose name be exalted, sent against the ship a wind, and the sea became black, and tossed the ship. And the master of the ship and the sailors were terrified and said: "Surely Allah sends this storm because for three months the young man has been tortured by this Magian!" Then they rose against the Magian to slay him, but he spoke to them softly, persuading them, and he loosed Hassan from his bonds, pulled off from him his tattered garments and clad him in fresh raiment.

He then made his peace with him saying: "O my son, be not offended with me, for I did these deeds to test thy patience! I am going to the Mountain of the Clouds, on which is an elixir which I use in my alchemy, and I swear to thee by the fire and the light that I will not harm thee in any way." So the heart of Hassan was comforted, and he rejoiced, and ate, and drank, and slept, and was content. Then the sailors rejoiced at Hassan's release, and the winds were stilled, and the darkness was withdrawn, and the voyage became pleasant.

They continued their voyage for three months more, and, at the end of that time, the vessel cast anchor on a long coast, beyond which was a desert interminable. The pebbles of that coast were white and yellow and blue and black and every other color. And the Magian arose, and took Hassan, and descended from the ship. They walked together until they were far from the ship and could no longer see the ship's crew. Then the Magian seated himself and took from his pocket a drum of copper and a drumstick covered with silk worked with gold, inscribed with talismans. He beat the drum, and instantly there appeared a dust from the further part of the desert. The dust dispersed, and there came toward them three she-camels. The Magian mounted one of them and Hassan mounted one, and they put their provisions on the third, and they proceeded for seven days. On the eighth day they beheld a cupola erected on four columns of red gold. They alighted from the she-camels, entered the cupola and ate, drank, and rested. Hassan happened to look about him, and he saw in the distance a lofty palace. "What is that, O my uncle?" he asked. The Magian answered: "That is the palace of mine enemy, and it is the abode of Genii, ghouls, and Devils." Then he beat the drum, and the she-camels approached and the two mounted and journeyed on until they arrived at a great and lofty mountain called the Mountain of Clouds.

Then Bahram the Magian alighted from his camel, and ordered Hassan to alight also. The Magian opened a leathern bag, and took forth from it a mill and a quantity of wheat. He ground the wheat in the mill, after which he kneaded the flour, and made of it three round cakes. He lighted a fire, and baked the cakes. He then took a camel, slaughtered it, and stripped off its skin. Then said he to Hassan: "Enter this skin and I will sew it up over thee. The Rocs will come, and carry thee off, and fly with thee to the summit of this mountain. Take this knife with thee, and when the birds set thee down on the mountain top, cut open the skin, and look down from the mountain, and I will tell thee what to do."

Then Bahram the Magian gave Hassan the three cakes and a leathern bottle of water, and he put him in the skin, and sewed him up. And the Rocs came, and carried him off, and flew with him to the summit of the mountain, and there put him down. So Hassan cut open the skin, and came forth, and spoke to the Magian, who on hearing his words rejoiced, and danced for joy. And he called to Hassan: "Behind thee thou wilt see many rotten bones, and beside them much wood. Make of the wood six bundles, and throw them down to me, for this wood I use in my alchemy." So Hassan threw down six bundles. And when the Magian saw that those bundles had come down to him, he cried out: "O young wretch, thou hast now accomplished all I desired! Remain upon this mountain and perish, or cast thyself down to the ground and perish there." Then the Magian departed.

Now Hassan found himself alone on the summit of the steep and lofty mountain, and he was filled with grief and despair. He looked to the right and left and walked along the summit until he came to the other side of the mountain, and at its foot he saw a blue sea, agitated with foamy waves, and every wave like a great mountain. He recited a portion of the Koran, and prayed to Allah for deliverance, and then cast himself into the sea. And, as Allah decreed, the waves bore Hassan along safely, and cast him up on the shore.

He then arose, and walked along searching for something to eat. And he walked for a while, and then he saw a great palace rising high in the air, and it was the same which Bahram the Magian had said belonged to his enemy, and was the abode of Genii, ghouls, and Devils. Hassan approached, and entered the palace, and saw a bench in the entrance-passage, and on the bench sat two damsels like moons, with a chess-table before them, and they were playing. And one of the damsels raised her head when she saw him. "O my sister," she cried out with joy, "here is a human being, and I imagine he is the youth whom Bahram the Magian brought this year!" And then Hassan cast himself down before the damsels. "O my mistresses," he entreated, "I am indeed that poor man!" Then said the younger damsel to her sister: "Bear witness, O my sister, that I take this young man for my brother by a covenant and compact before Allah. I will die for his death, and live for his life, rejoice for his joy, and mourn for his mourning." And the youngest damsel arose, and embraced Hassan, and kissed him, and taking him by the hand led him into the palace. She pulled off his tattered clothes, and brought him a suit of royal apparel, with which she clad him. She prepared for him viands of every kind and served him, and both she and her sister sat and ate with him.

Then said the damsels to Hassan: "Relate to us thine adventure with that wicked dog, the enchanter." And he related to them all that had befallen him. Then said the youngest damsel: "I will now relate to thee in return our whole story, so thou mayest know what manner of damsels we are."

"Know, O my brother," said the youngest damsel, "that we are of the daughters of the Kings. Our father is one of the Kings of the Genii, of great dignity, and he hath troops and guards and servants. Allah, whose name be exalted, blessed him with seven daughters, but our father was filled with such folly, jealousy and pride, that he would marry us to no one, therefore he had us conveyed to this palace which is named the Palace of the Mountain of Clouds. It is separated from the rest of the world, and none can gain access to it, neither of mankind nor of the Genii. Around it are trees, and fruits, and rivers and running water sweeter than honey and colder than snow. We have five sisters who have gone to hunt in the desert, for in it are wild beasts that cannot be numbered."

And even as the damsel spoke the five sisters returned from the chase, and the youngest damsel acquainted them with the case of Hassan. Whereupon the damsels rejoiced and congratulated him

on his safety. And he remained with them a year, passing the most pleasant life. And he used to go forth with them to the chase, and slaughter the game. He amused and diverted himself with the damsels in that decorated palace, and in the gardens and among the flowers, while the damsels treated him with courtesy and cheered him so that his sadness ceased.

Now, in the following year Bahram the Magian, the accursed, came again, having with him a comely young man, a Mohammetan, resembling the moon in its beauty, shackled, and tortured in the most cruel manner; and he alighted with him beneath the Palace of the Mountain of Clouds. Hassan was sitting by the river, beneath the trees when he beheld the Magian. In great anger he struck his hands together and said to the damsels: "O my sisters, aid me to slay this accursed wretch! He hath now falled into your hands, and with him is a young Mohammetan, a captive, whom he is torturing with painful torture." And the damsels replied: "We hear and obey Allah and thee, O Hassan." And they equipped themselves with armor and slung on the swords. They brought him a courser richly caparisoned, and they armed him with beautiful weapons.

Having done this, they proceeded all together, and they found that the Magian had slaughtered a camel, and skinned it, and was tormenting the young man, saying to him: "Enter this skin!" So Hassan came behind him, and cried out: "Withhold thy hand, O accursed! O enemy of Allah! O dog! O perfidious wretch! O thou who worshipest fire, and swearest by the shade and the heat!" The Magian looked around, and seeing Hassan, said to him: "O my son, how didst thou escape?" Hassan answered: "Allah delivered me! Thou hast been unfaithful to the bond of bread and salt, therefore hath Allah thrown thee into my power." And Hassan advanced and quickly smote him upon the shoulders, so that the sword came forth glittering from his vitals. And Bahram the Magian fell down dead.

Then Hassan took the leathern bag, opened it, and drew forth the drum and drumstick. He beat the drum, whereupon the camels came to him like lightning. He loosed the young man from his bonds, mounted him upon a camel, gave him the remaining food and water, and said to him: "Return thou in peace to thy home." And the young man departed rejoicing. Then the damsels, when they had seen Hassan smite the neck of the Magian, came around him admiring his courage, and thanking him for what he had done. And he and the damsels returned to the Palace of the Mountain of Clouds.

THE BIRD-DAMSELS

Hassan continued to reside with the damsels, passing a most pleasant life, and he forgot his mother. One morning there arose a great dust from the further part of the desert, and the sky was darkened. Then the damsels said to him: "Arise, Hassan, enter thy private chamber, and conceal thyself among the trees and grape-vines, and no harm shall befall thee." And he arose and went in and concealed himself in his private chamber.

After a while the dust dispersed, and there approached numerous troops like the roaring sea, sent from the King who was the father of the damsels. When the troops arrived, the damsels entertained them for three days, after which the commander of the troops said: "We have come from the King your father to summon you to him. One of the Kings celebrateth a marriage-festivity, and your father desireth that ye should be present that ye may divert yourselves." The damsels arose and went in to Hassan, and told him of the summons, and they said to him: "Verily this place is thy place, and our house is thy house. Be of good heart and cheerful eye, and fear not nor grieve, nor no one can come nigh unto thee in this place; therefore be of tranquil heart and joyful mind, until we come to thee again. These keys of our private chambers we leave with thee; but, O our brother, we beg thee by the bond of brotherhood that thou open not yonder door." Then they bade him farewell, and departed with the troops.

So Hassan remained in the palace alone. And he was solitary and sad, and he mourned for the damsels. He used to go alone to hunt in the desert, and bring back the game, and slaughter it, and eat alone. His gloominess and loneliness became excessive. So he arose, and went through the palace, and opened the private chambers, and he saw in them riches such as ravished his mind. And the fire of curiosity burned in his heart, and

made him long to open the secret door, which the damsels had forbidden him to go near. And he said to himself: "I will arise, and open this door, and see what is within, though within be death!"

Accordingly he took the key, and opened the door, and saw therein a flight of steps, vaulted with stones of onyx. He ascended the steps to the roof of the palace, and he looked down from one side of the palace upon a strange country, where were sown fields, gardens, and trees and flowers, and where wandered wild beasts, while birds warbled and proclaimed the perfection of Allah, the One, the Omnipotent. And he gazed from the other side of the palace upon a roaring sea, with foaming waves.

Now in the center of the roof of the palace Hassan saw a pavilion supported by four columns, and built of bricks of gold, silver, jacinth and emerald. In the middle of that pavilion was a pool of water, over which was a trellis of sandalwood and aloes-wood, ornamented with bars of red gold and oblong emeralds, and adorned with jewels and pearls, every bead of which was as large as a pigeon's egg. By the side of the pool was a couch of aloes-wood, adorned with large pearls and with jewels. And around the pavilion birds warbled, proclaiming the perfection of Allah, whose name be exalted. Hassan was amazed when he beheld it, and he sat in the pavilion, looking at what was around it.

And while he sat wondering at the beauty of the pavilion, and at the luster of the large pearls, lo, he beheld ten birds approach from the direction of the desert, coming to the pavilion and pool. So Hassan concealed himself, fearing lest they would see him, and fly away. The birds alighted on a great and beautiful tree which grew near the pavilion. And he saw among them a stately bird, the handsomest of them all. The ten birds seated themselves, and each proceeded to rend open its skin with its talons, and, lo, there came forth from the feathers, ten damsels more beautiful than the moon. They all descended into the pool, and washed, and played, and jested together. And, as Hassan gazed on the most beautiful damsel of them all, who had been the handsomest bird, he lost his reason, and his heart became entangled in the snare of her love. And he continued to gaze on the loveliness of the chief damsel, sighing and weeping, for she had hair blacker than night, a mouth like the seal of Solomon, eyes like those of gazelles, cheeks like anemones, lips like coral, and a figure like a willow-branch. And while he stood gazing, behold the damsels came up out of the pool, and each put on her dress of feathers and became a bird again, and they all flew away together.

And Hassan despaired at the disappearance of the damsels, and he descended to the lower part of the palace and dragged himself to his own chamber, where he lay upon his side, sick, without eating or drinking, and thus he remained for two days. Now, while he was in this state of violent grief, a dust arose from the desert, and but a little while elapsed when the troops of the damsels alighted, and surrounded the palace. The seven damsels also alighted, and entered the palace, and took off their arms and weapons of war, except the youngest damsel his sister, for when she saw not Hassan she searched for him. She found him in his chamber languid and wasted, his complexion was sallow and his eyes were sunk in his face because of the little food and drink he had taken. When his sister saw him in this state she sorrowed, and questioned him as to what had befallen. So he told her all that had happened to him. And she wept with pity and compassion, and bade him refrain from confiding his secret to the other damsels, lest they should slay him on account of his having opened the secret door, and she said to him: "O my brother, be of good heart and cheerful eye, for I will expose myself to peril for thee and will contrive a stratagem to help thee to gain that which thou desirest." So Hassan was comforted, and arose, and greeted the damsels.

Now at the end of a month the damsels mounted, and taking with them provisions for twenty days, went forth to hunt, but the youngest damsel remained in the palace with Hassan. When the sisters were far from the palace, the youngest damsel said to Hassan: "Arise, and show me the place where thou sawest the flying damsel." So he arose, opened the secret door, and went with her to the roof of the palace, where he showed her the pavilion and the pool. Then said his sister: "Know, O my brother, that this damsel is the daughter of the King of all the Genii. Her father hath dominion over men and Genii, en-

chanters and diviners, tribes and guards, and regions and cities in great numbers, and hath vast riches. He hath an army of damsels who smite with swords and thrust with spears, five and twenty thousand in number. He hath seven daughters to whom he hath assigned a vast kingdom, encompassed by a great river, so that no one can gain access to the palace, neither man nor Genie. And over this kingdom he hath set to rule his eldest daughter, the chief of her sisters, and she it is whom thou lovest. The damsels who were with her are the favorite ladies of her empire, and the feathered skins in which they fly are the work of the enchanters of the Genii. Now if thou desirest to marry this damsel thou must do all that I tell thee. On the first day of every month the Queen and her damsels come here to the pool to bathe. Sit thou in a place so thou shalt see them, but they shall not see thee. When they take off their dresses, seize thou the dress of feathers belonging to the chief damsel. When she imploreth thee with tender words, give not back her dress, or she will slay thee and fly away. But do thou grasp her by the hair, and drag her to thee, and lift her up, and carrying her descend to thine apartment. Take care of the dress of feathers, for as long as thou possessest that she is in thy power, and cannot fly away to her own country." So when Hassan heard these words of his sister he was comforted and he returned with her to the lower part of the palace and waited with patience for the first day of the following month.

Now, on the first day of the new moon Hassan opened the secret door, and ascended the steps to the roof of the palace. He hid himself near the pavilion and he saw ten birds approach like lightning. The birds alighted, opened their dresses and the damsels descended into the pool, where they played and sported together. And Hassan seized the feather dress of the chief damsel and hid it. When the damsels came forth from the pool, each put on her dress of feathers except his beloved, who found hers not. Upon this she cried out, and slapped her face, and tore her clothes. And when the others knew her dress was lost they wept, and cried out, then flew away and left her. Then Hassan heard the chief damsel implore: "O thou, who hast taken my dress I beg thee restore it to me!" But he rose from his place, and ran forward, and rushed upon her, and laid hold of her. Then lifting her he descended with her to the lower part of the palace, and placed her in his private chamber. He locked the door upon her, and went to his sister, and told her how he had gotten possession of the chief damsel, and had brought her down to his private chamber, and said he: "She is now sitting weeping and biting her hands."

His sister, when she heard his words, arose, and going into the private chamber, saw the King's daughter weeping and mourning. She kissed the ground before her, and saluted her and the chief damsel said: "Who are ye that do such evil deeds to the daughter of the King? Thou knowest that my father is a great King, and that the Kings of all the Genii fear his awful power, and that he hath under his authority enchanters, sages, diviners, Devils and Marids without number. How is it right for you, O daughter of the Genii, to lodge a human being in your palace, and to acquaint him with our customs? If ye did not so, how could this man have gained access to us?" So the sister of Hassan answered: "O daughter of the King, verily this human being is kindly and noble, and he loveth you." And she related to the chief damsel all that Hassan had done.

Then the sister of Hassan arose, and brought a sumptuous dress in which she clad the chief damsel. She also brought her food and drink, and ate with her, and comforted her, and appeased her terror. She ceased not to caress her with gentleness and kindness until she was content.

The sister of Hassan then went forth to him and said: "Arise, go in to her, and kiss her hands and feet." He therefore entered, and kissed her between the eyes, and said: "O mistress of beauties, and life of souls, be tranquil in heart. I desire to marry thee, and to journey to my country, and I will reside with thee in the city of Bagdad. I will purchase for thee female slaves and male slaves, and I have a mother, the best of women, who will be thy servant."

But while he was addressing her, the damsels, the mistresses of the palace, returned from the chase. They alighted from their horses and entered the palace. They brought with them an abundance of gazelles, and wild oxen and hares, and lions and hyenas, and other beasts. Hassan advanced to meet the eldest damsel and kissed

her hand, and the youngest damsel his sister said: "O my sisters, he hath caught a bird of the air and he desireth ye to aid him to make her his wife." And the eldest damsel said to Hassan: "Tell thy tale and conceal naught of it." So he related all that had happened. And she said: "Show her to us." So he conducted them to the private chamber in which was the King's daughter. When they saw her they kissed the ground before her, wondering at her beauty and her elegance. And they consented to the marriage, and drew up the contract, after which they celebrated the marriage festivities in a manner befitting the daughter of Kings. And for forty days the festivities continued with pleasure, happiness, delight and joy, and the damsels presented Hassan and his bride with many gifts and rarities.

Now, after forty days Hassan was sleeping, and he saw his mother mourning for him. So he woke from his sleep weeping and lamenting, the tears running down his cheeks like rain. In the morning he arose and calling the damsels acquainted them with his dream and implored them to hasten his departure. The damsels were moved with pity for his state, and they arose, and prepared the provisions. They adorned his bride with ornaments and costly apparel, and gave him rarities without number. After that they beat the drum, and the she-camels came to them from every quarter. They mounted the damsel and Hassan, and put upon the camels five and twenty chests full of gold and fifty of silver. And they bade him farewell with tears and embraces.

Hassan proceeded night and day, traversing with his wife the deserts and wastes and the valleys and rugged tracts, during midday-heat and early dawn, and Allah decreed them safety. So they were safe, and arrived at the city of Balsora, and they ceased not to pursue their way until they made their camels kneel at the door of his house. He dismissed the camels and advanced to the door to open it, and he heard his mother weeping with a soft voice. And Hassan wept when he heard his mother weeping and lamenting, and he knocked at the door with alarming violence. His mother said: "Who is at the door?" And he replied: "Open." Whereupon she opened the door and looked at him and fell down in a faint. He caressed her until she recovered, when he embraced her, and she embraced him and kissed him.

He conveyed his goods and property into the house, while the damsel looked at him and his mother. He told his mother all that had happened to him with the Persian and with his sisters in the Palace of the Mountain of Clouds. And when his mother heard his story she wondered, and gazing on the damsel she was amazed by her beauty and loveliness. She seated herself beside the damsel to comfort and welcome her.

Then said his mother to Hassan: "O my son, with this wealth we cannot live in this city, for the people know that we are poor, and they will accuse us of practicing alchemy. Therefore let us arise and go to the city of Bagdad, the Abode of Peace, that we may reside under the protection of the Caliph Haroun Al Raschid."

When Hassan heard these words he approved them. He arose immediately, sold his house, and summoned the she-camels, and put upon them all his riches and goods, together with his wife and his mother. He set forth and journeyed until he reached the city of Bagdad. He bought in that city a house ample and handsome for a hundred thousand pieces of gold. To this he removed his furniture, rarities, and chests of gold and silver. And he resided in ease with his wife for the space of three years during which he was blessed by her with two boys, named Nasir and Mansour.

Now, at the end of three years, Hassan remembered his sisters, the damsels of the Palace of the Mountain of Clouds, and he longed to see them. He went forth to the markets of the city and bought ornaments and costly stuffs, and dried fruits, the like of which his sisters had never seen nor known. And returning to his house he called his mother and said unto her: "Know, O my mother, I go on a long journey. In this closet, buried in the earth, is a chest in which is a dress of feathers belonging to my wife. Be careful lest she find it and take it and fly away with the children. Know also that she is the daughter of the King of the Genii. She is the mistress of her people, and the dearest thing that her father hath. Allow her not to go forth from the door, or to look from a window, or from over a wall, for if anything should befall her I shall slay myself on her account." And his wife heard his words to his mother, and they knew it not.

Hassan arose, went forth from the city and beat the drum and immediately the she-camels came to him. He laded twenty with rarities, after which he bade farewell to his wife and children. He then mounted and journeyed to his sisters. He pursued his journey night and day, traversing the valleys and the mountains, and the plains and the rugged tracts, for the space of ten days, and on the eleventh he arrived at the palace and went in to his sisters. And when they saw him they rejoiced at his arrival, and welcomed him exceedingly. He remained with them, entertained and treated with honor, for three months, and he passed his time in joy and happiness and in hunting.

Now, after Hassan had set forth on his journey, it happened one day that his wife longed to visit the public bath. So she entreated his mother, and gave her no rest until she arose, and prepared the things required and took the damsel and her two children, and went to the bath. When they entered all the women looked at the damsel, wondering at her beauty. Now, it happened there came to the bath that day one of the slave-girls of the Prince of the Faithful, the Caliph Haroun Al Raschid, called Tofeh, the lute player. She sat confounded at the sight of the damsel, who had made an end of washing, and had come forth, and had put on her clothes, when she appeared still more beautiful. The damsel then went forth to her abode.

Tofeh, the lute-player, the slave-girl of the Caliph, arose and went forth with the damsel until she knew her house. She then returned to the palace of the Caliph. She went into the Lady Zobeide, and kissed the ground before her, and said: "O my mistress, I have been to the bath, where I saw a wonder! A damsel having with her two young children like two moons. None hath beheld the like of her nor doth there exist the like of her in the whole world! I fear, O my mistress, that the Prince of the Faithful may hear of her and that he will disobey the law, and slay her husband, and marry her." "Is this damsel endowed with such beauty and loveliness!" said the Lady Zobeide. "Verily I must see her, and if she be not as thou hast described, I will give orders to strike off thy head, O thou wicked woman!"

So the Lady Zobeide summoned Mesrour, and

bade him bring quickly the damsel and the two children. And Mesrour replied: "I hear and obey." He went forth, and proceeded to the house of Hassan, and he took the wife and mother of Hassan, together with the two children, and brought them to the Lady Zobeide.

The damsel had her face covered, and the Lady Zobeide commanded her to remove her veil. She did so, and displayed a face of dazzling beauty, and the Lady Zobeide was amazed, and pressed the damsel to her bosom, and seated her with herself upon the couch. And she gave orders to bring a suit of the most magnificent apparel and a necklace of the most precious jewels, and she decked the damsel with them, saying: "O mistress of beauties! Thou hast filled mine eye with delight! What hast thou among thy treasures?" "I have a dress of feathers," the damsel answered. "If I were to put it on, thou wouldst see a thing of wonderful make!" "And where," said the Lady Zobeide, "is this dress?" "It is in the possession of the mother of my husband," she answered, "it is in a chest buried in a closet in my husband's house, his mother hath the key."

At this the Lady Zoebeide cried out to Hassan's mother, and took the key from her. She then called Mesrour, and bade him proceed immediately to the house of Hassan, enter the cupboard, dig up the chest, break it open, and bring her the dress of feathers. Mesrour took the key and did all that the Lady Zobeide commanded, and, wrapping the dress of feathers in a napkin, he brought it to her.

She gave it to the damsel, who rising with delight, took her children in her bosom, and wrapping herself in the dress of feathers, became a bird. She expanded her wings, and flew with her children through the window, saying: "O mother of Hassan, when thy son cometh, and sorrow and despair oppress him, bid him come to me in the Islands of Wak Wak." And she flew away with her children, and sought her country. And the mother of Hassan returned to her home, and would not be comforted. . . .

THE WHITE CAT / France

Rachel Field

This variant was made widely known by Madame d'Aulnoy in 1710. Similar tales are told throughout Europe, although the animal is sometimes a mouse or a frog. The youngest prince is, of course, "gay and well-mannered, handsome and accomplished." He and his two brothers are sent on three quests by their father. By serving a white cat for three years, he is able to surpass his brothers.

This tale also includes the motifs of transformation and disenchantment. By cutting off the cat's tail and head (a common method of breaking an enchantment), the prince restores her to her original human form—a beautiful queen.

Once upon a time there was a King who had three sons. The day came when they were grown so big and strong that he began to fear they would be planning to rule in his place. This would cause trouble among themselves and his subjects. Now the King was not so young as he once had been but nevertheless he had no notion of giving up his kingdom then and there. So after much thought he hit upon a scheme which should keep them too busily occupied to interfere in the affairs of state. Accordingly he called the three into his private apartments where he spoke to them with great kindliness and concern of his plans for the future.

"I am planning to retire from the affairs of state. But I do not wish my subjects to suffer from this change. Therefore, while I am still alive, I shall transfer my crown to one of you. I shall not follow the usual custom of leaving the crown to my eldest son, but whichever one of you shall bring me the handsomest and most intelligent little dog shall become my heir."

The Princes were greatly surprised by this strange request, but they could not very well refuse to humor their father's whim; and since there was luck in it for the two younger sons and the elder of the three was a timid, rather spiritless fellow, they agreed readily enough. The King then bade them farewell after first distributing jewels and money among them and adding that a year from that day at the same place and hour they should return to him with their little dogs.

Within sight of the city gates stood a castle where the three often spent many days in company with their young companions. Here they agreed to part and to meet again in a year before proceeding with their trophies to the King; and so having pledged their good faith, and changing their names that they might not be known, each set off upon a different road.

It would take far too long to recount the adventures of all three Princes so I shall tell only of those that befell the youngest, for a more gay and well-mannered Prince never lived, nor one so handsome and accomplished.

Scarcely a day passed that he did not buy a dog or two, greyhounds, mastiffs, bloodhounds, pointers, spaniels, water dogs, lapdogs; but the instant he found a handsomer one he let the first go and kept the new purchase, since it would have been impossible for him to carry them all on his journeyings. He went without fixed plan or purpose and so he continued for many days until at last darkness and a terrible storm overtook him at nightfall in a lonely forest. Thunder and lightning rumbled and flashed; rain fell in torrents; the trees seemed to close more densely about him until at last he could no longer find his way. When he had wandered thus for some time he suddenly saw a glint of light between the tree trunks. Feeling certain that this must mean a shelter of some sort he pressed on till he found himself approaching the most magnificent castle he had ever seen. The gate was of gold and covered with jewels of such brilliance that it was their light which had guided him to the spot. In spite of the rain and storm he caught glimpses of walls of finest porcelain decorated with pictures of the most famous fairies from the beginning of the world up to that very day: Cinderella, Graciosa, Sleeping Beauty, and a hundred others. As he admired all this magnificence he noticed a rabbit's foot fastened to the golden gates by a chain of diamonds. Marveling greatly at such a lavish display of precious gems, the young Prince pulled at the rabbit's foot and straightway an unseen bell of wonderful sweetness rang; the gate was opened by hundreds of tiny hands and others pushed him forward while he hesitated amazed upon the threshold. He moved on wonderingly, his hand on the hilt of his sword until he was reassured by two voices singing a welcome. Again he felt himself being pushed, this time toward a gate of coral opening upon an apartment of mother-of-pearl from which he passed into others still more richly decorated and alight with wax candles and great chandeliers sparkling with a thousand rainbows.

He had passed through perhaps sixty such rooms when the hands that guided him made a sign for him to stop. He saw a large armchair moving by itself toward a fireplace at the same moment that the fire began to blaze and the hands, which he now observed to be very small and white, carefully drew off his wet clothes and handed him others so fine and richly embroidered they seemed fit for a wedding day. The hands continued to dress him, until at last, powdered and attired more handsomely than he had ever been in his life before, the Prince was led into a banquet hall. Here the four walls were decorated solely with paintings representing famous cats, Puss-in-Boots and others whom he was quick to recognize. Even more astonishing than this was the table set for two with its gold service and crystal cups.

There was an orchestra composed entirely of cats. One held a music book with the strangest notes imaginable; another beat time with a little baton; and all the rest strummed tiny guitars.

While the Prince stared in amazement, each cat suddenly began to mew in a different key and to claw at the guitar strings. It was the strangest music ever heard! The Prince would have thought himself in bedlam had not the palace itself been so marvelously beautiful. So he stopped his ears and laughed heartily at the various poses and grimaces of these strange musicians. He was meditating upon the extraordinary sights he had already seen in the castle, when he beheld a little figure entering the hall. It was scarcely more than two feet in height and wrapped in a long gold crêpe veil. Before it walked two cats dressed in deep mourning and wearing cloaks and swords, while still others followed, some carrying rat-traps full of rats and mice in cages.

By this time the Prince was too astonished to think. But presently the tiny pink figure approached him and lifted its veil. He now beheld the most beautiful little white cat that ever was or ever will be. She had such a very youthful and melancholy air and a mewing so soft and sweet that it went straight to the young Prince's heart.

"Son of a King," she said to him, "thou art welcome; my mewing Majesty beholds thee with pleasure.

"Madam," responded the Prince, bowing as low as possible before her, "it is very gracious of you to receive me with so much attention, but you do not appear to me to be an ordinary little cat. The gift of speech which you have and this superb castle you inhabit are certainly evidence to the contrary."

"Son of a King," rejoined the White Cat, "I pray that you will cease to pay me compliments. I am plain in my speech and manners, but I have a kind heart. Come," she added, to her attendants, "let them serve supper and bid the concert cease, for the Prince does not understand what they are singing."

"And are they singing words, madam?" he asked incredulously.

"Certainly," she answered, "we have very gifted poets here, as you will see if you remain long enough."

Supper was then served to them by the same hands that had guided him there, and a very strange meal it was. There were two dishes of each course—one soup, for instance, being of savory pigeons while the other had been made of nicely fattened mice. The sight of this rather took away the Prince's appetite until his hostess, who seemed to guess what was passing in his mind, assured him that his own dishes had been specially prepared and contained no rats and mice of any kind. Her charming manners convinced the Prince that the little Cat had no wish to deceive him, so he began to eat and drink with great enjoyment. During their meal he happened to observe that on one paw she wore a tiny miniature set in a bracelet. This surprised him so that he begged her to let him examine it more closely. He had supposed it would be the picture of Master Puss, but what was his astonishment to find it the portrait of a handsome young man who bore a strange resemblance to himself! As he stared at it, the White Cat was heard to sigh so deeply and with such profound sadness that the Prince became even more curious; but he dared not question one so affected. Instead he entertained her with tales of court life, with which, to his surprise, he found her well acquainted.

After supper the White Cat led her guest into another Hall, where upon a little stage twelve cats and twelve monkeys danced in the most fantastic costumes. So the evening ended in great merriment; and after the Cat had bade the Prince a gracious good night the same strange hands conducted him to his own apartment, where in spite of the softness of his bed he spent half the night trying to solve the mystery of the castle and his extraordinary little hostess.

But when morning came he was no nearer to an answer to his questionings, so he allowed the pair of hands to help him dress and lead him into the palace courtyard. Here a vast company of cats in hunting costume were gathering to the sound of the horn. A fête day indeed! The White Cat was going to hunt and wished the Prince to accompany her. Now the mysterious hands presented him with a wooden horse. He made some objection to mounting it, but it proved to be an excellent charger, and a tireless galloper. The White Cat rode beside him on a monkey, the handsomest and proudest that ever was seen. She had thrown off her long veil and wore a military cap which made her look so bold that she frightened all the mice in the neighborhood. Never was there a more successful hunt. The cats outran all the rabbits and hares and a thousand skillful feats were performed to the gratification of the entire company. Tiring of the hunt at last the White Cat took up a horn no bigger than the Prince's little finger and blew upon it with so loud and clear a tone it could be heard ten leagues away. Scarcely had she sounded two or three flourishes when all the cats in the countryside seemed to appear. By land and sea and through the air they all came flocking to her call, dressed in every conceivable costume. So, followed by this extraordinary train, the Prince rode back with his hostess to the castle.

That night the White Cat put on her gold veil again and they dined together as before. Being very hungry the Prince ate and drank heartily, and this time the food had a strange effect upon him. All recollection of his father and the little dog he was to find for him slipped from his mind. He no longer thought of anything but of gossiping with the White Cat and enjoying her kind and gracious companionship. So the days passed in pleasant sport and amusement and the night in feasting and conversation. There was scarcely one in which he did not discover some new charm of the little White Cat. Now he had forgotten even the land of his birth. The hands continued to wait upon him and supply every want till he began to regret that he could not become a cat himself to live forever in such pleasant company.

"Alas," he confessed to the White Cat at last, "how wretched it makes me even to think of leaving you! I have come to love you so dearly. Could you not become a woman or else make me a cat?"

But though she smiled at his wish, the look she turned upon him was very strange.

A year passes away quickly when one has neither pain nor care, when one is merry and in good health. The Prince took no thought of time, but the White Cat was not so forgetful.

"There are only three days left to look for the little dog you were to bring to the King, your father," she reminded him. "Your two brothers have already found several very beautiful ones."

At her words the Prince's memory returned to him and he marveled at his strange forgetfulness.

"What spell would have made me forget what was most important to me in the whole world?" he cried in despair. "My honor and my fortune are lost unless I can find a dog that will win a kingdom for me and a horse swift enough to carry me home again in this short time!"

So, believing this to be impossible, he grew very sorrowful. Then the White Cat spoke to him with great reassurance.

"Son of a King," she said, "do not distress yourself so. I am your friend. Remain here another day, and though it is five hundred leagues from here to your country the good wooden horse will carry you there in less than twelve hours' time."

"But it is not enough for me to return to my father, dear Cat," said the Prince. "I must take him a little dog as well."

"And so you shall," replied she. "Here is a walnut which contains one more beautiful than the Dog Star."

"Your Majesty jests with me," he protested.

"Put the walnut to your ear then," insisted the Cat, "and you will hear it bark."

He obeyed her, and as he held the walnut to his ear a faint "Bow-wow" came from within, more tiny and shrill than a cricket on a winter night. The Prince could scarcely believe his ears or contain his curiosity to see so diminutive a creature. But he was wise enough to follow the White Cat's advice not to open the walnut till he should reach his father's presence.

It was a sad leave-taking between the Prince and the White Cat. A thousand times he thanked her, but though he urged her to return to court with him, she only shook her head and sighed deeply as upon the night of his arrival. So he galloped away at last on the wooden horse, which bore him more swiftly than the wind to the appointed place.

He reached the castle even before his two brothers and enjoyed the sight of their surprise at seeing a wooden horse champing at the bit in the courtyard. The two brothers were so busy telling of their various adventures that they took little note of their young brother's silence concerning his, but when the time came to show one another their dogs the two were vastly amused at sight of an ugly cur which the young Prince had brought along, pretending to consider it a marvel of beauty. Needless to say the elder Princes smiled with secret satisfaction to think how far superior were their own dogs, for though they wished their brother no ill luck, they had no wish to see him ruling over the kingdom.

Next morning the three set out together in the same coach. The two eldest brothers carried baskets filled with little dogs too delicate and beautiful to be touched, while the youngest carried the poor cur as if it also was precious. By no outward sign did he betray the presence of the walnut with its precious occupant which was safely hidden in his pocket. No sooner did the three set foot in the palace than all the court crowded around to welcome the returned travelers and see the results of their journeyings. The King received them with great joy, professing delight over the little dogs his two elder sons brought out for his inspection. But the more he studied their merits, the more puzzled he became, so nearly were they alike in beauty and grace. The two brothers were already beginning to dispute with one another as to which deserved the crown when the younger brother stepped forward, holding upon the palm of his hand the walnut so lately presented to him by the White Cat. Opening it without more ado, he revealed a tiny dog lying upon cotton. So perfectly formed was it and so small that it could pass through a little finger ring without touching any part of it. It was more delicate than thistledown and its coat shone with colors of the rainbow. Nor was this all; immediately it was released from its kennel, the little creature arose on its hind legs and began to go through the steps of a tarantella, with tiny castanets and all the airs and graces of a Spanish dancer!

The King was dumbfounded and even the two brothers were forced to acknowledge that such a beautiful and gifted dog had never been seen before. But their father was in no mood to give up his kingdom, so he announced that he had decided upon another test of their skill. This time he would give them a year to travel over land and sea in search of a piece of cloth so fine it would pass through the eye of the finest Venetian-point lace needle.

So the Prince remounted his wooden horse and set off at full speed, for now he knew exactly where he wanted to go. So great was his eagerness to see the beautiful White Cat once more that he could scarcely contain himself until her castle came into view. This time every window was alight to welcome him and the faithful pair of hands which had waited on him so well before were ready to take the bridle of the wooden horse and lead it back to the stable while the Prince hurried to the White Cat's private apartments.

He found her lying on a little couch of blue satin with many pillows. Her expression was sad until she caught sight of him. Then she sprang up and began to caper about him delightedly.

"Oh, dear Prince," cried she, "I had scarcely dared to hope for your return. I am generally so unfortunate in matters that concern me."

A thousand times must the grateful Prince caress her and recount his adventures, which perhaps she knew more about than he guessed. And now he told her of his father's latest whim—how he had set his heart upon having a piece of cloth that could pass through the eye of the finest needle. For his own part he did not believe it was possible to find such a thing, but he believed that if any one could help him in this quest it would be his dear White Cat. She listened attentively to all he told her and finally explained with a thoughtful air that this was a matter demanding careful consideration. There were, it seemed, some cats in her castle who could spin with extraordinary skill, and she added that she would also put a paw to the work herself so that he need not trouble himself to search farther.

The Prince was only too delighted to accept this offer and he and his charming hostess sat down to supper together, after which a magnificent display of fireworks was set off in his honor. And once more the days passed in enchanted succession. The ingenious White Cat knew a thousand different ways of entertaining her guest, so that he never once thought of missing human society. Indeed, he was probably the first person in the world to spend a whole year of complete contentment with only cats for company.

The second year slipped away as pleasantly as the first. The Prince could scarcely think of anything that the tireless hands did not instantly supply, whether books, jewels, pictures, old things or new. In short, he had but to say, "I want a certain gem that is in the cabinet of the Great Mogul, or the King of Persia, or such and such a statue in Corinth or any part of Greece," and he saw it instantly before him, without knowing how it came or who brought it. It is not unpleasant at all to find oneself able to possess any treasure in the world. No wonder our Prince was happy!

But the White Cat who was ever watchful of his welfare, warned him that the hour of departure was approaching and that he might make himself easy in his mind about the piece of cloth, for she had a most wonderful one for him. She added that it was her intention this time to furnish him with an equipage worthy of his high birth, and without waiting for his reply, beckoned him to the window overlooking the castle courtyard. Here he saw an open coach of gold and flame-color with a thousand gallant devices to please the mind and eye. It was drawn by twelve horses as white as snow, four-and-four abreast, with harnesses of flaming velvet embroidered with diamonds and gold. A hundred other coaches, each with eight horses and filled with superbly attired noblemen followed, escorted by a thousand bodyguards whose uniforms were so richly embroidered you could not see the material beneath. But the most remarkable part of this cavalcade was that a portrait of the White Cat was to be seen everywhere, in coach device, uniform, or worn as a decoration on the doublets of those who rode in the train, as if it were some newly created order that had been conferred upon them.

"Go now," said the White Cat to the Prince. "Appear at the court of the King, your father, in such mangificence that he cannot fail to be impressed and to bestow upon you the crown which you deserve. Here is another walnut. Crack it in his presence and you will find the piece of cloth you asked of me."

"Oh, dear White Cat," he answered tenderly, "I am so overcome by your goodness that I would gladly give up my hopes of power and future grandeur to stay here with you the rest of life."

"Son of a King," she answered, "I am convinced of your kindness of heart. A kind heart is a rare thing among princes who would be loved by all, yet not love any one themselves. But you are the proof that there is an exception to this rule. I give you credit for the affection you have shown to a little white cat that after all is good for nothing but to catch mice."

So the Princed kissed her paw and departed.

This time the two brothers arrived at their father's palace before him, congratulating themselves that their young brother must be dead or gone for good. They lost no time in displaying the cloths they had brought, which were indeed so fine that they could pass through the eye of a large needle but not through the small eye of the needle the King had already selected. At this there arose a great murmuring at court. The friends of the two Princes took sides among themselves as to which had fulfilled the bargain better. But this was interrupted by a flourish of trumpets announcing the arrival of their younger brother.

The magnificence of his train fairly took away the breath of the King and his court, but their astonishment grew even greater when, after saluting his father, the young Prince brought out the walnut. This he cracked with great ceremony only to find, instead of the promised piece of cloth, a cherry stone. At sight of this the King and the court exchanged sly smiles. Nothing daunted, the Prince cracked the cherry stone, only to find a kernel inside. Jeers and murmurs ran through the great apartment. The Prince must be a fool indeed! He made no answer to them, but even he began to doubt the white Cat's words as he found next a grain of wheat and within that the smallest millet seed. "Oh, White Cat, White Cat! Have you betrayed me?" he muttered between his teeth. Even as he spoke he felt a little scratch upon his hand, so sharp that it drew blood. Taking this to be some sort of sign, the Prince proceeded to open the millet seed. Before the incredulous eyes of the whole court he drew out of it a piece of cloth four hundred yards long and marvelously embroidered with colored birds and beasts, with trees and fruits and flowers, with shells and jewels and even with suns and moons and countless stars. There were also portraits of Kings and Queens of the past upon it and of their children and children's children, not forgetting the smallest child, and each dressed perfectly in the habit of his century.

The sight of this was almost too much for the King. He could scarcely find the needle. Through its eye the wonderful piece of cloth was able to pass not only once, but six times, before the jealous gaze of the two older Princes. But the King was still far from ready to give up his kingdom. Once more he turned to his children.

"I am going to put your obedience to a new

and final test," he told them. "Go and travel for another year and whichever one of you brings back with him the most beautiful Princess shall marry her and be crowned King on his wedding day. I pledge my honor that after this I shall ask no further favors of you."

So off the three went again, the youngest Prince still in a good humor although he had the least cause to be since he had twice been the acknowledged winner of the wager. But he was not one to dispute his father's will, so soon he and all his train were taking the road back to his dear White Cat. She knew the very day and hour of his arrival, and all along the way flowers had been strewn and perfume made the air sweet. Once more the castle gate was opened to him and the strange hands took him in charge while all the cats climbed into the trees to welcome their returning visitor.

"So, my Prince," said the White Cat when he reached her side at last, "once more you have returned without the crown. But no matter," she added as he opened his lips to explain. "I know that you are bound to take back the most beautiful Princess to court and I will find one for you, never fear. Meantime, let us amuse ourselves and be merry."

The third year passed for the young Prince as had the two others, and since nothing runs away faster than time passed without trouble or care, it is certain that he would have completely forgotten the day of his return to court had not the White Cat reminded him of it. This time, however, she told him that upon him alone depended his fate. He must promise to do whatever she asked of him. The Prince agreed readily enough until he heard her command him to cut off her head and tail and fling them into the fire.

"I!" cried the Prince, aghast, "I be so barbarous as to kill my dear White Cat? This is some trick to try my heart, but you should be sure of its gratitude."

"No, no, Son of a King," she answered, "I know your heart too well for that. But fate is stronger than either of us, and you must do as I bid you. It is the only way; and you must believe me, for I swear it on the honor of a Cat."

Tears came into the eyes of the Prince at the mere thought of cutting off the head of so amiable and pretty a creature. He tried to say all the most tender things he could think of, hoping to distract her. But she persisted that she wished to die by his hand because it was the only means of preventing his brothers from winning the crown. So pietously did she beg him that at last, all of a tremble, he drew his sword. With faltering hand he cut off the head and tail of his dear White Cat.

Next moment the most remarkable transformation took place before his very eyes. The body of the little White Cat suddenly changed into that of a young girl, the most graceful ever seen. But this was as nothing compared to the beauty and sweetness of her face, where only the shining brightness of the eyes gave any hint of the cat she had so recently been. The Prince was struck dumb with surprise and delight. He opened his eyes wider still to look at her, and what was his amazement to behold a troop of lords and ladies entering the apartment, each with a cat's skin flung over an arm. They advanced, and throwing themselves at the feet of their Queen, expressed their joy at seeing her once more restored to her natural form. She received them with great affection, but presently she desired them to leave her alone with the Prince.

"Behold, my dear Prince," she said as soon as they had done so, "I am released of a terrible enchantment, too long a tale to tell you now. Suffice it to say that this portrait which you saw upon my paw when I was a cat, was given to me by my guardian faries during the time of my trial. I supposed it was of my first, unhappy love who was so cruelly taken from me and whose resemblance to you is so striking. Conceive my joy then, to find that it is of the Prince who has my entire heart and who was destined to rescue me from my enchantment."

And she bowed low before our Prince, who was so filled with joy and wonder that he would have remained there forever telling her of his love, had she not reminded him that the hour for his return to his father's court was almost upon them. Taking him by the hands, she led him into the courtyard to a chariot even more magnificent than the one she had provided before. The rest were equally gorgeous, the horses shod with emeralds held in place by diamond nails, with such gold and jeweled trappings as were never seen before or since. But the young Prince had eyes for nothing beyond the beauty of his companion.

Just before they reached the outskirts of the city, they sighted the Prince's two brothers with their trains driving toward them from opposite directions. At this the Princess hid herself in a small throne of rock crystal and precious gems while the Prince remained alone in the coach. His two brothers, each accompanied by a charming lady, greeted him warmly but expressed surprise and curiosity that he should be alone. To these questions he replied that he had been so unfortunate as not to have met with any lady of sufficient beauty to bring with him to court. He added, however, that he had instead a very rare and gifted White Cat. At this the brothers laughed loudly and exchanged pleased glances, for now they were convinced that he was indeed a simpleton and they need have no fears of his outwitting them a third time.

Through the streets of the city the two elder Princes rode with their ladies in open carriages, while the youngest Prince came last. Behind him was borne the great rock crystal, at which every one gazed in wonder.

The two Princes eagerly charged up the palace stairs with their Princesses, so anxious were they for their father's approval. The King received

them graciously, but once more had difficulty in deciding which should have the prize. So he turned to his youngest son, who stood alone before him. "Have you returned empty-handed this time?" he asked.

"In this rock your Majesty will find a little White Cat," he answered, "one which mews so sweetly and has such velvet paws that you cannot but be delighted with it."

But before the surprised King could reach the crystal, the Princess touched an inner spring. It flew open revealing her in all her beauty, more dazzling than the sun itself. Her hair fell in golden ringlets; she was crowned with flowers and she moved with incomparable grace in her gown of white and rose-colored gauze. Even the King himself could not resist such loveliness, but hastened to acknowledge her undisputed right to wear the crown.

"But I have not come to deprive your Majesty of a throne which you fill so admirably," she said, bowing before him graciously. "I was born the heiress to six kingdoms of my own, so permit me to offer one to you and to each of your elder sons. I ask no other favors of you than your friendship and that your youngest son shall be my husband. Three kingdoms will be quite enough for us."

And so in truth they found them.

BEAUTY AND THE BEAST / France

Andrew Lang

Fairy tales are set in a dangerous world. Luckily there is good magic as well as bad, and enchantments can be broken. Transformations and their subsequent disenchantments provide the conflict for many folk narratives and are common motifs.

The Greek myth "Cupid and Psyche" appears to be related to these tales, as can be seen in the Scandinavian "East o' the Sun and West o' the Moon" and the French "Beauty and the Beast." In the "Cupid and Psyche" tradition a beautiful girl thinks she is married to a monster, comes to like him, disobeys his warning or command, and loses him after discovering she loves him. Many of these complex narratives include the motifs of a quest and the performance of difficult tasks before disenchantment is possible. In "Beauty and the Beast" the quest and tasks are omitted. In this allegory about the power of love, only her declaration of love and willingness to marry him are necessary to break the enchantment.

Once upon a time, in a far-off country, there lived a merchant who was enormously rich. As he had six sons and six daughters, however, who were accustomed to having everything they fancied, he did not find he had a penny too much. But misfortunes befell them. One day their house caught fire and speedily burned to the ground, with all the splendid furniture, books, pictures, gold, silver and precious goods it contained. The father suddenly lost every ship he had upon the sea, either by dint of pirates, shipwreck or fire. Then he heard that his clerks in distant countries, whom he had trusted entirely, had proved unfaithful. And at last from great wealth he fell into the direst poverty.

All that he had left was a little house in a desolate place at least a hundred leagues from the town. The daughters at first hoped their friends, who had been so numerous while they were rich, would insist on their staying in their houses, but they soon found they were left alone. Their former friends even attributed their misfortunes to their own extravagance and showed no intention of offering them any help.

So nothing was left for them but to take their departure to the cottage, which stood in the midst of a dark forest. As they were too poor to have any servants, the girls had to work hard, and the sons, for their part, cultivated the fields to earn their living. Roughly clothed, and living in the simplest way, the girls regretted unceasingly the luxuries and amusements of their former life. Only the youngest daughter tried to be brave and cheerful.

She had been as sad as anyone when misfortune first overtook her father, but soon recovering her natural gaiety, she set to work to make the best of things, to amuse her father and brothers as well as she could, and to persuade her sisters to join her in dancing and singing. But they would do nothing of the sort, and because she was not as doleful as themselves, they declared this miserable life was all she was fit for. But she was really far prettier and cleverer than they were. Indeed, she was so lovely she was always called Beauty.

After two years, their father received news that one of his ships, which he had believed lost, had come safely into port with a rich cargo. All the sons and daughters at once thought that their poverty was at an end and wanted to set out directly for the town; but their father, who was more prudent, begged them to wait a little, and though it was harvest time, and he could ill be spared, determined to go himself to make inquiries.

Only the youngest daughter had any doubt but that they would soon again be as rich as they were before. They all loaded their father with commissions for jewels and dresses which it would have taken a fortune to buy; only Beauty did not ask for anything. Her father, noticing her silence, said:

"And what shall I bring for you, Beauty?"

"The only thing I wish for is to see you come home safely," she answered.

But this reply vexed her sisters, who fancied she was blaming them for having asked for such costly things. Her father, however, was pleased, but as he thought she certainly ought to like pretty presents, he told her to choose something.

"Well, dear Father," she said, "as you insist upon it, I beg that you will bring me a rose. I have not seen one since we came here, and I love them so much."

The merchant set out, only to find that his former companions, believing him to be dead, had divided his cargo between them. After six months of trouble and expense he found himself as poor as when he started on his journey. To make matters worse, he was obliged to return in the most terrible weather. By the time he was within a few leagues of his home he was almost exhausted with cold and fatigue. Though he knew it would take some hours to get through the forest, he resolved to go on. But night overtook him, and the deep snow and bitter frost made it impossible for his horse to carry him any farther.

The only shelter he could get was the hollow

"Beauty and the Beast," from *The Blue Fairy Book.* Edited by Andrew Lang. Published by Longmans, Green & Co., Ltd.

trunk of a great tree, and there he crouched all the night, which seemed to him the longest he had ever known. The howling of the wolves kept him awake, and when at last day broke the falling snow had covered up every path, and he did not know which way to turn.

At length he made out some sort of path, but it was so rough and slippery that he fell down more than once. Presently it led him into an avenue of trees which ended in a splendid castle. It seemed to the merchant very strange that no snow had fallen in the avenue of orange trees, covered with flowers and fruit. When he reached the first court of the castle he saw before him a flight of agate steps. He went up them and passed through several splendidly furnished rooms.

The pleasant warmth of the air revived him, and he felt very hungry; but there seemed to be nobody in all this vast and splendid palace. Deep silence reigned everywhere, and at last, tired of roaming through empty rooms and galleries, he stopped in a room smaller than the rest, where a clear fire was burning and a couch was drawn up cosily before it. Thinking this must be prepared for someone who was expected, he sat down to wait till he should come and very soon fell into a sweet sleep.

When his extreme hunger wakened him after several hours, he was still alone; but a little table, with a good dinner on it, had been drawn up close to him. He lost no time in beginning his meal, hoping he might soon thank his considerate host, whoever it might be. But no one appeared, and even after another long sleep, from which he awoke completely refreshed, there was no sign of anybody, though a fresh meal of dainty cakes and fruit was prepared upon the little table at his elbow.

Being naturally timid, the silence began to terrify him, and he resolved to search once more through all the rooms; but it was of no use, there was no sign of life in the palace! Then he went down into the garden, and though it was winter everywhere else, here the sun shone, the birds sang, the flowers bloomed, and the air was soft and sweet. The merchant, in ecstasies with all he saw and heard, said to himself:

"All this must be meant for me. I will go this minute and bring my children to share all these delights."

In spite of being so cold and weary when he reached the castle, he had taken his horse to the stable and fed it. Now he thought he would saddle it for his homeward journey, and he turned down the path which led to the stable. This path had a hedge of roses on each side of it, and the merchant thought he had never seen such exquisite flowers. They reminded him of his promise to Beauty, and he stopped and had just gathered one to take to her when he was startled by a strange noise behind him. Turning round, he saw a frightful Beast, which seemed to be very angry and said in a terrible voice:

"Who told you you might gather my roses? Was it not enough that I sheltered you in my palace and was kind to you? This is the way you show your gratitude, by stealing my flowers! But your insolence shall not go unpunished."

The merchant, terrified by these furious words, dropped the fatal rose and, throwing himself on his knees, cried, "Pardon me, noble sir. I am truly grateful for your hospitality, which was so magnificent I could not imagine you would be offended by my taking such a little thing as a rose."

But the Beast's anger was not lessened by his speech.

"You are very ready with excuses and flattery," he cried. "But that will not save you from the death you deserve."

Alas, thought the merchant, if my daughter Beauty could only know into what danger her rose has brought me! And in despair he began to tell the Beast all his misfortunes and the reason of his journey, not forgetting to mention Beauty's request.

"A king's ransom would hardly have procured all that my other daughters asked for," he said. "But I thought I might at least take Beauty her rose. I beg you to forgive me, for you see I meant no harm."

The Beast said, in a less furious tone, "I will forgive you on one condition—that you will give me one of your daughters."

"Ah," cried the merchant, "if I were cruel enough to buy my own life at the expense of one of my children's, what excuse could I invent to bring her here?"

"None," answered the Beast. "If she comes at all she must come willingly. On no other condition will I have her. See if any of them is courageous enough, and loves you enough, to come and save your life. You seem to be an honest man so I will trust you to go home. I give you a month to see if any of your daughters will come back with you and stay here, to let you go free. If none of them is willing, you must come alone, after bidding them good-bye forever, for then you will belong to me. And do not imagine that you can hide from me, for if you fail to keep your word I will come and fetch you!" added the Beast grimly.

The merchant accepted this proposal. He promised to return at the time appointed, and then, anxious to escape from the presence of the Beast, he asked permission to set off at once. But the Beast answered that he could not go until the next day.

"Then you will find a horse ready for you," he said. "Now go and eat your supper and await my orders."

The poor merchant, more dead than alive, went back to his room, where the most delicious supper was already served on the little table drawn up before a blazing fire. But he was too terrified to eat and only tasted a few of the dishes, for fear the Beast should be angry if he did not obey his orders. When he had finished, the Beast warned him to remember their agreement and to prepare his daughter exactly for what she had to expect.

"Do not get up tomorrow," he added, "until you see the sun and hear a golden bell ring. Then you will find your breakfast waiting for you, and the horse you are to ride will be ready in the courtyard. He will also bring you back again when you come with your daughter a month hence. Farewell. Take a rose to Beauty, and remember your promise!"

The merchant lay down until the sun rose. Then, after breakfast, he went to gather Beauty's rose and mounted his horse, which carried him off so swiftly that in an instant he had lost sight of the palace. He was still wrapped in gloomy thoughts when it stopped before the door of his cottage.

His sons and daughters, who had been uneasy at his long absence, rushed to meet him, eager to know the result of his journey which, seeing him mounted upon a splendid horse and wrapped in a rich mantle, they supposed to be favorable. But he hid the truth from them at first, only saying sadly to Beauty as he gave her the rose:

"Here is what you asked me to bring you. Little you know what it has cost."

Presently he told them his adventures from beginning to end, and then they were all very unhappy. The girls lamented loudly over their lost hopes, and the sons declared their father should not return to the terrible castle. But he reminded them he had promised to go back. Then the girls were very angry with Beauty and said it was all her fault. If she had asked for something sensible this would never have happened.

Poor Beauty, much distressed, said to them, "I have indeed caused this misfortune, but who could have guessed that to ask for a rose in the middle of summer would cause so much misery? But as I did the mischief it is only just that I should suffer for it. I will therefore go back with my father to keep his promise."

At first nobody would hear of it. Her father and brothers, who loved her dearly, declared nothing should make them let her go. But Beauty was firm. As the time drew near she divided her little possessions between her sisters, and said good-bye to everything she loved. When the fatal day came she encouraged and cheered her father as they mounted together the horse which had brought him back. It seemed to fly rather than gallop, but so smoothly that Beauty was not frightened. Indeed, she would have enjoyed the journey if she had not feared what might happen at the end of it. Her father still tried to persuade her to go back, but in vain.

While they were talking the night fell. Then, to their great surprise, wonderful colored lights began to shine in all directions, and splendid fireworks blazed out before them; all the forest was illuminated. They even felt pleasantly warm, though it had been bitterly cold before. They reached the avenue of orange trees and saw that the palace was brilliantly lighted from roof to ground, and music sounded softly from the courtyard.

"The Beast must be very hungry," said Beauty, trying to laugh, "if he makes all this rejoicing over the arrival of his prey." But, in spite of her anxiety, she admired all the wonderful things she saw.

When they had dismounted, her father led her to the little room. Here they found a splendid fire burning, and the table daintily spread with a delicious supper.

Beauty, who was less frightened now that she had passed through so many room and seen nothing of the Beast, was quite willing to begin, for her long ride had made her very hungry. But they had hardly finished their meal when the noise of the Beast's footsteps was heard approaching, and Beauty clung to her father in terror, which became all the greater when she saw how frightened he was. But when the Beast really appeared, though she trembled at the sight of him, she made a great effort to hide her horror, and saluted him respectfully.

This evidently pleased the Beast. After looking at her he said, in a tone that might have struck terror into the boldest heart, though he did not seem to be angry:

"Good evening, old man. Good evening, Beauty."

The merchant was too terrified to reply, but Beauty answered sweetly, "Good evening, Beast."

"Have you come willingly?" asked the Beast. "Will you be content to stay here when your father goes away?"

Beauty answered bravely that she was quite prepared to stay.

"I am pleased with you," said the Beast. "As you have come of your own accord, you may remain. As for you, old man," he added, turning to the merchant, "at sunrise tomorrow take your departure. When the bell rings, get up quickly and eat your breakfast, and you will find the same horse waiting to take you home."

Then turning to Beauty, he said, "Take your father into the next room, and help him choose gifts for your brothers and sisters. You will find two traveling trunks there; fill them as full as you can. It is only just that you should send them something very precious as a remembrance."

Then he went away, after saying, "Good-bye, Beauty; good-bye, old man." Beauty was beginning to think with great dismay of her father's departure, but they went into the next room, which had shelves and cupboards all round it.

They were greatly surprised at the riches it contained. There were splendid dresses fit for a queen, with all the ornaments to be worn with them, and when Beauty opened the cupboards she was dazzled by the gorgeous jewels lying in heaps upon every shelf. After choosing a vast quantity, which she divided between her sisters —for she had made a heap of the wonderful dresses for each of them—she opened the last chest, which was full of gold.

"I think, Father," she said, "that, as the gold will be more useful to you, we had better take out the other things again, and fill the trunks with it."

So they did this, but the more they put in, the more room there seemed to be, and at last they put back all the jewels and dresses they had taken out, and Beauty even added as many more of the jewels as she could carry at once. Even then the trunks were not too full, but they were so heavy an elephant could not have carried them!

"The Beast was mocking us!" cried the merchant. "He pretended to give us all these things, knowing that I could not carry them away."

"Let us wait and see," answered Beauty. "I cannot believe he meant to deceive us. All we can do is to fasten them up and have them ready."

So they did this and returned to the little room where they found breakfast ready. The merchant ate his with a good appetite, as the Beast's generosity made him believe he might perhaps venture to come back soon and see Beauty. But she felt sure her father was leaving her forever, so she was very sad when the bell rang sharply.

They went down into the courtyard, where two horses were waiting, one loaded with the two trunks, the other for him to ride. They were pawing the ground in their impatience to start, and the merchant bade Beauty a hasty farewell. As soon as he was mounted he went off at such a pace she lost sight of him in an instant. Then Beauty began to cry and wandered sadly back to her own room. But she soon found she was very sleepy, and as she had nothing better to do she lay down and instantly fell asleep. And then she dreamed she was walking by a brook bordered with trees, and lamenting her sad fate, when a young prince, handsomer than anyone she had ever seen, and with a voice that went straight to heart, came and said to her:

"Ah, Beauty, you are not so unfortunate as you suppose. Here you will be rewarded for all you have suffered elsewhere. Your every wish shall be gratified. Only try to find me out, no matter how I may be disguised, for I love you dearly, and in making me happy you will find your own happiness. Be as true-hearted as you are beautiful, and we shall have nothing left to wish for."

"What can I do, Prince, to make you happy?" said Beauty.

"Only be grateful," he answered, "and do not trust too much to your eyes. Above all, do not desert me until you have saved me from my cruel misery."

After this she thought she found herself in a room with a stately and beautiful lady, who said to her, "Dear Beauty, try not to regret all you have left behind you; you are destined for a better fate. Only do not let yourself be deceived by appearances."

Beauty found her dreams so interesting that she was in no hurry to awake, but presently the clock roused her by calling her name softly twelve times. Then she rose and found her dressing-table set out with everything she could possibly want, and when her toilet was finished, she found dinner waiting in the room next to hers. But dinner does not take very long when one is alone, and very soon she sat down cosily in the corner of a sofa, and began to think about the charming prince she had seen in her dream.

"He said I could make him happy," said Beauty to herself. "It seems, then, that this horrible Beast keeps him a prisoner. How can I set him free? I wonder why they both told me not to trust to appearances? But, after all, it was only a dream, so why should I trouble myself about it? I had better find something to do to amuse myself."

So she began to explore some of the many rooms of the palace. The first she entered was lined with mirrors. Beauty saw herself reflected on every side and thought she had never seen such a charming room. Then a bracelet which was hanging from a chandelier caught her eye, and on taking it down she was greatly surprised to find that it held a portrait of her unknown admirer, just as she had seen him in her dream. With great delight she slipped the bracelet on her arm and went on into a gallery of pictures, where she soon found a portrait of the same handsome prince, as large as life, and so well painted that as she studied it he seemed to smile kindly at her.

Tearing herself away from the portrait at last, she passed into a room which contained every musical instrument under the sun, and here she amused herself for a long while in trying them and singing. The next room was a library, and she saw everything she had ever wanted to read as well as everything she had read. By this time it was growing dusk, and wax candles in diamond and ruby candlesticks lit themselves in every room.

Beauty found her supper served just at the time she preferred to have it, but she did not see anyone or hear a sound, and though her father had warned her she would be alone, she began to find it rather dull.

Presently she heard the Beast coming and wondered tremblingly if he meant to eat her now. However, he did not seem at all ferocious, and only said gruffly:

"Good evening, Beauty."

She answered cheerfully and managed to conceal her terror. The Beast asked how she had been amusing herself, and she told him all the rooms she had seen. Then he asked if she thought she could be happy in his palace; and Beauty answered that everything was so beautiful she would be very hard to please if she could not be happy. After about an hour's talk Beauty began to think the Beast was not nearly so terrible as she had supposed at first. Then he rose to leave her, and said in his gruff voice:

"Do you love me, Beauty? Will you marry me?"

"Oh, what shall I say?" cried Beauty, for she was afraid to make the Beast angry by refusing.

"Say yes or no without fear," he replied.

"Oh, no, Beast," said Beauty hastily.

"Since you will not, good night, Beauty," he said.

And she answered, "Good night, Beast," very glad to find her refusal had not provoked him. After he was gone she was very soon in bed and dreaming of her unknown prince.

She thought he came and said, "Ah, Beauty! Why are you so unkind to me? I fear I am fated to be unhappy for many a long day still."

Then her dreams changed, but the charming

prince figured in them all. When morning came her first thought was to look at the portrait and see if it was really like him, and she found it certainly was.

She decided to amuse herself in the garden, for the sun shone, and all the fountains were playing. She was astonished to find that every place was familiar to her, and presently she came to the very brook and the myrtle trees where she had first met the prince in her dream. That made her think more than ever he must be kept a prisoner by the Beast.

When she was tired she went back to the palace and found a new room full of materials for every kind of work—ribbons to make into bows and silks to work into flowers. There was an aviary full of rare birds, which were so tame they flew to Beauty as soon as they saw her and perched upon her shoulders and her head.

"Pretty little creatures," she said, "how I wish your cage was nearer my room that I might often hear you sing!" So saying she opened a door and found to her delight that it led into her own room, though she had thought it was on the other side of the palace.

There were more birds in a room farther on, parrots and cockatoos that could talk, and they greeted Beauty by name. Indeed, she found them so entertaining that she took one or two back to her room, and they talked to her while she was at supper. The Beast paid her his usual visit and asked the same questions as before, and then with a gruff good night he took his departure, and Beauty went to bed to dream of her mysterious prince.

The days passed swiftly in different amusements, and after a while Beauty found another strange thing in the palace, which often pleased her when she was tired of being alone. There was one room which she had not noticed particularly; it was empty, except that under each of the windows stood a very comfortable chair. The first time she had looked out of the window it seemed a black curtain prevented her from seeing anything outside. But the second time she went into the room, happening to be tired, she sat down in one of the chairs, when instantly the curtain was rolled aside, and a most amusing pantomime was acted before her. There were dances and colored lights, music and pretty dresses, and it was all so gay that Beauty was in ecstasies. After that she tried the other seven windows in turn, and there was some new and surprising entertainment to be seen from each of them so Beauty never could feel lonely any more. Every evening after supper the Beast came to see her, and always before saying good night asked her in his terrible voice: "Beauty, will you marry me?"

And it seemed to Beauty, now she understood him better, that when she said, "No, Beast," he went away quite sad. Her happy dreams of the handsome young prince soon made her forget the poor Beast, and the only thing that disturbed her was being told to distrust appearances, to let her heart guide her, and not her eyes. Consider as she would, she could not understand.

So everything went on for a long time, until at last, happy as she was, Beauty began to long for the sight of her father and her brothers and sisters. One night, seeing her look very sad, the Beast asked her what was the matter. Beauty had quite ceased to be afraid of him. Now she knew he was really gentle in spite of his ferocious looks and his dreadful voice. So she answered that she wished to see her home once more. Upon hearing this the Beast seemed sadly distressed, and cried miserably:

"Ah, Beauty, have you the heart to desert an unhappy Beast like this? What more do you want to make you happy? Is it because you hate me that you want to escape?"

"No, dear Beast," answered Beauty softly, "I do not hate you, and I should be very sorry never to see you any more, but I long to see my father again. Only let me go for two months, and I promise to come back to you and stay for the rest of my life."

The Beast, who had been sighing dolefully while she spoke, now replied, "I cannot refuse you anything you ask, even though it should cost me my life. Take the four boxes you will find in the room next to your own and fill them with everything you wish to take with you. But remember your promise and come back when the two months are over, for if you do not come in good time you will find your faithful Beast dead. You will not need any chariot to bring you back. Only say good-bye to all your brothers and sisters the night before you come away and, when you have gone to bed, turn this ring round upon your finger, and say firmly, 'I wish to go back to my palace and see my Beast again.' Good night, Beauty. Fear nothing, sleep peacefully, and before long you shall see your father once more."

As soon as Beauty was alone she hastened to fill the boxes with all the rare and precious things she saw about her, and only when she was tired of heaping things into them did they seem to be full. Then she went to bed, but could hardly sleep for joy. When at last she began to dream of her beloved prince she was grieved to see him stretched upon a grassy bank, sad and weary, and hardly like himself.

"What is the matter?" she cried.

But he looked at her reproachfully, and said, "How can you ask me, cruel one? Are you not leaving me to my death perhaps?"

"Ah, don't be so sorrowful!" cried Beauty. "I am only going to assure my father that I am safe and happy. I have promised the Beast faithfully I will come back, and he would die of grief if I did not keep my word!"

"What would that matter to you?" asked the prince. "Surely you would not care?"

"Indeed I should be ungrateful if I did not care for such a kind beast," cried Beauty indignantly. "I would die to save him from pain. I assure you it is not his fault he is so ugly."

Just then a strange sound woke her—someone was speaking not very far away; and opening her eyes she found herself in a room she had never seen before, which was certainly not as splendid as those she had seen in the Beast's palace. Where could she be? She rose and dressed hastily and then saw that the boxes she had packed the night before were all in the room. Suddenly she heard her father's voice and rushed out to greet him joyfully. Her brothers and sisters were astonished at her appearance, for they had never expected to see her again. Beauty asked her father what he thought her strange dreams meant and why the prince constantly begged her not to trust to appearances. After much consideration he answered:

"You tell me yourself that the Beast, frightful as he is, loves you dearly and deserves your love and gratitude for his gentleness and kindness. I think the prince must mean you to understand you ought to reward him by doing as he wishes, in spite of his ugliness."

Beauty could not help seeing that this seemed probable; still, when she thought of her dear prince who was so handsome, she did not feel at all inclined to marry the Beast. At any rate, for two months she need not decide but could enjoy herself with her sisters. Though they were rich now, and lived in a town again and had plenty of acquaintances, Beauty found that nothing amused her very much. She often thought of the palace where she was so happy, especially as at home she never once dreamed of her dear prince, and she felt quite sad without him.

Then her sisters seemed quite used to being without her, and even found her rather in the way, so she would not have been sorry when the two months were over but for her father and brothers. She had not the courage to say good-bye to them. Every day when she rose she meant to say it at night, and when night came she put it off again, until at last she had a dismal dream which helped her to make up her mind.

She thought she was wandering in a lonely path in the palace gardens, when she heard groans. Running quickly to see what could be the matter, she found the Beast stretched out upon his side, apparently dying. He reproached her faintly with being the cause of his distress, and at the same moment a stately lady appeared, and said very gravely:

"Ah, Beauty, see what happens when people do not keep their promises! If you had delayed one day more, you would have found him dead."

Beauty was so terrified by this dream that the very next evening she said good-bye to her father and her brothers and sisters, and as soon as she was in bed she turned her ring round upon her finger, and said firmly:

"I wish to go back to my palace and see my Beast again."

Then she fell asleep instantly, and only woke up to hear the clock saying, "Beauty, Beauty," twelve times in its musical voice, which told her she was really in the palace once more. Everything was just as before, and her birds were so glad to see her, but Beauty thought she had never known such a long day. She was so anxious to see the Beast again that she felt as if suppertime would never come.

But when it came no Beast appeared. After

listening and waiting for a long time, she ran down into the garden to search for him. Up and down the paths and avenues ran poor Beauty, calling him. No one answered, and not a trace of him could she find. At last, she saw that she was standing opposite the shady path she had seen in her dream. She rushed down it and, sure enough, there was the cave, and in it lay the Beast—asleep, so Beauty thought. Quite glad to have found him, she ran up and stroked his head, but to her horror he did not move or open his eyes.

"Oh, he is dead, and it is all my fault!" cried Beauty, crying bitterly.

But then, looking at him again, she fancied he still breathed. Hastily fetching some water from the nearest fountain, she sprinkled it over his face, and to her great delight he began to revive.

"Oh, Beast, how you frightened me!" she cried. "I never knew how much I loved you until just now, when I feared I was too late to save your life."

"Can you really love such an ugly creature as I am?" asked the Beast faintly. "Ah, Beauty, you came only just in time. I was dying because I thought you had forgotten your promise. But go back now and rest, I shall see you again by-and-by."

Beauty, who had half expected he would be angry with her, was reassured by his gentle voice and went back to the palace, where supper was awaiting her. And afterward the Beast came in as usual and talked about the time she had spent with her father, asking if she had enjoyed herself and if they had all been glad to see her.

Beauty quite enjoyed telling him all that had happened to her. When at last the time came for him to go, he asked, as he had so often asked before:

"Beauty, will you marry me?"

She answered softly, "Yes, dear Beast."

As she spoke a blaze of light sprang up before the windows of the palace; fireworks crackled and guns banged, and across the avenue of orange trees, in letters all made of fireflies, was written: *Long live the prince and his bride.*

Turning to ask the Beast what it could all mean, Beauty found he had disappeared, and in his place stood her long-loved prince! At the same moment the wheels of a chariot were heard upon the terrace, and two ladies entered the room. One of them Beauty recognized as the stately lady she had seen in her dreams; the other was so queenly that Beauty hardly knew which to greet first. But the one she already knew said to her companion:

"Well, Queen, this is Beauty, who has had the courage to rescue your son from the terrible enchantment. They love each other, and only your consent to their marriage is wanting to make them perfectly happy."

"I consent with all my heart," cried the queen. "How can I ever thank you enough, charming girl, for having restored my dear son to his natural form?" And then she tenderly embraced Beauty and the prince, who had meanwhile been greeting the fairy and receiving her congratulations.

"Now," said the fairy to Beauty, "I suppose you would like me to send for all your brothers and sisters to dance at your wedding?"

And so she did, and the marriage was celebrated the very next day with the utmost splendor, and Beauty and the prince lived happily ever after.

EAST O' THE SUN AND WEST O' THE MOON/Scandinavia

Peter Christen Asbjörnsen

Many theories have been developed to explain supernatural mates. They have been said to represent natural phenomena, totemistic and animistic beliefs, and to be remnants of pre-Christian rites. None of these theories adequately explains all the narratives that contain this popular motif.

"East o' the Sun and West o' the Moon" has much in common with "Beauty and the Beast," but a comparison of the two tales can lead to several insights. Through the differences in style, conclusions can be drawn about the literary histories of the Scandinavian and French stories reprinted in this book. Other points for comparison are the differences of plot and motifs in the two variants of the same story. It seems likely that these two tales and the Greek myth "Cupid and Psyche" developed from the same folk source, so a third comparison can be made of cultural modifications.

Once on a time there was a poor husbandman who had so many children that he hadn't much of either food or clothing to give them. Pretty children they all were; but the prettiest was the youngest daughter, who was so lovely there was no end to her loveliness.

So one day, 'twas on a Thursday evening late in the fall of the year, the weather was wild and rough outside. It was cruelly dark, and rain fell and wind blew, till the walls of the cottage shook again and again. There they all sat round the fire busy with this thing and that. Just then, all at once something gave three taps on the window-pane. The father went out to see what was the matter; and when he got out of doors, what should he see but a great big White Bear.

"Good evening to you," said the White Bear.

"The same to you," said the man.

"Will you give me your youngest daughter? If you will, I'll make you as rich as you are now poor," said the Bear.

Well, the man would not be at all sorry to be so rich; but still he thought he must have a bit of a talk with his daughter first; so in he went and told them how there was a great White Bear waiting outside, who had given his word to make them rich if he could only have the youngest daughter.

The lassie said "No!" outright. Nothing could get her to say anything else; so the man went out and settled it with the White Bear, that he should come again the next Thursday evening and get an answer. Meantime the man talked to his daughter and kept telling her of all the riches they would get; and how well off she would be herself. At last she thought better of it, and

"East o' the Sun and West o' the Moon," from Peter Christen Asbjörnsen, *Popular Tales from the Norse*, translated by G. W. Dasent. Published by Putnam, 1908.

washed and mended her rags, made herself as smart as she could, and was ready to start. I can't say her packing gave her much trouble.

Next Thursday evening came the White Bear to fetch her; and she got upon his back with her bundle, and off they went. When they had gone a bit of the way, the White Bear said,

"Are you afraid?"

"No," she said.

"Well! mind and hold tight by my shaggy coat, and there's nothing to fear," said the Bear.

So she rode a long, long way, till they came to a great steep hill. There on the face of it, the White Bear gave a knock; and a door opened, and they came into a castle, where there were many rooms lit up; rooms gleaming with silver and gold; and there was a table ready laid, and it was all as grand as it could be. The White Bear gave her a silver bell; and when she wanted anything, she had only to ring it, and she would get what she wanted at once.

Well, after she had eaten and drunk, and evening wore on, she got sleepy after her journey and thought that she would like to go to bed; so she rang the bell; and she had scarce taken hold of it before she came into a chamber where there were two beds made, as fair and white as any one could wish to sleep in, with silken pillows and curtains and gold fringe. All that was in the room was gold or silver; but when she had gone to bed, and put out the light, a man came in and lay down on the other bed. That was the White Bear, who threw off his beast shape at night; but she never saw him, for he always came after she put the light out, and before the day dawned he was up and gone again. So things went on happily for a while; but at last she began to grow silent and sorrowful; for she went about all day alone and she longed to go home and see her father and mother, and brothers and sisters, and that was why she was so sad and sorrowful, because she couldn't get to them.

"Well, well!" said the Bear, "perhaps there's a cure for all this; but you must promise me one thing, not to talk alone with your mother, but only when the rest are by to hear; for she will take you by the hand and try to lead you into a room alone to talk; but you must mind and not do that, else you'll bring bad luck to both of us."

So one Sunday, the White Bear came and said now they could set off to see her father and mother. Well, off they started, she sitting on his back; and they went far and long. At last they came to a grand house, and there her brothers and sisters were running about out of doors at play, and everything was so pretty, 'twas a joy to see.

"This is where your father and mother live now," said the White Bear; "but don't forget what I told you, else you'll make us both unlucky."

No, bless you, she'd not forget, and when she had reached the house, the White Bear turned right about and left her.

Then she went in to see her father and mother, and there was such joy, there was no end of it. None of them thought that they could thank her enough for all she had done for them. Now, they had everything they wished, as good as good could be, and they all wanted to know how she got on where she lived.

Well, she said, it was very good to live where she did; she had all she wished. What she said beside I don't know; but I don't think any of them had the right end of the stick, or that they got much out of her. But so in the afternoon, after they had finished their dinner, all happened as the White Bear had said. Her mother wanted to talk with her alone in her bed-room; but she minded what the White Bear had said, and wouldn't go upstairs.

"Oh, what we have to talk about will keep," she said, and put her mother off. But somehow or other, her mother got around her at last, and she had to tell the whole story. So she said, how every night, when she had gone to a bed, a man came and lay down on the other bed in her room as soon as she had put out the light, and how she

never saw him, because he was always up and away before the morning dawned; and how she went woeful and sorrowful, for she thought she should so like to see him, and how all day long she walked about there alone, and how dull, and dreary, and lonesome it was.

"My!" said her mother; "it may well be a Troll sleeping in your room! But now I'll teach you a lesson how to set eyes on him. I'll give you a bit of candle, which you can carry in your bosom. Just light that while he is asleep; but take care not to drop the tallow on him."

Yes, she took the candle, and hid it in her bosom, and as night drew on the White Bear came to fetch her away.

But when they had gone a bit of the way, the Bear asked her if all hadn't happened as he had said.

Well, she couldn't say it hadn't.

"Now mind," said he, "if you have listened to your mother's advice, you have brought bad luck on us both, and then all that has passed between us will be as nothing."

"No," she said, "I haven't listened to my mother's advice."

When she reached home, and had gone to bed, it was the old story over again. There came a man and lay down on the other bed; but at dead of night, when she heard him sleeping, she got up and struck a light, lit the candle, and let the light shine on him, and she saw that he was the loveliest Prince she had ever set eyes on and she fell so deep in love with him on the spot, that she thought that she couldn't live if she didn't give him a kiss then and there. And so she did; but as she kissed him, she dropped three hot drops of tallow on his shirt and he woke up.

"What have you done?" he cried; "now you have made us both unlucky, for had you held out only for this one year, I had been freed. For I have a stepmother who has bewitched me, so that I am a White Bear by day, and a Man by night. But now all ties are snapt between us; now I must set off from you to her. She lives in a castle which stands EAST O' THE SUN AND WEST O' THE MOON, and there, too, is a Princess with a nose three ells long, and she's the wife I must have now."

She wept and took it ill, but there was no help for it; go he must.

Then she asked him if she mightn't go with him.

No, she mightn't.

"Tell me the way, then," she said, "and I'll search you out; that surely I may get leave to do."

"Yes, you may do that," he said; "but there is no way to that place. It lies EAST O' THE SUN AND WEST O' THE MOON, and thither you'll never find your way."

The next morning when she awoke, both Prince and castle were gone, and there she lay on a little green patch in the midst of the gloomy thick wool, and by her side lay the same bundle of rags she had brought with her from her old home.

When she had rubbed the sleep out of her eyes, and wept till she was tired, she set out on her way, and walked many, many days, till she came to a lofty crag. Under it sat an old hag, and played with a gold apple which she tossed about. Her the lassie asked if she knew the way to the Prince, who lived with his stepmother in the castle that lay EAST O' THE SUN AND WEST O' THE MOON, and who was to marry the Princess with a nose three ells long.

"How did you come to know about him?" asked the old hag; "but maybe you are the lassie who ought to have had him?"

Yes, she was.

"So, so; it's you, is it?" said the old hag. "Well, all I know about him is, that he lives in the old castle that lies EAST O' THE SUN AND WEST O' THE MOON, and thither you'll come late or never; but still you may have the loan of my horse and on him you may ride to the next neighbor. Maybe she'll be able to tell you; and when you get there, just give the horse a switch under the left ear, and beg him to be off home; and, stay, this golden apple may you take with you."

So she got upon the horse and rode a long, long time, till she came to another crag, under which sat another old hag, with a gold carding-comb. Her the lassie asked if she knew the way to the castle that lay EAST O' THE SUN AND WEST O' THE MOON, and she answered, like the first old hag, that she knew nothing about it except it was east o' the sun and west o' the moon.

"And thither you'll come, late or never; but you shall have the loan of my horse to my next

neighbor; maybe she'll tell you all about it; and when you get there, just switch the horse under the left ear and beg him to be off home."

And this old hag gave her the golden carding-comb; it might be she'd find some use for it, she said. So the lassie got up on the horse, and rode a far, far way, and a weary time; and so at last she came to another great crag, under which sat another hag, spinning with a golden spinning-wheel. Her, too, the lassie asked if she knew the way to the Prince, and where the castle was that lay EAST 'O THE SUN AND WEST O' THE MOON. So it was the same thing over again.

"Maybe it's you who ought to have had the Prince?" said the old hag.

Yes, it was.

But she, too, didn't know the way a bit better than the others. East o' the sun and west o' the moon it was, she knew—that was all.

"And thither you'll come, late or never; but I'll lend you my horse, and then I think you'd best ride to the East Wind and ask him; maybe he knows those parts, and can blow you thither. But when you get to him, you need only to give the horse a switch under the left ear, and he'll trot home himself."

And so, too, she gave the girl the gold spinning-wheel. "Maybe you'll find use for it," said the old hag.

Then on she rode many, many days, a weary time, before she got to the East Wind's house; but at last she did reach it, and then she asked the East Wind if he could tell her the way to the Prince who dwelt east o' the sun and west o' the moon. Yes, the East Wind often heard tell of the Prince and the castle, but he couldn't tell the way for he had never blown so far.

"But if you will, I'll go to my brother, the West Wind; maybe he knows, for he is much stronger. So, if you'll just get on my back, I'll carry you thither."

Yes, she got on his back, and they went briskly along.

When they got there they went into the West Wind's house; and the East Wind said the lassie he had brought was the one who ought to have had the Prince who lived in the castle EAST O' THE SUN AND WEST O' THE MOON; and so she had set out to seek him, and how he had come with her, and would be glad to know if the West Wind knew how to get to the castle.

"Nay," said the West Wind, "so far I've never blown; but if you will, I'll go with you to our brother the South Wind, for he's much stronger than either of us, and he has flapped his wings far and wide. Maybe he'll tell you. You can get on my back, and I'll carry you to him."

Yes, she got on his back, and so they traveled to the South Wind and were not so very long on the way.

When they got there, the West Wind asked him if he could tell the lassie the way to the castle that lay East o' the Sun and West o' the Moon, for it was she who ought to have had the Prince who lived there.

"You don't say so! That's she, is it?" said the South Wind.

"Well, I have blustered about in most places in my time, but so far have I never blown; but if you will, I'll take you to my brother the North Wind; he is the strongest of the whole lot of us and if he doesn't know where it is, you'll never find any one in the world to tell you. You can get on my back and I'll carry you thither."

Yes! she got on his back and away he went from his house at a fine rate. And this time, too, she wasn't long on the way.

When they got to the North Wind's house, he was so wild and cross, cold puffs came from him a long way off.

"BLAST YOU BOTH, WHAT DO YOU WANT?" he roared out to them ever so far off, so that it struck them with an icy shiver.

"Well," said the South Wind, "you needn't be so foul-mouthed, for here I am, your brother, the South Wind, and here is the lassie who ought to have had the Prince who dwells in the castle that lies East o' the Sun and West o' the Moon; and now she wants to ask you if you ever were there, and can tell her the way, for she would be so glad to find him again."

"YES, I KNOW WELL ENOUGH WHERE IT IS," said the North Wind; "once in my life I blew an aspenleaf thither, but I was so tired I couldn't blow a puff for ever so many days after. But if you really wish to go thither, and aren't afraid to come along with me, I'll take you on my back and see if I can blow you thither."

Yes! with all her heart; she must and would get

thither if it were possible in any way; and as for fear, however madly he went, she wouldn't be at all afraid.

"Very well, then," said the North Wind, "but you must sleep here tonight, for we must have the whole day before us if we're to get thither at all."

Early the next morning the North Wind woke her, and puffed himself up, and blew himself out, and made himself so stout and big 'twas gruesome to look at him; and so off they went high through the air as if they would never stop till they got to the world's end.

Down below there was such a storm; it threw down long tracts of wood and many houses, and when it swept over the great sea ships foundered by the hundreds.

They tore on and on—no one can believe how far they went—and all the while they still went over the sea, and the North Wind got more and more weary, and so out of breath he could scarcely bring out a puff; and his wings drooped and drooped, till at last he sank so low that the crests of the waves dashed over his heels.

"Are you afraid?" said the North Wind.

No, she wasn't.

But they weren't very far from land; and the North Wind had still enough strength left in him that he managed to throw her up on the shore under the windows of the castle which lay East o' the Sun and West o' the Moon; but then he was so weak and worn out he had to stay there and rest many days before he could get home again.

Next morning the lassie sat under the castle window and began to play with the gold apple; and the first person she saw was the Long-nose who was to have the Prince.

"What do you want for your gold apple, you lassie?" said the Long-nose, and threw up the window.

"It's not for sale for gold or money," said the lassie.

"If it's not for sale for gold or money, what is it that you will sell it for? You may name your own price," said the Princess.

"Well! if I may get to the Prince who lives here and be with him tonight, you shall have it," said the lassie.

Yes! she might; that could be arranged. So the

Princess got the gold apple; but when the lassie came up to the Prince's bed-room at night he was fast asleep; she called him and shook him, and between whiles she wept sore; but for all she could do she couldn't wake him up. Next morning as soon as day broke, came the Princess with the long nose, and drove her out again.

So in the daytime she sat down under the castle windows and began to card with her golden carding-comb, and the same thing happened again. The Princess asked what she wanted for it; and she said it wasn't for sale for gold or money, but if she might get leave to go to the Prince and be with him for the night, the Princess should have it. But when she went up, she found him asleep again, and she called, and she shook him, and wept, and prayed, and she couldn't get life into him; and as soon as the first gray peep of day came, then came the Princess with the long nose, and chased her out again.

So in the daytime, the lassie sat down outside under the castle window, and began to spin with her golden spinning-wheel, and that, too, the Princess with the long nose wanted to have. So she raised the window and asked what the lassie wanted for it. The lassie said, as she had said before, it wasn't for sale for gold or money; but if she might go up to the Prince who was there, and be there alone that night, the Princess might have it.

Yes! she might do that and welcome. But now you must know there were some Christian folk who had been carried off thither, and as they sat in their room, which was next the Prince, they had heard how a girl had been in there, and wept and prayed, and called to him two nights running, and they told that to the Prince.

That evening when the Princess came with her sleeping potion, the Prince made as if he drank, but threw the drink over his shoulder for he could guess what kind of a drink it was. So when the lassie came in she found the Prince wide awake; and then she told him the whole story of how she came thither.

"Ah," said the Prince, "you've come just in the nick of time for tomorrow is to be our wedding-day; and now I won't have the Long-nose, for you are the only lassie in the world who can set me free. I'll say I want to see what my wife is fit for and beg her to wash the shirt which has the three

spots of tallow on it; she'll say yes, for she doesn't know 'tis you who put them there; but that's work for Christian folk, and not for a pack of Trolls; and so I'll say that I won't have any other for my bride than she who can wash them out, and ask you to do it."

The next day, when the wedding was to be, the Prince said,

"First of all, I want to see what my bride is fit for."

"Yes," said the stepmother with all her heart.

"Well," said the Prince, "I've got a fine shirt which I'd like for my wedding shirt; but somehow it has got the three spots of tallow on it which I must have washed out; and I have sworn never to take any other bride than the lassie who is able to do that. If she can't she's not worth having."

Well, that was no great thing, they said; so they agreed, and she with the long nose began to wash away as hard as ever she could, but the more she rubbed and scrubbed, the bigger the spots grew.

"Ah," said the old hag, her mother, "you can't wash; let me try."

But she hadn't long taken the shirt in hand before it got far worse than ever, and with all her rubbing, and wringing, and scrubbing, the spots grew bigger and blacker, and the darker and uglier the shirt.

Then all the other Trolls began to wash; but the longer it lasted, the blacker and uglier the shirt grew, till at last it was as black all over as if it had been up the chimney.

"Ah," said the Prince, "you're none of you worth a straw; you can't wash. Why there, outside, sits a beggar lassie. I'll be bound she knows how to wash better than the whole lot of you. *Come in, lassie!*" he shouted.

Well, in she came.

"Can you wash this shirt clean, lassie?" he said.

"I don't know," she said, "but I think I can."

And almost before she had taken it and dipped it in the water, it was as white as the driven snow, and whiter still.

"Yes, you are the lassie for me," said the Prince.

At that the old hag flew into such a rage, she

burst on the spot, and the Princess with the long nose did the same, and the whole pack of Trolls after her—at least I've never heard a word about them since.

As for the Prince and the Princess, they set free all the poor Christian folk who had been carried off and shut up there; and they took with them all the silver and gold, and flitted away as far as they could from the castle that lay EAST O' THE SUN AND WEST O' THE MOON.

THE WELL OF THE WORLD'S END / England

Joseph Jacobs

In contrast to the kindness and natural sweetness of heroines in "Beauty and the Beast" and "East o' the Sun, and West o' the Moon," the girl in "The Well of the World's End" keeps her promises to the frog with poor grace, uncommon in wonder tale heroines. It is an interesting variation in an otherwise predictable wonder tale which includes a beautiful girl, a cruel stepmother, the abused heroine, an impossible task, a talking animal, enchantment, and transformation, all standard motifs.

This version is part of a longer narrative called "The Frog King" or "Iron Henry," which is told from Germany to Russia and was made more widely known by the Grimm brothers. "The Well of the World's End" is written in a colloquial style delightful for storytelling.

Once upon a time, and a very good time it was, though it wasn't in my time, nor in your time, nor any one else's time, there was a girl whose mother had died, and her father married again. And her stepmother hated her because she was more beautiful than herself, and she was very cruel to her. She used to make her do all the servant's work, and never let her have any peace. At last, one day, the stepmother thought to get rid of her altogether; so she handed her a sieve and said to her: "Go, fill it at the Well of the World's End and bring it home to me full, or woe betide you." For she thought she would never be able to find the Well of the World's End, and, if she did, how could she bring home a sieve full of water?

Well, the girl started off, and asked every one she met to tell her where was the Well of the World's End. But nobody knew, and she didn't

"The Well of the World's End," from *English Fairy Tales* by Joseph Jacobs. Published by Putnam, 1892.

know what to do, when a queer little old woman, all bent double told her where it was, and how she could get to it. So she did what the old woman told her, and at last arrived at the Well of the World's End. But when she dipped the sieve in the cold, cold water, it all ran out again. She tried and she tried again, but every time it was the same; and at last she sat down and cried as if her heart would break.

Suddenly she heard a croaking voice, and she looked up and saw a great frog with goggle eyes looking at her and speaking to her.

"What's the matter, dearie?" it said.

"Oh, dear, oh dear," she said, "my stepmother has sent me all this long way to fill this sieve with water from the Well of the World's End, and I can't fill it no how at all."

"Well," said the frog, "if you promise me to do whatever I bid you for a whole night long, I'll tell you how to fill it."

So the girl agreed, and the frog said:

"Stop it with moss and daub it with clay,
    And then it will carry the water away";

and then it gave a hop, skip, and jump, and went flop into the Well of the World's End.

So the girl looked about for some moss, and lined the bottom of the sieve with it, and over that she put some clay, and then she dipped it once again into the Well of the World's End; and this time, the water didn't run out, and she turned to go away.

Just then the frog popped up its head out of the Well of the World's End, and said: "Remember your promise."

"All right," said the girl; for thought she, "what harm can a frog do me?"

So she went back to her stepmother, and brought the sieve full of water from the Well of the World's End. The stepmother was angry as angry, but she said nothing at all.

That very evening they heard something tap tapping at the door low down, and a voice cried out:

"Open the door, my hinny, my heart,
    Open the door, my own darling;
  Mind you the words that you and I spoke,
      Down in the meadow, at the World's End
          Well."

"Whatever can that be?" cried out the stepmother, and the girl had to tell her all about it, and what she had promised the frog.

"Girls must keep their promise," said the stepmother. "Go and open the door this instant." For she was glad the girl would have to obey a nasty frog.

So the girl went and opened the door, and there was the frog from the Well of the World's End. And it hopped, and it hopped, and it jumped, till it reached the girl, and then it said:

"Lift me to your knee, my hinny, my heart:
    Lift me to your knee, my own darling;
  Remember the words you and I spoke,
      Down in the meadow by the World's End
          Well."

But the girl didn't like to, till her stepmother said: "Lift it up this instant, you hussy! Girls must keep their promises!"

So at last she lifted the frog up on to her lap, and it lay there for a time, till at last it said:

"Give me some supper, my hinny, my heart,
    Give me some supper, my darling;
  Remember the words you and I spake,
      In the meadow, by the Well of the World's
          End."

Well, she didn't mind doing that, so she got it a bowl of milk and bread, and fed it well. And when the frog had finished, it said:

"Go with me to bed, my hinny, my heart,
    Go with me to bed, my own darling;
  Mind you the words you spake to me,
      Down by the cold well, so weary."

But that the girl wouldn't do, till her stepmother said: "Do what you promised, girl; girls must keep their promises. Do what you're bid, or out you go, you and your froggie."

So the girl took the frog with her to bed, and kept it as far away from her as she could. Well, just as the day was beginning to break what should the frog say but:

"Chop off my head, my hinny, my heart,
    Chop off my head, my own darling;
  Remember the promise you made to me,
      Down by the cold well so weary."

At first the girl wouldn't, for she thought of what the frog had done for her at the Well of the World's End. But when the frog said the words over again, she went and took an axe and chopped off its head, and lo! and behold, there stood before her a handsome young prince, who told her that he had been enchanted by a wicked magician, and he could never be unspelled till some girl would do his bidding for a whole night, and chop off his head at the end of it.

The stepmother was surprised indeed when she found the young prince instead of the nasty frog, and she wasn't best pleased, you may be sure, when the prince told her that he was going to marry her stepdaughter because she had unspelled him. But married they were, and went away to live in the castle of the king, his father, and all the stepmother had to console her was, that it was all through her that her stepdaughter was married to a prince.

SNOW-WHITE AND ROSE-RED/Germany

The Grimm brothers

It is not certain if "Snow-White and Rose-Red" is a variant of the "Cupid and Psyche" tradition or if it had an independent origin. Stith Thompson reports it is known primarily because the Grimm brothers reworked it from a German literary collection and included it in their books. Whatever its source, it has become a much loved tale of disenchantment.

There was once a poor widow who lived in a lonely cottage. In front of the cottage was a garden wherein stood two rose-trees, one of which bore white and the other red roses. She had two children who were like the two rose-trees, and one was called Snow-White, and the other Rose-Red. They were as good and happy, as busy and cheerful as ever two children in the world were, only Snow-White was more quiet and gentle than Rose-Red. Rose-Red liked better to run about in the meadows and fields seeking flowers and catching butterflies; but Snow-White sat at home with her mother, and helped her with her house-work, or read to her when there was nothing to do.

The two children were so fond of each other that they always held each other by the hand when they went out together, and when Snow-White said, "We will not leave each other," Rose-Red answered, "Never so long as we live," and their mother would add, "What one has she must share with the other."

They often ran about the forest alone and gathered red berries, and no beasts did them any harm, but came close to them trustfully. The little hare would eat a cabbage-leaf out of their hands, the roe grazed by their side, the stag leapt merrily by them, and the birds sat still upon the boughs, and sang whatever they knew.

No mishap overtook them; if they had stayed too late in the forest, and night came on, they laid themselves down near one another upon the

moss, and slept until morning came, and their mother knew this and had no distress on their account.

Once when they had spent the night in the wood and the dawn had roused them, they saw a beautiful child in a shining white dress sitting near their bed. He got up and looked quite kindly at them, but said nothing and went away into the forest. And when they looked round they found that they had been sleeping quite close to a precipice, and would certainly have fallen into it in the darkness if they had gone only a few paces further. And their mother told them that it must have been the angel who watches over good children.

Snow-White and Rose-Red kept their mother's little cottage so neat that it was a pleasure to look inside it. In the summer Rose-Red took care of the house, and every morning laid a wreath of flowers by her mother's bed before she awoke, in which was a rose from each tree. In the winter Snow-White lit the fire and hung the kettle on the wrekin. The kettle was of copper and shone like gold, so brightly was it polished. In the evening, when the snowflakes fell, the mother said, "Go, Snow-White, and bolt the door," and then they sat round the hearth, and the mother took her spectacles and read aloud out of a large book, and the two girls listened as they sat and span. And close by them lay a lamb upon the floor, and behind them upon a perch sat a white dove with its head hidden beneath its wings.

One evening, as they were thus sitting comfortably together, some one knocked at the door as if

"Snow-White and Rose-Red," from *Grimms' Household Tales*, translated by Margaret Hunt.

he wished to be let in. The mother said, "Quick, Rose-Red, open the door, it must be a traveller who is seeking shelter." Rose-Red went and pushed back the bolt, thinking that it was a poor man, but it was not; it was a bear that stretched his broad, black head within the door.

Rose-red screamed and sprang back, the lamb bleated, the dove fluttered, and Snow-White hid herself behind her mother's bed. But the bear began to speak and said, "Do not be afraid, I will do you no harm! I am half-frozen, and only want to warm myself a little beside you."

"Poor bear," said the mother, "lie down by the fire, only take care that you do not burn your coat." Then she cried, "Snow-White, Rose-Red, come out, the bear will do you no harm, he means well." So they both came out, and by-and-by the lamb and dove came nearer, and were not afraid of him. The bear said, "Here, children, knock the snow out of my coat a little;" so they brought the broom and swept the bear's hide clean; and he stretched himself by the fire and growled contentedly and comfortably. It was not long before they grew quite at home, and played tricks with their clumsy guest. They tugged his hair with their hands, put their feet upon his back and rolled him about, or they took a hazel-switch and beat him, and when he growled they laughed. But the bear took it all in good part, only when they were too rough he called out, "Leave me alive, children,

> "Snowy-White, Rosy-Red,
> Will you beat your lover dead?"

When it was bed-time, and the others went to bed, the mother said to the bear, "You can lie there by the hearth, and then you will be safe from the cold and the bad weather." As soon as day dawned the two children let him out, and he trotted across the snow into the forest.

Henceforth the bear came every evening at the same time, laid himself down by the hearth, and let the children amuse themselves with him as much as they liked; and they got so used to him that the doors were never fastened until their black friend had arrived.

When spring had come and all outside was green, the bear said one morning to Snow-White, "Now I must go away, and cannot come back for the whole summer." "Where are you going, then, dear bear?" asked Snow-White. "I must go into the forest and guard my treasures from the wicked dwarfs. In the winter, when the earth is frozen hard, they are obliged to stay below and cannot work their way through; but now, when the sun has thawed and warmed the earth, they break through it, and come out to pry and steal; and what once gets into their hands, and in their caves, does not easily see daylight again."

Snow-White was quite sorry for his going away, and as she unbolted the door for him, and the bear was hurrying out, he caught against the bolt and a piece of his hairy coat was torn off, and it seemed to Snow-White as if she had seen gold shining through it, but she was not sure about it. The bear ran away quickly, and was soon out of sight behind the trees.

A short time afterwards the mother sent her children into the forest to get fire-wood. There they found a big tree which lay felled on the ground, and close by the trunk something was jumping backwards and forwards in the grass, but they could not make out what it was. When they came nearer they saw a dwarf with an old withered face and a snow-white beard a yard long. The end of the beard was caught in a crevice of the tree, and the little fellow was jumping backwards and forwards like a dog tied to a rope, and did not know what to do.

He glared at the girls with his fiery red eyes and cried, "Why do you stand there? Can you not come here and help me?" "What are you about there, little man?" asked Rose-Red. "You stupid, prying goose!" answered the dwarf; "I was going to split the tree to get a little wood for cooking. The little bit of food that one of us wants gets burnt up directly with thick logs; we do not swallow so much as you coarse, greedy folk. I had just driven the wedge safely in, and everything was going as I wished; but the wretched wood was too smooth and suddenly sprang asunder, and the tree closed so quickly that I could not pull out my beautiful white beard; so now it is tight in and I cannot get away, and the silly, sleek, milk-faced things laugh! Ugh! how odious you are!"

The children tried very hard, but they could not pull the beard out, it was caught too fast. "I will run and fetch some one," said Rose-Red.

"You senseless goose!" snarled the dwarf; "why should you fetch some one? You are already two too many for me; can you not think of something better?" "Don't be impatient," said Snow-White, "I will help you," and she pulled her scissors out of her pocket, and cut off the end of the beard.

As soon as the dwarf felt himself free he laid hold of a bag which lay amongst the roots of the tree, and which was full of gold, and lifted it up, grumbling to himself, "Uncouth people, to cut off a piece of my fine beard. Bad luck to you!" and then he swung the bag upon his back, and went off without even once looking at the children.

Some time after that Snow-White and Rose-Red went to catch a dish of fish. As they came near the brook they saw something like a large grasshopper jumping towards the water, as if it were going to leap in. They ran to it and found it was the dwarf. "Where are you going?" said Rose-Red; "you surely don't want to go into the water?" "I am not such a fool!" cried the dwarf; "don't you see that the accursed fish wants to pull me in?" The little man had been sitting there fishing, and unluckily the wind had twisted his beard with the fishing-line; just then a big fish bit, and the feeble creature had not strength to pull it out; the fish kept the upper hand and pulled the dwarf towards him. He held on to all the reeds and rushes, but it was of little good, he was forced to follow the movements of the fish, and was in urgent danger of being dragged into the water.

The girls came just in time; they held him fast and tried to free his beard from the line, but all in vain, beard and line were entangled fast together. Nothing was left but to bring out the scissors and cut the beard, whereby a small part of it was lost. When the dwarf saw that he screamed out, "Is that civil, you toad-stool, to disfigure one's face? Was it not enough to clip off the end of my beard? Now you have cut off the best part of it. I cannot let myself be seen by my people. I wish you had been made to run the soles off your shoes!" Then he took out a sack of pearls which lay in the rushes, and without saying a word more he dragged it away and disappeared behind a stone.

It happened that soon afterwards the mother sent the two children to the town to buy needles and thread, and laces and ribbons. The road led them across a heath upon which huge pieces of rock lay strewn here and there. Now they noticed a large bird hovering in the air, flying slowly round and round above them; it sank lower and lower, and at last settled near a rock not far off. Directly afterwards they heard a loud, piteous cry. They ran up and saw with horror that the eagle had seized their old acquaintance the dwarf, and was going to carry him off.

The children, full of pity, at once took tight hold of the little man, and pulled against the eagle so long that at last he let his booty go. As soon as the dwarf had recovered from his first fright he cried with his shrill voice, "Could you not have done it more carefully! You dragged at my brown coat so that it is all torn and full of holes, you helpless clumsy creatures!" Then he took up a sack full of precious stones, and slipped away again under the rock into his hole. The girls, who by this time were used to his thanklessness, went on their way and did their business in the town.

As they crossed the heath again on their way home they surprised the dwarf, who had emptied out his bag of precious stones in a clean spot, and had not thought that any one would come there so late. The evening sun shone upon the brilliant stones; they glittered and sparkled with all colours so beautifully that the children stood still and looked at them. "Why do you stand gaping there?" cried the dwarf, and his ashen-grey face became copper-red with rage. He was going on with his bad words when a loud growling was heard, and a black bear came trotting towards them out of the forest. The dwarf sprang up in a fright, but he could not get to his cave, for the bear was already close. Then in the dread of his heart he cried, "Dear Mr. Bear, spare me, I will give you all my treasures; look, the beautiful jewels lying there! Grant me my life; what do you want with such a slender little fellow as I? You would not feel me between your teeth. Come, take these two wicked girls, they are tender morsels for you, fat as young quails; for mercy's sake eat them!" The bear took no heed of his words, but gave the wicked creature a single blow with his paw, and he did not move again.

The girls had run away, but the bear called to them, "Snow-White and Rose-Red, do not be afraid; wait, I will come with you." Then they knew his voice and waited, and when he came up to them suddenly his bearskin fell off, and he stood there a handsome man, clothed all in gold. "I am a King's son," he said, "and I was bewitched by that wicked dwarf, who had stolen my treasures; I have had to run about the forest as a savage bear until I was freed by his death. Now he has got his well-deserved punishment."

Snow-White was married to him, and Rose-Red to his brother, and they divided between them the great treasure which the dwarf had gathered together in his cave. The old mother lived peacefully and happily with her children for many years. She took the two rose-trees with her, and they stood before her window, and every year bore the most beautiful roses, white and red.

THE SLEEPING BEAUTY / France

Walter de la Mare

Perrault included this tale in his collection of Tales from the Past, with Morals, *better known as* Tales of My Mother Goose.

Very few of the stories commonly called "fairy tales" actually deal with fairies. While "Sleeping Beauty" is one such story, it does reveal that not all the fairy folk are kind; here the oldest of them all could be spiteful and cruel.

There lived long ago a King and a Queen, who, even though they loved one another, could not be wholly happy, for they had no children. But at last, one night in April—and a thin wisp of moon was shining in the light of the evening sky—a daughter was born to them. She was a tiny baby, so small that she could have been cradled in a leaf of one of the water-lilies in the moat of the castle. But there were no bounds to the joy of the King and Queen.

In due time they sent out horsemen all over the country, to invite the Fairy Women to her christening. Alas, that one of them should have been forgotten! There were wild hills and deep forests in that country, and it was some days before everything was ready. But then there was great rejoicing in the castle, and all day long the clattering of horses' hoofs across the drawbridge over the moat; and not only horses, but much

stranger beasts of burden, for some of the Fairy Women had journeyed from very far away. And each of them brought a gift—fine, rare, and precious—for the infant Princess.

When the merriment was nearly over, and most of the guests were gone, and the torches were burning low in the great hall, a bent-up old Fairy Woman—the oldest and most potent of them all—came riding in towards the castle on a white ass, with jangling bells upon its harness and bridle.

Without pausing or drawing rein, she rode on, over the drawbridge, and into the hall, nor stayed her ass until it stood beside the great chair where sat the chief nurse of the Princess, the infant asleep on a velvet cushion on her lap. The ass lifted its head and snuffed at the golden tassel of the cushion, as if it might be hay. Long and steadfastly this old Fairy Woman gazed down on the harmless child, lying asleep there, and her rage knew no bounds. At last she raised her eyes, and glaring round on the King and Queen from under the peak of her black mantle, she uttered these words:

"Plan as you may, the day will come,
When in spinning with spindle, she'll prick her
   thumb.
Then in dreamless sleep she shall slumber on
Till years a hundred have come and gone."

Then, mantling herself up again, she clutched at her bridle-rein, wheeled her jangling ass about in the hall, rode off, and was gone.

Now, if the King and Queen had remembered to invite this revengeful Fairy Woman to the Christening Feast, all might have been well. But to grieve at their folly was in vain. The one thing left to them was to keep unceasing watch over the child, and to do all in their power to prevent what the old Fairy Woman had foretold from coming true. The King sent messengers throughout his kingdom far and near, proclaiming that every spindle in his realm should be destroyed or brought at once to the castle. There they were burnt. Anyone after that who was found to be hiding a spindle away at once lost his head.

Many years went by, until the King and Queen seldom recalled what the evil-wishing Fairy Woman had said. The Princess, as she grew up, first into a child, then into a maid, became ever more beautiful; and she was of a gentle nature, loving and lovable. Indeed, because they feared to sadden her heart with the thought that anyone had ever boded ill of her, she was never told of what had happened after her christening, or of the Fairy Woman on the white ass.

Now, nothing more delighted the young Princess than to wander over the great castle and to look out of its many windows, and to peep out through the slits in its thick walls. But there was one turret into which for a long time she never succeeded in finding her way. She would look up at it from the green turf beneath and long to see into it. Everywhere else she had been, but not there.

However, one evening in April she came by chance to a secret door that she had never till then noticed. There was a key in its iron lock. Glancing over her shoulder, she turned the key, opened the door, and ran as fast as she could up the winding stone steps beyond it.

Every now and then appeared a windowslit, and at one she saw the bright, young, new moon in the sky, like a sickle of silver; and at another the first stars beginning to prickle into the East.

But at the top of the staircase she came to another door.

Here she stopped to peep through the latch-hole, and in the gloom beyond she saw an old, grey, stooping woman hunched up in a hood of lamb's wool. She was squatting on a stool, and now she leant a little this way and now she leant a little that way, for with her skinny fingers she was spinning flax with a spindle.

The Princess watched her intently, and at last, through she was unaware of it, breathed a deep sigh at the latch-hole, for the sight of the twirling spindle had so charmed her mind that her body had almost forgotten to breathe.

At sound of this sigh the old woman at once stayed in her spinning, and, without moving, apart from tremulous head and hand, called softly:

"If thou wouldst see an old woman spin,
   Lift up the latch and enter in!"

The Princess, knowing of no harm, lifted the latch and went in.

It was cold and dark in the thick-walled room, and when she drew near, the old woman began again to croon over her work; and these were the words she said:

"Finger and thumb you twirl and you twine,
   Twisting it smooth and sleek and fine."

She span with such skill and ease, her right hand drawing the strands from the cleft stick or distaff, while her left twisted and stayed, twisted and stayed, that the Princess longed to try too.

Then the old woman, laying her bony fingers that were cold as a bird's claws on the Princess's hand, showed her how to hold the spindle, and at last bade her take it away and practice with it, and to come again on the morrow. But never once did she raise her old head from beneath her hood or look into the Princess's face.

For some reason which she could not tell, the Princess hid the spindle in a fold of her gown as she hastened back to her room. But she had been gone longer than she knew, and already the King and Queen were anxiously looking for her and were now come for the second time to her room seeking her. When they saw her, safely returned, first they sighed with relief, and then they began to scold her for having been away so long without reason.

And the Princess said: "But surely, mother, what is there to be frightened of? Am I not old enough yet to take care of myself?"

She laughed uneasily as (with the spindle hidden in the folds of her gown) she sat on her bedside, her fair hair dangling down on to its dark-blue quilted coverlet.

The King said: "Old enough, my dear, why yes. But wise enough? Who can say?"

The Queen said, "What are you hiding in your hand, my dear, in the folds of your gown?"

The Princess laughed again and said it was a secret.

"Maybe," said the Princess, "it is a flower, or maybe it is a pin for my hair, or maybe it is neither of these; but this very night I will show it you." And again she laughed.

So for the moment they were contented, she was so gay and happy. But when the King and Queen had gone away and were closeted together in their own private room, their fears began to stir in them again, and they decided that the very next day they would tell the Princess of the Fairy Woman and warn her against her wiles.

But, alas! even when the King and Queen were still talking together, the Princess had taken out the spindle again, and was twisting it in her hand. It was a pretty, slender thing, made cunningly out of the wood of the coral-berried prickwood or spindle-tree, but at one end sharp as a needle. And as she twisted and stayed, twisted and stayed, wondering as she did so why her young fingers were so clumsy, there sounded suddenly in the hush of the evening the wild-yelling screech of an owl at her window. She started, the spindle twisted in her hand, and the sharp point pricked deep into her thumb.

Before even the blood had welled up to the size of a bead upon her thumb, the wicked magic of the Fairy Woman began to enter into her body. Slowly, drowsily, the Princess's eyelids began to descend over her dark blue eyes; her two hands slid softly down on either side of her; her head drooped lower and lower towards her pillow. She put out her two hands, as if groping her way; sighed; sank lower; and soon she had fallen fast, fast asleep.

Not only the Princess, either. Over the King and Queen, as they sat talking together, a dense, stealthy drowsiness began to descend, though they knew not what had caused it, and they too, in a little while, were mutely slumbering in their chairs. The Lord Treasurer, alone with his money bags, the Astronomer over his charts, the ladies in their chamber, the chief butler in his pantry, and the cooks with their pots and ladles, and the scullions at their basting and boiling, and the maids at their sewing and sweeping—over each and every one of them this irresistible drowsiness descended, and they too were soon asleep.

The grooms in the stables, the gardeners in the garden, the huntsmen and the beekeepers and the herdsmen and the cowmen and the goat-girl and the goose-girl; the horses feeding at their mangers, the hounds in their kennels, the pigs in their sties, the hawks in their cages, the bees in their skeps, the hens on their roosting sticks, the birds in the trees and bushes—even the wakeful robin hopping upon the newly-turned clods by the hedge-side, drooped and drowsed; and a deep slumber overwhelmed them one and all.

The fish in the fish-ponds, the flies crawling on the walls, the wasps hovering over the sweet-meats, the moths flitting in search of some old clout in which to lay their eggs, stayed one and all where the magic had found them. All, all were entranced—fell fast, fast asleep.

Throughout the whole castle there was no sound or movement whatsoever, but only the gentle sighings and murmurings of a deep, unfathomable sleep.

Darkness gathered over its battlements and the forests around it; the stars kindled in the sky; and then, at last, the April night gone by, came dawn and daybreak and the returning sun in the East. It glided slowly across the heavens and once more declined into the west; but still all slept on. Days, weeks, months, years went by. Time flowed on, without murmur or ripple, and, wonder of wonders, its passing brought no change.

The Princess, who had been young and lovely, remained young and lovely. The King and Queen aged not at all. They had fallen asleep talking, and the King's bearded mouth was still ajar. The Lord High Chancellor in his gown of velvet, his head at rest upon his money bags, looked not a moment older, though old indeed he looked. A fat scullion standing at a table staring at his fat cheeks and piggy eyes in the bottom of a copper pot continued to stand and stare, and the reflection of those piggy eyes and his tow-coloured mop at the bottom of it changed not at all. The flaxen-haired goose-girl with her switch and her ball of cowslips sat in the meadow as still and young and changeless as her geese. And so it was throughout the castle—the living slumbered on, time flowed away.

But with each returning spring the trees in the garden grew taller and greener, the roses and brambles flung ever wider their hooked and prickled stems and branches. Bindweed and bryony and woodbine and traveller's joy mantled walls and terraces. Wild fruit and bushes of mistletoe flaunted in the orchards. Moss, greener than samphire and seaweed, crept over the stones. The roots of the water-lilies in the moat swelled to the girth of Asian serpents; its water shallowed; and around the castle there sprang up, and every year grew denser, an immense thorny hedge of white-thorn and briar, which completely encircled it at last with a living wall of green.

At length, nine-and-ninety winters with their ice and snow and darkness had come and gone, and the dense thorn-plaited hedge around the castle began to show the first tiny knobs that would presently break into frail green leaf; the first of spring was come again once more. Wild sang the missel-thrush in the wind and rain. The white-thorn blossomed; the almond-tree; the wilding peach. Then returned the cuckoo, its *cuck-oo* echoing against the castle's walls; and soon the nightingale, sweet in the far thickets.

At last, a little before evening of the last day of April, a Prince from a neighboring country, having lost his way among mountains that were strange to him in spite of his many wanderings, saw from the hillside the distant turrets of a castle.

Now, when this Prince was a child his nurse had often told him of the sleeping Princess and of the old Fairy Woman's spell, and as he stared down upon the turrets from the hillside the thought came to him that this might be the very castle itself of this old story. So, with his hounds beside him, he came riding down the hill, until he approached and came nearer to the thicket-like hedge that now encircled it even beyond its

moat, as if in warning that none should spy or trespass further.

But, unlike other wayfarers who had come and gone, this Prince was not easily turned aside. Having tied his hunting-horn to a jutting branch, he made a circuit and rode round the hedge until he came again to the place from which he had started and where his horn was left dangling. But nowhere had he found any break or opening or makeway in the hedge. "Then," thought he, "I must hack my way through." So a little before dark he began to hack his way through with his hunting-knife.

He slashed and slashed at the coarse, prickly branches, pressing on inch by inch until his hands were bleeding and his hunting-gloves in tatters. Darkness came down, and at midnight he hadn't won so much as half-way through the hedge. So he rested himself, made a fire out of the dry twigs and branches, and, exhausted and wearied out, lay down intending to work on by moonlight. Instead, he unwittingly fell fast asleep. But while he slept, a little wind sprang up, and carried a few of the glowing embers of the Prince's fire into the tindery touchwood in the undergrowth of the hedge. There the old, dead leaves began to smoulder, then broke into flame, and by dawn the fire had burnt through the hedge and then stayed. So that when beneath the bright morning sky, wet with dew but refreshed with sleep, the Prince awoke, his way was clear.

He crept through the ashen hole into the garden beyond, full of great trees, many of them burdened with blossom. But there was neither note of bird nor chirp of insect. He made his way over the rotting drawbridge, and went into the castle. And there, as they had fallen asleep a hundred years ago, he saw the King's soldiers and retainers. Outside the guard-house sat two of them, mute as mummies, one with a dice-box between his fingers, for they had been playing with the dice when sleep had come over them a hundred years ago.

At last the Prince came to the bedchamber of the Princess; its door stood ajar, and he looked in. For a while he could see nothing but a green dusk in the room, for its stone windows were overgrown with ivy. He groped slowly nearer to the bed, and looked down upon the sleeper. Her faded silks were worn thin as paper and crumbled like tinder at a touch, yet Time had brought no change at all in her beauty. She lay there in her loveliness, the magic spindle still clasped in her fingers. And the Prince, looking down upon her, had never seen anything in the world so enchanting or so still.

Then, remembering the tale that had been told him, he stooped, crossed himself, and gently kissed the sleeper, then put his hunting-horn to his lips, and sounded a low, but prolonged clear blast upon it, which went echoing on between the stone walls of the castle. It was like the sound of a bugle at daybreak in a camp of soldiers. The Princess sighed; the spindle dropped from her fingers, her lids gently opened, and out of her dark eyes she gazed up into the young man's face. It was as if from being as it were a bud upon its stalk she had become suddenly a flower; and they smiled each at the other.

At this same moment the King, too, stirred, lifted his head, and looked about him uneasily, as if in search for something. But seeing the dark beloved eyes of the Queen moving beneath their lids, he put out his hand and said, "Ah, my dear!" as if he were satisfied. The Lord High Chancellor, lifting his grey beard from his money table, began to count again his money. The ladies began again to laugh and to chatter over their embroideries. The fat chief butler rose up from stooping over his wine-bottles in the buttery. The cooks began to stir their pots; the scullions began to twist their spits; the grooms began to groom their horses; the gardeners to dig and prune. The huntsmen rode out to their hunting; the cowman drove in his cows; the goat-girl her goats; and the goose-girl in the meadow cried "Ga! ga!" to her geese. There was a neighing of horses and a baying of hounds and a woofing of pigs and a mooing of cows. There was a marvellous shrill crowing of cocks and a singing of birds and a droning of bees and a flitting of butterflies and a buzzing of wasps and a stirring of ants and a cawing of rooks and a murmuration of starlings. The round-eyed robin hopped from clod to clod, and the tiny wren, with cocked-up tail, sang shrill as a bugle amid the walls of the orchards.

For all living things within circuits of the castle at sound of the summons of the Prince's horn had slipped out of their long sleep as easily as a seed of gorse in the hot summer slips out of its pod, or a fish slips from out under a stone. Hearts beat pit-a-pat, tongues wagged, feet clattered, pots clashed, doors slammed, noses sneezed: and soon the whole castle was as busy as a newly-wound clock.

The seventh day afterwards was appointed for the marriage of the Prince and the Princess. But when word was sent far and near, bidding all the Fairy Women to the wedding—and these think no more of time than fish of water—one of them again was absent. And since—early or late—she never came, it seems that come she couldn't. At which the King and Queen heartily rejoiced. The dancing and feasting, with music of harp and pipe and drum and tabor, continued till daybreak; for, after so long a sleep, the night seemed short indeed.

THE SLEEPING BEAUTY

Evelyn Andreas

In comparison with the previous tale, retold by Walter de la Mare, this version is nothing more than a sketchy outline of a beautiful story. The danger is that such a superficial, inartistic retelling can do no more than hint to children how much beauty and refreshment can be found in folk literature.

Once a lovely princess was born and twelve fairy godmothers came to the celebration of her birthday. They each gave the baby a gift. Suddenly a thirteenth fairy appeared. She said, "When the princess grows up, she will prick her finger with a spindle. Then something dreadful will happen to her."

One day when the princess was fifteen years old, she came upon a small door in a high tower of the castle. She pushed it open and saw an old woman busily spinning.

"What are you doing?" asked the princess. The old woman replied, "I am spinning. Would you like to try it?" The princess picked up the spindle and pricked her finger. At that moment she fell back onto the couch in a deep sleep.

Then a great stillness came upon the whole castle and everyone in it fell asleep. Outside a tall thorn hedge sprang up, hiding the castle from view. The magic spell lasted for a hundred years.

At the end of that time, a brave and handsome prince from a far country came to the castle. He wanted to rescue the Sleeping Beauty. He raised his sword to cut his way through the thorny hedge. Suddenly the hedge parted. A path of flowers spread out before the prince.

The prince walked up the marble stairway into the castle. At the top of the tower he found the Sleeping Beauty. She looked so lovely that he stooped to kiss her.

That kiss broke the enchantment. The princess opened her eyes and smiled up at the prince. Then the king and queen and everyone else awoke. The prince was greeted with joy by everyone in the castle.

That very day a great wedding feast was held and the Sleeping Beauty married the brave prince.

"The Sleeping Beauty," from *Fairy Tales Retold* by Evelyn Andreas. Coypright 1954 by Grosset & Dunlap, Inc., the publisher.

SNOW-WHITE / Germany

The Grimm brothers

Dwarfs are often portrayed as cruel and greedy creatures, but in "Snow White" they are kind and protective to the homeless child. Some of the motifs common to wonder tales are the cruel stepmother, the innocent, trusting girl who wins a prince's love, and the transformation of seeming death. The tale includes the human touch of showing that jealousy can be felt by a beautiful woman toward a more beautiful girl. Even today nonmagical mirrors can reveal unpleasant truths.

It was the middle of the winter, and the snowflakes were falling like feathers from the sky, and a queen sat at her window working, and her embroidery frame was of ebony. And as she worked, gazing at times out on the snow, she pricked her finger and there fell from it three drops of blood on the snow. When she saw how bright and red it looked, she said to herself, "Oh, that I had a child as white as snow, as red as blood, and as black as the wood of the embroidery frame!"

Not very long after, she had a daughter, with a skin as white as snow, lips as red as blood, and hair as black as ebony, and she was named Snow-White. And when she was born, the queen died.

After a year had gone by the king took another

"Snow-White," from *Fairy Tales of the Brothers Grimm*, translated by Mrs. Edgar Lucas, Published by J. B. Lippincott Company, 1902.

wife, a beautiful woman, but proud and overbearing, and she could not bear to be surpassed in beauty by any one. She had a magic looking glass, and she used to stand before it, and look in it and say,

"Mirror, Mirror on the wall,
Who is fairest of us all?"

And the glass answered,

"You are fairest of them all."

But Snow-White grew more and more beautiful, and when she was seven years old she was as beautiful as day, far more so than the queen herself. One day when the queen went to her glass and said,

"Mirror, Mirror on the wall,
Who is fairest of us all?"

It answered,

"Queen, you are full fair, 'tis true,
But Snow-White is fairer far than you."

This gave the queen a great shock, and she became yellow and green with envy, and from that hour her heart turned against Snow-White, and she hated her. At last she sent for a huntsman, and said, "Take the child into the woods so that I may never set eyes on her again. You must put her to death and bring me her heart for a token."

The huntsman led her away, but when he drew his knife to pierce her heart, she began to weep and begged him to spare her life. As she was so lovely, the huntsman had pity on her and said, "Well, run away, poor child." Wild animals would soon devour her, he thought, and it was as if a stone had rolled away from his heart when he made up his mind not to kill her, but leave her to her fate.

Now, when Snow-White found herself alone run, while the animals passed her by without in the woods, she was frightened and began to harming her. In the evening she came to a little house and went inside to rest because her little feet would carry her no farther.

Everything was very small, but as pretty and

clean as possible. On the table was spread a white cloth, and there were seven knives and forks and drinking cups. By the wall stood seven little beds, covered with clean white quilts. Snow-White, being quite hungry and thirsty, ate a little from each plate, and drank out of each cup. After that she felt so tired that she lay down on one of the beds, but it was too long, and another was too short. At last the seventh was just right and she lay down upon it, said her prayers, and fell asleep.

Presently the masters of the house came in. They were seven dwarfs, who lived among the mountains and searched for gold. When they had lighted their seven candles, they saw that someone must have been in, as everything was not in the same order in which they left it.

The first said, "Who has been sitting in my chair?"

The second said, "Who has been nibbling my bread?"

The third said, "Who has been tasting my porridge?"

The fourth said, "Who has been eating my vegetables?"

The fifth said, "Who has been using my fork?"

The sixth said, "Who has been cutting with my knife?"

The seventh said, "Who has been drinking out of my cup?"

Then the first looked and saw a hollow in his bed and cried, "Who has been lying on my bed?" And the others came running, and everyone cried out that someone had been on his bed too. When the seventh looked at his bed, he saw little Snow-White lying asleep, and he called the others, who came running with their candles to see her.

"Heavens! What a beautiful child!" they cried, but they were careful not to wake her. The seventh dwarf slept an hour at a time with each of his comrades until the night had passed.

When morning came, Snow-White awoke and, seeing the dwarfs, was very frightened, but they were kind and asked her name, and she told them her story. Then the dwarfs said, "If you will keep our house for us, cook, make beds, sew, knit, and keep everything neat and clean, you may stay with us and want for nothing."

"With all my heart," said Snow-White, and

she stayed with them and kept all things in order.

In the morning they went to the mountain to dig for gold; in the evening they came home, and their supper was ready for them. All day Snow-White was alone, and the dwarfs warned her, "Beware of the queen, for she will soon learn that you are here. Let no one enter the house."

The queen, thinking that Snow-White was surely dead, came to the mirror and said,

> "Mirror, Mirror on the wall,
> Who is fairest of us all?"

And the glass answered,

> "Queen, you are of beauty rare,
> But Snow-White living in the glen
> With the seven little men
> Is a thousand times more fair."

Then she was angry, for the glass always spoke the truth, and she knew the huntsman had deceived her. At last she thought of a plan. She painted her face and dressed up like an old peddler so no one would know her. In this disguise she went across the mountains to the house of the seven dwarfs.

She knocked at the door and cried, "Fine wares for sale."

Snow-White looked out the window and said, "Good-day, good woman, what have you to sell?"

"Good wares, fine wares," she answered, "laces of all colors," and she held up a piece.

"I need not be afraid of letting in this good woman," thought Snow-White, and she unbolted the door and bought the pretty lace.

"What a figure you are, child!" said the old woman. "Come and let me lace you properly for once."

Snow-White, suspecting nothing, stood before her, and let her lace her with the new lace; but the old woman laced so quickly and tightly that she took away Snow-White's breath, and she fell down as dead.

"Now I am the fairest," she said to herself as she hurried away.

In the evening the seven dwarfs returned and were horrified to see their dear Snow-White lying on the floor without stirring. When they saw she was laced too tight, they cut the lace, and she began to breathe, and soon came to life again. When the dwarfs heard what had happened, they said that the old peddler was no other than the wicked queen. "Take care not to let anyone in when we are not here," they said.

When the wicked woman got home, she went to her glass and said,

> "Mirror, Mirror on the wall,
> Who is fairest of us all?"

As usual it answered,

> "Queen, you are of beauty rare,
> But Snow-White living in the glen
> With the seven little men
> Is a thousand times more fair."

When she heard that, she was so struck with surprise that the blood left her heart, for she knew that Snow-White must still be living. "I must plan something different," she said. By means of witchcraft she made a poisoned comb. Then she dressed herself to look like another different sort of old woman.

When she reached the dwarfs' cottage, she knocked and cried out, "Good wares to sell!"

Snow-White looked out and said, "I must not let anybody in."

"But you are not forbidden to look," said the old woman, and she took the poisoned comb and held it up. It pleased the child so that she opened the door.

When the bargain was made, the old woman said, "For once I shall comb your hair properly." Poor Snow-White, thinking no harm, let the old woman have her way, but scarcely was the comb put into her hair than the poison began to work, and the poor girl fell down unconscious.

"Now, you paragon of beauty," said the wicked woman, "this is the end of you," and she went away.

Happily it was near the time when the seven dwarfs came home. When they saw Snow-White lying on the ground as dead, they searched till they found the poisoned comb. No sooner had they removed it than Snow-White came to herself and told what had happened. Once more they warned her to be on her guard and to open the door to no one.

The queen went home and stood before her glass and said,

> "Mirror, Mirror on the wall,
> Who is fairest of us all?"

And the looking-glass answered as before,

> "Queen, you are of beauty rare,
> But Snow-White living in the glen
> With the seven little men
> Is a thousand times more fair."

When she heard the glass speak thus, she trembled and shook with anger. "Snow-White shall die," she cried, "even if it cost me my life!" Then she went to a secret room, which no one ever entered but herself, and made a poisoned apple. Outwardly it was beautiful to look upon, pale with rosy cheeks, so that whoever saw it must long for it, but whoever ate even a bite must die. When the apple was ready, she painted her face and dressed like an old peasant woman and went over the mountain to the dwarfs' cottage.

When she knocked at the door, Snow-White put her head out the window and said, "I must not let anyone in; the seven dwarfs told me not to."

"All right," answered the woman. "I can easily get rid of my apples elsewhere. There, I will give you one."

"No," answered Snow-White, "I dare not take anything."

"Are you afraid of poison?" asked the woman. "Look here, I shall cut the apple in two pieces. You shall have the red side, and I shall keep the pale."

Now the apple was so cunningly made that the red half alone was poisoned. Snow-White longed for the beautiful apple, and as she saw the woman eating a piece, she stretched out her hand and took the poisoned half. Scarcely had she put a piece into her mouth than she fell to the earth as dead.

The queen looked with a fiendish glance, and laughingly cried, "White as snow, red as blood, and black as ebony! This time the dwarfs will not be able to bring you to life again."

And when she got home, she asked the looking glass,

> "Mirror, Mirror on the wall,
> Who is fairest of us all?"

At last it answered,

> "You, queen, are the fairest of them all."

Then her jealous heart was at rest as much as an envious heart can be.

The dwarfs, when they came home in the evening, found Snow-White lying on the ground, and not a breath escaped her lips; she looked quite dead. They lifted her up and looked to see if any poison was to be found, unlaced her dress, combed her hair, washed her with wine and water, but it was no use; the poor child was dead. They laid her on a bier, and all seven sat down and wept over her for three days. They they prepared to bury her, but she looked so fresh and living, and still had such beautiful rosy cheeks, that they said, "We cannot put her in the dark earth."

They made a coffin of clear glass and laid her in it, and wrote her name upon it in letters of gold, and that she was a king's daughter. Then they set the coffin out upon the mountain, and one of them always stayed by and watched it. And the birds came, too, and mourned for Snow-White, first an owl, then a raven, and lastly a dove.

Now Snow-White lay a long time in her coffin, looking as though she were asleep. It happened that a king's son rode through the woods and came to the dwarfs' house to pass the night. He saw the coffin on the mountain and lovely Snow-White inside and read what was written in golden letters. Then he said to the dwarfs, "Let me have the coffin. I will give you whatever you like for it."

But they said, "We will not give it up for all the gold of the world."

At last, however, they had pity on him and gave him the coffin, and the king's son called his servants and bade them carry it away on their shoulders. Now it happened that they stumbled over a bush and the shaking dislodged the poisoned apple from Snow-White's throat. In a short time she opened her eyes, lifted the lid of the coffin, and sat up. "Oh dear! where am I?" she cried.

The prince said, "You are near me," and he related what had happened, and then said, "I love you better than all the world. Come with me to my father's castle and be my wife."

Snow-White consented and went with him, and their wedding was held with great pomp and splendor.

To the feast was invited, among the rest, the wicked queen. When she had dressed herself in her beautiful clothes, she went to her looking glass and asked,

"Mirror, Mirror on the wall,
Who is fairest of us all?"

The glass answered,

"O queen, although you are of beauty rare,
The young queen is a thousand times more fair."

Then the wicked woman was beside herself with anger and disappointment. First she thought she would not go, but her envy and curiosity were so great she could not help setting out to see the bride. When she came in and recognized Snow-White, she was so filled with terror and rage that she fell down and died. Snow-White and the prince lived and reigned happily over that land for many, many years.

KING BARTEK / Poland

Greed for power or wealth is ridiculed and punished in wonder tales. There seems to be no tolerance for those whose ambition leads them to pursue good fortune too avidly. The next five stories illustrate this principle. In "King Bartek" the behavior of two beautiful sisters is contrasted. Bialka, so eager to marry wealth and position that she throws over her fiance for the king, is fittingly humiliated to discover her "royal" suitor is only the court jester in disguise. Spiewna, who with a true heart loves a handsome page, is rewarded by discovering he is the real king.

On the outskirts of a village, in a hut fallen almost to ruins, there lived a very poor widow with her two daughters, Bialka and Spiewna. Both of them were so beautiful that their fame spread over seven mountains, over seven seas. Even at the king's palace the rumors were heard. Many of the knights wished to go at once and woo the girls.

The King disliked to lose his knights, as he had planned a great war, and besides he did not have much faith in the rumors. Instead of granting permission to the knights to go, he sent some of his faithful messengers to see the maidens and bring back pictures of Bialka and Spiewna.

"King Bartek," pp. 63–73, from *The Jolly Tailor and Other Fairy Tales* translated from the Polish by Lucia Merecka Borski and Kate B. Miller. Copyright 1928 by Longmans, Green and Co. Copyright renewed 1956 by Lucia Merecka Borski and John F. Miller. Reprinted by permission of David McKay Company.

The rumors were true. The pictures brought back by the messengers exceeded everybody's expectations. Spiewna was a true sister to the lily; Bialka, to the red rose. The first had azure eyes, the other, eyes dark as the Black Sea; one was proud of her long, golden braids, the other of her raven black braids. The first one had the beauty of a sunny day in her face, the other, the charm of a May night. The knights became enamored of the maidens; no one could keep them from departing. Even the King himself, as he was young and thought of marriage, scratched himself behind the ear and looked at the pictures with great pleasure. The war was put off, the court was desolated, and only the King and his Jester Pieś, who was old and ugly like the seven mortal sins, were left there.

For a long, long time the knights did not come back. They were enjoying themselves; or it might be the other way around, Bialka and Spiewna, sure of their beauty might be taking their time picking and choosing, like sparrows in poppy seeds. The knights in love unwound entangled thread, killed partridges in the air, and sang serenades. Be it as it may, their long absence annoyed the King and he grew impatient and ill-tempered.

"Pieś," he once addressed the Jester, "do you know what I am thinking about?"

"I know, Your Lordship!"

"How?"

"Because our thoughts walk the same paths."

"I wonder!" laughed the King.

"Your Lordship wishes to go to the widow's daughters."

"You guessed!" cried the young King, rejoicing.

"Then we shall go together," said Pieś. "But we must change our places; I, a King; Your Lordship, a Jester."

"What an idea!" said the young ruler, shocked a bit.

"There won't be much of a difference," smiled the Jester.

"No, I shall not do it! You may, if you wish, become a King, but I shall put on a peasant's garb and call myself Bartek."

"As you please!" answered Pieś. "Something unpleasant may come of it though."

"Why?" asked the King, now Bartek.

"A King, be he as ugly and humpbacked as I am, will always have preference over Bartek. And then who knows? Your Highness may fall in love with either Spiewna or Bialka."

The youthful lord became alarmed.

"So much the better!" he said after a while, and added in a whisper, "The heart that loves will not fool itself."

They went on their journey.

In the meantime the widow's hut was as noisy as a beehive. One brought musicians, another singers. The hut changed into a music box adorned with garlands and flowers, as if in celebration of a holiday. The knights reveled, the girls danced, song followed song, and jokes, one after another. The mother's white bonnet swung on her white hair from one ear to the other from happiness.

Bialka liked Przegon (Pshegoń) more than all the others. Spiewna chose none as yet. Neither her mother's persuasion nor her sister's scoffs did any good. The girl's heart had not awakened yet, and without love she did not wish to marry even the richest of knights.

The betrothal of Przegoń to Bialka was announced. She had her wedding dress made, goods for which were brought by Przegoń. The Jewelry, one could not describe, it could be gathered in measures.

Bialka was overwhelmed with joy, was triumphant with her success. She looked down on her sister with haughtiness and consoled her mother with scornful words.

"Do not worry, Mother! Spiewna awaits a prince. She will become wiser when she has to grow rue, and then I, Przegoń's wife, will try to get her an organist. Also I shall find a suitable nook for you, Mother."

Her mother's heart grieved, but what could she answer?

Then one day a golden carriage drove up before the door. All three of them ran quickly to the window, and Bialka shouted:

"The King has come!"

Sudden confusion possessed the hut. The old widow trotted to the kitchen to prepare some fowl for His Majesty, the King, while Bialka snatched a hand-mirror and a comb and turning to her sister called in a commanding voice:

"Don't you dare to call the King's attention to yourself!"

Spiewna stopped in astonishment.

"Do you hear me?" shouted Bialka.

"I hear, but I don't understand."

"You don't understand—you don't understand!"

"For—how—" began Spiewna.

"Don't dare to call the King's attention to yourself!"

"What do you care about the King when you have Przegoń?

"Have I or not, that is nothing to you!" grumbled Bialka. "And better take my advice, otherwise—you shall see!"

His Majesty, the King, was far from good looking. He was ugly, old, his right arm was higher than the left, and he was also limping. But all this was covered with the golden crown, was concealed by the purple cloak and was straightened by the long robe richly embroidered with pearls. Upon seeing the sisters, he at once laid his royal gifts at their feet, and loaded them with compliments. Spiewna refused all the gifts, she accepted only a white rose, which she pinned into her hair.

"How beautiful he is!" whispered Bialka.

"How ridiculous he is!" replied Spiewna.

Bialka looked at her with anger.

Among the King's numerous attendants, there was a young and handsome page, called Bartek. Spiewna's eyes met the youth's gaze. Bartek, dazzled with the girl's beauty, did not take his eyes off her, and when the King offered jewels to Bialka, he came near Spiewna and said:

"All my riches is this fife. It plays beautifully and the time will come when I shall present you with its song."

Spiewna, standing on the threshold, blushed like a rose, and Bialka seeing this, maliciously whispered in her ear:

"Just the kind of a husband for you. Keep away from the King!"

"And Przegoń?" questioned Spiewna.

"You may have him," threw out Bialka.

Przegoń did not see the King, but he learned of his arrival and of his gifts to Bialka. He wished to speak to Bialka, but she, busy with her guest, who exaggerated his compliments and promised golden mountains, did not care to see him. He stayed away from his unfaithful sweetheart and waited to see what time would bring forth.

One night, and 'twas a night with the full moon, a scented intoxicating night, under the window of the room where both sisters slept, there came sounds of a guitar accompanied by a song.

"The King!" murmured Bialka and she jumped to the window.

The King sang:

> Out of the mist thou shalt have palaces,
> For thy comfort and pleasures I will care
> And pay with gold for thy every smile.
> Attired, bejewelled like a peacock
> Thou shalt be Queen in the royal gardens.

"Do you hear, do you hear?" said Bialka to Spiewna. "Thus sings the King!"

Then later under the window fluted the country fife. Bialka looked out of the window and noticed Bartek. Seeing her sister moved by the sad and sweet tones of the fife, she roared with laughter.

The fife stopped playing and they heard this song:

> Do not come to me with pretense
> But with love in thy pure eyes
> That knows another's love.
> Be not touched with a royal gown
> That is worn by a fool's soul,
> A soul that knows not what is love.

"Thus sings Bartek!" called Spiewna.

"Ha-ha-ha!" rang out Bialka's venomous laughter. She leaned over the window and called aloud into the silent night:

"Drive away the fool, Your Majesty, who has the boldness to interrupt your song and insult your royal soul! Order him away, for he steals from us this beautiful night!"

"I will punish him more severely than you think," was the answer, "because to-morrow he will marry your sister."

"And when we?" asked Bialka.

"Even now. Come to me!"

Bialka jumped out of the window, and there she met face to face with Przegoń.

"What are you doing here?" she asked him haughtily.

"I came to wish you happiness with this— king's Jester," replied Przegoń pointing to Pieś.

"What? What?" cried Bialka, looking with frightened eyes at the splendid dress, like a king's.

And in the room, where Spiewna remained, Bartek's fife rang out followed by a song:

> 'Tis hard to find true love
> Under an alluring purple gown,
> Infirmity shall remain in heart
> With all the roses torn aside.
> Ugly looks and lameness and a hump
> May all be covered with a royal cloak.
> The King wished for a true heart;
> The fool desired fun and laughter;
> And both are satisfied.
> Therefore the fool dressed like a King
> The King put on the peasant's garb.
> Now, maiden, cry for thy alluring loss
> And understand these prophesying words:
> That people are not judged by looks
> But by their hearts and deeds.

The golden carriage came to the door, a thousand torches were lighted, a thousand knights with Przegoń at the head surrounded the royal carriage, into which Spiewna was led with her bridesmaids, and they all went to the King's palace to celebrate the wedding. The mother rejoiced at Spiewna's happiness, but she grieved over the neglected Bialka, who had to grow sixteen beds of rue before she married an old organist.

THE FISHERMAN AND HIS WIFE / Germany

The Grimm brothers

Power is often given to characters of wonder tales, and when used well by kind, modest heroes and heroines the listener is pleased to see virtue rewarded. But not all recipients of supernatural help are grateful or careful, and their punishment is equally satisfying. This tale, known throughout Europe, shows how destructive the hunger for power can be. As does so much of folklore, "The Fisherman and His Wife" illustrates a psychological truth: some people can never find contentment but must always torment themselves and others by demanding more and more from life.

There was once a fisherman who lived with his wife in a miserable little hovel close to the sea. He went to fish every day, and he fished and fished, and at last one day as he was sitting looking deep down into the shining water, he felt something on his line. When he hauled it up, there was a big flounder on the end of the line.

The flounder said to him, "Listen, fisherman, I beg you not to kill me. I am no common flounder. I am an enchanted prince! What good will it do you to kill me? I shan't be good to eat. Put me back into the water and leave me to swim about."

"Ho! ho!" said the fisherman. "You need not make so many words about it. I am quite ready to put back a flounder that can talk." And so saying, he put back the flounder into the shining water and it sank down to the bottom, leaving a streak of blood behind it. Then the fisherman got up and went back to his wife in the hovel.

"Husband," she said, "have you caught anything today?"

"No," said the man. "All I caught was one flounder. And he said he was an enchanted prince, so I put him back into the water."

"Did you not wish for anything then?" asked the goodwife.

"No," said the man. "What was there to wish for?"

"Alas," said his wife, "isn't it bad enough always to live in this wretched hovel? You might at least have wished for a nice clean cottage. Go back and call him! Tell him I want a pretty cottage. He will surely give us that."

"Alas," said the man, "what am I to go back there for?"

"Well," said the woman, "it was you who caught him and let him go again. He will certainly do that for you. Be off now."

The man was still not very willing to go, but he did not want to vex his wife and at last he went back to the sea.

He found the sea no longer bright and shining, but dull and green. He stood by it and said:

"Flounder, flounder in the sea,
Prythee, hearken unto me:
My wife, Ilsebil, must have her own will,
And sends me to beg a boon of thee."

"The Fisherman and His Wife," from *Grimms' Fairy Tales*, translated by Mrs. E. V. Lucas, Lucy Crane, and Marian Edwards.

The flounder came swimming up and said, "Well, what do you want?"

"Alas," said the man, "I had to call you, for my wife said I ought to have wished for something as I caught you. She doesn't want to live in our miserable hovel any longer. She wants a pretty cottage."

"Go home again then," said the flounder. "She has her wish fully."

The man went home and found his wife no longer in the old hut, but a pretty little cottage stood in its place and his wife was sitting on a bench by the door.

She took him by the hand and said, "Come and look in here. Isn't this much better?"

They went inside and found a pretty sitting room, a bedroom with a bed in it, a kitchen, and a larder furnished with everything of the best in tin and brass and every possible need. Outside there was a little yard with chickens and ducks and a little garden full of vegetables and fruit.

"Look!" said the woman. "Is not this nice?"

"Yes," said the man, "and so let it remain. We can live here very happily."

"We will see about that," said the woman. With that they ate something and went to bed.

Everything went well for a week or more, and then the wife said, "Listen, husband, the cottage is too cramped and the garden is too small. The flounder could have given us a bigger house. I want to live in a big stone castle. Go to the flounder and tell him to give us a castle."

"Alas, wife," said the man, "the cottage is good enough for us. What should we do with a castle?"

"Never mind," said his wife. "You just go to the flounder and he will manage it."

"No, wife," said the man. "The flounder gave us the cottage. I don't want to go back. As likely as not he'll be angry."

"Go, all the same," said the woman. "He can do it easily enough and willingly into the bargain. Just go!"

The man's heart was heavy and he was very unwilling to go. He said to himself, "It's not right." But at last he went. He found the sea was no longer green: it was still calm, but dark violet and gray. He stood by it and said:

"Flounder, flounder in the sea,
Prythee, hearken unto me:
My wife, Ilsebil, must have her own will,
And sends me to beg a boon of thee."

"Now what do you want?" said the flounder.

"Alas," said the man, half scared, "my wife wants a big stone castle."

"Go home again," said the flounder. "She is standing at the door of it."

Then the man went away thinking he would find no house; but when he got back he found a great stone palace, and his wife was standing at the top of the steps waiting to go in. She took him by the hand and said, "Come in with me."

With that they went in and found a great hall paved with marble slabs, and numbers of servants in attendance who opened the great doors for them. The walls were hung with beautiful tapestries and the rooms were furnished with golden chairs and tables, while rich carpets covered the floors and crystal chandeliers hung from the ceilings. The tables groaned under every kind of delicate food and the most costly wines. Outside the house there was a great courtyard, with stables for horses and cows, and many fine carriages. Beyond this there was a great garden filled with the loveliest flowers and fine fruit trees. There was also a park half a mile long, and in it were stags and hinds and hares, and everything that one could wish for.

"Now," said the woman, "is not this worth having?"

"Oh yes," said the man, "and so let it remain. We will live in this beautiful palace and be content."

"We will think about that," said his wife, "and sleep upon it.

With that they went to bed.

Next morning the wife woke up first. Day was just dawning, and from her bed she could see the beautiful country around her. Her husband was still asleep, but she pushed him with her elbow and said, "Husband, get up and peep out of the window. See here, now, could we not be King over all this land? Go to the flounder. We will be King."

"Alas, wife," said the man, "why should we be King? I don't want to be King."

"Ah," said his wife, "if you will not be King, I will. Go to the flounder. I will be King."

"Alas, wife," said the man, "why do you want to be King? I don't want to ask the flounder."

"Why not?" said the woman. "Go you must. I insist I will be King."

So the man went, but he was quite sad because his wife would be King.

"It is not right," he said. "It is not right."

When he reached the sea, he found it dark, gray, and rough, and evil-smelling. He stood there and said:

"Flounder, flounder in the sea,
Prythee, hearken unto me:
My wife, Ilsebil, must have her own will,
And sends me to beg a boon of thee."

"Now what does she want?" said the flounder.

"Alas," said the man, "she wants to be King now."

"Go back. She is King already," said the flounder.

So the man went back, and when he reached the palace he found that it had grown much larger and a great tower had been added with handsome decorations. There was a sentry at the door and numbers of soldiers were playing drums and trumpets. As soon as he got inside the house he found everything was marble and gold, and the hangings were of velvet with great golden tassels. The doors of the salon were thrown wide open, and he saw the whole court assembled. His wife was sitting on a lofty throne of gold and diamonds. She wore a golden crown and carried in one hand a scepter of pure gold. On each side of her stood her ladies in a long row, every one a head shorter than the next.

He stood before her and said, "Alas, wife, are you now King?"

"Yes," she said. "Now I am King."

He stood looking at her for some time, and then he said, "Ah, wife, it is a fine thing for you to be King. Now we will not wish to be anything more."

"No, husband," she answered, quite uneasily, "I find that time hangs very heavy on my hands. I can't bear it any longer. Go back to the flounder. King I am, but I must also be Emperor."

"Alas, wife," said the man, "why do you now want to be Emperor?"

"Husband," she answered, "go to the flounder. Emperor I will be."

"Alas, wife," said the man, "Emperor he can't make you, and I won't ask him. There is only one emperor in the country, and Emperor the flounder cannot make you. That he can't."

"What?" said the woman. "I am King, and you are but my husband. To him you must go and that right quickly. If he can make a king, he can also make an emperor. Emperor I will be, so go quickly."

He had to go, but he was quite frightened. And as he went he thought, "This won't end well. Emperor is too shameless. The flounder will make an end of the whole thing."

With that he came to the sea, but now he found it quite black and heaving up from below in great waves. It tossed to and fro and a sharp wind blew over it, and the man trembled. So he stood there and said:

"Flounder, flounder in the sea,
Prythee, hearken unto me:
My wife, Ilsebil, must have her own will,
And sends me to beg a boon of thee."

"What does she want now?" said the flounder.

"Alas," he said, "my wife wants to be Emperor."

"Go back," said the flounder. "She is Emperor."

So the man went back, and when he got to the door he found that the whole palace was made of polished marble, with alabaster figures and golden decorations. Soldiers marched up and down before the doors, blowing their trumpets and beating their drums. Inside the palace, counts, barons, and dukes walked about as attendants, and they opened to him the doors, which were of pure gold.

He went in and saw his wife sitting on a huge throne made of solid gold. It was at least two miles high. She had on her head a great golden crown set with diamonds three yards high. In one hand she held the scepter, and in the other the orb of empire. On each side of her stood the gentlemen-at-arms in two rows, each one a little smaller than the other, from giants two miles high down to the tiniest dwarf no bigger than my little finger. She was surrounded by princes and dukes.

Her husband stood still and said, "Wife, are you now Emperor?"

"Yes," said she. "Now I am Emperor."

Then he looked at her for some time and said, "Alas, wife, how much better off are you for being Emperor?"

"Husband," she said, "what are you standing there for? Now I am Emperor, I mean to be Pope! Go back to the flounder."

"Alas, wife," said the man, "what won't you want next? Pope you cannot be. There is only one pope in Christendom. That's more than the flounder can do."

"Husband," she said, "Pope I will be, so go at once! I must be Pope this very day."

"No, wife," he said, "I dare not tell him. It's no good. It's too monstrous altogether. The flounder cannot make you Pope."

"Husband," said the woman, "don't talk nonsense. If he can make an emperor, he can make a pope. Go immediately. I am Emperor, and you are but my husband, and you must obey."

So he was frightened and went, but he was quite dazed. He shivered and shook and his knees trembled.

A great wind arose over the land, the clouds flew across the sky, and it grew as dark as night. The leaves fell from the trees, and the water foamed and dashed upon the shore. In the distance the ships were being tossed to and fro on the waves, and he heard them firing signals of distress. There was still a little patch of blue in the sky among the dark clouds, but towards the south they were red and heavy, as in a bad storm. In despair, he stood and said:

"Flounder, flounder in the sea,
Prythee, hearken unto me:
My wife, Ilsebil, must have her own will,
And sends me to beg a boon of thee."

"Now what does she want?" said the flounder.

"Alas," said the man, "she wants to be Pope!"

"Go back. Pope she is," said the flounder.

So back he went, and he found a great church surrounded with palaces. He pressed through the crowd, and inside he found thousands and thousands of lights. And his wife, entirely clad in gold, was sitting on a still higher throne with three golden crowns upon her head, and she was surrounded with priestly state. On each side of her were two rows of candles, from the biggest as thick as a tower down to the tiniest little taper. Kings and emperors were on their knees before her, kissing her shoe.

"Wife," said the man, looking at her, "are you now the Pope?"

"Yes," said she. "Now I am Pope."

So there he stood gazing at her, and it was like looking at a shining sun.

"Alas," he said, "are you better off for being Pope?"

At first she sat as stiff as a post, without stirring. Then he said, "Now, wife, be content with being Pope. Higher you cannot go."

"I will think about that," said the woman, and with that they both went to bed. Still she was not content and could not sleep for her inordinate desires. The man slept well and soundly, for he had walked about a great deal in the day. But his wife could think of nothing but what further grandeur she could demand. When the dawn reddened the sky she raised herself up in bed and looked out of the window, and when she saw the sun rise she said, "Ha! Can I not cause the sun and the moon to rise? Husband!" she cried, digging her elbow into his side, "wake up and go to the flounder. I will be Lord of the Universe."

Her husband, who was still more than half asleep, was so shocked that he fell out of bed. He thought he must have heard wrong. He rubbed his eyes and said, "Alas, wife, what did you say?"

"Husband," she said, "if I cannot be Lord of the Universe, and cause the sun and moon to set and rise, I shall not be able to bear it. I shall never have another happy moment."

She looked at him so wildly that it caused a shudder to run through him.

"Alas, wife," he said, falling on his knees before her. "The flounder can't do that. Emperor and Pope he can make, but this is indeed beyond him. I pray you, control yourself and remain Pope."

Then she flew into a terrible rage. Her hair stood on end. She kicked him and screamed, "I won't bear it any longer. Now go!"

Then he pulled on his trousers and tore away like a madman. Such a storm was raging that he could hardly keep his feet. Houses and trees quivered and swayed, and mountains trembled, and the rocks rolled into the sea. The sky was pitchy black. It thundered and lightened, and the sea ran in black waves mountains high, crested with white foam. He shrieked out, but could hardly make himself heard:

"Flounder, flounder in the sea,
  Prythee, hearken unto me:
  My wife, Ilsebil, must have her own will,
  And sends me to beg a boon of thee."

"Now what does she want?" asked the flounder.

"Alas," he said, "she wants to be Lord of the Universe."

"Now she must go back to her old hovel," said the flounder, "and there she is!" So there they are to this very day.

GODFATHER DEATH / Germany

The Grimm brothers

This powerful tale has an extensive literary history that reaches back to 1300. It is told throughout Europe and is also found in Iceland and Palestine as an oral tale. In the 1960s a Mexican film was made of the narrative.

Unlike most folktales, "Godfather Death" reveals the bitterness felt by many peasants toward a life in which they knew hunger and pain well. But, like "The Fisherman and His Wife," it also shows the danger of presuming too much on the supernatural being who offers favor but can also punish the unwise.

A poor man had twelve children and was forced to work night and day to give them even bread. When, therefore, the thirteenth came into the world, he knew not what to do in his trouble, but ran out into the great highway, and resolved to ask the first person whom he met to be godfather.

The first to meet him was the good God who already knew what filled his heart, and said to him:

"Poor man, I pity you. I will hold your child at its christening, and will take charge of it and make it happy on earth." The man said:

"Godfather Death" from *Grimm's Fairy Tales* translated by Janusz Grabianski. Copyright © 1962 by Verlag Carl Ueberreuter, Wein-Heidelberg. Reprinted by permission of Hawthorn Books, Inc., 70 Fifth Avenue, New York 10011.

"Who are you?"

"I am God."

"Then I do not desire to have you for a godfather," said the man. "You give it to the rich, and leave the poor to hunger." Thus spake the man, for he did not know how wisely God apportions riches and poverty. He turned therefore away from the Lord, and went farther. Then the Devil came to him and said:

"What do you seek? If you will take me as a godfather for your child, I will give him gold in plenty and all the joys of the world as well." The man asked:

"Who are you?"

"I am the Devil."

"Then I do not desire to have you for godfather," said the man. "You deceive men and lead them astray." He went onwards, and then came Death striding up to him with withered legs, and said:

"Take me as a godfather." The man asked:

"Who are you?"

"I am Death, and I make all equal." Then said the man:

"You are the right one. You take the rich as well as the poor, without distinction. You shall be godfather." Death answered:

"I will make your child rich and famous, for he who has me for a friend can lack nothing." The man said:

"Next Sunday is the christening; be there at the right time."

Death appeared as he had promised, and stood godfather quite in the usual way.

When the boy had grown up, his godfather one day appeared and bade him go with him. He led him forth into a forest, and showed him a herb which grew there, and said:

"Now shall you receive your godfather's present. I make you a celebrated physician. When you are called to a patient, I will always appear to you. If I stand by the head of the sick man, you may say with confidence that you will make him well again, and if you give him of this herb he will recover; but if I stand by the patient's feet, he is mine, and you must say that all remedies are in vain, and that no physician in the world could save him. But beware of using the herb against my will, or it might fare ill with you."

It was not long before the youth was the most famous physician in the whole world.

"He has only to look at the patient and he knows his condition at once, and if he will recover or must needs die," so they said of him, and from far and wide people came to him, sent for him when they had anyone ill, and gave him so much money that he soon became a rich man.

Now it so befell that the King became ill, and the physician was summoned, and was to say if recovery were possible. But when he came to the bed, Death was standing by the feet of the sick man, and the herb did not grow which could save him.

"If I could but cheat Death for once," said the physician, "he is sure to take it ill if I do, but as I am his godson, he will shut one eye. I will risk it." He therefore took up the sick man, and laid him the other way, so that now Death was standing by his head. Then he gave the King some of the herb, and he recovered and grew healthy again.

But Death came to the physician, looking very black and angry, threatened him with his finger, and said:

"You have overreached me; this time I will pardon it, as you are my godson; but if you venture it again, it will cost you your neck, for I will take you yourself away with me."

Soon afterwards the King's daughter fell into a severe illness. She was his only child, and he wept day and night, so that he began to lose the sight of his eyes, and he caused it to be made known that whosoever rescued her from death should be her husband and inherit the crown. When the physician came to the sick girl's bed, he saw Death by her feet. He ought to have remembered the warning given by his godfather, but he was so infatuated by the great beauty of the King's daughter, and the happiness of becoming her husband, that he flung all thought to the wind. He did not see that Death was casting angry glances on him, that he was raising his hand in the air, and threatening him with his withered fist. He raised up the sick girl, and placed her head where her feet had lain. Then he gave her some of the herb, and instantly her cheeks flushed red, and life stirred afresh in her.

When Death saw that for a second time he was defrauded of his own property, he walked up to the physician with long strides, and said:

"All is over with you, and now the lot falls on you," and seized him so firmly with his ice-cold hand that he could not resist, and led him into a cave below the earth. There he saw how thousands and thousands of candles were burning in countless rows, some large, others half-sized, others small. Every instant some were extinguished, and others again burnt up, so that the flames seemed to leap hither and thither in perpetual change.

"See," said Death, "these are the light of men's lives. The large ones belong to children, the half-sized ones to people in their prime, the little ones belong to old people; but children and young folks likewise have often only a tiny candle."

"Show me the light of my life," said the physician, and he thought that it would be still very tall. Death pointed to a little end which was just threatening to go out and said:

"Behold, it is here."

"Ah, dear Godfather," said the horrified physician, "light a new one for me, do it for love of me, that I may enjoy my life, be King, and the husband of the King's beautiful daughter."

"I cannot," answered Death, "one must go out before a new one is lighted."

"Then place the old one on a new one, that will go on burning at once when the old one has come to an end," pleaded the physician.

Death behaved as if he were going to fulfil his wish, and took hold of a tall new candle; but as he desired to revenge himself, he purposely made a mistake in fixing it, and the little piece fell down and was extinguished. Immediately the physician fell on the ground, and now he himself was in the hands of Death.

THE MOST PRECIOUS POSSESSION / Italy

Domenico Vittorini

This tale shows how luck can meet a man in unexpected places and ways. A merchant, blown off course to an island overrun with rats, freely gives the king his ship's cats and in return is richly rewarded. But a greedy merchant who hears of this is quite surprised at his reward when he visits the island hoping to be enriched.

There was a time when Italian traders and explorers, finding the way to the East blocked by the Turks, turned west in their search for new lands to trade with—a search that led to the discovery of the New World.

In those days there lived in Florence a merchant by the name of Ansaldo. He belonged to the Ormanini family, known not only for its wealth but for the daring and cunning of its young men. It happened that on one of his trips in search of adventure and trade, Ansaldo ventured beyond the Strait of Gibraltar and, after battling a furious storm, landed on one of the Canary Islands.

The king of the island welcomed him cordially, for the Florentines were well known to him. He ordered a magnificent banquet prepared and arranged to have it served in the sumptuous hall, resplendent with mirrors and gold, in which he had received Ansaldo.

When it was time to serve the meal, Ansaldo

noticed with surprise that a small army of youths, carrying long stout sticks, entered and lined up against the walls of the banquet hall. As each guest sat down, one of the youths took up a place directly behind him, the stick held in readiness to strike.

Ansaldo wondered what all this meant and wracked his brain for some clue to these odd goings-on. He didn't have long to wait. Suddenly, a horde of huge ferocious rats poured into the hall and threw themselves upon the food that was being served. Pandemonium broke loose as the boys darted here and there, wielding the sticks.

For many years the Florentines had enjoyed the reputation of being the cleverest people on earth, able to cope with any situation. Ansaldo saw a chance to uphold the tradition. He asked the king's permission to go back to his ship, and returned shortly with two big Persian cats. These animals were much admired and loved by the Florentines and Venetians who had first seen them in the East and who had brought many of them back to Italy. Ever since, one or two cats always completed the crew of a ship when it set out on a long journey.

Ansaldo let the cats go and before long the entire hall was cleared of the revolting and destructive rats.

The astonished and delighted king thought he was witnessing a miracle. He could not find words enough to thank Ansaldo whom he hailed as the saviour of the island, and when Ansaldo made him a present of the cats, his gratitude knew no bounds.

After a pleasant visit, Ansaldo made ready to sail for home. The king accompanied him to his ship and there he showered him with rich and rare gifts, much gold and silver, and many precious stones of all kinds and colors—rubies, topazes, and diamonds.

Ansaldo was overwhelmed not only by these costly gifts but by the king's gratitude and the praises he heaped upon him and on the cats. As for the latter, they were regarded with awe by all the islanders and as their greatest treasure by the king and the entire royal household.

When Ansaldo returned home he regaled his friends with the account of his strange adventure. There was among them a certain Giocondo de' Fifanti who was as rich in envy as he was poor in intelligence. He thought: "If the island king gave Ansaldo all these magnificent gifts for two mangy cats, what will he not give me if I present him with the most beautiful and precious things that our city of Florence has to offer?" No sooner said

than done. He purchased lovely belts, necklaces, bracelets studded with diamonds, exquisite pictures, luxurious garments and many other expensive gifts and took ship for the now famous Canary Islands.

After an uneventful crossing he arrived in port and hastened to the royal palace. He was received with more pomp than was Ansaldo. The king was greatly touched by the splendor of Giocondo's gifts and wanted to be equally generous. He held a long consultation with his people and then informed Giocondo happily that they had decided to let him share with his visitor their most precious possession. Giocondo could hardly contain his curiosity. However, the day of departure finally arrived and found Giocondo on his ship, impatiently awaiting the visit of the king. Before long, the king, accompanied by the entire royal household and half the islanders, approached the ship. The king himself carried the precious gift on a silken cushion. With great pride he put the cushion into Giocondo's outstretched greedy hands. Giocondo was speechless. On the cushion, curled up in sleepy, furry balls, were two of the kittens that had been born to the Persian cats Ansaldo had left on the island.

The old story does not go on to say whether Giocondo, on his return to Florence, ever regaled his friends with the tale of *his* adventure!

THE TONGUE-CUT SPARROW / Japan

Lafcadio Hearn

"The Tongue-cut Sparrow" is the Japanese version of a widely told tale in which the person who chooses the smallest object is rewarded, but the one whose greed causes him to take the largest is suitably punished. Such stories were obviously told to encourage unselfish behavior.

'Tis said that once upon a time a cross old woman laid some starch in a basin intending to put it in the clothes in her wash-tub; but a sparrow that a woman, her neighbor, kept as a pet ate

"The Tongue-cut Sparrow," from *Japanese Fairy Tales* by Lafcadio Hearn. Published by Liveright Publishing Corporation, 1924.

it up. Seeing this, the cross old woman seized the sparrow and saying, "You hateful thing!" cut its tongue and let it go.

When the neighbor woman heard that her pet sparrow had got its tongue cut for its offense, she was greatly grieved, and set out with her husband over mountains and plains to find where it had gone, crying: "Where does the tongue-cut sparrow stay? Where does the tongue-cut sparrow stay?"

At last they found its home. When the sparrow saw that its old master and mistress had come to see it, it rejoiced and brought them into its house and thanked them for their kindness in old times and spread a table for them, and loaded it with *sake* and fish till there was no more room, and made its wife and children and grandchildren all serve the table. At last, throwing away its drinking-cup, it danced a jig called the sparrow's dance. Thus they spent the day. When it began to grow dark, and they began to talk of going home, the sparrow brought out two wicker baskets and said: "Will you take the heavy one, or shall I give you the light one?" The old people replied: "We are old, so give us the light one: it will be easier to carry it." The sparrow then gave them the light basket and they returned with it to their home. "Let us open and see what is in it," they said. And when they had opened it and looked they found gold and silver and jewels and rolls of silk.

They never expected anything like this. The more they took out the more they found inside. The supply was inexhaustible. So that house at once became rich and prosperous. When the cross old woman who had cut the sparrow's tongue out saw this, she was filled with envy, and went and asked her neighbor where the sparrow lived, and all about the way. "I will go too," she said, and at once set out on her search.

Again the sparrow brought out two wicker baskets and asked as before: "Will you take the heavy one, or shall I give you the light one?"

Thinking the treasure would be great in proportion to the weight of the basket, the old woman replied: "Let me have the heavy one." Receiving this, she started home with it on her back; the sparrow laughing at her as she went. It was as heavy as a stone and hard to carry; but at last she got back with it to her house.

Then when she took off the lid and looked in, a whole troop of frightful devils came bouncing out from the inside and at once tore the old woman to pieces.

THE GREEDY RICH MAN / Eastern Russia

Babette Deutsch
Avrahm Yarmolinsky

In contrast to the two previous tales, this story mocks avarice gently. Rather than being punished, as the greedy usually are in wonder tales, this man learns his lesson and, the reader assumes, behaves much more reasonably ever after.

Once upon a time there was a rich man who was very greedy. He ate a lot. He drank a lot. He slept a lot. But work he did not, not even a little. Instead, he hired men to work for him while he was eating and drinking and sleeping.

He had only one worry. He was troubled because the day was too short. With such a short

day, how could his laborers get enough work done? If only, he said to himself, I could make the day longer! What plowing and planting and harvesting, what digging and building they would do for me then! True, I am rich. But if the day were only longer, how very rich I would be!

So he went in search of a wise man who could tell him how to make the day longer. Finally he found such a wise man. He was as poor as he was wise. His name was Lopsho Pedun.

"What trouble has brought you to my house?"

asked Lopsho Pedun. So rich a guest could come for nothing but advice.

"I am troubled because the day is too short," answered the greedy one. "Even in summer the day is shorter than a hare's tail. No sooner do my laborers take up their tools than the hens begin to perch for the night. And summer is the best time for work. Pray teach me, O wise one, how to make the summer day longer."

Lopsho Pedun looked at the greedy man with sly eyes, and said:

"I will teach you how to lengthen the summer day. But you must do exactly as I tell you."

"Thank you, O wise one," answered the rich man. "Only tell me, and I will do just as you say."

"Well, then," said Pedun, "go home and put on seventy-seven garments, and each garment must be good and warm. On top of these you must wear a heavy greatcoat. On your head you must have a fur cap. On your feet you must have woollen socks and thick felt boots. Then take a large bag full of provisions and carry it on your shoulders. And in your hand take a wooden pitchfork. When you have done all this, walk until you come to a tall birch tree and climb to the top. Lift up your pitchfork and hook the sun with it, and hold the sun steadily in one spot like a golden pancake. Then the sun will not be able to set, and the summer day will not come to an end."

"Good," said the rich man. "I will do just as you say. And in reward for your advice, here is a hundred rubles."

The poor wise man accepted the hundred rubles with a smile, and the greedy rich man went home to lengthen the summer day.

When he got home he put on seventy-seven warm garments, as the wise man had bidden him, and over them he put on a greatcoat. He set a fur cap on his head, and put woollen socks and thick felt boots on his feet. Then he piled a large bag of provisions on his shoulders, took a pitchfork in his hand, and went off to look for a tall birch tree. When he came to the tree he shifted the bag on his back, grasped the pitchfork firmly, and climbed to the top. It was not long before he

managed to hook the sun with his pitchfork. And there he perched at the top of the tree, holding the sun aloft.

"Hey, there!" he shouted to his laborers. "See that you don't quit until sundown."

For an hour the rich man crouched at the top of the tree, clad in his seventy-seven warm garments and his greatcoat and his fur cap and his woollen socks and felt boots, holding the sun on his pitchfork. It was hot. Another hour passed, and he was still there. It was very hot. The greedy man's arms were numb from holding the sun on the pitchfork. His feet were swollen with heat. His shoulders ached from the heavy bag of provisions. His body seemed to be on fire.

Suddenly he let go of the pitchfork. It got caught in the branches of the birch tree and the sun fell out of it. The greedy rich man wanted to climb down from the tree, but his arm was lame from holding the pitchfork and he could barely stir. When he tried to move, he tumbled, plop! onto the ground. Luckily, he fell on his back on top of the bag of provisions. Luckily, he wore a fur cap, heavy socks, and fur boots. Luckily, he was dressed in seventy-seven garments and a greatcoat. Otherwise he would have broken every bone in his body. As it was, he was only a little bruised.

He picked himself up, and as quickly as he could he took off the greatcoat and all but two of the seventy-seven garments. Oofff! he felt better. Now he knew why the poor wise man, Lopsho Pedun, had smiled at his question. Greedy as he was, and rich as he was, he must be content with a summer day that was no longer than a summer day. It was worth the hundred rubles that he had given Lopsho Pedun to learn that. So he went home.

He left the seventy-five garments where he had thrown them for any poor wayfarers to find. He left the bag of provisions to the small beasts of the field and the birds of the air. He was poorer by a hundred rubles, but he was richer in wisdom. His laborers had reason to be grateful to Lopsho Pedun. And the wise man smiled a wider smile than before.

RUMPELSTILTSKIN / Germany

The Grimm brothers

The next two tales reveal an interesting contrast of style in two variants of the same story. "Rumpelstiltskin" is written in a polished literary style, one that is pleasant to read. "Tom Tit Tot," however, has been put in the colloquial language of an untutored English nurse—even the king talks like a peasant. The predominant use of dialogue adds the humor and suspense which make "Tom Tit Tot" almost demand to be told aloud. A third variant, "Whippety Stourie," is included to show how one lady managed to avoid weaving permanently.

Stith Thompson in The Folktale *states that versions of this story are told in Scandinavia, Germany, Spain, Italy, and around the Baltic, as well as throughout the British Isles. Von Syndow, the Swedish folklorist, first believed it originated in Sweden, but in 1943 declared it went to Scandinavia from the British Isles.*

There was once a miller who was poor, but he had one beautiful daughter. It happened one day that he came to speak with the king, and, to give himself consequence, he told him that he had a daughter who could spin gold out of straw. The king said to the miller, "That is an art that pleases me well; if thy daughter is as clever as you say, bring her to my castle tomorrow, that I may put her to the proof."

When the girl was brought to him, he led her into a room that was quite full of straw, and gave her a wheel and spindle, and said, "Now set to work, and if by the early morning thou hast not spun this straw to gold thou shalt die." And he shut the door himself, and left her there alone.

And so the poor miller's daughter was left there sitting, and could not think what to do for her life; she had no notion how to set to work to spin gold from straw, and her distress grew so great that she began to weep. Then all at once the door opened, and in came a little man, who said, "Good evening, miller's daughter; why are you crying?"

"Oh!" answered the girl, "I have got to spin gold out of straw, and I don't understand the business."

Then the little man said, "What will you give me if I spin it for you?"

"My necklace," said the girl.

The little man took the necklace, seated himself before the wheel, and whirr, whirr, whirr! three times round and the bobbin was full; then he took up another, and whirr, whirr, whirr; three times round, and that was full; and so he went on till the morning, when all the straw had been spun, and all the bobbins were full of gold. At sunrise came the king, and when he saw the gold he was astonished and very much rejoiced, for he was very avaricious. He had the miller's daughter taken into another room filled with straw, much bigger than the last, and told her that as she valued her life she must ·spin it all in one night.

The girl did not know what to do, so she began to cry, and then the door opened, and the little man appeared and said, "What will you give me if I spin all this straw into gold?"

"The ring from my finger," answered the girl.

"Rumpelstiltskin," from Jakob and Wilhelm Grimms' *Household Stories*, translated by Lucy Crane. Published by The Macmillan Company, 1926.

So the little man took the ring, and began again to send the wheel whirring round, and by the next morning all the straw was spun into glistening gold. The king was rejoiced beyond measure at the sight, but as he could never have enough of gold, he had the miller's daughter taken into a still larger room full of straw, and said, "This, too, must be spun in one night, and if you accomplish it you shall be my wife." For he thought, "Although she is but a miller's daughter, I am not likely to find any one richer in the whole world."

As soon as the girl was left alone, the little man appeared for the third time and said, "What will you give me if I spin the straw for you this time?"

"I have nothing left to give," answered the girl.

"Then you must promise me the first child you have after you are queen," said the little man.

"But who knows whether that will happen?" thought the girl; but as she did not know what else to do in her necessity, she promised the little man what he desired, upon which he began to spin, until all the straw was gold. And when in the morning the king came and found all done according to his wish, he caused the wedding to be held at once, and the miller's pretty daughter became a queen.

In a year's time she brought a fine child into the world, and thought no more of the little man; but one day he came suddenly into her room, and said, "Now give me what you promised me."

The queen was terrified greatly, and offered the little man all the riches of the kingdom if he would only leave the child; but the little man said, "No, I would rather have something living than all the treasures of the world."

Then the queen began to lament and to weep, so that the little man had pity upon her.

"I will give you three days," said he, "and if at the end of that time you cannot tell my name, you must give up the child to me."

Then the queen spent the whole night in thinking over all the names that she had ever heard, and sent a messenger through the land to ask far and wide for all the names that could be found. And when the little man came next day, (beginning with Caspar, Melchior, Balthazar) she repeated all she knew, and went through the whole list, but after each the little man said, "That is not my name."

The second day the queen sent to inquire of all the neighbors what the servants were called, and told the little man all the most unusual and singular names, saying, "Perhaps you are called Roast-ribs, or Sheepshanks, or Spindleshanks?" But he answered nothing but "That is not my name."

The third day the messenger came back again, and said, "I have not been able to find one single new name; but as I passed through the woods I came to a high hill, and near it was a little house, and before the house burned a fire, and round the fire danced a comical little man, and he hopped on one leg and cried,

> "Today do I bake, tomorrow I brew,
>   The day after that the queen's child comes in;
> And oh! I am glad that nobody knew
>   That the name I am called is Rumpelstiltskin!"

You cannot think how pleased the queen was to hear that name, and soon afterwards, when the little man walked in and said, "Now, Mrs. Queen, what is my name?" she said at first, "Are you called Jack?"

"No," answered he.

"Are you called Harry?" she asked again.

"No," answered he. And then she said,

"Then perhaps your name is Rumpelstiltskin!"

"The devil told you that! the devil told you that!" cried the little man, and in his anger he stamped with his right foot so hard that it went into the ground above his knee; then he seized his left foot with both his hands in such a fury that he split in two, and there was an end of him.

TOM TIT TOT / England

Joseph Jacobs

Please see the introduction to "Rumpelstiltskin" for information pertinent to this tale.

Once upon a time there was a woman, and she baked five pies. And when they came out of the oven they were that overbaked the crusts were too hard to eat. So she says to her daughter:

"Darter," says she, "put you them there pies on the shelf, and leave 'em there a little, and they'll come again."—She meant, you know, the crust would get soft.

But the girl, she says to herself: "Well, if they'll come again, I'll eat 'em now." And she set to work and ate 'em all, first and last.

Well, come supper time the woman said: "Go you, and get one o' them there pies. I dare say they've come again now."

The girl went and she looked, and there was nothing but the dishes. So back she came and says she: "Noo, they ain't come again."

"Not one of 'em?" says the mother.

"Not one of 'em," says she.

"Well, come again, or not come again," said the woman, "I'll have one for supper."

"But you can't, if they ain't come," said the girl.

"But I can," says she. "Go you, and bring the best of 'em."

"Best or worst," says the girl, "I've ate 'em all, and you can't have one till that's come again."

Well, the woman she was done, and she took her spinning to the door to spin, and as she span she sang:

"My darter ha' ate five, five pies today.
My darter ha' ate five, five pies today."

The king was coming down the street, and he heard her sing, but what she sang he couldn't hear, so he stopped and said:

"What was that you were singing, my good woman?"

The woman was ashamed to let him hear what her daughter had been doing, so she sang, instead of that:

"My darter ha' spun five, five skeins today.
My darter ha' spun five, five skeins today."

"Stars o' mine!" said the king, "I never hear tell of any one that could do that."

Then he said: "Look you here, I want a wife, and I'll marry your daughter. But look you here," says he, "eleven months out of the year she shall have all she likes to eat, and all the gowns she likes to get, and all the company she likes to keep; but the last month of the year she'll have to spin five skeins every day, and if she don't I shall kill her."

"All right," says the woman; for she thought what a grand marriage that was. And as for the five skeins, when the time came, there'd be plenty of ways of getting out of it, and likeliest, he'd have forgotten all about it.

Well, so they were married. And for eleven months the girl had all she liked to eat, and all the gowns she liked to get, and all the company she liked to keep.

But when the time was getting over she began to think about the skeins and to wonder if he had 'em in mind. But not one word did he say about 'em, and she thought he'd wholly forgotten 'em.

However, the last day of the last month he takes her to a room she'd never set eyes on be-

"Tom Tit Tot," from *English Fairy Tales* by Joseph Jacobs. Published by G. P. Putnam's Sons, 1892.

fore. There was nothing in it but a spinning-wheel and a stool. And says he: "Now, my dear, here you'll be shut in tomorrow with some victuals and some flax, and if you haven't spun five skeins by the night your head'll go off."

And away he went about his business.

Well, she was that frightened, she'd always been such a gatless girl, that she didn't so much as know how to spin, and what was she to do tomorrow with no one to come nigh her to help her? She sat down on a stool in the kitchen, and law! how she did cry!

However, all of a sudden she heard a sort of a knocking low down on the door. She upped and opened it, and what should she see but a small little black thing with a long tail. That looked up at her right curious, and that said:

"What are you a-crying for?"

"What's that to you?" says she.

"Never you mind," that said, "but tell me what you're a-crying for."

"That won't do me no good if I do," says she.

"You don't know that," that said, and twirled that's tail round.

"Well," says she, "that won't do no harm, if that don't do no good," and she upped and told about the pies, and the skeins, and everything.

"This is what I'll do," says the little black thing, "I'll come to your window every morning and take the flax and bring it spun at night."

"What's your pay?" says she.

That looked out of the corner of that's eyes, and that said: "I'll give you three guesses every night to guess my name, and if you haven't guessed it before the month's up you shall be mine."

Well, she thought she'd be sure to guess that's name before the month was up. "All right," says she, "I agree."

"All right," that says, and law! how that twirled that's tail.

Well, the next day, her husband took her into the room, and there was the flax and the day's food.

"Now there's the flax," says he, "and if that ain't spun up this night off goes your head."

And then he went out and locked the door.

He'd hardly gone, when there was a knocking against the window.

She upped and she oped it, and there sure enough was the little old thing sitting on the ledge.

"Where's the flax?" says he.

"Here it be," says she. And she gave it to him.

Well, come the evening a knocking came again to the window. She upped and she oped it, and there was the little old thing with five skeins of flax on his arm.

"Here it be," says he, and he gave it to her.

"Now, what's my name?" says he.

"What, is that Bill?" says she.

"Noo, that ain't," says he, and he twirled his tail.

"Is that Ned?" says she.

"Noo, that ain't," says he, and he twirled his tail.

"Well, is that Mark?" says she.

"Noo, that ain't," says he, and he twirled his tail harder, and away he flew.

Well, when her husband came in there were the five skeins ready for him. "I see I shan't have to kill you tonight, my dear," says he; "you'll have your food and your flax in the morning," says he, and away he goes.

Well, every day the flax and the food were brought, and every day that there little black impet used to come mornings and evenings. And all the day the girl sat trying to think of names to say to it when it came at night. But she never hit on the right one. And as it got toward the end of the month, the impet began to look so maliceful, and that twirled that's tail faster and faster each time she gave a guess.

At last it came to the last day but one. The impet came at night along with the five skeins, and that said:

"What, ain't you got my name yet?"

"Is that Nicodemus?" says she.

"Noo, 'tain't," that says.

"Is that Samuel?" says she.

"Noo, 'tain't," that says.

"A-well, is that Methusalem?" says she.

"Noo, 'tain't that neither," that says.

Then that looks at her with that's eyes like a coal o'fire, and that says: "Woman, there's only tomorrow night, and then you'll be mine!" And away it flew.

Well, she felt that horrid. However, she heard

the king coming along the passage. In he came, and when he sees the five skeins, he says, says he:

"Well, my dear," says he, "I don't see but what you'll have your skeins ready tomorrow night as well, and as I reckon I shan't have to kill you, I'll have supper in here tonight." So they brought supper, and another stool for him, and down the two sat.

Well, he hadn't eaten but a mouthful or so, when he stops and begins to laugh.

"What is it?" says she.

"A-why," says he, "I was out a-hunting today, and I got away to a place in the wood I'd never seen before. And there was an old chalk-pit. And I heard a kind of a sort of a humming. So I got off my hobby, and I went right quiet to the pit, and I looked down. Well, what should there be but the funniest little black thing you ever set eyes on. And what was that doing, but that had a little spinning-wheel, and that was spinning wonderful fast, and twirling that's tail. And as that span that sang:

> " 'Nimmy Nimmy Not,
>   My name's Tom Tit Tot.' "

Well, when the girl heard this, she felt as if she could have jumped out of her skin for joy, but she didn't say a word.

Next day that there little thing looked so maliceful when he came for the flax. And when night came she heard that knocking against the window panes. She oped the window, and that come right in on the ledge. That was grinning from ear to ear, and Oo! that's tail was twirling round so fast.

"What's my name?" that says, as that gave her the skeins.

"Is that Solomon?" she says, pretending to be afraid.

"Noo, 'tain't," that says, and that came further into the room.

"Well, is that Zebedee?" says she again.

"Noo, 'taint," says the impet. And then that laughed and twirled that's tail till you couldn't hardly see it.

"Take time, woman," that says; "next guess and you're mine." And that stretched out that's black hands at her.

Well, she backed a step or two, and she looked at it, and then she laughed out, and says she, pointing her finger at it:

> "Nimmy Nimmy Not,
>   Your name's Tom Tit Tot."

Well, when that heard her, that gave an awful shriek and away that flew into the dark, and she never saw it any more.

WHIPPETY STOURIE / Scotland

Barbara Ker Wilson

Please see the introduction to "Rumpelstiltskin" for information pertinent to this tale.

On a day long ago, when the bracken sprang green and tender on the hills, a fine gentleman rode over the braeside to woo a fair lady. As the

"Whippety Stourie," from *Scottish Folk-Tales and Legends* by Barbara Ker Wilson. Used by permission of Henry Z. Walck, Inc., publisher, and Oxford University Press.

summer passed the lady came to love her suitor very dearly; and by the time that the bracken hung crisp and golden on the hills they were married with great rejoicing, and he took her away from her father's home to live in his own house.

The lady thought she had never been happier in all her life, for she had all that her heart desired: a great house, rich velvet gowns, and beautiful jewels. But one day her husband came to her and said:

"Now, wife, it is time you put your fair hand to the spinning-wheel; for a home is no home without the clack of a shuttle within its walls; and a wife is no wife unless she can spin fine thread for her husband's shirts."

The lady looked downcast at these words, and she displayed her hands imploringly.

"Alas," she said, "I have never spun a single thread in all my life, husband, for in my father's house it was not thought fitting that a maid of high degree should learn such a lowly occupation."

Then her husband's face grew dark and he replied:

"To sit by the spinning-wheel and spin fine thread is a womanly task that all good wives should perform. From now on you must spin me twelve hanks of thread each day—or, dear as you are to my heart, it will be the worse for you,"

"Truly, husband," his lady wept, "I am not too proud to do your bidding, for I would willingly obey your slightest wish. But I fear I shall never be able to spin one good hank of thread, let alone twelve. For how shall I set about my spinning, with no one to show me the way it should be done?"

But her husband would not listen to her pleading, and only replied that she must find out for herself how to spin. Then he ordered the servants to bring a spinning-wheel to his lady's room, and to provide her each day with sufficient flax to spin twelve hanks of thread.

During the week that followed, the lady rose early each morning and sat herself down before the spinning-wheel, with a heap of shining flax by her side. But though she turned the wheel from the time the sunlight first struck the heather on the hills until it grew dusk, she did not spin one good hank of thread. Every night when her husband came to her room, he would find her resting wearily on her stool and weeping bitterly. Then he would pick up the shuttle and see perhaps half a hank of ravelled and knotted thread.

"This is not the fine thread I want," he said, "but coarse stuff, fit for a crofter's garments. You must do better than this, wife—or, dear as you are to my heart, it will be the worse for you."

On the last night of the week he came to her and announced that he was going away on a journey.

"And when I come back," he said, "you must have spun a hundred hanks of fine thread. If you have not, then, dear as you are to my heart, I must surely cast you aside and find a new wife to spin for me."

(For you must know that in those days if a man was not satisfied with his first wife, he could cast her aside just so and get himself another instead.)

And he kissed his wife farewell and rode away.

"Alas, alas," the lady grieved, "what shall I do now? For I well know that I shall never manage to spin a hundred hanks of fine thread before my husband returns; and he will surely cast me aside and find a new wife."

She left her room and went out to the braeside to wander among the bracken and the heather, full of sorrowful thoughts. She had not gone far when she felt weary, and sat down on a flat grey stone in the shade of a scarlet-berried rowan-tree. By and by she heard a faint sound of music; and to her amazement it seemed to be coming from underneath the very stone where she sat.

"Now surely it is fairy music I can hear," she thought. "For I never heard a mortal piper play such a bonny tune."

And plucking a twig of the rowan-tree to protect herself, she jumped up and rolled away the stone, to find that it had concealed the entrance to a green cave in the hill-side. Peering inside the cave, she was surprised to see six wee ladies in green gowns, all sitting round in a circle. One of them had a little spinning-wheel before her, and as the shuttle clacked busily to and fro she sang:

> "Little kens my dame at hame
> That Whippety Stourie is my name."

Without taking a second thought, the lady stepped into the cave and greeted the Little Folk pleasantly. They nodded to her in reply; and she noticed that all their six mouths were as lop-sided as a fir-tree leaning against the wind. Now as soon as she saw the fine, fine thread that the wee lady called Whippety Stourie was spinning, the lady was reminded of all her troubles, and she could not stop the tears from trickling down her cheeks.

"Why do you weep?" one of the Little Folk asked her out of the side of her mouth. "For you seem a fine lady in your rich velvet gown and beautiful jewels, and should have nothing to weep for."

"Alas, good folk, my husband has gone away on a journey, and when he comes back I must have spun for him a hundred hanks of fine thread —or, dear as I am to his heart, he will surely kill me and find another wife. And I weep because I am not able to spin one good hank of thread, let alone a hundred; and so I cannot do his bidding."

Then the six wee ladies looked at each another out of their sharp bright eyes, and they all burst into lop-sided laughter.

"Och, is that all your trouble?" said Whippety Stourie. "You can forget your sorrow, fair lady, for we will help you. If you ask us to take supper with you in your fine house on the day appointed for your husband's return, you will find that you will have nothing more to worry about."

The lady looked at the six wee folk in their gowns of green, and she felt an upspringing of hope.

"Indeed, you are welcome to take supper in our house on the day that my husband returns," she said. "And if only you can help me, I will be grateful to you as long as I live."

Then she took her leave of them and rolled back the flat grey stone so that it once more concealed the entrance to their green cave in the hill-side. When she returned to her house, she sat no more at her spinning-wheel, and left untouched the heap of shining flax that lay in her room—for she knew that the Little Folk would keep their word and come to help her.

Her husband came riding home in the evening of the day appointed for his return. He greeted his wife fondly and seemed to have left his grouchy humour behind him on his travels. At every moment his lady was expecting him to ask her about her spinning; but he did not have time to do so before the servants announced that supper was ready.

"Why are there six more places made ready at the table, and six wee stools drawn up beside them?" her husband asked as they sat down.

"Och, I asked six wee ladies to come and take supper with us tonight, for I thought the company would cheer you on your return," the lady replied.

She had no sooner spoken than there was a scuttering of feet in the passage outside, and in came the six wee ladies in their gowns of green. The husband greeted them courteously, and bade them be seated. During the meal he talked and joked with them in high good humour, and his wife was pleased to see how well they agreed. Then there was a pause in their talk, and the husband looked at the six wee ladies curiously.

"Would you mind telling me," he asked them, "why it is that your mouths are all as lop-sided as a fir-tree leaning against the wind?"

Then the six wee ladies burst into loud, lop-sided laughter, and Whippety Stourie herself replied:

"Och, it's with our constant spin-spin-spinning. For we're all of us great ones for the spinning, and there's no surer way to a lop-sided mouth."

At these words the husband grew pale. He looked at his fair wife, and he glanced at the wee ladies, and his alarm was plain to see.

And when their six wee guests had taken their leave and departed, he put his arm round his lady's shoulders and called the servants to him.

"Burn the spinning-wheel that is in my wife's room," he told them, "and see that it perishes on a bright flame. I would not have my fair lady spin one more inch of thread, for fear she should spoil her bonny face. For there's no surer way to a lop-sided mouth than a constant spin-spin-spinning."

The lady's heart leapt for joy at her husband's words; and from that day onwards the two of them lived contentedly for the rest of their days, with never the clack of a shuttle to disturb their happiness.

THE PUGILIST AND HIS WONDERFUL HELPERS/Germany

Carl Withers

Action by supernatural powers is a common occurrence in wonder tales: The Twelve Months are able to bring spring and summer to a winter forest, turkeys richly clothe a poor girl so she can go to a dance, Boots has an axe that will hew by itself. But one type of folk narrative develops its plot around the possession by mortals of superhuman strength or powers. In some of these stories the powers are obviously impossible—a man is unharmed by fire, he is able to survive for days without air, or he has a neck so hard it dents the sword that tries to decapitate him. Some powers, however, are human abilities greatly exaggerated. Many people are swift or keen-sighted, but in these tales men can see objects hundreds of miles away and can outrun an arrow.

Many folk variants revolve around this motif of extraordinary powers. Some, such as "The Hunters and the Antelope" from Western Sudan, have only the one simple narrative motif. Others, illustrated in the following section by "The Seven Simeons," have a more involved plot structure with other motifs common to wonder tales.

The central idea of these powers may have originated in India. They are not only found in old Buddist literature but are also still a part of the Indian oral tradition. These tales can be found throughout all of Europe, Western Asia and, as Stith Thompson reports in The Folktale, *they have been taken to Indonesia, China, America, and Africa.*

Once upon a time a pugilist lived in Bremen who understood his art better than anyone else in the whole world. He had at last become so proficient in the ring that he could take on twenty-four opponents at once and win over them every time.

"Holla," he thought to himself, "I'll just take a trip and show my skill. Let others show off what they can do, for money. No one can perform wonders half so great as I can. Wherever I go, people will all hurry up to see my strength."

No sooner said than done. On a summer morning he flung his seven possessions onto his shoulders and walked out through the city gate.

Not far from the city he came to a huntsman

who had his gun raised high in the air and was pointing it very carefully, although not a bird could be seen or heard. Our pugilist looked at him a moment and then with great curiosity asked what he was about to shoot.

"Don't disturb me, friend," said the huntsman, without even looking down from the sky. Suddenly he fired his gun and said, "There it is!"

"There's what?" asked the other. "I can't see anything."

"That's quite possible," answered the huntsman, "since it *is* rather far away. I just shot a sparrow on the steeple of the cathedral in Strassburg."

"Shall we travel together?" asked the pugilist. "You're just the man for me. I, too, can do more than other people."

They quickly agreed to join forces, and set forth together very companionably. They had not gone a thousand paces when a fellow overtook them and swept on past as fast as a cannonball. They were amazed and watched him as far as their eyes could see him. But it wasn't over half a minute until even the huntsman, sharp as his eyes were, could no longer see him. They went along, still wondering at the man's great speed, but before they realized it he was back.

"Where have you been?" the two travelers asked.

"Not far," he answered. "Just to Rome. I had to deliver a letter there."

Their eyes opened wide when they heard that. It had been only ten minutes at the longest since he flew past.

"Will you travel with us?" they both asked him at the same time, and they told him about their own skills.

The runner thought a moment and agreed to go along with them. So now there were three traveling companions.

They hadn't gone over a mile further when they came to a big forest. At the edge of it stood a man with a rope in his hands that was tied around the whole forest. Just before they came up to him he gave the rope a big yank, and all the trees pulled out of the ground like turnips and fell over on one another. Only a very few trees remained standing, and the strong man reached out and grabbed them and pulled them out by the roots.

"Here's another man after our heart," said the travelers, and they asked him to go along with them. He accepted their invitation, and so all four went on together.

A little further on they came to a high mountain. On it stood a man with arms akimbo and his cheeks puffed out. He was blowing with all his strength. The travelers could feel the wind while they were still a good distance away from him, even though he was blowing in another direction. Curiosity drove the travelers up the mountain. They asked him where he was blowing and why he was blowing so terribly hard.

"I've got to!" he answered. "Don't you see the thirty-six windmills all round about? I have to keep them turning. When the wind helps me out by blowing even a little bit, my job isn't so hard. But today, unfortunately, no air is stirring and so I have a great labor." While he was talking to our travelers, all the windmills stopped. As soon as he blew again, they all started turning as before.

"We've got to take him along with us," the travelers whispered to each other. They asked him to join them, he accepted, and so they all started off—now five in number—toward Mainz.

Here they found everything in a sad uproar, because the duke lay ill. The doctors had completely given him up. The only means to save him, they said, was lacking. If they could get a certain herb, before noon, it might be possible to save the duke's life. But there was no hope of getting that herb in time because it grew only in the Swiss Alps. There was no way to fetch it so soon.

As soon as our travelers heard this they went to the castle and promised to get the needed herb within the time named if they were offered a suitable reward. Their message was taken in to the duke and he said that for this service he would give as much gold and silver as the strongest man could carry. The five friends were delighted with his offer and in a wink the fast runner was off to fetch the herb.

When an hour had passed the others began to be very impatient for their friend's return. It was already ten o'clock and he wasn't back. They waited another half hour, and when he didn't come they began to be scared. They sent the huntsman up onto the castle tower to look around for him with his sharp eyes. At first he couldn't see him anywhere. Then he saw him far off beyond Basel.

"The lazy rascal is lying there asleep!" he cried. "Just wait, we'll wake you up."

With that he loaded his gun and shot the hat off the fast runner's head. He was on his legs in a flash, and before the huntsman could climb down from the steeple he was there with the herb. This was carried in to the duke, who took it and was hale and hearty in an instant. Now he told the travelers that they could send someone in to take away the money. They knew no one better to do this than the strong man who had torn down the whole forest. So he went to the castle, went down into the treasury, and packed up everything that was there, so that not even a single coin remained. He wasn't content with this, however, but went round all over the castle and gathered up all the gold and silver he could find anywhere and carried it all away. Who could be happier than the other four men, when they saw the incredible amount of gold and silver? To lighten the strong man's load a little, they loaded themselves with part of the treasure. Then they all started walking toward the city gate in order to seek their fortune somewhere else.

Meanwhile, the duke learned how completely his castle had been plundered. He summoned two regiments of soldiers and sent them after the travelers to take back part of the money and valuables they were carrying away. They were only about a mile outside the gate when they saw the soldiers on their tracks. They saw at once that what they most needed was good advice.

"If it were only twenty-four men," said the pugilist, "I could make short shrift of them. But two regiments! That's too much for me."

"If I only had my rope," said the strong man who had pulled down the forest, "I would tie them all together so they couldn't even move, but—"

"What can I do?" asked the huntsman. "I can easily shoot down one man with every shot. But I don't have enough shells to shoot very many of them."

"I have nothing to fear," said the fast runner. "They won't get me because I can rely on my legs to carry me out of danger."

"What kind of a problem is this?" asked the man with strong lungs. "There's really nothing much to it."

So he set his arms akimbo and blew with might and main. Within a very few minutes he had blown the two regiments far, far away. And to this day nobody knows where they went.

TWO IMPROBABLE TALES / Western Sudan

Leo Frobenius
Douglas C. Fox

Please see the introduction to the preceding tale, "The Pugilist and His Wonderful Helpers," for information pertinent to these anecdotes.

THE HUNTERS AND
THE ANTELOPE

Two youths went hunting and they saw an antelope. The younger drew his bow and shot an arrow at the antelope. At the very instant he shot, the older youth jumped up, ran to the antelope, killed it, skinned it, and cut it up, laid the hide to dry in the sun, and packed the meat in a carrying sack. Just as he finished, the arrow arrived through the air. He caught it with one hand and shouted to his younger companion, "Hey,

"Two Improbable Tales," by permission of Stackpole Books, from *African Genesis* by Leo Frobenius and Douglas C. Fox.

there! What do you mean by trying to shoot holes in my sack?"

WHO WAS MOST
SKILLFUL?

Three young men set out on a journey. One had been turned out by his father because he heard so well. The second had been turned out by his father because he counted so well, and the third had been turned out by his father because he saw so well.

The three young men had a sack of millet. They loaded the grain on a boat. As they were in midstream the one who heard so well said: "A grain of millet has just fallen into the water. I heard it distinctly." The one who saw so well said: "I'll look for it at once," and jumped overboard. The one who counted so well counted all the grain in the sack of millet and said "He is right. There is one grain missing." In the same second the young man who saw so well reappeared on the surface of the water and said: "Here it is."

THE SEVEN SIMEONS, FULL BROTHERS / Russia

Jeremiah Curtin

In some variants of this widely told tale the men with the extraordinary abilities help a central figure find the princess. She falls in love with her kidnapper, tricks the king, and marries the hero. In a tale with seven heroes and only one princess, such an ending could cause complications. Indeed, such complications are included in some versions.

Please see the introduction to "The Pugilist and His Wonderful Helpers" for more information pertinent to this tale.

There lived an old man and his old wife; they lived many years, to a great age. Then they began to pray to God to give them a child who in their old age might help them to work. They prayed a year, they prayed a second, they prayed a third and fourth, they prayed a fifth and a sixth, and did not receive a child; but in the seventh year the Lord gave them seven sons, and they called them all Simeon. When the old man with the old woman died, the Simeons were left orphans all in their tenth year.

They ploughed their own land, and were not worse than their neighbors. It happened one time to Tsar Ador, the ruler of all that country, to pass their village, and he saw the Seven Simeons working in the field. He wondered greatly that such small boys were plowing and harrowing. Therefore he sent his chief boyar to inquire whose children they were. When the boyar came to the Simeons, he asked why they, such small children, were doing such heavy work.

"The Seven Simeons, Full Brothers," from *Myths and Folk-Tales of the Russians, Western Slavs and Magyars* by Jeremiah Curtin. Published by Little, Brown & Company, 1890.

The eldest Simeon answered that they were orphans, that there was no work for them, and said at the same time that they were all called Simeon. The boyar left them and told this to the Tsar, who wondered greatly that so many small boys, brothers, should be called by one name. Therefore he sent the same boyar to take them to the palace. The boyar carried out the command of the Tsar and took all the Simeons with him. When the Tsar came to the palace, he assembled the boyars and men of counsel and asked advice in the following words:

"My boyars and men of counsel, ye see these seven orphans who have no relatives; I wish to make of them men who may be grateful to me hereafter; therefore I ask counsel of you. In what science or art should I have them instructed?"

To this all answered as follows: "Most Gracious Sovereign, as they are now grown somewhat and have reason, dost thou not think it well to ask each one of them separately with what science or art he would like to occupy himself?"

The Tsar accepted this advice gladly, and began by asking the eldest Simeon: "Listen to me, my friend; with what science or art thou wishest to occupy thyself, in that I will have thee instructed."

Simeon answered: "Your Majesty, I have no wish to occupy myself with any science or art; but if you would command to build a forge in the middle of the courtyard, I would forge a pillar reaching to the sky."

The Tsar saw that there was no reason to teach this Simeon, for he knew well enough the art of a blacksmith; still, he did not believe that the boy could forge a pillar to the very sky; therefore he gave command to build in quick time a forge in the middle of the courtyard. After the first, the called the second Simeon. "And thou, my friend, whatever science or art thou wishest to study, in that will I give thee to be taught."

Then that Simeon answered: "Your Majesty, I do not wish to study any science or art; but if my eldest brother will forge a pillar to the sky, then will I climb that pillar to the top, and will look at all lands, and tell you what is going on in each one of them."

The Tsar considered that there was no need to teach this Simeon either, because he was wise already. Then he asked the third Simeon: "Thou, my friend, what science or art dost thou wish to learn?"

Simeon answered: "Your Majesty, I do not wish to learn any science or art; but if my eldest brother will make me an ax, with the ax I will strike once, twice; that moment there will be a ship."

Then the king answered: "I need shipwrights, and thou shouldst not be taught anything else." Next he asked the fourth: "Thou, Simeon, what science or art dost thou wish to know?"

"Your Majesty," answered he, "I do not wish to learn any science; but if my third brother should make a ship, and if it should happen to that ship to be at sea, and an enemy should attack it, I would seize it by the prow and take the ship to the underground kingdom; and when the enemy had gone away I would bring it back to the surface of the sea."

The Tsar was astonished at these great wonders of the fourth Simeon, and he said: "There is not need to teach thee either." Then he asked the fifth Simeon: "And thou, Simeon, what science or art dost thou wish to learn?"

"I do not wish to learn any," said he; "but if my eldest brother will make me a gun, with that gun, if I see a bird, I will hit it, even one hundred versts distant."

"Well, thou wilt be a splendid sharpshooter for me," said the Tsar. Then he asked the sixth Simeon: "Thou, Simeon, what science dost thou wish to begin?"

"Your Majesty," said Simeon, "I have no wish to begin any science or art; but if my fifth brother will shoot a bird on the wing, I will not let it reach the earth, but will catch it and bring it to you."

"Thou'rt very cunning," said the Tsar; "thou wilt take the place of a retriever for me in the field." Then the Tsar asked the last Simeon: "What art or science dost thou wish to learn?"

"Your Majesty," answered he, "I do not wish to learn any science or art, because I have a most precious craft."

"But what is thy craft? Tell me, if it pleases thee."

"I know how to steal dexterously," said Simeon, "so that no man can steal in comparison with me."

The Tsar became greatly enraged, hearing of such an evil art, and said to his boyars and men of counsel:

"Gentlemen, how do ye advise me to punish this thief Simeon? Tell me what death should he die?"

"Your Majesty," said they all to him, "why put him to death? He is a thief in name, but a thief who may be needed on an occasion."

"For what reason?" asked the Tsar.

"For this reason: your Majesty is trying now these ten years to get Tsarevna Yelena the Beautiful, and you have not been able to get her; and besides, have lost great forces and armies, and spent much treasure and other things. Mayhap this Simeon, the thief, may in some way be able to steal Yelena the Beautiful for your Majesty."

The Tsar said in answer: "My friends, ye tell me the truth." Then he turned to Simeon, the thief, and asked: "Well, Simeon, canst thou go to the thrice-ninth land, to the thirtieth kingdom and steal for me Yelena, the Beautiful? I am strongly in love with her, and if thou canst steal her for me I'll give thee a great reward."

"Stealing is my art, your Majesty," answered the seventh Simeon, "and I will steal her for you; only give the command."

"Not only do I give the command, but I beg thee to do it; and delay no longer at my court, but take for thyself troops and money, whatever is needed."

"Neither troops nor treasure do I need," answered he. "Let all of us brothers go together, and I will get Tsarevna Yelena the Beautiful."

The Tsar did not like to part with all the Simeons; still, though he regretted it, he was obliged to let them all go together. Meanwhile the forge was built in the court, and the eldest Simeon climbed on that pillar to the top, and looked in the direction in which was the kingdom of the father of Yelena the Beautiful. After he had looked he cried from the top of the pillar: "Your Majesty, I see Yelena the Beautiful sitting beyond the thrice-ninth land in the thirtieth kingdom under a window."

Now the Tsar was still more enticed by her beauty, and said to the Simeons in a loud voice: "My friends, start on your journey at once, for I cannot live without Yelena, the beautiful Tsarevna."

The eldest Simeon made an ax for the third, and for the fifth he made a gun; and after that they took bread for the journey, and Simeon, the Thief, took a cat, and they went their way. Simeon the Thief had made the cat so used to him that she ran after him everywhere like a dog; and if he stopped on the road, or in any other place, the cat stood on her hind legs, rubbed against him, and purred. So the brothers went their way for some time, and at last came to the sea, which they had to cross, and there was nothing to cross upon. They walked along the shore and looked for a tree of some kind to make a vessel, and they found a very large oak. The third Simeon took his ax and cut the oak at the very root, and then with one stroke and another he made straightway a ship, which was rigged, and in the ship were costly goods. All the Simeons sat on that ship and sailed on their journey.

In a few months they arrived safely at the place where it was necessary for them to go. When they entered the harbor, they cast anchor at once. On the following day Simeon the Thief took his cat and went into the town, and coming to the Tsar's palace he stood opposite the window of Yelena the Beautiful. At that moment the cat stood on her hind legs and began to rub against him and to purr. It is necessary to say that in that kingdom they knew nothing of cats, and had not heard what kind of beast the cat is.

Tsarevna Yelena the Beautiful was sitting at the window; and seeing the cat, sent straightway her nurses and maidens to ask Simeon what kind of beast that was, would he not sell it, and what price would he take. The maidens and nurses ran out in the street and asked Simeon what kind of beast that was, and would he not sell it?

Simeon answered: "My ladies, be pleased to relate to her Highness, Yelena the Beautiful, that this little beast is called a cat, that I will not sell it, but if she wishes to have it I will give it to her without price."

The maidens and nurses ran straight to the palace and told what they had heard from Simeon.

Tsarevna Yelena the Beautiful was rejoiced beyond measure, ran out herself, and asked Simeon would he not sell the cat.

Simeon said: "Your Highness, I will not sell the cat; but if you like her, then I make you a present of her."

The Tsarevna took the cat in her arms and went to the palace, and Simeon she commanded to follow. When she came to the palace, the Tsarevna went to her father, and showed him the cat, explaining that a certain foreigner had given it to her as a present.

The Tsar, seeing such a wonderful little beast, was greatly delighted, and gave orders to call Simeon the Thief; and when he came, the Tsar wished to reward him with money for the cat; but as Simeon would not take it, he said: "My friend, live for the time in my house, and meanwhile, in your presence, the cat will become better used to my daughter."

To this Simeon did not agree, and said to the Tsar: "Your Majesty, I could live with great delight in your house if I had not the ship on which I came to your kingdom, and which I cannot commit to anyone; but if you command me, I will come every day and teach the cat to know your daughter."

The Tsar commanded Simeon to come every

day. Simeon began to visit Tsarevna Yelena the Beautiful. One day he said to her: "Gracious lady, often have I come here; I see that you are not pleased to walk anywhere; you might come to my ship, and I would show you such costly brocades as you have not seen till this day."

The Tsareva went straightway to her father and began to beg permission to go to the ship wharf. The Tsar permitted her, and told her to take nurses and maidens, and go with Simeon.

As soon as they came to the wharf, Simeon invited her to his ship, and when she entered the ship Simeon and his brothers began to show the Tsarevna various rich brocades. Then Simeon the Thief said to Yelena the Beautiful: "Now be pleased to tell your nurses and maidens to leave the ship, because I wish to show you things so costly that they should not see them."

The Tsarevna commanded her maidens and nurses to leave the ship. As soon as they had gone, Simeon the Thief ordered his brothers in silence to cut off the anchor and go to sea with all sail. Meanwhile he showed the Tsarevna rich goods and made her presents of some. About two hours had passed while he was showing the stuffs. At last she said it was time for her to go home; the Tsar, her father, would expect her to dinner.

Then she went out of the cabin and saw that the ship was under sail and land no longer in sight.

She struck herself on the breast, turned into a swan, and flew off. The fifth Simeon took his gun that minute and wounded the swan; the sixth Simeon did not let her fall to the water, but brought her back to the ship, where she became a maiden as before.

The nurses and maidens who were at the wharf, seeing the ship move away from the shore with the Tsarevna, ran straight to the Tsar and told him of Simeon's deceit. Then the Tsar sent a whole fleet in pursuit. When the fleet coming up was very near the ship of the Simeons, the fourth Simeon seized the prow and conducted the ship to the underground kingdom. When the ship had become entirely invisible, the commanders of the fleet thought it was lost, with the Tsarevna; therefore they returned, and reported to the Tsar that Simeon's ship had gone to the bottom with Yelena the Beautiful.

The Simeons arrived at their own kingdom successfully, delivered Yelena the Beautiful to Tsar Ador, who for such a mighty service of the Simeons gave liberty to them all, and plenty of gold, silver, and precious stones, married Yelena the Beautiful and lived with her many years.

THE FIVE QUEER BROTHERS / China

Lim Sian-Tek

The amazing abilities differ in each variant but the problems encountered by the heroes always fit their superhuman powers. Please see the introduction to "The Pugilist and His Wonderful Helpers" for information pertinent to this tale.

Once upon a time there lived a good Chinese woman who had five sons, who looked exactly alike. No one but the mother could tell them apart.

The oldest could gulp up the water of the sea at a mouthful; the second had a body as hard as

steel; the third had legs that could be stretched to any length; the fourth could not be burned; and the fifth could live without breathing for many days.

One day the oldest brother took along some children of the village to the seashore to play. He gulped up the sea water in his mouth, to allow the children to wade in the dry bottom of the sea and catch fish. They were so happy catching fish that they waded far out and would not pay any attention to the man when he motioned for them to return. Finally when the man with the sea in his mouth could not hold the water any longer, he let it flow back into the sea, thus drowning the children.

The parents were so angry when he returned without the children that they had him arrested and put in prison. On the day of his trial, the Judge sentenced the poor man to have his head cut off.

"Oh, worthy Judge," said the man, "at home I have an old mother to whom I must say good-by. Please let me go home, and upon my word of honor I promise to return tomorrow for my punishment."

But it was the second brother who returned and took the oldest brother's place. When the people gathered to witness the execution, the sharp knife of the executioner fell on the man's neck and nicked the blade, but did not harm the man. Then he got up and smiled. The Judge at once ordered him to be killed by drowning.

When the morning arrived for the drowning, this second brother pleaded, "Sir, please let me go home to bid my old mother good-by," and the kind-hearted Judge consented.

When this prisoner came back, it was the third brother, who had taken his second brother's place. The officers took him out in a boat to the deepest part of the sea and dumped him, but he stretched his legs to touch the bottom and would not drown.

By this time the people were getting angry, and they cried out, "Let's roast him alive!" So the Judge ordered the man to be burned.

When the day arrived, the poor condemned man asked the Judge, "Please, sir, won't you let me go home and bid my dear old mother good-by?"

Again instead of this brother's returning, it was the fourth, whom fire could not touch, that came back. The officers tied him to a stake and set fire to the kindling, expecting to see him burned to death. But he only smiled, saying, "This is fine!" and even sang. The people cried out, "Get more wood," but still the Chinese brother declared that he was quite comfortable.

The Judge was exasperated. What could he do to carry out the sentence? He then decided that no man could live without air, and so he ordered that the man be buried alive. Again this man begged so earnestly, "Most Honored Sir! Let me go home to see my mother for the last time," until the Judge consented.

When the man came back, it was the youngest of the five brothers, who had come in place of his condemned brother. Many people helped dig the hole to bury his brother. To be sure this time, they covered him with loads of earth and set soldiers on guard.

But this man could live many days without breathing. And when the soldiers left, the other brothers came and dug the man out of his grave.

Finally the Judge said, "We have tried every possible way, and still we cannot kill you. It must be that you are innocent." Thus the last of the five brothers was released, and the five Chinese brothers were reunited and lived happily with their mother.

THE CEABHARNACH / Scotland

Sorche Nic Leodhas

The Ceabharnach is an interesting combination of the clever rogue and the magical benefactor. He is the son of a poor man and yet he makes his own fortune and those of two other poor men. He is a mortal and no fairy folk help him, yet his powers are more than human skill or luck can explain. And, in an unusual ending, he refuses to marry the king's daughter.

Once there was a man of Islay who had a very intelligent son. Even as a wee bairn he was so full of liveliness and mischief that the folk thereabouts took to calling him the Ceabharnach, that is, the Naughty Breeze, and the name suited him so well that soon few remembered that he had ever had another name. The father was not greatly blessed with the world's goods, but he saw that the lad had a very good mind, so he sent him to school and put him in the way of getting as much learning as he could afford. When the Ceabharnach came to the age of fourteen years, he told his father that he had learned all the schoolmaster could teach him, and a lot more that he had picked up here and there for himself.

"I've had enough of schooling," he said to his father. "And if there is any knowledge I lack, I can get it as I go along. You're wearing the life clean out of yourself fending for me. It's high time I was doing for myself."

So he got his father's blessing and bade him farewell till he came back again, and he promised that when he returned he'd have both their fortunes made.

It came into the mind of the Ceabharnach that he'd like to go to Erin, so he traveled along until he reached the sea, and there across the water the land of Erin lay. There was a garden not far from the sea in which there were trees upon which grew apples, so he plucked sixteen apples from the trees and went down to the shore. He threw one of the apples into the sea and set a foot upon it, then he threw another apple into the sea and set his other foot upon it. Then one by one, he threw the other apples into the sea before him, and set his feet upon them, one after the other, and when he stepped upon the sixteenth apple it brought him to Erin and he stepped off the apple onto the shore.

Then he went along the road, with his two elbows poking through the holes in his old coat sleeves; with his two ears poking through the holes in his old hat; with his square feet going clippety-cloppety, trippety-tattery in his old brogues with the cold ditch water running in and out of them;

and with his old long sword sticking an ell's length out of a hole in the scabbard that hung crosswise at his backside. He went on until he came to the castle of the O'Donnell, and when he got there he took off in a great flying leap that lifted him over the walls, and over the towers, and brought him down in the middle of the courtyard where the O'Donnell was taking his ease.

"Och, wow!" cried the O'Donnell. "What in the world will that be, now?" He blinked his eyes twice and opened them thrice, and looked at the young lad standing before him.

"May the luck be easy on you, O'Donnell," said the lad.

"And to you the same," replied the O'Donnell. "And will you kindly tell me who are you and whence do you come?"

"I am the Ceabharnach," answered the lad. "I am master of all the arts, and I come from Scotland."

"Are you, now!" said the O'Donnell. "And what art can you be doing, then?"

"I can do harping," said the Ceabharnach.

"'Tis the wrong place entirely what you've come to," said the O'Donnell. "For it's myself that has five-fifths of all the best harpers in Erin. Have I not Rory O'Calahan, and Tommy O'Gilligan, and Sean Cooney, as well as twelve others?"

Then the O'Donnell called his harpers to him and bade them all harp for the Ceabharnach to hear.

When they had finished, "Is that not harping?" the O'Donnell asked proudly.

"Well enough, if you like it," said the Ceabharnach. "But on my way over to Erin from Scotland I passed by the Isle of Cats, and the miauling and caterwauling of the creatures there sounded better to my ears than the harping of your pipers here." And with those words the lad seized all the harps from the harpers, and breaking them up he made a fire of them, and stood over the fire warming his hands and feet at the blaze.

Then the O'Donnell was angry and leapt up to fight the Ceabharnach for losing him his harps. But the lad held him off, saying, "Peace, man! Do the harps mean so much to you?"

"I would give five marks for each of them, to

have them whole and unburned!" the O'Donnell said.

" 'Twill be no harder to bring them back than it was to burn them," the Ceabharnach told him. "Put the marks in my hand, and you shall have your harps."

So the O'Donnell fetched a bag of money from his treasure room, and counted seventy-five marks, five for each harp, into the Ceabharnach's hand. The Ceabharnach stowed the money away in his sporran, then he took up a handful of ashes from the harps he had burned and rolled them and twisted them between his fingers, and they became a harp. And as good a harp it was, and even better, than the one he had burned. Then he did so again and again, until he had made harps for Rory O'Calahan, Tommy O'Gilligan, Sean Cooney, and the other twelve harpers as well, and put the harps into the harpers' hands.

But the harpers were angry because of the insult the Ceabharnach had put upon them when he compared their harping to the howling of the creatures on the Isle of Cats, so they all rushed at him to kill him. But he whipped his long old sword out of its scabbard and cut their heads off as they came at him, one by one.

"Ochone! Och, ochone!" lamented the O'Donnell. "Look at what you have done to me, O Ceabharnach! What shall I do for harpers now?"

"That you must answer for yourself," said the Ceabharnach. "I have tarried here long enough. I bid you good day."

And off he went, leaving the O'Donnell behind him mourning for his dead harpers who lay neatly in a row with their bodies on one side and their heads on the other, at O'Donnell's feet.

The Ceabharnach went out of the castle and as he passed through the village below the wall, he met a fisherman with a half-empty creel of fish.

"Fáilte," said the Ceabharnach, giving an eye to the fish. "The luck is bad today?"

"Is it not always bad, today or any day?" answered the fisherman, showing his meager catch.

"In that case, would you like to be making your fortune?" the Ceabharnach asked.

"And why would I not?" the fisherman said.

"Well, then," said the Ceabharnach. "In the court of the castle of the O'Donnell there are fifteen men lying with their heads cut off. You shall go to the castle and put their heads back upon their bodies and bring them to life again. But before you do it, demand a peck of gold and a peck of silver from the O'Donnell for doing the deed, and until you get it do nothing at all."

"Glory be to heaven!" the fisherman exclaimed. "I will do as you say. But how will I bring them alive again after their heads are on?"

"Pluck yourself a bunch of grass from the kirkyard," said the Ceabharnach. "When their heads and bodies are together again, dip the grass in water and sprinkle the lot of them well. They'll leap up in a trice, as well and strong as ever they were."

The fisherman got a bunch of grass from the kirkyard and rushed off to the castle of the O'Donnell, who gladly paid him the peck of gold and the peck of silver for which he asked. The fisherman did as the Ceabharnach had told him to do, and brought the fifteen harpers back to life again. Then all was joy in the castle of the O'Donnell, for the O'Donnell had his harpers and the fisherman's fortune was made.

The Ceabharnach went along the road again with his two elbows poking through the holes in his old coat sleeves; with his two ears poking through the holes in his old hat; with his square feet going clippety-cloppety, trippety-tattery in his old brogues with the cold ditch water running in and out of them; and with his old long sword sticking an ell's length out of a hole in the scabbard that hung crosswise at his backside. And he came to the house of Sean Mor Eilean and knocked boldly at the door.

"Who knocks at my door to open it?" Sean Mor Eilean called out. "Come into the house, for no man stands on my doorstep who is not bidden to enter." So the lad went into the house.

"Blessed be the day to you, Sean Mor Eilean," said the Ceabharnach.

"And to you the same," returned Sean Mor Eilean. "Who are you, and whence do you come?"

"I am the Ceabharnach, and I am master of all the arts, and I have come to Erin from Scotland," the Ceabharnach told him.

"What arts can you be doing then, O Ceabharnach?" asked Sean Mor Eilean.

"I can do a juggle," the Ceabharnach said.

"You have come to the wrong house entirely," said Sean Mor Eilean. "I have five-fifths of the best jugglers in Erin, for I have Coltan O'Ballachan, and I have Tighe O'Kelly, and better jugglers than those two never drew mortal breath."

"We have better in Scotland," the Ceabharnach said.

"Let me see you do a juggle then," said Sean Mor Eilean.

The Ceabharnach took three straws and threw them into the air, and blew upon them to send them high, then caught them upon the back of his hand as they fell. Then he made his hand into a fist and blew the straws off again.

"Hah!" laughed Tighe O'Kelly. "That is a juggle for babes to do. I can do the like myself."

Then Tighe threw the straws up in the air and caught them, and made his hand into a fist. But when he blew upon the straws, his fist blew off with the straws, and there he stood, surprised and dismayed, with only one hand left.

"I will do another juggle," said the Ceabharnach, not waiting to be asked. He took hold of one of his ears and pulled it until he touched it to his nose, and when he let it go again, his ear sprang back into place.

"I can do that same juggle," said Coltan O'Ballachan. "Any fool could do the like." And Coltan took hold of his own ear, but he pulled at his ear so hard that his head came off, and there stood Coltan O'Ballachan, holding his head in his hand by his ear, and his head clean off his shoulders and a surprised look on his face.

Sean Mor Eilean looked at his two jugglers, one without a hand and the other without a head. "I'll grant that you have won with the juggling this day, O Ceabharnach," he said sadly.

"I have so," said the Ceabharnach. "Well, having bested both your men who are five-fifths of all the best jugglers in Erin, I see no need for staying with you any longer, so I'll be on my way."

"Och, nay! Nay!" cried Sean Mor Eilean. "You'll not be leaving my men in such a sorry state. Will you not mend them before you go?"

"I haven't the time to spare for it today," the Ceabharnach said. "Happen I'll be coming this way in another twelvemonth or so, and if I do I'll stop by and mend them, but if I do not you will have to keep them as they are."

Then the Ceabharnach walked out of the great house of Sean Mor Eilean and left him sorrowing over his jugglers there.

The Ceabharnach went through the village that lay beyond the great house, and when he got to the end of it he met a farmer with a sack over his shoulder, and it no more than half full.

"Fáite," said the Ceabharnach. "What is it that you have there?"

"A bushel of corn," said the farmer. "And it is the whole of my harvest for this year. The times are bad for the crops."

"Would you like to be making your fortune?" the Ceabharnach asked.

"Och, aye!" said the farmer. "And who would not?"

"In the great house of Sean Mor Eilean are his two jugglers, one without a hand and the other without a head, and himself sitting sorrowing beside them. If you mend them for him he will make you a rich man for the rest of your life."

"I'd not mind being rich at all," said the farmer. "But how can men in such a state be mended, I'd like to know?"

"Pluck a tuft of grass from the kirkyard," said the Ceabharnach, "and carry it up to the great house with you. When you get to the house strike a bargain with Sean Mor Eilean for a peck of gold and a peck of silver to mend his men, and make them whole again. When you have the money safe in your sack, put the head on the shoulders of the man who lacks it, and the hand on the wrist of the man who has but one hand. Dip the kirkyard grass into water and sprinkle the two of the men with the water. As soon as you do that both of the men will be as well as ever they were."

The farmer ran off to the great house of Sean Mor Eilean with the bunch of grass in his sack. He made a bargain with Sean Mor Eilean for a peck of gold and a peck of silver, and when the money was safe in his sack, the farmer did as the Ceabharnach had told him to do, and mended Sean Mor Eilean's men. Then everybody was happy in the great house of Sean Mor Eilean, because Sean Mor Eilean had his jugglers again and the farmer had made his fortune and was a rich man for life.

So the Ceabharnach went along the road again with his two elbows poking through the holes in his old hat; with his square feet going clippety-cloppety, trippety-tattery in his old brogues with the cold ditch water running in and out of them; with his old long sword sticking an ell's length out of a hole in the scabbard that hung crosswise at his backside.

Then he came to the kingdom of the king of Leinster, and he met the king and his huntsmen and his nobles riding out of the castle, going to the chase. The Ceabharnach stood in the road so that the king could not go by, neither to the left of him nor to the right of him, so the king and his party stopped.

"Fáilte, King of the Kingdom of Leinster," said the Ceabharnach. "May the hunting go well for you this day!"

"To you the blessing of luck, also," said the king. "Who are you, and whence do you come?"

"I am the Ceabharnach," said the lad. "I am a master of all the arts and I come from Scotland."

"What art will you be doing now?" asked the king.

"I will be at the art of hunting," the Ceabharnach said.

"Hunting?" exclaimed the king. "What would your age be, lad?"

"I am fourteen years of age, and soon will be fifteen," said the Ceabharnach.

"You must bide a few years," the king said, laughing. "You are not yet man enough to go hunting with me."

"If I do a man's share, will you give me a man's honors?" asked the Ceabharnach.

The king of Leinster liked the lad's spirit. He stopped laughing and had another look at the Ceabharnach. "Och, well, you might as well come along," said he. "And you'll be given whatever you earn." Then he turned to his huntsmen and bade one of them find the lad a horse.

"I have no need of a horse," said the Ceabharnach. "I will run with you on my two feet, and there will be no horse here today which will outrun me."

All day the king of Leinster and his men hunted, and the Ceabharnach hunted with them, and no horse outran him in the chase. But when the day was nearly over they had not yet brought down one stag. Fast before them the drove raced and twisted and turned, and the king and his men could not take so much as one deer of them all.

Then the king of Leinster wiped the sweat from his brow and cried out, "The curse of the devil is on this day and the hunting! We'll do as well to give it up and ride home."

The Ceabharnach, who was running beside the horse of the king, looked up at him and said, "I have a mind to show you the art of hunting. If I catch the drove and turn it to you, will you give me half of the value in gold of all the spoil you take?"

"That I will, O Ceabharnach," answered the king of Leinster. "Not only the half of the worth of the hunt will I give you, but my daughter to you in marriage, as well."

Then the Ceabharnach cut himself a whistle from the twig of a tree nearby, and told the king to bid his huntsmen stretch out their line to catch the deer as he drove them toward them. The Ceabharnach ran toward the drove and the deer took flight, but if they ran fast, the Ceabharnach ran faster, for he could catch the wind, but the wind could not catch him. He outran the deer, and getting before them, blew his whistle, and at the sound of the whistle the drove turned, and the Ceabharnach herded them all like kyne into the hands of the king and his men, and many a deer was slain in that day's hunting.

The king of Leinster was a man of his word. He gave the Ceabharnach a man's full honors for his share of the hunt, and of gold he gave half the worth of the great spoil that was won that day in the hunting, as he had promised to do. Then the king gave orders that preparations should be made for the wedding of his daughter to the Ceabharnach, which was to take place in two days' time.

On the morning of the wedding day, while the bride was being dressed and guests were riding in from all directions, the Ceabharnach put his gold, and the seventy-five marks he had got from the O'Donnell, into a sack and took the sack upon his shoulder and out of the castle he ran. Somebody caught sight of him and gave the alarm, and all came running after, the king, the queen, the nobles, the bride, and the guests and all. They chased him all the way down to the sea, but they never caught him, and how could they, if the wind itself could never catch him?

There was a boat there by the shore, and he got into it, and pushed away from the shore. Then he shouted out to those who came after him, "Somebody else may marry the daughter of the king of Leinster this day, but it will not be me!" With that, he picked up the oars and tore the sea to pieces in his haste to get back to the land of Scotland on the other side.

When he got across the water, he landed on the shore of Islay, and, taking his sack of gold upon his shoulder, he started off for home. He went along the road with his two elbows poking through the holes in his old coat, with his two ears poking through the holes in his old hat, with his square feet going clippety-cloppety, trippety-tattery in his old brogues with the cold ditch water running in and out of them, and with his old long sword sticking an ell's length out of a hole in the scabbard that hung crosswise at his backside, and he never stopped until he was under his father's roof once more.

Then to his father he said, "I have walked the roads of Erin from the castle of the O'Donnell to the kingdom of the king of Leinster, and I have made the fortunes of a fisherman and a farmer, and I have made yours and mine!"

"Did you now!" said his father. "Och, well, everybody has always said that I had a very intelligent son."

So the Ceabharnach and his father lived very merrily at ease on the Isle of Islay all the rest of their days.

Tales of Trickery

In wonder tales the virtuous and the kind are rewarded while those who go against social or moral standards are punished. Surprisingly, however, not all folktales hold honesty as an important virtue. There are many narratives whose heroes are clever deceivers and thieves, in direct contrast to wonder tales. Almost every culture has developed and adopted tales that glorify the ingenious rascal. Such narratives have a loose structure that permits easy expansion and adaptation of incidents, thus creating many variants of the same tale.

Some trickster heroes use their cleverness to escape danger, as Odysseus did to outwit the one-eyed Cyclops who held him and his men captive. Others, like Robin Hood, are shown robbing the rich to help the poor. Still others, like Till Eulenspiegel, poke fun at the pompous. It is natural for the socially disadvantaged to enjoy and approve exploits that hurt or humiliate the rich and powerful. Some groups, like the American Negro slaves, even developed a Culture Hero, Brer Rabbit, around such a wish fulfillment figure.

Yet not only the powerful are duped in these tales; in many, a gullible but innocent man is tricked. A different set of ethics operates in tales of trickery. The clever seem to have a right to success while fools seem to deserve to be duped. In wonder tales the youngest child is the hero for no other reason than that he is youngest: because he is the youngest he is virtuous. This is a recognized and accepted convention of the genre. So, too, there are narratives in which the trickster is hero for no reason other than that he is more clever than most people. That is another convention of folklore. So it is, that even though in "Hudden, Dudden and Donald O'Neary" Donald exchanges places with a naïve farmer, who is then

drowned, the audience admires Donald for his cleverness rather than being horrified at his cruel deception. Let the fool beware.

Most trickster tales operate in the everyday world familiar to the audience. Instead of relying on the supernatural help of wonder tales, the hero's wit and intelligence bring him success. In many such narratives the plot is less interesting

Illustration by Gustave Doré for Perrault's *Fairy Tales*.

than the intricate steps by which the deception is accomplished. "The Clever Lad from Skye" is such a tale. The reader is most interested in the details of each theft. Instead of being shocked by thievery, he hopes the hero will succeed and admires his intelligence. The teller has softened this story by having the lad return the money, an unusual development in a trickster tale.

The following section includes several opportunities for comparison. This type of folktale can be contrasted with wonder tales to see not only the differences but also how many common motifs are developed. As can be seen in the other types of folklore, not all tales of deception glorify the trickster. The first tale in this section, "The Rubber Man," is such a type and has been included to illustrate the difference between the trickster-hero and the trickster-villain.

THE RUBBER MAN / Africa—the Hausa

Kathleen Arnott

The Jakata contains the earliest record of the Tarbaby story which has been found in Africa, Europe, and America. More than 265 versions have been recorded, 39 in Africa.

This variant, which could have been grouped with Animal Tales, has been placed here for comparison with the other tales of trickery. Unlike the tricksters of the other stories in this section, Spider is not a hero; he is a thief whose punishment pleases the audience. In contrast, the clever lad from Skye, in the next tale, is also a thief, but he has the reader's sympathy and admiration.

Narratives similar to "The Rubber Man" were brought to this country by captured Negroes and entered American folklore through the slaves' tales. Joel Chandler Harris helped preserve a version of this narrative. He scorned the tales told by Negroes as being "old darkey's poor little stories" and "uncouth." This was not an intelligent judgment for, as this narrative illustrates, African tales not only are as interesting as the European, but many developed from the same Indian source.

Another interesting comparison can be made by comparing "The Rubber Man" with "The Wonderful Tarbaby" in Chapter 4, Hero Tales. The slaves adapted Spider's personality by changing him into a Culture Hero at the mercy of stronger folk, as were the Negroes. Brer Rabbit's cleverness helped him not only to survive but covertly to laugh at those more powerful than himself.

Spider was a lazy fellow. The rainy season had come and everybody except Spider was working on the farms—hoeing, digging, and planting. Every morning Spider lay long in bed, only rising at mid-day, to eat a leisurely meal and spend the afternoon resting under a shady tree.

Now his wife knew that the other people in the village had almost finished their planting, and each day she would say hesitantly:

'Don't forget to tell me when you want my help on the farm,' for she dared say no more than that.

Spider would reply, 'Oh, there's plenty of time yet. The rains have scarcely begun.'

But as the days went by and people passing on

the road called out to Spider, asking him when he was going to begin work on his farm, he decided on a plan.

'Today I shall begin clearing the weeds and tomorrow I shall plant ground-nuts,' he said to his wife one morning. 'Go to the market and buy a sackful, then roast them and salt them and have them ready for me to plant in the morning.'

'But husband,' objected his wife, 'whoever heard of ground-nuts being roasted and salted except for eating?'

'Don't argue with me, woman,' said Spider. 'I know what I am doing. Surely you understand that if we plant ground-nuts prepared in this way, then the fresh crop they produce will be already roasted and salted and we shall be able to eat them as soon as they are ripe, without cooking them at all.'

'How clever you are,' said his simple wife, as she set off for the market, while Spider went deep into the bush where no one could see him, and had a good sleep.

That evening Spider returned and told his wife how hard he had worked on the farm, while he watched her shelling, roasting, and salting the ground-nuts.

As soon as the sun rose, Spider took the sack of nuts and pretended to go to his farm. Along the little winding paths he went, until he was far away from the village and the farms. Then, sitting down beneath a tree, he had a wonderful feast and ate every single nut. He followed this with a drink of water from a nearby stream, then, curling up in the shade of a tree, slept soundly until sunset.

Hurrying home he called to his wife, 'Isn't supper ready yet? We men have a hard life! Here have I been working all day in the fields and you, with nothing to do except cook my supper, haven't even got it ready yet!'

'It's just coming,' replied his wife, as she brought him his meal. 'And I will put some water on the fire now, so that you can wash with warm water before you go to bed.'

Every day the same thing happened. Spider said good-bye to his wife in the morning and pretended to go to his farm, but instead of hoeing and weeding like the other men he found a quiet, lonely spot and went to sleep. When evening came, he went back to his wife, complaining of

his tired limbs and aching back, and after a well-cooked supper and a good wash he went to bed.

Time passed until, one by one, the other husbands began to bring home their harvest. But Spider brought nothing. At last his wife said:

'Surely our ground-nuts are ready by now? Nearly everyone in the village is harvesting.'

'Ours are slower than the others,' replied Spider. 'Wait a little longer.'

At last his wife changed her tactics and suggested:

'I'll come to the farm with you tomorrow and help with the harvest. I'm sure our nuts are ready now.'

'I don't want you working on the farm like a poor man's wife,' replied Spider. 'Have patience for a few more days and I'll harvest the ground-nuts myself and bring them home.'

Now Spider was indeed in a fix! How could he bring home ground-nuts to his wife when he had not even got a farm? There was only one solution. He must steal some.

That night, when his wife was asleep, he crept out of the house and made his way to the biggest farm of all, the chief's farm which still had row upon row of ground-nuts unharvested. As quickly as he could, he filled his leather bag with nuts which he dug from the ground, and hiding the bag in a tree some distance away, he returned home.

Early next morning he announced cheerfully to his wife:

'Aha! Today I go to the farm to harvest the first of our nuts. Mind you have a good supper waiting for me when I come home tired and weary.'

'Oh yes, husband, I will,' exclaimed his delighted wife, little knowing that Spider was going straight to the tree where he had hidden his bag and would sleep there all day. She had supper ready for him when he came home, complaining of exhaustion and describing how hard he had worked digging up the nuts, which he handed to her.

Joyfully she cracked open a nut and put it in her mouth. Then her face fell and she cried:

'But these are ordinary nuts! Did you not say that they would grow already roasted and salted?'

'I remember saying no such thing,' replied Spider. 'The reason we salted the nuts was to keep the ants from eating them, once I had planted them in the soil. What a stupid woman you are to think nuts can grow which are roasted and salted already!'

'I see,' said his wife. 'I must have misunderstood you,' and being a very simple woman she thought no more about it.

That night, and a number of following nights, Spider went back to the chief's farm, stole a bagful of ground-nuts and hid them in a tree. Then when morning came he pretended to go to his farm, had a long, deep sleep and returned to his wife with the stolen goods in the evening.

But alas! The chief's servant soon noticed that somebody was stealing his master's nuts and was determined to catch him, so taking several large calabashes, he went into the bush until he found some gutta-percha trees. Then, making long slashes in the bark, he left a calabash at the foot of each tree to catch the sap as it trickled out, and next day when he returned he found they were full of sticky, brown rubber. This he took back to the farm and made into the shape of a man which he placed in the middle of the chief's ground-nut field. Then he rubbed his hands together with glee and said to himself, 'Aha! Now I shall soon know who the thief is!'

When all was dark and the villagers were asleep in bed, Spider crept out of his house as usual and made his way silently to the chief's farm. He was just about to begin digging when he saw what he thought was the figure of a man, only a few yards away.

'Oh!' he gasped. 'What do you want here?' But there was no reply.

Spider became frightened and angry, so lifting his hand he struck the man a hard blow on the cheek, saying:

'Why don't you answer me?'

Now the rubber man had been standing in the sun all day and was still extremely sticky, and Spider found that he could not pull his hand away from the man's face.

'Let me go at once!' he spluttered. 'How dare you hold on to me like that!' And he hit him with the other hand. Now Spider really was in a fix as *both* hands were stuck, and he began to realize that this was no ordinary man. Lifting his knees he tried to free himself by pushing them against the man's body, only to find that they too were held fast.

Frantically he battered his head against the man's chest—and now he could not move at all!

'How foolish I am,' he said to himself. 'I shall have to stay here all night and everybody will know I am a thief.'

Sure enough when the morning came, the chief's servant hurried to the farm to see who had been caught. How he laughed when he saw Spider stuck to the rubber man—head, hands, knees and all.

'So you were the thief!' he exclaimed. 'I might have guessed it.'

Poor Spider! How ashamed he was when the chief's servant managed to get him away from the sticky rubber and brought him before the chief. For weeks afterwards he hid among the rafters of his house seeing and speaking to nobody, and ever since that day his descendants have always hidden in corners.

THE CLEVER LAD FROM SKYE / Scotland

Sorche Nic Leodhas

Tales of thievery often include much greater detail than do wonder tales, where Cinderella dazzles the Prince and Beauty comes to love Beast, no matter how. In tales of trickery, the reader wants to know exactly how such deeds as stealing a well-guarded horse and daughter could be accomplished. How could the lad from Skye steal the gentleman himself? The primary interest of this tale is the thief's cunning, the logic and plausibility of his schemes. Not everyone can humble the arrogant, but it is exciting to see just how the clever lad from Skye did it.

There was once a lad, Tormod MacLeod his name was, and he was one of the clan of Mac-Leods that lived on the Isle of Skye. Being the least one of a family of ten, his father had little to give him, so Tormod took it into his mind to go over to the mainland to make his fortune in one of the big towns there. He wandered from place to place until he came to Glasgow, and there he was lucky enough to find himself a place with a blacksmith who had need of a pair of hands to help him. As Tormod was willing and able he did well at the work, and his master being satisfied with him, he settled down to learn the trade. He was so quick and clever at his work that the blacksmith often blessed the day he came.

But if Tormod's hand was quick, his wits were quicker. There was little that happened about the town that he missed. As he had come over from Skye to make his fortune, he had his eye out to find a chance to do the same.

There was a Glasgow gentleman who had a horse that he was terribly fond of, and with justice, for it was a very fine steed. The gentleman brought it into the smithy one day to have it shod, and the blacksmith gave the job to Tormod to do. While Tormod was shoeing the creature he said to the gentleman, "That's a grand horse you have there."

"Aye, that it is," the gentleman said.

"What will you take for the beast?" asked Tormod.

"There's no amount of money could buy him," the gentleman said. "I'd not part with him for any amount of gold."

"Are you not afraid some thieving body will come along and carry him off, and him so valuable?" Tormod asked.

The gentleman laughed aloud at that. "It could not be done," said he. "Och, he has his

"The Clever Lad from Skye," from *Sea-Spell and Moor-Magic* by Sorche Nic Leodhas. Copyright © 1968 by Leclaire G. Alger. Reprinted by permission of Holt, Rinehart and Winston, Inc.

own stable to stay in, with four strapping big fellows to guard him, and with bells and gongs and horns to give the alarm and bring more, should anyone try to take him away."

"Och, away with your guards and bells and gongs and all!" scoffed Tormod. "And with your big fellows, too. I could steal him out of your stable if I had a mind to, before another week was out. And you'd know naught about it until you found him gone!"

At that the gentleman grew angry. "I've a hundred pounds here in my pocket that says that you cannot get him out of my stable without getting caught at it," he shouted. "Och, if you manage to do it, you may keep the horse!"

"D'ye mean that?" Tormod asked.

"Aye, and I do!" the gentleman said.

Then Tormod turned to the blacksmith who was standing by with his ears and his mouth wide open, and bade him witness that the gentleman had agreed that if Tormod could get the horse out of the gentleman's stable and into their own without getting caught at it, he was to have the horse to keep and a hundred pounds in money beside. So the bargain was made, and then the gentleman went off with his horse, which by this time was well shod, and Tormod went on with his work.

Tormod was not the sort of lad to slack his work, but when his day at the smithy was over he went off on his own. Up to the gentleman's house he went, to see how the land lay. Spying around, he found that it was just as the gentleman said. Behind the gentleman's house there was a tidy wee stable away from the big one, with a court-yard of its own, and there were four great strong ghillies watching the horse, and tending to it, and along the walls of the stable there were bells and gongs and horns galore, to give the alarm if help was needed. All that did not discourage Tormod in the least.

Well, the horse stayed safe in his stable, and Tormod stayed in the smithy for the first few days of the week. But on the fourth day Tormod made ready to take away the gentleman's horse. He had noticed that when the gentleman was away from home, riding upon his fine horse, the four ghillies were usually found at the tavern near the smithy, and from what Tormod had seen of them, he thought the lot of them were fonder of drinking than they ought to have been. "Och, well," said Tormod, "their weakness will be my strength."

That night he went to the tavern and bought three bottles of good strong drink. He put one in the pocket on either side of his jacket, but the third he kept in his hand. When he got to the gentleman's house he poured a bit from the bottle on to his clothes, then corked the bottle up again. He went around the horse and into the courtyard of the stable where the fine horse was kept. He could see, through the open door, the four fellows tending to the horse by the light of a lantern that hung by its stall.

Tormod began to stagger about the courtyard, waving his bottle and singing foolish snatches of song, and muttering to himself. The four ghillies came running to find out what the commotion was, and as the first one came from the stable Tormod pretended to fall upon the ground as if he had slipped into a drunken sleep. There he lay, snoring and groaning loud enough to wake the dead. The four fellows bent over him scolding and shaking him, but he paid them no heed and only snored the louder. "Och!" said one of the ghillies. " 'Tis naught but a drunken lout that's strayed into the place. Pah! He fair reeks o'whuskey!" said he, as he got a whiff of the liquor Tormod had spilled on his clothes.

"Leave him be," said another. "He'll be able to do no harm the way he is, and when he comes round to himself in the morn, we'll hustle him out."

Then a third man saw the bottle of whiskey in Tormod's hand. "He'll have no need for this," he said, reaching down and taking the bottle away. "And we can very well use it."

So back to the stable they went to share the bottle among them. Tormod remained lying on the stones of the courtyard, pretending to be asleep.

When the bottle was empty, one of the ghillies said to the others, "That was well enough in

its way, but it gives one a thirst for more. I'm thinking I felt another bottle in his pocket when I shook him." So they trooped out and felt in Tormod's pocket and there they found the second bottle, which they took back and shared, too. By the time the second bottle was empty every man of them was terribly unsteady upon his legs, and not as steady in his head as he should have been, but they were still thirsty. So out they went and found the last of the bottles Tormod had brought. By this time they'd never have known if Tormod was asleep or not, and when the last bottle was empty they had entirely forgotten that he was there. One by one, they settled down on the stable floor and fell asleep.

Tormod lifted his head to watch them, and when all four were snoring loudly, he leaped to his feet and went into the stable.

"Losh!" he said. "If with all that music you lads are making you do not wake each other, nothing that I do will rouse you, to be sure!" So he went boldly over to the horse and bridled and saddled it, and got up on its back. Then he rode out of the stable and out of the courtyard and down the road, and never stopped until he got back to the smithy. There he put the horse in a stall in the blacksmith's stable, and then he went to bed.

The gentleman came down to his stable in the morning to get his fine horse, intending to ride out upon it, to take the early fresh air. When he found the horse gone and the ghillies lying asleep on the floor of the stable he flew into a rage. He roused the ghillies by throwing a pail of cold water upon them, but even then they were so dazed and drowsy that they could tell him nothing at all. But the gentleman had no need to be told, for a moment's thought told him that Tormod MacLeod, the blacksmith's helper, had gotten away with his horse. So he had one of his other horses saddled, and it was much inferior to the fine one he'd lost. Off he galloped to the smithy. Tormod was there, and the blacksmith with him, both busy at their day's work. The horse was there, too, in the blacksmith's stable, contentedly eating some oats.

"You thief! You rogue!" the gentleman cried. "The sheriff shall take you up this day and jail you for stealing my horse."

"Not so fast!" Tormod said calmly. "I did not

steal your horse, as you well know. Did we not make a bargain that if I could take the creature out of the stable without being caught, then I might keep it, with the blacksmith standing as witness when the bargain was made?"

"Aye!" said the blacksmith, well pleased to have such a clever lad as his helper. "And there was the matter of a hundred pounds, to boot, which I will thank you to hand over to the lad."

The gentleman fussed and fumed but there was naught he could do about it. The blacksmith stood firm. A bargain was a bargain. So in the end the gentleman had to put a hundred pounds of good money in Tormod's hand. "You'll ne'er get the better of me again!" the gentleman said, glowering at Tormod as he paid over the money.

"I'd not say that," said Tormod. "They tell me you've a bonnie young daughter that you're wanting to wed to a rich old laird. I hear that the lass does not see eye-to-eye with you about it, so you're keeping her pent up in her room until she changes her mind and agrees to wed the old coof. I've half a mind to go and get her and marry her myself!"

The gentleman nearly burst with rage. When he could speak, he said, "You ne'er could do so! I've got her shut up in a room at the top of the house, and from the front door to the door of the room she's in there are sluaghs of servants to make sure she doesn't run off before I get her wed to the laird."

"Och, the poor lass!" said Tormod. "But I could take her out of the house just the same, with nobody stopping me the while I did so."

"If you can get her out and not be stopped, you may have her and welcome," the gentleman told Tormod. "But I have five hundred pounds of good money here in my pocket that says you cannot do it."

"Is it a bargain?" Tormod asked.

The blacksmith stepped up then and said to the gentleman. "Come now, have a care, for my helper here is a clever fellow, and what he says he's going to do, he's not likely to leave undone. You could lose your daughter to him, and your money as well." But the gentleman would not heed the blacksmith's good advice.

"Aye!" he said. " 'Tis a bargain!"

So the blacksmith stood again as witness to a bargain between the gentleman and Tormod. The way the bargain stood was, if Tormod could take the gentleman's daughter out of his house, and not be caught at it, he might marry the lass if he liked, and have five hundred pounds of the gentleman's money forbye!

Then the gentleman went away, and the blacksmith and Tormod got busy at their day's work.

Carrying off the gentleman's daughter was not going to be as easy as taking his horse had been. It took Tormod a fortnight to think how it could be done.

"The gentleman's fashing himself about the way you're going to steal his lass," the blacksmith told Tormod one day. "He's given out word that his daughter will be wedding the auld laird he's picked for her, and he's set the date of the wedding day."

Tormod only grinned at the blacksmith's news, for his plans were made, and he thought it very unlikely the gentleman's daughter would be marrying anyone but himself. So he took the next day off from his work, with his master's leave, and went off to the town's best dressmaker. There he so coaxed and beguiled her that she consented to sell him the gown and the bonnet that she was accustomed to wear as she went on her errands about the town, and the shawl and skirt and apron of the maid who usually accompanied her when she went out, as well. That wasn't all he got from her, for he cajoled her into lending him one of the big wicker dress-baskets that she used for carrying the fine garments she made to her customers, and she even found him a couple of caddies to carry the dress-basket for him, too. Although she bridled at his boldness, and said he had a great cheek to behave so sly, she gave him everything he wanted, and never asked what he was going to do with what she gave him.

Tormod had a good friend who was willing to help him. He had set his friend to watching the gentleman's house to discover when the gentleman would be going away from the town. Tormod's friend came back the very day that Tormod went to the dressmaker's house, and brought good news. "The gentleman's off and away," he told Tormod, "and he'll not be back this day again, for he has taken his luggage with him. Where he went to, I was not able to learn."

"Where he went to does not matter at all," said Tormod. "As long as he is not at home."

So Tormod got into the dressmaker's gown, and put her bonnet on his head, with a veil to hang down from it, and cover her face. The friend put on the maid's skirt and apron, and arranged the shawl over his head so as to hide his face. Then the two of them came out of the house where Tormod lived, and there were the caddies, waiting in the street, with the dress-basket, ready to go. Tormod started up the road toward the gentleman's house, and Tormod's friend followed him, walking respectfully a little behind him, and at the end of the procession came the two caddies carrying the wicker hamper between them. All the people they met on the way nodded or bowed, for they thought it was the dressmaker and her servant, whom they knew well, so good was their disguise. And Tormod nodded and bowed back, very well pleased with the success of his plan as far as it had gone. "May it go well to the end!" said Tormod to himself.

When they got to the house of the gentleman, Tormod knocked at the door. A servant opened it to him and Tormod spoke to him, making his voice high and mincing, and so much like the dressmaker's that if she had heard it, she'd have thought it was herself that spoke. "I've come to try the wedding dress on the gentleman's daughter," Tormod said. "There's very little time left ere the wedding day, and the fitting of the gown is important, in case there are changes that must be made."

"Och, aye!" said the servant. "Well, ye've been here before, so you'll be knowing the way. The lass is on the top floor, in the room at the head of the stairs." Then he left them to find their own way, and went about his work.

So up the stairs the lot of them went, Tormod first, in the dressmaker's gown, then his friend in the maid's clothes, with the two caddies, bearing the hamper, coming along behind. Many a servant they passed on their way, but not one of them gave them a second glance. Och, the servants all thought as they passed by. 'Tis naught but the seamstress and her lass.

When Tormod came to the room at the top of the stairs, he opened the door and they all went in. After the caddies had set the dress-basket down in the middle of the floor, Tormod told them to wait in the hall outside until they were needed again, because it would not be seemly for them to stay in the room while the lady was changing her gown. So out they went, and Tormod shut the door behind them.

The lass whirled around from the window where she had been standing looking down at the street. Her eyes and her poor little nose were red from weeping, but still she was bonnier than any lass that Tormod had ever seen. Thinking Tormod was the dressmaker herself, the lass stamped her foot. "You may just take the gown away," said she. "For I'll ne'er wear it. I've said it before and I'll say it again. I will not marry that silly old laird!"

"You'll not, to be sure," said Tormod, speaking to her with his own voice. "Have I not come to make sure that you do not?" And he took off the dressmaker's bonnet and veil and laid them aside.

When the lass saw that it was a man who wore the dressmaker's gown, she started back in terror. It was lucky for Tormod that she was too frightened to find her voice and scream, and bring the servants on the run. But Tormod talked to her so kindly and so gently that soon she listened to what he said. When she understood that he had come to save her from wedding the rich old laird, she was willing to do whatever Tormod told her to do. So Tormod popped her into the dressmaker's hamper and fastened the top down tight. Then he called the caddies and told them he was ready to leave. When the caddies came in from the hall and picked up the hamper, Tormod was at the mirror, fixing the veil of the bonnet, which he had put on again. If the caddies noticed the lass was not in the room they asked no questions about her, and if the hamper seemed heavier going out than coming in, they did not mention that at all. Out of the room they all went, Tormod with his bonnet and his veil hiding his face, then his friend, well-muffled in the maid's shawl, and last of all, the two caddies bearing the wicker hamper between them. They went down the stairs and all the servants they passed looked at them quickly and looked away again. "Och," they said to themselves. "'Tis naught but the seamstress and her serving maid, going back home again."

When they got down to the front door, there was the servant who had let them into the house. He opened the door for them and as they went out of the house, he bade them a polite "Good e'en," and then he closed the door after them, and there was not one of the servants who had seen Tormod that day who had not been well fooled by the clever lad.

Tormod lost no time in leading his crew back to the smithy. When they got there Tormod bade the caddies to set the hamper down, saying that there was a strap with a buckle that wanted mending. The blacksmith would take care of it, and see that the hamper got home safe when the job was done. He paid them for their trouble and they ran off very well pleased with what he gave them, and Tormod called to the blacksmith, who came out of the smithy and gave him a hand. They carried the dress-basket in and set it down on the floor, and Tormod unfastened the straps and lifted up the cover. There lay the lass, as snug as a kitten in a basket, and not in the least harmed by her travels, and when Tormod held out his hands to her, she sprang up and out of the basket into Tormod's arms. Then he asked if she would wed him, instead of the old laird, and she said she was willing, so off they went to the priest that very night. So Tormod married the gentleman's daughter, as he had said he would, and the blacksmith and Tormod's friend stood up with them as witnesses when they were wed.

The next day the gentleman came home from wherever he had been and found the house in a terrible state. The gentleman's daughter had disappeared the day before, and, for the life of them, none of them could say how she got away. 'Twas not by the hall, for some of them had been watching there all the day. 'Twas not by the window, for that was too high, and there was naught she could climb down by. They'd searched the house from top to bottom, and she was not hiding anywhere within it. However she got away, she was gone, and that they'd swear to, for there wasn't a sight or a sound of her to be found.

The gentleman was so angry that sparks fair flew from his eyes. The first thing that came into his head was the bargain that he had made with the blacksmith's lad.

"Was there a great lout came to the house here yesterday?" he asked.

"Och, nay," the servants said. "There was not. De'il a body come to the hoose the whole day long," they told him. "That is, except for the dressmaker with her maid, who came to try the wedding gown on your lass."

"Wedding gown!" said the gentleman. "There's been no wedding gown ordered as yet. De'il take you all for a pack o' fools! I'll warrant that it was not the dressmaker yesterday at all, but the blacksmith's helper decked out in the dressmaker's clothes, and by some trick he's spirited my lass away."

Away to the smithy he rushed, and there were the blacksmith and Tormod, as busy as busy could be. There was his daughter, too, smiling and happy, watching the men as they worked. The gentleman made for his daughter, shouting, "Och, you graceless hizzy, come home wi' me now! I'll promise you'll not get away again, until I've seen you wed to the laird."

But Tormod stepped between the lass and her father, and would not let him come near her.

Then the blacksmith spoke up. "A bargain's a bargain," said he. "The agreement between the two of you was made plain and fair, and although I warned you against it, you would have your own way. The bargain was that if my helper could take your daughter out of your house without being caught, then he could keep her. And as he has done so, to my way of thinking the lass belongs to him."

Then the lass told her father, "I cannot marry your rich old laird, anyway, because I'm already married to Tormod here."

Well, the gentleman had to admit that Tormod had got the better of him again. But there was more misfortune to come for him.

"There's a little matter of some money ye're owing the lad," the blacksmith said, picking up a monstrous big sledge hammer from the anvil against which it was leaning, and hefting it thoughtfully in his hand. "Five hundred pounds, it was, and I'll be thanking you to pay it to him without delay."

The gentleman looked at the sledge hammer and then he looked at the blacksmith, who was eying him in a fashion he did not care for at all. There was naught he could do but take out his purse and pay the five hundred pounds into Tormod's hand.

"Make the most of it!" he growled. "For you've got the best o' me for the last time," and he turned his back and walked away from them all.

Then Tormod, grinning all over his face, called after him. "Och, I'd ne'er say that. Why, I could take yourself out of your own house, as easy as I did your horse and your daughter, and you coming with me as easy and gentle-like as a led lamb."

The gentleman spun around on his heel and back he came to the door of the smithy. "Ye're daft!" said he. "I would not come willingly with you the length of six paces from my front door."

"Aye, but I could," Tormod said.

"Och, now," said the smith to the gentleman. "Have ye no sense at all? This business has gone far enough. Can you not see that you are no match for this clever lad o' mine? Whatever he says he'll do, I promise you, he'll be bound to do it. Leave it alone and make no more bargains with him!"

But the blacksmith might have saved his breath to cool his porridge, for all the good he did. The gentleman was not to hold or to bind.

"There's a thousand pounds in my kist at home that says you can never do so!" he shouted, brandishing his fist at Tormod. "If you can make me go anywhere with you, and me willing to go, you may have the gold."

"Is it a bargain, then?" asked Tormod.

"A bargain it is!" the gentleman said.

"Och, well," sighed the blacksmith. "If ye'll not see reason, I'll be witness to it again."

So it was agreed that if Tormod could make the gentleman come out of his house and go with Tormod willingly, Tormod could have the gentleman's money and welcome to it, so the gentleman said.

Well, the days went by and turned into weeks, and weeks turned into months. The lass was happy and Tormod was happy and all went well. It might have been thought that Tormod had forgotten the bargain he had made with the gentleman, and as for the gentleman, the matter had slipped completely from his mind. But Tormod had not forgotten. He was just biding his time.

Well, at the turn of the year there was going to be a grand celebration in the town to honor some person of great distinction who was visiting there. There was going to be a big dinner, with all the gentry invited, and among the guests who were asked to attend was the gentleman whose horse and whose daughter Tormod had stolen away. When Tormod heard about it, he laughed loud and long. This was the sort of chance he'd been waiting for all this time.

Tormod started to get ready long before the day. In the first place, he had to persuade his wife to pay a visit to his mother on Skye.

"'Tis a sin and a shame the two of you have had no chance to get acquainted," he told her. "Och, she's always begging me to send you to see her, and it would not look well to put it off any longer. She'll be thinking you're not wanting to know her, you see."

So his wife consented to go to the Isle of Skye and stay until the New Year for the Hogmanay holiday and maybe a fortnight or two longer, until Tormod came to fetch her home. But it was not so much to please his mother that Tormod wanted her to go, as it was that Tormod knew full well that his wife would ne'er put up with the trick he intended to play on her father, so it was best to keep her out of the way.

When she had gone, Tormod began to lay his plans for taking the gentleman away with him. He could count on the help of the blacksmith and the friend who had aided him before, but he'd be needing more than the two of them this time. He'd be needing a couple of fellows with trumpets, and maybe a dozen young caddies who looked to be lively and full of fun. He found them without too much bother, and gathered them together at the smithy, and a spry lot of *gavallachans* they were, to be sure. He had chosen them wisely, for they were just the lads to be ready for a bit of fun. When they heard what Tormod was up to, there was not one of them who would not have done his best at the job, without being paid for his trouble at all. It tickled them well to be playing a trick on a gentleman of the town, and such a fine gentleman, too. So Tormod set the date and the hour for them to meet him again and sent them on their way.

When the night of the great celebration came, all the lairds and the gentry of the town assembled about the table in the grand hall where the dinner was being held, and brave and bold among them, to be sure, was the gentleman whom Tormod was going to carry away. While the fine folk were feasting and passing the wine around the table, Tormod and his rascals were gathered together at the smithy, where Tormod was making certain that each man knew the part he must play.

One of the caddies had been sent to watch outside the hall, ready to bring word to Tormod when the dinner was over, and now he came running to say that the gentry were coming out of the hall. Tormod had managed to persuade the dressmaker to make him two long white robes with hoods to them, such as the old monks used to wear. One of these he put on himself, and folded the other over his arm. The blacksmith and the friend were left at the smithy to prepare for his return, while Tormod went off to the gentleman's house, taking his two trumpeters and the pack of caddies along with him.

'Twas the dark of the moon and the winter's night was black and cloudy, with never the twinkle of a star to be seen in the sky. When they got to the place, Tormod sent his companions to hide themselves nearby where they would not be seen. Tormod himself crouched behind a bush in the little garden, just outside the front door.

As soon as the gentleman turned toward his house door, Tormod was after him, stealing along close behind, so silently that the gentleman never knew he was there. When the gentleman opened his front door and went into his house, Tormod slipped in with him, and what with it being so dark, and with the gentleman paying no heed because his thoughts were taken up with the evening's pleasures, Tormod had no trouble at all getting past him into the house and taking his stand at the foot of the stairs. The gentleman felt around until he found a candle on a table against the wall in the hall, and having lit the candle, he turned to go up to his bed. His jaw dropped and his eyes goggled, for there at the foot of the staircase stood a tall figure all in white from head to foot. The gentleman took the apparition to be a ghost, and it scared what wits he had left clean out of his head.

"What's that!" he asked, his voice shaking with fright.

Tormod, standing tall in his long white robe, lifted an arm and pointed at the gentleman. "Wretched mortal!" he said, making his voice so deep and loud that it rumbled through the hall. "I have come to warn you! The end of the world is at hand and you must suffer judgment for the evil you have done in this world."

"Och, nay! Nay!" the gentleman cried, and his knees began to shake. "I am not ready to be judged yet."

"Ready or not," said Tormod sternly. "You'll be judged just the same."

"I've been none so bad," the gentleman wept, and he began to beg for help. "Och, if you are one of the blessed saints, as I take it you are, can you not save me?"

"I can not stay with you," Tormod said. "Soon the trumpets of doom will be blowing, and I shall be needed elsewhere."

"Take me with you, then," the gentleman pleaded. "I shall be safe if I am by your side."

"Happen you would," said Tormod doubtfully. "That is, if the fiends did not come and drag you away from me. They'd know you at once upon seeing you, you may be sure."

"Oh, woe, woe!" wept the gentleman. "Save me, save me, blessed one!"

"Och, well—poor soul, I'll do what I can," said Tormod. "But are you willing to put yourself in my hands, and come with me?"

"Willing!" the gentleman said. "Och, and that I am! I'll go gladly where'er you take me."

"You'll not get far, clad as you are" said Tormod. "But here is a robe like my own. You and me will look the same as two peas out of the same pod when you get into it, and it will suit you fine for a disguise." And Tormod took the second white robe that he carried folded over his arm, and bundled the gentleman into it, taking care to pull the hood well down over the gentleman's face. "It will be best if they cannot make out who you are at all," Tormod said. "Lest they lay hands upon you to punish you for your sins."

The gentleman agreed to that, but if his face could not be seen, neither could he see. He groped about with his hands, trying to feel his way. "Give me your hand," said Tormod. "I'll lead you. My eyes will do for the two of us, never fear."

So the gentleman put his hand into Tormod's and off they started. The moment the two stepped out of the house the trumpeters in the garden let out a mighty blast on their horns, as Tormod had arranged that they should do.

"Och! Heaven save us! What's that?" shrieked the gentleman, frantically clutching Tormod's arm in his fright.

"'Tis the Angel Gabriel, blowing the trump o' doom," said Tormod. "He'll be marking the beginning of the Judgement Day."

Then on all sides there was the sound of screeching and wailing, and fleeing feet and wild laughter. Tormod had to half carry and half drag the gentleman along the road, he was so weak with fright. With his eyes covered by the folds of the heavy cloth of the hood the poor wretch could see not a thing, but that was satisfactory to him, for he had no wish to see. To hear was bad enough, to his mind.

At last they reached the smithy and Tormod led the gentleman inside. The blacksmith and Tormod's friend were there, throwing fuel on the fire by the forge until it blazed nearly to the roof. There was such a clashing and glee-glashing of iron as you never heard in your life, as they knocked pokers and hammers and shovels together, while the shouting and shrieking of the caddies outside came nearer and nearer all the time. Although the gentleman could not see, he could feel the heat, and hear the crackling and roaring of the fire above the uproar outside the smithy.

"Och!" he cried out to Tormod. "In heaven's name, what are those awful sounds? What is that terrible heat I feel?"

"'Tis the flames of the fiery pit you're feeling," Tormod said. "And the noise is the gates of doom as they open and close, and the shrieks of the poor lost sinners as they are carried in."

Then Tormod said to the gentleman, "I can stay no longer. I must be on my way. Before I go I will take you to a place where, if you truly repent your sins, you will, no doubt, be safe."

Then he led the gentleman past the fire and into the wee room behind the forge where the horses' food and other stores were kept. The gentleman fell on his knees on the floor, and Tormod left him kneeling there, saying his prayers.

All night long the blacksmith and Tormod's friend kept the fire roaring high and the fire irons crashing, and all night long the trumpeters and the caddies shrieked and screamed and leaped about the blacksmith shop. Why the neighbors did not send for the sheriff because of the wild carouse I cannot tell you, but happen Tormod had made it all right with them in advance. When daybreak came, Tormod called a halt to the racket, and laid his white robe aside. The blacksmith and Tormod's friends let the fire go down, and the trumpeters and the caddies left off their shrieking and gamboling, and were not sorry to do so, for they were fair winded by that time. Tormod paid them all well, for they had earned it, and sent them home.

It was suddenly very still in the blacksmith shop. Tormod opened the door of the storeroom. There was the gentleman still kneeling on the floor, in the white robe that Tormod had clad him in, and with the hood still well over his face.

"Och, you can come out now," Tormod said.

The gentleman recognized Tormod's voice, and for a few minutes he stayed as he was, stock still. Then he pushed the hood from his face and looked about him and saw the sacks of corn, and the hides and nails and suchlike things that were stored in the wee room. He got to his feet slowly, rubbing his knees which were stiff from the night's long kneeling, and then he walked past Tormod, out of the storeroom into the smithy, and all the time he said not one word.

"Well, and did I take you out of your house?" asked Tormod.

"You did," the gentleman said.

"And did you come with me willingly?" asked Tormod.

"I did," the gentleman said. And then, without another word, he walked out of the smithy, still wearing the long white robe, and home he went.

Neither the gentleman nor Tormod said a word about making another bargain between them. That day, before noontide, the gentleman's man of business came to the smithy and gave Tormod a bundle, and when Tormod opened it up he found in it the white robe the gentleman had worn, and the thousand pounds that Tormod had won.

But that is not the end of the story. Tormod fetched his wife back from Skye, and now that his mischief was over, Tormod told her what he had done to her father on Hogmanay night. Very vexed she was, too, but in the end she said that happen it would teach her father to stop trying to get the best of Tormod with his old bargains, which would be a very good thing, for she did not hold with betting and gambling forbye. And if Tormod would promise to play no more tricks upon her poor old father, she supposed she'd have to forgive him this time.

Early one morn, a few days later, Tormod called his wife to him. "You know that fine horse I got from your father?" said he. "Well, now, you're to be taking it back to him, and tell him that I said 'twas a very grand creature, but that I do not care to keep it any longer, so he'd better have it back."

His wife looked surprised, but said nothing, and as she started away to get ready to go, Tormod called her back to him. "That's not all," said he. And into her hand he put fifteen hundred pounds, and that was the five hundred he had got when he carried her off, and the thousand the gentleman had sent after he had been carried off

himself. As for the hundred pounds Tormod had got for carrying off the horse, he no longer had that, for the dressmaker and the two trumpeters and the caddies got all of that.

"Tell your father I thank him for the use of his money, but as I'm not needing it any more, he might as well have it, too." So his wife did as Tormod told her, and took the horse and the money back to the gentleman and told him what Tormod had said.

When their first child was born, and it a son, Tormod would have it no other way than that it should be called after his wife's father, which gave the gentleman a great deal of pleasure. It wasn't long after that that he was heard bragging that Tormod MacLeod, his son-in-law, was a very fine fellow, and there wasn't a man in all Scotland who could match him for cleverness. But of course he never told anybody why he thought the same.

As for Tormod, who had come all the way from the Isle of Skye to Glasgow to find his fortune, he was entirely satisfied. He had a good trade and a good master, a bonnie wife and a grand wee son—and what better fortune could any man want?

FIN M'COUL AND THE GIANT / Ireland

Joseph Jacobs

In this tale, neither Fin nor Cuchullin have the heroic stature they possess in so many Irish and Scottish tales. Here they are merely giants, and the great M'Coul must resort to trickery. Compare this tale with the legends about each in Chapter 4, Hero Tales.

What Irish man, woman, or child has not heard of our renowned Hibernian Hercules, the great and glorious Fin M'Coul? Not one, from Cape Clear to the Giant's Causeway, nor from that back again to Cape Clear. And, by the way, speaking of the Giant's Causeway brings me at once to the beginning of my story.

"Fin M'Coul and the Giant," from *Celtic Fairy Tales* by Joseph Jacobs. Published by Blue Ribbon Books, 1899.

Well, it so happened that Fin and his men were all working at the Causeway, in order to make a bridge across to Scotland; when Fin, who was very fond of his wife Oonagh, took it into his head that he would go home and see how the poor woman got on in his absence. So, accordingly, he pulled up a fir tree, and, after lopping off the roots and branches, made a walking stick of it, and set out on his way to Oonagh.

Oonagh, or rather Fin, lived at this time on the very tiptop of Knockmany Hill, which faces a cousin of its own that rises up, half-hill, half-mountain, on the opposite side.

There was at that time another giant, named Cuhullin—some say he was Irish, and some say he was Scotch—but whether Scotch or Irish, no other giant of the day could stand before him. Such was his strength that, when well-vexed, he could give a stamp that shook the country about him.

The fame and name of Cuhullin went far and near, and nothing in the shape of a man, it was said, had any chance with him in a fight. By one blow of his fists he flattened a thunderbolt and kept it in his pocket, in the shape of a pancake, to show to his enemies when they were about to fight him.

Undoubtedly Cuhullin had given every giant in Ireland a considerable beating, barring Fin M'Coul himself. He swore that he would never rest, night or day, winter or summer, till he would serve Fin with the same sauce, if he could catch him.

The short and long of it was that Fin had heard Cuhullin was coming to the Causeway to have a trial of strength with him. So at once he was seized with a very warm and sudden fit of affection for his wife, poor woman, leading a very lonely life in his absence. He accordingly pulled up the fir tree, as I said before, and having made it into a walking stick, set out to see his wife on the top of Knockmany Hill.

In truth, many people had wondered very much why it was that Fin had selected such a windy spot for his dwelling-house, and they even went so far as to tell him as much.

"What can you mane, Mr. M'Coul," said they, "by living on the top of Knockmany, where you are never without a breeze, day or night, winter or summer, and where there's sorrow's own want of water?"

"Why," said Fin, "ever since I was the height of a round tower, I was known to be fond of a good view. Where, neighbors, could I find a better spot for a good view than the top of Knockmany? As for water, I am sinking a pump, and, please goodness, as soon as the Causeway's made, I intend to finish it."

Of course the real state of the case was that he lived on the top of Knockmany Hill in order that he might be able to see Cuhullin coming towards the house. All we have to say is, that if he wanted a spot from which to keep a sharp lookout—and, between ourselves, he did want it grievously—he could not have found a neater or more convenient location for it.

"God save all here!" said Fin, good-humoredly, putting his honest face into his own door.

"Fin, an' you're welcome home, you darlin' bully!" said Oonagh. There followed a smack that is said to have made the waters of the lake at the bottom of the hill curl, as it were, with kindness and sympathy.

Fin spent two or three happy days with Oonagh, and felt himself very comfortable considering the dread he had of Culhullin. This, however, grew upon him so much that his wife could not but see there was something on his mind which he kept altogether to himself. Let a woman alone, and she will wheedle a secret out of her good man. Fin proved this.

"It's this Cuhullin," said he, "that's troubling me. When the fellow gets angry, and begins to stamp, he shakes a whole town. It's well known that he can stop a thunderbolt, for he always carries one about him in the shape of a pancake, to show to anyone that might misdoubt it."

As he spoke, he clapped his thumb into his mouth, which he always did when he wanted to find out something. His wife asked him what he did it for.

"He's coming," said Fin. "I see him below Dungannon."

"An' who is it, dear?"

"That Cuhullin," replied Fin. "And how to manage I don't know. If I run away, I am disgraced; but I know that sooner or later I must meet him, for my thumb tells me so."

"When will he be here?" asked Oonagh.

"Tomorrow, about two o'clock," replied Fin, with a groan.

"Well, my bully, don't be cast down," said Oonagh. "Depend on me, and maybe I'll bring you out of this scrape better than ever you could bring yourself, by your rule o'thumb."

She then made a high smoke on the top of the hill, after which she put her finger in her mouth, and gave three whistles. By that Cuhullin knew he was invited to Knockmany—for this was the way that the Irish long ago gave a sign to all strangers and travelers, to let them know they were welcome to come and take share of whatever was in the house.

In the meantime, Fin was very melancholy, and did not know what to do, or how to act at all. Cuhullin was an ugly customer to meet with; and, the idea of the pancake flattened Fin's very heart.

What chance could he have, strong and brave though he was, with a man who could, when put in a passion, walk the country into earthquakes and knock thunderbolts into pancakes? Fin knew not on what hand to turn. Right or left—backward or forward—where to go he could form no guess whatsoever.

"Oonagh," said he, "can you do nothing for me? Where's all your invention? Am I to be skivered like a rabbit before your eyes, and to have my name disgraced forever in the sight of all my tribe, and me the best man among them? How am I to fight this man-mountain—this huge cross between an earthquake and a thunderbolt? With a pancake in his pocket that was once—"

"Be easy, Fin," replied Oonagh. "I'm ashamed of you. Talking of pancakes, maybe, we'll give him as good as any he brings with him—thunderbolt or otherwise. If I don't treat him to as smart feeding as he's had this many a day, never trust Oonagh again. Leave him to me, and do just as I bid you."

This relieved Fin very much; for, after all, he had great confidence in his wife, knowing, as he did, that she had got him out of many a difficulty before.

Then Oonagh sent round to the neighbors and borrowed one and twenty iron griddles. She took the griddles and kneaded them into the middle of one and twenty cakes of bread. She baked the cakes on the fire in the usual way, setting them aside in the cupboard as they were done. She then took a large pot of new milk and made curds and whey.

Having done all this, Oonagh sat down quite contented, waiting for Cuhullin's arrival on the next day about two o'clock. That was the hour at which he was expected. Fin knew as much by his thumb; that was a curious property that Fin's thumb had.

At length, the next day, Cuhullin was seen coming across the valley. Now Oonagh knew that it was time to commence operations. She immediately brought the cradle, and made Fin lie down in it, and cover himself up with the bedclothes.

"You must pass for your own child," she said. "So just lie there snug, and say nothing, but be guided by me."

About two o'clock, as he had been expected, Cuhullin came in. "God save all here!" said he. "Is this where the great Fin M'Coul lives?"

"Indeed it is, honest man," replied Oonagh. "Won't you be sitting?"

"Thank you, ma'am," said he, sitting down. "You're Mrs. M'Coul, I suppose?"

"I am," said she, "and I have no reason, I hope, to be ashamed of my husband."

"No," said the other, "he has the name of being the strongest and bravest man in Ireland; but for all that, there's a man not far from you that's very desirous of seeing him. Is he at home?"

"Why, no," she replied. "And if ever a man left his house in a fury, he did. It appears that someone told him of a giant called Cuhullin being down at the Causeway looking for him, and so he set out to try to catch him. I hope, for the poor giant's sake, he won't meet with him; for if he does, Fin will make paste of him at once."

"Well," said the other, "I am Cuhullin, and I have been seeking him these twelve months, but he always kept clear of me; and I will never rest night or day till I lay my hands on him."

At this Oonagh set up a loud laugh of great contempt, and looked at him as if he were only a mere handful of a man.

"Did you ever see Fin?" she said, changing her manner all at once.

"How could I?" said he. "He always took care to keep his distance."

"I thought so," she replied. "I judged as much. And if you take my advice, you poor-looking creature, you'll pray night and day that you may never see him; for I tell you it will be a black day for you when you do. But, in the meantime, you see that the wind's changed and is blowing in the door. As Fin himself is away from home, maybe you'd be so civil as to turn the house. That's what Fin always does when the wind changes."

This was a startler even to Cuhullin; but he

got up, however, went outside, and getting his arms about the house, turned it as she had wished. When Fin saw this, he felt the sweat of fear oozing out through every pore of his skin; but Oonagh, depending upon her woman's wit, felt not a whit daunted.

"Well, then," she said, "as you are so civil, maybe you'd do another obliging turn for us, as Fin's not here to do it himself. You see, after this long stretch of dry weather we've had, we feel very badly off for want of water. Now, Fin says there's a fine spring somewhere under the rocks behind the hill here below. It was his intention to pull the rocks asunder; but having heard of you, he left the place in such a fury, that he never thought of it. Now, if you would try to find the spring, I'd feel it a kindness."

She brought Cuhullin down to see the place, which was then all one solid rock. After looking at it for some time, Cuhullin stooped down and tore a cleft in the rock about four hundred feet deep and a quarter of a mile long. If you go there, you can see it, for it has since been christened by the name of Lumford's Glen.

After that was done Oonagh said politely, "Now come in and eat a bit of such humble fare as we can give you. Even though you and Fin are enemies, he would scorn not to treat you kindly in his own house. Indeed, if I didn't do it in his absence, he would not be pleased with me."

She accordingly brought him into the house, and placed before him half a dozen of the cakes she had baked. She brought out also a can of butter, a side of boiled bacon, and a stack of cabbage; for this, be it known, was long before the invention of potatoes. She urged him to help himself.

Cuhullin put one of the cakes in his mouth to take a huge whack out of it. Then he made a thundering noise, something between a growl and a yell. "Blood and fury!" he shouted! "What is this? Here are two of my teeth out! What kind of bread is this you gave me?"

"What's the matter?" said Oonagh coolly.

"Matter!" shouted the other again. "Why, here are the two best teeth in my head gone."

"Why," she said, "that's Fin's bread, the only bread he ever eats when at home. But, indeed, I forgot to tell you that nobody can eat it but himself and that child in the cradle there. I thought, however, that as you were reported to be rather a stout little fellow of your size, you might be able to manage it. I did not wish to affront a man that thinks himself able to fight Fin. Here's another cake; maybe it's not so hard as that."

Cuhullin at the moment was not only hungry, but ravenous; so he accordingly made a fresh try at the second cake. Immediately another yell was heard twice as loud as the first. "Thunder and gibbets!" he roared. "Take your bread away, or I will not have a tooth in my head. There's another pair of them gone!"

"Well, honest man," replied Oonagh, "if you're not able to eat the bread, say so quietly, and don't be waking the child in the cradle there. There now, he's awake!"

Fin now gave a howl that startled the giant, as coming from such a youngster as he was supposed to be. "Mother," said he, "I'm hungry. Get me something to eat."

Oonagh went over, and put into his hand a cake that had no griddle in it. Fin, whose appetite in the meantime had been sharpened by seeing eating going on, soon swallowed it. Cuhullin was thunderstruck, and secretly thanked his stars that he had the good fortune to miss meeting Fin. He said to himself, "I would have no chance with a man who could eat such bread as that. Bread which even his son that's but in his cradle can munch before my eyes!"

"I'd like to take a glimpse at the lad in the cradle," said he to Oonagh. "For I can tell you that the infant who can manage that nutriment is no joke to look at."

"With all my heart," replied Oonagh. "Get up, dear, and show this decent little man something that won't be unworthy of your father, Fin M'Coul."

Fin, who was dressed for the occasion as much like a baby as possible, got up, and said to Cuhullin. "Are you strong?"

"Thunder an' 'ounds!" exclaimed the other. "What a voice in so small a chap!"

"Are you strong?" said Fin again. "Are you able to squeeze water out of that white stone?" he asked, putting one into Cuhullin's hand. The later squeezed and squeezed the stone, but in vain.

"Ah! You're a poor creature!" said Fin. "You a

giant! Give me the stone here, and when I show what Fin's little son can do, you may judge of what my daddy himself is."

Fin then took the stone, and exchanging it for the curds, he squeezed the latter until the whey, as clear as water, oozed out in a little shower from his hand.

"I'll now go back," said he, "to my cradle; for I scorn to lose my time with anyone that's not able to eat my daddy's bread, or squeeze water out of a stone. You had better be off before he comes back. If he catches you, he'll make flummery out of you in two minutes."

Cuhullin, seeing what he had seen, was of the same opinion himself. His knees knocked together with the terror of Fin's return. He accordingly hastened to bid Oonagh farewell, and to assure her that from that day on, he never wished to hear of, much less to see, her husband.

"I admit fairly that I'm not a match for him," said he, "strong as I am. Tell him I will avoid him as I would the plague, and that I will make myself scarce in this part of the country as long as I live."

Fin, in the meantime, had got back into the cradle, where he lay very quietly. His heart was in his mouth with delight that Cuhullin was about to take his departure, without discovering the tricks that had been played on him.

"It's well for you," said Oonagh to Cuhullin, "that Fin doesn't happen to be here, for it's nothing but hawk's meat he'd make of you."

"I know that," said Cuhullin. "Never a thing else he'd make of me; so I'll be going."

Thus did Fin, through the wit and invention of Oonagh, his wife, succeed in overcoming his enemy by cunning, which he never could have done by force.

JACK AND THE KING WHO WAS A GENTLEMAN / Ireland

Seumas MacManus

Many tales are told in Europe about winning the princess by making her or her father call the hero a liar. This plot motif is especially popular in Ireland.

Compare the use of idioms and the nonstandard spelling in this story with that in Joseph Jacobs' "Tom Tit Tot" and Richard Chase's "Jack in the Giants' Newground." Colloquialisms, dialect, and phonetic spelling add flavor by giving a sense of the oral version. Yet when too closely followed these same devices can create difficulties for the reader. For the modern storyteller with an understanding of the Irish dialect, "Jack and the King Who Was a Gentleman" will provide a wonderful base for an oral retelling, but to most young children the language will be strange and difficult. Few will struggle through this story and so will miss the humor of Jack's tall tales. Hopefully teachers and librarians will tell or read this delightful tale aloud.

Well, childre: wanst upon a time, when pigs was swine, there was a poor widdy woman lived all alone with her wan son Jack in a wee hut of a house, that on a dark night ye might aisily walk over it by mistake, not knowin' at all, at all, it was there, barrin' ye'd happen to strike yer toe again' it. An' Jack an' his mother lived for lee an' long, as happy as hard times would allow them, in this wee hut of a house, Jack sthrivin' to 'arn a little

"Jack and the King Who Was a Gentleman," from *In Chimney Corners* by Seumas MacManus. Published by Doubleday, 1899.

support for them both by workin' out, an' doin' wee turns back an' forrid to the neighbors. But there was one winter, an' times come to look black enough for them—nothin' to do, an' less to ate, an' clothe themselves as best they might; an' the winther wore on, gettin' harder an' harder, till at length when Jack got up out of his bed on a mornin', an' axed his mother to make ready the drop of stirabout for their little brakwus as usual, "Musha, Jack, *a mhic*," says his mother, says she, "the malechist—thanks to be to the Lord!—is as empty as Paddy Ruadh's donkey that used to ate his brakwus at supper-time. It stood out long an' well, but it's empty at last, Jack, an' no sign of how we're goin' to get it filled again—only we trust in the good Lord that niver yet disarted the widow and the orphan—He'll not see us wantin', Jack."

"The Lord helps them that help themselves, mother," says Jack back again to her.

"Thrue for ye, Jack," says she, "but I don't see how we're goin' to help ourselves."

"He's a mortial dead mule out an' out that hasn't a kick in him," says Jack. "An', mother, with the help of Providence—not comparin' the Christian to the brute baste—I have a kick in me yet; if you thought ye could only manage to sthrive along the best way you could for a week, or maybe two weeks, till I get back again off a little journey I'd like to undhertake."

"An' may I make bound to ax, Jack," says his mother to him, "where would ye be afther makin' the little journey to?"

"You may that, then, Mother," says Jack. "It's this: You know the King of Munsther is a great jintleman entirely. It's put on him, he's so jintlemanly, that he was niver yet known to make use of a wrong or disrepectable word. An' he prides himself on it so much that he has sent word over all the known airth that he'll give his beautiful daughter—the loveliest picthur in all Munsther, an' maybe in all Irelan', if we'd say it—an' her weight in goold, to any man that in three trials will make him use the unrespectful word, an' say, 'Ye're a liar!' But every man that tries him, an' fails, loses his head. All sorts and descriptions of people, from prences an' peers down to bagmen an' beggars, have come from all parts of the known world to thry for the great prize, an' all of them up to this has failed, an' by consequence

lost their heads. But, mother dear," says Jack, "where's the use in a head to a man if he can't get mail for it to ate? So I'm goin' to thry me fortune, only axin' your blissin' an' God's blissin' to help me on the way."

"Why, Jack, a *thaisge*," says his mother, "it's a dangersome task; but as you remark, where's the good of the head to ye when ye can't get mail to put in it? So, I give ye my blissin', an' night, noon, an' mornin' I'll be prayin' for ye to prosper."

An' Jack set out, with his heart as light as his stomach, an' his pocket as light as them both together; but a man 'ill not travel far in ould Irelan' (thanks be to God!) on the bare-footed stomach—as we'll call it—or it'll be his own fault if he does; an' Jack didn't want for plenty of first-class aitin' an' dhrinkin' lashin's an' laivin's, and pressin' him to more. An' in this way he thravelled away afore him for five long days till he come to the King of Munsther's castle. And when he was comed there he rattled on the gate, an' out come the king.

"Well, me man," says the king, "what might be your business here?"

"I'm come here, your Kingship," says Jack, mighty polite, an' pullin' his forelock, be raison his poor ould mother had always insthructed him in the heighth of good breedin'—"I'm come here, your R'yal Highness," says Jack, "to thry for yer daughter."

"Hum!" says the king. "Me good young man," says he, "don't ye think it a poor thing to lose yer head?"

"If I lose it," says Jack, "sure one consolation 'ill be that I'll lose it in a glorious cause."

An' who do ye think would be listenin' to this same deludherin' speech of Jack's, from over the wall, but the king's beautiful daughter herself. She took an eyeful out of Jack, an' right well plaised she was with his appearance, for—

"Father," says she at once, "hasn't the boy as good a right to get a chance as another? What's his head to you? Let the boy in," says she.

An' sure enough, without another word, the King took Jack within the gates, an' handin' him over to the sarvints, tould him to be well looked afther an' cared for till mornin'.

Next mornin' the King took Jack with him an' fetched him out into the yard. "Now then, Jack," says he, "we're goin' to begin. We'll drop into the stables here, and I'll give you your first chance."

So he took Jack into the stables an' showed him some wondherful big horses, the likes of which poor Jack never saw afore, an' everyone of which was the heighth of the side wall of the castle an' could step over the castle walls, which were twenty-five feet high, without strainin' themselves.

"Them's purty big horses, Jack," says the King. "I don't suppose ever ye saw as big or as wondherful as them in yer life."

"Oh, they're purty big indeed," says Jack, takin' it as cool as if there was nothin' whatsomever astonishin' to him about them. "They're purty big indeed," says Jack, *for this counthry*. But at home with us in Donegal we'd only count them little nags, shootable for the young ladies to dhrive in pony-carriages."

"What!" says the King, "do ye mane to tell me ye have seen bigger in Donegal?"

"Bigger!" says Jack. "Phew! Blood alive, yer Kingship, I seen horses in my father's stable that could step over your horses without thrippin'. My father owned one big horse—the greatest, I believe, in the world again."

"What was he like?" says the King.

"Well, yer Highness," says Jack, "it's quite beyond me to tell ye what he was like. But I know when we wanted to mount it could only be done by means of a step-laddher, with nine hundred and ninety steps to it, every step a mile high, an' you had to jump seven mile off the topmost step to get on his back. He ate nine ton of turnips, nine ton of oats, an' nine ton of hay, in the day an' it took ninety-nine men in the daytime, an' ninety-nine more in the night-time, carrying his feeds to him; an' when he wanted a drink, the ninety-nine men had to lead him to a lough that was nine mile long, nine mile broad, an' nine mile deep, an' he used to drink it dry every time," says Jack, an' then he looked at the King, expectin' he'd surely have to make a liar of him for that.

But the King only smiled at Jack, an' says he, "Jack, that was a wonderful horse entirely, an' no mistake."

Then he took Jack with him out into the garden for his second trial, an' showed him a bees-kep, the size of the biggest rick of hay ever Jack had seen; an' every bee in the skep was the size of a thrush, an' the queeny bee as big as a jackdaw.

"Jack," says the King, says he, "isn't them wondherful bees? I'll warrant ye, ye never saw anything like them?"

"Oh, they're middlin'—middlin' fairish," says Jack—"*for this counthry*. But they're nothin' at all to the bees we have in Donegal. If one of our bees was flying across the fields," says Jack, "and one of your bees happened to come in its way, an' fall into our bee's eye, our bee would fly to the skep, an' ax another bee to take the mote out of his eye."

"Do you tell me so, Jack!" says the King. "You must have great monsthers of bees."

"Monsthers," says Jack. "Ah, yer Highness, monsthers is no name for some of them. I remimber," says Jack, says he, "a mighty great breed of bees me father owned. They were that big that when my father's new castle was a-buildin' (in the steddin' of the old one which he consaived to be too small for a man of his mains), and when the workmen closed in the roof, it was found there was a bee inside, an' the hall door not bein' wide enough, they had to toss the side wall to let it out. Then the queeny bee—ah! she was a wondherful baste entirely!" says Jack. "Whenever she went out to take the air she used to overturn all the ditches and hedges in the country; the wind of her wings tossed houses and castles; she used to swallow whole flower gardens; an' one day she flew against a ridge of mountains nineteen thousand feet high and knocked a piece out from top to bottom, an' it's called Barnesmore Gap to this day. This queeny bee was a great trouble an' annoyance to my father, seein' all the harm she done the naybours round about; and once she took it in her head to fly over to England, an' she created such mischief an' disolation there that the King of Englan' wrote over to my father if he didn't come immaidiately an' take home his queeny bee that was wrackin' an' ruinin' all afore her he'd come over himself at the head of all his army and wipe my father off the face of the airth. So my father ordhered me to mount our wondherful big horse that I tould ye about, an' that could go nineteen mile at every step, an' go over to Englan' an' bring home our queeny bee. An' I mounted the horse an' started, an' when I come as far as the sea I had to cross to get over to Englan', I put the horse's two fore feet into my hat, an' in that way he thrashed the sea dry all the way across an' landed me safely. When I come to the King of Englan' he had to supply me with nine hundred and ninety-nine thousand men an' ninety-nine thousand mile of chains an' ropes to catch the queeny bee an' bind her. It took us nine years to catch her, nine more to tie her, an' nine years and nine millions of men to drag her home, an' the King of Englan' was a beggar after from that day till the day of his death. Now what do ye think of that bee?" says Jack, thinkin' he had the King this time sure enough.

But the King was a cuter one than Jack took him for, an' he only smiled again, an' says he,—

"Well, Jack, that was a wondherful great queeny bee entirely."

Next, for poor Jack's third an' last chance, the King took him to show him a wondherful field of beans he had, with every beanstalk fifteen feet high an' every bean the size of a goose's egg.

"Well, Jack," says the King, says he, "I'll engage ye never saw more wondherful beanstalks than them?"

"Is it them?" says Jack. "Arrah, man, yer Kingship," says he, "they may be very good—*for this counthry*; but sure we'd throw them out of the ground for useless afther-shoots in Donegal. I mind one bean-stalk in partickler, that my father had for a show an' a cur'osity, that he used to show as a great wondher entirely to sthrangers. It stood on ninety-nine acres of ground, it was nine hundred mile high, an' every leaf covered nine acres. It fed nine thousand horses, nine thousand mules, an' nine thousand jackasses for nineteen years. He used to send nine thousand harvestmen up the stalk in spring to cut and gather off the soft branches at the top. They used to cut these off when they'd reach up as far as them (which was always in the harvest time), an' throw them down, an' nine hundred and ninety-nine horses an' carts were kept busy for nine months carting

the stuff away. Then the harvestmen always reached down to the foot of the stalk at Christmas again."

"Faix, Jack," says the King, "it was a wondherful bean-stalk, that, entirely."

"You might say that," says Jack, trying to make the most of it, for he was now on his last leg. "You might say that," says he. "Why, I mind one year I went up the stalk with the harvestmen, an' when I was nine thousand mile up, doesn't I miss my foot, and down I come. I fell feet foremost, and sunk up to my chin in a whinstone rock that was at the foot. There I was in a quandhary—but I was not long ruminatin' till I hauled out my knife, an' cut off my head, an' sent it home to look for help. I watched after it, as it went away, an' lo an' behould ye, afore it had gone half a mile I saw a fox set on it, and begin to worry it. 'By this an' by that,' says I to meself, 'but this is too bad!'—an' I jumped out an' away as hard as I could run, to the assistance of my head. An' when I come up, I lifted my foot, an' give the fox three kicks, an' knocked three kings out of him—every one of them a nicer an' a better jintleman than you."

"Ye're a liar, an' a rascally liar," says the King.

"More power to ye!" says Jack, givin' three buck leaps clean into the air, "an' it's proud I am to get you to confess it; for I have won yer daughter."

Right enough the King had to give up to Jack the daughter—an' be the same token, from the first time she clapped her two eyes on Jack she wasn't the girl to gainsay him—an' her weight in goold. An' they were both of them marrid, an' had such a weddin' as surpassed all the weddin's ever was heerd tell of afore or since in that counthry or in this. An' Jack lost no time in sendin' for his poor ould mother, an' neither herself nor Jack ever after knew what it was to be in want. An' may you an' I never know that same naither.

JACK IN THE GIANT'S NEWGROUND/United States—Appalachia

Richard Chase

The stories in The Jack Tales *edited by Richard Chase are much closer to the oral folk tradition than any of the other narratives in this book. In the late 1930s, Mr. Chase visited Beech Creek, North Carolina, and recorded a number of tales from the Jack cycle that were still being told in the southern Appalachian region.*

The printed version of "Jack in the Giants' Newground" is a retelling by Mr. Chase of the best elements from the tales told to him by R. M. Ward, Martha Ward Presnell, Roby Hicks, and Ben Hicks. In his introduction, the editor explains that the dialect has been changed somewhat to permit ease of reading but that the regional idioms have been retained.

The Jack tales offer interesting comparisons with European stories. Notice that while a king is still present, his behavior, language, and power are quite different from that of rulers in German and Oriental tales. Numerous motifs from the European-Asian tradition occur: the giant's wife being burned to death, squeezing milk from a stone, slitting a bag under the clothes. They have, however, been given a uniquely American flavor. And, as Mr. Chase points out in his foreword, this Jack is quite different from the cocky hero of English and Irish tales. An interesting comparison can be made between this contemporary American variant and "The History of Jack and the Giants," an eighteenth-century English chapbook, an excerpt from which can be found in Chapter 1, Yesterday and Today.

One time away back years ago there was a boy named Jack. He and his folks lived off in the mountains somewhere and they were awful poor, just didn't have a thing. Jack had two brothers, Will and Tom, and they are in some of the Jack Tales, but this one I'm fixin' to tell you now, there's mostly just Jack in it.

Jack was awful lazy sometimes, just wouldn't do ary lick of work. His mother and his daddy kept tryin' to get him to help, but they couldn't do a thing with him when he took a lazy spell.

Well, Jack decided one time he'd pull out from there and try his luck in some other section of the country. So his mother fixed him up a little snack of dinner, and he put on his old raggedy hat and lit out.

Jack walked on, walked on. He eat his snack 'fore he'd gone very far. Sun commenced to get awful hot. He traveled on, traveled on, till he was plumb out of the settle-ment what he knowed. Hit got to be about twelve, sun just a-beatin' down, and Jack started gettin' hungry again.

He came to a fine smooth road directly, decided he'd take that, see where it went, what kind of folks lived on it. He went on, went on, and pretty soon he came to a big fine stone house up above the road. Jack stopped. He never had seen such a big house as that before. Then he looked at the gate and saw it was made out of gold. Well, Jack 'lowed some well-doin' folks must live there, wondered whether or no they'd give him his dinner. Stepped back from the gate, hollered, "Hello!"

A man came to the door, says, "Hello, stranger. What'll ye have?"

"I'm a-lookin' for a job of work."

"Don't know as I need to hire anybody right now. What's your name?"

"Name's Jack."

"Come on up, Jack, and sit a spell. Ain't it pretty hot walkin'?"

"Pretty hot," says Jack.

"Come on up on the porch and cool off. You're not in no hurry, are ye?"

Jack says, "Well, I'll stop a little while, I reckon."

Shoved back that gold gate and marched on in. The man reached in the door and pulled out a couple of chairs. Jack took one and they leaned back, commenced smokin'. Directly Jack says to that man, "What did you say your name was, mister?"

"Why, Jack, I'm the King."

"Well, now, King," says Jack, "hit looks like you'd be a-needin' somebody with all your land. I bet you got a heap of land to work."

"Are ye a hard worker, Jack?"

"Oh, I'm the workin'est one of all back home yonder."

"You a good hand to plow?"

"Yes sir!"

"Can ye clear newground?"

"Why, that's all I ever done back home."

"Can ye kill giants?"

"Huh?" says Jack, and he dropped his pipe. Picked it up, says, "Well, I reckon I could try."

The old King sort of looked at Jack and how little he was, says, "Well, now, Jack, I have got a little piece of newground I been tryin' for the longest to get cleared. The trouble is there's a gang of giants live over in the next holler, been disputin' with me about the claim. They kill ever' Englishman goes up there, kill 'em and eat 'em. I reckon I've done hired about a dozen men claimed to be giantkillers, but the giants killed them, ever' last one."

"Are these here giants very big 'uns?" says Jack.

"Well, they're all about six times the size of a natural man, and there's five of 'em. The old man has got four heads and his old woman has got two. The oldest boy has got two heads, and there's a set of twins has got three heads a-piece."

Jack didn't say nothin', just kept studyin' about how hungry he was.

King says, "Think ye can clear that patch, Jack?"

"Why, sure!" says Jack. "All I can do is get killed, or kill them, one."

"All right, son. We'll make arrange-ments about the work after we eat. I expect my old woman's about got dinner ready now. Let's us go on in to the table."

"Thank ye, King," says Jack. "I hope it won't put ye out none."

"Why, no," says the King. "Hit ain't much, but you're welcome to what we got."

Well, Jack eat about all the dinner he could hold, but the King's old woman kept on pilin' up his plate till he was plumb foundered. His dish set there stacked up with chicken and cornbread and beans and greens and pie and cake, and the Queen had done poured him milk for the third time. The old King kept right on, and Jack didn't want them to think he couldn't eat as much as anybody else, so directly he reached down and took hold on the old leather apron he had on and doubled that up under his coat. Then he'd make like he was takin' a bite, but he'd slip it down in that leather apron. He poured about four glasses of milk down there, too. Had to fasten his belt down on it so's it 'uld hold.

Well, directly the King pushed his chair back, and then he and Jack went on out and sat down again, leaned back against the house and lit their pipes.

King says to Jack, says, "If you get that patch cleared, Jack, I'll pay ye a thousand dollars a-piece for ever' giant's head you bring down, and pay ye good wages for gettin' that patch cleared: ten cents a hour."

Jack said that suited him all right, and he got the King to point him out which ridge it was. Then Jack says to the King, "You say them giants live over in the other holler?"

King said they did.

Jack says, "Can they hear ye when ye start hackin'?"

"They sure can," says the King.

Jack didn't say nothin'.

The King says to him, "You don't feel uneasy now, do ye, Jack?"

"Why, no, bedads!" says Jack. "Why, I may be

the very giantkiller you been lookin' for. I may not kill all of 'em today, but I'll try to get a start anyhow."

So the King told him maybe he'd better go on to work. Said for him to go on out past the woodpile and get him a axe, says, "You might get in a lick or two 'fore them giants come. You'll find a tree up there where them other men have knocked a couple of chips out'n. You can just start in on that same tree."

So Jack started on out to the woodpile. The King watched him, saw him lean over and pick up a little old Tommy hatchet, says, "Hey, Jack! You'll need the axe, won't ye?"

"Why, no," says Jack. "This here'll do me all right." He started on off, turned around, says, "I'll be back about time for supper."

The old King just grinned and let him go on.

When Jack fin'ly got up on that ridge, he was scared to death. He sat down on a log and studied awhile. He knowed if he started in cuttin', them giants would come up there; and he knowed if he didn't, the King 'uld know he hadn't done no work and he'd likely get fired and wouldn't get no supper. So Jack thought about it some more, then he picked out the tallest poplar he could see, and cloomb up in it, started in choppin' on the limbs way up at the very top . . .

Hack! Hack! Hack!

Heard a racket directly, sounded like a horse comin' up through the bresh. Jack looked down the holler, saw a man about thirty foot high comin' a-stompin' up the mountain, steppin' right over the laurel bushes and the rock-clifts. Jack was so scared he like to slipped his hold.

The old giant came on up, looked around till he fin'ly saw where Jack was settin', came over there under him, says, "Hello, stranger."

"Howdy do, daddy."

"What in the world you a-doin' up there?"

"I'm a-clearin' newground for that man lives back down yonder."

"Clearin' land? Well, I never seen such a fool business, start in clearin' newground in the top of a tree! Ain't ye got no sense?"

"Why, that's allus the way we start in clearin' back home."

"What's your name, son?"

"My name's Jack."

"Well, you look-a-here, Jack. This patch of land is ours and we don't aim to have it cleared. We done told the King so."

"Oh, well, then," says Jack, "I didn't know that. If I'd 'a knowed that I'd 'a not started."

"Come on down, Jack. I'll take ye home for supper."

Didn't think Jack 'uld know what he meant. Jack hollered back, says, "All right, daddy. I'll be right down."

Jack cloomb down a ways, got on a limb right over the old giant's head, started in talkin' to him, says, "Daddy, they tell me giants are awful stout. Is that so?"

"Well, some," says the old giant. "I can carry a thousand men before me."

"Well, now, daddy, I bet I can do somethin' you can't do."

"What's that, Jack?"

"Squeeze milk out'n a flint rock."

"I don't believe ye."

"You throw me up a flint rock here and I'll show ye."

So while the old giant hunted him up a flint rock, Jack took his knife and punched a little hole in that old leather apron. The giant chunked the rock up to him and Jack squeezed down on it, pushed up against his apron, and the milk commenced to dreen out . . .

Dreep, dreep, dreep.

"Do it again, Jack!"

So Jack pushed right hard that time, and hit just went like milkin' a cow.

The old giant hollered up to Jack, says, "Throw me down that rock."

He took the rock and squeezed and squeezed till fin'ly he got so mad he mashed down on it and they tell me he crumbled that flint rock plumb to powder.

Then Jack hollered down to him again, says, "I can do somethin' else you can't do."

"What's that, Jack?"

"I can cut myself wide open and sew it back up. And it won't hurt me none."

"Aw, shucks, Jack. I know you're lyin' now."

"You want to see me do it?"

"Go ahead."

Jack took his knife and ripped open that

leather apron, took a piece of string he had, punched some holes, and sewed it back up, says, "See, daddy? I'm just as good as I ever was."

Well, the old giant just couldn't stand to let Jack out-do him, so he hollered up, says, "Hand here the knife, Jack."

Took Jack's knife and cut himself wide open, staggered around a little and fin'ly querled over on the ground dead. Well, Jack, he scaled down the tree and cut off the old giant's heads with that little Tommy hatchet, took 'em on back to the King's house.

II

The King paid Jack two thousand dollars like he said he would. Jack eat him a big supper and stayed the night. Next mornin', after he eat his breakfast, Jack told the King he reckoned he'd have to be a-gettin' on back home. Said his daddy would be a-needin' him settin' out tobacco.

But the King says, "Oh, no, Jack. Why, you're the best giantkiller I ever hired. There's some more of that giant gang yet, and I'd like awful well to get shet of the whole crowd of 'em."

Jack didn't want to do it. He figgered he'd done made him enough money to last him awhile, and he didn't want to get mixed up with them giants any more'n he could help. But the King kept on after him till Jack saw he couldn't get out of it very handy. So he went and got the Tommy hatchet, started on up to the newground again.

Jack hadn't hardly got up there that time 'fore he heard somethin' comin' up the holler stompin' and breakin' bresh, makin' the awfulest racket. He started to climb him a tree like he done before, but the racket was gettin' closer and closer, and Jack looked and saw it was them twin giants that had three heads a-piece. Jack looked up, saw them six heads a-comin' over the tree tops, says, "Law me! I can't stand that! I'll hide!"

He saw a big holler log down the hill a ways, grabbed him up a shirt-tail full of rocks and shot in that log like a ground squirrel. Hit was pretty big inside there. Jack could turn right around in it.

The old giants fin'ly got there. Jack heard one of 'em say to the other'n, "Law! Look a-yonder! Somebody's done killed brother."

"Law, yes! Now, who you reckon could 'a done that? Why, he could 'a carried a thousand Englishmen before him, singlehanded. I didn't hear no racket up here yesterday, did you?"

"Why, no, and the ground ain't tromped none, neither. Who in the world you reckon could 'a done it?"

Well, they mourned over him awhile, then they 'lowed they'd have to take him on down and fix up a buryin'. So they got hold on him, one by the hands and the other by the feet, started on down.

"Poor brother!" says one of 'em. "If we knowed who it was killed him, we'd sure fix them!"

The other'n stopped all at once, says, "Hold on a minute. There ain't a stick of wood to the house. Mother sent us up here after wood; we sure better not forget that. We'll have to have plenty of wood too, settin' up with brother tonight."

"We better get about the handiest thing we can find," says the other'n. "Look yonder at that holler log. Suppose'n we take that down."

Well, they laid the old dead giant down across the top of that log and shouldered it up. Jack got shook around right considerable inside the log, but after he got settled again, he looked and saw the old giant in front had the log restin' right betwixt his shoulders. And directly Jack happened to recollect he had all them rocks. So after they'd done gone down the holler a little piece, Jack he picked him out a rock and cut-drive at the giant in front—fumped him right in the back of the head. Old giant stumbled, and stopped and hollered back at his brother, says, "You look-a-here! What you a-throwin' rocks at me for?"

"I never so throwed no rocks at you."

"You did so! You nearly knocked me down!"

"Why, I never done it!"

They argued awhile, fin'ly started on down again.

Jack waited a minute or two, then he cut loose with another good-sized rock. *Wham!*

"You con-founded thing! You've done hit me again!"

"I never done no such a thing!"

"You did too!"

"I never teched ye!"

"You're the very one. You needn't try to lie

out of it neither. You can see as good as I can there ain't nobody else around here to throw no rocks. You just hit me one other time now, and I'll come back there and smack the fire out-a you!"

They jawed and cussed a right smart while till fin'ly they quit and got started on down again.

Well, this time Jack picked out the sharpest-edged rock he had, drew back and clipped him again right in the same place. *Pow!* The old giant in front hollered so loud you could 'a heard him five miles, throwed that log off'n his shoulder and just made for the other'n, says, "That makes three times you've done rocked me! And you'll just take a beatin' from me now or know I can't do it!"

Them twin giants started in to fightin' like horses kickin'. Beat any fightin' ever was seen: pinchin' and bitin' and kickin' and maulin' one another; made a noise like splittin' rails. They fit and scratched and scratched and fit till they couldn't stand up no more. Got to tumblin' around on the ground, knockin' down trees and a-kickin' up rocks and dirt. They were clinched so tight couldn't neither one break loose from the other'n, and directly they were so wore out they just lay there all tangled up in a pile, both of 'em pantin' for breath.

So when Jack saw there wasn't no danger in 'em, he crawled out from that log and chopped off their heads, put 'em in a sack and pulled on back to the King's house.

III

Well, the old King paid Jack six thousand dollars for that load of heads. Then Jack said he just had to get on in home. Said his folks would be uneasy about him, and besides that they couldn't get the work done up unless he was there.

But the King says to him, says, "Why, Jack, there ain't but two more of 'em now. You kill them for me and that'll wind 'em up. Then we won't have no trouble at all about that newground."

Jack said he'd see what he could do: went on back that same evenin'.

This time Jack didn't climb no tree or nothin'. Went to work makin' him a bresh pile, made all

the racket he could. The old four-headed giant come a-tearin' up there in no time. Looked around, saw the other giants lyin' there dead, came over to where Jack was, says, "Hello, stranger."

"Hello, yourself."

"What's your name, buddy?"

"My name's Jack—Mister Jack."

"Well, Mister Jack, can you tell me how come all my boys layin' here dead?"

"Yes, bedads, I can tell ye," says Jack. "They came up here cussin' and 'busin' me, and I had to haul off and kill 'em. You just try and sass me ary bit now, and I'll kill you too!"

"Oh pray, Jack, don't do that! There's only me and the old woman left now, and she's got to have somebody to get in her stovewood and tote up water."

"You better be careful what ye say then. I ain't goin' to take nothin' off nobody."

"Well, now, I don't want to have no racket with ye at all, Mister Jack. You come on down and stay the night with us, help set up with our dead folks, and we'll get fixed to have a buryin' tomorrow."

"Well, I'll go," says Jack, "but you sure better watch out what you say."

"Oh, I'll not say nothin'," says the old giant. Says, "Law, Jack, you must be the awfulest man!"

So the old giant stuck the dead 'uns under his arm and he and Jack started on down. When they got close to the house, the giant stopped, says to Jack, "Now, Jack, you better wait till I go and tell the old lady you've come down for supper. She might cut a shine. She'll be mad enough already about her boys bein' killed."

He went on in and shut the door. Jack slipped up and laid his ear to the keyhole so's he could hear what they said. Heard him tell his old lady, says, "I've got Jack here, claims to be a giantkiller. I found the boys up yonder at the newground with their heads cut off, and this here Jack says he's the one done it."

The old woman just carried on. Fin'ly the old giant got her hushed, says, "He don't look to me like he's so stout as all that. We'll have to test him out a little, and see whe'er he's as bad as he claims he is."

Directly Jack heard him a-comin' to the door

rattlin' buckets. So he stepped back from the house and made like he was just comin' up. The old giant came on out, says, "There ain't a bit of water up, Jack. The old woman wants you and me to tote her some from the creek."

Jack saw he had four piggins big as wash tubs, had rope bails fixed on 'em, had 'em slung on one arm. So they went on down to the creek and the old giant set the piggins down. Stove his two in, got 'em full and started on back. Jack knowed he couldn't even tip one of them things over and hit empty. So he left his two piggins a-layin' there, waded out in the creek and started rollin' up his sleeves. The old giant stopped and looked back, saw Jack spit in his hands and start feelin' around under the water.

"What in the world ye fixin' to do, Jack?"

"Well, daddy," says Jack, "just as soon as I can find a place to ketch a hold, I'm a-goin' to take the creek back up there closer to the house where your old woman can get her water everwhen she wants it."

"Oh, no, Jack! Not take the creek back. Hit'll ruin my cornfield. And besides that, my old lady's gettin' sort-a shaky on her feet; she might fall in and get drownded."

"Well, then," says Jack, "I can't be a-wastin' my time takin' back them two little bitty bucket-fulls. Why, I'd not want to be seen totin' such little buckets as them."

"Just leave 'em there, then, Jack. Come on, let's go back to the house. Mind, now, you come on here and leave the creek there where it's at."

When they got back, he told his old woman what Jack had said. Says, "Why, Law me! I had a time gettin' him to leave that creek alone."

He came on out again, told Jack supper wasn't ready yet, said for him to come on and they'd play pitch-crowbar till it was time to eat. They went on down to the level field, the old giant picked up a crowbar from the fence corner. Hit must 'a weighed about a thousand pounds. Says, "Now, Jack, we'll see who can pitch this crowbar the furthest. That's a game me and the boys used to play."

So he heaved it up, pitched it about a hundred yards, says, "You run get it now, Jack. See can you pitch it back here to where I'm at."

Jack ran to where it fell, reached down and took hold on it. Looked up 'way past the old giant, put his hand up to his mouth, hollers, "Hey, Uncle! Hey, Uncle!"

The old giant looked all around, says, "What you callin' me Uncle for?"

"I ain't callin' you. —Hey! *Uncle!*"

"Who are ye hollerin' at, Jack?"

"Why, I got a uncle over in Virginia," says Jack. "He's a blacksmith and this old crowbar would be the very thing for him to make up into horseshoes. Iron's mighty scarce over there. I thought I'd just pitch this out there to him.— Hey! UNCLE!"

"Oh, no, Jack. I need that crowbar. Pray don't pitch it over in Virginia."

"Well, now," says Jack, "I can't be bothered with pitchin' it back there just to where you are. If I can't pitch it where I want, I'll not pitch it at all."

"Leave it layin' then, Jack. Come on let's go back to the house.—You turn loose of my crow-bar now."

They got back, the giant went in and told his old woman he couldn't find out nothin' about Jack. Said for her to test him awhile herself. Says, "I'll go after firewood. You see can't you get him in the oven against I get back, so's we can eat."

Went on out, says to Jack, "I got to get a turn of wood, Jack. You can go on in the house and get ready for supper."

Jack went on in, looked around, didn't see a thing cookin', and there set a big old-fashioned clay oven with red-hot coals all across it, and the lid layin' to one side.

The old giant lady came at him, had a wash rag in one hand and a comb in the other'n, says, "Come here now, Jacky. Let me wash ye and comb ye for supper."

"You're no need to bother," says Jack. "I can wash."

"Aw, Jack. I allus did wash my own boys before supper. I just want to treat ye like one of my boys."

"Thank ye, ma'am, but I gen'ally wash and comb myself."

"Aw, please, Jack. You let me wash ye a little now, and comb your head. Come on, Jacky, set up here on this shelf so's I won't have to stoop over."

Jack looked and saw that shelf was right on

one side of the big dirt oven. He cloomb on up on the scaffle, rocked and reeled this-a-way and that-a-way. The old woman kept tryin' to get at him with the rag and comb, but Jack kept on teeterin' around till he slipped off on the wrong side. He cloomb back up and he'd rockle and reel some more. The old woman told him, says, "Sit straight now, Jack. Lean over this way a little. Sakes alive! Don't ye know how to sit up on a shelf?"

"I never tried sittin' on such a board before," says Jack. "I don't know how you mean."

"You get down from there a minute. I reckon I'll have to show ye."

She started to climb up there on the scaffle, says, "You put your shoulder under it, Jack. I'm mighty heavy and I'm liable to break it down."

Jack put his shoulder under the far end, and when the old woman went to turn around and sit, Jack shoved up right quick, fetched her spang in the oven. Grabbed him up a hand-spike and prized the lid on. Then he went and hid behind the door.

Old giant came in directly. Heard somethin' in the oven just a-crackin' and a-poppin'.

"Old woman! Hey, old woman! Jack's a-burnin'."

When she didn't answer, the old giant fin'ly lifted the lid off and there was his old lady just about baked done, says, "Well, I'll be confounded! That's not Jack!"

Jack stepped out from behind the door, says, "No, hit sure ain't. And you better mind out or I'll put you in there too."

"Oh, pray, Jack, don't put me in there. You got us licked, Jack. I'm the only one left now, and I reckon I better just leave this country for good. Now, you help me get out of here, Jack, and I'll go off to some other place and I'll promise not to never come back here no more."

"I'd sure like to help ye, daddy, but I don't think we got time now. Hit's too late."

"Too late? Why, how come, Jack?"

"The King told me he was goin' to send a army of two thousand men down here to kill ye this very day. They ought to be here any minute now."

"Two thousand! That many will kill me sure. Law, what'll I do? Pray, Jack, hide me somewhere."

Jack saw a big chest there in the house, told the old giant to jump in that. Time he got in it and Jack fastened the lid down on him, Jack ran to the window and made-out like that army was a-comin' down the holler, says, "Yonder they come, daddy. Looks to me like about three thousand. I'll try to keep 'em off, though. You keep right still now and I'll do my best not to let 'em get ye."

Jack ran outside the house and commenced makin' a terrible racket, bangin' a stick on the walls, rattlin' the windows, shoutin' and a-hollerin', a-makin'-out like he was a whole army. Fin'ly he ran back in the house, knocked over the table and two or three chairs, says, "You quit that now and get on out of here! I done killed that old giant! No use in you a-breakin' up them chairs. He ain't here I tell ye!"

Then Jack 'uld tumble over some more chairs and throw the dishes around considerable, says, "You all leave them things alone now, 'fore I have to knock some of ye down."

Then he'd run by that chest and beat on it, says, "He ain't in there. You all leave that chest alone. He's dead just like I told ye. Now you men march right on back to the King and tell him I done got shet of them giants and there ain't ary one left."

Well, Jack fin'ly made like he'd done run the army off. Let the old giant out the chest. He was just a-shakin', says, "Jack, I sure do thank ye for not lettin' all them men find out where I was at."

So Jack took the old giant on down to the depot, put him on a freight train, and they hauled him off to China.

The King paid Jack two thousand dollars for bakin' the old giant lady, but he said he couldn't allow him nothin' on the old giant because the trade they'd made was that Jack had to bring in the heads.

Jack didn't care none about that, 'cause his overhall pockets were just a-bulgin' with money when he got back home. He didn't have to clear that newground for the King, neither. He paid his two brothers, Will and Tom, to do it for him.

And the last time I went down to see Jack he was a-doin' real well.

THE SILENT MAIDEN / East Africa

Eleanor B. Heady

This tale goes back at least to the sixth century A.D., *for it is found in* The Panchatantra. *In most versions, however, the girl cannot or will not laugh and, as in "Lazy Jack" and the Grimm brothers' "The Golden Goose," is won by the man whose actions cause her to laugh. The silent girl who must be made to talk is a relatively rare variation of the plot. Unlike the two previously mentioned stories in which the heroes made no conscious effort to win the girls, Fupajena deliberately tricks Mepo into talking.*

Once very long ago, there was a beautiful young maiden called Mepo. She was the daughter of the great chief, Amagogo. Mepo was good and handsome, with skin like black velvet, teeth like flashing pearls, eyes with a dark diamond brightness. Her smile made all who saw her love her. Because of her great beauty she was her father's favorite daughter.

When it came time for Mepo to marry, she went to her father and said, "Father, please, do not give me to the first man who offers you a great reward, nor to any man you fancy, but let me choose my own husband. He must be handsome, a valiant warrior, a fine hunter, and clever."

"A man like that would make a very good husband indeed. If you are looking for such a man, you may certainly choose for yourself," said the chief.

So word came out to the other villages that the young men of the tribe might pay court to Mepo, the beautiful daughter of the chief, Amagogo. They came from miles around, short men, tall men, lean men, fat men, young men, and old men. All of them tried so hard to please the girl that she became very tired of their constant attentions. At last she refused to speak to any of them.

"Daughter, why do you behave so?" asked her father. "Your mother and I are worried because you do not speak."

Mepo shook her head wearily and refused to say a word.

Still the young men and the old men came. For weeks the spears stuck into the ground at the door of the chief's house told all who passed by that there were many men visiting Mepo. But she only sat in the center of the admiring circle and smiled sadly. They brought her gifts of ripe fruit, melons, choice meat, and beads of many colors; still she refused to speak to anyone or to choose between them.

Finally her father tired of this stubborn behavior. He sent out word to the villages that he would give Mepo in marriage to anyone who could make her speak.

In the village far away across the great river lived a brave young chief of another tribe. His name was Fupajena. He heard of the silent maiden and of her father's offer. He went to her village and asked at the house of Amagogo for permission to meet her. The old chief welcomed him. Such a strong and handsome young man would make a fine husband for his daughter.

"How I hope you can make her speak," said Amagogo. "I'm sure she would be happy with you."

Fupajena was shown into the chief's hut. Mepo looked up wearily from her basket making.

"Great beauty is yours, lovely Mepo," said Fupajena with a low bow. "Will you be my wife?"

Mepo lowered her eyes and refused to say a word.

Fupajena had come a long way to pay court to the beautiful maiden. Amagogo had a bed of skins made for him inside one of the houses and invited him to spend the night.

It was weeding time, for the rains had just passed. Early the next morning, Mepo took her hoe and went to weed her maize field.

Fupajena watched her go, then quietly followed. When they reached the field, Fupajena again said to her, "Please beautiful Mepo, be my wife."

Mepo did not answer, but handed him the hoe and went and sat in the shade of a tree. The young chief began hoeing with quick sure strokes. "Look, Mepo," he called. "I have finished."

Mepo looked at the field. She shouted angrily, "Punda, donkey! You have ruined my crop. You hoed up the maize and left the weeds standing!"

Fupajena threw down the hoe and began to dance and laugh. Mepo became angrier and shouted louder than before. "How could anyone be so stupid?"

In mock fright, the young chief ran toward Amagogo's house. Mepo followed, still shouting. Her father and mother hearing the noise, met them outside. They were overjoyed that someone had made their daughter speak.

After her anger cooled, Mepo knew that Fupajena had been clever enough to make her forget her silence. She gladly went home with him to be his wife and was never silent again.

THE HODJA AND THE CAULDRON / Turkey

Charles Downing

The Hodja is not always a numbskull at a loss for words. In many anecdotes humor comes from his clever wit and tricks. Please see the introduction to "Three Tales of the Hodja" in Chapter 6, Drolls, for more information pertinent to this story.

Once the Hodja borrowed a large cauldron from his neighbour, and when some time had passed, he placed a small metal coffee-can in it and took it back to its owner.

'What is that?' said the latter, pointing to the small can.

'Oh, your cauldron gave birth to that while it was in my possession.'

The neighbour was delighted, and took both the cauldron and the coffee-can.

Some days later, the Hodja again asked his neighbour to lend him his cauldron, which he did. This time a few weeks passed, and when the neighbour felt he could do without his cauldron no longer, he went to the Hodja, and asked him to return it.

'I cannot,' replied the Hodja. 'Your cauldron has died.'

'Died?' cried the neighbour. 'How can a cauldron die?'

'Where is the difficulty?' said the Hodja. 'You believed it could give birth. Why will you not believe it can die?'

HUDDEN AND DUDDEN AND DONALD O'NEARY/Ireland

Joseph Jacobs

Through diffusion, the tale of the Rich and the Poor Peasant has been carried to Iceland, Russia, the Dutch East Indies, Africa, and North and South America. Hans Christian Andersen retold it in "Big Claus and Little Claus." This Irish version is shorter than many of the tales, yet is true to the basic pattern.

There was once upon a time two farmers, and their names were Hudden and Dudden. They had poultry in their yards, sheep on the uplands, and scores of cattle in the meadowland alongside the river. But for all that they weren't happy. For just between their two farms there lived a poor man by the name of Donald O'Neary. He had a hovel over his head and a strip of grass that was barely enough to keep his one cow, Daisy, from starving, and, though she did her best, it was but seldom that Donald got a drink of milk or a roll of butter from Daisy. You would think there was little here to make Hudden and Dudden jealous, but so it is, the more one has the more one wants, and Donald's neighbors lay awake of nights scheming how they might get hold of his little strip of grassland. Daisy, poor thing, they never thought of; she was just a bag of bones.

One day Hudden met Dudden, and they were soon grumbling as usual, and all to the tune of "If only we could get that vagabond Donald O'Neary out of the country."

"Let's kill Daisy," said Hudden at last; "if that doesn't make him clear out, nothing will."

No sooner said than agreed, and it wasn't dark before Hudden and Dudden crept up to the little shed where lay poor Daisy trying her best to chew the cud, though she hadn't had as much grass in the day as would cover your hand. And when Donald came to see if Daisy was all snug for the

night, the poor beast had only time to lick his hand once before she died.

Well, Donald was a shrewd fellow, and down-hearted though he was, began to think if he could get any good out of Daisy's death. He thought and he thought, and the next day you could have seen him trudging off early to the fair, Daisy's hide over his shoulder, every penny he had jingling in his pockets. Just before he got to the fair he made several slits in the hide, put a penny in each slit, walked into the best inn of the town as bold as if it belonged to him, and, hanging the hide up to a nail in the wall, sat down.

"Some of your best whisky," says he to the landlord. But the landlord didn't like his looks. "Is it fearing I won't pay you, you are?" says Donald; "why I have a hide here that gives me all the money I want." And with that he hit it a whack with his stick and out hopped a penny. The landlord opened his eyes, as you may fancy.

"What'll you take for that hide?"

"It's not for sale, my good man."

"Will you take a gold piece?"

"It's not for sale, I tell you. Hasn't it kept me and mine for years?" and with that Donald hit the hide another whack and out jumped a second penny.

Well, the long and the short of it was that Donald let the hide go and, that very evening, who but he should walk up to Hudden's door?

"Good-evening, Hudden. Will you lend me your best pair of scales?"

"Hudden and Dudden and Donald O'Neary," from *Celtic Fairy Tales* by Joseph Jacobs. Published by Blue Ribbon Books, 1899.

Hudden stared and Hudden scratched his head, but he lent the scales.

When Donald was safe at home, he pulled out his pocketful of bright gold and began to weigh each piece in the scales. But Hudden had put a lump of butter at the bottom, and so the last piece of gold stuck fast to the scales when he took them back to Hudden.

If Hudden had stared before, he stared ten times more now, and no sooner was Donald's back turned, than he was off as hard as he could pelt to Dudden's.

"Good evening, Dudden. That vagabond, bad luck to him—"

"You mean Donald O'Neary?"

"And who else should I mean? He's back here weighing out sackfuls of gold."

"How do you know that?"

"Here are my scales that he borrowed, and here's a gold piece still sticking to them."

Off they went together, and they came to Donald's door. Donald had finished making the last pile of ten gold pieces. And he couldn't finish because a piece had stuck to the scales.

In they walked without an "If you please" or "By your leave."

"Well, *I* never!" that was all *they* could say.

"Good evening, Hudden; good evening, Dudden. Ah! you thought you had played me a fine trick, but you never did me a better turn in all your lives. When I found poor Daisy dead, I thought to myself, 'Well, her hide may fetch something;' and it did. Hides are worth their weight in gold in the market just now."

Hudden nudged Dudden, and Dudden winked at Hudden.

"Good evening, Donald O'Neary."

"Good evening, kind friends."

The next day there wasn't a cow or a calf that belonged to Hudden or Dudden but her hide was going to the fair in Hudden's biggest cart drawn by Dudden's strongest pair of horses.

When they came to the fair, each one took a hide over his arm, and they were walking through the fair, bawling out at the top of their voices: "Hides to sell! hides to sell!"

Out came the tanner:

"How much for your hides, my good men?"

"Their weight in gold."

"It's early in the day to come out of the tav-

ern." That was all the tanner said, and back he went to his yard.

"Hides to sell! Fine fresh hides to sell!"

Out came the cobbler.

"How much for your hides, my men?"

"Their weight in gold."

"It is making game of me you are! Take that for your pains," and the cobbler dealt Hudden a blow that made him stagger.

Up the people came running from one end of the fair to the other. "What's the matter? What's the matter?" cried they.

"Here are a couple of vagabonds selling hides at their weight in gold," said the cobbler.

"Hold 'em fast; hold 'em fast!" bawled the innkeeper, who was the last to come up, he was so fat. "I'll wager it's one of the rogues who tricked me out of thirty gold pieces yesterday for a wretched hide."

It was more kicks than halfpence that Hudden and Dudden got before they were well on their way home again, and they didn't run the slower because all the dogs of the town were at their heels.

Well, as you may fancy, if they loved Donald little before, they loved him less now.

"What's the matter, friends!" said he, as he saw them tearing along, their hats knocked in, and their coats torn off, and their faces black and blue. "Is it fighting you've been? or mayhap you met the police, ill luck to them?"

"We'll police you, you vagabond. It's mighty smart you thought yourself, deluding us with your lying tales."

"Who deluded you? Didn't you see the gold with your own two eyes?"

But it was no use talking. Pay for it he must, and should. There was a meal-sack handy, and into it Hudden and Dudden popped Donald O'Neary, tied him up tight, ran a pole through the knot, and off they started for the Brown Lake of the Bog, each with a pole-end on his shoulder, and Donald O'Neary between.

But the Brown Lake was far, the road was dusty, Hudden and Dudden were sore and weary, and parched with thirst. There was an inn by the roadside.

"Let's go in," said Hudden; "I'm dead beat. It's heavy he is for the little he had to eat."

If Hudden was willing, so was Dudden. As for

Donald, you may be sure his leave wasn't asked, but he was lumped down at the inn door for all the world as if he had been a sack of potatoes.

"Sit still, you vagabond," said Dudden; "if we don't mind waiting, you needn't."

Donald held his peace, but after a while he heard the glasses clink, and Hudden singing away at the top of his voice.

"I won't have her, I tell you; I won't have her!" said Donald. But nobody heeded what he said.

"I won't have her, I tell you; I won't have her!" said Donald, and this time he said it louder; but nobody heeded what he said.

"I won't have her, I tell you; I won't have her!" said Donald; and this time he said it as loud as he could.

"And who won't you have, may I be so bold as to ask?" said a farmer, who had just come up with a drove of cattle, and was turning in for a glass.

"It's the king's daughter. They are bothering the life out of me to marry her."

"You're the lucky fellow. I'd give something to be in your shoes."

"Do you see that now! Wouldn't it be a fine thing for a farmer to be marrying a princess, all dressed in gold and jewels?"

"Jewels, do you say? Ah, now, couldn't you take me with you?"

"Well, you're an honest fellow, and as I don't care for the king's daughter, though she's as beautiful as the day, and is covered with jewels from top to toe, you shall have her. Just undo the cord, and let me out; they tied me up tight, as they knew I'd run away from her."

Out crawled Donald; in crept the farmer.

"Now lie still, and don't mind the shaking; it's only rumbling over the palace steps you'll be. And maybe they'll abuse you for a vagabond, who won't have the king's daughter; but you needn't mind that. Ah! it's a deal I'm giving up for you, sure as it is that I don't care for the princess."

"Take my cattle in exchange," said the farmer; and you may guess it wasn't long before Donald was at their tails driving them homeward.

Out came Hudden and Dudden, and the one took one end of the pole, and the other took the other.

"I'm thinking he's heavier," said Hudden.

"Ah, never mind," said Dudden; "it's only a step now to the Brown Lake."

"I'll have her now! I'll have her now!" bawled the farmer, from inside the sack.

"By my faith, and you shall though," said Hudden, and he laid his stick across the sack.

"I'll have her! I'll have her!" bawled the farmer, louder than ever.

"Well, here you are," said Dudden, for they were now come to the Brown Lake, and, unslinging the sack, they pitched it plump into the lake.

"You'll not be playing your tricks on us any longer," said Hudden.

"True for you," said Dudden. "Ah, Donald, my boy, it was an ill day when you borrowed my scales."

Off they went, with a light step and an easy heart, but when they were near home, who should they see but Donald O'Neary, and all around him the cows were grazing, and the calves were kicking up their heels, and butting their heads together.

"Is it you, Donald?" said Dudden. "Faith, you've been quicker than we have."

"True for you, Dudden, and let me thank you kindly; the turn was good, if the will was ill. You'll have heard, like me, that the Brown Lake leads to the Land of Promise. I always put it down as lies, but it is just as true as my word. Look at the cattle."

Hudden stared and Dudden gaped; but they couldn't get over the cattle; fine fat cattle they were, too.

"It's only the worst I could bring up with me," said Donald O'Neary; "the others were so fat there was no driving them. Faith, too, it's little wonder they didn't care to leave, with grass as far as you could see, and as sweet and juicy as fresh butter."

"Ah, now, Donald, we haven't always been friends," said Dudden, "but, as I was just saying, you were ever a decent lad, and you'll show us the way, won't you?"

"I don't see that I'm called upon to do that; there is a power more cattle down there. Why shouldn't I have them all to myself?"

"Faith, they may well say, the richer you get, the harder the heart. You always were a neighborly lad, Donald. You wouldn't wish to keep the luck all to yourself?"

"True for you, Hudden, though 'tis a bad example you set me. But I'll not be thinking of old times. There is plenty for all there; so come along with me."

Off they trudged, with a light heart and an eager step. When they came to the Brown Lake the sky was full of little white clouds, and, if the sky was full, the lake was as full.

"Ah! now, look, there they are," cried Donald, as he pointed to the clouds in the lake.

"Where? where?" cried Hudden, and "Don't be greedy!" cried Dudden, as he jumped his hardest to be up first with the fat cattle. But if he jumped first, Hudden wasn't long behind.

They never came back. Maybe they got too fat, like the cattle. As for Donald O'Neary, he had cattle and sheep all his days to his heart's content.

MASTER AND MAN / Armenia

Babette Deutsch
Avrahm Yarmolinsky

This tale must have been used to show what can happen to those who try to take unfair advantage of others. The inclusion of a moral makes its instructive purpose plain: "Don't dig a pit for another, lest you fall into it yourself." The master's cleverness brings him success until he meets a more intelligent man, the younger son in true folktale tradition.

Like many tales of trickery the audience's primary interest is in the clever methods used to make the master lose his temper.

Once upon a time there were two brothers who lived together. They were very poor. The elder brother decided to mend matters.

"I am going to hire myself out as a farm hand," he said to the younger brother. "You stay here and take care of things at home. When I have earned my wages I will bring them back with me, and we shall live well."

And so it was arranged. The younger brother stayed behind to look after their little house. The elder went off and hired himself out to a rich farmer.

It was agreed between him and his master that he should work until the following spring, then he should receive his wages and would be free to leave. But the master set one condition.

"If one of us should lose his temper before spring comes," said the master, "he must pay a fine. If you get angry, you pay me a thousand silver coins. If I get angry, I pay you a thousand."

"Where would a poor fellow like me get so much money?" asked the elder brother.

"Don't worry about that. You can earn it by working for me ten more years."

At first the elder brother wanted to refuse. But then he thought it over and decided to accept the condition. "No matter what happens," he said to himself, "I shall keep my temper. And if the master gets angry, why, then he will have to pay me a thousand silver coins. That is a fine sum! What couldn't my brother and I do with a thousand silver coins!" So he agreed, and the two shook hands on it.

Early next morning the rich farmer sent his new hired man out into the field.

"Go out with your scythe," he said, "and work as long as it is light."

The field hand worked hard the whole day. He was heartily glad when dusk fell and he could return to the farmhouse to rest. But when he got there the farmer asked him:

"Why have you come back?"

"And why not?" asked the field hand. "You told me to work as long as it was light. But now the sun has set."

"Oh, no, this won't do at all," said the farmer. "I did indeed tell you to work as long as there was light. But if the sun has set, his sister, the moon, has risen. You must work by moonlight."

"Am I to have no rest at all?" asked the field hand, astonished.

"Are you getting angry?" the farmer wanted to know.

"Not at all," said the field hand quickly. "But I am very tired."

He was hardly able to move, but he remembered the agreement, and he went back to the field. He worked all night, until the moon set. But the moon had no sooner left the sky than the sun rose. The man could bear it no longer. He dropped to the ground, worn out.

"A curse on your field, your crops, and your money!" he gasped.

The words were barely out of his mouth when the farmer appeared, as if by magic.

"I see you have lost your temper," he said. "You remember our agreement. Either you pay me a thousand silver coins or you work for me ten more years."

The field hand did not know what to do. He had no money with which to pay the fine. But how could he undertake to work ten years for such a slave driver? At last he told the farmer that he would pay him the money as soon as he had earned it elsewhere. It was hard to make the farmer agree to this. But at last he let the poor man go to earn the sum by working in another place.

Tired, discouraged, empty-handed, the poor man returned home.

"How did you make out?" asked the younger brother.

The elder told him the whole story.

"What's to be done?" he asked, when he had finished. "Where shall I earn a thousand silver coins? And if I don't give the farmer the money soon, he will have me punished for not paying my debt."

"Don't take it to heart," said the younger brother. "You stay here and look after the house. I will go and hire myself out. I am young and strong. I can soon earn a good sum."

So the younger brother went off and hired himself out to the same rich farmer. The farmer wanted to set the same condition. If he lost his temper, he would pay the field hand a thousand silver coins and release him. If the field hand lost his temper, he would pay the farmer a thousand silver coins or work for ten years without wages.

"No," said the younger brother. "The sum is not large enough. If you get angry, you pay me two thousand silver coins. And the same holds for me, or I'll work twenty years without wages."

"That suits me capitally," said the rich, greedy farmer.

And so the younger brother entered his service.

When the sun rose early the next morning the young field hand was still asleep.

"Get up!" cried the farmer, prodding him. "It will be midday before you know it, and here you are still lying abed!"

"What's the matter?" asked the field hand, rubbing his eyes. "Are you angry at me?"

"Not at all," said the farmer hastily. "I only wanted to tell you that it's time to go out into the field and get in the crop."

"All right," drawled the field hand, yawning, and he got up, ever so slowly, and slowly began to draw on his clothes.

"Hurry, man, hurry! It's late!" cried the farmer.

"You're not angry, are you?" asked the field hand.

"No, no, I just want to remind you of the hour," said the farmer.

"That's all right, then. Only be sure to remember our agreement," said the field hand.

He dawdled so that it was nearly noon before he was ready to go out to the field.

"Is it worth while starting work now?" he asked the farmer. "You see, people are eating dinner at this hour. Let's sit down and have our dinner properly, too."

The farmer bit his lip with vexation, but he agreed, and they made a good meal. After dinner, as they were setting out for the field, the hired man turned to the farmer with a yawn.

"We are working people," he said. "It is only right that we should take a nap after dinner. Then we'll have more strength with which to work."

With that he lay down under a shady tree, fell asleep, and slept till evening.

"This is too much!" cried the farmer. He strode over to the field hand and shook him by the arm. "In heaven's name, wake up! Here it is already dusk and not a stroke of work have your done!"

"You're really angry with me, eh?" said the field hand sleepily.

"No, no. I'm not at all angry," replied the farmer, remembering his agreement. "I just wanted to tell you that it's getting dark and it's time to go home."

"Very well," said the field hand pleasantly, and returned to the house with his master.

When they reached the farmhouse, the farmer found a guest waiting for him. So he sent the hired man out to butcher a sheep, that he might prepare a feast for his guest.

"Which sheep shall I butcher?" asked the hired man.

"Any that comes your way," answered the farmer hastily. He was happy to think that he was getting some work out of the man at last.

The hired man went off, and the farmer sat down with his guest for a good talk. Time passed, and the hired man did not return. The farmer began to grow uneasy. Suddenly he heard a clamor in the yard. It was crowded with neighbors; they were making a great to-do.

"Your hired man has lost his mind!" they cried. "He is butchering one sheep after another!"

The farmer rushed out to the sheep pen and saw that in truth the hired man had slaughtered the whole flock.

"What have you done, you good-for-nothing?" shouted the farmer. "Devil take you!"

"I only did what you ordered," answered the hired man quietly. "You told me to butcher any

sheep that came my way. But you see, when one sheep came my way, all the rest followed. So I had to butcher them all. It's a pity, because now you are really angry."

"No, no!" insisted the farmer. "I'm not angry. I'm only sorry to see that you've done away with the whole flock."

"Oh, if you are not angry, I'll keep my part of the bargain and go on working for you until spring," said the hired man.

The farmer did not know whether to be glad or sorry about this. Indeed, during the next few months the hired man nearly drove him to despair. It was understood that they were to part in the spring as soon as they heard the first call of the cuckoo. But spring was still far off and the call of the cuckoo would not be heard for a long time. Finally the farmer thought up a scheme that would rid him of his unwanted helper.

He took his wife to the woods, had her climb a tree, and told her that as soon as she saw him again she should give the call of the cuckoo. Then he went home and told the hired man to fetch his gun: they were going hunting.

No sooner had they entered the woods than the farmer's wife saw them coming and began to call:

"Cuckoo, cuckoo, cuckoo!"

"Congratulations!" said the farmer. "The cuckoo is calling. That means your time is up."

But the hired man protested.

"Impossible!" he said. "A cuckoo calling in winter! I must fetch that bird down with a shot and see what sort it is."

He raised his rifle and took aim at the top of the tree where the farmer's wife was perched.

"Stop!" cried the farmer.

"I must shoot," insisted the man.

"Devil take you!" cried the farmer. "Will you never do what I want!"

"Ah, now you've lost your temper for fair," said the hired man.

"Temper or no temper, be off with you!" shouted the farmer.

"Gladly," answered the hired man. "But first you must give me the two thousand silver coins you promised me if you got angry before my time was up."

"Take your two thousand and get out," said

the farmer. "Now I understand the saying: 'Don't dig a pit for another, lest you fall into it yourself.'"

So the younger brother got the two thousand silver coins and took them home. What cheer there was then in the little house! The elder brother was able to pay his debt to the greedy farmer, and the brothers still had a thousand silver coins on which to live happily for many a long day.

THE PEASANT AND THE DEVIL / Germany

The Grimm Brothers

Many tales are told about deceptive crop divisions. Sometimes the objects are pigs, with the trickster taking all the ones with curly tails and the dupe all those whose tails are straight. Whether told about people, animals, or as in this tale, a man and the devil, these anecdotes are about cleverness and stupidity.

The devil in this tale is not related to the Biblical Satan. In most German tales he is little more than a stupid ogre.

There was once upon a time a peasant who had been working in his field, and as twilight had set in, he was making ready for the journey home, when he saw a heap of burning coals in the middle of his field, and when, full of astonishment, he went up to it, a little black devil was sitting on the live coals.

"Do you sit upon a treasure?" inquired the peasant.

"Yes, in trust," replied the Devil, "on a treasure which contains more gold and silver than you have ever seen in your life!"

"The treasure lies in my field and belongs to me," said the peasant.

"It is yours," answered the Devil, "if you will for two years give me the half of everything your field produces. Money I have enough of, but I have a desire for the fruits of the earth."

The peasant agreed to the bargain.

"In order, however, that no dispute may arise about the division," said he, "everything that is above ground shall belong to you, and what is under the earth to me."

The Devil was quite satisfied with that, but the cunning peasant had sown turnips. Now when the time for harvest came, the Devil appeared and wanted to take away his crop; but he found nothing but the yellow withered leaves, while the peasant, quite pleased, was digging up his turnips.

"You have had the best of it for once," said the Devil, "but the next time that won't do. What grows above ground shall be yours, and what is under it, mine."

"I am willing," replied the peasant. When, however, the time came to sow, the peasant did not again sow turnips, but wheat.

The grain became ripe, and the peasant went into the field and cut the full stalks down to the ground. When the Devil came, he found nothing but the stubble, and went away in a fury down into a cleft in the rocks.

"That is the way to cheat the Devil," said the peasant, and went and fetched away the treasure.

MICHAEL SCOTT AND THE DEMON / Scotland

Sorche Nic Leodhas

This demon, unlike the devil in the preceding anecdote, is related to Satan and yet there is no sense of danger in this humorous tale. The demon's only deeds are acts of michief—overturning pots and making the fire smoke. However, he is proud and, as folktales show, the proud must be humbled.

There was a man and his name was Michael Scott and he was a wizard. He had the knowledge on him of black magic and white magic and the whole of the shades between and he was a great man entirely.

This same Michael Scott it was who stopped the plague, when it got to Scotland, by gathering a lot of it up into his bag and shutting it tight within. As the plague was the De'il's own work, he put the bag where the De'il would not be getting at it to let it loose again. And that was in a vault at Glenluce Abbey in Galloway where the De'il would not be liking to go, it being too holy a place for the likes of him.

That put the De'il against Michael Scott, so he sent one of his demons to be troubling him at his work.

It was just the sort of a job for the demon, he being young and full of mischief. So Michael Scott had a terrible time of it after the demon came. What with his pots being o'erturned, his cauldron boiling over, his fire smoking, and one thing and another, he'd have had less time wasted if he had just sat with his hands folded.

It was beyond bearing! So Michael Scott set his mind to mend matters, so that he could go on with his magic arts in peace.

First, he tried to catch the demon, but that one was too nimble and couldn't be caught. Then he tried to set a spell on him, but spells only seemed to make the demon livelier. So at last

Michael Scott had the idea of trying to make a bargain with him.

One day, when the demon was hopping around doing whatever mischief he could, Michael Scott said to him, "Och, now, 'tis weary work this must be for you what with all the flitting around you've got to do. Sit ye down and rest yourself for a while and let's have a gab together."

"Och, I'm not weary at all," the demon said. "It suits me fine to be busy." But being willing to oblige Michael, he perched himself on the edge of the hob, anyway.

"I can see that fine," said Michael Scott. "But can you not go and be busy elsewhere?"

"That I cannot," said the demon, "because my master has sent me to attend to you."

" 'Tis sad," said Michael Scott. "Such a wearying job for a braw young lad like yourself. Is there no way you could be getting out of it?"

"There is not," said the demon cheerfully. "But it suits me fine, anyway."

"Och, aye," said Michael Scott. "But that is for now whilst it's all new to you. However, I'm none so old and 'tis likely I'll live long. The heart of me aches to think of the long weary years you have ahead of you. It does indeed!"

The demon stopped looking so cheerful. "That may be so," said he, "but nevertheless I must just make the best of it."

"Aye," sighed Michael Scott. "So you must. And there's no way at all that you could be rid of the job?"

"None," said the demon, sighing, too, in spite of himself. "Barring one."

"And what would that one be?" Michael asked kindly, taking care not to seem too interested and eager.

"Well, if you could be setting me a task that was too much for me so I'd not be able to do it," the demon told him. Then he laughed, and added, "Never fear! That you ne'er could do."

"Well, 'tis worth trying," said Michael Scott. "We could make sort of a game of it. 'Twould be a change for us both and make time pass quicker."

Well, the demon could see the sense of that. He'd been overturning pots and smothering fires and the like for a fortnight past. It was a bit monotonous, if you came to look at it straight. And it could get more so as years went by. He would like a change himself for a bit of diversion.

"Give us a task then!" he said with a chuckle, being terribly sure of himself.

Michael Scott thought for a minute or two. Then he said, "River Tweed does need a cauld to it up by Kelso Town. No man's ever been able to build one, for the water there runs too fast and deep. Would you like to be taking that in hand?"

"I will so!" said the demon, and off he went.

Michael Scott had one night to work in peace, but no more than that. The next morn, in came the demon very full of himself with his chest stuck out and a grin on his face that stretched from ear to ear.

" 'Tis done!" said he, putting a foot on the fire to set it smoking, and o'erturning a pot or two.

"Is it now?" said Michael Scott, hiding his disappointment as well as he could. "Och! 'Tis something harder I should have asked you to do, for I'd have been able to do that myself."

"Have another try!" said the demon, laughing at him.

"That I will," said Michael Scott. "You'll be knowing Ercildoune Hill where it sets in the plain like a big sugar loaf? Well then! Break it up and make three hills of it, if you can."

"I'll be at it at once!" the demon said. "I'll be finding it easier far than last night's work."

So Michael Scott had another night's peace. He did no work in it but he set his wits to work for him. He sat in his chair and thought and thought and thought. He misdoubted that the demon would be back on the morrow's morn, and

he wanted to be ready with a task that would free him from the demon for good and all.

Well, back the demon came the next morning, and the grin on his face was wide enough to near split his head in two.

" 'Twas no trouble at all," he told Michael Scott gleefully. "I'd have been back long ere this, did I not stop to hear the commotion of the people to see three hills this morn where only one was the night before. 'Tis sore befuddled and bemazed they are, to be sure!" And he screeched with laughter at the memory.

"I'm hoping you'll have something as easy and entertaining for me to do next," he told Michael Scott.

"Och," said Michael Scott, putting on a doleful air. "I fear you are too much for me. 'Tis past believing the wonders you can bring about. I'm just at the point of giving it all up."

"Och, come now," said the demon kindly. "Give it another try, anyway." He looked pleased at the praise Michael had given him.

"Happen 'tis too trifling a task for a lad with powers like your own," Michael Scott said reluctantly.

"Nay! Nay!" said the demon. "Tell me then. I'll not be offended."

"Well then," said Michael hesitating-like, " 'Tis not much, but I'd like it fine if you'd go down by the sea and make me a few fathom of rope from the sand on the shore there."

"I will so!" cried the demon happily. "And be back in time for my tea. 'Tis the softest task of them all!"

So off he went and left Michael Scott with a promise that he'd not be long gone.

But he never came back again. For Michael's last bidding had stumped him entirely. To this very day the demon is still there by the sea trying to make ropes of sand, and all in vain.

When the wind blows high and the waves beat the shore, if you listen you'll hear him whispering, "R-r-r-r-ropes of s-s-s-s-sand! R-r-r-r-ropes of s-s-s-s-sand!" as he works away at the task he ne'er can do.

So Michael Scott had peace at his magic for all the rest of his days. Even the De'il himself did not bother him any more, for he was afraid if he did, Michael Scott would get the best of him, too.

THE TRANSFORMED DONKEY / England

Carl Withers

This anecdote illustrates the relationship between literary and oral folk traditions. Stith Thompson in The Folktale *reports it originated as an Oriental literary tale but is now told throughout Europe. It also illustrates how the ethics of tales of trickery differ from ethics in wonder tales.*

Three or four mischievous Oxford scholars, walking one day near Abingdon, saw a man asleep in a ditch, holding by the bridle a donkey loaded with earthen crockery.

"Help me," said one to the rest, "and I'll get us a little money! We'll sell this donkey at Abingdon Fair. Shift the donkey's baskets onto my back and put the bridle over my head. Then lead the donkey away and sell it, and leave me with the old man."

This was done and in a little while the man awoke and was surprised to see his donkey thus changed.

"Oh!" pleaded the scholar, "take this bridle out of my mouth and this load from my back!"

"Heavens! how came you here?" asked the astonished old man.

"Why," said the scholar, "my father is a great magician, and at something I did which displeased him he turned me into a donkey. But now his heart has relented and I have returned to my own shape again. I beg you to let me go home and thank him."

"By all means," said the crockery merchant. "I want nothing to do with conjuration!" So he set the scholar at liberty, who went directly to his fellows. By this time they were making merry with the money they had sold the donkey for.

The next day the old man went to the fair to look for a new donkey, and after he had seen several others, he saw his own. It was shown to him as a very good one.

"Oh, no!" said he. "Have he and his father quarreled again already! No, no, I'll have nothing to do with him."

HOW TILL BECAME PAINTER TO THE EARL OF HESSE/Germany

Godfrey Freeman

Till Eulenspiegel (pronounced oil-en-shpee-gel) is as clever a trickster as can be found in all folklore, and it is a shame he is not better known by North American children. The following tale was the source for Hans Christian Andersen's "The Emperor's New Clothes," which is the next story in this

*section. A comparison of the two tales will offer many insights on how folk
and literary tales differ and how an artist can create an original story even
when drawing from an existing narrative.*

Till's adventures at last forced him to leave the land of Saxony for a while, for he had become too well known there and he felt that the people had seen enough of him for the time being. At length chance brought him to the land of Hesse, and soon he made his way to the court of the earl in Marburg. The earl at once asked him his business, and Till, remembering that somewhere in his baggage were a few old Flemish pictures, replied that he was a painter, and, what was more, that he could paint pictures of a magical kind.

Now it so happened that the earl of Hesse was much interested in alchemy, that is, a sort of old-fashioned mixture of magic and chemistry, and as soon as he heard Till speak of magic, he was overjoyed and at once invited him to come and paint for him. "But," he said thoughtfully, "I should like first to see some examples of your work."

Till carelessly dropped a few of the Flemish paintings onto the table and shrugged his shoulders modestly. "Of course," he said, "these are not the best I can do. They are only a few samples that I have painted for practice."

The earl stared at the masterpieces and his mouth fell open in astonishment. "My good fellow," he exclaimed, "if these are only rough practice pieces, what must your magical ones be like?"

"What indeed!" replied Till with pride. "I can promise you faithfully that you have never seen the like of them before—nor indeed will ever see the like of them again."

"Excellent!" cried the earl, rubbing his hands together in glee. "And magical, too, eh? You shall start work for me this every day. Tell me, what is your fee?"

"Four hundred guilders," answered Till, for he thought, "The earl is a rich man, and if I ask for less, he will think the less of me."

"Done!" said the earl at once, and felt that he was getting a really good bargain. And he gave

Till a hundred guilders in advance to buy any special paints or brushes he might need.

Till lost no time in settling down in the earl's court and chose for his place of work a long passage with a door at either end. By special arrangement he kept both doors locked so that he would not be disturbed, and he persuaded the earl, who was a ready believer in magic of any kind, that if anyone besides Till himself should open the doors, the magic spell would be broken forever.

For nearly a month Till lived in ease and luxury, ordering whatever food or drink he might fancy and rising or sleeping whenever he chose. At last the earl grew impatient and called Till to speak with him in front of all the nobles. "Ah, my good master painter," he cried, "we are all full of eagerness to see your work. I pray you to lift the magic spell and let us come and see your paintings."

"As your Grace wishes," replied Till, bowing deeply, "but there is one thing of which I must warn you. The paintings are, as you know, of a magical nature. If any of your courtiers are not born of noble families, then I very much regret that, however hard they try, they will see nothing of the pictures I have completed."

The earl was delighted. "Marvelous! Marvelous!" he exclaimed. "This is better than any of us could have expected—eh my friends?" and although several of the courtiers began to feel uneasy, they all nodded and smiled in agreement.

Till led them all to the passage, muttered a few words of magic, and then flung open the door.

All down the length of one wall he had hung a long linen cloth like a curtain. This he now drew aside, and picking up a long paintbrush, he pointed to the wall.

"Your Grace," he began with a bow, "gentlemen; here we have the first earl of Hesse, who later became emperor. And this," he continued, "is his lady wife, daughter of Justinian the Mild, and herself an archduchess of Bavaria. Next to Her," he went on, moving slowly along the wall

"How Till Became Painter to the Earl of Hesse," from *The Owl and the Mirror* by Godfrey Freeman. By permission of Basil Blackwell & Mott, Ltd.

as he spoke, "stands Adolfus the Mighty, and there you can just see his little son William the Black. Just along here is Ludwig the Pious, and if you look carefully, Your Grace, you can follow the whole family tree down to your noble self, standing at the end of the line.

"Well, gentleman," finished Till, "I am a humble man, but I think I can say that these paintings are unlike anything you have ever seen before, and that the colors, especially, are of—shall we say?—an unusual beauty."

The earl strained his eyes as Till talked, but for all his pains he could see nothing but a blank white wall. "But if I admit that," he thought, "I shall be disgraced forever in front of all my courtiers," so he spoke instead in a loud voice. "Good master painter," he said, "your work does indeed satisfy all of us. If there is any fault, it is ours, that we do not have the wisdom to understand your paintings properly." With these words he left hurriedly and went off to find his wife.

The countess was waiting to hear news of the pictures and she asked her husband what he thought of them. "Tell me," she asked, "what is his work really like? I myself have begun to fear trickery."

"Have no fear," replied the earl uncomfortably. "His work is excellent and I am well satisfied."

"I am very glad to hear it," said the countess, "and may I now be allowed to see it?"

"Certainly, certainly," answered the earl, for he could think of no way of stopping her that would not make her suspicious, "but of course you must ask the painter first, or the magic spell will be broken."

Without further delay the countess made her way to Till's picture gallery, taking eight of her maidservants with her, and soon she was listening to the same explanation of the magic and of how it was impossible for anyone not of noble birth to see the pictures at all. Till drew back his cloth as

before and once again recited the names of the ancestors whose portraits were supposed to be painted on the wall. The women, however, kept silent, neither praising nor finding fault, until suddenly one of the maidservants began to cry. "Oh, master painter," she sobbed, "it is true, it is true. I am an orphan and can see nothing on the wall. It is plain that my dear father and mother cannot have been of noble birth."

This upset Till greatly, for it was never his wish to hurt the truly innocent, and moreover he was in danger of being found out before he could escape. To his great relief, all the women swept out silently in a body, and as soon as night had fallen Till collected together his belongings and made off in the darkness with what few guilders were left to him.

In the meantime, however, the earl had made up his mind to put his whole court to the test, and the next morning all those who had not already seen the paintings were herded together in Till's picture gallery. "Now," called the earl, when they had all arrived, "if anyone here can see a picture on the wall—say so at once!"

There was silence for a full two minutes, and then the earl spoke again. "So!" he exclaimed, his rage growing as he uttered the words. "It is clear to me now that we have been outrageously cheated by that rogue and villain Eulenspiegel!" and he went off in a black fury to send his soldiers in search of Till. The poor fellows searched for two whole days, but whenever they mentioned to passers-by that they were hunting for Eulenspiegel, the only answers they received were hoots of laughter.

For long after that, the courtiers used to jeer at each other for not daring to speak the truth; all of them, that is, except the little orphan maid servant. And she, it is strange to say, was often seen smiling to herself after that, though nobody could ever guess exactly why.

THE EMPEROR'S NEW CLOTHES/Denmark

Hans Christian Andersen

Hans Christian Andersen's stories reveal he had a poor opinion of man's nature. His narratives lack the sense of tolerant humor common to many tales of trickery. There is no satisfaction in the human imagination and wit, such as is present in "The Clever Lad from Skye," or innocent pleasure that the proud have been tripped up, as in "Michael Scott and the Demon." Andersen treats both the dupe and his deceivers with disdain. Although this is true of "The Emperor's New Clothes," it is one of the few tales written by Andersen appropriate for children.

Many years ago there was an Emperor who was so excessively fond of new clothes that he spent all his money on them. He cared nothing about his soldiers, nor for the theater, nor for driving in the woods except for the sake of showing off his new clothes. He had a costume for every hour in the day. Instead of saying as one does about any other king or emperor, "He is in his council chamber," the people here always said "The Emperor is in his dressing room."

Life was very gay in the great town where he lived. Hosts of strangers came to visit it every day, and among them one day were two swindlers. They gave themselves out as weavers and said that they knew how to weave the most beautiful fabrics imaginable. Not only were the colors and patterns unusually fine, but the clothes that were made of this cloth had the peculiar quality of becoming invisible to every person who was not fit for the office he held, or who was impossibly dull.

"Those must be splendid clothes," thought the Emperor. "By wearing them I should be able to discover which men in my kingdom are unfitted for their posts. I shall distinguish the wise men from the fools. Yes, I certainly must order some of that stuff to be woven for me."

The Emperor paid the two swindlers a lot of money in advance, so that they might begin their work at once.

They did put up two looms and pretended to weave, but they had nothing whatever upon their shuttles. At the outset they asked for a quantity of the finest silk and the purest gold thread, all of which they put into their own bags while they worked away at the empty looms far into the night.

"I should like to know how those weavers are getting on with their cloth," thought the Emperor, but he felt a little queer when he reflected that anyone who was stupid or unfit for his post would not be able to see it. He certainly thought that he need have no fears for himself, but still he thought he would send somebody else first to see how it was getting on. Everybody in the town knew what wonderful power the stuff possessed, and everyone was anxious to see how stupid his neighbor was.

"I will send my faithful old minister to the weavers," thought the Emperor. "He will be best able to see how the stuff looks, for he is a clever man and no one fulfills his duties better than he does."

So the good old minister went into the room where the two swindlers sat working at the empty loom.

"Heaven help us," thought the old minister, opening his eyes very wide. "Why, I can't see a thing!" But he took care not to say so.

Both the swindlers begged him to be good

"The Emperor's New Clothes," from *Andersen's Fairy Tales* by Hans Christian Andersen, translated by Mrs. E. V. Lucas. Everyman's Library text. Reprinted by permission of J. M. Dent & Sons, Ltd.

enough to step a little nearer, and asked if he did not think it a good pattern and beautiful coloring. They pointed to the empty loom. The poor old minister stared as hard as he could, but he could not see anything, for of course there was nothing to see.

"Good heavens," thought he. "Is it possible that I am a fool? I have never thought so, and nobody must know it. Am I not fit for my post? It will never do to say that I cannot see the stuff."

"Well, sir, you don't say anything about the stuff," said the one who was pretending to weave.

"Oh, it is beautiful—quite charming," said the minister, looking through his spectacles. "Such a pattern and such colors! I will certainly tell the Emperor that the stuff pleases me very much."

"We are delighted to hear you say so," said the swindlers, and then they named all the colors and described the peculiar pattern. The old minister paid great attention to what they said, so as to be able to repeat it when he got home to the Emeror.

Then the swindlers went on to demand more money, more silk, and more gold, to be able to proceed with the weaving. But they put it all into their own pockets. Not a single strand was ever put into the loom, but they went on as before, weaving at the empty loom.

The Emperor soon sent another faithful official to see how the stuff was getting on and if it would soon be ready. The same thing happened to him as to the minister. He looked and looked, but as there was only the empty loom, he could see nothing at all.

"Is not this a beautiful piece of stuff?" said both the swindlers, showing and explaining the beautiful pattern and colors which were not there to be seen.

"I know I am no fool," thought the man, "so it must be that I am unfit for my good post. It is very strange, though. However, one must not let it appear." So he praised the stuff he did not see, and assured them of his delight in the beautiful colors and the originality of the design.

"It is absolutely charming," he said to the Emperor. Everybody in the town was talking about this splendid stuff.

Now the Emperor thought he would like to see it while it was still on the loom. So, accompanied by a number of selected courtiers, among whom were the two faithful officials who had already seen the imaginary stuff, he went to visit the crafty impostors, who were working away as hard as ever they could at the empty loom.

"It is magnificent," said both the honest officials. "Only see, Your Majesty, what a design! What colors!" And they pointed to the empty loom, for they each thought no doubt the others could see the stuff.

"What?" thought the Emperor. "I see nothing at all. This is terrible! Am I a fool? Am I not fit to be Emperor? Why, nothing worse could happen to me!"

'Oh, it is beautiful," said the Emperor. "It has my highest approval." And he nodded his satisfaction as he gazed at the empty loom. Nothing would induce him to say that he could not see anything.

The whole suite gazed and gazed, but saw nothing more than the others. However, they all exclaimed with His Majesty, "It is very beautiful." And they advised him to wear a suit made of the wonderful cloth on the occasion of a great procession which was just about to take place. "Magnificent! Gorgeous! Excellent!" went from mouth to mouth. They were all equally delighted with it. The Emperor gave each of the rogues an order of knighthood to be worn in their buttonholes and the title of "Gentleman Weaver."

The swindlers sat up the whole night before the day on which the procession was to take place, burning sixteen candles, so that people might see how anxious they were to get the Emperor's new clothes ready. They pretended to take the stuff off the loom. They cut it out in the air with a huge pair of scissors, and they stitched away with needles without any thread in them.

At last they said, "Now the Emperor's new clothes are ready."

The Emperor with his grandest courtiers went to them himself, and both swindlers raised one arm in the air, as if they were holding something. They said, "See, these are the trousers. This is the coat. Here is the mantle," and so on. "It is as light as a spider's web. One might think one had nothing on, but that is the very beauty of it."

"Yes," said all the courtiers, but they could not see anything, for there was nothing to see.

"Will Your Imperial Majesty be graciously pleased to take off your clothes?" said the impostors. "Then we may put on the new ones, along here before the great mirror."

The Emperor took off all his clothes, and the impostors pretended to give him one article of dress after the other of the new ones which they had pretended to make. They pretended to fasten something around his waist and to tie on something. This was the train, and the Emperor turned round and round in front of the mirror.

"How well His Majesty looks in the new clothes! How becoming they are!" cried all the people round. "What a design, and what colors! They are most gorgeous robes."

"The canopy is waiting outside which is to be carried over Your Majesty in the procession," said the master of the ceremonies.

"Well, I am quite ready," said the Emperor. "Don't the clothes fit well?" Then he turned round again in front of the mirror, so that he should seem to be looking at his grand things.

The chamberlains who were to carry the train stooped and pretended to lift it from the ground with both hands, and they walked along with their hands in the air. They dared not let it appear that they could not see anything.

Then the Emperor walked along in the procession under the gorgeous canopy, and everybody in the streets and at the windows exclaimed, "How beautiful the Emperor's new clothes are! What a splendid train! And they fit to perfection!" Nobody would let it appear that he could see nothing, for then he would not be fit for his post, or else he was a fool.

None of the Emperor's clothes had been so successful before.

"But he has got nothing on," said a little child.

"Oh, listen to the innocent," said its father. And one person whispered to the other what the child had said. "He has nothing on—a child says he has nothing on!"

"But he has nothing on!" at last cried all the people.

The Emperor writhed, for he knew it was true. But he thought "The procession must go on now." So he held himself stiffer than ever, and the chamberlains held up the invisible train.

THE NIGHTINGALE/Denmark

Hans Christian Andersen

This is a moralistic tale difficult to classify. It is not a wonder tale; perhaps it is closest to the fable in intent. Because the Emperor of China is tricked by his lack of true values, it is placed in this section. Although Andersen's cynicism is revealed in his belief that men prefer mechanical objects which do man's bidding to live objects in nature, the gentle charm of this story makes it one of his most pleasant.

This story happened a good many years ago, but that's just why it's worthwhile to hear it, before it is forgotten.

The palace of the Emperor of China was the most splendid in the world; entirely and altogether made of porcelain, so costly, but so brittle,

"The Nightingale," reprinted with permission of The Macmillan Company from *Fairy Tales and Stories* by Hans Christian Anderson. Copyright 1921 by The Macmillan Company, renewed 1953 by The Macmillan Company.

so difficult to handle that one had to be terribly careful. In the garden were to be seen the strangest flowers. To the most splendid of them silver bells were tied, and the bells tinkled so that nobody could pass by without noticing the flowers.

The Emperor's garden extended so far that the gardener himself didn't know where the end was. If you went on and on, you came to the loveliest forest with high trees and deep lakes. The forest went right down to the sea, which was blue and deep. Tall ships could sail right in under the branches of the trees. In the trees lived a Nightingale. It sang so sweetly that even the poor fisherman, who had gone out at night to take up his nets, heard it and stopped to listen.

"How beautiful it is!" he said; but he had to attend to his business, and forgot the bird. But the next night when the bird sang again, and the fisherman heard it, he said again, "How beautiful it is!"

From all the countries of the world travelers came to the city of the Emperor, and admired it, and the palace, and the garden. But when they heard the Nightingale, they said, "That is the best of all!"

Travelers told about it when they went home. Learned men wrote many books about the city, the palace, and the garden, and they did not forget the Nightingale; that was placed highest of all. Those who were poets wrote poems about the Nightingale in the forest by the sea.

The books went through all the world, and a few of them came to the Emperor of China. He sat in his golden chair, and read, and read. Every moment he nodded his head, for it pleased him to read the splendid descriptions of the city, the palace, and the garden. "But the Nightingale is the best of all," it stood written there.

"What's that?" said the Emperor. "The Nightingale? I don't know that at all! Is there such a bird in my empire, and even in my own garden? I've never heard of it. I had to find it in a book!"

He called his cavalier.

"They tell me that we have here a highly remarkable bird called a Nightingale!" said the Emperor. "They say it is the best thing in all my great empire. Why haven't I ever been told about this?"

"I have never before heard anybody mention it," said the cavalier. "It has never been presented at court."

"I command that it shall appear this evening, and sing before me," said the Emperor. "It seems that all the world knows what I possess, except myself."

"I have never heard it mentioned," said the cavalier. "I will look for it. I will find it."

But where was it to be found? The cavalier ran up and down all the stairs, through halls and corridors, but no one among all those whom he met had ever heard of the Nightingale. And the cavalier ran back to the Emperor, and said that it must be a fable invented by the writers of books.

"Your Imperial Majesty mustn't believe the things people write!" he said.

"But the book in which I read this," said the Emperor, "was sent to me by the high and mighty Emperor of Japan, and therefore it cannot be a lie. I *will* hear the Nightingale! It must be here this evening! It has my imperial favor; and if it does not come, the whole court will be punched in the stomach after the court has eaten its supper!"

Again the cavalier ran up and down all the stairs, and through all the halls and corridors; and half the court ran with him, because they didn't want to be punched in the stomach.

Ever so many questions were asked about this remarkable Nightingale, which all the world knew excepting the people at court.

At last they met a poor little girl in the kitchen.

"The Nightingale?" she said. "I know it very well. Yes, it certainly can sing! Every evening I am allowed to carry my poor sick mother the scraps from the table. She lives down by the shore, and when I walk back and am tired, and rest in the wood, then I hear the Nightingale sing. The tears come into my eyes, and it is just as if my mother kissed me!"

"Little kitchen maid," said the cavalier, "I will get you a permanent appointment in the kitchen, with permission to see the Emperor dine, if you will lead us to the Nightingale, for it is announced for this evening."

So they all went out into the wood where the Nightingale usually sang; half the court went along. When they were in the midst of their journey a cow began to low.

"Oh," said all the court cavaliers, "there it is! That's really a remarkable power in so small a creature! I have certainly heard it before."

"No, those are cows lowing," said the little kitchen maid. "We are a long way from the place yet."

Now the frogs began to croak in the pool.

"Glorious!" said the cavalier. "Now I can hear it. It sounds just like little church bells."

"No, those are frogs," said the little kitchen maid. "But now I think we shall soon hear it."

And the Nightingale began to sing.

"That is it!" said the little girl. "Listen, listen! It's sitting there!"

And she pointed to a little gray bird up in the boughs.

"Is it possible?" said the cavalier. "I should never have thought it looked like that! How plain it is! I suppose it has lost its color at seeing so many aristocratic visitors."

"Little Nightingale!" called the little kitchen maid, quite loudly. "Our gracious Emperor would so like you to sing for him."

"With the greatest pleasure!" said the Nightingale, and began to sing most delightfully.

"It sounds just like glass bells!" said the cavalier. "And look at its little throat, how it's working! It's strange we've never heard it before. It will be a great success at court."

"Shall I sing once more for the Emperor?" asked the Nightingale, for it thought the Emperor was present.

"My excellent little Nightingale," said the cavalier, "I have great pleasure in inviting you to a court festival this evening, when you shall enchant His High and Imperial Majesty with your singing."

"My song sounds best in the green wood!" said the Nightingale. Still it came willingly when it heard that the Emperor wanted it.

In the palace everything was brightly lighted. The walls and the flooring, which were of porcelain, gleamed in the rays of thousands of golden lamps. The loveliest flowers, those that tinkled best, had been placed in the passages. There was a running to and fro, and a draught, and then all the bells rang so loudly that one could not hear oneself speak.

In the midst of the great hall, where the Emperor sat, a golden perch had been placed, on which the Nightingale was to sit. The whole court was there, and the little kitchen maid had been allowed to stand behind the door, as she had now received the title of Regular Cook. All the court was in full dress, and all looked at the little gray bird, to which the Emperor nodded.

And the Nightingale sang so beautifully that the tears came into the Emperor's eyes, and the tears ran down over his cheeks. Then the Nightingale sang still more sweetly, so that its song went straight to the heart. The Emperor was so much pleased that he said the Nightingale should have his golden slipper to wear around its neck. But the Nightingale thanked him and said it had already had reward enough.

"I have seen tears in the Emperor's eyes—there is no richer treasure for me. An Emperor's tears have a strange power. I am rewarded enough!" And then it sang again with its marvelously sweet voice.

"Isn't it too darling?" said the ladies who stood around. They took water in their mouths to gurgle when any one spoke to them; then they thought they were nightingales too. And the lackeys and chambermaids reported that they were satisfied too; and that was saying a good deal, for they are the most difficult to please. In short, the Nightingale was a real success.

It was now to remain at court, to have its own cage, with liberty to go out twice every day and once at night. Twelve servants came along when the Nightingale went out, each of whom had a silken string fastened to the bird's leg, which they held very tight. There was really no pleasure in an excursion of that kind.

The whole city spoke of the remarkable bird. When two people met, one said nothing but "Nightin," and the other said "gale"; and then they sighed, and understood one another. Eleven grocers' children were named after the bird, but not one of them could sing a note.

One day the Emperor received a large parcel, on which was written, "The Nightingale."

"Here we have a new book about this celebrated bird," said the Emperor.

But it was not a book. It was a little work of art, lying in a box—an artificial nightingale, which was supposed to look like the living one, but it was decorated with diamonds, rubies, and sapphires. When the artificial bird was wound up, it could sing one of the pieces that the real one sang, and then its tail moved up and down, and glittered with silver and gold. Round its neck hung a little ribbon, and on that was written, "The Emperor of Japan's nightingale is poor compared to that of the Emperor of China."

"Isn't that lovely?" they all said, and he who

had brought the artificial bird immediately received the title, Imperial Head-Nightingale-Bringer.

"Now they must sing together; what a duet that will be!"

And so they had to sing together; but it did not sound very well, for the real Nightingale sang in its own way, and the artificial bird sang a waltz.

"That's not its fault," said the music master. "It keeps perfect time and very much in my style."

Now the artificial bird was to sing alone. It made just as much of a hit as the real one, and then it was much handsomer to look at. It shone like bracelets and breast-pins.

Three and thirty times over it sang the same piece, still it was not tired. The people would gladly have heard it again, but the Emperor said that the living Nightingale ought to sing something now. But where was it? No one had noticed that it had flown away out of the open window, back to the green wood.

And all the courtiers scolded the Nightingale, and declared that it was a very ungrateful creature.

"We have the best bird, after all," they said.

So the artificial bird had to sing again, and that was the thirty-fourth time that they listened to the same piece, but still they didn't know it quite by heart, for it was so very difficult. The music master praised the bird very highly; yes, he declared that it was better than the real Nightingale, not only with regard to its plumage and the many beautiful diamonds, but inside as well.

"For you see, ladies and gentlemen, and above all, Your Imperial Majesty, with a real Nightingale one can never calculate what is coming, but in this artificial bird everything is settled. It is this way, and no other! One can explain it; one can open it and show where the music comes from and how it is made!"

"That's just what I was thinking," they all said.

The music master received permission to show the bird to the people on the next Sunday. The people were to hear it sing, too, the Emperor commanded. And they did hear it, and were so much pleased that they all said, "Oh!" and held up their forefingers and nodded.

But the poor fisherman who had heard the real Nightingale said, "It sounds pretty enough, but there's something missing; I don't know what it is."

The real Nightingale was banished from the country. The artificial bird had its place on a silken cushion close to the Emperor's bed. All the presents it had received, gold and precious stones, lay around it. The music master wrote a work of five and twenty volumes about the artificial bird. It was very learned and very long, and full of the most difficult words.

So a whole year went by. The Emperor, the court, and all the people knew every little gurgle in the artificial bird's song by heart. And that was just why they liked it; then they could sing it too, and they did. The street boys sang it, and the Emperor himself sang it too! Oh, it was certainly wonderful!

But one evening, when the artificial bird was singing its best, and the Emperor lay in bed listening to it, something inside the bird said, "Whizz!" Something cracked. "Whir-r!" All the wheels ran round, and then the music stopped.

The Emperor jumped out of bed right away and sent for his own doctor; but what could he do? Then they sent for a watchmaker, and after a good deal of talking and looking, the bird was put into something like order. But the watchmaker said that the bird must be carefully treated, for the pivots were worn, and it would be impossible to put his new ones in in such a manner that the music would go. There was great lamentation; only once in a year was it permitted to let the bird sing, and that was almost too much. But then the music master made a little speech, full of difficult words, and said it was just as good as before—and so of course it was as good as before.

Now five years had gone by, and a real grief came to the whole nation. The people did, after all, like their Emperor very much, and now he was ill, and the doctors said he couldn't live much longer. Already a new Emperor had been chosen, and the people stood out in the street and asked the cavalier how their old Emperor was.

He shook his head.

Cold and pale the Emperor lay in his big gorgeous bed. The whole court thought him dead, and each one ran to bow to the new Emperor. Everywhere, in all the halls and passages, cloth had been laid down so that no footstep could be heard, and therefore it was so still, so still. But the Emperor was not dead, though he lay still and pale on the gorgeous bed with the long velvet curtains and the heavy gold tassels. High up, a window stood open, and the moon shone in on the Emperor and the artificial bird.

The poor Emperor could scarcely breathe; it was just as if something sat on his chest. He opened his eyes, and then he saw that it was Death who sat on his chest, and had put on his golden crown, and held in one hand the Emperor's gold sword, and in the other his beautiful banner. And all around, from the folds of the big velvet bed curtains, strange heads peered forth; some ugly, others lovely and mild. These were all the Emperor's bad and good deeds looking at him.

"Do you remember this?" whispered one after the other, "Do you remember that?" And then they told him so much that the sweat ran from his forehead.

"I never knew that!" said the Emperor. "Music, music! The big drum!" he called. "So that I won't hear what they say!"

But they kept on.

"Music, music!" cried the Emperor. "My blessed little golden bird sing, sing! I have given you gold and costly presents; I have even hung my golden slipper around your neck. Sing, now, sing!"

But the bird stood still; no one was there to wind it up, and it couldn't sing without that.

Just then the loveliest song sounded close by the window. It was the little live Nightingale, that sat outside on a spray. It had heard of the Emperor's danger, and had come to sing to him of comfort and hope. And as it sang, the specters grew paler and paler; the blood ran quicker and quicker through the Emperor's weak body.

Even Death listened, and said, "Go on, little Nightingale, go on!"

"But will you give me that splendid golden sword? Will you give me that rich banner? Will you give me the Emperor's crown?" said the Nightingale.

And Death gave up each treasure for a song. The Nightingale sang on and on. Then Death felt a longing for the garden, and floated like a cold white mist out of the window.

"I thank you, thank you!" said the Emperor. "You heavenly little bird! I know you well. I drove you from my country, and yet you have sung away the evil faces from my bed, and taken Death from my heart! How can I reward you?"

"You have rewarded me!" said the Nightingale. "I have drawn tears from your eyes, when I sang the first time—I shall never forget that. Those are the jewels that do a singer's heart good. But now sleep and grow fresh and strong again. I will sing for you."

And it sang, and the Emperor fell into a sweet sleep. Ah, how mild and refreshing that sleep was! The sun shone on him through the windows when he woke up strong and well. Not one of his servants had come back yet, for they all thought he was dead; only the Nightingale still sat beside him and sang.

"You must always stay with me," said the Emperor. "You shall sing only when you please; and I'll break the artificial bird into a thousand pieces."

"Don't do that," said the Nightingale. "It did as well as it could; keep it as you have done till now. I cannot live in the palace, but let me come when I want to. Then I will sit in the evening on the branch there by the window, and sing you something, so that you may be glad and thoughtful at once. I will sing of those who are happy and of those who suffer. I will sing of the good and the evil that people hide from you. The little singing bird flies far around, to the poor fisherman, to the peasant's roof, to everyone who dwells far away from you and your court. I will come, I will sing to you—but one thing you must promise me."

"Everything!" said the Emperor; and he stood there in his imperial robes, which he had put on himself, and pressed the sword which was heavy with gold to his heart.

"One thing I beg of you," said the Nightingale, "tell no one that you have a little bird who tells you everything. Then things will be even better."

And the Nightingale flew away.

The servants came in to look at their dead Emperor, and—well, there they were, and the Emperor said, "Good morning!"

THE PRINCESS AND THE PEA/Denmark

Hans Christian Andersen

Hans Christian Andersen not only rewrote many traditional folktales but also utilized their form to express his personal philosophy. These original literary tales reveal great genius but few are suitable for children because Andersen's cynicism gives them a bitter quality. Most can be understood only by a mature mind.

"The Real Princess" is such a story. Andersen's sarcasm is not primarily against the Princess but against those who make such superficial judgments. This is not applicable or appropriate for children. Realism has a definite place in their literature, but not bitterness.

There was once a prince, and he wanted a princess, but then she must be a *real* princess. He travelled right round the world to find one, but there was always something wrong. There were plenty of princesses, but whether they were real princesses he had great difficulty in discovering; there was always something which was not quite right about them. So at last he had to come home again, and he was very sad because he wanted a real princess so badly.

One evening there was a terrible storm; it thundered and lightened and the rain poured down in torrents; indeed it was a fearful night.

In the middle of the storm somebody knocked at the town gate, and the old King himself went to open it.

It was a princess who stood outside, but she was in a terrible state from the rain and the storm. The water streamed out of her hair and her clothes, it ran in at the top of her shoes and

out at the heel, but she said that she was a real princess.

"Well, we shall soon see if that is true," thought the old Queen, but she said nothing. She went into the bedroom, took all the bedclothes off and laid a pea on the bedstead; then she took twenty mattresses and piled them on the top of the pea, and then twenty feather beds on the top of the mattresses. This was where the princess was to sleep that night. In the morning they asked her how she had slept.

"Oh, terribly badly!" said the princess. "I have hardly closed my eyes the whole night! Heaven knows what was in the bed. I seemed to be lying upon some hard thing, and my whole body is black and blue this morning. It is terrible!"

They saw at once that she must be a real princess when she had felt the pea through twenty mattresses and twenty feather beds. Nobody but a real princess could have such a delicate skin.

So the prince took her to be his wife, for now he was sure that he had found a real princess, and the pea was put into the Museum, where it may still be seen if no one has stolen it.

Now this is a true story.

"The Princess and the Pea" from *Fairy Tales* by Hans Christian Andersen, translated by Mrs. Edgar Lucas. Children's Illustrated Classics. Published by E. P. Dutton & Co., Inc. and J. M. Dent & Sons Ltd. and reprinted with their permission. 1899.

Animal Tales

The early tellers of tales did not make modern man's sharp distinction between the animal world and the world of men. Anthropomorphism, the endowing of human characteristics to nonhuman forms of life and inanimate objects, is common among prescientific groups. This is readily observable today among young children, who believe their pets have human feelings and thoughts.

The anthropomorphic view of life can explain the prominent role animals play in folklore. Although scientific reasoning recognizes the differences between animals and men, the convention of talking animals is still accepted in the old tales as well as in the creation of new folk and fantasy narratives.

Beasts and men talk and act together with no sense of strangeness in many stories. A number of tales have talking animals who reason and act as man does. See, for example, "The Master Cat" and "The Traveling Musicians." Some animals are transformed people who need to be loved in order to regain their human forms, as in "Beauty and the Beast" and "The White Cat." In other wonder tales, real animals reward people's kindnesses by threshing grain or recovering lost possessions. Many tales of trickery have animals as the central characters: one example is "The Rubber Man." Most fables use animals to represent human virtues and vices. A story may use only animals as characters in one version, people in another, and a combination of people and animals in a third variant.

While all types of folklore have narratives that include animals, there are some stories that can be classified as animal tales. These are the narratives in which the animal's deeds are not only

From *A Frog He Would A-wooing Go,* illustrated by Randolph Caldecott. Published by George Routledge & Sons, Ltd., 1883.

central to the plot but are, in fact, the primary interest. One such tale is "The Master Cat," in which the clever cat is able to raise his master from poverty to riches greater than the king's.

In these tales the animals do not always act in accordance to their true nature. Grain eaters may devour meat and natural enemies may live together in peace. A lion may be the "king of beasts," brave and powerful, or he may be portrayed as a bully and braggart. In the European tales a few animals have been typed: the donkey or ass is stupid, as is the bear, the fox is cunning, and the rabbit quick and clever. However, stereotypes of animal nature vary between cultures. The wily fox of Europe becomes the stupid animal who is always duped by Brer Rabbit in America.

Stith Thompson reports that animal tales originated from four sources: the Indian literary fables, of which *The Panchatantra* is the most well known; the Aesopic fables;[1] Baltic regional tales

[1] See the introduction to Fables, Chapter 5, for more detailed information.

told over a thousand years ago, and the Reynard cycle. These traveled throughout Europe, to Africa, and then with the slaves to America.

In the middle ages a number of the Baltic tales were formed into the satiric Reynard the Fox literary cycle. One series of Reynard tales pits a stupid bear or wolf against a sly fox. These stories usually involve a deception that is quite cruel, and many variants picture Reynard with no likeable characteristics. He is a thoroughly detestable trickster more like the fable villains than a folktale central figure. Some of the Reynard incidents have become independent *pourquoi* stories. The second tale in this section, "Why the Bear's Tale Is Short," is such an example.

The following section includes selections from Asia, Europe, the Near East, and Africa. These will permit an understanding of the universality of animal tales as well as a comparison of motifs and themes. No poorly written examples are included for stylistic comparisons because these have already been made in the Wonder Tales section.

BRUIN THE BEAR AND THE HONEYCOMBS / France

Roy Brown

Every year the animals gathered at King Lion's palace for a feast. One year, however, the banquet turned into an angry protest against Reynard the fox, the wily robber and deceiver. After many animals detail his treachery, Lion decides to bring him to trial. First, however, Reynard must be brought to the court. The Bear is sent to fetch him.

For information on the Reynard cycle, please see the introduction to this chapter.

In due course, Bruin the Bear arrived at Reynard's chief fortress which lay beyond a dark forest on the other side of a high mountain. The Bear found the gate locked and barred, so he sat on his tail and called out, "Hail, Cousin Fox. I bring a summons from his Majesty, King of beasts. You are to come with me to the palace,

"Bruin the Bear and the Honeycombs" from *Reynard the Fox*, retold by Roy Brown. Published by Abelard-Schuman, © 1969.

where you must answer those who accuse you of many wicked deeds. It is best that we go at once, or the king will be angry. Sir Reynard, can you hear me?"

Reynard the Fox had heard every word for he was crouched just on the other side of the fence where he had been sunning himself most pleasantly. But instead of answering the Bear, he darted into one of his tunnels to think out some way of avoiding this latest predicament.

Presently he came out of the hole, opened the gate and said, "My dear Bruin, do forgive my rudeness in not coming more quickly. As it happens I was saying my morning prayers. You are most welcome, but I wonder why King Lion sent an important person such as you to fetch me to court? Why didn't he choose a more humble messenger, such as a sparrow? In any case, I'm afraid our journey will be a slow one as I am not at all well today. It must be something I ate. You see, since I gave up meat I have had to swallow so many strange and unwholesome kinds of food."

"How dreadful!" said the Bear. "What exactly have you been eating?"

"Honeycombs! We poor foxes are not so high and mighty that we can pick and choose, you know. It was either honeycombs or starve."

"Honeycombs!" cried the Bear, for there is no delicacy more loved by his kind. "My dear Fox, you speak as though honeycombs were not fit to taste, yet surely you know there is no food more suitable for an emperor's feast. Just show *me* some honeycombs and I will be your devoted friend forever."

The Fox chuckled. "Oh, you bears will have your little jokes!"

Bruin began to slobber with greed. "One does not make jokes about honeycombs, Fox. Are you trying to tell me that you actually know where some of this delicious food is to be found?"

"Enough for *ten* bears, and you will be very welcome to it. I hope I never have to taste it again! Look, not far away there lives a carpenter by the name of Lanfert. I happen to know that he has so much honey that it would take even a big fellow like you seven years to eat it. You may have every drop, and that shows how warm is my affection for you."

The Bear was pleased and flattered. How could he guess that the wicked Fox was thinking: "What luck! Why, the stupid creature laughs and sighs! Imagine what a different sort of tune he'll be humming soon!"

They set out at once for the carpenter's house. Only that morning, the man had dragged in a huge oak trunk from the forest, taken his axe and cut a great slit in it to enable the sun and air to dry out the inside. The slit was held wide open by means of two wedges, and the Fox

chortled to himself when he pictured what would soon happen.

"There you are, Bruin," whispered Reynard as they crouched under some bushes. "In the oak trunk the honeycombs are packed so tightly that they are like peas in a pod." The Bear's eyes bulged. "But take care not to eat too much all at once. Honey is such rich food. I would never forgive myself if it made you ill!"

The Bear placed his feet firmly apart, leaned over the tree trunk, then with a mighty thrust of his hairy body, drove his head into the slit. No sooner had it vanished into the tree than Reynard artfully removed the stout wedges. The slit snapped shut, like jaws, trapping the Bear, who kicked out his great hind legs and bellowed frantically.

"Enjoy your feast, dear Bruin," cried Reynard from the bushes. "If the honey sticks in your throat, beg the farmer to bring you a drink of water to wash it down. Whatever you do, don't gobble *all* the honey because it will make you too fat to run back to the palace!"

Then the Fox, well pleased with his morning's work, slunk off to his fortress. Meanwhile, the carpenter, hearing the pitiful bellowings, came from his house. Seeing the Bear stuck in the tree, ears and all, he called upon his neighbors to help him. Eventually, the entire town was aroused, and people came along armed with any weapons they could lay their hands on: goads, rakes, brooms—and, making a ring around the poor trapped Bear, they beat him until he was half-dead.

Bruin the Bear, terrified and in agony, bellowed even louder. When he got loose, at last, it was only at the cost of much skin and both ears, which he left behind in the tree trunk together with the fur from his front paws. Finally, he managed to reach the river. One of his pursuers struck him such a blow on the head that he was stunned and blinded. He lashed out in all directions, and that was how he accidentally knocked the priest's wife into the river. She couldn't swim, so the people had to rescue her instead of paying attention to the Bear. Bruin escaped by swimming to the far bank where, in utter misery, he threw himself down on the ground.

Even then his ordeal was not over. Reynard,

thinking he was safe now, had been cheerfully catching chickens. He was on his way home, singing, when he saw Bruin lying on the riverbank. "That fool of a carpenter!" he muttered to himself. "To think that he had such a fine lump of bear meat under his very nose, and he let it escape."

The Bear saw him and moaned, "Oh, red villain, what have you done to me?"

The Fox sounded most indignant. "What are you grumbling about? It was *you* that stole the honeycombs and I don't suppose you paid even a penny for them! And what on earth are you lying there for, with your ears cropped and half your skin missing from your head and paws? Have you mislaid your cap and gloves?"

Then, with many more taunts, the Fox went singing on his way. As for the Bear, finding it far too painful to walk, he proceeded to roll head over heels all the way back to the palace, pushing himself along with his tail.

The King of Beasts was furious when he heard what had happened. He called his advisers to decide what should be done next, and that was how Tibert the Cat came to be chosen as the second messenger.

WHY THE BEAR'S TAIL IS SHORT / Lapland

Babette Deutsch
Avrahm Yarmolinsky

This same tale occurs in the medieval cycle about Reynard, the sly and dangerous fox. While the Lapps tell the story about a female, she has Reynard's cunning and cruel sense of humor.

The title prepares the reader for a pourquoi story but, as in many animal tales, the explanation is secondary to the fox's memorable tricks.

This happened on a very cold day. It was so cold that no creature dared stir out of its hole but the fox. The fox was hungry, and so, in spite of the weather, she went trotting down the road, looking for something to eat. But there was nothing to be found. Not a bird was flying in the icy wind. Not a mouse was creeping across the snow-covered earth.

Suddenly the fox noticed that a string of sledges, driven by a Lapp, was coming along the road. And on the last of the sledges was a fine load of fish.

At once the fox lay down on the road and stretched out her legs as though she were frozen stiff. When the Lapp drove up, he saw the fox lying there.

"Aha!" he said to himself. "This is a find, indeed! I will take that fox home to my wife, and she will make a coat for our little son out of the foxskin and trim his cap with her bushy tail."

The Lapp halted his reindeer, got down, placed the fox on the sledge behind him, and drove merrily on.

In a little while the fox dropped off the sledge. The Lapp got down, picked her up, and placed her on the second sledge. This went on, with the fox dropping off and the Lapp placing her on the next sledge, until finally the fox found herself on the last sledge of all, which was loaded with fish.

Very quietly and very steadily the fox began to gnaw at the rope that fastened the sledge to the one ahead. At last she gnawed the rope through: the sledge loaded with fish stood still in its tracks, while the rest of the sledges went merrily on. The Lapp did not notice his loss, and the fox settled down for a feast.

When she had eaten her fill, she took a fine fat fish in her mouth so that she would have something for her supper, and trotted off into the forest.

She had not gone far when she met the bear.

"Ah, Mistress Fox," said the bear, "wherever did you get that fine fat fish?"

"I caught it," said the fox.

"And how did you catch it?" asked the bear.

"Oh, it was simple," answered the fox. "I went to the river and stuck in my tail. The fish swam up and caught hold of it, and so I drew my supper out of the water."

"Show me how to do it," begged the bear. For though he had not so thick and bushy a hind-piece as the fox, in those days the bear, too, had a long, respectable tail.

"Come along," said the fox with a grin. She loved a joke better than anything except a good meal.

The fox led the bear to the river and knocked a small hole in the ice for him. The bear stuck his long, respectable tail into the hole and waited for a fish to bite.

"Good fishing," said the fox, and went about her own affairs.

After a while, however, the fox thought that she really must see how the bear was getting on, and she returned to the river. There stood the bear, patiently holding his long, respectable tail in the ice hole. But, as you know, it was a very cold day, even for Lapland, and by this time the bear's long, respectable tail was frozen fast in the ice.

"Oh, Master Bear!" cried the fox. "Your tail is frozen!"

The bear roared with dismay and tried to pull his long, respectable tail out of the ice hole. The harder he pulled, the louder he roared, but it did not help. At last he managed to get his tail out. But it was not a long, respectable tail any more. Most of it had stuck fast in the ice, and only a short stub remained to him.

From that day to this the bear has worn his tail short. Besides, he has lost his taste for fish. He prefers to eat honey. After all, you can get plenty of honey without having a long, respectable tail.

WHY THE DOG AND THE CAT ARE ENEMIES/China

Many groups have pourqoui *stories about the origin of the enmity between cats and dogs. Unlike "Why the Bear's Tail Is Short," this brief tale from China is little more than a* pourquoi *explanation.*

"Why the Dog and the Cat Are Enemies" includes the quest for a missing ring. This is a common motif which is often included as a small element in many longer tales although, as in "Aladdin and His Wonderful Lamp," the magical object is not always a ring.

A man and his wife owned a golden ring. It was a lucky ring: whoever possessed it would always have enough to live on. But the man and his wife did not know this, so they sold the ring to get a little money. Scarcely was the ring out of the house than they became poorer and poorer, until finally they were desperate to know how they could buy enough to eat. They also had a

"Why the Dog and the Cat Are Enemies," from *The Big Book of Animal Fables*, edited by Margaret Green. By permission of Dobson Books Ltd, London.

dog and a cat, who, of course, were obliged to suffer hunger with them. These animals went into a conference to see how they could bring their master and mistress back to their old happiness. Finally the dog hit on an idea.

"We must get the ring back again," he told the cat. The cat said, "But the ring is carefully guarded in a box. Nobody can get to it."

"Catch a mouse, then," the dog advised her. "The mouse will have to gnaw a hole in the box and get the ring out. Tell her that if she won't do this you'll bite her to death; *then* she'll do it, you can be certain."

This advice pleased the cat, so she caught a mouse. Then the cat and the dog and the mouse set off together to the house where the box was. After a while they came to a large river. As the cat could not swim, the dog took her on his back and swam across with her. The cat carried the mouse to the house where the box was. The mouse gnawed a hole in the box and pulled out the ring. The cat took the ring in her mouth, and returned to the river where the dog was waiting,

and they swam back. Then they started home together to bring the lucky ring to their master and mistress.

But the dog was only able to run along the ground; if there was a house in the way, he had always to go round it. The cat, however, could climb nimbly over the roofs, so she got back much quicker than the dog.

She brought the ring to her master and then the master said to his wife, "The cat is a good animal. We'll always give her something to eat and look after her as if she were our own child."

When the dog arrived at the house, they beat and scolded him because he had not helped to bring the ring home again. The cat sat by the fire, watching and purring and saying nothing. So the dog was angry with the cat because she had cheated him of his reward, and when next she came out of the house, the dog chased her and tried to catch and bite her.

Ever since then, dogs and cats have been enemies.

THE MASTER CAT / France

Andrew Lang

In European folktales cats are often portrayed as helpful animals. They have the fox's cleverness without his cruelty. Compare this cat's cunning with that of the fox in "Why the Bear's Tail Is Short." Though definitely an animal tale, "The Master Cat" includes motifs common to tales of trickery and wonder tales. A comparison of this tale with tales of these other two types will reveal how differences in emphasis of the same motifs help determine the categorization of folktales.

There was a miller who left no more estate to the three sons he had than his mill, his donkey and his cat. The division was soon made. Neither scrivener nor attorney was sent for; they would soon have eaten up all the poor patrimony. The

"The Master Cat," from *The Blue Fairy Book*. Edited by Andrew Lang. Published by Longmans, Green & Co., Ltd.

eldest had the mill, the second the donkey, and the youngest nothing but the cat. The poor young fellow was quite comfortless at having so poor a lot.

"My brothers," said he, "may get their living handsomely enough by joining their stocks together. But for my part, when I have eaten my cat, and made me a muff of his skin, I must die of hunger."

The cat, who heard all this, said to him with a grave and serious air, "Do not thus afflict yourself, my good master. You need only give me a bag, and have a pair of boots made for me that I may scamper through the brambles. You shall see you have not so bad a portion with me as you imagine."

The cat's master had often seen him play a great many cunning tricks to catch rats and mice; he used to hide himself in the meal, and make as if he were dead; so he did not altogether despair. When the cat had what he asked for, he booted himself very gallantly, and putting his bag about his neck he held the strings of it in his two forepaws and went into a warren where was a great abundance of rabbits. He put bran and lettuce into his bag and, stretching out at length as if he were dead, he waited for some young rabbits, not yet acquainted with the deceits of the world, to come and rummage for what he had put into his bag.

Scarce had he lain down but he had what he wanted: a rash and foolish young rabbit jumped into his bag. Monsieur Puss, immediately drawing close the strings, killed him without pity. Proud of his prey, he went with it to the palace, and asked to speak with his majesty. He was shown into the king's apartment and making a low reverence, said to him:

"I have brought you, sir, a rabbit from the warren, which my noble lord, the Master of Carabas"—for that was the title Puss was pleased to give his master—"has commanded me to present to Your Majesty from him."

"Tell your master," said the king, "that I thank him, and that he gives me a great deal of pleasure."

Another time the cat hid himself among some standing corn, holding his bag open. When a brace of partridges ran into it, he drew the strings and so caught them both. He made a present of these to the king as he had the rabbit. The king, in like manner, received the partridges with great pleasure, and ordered some money to be given to him.

The cat continued thus for two or three months to carry to his majesty, from time to time, game of his master's taking. One day in particu-

lar, when he knew for certain that the king was to take the air along the riverside with his daughter, the most beautiful princess in the world, he said to his master:

"If you will follow my advice your fortune is made. You have nothing to do but wash yourself in the river, where I shall show you, and leave the rest to me."

The Marquis of Carabas did what the cat advised him to do, without knowing why or wherefore. While he was washing, the king passed by, and the cat began to cry out:

"Help! Help! My Lord Marquis of Carabas is going to be drowned."

At this the king put his head out of the coach window, and finding it was the cat who had so often brought him such good game, he commanded his guards to run immediately to the assistance of his lordship the Marquis of Carabas. While they were drawing him out of the river, the cat came up to the coach and told the king that, while his master was washing, there came by some rogues, who went off with his clothes, though he had cried out, 'Thieves! Thieves!' several times, as loud as he could.

This cunning cat had hidden them under a great stone. The king immediately commanded the officers of his wardrobe to run and fetch one of his best suits for the Marquis of Carabas.

The fine clothes set off his good mien, for he was well made and very handsome in his person. The king's daughter took a secret inclination to him, and the Marquis of Carabas had no sooner cast two or three respectful and tender glances upon her than she fell in love with him to distraction. The king would needs have him come into the coach and take the air with them. The cat, quite overjoyed to see his project begin to succeed, marched on before, and meeting with some countrymen, who were mowing a meadow, he said to them:

"Good people, you who are mowing, if you do not tell the king that the meadow you mow belongs to my Lord Marquis of Carabas, you shall be chopped as small as herbs for the pot."

The king did not fail to ask the mowers to whom the meadow belonged.

"To my Lord Marquis of Carabas," they answered altogether, for the cat's threat had made them terribly afraid.

"You see, sir," said the marquis, "this is a meadow which never fails to yield a plentiful harvest every year."

The Master Cat, who still went on before, met with some reapers, and said to them, "Good people, you who are reaping, if you do not tell the king that all this corn belongs to the Marquis of Carabas you shall be chopped as small as herbs for the pot."

The king, who passed by a moment after, wished to know to whom all that corn belonged.

"To my Lord Marquis of Carabas," replied the reapers, and the king was very well pleased with it, as well as with the marquis, whom he congratulated thereupon. The Master Cat, who went always before, said the same words to all he met, and the king was astonished at the vast estates of the Marquis of Carabas.

Monsieur Puss came at last to a stately castle, the master of which was an ogre, the richest ever known. All the lands which the king had then gone over belonged to this ogre. The cat, who had taken care to inform himself who this ogre was and what he could do, asked to speak with him, saying he could not pass so near his castle without paying his respects to him.

The ogre received him as civilly as an ogre could and made him sit down.

"I have been assured," said the cat, "that you have the gift of being able to change yourself into any sort of creature. You can, for example, transform yourself into a lion or elephant and the like."

"That is true," answered the ogre briskly, "and to convince you, you shall see me now become a lion."

Puss was so badly terrified at the sight of a lion so near him that he immediately got into the rain gutter, not without abundance of trouble and danger, because of his boots. They were of no use walking upon the tiles. A little while after, when Puss saw that the ogre had resumed his natural form, he came down and owned he had been very much frightened.

"I have been moreover informed," said the cat, "but I know not how to believe it, that you have also the power to take on the shape of the smallest animal; for example, to change yourself into a rat or a mouse; but I must own to you I take this to be impossible."

"Impossible!" cried the ogre. "You shall see that presently."

At the same time he changed himself into a mouse and began to run about the floor. Puss no sooner perceived this than he fell upon him and ate him up.

Meanwhile the king, who saw, as he passed, this fine castle of the ogre's, had a mind to go into it. Puss, who heard the noise of his majesty's coach running over the drawbridge, ran out, and said to the king:

"Your Majesty is welcome to this castle of my Lord Marquis of Carabas."

"What, my Lord Marquis!" cried the king. "And does this castle also belong to you? There can be nothing finer than this court and all the stately buildings which surround it. Let us go in, if you please."

The marquis gave his hand to the princess and followed the king, who went first. They passed into a spacious hall, where they found a magnificent collation, which the ogre had prepared for his friends, who were that very day to visit him, but dared not enter, knowing the king was there. His majesty was charmed with the good qualities of the Lord Marquis of Carabas, as was his daughter, and seeing the vast estate he possessed, said to him:

"It will be owing to yourself only, my Lord Marquis, if you are not my son-in-law."

The marquis, making several low bows, accepted the honor which his majesty conferred upon him, and forthwith, that very same day, married the princess.

Puss became a great lord, and never ran after mice any more.

THE COUNTRY OF MICE / Tibet

L. C. Hume

The motif of the weak helping the strong occurs in the folklore of most cultures. This tale from Tibet has some similarities with the Aesopic fable about the lion and the mouse. However it differs from the fable not only in its elaboration of plot and detail but also in its use of humor, which is rare in the Aesopic fables.

An intriguing touch is the mention of enemy soldiers' muskets. They indicate that the tale is either of recent origin or, a more probable explanation, that this version has been adapted by the teller to include objects familiar to his audience. Such modifications are common and help to explain the existence of multiple variants.

Once there was a king who ruled over a large country in which there lived a great number of mice. Generally these mice were very prosperous, with plenty to eat, but one year it happened that the country's crops were poor and the mice, who depended upon the spare grains left after harvest, found their stores running short before spring. The king of the mice, having determined upon a personal appeal to the king of the country, dressed up in his best gray suit and set off one morning to the king's palace. When the doorman announced to the king of the country that a mouse was asking to see him, His Majesty was greatly amused and ordered him admitted.

The mouse entered the audience chamber carrying a little silk thread which he presented to the king in place of the usual ceremonial scarf. "Good morning, Brother Mouse," said the king courteously. "What can I do for you?" The mouse bowed nicely and replied: "Oh King, as you know, this year our crops are short and we mice are threatened with famine unless we can borrow enough grain to see us through the winter. If you will loan us what we need, we will repay you with interest at the next harvest."

"Well," said the king, stroking his chin, "how much grain do you want?" Said the mouse: "We will require one of your big barns full." "How would you carry it away?" said the king. "Leave that to us," said the mouse. So the king ordered a large granary to be thrown open to the mice with no interference whatsoever.

That night the king of the mice summoned all his subjects together and by the hundreds of thousands they invaded the barn. Each one picked up as much grain as he could carry in his mouth, on his back, and curled up in his tail; and when they were all through, the barn was empty and not a single grain of barley was left.

Next morning, when the king went out to look at his barn, he was astonished to find that the mice had been able to empty it so efficiently and he conceived a high opinion of their abilities. And when, at the following harvest, the king of the mice redeemed his promise by repaying the loan with interest, the king of the country was prepared to admit that the mice were trustworthy as well as clever.

Now it happened that shortly after this, the king of the country was forced to go to war with a neighboring kingdom that lay on the opposite shore of the river bordering the two countries. This other country was far richer and more powerful than the country where the mice lived, and its king soon assembled a huge army on the opposite bank of the river and began making preparations for invasion. The mice soon heard about this state of affairs and were distressed, for they feared living under a strange and unsympathetic ruler. So once more the mouse king set out for the king's palace to offer the help of the mice. Despite his worries, the king was amused and asked how mice could help him when he couldn't even muster enough men to repel the enemy. "Leave it to us," replied the mouse; and the king, not knowing what else to do, agreed.

Next evening at dusk, the mouse king led several hundred thousand of his subjects to the river bank, where they found lined up a hundred thousand foot-long sticks which, at the mouse king's request, the king of the country had agreed to place there. The mice used these sticks as rafts to carry them across the river to the enemy camp, where the soldiers were all sound asleep. At a command from their king, the mice scattered over the camp and went to work, quietly doing as much destruction as possible. Some nibbled at the bowstrings and slings of the soldiers' muskets; others gnawed the slow matches and fuses; still others bit off the clothes and pigtails of the sleeping men. In fact, they nibbled everything and left shreds and confusion in every direction. After a couple of hours' work, they reassembled at the river bank and re-embarked on their sticks, sailing noiselessly back to their own shore without having been detected by the enemy or having raised any alarm.

Next morning at daybreak a huge outcry arose from the enemy camp as each man, arising from sleep, found himself in sorry state—his clothes in tatters, his bow without a string, his rifle without a sling (and with no fuse or slow match to fire it), and no provisions for breakfast. As each accused the other of treachery, the whole camp was soon in an uproar. In the midst of the clamor, some shots were fired and bugles sounded on the opposite bank, and, thinking they were about to be overtaken, the whole army took to its heels. In a few minutes not a man was to be seen.

The king of the country of the mice was naturally elated at this easy victory, and quickly summoned the king of the mice to thank him for his good services. And in accordance with a bargain made at the time the mice offered their assistance, he quickly set about to rid the country of the two things most harmful to mice—floods and cats. Since the burrows of the mice were in low land near the river, a small rise in the water always overflowed the level land and flooded their nests. The king of the country had a strong embankment built all along the river to ensure that water would, in future, be kept out. Cats are always, of course, persecutors of mice, and so the king banished them forever from the country, issuing an edict forbidding all persons henceforth, on pain of death, to keep cats of any kind. These rewards pleased the mice very much. The king of the country and the king of the mice each knew that the other was to be trusted and counted upon in all emergencies; and everyone lived together in that land very happily for the rest of their lives. Except cats.

THE TRAVELING MUSICIANS / Germany

The Grimm brothers

Narratives similar to "The Traveling Musicians" are told throughout Europe and Asia. The Asian tales, however, involve the adventures of a group of objects rather than animals. An egg, a needle, a scorpion, a mortar, and a piece of dung travel together to find a home. While European variants deal with animals, both versions include the incident of driving the owners from the house. This tale is often entitled "The Bremen Town Musicians."

A farmer once had a donkey that had been a faithful servant to him a great many years, but was now growing old and every day more and more unfit for work. His master, therefore, was tired of keeping him and began to think of putting an end to him. But the donkey, who saw that some mischief was in the wind, took himself slyly off and began to journey toward the great city.

"For there," thought he, "I may turn musician."

After he had traveled a little way, he spied a dog lying by the roadside and panting as if he were very tired.

"What makes you pant so, my friend?" said the donkey.

"Alas!" said the dog. "My master said he would not keep me because I am old and weak and can no longer make myself useful to him in hunting. So I ran away. But what can I do to earn my living?"

"Oh," said the donkey, "I am going to the great city to turn musician! Suppose you go with me and try what you can do in the same way?"

The dog said he was willing, and they jogged on together.

Before they had gone far, they saw a cat sitting in the middle of the road and looking very sad.

"Pray, my good lady," said the donkey, "what's the matter with you? You look quite out of spirits!"

"Ah, me!" said the cat. "How can one be in good spirits when one's life is in danger? Because I am beginning to grow old and had rather lie at my ease by the fire than run about the house after mice, my mistress was going to drown me. Though I have been lucky enough to get away from her, I do not know what I am going to do."

"Oh," said the donkey, "by all means go with us to the great city! You are a good night singer and may make your fortune as a musician."

The cat was pleased with the thought and joined the party.

Soon afterwards, as they were passing by a farmyard, they saw a cock perched upon a gate, screaming out with all his might and main.

"Bravo!" said the donkey. "Upon my word you

make a famous noise! Pray, what is all this about?"

"Why," said the cock, "I was just now saying that we should have fine weather for our washing day. Yet my mistress and the cook don't thank me for my pains but threaten to cut off my head tomorrow and make broth of me for the guests that are coming on Sunday."

"Well, then," said the donkey, "come with us. It will be better than staying here to have your head cut off! Besides, who knows? If we take care to sing in tune, we may get up some kind of concert. So come along with us."

"With all my heart," said the cock.

So they all four went on together.

They could not, however, reach the great city the first day. When night came, they went into a wood to sleep. The donkey and the dog laid themselves down under a great tree, and the cat climbed up into the branches. The cock, thinking that the higher he sat the safer he would be, flew up to the very top of the tree; and then, according to his custom, before he went to sleep, looked out on all sides of him to see that everything was well. In doing this, he saw afar off something bright and shining.

The cock called to his companions, "There must be a house no great way off, for I see a light."

"If that is the case," said the donkey, "we had better change our quarters. Lodging would be better there than here in the wood."

"Besides," added the dog, "I should not be the worse for a bone or two, or a bit of meat."

So they walked off together toward the spot where the cock had seen the light. As they drew near, it became larger and brighter, till they at last came close to a house.

The donkey, being the tallest of the company, marched up to the window and peeped in.

"Well, Donkey," said the cock, "what do you see?"

"What do I see?" replied the donkey. "Why, I see a table spread with all kinds of good things, and robbers sitting around it making merry."

"That would be a noble lodging for us," said the cock.

"Yes," said the donkey, "if we could only get in."

So they consulted together how they could get

"The Traveling Musicians," translated by Edgar Taylor from *Grimms' Popular Stories*, 1856.

the robbers out, and at last they hit upon a plan. The donkey placed himself upright on his hind legs, with his forefeet resting against the window. The dog got upon his back, the cat scrambled up to the dog's shoulders, and the cock flew up and sat upon the cat's head. When all was ready, a signal was given, and they began their music. The donkey brayed, the dog barked, the cat mewed, and the cock crowed. Then they all broke through the window at once and came tumbling into the room amongst the broken glass, with a most hideous clatter!

The robbers, who had been not a little frightened by the opening concert, had now no doubt that some frightful hobgoblin had broken in upon them, and scampered away as fast as they could.

The coast once clear, our travelers soon sat down and ate what the robbers had left, with as much eagerness as if they did not expect to eat again for a month. Then they put out the lights and each once more sought out a resting place to his own liking. The donkey laid himself down upon a heap of straw in the yard; the dog stretched himself upon a mat behind the door; the cat rolled herself up on the hearth before the warm ashes; the cock perched upon the roof of the house. As they were all rather tired from their journey, they soon fell asleep.

About midnight, the robbers saw from afar that the lights were out and that all seemed quiet, so they began to think that they had been in too great a hurry to run away. One of them, who was bolder than the rest, went to see what was going on. Finding everything still, he marched into the kitchen and groped about till he found a match in order to light a candle. Then seeing the glittering fiery eyes of the cat, he mistook them for live coals and held the match to them to light it. But the cat, not understanding the joke, sprang at his face, and spit, and scratched him. This frightened the robber dreadfully, and away he ran to the back door; but there the dog jumped up and bit him in the leg; and as he was crossing the yard, the donkey kicked him; and the cock, who had been awakened by the noise, crowed with all his might.

At this the robber ran back as fast as he could to his comrades and told the captain how a horrid witch had got into the house and had spit at him and scratched his face with her long bony fingers; how a man with a knife in his hand had hidden himself behind the door and stabbed him in the leg; how a black monster stood in the yard and struck him with a club; how a ghost sat upon the top of the house and cried out, "Throw the rascal up here!"

After this the robbers never dared to go back to the house. But the musicians were so pleased with their quarters that they took up their home there; and there they are, I dare say, to this very day.

THE RAM AND THE PIG WHO WENT INTO THE WOODS
Scandinavia

Peter Christen Asbjörnsen

A variant of "The Traveling Musicians," this Scandinavian version has been modified more than "Jack and His Friends," the next tale. Compare not only their plot differences but also the differences in language. The excessive use of folk wisdom, often cliches, adds humor for the sophisticated reader although the slower action may bore young children. "The Ram and the Pig Who Went into the Woods" also has elements of the cumulative tale. Each time a new animal is added to the group a pattern of questions and responses occur.

There was once upon a time a ram, who was being fattened up for killing. He had therefore plenty to eat, and he soon became round and fat with all the good things he got. One day the dairymaid came, and gave him some more food.

"You must eat, ram," she said; "you'll not be long here now, for tomorrow we are going to kill you."

"There's an old saying, that no one should sneer at old women's advice, and that advice and physic can be had for everything except death," thought the ram to himself; "but perhaps I might manage to escape it this time."

And so he went on eating till he was full, and when he was quite satisfied he ran his horns against the door, burst it open, and set off to the neighboring farm. There he made straight for the pigsty, to look for a pig with whom he had struck up an acquaintance on the common, since when they had always been good friends and got on well together.

"Good day, and thanks for your kindness last time we met," said the ram to the pig.

"Good day, and thanks to you," said the pig.

"Do you know why they make you so comfortable, and why they feed you and look after you so well?" said the ram.

"No," said the pig.

"There are many mouths to feed on this farm, you must know," said the ram; "they are going to kill you and eat you."

"Are they?" said the pig. "Well, much good it may do them!"

"If you are of the same mind as I, we will go into the woods and build a house and live by ourselves; there is nothing like having a home of your own, you know," said the ram.

Yes, the pig was quite willing. "It's nice to be in fine company," said he, and off they started.

When they had got a bit on the way they met a goose.

"Good day, my good people, and thanks for your kindness last time we met," said the goose. "Where are you off to?"

"Good day, and thanks to you," said the ram.

"The Ram and the Pig Who Went into the Woods," from *Popular Tales from the Norse* by Peter Christen Asbjörnsen, translated by G. W. Dasent. Published by G. P. Putnam's Sons, 1908.

"We had it altogether too comfortable at our place, so we are off to the woods to live by ourselves. In your own house you are your own master, you know," said he.

"Well, I'm very comfortable where I am," said the goose; "but why shouldn't I join you? Good company makes the day shorter," said she.

"But neither hut nor house can be built by gabbling and quacking," said the pig. "What do you think you can do?"

"Good counsel and skill may do as much as a giant's will," said the goose. "I can pluck moss and stuff it into the crevices, so that the house will be warm and comfortable."

Well, she might come with them, thought the pig, for he liked the place to be warm and cozy.

When they had gone a bit on the way—the goose was not getting along very fast—they met a hare, who came scampering out of the wood.

"Good day, my good people, and thanks for your kindness the last time we met," said the hare. "How far are you going today?" said he.

"Good day, and thanks to you," said the ram; "we had it altogether too comfortable at our place, so we are off to the woods to build a house and live by ourselves. When you have tried both East and West, you'll find that a home of your own is after all the best," said he.

"Well, I have, of course, a home in every bush," said the hare; "but I have often said to myself in the winter that if I lived till the summer I would build a house, so I have a good mind to go with you and build one after all," said he.

"Well, if the worst comes to the worst, we might take you with us to frighten the dogs away," said the pig, "for you couldn't help us to build the house, I should say."

"There is always something for willing hands to do in this world," said the hare. "I have teeth to gnaw pegs with, and I have paws to knock them into the walls, so I'll do very well for a carpenter; for 'good tools make good work,' as the man said, when he skinned his mare with an auger," said the hare.

Well, he might come with them and help to build the house; there could be no harm in that.

When they had got a bit farther on the way they met a cock.

"Good day, my good people, and thanks for your kindness last time we met," said the cock; "where are you all going today?" he said.

"Good day, and thanks to you," said the ram; "we had it altogether too comfortable at our place, so we are off to the woods to build a house and live by ourselves. 'For unless at home you bake, you'll lose both fuel and cake,' " said he.

"Well, I am comfortable enough, where I am," said the cock, "but it's better to have your own roost than to sit on a stranger's perch and crow; and that cock is best off who has a home of his own," said he. "If I could join such fine company as yours, I too would like to go to the woods and build a house."

"Well, flapping and crowing is all very well for noise, but it won't cut joists," said the pig. "You can't help us to build a house," he said.

"It is not well to live in a house where there is neither dog nor cock," said the cock; "I am early to rise and early to crow."

"Yes, 'early to rise makes one wealthy and wise,' so let him come with us!" said the pig. He was always the heaviest sleeper. "Sleep is a big thief, and steals half one's life," he said.

So they all set off to the woods and built the house. The pig felled the trees and the ram dragged them home; the hare was the carpenter, and gnawed pegs and hammered them into walls and roof; the goose plucked moss and stuffed it into the crevices between the logs; the cock crew and took care that they did not oversleep themselves in the mornings, and when the house was ready and the roof covered with birch-bark and thatched with turf, they could at least live by themselves, and they were all both happy and contented.

"It's pleasant to travel both East and West, but home is, after all, the best," said the ram.

But a bit farther into the wood two wolves had their lair, and when they saw that a new house had been built hard by they wanted to know what sort of folks they had got for neighbors. For they thought, "a good neighbor is better than a brother in a foreign land, and it is better to live among good neighbors than to be known far and wide."

So one of them made it his business to call there and ask for a light for his pipe. The moment he came inside the door the ram rushed at him, and gave him such a butt with his horns that the wolf fell on his head into the hearth; the pig snapped and bit, the goose nipped and pecked, the cock flew up on a rafter and began to crow and cackle, and the hare became so frightened that he scampered and jumped about, both high and low, and knocked and scrambled about from one corner of the room to the other.

At last the wolf managed to get out of the house.

"Well, to know one's neighbors is to add to one's wisdom," said the wolf who was waiting outside; "I suppose you had a grand reception, since you stayed so long. But what about the light? I don't see either pipe or smoke," said he.

"Yes, that was a nice light I got, and a nice lot of people they were," said he who had been inside. "Such treatment I never met with before, but 'as you make your bed so you must lie,' and 'an unexpected guest must put up with what he gets,' " said the wolf. "No sooner had I got inside the door than the shoemaker threw his last at me, and I fell on my head in the middle of the forge; there sat two smiths, blowing bellows and pinching and snipping bits of flesh off me with red-hot tongs and pincers; the hunter rushed about the room looking for his gun, but as luck would have it, he couldn't find it. And up on the rafters sat some one beating his arms about and shouting: 'Let's hook him! let's hook him! Sling him up! sling him up!' and if he had only got hold of me I should never have got out alive."

JACK AND HIS FRIENDS / Ireland

F. M. Pilkington

Obviously another variant of "The Traveling Musicians," "Jack and His Friends" has some interesting differences in language and plot. It illustrates how a tale may be about animals in one country but include people in another. While Edgar Taylor retold the previous tale in very formal language with no hint of colloquialisms, F. M. Pilkington has deliberately included echoes of Irish speech rhythms to make his variant seem closer to the oral tradition.

"Jack and His Friends" has some similarities to wonder tales: a poor boy's kindness to animals gains him their help. However, compare Jack's reward with the endings of the wonder tales.

There was once a poor widow with an only son named Jack, and poverty was no stranger in their house. But there came a year when even the potato crop failed and they had to go hungry, and one evening Jack said to his mother, "I'm off tomorrow to make a fortune for the two of us, so give me your blessing."

"You can have a thousand blessings," said his mother, "and good luck go with you."

Next day he set off and walked for miles. At last he came to a bog and saw an ass struggling in the mire.

"Help me out or I'll drown," he called to Jack.

So Jack threw stones and clods of turf into the bog and made a firm place for the ass to step on, and so he got out.

"Thank you," says he, "and where are *you* going?"

"I'm seeking my fortune," says Jack.

"Let me come along with you then," says the ass; and so it was agreed.

Not long after his they passed through a village and a crowd of boys were tormenting a poor dog with a kettle tied to his tail. When Jack and the ass saw what they were at, the ass let out such a terrible roaring, and Jack gave them such a drubbing with his stout stick that the wretches ran off as if the devil were at their heels.

"It's myself that is grateful to you both," said the dog, "and may I travel in your company?"

Jack and the ass agreed, and they all made off to find a cool, quiet place to eat their dinner.

While they were sitting under a shady tree, a poor thin cat came by.

"Come and share our dinner before you faint with the hunger," called Jack.

"Heaven's blessing on you all," said the cat, "'tis hungry I am indeed, And might I ask where you are going?"

"We're seeking our fortune in the wide world," said the ass.

"Then I'd be glad to join you," said the cat.

So off they went, all four; and just as evening fell they heard a queer sort of crowing, and suddenly, out of a field into the road came a fox with a black cock held fast in his mouth.

"Oh, the wretch," brayed the ass at the top of his voice.

"At him, good dog," says Jack; and in a second the dog was after the fox, and foxie dropped the cock like a hot potato and was gone in a flash.

The cock fluttered up to Jack and his friends, trembling and shaking down its feathers.

"Oh, glory be to goodness, wasn't it a lucky

thing that you were on this road," he said, "and I'll never forget the help you gave me. But where are you all going?"

"We're off to seek a fortune and we'd be glad for you to join us if you wish," said Jack.

By then it was nearly dark, and not a house to be seen; so they went into a hayfield and made themselves comfortable in the dry, warm hay. They were no sooner asleep than the cock took to crowing, and woke them up again. When they asked crossly what was the matter, he said, "It's the dawn over yonder, can't you see it?"

"That's candlelight, not daylight," says Jack, "but we might as well go and ask for a night's shelter."

So they all got up, and stumbled over the field, and down into a little hollow, and there the light shone brightly and they could hear laughter and singing.

Jack whispered to the others to be very quiet, and they crept nearer and saw a fine cottage with a window just above their heads. So Jack climbed on to the ass's back and looked in, and there were six robbers all armed with pistols sitting at a table eating and drinking.

"That was a fine haul we got at Lord Dunlavin's," shouts an ugly fellow.

"And we owe it all to the porter, so here's to his health," bellows another.

Then Jack made signs to his friends, and the ass put his front hoofs up on the window-ledge; the dog stood on the ass's head, the cat on the dog's head, and the cock on the cat's head. And suddenly they all sung out together at the tops of their voices.

"Hee-haw," cried the ass; "Bow-wow," barked the dog; "Meow, meow," cried the cat; "Cock-a-doodle-do," crowed the cock.

"Have at them," cried Jack, "get your guns ready!" And with that he lifted his foot, gave a good kick, and smashed all the window panes.

The robbers were so frightened that they blew out the light, and ran out of the back door, and never stopped until they were five miles away.

So Jack and his friends went inside, lighted the candles, closed the shutters, and made a good meal. Then they settled themselves for the night, Jack in a bed, the ass in the stable, the dog on a mat, the cat near the fire, and the cock up over the front door.

Now when the robbers found that no one was coming after them, they began to wish that they hadn't run away. And after talking it over among themselves, the leader of the band offered to go back and try to recover the sack of stolen silver.

When he got to the house, all was in darkness; so he crept in at the back door and made for the wee glimmer of firelight. Suddenly he stumbled over the cat, which sprang up into his face and scratched and clawed until he shouted with the pain. Then he tried to find a cupboard to get a candle, but he tripped over the dog and was bitten on his legs and arms.

"Och, I wish I'd never come into the place," he muttered, as he groped his way to the front door. Just as he got it open, the cock dropped onto his shoulders and began to peck at his nose.

"There must be a pack of demons about," he thought, terrified, and shaking off the cock, he ran for the shelter of the stable, but the ass was waiting and gave him such a kick that he flew through the air like a feather and landed on the dung-heap.

As soon as he was able to crawl, the poor man dragged himself wearily through the wood and over the fields, and rejoined his comrades; and when they saw his cuts and bruises, and his tattered clothes, and heard his tale, nothing in all the world would have persuaded them to go near that house again.

At sunrise next morning, Jack and his friends were up and made a hearty breakfast. Then Jack took up the sack of silver stolen by the robbers, tied it firmly on the ass's back, and they all set off for Lord Dunlavin's castle.

It was a long journey, but at last they came to the castle door, and when they knocked, it was opened by the porter who had let the robbers in the night before.

"We don't want the likes of you here," says he rudely, when his eye fell on Jack and his companions, "what's your business?"

"We've come to see his lordship," says Jack, short and sharp.

"Be off, you rascals, or I'll set the dogs on you," answered the porter.

"Who opened the door for the robbers, can

you tell us that?" says the cock shrilly from his perch on the ass's head.

"And what is your answer, Barney?" said another voice from behind the porter—and there stood Lord Dunlavin and his daughter.

"Ah, don't believe a word of it, your lordship," stammered the porter, his face as white as his shirt front. "Would I be likely to open the door to six desperate men?"

"And how did you know there were six, you villain?" asked Lord Dunlavin.

Then Jack spoke up, and he said, "We've got all your silver here in this sack, sir, and we'd be glad if you'd spare us a bit of supper and beds for the night, after our long journey."

"You can have that and more," said Lord Dunlavin, "for I'll see that none of you ever knows want again in all your lives."

So they had a grand welcome; the ass, the dog, and the cock got the best places in the farmyard, and the cat was given possession of the kitchen.

As for Jack, he was dressed in new clothes from head to foot, and given a snug little cottage near the castle for himself and his mother. And they lived there happy ever after.

RUBA AND THE STORK / Iran

Anne Sinclair Mehdevi

To break bread and taste salt in the past was a pledge of friendship, and to give such an invitation with secret, vicious intent was villainous. "Ruba and the Stork" proves that the sly, cruel fox of Europe was known in the Near East.

This tale is an illustration of how a story similar to an Aesopic fable has been treated by an eastern culture. In contrast to the Aesopic characteristics of brevity and sparseness of detail, "Ruba and the Stork" gives greater motivation for the animals' behavior as well as a more involved plot. Compare this tale with "The Fox and the Stork" in Chapter 5, Fables.

There was a time and there wasn't a time in the long ago when Ruba, the fox, lived in a hole at the foot of a tall pine tree. Though Ruba was small, he was quick and cunning, and he cared for nothing but looking out for himself.

One day, he saw a stork building its nest at the top of the tall pine tree. Ruba smiled to himself and licked his chops. "Soon this busy Madam Stork will have a nest full of succulent baby storks," he said to himself. "I must make friends with her."

So, every morning, Ruba called out "Salaam" in a honey-sweet voice as the stork flew past him. And the stork, who was a neighborly sort of person, began answering "Salaam." In this way, they became friends.

One day Ruba said, "Dear Madam Stork, we have been friends and neighbors for a week now. Yet we have not broken bread nor tasted salt together. Why don't you come to my fox-hole for the noonday meal tomorrow?"

The stork said, "Thank you, Friend Ruba, I should be glad to come and taste of your bread and salt."

"I am honored, Madam Stork," said Ruba, smiling to himself and thinking of the days ahead when he would invite the stork babies to his fox-hole for a meal—for his meal.

The stork said, "Excuse me, Friend Ruba. You will not be angry, I hope, if I correct you? I am not Madam Stork.

"And are you not married?" asked Ruba.

"As yet I have not been blessed with a companion and wife," said Mr. Stork. And politely taking his leave, he flew away to his nest at the top of the tall pine tree.

Ruba, the fox, was in a fury. "I am not in the mood to give food to a neighbor who is of no use to me," he thought. "Mr. Stork, indeed! Well, I shall make sure that, after tomorrow, he never comes to my house again for a meal."

At noon the next day, Mr. Stork flew down from the pine treetop to visit Ruba. The fox and the stork sat down on either side of the table and Ruba brought out the food. He had prepared two large flat plates of honey. The honey was spread smoothly and evenly over each plate. Ruba began at once to lick up the honey on his plate with his tongue. Mr. Stork pecked and pecked at his plate with his long pointed beak, but he was unable to get even a bite. Soon the tip of his beak was sore, but still he couldn't pick up a single drop of the delicious honey.

Mr. Stork was too well-mannered to say anything. He thanked Ruba for the meal and flew up to his nest thinking, "I shall get even with that cunning fox."

A few days later, Mr. Stork saw Ruba sunning himself in front of his foxhole and said, "Haven't your heard that each invitation deserves a return invitation? I visited you in your house and now it is your turn to visit me and taste my bread and salt."

Ruba said, "Thank you, Friend Stork. You know I would sacrifice my eyes for you but, unfortunately, I cannot climb the pine tree, so I'll have to refuse." To himself, Ruba was saying, "I won't waste my time being friendly with a stork who isn't even married and therefore can't provide me with succulent baby storks to fill my belly."

The stork said, "Friend Ruba, do not despair. I will spread my wings and carry you to the top of the pine tree."

"Thank you, Friend Stork, you are indeed thoughtful," said Ruba. And to himself, he added, "Why not?"

At noon the next day, Mr. Stork put Ruba, the fox, on his back and flew into the sky. Ruba looked around in astonishment. He was high above the treetops. He could see into all the birds' nests. He saw nests full of magpie babies and hoopoe babies and eaglets and thrushlings and baby sparrows, and his mouth watered.

Then Mr. Stork gently settled on the edge of his own nest at the top of the tall pine tree. Ruba, the fox, sat on one edge of the nest and Mr. Stork sat on the other. Then Mr. Stork placed two long-necked jugs on the table between them. The jugs were filled with roasted grains of wheat. Mr. Stork dipped his long pointed beak down the narrow neck of his jug and began to eat. But Ruba could not get his tongue down through the neck of his jug. He stretched his tongue as far as he could, but he was unable to touch even a grain of wheat. Mr. Stork finished the wheat in his jug while Ruba had not had so much as a taste.

"Is this the proper way to treat a guest?" said Ruba.

Mr. Stork replied, "I learned this from you."

After that, Ruba and Mr. Stork did not greet each other. Then, one day, Ruba noticed that a second stork had come to the nest. "I am lucky after all," said the cunning fox to himself. "Mr. Stork has brought a wife to his nest and soon there will be a nestful of succulent baby storks. I must make friends again."

When Mr. Stork flew past him, Ruba called out, "Salaam, Friend Stork. Let us forget the past. Let us be friends again."

"All right," said the stork.

"You should introduce me to your pretty wife, Friend Stork," said Ruba, the fox. "Neighbors, as you know, should help each other, but how can I help your wife if I haven't met her?"

So, Mr. Stork called Madam Stork down from the nest and said to her, "This is our neighbor, Friend Ruba, who has offered to help you if you are in trouble when I am away from home."

Days passed, and soon the storks' nest was filled with eggs. The eggs hatched and three baby storks began to lift their beaks to be fed. Ruba watched, licking his chops, as the baby storks grew bigger and bigger, and fatter and fatter. Mr. Stork and Madam Stork were busy from sunrise to sunset gathering food for their fledglings.

One day, Ruba was lying in front of his foxhole sunning himself when Madam Stork flew past. "Salaam, Madam Stork," said Ruba pleasantly. "It burns my heart to see you working so hard. May I offer to help you?"

"What can you do?" she asked.

"I can do nothing here on the ground," he said. "But if you lift me up to your nest, I could guard your fledglings from danger while you are away looking for food."

"All right," she said. She put Ruba, the fox, on her back and flew up to her nest at the top of the tall pine tree. Ruba was faint with delight when he found himself sitting in the nest surrounded by three fat baby storks. "What fat, juicy fledglings you have," he said to Madam Stork, licking his chops.

"Guard them well," said Madam Stork and flew away.

The moment she was out of sight, Ruba gobbled up the fattest and largest of the three stork fledglings.

When Mr. Stork and Madam Stork came home, they saw that one of their fledglings was missing. Mr. Stork said, "Friend Ruba, where is my eldest fledgling, the light of my eyes, the crown of my head?"

"He flew away," said Ruba. "And, as I am a fox and cannot fly, I could not bring him back."

But Mr. Stork saw that there were feathers sticking out on either side of Ruba's wicked, smiling snout—baby stork feathers. Mr. Stork understood, at once, that the cunning Ruba had eaten up his eldest fledgling, and he said to himself:

"This cunning fox will think of tricks to eat up all my fledglings if I do not get rid of him."

"Friend Ruba," said Mr. Stork, "we must go and look for my fledgling."

"Unfortunately, I cannot fly," said the fox. "Otherwise, I would sacrifice my eyes for you."

"You shall ride on my back," said Mr. Stork.

"All right," agreed Ruba, for he remembered the last time he had taken a ride on Mr. Stork's back, and he remembered all the baby birds he had seen from the sky—the magpie babies and the hoopoe babies, the eaglets and the thrushlings, and the baby sparrows—and his mouth watered.

Ruba climbed on Mr. Stork's back, and soon they rose high into the sky. "Look well for my child, Friend Ruba," said Mr. Stork. "What do you see?"

"I see people in their houses and in the streets. I see hens and roosters and ducklings and geese. How fortunate you are to be able to look at the world like this."

The stork flew higher and again asked, "What do you see, Friend Ruba?

The fox answered, "I can still see people in their houses and in the streets, but they have grown smaller. And I still see the hens and roosters and ducklings and geese, but they are no bigger than ants."

The stork flew higher and again asked, "What do you see, Friend Ruba?"

Ruba said, "My eyes are blurred. I feel dizzy. Go no higher for I can no longer see anything of interest. I cannot see any hens or roosters or ducklings or geese. And even the people look like ants."

Mr. Stork said, "You wish to go down?"

"Yes."

"You shall have your wish," said Mr. Stork, and he shook his wings and he shook his tail and he shook his neck, and he began to swoop up and down and around through the air. Soon he shook Ruba, the fox, off his back. And, thus, he got rid of the wicked fox who had falsely shared bread and salt with him and betrayed his friendship.

HARE AND THE HYENA / Africa—the Bantu

Kathleen Arnott

Most cultures tell warning stories about what happens to the greedy. This is one such narrative told by the Bantu. The last sentence of this tale brings to mind the picture of a mother telling this story to her child to restrain his natural propensity toward greediness.

One day, a long time ago when there was a famine in a certain part of Africa, Hare met Hyena.

'How thin you are looking,' said Hare.

'You look as though you would not say 'No' to a good meal either,' replied Hyena.

The two animals continued on the road together until they came to a farmer, who was grumbling because all his servants had left him.

'We'll work for you if you will feed us,' suggested Hare.

The farmer willingly agreed, and, giving the two animals a pot of beans to cook, showed them the part of his farm where they must weed.

First of all they made a fire, and fetching three large stones, they rested the pot on them to cook their meal while they set to work. When the sun was high in the sky and it was time for the midday rest, Hyena told Hare to keep an eye on the cooking-pot while he himself went down to the river to wash.

Hare sat by the pot, stirring it with a stick and longing to begin his meal, while Hyena, as soon as he was out of sight of Hare, stripped off his skin. He looked the most horrible spectacle, and ran back to Hare uttering strange cries. Poor Hare was terrified.

'Help! Help!' he squealed, as he ran for his life. 'Never have I seen such a terrible creature! It must be a very bad juju.'

Hyena quickly sat down and ate all the food, which was scarcely enough for one in any case, and then he went back to the river, found his skin and put it on again. He strolled slowly up the bank to the place where the cooking-pot stood, and found Hare returning cautiously.

'O Hyena!' gasped Hare. 'Did you see it too?'

'See what?' asked the deceitful animal.

'That terrible demon,' explained Hare.

'I saw nothing. But come, let us eat now,' said Hyena calmly, as he walked towards the cooking-pot and looked inside it.

"Hare and the Hyena," from *African Myths and Legends.* © 1962 Kathleen Arnott. Used by permission of Henry Z. Walck, Inc., publisher, and Oxford University Press.

'Where is it? Where is my food? What has happened to it?' cried Hyena, pretending to be in a fine rage.

Hare looked at the empty pot.

'It was that horrible demon,' he explained. 'It frightened me away so that it could eat our food.'

'Rubbish! You ate it yourself while I was washing at the river,' shouted Hyena, and no amount of protestations by poor Hare had any effect.

'Well,' said Hare. 'I know what I shall do. I shall make a fine bow and arrow and if the creature comes again I shall shoot it.'

The next day the farmer again gave them a pot of beans, but instead of working while it cooked, Hare took a supple branch and began to make himself a bow.

The cunning hyena watched him as he shaped the wood with his knife, and when it was almost finished, he said:

'Give me your bow, Hare. My father taught me a special way of cutting bows to make them better than any others. I'll finish that for you.'

The unsuspecting Hare gave up his bow and knife and Hyena began cutting it in a special way, making it so weak in one place that it was bound to break as soon as it was used.

'There you are! Keep this beside you while I go and wash, in case that creature comes again,' said Hyena, as he bounded off to the river, to remove his skin once more.

Hare, waiting beside the pot of beans, was just considering whether he could take a mouthful, so great was his hunger, when once again the most repulsive-looking animal he had ever seen bounded towards him. Seizing his bow, he put an arrow in it and pulled. Snap! It broke in his hands, and as the horrible creature came closer and closer, Hare fled.

So, of course, Hyena had all the food once more, and then went back to the river and put on his skin. He returned to accuse Hare of stealing the beans. Hare denied having even a taste of food, but looking closely at Hyena he thought he saw a little piece of bean stuck in his teeth as he spoke.

'Aha!' said Hare to himself. 'If that's the way it is, I shall be ready for you tomorrow, my friend.'

That night while Hyena was sleeping, Hare made another bow. It was a good strong bow with no weak spots at all, and had three sharp arrows to go with it. Then the hare, feeling ravenous by now, crept to the spot where they cooked their food, hid the bow and arrows in some nearby long grass and, returning to find Hyena still asleep, he lay down close by him.

The next day, everything happened as Hare had expected. The two animals worked hard all the morning while the cooking-pot boiled nearby, and at mid-day Hyena went to the river to wash.

Hare waited, his new bow in his hand. Presently the loathsome-looking creature came towards him. Hare raised his bow and shot. Straight into the creature's heart went the arrow and Hyena fell dead on the ground. Hare bent over the body and was not surprised when he saw it really was Hyena.

'O well,' he remarked, as he ate the first good meal he had had for days, 'my mother always told me that greed did not pay, and now I know she was right.'

THE ELEPHANT'S CHILD

Rudyard Kipling

Rudyard Kipling's pourquoi Just So Stories *are still favorites with children. His play with words and sounds delight them: "'satiable curtiosity," "dretful," "the great grey-green, greasy Limpopo River," and the Python's "scalesome, flailsome tail." They especially enjoy stories like "The Elephant's Child" in which a child is able to dominate adults.*

In the High and Far-Off Times the Elephant, O Best Beloved, had no trunk. He had only a blackish, bulgy nose, as big as a boot, that he could wriggle about from side to side; but he couldn't pick up things with it. But there was one Elephant—a new Elephant—an Elephant's Child—who was full of 'satiable curtiosity, and that means he asked ever so many questions. *And* he lived in Africa, and he filled all Africa with his 'satiable curtiosities. He asked his tall aunt, the Ostrich, why her tail-feathers grew just so, and his tall aunt the Ostrich spanked him with her hard, hard claw. He asked his tall uncle, the Giraffe, what made his skin spotty, and his tall uncle, the Giraffe, spanked him with his hard, hard hoof. And still he was full of 'satiable curtiosity! He

asked his broad aunt, the Hippopotamus, why her eyes were red, and his broad aunt, the Hippopotamus, spanked him with her broad, broad hoof; and he asked his hairy uncle, the Baboon, why melons tasted just so, and his hairy uncle, the Baboon, spanked him with his hairy, hairy paw. And *still* he was full of 'satiable curtiosity! He asked questions about everything that he saw, or heard, or felt, or smelt, or touched, and all his uncles and his aunts spanked him. And still he was full of 'satiable curtiosity!

One fine morning in the middle of the Precession of the Equinoxes this 'satiable Elephant's Child asked a new fine question that he had never asked before. He asked, 'What does the Crocodile have for dinner?' Then everybody said, 'Hush!' in a loud and dretful tone, and they spanked him immediately and directly, without stopping, for a long time.

By and by, when that was finished, he came

upon Kolokolo Bird sitting in the middle of a wait-a-bit thornbush, and he said, 'My father has spanked me, and my mother has spanked me; all my aunts and uncles have spanked me for my 'satiable curtiosity; and *still* I want to know what the Crocodile has for dinner!'

Then Kolokolo Bird said, with a mournful cry, 'Go to the banks of the great grey-green, greasy Limpopo River, all set about with fever-trees, and find out.'

That very next morning, when there was nothing left of the Equinoxes, because the Precession had preceded according to precedent, this 'satiable Elephant's Child took a hundred pounds of bananas (the little short red kind), and a hundred pounds of sugar-cane (the long purple kind), and seventeen melons (the greeny-crackly kind), and said to all his dear families, 'Goodbye. I am going to the great grey-green, greasy Limpopo River, all set about with fever-trees, to find out what the Crocodile has for dinner.' And they all spanked him once more for luck, though he asked them most politely to stop.

Then he went away, a little warm, but not at all astonished, eating melons, and throwing the rind about, because he could not pick it up.

He went from Graham's Town to Kimberley, and from Kimberley to Khama's Country, and from Khama's Country he went east by north, eating melons all the time, till at last he came to the banks of the great grey-green, greasy Limpopo River, all set about with fever-trees, precisely as Kolokolo Bird had said.

Now you must know and understand, O Best Beloved, that till that very week, and day, and hour, and minute, this 'satiable Elephant's Child had never seen a Crocodile, and did not know what one was like. It was all his 'satiable curtiosity.

The first thing that he found was a Bi-Coloured-Python-Rock-Snake curled round a rock.

''Scuse me,' said the Elephant's Child most politely, 'but have you seen such a thing as a Crocodile in these promiscuous parts?'

'*Have* I seen a Crocodile?' said the Bi-Coloured-Python-Rock-Snake, in a voice of dretful scorn. 'What will you ask me next?'

''Scuse me,' said the Elephant's Child, 'but could you kindly tell me what he has for dinner?'

Then the Bi-Coloured-Python-Rock-Snake uncoiled himself very quickly from the rock, and spanked the Elephant's Child with his scalesome, flailsome tail.

'That is odd,' said the Elephant's Child, 'because my father and my mother, and my uncle and my aunt, not to mention my other aunt, the Hippopotamus, and my other uncle, the Baboon, have all spanked me for my 'satiable curtiosity—and I suppose this is the same thing.'

So he said good-bye very politely to the Bi-Coloured-Python-Rock-Snake, and helped to coil him up on the rock again, and went on, a little warm, but not at all astonished, eating melons, and throwing the rind about, because he could not pick it up, till he trod on what he thought was a log of wood at the very edge of the great grey-green, greasy Limpopo River, all set about with fever-trees.

But it was really the Crocodile, O Best Beloved, and the Crocodile winked one eye—like this!

''Scuse me,' said the Elephant's Child most politely, 'but do you happen to have seen a Crocodile in these promiscuous parts?'

Then the Crocodile winked the other eye, and lifted half his tail out of the mud; and the Elephant's Child stepped back most politely, because he did not wish to be spanked again.

'Come hither, Little One,' said the Crocodile. 'Why do you ask such things?'

''Scuse me,' said the Elephant's Child most politely, 'but my father has spanked me, my mother has spanked me, not to mention my tall aunt, the Ostrich, and my tall uncle, the Giraffe, who can kick ever so hard, as well as my broad aunt, the Hippopotamus, and my hairy uncle, the Baboon, *and* including the Bi-Coloured-Python-Rock-Snake, with the scalesome, flailsome tail, just up the bank, who spanks harder than any of them; and *so*, if it's quite all the same to you, I don't want to be spanked any more.'

'Come hither, Little One,' said the Crocodile, 'for I am the Crocodile,' and he wept crocodile-tears to show it was quite true.

Then the Elephant's Child grew all breathless, and panted, and kneeled down on the bank and said, 'You are the very person I have been looking for all these long days. Will you please tell me what you have for dinner?'

'Come hither, Little One,' said the Crocodile, 'and I'll whisper.'

Then the Elephant's Child put his head down close to the Crocodile's musky, tusky mouth, and the Crocodile caught him by his little nose, which up to that very week, day, hour, and minute, had been no bigger than a boot, though much more useful.

'I think,' said the Crocodile—and he said it between his teeth, like this—'I think to-day I will begin with Elephant's Child!'

At this, O Best Beloved, the Elephant's Child was much annoyed, and he said, speaking through his nose, like this, 'Led go! You are hurtig be!'

Then the Bi-Coloured-Python-Rock-Snake scuffled down from the bank and said, 'My young friend, if you do not now, immediately and instantly, pull as hard as ever you can, it is my opinion that your acquaintance in the large-pattern leather ulster' (and by this he meant the Crocodile) 'will jerk you into yonder limpid stream before you can say Jack Robinson.'

This is the way Bi-Coloured-Python-Rock-Snakes always talk.

Then the Elephant's Child sat back on his little haunches, and pulled, and pulled, and pulled, and his nose began to stretch. And the Crocodile floundered into the water, making it all creamy with great sweeps of his tail, and *he* pulled, and pulled, and pulled.

And the Elephant's Child's nose kept on stretching; and the Elephant's Child spread all his little four legs and pulled, and pulled, and pulled, and his nose kept on stretching; and the Crocodile threshed his tail like an oar, and *he* pulled, and pulled, and pulled, and at each pull the Elephant's Child's nose grew longer and longer—and it hurt him hijjus!

Then the Elephant's Child felt his legs slipping, and he said through his nose, which was now nearly five feet long, 'This is too butch for be!'

Then the Bi-Coloured-Python-Rock-Snake came down from the bank, and knotted himself in a double-clove-hitch round the Elephant's Child's hind legs, and said, 'Rash and inexperienced traveller, we will now seriously devote ourselves to a little high tension, because if we do not, it is my impression that yonder self-propelling man-of-war with the armour-plated upper deck' (and by this, O Best Beloved, he meant the Crocodile), 'will permanently vitiate your future career.'

That is the way all Bi-Coloured-Python-Rock-Snakes always talk.

So he pulled, and the Elephant's Child pulled, and the Crocodile pulled; but the Elephant's Child and the Bi-Coloured-Python-Rock-Snake pulled hardest; and at last the Crocodile let go of the Elephant's Child's nose with a plop that you could hear all up and down the Limpopo.

Then the Elephant's Child sat down most hard and sudden; but first he was careful to say 'Thank you' to the Bi-Coloured-Python-Rock-Snake; and next he was kind to his poor pulled nose, and wrapped it all up in cool banana leaves, and hung it in the great grey-green, greasy Limpopo to cool.

'What are you doing that for?' said the Bi-Coloured-Python-Rock-Snake.

' 'Scuse me,' said the Elephant's Child, 'but my nose is badly out of shape, and I am waiting for it to shrink.'

'Then you will have to wait a long time,' said the Bi-Coloured-Python-Rock-Snake. 'Some people do not know what is good for them.'

The Elephant's Child sat there for three days waiting for his nose to shrink. But it never grew any shorter, and, besides, it made him squint. For, O Best Beloved, you will see and understand that the Crocodile had pulled it out into a really truly trunk same as all Elephants have today.

At the end of the third day a fly came and stung him on the shoulder, and before he knew what he was doing he lifted up his trunk and hit that fly dead with the end of it.

' 'Vantage number one!' said the Bi-Coloured-Python-Rock-Snake. 'You couldn't have done that with a mere-smear nose. Try and eat a little now.'

Before he thought what he was doing the Elephant's Child put out his trunk and plucked a large bundle of grass, dusted it clean against his fore-legs, and stuffed it into his own mouth.

' 'Vantage number two!' said the Bi-Coloured-Python-Rock-Snake. 'You couldn't have done that with a mere-smear nose. Don't you think the sun is very hot here?'

'It is,' said the Elephant's Child, and before he thought what he was doing he schlooped up a schloop of mud from the banks of the great grey-green, greasy Limpopo, and slapped it on his head, where it made a cool schloopy-sloshy mud-cap all trickly behind his ears.

''Vantage number three!' said the Bi-Coloured-Python-Rock-Snake. 'You couldn't have done that with a mere-smear nose. Now how do you feel about being spanked again?'

''Scuse me,' said the Elephant's Child, 'but I should not like it at all.'

'How would you like to spank somebody?' said the Bi-Coloured-Python-Rock-Snake.

'I should like it very much indeed,' said the Elephant's Child.

'Well,' said the Bi-Coloured-Python-Rock-Snake, 'you will find that new nose of yours very useful to spank people with.'

'Thank you,' said the Elephant's Child, 'I'll remember that; and now I think I'll go home to all my dear families and try.'

So the Elephant's Child went home across Africa frisking and whisking his trunk. When he wanted fruit to eat he pulled fruit down from a tree, instead of waiting for it to fall as he used to do. When he wanted grass he plucked grass up from the ground, instead of going on his knees as he used to do. When the flies bit him he broke off the branch of a tree and used it as a fly-whisk; and he made himself a new, cool, slushy-squshy mud-cap whenever the sun was hot. When he felt lonely walking through Africa he sang to himself down his trunk, and the noise was louder than several brass bands. He went especially out of his way to find a broad Hippopotamus (she was no relation of his), and he spanked her very hard, to make sure that the Bi-Coloured-Python-Rock-Snake had spoken the truth about his new trunk. The rest of the time he picked up the melon rinds that he had dropped on his way to the Limpopo—for he was a Tidy Pachyderm.

One dark evening he came back to all his dear families, and he coiled up his trunk and said, 'How do you do?' They were very glad to see him, and immediately said, 'Come here and be spanked for your 'satiable curtiosity.'

'Pooh,' said the Elephant's Child. 'I don't think you peoples know anything about spanking; but *I* do, and I'll show you.'

Then he uncurled his trunk and knocked two of his dear brothers head over heels.

'O Bananas!' said they, 'where did you learn that trick, and what have you done to your nose?'

'I got a new one from the Crocodile on the banks of the great grey-green, greasy Limpopo River,' said the Elephant's Child. 'I asked him what he had for dinner, and he gave me this to keep.'

'It looks very ugly,' said his hairy uncle, the Baboon.

'It does,' said the Elephant's Child. 'But it's very useful,' and he picked up his hairy uncle, the Baboon, by one hairy leg, and hove him into a hornet's nest.

Then that bad Elephant's Child spanked all his dear families for a long time, till they were very warm and greatly astonished. He pulled out his tall Ostrich aunt's tail-feathers; and he caught his tall uncle, the Giraffe, by the hind-leg, and dragged him through a thorn-bush; and he shouted at his broad aunt, the Hippopotamus, and blew bubbles into her ear when she was sleeping in the water after meals; but he never let any one touch Kolokolo Bird.

At last things grew so exciting that his dear families went off one by one in a hurry to the banks of the great grey-green, greasy Limpopo River, all set about with fever-trees, to borrow new noses from the Crocodile. When they came back nobody spanked anybody any more; and ever since that day, O Best Beloved, all the Elephants you will ever see, besides all those that you won't, have trunks precisely like the trunk of the 'satiable Elephant's Child.

Drolls

Stories about the absurd actions of numbskulls have a long history. They are popular throughout the world because the "dümmling" figure seems to be as universal as the abused child, the trickster, and the Culture Hero. There is a bit of the fool in most people; everyone is occasionally forgetful, illogical, or naïve. And it is common for an individual to joke about his foolish behavior. In listening to folktales about numbskulls and simpletons—the hearer feels a sense of relief—as silly as he behaves at times, at least he is not as stupid as Hans Hansen's hired girl or lazy Jack.

Many drolls poke gentle fun, but some are harsher, more satiric. Compare the tone of "Lazy Jack" with that of "A Time for Everything," two stories about the problems that arise from having a too literal mind. Jack's mother calls him a "stupid lout" while the other mother calls her son "my darling." There is gentle fun in "A Time for Everything" as well as a feeling that the dümmling will mature and learn, but the teller of "Lazy Jack" obviously considers him a hopeless, although lucky, fool. Two other tales that can be compared are "Gudbrand on the Hill-side" and "The Husband Who Was To Mind the House." The satiric drolls are often less popular than the more gentle ones because their tone can make listeners feel uncomfortable.

In addition to the problems caused by a too literal mind, the relationship between men and women is a favorite topic of drolls. Old men who want young wives have long been considered absurd, as the Scandinavian tale "The Squire's Bride" illustrates. The roles of husband and wife are central to a large number of humorous narratives. In "Gudbrand on the Hill-side" a simple farmer sets off to sell his cow. He exchanges it for a horse and continues to make trades, each time

receiving something less valuable. Eventually he receives a shilling which he spends for food. Arriving home he recounts his adventures and not only receives his wife's complete approval for each action but also the hundred dollars his neighbor had wagered on the wife's reaction. Less fortunate is the man in "The Husband Who Was To

From *Thistle and Thyme* by Sorche Nic Leodhas. Illustrated by Evaline Ness. Copyright © 1962 by Leclaire G. Alger. Reproduced by permission of Holt, Rinehart and Winston, Inc.

Mind the House." Exchanging roles with his wife proves disastrous for him, the cow, the ale, and the house. A North African tale about husbands and wives, "Stubborn Husband, Stubborn Wife," is also included in the following section.

In folklore most plot incidents and motifs are quite flexible; they can stand alone in simple anecdotes or be included in longer, more complex narratives. To illustrate, "Hans Hansen's Hired Girl" and "Clever Elsie" have been placed side by side for comparison in the following collection. Another example of this process can be seen in the eastern anecdote, "The Hodja and the Moon," a short droll concerning the Hodja's attempt to fish the moon out of a well and throw it back to the sky. The same motif plays a minor role in "The Three Sillies," an English tale about an amazing set of fools.

The history of drolls is interesting because of the relationship between the oral and the literary traditions. While many are part of oral folklore, most of the narratives are known because of literary sources. Stories about numbskulls have been compiled in jestbooks ever since the Renaissance. These collections have in turn influenced oral tales, and many seemingly new drolls are simply reworkings of these old sources. Regardless of their origin, folk or literary, narratives about human absurdities provide needed laughter and entertainment in a troubled world.

THREE TALES OF THE HODJA / Turkey

Charles Downing

Tales of the Hodja are told in the Middle East, the Balkans, and Greece. In Turkey, "Hodja" is a title of respect given to a scholar of the Qoran, Koran, and religious law. The holder wore a large headdress called a kavuk that indicated his learning. He was wise, and in some of the traditional tales about the Hodja he does so appear, as can be seen in the selection in Tales of Trickery. The Hodja is able to give witty repartee to Timur Leng in the jokes about this Mongol conquerer of Turkey in the early fifteenth century.

However, the Hodja has another side to him: at times he finds himself in embarrassing situations, as when caught stealing, and often reveals himself to be a gullible fool, as when he believes he is dead.

These short anecdotes about everyday life may have originated in India, Persia, Syria, or Arabia, but they have long been a part of the Turkish culture. The Turks consider them to be about a historical personage, Nasr-ed-Dīn Hodja, and many areas claim to be his birthplace. However, some of the stories told about the Hodja are found in eleventh-century Persian literature about an Arab named Djuhā. It is likely that as the Hodja cycle developed, all jests and humorous tales were put under his name, much like many timber tales were ascribed to Paul Bunyan.

It is unfortunate that these stories are not better known in the West because their humor has never been surpassed.

One morning the Hodja entered a vegetable garden, and began to fill his sack with everything

From *Tales of the Hodja*, © Charles Downing 1964. Used by permission of Henry Z. Walck, Inc., publisher, and Oxford University Press.

he could lay his hands on—carrots, marrows, aubergines, beans, and melons. Suddenly the owner appeared.

'What are you doing in there?' he said.

'Yesterday evening,' replied the Hodja, 'a terrible whirlwind swept me away and deposited me in this garden.'

'And who picked all these vegetables?' said the owner, pointing to the abundant contents of the sack.

'Ah. The whirlwind threw me with great force from side to side and in order to remain on the ground, I seized hold of whatever I could, and it came away in my hand.'

'All right,' said the owner, grimly. 'And who put them in that sack?'

'Not so fast,' said the Hodja. 'I am still working on that one!'

One day a friend entrusted a jar to the Hodja and asked him to keep it for him until he came back. A few days passed, and the Hodja, who had been very curious to know what was in the jar, grew more and more impatient. Finally he took off the lid, and looked inside. The jar was full of honey. The Hodja dipped his finger in, and tasted the honey. It was excellent. The Hodja replaced the lid, and went about his business. It was not long, however, before his mind returned to the delicious honey. Off came the lid, in went the finger, on went the lid, and the Hodja went about his business. So it continued until the jar was wiped clean of any trace of honey. The owner returned and asked for the jar he had entrusted to the Hodja. It felt rather light, and he looked inside.

'Hodja!' he exclaimed. 'Where is my honey?'

'How nice it would be if you hadn't asked that question,' sighed the Hodja, 'and I didn't have to reply!'

The Hodja was sitting up a tree cutting wood. A passerby observed that the Hodja was sawing away at the branch upon which he was sitting between himself and the tree.

'You will fall down if you continue like that!' he called up.

The Hodja shrugged his shoulders, took no notice, and carried on. Suddenly the branch creaked and cracked, and the Hodja fell with a thud to the ground.

Jumping up, he ran after the man as fast as his bruises would allow him. Catching him up, he said:

'I see you are a prophet, effendi. If you knew when I should fall off a tree, you will know when I shall die.'

The stranger, not wishing to go into a long rigmarole of explanations for a man who had proved he could not see sense, cut matters very short by saying:

'When your donkey brays once, half of your soul will leave your body. When it brays for the second time, you will die!'

The Hodja, much chastened, returned to his donkey, loaded it with the firewood he had cut, and began to make his way home.

On the way, his donkey brayed. The Hodja felt very, very ill. Then the donkey brayed a second time.

'I am dead!' cried Nasreddin, and lying down on the road, he shut his eyes.

After a little time, a group of villagers passed by. Seeing the pale and prostrate Hodja, they fetched a rough wooden coffin, and started to carry him towards his house. On the way through the forest, they came to a fork in the road, and not knowing which branch to take, they began to argue.

The Hodja, already put out by the jostling he had received in the uncomfortable coffin and very much disappointed with his eternal rest, could bear it no longer.

He lifted up his head.

'When I was alive,' he snapped, 'I took the left fork!'

GUDBRAND ON THE HILL-SIDE / Scandinavia

Peter Christen Asbjörnsen

The structure of this story is reminiscent of cumulative tales, but the reader's interest is on the foolish trades and the wife's reactions rather than on the pattern.

Compare the teller's attitude toward Gudbrand with that of the feeling about numbskulls in the next two tales.

Once on a time there was a man whose name was Gudbrand; he had a farm which lay far, far away, upon a hill-side, and so they called him Gudbrand on the Hill-side.

Now, you must know this man and his good-wife lived so happily together, and understood one another so well, that all the husband did the wife thought so well done, there was nothing like it in the world, and she was always glad whatever he turned his hand to. The farm was their own land, and they had a hundred dollars lying at the bottom of their chest, and two cows tethered up in a stall in their farmyard.

So one day his wife said to Gudbrand,

"Do you know, dear, I think we ought to take one of our cows into town and sell it; that's what I think; for then we shall have some money in hand, and such well-to-do people as we ought to have ready money like the rest of the world. As for the hundred dollars at the bottom of the chest yonder, we can't make a hole in them, and I'm sure I don't know what we want with more than one cow. Besides, we shall gain a little in another way, for then I shall get off with only looking after one cow, instead of having, as now, to feed and litter and water two."

Well, Gudbrand thought his wife talked right good sense, so he set off at once with the cow on his way to town to sell her; but when he got to the town, there was no one who would buy his cow.

"Well! well! never mind," said Gudbrand, "at the worst, I can only go back home again with my cow. I've both stable and tether for her, I should think, and the road is no farther out than in"; and with that he began to toddle home with his cow.

But when he had gone a bit of the way, a man met him who had a horse to sell, so Gudbrand thought 'twas better to have a horse than a cow, so he swopped with the man. A little farther on, he met a man walking along, and driving a fat pig before him, and he thought it better to have a fat pig than a horse, so he swopped with the man. After that he went a little farther, and a man met him with a goat; so he thought it better to have a goat than a pig, and he swopped with the man that owned the goat. Then he went on a good bit till he met a man who had a sheep, and he swopped with him too, for he thought it always better to have a sheep than a goat. After a while he met a man with a goose, and he swopped away the sheep for the goose; and when he had walked a long, long time, he met a man with a cock, and he swopped with him, for he thought in this wise, "'Tis surely better to have a cock than a goose." Then he went on till the day was far spent, and he began to get very hungry, so he sold the cock for a shilling, and bought food with the money, for, thought Gudbrand on the Hill-side, "'Tis always better to save one's life than to have a cock."

After that he went on home till he reached his nearest neighbour's house, where he turned in.

"Well," said the owner of the house, "how did things go with you in town?"

"Rather so so," said Gudbrand. "I can't praise my luck, nor do I blame it either"; and with that he told the whole story from first to last.

"Gudbrand on the Hill-side," from *Popular Tales from the Norse* by Peter Christen Asbjörnsen, translated by G. W. Dasent. Published by G. P. Putnam's Sons, 1908.

"Ah!" said his friend, "you'll get nicely hauled over the coals, that one can see, when you get home to your wife. Heaven help you, I wouldn't stand in your shoes for something."

"Well!" said Gudbrand on the Hill-side, "I think things might have gone worse with me; but now, whether I have done wrong or not, I have so kind a goodwife, she never has a word to say against anything that I do."

"Oh!" answered his neighbour, "I hear what you say, but I don't believe it for all that."

"Shall we lay a bet upon it?" asked Gudbrand on the Hill-side. "I have a hundred dollars at the bottom of my chest at home; will you lay as many against them?"

Yes, the friend was ready to bet; so Gudbrand stayed there till evening, when it began to get dark, and then they went together to his house, and the neighbour was to stand outside the door and listen, while the man went in to see his wife.

"Good evening!" said Gudbrand.

"Good evening!" said the goodwife. "Oh! is that you? Now, God be praised!"

Yes, it was he. So the wife asked how things had gone with him in town.

"Oh! only so so," answered Gudbrand; "not much to brag of. When I got to the town there was no one who would buy the cow, so you must know I swopped it away for a horse."

"For a horse!" said his wife; "well, that is good of you; thanks with all my heart. We are so well-to-do that we may drive to church, just as well as other people; and if we choose to keep a horse we have a right to get one, I should think. So run out, child, and put up the horse."

"Ah!" said Gudbrand, "but you see I've not got the horse after all; for when I got a bit farther on the road, I swopped it away for a pig."

"Think of that, now!" said the wife; "you did just as I should have done myself; a thousand thanks! Now I can have a bit of bacon in the house to set before people when they come to see me, that I can. What do we want with a horse? People would only say we had got so proud that we couldn't walk to church. Go out, child, and put up the pig in the stye."

"But I've not got the pig either," said Gudbrand; "for when I got a little farther on, I swopped it away for a milch goat."

"Bless us!" cried his wife, "how well you manage everything! Now I think it over, what should I do with a pig? People would only point at us and say, 'Yonder they eat up all they have got.' No! now I have got a goat, and I shall have milk and cheese, and keep the goat too. Run out, child, and put up the goat."

"Nay, but I haven't got the goat either," said Gudbrand, "for a little farther on I swopped it away, and got a fine sheep instead."

"You don't say so!" cried his wife; "why you do everything to please me, just as if I had been with you; what do we want with a goat? If I had it I should lose half my time in climbing up the hills to get it down. No! if I have a sheep, I shall have both wool and clothing, and fresh meat in the house. Run out, child, and put up the sheep."

"But I haven't got the sheep any more than the rest," said Gudbrand, "for when I had gone a bit farther, I swopped it away for a goose."

"Thank you! thank you! with all my heart!" cried his wife; "what should I do with a sheep? I have no spinning-wheel, nor carding-comb, nor should I care to worry myself with cutting, and shaping, and sewing clothes. We can buy clothes now, as we have always done; and now I shall have roast goose, which I have longed for so often; and, besides, down to stuff my little pillow with. Run out, child, and put up the goose."

"Ah!" said Gudbrand, "but I haven't the goose either; for when I had gone a bit farther I swopped it away for a cock."

"Dear me!" cried his wife, "how you think of everything! just as I should have done myself! A cock! think of that! why, it's as good as an eight-day clock, for every morning the cock crows at four o'clock, and we shall be able to stir our stumps in good time. What should we do with a goose? I don't know how to cook it; and as for my pillow, I can stuff it with cotton-grass. Run out, child, and put up the cock."

"But, after all, I haven't got the cock," said Gudbrand; "for when I had gone a bit farther, I got as hungry as a hunter, so I was forced to sell the cock for a shilling, for fear I should starve."

"Now, God be praised that you did so!" cried his wife; "whatever you do, you do it always just after my own heart. What should we do with a cock? We are our own masters, I should think, and can lie a-bed in the morning as long as we like. Heaven be thanked that I have got you safe back again! you do everything so well that I want neither cock nor goose; neither pigs nor kine."

Then Gudbrand opened the door and said, "Well, what do you say now? Have I won the hundred dollars?" and his neighbour was forced to allow that he had.

MR. VINEGAR / England

James Orchard Halliwell

As "Mr. Vinegar" illustrates, variants of the same tale often have different introductions. The English tale, unlike "Gudbrand on the Hill-side," begins with the incident of the door dropping on robbers. This anecdote is often told about the literal-minded woman who, being told to guard the door, carries it with her in her travels. The real point of "Mr. Vinegar," however, is the "dümmling's" lack of business sense.

Mr. and Mrs. Vinegar lived in a vinegar bottle. Now, one day when Mr. Vinegar was away from home and Mrs. Vinegar, who was a very good housewife, was busily sweeping her house, an unlucky thump of the broom brought the whole house clitter-clatter about her ears.

In great grief she rushed forth to meet her husband. On seeing him she exclaimed, "Oh, Mr. Vinegar, Mr. Vinegar, we are ruined, we are ruined! I have knocked the house down, and it is all in pieces!"

Mr. Vinegar said, "My dear, let us see what can be done. Here is the door; I will take it on my back, and we will go forth to seek our fortune."

They walked all that day and at nightfall entered a thick forest. They were both tired.

Mr. Vinegar said, "My love, I will climb up into a tree, drag up the door, and you shall follow."

He did so, and they both stretched their weary limbs on the door and fell fast asleep.

In the middle of the night Mr. Vinegar was disturbed by the sound of voices beneath the tree. To his dismay he saw that a party of thieves had met there to divide their booty.

"Here, Jack," said one, "here's five pounds for

"Mr. Vinegar," from *Nursery Rhymes and Nursery Tales of England* by James Orchard Halliwell, 1849.

you. Here, Bill, here's ten pounds for you. Here, Bob, here's three pounds for you."

Mr. Vinegar could listen no longer. He was so afraid and he trembled so violently that he shook the door down on their heads. Away scampered the thieves, but Mr. Vinegar dared not come down out of the tree till broad daylight. He then scrambled down and went to lift up the door. What did he see under the door but a number of golden guineas!

"Come down, Mrs. Vinegar!" he cried. "Come down, I say; our fortune's made! Come down, I say."

Mrs. Vinegar got down as fast as she could and saw the money with equal delight.

"Now, my dear," said she, "I'll tell you what you shall do. There is a fair at the neighboring town; you shall take these forty guineas and buy a cow. I can make butter and cheese, which you shall sell at market, and we shall then be able to live very comfortably."

Mr. Vinegar agreed and took the money and went off to the fair. When he arrived, he walked up and down and at length saw a beautiful red cow. It was an excellent milker and perfect in every respect.

"Oh," thought Mr. Vinegar, "if I had that cow, I should be the happiest man alive!"

So he offered the forty guineas for the cow,

and the owner declaring that, as he was a friend, he'd oblige him, the bargain was made. Proud of his purchase, he drove the cow backwards and forwards to show it off.

By and by Mr. Vinegar saw a man playing some bagpipes—*tweedle-dum, tweedle-dee.* The children followed the man about, and he appeared to be pocketing money on all sides.

"Well," thought Mr. Vinegar, "if I had that beautiful instrument, I should be the happiest man alive. My fortune would be made."

So he went up to the man.

"Friend," said he, "what a beautiful instrument that is, and what a deal of money you must make!"

"Why, yes," said the man, "I make a great deal of money, to be sure, and it is a wonderful instrument."

"Oh," cried Mr. Vinegar, "how I should like to possess it!"

"Well," said the man, "as you are a friend, I don't much mind parting with it; you shall have it for that red cow."

"Done!" said the delighted Mr. Vinegar. So the beautiful red cow was given for the bagpipes.

Mr. Vinegar walked up and down with his purchase; but in vain he attempted to play a tune. Instead of his pocketing pence, the boys followed him hooting and laughing.

Poor Mr. Vinegar, his fingers grew very cold! Heartily ashamed and mortified, he was leaving the town, when he met a man with a fine thick pair of gloves.

"Oh, my fingers are so very cold!" said Mr. Vinegar to himself. "If I had those beautiful gloves. I should be the happiest man alive."

He went up to the man. "Friend," said he, "you seem to have a capital pair of gloves there."

"Yes, truly," said the man, "and my hands are as warm as possible this cold November day."

"Well," said Mr. Vinegar, "how I should like to have them!"

"What will you give?" said the man. "As you are a friend, I don't much mind letting you have them for those bagpipes."

"Done!" cried Mr. Vinegar. He put on the gloves and felt perfectly happy as he trudged homewards.

At last he grew very tired. Just then he saw a man coming towards him with a good stout stick in his hand.

"Oh," said Mr. Vinegar, "if I had that stick, I should be the happiest man alive."

"Friend," he said to the man, "what a rare good stick you have!"

"Yes," said the man, "I have used it for many a long mile, and a good friend it has been. But if you have a fancy for it, and as you are a friend, I don't mind giving it to you for the pair of gloves."

Mr. Vinegar's hands were so warm and his legs so tired, that he gladly exchanged.

As he drew near to the wood where he had left his wife, he heard a parrot on a tree calling out his name.

"Mr. Vinegar, you foolish man!" said the parrot. "You went to the fair and laid out all your money in buying a cow. Not content with that, you changed it for bagpipes, on which you could not play and which were not worth one-tenth of the money. You had no sooner got the bagpipes than you changed them for gloves, which were not worth one-quarter of the money. When you had got the gloves, you changed them for a poor miserable stick. Now for your forty guineas, cow, bagpipes, and gloves, you have nothing to show but that poor miserable stick, which you might have cut in any hedge."

At this the bird laughed, and Mr. Vinegar, falling into a violent rage, threw the stick at its head. The stick lodged in the tree. So Mr. Vinegar returned to his wife without money, cow, bagpipes, gloves, or stick.

THE HUSBAND WHO WAS TO MIND THE HOUSE/Scandinavia

Peter Christen Asbjörnsen

Some women may feel that any man who believes his wife has an easy life deserves what happens to this husband, but most readers will think the man's disasters are like a bad dream. The tone of this version is rather cruel in its punishment of a common masculine attitude. Compare this teller's view of the husband–wife relationship with that in "Gudbrand on the Hill-side" and "Stubborn Husband, Stubborn Wife."

Once upon a time there was a man so surly and cross, he never thought his wife did anything right in the house. So, one evening in haymaking time, he came home, scolding and swearing, and showing his teeth and making a dust.

"Dear love, don't be so angry; there's a good man," said his goody; "to-morrow let's change our work. I'll go out with the mowers and mow, and you shall mind the house at home."

Yes, the husband thought that would do very well. He was quite willing, he said.

So, early next morning his goody took a scythe over her neck, and went out into the hay-field with the mowers and began to mow; but the man was to mind the house, and do the work at home.

First of all he wanted to churn the butter; but when he had churned a while, he got thirsty, and went down to the cellar to tap a barrel of ale. So, just when he had knocked in the bung, and was putting the tap into the cask, he heard overhead the pig come into the kitchen. Then off he ran up the cellar steps, with the tap in his hand, as fast as he could, to look after the pig, lest it should upset the churn; but when he got up, and saw that the pig had already knocked the churn over, and stood there, routing and grunting amongst the cream which was running all over the floor, he got so wild with rage that he quite

forgot the ale-barrel, and ran at the pig as hard as he could. He caught it, too, just as it ran out of doors, and gave it such a kick that piggy lay for dead on the spot. Then all at once he remembered he had the tap in his hand; but when he got down to the cellar, every drop of ale had run out of the cask.

Then he went into the dairy and found enough cream left to fill the churn again, and so he began to churn, for butter they must have at dinner. When he had churned a bit, he remembered that their milking cow was still shut up in the byre, and hadn't had a bit to eat or a drop to drink all the morning, though the sun was high. Then all at once he thought 'twas too far to take her down to the meadow, so he'd just get her up on the housetop—for the house, you must know, was thatched with sods, and a fine crop of grass was growing there. Now their house lay close up against a steep down, and he thought if he laid a plank across to the thatch at the back he'd easily get the cow up.

But still he couldn't leave the churn, for there was his little babe crawling about on the floor, and "if I leave it," he thought, "the child is sure to upset it." So he took the churn on his back, and went out with it; but then he thought he'd better first water the cow before he turned her out on the thatch; so he took up a bucket to draw water out of the well; but, as he stooped down at the well's brink, all the cream ran out of the churn over his shoulders, and so down into the well.

"The Husband Who Was To Mind the House," from *Popular Tales from the Norse* by Peter Christen Asbjörnsen, translated by G. W. Dasent. Published by G. P. Putnam's Sons, 1908.

Now it was near dinner-time, and he hadn't even got the butter yet; so he thought he'd best boil the porridge, and filled the pot with water, and hung it over the fire. When he had done that, he thought the cow might perhaps fall off the thatch and break her legs or her neck. So he got up on the house to tie her up. One end of the rope he made fast to the cow's neck, and the other he slipped down the chimney and tied round his own thigh; and he had to make haste, for the water now began to boil in the pot, and he had still to grind the oatmeal.

So he began to grind away; but while he was hard at it, down fell the cow off the housetop after all, and as she fell, she dragged the man up the chimney by the rope. There he stuck fast; and as for the cow, she hung halfway down the wall, swinging between heaven and earth, for she could neither get down nor up.

And now the goody had waited seven lengths and seven breadths for her husband to come and call them home to dinner; but never a call they had. At last she thought she'd waited long enough, and went home. But when she got there and saw the cow hanging in such an ugly place, she ran up and cut the rope in two with her scythe. But as she did this, down came her husband out of the chimney; and so when his old dame came inside the kitchen, there she found him standing on his head in the porridge-pot.

STUBBORN HUSBAND, STUBBORN WIFE / Iran

Anne Sinclair Mehdevi

The English ballad "Get Up and Bar the Door," Chapter 15, Ballads, uses the same plot, two stubborn people who will not talk no matter what happens. It leads to amusing situations.

There was a time and there wasn't a time in the long ago when a man and wife lived together in a small house in the city of Hamadan. The wife was industrious and hard-working and was busy from morning till night. The man was lazy and good-for-nothing. They argued and quarreled all day long.

One day, the wife said, "It's a disgrace the way you sit all day on the bench in front of the house staring at the sky and doing nothing at all. Are you afraid to move for fear that the wind will blow off your beard?"

The man said, "What is there for me to do? I inherited a flock of sheep from my father and I gave them to a shepherd. In return, he gives us cheese and milk and wool, and with this we eat

the man folded his arms and stared at the sky.

The wife said, "What about the calf in the stable? Every day I give the calf its water. That is man's work. I will not do it any more. You will and clothe ourselves. You are strong and able to do the cooking and cleaning and washing." Then have to break a rib, now and then, and water the calf yourself."

The man said, "If you can't do a little job like watering the calf, then what are you good for?"

The wife answered, "I am good for a woman's work. I cook for you and sew for you. I wash for you and dry for you. But I will not water the calf."

The man said, "That is not right. I brought you to my house to do what I tell you, even if I tell you to throw yourself off the roof. It has been said by the poets that men are the masters of women. Whatever a man orders, a woman must do."

At these words, the wife grew angry and said, "Yes, the poets have written those words about real men, brave men, not about donkey droppings like you."

And so they argued and quarreled about who would water the calf. At last, they reached an agreement. The wife said she would water the calf that day. But, starting tomorrow, they agreed that whoever spoke the first word in the morning would have to water the calf forever after. If the wife should speak first, she agreed to water the calf without complaining. And if the man should speak first, he agreed to water it.

And so they went to bed, each promising himself that, on the next day, he would refuse to utter a word until the other had spoken.

The next morning, the woman got up early, rolled up her mattress, swept the house, prepared the breakfast, but said nothing. The man too, got up, put on his clothes, ate his breakfast, and said nothing.

The woman watched angrily as her husband prepared to go out as usual and sit on the bench and stare at the sky. Ten times in ten minutes she wanted to shout at him in anger. At last, she put on her veil and went to the neighbor's house so she would be away from him and couldn't speak to him even if she wanted to.

The man watched his wife as she put on her cloak and left the house and walked over to the neighbor's house. He wondered what she was up to, but he did not say a word. After she had gone, he went outside and sat on the stone bench in front of the house and began to look at the sky.

Soon a beggar came along. Seeing the man sitting there, the beggar approached and said, "In the name of Allah, a piece of bread and a slice of onion, master, and may your shadow never grow shorter."

The man said nothing, so the beggar raised his voice and asked again for a piece of bread or a few pennies. Still the man gave no answer.

"This is strange," the beggar said to himself. "This man is moving and breathing, but he doesn't talk. Maybe he is deaf." So, the beggar began to shout.

Still the man said not a word, for he was thinking, "My wife has sent this beggar to make me talk. As soon as I open my mouth, she will come out of the neighbor's house and say, 'You spoke first. Hurry up and water the calf.' I won't be taken in by her tricks. If earth flies up to heaven or if heaven falls down to earth, I will not move my tongue in my mouth."

By this time, the beggar saw that the man was not going to say anything, so he walked past the man and went into the house. He filled his beggar's bowl with all the bread and cheese he could find and then went away. The man saw all this, but said nothing, because he was afraid that if he spoke, he would have to water the calf every day.

Soon a traveling barber came walking down the street. When he saw the man sitting on the bench, he said, "Do you want me to give your beard a trim?"

The man said nothing. So, the barber thought to himself, "If he didn't want me to fix up his hair and trim his beard, he would have spoken up. So, I guess he wants me to work on him."

The barber began to sharpen his razor against his whetstone and soon he had trimmed the man's beard and cut his hair short. Then the barber held out his hand for payment.

The man said nothing. The barber asked for his money three times, but got no answer. This made him angry. "Pay me!" he shouted. "Or I will shave off your beard so you'll look like a woman, and I'll fix your hair to look like a duck's tail." When the man still didn't answer, the barber flew into a rage. He took out his razor and shaved off the man's beard until the man's face was as smooth as the palm of his hand. And he fixed the man's hair to look like a duck's tail. Then the barber went away.

Soon an old woman came hobbling down the street. She was a seller of paint and powder for ladies. As soon as she saw the man with his face all shaven, she thought he was a woman. She said, "My lady, why are you sitting here without your veil? And why have you cut your hair so short?"

The man did not answer, so the old woman reached in her knapsack and took out her pots of paint and powder and some false hair besides. "My lady," she said, coming closer, "you will shame your husband sitting here like this with your hair short and without your veil." The old woman put false hair on the man's head. Then she put rouge on his cheeks and berry juice on his lips and powdered his face all over. When she had finished, she wanted to be paid.

The man said nothing, so the old woman reached in his pocket and took all his money and went away.

Now a clever thief came along. He saw what he thought was a woman sitting on the bench in front of the house and he saw the door wide open. He stopped and said in a sweet voice. "My lady, why have you left your door open? Do you not know that thieves are all around? And why are you sitting outside your house without your veil? Is your husband not at home to keep you safe inside?"

When the thief received no answer, he said to himself, "This woman is deaf and dumb." So he said, "My lady, since your door is open, do you mind if I step inside for a word with your husband?"

The man still said nothing. He was thinking, "My wife has sent this person to make me open my mouth, just as she sent all the others. I know my wife. She is hiding behind the neighbor's window and listening. As soon as I speak, she will run out and say, 'You spoke first. Hurry up and water the calf.' But I am not going to give in just because of a few troubles."

Now the thief saw that whatever he said, not a sound came from the woman sitting on the bench. So, the thief went into the house. When he saw that no one was home, he searched the house and gathered up everything that had a light weight and a heavy price. He put the rugs, the pots and pans, and all the clothing he could find into his satchel and went away.

All this time, the calf in the stable was weak with thirst. The poor calf began to bang its head against the stable door in despair and soon knocked the door down. It ran through the house and out into the street, and began bawling for water.

When the man saw the calf he said to himself, "That wicked wife of mine has even told the calf to come out and start bawling so that I will be forced to speak. But I haven't answered any of the others and I won't answer the calf, either."

Just at this moment, the wife looked out of the neighbor's window and saw the calf running away down the street to the stream. She hurried out of the neighbor's house and caught the calf and took it home. As she came to her house, leading the calf, she suddenly saw her husband sitting on the stone bench wearing false hair, with rouge on his cheeks and berry juice on his lips and powder on his face. She did not recognize him and thought to herself, "That wicked husband of mine has married another wife and brought her here in my place because I refused to water the calf."

She went over to her husband said, "O woman, who told you to come here and sit before my house?"

With a shout of joy, the man jumped up and said, "You spoke first! Hurry up and water the calf." Then he took off his false hair and laughed and laughed.

When the woman saw that this strange creature was her husband, with his face shaven and his cheeks painted, she said, "Dust on your head. Who has done this to you? Who has shaved you?"

She ran into the house in a rage. She saw all the boxes thrown about, the shelves empty, the rugs gone, and she realized that a thief had come and taken everything. She ran outside again and said to her husband, "What was the matter with you? Were you dead or sleeping that you didn't protest?"

The man said, "I was neither dead nor sleeping, but I knew you told all those people to come and force me to talk so I would have to water the calf."

The woman said, "Dust on your stubborn head! You lost what you had and what you'll never have. You lost your face, you lost your money, you lost your rugs—and all because of your stubbornness. And yet you are happy because you don't have to water the calf."

The man smiled and said, "The wise men have said that when a man orders, a woman must obey."

The wife said, "O stubborn man, you have lost your wife too. I am going away and I shall take the calf, since you refuse to water it." So, the woman ran off down the street and the calf followed her.

When she came to the edge of town, she asked some children who were playing, "Did you see a man with a satchel coming out of my house?" The children told her that a man with a satchel had passed them half an hour ago and that he had taken the road across the desert.

The woman took the calf's halter in her hand and started out across the desert. Soon she saw a man with a satchel walking ahead of her. She knew he was the thief, so she hurried to catch up with him. She walked very fast and soon she came up to the thief and passed him.

The thief called, "Where are you going, sister?"

The woman said in a weak voice, "O stranger, I am going to my home."

"Why do you walk so fast?"

She said, "I must get to a caravanserai before it is dark, as I am afraid to spend the night alone in the desert with no one to guard me but the calf. If I had someone to protect me, I would walk slower."

The thief saw that she was very pretty, so he said, "If you walk slower, we can walk together and I will protect you."

"I don't mind," she said, smiling very sweetly at him.

So the wife and the thief walked on together and the woman began to give him tender glances. "O stranger," she said, "how lucky I was to meet a fine, strong man to protect me and care for me." And she smiled even more sweetly and gave him a thousand loving glances from her dark eyes.

The thief said to himself, "She is not bad looking." Then he asked, "Lady sister, don't you have a husband?"

She said, "If I had a husband, would I be all alone in the desert with a calf?"

So, they walked on, and all the time the wife kept sighing and sending loving glances at the thief. Before the afternoon was half over, he asked her to be his wife and she agreed to go with him to the headman in the next town and get married.

Now the wife did not love the thief at all and certainly did not want to marry a thief. In fact, the farther she got from home, the more she thought of her stubborn husband and her heart burned for him. But she had a plan.

She said to the thief, "And when we are married, how will you feed me and clothe me?"

The thief said, "In my satchel there is money enough and clothes enough."

The woman said, "Let me see in your satchel."

But the thief said, "Not now. You shall see when we are married."

They walked on until the sun set, when they came to the next village. They went to the headman's house and asked if he could marry them. The headman agreed and promised to marry them in the morning. He gave them supper and prepared a bedroll for the night. "I have only one guest room," the headman said. "Lady, you may sleep this night on the bedroll of my guest room and your beloved will sleep on the floor next to you. Tomorrow, you will be married at dawn, and then you will go on your journey as man and wife."

So, the wife lay down on the bedroll and the thief stretched out on the floor, and the headman went off to sleep in his own room. Before the thief went to sleep, he placed his satchel next to the door.

Very soon, the thief's snores were so loud they reached the sky. The wife quietly got up and tiptoed to the headman's kitchen. She took a handful of flour and mixed it with water and cooked it over a candle flame until it was paste. Then she poured the paste into the headman's shoes and into the thief's shoes.

Next, she went to get the satchel, but it was too heavy for her to carry, so she dragged it out of the house where she found the calf tied to a post. She put the satchel on the calf's back and started home across the desert just as the sun peeped above the horizon.

At this time, the headman woke up, stretched himself and went to put on his shoes. The paste had hardened and he couldn't get his feet inside. "I cannot marry my guests without shoes," he said to himself, "I wonder what has happened."

He went to his guests' room in his bare feet and there he found the door open and the woman gone. Only the man remained, sound asleep on the floor. The headman shouted, "Say, uncle! Where is your bride?"

The thief woke up and saw that the wife was gone and the satchel, too. He jumped up and ran to put on his shoes but the paste inside them had hardened and he couldn't get his feet inside. Without saying a word to the headman, the thief ran out of the house and down the road to the desert in his bare feet. He ran as fast as he could, but he had gone no more than a league when he had to stop. His feet were sore and bleeding and he couldn't run a step farther. In a rage, he sat down by the roadside and said to himself, "I shall never again see my satchel, but at least I have learned a lesson. Never trust a flirting woman."

Meanwhile, the woman arrived home with the calf and the satchel. As she entered the courtyard, she called, "Husband, I have returned and I will never leave you again. I have brought the calf and I have brought all the things the thief stole from us."

There was no answer to her call. So, she tied the calf to a post and ran inside. There she found her husband sweeping the floor. She looked around in amazement. The breakfast was made, the fire was lit, and the washing was hanging on the bushes to dry.

"O stubborn man," she cried. "What has happened to you? Why are you not sitting on your bench staring at the sky?"

The husband said, "I lost my fortune, I lost my face, and I lost my wife because I was so stubborn."

At once, the wife took the broom and began to sweep. "Go and sit on your bench," she said. "It is for man to order and for woman to obey."

At that moment, the calf, who had not been fed all day, began to bawl. The husband said, "I shall water the calf."

The woman said, "No, I shall do it."

The husband said, "It is for man to order and woman to obey. You shall not water the calf. That is man's work."

And so he watered the calf that day and every day thereafter, and the husband and wife never quarreled again.

THE SQUIRE'S BRIDE / Scandinavia

This tale could be categorized as a tale of trickery as well as a droll. Its humor is not just that of an old man desiring a young girl, but comes from the confusion caused by the squire's orders to dress the bride. He assumes the servant has returned with the girl while the servant believes the squire is talking about a horse.

Once upon a time there was a rich squire who owned a large farm, and had plenty of silver at the bottom of his chest and money in the bank besides; but he felt there was something wanting, for he was a widower.

One day the daughter of a neighboring farmer was working for him in the hayfield. The squire saw her and liked her very much, and as she was the child of poor parents, he thought if he only hinted that he wanted her she would be ready to marry him at once.

So he told her he had been thinking of getting married again.

"Ay! one may think of many things," said the girl, laughing slyly. In her opinion the old fellow ought to be thinking of something that behoved him better than getting married.

"Well, you see, I thought that you should be my wife!"

"No, thank you all the same," said she; "that's not at all likely."

The squire was not accustomed to be gainsaid, and the more she refused him the more determined he was to get her.

But as he made no progress in her favor he sent for her father and told him that if he could arrange the matter with his daughter he would forgive him the money he had lent him, and he would also give him the piece of land which lay close to his meadow into the bargain.

"Yes, you may be sure I'll bring my daughter to her senses," said the father. "She is only a child, and she doesn't know what's best for her."

"The Squire's Bride," from *Fairy Tales from the Far North*, translated by H. L. Braekstad, 1897.

But all his coaxing and talking did not help matters. She would not have the squire, she said, if he sat buried in gold up to his ears.

The squire waited day after day, but at last he became so angry and impatient that he told the father, if he expected him to stand by his promise, he would have to put his foot down now, for he would not wait any longer.

The man knew no other way out of it but to let the squire get everything ready for the wedding; and when the parson and the wedding guests had arrived the squire should send for the girl as if she were wanted for some work on the farm. When she arrived she would have to be married right away, so that she would have no time to think it over.

The squire thought this was well and good, and so he began brewing and baking and getting ready for the wedding in grand style. When the guests had arrived the squire called one of his farm lads and told him to run down to his neighbor and ask him to send him what he had promised.

"But if you are not back in a twinkling," he said, shaking his fist at him, "I'll—"

He did not say more, for the lad ran off as if he had been shot at.

"My master has sent me to ask for that you promised him," said the lad, when he got to the neighbor, "but there is no time to be lost, for he is terribly busy today."

"Yes, yes! Run down into the meadow and take her with you. There she goes!" answered the neighbor.

The lad ran off and when he came to the meadow he found the daughter there raking the hay.

"I am to fetch what your father has promised my master," said the lad.

"Ah, ha!" thought she. "Is that what they are up to?"

"Ah, indeed!" she said. "I suppose it's that little bay mare of ours. You had better go and take her. She stands there tethered on the other side of the pea field," said the girl.

The boy jumped on the back of the bay mare and rode home at full gallop.

"Have you got her with you?" asked the squire.

"She is down at the door," said the lad.

"Take her up to the room my mother had," said the squire.

"But, master, how can that be managed?" said the lad.

"You must just do as I tell you," said the squire. "If you cannot manage her alone you must get the men to help you," for he thought the girl might turn obstreperous.

When the lad saw his master's face he knew it would be no use to gainsay him. So he went and got all the farm-tenants who were there to help him. Some pulled at the head and the forelegs of the mare and others pushed from behind, and at last they got her up the stairs and into the room. There lay all the wedding finery ready.

"Now, that's done, master!" said the lad; "but it was a terrible job. It was the worst I have ever had here on the farm."

"Never mind, you shall not have done it for nothing," said his master. "Now send the women up to dress her."

"But I say, master!—" said the lad.

"None of your talk!" said the squire. "Tell them they must dress her and mind and not forget either wreath or crown."

The lad ran into the kitchen.

"Look here, lasses," he said; "you must go upstairs and dress up the bay mare as a bride. I expect the master wants to give the guests a laugh."

The women dressed the bay mare in everything that was there, and then the lad went and told his master that now she was ready dressed, with wreath and crown and all.

"Very well then, bring her down!" said the squire. "I will receive her myself at the door," said he.

There was a terrible clatter on the stairs; for that bride, you know, had no silken shoes on.

When the door opened, and the squire's bride entered the parlor, you can imagine there was a good deal of tittering and grinning.

And as for the squire, you may be sure he had had enough of that bride, and they say he never went courting again.

THE THREE SILLIES / England

Edwin S. Hartland

*The following tale is the English version of a popular narrative told through-
out Europe and even in Siberia. In some stories the incidents of stupidity
found on the quest are told in detail, creating a much longer episodic tale.*

    *Trying to graze a cow on the roof is also found in "The Husband Who
Was To Mind the House." It is a common European anecdote that can stand
alone or be joined to other illustrations of foolish stupidity.*

Once upon a time there was a farmer and his wife who had one daughter, and she was courted by a gentleman. Every evening he used to come and see her, and stop to supper at the farmhouse, and the daughter used to be sent down into the cellar to draw the beer for supper. So one evening she was gone down to draw the beer, and she happened to look up at the ceiling while she was drawing, and she saw an axe stuck into one of the beams. It must have been there a long, long time, but somehow or other she had never noticed it before, and she began thinking. And she thought it was very dangerous to have that axe there, for she said to herself, "Suppose him and me was to be married, and we was to have a son, and he was to grow up to be a man, and come down into the cellar to draw the beer, as I'm doing now, and the axe was to fall on his head and kill him, what a dreadful thing it would be!" And she put down the candle and the jug, and sat herself down and began crying.

Well, they began to wonder upstairs how it was that she was so long drawing the beer, and her mother went down to see after her, and found her crying, and the beer running over the floor. "Why, whatever is the matter?" said her mother.

"Oh, mother!" says she, "look at that horrid axe! suppose we was to be married, and was to have a son, and he was to grow up, and was to come down to the cellar to draw the beer, and

the axe was to fall on his head and kill him, what a dreadful thing it would be!"

"Dear, dear! what a dreadful thing it would be!" said the mother, and she sat her down beside the daughter and started crying too.

Then after a bit the father began to wonder that they didn't come back, and he went down into the cellar to look after them himself, and there the two sat crying, and the beer running all over the floor. "Whatever is the matter?" says he.

"Why," says the mother, "look at that horrid axe. Just suppose, if our daughter and her sweetheart was to be married and was to have a son, and he was to grow up, and was to come down into the cellar to draw the beer, and the axe was to fall on his head and kill him, what a dreadful thing it would be!"

"Dear, dear, dear! so it would!" said the father, and he sat himself down beside the other two, and started crying.

Now the gentleman got tired of stopping in the kitchen by himself, and at last he went down into the cellar, too, to see what they were after. There they three sat crying side by side, and the beer running all over the floor. And he ran straight and turned the tap. Then he said, "Whatever are you three doing, sitting there crying, and letting the beer run all over the floor?"

"Oh!" says the father, "look at that horrid axe! Suppose you and our daughter were to be married, and was to have a son, and he was to grow up, and was to come down into the cellar to draw the beer, and the axe was to fall on his head and

"The Three Sillies," from *English Fairy and Folk Tales*
by Edwin S. Hartland. Published by Charles Scribner's
Sons, 1880.

kill him!" And then they all started crying worse than before. But the gentleman burst out laughing, and reached up and pulled out the axe, and then he said, "I've traveled many miles and I never met three such big sillies as you three before; but now I shall start out on my travels again, and when I can find three bigger sillies than you three, then I'll come back and marry your daughter." So he wished them good-by, and started off on his travels, and left them all crying because the girl had lost her sweetheart.

Well, he set out, and he traveled a long way, and at last he came to an old woman's cottage that had some grass growing on the roof. And the old woman was trying to get her cow to go up a ladder to the grass, and the poor thing would not go. So the gentleman asked the old woman what she was doing. "Why, look ye," she said, "look at all that beautiful grass. I'm going to get the cow on to the roof to eat it. She'll be quite safe, for I shall tie a string round her neck, and pass it down the chimney, and tie it to my wrist as I go about the house, so she can't fall off without my knowing it."

"Oh, you poor old silly!" said the gentleman, "you should cut the grass and throw it down to the cow!" But as the old woman thought it was easier to get the cow up the ladder than to get the grass down, she pushed her and coaxed her and got her up and tied a string around her neck, and passed it down the chimney, and fastened it to her own wrist. And the gentleman went on his way, but he hadn't gone far when the cow tumbled off the roof, and hung by the string tied round her neck, and it strangled her. And the weight of the cow tied to her wrist pulled the old woman up the chimney, and she stuck fast halfway, and was smothered in the soot.

Well, that was one big silly.

And the gentleman went on and on, and he went to an inn to stop the night, and they were so full at the inn that they had to put him in a double-bedded room, and another traveler was to sleep in the other bed. The other man was a very pleasant fellow, and they got very friendly together; but in the morning, when they were both getting up, the gentleman was surprised to see the other hang his trousers on the knobs of the chest of drawers and run across the room and try to jump into them, and he tried over and over again, and couldn't manage it; and the gentleman wondered whatever he was doing it for. At last he stopped and wiped his face with his handkerchief. "Oh dear," he says, "I do think trousers are the most awkward kind of clothes that ever were. I can't think who could have invented such things. It takes me the best part of an hour to get into mine every morning, and I get so hot! How do you manage yours?" So the gentleman burst out laughing, and showed him how to put them on; and he was very much obliged to him, and said he never should have thought of doing it that way.

So that was another big silly.

Then the gentleman went on his travels again; and he came to a village; and outside the village there was a pond, and round the pond was a crowd of people. And they had got rakes, and brooms and pitchforks, reaching into the pond; and the gentleman asked what was the matter. "Why," they says, " matter enough! Moon's tumbled into the pond, and we can't get her out anyhow!" So the gentleman burst out laughing, and told them to look up into the sky, and that it was only the shadow in the water. But they wouldn't listen to him, and abused him shamefully, and he got away as quick as he could.

So there was a whole lot of sillies bigger than the three, and the gentleman turned back home again and married the farmer's daughter.

CLEVER ELSIE / Germany

The Grimm brothers

A numbskull's logic is quite unlike most people's. It never occurs to him to remove the pickaxe and go about his business; instead he bewails what may never occur. Unlike the gentleman in "The Three Sillies," Hans is impressed with Elsie's cleverness. In the end, however, it is Hans who rejects the dümmling.

Compare this version with the previous tale as well as with "Hans Hansen's Hired Girl."

There was once a man who had a daughter who was called Clever Elsie. And when she had grown up her father said, "We will get her married." "Yes," said the mother, "if only any one would come who would have her." At length a man came from a distance and wooed her, who was called Hans; but he stipulated that Clever Elsie should be really wise. "Oh," said the father, "she's sharp enough"; and the mother said, "Oh, she can see the wind coming up the street, and hear the flies coughing," "Well," said Hans, "if she is not really wise, I won't have her." When they were sitting at dinner and had eaten, the mother said, "Elsie, go into the cellar and fetch some beer."

Then Clever Elsie took the pitcher from the wall, went into the cellar, and tapped the lid briskly as she went, so that the time might not appear long. When she was below she fetched herself a chair, and set it before the barrel so that she had no need to stoop, and did not hurt her back or do herself any unexpected injury. Then she placed the can before her, and turned the tap, and while the beer was running she would not let her eyes be idle, but looked up at the wall, and after much peering here and there, saw a pick-axe exactly above her, which the masons had accidently left there.

Then Clever Elsie began to weep and said, "If I get Hans, and we have a child, and he grows

"Clever Elsie," from *Grimms' Household Tales,* translated by Margaret Hunt.

big, and we send him into the cellar here to draw beer, then the pick-axe will fall on his head and kill him." Then she sat and wept and screamed with all the strength of her body, over the misfortune which lay before her. Those upstairs waited for the drink, but Clever Elsie still did not come. Then the woman said to the servant, "Just go down into the cellar and see where Elsie is." The maid went and found her sitting in front of the barrel, screaming loudly. "Elsie, why do you weep?" asked the maid. "Ah," she answered, "have I not reason to weep? If I get Hans, and we have a child, and he grows big, and has to draw beer here, the pick-axe will perhaps fall on his head, and kill him." Then said the maid, "What a clever Elsie we have!" and sat down beside her and began loudly to weep over the misfortune.

After a while, as the maid did not come back, and those upstairs were thirsty for the beer, the man said to the boy, "Just go down into the cellar and see where Elsie and the girl are." The boy went down, and there sat Clever Elsie and the girl both weeping together. Then he asked, "Why are you weeping?" "Ah," said Elsie, "have I not reason to weep? If I get Hans, and we have a child, and he grows big, and has to draw beer here, the pick-axe will fall on his head and kill him." Then said the boy, "What a clever Elsie we have!" and sat down by her, and likewise began to howl loudly.

Upstairs they waited for the boy, but as he still

did not return, the man said to the woman, "Just go down into the cellar and see where Elsie is!" The woman went down, and found all three in the midst of their lamentations, and inquired what was the cause; then Elsie told her also that her future child was to be killed by the pick-axe, when it grew big and had to draw beer, and the pick-axe fell down. Then said the mother likewise, "What a clever Elsie we have!" and sat down and wept with them.

The man upstairs waited a short time, but as his wife did not come back and his thirst grew ever greater, he said, "I must go into the cellar myself and see where Elsie is." But when he got into the cellar, and they were all sitting together crying, and he heard the reason, and that Elsie's child was the cause, and that Elsie might perhaps bring one into the world some day, and that he might be killed by the pick-axe, if he should happen to be sitting beneath it, drawing beer just at the very time when it fell down, he cried, "Oh, what a clever Elsie!" and sat down, and likewise wept with them.

The bridegroom stayed upstairs alone for a long time; then as no one would come back he thought, "They must be waiting for me below: I too must go there and see what they are about." When he got down, the five of them were sitting screaming and lamenting quite piteously, each out-doing the other. "What misfortune has happened then?" asked he. "Ah, dear Hans," said Elsie, "if we marry each other and have a child, and he is big, and we perhaps send him here to draw something to drink, then the pick-axe which has been left up there might dash his brains out if it were to fall down, so have we not reason to weep?" "Come," said Hans, "more understanding than that is not needed for my household, as you are such a clever Elsie, I will have you," and he seized her hand, took her upstairs with him, and married her.

After Hans had had her some time, he said, "Wife, I am going out to work and earn some money for us; go into the field and cut the corn that we may have some bread." "Yes, dear Hans, I will do that." After Hans had gone away, she cooked herself some good broth and took it into the field with her. When she came to the field she said to herself, "What shall I do; shall I cut first, or shall I eat first? Oh, I will eat first." Then she drank her cup of broth, and when she was fully satisfied, she once more said, "What shall I do? Shall I cut first, or shall I sleep first? I will sleep first." Then she lay down among the corn and fell asleep. Hans had been at home for a long time, but Elsie did not come; then said he, "What a clever Elsie I have; she is so industrious that she does not even come home to eat."

But when evening came and she still stayed away, Hans went out to see what she had cut, but nothing was cut, and she was lying among the corn asleep. Then Hans hastened home and brought a fowler's net with little bells and hung it round about her, and she still went on sleeping. Then he ran home, shut the house-door, and sat down in his chair and worked.

At length, when it was quite dark, Clever Elsie awoke and when she got up there was a jingling all round about her, and the bells rang at each step which she took. Then she was alarmed, and became uncertain whether she really was Clever Elsie or not, and said, "Is it I, or is it not I?" But she knew not what answer to make to this, and stood for a time in doubt; at length she thought: "I will go home and ask if it be I, or if it be not I, they will be sure to know." She ran to the door of her own house, but it was shut; then she knocked at the window and cried, "Hans, is Elsie within?" "Yes," answered Hans, "she is within." Hereupon she was terrified, and said, "Ah, heavens! Then it is not I," and went to another door; but when the people heard the jingling of the bells they would not open it, and she could get in nowhere. Then she ran out of the village, and no one has seen her since.

HANS HANSEN'S HIRED GIRL / Germany

Carl Withers

This anecdote makes an interesting comparison with the previous more complex tale.

Hansen's Trina was lazy and wouldn't do anything. She said to herself, "Shall I eat or shall I sleep or shall I work? Oh, I shall eat first."

When she had eaten she said again, "Shall I work or shall I sleep? Oh, I shall sleep a little first." Then she lay down and slept, and when she woke, it was night and she could no longer go out to the field to work. And so went all the days.

One afternoon Hans came to the house and found Trina lying in her bed sleeping, so he took out his knife and cut her dress off up to her knees.

Trina woke up and thought, "Now I must go out and work."

When she had gone out and saw that her dress was now so short, she was frightened and wondered if she was really Trina.

She said to herself, "Am I I, or am I not I?" But she did not know how to answer herself.

She stood there in doubt a moment and then she thought, "I must go to the house and ask whether or not I am I. They will know."

So she went to the house, knocked at the window, and called in, "Is Hansen's Trina in there?"

They answered, "Yes, she is lying in her room asleep."

"Then I am not I," said Trina gaily. So she went to the village and didn't come back and Hans no longer had Trina as hired girl.

THE HODJA AND THE MOON / Turkey

Charles Downing

Please see the introduction to the three previous "Tales of the Hodja," page 375, for information pertinent to this anecdote.

One evening the Hodja was drawing water when he saw the reflection of the moon at the bottom of the well.

'The moon has fallen down my well,' said the Hodja. 'If I do not get it out, it will be the end of the world, and everyone will blame me!'

He tied a large iron hook to the end of a piece

of rope, and let it down the well. When he judged that he could hook the moon, he began to pull on the rope. The hook, however, had caught under a stone on the bottom of the well. The Hodja strained and pulled, until the hook suddenly dislodged the stone and flew up the well-shaft. The Hodja fell flat on his back.

'Allah be praised!' he said, seeing the moon in the sky. 'It was a great effort, but I have got it back where it belongs!'

LAZY JACK / England

Joseph Jacobs

This poor child tries to survive in the world by carefully following his mother's advice, but in each instance his lack of understanding leads to unpleasant results. Yet, reminiscent of wonder tales, Jack wins the rich man's daughter by making her laugh.

Stith Thompson in The Folktale *states that this narrative is found in a Chinese Buddhist literary collection and several Renaissance jest books. It is told not only throughout Europe and Africa but also in Indonesia and Japan.*

Once upon a time there was a boy whose name was Jack, and he lived with his mother on a dreary common. They were very poor, and the old woman got her living by spinning, but Jack was so lazy that he would do nothing but lie in the shade in hot weather and sit by the corner of the hearth in the winter. His mother could not persuade him to do anything for her, and was forced to tell him at last that if he did not begin to work she would turn him out of the home.

This threat at length roused Jack, and he went out and hired himself to a farmer for a penny. As he was coming home, never having had any money before, he lost it in passing over a brook. "You stupid boy," said his mother, "you should have put it in your pocket."

"I'll do so another time," replied Jack.

The next day Jack went again and hired himself to a cowherd, who gave him a jar of milk for his day's work. Jack took the jar and put it into the large pocket of his jacket, spilling it all long before he got home.

"Dear me!" said the old woman. "You should have carried it on your head."

"I'll do so another time," replied Jack.

The following day Jack hired himself again to a farmer, who agreed to give him a cream cheese for the services. In the evening, Jack took the cheese, and went home with it on his head. By the time he got home the cheese was completely spoiled, part of it being lost, and part matted with his hair.

"You stupid lout," said his mother, "you should have carried it very carefully in your hands."

"I'll do so another time," replied Jack.

The day after this Jack again went out, and hired himself to a baker, who would give him nothing for his work but a large tomcat. Jack took the cat, and began carrying it very carefully in his hands, but in a short time the cat scratched him so much that he was compelled to let it go.

When he got home, his mother said to him, "You silly fellow, you should have tied it with a string, and dragged it along after you."

"I'll do so another time," said Jack.

The next day Jack hired himself to a butcher, who rewarded his labors by a handsome present of a shoulder of mutton. Jack took the mutton, tied it to a string, and trailed it along after him in the dirt, so by the time he reached home the meat was completely spoiled.

His mother was this time quite out of patience with him, for the next day was Sunday, and she was obliged to content herself with cabbage for her dinner. "You ninnyhammer," said she, "you should have carried it on your shoulder."

"I'll do so another time," replied Jack.

On the Monday Jack went once more, and

"Lazy Jack," from *English Fairy Tales* by Joseph Jacobs. Published by G. P. Putnam's Sons, 1892.

hired himself to a cattlekeeper, who gave him a donkey for his work. Although Jack was very strong, he found some difficulty in hoisting the donkey on his shoulders, but at last he did, and began walking slowly home with his prize. Now it happened that in the course of his journey, there lived a rich man with his only daughter, a beautiful girl, but unfortunately deaf and dumb; she had never laughed in her life, and the doctors said she would never recover until somebody made her laugh. Many tried without success, and at last her father, in despair, offered her in marriage to the first man who could make her laugh. This young lady happened to be looking out of the window when Jack was passing with the donkey on his shoulders, the legs sticking up in the air, and the sight was so comical and strange that she burst out into a great fit of laughter, and immediately recovered her speech and hearing. Her father was overjoyed, and fulfilled his promise by marrying her to Jack, who was thus made a rich gentleman. They lived in a large house, and Jack's mother lived with them in great happiness until she died.

A TIME FOR EVERYTHING / Russia

Babette Deutsch
Avrahm Yarmolinsky

This Russian version of the "Lazy Jack" tale uses the cumulative pattern. Compare the tone of "Lazy Jack" with that of "A Time for Everything." The inclusion of philosophy through a paraphrase of a Biblical passage adds a depth unusual to drolls.

Once there was a poor widow who had only one son. He was not very little, but he was not very big either.

One morning she called him to her and said:

"Child, it is time that you stopped hanging onto my apron strings. You must go out and see what is to be seen. You must rub elbows with people. That is the way to learn."

"Go out and rub elbows with people?" repeated the boy.

"Just so, my darling," said his mother, and with a little shove she sent him out-of-doors.

The boy wandered off and before long he came to a threshing ground. Men and women were busily using their flails, making the chaff fly. The good grain they piled into carts.

The boy stepped right in among the threshers and went from one to another, his arms akimbo, carefully rubbing elbows now with this one and now with that.

It is not easy to use a flail when someone is just at your elbow, and rubbing it into the bargain. The threshers, at first astonished, soon grew angry.

"What are you doing? Be off with you!" they cried.

The boy did not stop rubbing elbows, however, for he remembered what his mother had told him. So they began using their flails on his back, and they spanked him hard and long till the tears came. It was plain that he was not wanted there.

He ran home to his mother, and the tears were still wet on his cheeks as he shot through the door.

"Child, child, what has happened to you?" cried his mother.

So he told her the story.

"Ah, my chick, you should not have done that!" said his mother sadly. "You should have taken a flail and threshed the buckwheat with the others. And then they would have been glad of your company. Or, if you had no flail, you should have cheered them on and wished them well. They might even have given you some buckwheat and I would have cooked it for you and put a lump of fat into it. We would have had a good meal. You should have said to them: 'Good! Good! May you have this load and more, too! May there be no end to your carting!'"

"Is that what I should have said?" asked the boy.

"Just so, my darling!" said his mother.

By the next day the boy had got over his beating and he wandered off again.

The first thing he met was a funeral procession. The mourners marched along slowly, with bowed heads, behind the cart on which the coffin was being carried.

The boy ran up to them and called out in a clear voice:

"Good! Good! May you have this load and more, too!"

The mourners stopped in their tracks, astonished. The cart with the coffin halted.

"Good! Good!" cried the boy. "May there be no end to your carting!"

At this the mourners cried out, not with grief but with anger. And one of them, a tall, sturdy man, turned on the boy and gave him a thorough spanking. It was plain to him that he was not wanted here.

He ran home to his mother, and the tears were still wet on his cheeks as he shot through the door.

"Child, child, what has happened to you?" asked his mother.

So he told her the story.

"Ah, my chick, you should not have done that!" said his mother sadly. "You should have taken off your cap and crossed yourself. You should have wept for the good old man that was gone. You should have lifted up your voice and cried: 'Oh, the pity of it! Oh, the pity!' Then they would have taken you with them in the procession and afterward you would have been invited to the funeral feast. You would have filled

your stomach with pancakes and other good things, and maybe even brought some home in your pockets for me. You should have wept and wailed."

"Wept and wailed?" repeated the boy.

"Just so, my darling," said his mother.

By the next day the boy had got over his beating and he wandered off again. Before long he came upon another procession. His eyes brightened, for this was much finer than the first, and ever so jolly. It was a wedding procession. The bride and groom and the parents of the groom, and their sisters and their brothers and their cousins and their aunts and their uncles, all gaily dressed in their best, were marching along to the playing of pipes and accordions.

The boy stared for a moment in wonder. Then he went up to the wedding party, and keeping step with the bride, he began to weep and to wail.

"Oh, the pity of it!" he cried.

The bride stopped in her tracks, astonished. And the rest of the procession: the groom, and the old people and the young people, and the pipers and the accordion players stopped, too.

Thereupon the boy wailed more loudly than before:

"Oh, the pity of it! Oh, the pity!"

At this the groom's father, a great bearded man, seized the boy and gave him a box on the ear that made it sting.

"What bad luck are you bringing on this pair! The pity of it, indeed! You'll be needing pity, you idiot!"

It was plain to the boy that he was not wanted here.

He ran home to his mother, and his ear still stung as he shot through the door.

She heard his story through, and then she said sadly:

"Ah, my chick, you should not have done that! You should have taken a pipe with the others, and gone dancing and piping with them along the road. Then you would have seen the fine doings at church and you would have been invited to the wedding feast. You would have filled your stomach with bride-cake, and perhaps taken some home in your pockets for me."

"I should have piped and danced?" repeated the boy.

"Just so, my darling," said his mother.

By the next day the boy was ready to wander off once more.

After he had trotted quite a distance he noticed a cloud of smoke off to the right, and hastening his steps, he came to a burning barn. The peasant whose barn was on fire kept throwing pailfuls of water onto the flaming timbers, but the barn was of wood, after all, and filled with dry hay, and the buckets of water did not move as fast as the wind that made the blaze greater.

The boy pulled a hollow reed out of his pocket and began leaping about in a kind of dance, and piping the merriest tune he knew.

When the peasant noticed the boy apparently rejoicing at his misfortune, he got so angry that he wasted a whole pail of water on him. The boy was drenched to the skin. Clearly he was not wanted here.

He ran home, dripping wet, and some of the water was salt because it came from his eyes.

"Child, child, what has happened?" cried his mother.

So he told her the story.

"Ah, my chick, you should not have done that," she said sadly, as she rubbed him and patted him, and brought out some dry clothes. "You should have taken a bucket of water and thrown it on the burning barn. Yes, indeed, a bucket of water was what was needed."

"A bucket of water?" repeated the boy.

"Just so, my darling," said his mother. "Now are you quite dry again?"

The boy nodded.

"Then run along and don't bother me while I cook dinner. Here's a piece of bread to eat on the way." And she sent him out-of-doors again with a little shove.

The boy set off, munching his bread and looking about him as he walked. He had swallowed his last crumb when he came to a farmyard. The farmer had just finished slaughtering a hog. He had placed the hog on a spit over a fire so as to singe off its bristles before preparing it for meat. The fire was just beginning to burn nicely. Just then the farmer's wife came from the well carrying a wooden yoke on her shoulders, with a bucket of water suspended at either end of the yoke.

The boy did not hesitate a moment. He leaped for a bucket and poured the water over the fire where the farmer was singeing the hog.

The farmer did not hesitate a moment. He seized the boy and spanked him long and hard.

It was clear to him that he was not wanted here. He ran home to his mother, and he was still crying as he shot through the door.

"Child, child, what has happened to you now?" she exclaimed.

So he told her the story.

"Ah, my chick, you should not have done that," she sighed.

"But you said . . ." the boy began, when his mother interrupted:

"There is a time for everything: a time to throw water on the fire and a time to let it burn, a time to weep and a time to dance, a time when we wish carts would carry their loads endlessly and a time when we wish there were no load at all. On, my chick, my child, my darling, when will you learn what the right time is?"

"I don't know, Mother," answered the boy slowly, "but I know what time it is now."

"Yes?" asked his mother eagerly.

"Time for dinner," said the boy.

And so it was.

THE WITCHES' RIDE / Costa Rica

Lupe de Osma

Most drolls take place in the real world of everyday life. "The Witches' Ride" is unusual in its use of magical objects and supernatural beings.

Not all dümmlings are unlucky; some achieve unexpected success, as can be seen in "Lazy Jack" and "The Witches' Ride."

Once, in the days of long ago, there lived in Costa Rica a widow who had an only son. Now this son was considered a *bobo*, or simpleton, because he was lazy and, more than that, because in one way or another he muddled everything he set out to do.

One day the bobo's mother was preparing to cook the *chayote* hash and rice which were to be their supper. She went to the shed for wood to burn in the stove, but the shed was empty. So she told the bobo to go to the forest yonder and bring her some sticks for the fire.

Since it was already late afternoon and a chill wind was blowing, the bobo wrapped himself up in a coarse old blanket, wearing it like a cape. Then he set off. He soon entered the forest, but there were no broken branches at hand and since he had no machete, or long, sharp knife, with him to cut branches from the trees, he went on farther and farther, from one thicket to another. Before long he was deep in the forest.

Soon it grew dark and he lost the path. As he groped his way through the dense underbrush and hanging vines, not knowing which way to turn, he suddenly came upon a hut. He was glad to find a shelter and knocked a good round knock. No one answered. So he opened the door and went in. Finding the hut deserted, he proceeded to make himself at home. In a corner behind a pile of straw he found an old mat woven of reeds, and there he snuggled down. Soon, in good comfort, he was fast asleep.

He slept and slept till at the hour of midnight he was awakened with a start by the sound of merry voices. He raised his head a wee bit and looked around with one eye.

Through the open window of the hut the moonlight shone on the clay floor, turning it white. There the bobo saw twelve black shadows —the shadows of twelve old witches. They were jesting and laughing and having altogether a merry time as each witch took a sip from a big drinking gourd, then smacked her lips and passed it on.

Meantime, the bobo lay quiet and still behind the pile of straw, scarcely daring to draw his

breath lest the witches find him and change him into some bird or beast.

And the riot and revelry went on until the gourd ran dry. Then without any warning at all, a witch cried out in a croaking voice, "Time to be off!" At the same moment she picked up a broom from a pile on the floor, placed herself nimbly upon it, and said these magic words:

> "Fly me faster than a fairy,
>   Without God—without Saint Mary!"

Away out of the window she flew and soared gracefully up into the air. The others followed quickly—each pouncing upon a broomstick from the pile, then repeating the magic words.

High in the night sky they flew, one behind the other, like a long black waving ribbon. They circled once and again around the big yellow moon and then vanished swiftly from sight beyond the tall mountain peaks.

"A week of Sundays!" cried the bobo in surprise. "Wasn't the neatly done! I wouldn't mind doing it myself! And why not?"

Well, as soon as the last witch had disappeared, up sprang the bobo from the reed mat and straightway went to the corner where the pile of brooms had been. He hoped that the witches might have left one behind. And they had! He snatched it up, and fastening the blanket around his shoulders good and tight, he placed himself upon the stick. Then he shouted with all his might:

> "Fly me faster than a fairy,
>   Without God—without Saint Mary!"

These words were scarcely out of his mouth when up he shot into the air like a whizzing arrow, and out of the window he flew. Faster and faster he soared, low over the treetops and high toward the moon, like a bird. And he flew and flew and flew, and the higher he went, the more he liked it—so much that every once in a while he would say the magic words again to the broom.

But, alas, he was not called a bobo for nothing. In his great glee he muddled the words, and said to the broomstick:

> "Fly me faster than a fairy,
>   Fly with God and good Saint Mary!"

"The Witches' Ride," from *The Witches' Ride and Other Tales from Costa Rica*, told and illustrated by Lupe de Osma. Reprinted by permission of William Morrow and Company, Inc. Copyright © 1957 by Lupe de Osma.

No sooner were these words out of his mouth than the broom began to fall. Fast—and faster than fast—it dropped. The poor bobo had no time to think of the right magic words as he tumbled and somersaulted through the air.

Now then, it so happened that some robbers were hiding at the edge of the forest that night. Their booty was spread out on a large cloth, and they were seated around it, counting out each one's share of the treasure by the weak light of their lantern.

"Ho! The Devil himself must have been with us today," cried one of the robbers in delight. "Hope he doesn't take a fancy to drop in for his share!"

And at this very moment the bobo, who was coming down full tilt, saw the group and shouted, "Out of the way! Look out there, all of you! Make way for this poor devil!"

The robbers looked up, each and all of them afraid of the strange sight the bobo made. For his blanket flapped and danced behind him like two big black wings as he plunged down upon them. They sprang up in great fear, thinking they had the Devil on their backs.

"The Devil! The Devil is loose! Here he comes!" they cried in terror. "Run! Let us fly! Away . . . away!" They took to their heels as if they were running a race. And they left their booty behind.

The bobo came down in one enormous swoop upon the pile of riches—*plump*! There he sat, gazing rapturously at the heap of gold and silver coins. "Bless my soul! Bless my little soul!" he cried.

Straightway he jumped up and piled the coins together again in the center of the large cloth. Then he made a bundle out of it, slung it over his shoulder, and hobbled home very happy, humming a merry tune.

And as for the robbers, they were never seen again.

ALI AND THE CAMELS / North Africa

Robert Gilstrap
Irene Estabrook

Numbskulls have great trouble in counting. In other versions of this tale a dümmling believes one member of his group is dead because he has not counted himself. Most tales of foolish calculations have literary origins, although a few have entered the oral tradition.

In the long-ago days when these tales were lived rather than told, Tripoli was well known for many things. But no one thing and no one person was better known than the great and illustrious Caliph, Ahmed Ben Hamed of Tripoli. One day the great Caliph decided to send some of his most handsome camels to the Sultan of Egypt as

"Ali and the Camels," from *The Sultan's Fool and Other North African Tales* by Robert Gilstrap and Irene Estabrook. Copyright © 1958 by Robert Gilstrap and Irene Estabrook. Reprinted by permission of Holt, Rinehart and Winston, Inc.

a symbol of his friendship. He called his faithful servant, Ramadan, to his throne room.

"I wish to send ten of my finest camels to the Sultan of Egypt," he told the servant. "Choose them well for they must please the Sultan. Then prepare yourself for the journey and be ready to start when the sun appears again in the sky."

Ramadan was astonished by his master's command, for he knew little of desert life.

"I pray that you will let me find someone who knows more about desert life than I," Ramadan said humbly. "Let me find a desert Arab who knows the stars and who can follow the course of the sun. Such a person would not lose your camels as I might."

"Very well," the Caliph said. "Find such a man and send him on his way."

And so it was that Ramadan wandered through all the bazaars of the city looking for a man of the desert. Finally, when his search seemed hopeless and he was about to give up in despair, he saw a man wearing the robes of a desert tribe, sitting against the wall.

"Are you from the desert, my friend?" Ramadan asked.

"Yes," the Arab replied. "My name is Ali. I came to the city to find work. My sheep have died. My crops have failed. If I do not find a job my family will starve."

"Then I have a job for you," the servant said. "My master needs someone to take ten camels to Cairo as a gift to the Sultan. He will pay you well —in gold. If you know your way through the desert and can follow the course of the sun and the stars you can have the job."

"Oh, yes," Ali shouted for joy. "I have lived all my years in the desert and know it well."

The servant was pleased and he took Ali with him to the Caliph's palace. Once there he showed him the camel stables and said, "Here are the ten camels. You are to take them to Cairo and give them to the Sultan."

Ali looked at the camels and then scratched the small white cap he wore on his head. "You say there are ten camels here," he said, "but let me count them to see if you are not trying to fool me."

Quickly Ali arranged the camels in a straight line. "Now I will count them," he said. "One-two-three-four-five-six-five-seven-six-eight. Eight! Ah-hah! There are only eight camels here. You rascal. You said there were ten. You have tried to trick me."

Realizing then that Ali could not count, Ramadan did not become upset. Instead he suggested another way of counting so that Ali could understand how many camels were before him.

"I have not tricked you," Ramadan said gently. "But because you have difficulty counting the camels, let us try another way. Try this. Pat each camel on the nose, and as you do so, bend a finger

down like this. Then you will know how many camels you have."

To help Ali, Ramadan patted each camel on the nose, bent down each finger, and said, "See, I have patted the noses of all the camels and all my fingers are bent!"

Then Ali tried to follow Ramadan's example, and when he had finished, he found that all of his fingers were bent, also.

"Now," said Ramadan hopefully. "Your fingers are all bent. How many camels are there?"

"Two handsful," Ali replied. "But I don't know how many in numbers because I don't know how many fingers I have!"

Ramadan tried not to get angry, but he was losing his patience. "Open your fingers slowly," he said firmly. "And say a number as you open each one. Then you will know the number."

Slowly Ali opened his fingers. "Ten-nine-eight-seven-six-five-four-three-two-one-none. Well, I'll be! According to this way of counting, there are no camels at all. But I can see them right before me as plain as I see the moon at night."

Ramadan was almost ready to dismiss Ali and look for another Arab to take the camels to the Sultan of Egypt. But it was late and desert Arabs were scarce, and his master had ordered him to have the camels on their way by morning.

So he decided to try one more time. He took a piece of string and put ten beads on it. He knotted both ends well.

"Now," he said. "Do not concern yourself with counting the camels. On this string I have placed beads, one for each animal. Now pat each camel on the nose and pass a bead from the top of the string to the bottom as you do so. When you have finished with the counting, all the beads will be at the bottom, and the count will be right."

"If you should have a bead left over, then you have lost a camel," Ramadan continued. "And if you have a camel left over, then Allah has given it to you and you may do with it what you wish!"

Understanding this method, Ali took the string with the ten beads on it, and the ten camels, and enough food and water for many days, and began his long journey to Cairo.

After traveling through the desert sands for several hours Ali became very hot and tired. The sand was deep and burned his feet, and he could go only short distances before he was forced to stop and rest. Finally, as he stopped at an oasis to drink and count the camels, he had an idea.

Why should I walk through this hot, deep sand, he thought. I have ten camels right here and I could be riding one. Camels do not mind walking in the sand. Their feet are made for it. As for me, my poor feet are getting burned with every step I take. I think I shall ride a camel.

So Ali mounted the first camel, and led the others after him.

After some time he counted the camels again, letting one bead go from the top of the string to the bottom each time he patted the nose of a camel. He started counting, however, with the second camel, completely forgetting the one he was riding. Thus he discovered he had one bead left over.

When Ali saw the extra bead, he was frightened. The rope must have broken, he thought, and a camel must have strayed. I must go back to the last place I counted to see if I can find it.

So Ali turned the camels around and headed back over the burning sand to the small oasis. But he found no camel.

This can mean only one thing, Ali thought. The great Allah has given me an extra bead.

So he took the bead off the string and to Ali the number of beads and the number of camels were again the same.

Ali turned his camels around and started again on his journey. He traveled until the sun was sinking in the west and the desert was getting cool. Soon he came to an oasis where a small spring of cold water flowed, and the palm trees swayed in the slight breeze. A few tents belonging to other travelers surrounded the area.

Ali got down from his camel, got out his piece of string, and began to count the animals. This time he had the camels in a half circle around him so he started with the one he had been riding. Thus he found that he had one camel for which there was no bead.

"Praise be to Allah!" Ali shouted. "He has seen fit to send me a camel for my food tonight, and I may share it with the others who are gathered here. Praise be to Allah!"

So Ali took out his long knife and killed the camel for which there was no bead. Then he called the other travelers and invited them to feast with him.

The next morning before Ali started on his journey, he counted the camels, and the number of beads and camels were just the same. Then he climbed up on the first camel and moved out into the desert.

After several hours had passed, he once again took out his string and checked the number of animals. Overlooking the camel he was riding, Ali found that there was one bead more than camels. So he threw the bead away.

That same evening when he made camp he stood on the sand and counted the camels just as he had done the night before. This time he found that there was one camel too many. Given to me by Allah, he thought. So he killed the camel and called the other travelers to join him in feast.

And so it was on the next day, and on the next, and on each day that followed. Ali found himself during the day with an extra bead, which he threw away, and at night with an extra camel, which he ate.

Finally, on the eleventh day of his journey, Ali walked into the city of Cairo holding only a piece of string in his dirty hand. Not understanding what he had done, he still proceeded to the Sultan's palace and asked to see the great ruler.

"This piece of string," Ali said, as he bowed before the Sultan, "is from the Caliph of Tripoli. He sends it with his greetings. He also said something about camels and beads, but it must have been very unimportant, for I have forgotten the exact message."

Naturally the Sultan was surprised by the Caliph's gift and able to make very little sense from Ali's words. Thinking that the heat of the desert must have affected the man's mind, the Sultan ordered food and drink.

Although Ali appreciated the Sultan's kindness, he was able to eat very little of the food which was set before him. To be truthful, he was much too full of camel meat.

ALLAH WILL PROVIDE / North Africa

Robert Gilstrap
Irene Estabrook

Bou Azza obviously is a fool when he suddenly refuses to work. He will not even help his wife carry the pot of gold she discovers. And yet is Bou Azza really a dümmling? Allah did provide. Here again is a fortunate numbskull. The motif of undeserved luck which is central to wonder tales occasionally occurs in drolls.

Bou Azza was an honest woodcutter who worked hard each day cutting down trees which he sold in the market place of a small North African village. His efforts were not highly rewarded, however, for he earned barely enough money to keep his young wife and himself in food and clothing.

Because he was getting old in body, Bou Azza wondered with each passing day how much longer he would be able to work and who would take care of him and his wife when he was too old to do so.

One afternoon as the hot sun beat down on him, Bou Azza gathered together the logs he had cut that morning, fastened them with a piece of rope, and slung them over his shoulder. Then he set out down the hill toward his tiny house on the outskirts of the village.

Before reaching his home, Bou was forced to stop and rest beneath an olive tree near the road. As he wiped the perspiration from his forehead he suddenly noticed a horned viper curled up on the ground a few feet away from him. At first the old woodcutter was very frightened for he knew that a bite from this reptile would surely kill him. Carefully he climbed up to a high branch of the olive tree. But after watching the snake for a few seconds, Bou Azza realized that he had nothing to fear. The snake had other interests.

On one of the lower branches of the tree, not far from where Bou Azza was sitting, there was a small bird. The snake was staring at the bird with his beady black eyes, swaying its long, slender body back and forth, and occasionally spitting out its evil-looking, forked tongue.

At first the bird did not notice the snake, but when she did, her small feathery body was seized with helpless terror. Gripping the fragile little twig on which she rested, she tried to move her wings, but they were frozen with fear. She also tried to sound an alarm, but her beak opened and shut without a sound coming out.

As the snake swayed back and forth, Bou Azza realized that the bird had been hypnotized by the viper's movements, and he watched the two animals with weird fascination.

As Bou Azza looked down, the viper held the bird in its merciless stare, swaying from side to side like the pendulum of a clock, while the helpless victim became more and more paralyzed. Then suddenly the little bird fell from the branch and landed just a few inches from the snake. As Bou Azza watched, the snake ate its prey whole —feathers and all. Then, satisfied, it crawled away looking for new victims.

Bou Azza, rested from his journey, but sickened by what he had just witnessed, headed for home with his wood on his back, and an idea in his head.

As Bou Azza walked home in the twilight, he thought more and more about his idea. After a time he said to himself, "I am a fool! The serpent finds much food without really working for it, thanks to Allah. Whereas I, a man, must work very hard in the hottest part of the day to earn just a mouthful of food. Allah alone is good, and with His help I will be like the serpent. No longer will I work so hard to get food when the serpent gets it for nothing. So shall it be."

And continuing on his way home, Bou Azza wore an expression of contentment over the new way of life that the serpent had revealed to him.

On the following morn, instead of rising before the sun made its way into the sky, Bou Azza stayed in bed until noon. Then he took his grass mat to the rear of the house where he sat under a fig tree.

His wife became worried at his strange behavior, and when she saw that he obviously had no plans to work for the day she went to him and said, "Bou Azza! What is wrong with you today? Are you not going to cut wood to sell in the market?"

"No, wife," said Bou Azza as he stretched in the sun. "I will not leave my mat even if I die of hunger. Yesterday I saw a serpent finding his food without working, and I have decided that if Allah feeds the serpents he will provide me with my bread."

His anxious wife had no idea what her husband was talking about and thought he had gone mad.

"Please get up," she cried, and she tugged at his clothing. But nothing she said or did made any difference, and when twilight came to Bou Azza's home, he was still resting on his mat.

The poor woman was sick with worry for she had always counted on her husband for food and money. But when she realized that he would not change his mind, she hurried to the woods while there was still light to see and looked for mushrooms to sell at the market in the village.

She looked for hours, scraping away leaves, digging under fallen logs, searching everywhere. Suddenly, as she dug into some soft earth her knife hit something hard buried beneath the surface of the ground. Rapidly she dug the dirt away and uncovered a metal cooking pot with a lid. After working for some time she pried the lid off and discovered that the pot was filled with shimmering gold pieces.

The animals of the forest drew close to watch her struggle helplessly with the giant pot as she shouted with excitement. But it was too heavy for

her to lift. She ran as fast as she could to the house crying with happiness. "Oh, Bou Azza," she shouted. "I have found a whole pot of gold. Come with me. Help me bring it to the house."

Actually Bou Azza was impressed with the thought of the gold. But he had made a promise to himself not to move, and now he could not lift his finger.

"Oh, wife," he said, without opening his eyes. "If Allah saw fit to let you find such a treasure surely he will give you the strength to carry it home. Personally I have decided not to move an inch!"

This reply made his wife furious. And she ran to the house of her brothers to see if they would help her carry the pot home. Naturally her brothers were delighted with the prospect of sharing so much gold, and they ran with Bou Azza's wife to the forest and helped her carry it home.

When she and her brothers reached her house, with the giant pot spilling over with gold, she felt sure that her husband would get off his mat and help her count their fortune.

"Get up, you lazy lout!" she shouted, as she stood over her husband who slept peacefully on his straw bed. "I hope you have enough energy to come and count your riches."

"Did I not tell you?" he said sleepily. "I am not going to lift a finger until Allah drops fortunes on my head just as he showered gifts on the serpent."

"Just as you like," the angry wife said, as she filled her skirt with hundreds of heavy gold pieces and poured them over her husband's head.

"Praise be to Allah!" her husband shouted as the gold pieces fell around him. "Praise be to the one and only Allah! Do you not now see, my wife, that serpents and men are all his creatures and he does provide for all of us?"

His wife did not understand, but she did know that for the rest of their lives she and her husband would live in luxury and that Bou Azza would never have to work again.

And every time someone came to visit them, Bou Azza told them this story, ending each time with the words, "Why work? Allah will provide."

And although his listeners felt that he was wrong, no one could contradict him.

MASTER OF ALL MASTERS / England

Joseph Jacobs

This type of nonsense goes back at least to Straparola, a sixteenth-century Italian writer. It is told throughout Europe but is little known elsewhere. England alone has five versions.

Like cumulative tales, this droll is a challenge to both the teller's and the listener's memories. The more quickly and surely the last paragraph of "Master of All Masters" is told, the more hilarious the effect.

A girl once went to the fair to hire herself for servant. At last a funny-looking old gentleman engaged her, and took her home to his house. When she got there, he told her that he had something to teach her, for that in his house he had his own names for things.

He said to her: "What will you call me?"

"Master or mister, or whatever you please, sir," says she.

He said: "You must call me 'master of all masters.' And what would you call this?" pointing to his bed.

"Bed or couch, or whatever you please, sir."

"No, that's my 'barnacle.' And what do you call these?" said he pointing to his pantaloons.

"Breeches or trousers, or whatever you please, sir."

"You must call them 'squibs and crackers.' And what would you call her?" pointing to the cat.

"Cat or kit, or whatever you please, sir."

"You must call her 'white-faced simminy.' And this now," showing the fire, "what would you call this?"

"Fire or flame, or whatever you please, sir."

"You must call it 'hot cockalorum,' and what this?" he went on, pointing to the water.

"Water or wet, or whatever you please, sir."

"No, 'pondalorum' is its name. And what do you call all this?" asked he as he pointed to the house.

"House or cottage, or whatever you please, sir."

"You must call it 'high topper mountain.' "

That very night the servant woke her master up in a fright and said: "Master of all masters, get out of your barnacle and put on your squibs and crackers. For white-faced simminy has got a spark of hot cockalorum on its tail, and unless you get some pondalorum, high topper mountain will be all on hot cockalorum". . . . . .
. . . . That's all.

"Master of all Masters," from *English Fairy Tales* by Joseph Jacobs. Published by G. P. Putnam's Sons, 1892.

Cumulative
Tales

Young children, preschoolers and primary-graders, enjoy relatively little folk literature. Aesopic fables are too abstract for them, mythology explains truths they are not yet interested in, and most wonder tales and tales of trickery deal with subjects beyond their ken. Cumulative stories, however, are loved by almost everyone, from the three-year-old to the adult with enough imagination still to have a child's appreciation of the humorous.

Cumulative tales are distinguished by a reliance on repetition of actions, details, and verbal patterns. Some have quite simple plots, such as "Teeny-Tiny," in which the adventures of a "teeny-tiny woman" and a "teeny-tiny bone" are told with the words of the title repeated so often they produce a hilarious effect. "The Pancake" is a better known cumulative tale. Here the very simple plot of a pancake's escape and eventual destruction is less interesting than the rhythmical repetition of action and verbal responses.

Incremental repetition, in which each repetition builds on and adds to the last, is common to cumulative tales. It is this that creates the tension in "The Old Woman and Her Pig." To force her pig over the stile, an old woman goes to a stick, to force the stick to beat her pig she goes to a fire, to force the fire to burn the stick to force it to beat the pig she goes to water. . . . And so on until she is finally successful; then the story quickly unwinds:

As soon as the cat had lapped up the milk, the cat began to kill the rat; the rat began to gnaw the rope; the rope began to hang the butcher; the butcher began to kill the ox; the ox began to drink the water; the water began to quench the fire; the fire began to burn the stick; the stick began to beat the dog; the dog began to bite the pig; the little pig in a fright jumped over the stile; and so the old woman got home that night.

The hearer of such a tale is less interested in the old woman's adventures than in the storyteller's memory. Telling such narratives is an act of oral dexterity, a challenge enjoyed by the audi-

From *A World of Nonsense* by Carl Withers. Illustrated by John E. Johnson. Copyright © 1968 by Holt, Rinehart and Winston, Inc. Reproduced by permission of Holt, Rinehart and Winston, Inc.

ence, which is forced to listen carefully to see if the correct order of events is followed. As with "Teeny-Tiny," the more rapid the teller's pace the more amusing the story. Cumulative tales must be heard to really be appreciated, for they lose much of their delight and almost all of their rhythm when read silently from a printed page.

Not all tales that accumulate incident upon incident and rely on repetition have the simple plot structure of the above narratives. The African story "Why the Bush Fowl Calls at Dawn and Why Flies Buzz" is a cumulative tale of some complexity. A small black fly sets off a chain of events that finally leads to the sun not being awakened. The story does not end here. Each animal or person involved in the sequence of events is questioned by the Great Spirit of Heaven, and the narrative slowly unwinds as each character repeats, in reverse, the events that occurred. In addition to incremental repetition, this tale has a *pourquoi* motif, which is introduced to explain why flies cannot talk but only buzz.

Cumulative tales are told throughout Europe, Asia, and Africa as the following selections illustrate. While such narratives vary in complexity, their primary interest comes from the pleasing

rhythm created by both their stylistic devices and the repetition of action and details.

Interesting comparisons can be made by observing the similarities of "Plop!" from Tibet and "Henny Penny" from England with "The Hare That Ran Away" from India. This last tale is from the *Jātaka*, one of the early Buddhist literary collections which contains many traditional European tales. The similarities are naturally much greater between the narratives from India and Tibet, although there are some significant differences. "Henny Penny" illustrates the changes that can occur when a tale is retold by people who know nothing of its original cultural context. "The Pancake," "The Wonderful Cake," and "The Gingerbread Boy" also invite comparison and illustrate folktale diffusion. As often happens, a narrative's beginning and ending are easily varied but the basic plot and theme remain the same.

Cumulative tales are usually left to children today; adults seem less interested in them than in the more sophisticated types of folklore. Yet, as "The Hare That Ran Away" reveals, such tales have not only provided entertainment for centuries, but some have played a part in man's moral instruction.

TEENY-TINY / England

Joseph Jacobs

The plot of the following tale is not only secondary to but almost hidden by the repetition of "teeny-tiny." Yet the progressively louder demands of the bone and the old woman's unexpectedly defiant answer add additional humor to one of the most delightful-to-tell English folktales.

Once upon a time there was a teeny-tiny woman who lived in a teeny-tiny house in a teeny-tiny village. Now, one day this teeny-tiny woman put on her teeny-tiny bonnet and went out of her teeny-tiny house to take a teeny-tiny walk. And when this teeny-tiny woman had gone

"Teeny-Tiny," from *English Fairy Tales*, by Joseph Jacobs. Published by Putnam, 1892.

a teeny-tiny way, she came to a teeny-tiny gate; so the teeny-tiny woman opened the teeny-tiny gate and went into a teeny-tiny churchyard. And when this teeny-tiny woman had got into the teeny-tiny churchyard, she saw a teeny-tiny bone on a teeny-tiny grave, and the teeny-tiny woman said to her teeny-tiny self, "This teeny-tiny bone will make me some teeny-tiny soup for my teeny-tiny supper." So the teeny-tiny woman put the teeny-tiny bone into her teeny-tiny pocket and went home to her teeny-tiny house.

Now when the teeny-tiny woman got home to her teeny-tiny house, she was a teeny-tiny bit tired; so she went up her teeny-tiny stairs to her teeny-tiny bed and put the teeny-tiny bone into a teeny-tiny cupboard. And when this teeny-tiny woman had been to sleep a teeny-tiny time, she was awakened by a teeny-tiny voice from the teeny-tiny cupboard, which said,

"Give me my bone!"

And this teeny-tiny woman was a teeny-tiny frightened; so she had her teeny-tiny head under the teeny-tiny clothes and went to sleep again. And when she had been to sleep again a teeny-

tiny time, the teeny-tiny voice again cried out from the teeny-tiny cupboard a teeny-tiny louder,

"Give me my bone!"

This made the teeny-tiny woman a teeny-tiny more frightened; so she hid her teeny-tiny head a teeny-tiny farther under the teeny-tiny clothes. And when the teeny-tiny woman had been to sleep again a teeny-tiny time, the teeny-tiny voice from the teeny-tiny cupboard said again a teeny-tiny louder,

"Give me my bone!"

And this teeny-tiny woman was a teeny-tiny more frightened, but she put her teeny-tiny head out of the teeny-tiny clothes and said in her loudest teeny-tiny voice,

"TAKE IT!"

THE PANCAKE / Scandinavia

Peter Christen Asbjörnsen
Jörgen Moe

Incremental repetition is effectively used by each hungry bairn as well as by the pancake as he responds to each would-be devourer. But the pancake's quickness does not save him from being taken in, both literally and figuratively, by the pig.

Once on a time there was a goody who had seven hungry bairns, and she was frying a pancake for them. It was a sweet-milk pancake, and there it lay in the pan bubbling and frizzling so thick and good, it was a sight for sore eyes to look at. And the bairns stood round about, and the goodman sat by and looked on.

"Oh, give me a bit of pancake, mother, dear; I am so hungry," said one bairn.

"Oh, darling mother," said the second.

"Oh, darling, good mother," said the third.

"Oh, darling, good, nice mother," said the fourth.

"Oh, darling, pretty, good, nice mother," said the fifth.

"The Pancake," from *Tales From the Fjeld* by Peter Christen Asbjörnsen and Jörgen Moe, translated by G. W. Dasent. Published by G. P. Putnam's Sons.

"Oh, darling, pretty, good, nice, clever mother," said the sixth.

"Oh, darling, pretty, good, nice, clever, sweet mother," said the seventh.

So they begged for the pancake all round, the one more prettily than the other; for they were so hungry and so good.

"Yes, yes, bairns, only bide a bit till it turns itself,"—she ought to have said, "till I can get it turned,"—"and then you shall all have some—a lovely sweet-milk pancake; only look how fat and happy it lies there."

When the pancake heard that it got afraid, and in a trice it turned itself all of itself, and tried to jump out of the pan; but it fell back into it again t'other side up, and so when it had been fried a little on the other side too, till it got firmer in its flesh, it sprang out on the floor, and rolled off like a wheel through the door and down the hill.

"Holloa! Stop, pancake!" and away went the goody after it, with the frying-pan in one hand and the ladle in the other, as fast as she could, and her bairns behind her, while the goodman limped after them last of all.

"Hi! won't you stop? Seize it. Stop, pancake," they all screamed out, one after the other, and tried to catch it on the run and hold it; but the pancake rolled on and on, and in the twinkling of an eye it was so far ahead that they couldn't see it, for the pancake was faster on its feet than any of them.

So when it had rolled awhile it met a man.

"Good day, pancake," said the man.

"God bless you, Manny Panny!" said the pancake.

"Dear pancake," said the man, "don't roll so fast; stop a little and let me eat you."

"When I have given the slip to Goody Poody, and the goodman, and seven squalling children, I may well slip through your fingers, Manny Panny," said the pancake, and rolled on and on till it met a hen.

"Good day, pancake," said the hen.

"The same to you, Henny Penny," said the pancake.

"Pancake, dear, don't roll so fast; bide a bit and let me eat you up," said the hen.

"When I have given the slip to Goody Poody, and the goodman, and seven squalling children, and Manny Panny, I may well slip through your claws, Henny Penny," said the pancake, and so it rolled on like a wheel down the road.

Just then it met a cock.

"Good day, pancake," said the cock.

"The same to you, Cocky Locky," said the pancake.

"Pancake, dear, don't roll so fast, but bide a bit and let met eat you up."

"When I have given the slip to Goody Poody, and the goodman, and seven squalling children, and to Manny Panny, and Henny Penny, I may well slip through your claws, Cocky Locky," said the pancake, and off it set rolling away as fast as it could; and when it had rolled a long way it met a duck.

"Good day, pancake," said the duck.

"The same to you, Ducky Lucky."

"Pancake, dear, don't roll away so fast; bide a bit and let me eat you up."

"When I have given the slip to Goody Poody, and the goodman, and seven squalling children, and Manny Panny, and Henny Penny, and Cocky Locky, I may well slip through your fingers, Ducky Lucky," said the pancake, and with that it took to rolling and rolling faster than ever; and when it had rolled a long, long while, it met a goose.

"Good day, pancake," said the goose.

"The same to you, Goosey Poosey."

"Pancake, dear, don't roll so fast; bide a bit and let me eat you up."

"When I have given the slip to Goody Poody, and the goodman, and seven squalling children, and Manny Panny, and Henny Penny, and Cocky Locky, and Ducky Lucky, and Goosey Poosey, I your feet, Goosey Poosey," said the pancake, and off it rolled.

So when it had rolled a long, long way farther, it met a gander.

"Good day, pancake," said the gander.

"The same to you, Gander Pander," said the pancake.

"Pancake, dear, don't roll so fast; bide a bit and let me eat you up."

"When I have given the slip to Goody Poody, and the goodman, and seven squalling children, and Manny Panny, and Henny Penny, and Cocky Locky, and Ducky Lucky, and Goosey Poosey, I may well slip through your feet, Gander Pander," said the pancake, which rolled off as fast as ever.

So when it had rolled a long, long time, it met a pig.

"Good day, pancake," said the pig.

"The same to you, Piggy Wiggy," said the pancake, which, without a word more, began to roll and roll like mad.

"Nay, nay," said the pig, "you needn't be in such a hurry; we two can then go side by side and see one another over the wood; they say it is not too safe in there."

The pancake thought there might be something in that, and so they kept company. But when they had gone awhile, they came to a brook. As for Piggy, he was so fat he swam safe across, it was nothing to him; but the poor pancake couldn't get over.

"Seat yourself on my snout," said the pig, "and I'll carry you over."

So the pancake did that.

"Ouf, ouf," said the pig, and swallowed the pancake at one gulp; and then, as the poor pancake could go no farther, why—this story can go no farther either.

THE WONDERFUL CAKE / Ireland

F. M. Pilkington

The beginning of this variant is similar to "The Little Red Hen," in which a hen can find no one to help her bake bread but many who wish to help her eat it. The hen in "The Wonderful Cake" has a way of putting the rat and mouse in their place with a "Dickens a bit you shall." Instead of a pig, as in "The Pancake," this version relies on the fox, the traditional sly fellow, to bring the cake to its just end. Even in cumulative tales pride is punished.

A mouse, a rat, and a little red hen once lived together in the same cottage, and one day the little red hen said, "Let us bake a cake and have a feast."

"Let us," says the mouse, and, "Let us," says the rat.

"Who'll get the wheat ground?" says the hen.

"I won't," says the mouse.

"I won't," says the rat.

"I will go myself," says the little red hen. "Who'll make the cake?"

"I won't," says the mouse.

"I won't," says the rat.

"I will make it myself," says the little red hen.

So the little red hen baked the cake, and when it was baked, she asked, "Who'll eat the cake?"

"I will," said the mouse, and "I will," said the rat.

"Dickens a bit you shall," said the little red hen.

Well, while they argued—hey presto! out rolled the cake from the cottage, and after it ran the mouse, the rat, and the little red hen.

When it was running away it went by a barn full of threshers, and they asked it where it was running.

"Oh," says it, "I'm running away from the mouse, the rat, and the little red hen, and from you too, if I can."

So they rushed away after it with their flails, and it ran, and it ran till it came to a ditch full of ditchers, and they asked it where it was running.

"Oh, I'm running away from the mouse, the rat, and the little red hen, and from a barn full of threshers, and from you, too, if I can."

Well, they all ran after it along with the rest, till it came to a well full of washers, and they asked the same question, and it returned the same answer, and after it they went.

At last it came to a ford where it met with a fox, and he asked where it was running.

"Oh, I'm running away from the mouse, the rat, and the little red hen, from a barn full of threshers, a ditch full of ditchers, a well full of washers, and from you, too, if I can."

"But you can't cross the ford," says the fox.

"And can't you carry me over?" says the cake.

"What'll you give me?" says the fox.

"A kiss at Christmas and an egg at Easter," says the cake.

"Very well," says the fox, "up with you."

So he sat on his haunches with his nose in the air, and the cake got up by his tail till it sat on his crupper.

"Now, over with you," says the cake.

"You're not high enough," says the fox.

Then it scrambled up on his shoulder.

"Up higher still," says he; "you wouldn't be safe there."

"Am I right now?" says the cake.

"You'll be safer on the ridge pole of my nose."

"Well," says the cake, "I think I can go no further."

"Oh, yes," says he, and he shot it up in the air, caught it in his mouth, and sent it down the Red Lane. And that was the end of the cake.

THE GINGERBREAD BOY / United States

The motif of a childless couple who long for a son is used to begin this variant of "The Pancake." Compare the effectiveness of the ending of this tale with the two previous versions.

Now you shall hear a story that somebody's great-great-grandmother told a little girl ever so many years ago:

There was once a little old man and a little old woman, who lived in a little old house in the edge of a wood. They would have been a very happy old couple but for one thing—they had no little child, and they wished for one very much. One day, when the little old woman was baking gingerbread, she cut a cake in the shape of a little boy, and put it into the oven.

Presently, she went to the oven to see if it was baked. As soon as the oven door was opened, the little gingerbread boy jumped out, and began to run away as fast as he could go.

The little old woman called her husband, and they both ran after him. But they could not catch him. And soon the gingerbread boy came to a barn full of threshers. He called out to them as he went by, saying

"I've run away from a little old woman,
    A little old man,
    And I can run away from you, I can!"

Then the barn full of threshers set out to run after him. But, though they ran fast, they could not catch him. And he ran on till he came to a field full of mowers. He called out to them:

"I've run away from a little old woman,
    A little old man,
    A barn full of threshers,
    And I can run away from you, I can!"

"The Gingerbread Boy," from *St. Nicholas Magazine*, May 1875.

Then the mowers began to run after him, but they couldn't catch him. And he ran on till he came to a cow. He called out to her:

"I've run away from a little old woman,
    A little old man,
    A barn full of threshers,
    A field full of mowers,
    And I can run away from you, I can!"

But, though the cow started at once, she couldn't catch him. And soon he came to a pig. He called out to the pig:

"I've run away from a little old woman,
    A little old man,
    A barn full of threshers,
    A field full of mowers,
    A cow
    And I can run away from you, I can!"

But the pig ran, and couldn't catch him. And he ran till he came across a fox, and to him he called out:

"I've run away from a little old woman,
    A little old man,
    A barn full of threshers,
    A field full of mowers,
    A cow and a pig,
    And I can run away from you, I can!"

Then the fox set out to run. Now foxes can run very fast, and so the fox soon caught the gingerbread boy and began to eat him up.

Presently the gingerbread boy said: "Oh, dear! I'm quarter gone!" And then: "Oh, I'm half gone!" And soon: "I'm three-quarters gone!" And at last: "I'm all gone!" and never spoke again.

THE OLD WOMAN AND HER PIG / England

Joseph Jacobs

The use of incremental repetition in this tale can be compared with that in "The Pancake" and "Why the Bush-Fowl Calls at Dawn and Why Flies Buzz." In "The Old Woman and Her Pig" it plays a more important role than in the other two stories. Similar narratives are told in Europe, Africa, Asia, and America, although the details vary a great deal.

An old woman was sweeping her house, and she found a little crooked sixpence. "What," said she, "shall I do with this little sixpence? I will go to market, and buy a little pig."

As she was coming home, she came to a stile: but the piggy wouldn't go over the stile.

She went a little further, and she met a dog. So she said to him: "Dog! dog! bite pig; piggy won't go over the stile; and I shan't get home to-night." But the dog wouldn't.

She went a little further, and she met a stick. So she said: "Stick! stick! beat dog! dog won't bite pig; piggy won't get over the stile; and I shan't get home to-night." But the stick wouldn't.

She went a little further, and she met a fire. So she said: "Fire! fire! burn stick; stick won't beat dog; dog won't bite pig; piggy won't get over the stile; and I shan't get home to-night." But the fire wouldn't.

She went a little further, and she met some water. So she said: "Water! water! quench fire; fire won't burn stick; stick won't beat dog; dog won't bite pig; piggy won't get over the stile; and I shan't get home to-night." But the water wouldn't.

She went a little further, and she met an ox. So she said: "Ox! ox! drink water; water won't quench fire; fire won't burn stick; stick won't beat dog; dog won't bite pig; piggy won't get over the

"The Old Woman and Her Pig," from *English Fairy Tales* by Joseph Jacobs. Published by G. P. Putnam's Sons, 1892.

stile; and I shan't get home to-night." But the ox wouldn't.

She went a little further, and she met a butcher. So she said: "Butcher! butcher! kill ox; ox won't drink water; water won't quench fire; fire won't burn stick; stick won't beat dog; dog won't bite pig; piggy won't get over the stile; and I shan't get home to-night." But the butcher wouldn't.

She went a little further, and she met a rope. So she said: "Rope! rope! hang butcher; butcher won't kill ox; ox won't drink water; water won't quench fire; fire won't burn stick; stick won't beat dog; dog won't bite pig; piggy won't get over the stile; and I shan't get home to-night." But the rope wouldn't.

She went a little further, and she met a rat. So she said: "Rat! rat! gnaw rope; rope won't hang butcher; butcher won't kill ox; ox won't drink water; water won't quench fire; fire won't burn stick; stick won't beat dog; dog won't bite pig; piggy won't get over the stile; and I shan't get home to-night." But the rat wouldn't.

She went a little further, and she met a cat. So she said: "Cat! cat! kill rat; rat won't gnaw rope; rope won't hang butcher; butcher won't kill ox; ox won't drink water; water won't quench fire; fire won't burn stick; stick won't beat dog; dog won't bite pig; piggy won't get over the stile; and I shan't get home to-night." But the cat said to her, "If you will go to yonder cow, and fetch me a saucer of milk, I will kill the rat." So away went the old woman to the cow.

But the cow said to her: "If you will go to yonder hay-stack, and fetch me a handful of hay, I'll give you the milk." So away went the old woman to the hay-stack; and she brought the hay to the cow.

As soon as the cow had eaten the hay, she gave the old woman the milk; and away she went with it in a saucer to the cat.

As soon as the cat had lapped up the milk, the cat began to kill the rat; the rat began to gnaw the rope; the rope began to hang the butcher; the butcher began to kill the ox; the ox began to drink the water; the water began to quench the fire; the fire began to burn the stick; the stick began to beat the dog; the dog began to bite the pig; the little pig in a fright jumped over the stile; and so the old woman got home that night.

WHY THE BUSH-FOWL CALLS AT DAWN AND WHY FLIES BUZZ / Nigeria—the Ekoi

Kathleen Arnott

Some cumulative tales do not clearly illustrate that one thing leads to another. However, anyone who has been bothered by a fly will understand how all of the following could occur. The inclusion of the pourquoi *motif in a cumulative tale is rather unusual.*

One day a man and his wife went into the bush to collect nuts. They found a palm tree with clusters of ripe nuts growing among the large green leaves, and telling his wife to wait below, the man soon climbed to the top of the tree, with his knife in his belt.

He was hacking away at the heavy clusters of palm nuts when a small black fly buzzed round his face, tickling his nose and trying to get into the corner of his eye. As he hastily brushed it away, his hand slipped and the knife began to fall.

'Wife!' he called. 'Move away! The knife is falling.'

The woman quickly leapt aside so that the knife missed her, but as she did so she jumped over a snake which was sleeping under the dead leaves. This so frightened the snake that it dived into the nearest place of refuge it could see, which happened to be a rat's hole.

The poor rat was terrified, and dashing past the snake he managed to get out of his hole and ran up the nearest tree for safety.

Unfortunately the rat had chosen a tree where the plaintain-eater bird had built her nest, and thinking that the rat was after her eggs, she set up such a cackling and a screaming that the monkey in another tree was almost frightened out of his wits. He had been just about to eat a nice juicy mango which he had picked, but in his terror he dropped it.

The mango fell with a thud on to the back of an elephant who was walking quietly below, minding his own business. Imagining that he was being attacked by hunters he rushed madly away, catching his head in a flowering creeper which was climbing up a tree and dragging it through the bush in his flight.

The creeper had a strong stem which became entwined round a tall earthen ant heap, pulling it to the ground, where it fell on to a nest full of bush-fowl's eggs and broke them all.

'Kark!' squawked the poor mother bush-fowl. 'Look what you've done to my eggs,' and spreading her feathers over the ruined nest she collapsed in misery and uttered not another sound for two whole days and nights.

Now everyone knows that the bush-fowl is always the first to wake among the wild creatures, and that when the sun hears her loud and raucous cries, he rises from his bed and a new day begins. But since the bush-fowl was silently brooding over her loss, she had not called the sun, and the sky remained dark. The other animals wondered why the daylight did not come, and cried out to the Great Spirit of the Heavens, asking him what had happened.

So the Great Spirit summoned all the animals together, and even the bush-fowl had to answer his call.

'Why have you not wakened the sun these last two mornings?' the Spirit asked the bush-fowl, who stood before all the other animals and answered:

> 'My eggs were broken by the falling ant heap
>   which was pulled over by the creeper,
> Which was dragged down by the elephant,
> Who was hit by a mango,
> Which was dropped by a monkey,
> Who was startled by a bird,
> Who was frightened by a rat,
> Who was scared by a serpent,
> Who was wakened by a woman,
> Who was running from a knife,
> Which was dropped by her husband,
> Who was tickled by a black fly
> Up a palm tree.'

So the Great Spirit turned to the ant heap and asked: 'Why were you so careless as to fall and break the bush-fowl's eggs?'

The ant heap, which had by now collected itself together, replied:

> 'I was pulled over by the creeper,
> Which was dragged down by the elephant,
> Who was hit by a mango,
> Which was dropped by a monkey,
> Who was startled by a bird,
> Who was frightened by a rat,
> Who was scared by a serpent,
> Who was wakened by a woman,
> Who was running from a knife,
> Which was dropped by her husband,
> Who was tickled by a black fly
> Up a palm tree.'

Then the Great Spirit said to the flowering creeper: 'Why were you so careless as to pull over the ant heap?'

So the creeper replied:

> 'I was dragged down by the elephant,
> Who was hit by a mango,
> Which was dropped by a monkey,
> Who was startled by a bird,
> Who was frightened by a rat,
> Who was scared by a serpent,
> Who was wakened by a woman,
> Who was running from a knife,
> Which was dropped by her husband,
> Who was tickled by a black fly
> Up a palm tree.'

The Great Spirit turned to the elephant. 'Why were you so careless as to pull down the flowering creeper?' he asked.

The elephant answered:

> 'I was hit by a mango,
> Which was dropped by a monkey,
> Who was startled by a bird,
> Who was frightened by a rat,
> Who was scared by a serpent,
> Who was wakened by a woman,
> Who was running from a knife,
> Which was dropped by her husband,
> Who was tickled by a black fly
> Up a palm tree.'

The mango was still lying on the ground where it had bounced off the elephant's back, so the Great Spirit asked it why it had fallen so heavily and frightened the big creature.

> 'I was dropped by a monkey,
> Who was startled by a bird,
> Who was frightened by a rat,
> Who was scared by a serpent,
> Who was wakened by a woman,
> Who was running from a knife,
> Which was dropped by her husband,
> Who was tickled by a black fly
> Up a palm tree,'

replied the mango.

'That was very careless of you, Monkey,' said the Great Spirit. So the monkey chattered and said:

> 'I was startled by a bird,
> Who was frightened by a rat,

Who was scared by a serpent,
Who was wakened by a woman,
Who was running from a knife,
Which was dropped by her husband,
Who was tickled by a black fly
Up a palm tree.'

'And what have you to say for yourself?' the Great Spirit asked the bird, who replied:

'I was frightened by a rat,
Who was scared by a serpent,
Who was wakened by a woman,
Who was running from a knife,
Which was dropped by her husband,
Who was tickled by a black fly
Up a palm tree.'

'Rat! Rat! Why did you frighten the plantain-eating bird?' asked the Great Spirit.

'I was scared by a serpent,
Who was wakened by a woman,
Who was running from a knife,
Which was dropped by her husband,
Who was tickled by a black fly
Up a palm tree,'

said the rat.

Then the Great Spirit called upon the snake to explain why he had alarmed the rat.

'I was wakened by a woman,
Who was running from a knife,
Which was dropped by her husband,
Who was tickled by a black fly
Up a palm tree,'

replied the snake.

'Woman! Come here and tell me why you wakened the serpent,' commanded the Great Spirit, and the woman explained:

'I was running from a knife,
Which was dropped by her husband,
Who was tickled by a black fly
Up a palm tree.'

'Then the knife must explain why he made you run,' said the Great Spirit, and a little voice piped up from the man's belt, saying:

'I was dropped by her husband
Who was tickled by a black fly
Up a palm tree.'

'It is a dangerous thing to drop knives,' said the Great Spirit to the man. 'Why did you do so?'

'I was tickled by a black fly
Up a palm tree,'

replied the man.

'Then it seems to me,' said the Great Spirit, 'that all this trouble was caused by the black fly. Why did you tickle the man's face while he was up the palm tree, O black fly?'

But instead of answering courteously, as the others had done, the black fly flew about their heads and would only say, 'Buzz! Buzz! Buzz!'

The Great Spirit repeated his question, and again the only answer he got was 'Buzz! Buzz! Buzz!' for the fly refused to say a word. Then the Great Spirit was angry, and exclaimed:

'Because you have refused to answer my questions, I have taken away your power of speech. From now onwards, you will only be able to buzz.'

Then turning to the bush-fowl, the Great Spirit said:

'Never again must you neglect to call the sun at dawn, whatever may have happened to your eggs.'

The bush-fowl hung her head and promised she would never forget, and, as you know, she never has. Neither has the black fly ever got back his voice and you can still hear him and his brothers flying about the world saying nothing but 'Buzz! Buzz! Buzz!'

THE HARE THAT RAN AWAY / India

Marie Shedlock

This story is from the Jātaka, *a literary collection of animal tales. The Buddha is said to have been incarnated as animals before becoming a man. In each tale about a particular animal he exemplifies kindness and wisdom. The general tone is instructive, yet this narrative is not so moralistic that it should be classified as a fable.*

The Jātaka, *like* The Panchatantra, *contains the ancestors of some traditional European, African, and Asian tales. Compare the differences in tone and plot between this story and the next two variants.*

And it came to pass that the Buddha (to be) was born again as a Lion. Just as he had helped his fellow-men, he now began to help his fellow-animals, and there was a great deal to be done. For instance, there was a little nervous Hare who was always afraid that something dreadful was going to happen to her. She was always saying: "Suppose the Earth were to fall in, what would happen to me?" And she said this so often that at last she thought it really was about to happen. One day, when she had been saying over and over again, "Suppose the Earth were to fall in, what would happen to me?" she heard a slight noise: it really was only a heavy fruit which had fallen upon a rustling leaf, but the little Hare was so nervous she was ready to believe anything, and she said in a frightened tone: "The Earth *is* falling in." She ran away as fast as she could go, and presently she met an old brother Hare, who said: "Where are you running to, Mistress Hare?"

And the little Hare said: "I have no time to stop and tell you anything. The Earth is falling in, and I am running away."

"The Earth is falling in, is it?" said the old brother Hare, in a tone of much astonishment;

and he repeated this to *his* brother hare, and *he* to *his* brother hare, and *he* to *his* brother hare, until at last there were a hundred thousand brother hares, all shouting: "The Earth is falling in." Now presently the bigger animals began to take the cry up. First the deer, and then the sheep, and then the wild boar, and then the buffalo, and then the camel, and then the tiger, and then the elephant.

Now the wise Lion heard all this noise and wondered at it. "There are no signs," he said, "of the Earth falling in. They must have heard something." And then he stopped them all short and said: "What is this you are saying?"

And the Elephant said: "I remarked that the Earth was falling in."

"How do you know this?" asked the Lion.

"Why, now I come to think of it, it was the Tiger that remarked it to me."

And the Tiger said: "I had it from the Camel," and the Camel said: "I had it from the Buffalo." And the buffalo from the wild boar, and the wild boar from the sheep, and the sheep from the deer, and the deer from the hares, and the Hares said: "Oh! *we* heard it from *that* little Hare."

And the Lion said: "Little Hare, *what* made you say that the Earth was falling in?"

And the little Hare said: "I saw it."

"You saw it?" said the Lion. "Where?"

"Yonder by the tree."

"Well," said the Lion, "come with me and I will show you how——"

"No, no," said the Hare, "I would not go near that tree for anything, I'm *so* nervous."

"But," said the Lion, "I am going to take you on my back." And he took her on his back, and begged the animals to stay where they were until they returned. Then he showed the little Hare how the fruit had fallen upon the leaf, making the noise that had frightened her, and she said:

"Yes, I see—the Earth is *not* falling in." And the Lion said: "Shall we go back and tell the other animals?"

And they went back. The little Hare stood before the animals and said: "The Earth is *not* falling in." And all the animals began to repeat this to one another, and they dispersed gradually, and you heard the words more and more softly:

"The Earth is *not* falling in," etc., etc., etc., until the sound died away altogether.

PLOP! / Tibet

Carl Withers

The most significant difference between "Plop!" and "The Hare That Ran Away" is that no mention of Buddha is made in "Plop!" Although this lion is not so tolerant, the two lions are remarkably similar in their calm search for the truth. The basic tale was adopted by the Tibetan tellers of tales with little adaptation. This is not true of "Henny Penny," the English variant of the same tale.

Many, many years ago there were six rabbits who lived on the shore of a lake, in a forest. One fine day, a big ripe fruit on one of the biggest trees fell down into the lake, making a loud "plop!" when it hit the water. The rabbits were terrified, not knowing what the noise could be, and at once made off as fast as their four legs could carry them.

A fox saw them fleeing and called out, "Why are you flying?" The rabbits said, "Plop is coming!" When the fox heard this, he immediately started to flee with them. Next they ran into a monkey, who queried, "Why are you in such a hurry?" "Plop is coming!" replied the fox. So the monkey also joined in their flight.

Thus the news spread from mouth to mouth until a deer, a pig, a buffalo, a rhinoceros, an elephant, a black bear, a brown bear, a leopard, a

tiger, and a lion were all running away, helter-skelter.

They had no thought at all, except to fly. The faster they ran, the more frightened they became.

At the foot of the hill there lived a lion with a great long mane. When he caught sight of the other lion running, he roared to him, "Brother, you have claws and teeth and you are the strongest of all animals. Why are you running like mad?"

"Plop is coming!" the running lion panted.

"Who's Plop? What is he?" the lion with the long mane demanded.

"Well, I really don't know," he faltered.

"Why make such a fuss then?" the long-maned lion went on. "Let's find out what it is first. Who told you about it?"

"The tiger told me."

The inquisitive lion with the long mane asked the tiger, who said that the leopard had told him, so the lion turned to the leopard, and the leopard answered that he had heard it from the brown bear. The question was passed on to the brown bear, who said he had heard it from the black bear. In this way, the black bear, the elephant, the rhinoceros, the buffalo, the pig and the deer were all asked, one by one, and each of them said he was told by someone else. Finally it came down to the fox's testimony, and he said, "The rabbits told me." Then the lion went up to the rabbits, who squeaked in chorus:

"All six of us heard this terrible Plop with our own ears. Come with us, we'll show you where we heard him."

They led him to the forest, and pointing at it, they said, "The terrible Plop is there."

Just at this moment another big fruit fell from the tree and dropped into the water with a deep "plop!"

The lion sneered. "Now, look, all of you!" he said. "You've all seen what that plop is. It's only the sound of a fruit dropping into the water. What is so terrifying about that? You almost ran your legs off!"

They breathed a sigh of relief. The panic was all for naught.

HENNY-PENNY / England

Joseph Jacobs

The western storytellers had no understanding of Buddhism and no interest in preserving the wise lion figure of the previous two narratives. The sly fox is introduced in the English tale and shows a harsher result of panic. Only the witless Henny-Penny escapes, but because she created the mixup that led to her friends' deaths, it is a vaguely unsatisfactory ending.

The English enjoment of incremental repetition is apparent in this variant of "The Hare That Ran Away" and almost hides the basic theme of foolish fear. It is this language play that has made "Henny-Penny" popular with children.

One day Henny-Penny was picking up corn in the cornyard when—whack!—something hit her upon the head. "Goodness gracious me!" said Henny-Penny; "the sky's a-going to fall; I must go and tell the king."

So she went along, and she went along, and she went along till she met Cocky-Locky. "Where are you going, Henny-Penny?" says Cocky-Locky. "Oh! I'm going to tell the king the sky's a-falling," says Henny-Penny. "May I come with you?" says Cocky-Locky. "Certainly," says Henny-Penny. So Henny-Penny and Cocky-Locky went to tell the king the sky was falling.

They went along, and they went along, and they went along till they met Ducky-Daddles.

"Where are you going to, Henny-Penny and Cocky-Locky?" says Ducky-Daddles. "Oh! we're going to tell the king the sky's a-falling," said Henny-Penny and Cocky-Locky. "May I come with you?" says Ducky-Daddles. "Certainly," said Henny-Penny and Cocky-Locky. So Henny-Penny, Cocky-Locky, and Ducky-Daddles went to tell the king the sky was a-falling.

So they went along, and they went along, and they went along, till they met Goosey-Poosey. "Where are you going to, Henny-Penny, Cocky-Locky, and Ducky-Daddles?" said Goosey-Poosey. "Oh! we're going to tell the king the sky's a-falling," said Henny-Penny and Cocky-Locky and Ducky-Daddles. "May I come with you?" said Goosey-Poosey. "Certainly," said Henny-Penny, Cocky-Locky, and Ducky-Daddles. So Henny-

"Henny Penny," from *English Fairy Tales* by Joseph Jacobs. Published by G. P. Putnam's Sons, 1892.

Penny, Cocky-Locky, Ducky-Daddles, and Goosey-Poosey went to tell the king the sky was a-falling.

So they went along, and they went along, and they went along, till they met Turkey-Lurkey. "Where are you going, Henny-Penny, Cocky-Locky, Ducky-Daddles, and Goosey-Poosey?" says Turkey-Lurkey. "Oh! we're going to tell the king the sky's a-falling," said Henny-Penny, Cocky-Locky, Ducky-Daddles, and Goosey-Poosey. "May I come with you, Henny-Penny, Cocky-Locky, Ducky-Daddles, and Goosey-Poosey?" said Turkey-Lurkey. "Oh, certainly, Turkey-Lurkey," said Henny-Penny, Cocky-Locky, Ducky-Daddles, and Goosey-Poosey. So Henny-Penny, Cocky-Locky, Ducky-Daddles, Goosey-Poosey, and Turkey-Lurkey all went to tell the king the sky was a-falling.

So they went along, and they went along, and they went along, till they met Foxy-Woxy, and Foxy-Woxy said to Henny-Penny, Cocky-Locky, Ducky-Daddles, Goosey-Poosey, and Turkey-Lurkey: "Where are you going, Henny-Penny, Cocky-Locky, Ducky-Daddles, Goosey-Poosey, and Turkey-Lurkey?" And Henny-Penny, Cocky-Locky, Ducky-Daddles, Goosey-Poosey, and Turkey-Lurkey said to Foxy-Woxy: "We're going to tell the king the sky's a-falling." "Oh! but this is not the way to the king, Henny-Penny, Cocky-Locky, Ducky-Daddles, Goosey-Poosey, and Turkey-Lurkey," said Foxy-Woxy; "I know the proper way; shall I show it you?" "Oh, certainly, Foxy-Woxy," said Henny-Penny, Cocky-Locky, Ducky-Daddles, Goosey-Poosey, and Turkey-Lurkey. So Henny-Penny, Cocky-Locky, Ducky-Daddles, Goosey-Poosey, Turkey-Lurkey, and Foxy-Woxy all went to tell the king the sky was a-falling. So they went along, and they went along, and they went along, till they came to a narrow and dark hole. Now this was the door of Foxy-Woxy's cave. But Foxy-Woxy said to Henny-Penny, Cocky-Locky, Ducky-Daddles, Goosey-Poosey, and Turkey-Lurkey: "This is the short way to the king's palace; you'll soon get there if you follow me. I will go first and you come after, Henny-Penny, Cocky-Locky, Ducky-Daddles, Goosey-Poosey, and Turkey-Lurkey." "Why of course, certainly, without doubt, why not?" said Henny-Penny, Cocky-Locky, Ducky-Daddles, Goosey-Poosey, and Turkey-Lurkey.

So Foxy-Woxy went into his cave, and he didn't go very far, but turned round to wait for Henny-Penny, Cocky-Locky, Ducky-Daddles, Goosey-Poosey, and Turkey-Lurkey. So at last at first Turkey-Lurkey went through the dark hole into the cave. He hadn't got far when "Hrumph," Foxy-Woxy snapped off Turkey-Lurkey's head and threw his body over his left shoulder. Then Goosey-Poosey went in, and "Hrumph," off went her head and Goosey-Poosey was thrown beside Turkey-Lurkey. Then Ducky-Daddles waddled down, and "Hrumph," snapped Foxy-Woxy, and Ducky-Daddles' head was off and Ducky-Daddles was thrown alongside Turkey-Lurkey and Goosey-Poosey. Then Cocky-Locky strutted down into the cave, and he hadn't gone far when "Snap, Hrumph!" went Foxy-Woxy and Cocky-Locky was thrown alongside of Turkey-Lurkey, Goosey-Poosey, and Ducky-Daddles.

But Foxy-Woxy had made two bites at Cocky-Locky; and when the first snap only hurt Cocky-Locky, but didn't kill him, he called out to Henny-Penny. But she turned tail and off she ran home; so she never told the king the sky was a-falling.

THE STORY OF THE THREE LITTLE PIGS / England

Joseph Jacobs

Many people assume "fairy tales" begin, "Once upon a time." The rhyme that begins this story is much more interesting and certainly more appropriate to the mood of the tale.

While an adult may find echoes here of the parable about the man who built his house on sand, children are less interested in moralizing about good, strong houses than in the way the last pig outwits the wolf. Unlike the fox in "Henny-Penny," this wolf is not too bright.

Once upon a time when pigs spoke rhyme,
And monkeys chewed tobacco,
And hens took snuff to make them tough,
And ducks went quack, quack, quack, O!

There was an old sow with three little pigs, and as she had not enough to keep them, she sent them out to seek their fortune. The first that went off met a man with a bundle of straw, and said to him:

"Please, man, give me that straw to build me a house."

Which the man did, and the little pig built a house with it. Presently came along a wolf, and knocked at the door, and said:

"Little pig, little pig, let me come in."

To which the pig answered:

"No, no, by the hair of my chinny chin chin."

The wolf then answered to that:

"Then I'll huff, and I'll puff, and I'll blow your house in."

So he huffed, and he puffed, and he blew his house in, and ate up the little pig.

The second little pig met a man with a bundle of furze and said:

"Please, man, give me that furze to build a house."

Which the man did, and the pig built his house. Then along came the wolf, and said:

"Little pig, little pig, let me come in."

"No, no, by the hair of my chinny chin chin."

"Then I'll puff, and I'll huff, and I'll blow your house in."

So he huffed, and he puffed, and he puffed and he huffed, and at last he blew the house down, and he ate up the little pig.

The third little pig met a man with a load of bricks, and said:

"Please, man, give me those bricks to build a house with."

So the man gave him the bricks, and he built his house with them. So the wolf came, as he did to the other little pigs, and said:

"Little pig, little pig, let me come in."

"No, no, by the hair of my chinny chin chin."

"Then I'll huff, and I'll puff, and I'll blow your house in."

Well, he huffed, and he puffed, and he huffed and he puffed, and he puffed and huffed; but he could *not* get the house down. When he found that he could not, with all his huffing and puffing, blow the house down, he said:

"Little pig, I know where there is a nice field of turnips."

"Where?" said the little pig.

"Oh, in Mr. Smith's home-field, and if you will be ready to-morrow morning I will call for you, and we will go together, and get some for dinner."

"Very well," said the little pig, "I will be ready. What time do you mean to go?"

"Oh, at six o'clock."

Well, the little pig got up at five and got the turnips before the wolf came (which he did about six), who said:

"Little pig, are you ready?"

The little pig said, "Ready! I have been and come back again and got a nice potful for dinner."

The wolf felt very angry at this, but thought that he would be up to the little pig somehow or other, so he said:

"Little pig, I know where there is a nice apple-tree."

"Where?" said the pig.

"Down at Merry-Garden," replied the wolf, "and if you will not deceive me, I will come for you at five o'clock to-morrow and get some apples."

Well, the little pig bustled up the next morning at four o'clock, and went off for the apples, hoping to get back before the wolf came; but he had further to go and had to climb the tree, so

"The Story of the Three Little Pigs," from *English Fairy Tales* by Joseph Jacobs. Published by G. P. Putnam's Sons 1892.

that just as he was coming down from it, he saw the wolf coming, which, as you may suppose, frightened him very much. When the wolf came up he said:

"Little pig, what! are you here before me? Are they nice apples?"

"Yes, very," said the little pig. "I will throw you down one."

And he threw it so far, that, while the wolf was gone to pick it up, the little pig jumped down and ran home. The next day the wolf came again and said to the little pig:

"Little pig, there is a fair at Shanklin this afternoon; will you go?"

"Oh, yes," said the pig, "I will go; what time shall you be ready?"

"At three," said the wolf. So the little pig went off before the time as usual and got to the fair and bought a butter-churn, which he was going home with, when he saw the wolf coming. Then he could not tell what to do. So he got into the churn to hide, and by so doing turned it round, and it rolled down the hill with the pig in it, which frightened the wolf so much, that he ran home without going to the fair. He went to the little pig's house and told him how frightened he had been by a great round thing which came down the hill past him. Then the little pig said:

"Hah, I frightened you then. I had been to the fair and bought a butter-churn; and when I saw you, I got into it, and rolled down the hill."

Then the wolf was very angry indeed and declared he *would* eat up the little pig, and that he would get down the chimney after him. When the little pig saw what he was about, he hung on the pot full of water and made up a blazing fire, and, just as the wolf was coming down, took off the cover, and in fell the wolf; so the little pig put on the cover again in an instant, boiled him up, and ate him for supper and lived happy ever afterwards.

THE THREE BILLY GOATS GRUFF / Scandinavia

Peter Christen Asbjörnsen

Few folktales are as popular with kindergarten children as "The Three Billy Goats Gruff." Children enjoy the way the first two goats escape being eaten, they repeat the "trip, trap! trip, trap!," they squeal with each louder "WHO'S THAT tripping over my bridge?," and they triumph with the Big Billy Goat when he pokes and crushes and tosses. All in all, it is a participation story par excellence.

Once upon a time there were three Billy Goats who wanted to go up to the hillside to make themselves fat, and the name of all the three was "Gruff."

On the way up, they had to cross a bridge over a brook; and under the bridge lived a great ugly Troll, with eyes as big as saucers and a nose as long as a poker.

"The Three Billy Goats Gruff," from *Popular Tales from the Norse* by Peter Christen Asbjörnsen, translated by G. W. Dasent. Published by Putnam, 1908.

First of all came the youngest Billy Goat Gruff to cross the bridge.

"TRIP, TRAP! TRIP, TRAP!" went the bridge.

"WHO'S THAT tripping over my bridge?" roared the Troll.

"Oh! It is only I, the tiniest Billy Goat Gruff, and I'm going up to the hillside to make myself fat," said the Billy Goat in such a small voice.

"Now, I'm coming to gobble you up," said the Troll.

"Oh, no! Pray don't take me. I'm too little,

that I am," said the Billy Goat. "Wait a bit till the second Billy Goat Gruff comes; he's much bigger."

"Well! Be off with you," said the Troll.

A little while after, came the second Billy Goat Gruff to cross the bridge.

"TRIP, TRAP! TRIP, TRAP! TRIP, TRAP!" went the bridge.

"WHO'S THAT tripping over my bridge?" roared the Troll.

"Oh! It's the second Billy Goat Gruff, and I'm going up to the hillside to make myself fat," said the Billy Goat, who hadn't such a small voice.

"Now, I'm going to gobble you up," said the Troll.

"Oh, no! Don't take me. Wait a bit till the big Billy Goat Gruff comes; he's much bigger."

"Very well! Be off with you," said the Troll.

Just then up came the big Billy Goat Gruff.

"TRIP, TRAP! TRIP, TRAP! TRIP, TRAP! TRIP, TRAP!" went the bridge, for the big Billy Goat was so heavy that the bridge creaked and groaned under him.

"WHO'S THAT tramping over my bridge?" roared the Troll.

"It's I! THE BIG BILLY GOAT GRUFF!" said the Billy Goat, who had an ugly hoarse voice of his own.

"Now, I'm coming to gobble you up," roared the Troll.

Then the Big Billy Goat Gruff said:

"Well, come along! I've got two spears,
And I'll poke your eyeballs out at your ears;
I've got besides two curling-stones,
And I'll crush you to bits, body and bones."

That was what the big Billy Goat said. And so he flew at the Troll and poked his eyes out with his horns, and crushed him to bits, body and bones, and tossed him into the brook. After that he went up to the hillside. There the Billy Goats got so fat they were hardly able to walk home again; and if the fat hasn't fallen off them, why they're still fat; and so—

Snip, snap, snout,
This tale's told out.

THE THREE BEARS / England

Flora Annie Steel

A common motif in folktales is a confrontation with a monster: the troll in "The Three Billy Goats Gruff" and the bear in "East o' the Sun and West o' the Moon," for example. Children identify with Goldilocks and may consider the bears as frightening as she did. Adults, however, may wonder who represents the monster, the surprised bears or the trespassing child. Earlier versions were more clear. Instead of a fair-haired child, the bears' home was invaded by a rude old woman.

Once upon a time there were three Bears, who lived together in a house of their own in a wood. One of them was a Little Wee Bear, and one was a Middle-sized Bear, and the other was a Great Big Bear.

They had each a bowl for their porridge; a little bowl for the Little Wee Bear; and a middle-sized bowl for the Middle-sized Bear; and a great big bowl for the Great Big Bear.

They had each a chair to sit in; a little chair for the Little Wee Bear; and a middle-sized chair for the Middle-sized Bear; and a great big chair for the Great Big Bear.

They had each a bed to sleep in; a little bed for the Little Wee Bear; and a middle-sized bed for the Middle-sized Bear; and a great big bed for the Great Big Bear.

One day, after they had made the porridge for their breakfast and poured it into their porridge bowls, they walked out into the wood while the porridge was cooling. And while they were away a little girl called Goldilocks, who lived at the other side of the wood and had been sent on an errand by her mother, passed by the house and looked in at the window. And then she peeped in at the keyhole. Then seeing nobody in the house, she lifted the latch. The door was not fastened, so Goldilocks opened the door and went in; and well pleased was she when she saw the porridge on the table.

First she tasted the porridge of the Great Big Bear, and that was too hot for her. Next she tasted the porridge of the Middle-sized Bear, but that was too cold for her. And then she went to the porridge of the Little Wee Bear and tasted it, and that was neither too hot nor too cold, but just right; and she liked it so well that she ate it all up.

Then Goldilocks sat down in the chair of the Great Big Bear, but that was too hard for her. And then she sat down in the chair of the Middle-sized Bear, and that was too soft for her. But when she sat down in the chair of the Little Wee Bear, that was neither too hard, nor too soft, but just right. So she seated herself in it, and there she sat till the bottom of the chair came out, and down she came, plump! upon the ground.

Now Goldilocks went into the bedchamber in which the three Bears slept. And first she lay down upon the bed of the Great Big Bear, but that was too high at the head for her. And next she lay down upon the bed of the Middle-sized Bear, and that was too high at the foot for her. And then she lay down upon the bed of the Little Wee Bear, and that was neither too high at the head, nor at the foot, but just right. So she covered herself up, and lay there till she fell fast asleep.

By this time the three Bears thought their porridge would be cool enough for them to eat it

properly, so they came home to breakfast. Now Goldilocks had left the spoon of the Great Big Bear standing in his porridge.

"SOMEBODY HAS BEEN AT MY POR-RIDGE!" said the Great Big Bear in his great, rough, gruff voice.

Then the Middle-sized Bear looked at his porridge and saw the spoon standing in it too.

"SOMEBODY HAS BEEN AT MY PORRIDGE!" said the Middle-sized Bear in his middle-sized voice.

Then the Little Wee Bear looked at his porridge. There was the spoon in the porridge bowl; but the porridge was all gone!

"SOMEBODY HAS BEEN AT MY PORRIDGE—AND HAS EATEN IT ALL UP!" said the Little Wee Bear in his little wee voice.

At this the three Bears, seeing that some one had entered their house and eaten up the Little Wee Bear's breakfast, began to look about them. Now Goldilocks had not put the cushion straight when she rose from the chair of the Great Big Bear.

"SOMEBODY HAS BEEN SITTING IN MY CHAIR!" said the Great Big Bear in his great, rough, gruff voice.

And Goldilocks had not put the cushion straight when she rose from the chair of the Middle-sized Bear.

"SOMEBODY HAS BEEN SITTING IN MY CHAIR!" said the Middle-sized Bear in his middle-sized voice.

"SOMEBODY HAS BEEN SITTING IN MY CHAIR—AND HAS SAT THE BOTTOM THROUGH!" said the Little Wee Bear in his little wee voice.

Then the three Bears thought they had better look further, so they went into their bedchamber. Now Goldilocks had pulled the pillow of the Great Big Bear out of its place.

"SOMEBODY HAS BEEN LYING IN MY BED!" said the Great Big Bear in his great, rough, gruff voice.

And Goldilocks had pulled the pillow of the Middle-sized Bear out of its place.

"SOMEBODY HAS BEEN LYING IN MY BED!" said the Middle-sized Bear in his middle-sized voice.

But when the Little Wee Bear came to look at his bed, there was the pillow in its place!

And upon the pillow——?

There was Goldilocks' yellow head.

"SOMEBODY HAS BEEN LYING IN MY BED—AND HERE SHE IS STILL!" said the Little Wee Bear in his little wee voice.

Now Goldilocks had heard in her sleep the great, rough, gruff voice of the Great Big Bear; but she was so fast asleep that it was no more to her than the roaring of wind, or the rumbling of thunder. And she had heard the middle-sized voice of the Middle-sized Bear, but it was only as

if she had heard some one speaking in a dream. But when she heard the little wee voice of the Little Wee Bear, it was so sharp, and so shrill, that it awakened her at once.

Up started Goldilocks; but when she saw the three Bears on one side of the bed, she tumbled herself out at the other and ran to the window. The window was open and out Goldilocks jumped; away she ran like the wind. The three Bears never saw anything more of her.

Related Reading

References for Adults

Arbuthnot, May Hill. *Children and Books*, 3d ed. Glenview, Ill.: Scott, Foresman, 1964. See notation under Mythology.

Botkin, B. A. *A Treasury of American Folklore, Stories, Ballads and Traditions of the People.* Foreword by Carl Sandburg. New York: Crown, 1944. Extensive collection of American folklore selected by the keeper of The Archive of American Song of the Library of Congress. Many of the tales and songs can be read to elementary school children and read by secondary school students. The background information is especially interesting.

Clarke, Kenneth and Mary. *Introducing Folklore.* New York: Holt, Rinehart and Winston, 1963. An interesting introduction to folk literature and beliefs; written for the beginning student and the general reader.

Colwell, Eileen, compiler. *A Second Storyteller's Choice.* Illustrated by Prudence Seward. New York: Walck, 1962. A collection of tales, mostly traditional, with an afterword of suggestions for the storyteller: appropriate age groups, length of telling time, and background information for each tale.

Folktales of the World Series. University of Chicago Press.

All of the books in this series have forewords by Richard M. Dorson on the history of folklore in the country from which the tales were collected. These are of great value to the student of folklore and for the serious storyteller. Many of these tales have never been published in English before.

Briggs, Katharine M., and Ruth L. Tongue, eds. *Folktales of England*, 1965.

Christiansen, Reidar Th., ed. *Folktales of Norway.* Translated by Pat Shaw Iverson, 1964.

Dégh, Linda, ed. *Folktales of Hungary*, 1965.

Eberhard, Wolfram, ed. *Folktales of China*, rev. ed., 1965.

Nov, Dov, ed. *Folktales of Israel*, 1963.

O'Sullivan, Sean, editor-translator. *Folktales of Ireland*, 1966.

Ranke, Kurt, ed. *Folktales of Germany.* Translated by Lotte Baumann, 1966.

Seki, Keigo, ed. *Folktales of Japan.* Translated by R. J. Adams, 1963.

Huck, Charlotte S., and Doris Young Kuhn. *Children's Literature in the Elementary School*, 2d ed. New York: Holt, Rinehart and Winston, 1968. See notation in Mythology.

O'Faolain, Eileen, compiler-translator. *Children of the Salmon and Other Irish Folktales.* Illustrated by Trina Hyman. New York: Little, Brown, 1965. 349 pages of Irish lore make an excellent sourcebook for storytellers.

Ramsey, Eloise, compiler. *Folklore for Children and Young People: A Critical and Descriptive Bibliography for Use in the Elementary and Intermediate School.* Philadelphia: The American Folklore Society, 1952. Kraus Reprint Co., 1970. The annotations are quite helpful for the relatively few books listed. A great weakness is that it has not been updated to include the many new collections that have been printed since 1952.

Smith, Lillian. *The Unreluctant Years*. Chicago: American Library Association, 1953. Chapter 3, "The Art of the Fairy Tale," is very helpful for teachers and librarians.

Tashjian, Virginia A., compiler. *Juba This and Juba That: Story Hour Stretches for Large or Small Groups*. Illustrated by Victoria de Larrea. Boston: Little, Brown, 1969. A collection of riddles, tongue-twisters, chants, finger plays, and songs for the story teller to intersperse among her tales. Advice for the adult accompanies each selection. (Grades 1–4)

Thompson, Stith. *The Folktale*. New York: Holt, Rinehart and Winston, 1946. An excellent study of the origin and development of folklore. Everyone interested in folktales should read this book.

Ullom, Judith C., compiler. *Folklore of the North American Indians: An Annotated Bibliography*. Washington, D.C.: Library of Congress, 1969. An annotated bibliography of "the best materials for the compiler or reteller of these folktales, for the storyteller or librarian serving children, and for the child's own reading. . . ." Scholarly studies and retellings for children are both included. The foreword is by Virginia Haviland.

General Collections for Children

Arbuthnot, May Hill. *The Arbuthnot Anthology of Children's Literature*. Illustrated by Arthur Paul and others. Glenview, Ill.: Scott, Foresman, 1969. Includes a collection of folktales from many countries. (Grades 1–7)

————. *Time for Fairy Tales, Old and New*, rev. ed. Illustrated by John Averill and others. Glenview, Ill.: Scott, Foresman, 1961b. The same stories that are reprinted in *The Arbuthnot Anthology of Children's Literature* are here published separately. (Grades 1–7)

Courlander, Harold, editor. *Ride with the Sun: An Anthology of Folktales and Stories from the United Nations*. Illustrated by Roger Duvoisin. The United Nations Women's Guild. New York: McGraw-Hill, 1955. Sixty well-told tales from as many countries; each approved by the U.N. delegation from the country of origin. (Grades 5–7)

Dalgliesh, Alice. *The Enchanted Book*. Illustrated by Concetta Cacciola. New York: Scribner, 1958. Interesting tales from many lands; well illustrated. (Grades 4–6)

de la Mare, Walter. *Tales Told Again*. Illustrated by Alan Howard. New York: Knopf, 1927, 1959. Excellently written versions of some of the most popular of folktales. (Grades 4–7)

Deutsch, Babette, and Avrahm Yarmolinsky. *More Tales of Faraway Folk*. Illustrated by Janina Domanska. New York: Harper & Row, 1963. Short tales from the Caucasus, central Asia, Karelia, Estonia, and eastern Russia; simply but beautifully retold. Helpful introductions for each tale. (Grades 2–5)

Hutchinson, Veronica. *Chimney Corner Fairy Tales*. Illustrated by Lois Lenski. New York: Minton, Balch (Putnam), 1926. Slight adaptations of favorite folktales from many countries. (Grades 3–5)

Lang, Andrew. *The Blue Fairy Book*. Illustrated by H. J. Ford and G. P. Jacomb Hood. New York: McGraw-Hill, 1965 (unabridged). Andrew Lang's many interesting collections of folktales are enjoyed by all children.

————. *The Crimson Fairy Book*. Illustrated by Ben Kutcher. Foreword by Mary Gould Davis. New York: Longmans, 1903, 1947.

————. *The Green Fairy Book*. Illustrated by Dorothy Lake Gregory. Foreword by Mary Gould Davis. New York: Longmans, 1899, 1948.

————. *The Olive Fairy Book*. Illustrated by Anne Vaughan. Foreword by Mary Gould Davis. New York: Longmans, 1907, 1949.

————. *The Orange Fairy Book*. Illustrated by Christine Price. Foreword by Mary Gould Davis. New York: Longmans, 1906, 1949.

————. *The Red Fairy Book*. Illustrated by Marc Simont. Foreword by Mary Gould Davis. New York: Longmans, 1901, 1948.

————. *The Violet Fairy Book*. Illustrated by Dorothy Lake Gregory. Foreword by Mary Gould Davis. New York: Longmans, 1901, 1947.

————. *The Yellow Fairy Book*. Illustrated by Janice Holiand. Foreword by Mary Gould Davis. New York: Longmans, 1894, 1948. Interesting collections, still enjoyed by children. (Grades 4–6)

Nic Leodhas, Sorche. *Ghosts Go Hunting*. Illustrated by Nonny Hogrogian. New York: Holt, Rinehart and Winston, 1965. Ghost stories from many countries. (Grades 4–6)

Rackham, Arthur, compiler-illustrator. *The Arthur Rackham Fairy Book: A Book of Old Favorites with New Illustrations.* Philadelphia: Lippincott, 1950. Rackham's illustrations, fifty-three black and white and eight color, perfectly complement twenty-three traditional tales. (Grades 3–5)

Withers, Carl. *I Saw a Rocket Walk a Mile.* Illustrated by John E. Johnson. New York: Holt, Rinehart and Winston, 1965. A collection of humorous "formula" lore: stories, poems, songs, and chants in which the pattern is more important than the content. Several selections from the book are included in this anthology. (Grades K–4)

————. *A World of Nonsense: Strange and Humorous Tales from Many Lands.* Illustrated by John E. Johnson. New York: Holt, Rinehart and Winston, 1968. A humorous collection of anecdotes. (Grades 4–7)

Regional Collections of Folktales

AFRICA

Courlander, Harold, and George Herzog. *The Cow Tail Switch and Other West African Stories.* Illustrated by Madye Lee Chastain. New York: Holt, Rinehart and Winston, 1947. (Grades 4–6)

————. *The Fire on the Mountain and Other Ethiopian Stories.* Illustrated by Robert W. Kane. New York: Holt, Rinehart and Winston, 1950. (Grades 5–7) Both books contain entertaining tales that are little known in America.

Courlander, Harold, with Ezekiel A. Eshugbayi. *Olode the Hunter and Other Tales from Nigeria.* Illustrated by Enrico Arno. New York: Harcourt, 1968. *Pourquoi* myths, trickster tales, and legends from the Yoruba, Ibo, and Hausa tribes of what is now Nigeria. (Grades 3 and up)

Courlander, Harold, and Albert Kofi Prempeh. *The Hat-Shaking Dance, and Other Tales from the Gold Coast.* Illustrated by Enrico Arno. New York: Harcourt, 1957. Twenty-one African narratives about Anansi, the trickster spider. (Grades 4–6)

Gilstrap, Robert, and Irene Estabrook. *The Sultan's Fool and Other North African Tales.* Illustrated by Robert Greco. New York: Holt, Rinehart and Winston, 1958. Amusing retellings of traditional tales. See Chapter 6, Drolls, for a selection from this book. (Grades 3–5)

Heady, Eleanor B. *Jambo, Sungura: Tales from East Africa.* Illustrated by Robert Frankenburg. New York: Norton, 1965. These tales of trickery are not only entertaining, but also of interest as examples of African ancestors to some of the Brer Rabbit tales. (Grades 2–4)

Walker, Barbara K. *Once There Was and Twice There Wasn't.* Illustrated by Gordon Kibbee. Chicago: Follett, 1968. (Grades 3–5)

————. *Watermelons, Walnuts and the Wisdom of Allah and Other Tales of the Hoca.* New York: Parents Institute, 1967. Both titles by this author are excellent collections of Turkish folktales. The hero of the first book, the bald-headed Keloglan, is similar to the Northern European Jack; the hero of the second is the Middle Eastern numbskull-trickster also known as the Hodja. (Grades 3–5)

CANADA

Barbeau, Marius. *The Golden Phoenix and Other French-Canadian Fairy Tales.* Retold by Michael Hornansky. Illustrated by Arthur Price. New York: Walck, 1958. Retellings interesting not only in their own right but also as examples of literary interpretations of Canadian variants of traditional European tales. (Grades 4–7)

Macmillan, Cyrus. *Glooskap's Country and Other Indian Tales.* Illustrated by John A. Hall. New York: Oxford, 1955; Walck, 1956. Canadian Indian folktales about the supernatural hero of the Micmacs. Taken from the author's *Canadian Wonder Tales* (1918) and *Canadian Fairy Tales* (1922). (Grades 3–6)

CARIBBEAN

Alegría, Ricardo E., compiler. *The Three Wishes, a Collection of Puerto Rican Folktales.* Translated by Elizabeth Culbert. Illustrated by Lorenz Homar. New York: Harcourt, 1969. An excellent collection of Puerto Rican tales written with the humor and rhythm typical of those told in their country of origin. (Grades 4–6)

Courlander, Harold. *The Piece of Fire and Other Haitian Tales.* Illustrated by Beth and Joe Krush. New York: Harcourt, 1964. Twenty-six simply told tales; helpful to the storyteller and interesting to children. (Grades 4–6)

Sherlock, Philip M. *Anansi the Spider Man, Jamaican Folk Tales.* Illustrated by Marcia Brown. New York: Crowell, 1954. Interesting retellings of Caribbean variants of West African folktales. (Grades 4–6)

—————. *West Indian Folk Tales*. Illustrated by Joan Kiddell-Monroe. New York: Walck, 1966. Traditional narratives of the Caribs, the Arawaks, and the African slaves are intertwined. (Grades 4–6)

EASTERN TALES

The Far East

Carpenter, Frances. *Tales of a Chinese Grandmother*. Illustrated by Malthe Hasselriis. New York: Doubleday, 1949.

—————. *The Elephant's Bathtub: Wonder Tales from the Far East*. Illustrated by Hans Guggenheim. New York: Doubleday, 1962. Well-told tales that retain their eastern flavor. (Grades 4–7)

Courlander, Harold. *The Tiger's Whisker and Other Tales and Legends from Asia and the Pacific*. Illustrated by Enrico Arno. New York: Harcourt, 1959. Interesting and well-told collection of tales from several eastern countries. (Grades 4–6)

Haviland, Virginia, reteller. *Favorite Fairy Tales Told in Japan*. Illustrated by George Suyeoka. Boston: Little, Brown, 1967. An excellent introduction to the folk literature of Japan. (Grades 2–5)

Hitchcock, Patricia. *The King Who Rides a Tiger and Other Folk Tales from Nepal*. Illustrated by Lillian Sader. Berkeley, Calif.: Parnassus, 1966. Twelve tales told by the Nepalese hill people accompanied by notes about the beliefs and customs that are a part of these tales. (Grades 3–7)

Jacobs, Joseph, ed. *Indian Folk and Fairy Tales*. Illustrated by John D. Batten. New York: Putnam, n.d. Originally published in 1892 as *Indian Fairy Tales*. Jacobs wrote in his preface that he had "selected those stories which throw most light on the origin of Fable and Folk-tales, and at the same time are most likely to attract English children." (Grades 4–6)

Macfarlane, Iris, compiler. *Tales and Legends from India*. Illustrated by Eric Thomas. New York: Watts, 1966. Stories told by villagers in the Assam hills. (Grades 4–6)

Uchida, Yoshiko. *The Dancing Kettle and Other Japanese Folk Tales*. Illustrated by Richard C. Jones. New York: Harcourt, 1949.

—————. *The Magic Listening Cap; More Folk Tales from Japan*. Retold and illustrated by Yoshiko Uchida. New York: Harcourt, 1955.

—————. *The Sea of Gold and Other Tales from Japan*. Illustrated by Marianne Yamaguchi. New York: Scribner, 1965. Traditional Japanese tales, heard by the author in her childhood, have been adapted for the American reader and yet retain a distinctive Japanese quality. (Grades 3–5)

The Middle East

Colum, Padraic. *The Arabian Nights*. Illustrated by Lynd Ward. New York: Macmillan, 1953. Fine retellings of nine tales; retain oriental flavor. (Grades 5–7)

Downing, Charles. *Tales of the Hodja*. Illustrated by William Papas. New York: Walck, 1965. So good that every classroom should have a copy. See Chapter 6, Drolls, for selections from this book. (Grade 4–up)

Hodges, Elizabeth Jamison. *Serendipity Tales*. Illustrated by June Atkin Corwin. New York: Atheneum, 1966. Seven old tales are told by the Princes of Serendip: each was heard by one of them in the seven palaces of the Emperor Vahram. (Grades 3–7)

Kelsey, Alice Geer. *Once the Hodja*. Illustrated by Frank Dobias. New York: Longmans, 1943. Turkish drolls about Nasr-ed-Din Hodja. (Grades 4–6)

Lang, Andrew. *Arabian Nights*. Illustrated by Vera Bock. Foreword by Mary Gould Davis. New York: Longmans, 1946. Revision of Lang's 1898 edition with some tales omitted and a few added. Enjoyable style. (Grades 5–7)

Mehdevi, Anne Sinclair. *Persian Folk and Fairy Tales*. Illustrated by Paul Kennedy. New York: Knopf, 1965. Stories from the author's childhood told in a readable style; excellent introduction to the folklore of the Near East. (Grade 5–up)

Tashjian, Virginia A. *Once There Was and Was Not*. Based on stories by Hovhannes Toumanian. Illustrated by Nonny Hogrogian. Boston: Little, Brown, 1966. Armenian folktales presented in an enjoyable, tellable style. (Grades 1–3)

EUROPE

Boggs, Ralph Steele, and Mary Gould Davis. *Three Golden Oranges and Other Spanish Folk Tales*. Illustrated by Emma Brock. New York: Longmans, 1936. Ten Spanish tales that retain the atmosphere of their origin. (Grades 4–6)

Brown, Roy, reteller. *Reynard the Fox*. Based on Joseph Jacob's version. Illustrated by John Vernon Lord. New York: Abelard, 1969. A welcome addition to folklore for children. See Chapter 6, Tales of Trickery for a story about Reynard. (Grades 3–6)

Durham, Mae, reteller. *Tit for Tat and Other Latvian Folk Tales*. From the translation of Skaidrite

Rubene-Koo. Illustrated by Harriet Pincus. New York: Harcourt, 1967. Many universal motifs and themes occur in these tales. Notes for each narrative identify it as to type and give variants. (Grades 3–5)

Duvoisin, Roger, author-illustrator. *The Three Sneezes and Other Swiss Tales*. New York: Knopf, 1941. Retellings of traditional tales and legends by an author who heard them as a child in Switzerland. (Grades 4–6)

Grimm, Jacob and William. *Grimm's Fairy Tales*. Chicago: Follett, 1968. Based on the Frances Jenkins Olcott edition of the 1884 English translation by Margaret Hunt. An introduction by Frances Clarke Sayers. Illustrated with color painting by children from fifteen countries. Fifty-four Grimm brothers' tales are well told. The Hunt translation is often considered the best. (Grade 3–up)

————. *Grimm's Fairy Tales*. Illustrated by Janusz Grabianski. New York: Duell, Sloan and Pearce-Meredith Press, 1962. Many lesser known tales are included. A fine collection, but one with no indication of translator. (Grade 3–up)

————. *Household Stories: From the Collection of the Bros. Grimm*. Translated by Lucy Crane. Illustrated by Walter Crane. New York: McGraw-Hill, 1966. Unabridged republication of the 1886 edition published by Macmillan. Over fifty tales; excellent black and white illustrations. (Grades 3–9)

————. *More Tales from Grimm*. Retold and illustrated by Wanda Gág. New York: Coward-McCann, 1947. (Grades 4–6)

————. *Tales from Grimm*. Translated and illustrated by Wanda Gág. New York: Coward-McCann, 1936. Robust translations with a feel of the folk tradition that is appropriate for the humorous tales, yet not as satisfying for the wonder tales as Margaret Hunt's or Lucy Crane's translations from the last century. (Grades 4–6)

————. *Three Gay Tales from Grimm*. Translated and illustrated by Wanda Gág. New York: Coward-McCann, 1943. "The Clever Wife," "The Three Feathers," and "Goose Hans." Three lesser known drolls well illustrated and translated. (Grades 2–5)

Haviland, Virginia, ed. *Favorite Fairy Tales Told in Czechoslovakia*. Illustrated by Trina Schart Hyman. Boston: Little, Brown, 1966. (Grades 2–6)

————. *Favorite Fairy Tales Told in France*. Illustrated by Roger Duvoisin. Boston: Little, Brown, 1959. (Grades 2–6)

————. *Favorite Fairy Tales Told in Germany*. Illustrated by Susanne Suba. Boston: Little, Brown, 1959. (Grades 2–6)

————. *Favorite Fairy Tales Told in Greece*. Illustrated by Nonny Hogrogian. Boston: Little, Brown, 1970. Eight well-told folktales that are unrelated to Greek mythology. (Grades 2–6)

————. *Favorite Fairy Tales Told in Italy*. Illustrated by Evaline Ness. Boston: Little, Brown, 1965. (Grades 2–6) Valuable collections of folktales.

Hurlimann, Bettina. *William Tell and His Son*. Translated and adapted from the German by Elizabeth D. Crawford. Illustrated by Paul Nussbaumer. New York: Holt, Rinehart and Winston, 1967. A retelling of the William Tell legend for younger children; excellently illustrated with striking full page, color pictures. (Grades 3–6)

Jagendorf, M. A. *The Priceless Cats and Other Italian Folk Stories*. Illustrated by Gioia Fiammenghi. New York: Vanguard, 1956. See Chapter 6, Wonder Tales for "The Priceless Cat." (Grades 3–5)

Picard, Barbara Leonie, reteller. *French Legends, Tales and Fairy Stories*. Illustrated by Joan Kiddell-Monroe. New York: Walck, 1958. Twenty-four well told tales. Sources are traditional French epics, provincial tales, courtly tales, and folk narratives. (Grades 5–7)

Pridham, Radost. *A Gift from the Heart: Folk Tales from Bulgaria*. Illustrated by Pauline Baynes. Cleveland: World Publishing, 1967. Humorous tales, some very short. Style excellent for reading aloud or for telling. (Grades K–6)

Spicer, Dorothy Gladys. *The Owl's Nest: Folktales from Friesland*. Illustrated by Alice Wadowski-Bak. New York: Coward-McCann, 1968. Seven well told tales from the seamen and farmers of northern Holland. (Grades 3–7)

GREAT BRITAIN

Haviland, Virginia. *Favorite Fairy Tales Told in England*. Retold from Joseph Jacobs. Illustrated by Bettina. Boston: Little, Brown, 1959.

————. *Favorite Fairy Tales Told in Scotland*. Illustrated by Adrienne Adams. Boston: Little, Brown, 1963. Interesting and useful collections of tales. (Grades 2–5)

Jacobs, Joseph. *Celtic Fairy Tales*. Illustrated by John D. Batten. New York: Putnam, 1892. (Grades 4–6)

————. *English Fairy Tales*. Illustrated by John D. Batten. 3d rev. ed. New York: Putnam, 1902. (Grades 4–6)

————. *More English Fairy Tales*. Illustrated by John D. Batten. New York: Putnam, n.d. (Grades

4–6) Few authors have equalled and none surpassed Jacob's style in retelling English folktales.

Nic Leodhas, Sorche. *Gaelic Ghosts.* Illustrated by Nonny Hogrogian. New York: Holt, Rinehart and Winston, 1964. Ten stories concerning ghosts, ghost giants and dogs among others. Excellent for storytelling as well as reading aloud.

———. *Heather and Broom, Tales of the Scottish Highlands.* Illustrated by Consuelo Joerns. New York: Holt, Rinehart and Winston, 1960. (Grades 4–6)

———. *Sea-Spell and Moor-Magic: Tales of the Western Isles.* Illustrated by Vera Bock. New York: Holt, Rinehart and Winston, 1968. Nine tales from the Scottish Hebrides and one from an imaginary Island of Youth. Excellent for oral reading or telling. Glossary gives the pronunciation of the Gaelic words. (Grades 4–7)

———. *Thistle and Thyme, Tales and Legends From Scotland.* Illustrated by Evaline Ness. New York: Holt, Rinehart and Winston, 1962. (Grades 4–6) Interesting collections of Scottish tales.

Pilkington, F. M., compiler. *Shamrock and Spear: Tales and Legends from Ireland.* Illustrated by Leo and Diane Dillon. New York: Holt, Rinehart and Winston, 1966. Twenty-three Irish tales. Rhythm of Irish speech retained, but no dialect. (Grades 4–6)

ICELAND

Boucher, Alan. *Mead Moondaughter & Other Icelandic Folk Tales.* Illustrated by Karolina Larusdottir. Philadelphia: Chilton, 1967. New translation in style similar to oral retellings. Much background information. Title story is a Cinderella variant. (Grades 6 and up)

JEWISH

Singer, Isaac Bashevis. *When Schlemiel Went to Warsaw & Other Stories.* Illustrated by Margot Zemach. Translated by the author and Elizabeth Shub. New York: Farrar, Straus, 1968. Eight stories: four traditional Jewish folktales and four original stories in the folktale pattern. Style excellent for reading aloud. (Grades 4–7)

———. *Zlateh the Goat and Other Stories.* Translated from the Yiddish by the author and Elizabeth Shub. Illustrated by Maurice Sendak. New York: Harper & Row, 1966. Seven stories about middle-European Jewish life in the early years of this century. Devils and real people, the clever and the schlemiels inhabit these stories told in Mr. Singer's excellent style. (Grades 1–6)

SCANDINAVIA

Asbjörsen, P. C., and Jorgen E. Moe. *East o' the Sun and West o' the Moon and Other Tales.* Illustrated by Tom Vroman. New York: Macmillan, 1963. (Grades 4–7)

———. *Norwegian Folk Tales.* Illustrated by Erik Werenskiold and Theodor Kettelsen. Translated by Pat Shaw Iversen and Carl Norman. New York: Viking, 1960. Two fine collections of the most popular Scandinavian folktales. All children should hear and read these tales. (Grades 4–7)

Bowman, James Cloyd, and Margery Bianco. *Tales from a Finnish Tupa.* From the translation of Aili Kolehmainen. Illustrated by Laura Bannon. Racine, Wis.: Whitman, 1936. Forty-three tales, some of which are variants of better known European tales; others are unique. (Grades 5–7)

Hatch, Mary C., reteller. *More Danish Tales.* Illustrated by Edgun. New York: Harcourt, 1949.

———. *13 Danish Tales.* Illustrated by Edgun. New York: Harcourt, 1947. Two delightful collections of humorous Danish folktales. (Grades 3–5)

Haviland, Virginia, ed. *Favorite Fairy Tales Told in Sweden.* Illustrated by Ronni Solbert. Boston: Little, Brown, 1966. Six tales pleasantly retold. (Grades 2–5)

Undset, Sigrid. *True and Untrue and Other Norse Tales.* Illustrated by Frederick T. Chapman. New York: Knopf, 1945. Twenty-seven Norwegian narratives from the Asbjörnsen and Moe Collections. Attractive and enjoyable book. (Grades 4–7)

SOUTH AMERICA

Finger, Charles. *Tales from Silver Lands.* Illustrated by Paul Honoré. New York: Doubleday, 1924. Retellings of South American Indian stories heard by the author during his travels. Winner of the 1925 Newbery Award. (Grades 5–7)

SOVIET UNION

Almedingen, E. M. *Russian Folk and Fairy Tales.* Illustrated by Simon Jeruchim. New York: Putnam, 1963. Reworkings of old Russian tales. Interesting to all children. (Grades 3–6)

Downing, Charles. *Russian Tales and Legends.* Illustrated by Joan Kiddell-Monroe. New York: Oxford, 1957. Tales from many areas of Russia. (Grades 3–6)

Haviland, Virginia. *Favorite Fairy Tales Told in Russia.* Illustrated by Herbert Danska. Boston: Little, Brown, 1961. Five tales skillfully retold. (Grades 2–5)

Rudchenko, Ivan, and Maria Lukiyanenko. *Ukrainian Folk Tales*. Translated by Marie Halun Bloch. Illustrated by J. Hnizdovsky. New York: Coward-McCann, 1964. Twelve traditional tales with motifs found in other European collections presented

UNITED STATES

Chase, Richard, ed. *Grandfather Tales*. Illustrated by Berkely Williams. Boston: Houghton Mifflin, 1948. Amusing folktales.

————. *The Jack Tales*. Illustrated by Berkely Williams. Boston: Houghton Mifflin, 1943. Every child should be acquainted with these books. See Chapter 6, Tales of Trickery, for a selection from *The Jack Tales*. (Grade 4–8)

Cothran, Jean. *With a Wig, and a Wag, and Other American Folk Tales*. Illustrated by Clifford N. Geary. New York: McKay, 1954. Fine retellings, many of which are not available in other sources. A number of Indian tales also included. (Grades 3–5)

Courlander, Harold. *Terrapin's Pot of Sense*. Illustrated by Elton Fax. New York: Holt, Rinehart and Winston, 1957. American Negro tales collected by Mr. Courlander in Alabama, New Jersey, and Michigan. Dialect modified for ease of reading, but rhythm and sentence patterns retained for flavor. (Grades 4–6)

Credle, Ellis. *Tall Tales from the High Hills and Other Stories*. Illustrated by Richard Bennett. Camden, N.J.: Nelson, 1957. Folktales of the Blue Ridge Mountain country. (Grades 5–7)

Leach, Maria. *The Rainbow Book of American Folk Tales and Legends*. Illustrated by Marc Simont. Cleveland: World Publishing, 1958. Includes tales and legends from each state as well as narratives told by North, Central, and South American Indians. (Grades 5–7)

Malcolmson, Anne. *Yankee Doodle's Cousins*. Illustrated by Robert McCloskey. Boston: Houghton Mifflin, 1941. Tall tales no elementary school child should miss. (Grades 4–7)

Poulakis, Peter, ed. *American Folklore*. Illustrated by

with strong Slavic characteristics and flavor. (Grades 3–7)

Wheeler, Post. *Russian Wonder Tales*. Illustrated by Bilibin. New York: Beechhurst Press, 1946. Excellent discussion on folklore in the foreword. Sixteen tales that will delight children. (Grades 5–7)

Marian Ebert. American Character Series. New York: Scribner, 1969. Interesting collection of American folklore. (Grades 6–9)

American Indian

Courlander, Harold. *People of the Short Blue Corn, Tales and Legends of the Hopi Indians*. Illustrated by Enrico Arno. New York: Harcourt, 1970. Seventeen folktales, all but one directly collected from Hopi storytellers. Background information about Hopi beliefs, folklore, and history are given in addition to information about each tale. (Grades 4–7)

Curry, Jane Louise. *Down from the Lonely Mountain: California Indian Tales*. Illustrated by Enrico Arno. New York: Harcourt, 1965. Twelve animal tales of trickery written in language appropriate for reading aloud or telling. (Grades 4–6)

Gillham, Charles E. *Beyond the Clapping Mountains*. Illustrated by Chanimun. New York: Macmillan, 1964. (Grades 4–6)

————. *Medicine Men of Hooper Bay*. Illustrated by Chanimun. New York: Macmillan, 1966. Two collections of Eskimo folklore excellent for retelling or reading aloud. (Grades 4–6)

Harris, Christie. *Once Upon a Totem*. Illustrated by John Frazer Mills. New York: Atheneum, 1963. Five Northwest Indian legends with background notes. Striking woodcuts. (Grades 4–6)

Rushmore, Helen, and Wolf Robe Hunt. *The Dancing Horses of Acoma and Other Acoma Indian Stories*. Illustrated by Wolf Robe Hunt. Cleveland: World Publishing, 1963. Twelve complex stories from New Mexico mesa Indian tribe. (Grades 5–9)

Picture Books

Ambrus, Victor G., author-illustrator. *The Three Poor Tailors*. New York: Harcourt, 1966. A wildly amusing Hungarian folktale about three penniless tailors who extravagantly entertain themselves at an inn during their first visit to the town. (Grades K–3)

Andersen, Hans Christian. *The Nightingale*. Translated by Eva Le Gallienne. Illustrated by Nancy Ekholm Burkert. New York: Harper & Row, 1965. Exquisitely beautiful illustrations accompany fine translation. (Grades 2–6)

Asbjörnsen, Peter Christen, and Jorgen E. Moe. *The Three Billy Goats Gruff*. Illustrated by Marcia Brown. New York: Harcourt, 1957. One of the most popular of Scandinavian folktales is excellently illustrated. (Grades K–4)

Bontemps, Arna, and Jack Conroy. *The Fast Sooner Hound*. Illustrated by Virginia Lee Burton. Boston: Houghton Mifflin, 1942. Tall tale of dog who would sooner run than eat. (Grades 3–6)

Brown, Marcia, adapter-illustrator. *Dick Whittington and His Cat*. New York: Scribner, 1950. Famous English legend is well told. Linoleum block illustrations complement the story and add atmosphere. (Grades K–5)

————. *The Flying Carpet*. New York: Scribner, 1956. An *Arabian Nights* story, based on Richard Burton's translation of "Prince Ahmed and the Fairy Paribanou." Illustrated in rich color. (Grades 2–5)

————. *Stone Soup; An Old Tale*. New York: Scribner, 1947. French story of how three hungry soldiers trick villagers into providing them with soup. Excellent prose and illustrations. (Grades K–5)

Bryant, Sara Cone. *The Burning Rice Fields*. Illustrated by Mamoru Funai. New York: Holt, Rinehart and Winston, 1963. Japanese legend about a village threatened by a tidal wave. Stylized illustrations. (Grades K–3)

Cooney, Barbara, adapter-illustrator. *The Little Juggler*. New York: Hastings House, 1961. French legend about poor juggler boy who has no gift for the Christ child except his ability to juggle. (Grades 3–6)

Fournier, Catharine, adapter. *The Coconut Thieves*. Illustrated by Janina Domanska. New York: Scribner, 1964. African folktale in which Turtle and Dog outwit selfish Tiger. Illustrations help create African atmosphere. (Grades 1–4)

Galdone, Paul, illustrator. *The Old Woman and Her Pig*. New York: McGraw-Hill, 1960. Delightful pictures accompany a favorite tale. (Grades K–2)

Grimm, the Brothers. *Jorinda and Joringel*. Translated by Elizabeth Shub. Illustrated by Adrienne Adams. New York: Scribner, 1968. The story of a wicked witch who turns beautiful girls into birds and the young man who must rescue his beloved. Dramatic pictures and a well-written text suitable for reading aloud or for storytelling. (Grades K–4)

Grimm, Jacob and Wilhelm. *Rapunzel*. Illustrated by Felix Hoffman. New York: Harcourt, 1961. Striking picture book of the story of the beautiful girl held prisoner in a tower by a witch. (Grades 2–4)

————. *The Shoemaker and the Elves*. Illustrated by Adrienne Adams. New York: Scribner, 1960.

Popular tale translated by Wayne Andrews in good style for storytelling. Lovely watercolor illustrations. (Grades K–3)

————. *Snow White and Rose Red*. Illustrated by Adrienne Adams. New York: Scribner, 1964. Well-known folktale is given interesting illustrations that will please young children. (Grades 1–3)

————. *Snow-White and Rose-Red*. Retold and illustrated by Barbara Cooney. New York: Delacorte, 1966. Lovely pink washed charcoal pictures illustrate this favorite fairy tale. (Grades 1–4)

————. *Snow White and the Seven Dwarfs*. Translated and illustrated by Wanda Gág. New York: Coward-McCann, 1938. A favorite fairy tale is presented in a new translation by a fine storyteller-illustrator. (Grades 1–4)

————. *The Traveling Musicians*. Illustrated by Hans Fischer. New York: Harcourt, 1955. (Grades 2–4)

————. *The Wolf and the Seven Little Kids*. Illustrated by Felix Hoffman. New York: Harcourt, 1959. Two distinguished picture books of tales by the Grimm brothers. (Grades K–3)

Hodges, Margaret. *The Wave*. Adapted from Lafcadio Hearn's *Gleanings in Buddha-Fields*. Illustrated by Blair Kent. Boston: Houghton Mifflin, 1964. Japanese legend about old man who sets his rice fields on fire to warn villagers of danger. Illustrations help create Japanese atmosphere. (Grades K–5)

Jacobs, Joseph. *Jack and the Beanstalk*. Retold and illustrated by William Stobbs. New York: Delacorte, 1969. A striking picture book treatment of the popular English fairy tale. (Grades K–3)

————. *Tom Tit Tot*. Illustrated by Evaline Ness. New York: Scribner, 1965. Striking woodcuts illustrate this humorous English variant of "Rumpelstiltskin." Illustrations of the greedy king and the imp are especially apt. (Grades K–3)

Lang, Andrew. *The Twelve Dancing Princesses*. Illustrated by Adrienne Adams. New York: Holt, Rinehart and Winston, 1966. Lang's version from a French source, as is typical, is romantic and detailed. Miss Adams' stylized illustrations complement Lang's style. (Grades 2–4)

Lines, Kathleen, reteller. *Dick Whittington*. Illustrated by Edward Ardizzone. New York: Walck, 1970. A retelling as well written as Marcia Brown's *Dick Whittington and His Cat*. Notes add information about the real Richard Whittington. (Grades 1–4)

Ness, Evaline, illustrator. *Tom Tit Tot*. New York: Scribner, 1965. Striking presentation of the humorous English variant of the Rumpelstiltskin story. Great fun. (Grades K–3)

Nic Leodhas, Sorche. *Always Room for One More.* Illustrated by Nonny Hogrogian. New York: Holt, Rinehart and Winston, 1965. An amusing revision of a traditional Scottish folk song about a remarkably hospitable Scotsman. (Grades K–3)

————. *Kellyburn Braes.* Illustrated by Evaline Ness. New York: Holt, Rinehart and Winston, 1968. A Scottish droll about the "auld" wife who drives the Devil and his demons mad. Dramatic illustrations add to the humor. (Grades K–3)

Perrault, Charles. *Cinderella: Or, The Little Glass Slipper.* Illustrated by Marcia Brown. New York: Scribner, 1954. Graceful presentation of the most popular of fairy tales. Winner of 1955 Caldecott Medal. See Chapter 2, color plates, for an illustration from this book. (Grades K–4)

————. *Puss in Boots.* Illustrated by Marcia Brown. New York: Scribner, 1952. Brilliant colors enhance this "free translation" of a traditional French tale. The Master Cat is especially well characterized. (Grades K–4)

Ransome, Arthur. *The Fool of the World and the Flying Ship.* Illustrated by Uri Shulevitz. New York: Farrar, Straus, 1968. Russian wonder tale about the adventures of a kind, but underestimated youngest son, Fool of the World. Winner of the 1969 Caldecott Medal. (Grades K–4)

Reyher, Becky. *My Mother Is the Most Beautiful Woman in the World.* Illustrated by Ruth Gannett. New York: Lothrop, 1945. A Russian tale about a little lost girl whose "beautiful" mother appears very ugly to those who do not love her. Illustrates the proverb: "We do not love people because they are beautiful, but they seem beautiful to us because we love them." (Grades 2–4)

Robbins, Ruth, adapter. *Baboushka and the Three Kings.* Illustrated by Nicolas Sidjakov. Berkeley, Calif.: Parnassus, 1960. Russian Christmas story, beautifully illustrated. Winner of the 1961 Caldecott Medal. (Grades 2–5)

Sawyer, Ruth. *Journey Cake, Ho!* Illustrated by Robert McCloskey. New York: Viking, 1953. Modern version of the Pancake story. (Grades K–3)

Tresselt, Alvin, reteller. *The Mitten.* Illustrated by Yaroslava. Adapted from the version by E. Rachev. New York: Lothrop, 1964. Attractively illustrated traditional Ukrainian folktale. (Grades K–2)

Tresselt, Alvin, and Nancy Cleaver. *The Legend of the Willow Plate.* Illustrated by Joseph Low. New York: Parents Institute, 1968. Illustrations and text beautifully retell the Chinese legend of the willow plate, the love of a mandarin's daughter and a poor clerk who wishes to be a poet. (Grades 1–5)

Zemach, Harve. *The Judge: An Untrue Tale.* Illustrated by Margot Zemach. New York: Farrar, Straus, 1969. An original verse story written in the style of a cumulative folktale. Amusing; will delight both elementary school children and adults. (Grades K–3)

Zemach, Harve, reteller. *Nail Soup.* Illustrated by Margot Zemach. Chicago: Follett, 1964. Swedish tale of trickery; tramp tricks stingy woman into making soup. (Grades K–3)

————. *Salt.* Illustrated by Margot Zemach. Chicago: Follett, 1965. A Russian tale about the adventures of Ivan the Fool who eventually marries a beautiful princess. (Grades 1–3)

Part III

FICTION

Most children want to read a book that has an interesting story about characters they like and with whom they can identify. This does not mean that children are consciously concerned about well-developed plots or characters. The long-lasting popularity of the *Nancy Drew* series proves that fast action and suspense can hold generations of readers and that children can be interested in stereotyped characters. But although children may not consciously be concerned with literary quality, if they read only mediocre books whose sole strength is suspense they are quite likely to join the extraordinarily large number of reluctant readers in this country.

WHAT MAKES GOOD FICTION?

Too many adults today turn to slick stories with stereotyped plots and characters or drug their evenings with TV programs that imitate the worst aspects of poor literature: swift, often illogical, action and shallow character delineation. These are poor substitutes for the relaxation, the recreation, the stimulation given by a well-written book. Adults will turn to books for something more than escape if as children they had experiences with excellent literature. Perhaps the people who refuse to read do so because they have never experienced good literature. Even those who are not consciously aware of the formal elements of good writing turn to books if they have known through personal experience how enjoyable reading can be.

Teachers, librarians, parents, and other friends of children must be able to recognize the well-written, must know both children and their literature so they can answer the most important question concerning a child's book: is it good enough for a young reader? The answer can only be found in a mature and careful reading of childrens' literature. This is no hardship—adults can learn a great deal about early English history from Rosemary Sutcliff's books, discover more about what it's like to be black by reading Dorothy Sterling's *Mary Jane*, and realize how it feels to be a migrant worker by reading Louisa R. Shotwell's *Roosevelt Grady*. Even adults will find delight in reading *Mary Poppins* or *The Wind in the Willows*. Some of the most enjoyable and entertaining books that have ever been written were written for children.

Yet studying children's literature can not be an easy, thought-free act. If children deserve the best literature, if poorly written books can drive them away from reading, if one of the most important functions of our schools is to develop literacy and create life-time readers (and most people believe all of these "ifs" are true), then a deep understanding of literary elements as they apply to young people's books must be developed by all who work with children. While that understanding can come through the pleasant experiences of reading books, students of children's literature should read thoughtfully, with a concern for plot development and unity, character-plot interrelationship, character development, theme, and style. A knowledge of these aspects of fiction is essential for the adult who wants to introduce children to memorable books and so develop in them a love of reading.

The following discussion of these elements of fiction is presented to facilitate comparisons between examples of children's literature. Evaluative skills can only develop from an understanding of the differences between well-written books and the less satisfactory.

THE DIFFERENCE BETWEEN ACTION AND PLOT

A basic aspect of a novel is its action, and this is all many readers are aware of in a book. Action is simply the sequence of events, one thing occurring after another. Interesting action depends on suspense and the reader's curiosity to discover what happens next. Plot, however, goes beyond the sequence of events, for its emphasis is on not what happens next but *why* it happened. The following examples illustrate the difference between these two aspects of fiction. A sequence of events is: A dog bit a man. The man kicked the dog. The man died and the dog died. Causality is emphasized in the following: That man kicked the dog because the dog bit him. The man died of the bite and the dog died of the kick.

While action is necessary to hold a child's interest, there must be an interrelationship between the action, the characters, and the theme in children's fiction. It is this interrelationship that creates the causality essential for plot. Superficial novels are often written when the author's only ability is to create suspense by producing one cliff hanger after another. In many of these books both the action and suspense are poorly contrived or extraneous. Once the ending is known and the suspense is over, unless the characters are memorable and their actions believable, the reader will feel vaguely dissatisfied and quickly forget the book.

In good novels the plots grow out of the characters' actions and reactions. For a plot to be convincing those actions must seem probable, and for actions to seem probable the people involved in them must be believable. No matter how much suspense there is, unless the characters are real the action will seem forced and contrived because action is believable only when it seems logical for people to act as they do. While a story with a great deal of suspense and action may carry the reader along, unconvincing characters will prevent the book from being memorable.

FLAT AND ROUND CHARACTERS

In early novels for children the characters were types, not individuals. They were used to sugar-coat religious, moral, social, or philosophical truths. Because these truths were more important than the actions and the characters, plot and character were not related. Authors used artificial plots and flat people who represented specific virtues and vices as devices to interest the child-reader in the message.

A flat character illustrates one facet of man. It can have little depth because it represents only one personality trait. Its behavior is always consistent, easily predictable, uncomplicated; and because it is so easily understood it is boring when encountered for any length of time. Characters that are all good or all bad are not believable; they are mouthpieces or symbols for sermons and tracts. Since in real life people are complex, fictional characters must be shown with contradictions and complexities to be believable and to give the illusion of reality.

HOW IS CHARACTERIZATION REVEALED?

Round characters, in contrast to flat characters, are those that are both familiar and unique. They are moved by universal human drives and so are recognizable; yet they are unique because the author has given them individualizing character traits. The good writer understands his main characters so well that through a careful selection of details he makes the reader know and care about these fictional people. Through involvement with their motivations and emotions the reader is able to experience the story and become deeply interested in the book.

The poor writer, or the creator of stereotypes, tells the reader what to think of the characters: he labels each one as being a sweet, beautiful, trustworthy girl or a powerful, stocky bully, for example. Like Liza Doolittle in "My Fair Lady," the reader does not want to be told, he wants to be shown. Rather than talking about their characters, good writers reveal them through action and dialogue. This does not mean an author cannot give his reader information about the characters; his insights, however, need to be substantiated by believable and logical dialogue and action.

In the following examples from Kenneth Grahame's *The Wind in the Willows*, notice how the characters react to, discuss, and treat each other. In the first example Water Rat is taking Mole on his first boat ride. Mole's naïvete and Rat's imperturbability are revealed by their conversation and their actions.

'This has been a wonderful day!' said he, as the Rat shoved off and took to the sculls again. 'Do you know, I've never been in a boat before in all my life.'

'What?' cried the Rat, open-mouthed: 'Never been in a—you never—well, I—what have you been doing, then?'

'Is it so nice as all that?' asked the Mole shyly, though he was quite prepared to believe it as he leant back in his seat and surveyed the cushions, the oars, the rowlocks, and all the fascinating fittings and felt the boat sway lightly under him.

'Nice? It's the *only* thing,' said the Water Rat solemnly, as he leant forward for his stroke. 'Believe me, my young friend, there is *nothing*—absolutely nothing—half so much worth doing as simply messing about in boats. Simply messing,' he went on dreamily: 'messing—about—in—boats; messing—'

'Look ahead, Rat!' cried the Mole suddenly.

It was too late. The boat struck the bank full tilt. The dreamer, the joyous oarsman, lay on his back at the bottom of the boat, his heels in the air.

'—about in boats—or *with* boats,' the Rat went on composedly, picking himself up with a pleasant laugh. 'In or out of 'em, it doesn't matter. Nothing seems really to matter, that's the charm of it. Whether you get away, or whether you don't; whether you arrive at your destination or whether you reach somewhere else, or whether you never get anywhere at all, you're always busy, and you never do anything in particular; and when you've done it there's always something else to do, and you can do it if you like, but you'd much better not. Look here! If you've really nothing else on hand this morning, supposing we drop down the river together, and have a long day of it?'

The Mole waggled his toes from sheer happiness, spread his chest with a sign of full contentment, and leaned back blissfully into the soft cushions. 'What a day I'm having!' he said. 'Let us start at once!'[1]

Later in the story, Ratty's reaction to Mole's foolish behavior which capsized the boat shows Ratty's thoroughly kind nature:

So the dismal Mole, wet without and ashamed within, trotted about till he was fairly dry, while the Rat plunged into the water again, recovered the boat, righted her and made her fast, fetched his floating property to shore by degrees, and finally dived successfully for the luncheon-basket and struggled to land with it.

When all was ready for a start once more, the Mole, limp and dejected, took his seat in the stern of the boat; and as they set off, he said in a low voice, broken with emotion, 'Ratty, my generous friend! I am very sorry indeed for my foolish and ungrateful conduct. My heart quite fails me when I think how I might have lost that beautiful luncheon-basket. Indeed, I have been a complete ass, and I know it. Will you overlook it this once and forgive me, and let things go on as before?'

'That's all right, bless you!' responded the Rat cheerily. 'What's a little wet to a Water Rat? I'm more in the water than out of it most days. Don't you think any more about it; and, look here! I really think you had better come and stop with me for a little time. It's very plain and rough, you know—not like Toad's house at all—but you haven't seen that yet; still, I can make you comfortable. And I'll teach you to row, and to swim, and you'll soon be as handy on the water as any of us.'[2]

For dialogue to effectively reveal character it must seem natural and spontaneous, never stilted or artificial. Compare the previous examples of Mole and Rat's conversations with the following selection from *The City under Ground* by Suzanne Martel, a French-Canadian book translated by Norah Smaridge. While each of Grahame's animals has his own way of speaking, no distinction is made in *The City under Ground* between the ways in which a young boy and a mature, important adult speak.

"Bernard! What are you doing here at the Power Center? I thought you were in bed with an injured hand."

"Oh no, Chief, I'm better now. I've just come from the doctor's. He put my hand under the curative-ray machine, and now there's nothing left but a pink scar."

"And aren't you enjoying a holiday with your friends?"

"Well, no, Chief. I can't take a holiday when our work isn't finished."

"You're right about that. We've been talking about it all night."

[1] Reprinted with the permission of Charles Scribner's Sons from *The Wind in the Willows* by Kenneth Grahame.

[2] Reprinted with the permission of Charles Scribner's Sons from *The Wind in the Willows* by Kenneth Grahame.

"I thought maybe I could still be useful. . . . we have to know what's hidden behind that patch soldered in the pipe."

"We've thought of that, son. We're looking for a way of clearing up the mystery. Your father is with the experts right now, trying to find a way of seeing things from a long distance."

"But—what about *me?* Can't I go back into the conduits?"[3]

This is an example of contrived dialogue; dialogue that does not develop believable characters. Such artificial dialogue destroys a reader's acceptance of the characters and the situation and thus inhibits any sense of reality. Effective dialogue advances action and makes that action seem more believable by creating a sense of drama and reality.

A person's actions can reveal his character as effectively as dialogue. An author may develop a small incident for this purpose as Rosemary Sutcliff does in her historical novel about Roman Britan, *The Silver Branch.*

"Who is the tall very fair man?" he murmured to Flavius. "The Emperor called him Allectus, I think."

"Carausius's Finance Minister and general righthand man. He has a vast following among the troops, as well as the merchants and moneyers, so that I suppose after Carausius he's the most powerful man in Britain. But he's a good enough fellow, in spite of looking as though he'd been reared in a dark closet."

And then, a few moments later, something happened; something so slight and so ordinary that afterwards Justin wondered if he had simply let his imagination run away with him—and yet he could never quite forget it, nor the sudden sense of evil that came with it. Roused perhaps by the warmth rising from the lamps, a big, soft-winged night moth had come fluttering down from the rafters to dart and hover and swerve about the table. Everyone's attention was turned towards the Emperor, who was at that moment preparing to pour the second Libation to the gods. Everyone, that is, save Justin and Allectus. For some unknown reason, Justin had glanced again at Allectus; and Allectus was watching the moth.

The moth was circling wildly nearer and nearer to one of the lamps which stood directly before the Finance Minister, its blurred shadow flashing about the table as it swooped and spun in dizzy spirals about the bright and beckoning flame, closer and closer, until the wild, ecstatic dance ended in a burst of shadows, and the moth spun away on singed wings, to fall with a pitiful, maimed fluttering close beside Allectus' wine-cup. And Allectus, smiling faintly, crushed out its life under one deliberate finger.

That was all. Anybody would crush a singed moth—it was the obvious, the only thing to do. But Justin had seen the pale man's face as he watched the dancing moth, waiting for it to dance too near, seen it in the unguarded instant as he stretched out that precise forefinger to kill.[4]

As the above selections illustrate, characters are revealed by what they do and say. Good characterization gives a sense of reality, makes the plot believable, and unifies the action. If characters are not believable their actions will not seem real, because for action to be logical it must grow out of the characters' motives and emotions. It is their confrontation with conflict that initiates and resolves the plot. In this confrontation the action must be consistent with as well as reveal the characters' personalities and motivations. Both must be accomplished if an illusion of reality is to be developed and sustained. As the main characters are revealed the plot moves, and as the plot develops the characters are revealed more fully.

This does not mean that a book must be complex or long to have a causal relationship. Young children are often confused by complex characters and involved or complicated plots. Yet even in books for these children characterization should be revealed through action and dialogue, and action should grow out of the characters' personalities and motivations. If character and action are two unrelated elements in even the most simple books, then all but the very youngest will soon become bored because the book has no unity or reality. Even young children know that something nice will happen, perhaps a smile or a hug, if they have been good, and they know something not as nice will happen if they do something they should not; this knowledge they bring to their understanding of books.

Young children may not have a highly verbalized or sophisticated sense of causality, yet they

[3] From *The City under Ground* by Suzanne Martel. Copyright © 1964 by The Viking Press Inc. Reprinted by permission of The Viking Press Inc.

[4] From *The Silver Branch* by Rosemary Sutcliff. Used by permission of Henry Z. Walck, Inc., publishers, and Oxford University Press.

enjoy the relationship between Yertle's ambition and his fall into the mud in *Yertle the Turtle* by Dr. Seuss. And they chuckle over the effect of Mac's burp. Older children can understand the causality in *Johnny Tremain*. They can clearly see that Johnny's arrogance is related to his accident as well as understand the effect of his maimed hand on his life and how it slowly changes his personality. Even Johnny learns about cause and effect when he is doused by the Hancock's maid; he learns that people treat him kindly when he is not rude. These are two examples of causality, one simple, the other complex, yet without them both books would suffer.

THEME

There has been an unfortunate tendency in discussions of children's literature to confuse theme with plot. To say that *The Loner* by Esther Wier is about a boy who belongs to no one and has no name is to tell only the initial situation which starts the action. To say that the theme of *The Ark* by Margot Benary-Isbert is a German family's search for a place to live after World War II is again to confuse the problem with the theme. *The Loner* deals with the universal need to belong and with the responsibilities that come with belonging. *The Ark*'s theme centers around another type of belonging—the need for a secure home after much insecurity and wandering.

Theme is correctly defined as:

the central idea or dominating idea in a literary work. . . . the abstract concept which is made concrete through its representation in person, action, and image in the work.[5]

The theme's role in unifying plot and character cannot be minimized. A book is written because an author has something to say. If all he has to offer is a series of incidents, the novel will lack depth. But when those incidents are colored by the author's insights, the story has an underlying idea that provides unity and gives meaning to the plot and characters. The author's arrangement of the action and his attitude toward his characters depend on his point of view. This point of view grows out of his personal insights and beliefs about life.

The theme's complexity is related to the maturity of the audience for whom the book is written. Dorothy Sterling's belief in the value and similarity of all people is conveyed in *Mary Jane*. In *Johnny Tremain* Esther Forbes parallels Johnny's search for freedom with America's. Johnny is not free when dominated by arrogance, nor is he free when shame for his crippled hand directs his actions. He is free, he can "stand up," only when he has control of himself and accepts responsibility.

The themes of the above books are handled subtly. They grow logically out of the plot and are revealed by the characters' personalities and actions. There is never any sense that the authors have didactic messages or that they are trying to lecture their readers. Both authors want to tell a good story, and do so, but add depth through a well-integrated theme.

A comparison of Walter Farley's *The Black Stallion* and Armstrong Sperry's *Call It Courage* will show how a significant theme adds depth. *The Black Stallion* is basically an adventure story about a young boy and an untamed stallion trapped on an uninhabited island. Its primary strength is suspense and so most chapters end with cliff-hangers. *Call It Courage* is also about a boy trapped on a deserted island, but Sperry's hero is there in an attempt to conquer his fear of the sea. The theme that fear can be met and conquered lifts *Call It Courage* far beyond *The Black Stallion*.

Some writers sacrifice plot and character development to stress a message. When this occurs the novel deteriorates into didacticism. Such a book is usually rejected by today's children who rightly expect to be entertained by novels, not "improved."

Literature for children began as a vehicle for teaching and preaching. Early books were little more than slightly disguised social or religious tracts. Three hundred years have passed, but there are still writers who feel literature should be used to change children. Munro Leaf's heavy theme in *Manners Can Be Fun* is, "Don't be as nasty as the Whineys, Pigs, and Me Firsts." Many adults in the 1940s and 1950s bought his

[5] Thrall, Hibbard, Holman, *A Handbook to Literature.* New York: The Odyssey Press, 1936, 1960, p. 486.

books to "improve" their children's behavior, but few children appreciated either his classifications or his humor. Few children enjoy sermons disguised as entertainment.

Well-written books that combine interesting plots, believable characters, and subtle themes bring enjoyment and insight. Children need the insights good writers can give to make growing up more comprehensible. Books can give perspective to life, which in its complex reality may seem confusing. Subtle themes in novels that show fictional children acquiring self-understanding, accepting responsibility, overcoming handicaps, solving problems, and maturing help children understand their own lives. Yet, to do this a theme must grow out of and be integral to the story's characters and plot. When it is arbitrarily imposed the book is unsatisfactory and the "message" is usually ineffective.

THE IMPORTANCE OF STYLE

Children may seldom be aware of good prose style, but the awkwardly written book is unsatisfactory even to the inexperienced reader. Basically, style is the way an author uses words to convey his ideas, to create the mood and understanding he is striving for. It involves matching the cadence, the flow and rhythm, of his sentences and the selection of words to his mood and scene. Cadence is used effectively in *Island of the Blue Dolphins* by Scott O'Dell. His restraint and tightness of language reflect the girl's Indian stoicism and need to keep her emotions in check after her brother's death:

> All night I sat there with the body of my brother and did not sleep. I vowed that someday I would go back and kill the wild dogs in the cave. I would kill all of them. I thought of how I would do it, but mostly I thought of Ramo, my brother.[6]

In addition to the effective use of cadence, an author also accomplishes his purpose by using exact words and phrases rather than trite expressions and generalities. Scott O'Dell is careful not

to slip into sentimentality to move the reader. The passage from *Island of the Blue Dolphin* shows the effectiveness of simplicity. The stylistic complexities in some of Henry James and William Faulkner's writings delight many mature readers, but extreme complexity has no place in children's literature.

In contrast to the previous quote is Kenneth Grahame's description of Mole's introduction to the river in *The Wind in the Willows*.

> Never in his life had he seen a river before— this sleek, sinuous, full-bodied animal, chasing and chuckling, gripping things with a gurgle and leaving them with a laugh, to fling itself on fresh playmates that shook themselves free, and were caught and held again. All was a-shake and a-shiver—glints and gleams and sparkles, rustle and swirl, chatter and bubble. The Mole was bewitched, entranced, fascinated. By the side of the river he trotted as one trots, when very small, by the side of a man who holds one spellbound by exciting stories; and when tired at last, he sat on the bank, while the river still chattered on to him, a babbling procession of the best stories in the world, sent from the heart of the earth to be told at last to the insatiable sea.[7]

This is not complexity for its own sake but a joyous use of language, with all stops out. While kind but simple Mole could never have described the river at all, this expresses what the river meant to him. Grahame conveys the sense of wonder by the literary devices of personification, alliteration, balance, and metaphor. And these are as appropriate for expressing Mole's mood as is the restraint used by O'Dell.

Notice how Grahame is able to develop a totally different mood when Mole enters the Wild Wood for the first time. When Ratty is evasive about going to visit Badger, Mole sets out alone without Rat's knowledge.

> Then the whistling began.
> Very faint and shrill it was, and far behind him, when first he heard it; but somehow it made him hurry forward. Then, still very faint and shrill, it sounded far ahead of him, and made him hesitate and want to go back. As he halted in indecision it broke out on either side, and seemed to be caught up and passed on throughout the

---

[6] From *Island of the Blue Dolphins* by Scott O'Dell. Reprinted by permission of the publisher, Houghton Mifflin Company.

[7] Reprinted with the permission of Charles Scribner's Sons from *The Wind in the Willows* by Kenneth Grahame.

whole length of the wood to its farthest limit. They were up and alert and ready, evidently, whoever they were! And he—he was alone, and unarmed, and far from any help; and the night was closing in.

Then the pattering began.

He thought it was only falling leaves at first, so slight and delicate was the sound of it. Then as it grew it took a regular rhythm, and he knew it for nothing else but the pat-pat-pat of little feet, still a very long way off. Was it in front or behind? It seemed to be first one, then the other, then both. It grew and it multiplied, till from every quarter as he listened anxiously, leaning this way and that, it seemed to be closing in on him.[8]

Another way to develop mood is illustrated by the following excerpt from *Johnny Tremain*. Esther Forbes has used carefully selected images to produce a profound sense of isolation and rejection. Notice how they build: mud flats, gallows, graves of suicides, salt marshes, the pest house, and on and on. The only weakness here is the sentence, "He felt his heart was broken," which is unnecessary; the rest of the passage says it so much more effectively. But by the end of the scene, through her careful selection of detail, Miss Forbes has demonstrated Johnny's heartbreak in a remarkably powerful way.

The nervous child went on screaming. 'Go away, Johnny, go away! I hate your hand.' Cilla slapped her and she burst into tears.

So he went away.

Now he was sure that what they all felt Isannah had been young enough to say. He felt his heart was broken. Once again he started to walk until he was so tired he could not think. The long, late-September night had already begun before he reached the town gates on the Neck. Beyond him, in the semidarkness, running across mud flats, was the one road which connected Boston with the mainland. And here the gallows—on which Mrs. Lapham promised him to end. He turned back from the lonely place. The gallows and the graves of suicides frightened him a little. He wandered about through the salt marshes at the foot of the Common, circling until he came out on Beacon Hill. There he sat in an orchard for quite a while. It was either Mr. Lyte's or Mr. Hancock's, for the houses stood side by side. He saw the glitter of candles throughout the great mansions, guests coming and going, heard the music of a spinet.

Isannah's words rang in his ears. He who had struggled hard never to cry now wished that he could. Then he walked off into sparsely settled West Boston. Behind the pesthouse by lantern light men were digging a hurried grave. He left West Boston and, skirting dirty Mill Cove, came at last into his own North Boston. On Hull Street he heard the staves of the town watch and the feet of the watchmen clumping on cobbles. By law no apprentice was allowed out so late. He slipped into Copp's Hill graveyard to hide until they were gone.[9]

Compare the way Forbes builds her mood with this scene from Suzanne Martel's science fiction book *The City under Ground*. Luke has a broken leg and has lain alone in great pain without hope of rescue. He is finally found by his brother, but their dialogue has no suggestion of any tension two boys lost in an unknown wilderness would naturally feel.

To distract him, Paul asked Luke how he had discovered the outer world and learned to his astonishment about the rescue mission on which Luke had set out.

"It's much farther than I thought," Luke said, crestfallen. "And then the night fell."

"And you, too!"

Luke chuckled faintly. "Fortunately I didn't lose my ray helmet. I would have died of fear in the dark."

"What about your mask?"

"First I thought I'd suffocate. But I found I could breathe quite well—fresh air smells good, you know. Paul, do you think the air could have become pure after such a long time?"[10]

Carl Sandburg is best known as a poet, but that he was a master of prose language is revealed by the excellent style of "The Huckabuck Family and How They Raised Popcorn in Nebraska and Quit and Came Back" in which he had great fun playing with words.

"I know where you have been," Mama Mama Huckabuck would say of an evening to Pony Pony Huckabuck. "You have been down to the watch factory watching your father watch the watches."

[8] Reprinted with the permission of Charles Scribner's Sons from *The Wind in the Willows* by Kenneth Grahame.

[9] From *Johnny Tremain*. Copyright 1943 by Esther Forbes Hoskins. Reprinted by permission of the publisher, Houghton Mifflin Company.

[10] From *The City under Ground* by Suzanne Martel. Copyright © 1964 by The Viking Press Inc. Reprinted by permission of The Viking Press Inc. See the Fantasy section for a longer passage from *The City under Ground*.

"Yes," said Pony Pony. "Yes, and this evening when I was watching father watch the watches in the watch factory, I looked over my left shoulder and I saw a policeman with a star and brass buttons and he was watching me to see if I was watching father watch the watches in the watch factory."[11]

Wanda Gág's *Millions of Cats* is a story for primary children about a little old lady who wanted a cat and a little old man who set out to find one.

> And he set out over the hills to look for one. He climbed over the sunny hills. He trudged through the cool valleys. He walked a long, long time and at last he came to a hill which was quite covered with cats.
> Cats here, cats there,
> Cats and kittens everywhere,
>   Hundreds of cats,
>   Thousands of cats,
> Millions and billions and
> trillions of cats.[12]

As they were each so lovely, he chose them all, and the cadenced refrain is varied and repeated through the story. The musical quality of the refrain produces the delights, for both children and adults, of recognition and pleasure.

Style is extremely important to the quality of a book—any book, whether written for children or adults. But the only way to develop a sense of style is to read those books that have been written by the best writers. The examples of good writing that have been given here can only begin a study of style. A variety of styles has been used to show that there is no "best" style nor is there any formula that should be followed in children's literature. Simplicity and complexity are both appropriate when they fit the mood and scene. Style differs from author to author and is good or bad depending on how effectively it conveys the author's intention in a way that seems pleasing and appropriate to the reader.

THE SELECTIONS

As you read the following selections, evaluate each writer's style. Since this anthology uses a comparative approach, some works have been included that are representative of mediocre writing. It is important to remember that, whatever the style or genre, whatever the level of complexity, children deserve better literature than the artificial, the sentimental, the patronizing, and the moralizing.

The following examples from children's fiction have been selected for purposes of historical and critical comparisons. There are selections from the eighteenth and nineteenth centuries to show not only what early children's literature was like but also to illustrate how contemporary fiction has developed. A few examples, such as *Alice's Adventures in Wonderland*, reveal that not all children's books from past centuries were didactic or without charm. Critical comparisons of style, plot and character development, and theme are possible through the inclusion of a few examples of mediocre works. These can be contrasted with the well-written selections to build a greater understanding of the elements of fiction and give practice in developing evaluation skill.

[11] From "The Huckabuck Family and How They Raised Popcorn in Nebraska and Quit and Came Back." From *Rootabaga Stories* by Carl Sandburg, copyright, 1922, 1923, by Harcourt Brace Javonovich, Inc.; renewed 1950, 1951, by Carl Sandburg. Reprinted by permission of the publishers.
[12] Reprinted by permission of Coward-McCann Inc. from *Millions of Cats* by Wanda Gág. Copyright © 1928, 1956 by Wanda Gág.

Chapter 7
Domestic Fiction

From *The Adventures of Huckleberry Finn* by Mark Twain, illustrated by E. W. Kemble. Chatto & Windus, 1884. Reprinted in *Illustrations of Children's Books, 1744–1945* by Bertha E. Mahony et al., 1958. Courtesy of The Horn Book, Inc.

In addition to the general requirements of good fiction that have already been discussed, plausibility is especially essential in realistic novels. It is not enough that something unlikely might possibly happen; the reader must believe that its occurrence and the character's response logically develop from previous action and characterization. This does not occur in the eighteenth-century *History of Miss Sally Spellwell*. Here a deserving girl is saved from poverty by the sudden appearance of the rich widow of a former friend of Sally's long dead father. While the reader is pleased at Sally's rescue, the events leading to it lack believability. Fairy godmothers in the form of benevolent, rich widows are seldom found in real life, so their presence in fiction gives a sense of unreality. When an author uses a *deus ex machina* or a fairy godmother to solve the hero's problem, or if the solution is too easy, the reader feels let down.

Whether realistic fiction is about animals or people, the past or the present, America or other countries, the most interesting characters face and solve their own problems. In the excerpt from *The Loner* by Ester Wier, included in this chapter, Boss rescues a homeless, lost, boy. Unlike the rescue of Sally Spellwell, this is not the unbelievable ending of all his problems. The boy's new, secure home itself creates emotional conflicts as he learns to trust others and to accept responsibility. Here no one "rescues" him or makes the struggle easier; he must find his own way. Because he does it himself, the reader becomes involved with the boy's life.

The complexity of plot and character depends on the age group for which the book is written. The short length of books for preschool and kindergarten children does not permit much charac-

ter development, yet skillful writers are able to create interesting characters. Rebecca Caudill does this in A *Pocketful of Cricket*.

Some books for young children have almost no plot, as in *White Snow, Bright Snow* by Alvin Tresselt where the beauty of language complements the wonder of snow. Very young children enjoy reading books about experiences with which they are familiar.

As children develop wider interests and enjoy reading books about lives and experiences beyond their own, novels for them can have more involved plots and greater depth of characterization. Regardless of the simplicity or complexity of the situation, well-written books of realistic fiction can give the reader insights into life in the actual world.

In the 1960s a number of books touching on controversial issues were written for older children: an unfit mother in *The Long Secret* and lying in *Harriet the Spy*, both by Louisa Fitzhugh, dope in *The Acid Nightmare* by M. E. Chaber and *Tuned Out* by Maia Wojciechowska, a boy's hatred and fear of his father in *False Start* by Gil Rabin, realistic portrayals of minority life in *The Winners* by Ester Wier.

When well written, like *False Start* and *Harriet the Spy*, such novels can give children a greater understanding of contemporary life. Yet when the plot and characters are poorly developed, as in *The Acid Nightmare*, the reader receives little insight. A number of books written about controversial topics, like *The Acid Nightmare*, are so moralistic they seem thinly disguised sermons whose main purpose is to show the young reader what will happen to him if he breaks any of society's codes. While adults approve such themes, most children and teen-agers reject didacticism. To be successful, messages need to be subtle and grow out of believable stories and characters.

Some adults believe children should not read books that deal with controversial subjects, yet works that reveal contemporary life in its complexity, that do not oversimplify it, can help today's youngsters understand their troubled world. When judging such books it is well to remember that Mark Twain's *Huckleberry Finn* and *Tom Sawyer* were once banned from some libraries and even Louisa May Alcott's *Little Women* once was considered by some adults to be unsuitable for children.

Realistic Literature has been grouped in this anthology into four categories: Domestic Literature, American Minority Literature (racial, religious, and economic), Life in Other Countries, and Historical Fiction. In each selection of realistic fiction examples of early children's literature have been given for historical perspective and comparative purposes. There are also a few examples of mediocre writing that can be contrasted with the many well-written selections.

THE HISTORY OF LITTLE GOODY TWO-SHOES

Anonymous

For the significance of Little Goody Two-Shoes *in the history of children's literature please see Chapter 1, A History of Children's Literature.*

Although there is a great deal of moralizing in the book, the character of Goody Two-Shoes has a charm and a life unlike any of the children in books before this novel and quite unlike characters in most of the children's books written after this first juvenile novel. Certain passages have enough suspense and humor to hold today's reader.

The plot of Little Goody Two-Shoes *is universally popular: the rise from rags to riches. Sir Timothy Gripe and Farmer Graspall destroy Little Goody's father by causing him to lose his farm. When both parents die, Margery and her brother are left alone. After many difficulties, Little Two-Shoes is rewarded for her goodness by being made Principal of a country school.*

Her happiness and security lasted a long while but through a country man's ignorance she was called into court as a witch. Not only was she cleared of the charge, but this action brought her to the attention of Sir Charles Jones, a rich gentleman who later married her. At the wedding Mrs. Margery was reunited with her brother Tom, now a man with a large fortune. Mrs. Margery, or Lady Jones, spent the rest of her life giving aid to those in distress.

THE HISTORY OF
LITTLE GOODY TWO-SHOES,
OTHERWISE CALLED
MRS. MARGERY TWO-SHOES
With
The Means by which she acquired her Learning and Wisdom, and in consequence thereof her Estate, set forth at large for the Benefit of those,
Who from a State of Rags and Care,

And having Shoes but half a Pair;
Their Fortune and their Fame would fix,
And gallop in a Coach and Six.
See the Original Manuscript in the Vatican at Rome, and the Cuts by Michael Angelo. Illustrated with the Comments of our great modern Critics.

The Third Edition
London

Printed for J. Newbery, at the Bible and Sun in St. Paul's Church-Yard, 1766

To All Young Gentlemen and Ladies, Who are good, or intend to be good, This BOOK is inscribed by Their old Friend in St. Paul's Church-Yard.

[Price Six-pence.][1]

CHAP. I
HOW AND ABOUT
LITTLE MARGERY
AND HER BROTHER

Care and Discontent shortened the Days of Little *Margery's* Father.—He was forced from his Family, and seized with a violent Fever in a Place where Dr. *James's* Powder was not to be had, and where he died miserably. *Margery's* poor Mother survived the Loss of her Husband but a few Days, and died of a broken Heart, leaving *Margery* and her little Brother to the wide World; but, poor Woman, it would have melted your Heart to have seen how frequently she heaved up her Head, while she lay speechless, to survey with languishing Looks her little Orphans, as much as to say, *Do Tommy, do Margery, come with me.* They cried, poor Things, and she sighed away her Soul; and I hope is happy.

It would both have excited your Pity, and have done your Heart good, to have seen how fond these two little ones were of each other, and how, Hand in Hand, they trotted about. Pray see them.

They were both very ragged, and *Tommy* had two Shoes, but *Margery* had but one. They had nothing, poor Things, to support them (not being in their own Parish) but what they picked from the Hedges, or got from the poor People, and they lay every Night in a Barn. Their Relations took no Notice of them; no, they were rich, and ashamed to own such a poor little ragged Girl as *Margery*, and such a dirty little curl-pated Boy as *Tommy*. Our Relations and Friends seldom take Notice of us when we are poor, but as we grow rich they grow fond. And this will always be the Case, while People love Money better than Virtue, or better than they do God Almighty. But

such wicked Folks, who love nothing but Money, and are proud and despise the Poor, never come to any good in the End, as we shall see by and by.

CHAP. II
HOW AND ABOUT
MR. SMITH

Mr. *Smith* was a very worthy Clergyman, who lived in the Parish where Little *Margery* and *Tommy* were born; and having a Relation come to see him, who was a charitable good Man, he sent for these Children to him. The Gentleman ordered Little *Margery* a new Pair of Shoes, gave Mr. *Smith* some Money to buy her Cloathes; and said, he would take *Tommy* and make him a little Sailor; and accordingly had a Jacket and Trowsers made for him, in which he now appears. Pray look at him.

After some Days the Gentleman intended to go to *London*, and take little *Tommy* with him, of whom you will know more by and by, for we shall at a proper Time present you with some Part of his History, his Travels and Adventures.

The Parting between these two little Children was very affecting, *Tommy* cried, and *Margery* cried, and they kissed each other an hundred Times. At last *Tommy* thus wiped off her Tears with the End of his Jacket, and bid her cry no more, for that he would come to her again, when he returned from Sea. However, as they were so very fond, the Gentleman would not suffer them to take Leave of each other; but told *Tommy* he should ride out with him, and come back at Night. When night came, Little *Margery* grew very uneasy about her Brother, and after sitting up as late as Mr. *Smith* would let her, she went crying to Bed.

CHAP. III
HOW LITTLE MARGERY
OBTAINED THE NAME
OF GOODY TWO-SHOES,
AND WHAT HAPPENED
IN THE PARISH

As soon as Little *Margery* got up in the Morning, which was very early, she ran all round the Village, crying for her Brother; and after

---

[1] From the facsimile reproduction of the edition of 1766 by Griffith and Farrar, Successors to Newbery and Harris, 1881. By the courtesy of the University of Washington Library.

some Time returned greatly distressed. However, at this Instant, the Shoemaker very opportunely came in with the new Shoes, for which she had been measured by the Gentleman's Order.

Nothing could have supported Little *Margery* under the Affliction she was in for the Loss of her Brother, but the Pleasure she took in her *two Shoes*. She ran out to Mrs. *Smith* as soon as they were put on, and stroking down her ragged Apron thus, cried out, *Two-Shoes, Mame, see two Shoes.* And so she behaved to all the People she met, and by that Means obtained the Name of *Goody Two-Shoes*, though her Playmates called her *Old Goody Two-Shoes*.

Little *Margery* was very happy in being with Mr. and Mrs. *Smith*, who were very charitable and good to her, and had agreed to breed her up with their Family; but as soon as that Tyrant of the Parish, that *Graspall*, heard of her being there, he applied first to Mr. *Smith*, and threatened to reduce his Tythes if he kept her; and after that he spoke to Sir *Timothy*, who sent Mr. *Smith* a peremptory Message by his Servant, that *he should send back* Meanwell's *Girl to be kept by her Relations, and not harbour her in the Parish.* This so distressed Mr. *Smith* that he shed Tears, and cried, *Lord have Mercy on the Poor!*

The Prayers of the Righteous fly upwards, and reach unto the Throne of Heaven, as will be seen in the Sequel.

Mrs. *Smith* was also greatly concerned at being thus obliged to discard poor Little *Margery*. She kissed her and cried; as also did Mr. *Smith*, but they were obliged to send her away; for the People who had ruined her Father could at any Time have ruined them.

CHAP. IV
HOW LITTLE MARGERY
LEARNED TO READ,
AND BY DEGREES
TAUGHT OTHERS

Little *Margery* saw how good, and how wise Mr. *Smith* was, and concluded, that this was owing to his great Learning, therefore she wanted of all Things to learn to read. For this Purpose she used to meet the little Boys and Girls as they came from School, to borrow their Books, and sit down and read till they returned. By this Means

she soon got more Learning than any of her Playmates, and laid the following Scheme for instructing those who were more ignorant than herself. She found, that only the following Letters were required to spell all the Words in the World; but as some of these Letters are large and some small, she with her Knife cut out of several Pieces of Wood ten Setts of each of these:

abcdefghijklmnopqrstuvwxyz.

And six Setts of these:

ABCDEFGHIJKLMNOPQRST
UVWXYZ.

And having got an old Spelling-Book, she made her Companions set up all the Words they wanted to spell, and after that she taught them to compose Sentences. You know what a Sentence is, my Dear, *I will be good*, is a Sentence, and is made up, as you see, of several Words.

The usual Manner of Spelling, or carrying on the Game, as they called it, was this: Suppose the Word to be spelt was Plum Pudding (and who can suppose a better) the Children were placed in a Circle, and the first brought the Letter *P*, the next *l*, the next *u*, the next *m*, and so on till the Whole was spelt; and if anyone brought a wrong Letter, he was to pay a Fine, or play no more. This was at their Play; and every Morning she used to go round to teach the Children with these Rattle-traps in a Basket. I once went her Rounds with her, and was highly diverted, as you may be, if you please to look into the next Chapter.

CHAP. V
HOW LITTLE TWO-SHOES
BECAME A TROTTING
TUTORESS, AND HOW
SHE TAUGHT HER
YOUNG PUPILS

It was about seven o'Clock in the Morning when we set out on this important Business, and the first House we came to was Farmer *Wilson's*. Here *Margery* stopped, and ran up to the Door, *Tap, tap, tap.* Who's there? Only little goody *Two-Shoes*, answered *Margery*, come to teach *Billy*. Oh Little *Goody*, says Mrs. *Wilson*, with Pleasure in her Face, I am glad to see you, *Billy* wants you sadly, for he has learned all his Lesson. Then out came the little Boy. *How do doody Two-Shoes*, says he, not able to speak plain. Yet this little Boy had learned all his Letters; for she threw down this Alphabet mixed together thus:

bdfhkmoqsuwyzsacegilnprtvxj

and he picked them up, called them by their right Names, and put them all in order thus:

abcdefghijklmnopqrstuvwxyz.

She then threw down the Alphabet of Capital Letters in the Manner you here see them.

BDFHKMOQSUWYZACEGILN
PRTVXJ

and he picked them all up, and having told their Names, placed them thus:

ABCDEFGHIJKLMNOPQRST
UVWXYZ.

Now, pray little Reader, take this Bodkin, and see if you can point out the Letters from these mixed Alphabets, and tell how they should be placed as well as little Boy *Billy*.

The next Place we came to was Farmer *Simpson's*. Bow, wow, wow, says the Dog at the Door. Sirrah, says his Mistress, what do you bark at Little *Two-Shoes*. Come in *Madge*; here, *Sally* wants you sadly, she has learned all her Lesson. Then out came the little one: So *Madge*! says she; so *Sally*! answered the other, have you learned your Lesson? Yes, that's what I have, replied the little one in the Country Manner; and immediately taking the Letters she set up these Syllables:

ba be bi bo bu, ca ce ci co cu, da de di do du,
fa fe fi fo fu

and gave them their exact Sounds as she composed them; after which she set up the following:

ac ec ic oc uc, ad ed id od ud, af ef if of uf,
ag eg ig og ug.

And pronounced them likewise. She then sung the Cuzz's Chorus (which may be found in the *Little Pretty Play Thing*, published by Mr. Newbery) and to the same Tune to which it is there set.

After this, Little *Two-Shoes* taught her to spell Words of one Syllable, and she soon set up Pear, Plum, Top, Ball, Pin, Puss, Dog, Hog, Fawn, Buck, Doe, Lamb, Sheep, Ram, Cow, Bull, Cock, Hen, and many more.

The next Place we came to was *Gaffer Cook's* Cottage.

Here a number of poor Children were met to learn, who all came round Little *Margery* at once; and, having pulled out her Letters, she asked the little Boy next her, what he had for Dinner? Who answered, *Bread*. (The poor Children in many Places live very hard.) Well then, says she, set the first Letter. He put up the Letter B, to which the next added r, and the next e, the next a, the next d, and it stood thus, *Bread*.

And what had you *Polly Comb* for your Dinner? *Apple-pye*, answered the little Girl: Upon which the next in Turn set up a great A, the two next a p each, and so on till the two Words Apple and Pye were united and stood thus, *Apple-Pye*.

The next had *Potatoes*, the next *Beef and Turnip* which were spelt with many others, till the Game of Spelling was finished. She then set them another Task, and we proceeded.

The next Place we came to was Farmer *Thompson's*, where there were a great many little ones waiting for her.

So little Mrs. *Goody Two-Shoes*, says one of them, where have you been so long? I have been teaching, says she, longer than I intended, and am afraid I am come too soon for you now. No, but indeed you are not, replied the other; for I have got my Lesson, and so has *Sally Dawson*, and so has *Harry Wilson*, and so we have all; and they capered about as if they were overjoyed to see her. Why then, says she, you are all very good, and God Almighty will love you; so let us begin our Lessons. They all huddled around her, and though at the other Place they were employed about Words and Syllables, here we had People of much Greater Understanding who dealt only in Sentences.

The Letters being brought upon the Table, one of the little ones set up the following Sentence.

The Lord have Mercy upon me, and grant that I may be always good, and say my Prayers, and love the Lord my God with all my Heart, with all my Soul, and with all my Strength; and honour the King, and all good Men in Authority under him.

Then the next took the Letters and composed this Sentence.

Lord have Mercy upon me, and grant that I may love my Neighbour as myself, and do unto all Men as I would have them do unto me, and tell no Lies; but be honest and just in all my Dealings.

The third composed the following Sentence.

The Lord have Mercy upon me, and grant that I may honour my Father and Mother, and love my Brothers and Sisters, Relations and Friends, and all my Playmates, and every Body, and endeavour to make them happy.

The fourth composed the following.

I pray God to bless this whole Company, and all our Friends, and all our Enemies.

To this last *Polly Sullen* objected, and said, truly, she did not know why she should pray for her Enemies? Not pray for your Enemies, says little *Margery*; yes, you must, you are no Christian, if you don't forgive your Enemies, and do Good for Evil. *Polly* still pouted; upon which little *Margery* said, though she was poor, and obliged to lie in a Barn, she would not keep Company with such a naughty, proud, perverse Girl as *Polly*; and was going away; however the Difference was made up, and she set them to compose the following

LESSONS

For the Conduct of LIFE

LESSON 1

He that will thrive,
Must rise by Five.
He that hath thriv'n,
May lie till Seven.
Truth may be blam'd,
But cannot be sham'd.
Tell me with whom you go;
And I'll tell what you do.
A Friend in your Need,
Is a Friend indeed.
They ne'er can be wise,
Who good Counsel despise.

* * *

LESSON III

A Lie stands upon one Leg, but Truth upon two.
When a Man talks much, believe but half what
      he says.
Fair Words butter no Parsnips.
Bad Company poisons the Mind.
A covetous Man is never satisfied.
Abundance, like Want, ruins many.
Contentment is the best Fortune.
A contented Mind is a continual Feast.

A LESSON IN RELIGION

Love God, for he is good.
Fear God, for he is just.
Pray to God, for all good Things come from him.
Praise God, for great is his Mercy towards us, and
      wonderful are all his Works.
Those who strive to be good, have God on their
      Side.
Those who have God for their Friend, shall want
      nothing.
Confess your Sins to God, and if you repent he
      will forgive you.
Remember that all you do, is done in the Presence of God.
The Time will come, my Friends, when we must
      give
Account to God, how we on Earth did live.

* * *

CHAP. VI
HOW THE WHOLE PARISH WAS FRIGHTED

Who does not know Lady *Ducklington*, or who does not know that she was buried at this Parish Church? Well, I never saw so grand a Funeral in all my Life; but the Money they squandered away, would have been better laid out in little Books for Children, or in Meat, Drink, and Cloaths for the Poor.

This is a fine Hearse indeed, and the nodding Plumes on the Horses look very grand; but what End does that answer, otherwise than to display the Pride of the Living, or the Vanity of the Dead. Fie upon such Folly, say I, and Heaven grant that those who want more Sense may have it.

But all the Country round came to see the

Burying, and it was late before the Corpse was interred. After which, in the Night, or rather about Four o'Clock in the Morning, the Bells were heard to jingle in the Steeple, which frightened the People prodigiously, who all thought it was Lady *Ducklington's* Ghost dancing among the Bell-ropes. The People flocked to *Will Dobbins* the Clerk, and wanted him to go and see what it was; but *William*, said he was sure it was a Ghost, and that he would not offer to open the Door. At length Mr. *Long* the Rector, hearing such an Uproar in the Village, went to the Clerk, to know why he did not go into the Church, and see who was there. I go, Sir, says *William*, why the Ghost would frighten me out of my Wits.—Mrs. *Dobbins* too cried, and laying hold of her Husband said, he should not be eat up by the Ghost. A Ghost, you Blockheads, says Mr. *Long* in a Pet, did either of you ever see a Ghost, or know any Body that did? Yes, says the Clerk, my Father did once in the Shape of a Windmill, and it walked all round the Church in a white Sheet, with Jack Boots on, and had a Gun by its Side instead of a Sword. A fine Picture of a Ghost truly, says Mr. *Long*, give me the Key of the Church, you Monkey; for I tell you there is no such Thing now, whatever may have been formerly. Then taking the Key, he went to the Church, all the people following him. As soon as he had opened the Door, what Sort of a Ghost do ye think appeared? Why Little *Two-Shoes*, who being weary, had fallen asleep in one of the Pews during the Funeral Service, and was shut in all Night. She immediately asked Mr. *Long's* Pardon for the Trouble she had given him, told him, she had been locked into the Church, and said, she should not have rung the Bells, but that she was very cold, and hearing Farmer *Boult's* Man go whistling by with his Horses, she was in Hopes he would have went to the Clerk for the Key to let her out.

CHAP. VII
CONTAINING AN ACCOUNT
OF ALL THE SPIRITS,
OR GHOSTS, SHE SAW
IN THE CHURCH

The People were ashamed to ask Little *Madge* any Questions before Mr. *Long*, but as soon as he was gone, they all got round her to satisfy their Curiosity, and desired she would give them a particular Account of all that she had heard and seen.

Her Tale

I went to the Church, said she, as most of you did last Night, to see the Burying, and being very weary, I sate me down in Mr. *Jones's* Pew, and fell fast asleep. At Eleven of the Clock I awoke; which I believe was in some measure occasioned by the Clock's striking, for I heard it. I started up, and could not at first tell where I was; but after some Time I recollected the Funeral, and soon found that I was shut in the Church. It was dismal dark, and I could see nothing; but while I was standing in the Pew, something jumped up upon me behind, and laid, as I thought, its Hands over my Shoulders.—I own, I was a little afraid at first; however, I considered that I had always been constant at Prayers and at Church, and that I had done nobody any Harm, but had endeavoured to do what Good I could; and then thought I, what have I to fear? yet I kneeled down to say my Prayers. As soon as I was on my Knees something very cold, as cold as Marble, ay, as cold as Ice, touched my Neck, which made me start; however, I continued my Prayers, and having begged Protection from Almighty God, I found my Spirits come, and I was sensible that I had nothing to fear; for God Almighty protects not only all those who are good, but also all those who endeavour to be good.—Nothing can withstand the Power, and exceed the Goodness of God Almighty. Armed with the Confidence of his Protection, I walked down the Church Isle, when I heard something, pit pat, pit pat, pit pat, come after me, and something touched my Hand, which seemed as cold as a Marble Monument. I could not think what this was, yet I knew it could not hurt me, and therefore I made myself easy, but being very cold, and the Church being paved with Stone, which was very damp, I felt my Way as well as I could to the Pulpit, in doing which something brushed by me, and almost threw me down. However I was not frightened, for I knew, that God Almighty would suffer nothing to hurt me.

At last, I found out the Pulpit, and having

shut to the Door, I laid me down on the Mat and Cushion to sleep; when something thrust and pulled the Door, as I thought for Admittance, which prevented my going to sleep. At last it cries, *Bow, wow, wow*; and I concluded it must be Mr. *Saunderson's* Dog, which had followed me from their House to Church, so I opened the Door, and called *Snip, Snip*, and the Dog jumped up upon me immediately. After this *Snip* and I lay down together, and had a most comfortable Nap; for when I awoke again it was almost light. I then walked up and down all the Isles of the Church to keep myself warm; and though I went into the Vault, and trod on Lady *Ducklington's* Coffin, I saw no Ghost, and I believe it was owing to the Reason Mr. *Long* has given you, namely, that there is no such thing to be seen. As to my Part, I would as soon lie all Night in the Church as in any other Place; and I am sure that any little Boy or Girl, who is good, and loves God Almighty and keeps his Commandments, may as

safely lie in the Church, or the Church-yard, as anywhere else, if they take care not to get Cold, for I am sure there are no Ghosts, either to hurt or to frighten them; though anyone possessed of Fear might have taken Neighbour *Saunderson's* Dog with his cold Nose for a Ghost; and if they had not been undeceived, as I was, would never have thought otherwise. All the Company acknowledged the Justness of the Observation, and thanked Little *Two-Shoes* for her Advice.

Reflection

After this, my dear Children, I hope you will not believe any foolish Stories that ignorant, weak, or designing People may tell you about Ghosts; for the Tales of Ghosts, Witches, and Fairies, are the Frolicks of a distempered Brain. No wise Man ever saw either of them. Little *Margery* you see was not afraid; no, she had *good Sense*, and a *good Conscience*, which is a Cure for all these imaginary Evils.

SANDFORD AND MERTON

Thomas Day

Tommy Merton is one of the most spoiled, idle children in all of literature; and Harry Sandford is one of the best behaved, knowledgeable children. To-day, readers might think Harry a prig and Tommy a fool, but many generations of readers enjoyed the three volumes Thomas Day wrote about these boys in 1783, 1786, and 1789. In 1907 Eva March Tappan, editor of The Children's Hour, Old Fashioned Stories and Poems, *wrote that children loved books like* Sanford and Merton, *"read them over and over, and talked about them until the characters seemed almost as real as their flesh and blood play-mates. . . . They found out with 'Tommy' that it is good to know a little arithmetic; . . . with 'Fanny,' the heroine of 'The Sore Tongue,' that it is well to think before you speak. In short, these entertaining little stories were not only amusing, but they were a real power and inspiration to the children to be studious and thoughtful and truthful and kind-hearted. . . . When these children were grown up and had children of their own, those children read the stories, and the children of those children read them; and even today we find them interesting."[2] John Masefield, a respected twentieth-century poet, declared his enjoyment of* Sandford and Merton *in his* So Long To Learn.[3]*

While such novels now seem boring and moralistic it is important to re-member they were once considered great fun. Their didactic instruction was accepted by readers of former times and, Miss Tappan says, the children would have been surprised if their stories did not have lectures and instructional passages.

The change in children's books from religious didacticism to instruction about the natural world was influenced by Rousseau's theories of education. He believed schools and books contaminated children, who could be better taught by wise adults who answered all their questions. That Thomas Day was influenced by Rousseau's ideas is apparent in the following selection. Mr. Barlow is Tommy and Harry's wise tutor who seizes upon the boys' slightest interest to introduce lessons.

Harry, as the country boy uncorrupted by wealth, epitomizes the Rousseauian child, while Tommy, corrupted by luxury, must be remade in Harry's image. Tommy does not have an easy time, but in the end repents, recognizes his errors, and reforms.

TOMMY DECIDES TO STUDY ARITHMETIC

The little boys returned to a diversion they had been amusing themselves with for several days,—the forming of a prodigious snowball. They had begun by making a small globe of snow with their hands, which they turned over and over, till, by continually collecting fresh matter, it grew so large that they were unable to roll it any farther. Here Tommy observed that their labors must end, "for it was impossible to turn it any longer." "No," said Harry, "I know a remedy for that." So he ran and fetched a couple of thick sticks, about five feet long, and giving one of them to Tommy, he took the other himself. He then desired Tommy to put the end of his stick under the mass, while he did the same on his side, and then, lifting at the other end, they rolled the heap forward with the utmost ease.

Tommy was extremely surprised at this, and said, "How can this be? We are not a bit stronger than we were before, and yet now we are able to roll this snowball along with ease, which we could not even stir before."

"That is very true," answered Harry, "but it is owing to these sticks. This is the way that the laborers move the largest trees, which, without

this contrivance, they would not be able to stir." "I am very much surprised at this," said Tommy; "I never should have imagined that the sticks would have given us more strength than we had before."

Just as he had said this, by a violent effort both their sticks broke short in the middle. "This is no great loss," observed Tommy, "for the ends will do just as well as the whole sticks."

They then tried to force the ball again with the truncheons which remained in their hands; but, to the new surprise of Tommy, they found they were unable to effect their object. "That is very curious indeed," said Tommy; "I find that only long sticks are of any use." "That," said Harry, "I could have told you before; but I had a mind you should find it out yourself. The longer the stick is, provided it be sufficiently strong, and you can manage it, the more easily will you succeed." "This is really very strange," replied Tommy: "but I see some of Mr. Barlow's laborers at work a little way off; let us go to them, and request them to cut us two longer sticks, that we may try their effect."

They then went up to the men who were at work, but here a new subject of admiration presented itself to Tommy's mind. There was a root of a prodigious oak tree, so large and heavy, that half a dozen horses would scarcely have been able to draw it along; besides, it was so tough and knotty, that the sharpest axe could hardly make any impression upon it. This a couple of old men were attempting to cleave in pieces, in order to make billets for Mr. Barlow's fire.

Tommy, who thought their strength totally dis-

---

[2] From *Old Fashioned Stories and Poems* edited by Eva March Tappan. Boston: Houghton Mifflin, 1907, p. xiii.
[3] John Masefield, *So Long To Learn.* New York: Macmillan, 1952, p. 39.

"Tommy Decides To Study Arithmetic," from *Sanford and Merton* by Thomas Day (three volumes, 1783, 1786, 1789).

proportionate to such an undertaking, could not help pitying them, and observing that certainly Mr. Barlow "did not know what they were about, or he would have prevented such poor weak old men from fatiguing themselves about what they never could perform." "Do you think so?" replied Harry; "what would you then say, if you were to see me, little as I am, perform this wonderful task, with the assistance of one of these good people?" So he took up a wooden mallet,—an instrument which, although much larger, resembles a hammer,—and began beating the root, which he did for some time, without making the least impression. Tommy, who imagined that for this time his friend Harry was caught, began to smile, and told him "that he would break a hundred mallets to pieces before he made the least impression upon the wood." "Say you so?" answered Harry smiling; "then I believe I must try another method." So he stooped down, and picked up a small piece of rough iron, about six inches long, which Tommy had not observed before, as it lay upon the ground. This iron was broad at the top, but gradually sloped all the way down, till it came to a thin edge at the bottom. Harry then took it up, and with a few blows drove it a little way into the body of the root. The old man and he then struck alternately with their mallets upon the head of the iron, till the root began to gape and crack on every side, and the iron was totally buried in the wood.

"There," said Harry, "this first wedge has done its business very well; two or three more will finish it." He then took up another larger wedge, and inserting the bottom of it between the wood and the top of the former one, which was now completely buried in the root, began to beat upon it as he had done before. The root now cracked, and split on every side of the wedges, till a prodigious cleft appeared quite down to the bottom. Thus did Harry proceed, still continuing his blows, and inserting new and larger wedges, as fast as he had driven the former down, till he had completely affected what he had undertaken, and entirely separated the immense mass of wood into two unequal parts.

Harry then said, "Here is a very large log, but I think you and I can carry it in to mend the fire; and I will show you something else that will surprise you." So he took a pole of about ten feet long, and hung the log upon it by a piece of cord which he found there; then he asked Tommy which end of the pole he chose to carry? Tommy, who thought it would be most convenient to have the weight near him, chose that end of the pole near which the weight was suspended, and put it upon his shoulder, while Harry took the other end. But when Tommy attempted to move, he found that he could hardly bear the pressure; however, as he saw Harry walk briskly away under his share of the load, he determined not to complain.

As they were walking in this manner, Mr. Barlow met them; and seeing poor Tommy laboring under his burden, asked him who had loaded him in that manner? Tommy said it was Harry. Upon this Mr. Barlow smiled, and said, "Well, Tommy, this is the first time I ever saw your friend Harry attempt to impose upon you; but he is making you carry about three times the weight which he supports himself." Harry replied "that Tommy had chosen that himself, and that he should directly have informed him of his mistake, but that he had been so surprised at seeing the common effects of a lever, that he wished to teach him some other facts about it"; then, shifting the ends of the pole, so as to support that part which Tommy had done before, he asked him "if he found his shoulder anything easier than before?" "Indeed, I do," replied Tommy; "but I cannot conceive how, for we carry the same weight between us that we did before, and just in the same manner." "Not quite in the same manner," answered Mr. Barlow; "for, if you observe, the log is a great deal farther from your shoulder than from Harry's; by which means he now supports just as much as you did before, and you, on the contrary, as little as he did when I met you." "This is very extraordinary, indeed," said Tommy; "I find there are a great many things that I did not know, nor even my mamma, nor any of the fine ladies that come to our house." "Well," replied Mr. Barlow, "if you have acquired so much useful knowledge already, what may you expect to do in a few years more?"

Mr. Barlow then led Tommy into the house, and showed him a stick of about four feet long, with a scale hung at each end. "Now," said he, "if you place this stick over the back of a chair, so that it may rest exactly upon the middle, you see the two scales will just balance each other. So, if I put into each of them an equal weight they will still remain suspended. In this method we weigh everything that is bought; only, for the greater convenience, the beam of the scale, which is the same thing as this stick, is generally hung up to something else by its middle. But let us now move the stick, and see what will be the consequence." Mr. Barlow then pushed the stick along in such a manner that, when it rested upon the back of the chair, there were three feet of it on one side, and only one on the other. That side which was the longer instantly came to the ground as heavier. "You see," said Mr. Barlow, "if we would now balance them, we must put a greater weight on the shorter side;" so he kept adding weights, till Tommy found that one pound on the longer side would exactly balance three on the shorter; for as much as the longer side exceeded the shorter in length, so much did the weight which was hung at that end require to exceed that on the longer side.

"This," said Mr. Barlow, "is what they call a *lever*, and all the sticks that you have been using to-day are only levers of a different construction. By these short trials you may conceive the prodigious advantage which they are of to men; for thus can one man move a weight which half a dozen would not be able to move with their hands alone; thus may a little boy like you do more than the strongest man could effect, who might not be acquainted with these secrets. As to that instrument by which you were so surprised that Harry could cleave such a vast body of wood, it is called a *wedge*, and is almost equally useful with the lever. The whole force of it consists in its being gradually narrower and narrower, till at last it ends in a thin edge capable of penetrating the smallest chink. By this we are enabled to overthrow the largest oaks, to cleave their roots, almost as hard as iron itself, and even to split the solid rocks." "All this," said Tommy, "is wonderful indeed! and I need not ask the use of these instruments, because I see it plainly in the experiments I have made to-day."

"One thing more," added Mr. Barlow; "as we are upon this subject, I will show you." So he led them into the yard, to the bottom of his granary, where stood a heavy sack of corn. "Now," said Mr. Barlow, "if you are so stout a fellow as you imagine, take up this sack of corn, and carry it up the ladder into the granary." "That," replied Tommy, laughing, "is impossible; and I doubt, sir, whether you could do it yourself." "Well," said Mr. Barlow, "we will at least try what is to be done." He then led them up into the granary, and showing them a middle-sized wheel with a handle fixed upon it, desired the boys to turn it round. They began to turn it with some little difficulty; and Tommy could hardly believe his eyes, when, presently after, he saw the sack of corn, which he had despaired of moving, mounted up into the granary, and safely landed upon the floor. "You see," said Mr. Barlow, "here is another ingenious contrivance, by which the weakest person may perform the work of the strongest. This is called the *wheel* and *axis*. You see this wheel, which is not very large, turns round an axle which goes into it, and is much smaller; and at every turn, the rope to which the weight is fixed that you want to move, is twisted round the axle. Now, just as much as the breadth of the whole wheel is greater than that of the axle which it turns round, so much greater is the weight that the person who turns it can move, than he could do without it!" "Well," said Tommy, "I see it is a fine thing, indeed, to acquire knowledge; for by these means one not only increases one's understanding, but one's bodily strength. But are there no more, sir, of these ingenious contrivances? for I should like to understand them all." "Yes," answered Mr. Barlow, "there are more; and all of them you shall be perfectly acquainted with in time; but for this purpose, you should be able to write, and comprehend something of arithmetic." —*Tommy.* What is arithmetic, sir? —*Mr. Barlow.* That is not so easy to make you understand at once; I will, however, try to explain it. Do you see the grains of wheat, which lie scattered in the window? —*T.* Yes, sir. —*Mr. B.* Can you count how many there are? —*T.* There are just five-and-twenty of them. —*Mr. B.* Very well. Here is another parcel; how many grains are there? —*T.* Just fourteen. —*Mr. B.* If there are fourteen grains in one heap, and twenty-five in the other, how many grains are there in all? or, how many do fourteen and twenty-five make?

Tommy was unable to answer, and Mr. Barlow proposed the same question to Harry, who answered that together they made thirty-nine. "Again," said Mr. Barlow, "I will put the two heaps together; and then how many will there be?" —*T.* Thirty-nine. —*Mr. B.* Now look, I have just taken away nineteen from the number; how many do you think remain? —*T.* I will count them. —*Mr. B.* And cannot you tell without counting? How many are there, Harry? —*Harry.* Twenty, sir. —*Mr. B.* All this is properly the art of arithmetic; which is the same as that of counting, only it is done in a much shorter and easier way, without the trouble of having the things always before you. Thus, for instance, if you wanted to know how many barleycorns were in this sack, you would perhaps be a week in counting the whole number. —*T.* Indeed, I believe I should. —*Mr. B.* If you understood arithmetic, you might do it in five minutes. —*T.* That is extraordinary, indeed; I can hardly conceive it possible. —*Mr. B.* A bushel of corn weighs about fifty pounds: this sack contains four bushels; so that there are just two hundred pounds' weight in all. Now every pound contains sixteen ounces; and sixteen times two hundred makes thirty-two hundred ounces. So that you have nothing to do but to count the number of grains in a single ounce, and there will be thirty-two hundred times that number in the sack. —*T.* I declare this is curious, indeed; and I should like to learn arithmetic. Will Harry and you teach me, sir? —*Mr. B.* You know we are always ready to improve you. But before we leave this subject, I must tell you a little story. There was a gentleman who was extremely fond of beautiful horses, and did not grudge to give the highest prices for them. One day a horse courser came to him, and showed him one so handsome that he thought it superior to all he had ever seen before. He mounted him, and found his paces equally excellent; for, though he was full of spirit, he was gentle and tractable as could be wished. So many perfections delighted the gentleman, and he eagerly demanded the price. The horse courser answered, that he would abate nothing of two hundred guineas; the gentleman, although he admired the horse, would not consent to give it; and they were just on the point of parting. As the man was turning his back, the gentleman called out to him, and said, "Is there no possible way of our agreeing? for I would give you anything in reason for such a beautiful creature." "Why," replied the dealer, who was a shrewd fellow, and perfectly understood calculation, "if you do not like to give me two hundred guineas, will you give me a farthing for the first nail the horse has in his shoe, two farthings for the second, four for the third, and so go doubling throughout the whole twenty-four? for there are no more than twenty-four nails in his shoes." The gentleman gladly accepted the condition, and ordered the horse to be led away to his stables. —*T.* This fellow must have been a very great blockhead, to ask two hundred guineas, and then to take a few farthings for this horse. —*Mr. B.* The gentleman was of the same opinion; however, the horse courser added, "I do not mean, sir, to tie you down to this last proposal, which, upon consideration, you may like as little as the first; all that I require is, that, if you are dissatisfied with your bargain, you will promise to pay me down the two hundred guineas which I first asked." This the gentleman willingly agreed to, and then called the steward to calculate the sum, for he was too much of a gentleman to be able to do it himself. The steward sat down with his pen and ink, and after some time gravely wished his master joy, and asked him "in what part of England the estate was situated that he was going to purchase." "Are you mad?" replied the gentleman: "it is not an estate, but a horse, that I have just bargained for; and here is the owner of him, to whom I am going to pay the money." "If there be any madness, sir," replied the steward, "it certainly is not on my side: the sum you have ordered me to calculate comes just to seventeen thousand four hundred and seventy-six pounds, besides some shillings and pence, and surely no man in his senses would give this price for a horse." The gentleman was more surprised than he had ever been before, to hear the assertion of his steward; but when, upon examination, he found it no more than the truth, he was very glad to compound for his foolish agreement, by giving the horse courser the two hundred guineas, and dismissing him. —*T.* This is quite incredible, that a farthing just doubled a few times, should amount to such a prodigious sum: however, I am determined to learn arithmetic, that I may not be imposed upon in this manner; for I think a gentleman must look very silly under such circumstances.

HENRY

Anonymous

[*From* A Cup of Sweets that can never Cloy; or Delightful Tales for Good Children. *By a London Lady: J. Harris, successor to E. Newbery, corner of St. Paul's Churchyard. 1804.*]

There must have been many willful children in the nineteenth century because much of the horrific children's literature develops around the theme of "this is what will happen to YOU, dear reader, if you don't obey your elders." Henry is a "good-natured" child, but he has a mind of his own— seemingly an unforgivable childhood trait in the nineteenth century.

While few twentieth-century writers have continued this style, stories like "Henry" are the direct ancestors of Munro Leaf's Fun Books. Many of today's adults were raised on these didactic social sermons rather like "Henry."

Henry was the son of a merchant of Bristol; he was a very good-natured, obliging boy, and loved his papa and mamma, and his brothers and sisters, most affectionately; but he had one very disagreeable fault, which was, that he did not like to be directed or advised.

He was the most amiable boy in the world, if you would let him have his own way: but the moment he was told not to stand so near the fire, or not to jump down two or three stairs at a time, not to climb upon the tables, or to take care he did not fall out of the window, he grew directly angry, and asked if they thought he did not know what he was about—said he was no longer a baby, and that he was certainly big enough to take care of himself.

A lady, who visited his mamma, and who was extremely fond of him, met him in the hall on new year's day, and gave him a seven-shilling piece to purchase something to amuse himself. Henry was delighted at having so much money, but instead of informing his parents of the present he had received, and asking them to advise him how to spend it, he determined to do as he liked with it, without consulting anybody; and having long had a great desire to amuse himself

with some gunpowder, he began to think (now he was so rich) whether it might not be possible to contrive to get some. He had been often told of the dreadful accidents which have happened by playing with this dangerous thing, but he fancied *he* could take care, *he* was old enough to amuse himself with it, without any risk of hurting himself; and meeting with a boy who was employed about the house by the servants, he offered to give him a shilling for his trouble, if he would get him what he desired; and as the boy cared very little for the danger to which he exposed Henry, of blowing himself up, so as he got but the shilling, he was soon in possession of what he wished for.

A dreadful noise was, some time afterwards, heard in the nursery. The cries of children, and the screams of their maid, brought the whole family upstairs: but, oh! what a shocking sight was presented to their view on opening the door! There lay Henry by the fireside, his face black, and smeared with blood; his hair burnt, and his eyes closed: one of his little sisters lay by him, nearly in the same deplorable condition; the others, some hurt, but all frightened almost to death, were got together in a corner, and the maid was fallen on the floor in a fit.

It was very long before either Henry or his sister could speak, and many months before they

"Henry," anon. Published by J. Harris, 1804. Reprinted in *Stories from Old Fashioned Children's Books,* edited by Andrew W. Tuer. The Leadenhall Press, 1899–1900, London. Reissued by Singing Tree Press (no © date).

were quite restored to health, and even then with the loss of one of poor Henry's eyes. He had been many weeks confined to his bed in a dark room, and it was during that time that he had reflected upon his past conduct: he now saw that he had been a very conceited, wrong-headed boy, and that children would avoid a great many accidents which happen to themselves, and the mischiefs they frequently lead others into, if they would listen to the advice of their elders, and not fancy they are capable of conducting themselves without being directed; and he was so sorry for what he had done, and particularly for what he had made his dear little Emma suffer, that he never afterwards did the least thing without consulting his friends: and whenever he was told not to do a thing, though he had wished it ever so much, instead of being angry, as he used to be, he immediately gave up all desire of doing it, and never after that time got into any mischief.

AFFECTING ACCOUNT OF A LITTLE BOY, WHO WAS KILLED IN INDIA BY A MAD DOG

From the Missionary Register—*London*

Children often died young in Victorian literature, but they died joyfully and at peace with God. The Victorians believed stories should be used to instill proper religious beliefs and social behavior in their children. This approach created hundreds of sentimental stories. While such didactic religious tracts are unattractive now because the church no longer uses God to frighten children into forms of behavior, they seem to have been quite effective and popular among the poorer people of those days. The following selection is included here as a characteristic example of these religious tracts from the early years of the Victorian period.

I will offer to your notice a very interesting account of a Little Boy who was, in his earliest infant days, blessed with the superintending care of a pious mother, who had learnt to know that the almighty God was a refuge in the hour of calamity, and his word a sure support. Strange, but delightful sight! to behold a child of five years of age, so thoroughly aware of the truth of the Bible, and so experimentally alive to its promises.

He was playing at his father's door, with his bearer, when a large dog passing by, fiercely attacked him, seized hold of his cheek, and inflicted a severe and ghastly wound, the fangs of the brute entering into the child's mouth: medical aid was obtained, and the wound gradually healed; and there seemed no further evil consequences to be apprehended. About a month subsequent to this misfortune, the poor little fellow was affected, as his affectionate mother supposed, with only a common fever, and medicine was, in consequence, administered; but on the following day, some spasmodic difficulty was perceptible on the child's attempting to drink water; these symptoms were removed by medicine, and he appeared better, and in good spirits. About twelve o'clock at night, the surgeon, who slept by his side, observed an alarming recurrence of the unfavourable symptoms, the urgency of which had been temporarily relieved by leeches. At five the following morning, the poor little patient fell into dreadful paroxysms, shortly after leaving the hot bath, and seemed like one making plunging efforts to escape drowning, crying out every instant with alarm. Convulsive struggles continued after he was in bed, and he foamed at the mouth considerably. He was, however, perfectly sensible, and inquired, in hurried accents, what it could possibly be that induced such agony when in the water.—'Can it be saltpetre?' His anxious mother, in the greatest distress, now plainly perceived that hydrophobia was actually confirmed in her child; and made up her mind at once to understand that this her beloved one must be resigned into the arms of the almighty Jesus.

And now she felt how good it was that she could speak even to this young creature on the nature of the change that soon awaited him, with some confidence of being understood; for he had been early taught, and always loved the Bible,—listening with peculiar interest to the narratives recorded therein—and dwelling on her remarks and explanations of his parent on the various characters brought to his notice, with remarkable pleasure, and selecting particular passages and men as his favourites.

Presuming on the known state of the child's mind, she at once told him not to be alarmed, but that he was going to the Almighty! 'You are now going to heaven, my love.' He immediately caught the words; and, in the very midst of his convulsive efforts, interrogated quickly, 'To die? To the Almighty? To heaven?' As the spasms gradually lessened on the little sufferer, he repeatedly and very tenderly exclaimed, 'Mamma, don't cry! Papa, don't cry! I shall not go to hell—shall I?' He was assured to the contrary, and told that God for Christ's sake loved him, and would not suffer him to go to hell! 'You are going,' exclaimed the sorrowing father, 'my dear child, to Abraham's bosom, to Jesus Christ.' 'Yes,' replied this interesting young disciple, 'to Abraham's bosom—to Christ—to Elijah!'

The fits now recurred with condsiderable violence, yet he again entreated his parents not to weep, but to call on God's angels to come and take him. His mother urged him to pray—'I have prayed, my mamma—I do pray!' The convulsions became more powerful, and the respiration spasmodically quick and hurried, when he supplicated 'O Lord, have mercy. O Lord have mercy!' The voice was sweet and harmonious, and great emphasis and precision were given to the words 'Have mercy.' 'Oh papa, pray for me! dear mamma, pray for me.' Dreadful to witness were the struggles of the body; yet the soul seemed in perfect peace, and as if the body was enabled to bear its abounding sufferings by the abounding mercies of an indwelling Christ.

Again he exclaimed, 'O Elijah! O Lord! O my God!' His father assured him, 'You will soon be happy, and at rest, Johnny!' He replied, 'Oh yes, very happy!' Another awful struggle followed. The earthly shell seemed to cling fast hold of its imprisoned tenant, while the struggling soul seemed fighting to escape through the dark shadow of death, constantly ejaculating supplications for mercy.

United prayers were now offered up to the throne of grace and mercy, to take this young and beautiful plant—a flower of the Lord's own cherishing—to its kindred heaven; and our prayers were heard. The disease generally lasts eight days: here it only actually raged three hours. The fits seemed now less severe. As we were looking at and watching the little sufferer at the foot of the bed, he called out to me in a clear firm voice, 'Come here, sir, and shut my eyes! Aha! Aha!' said he, 'There! there! it is now over, papa, don't cry! mamma, don't cry!' He paused a moment—'Papa! mamma!' 'We are close at your side, love!' He summoned me by name, also, to come near to him, and softly sighed out his soul into the hands of his Maker, with the affecting words, 'Mercy! Mercy! Happy! Happy!'

LITTLE WOMEN

Louisa May Alcott

This American classic was almost not published. A Boston publisher asked Louisa May Alcott to write a book for children, but when he read the first half of Little Women *he refused it. Fortunately he asked several young girls to confirm his opinion; instead they were enthusiastic, which persuaded him to reconsider.*

Little Women was one of the first American books to portray characters that seemed real to the children who read it. In breaking with the established tradition of stereotyped, idealized fictional children, Louisa May Alcott created sisters so memorable that Little Women is still popular today. While all girls cry a little over Beth's death, it is Jo's life that most interests them. Jo has always been the favorite March sister because hers is the most rounded character. The reader sees Jo struggle against her tomboy nature, trying to be ladylike.

THE LAURENCE BOY

Jo! Jo, where are you?" cried Meg, at the foot of the garret stairs.

"Here!" answered a husky voice from above; and, running up, Meg found her sister eating apples and crying over the "Heir of Redclyffe," wrapped up in a comforter on an old three-legged sofa by the sunny window. This was Jo's favorite refuge; and here she loved to retire with half a dozen russets and a nice book, to enjoy the quiet and the society of a pet rat who lived near by, and didn't mind her a particle. As Meg appeared, Scrabble whisked into his hole. Jo shook the tears off her cheeks, and waited to hear the news.

"Such fun! only see! A regular note of invitation from Mrs. Gardiner for tomorrow night!" cried Meg, waving the precious paper, and then proceeding to read it, with girlish delight.

" 'Mrs. Gardiner would be happy to see Miss March and Miss Josephine at a little dance on New Year's Eve.' Marmee is willing we should go; now what *shall* we wear?"

"What's the use of asking that, when you know we shall wear our poplins, because we haven't got anything else?" answered Jo, with her mouth full.

"If I only had a silk!" sighed Meg. "Mother says I may when I'm eighteen, perhaps; but two years is an everlasting time to wait.

"I'm sure our pops look like silk, and they are nice enough for us. Yours is as good as new, but I forgot the burn and the tear in mine. Whatever shall I do? This burn shows badly, and I can't take any out."

"You must sit still all you can, and keep your back out of sight; the front is all right. I shall have a new ribbon for my hair, and Marmee will lend me her little pearl pin, and my new slippers are lovely, and my gloves will do, though they aren't as nice as I'd like."

"Mine are spoilt with lemonade, and I can't get any new ones, so I shall have to go without," said Jo, who never troubled herself much about dress.

"You *must* have gloves, or I won't go," cried Meg decidedly. "Gloves are more important than anything else; you can't dance without them, and if you don't I should be *so* mortified."

"Then I'll stay still. I don't care much for company dancing; it's no fun to go sailing round; I like to fly about and cut capers."

"You can't ask mother for new ones, they are so expensive, and you are so careless. She said, when you spoilt the others, that she shouldn't get you any more this winter. Can't you make them do?" asked Meg anxiously.

"I can hold them crumpled up in my hand, so no one will know how stained they are; that's all I can do. No! I'll tell you how we can manage— each wear one good one and carry a bad one; don't you see?"

"Your hands are bigger than mine, and you will stretch my glove dreadfully," began Meg, whose gloves were a tender point with her.

"Then I'll go without. I don't care what people say!" cried Jo, taking up her book.

"You may have it, you may! Only don't stain it, and do behave nicely. Don't put your hands behind you, or stare, or say 'Christopher Columbus!' will you?"

"Don't worry about me; I'll be as prim as I can, and not get into any scrapes, if I can help it. Now go and answer your note, and let me finish this splendid story."

So Meg went away to "accept with thanks,"

look over her dress, and sing blithely as she did up her one real lace frill; while Jo finished her story, her four apples, and had a game of romps with Scrabble.

On New Year's Eve the parlor was deserted, for the two younger girls played dressing maids, and the two elder were absorbed in the all-important business of "getting ready for the party." Simple as the toilettes were, there was a great deal of running up and down, laughing and talking, and at one time a strong smell of burnt hair pervaded the house. Meg wanted a few curls about her face, and Jo undertook to pinch the papered locks with a pair of hot tongs.

"Ought they to smoke like that?" asked Beth, from her perch on the bed.

"It's the dampness drying," replied Jo.

"What a queer smell! It's like burnt feathers," observed Amy, smoothing her own pretty curls with a superior air.

"There, now I'll take off the papers and you'll see a cloud of little ringlets," said Jo, putting down the tongs.

She did take off the papers, but no cloud of ringlets appeared, for the hair came with the papers, and the horrified hairdresser laid a row of little scorched bundles on the bureau before her victim.

"'Oh, oh, oh! What *have* you done? I'm spoilt! I can't go! My hair, oh, my hair!" wailed Meg, looking with despair at the uneven frizzle on her forehead.

"Just my luck! You shouldn't have asked me to do it; I always spoil everything. I'm so sorry, but the tongs were too hot, and so I've made a mess," groaned poor Jo, regarding the black pancakes with tears of regret.

"It isn't spoilt; just frizzle it, and tie your ribbon so the ends come on your forehead a bit, and it will look like the last fashion. I've seen many girls do it so," said Amy consolingly.

"Serves me right for trying to be fine. I wish I'd let my hair alone," cried Meg petulantly.

"So do I, it was so smooth and pretty. But it will soon grow out again," said Beth, coming to kiss and comfort the shorn sheep.

After various lesser mishaps, Meg was finished at last, and by the united exertions of the family Jo's hair was got up and her dress on. They looked very well in their simple suits—Meg in

silvery drab, with a blue velvet snood, lace frills, and the pearl pin; Jo in maroon, with a stiff, gentlemanly linen collar, and a white chrysanthemum or two for her only ornament. Each put on one nice light glove, and carried one soiled one, and all pronounced the effect "quite easy and fine." Meg's highheeled slippers were very tight, and hurt her, though she would not own it, and Jo's nineteen hairpins all seemed stuck straight into her head, which was not exactly comfortable; but, dear me, let us be elegant or die!

"Have a good time, dearies!" said Mrs. March, as the sisters went daintily down the walk. "Don't eat much supper, and come away at eleven, when I send Hannah for you." As the gate clashed behind them, a voice cried from a window:

"Girls, girls! *Have* you both got nice pocket handkerchiefs?"

"Yes, yes, spandy nice, and Meg has cologne on hers," cried Jo, adding, with a laugh, as they went on, "I do believe Marmee would ask that if we were all running away from an earthquake."

"It is one of her aristocratic tastes, and quite proper, for a real lady is always known by neat boots, gloves, and handkerchief," replied Meg, who had a good many little "aristocratic tastes" of her own.

"Now don't forget to keep the bad breadth out of sight, Jo. Is my sash right? And does my hair look *very* bad?" said Meg, as she turned from the glass in Mrs. Gardiner's dressing room, after a prolonged prink.

"I know I shall forget. If you see me doing anything wrong, just remind me by a wink, will you?" returned Jo, giving her collar a twitch and her head a hasty brush.

"No, winking isn't ladylike; I'll lift my eyebrows if anything is wrong, and nod if you are all right. Now hold your shoulders straight, and take short steps, and don't shake hands if you are introduced to anyone: it isn't the thing."

"How *do* you learn all the proper ways? I never can. Isn't that music gay?"

Down they went, feeling a trifle timid, for they seldom went to parties, and, informal as this little gathering was, it was an event to them. Mrs. Gardiner, a stately old lady, greeted them kindly, and handed them over to the eldest of her six daughters. Meg knew Sallie, and was at her ease very soon; but Jo, who didn't care much for girls or girlish gossip, stood about with her back carefully against the wall, and felt as much out of place as a colt in a flower garden. Half a dozen jovial lads were talking about skates in another part of the room, and she longed to go and join them, for skating was one of the joys of her life. She telegraphed her wish to Meg, but the eyebrows went up so alarmingly that she dared not stir. No one came to talk to her, and one by one the group near her dwindled away, till she was left alone. She could not roam about and amuse herself, for the burnt breadth would show, so she stared at people rather forlornly till the dancing began. Meg was asked at once, and the tight slippers tripped about so briskly that none would have guessed the pain their wearer suffered smilingly. Jo saw a big redheaded youth approaching her corner, and fearing he meant to engage her, she slipped into a curtained recess, intending to peep and enjoy herself in peace. Unfortunately, another bashful person had chosen the same refuge; for, as the curtain fell behind her, she found herself face to face with the "Laurence boy."

"Dear me, I didn't know anyone was here!" stammered Jo, preparing to back out as speedily as she had bounced in.

But the boy laughed, and said pleasantly, though he looked a little startled:

"Don't mind me; stay, if you like."

"Shan't I disturb you?"

"Not a bit; I only came here because I don't know many people, and felt rather strange at first, you know."

"So did I. Don't go away, please, unless you'd rather."

The boy sat down again and looked at his pumps, till Jo said, trying to be polite and easy:

"I think I've had the pleasure of seeing you before; you live near us, don't you?"

"Next door"; and he looked up and laughed outright, for Jo's prim manner was rather funny when he remembered how they had chatted about cricket when he brought the cat home.

That put Jo at her ease; and she laughed too, as she said, in her heartiest way:

"We did have such a good time over your nice Christmas present."

"Grandpa sent it."

"But you put it into his head, didn't you, now?"

"How is your cat, Miss March?" asked the boy, trying to look sober, while his black eyes shone with fun.

"Nicely, thank you, Mr. Laurence; but I am not Miss March, I'm only Jo," returned the young lady.

"I'm not Mr. Laurence, I'm only Laurie."

"Laurie Laurence—what an odd name!"

"My first name is Theodore, but I don't like it, for the fellows called me Dora, so I made them say Laurie instead."

"I hate my name, too—so sentimental! I wish everyone would say Jo, instead of Josephine. How did you make the boys stop calling you Dora?"

"I thrashed 'em."

"I can't thrash Aunt March, so I suppose I shall have to bear it"; and Jo resigned herself with a sigh.

"Don't you like to dance, Miss Jo?" asked Laurie, looking as if he thought the name suited her.

"I like it well enough if there is plenty of room, and everyone is lively. In a place like this I'm sure to upset something, tread on people's toes, or do something dreadful, so I keep out of mischief, and let Meg sail about. Don't you dance?"

"Sometimes; you see I've been abroad a good many years, and haven't been into company enough yet to know how you do things here."

"Abroad!" cried Jo. "Oh, tell me about it! I love dearly to hear people describe their travels."

Laurie didn't seem to know where to begin; but Jo's eager questions soon set him going, and he told her how he had been at school in Vevay, where the boys never wore hats, and had a fleet of boats on the lake, and for holiday fun went walking trips about Switzerland with their teachers.

"Don't I wish I'd been there!" cried Jo. "Did you go to Paris?"

"We spent last winter there."

"Can you talk French?"

"We were not allowed to speak anything else at Vevay."

"Do say some! I can read it, but can't pronounce."

"Quel nom a cette jeune demoiselle en les pantoufles jolis?" said Laurie good-naturedly.

"How nicely you do it! Let me see—you said, 'Who is the young lady in the pretty slippers,' didn't you?"

"Oui, mademoiselle."

"It's my sister Margaret, and you knew it was! Do you think she is pretty?"

"Yes; she makes me think of the German girls, she looks so fresh and quiet, and dances like a lady."

Jo quite glowed with pleasure at this boyish praise of her sister, and stored it up to repeat to Meg. Both peeped and criticized and chatted, till they felt like old acquaintances. Laurie's bashfulness soon wore off, for Jo's gentlemanly demeanor amused and set him at his ease, and Jo was her merry self again, because her dress was forgotten, and nobody lifted their eyebrows at her. She liked the "Laurence boy" better than ever, and took several good looks at him, so that she might describe him to the girls; for they had no brothers, very few male cousins, and boys were almost unknown creatures to them.

"Curly black hair; brown skin; big black eyes; handsome nose; fine teeth; small hands and feet; taller than I am; very polite, for a boy, and altogether jolly. Wonder how old he is?"

It was on the tip of Jo's tongue to ask; but she checked herself in time, and, with unusual tact, tried to find out in a roundabout way.

"I suppose you are going to college soon? I see you pegging away at your books—no, I mean studying hard"; and Jo blushed at the dreadful "pegging" which had escaped her.

Laurie smiled, but didn't seem shocked, and answered, with a shrug:

"Not for a year or two; I won't go before seventeen, anyway."

"Aren't you but fifteen?" asked Jo, looking at the tall lad whom she had imagined seventeen already.

"Sixteen, next month."

"How I wish I was going to college! You don't look as if you liked it."

"I hate it! Nothing but grinding or skylarking. And I don't like the way fellows do either, in this country."

"What do you like?"

"To live in Italy, and to enjoy myself in my own way."

Jo wanted very much to ask what his own way was; but his black brows looked rather threatening as he knit them; so she changed the subject by saying, as her foot kept time, "That's a splendid polka! Why don't you go and try it?"

"If you will come too," he answered, with a gallant little bow.

"I can't; for I told Meg I wouldn't, because—" There Jo stopped, and looked undecided whether to tell or to laugh.

"Because what?" asked Laurie curiously.

"You won't tell?"

"Never!"

"Well, I have a bad trick of standing before the fire, and so I burn my frocks, and I scorched this one; and, though it's nicely mended, it shows, and Meg told me to keep still, so no one would see it. You may laugh, if you want to; it is funny, I know."

But Laurie didn't laugh; he only looked down a minute, and the expression of his face puzzled Jo, when he said very gently:

"Never mind that; I'll tell you how we can manage: there's a long hall out there, and we can dance grandly, and no one will see us. Please come?"

Jo thanked him, and gladly went, wishing she had two neat gloves, when she saw the nice, pearl-colored ones her partner wore. The hall was empty, and they had a grand polka; for Laurie danced well, and taught her the German step, which delighted Jo, being full of swing and spring. When the music stopped, they sat down on the stairs to get their breath; and Laurie was in the midst of an account of a students' festival at Heidelberg, when Meg appeared in search of her sister. She beckoned, and Jo reluctantly followed her into a side room, where she found her on a sofa, holding her foot, and looking pale.

"I've sprained my ankle. That stupid high heel turned and gave me a sad wrench. It aches so I can hardly stand, and I don't know how I'm ever going to get home," she said, rocking to and fro in pain.

"I knew you'd hurt your feet with those silly shoes. I'm sorry. But I don't see what you can do, except get a carriage, or stay here all night," answered Jo, softly rubbing the poor ankle as she spoke.

"I can't have a carriage, without its costing ever so much. I dare say I can't get one at all; for most people come in their own, and it's a long way to the stable, and no one to send."

"I'll go."

"No, indeed! It's past nine, and dark as Egypt. I can't stop here, for the house is full. Sallie has some girls staying with her. I'll rest till Hannah comes, and then do the best I can."

"I'll ask Laurie; he will go," said Jo, looking relieved as the idea occurred to her.

"Mercy, no! Don't ask or tell anyone. Get me my rubbers, and put these slippers with our things. I can't dance any more; but as soon as supper is over, watch for Hannah, and tell me the minute she comes."

"They are going out to supper now. I'll stay with you; I'd rather."

"No, dear, run along, and bring me some coffee. I'm so tired, I can't stir!"

So Meg reclined with rubbers well hidden, and Jo went blundering away to the dining room, which she found after going into a china closet, and opening the door of a room where old Mr. Gardiner was taking a little private refreshment. Making a dart at the table, she secured the coffee, which she immediately spilt, thereby making the front of her dress as bad as the back.

"Oh, dear, what a blunderbuss I am!" exclaimed Jo, finishing Meg's glove by scrubbing her gown with it.

"Can I help you?" said a friendly voice; and there was Laurie, with a full cup in one hand and a plate of ice in the other.

"I was trying to get something for Meg, who is very tired, and someone shook me; and here I am, in a nice state," answered Jo, glancing dismally from the stained skirt to the coffee-colored glove.

"Too bad! I was looking for someone to give this to. May I take it to your sister?"

"Oh, thank you! I'll show you where she is. I don't offer to take it myself, for I should only get into another scrape if I did."

Jo led the way; and, as if used to waiting on ladies, Laurie drew up a little table, brought a second installment of coffee and ice for Jo, and

was so obliging that even particular Meg pronounced him a "nice boy." They had a merry time over the bonbons and mottoes, and were in the midst of a quiet game of "Buzz," with two or three other young people who had strayed in, when Hannah appeared. Meg forgot her foot, and rose so quickly that she was forced to catch hold of Jo, with an exclamation of pain.

"Hush! Don't say anything," she whispered, adding aloud, "It's nothing. I turned my foot a little, that's all," and limped upstairs to put her things on.

Hannah scolded, Meg cried, and Jo was at her wits' end, till she decided to take things into her own hands. Slipping out, she ran down, and, finding a servant, asked if he could get her a carriage. It happened to be a hired waiter, who knew nothing about the neighborhood; and Jo was looking round for help, when Laurie, who had heard what she said, came up, and offered his grandfather's carriage, which had just come for him, he said.

"It's so early! You can't mean to go yet?" began Jo, looking relieved, but hesitating to accept the offer.

"I always go early—I do, truly! Please let me take you home. It's all on my way, you know, and it rains, they say."

That settled it; and, telling him of Meg's mishap, Jo gratefully accepted, and rushed up to bring down the rest of the party. Hannah hated rain as much as a cat does; so she made no trouble, and they rolled away in the luxurious closed carriage, feeling very festive and elegant. Laurie went on the box; so Meg could keep her foot up, and the girls talked over their party in freedom.

"I had a capital time. Did you?" asked Jo, rumpling up her hair, and making herself comfortable.

"Yes, till I hurt myself. Sallie's friend, Annie Moffat, took a fancy to me, and asked me to come and spend a week with her, when Sallie does. She is going in the spring, when the opera comes; and it will be perfectly splendid, if mother only lets me go," answered Meg, cheering up at the thought.

"I saw you dancing with the redheaded man I ran away from. Was he nice?"

"Oh, very! His hair is auburn, not red; and he was very polite, and I had a delicious redowa with him."

"He looked like a grasshopper in a fit, when he did the new step. Laurie and I couldn't help laughing. Did you hear us?"

"No; but it was very rude. What *were* you about all that time, hidden away there?"

Jo told her adventures, and, by the time she had finished, they were at home. With many thanks, they said "Good night," and crept in, hoping to disturb no one; but the instant their door creaked, two little nightcaps bobbed up, and two sleepy but eager voices cried out:

"Tell about the party! Tell about the party!"

With what Meg called "a great want of manners" Jo had saved some bonbons for the little girls; and they soon subsided, after hearing the most thrilling events of the evening.

"I declare, it really seems like being a fine young lady, to come home from the party in a carriage, and sit in my dressing gown, with a maid to wait on me," said Meg, as Jo bound up her foot with arnica, and brushed her hair.

"I don't believe fine young ladies enjoy themselves a bit more than we do, in spite of our burnt hair, old gowns, one glove apiece, and tight slippers that sprain our ankles when we are really silly enough to wear them." And I think Jo was quite right.

THE ADVENTURES OF TOM SAWYER

Samuel Clemens (Mark Twain)

Tom Sawyer is one of the great books written for children; one so memorable that many adults reread it with as much pleasure as when they were young. It is one of those exceptional books enjoyed by all ages. First published in 1876, Tom Sawyer *deals with many things that still appeal to children in the last decades of the twentieth century: caves, rivers, running away, fooling adults, mischief, secret gangs. But its greatness goes beyond these elements and lies in the excellent character and plot development.*

Tom Sawyer is important not only because it is one of the best American books written for adolescents but also because it was one of the first children's books to have believable, rounded characters. Tom is all boy and even Huck, with his lack of social graces and respectability, is a rounded person. They are not the stereotypes used by most of Twain's contemporaries. In the nineteenth century this was a remarkable break from the standard didactic novels. Tom Sawyer *helped begin a new era in American children's literature.*

TOM MEETS BECKY

Monday morning found Tom Sawyer miserable. Monday morning always found him so—because it began another week's slow suffering in school. He generally began that day with wishing he had had no intervening holiday, it made the going into captivity and fetters again so much more odious.

Tom lay thinking. Presently it occurred to him that he wished he was sick; then he could stay home from school. Here was a vague possibility. He canvassed his system. No ailment was found, and he investigated again. This time he thought he could detect colicky symptoms, and he began to encourage them with considerable hope. But they soon grew feeble, and presently died wholly away. He reflected further. Suddenly he discovered something. One of his upper front teeth was loose. This was lucky; he was about to begin to groan, as a "starter," as he called it, when it occurred to him that if he came into court with that argument, his aunt would pull it out, and that would hurt. So he thought he would hold the tooth in reserve for the present, and seek further. Nothing offered for some little time, and then he remembered hearing the doctor tell about a certain thing that laid up a patient for two or three weeks and threatened to make him lose a finger. So the boy eagerly drew his sore toe from under the sheet and held it up for inspection. But now he did not know the necessary symptoms. However, it seemed well worth while to chance it, so he fell to groaning with considerable spirit.

But Sid slept on unconscious.

Tom groaned louder, and fancied that he began to feel pain in the toe.

No result from Sid.

Tom was panting with his exertions by this time. He took a rest and then swelled himself up and fetched a succession of admirable groans.

Sid snored on.

Tom was aggravated. He said, "Sid, Sid!" and shook him. This course worked well, and Tom began to groan again. Sid yawned, stretched, then brought himself up on his elbow with a snort, and began to stare at Tom. Tom went on groaning. Sid said:

"Tom! Say, Tom! [No response.] Here, Tom! *Tom*! What is the matter, Tom?" And he shook him and looked in his face anxiously.

Tom moaned out:

"Oh, don't Sid. Don't joggle me."

"Why, what's the matter, Tom? I must call Auntie."

"No—never mind. It'll be over by and by, maybe. Don't call anybody."

"But I must! *Don't* groan so, Tom, it's awful. How long you been this way?"

"Hours. Ouch! Oh, don't stir so, Sid, you'll kill me."

"Tom, why didn't you wake me sooner? Oh, Tom, *don't*! It makes my flesh crawl to hear you. Tom, what *is* the matter?"

"I forgive you everything, Sid. [Groan.] Everything you've ever done to me. When I'm gone——"

"Oh, Tom, you ain't dying, are you? Don't, Tom—oh, don't. Maybe—"

"I forgive everybody, Sid. [Groan.] Tell 'em so, Sid. And Sid, you give my windowsash, and my cat with one eye to that new girl that's come to town, and tell her——"

But Sid had snatched his clothes and gone. Tom was suffering in reality, now, so handsomely was his imagination working, and so his groans had gathered quite a genuine tone.

Sid flew downstairs and said:

"Oh, Aunt Polly, come! Tom's dying!"

"Dying!"

"Yes'm. Don't wait—come quick!"

"Rubbage! I don't believe it!"

But she fled upstairs, nevertheless, with Sid and Mary at her heels. And her face grew white, too, and her lip trembled. When she reached the bedside she gasped out:

"You, Tom! Tom, what's the matter with you?"

"Oh, Auntie, I'm——"

"What's the matter with you—what *is* the matter with you, child?"

"Oh, Auntie, my sore toe's mortified!"

The old lady sank down into a chair and laughed a little, then cried a little, then did both together. This restored her and she said:

"Tom, what a turn you did give me! Now you shut up that nonsense and climb out of this."

The groans ceased and the pain vanished from the toe. The boy felt a little foolish, and he said:

"Aunt Polly, it *seemed* mortified, and it hurt so I never minded my tooth at all."

"Your tooth, indeed! What's the matter with your tooth?"

"One of them's loose, and it aches perfectly awful."

"There, there, now, don't begin that groaning again. Open your mouth. Well—your tooth *is* loose, but you're not going to die about that. Mary, get me a silk thread, and a chunk of fire out of the kitchen."

Tom said:

"Oh, please, Auntie, don't pull it out! It don't hurt any more. I wish I may never stir if it does. Please don't, Auntie. *I* don't want to stay home from school."

"Oh, you don't, don't you? So, all this row was because you thought you'd get to stay home from school and go a-fishing? Tom, Tom, I love you so, and you seem to try every way you can to break my old heart with your outrageousness." By this time the dental instruments were ready. The old lady made one end of the silk thread fast to Tom's tooth with a loop and tied the other to the bedpost. Then she seized the chunk of fire and suddenly thrust it almost into the boy's face. The tooth hung dangling by the bedpost, now.

But all trials bring their compensations. As Tom wended to school after breakfast, he was the envy of every boy he met because the gap in his upper row of teeth enabled him to expectorate in a new and admirable way. He gathered quite a following of lads interested in the exhibition; and one that had cut his finger and had been a center of fascination and homage up to this time now found himself suddenly without an adherent and shorn of his glory. His heart was heavy, and he said with a disdain which he did not feel that it wasn't anything to spit like Tom Sawyer; but another boy said "Sour grapes!" and he wandered away a dismantled hero.

Shortly Tom came upon the juvenile pariah of the village, Huckleberry Finn, son of the town drunkard. Huckleberry was cordially hated and dreaded by all the mothers of the town, because he was idle and lawless and vulgar and bad—and because all their children admired him so, and delighted in his forbidden society, and wished they dared to be like him. Tom was like the rest of the respectable boys, in that he envied Huckleberry his gaudy outcast condition, and was under strict orders not to play with him. So he played with him every time he got a chance. Huckleberry was always dressed in the cast-off clothes of full-grown men, and they were in perennial bloom and fluttering with rags. His hat was a vast ruin with a wide crescent lopped out of its brim; his coat, when he wore one, hung nearly to his heels and had the rearward buttons far down the back; but one suspender supported his trousers; the seat of the trousers bagged low and contained nothing; the fringed legs dragged in the dirt when not rolled up.

Huckleberry came and went, at his own free will. He slept on doorsteps in fine weather and in empty hogsheads in wet; he did not have to go to

school or to church, or call any being master or obey anybody; he could go fishing or swimming when and where he chose, and stay as long as it suited him; nobody forbade him to fight; he could sit up as late as he pleased; he was always the first boy that went barefoot in the spring and the last to resume leather in the fall; he never had to wash, nor put on clean clothes; he could swear wonderfully. In a word, everything that goes to make life precious that boy had. So thought every harassed, hampered, respectable boy in St. Petersburg.

Tom hailed the romantic outcast:

"Hello, Huckleberry!"

"Hello yourself, and see how you like it."

"What's that you got?"

"Dead cat."

"Lemme see him, Huck. My, he's pretty stiff. Where'd you get him?"

"Bought him off'n a boy."

"What did you give?"

"I give a blue ticket and a bladder that I got at the slaughter-house."

"Where'd you get the blue ticket?"

"Bought it off'n Ben Rogers two weeks ago for a hoopstick."

"Say—what is dead cats good for, Huck?"

"Good for? Cure warts with."

"No! Is that so? I know something that's better."

"I bet you don't. What is it?"

"Why, spunk-water."

"Spunk-water! I wouldn't give a dern for spunk-water."

"You wouldn't, wouldn't you? D'you ever try it?"

"No, I hain't. But Bob Tanner did."

"Who told you so?"

"Why, he told Jeff Thatcher, and Jeff told Johnny Baker, and Johnny told Jim Hollis, and Jim told Ben Rogers, and Ben told a nigger, and the nigger told me. There now!"

"Well, what of it? They'll all lie. Leastways all but the nigger. I don't know *him*. But I never see a nigger that *wouldn't* lie. Shucks! Now you tell me how Bob Tanner done it, Huck."

"Why, he took and dipped his hand in a rotten stump where the rainwater was."

"In the daytime?"

"Certainly."

"With his face to the stump?"

"Yes. Least I reckon so."

"Did he *say* anything?"

"I don't reckon he did. I don't know."

"Aha! Talk about trying to cure warts with spunk-water such a blame-fool way as that! Why, that ain't a-going to do any good. You got to go all by yourself, to the middle of the woods, where you know there's a spunk-water stump, and just as it's midnight you back up against the stump and jam your hand in and say:

Barley-corn, barley-corn, injun-meal shorts,
Spunk-water, spunk-water, swaller these warts,

and then walk away quick, eleven steps, with your eyes shut, and then turn around three times and walk home without speaking to anybody. Because if you speak the charm's busted."

"Well, that sounds like a good way; but that ain't the way Bob Tanner done."

"No, sir, you can bet he didn't, becuz he's the wartiest boy in this town; and he wouldn't have a wart on him if he'd knowed how to work spunk-water. I've took off thousands of warts off of my hands that way, Huck. I play with frogs so much that I've always got considerable many warts. Sometimes I take 'em off with a bean."

"Yes, bean's good. I've done that."

"Have you? What's your way?"

"You take and split the bean, and cut the wart so as to get some blood, and then you put the blood on one piece of the bean and take and dig a hole and bury it 'bout midnight at the cross-roads in the dark of the moon, and then you burn up the rest of the bean. You see that piece that's got the blood on it will keep drawing and drawing, trying to fetch the other piece to it, and so that helps the blood to draw the wart, and pretty soon off she comes."

"Yes, that's it, Huck—that's it; though when you're burying it if you say. 'Down bean; off wart; come no more to bother me!' it's better. That's the way Joe Harper does, and he's been nearly to Coonville and most everywheres. But say—how do you cure 'em with dead cats?"

"Why, you take your cat and go and get in the graveyard 'long about midnight when somebody that was wicked has been buried; and when it's midnight a devil will come, or maybe two or three, but you can't see 'em, you can only hear something like the wind, or maybe hear 'em talk; and when they're taking that feller away, you heave your cat after 'em and say, 'Devil follow corpse, cat follow devil, warts follow cat, *I'm* done with ye!' That'll fetch *any* wart."

"Sounds right. D'you ever try it, Huck?"

"No, but old Mother Hopkins told me."

"Well, I reckon it's so, then. Becuz they say she's a witch."

"Say! Why, Tom, I *know* she is. She witched Pap. Pap says so his own self. He come along one day, and he see she was a-witching him, so he took up a rock, and if she hadn't dodged, he'd 'a' got her. Well, that very night he rolled off'n a shed wher' he was a-layin' drunk, and broke his arm."

"Why, that's awful. How did he know she was a-witching him?"

"Lord, Pap can tell easy. Pap says when they keep looking at you right stiddy, they're a-witching you. 'Specially if they mumble. Becuz when they mumble, they're saying the Lord's Prayer back'ards."

"Say, Hucky, when you going to try the cat?"

"Tonight. I reckon they'll come after old Hoss Williams tonight."

"But they buried him Saturday. Didn't they get him Saturday night?"

"Why, how you talk! How could their charms work till midnight?—and *then* its Sunday. Devils don't slosh around much of a Sunday, I don't reckon."

"I never thought of that. That's so. Lemme go with you?"

"Of course—if you ain't afeard."

"Afeard! 'Tain't likely. Will you meow?"

"Yes—and you meow back, if you get a chance. Last time, you kep' me a-meowing around till old Hays went to throwing rocks at me and says 'Dern that cat!' and so I hove a brick through his window—but don't you tell."

"I won't. I couldn't meow that night, becuz Auntie was watching me, but I'll meow this time. Say—what's that?"

"Nothing but a tick."

"Where'd you get him?"

"Out in the woods."

"What'll you take for him?"

"I don't know. I don't want to sell him."

"All right. It's a might small tick, anyway."

"Oh, anybody can run a tick down that don't belong to them. I'm satisfied with it. It's a good enough tick for me."

"Sho, there's ticks a-plenty. I could have a thousand of 'em if I wanted to."

"Well, why don't you? Becuz you know mighty well you can't. This is a pretty early tick, I reckon. It's the first one I've seen this year."

"Say, Huck—I'll give you my tooth for him."

"Less see it."

Tom got out a bit of paper and carefully unrolled it. Huckleberry viewed it wistfully. The temptation was very strong. At last he said:

"Is it genuwyne?"

Tom lifted his lip and showed the vacancy.

"Well, all right," said Huckleberry, "it's a trade."

Tom enclosed the tick in the percussion-cap box that had lately been the pinch-bug's prison, and the boys separated, each feeling wealthier than before.

When Tom reached the little isolated frame schoolhouse, he strode in briskly, with the manner of one who had come with all honest speed. He hung his hat on a peg and flung himself into his seat with businesslike alacrity. The master, throned on high in his great splint-bottom armchair, was dozing, lulled by the drowsy hum of study. The interruption roused him.

"Thomas Sawyer!"

Tom knew that when his name was pronounced in full, it meant trouble.

"Sir!"

"Come up here. Now, sir, why are you late again, as usual?"

Tom was about to take refuge in a lie, when he saw two long tails of yellow hair hanging down a back that he recognized by the electric sympathy of love; and by that form was *the only vacant place* on the girls' side of the schoolhouse. He instantly said:

"I STOPPED TO TALK WITH HUCKLEBERRY FINN!"

The master's pulse stood still, and he stared helplessly. The buzz of study ceased. The pupils wondered if this foolhardy boy had lost his mind. The master said:

"You—you did what?"

"Stopped to talk with Huckleberry Finn."

There was no mistaking the words.

"Thomas Sawyer, this is the most astounding confession I have ever listened to. No mere ferule will answer for this offense. Take off your jacket."

The master's arm performed until it was tired and the stock of switches notably diminished. Then the order followed:

"Now, sir, go and sit with the *girls*! And let this be a warning to you."

The titter that rippled around the room appeared to abash the boy, but in reality that result was caused rather more by his worshipful awe of his unknown idol and the dread pleasure that lay in his high good fortune. He sat down upon the end of the pine bench and the girl hitched herself away from him with a toss of her head. Nudges and winks and whispers traversed the room, but Tom sat still, with his arms upon the long, low desk before him, and seemed to study his book.

By and by attention ceased from him, and the accustomed school murmur rose upon the dull air once more. Presently the boy began to steal furtive glances at the girl. She observed it, "made a mouth" at him and gave him the back of her head for the space of a minute. When she cautiously faced around again, a peach lay before her. She thrust it away. Tom gently put it back. She thrust it away again, but with less animosity. Tom patiently returned it to its place. Then she let it remain. Tom scrawled on his slate, "Please take it —I got more." The girl glanced at the words, but made no sign. Now the boy began to draw something on the slate, hiding his work with his left hand. For a time the girl refused to notice; but her human curiosity presently began to manifest itself by hardly perceptible signs. The boy worked on, apparently unconscious. The girl made a sort of non-committal attempt to see it, but the boy did not betray that he was aware of it. At last she gave in and hesitatingly whispered:

"Let me see it."

Tom partly uncovered a dismal caricature of a house with two gable ends to it and a corkscrew of smoke issuing from the chimney. Then the girl's interest began to fasten itself upon the work and she forgot everything else. When it was finished, she gazed a moment, then whispered:

"It's nice—make a man."

The artist erected a man in the front yard, that resembled a derrick. He could have stepped over the house; but the girl was not hypercritical; she was satisfied with the monster, and whispered:

"It's a beautiful man—now make me coming along."

Tom drew an hour-glass with a full moon and straw limbs to it and armed the spreading fingers with a portentous fan. The girl said:

"It's ever so nice—I wish I could draw."

"It's easy," whispered Tom, "I'll learn you."

"Oh, will you? When?"

"At noon. Do you go home to dinner?"

"I'll stay if you will."

"Good—that's a whack. What's your name?"

"Becky Thatcher. What's yours? Oh, I know. It's Thomas Sawyer."

"That's the name they lick me by. I'm Tom when I'm good. You call me Tom, will you?"

"Yes."

Now Tom began to scrawl something on the slate, hiding the words from the girl. But she was not backward this time. She begged to see. Tom said:

"Oh, it ain't anything."

"Yes, it is."

"No, it ain't. You don't want to see."

"Yes, I do, indeed I do. Please let me."

"You'll tell."

"No, I won't—deed and deed and double deed I won't."

"You won't tell anybody at all? Ever, as long as you live?"

"No, I won't ever tell *any*body. Now let me."

"Oh, *you* don't want to see!"

"Now that you treat me so, I *will* see." And she put her small hand upon his and a little scuffle ensued, Tom pretending to resist in earnest, but letting his hand slip by degrees till these words were revealed: "*I love you.*"

"Oh, you bad thing!" And she hit his hand a smart rap, but reddened and looked pleased, nevertheless.

Just at this juncture the boy felt a slow, fateful grip closing on his ear, and a steady lifting impulse. In that vise he was borne across the house and deposited in his own seat, under a peppering fire of giggles from the whole school. Then the master stood over him during a few awful moments, and finally moved away to his throne without saying a word. But although Tom's ear tingled, his heart was jubilant.

As the school quieted down, Tom made an honest effort to study, but the turmoil within him was too great. In turn he took his place in the reading class and made a botch of it; then in the geography class and turned lakes into mountains, mountains into rivers, and rivers into continents, till chaos was come again; then in the spelling class, and got "turned down," by a succession of mere baby words, till he brought up at the foot and yielded up the pewter medal which he had worn with ostentation for months.

HENRY HUGGINS

Beverly Cleary

Henry Huggins is representative of the many children's books that lack well-developed characters and plots. Instead they rely on mildly humorous episodes that exaggerate incidents from daily life. Many are set in suburban America of the 1940s and show a way of life unknown to most contemporary children. These harmless but mediocre novels should not be an important part of a child's reading; they seem shallow and boring not only to most adults but also to those children able to read books that are better written.

Henry Huggins, the first book of a series, begins with Henry struggling to get home the skinny, lost dog he has found. Another chapter shows the problems caused when guppies multiply and multiply. One chapter is about a dog show. In the last chapter, Ribsy's original owner appears and Henry fears he will lose his dog. Although one chapter may seem amusing, the total effect is monotonous.

HENRY AND RIBS

Henry Huggins was in the third grade. His hair looked like a scrubbing brush and most of his grown-up front teeth were in. He lived with his mother and father in a square white house on Klickitat Street. Except for having his tonsils out when he was six and breaking his arm falling out of a cherry tree when he was seven, nothing much happened to Henry.

I wish something exciting would happen, Henry often thought.

But nothing very interesting ever happened to Henry, at least not until one Wednesday afternoon in March. Every Wednesday after school Henry rode downtown on the bus to go swimming at the Y.M.C.A. After he swam for an hour, he got on the bus again and rode home just in time for dinner. It was fun but not really exciting.

When Henry left the Y.M.C.A. on this particular Wednesday, he stopped to watch a man tear down a circus poster. Then, with three nickels and one dime in his pocket, he went to the corner drugstore to buy a chocolate ice cream cone, get on the bus, drop his dime in the slot, and ride home.

That is not what happened.

He bought the ice cream cone and paid for it with one of his nickels. On his way out of the drugstore he stopped to look at funny books. It was a free look, because he had only two nickels left.

He stood there licking his chocolate ice cream cone and reading one of the funny books when he heard a thump, thump, thump. Henry turned, and there behind him was a dog. The dog was scratching himself. He wasn't any special kind of

dog. He was too small to be a big dog but, on the other hand, he was much too big to be a little dog. He wasn't a white dog, because parts of him were brown and other parts were black and in between there were yellowish patches. His ears stood up and his tail was long and thin.

The dog was hungry. When Henry licked, he licked. When Henry swallowed, he swallowed.

"Hello, you old dog," Henry said. "You can't have my ice cream cone."

Swish, swish, swish went the tail. "Just one bite," the dog's brown eyes seemed to say.

"Go away," ordered Henry. He wasn't very firm about it. He patted the dog's head.

The tail wagged harder. Henry took one last lick. "Oh, all right," he said. "If you're that hungry, you might as well have it."

The ice cream cone disappeared in one gulp.

"Now go away," Henry told the dog. "I have to catch a bus for home."

He started for the door. The dog started, too.

"Go away, you skinny old dog." Henry didn't say it very loudly. "Go on home."

The dog sat down at Henry's feet. Henry looked at the dog and the dog looked at Henry.

"I don't think you've got a home. You're awful thin. Your ribs show right through your skin."

Thump, thump, thump replied the tail.

"And you haven't got a collar," said Henry.

He began to think. If only he could keep the dog! He had always wanted a dog of his very own and now he had found a dog that wanted him. He couldn't go home and leave a hungry dog on the street corner. If only he knew what his mother and father would say! He fingered the two nickels in his pocket. That was it! He would use one of the nickels to phone his mother.

"Come on, Ribsy. Come on, Ribs, old boy. I'm going to call you Ribsy because you're so thin."

The dog trotted after the boy to the telephone booth in the corner of the drugstore. Henry shoved him into the booth and shut the door. He had never used a pay telephone before. He had to put the telephone book on the floor and stand on tiptoe on it to reach the mouthpiece. He gave the operator his number and dropped his nickel into the coin box.

"Hello—Mom?"

"Why, Henry!" His mother sounded surprised. "Where are you?"

"At the drugstore near the Y."

Ribs began to scratch. Thump, thump, thump. Inside the telephone booth the thumps sounded loud and hollow.

"For goodness' sake, Henry, what's that noise?" his mother demanded. Ribs began to whimper and then to howl. "Henry," Mrs. Huggins shouted, "are you all right?"

"Yes, I'm all right," Henry shouted back. He never could understand why his mother always thought something had happened to him when nothing ever did. "That's just Ribsy."

"Ribsy?" His mother was exasperated. "Henry, will you please tell me what is going on?"

"I'm trying to," said Henry. Ribsy howled louder. People were gathering around the phone booth to see what was going on. "Mother, I've found a dog. I sure wish I could keep him. He's a good dog and I'd feed him and wash him and everything. Please, Mom."

"I don't know, dear," his mother said. "You'll have to ask your father."

"Mom!" Henry wailed. "That's what you always say!" Henry was tired of standing on tiptoe and the phone booth was getting warm. "Mom, please say yes and I'll never ask for another thing as long as I live!"

"Well, all right, Henry. I guess there isn't any reason why you shouldn't have a dog. But you'll have to bring him home on the bus. Your father has the car today and I can't come after you. Can you manage?"

"Sure! Easy."

"And Henry, please don't be late. It looks as if it might rain."

"All right, Mom." Thump, thump, thump.

"Henry, what's that thumping noise?"

"It's my dog, Ribsy. He's scratching a flea."

"Oh, Henry," Mrs. Huggins moaned.

"Couldn't you have found a dog without fleas?"

Henry thought that was a good time to hang up. "Come on, Ribs," he said. "We're going home on the bus."

When the big green bus stopped in front of the drugstore, Henry picked up his dog. Ribsy was heavier than he expected. He had a hard time getting him into the bus and was wondering how he would get a dime out of his pocket when the driver said, "Say, sonny, you can't take that dog on the bus."

"Why not?" asked Henry.

"It's a company rule, sonny. No dogs on buses."

"Golly, Mister, how'm I going to get him home? I just have to get him home."

"Sorry, sonny. I didn't make the rule. No animal can ride on a bus unless it's inside a box."

"Well, thanks anyway," said Henry doubtfully, and lifted Ribsy off the bus.

"Well, I guess we'll have to get a box. I'll get you onto the next bus somehow," promised Henry.

He went back into the drugstore followed closely by Ribsy. "Have you got a big box I could have, please?" he asked the man at the toothpaste counter. "I need one big enough for my dog."

The clerk leaned over the counter to look at Ribsy. "A cardboard box?" he asked.

"Yes, please," said Henry, wishing the man would hurry. He didn't want to be late getting home.

The clerk pulled a box out from under the counter. "This hair tonic carton is the only one I have. I guess it's big enough, but why anyone would want to put a dog in a cardboard box I can't understand."

The box was about two feet square and six inches deep. On one end was printed, "Don't Let Them Call You Baldy," and on the other, "Try Our Large Economy Size."

Henry thanked the clerk, carried the box out to the bus stop, and put it on the sidewalk. Ribsy padded after him. "Get in, fellow," Henry commanded. Ribsy understood. He stepped into the box and sat down just as the bus came around the corner. Henry had to kneel to pick up the box. It was not a very strong box and he had to put his arms under it. He staggered as he lifted it, feeling like the strong man who lifted weights at the circus. Ribsy lovingly licked the face with his wet pink tongue.

"Hey, cut that out!" Henry ordered. "You better be good if you're going to ride on the bus with me."

The bus stopped at the curb. When it was Henry's turn to get on, he had trouble finding the step because he couldn't see his feet. He had to try several times before he hit it. Then he discovered he had forgotten to take his dime out of his pocket. He was afraid to put the box down for fear Ribsy might escape.

He turned sideways to the driver and asked politely, "Will you please take the dime out of my pocket for me? My hands are full."

The driver pushed his cap back on his head and exclaimed, "Full! I should say they *are* full! And just where do you think you're going with that animal?"

"Home," said Henry in a small voice.

The passengers were staring and most of them were smiling. The box was getting heavier every minute.

"Not on this bus, you're not!" said the driver.

"But the man on the last bus said I could take the dog on the bus in a box," protested Henry, who was afraid he couldn't hold the dog much longer. "He said it was a company rule."

"He meant a big box tied shut. A box with holes punched in it for the dog to breathe through."

Henry was horrified to hear Ribsy growl. "Shut up," he ordered.

Ribsy began to scratch his left ear with his left hind foot. The box began to tear. Ribsy jumped out of the box and off the bus and Henry jumped after him. The bus pulled away with a puff of exhaust.

"Now see what you've done! You've spoiled everything." The dog hung his head and tucked his tail between his legs. "If I can't get you home, how can I keep you?"

Henry sat down on the curb to think. It was so late and the clouds were so dark that he didn't want to waste time looking for a big box. His mother was probably beginning to worry about him.

People were stopping on the corner to wait for the next bus. Among them Henry noticed an elderly lady carrying a large paper shopping bag full of apples. The shopping bag gave him an idea. Jumping up, he snapped his fingers at Ribs and ran back into the drugstore.

"You back again?" asked the toothpaste clerk. "What do you want this time? String and paper to wrap your dog in?"

"No, sir," said Henry. "I want one of those big nickel shopping bags." He laid his last nickel on the counter.

"Well, I'll be darned," said the clerk, and handed the bag across the counter.

Henry opened the bag and set it up on the floor. He picked up Ribsy and shoved him hind feet first into the bag. Then he pushed his front feet in. A lot of Ribsy was left over.

The clerk was leaning over the counter watching. "I guess I'll have to have some string and paper, too," Henry said, "if I can have some free."

"Well! Now I've seen everything." The clerk shook his head as he handed a piece of string and a big sheet of paper across the counter.

Ribsy whimpered, but he held still while Henry wrapped the paper loosely around his head and shoulders and tied it with the string. The dog made a lumpy package, but by taking one handle of the bag in each hand Henry was able to carry it to the bus stop. He didn't think the bus driver would notice him. It was getting dark and a crowd of people, most of them with packages, was waiting on the corner. A few spatters of rain hit the pavement.

This time Henry remembered his dime. Both hands were full, so he held the dime in his teeth and stood behind the woman with the bag of apples. Ribsy wiggled and whined, even though Henry tried to pet him through the paper. When the bus stopped, he climbed on behind the lady, quickly set the bag down, dropped his dime in the slot, picked up the bag, and squirmed through the crowd to a seat beside a fat man near the back of the bus.

"Whew!" Henry sighed with relief. The driver was the same one he had met on the first bus! But Ribs was on the bus at last. Now if he could only keep him quiet for fifteen minutes they would be home and Ribsy would be his for keeps.

The next time the bus stopped Henry saw Scooter McCarthy, a fifth grader at school, get on and make his way through the crowd to the back of the bus.

Just my luck, thought Henry. I'll bet he wants to know what's in my bag.

"Hi," said Scooter.

"Hi," said Henry.

"Whatcha got in that bag?" asked Scooter.

"None of your beeswax," answered Henry.

Scooter looked at Henry. Henry looked at Scooter. Crackle, crackle, crackle went the bag. Henry tried to hold it more tightly between his knees.

"There's something alive in that bag!" Scooter said accusingly.

"Shut up, Scooter!" whispered Henry.

"Aw, shut up yourself!" said Scooter. "You've got something alive in that bag!"

By this time the passengers at the back of the bus were staring at Henry and his package. Crackle, crackle, crackle. Henry tried to pat Ribsy again through the paper. The bag crackled even louder. Then it began to wiggle.

"Come on, tell us what's in the bag," coaxed the fat man.

"N-n-n-nothing," stammered Henry. "Just something I found."

"Maybe it's a rabbit," suggested one passenger. "I think it's kicking."

"No, it's too big for a rabbit," said another.

"I'll bet it's a baby," said Scooter. "I'll bet you kidnaped a baby!"

"I did not!"

Ribs began to whimper and then to howl. Crackle, crackle, crackle. Thump, thump, thump. Ribsy scratched his way out of the bag.

"Well, I'll be doggoned!" exclaimed the fat man and began to laugh. "I'll be doggoned!"

"It's just a skinny old dog," said Scooter.

"He is not! He's a good dog."

Henry tried to keep Ribsy between his knees. The bus lurched around a corner and started to go uphill. Henry was thrown against the fat man. The frightened dog wiggled away from him, squirmed between the passengers, and started for the front of the bus.

"Here, Ribsy, old boy! Come back here," called Henry and started after him.

"E-e-ek! A dog!" squealed the lady with the bag of apples. "Go away, doggie, go away!"

Ribsy was scared. He tried to run and crashed into the lady's bag of apples. The bag tipped over and the apples began to roll toward the back of the bus, which was grinding up a steep hill. The apples rolled around the feet of the people who were standing. Passengers began to slip and slide. They dropped their packages and grabbed one another.

Crash! A high-school girl dropped an armload of books.

Rattle! Bang! Crash! A lady dropped a big paper bag. The bag broke open and pots and pans rolled out.

Thud! A man dropped a coil of garden hose. The hose unrolled and the passengers found it wound around their legs.

People were sitting on the floor. They were sitting on books and apples. They were even sitting on other people's laps. Some of them had their hats over their faces and their feet in the air.

Skree-e-etch! The driver threw on the brakes and turned around in his seat just as Henry made his way through the apples and books and pans and hose to catch Ribsy.

The driver pushed his cap back on his head. "O.K., sonny," he said to Henry. "Now you know why dogs aren't allowed on buses!"

"Yes, sir," said Henry in a small voice. "I'm sorry."

"You're sorry! A lot of good that does. Look at this bus! Look at those people!"

"I didn't mean to make any trouble," said Henry. "My mother said I could keep the dog if I could bring him home on the bus."

The fat man began to snicker. Then he chuckled. Then he laughed and then he roared. He laughed until tears streamed down his cheeks and all the other passengers were laughing too, even the man with the hose and the lady with the apples.

The driver didn't laugh. "Take that dog and get off the bus!" he ordered. Ribsy whimpered and tucked his tail between his legs.

The fat man stopped laughing. "See here, driver," he said, "you can't put that boy and his dog off in the rain."

"Well, he can't stay on the bus," snapped the driver.

Henry didn't know what he was going to do. He guessed he'd have to walk the rest of the way home. He wasn't sure he knew the way in the dark.

Just then a siren screamed. It grew louder and louder until it stopped right alongside the bus.

A policeman appeared in the entrance. "Is there a boy called Henry Huggins on this bus?" he asked.

"Oh boy, you're going to be arrested for having a dog on the bus!" gloated Scooter. "I'll bet you have to go to jail!"

"I'm him," said Henry in a very small voice.

"I am he," corrected the lady with the apples, who had been a schoolteacher and couldn't help correcting boys.

"You'd better come along with us," said the policeman.

"Boy, you're sure going to get it!" said Scooter.

"Surely going to get it," corrected the apple lady.

Henry and Ribsy followed the policeman off the bus and into the squad car, where Henry and the dog sat in the back seat.

"Are you going to arrest me?" Henry asked timidly.

"Well, I don't know. Do you think you ought to be arrested?"

"No, sir," said Henry politely. He thought the policeman was joking, but he wasn't sure, it was hard to tell about grownups sometimes. "I didn't mean to do anything. I just had to get Ribsy home. My mother said I could keep him if I could bring him home on the bus."

"What do you think?" the officer asked his partner, who was driving the squad car.

"We-e-ell, I think we might let him off this time," answered the driver. "His mother must be pretty worried about him if she called the police, and I don't think she'd want him to go to jail."

"Yes, he's late for his dinner already. Let's see how fast we can get him home."

The driver pushed a button and the siren began to shriek. Ribsy raised his head and howled. The tires sucked at the wet pavement and the wind-shield wipers splip-splopped. Henry began to enjoy himself. Wouldn't this be something to tell the kids at school! Automobiles pulled over to the curb as the police car went faster and faster. Even the bus Henry had been on had to pull over and stop. Henry waved to the passengers. They waved back. Up the hill the police car sped and around the corner until they came to Klickitat Street and then to Henry's block and then pulled up in front of his house.

Henry's mother and father were standing on the porch waiting for him. The neighbors were looking out of their windows.

"Well!" said his father after the policeman had gone. "It's about time you came home. So this is Ribsy! I've heard about you, fellow, and there's a big bone and a can of Feeley's Flea Flakes waiting for you."

"Henry, what *will* you do next?" sighed his mother.

"Golly, Mom, I didn't do anything. I just brought my dog home on the bus like you said."

Ribsy sat down and began to scratch.

SKINNY

Robert Burch

Children need novels that deal with light subjects for humorous enjoyment but they also need those that deal realistically with childhood and adolescence and so provide insights into life.

The most significant aspect about Skinny is its honest ending. This well-written book shows that there are problems, for both children and adults, that cannot be solved—not even by main characters who try hard and deserve to win. Although the novel ends with failure, there is no sense of defeat. Skinny goes to the orphanage he has tried so hard to avoid, Miss Bessie loses the man she loves and the child she wants to adopt. And yet they know, and the reader knows, they will be together for vacations; they are a family regardless of the law's technicality that a single woman cannot adopt a child.

From this book young readers can learn a great deal about trying to make a dream become reality and about living with disappointment.

Skinny took the big bell from the dining room and went upstairs. He rang it as he walked along, calling, "Suppertime! Come to supper!" Downstairs he rang it as he passed the parlor, and the guests there began to rise. He opened the screen door that led to the front porch, clanged the bell once more, and announced loudly, "SUPPER'S SERVED!"

Two of the highway engineers and Miss Clydie Essex, the town's beauty-parlor operator, were seated at the end of the porch. Miss Clydie didn't board at the hotel but ate supper there one night a week when she kept evening hours at her shop. One of the men said to Skinny, "Were you talking to us or to somebody across the street?"

The other one asked, "What'd you say, anyhow?"

"I said, 'supper's served,'" Skinny explained. "It means supper's ready, that's all it means. I've heard tell that's the way they say it in city hotels."

The group walked across the porch. One man said, "In city hotels the dining room is open 'most all the time, and folks go in and out and order whatever they please."

Skinny sniffed. "Seems like a poor arrangement," he said, holding the door open for the trio to enter. "How do they know how many to fix for?"

Miss Clydie Essex said, "Pay him no mind, Skinny. I've been in some of those big hotels and the food's not near as good as it is here."

"Why, thank you, Miss Clydie," said Skinny. He started to bow to her as she walked inside, but one of the men gave a friendly poke at his stomach and he had to jump back.

After the blessing Roman passed hot biscuits

and brought out extra platters of food, and Skinny began asking guests what they would like to drink. "Buttermilk, sweet milk, or iced tea?" When he received orders for as many glasses as he could handle, he would go to the kitchen. When he came to the couple who had arrived that day, he asked, "Buttermilk, sweet milk, or iced tea?" and the woman answered, "Coffee."

"Oh, we don't have coffee in the summertime," Skinny said. "Most folks like something cold."

"Well, I don't."

"We have coffee for breakfast," Skinny said proudly. "Every morning we have it."

The woman said, "Well, I'd like some now."

Miss Bessie, who had been chatting with the people at her table, looked across and asked, "Is something wrong?"

Skinny said, "I was just explaining that we don't have coffee at night."

Miss Bessie smiled at the woman. "That's right," she said. Then she added, "Except when we have fish. I think fish calls for coffee, no matter how hot the weather gets."

A man sitting near her said that he thought so too, and Miss Bessie turned back to her table. A discussion was soon under way about all the fish caught recently at Shallow Creek by local men.

Skinny stood very straight, holding his shoulders back so far that his white coat almost fell off. He said to the woman who was displeased about the choice of drinks, "Buttermilk, sweet milk, or iced tea?"

"Water," the woman answered, and Skinny quickly brought her a large glass of it filled with chunks of ice.

When supper was over he hurried along with his chores. "Ain't the knives and forks scrubbed yet?" he asked, agitating for Peachy to get on with the dishwashing. "How can I set the tables for tomorrow without knives and forks?" Most nights he wasn't in a rush to be finished with the after-supper chores. But most nights he wasn't going to a watermelon-cutting afterward.

Peachy sighed. "It's too hot a night to rush, child."

Roman, who was stacking away clean saucers, said, "Ain't no hotter than it was during your Revival Week." He was reminding her that the dishwashing was not likely to be as drawn-out when she was in a hurry to get away.

"One of these times you're gonna say the wrong thing," said Peachy, lowering her voice. "And I'll take this butcher knife and you'll wish you were back in the chain gang."

Roman and Skinny laughed. Miss Bessie, at the icebox rearranging shelves, asked, "What's so funny?"—but nobody could remember.

At last the dishwashing picked up to almost Revival Week speed, and the work was soon finished. Peachy took off her apron and went home; Roman went to the back porch, saying he would stay awake and listen out for guests who might need anything; and Miss Bessie and Skinny walked across town to the watermelon-cutting.

At the entrance to the long walkway in front of the Baptist church, they paid their admission fee to Mrs. Spunky Edison. She put the money into a cigar box she held in her lap. Miss Bessie looked toward the people gathered farther up the walk and in the pine grove to one side of it. "Seems like a good turnout," she said.

"All the Baptists," replied Mrs. Edison, "and half the Methodists."

Miss Trudy Boylan, who was assisting in taking up the money, added, "And we expect the other half of them when their choir practice lets out."

Skinny and Miss Bessie went on up the walk. "Reckon they planned for this big a crowd?" asked Skinny, sounding worried. "What if they run out of watermelons?"

Miss Bessie assured him there would be plenty. On a hot summer night, with nothing else going on in the community except the choir practice at the church across town, the Baptists naturally expected a lot of people.

"I hope so," Skinny said, "because my system sure is craving watermelon."

"I think it would be all right if you just said you were hungry for watermelon," suggested Miss Bessie.

"That's a good idea," Skinny agreed as they reached the edge of the crowd. "Goodness me!" he said. "It's as light as day out here." And he stopped to admire the extension lights that were swung from branches of the trees.

Miss Bessie told him to walk around and have himself a good time; she said she believed she would go over and visit with the ladies.

Mr. Barton Grice, the superintendent of the Sunday school, saw Skinny and asked if he wouldn't like to go across the yard and join in the games.

"No, sir," said Skinny, "I don't care too much for games."

Mr. Grice smiled. "All the children are there. Wouldn't you like to play with them?"

"No, sir," said Skinny. "I don't care too much for children." He didn't explain that he had never known other children very well and had seldom played with them.

A moment later one of the teachers he knew from Sunday school came over. "Come on, Skinny," she said. "Join in the fun."

"Thank you," said Skinny, "but I think I'll just stand around."

"Of course you won't," said the woman good-naturedly. She put her hand on his neck and urged him forward to where the children were playing.

He recognized members of his Sunday-school class and soon was enjoying the game. It was "'Tis but a Simpleton," and he was first to figure it out. He guessed right off what was required in order not to be a simpleton.

Next a game of "Cross Questions and Crooked Answers" got under way. One of the teachers from the Junior Department handed out questions on slips of paper to all the boys, and the girls were given answers. The boys stood on one side and the girls on the other.

The player at the head of each line stepped to the center, and the game began. The boy's question was: "Who was the first President of the United States?" The girl read her answer, which turned out to be: "I prefer pumpkin pie." They went through it three times. The boy remained solemn, but the girl giggled, so they both had to go to the ends of their lines.

The next question read was: "Shall I sing you a song?" and the answer was: "Underneath a washpot." Everybody laughed, including the two who were having their turn. They were sent to the ends of the lines, and the game continued.

Skinny was having a good time, and it would soon be his turn in the center. Then he realized that there he was, with his slip of paper—and not able to read what was on it. He thought of asking somebody to tell him what it said. But after he had won the last game himself, and everybody had said how smart he was to figure it out, this was no time to admit a weakness—even something as unimportant as not knowing how to read.

He kept his place in line and, when his turn came, stepped to the center to meet the girl across from him. He looked down at the paper and, pretending to read, said, "Who was the *second* President of the United States?"

The girl snickered. Skinny wondered if it had been a mistake for him to make up a question. The girl then began to giggle hysterically.

The teacher said, "Why, Cloris, you laughed before you even read your answer. Scoot to the end of the line." Then she added, "But I don't think it was quite fair to Skinny. Shouldn't he have another chance?"

The players agreed, and the woman handed him a piece of paper. "Here's another question," she said.

"Thank you," said Skinny, smiling as he accepted it.

"Now just stay in the center," continued the woman. "And, let's see, it's Lora's turn from the girls' side."

At that a pretty thin-faced girl came forward, and everyone waited quietly for Skinny to read the question. Suddenly his face turned red and beads of perspiration appeared at the top of his forehead. He clenched his fists and cleared his throat but said nothing.

The teacher asked, "Is something wrong?"

"No, ma'am," said Skinny. He hesitated. "It's just that—I mean—" And then his eyes brightened and he pointed toward the walkline. "There's a boy over yonder who got here late," he said. "I don't feel right about reading so many questions when he hasn't had a one." He called out, "Howdy, over there! You can take my place if you want to."

The boy quickly accepted, asking as he took the question, "Are you tired of playing?"

"Yes," said Skinny, walking away, "I'd rather stand around." He went near a gathering of grown people and stood by himself.

Mr. Grice walked across to him. "You look worried, young man. What's on your mind?"

Skinny didn't like to talk about not knowing how to read and write. "I was just thinking," he said. "I mean I was sort of concerned about where the watermelons are. I don't see any here."

"Oh," said Mr. Grice, "they're at the icehouse—a truckload of 'em. They'll be brought over now directly."

Before Skinny could reply, Mr. Murray Huff came to speak to them. He owned the land where Skinny and his father had been sharecroppers until the old man died. "Well, Skinny-boy!" said Mr. Huff, sort of half chuckling, "with your face washed and clean clothes on I almost didn't know you. You're looking better."

"Yes, sir," said Skinny. "I think I do very well."

The men laughed, and Mr. Huff said, "I was out at the old place today."

"Who lives there now?" Skinny asked.

"Nobody. I can't find anybody worth a cuss, so I'm gonna store corn in the house. That's about all it's fit for."

"Why, it's a fine place," said Skinny, shocked to hear such a comment about the house that had been his home until two months ago. Then he smiled, as a thought occurred to him. "I'll make a crop for you," he said.

Mr. Huff laughed, but Skinny continued, "I could do it. I ain't awful big, but I'm strong." He rushed on as if he were sure the plan would work out if he put it in words soon enough. "If you'd just get me up a mule and stake me to a few supplies, you'd be plumb surprised at what all I can do."

When he stopped, Mr. Huff laughed more and didn't even comment on the idea. Instead he asked, "Remember that little rat-terrier-looking dog you used to have?"

"Sure," said Skinny. "That was R.F.D."

This time it was Mr. Grice who laughed. "How'd a dog get a name like that?"

"On account of the mailman gave him to me. R.F.D. stands for Rural Free Delivery. Did you know that?"

"I'd heard it," said Mr. Grice, and Skinny continued, "Pa wasn't feeling well one night and ran him off. Threw rocks at that poor dog and chased him into the woods. I tried to find him but couldn't."

"Your pa was a mite cantankerous at times," said Mr. Huff, "especially when he was drunked-up."

"No, sir," said Skinny, "he wasn't cantankerous. He just didn't feel well sometimes. But I genuinely hated for him to chase off R.F.D."

"Well," said Mr. Huff, "what I set out to tell you was that the dog has turned up again. He was sitting on the back steps when I drove up today. I didn't throw a rock at him, but he lit out for the woods so fast you'd have thought I did."

"What?" Skinny said. "He's back? I always figured Pa hurt him worse than he meant to and drove him to take up with somebody else."

"He better take up with somebody else," said Mr. Huff, "'cause there sho ain't nobody out there now."

"No, sir," agreed Skinny, "there sho ain't. And I'm obliged to you for telling me you saw him." He started away from the two men then but, instead of going toward the crowd, turned and walked in the opposite direction.

At the end of the walkway Mrs. Edison was collecting admission money from latecomers. She noticed Skinny and asked, "Aren't you staying for the cutting?"

"No, ma'am," answered Skinny, heading into the dark. "I don't crave watermelon as much as I thought I did."

THE LONER

Ester Wier

Ester Wier's sophisticated style evokes the boy's desperation and lostness. She is especially good at description, showing the woman, the dog, and the land without halting the story. The reader learns a great deal about the boy and Boss with no sense of being told. Character, scene, plot, and theme are all effectively intertwined in this well-written book about the need to belong and the demands of responsibility.

The boy has no parents, cannot really remember having had parents, and has survived only because other migrant workers have allowed him to travel with them in exchange for his wages. He accepts this, knowing no other relationships. Only one person, a girl his age named Raidy, has ever cared about him. She is the only one who is bothered that he has no name and decides to choose one for him. Before she can tell him her choice, she is caught in a picking machine and killed. After this the boy withdraws from people even more. Becoming ill, he is left behind. After he recovers he struggles to follow the crops but loses his way in the Idaho sheep country.

The boy stood in the middle of the road, gazing up at the wedge of wild geese high in the sky above him. Their noisy honking broke the immense quiet that lay like a blanket, spread from the mountains beyond to the endless plains far below. He turned slowly, watching the birds disappear to the south, thinking how Raidy would

Chapter 2, pp. 15–28, from *The Loner* by Ester Wier. Copyright © 1963 by Ester Wier. Reprinted by permission of David McKay Company, Inc.

have liked seeing them. She would have made up something about them, like saying they were an Indian arrowhead flung across the sky by some unseen arm behind the mountains.

He shook his head dully, pushing Raidy out of his mind, and looked down at his feet. There was little left of the sneakers now, only the ragged canvas around his ankles, the raveled strings which held them on, and what had not been gouged from the soles on the long walk from the highway many miles behind him now.

A late afternoon wind was rising, biting into his legs through the threadbare dungarees and into his body under the worn flannel shirt. The crack in his lower lip opened again and his tongue, touching it, tasted blood. He put a chapped hand against his lip and pressed hard. Every inch of his body ached, ached with weariness and hunger and the terrible emptiness of losing Raidy.

Beyond him the road climbed another hill and upon the crest spruce trees bent in the wind and shadows spread like dark water seeping from the mountainside. The ruffled edges of the clouds had turned gold and for a moment it seemed that the whole world had become golden, the dried slopes about him reflecting the coming sunset. He was used to being out of doors at all hours but he had never seen anything like this and he stood, swaying wearily, caught by its splendor. In the distance, off to his right, a herd of deer driven from the higher ridges by the first signs of winter, moved slowly across the bronze grass. Except for birds, they were the first signs of life he had seen in days of struggling through this country, and suddenly the enormity of the space around him and the loneliness of its silence became more than he could stand and he found himself running toward the animals, leaving the road and scrambling over sun-scorched pasture land in a fury of haste.

"Wait!" he called, fighting through bushes and over hillocks. "Wait!" he shouted foolishly with all his strength, his voice carrying through the thin air. The deer poised for a moment and faded into the landscape. He watched them go, still calling frantically and running toward them. They were alive and at this moment he needed to be near something living, something besides endless stretches of hills and plains.

When he realized they were gone, his breath began to come in long shaking sobs. The reserve strength he had called on in trying to reach them left him and he fell headlong on the earth beside a cluster of pale-gold serviceberry bushes. The impact knocked the air out of him and he lay without moving, his tear-streaked face pressed into the rough dry grass.

A Montana mountain rat, busy on an errand of nest making, paused and sat on her haunches looking at him before scurrying on across the fields, and a flock of crows flew above him, seeking their roost for the night.

Finally the boy tried to raise his body, his shaggy brown hair falling over his eyes. He couldn't go any farther. He was through, finished, beaten. How long had it been since he left potato fields and started off on his own across this unfamiliar country? How many rides had he hitched on the highway? Which way was he headed now? How many meals had he made on berries and raw potatoes he carried in his pockets? He didn't know. He didn't care. Nothing mattered now.

He lay quietly until the sobs began again, deep and racking. Above him the sky turned from gold to dark blue and the clouds drifted to the south. He burrowed deeper into the earth, rolling his body into a ball against the bushes, the weariness spreading through him like a soothing syrup. He cried himself out and slowly his hands relaxed and his eyes closed. Like a small animal seeking the warmth of the earth, he pressed his face against the grass and slept.

The woman, waiting on the rise of the hill, stood six-foot-two in her boots. They were sturdy leather boots, laced to the knee. Above them she wore wool trousers and a heavy wool-lined jacket. On her head was a man's old felt hat, pulled down to cover her ears and the gray hair cut short all over her head. From a distance it would have been hard to tell she was a woman, for her body was powerful and she stood with the grace of an athlete, relaxed yet disciplined. She lifted a hand and called, "Come!" and the dog, below the hill beside some serviceberry bushes, raised his head and looked at her. The rough coat of the collie was black with white markings on the chest, the neck, the legs and the feet. He stood thirty inches at the shoulder and his weight was nearly eighty pounds. The bigness of his mistress would have dwarfed most dogs, but not Jupiter. He came from a line of the finest sheep dogs of northern Scotland and it showed in his deep chest, his remarkable height, his proud balance of body.

He looked at the woman and took a few steps toward her, then flung his head high and growled low in his throat. He retraced his steps to the bushes and looked at her again. Barking for a sheep dog was always the last resort in an emergency and one sure to excite the sheep, so he held his voice deep in his throat and the sound carried no farther than to the woman on the hill.

"What is it, Jup?" she asked, watching him. "If I walk down there and find it's only a rabbit, I'll skin you alive."

The dog, hearing her voice, started toward her again, then stopped and flung his head high.

"All right, all right," she said, "I'm coming."

He met her halfway and led her back to the bushes where the boy lay. There was no surprise on the woman's face. She had lived too long in this vast and unpredictable land to question what happened here. Although her son's death two years before had shaken the very foundations on which her life was built, she still held to her belief in a wisdom greater than man's. "God moves in a mysterious way His wonders to perform," she marveled now. How else had the boy been led here, a stone's throw from the only human being within miles?

"Well," she said at last, "if it were a sheep and as scrawny as this, I'd say it was hardly worth the finding. How do you suppose he got here, Jup? Where does he belong? Hardly enough clothes or flesh on him to cover his bones. You found a real stray this time."

The wind from the mountains carried the icy threat of snows soon to come. The sunset was over and night blue had spread across the sky. The first stars appeared and the chill turned to raw cold.

"Back to the sheep, Jup," the woman said. "I'll handle this." The collie hesitated for a moment in leavetaking, then sped off toward the bed-ground, the white tip of his tail moving through the fast-falling darkness.

The woman bent over the sleeping boy. Traces of tears were on his face, streaks through the dust and dirt. His thin body was curled against the cold, and the straight brown hair hung ragged against his neck. "What a miserable little critter," she said softly. "I won't let a sheep get into such a wretched condition." She studied for a while how to move him, and decided against awakening him. Carefully she placed an arm underneath and slowly raised him so that he lay against her, reminding her of stray lambs she had so often carried back to the fold. He stirred, a long convulsive shudder running through his body, then lay quietly in her arms.

She carried him up the hill and across the hundred yards to the sheep wagon. Jup was waiting for her, his head turned toward her yet his senses alert for any movement among the sheep on the bed-ground. They lay, over 900 of them, close together on a slanting rise beside the wagon. Around the bed-ground, several feet apart, stood the flags to scare off marauding animals.

The other dog, Juno, sniffed daintily, her nose pointed up at the boy. Her rough white coat moved in the wind and her dark mahogany-colored ears stood three-quarters erect, with the ends tipping forward.

"It's all right," the woman assured her. "Now you two get back to your posts and keep a sharp lookout for coyotes. If they get a sheep tonight, I'll skin you both alive." Jup whined softly and moved toward the sheep, Juno following a parallel course on the opposite side of the flock.

Smoke curled from the stovepipe atop the sheep wagon, drifting south with the wind. The woman mounted the steps to the door, pulling it open carefully so as not to disturb the boy. Once in, she shut it behind her and looked about. The benches on either side of the long narrow room were hard and bare, so she carried the boy to the end where her bed was built crosswise into the wagon. She pushed aside the soogan, the heavy square comforter, and laid him on top of the blankets. The room was warm and the boy sighed as he turned over and adjusted himself to the softness.

The woman took off her heavy coat and old felt hat, and went to the kerosene stove which stood to the right of the door. Taking a kettle, she poured water into it from a bucket, salted it, and set it on the flame. She seemed to fill the end of the wagon, her head clearing the ceiling by only a few inches. While the water came to a boil, she raised a trapdoor in the long bench on the left and pulled out two wool sacks stuffed with straw, two blankets, and another soogan. She made up a bed quickly on the bench, then returned to the stove and poured cornmeal into the boiling water. When the mush was ready she put it into a bowl and punctured a can of milk. She looked at the sugar and hesitated. She didn't hold with spoiling children with sweets. Even her own son had never been allowed sugar on his mush. Life was a hard business and indulgences led only to softness, and softness to weakness. She didn't believe in weakness. She left the bowl on the stove to keep warm and went back to the bed where the boy lay.

"Come," she said, rousing him. The boy's eyes flew open and he lay staring up at her. Confusion was on his face and a wary look about his eyes. "Here's some food," she said, "You look as if you could stand it." She went back to the stove and picked up the bowl.

The boy sat up and backed into a corner of the bed. He looked around the strange room and then up at the woman again. "Who're you?" he asked.

The woman handed him the bowl and poured milk on the mush. "Eat," she said. "I'll talk while you fill your stomach." She wanted to wash his hands and face before he ate but she knew at the moment his need was more for nourishment than for cleanliness.

"Eat!" she said again. The boy stared at her, then dropped his eyes to the bowl. Picking up the spoon, he began to eat, placing the hot mush in his mouth and swallowing hungrily.

"Take it slow," she said. "There's more if you want it." She sat on the bench and leaned forward. "My dog found you a while ago, and I carried you here and put you to bed. I figured you must be hungry so I fixed you something to eat. And I wanted you to know where you were so that when you woke up in the morning you wouldn't be scared to find yourself here."

The boy listened as he ate. "Who're you?" he asked again.

"You can call me Boss, I guess. It's been years since anyone called me anything else. I've got a flock of sheep outside and this is my wagon, and it's resting on the winter range."

The boy finished the mush and raising the bowl to his mouth licked it clean. The woman refilled it for him.

"Now, suppose you tell me what to call you," she said.

The boy looked at her silently for a long time. Distrust and caution played over his face and Boss had the notion that if he could squirm out of the corner and past her, he would make a dash for the door.

"This ain't a home for children?" he asked.

Boss laughed. "It's a home for me, that's what it is. Now, what's your name?"

The boy's eyes narrowed. "Boy," he said. "That's what folks call me, unless they're mad at me."

The woman knew she had been right about his being a stray. He was underfed, uncared for, and didn't even have a name. Right now he looked like a hunted animal, a lonely animal fighting for its life in a world where nobody care about it. It made her mad all over.

"All right," she said, "I'll call you Boy for now," She knew there was no use asking him questions. Let him settle down and relax first. There would be time enough to find out where he belonged and decide what to do with him later.

She took the bowl back to the stove and filled a pan with water from the kettle. In a corner of the dish cupboard beside the stove she found a towel. She got some soap and carried it all back to him.

"Wet a corner of the towel and wash your face. Then scrub your hands," she said. "And use the soap! I'll find something for you to sleep in."

The boy looked at the water and soap. "Is it Saturday?" he asked. In the crop-pickers' camps no one ever bathed except on Saturday evening.

"No, it isn't Saturday but I want you clean because I'm letting you sleep in my bed tonight. I won't have it messed up with a lot of dirt. Now, get to washing!"

She turned her back on him, lifted the bed she had made to get to the trapdoor of the bench again. When she found the garment she wanted, she came back to him and dropped it on the bed. He had rubbed the wet towel across his face, leaving his neck and ears grimy with dirt. She saw that the palms of his hands were heavily calloused, as though they had blistered and healed again and again, forming heavy pads of thickened skin. "Wipe your hands and get into this shirt."

The boy picked up the nightshirt in surprise. "Take off my clothes? Why?"

"So you'll sleep better," she answered. "Take off everything and put it on. I won't watch you."

She took the pan to the door, opened it, and flung the water out upon the ground. Then she refilled the pan and washed the bowl and spoon he had used. "All right to look now?"

The answer was muffled and she turned to see him struggling into the flannel shirt, his head coming slowly through the open neck.

"It's big," he said. "Is it yours?"

She shook her head. "Belonged to old Bezeleel who used to live here. I found it when I moved in. It's clean."

He pulled the nightshirt around him. "Take off your shoes," she said, "and don't ask me why again." He did as he was told.

"Where you sleeping?" he asked.

She pointed to the wool sacks on the bench. "I'll sleep here tonight, soon as I get my boots off."

"You going to wash and take off your clothes too?"

"I've already washed. I do that as soon as I come in from the range and get the sheep settled. And I don't undress because a good herder never takes his clothes off at night. He sleeps with one ear on the sheep and the other on the dogs, and never knows from one minute to the next when he'll have to get out there and scare off a coyote or two."

"That why Beze—the other sheepherder ain't here no more? Cause he took off his clothes and used this nightshirt?"

Boss laughed. He was quick all right . . . "No, that's not why." She stood up and straightened her bed.

"You'd be a good crop-picker," the boy said, studying her. "You're bigger than most men and

you could lift a sack of potatoes easy, or even a full hamper of beans."

The woman knew he had paid her a compliment. So that's where he had come from, she thought. Probably from the potatoe fields in Idaho. But why is he here and who does he belong to?

She raised the blankets on his bed and told him to crawl under. "It's going to be cold when I turn off the stove, so dig down deep and keep the potatoes warm." She picked up a sack of potatoes and put them under the covers beside him. "When you sleep in his bed, that chore goes with it."

He looked at her as though she were crazy. "Sleep with potatoes? Why?"

"So they won't freeze. Now, no more questions. I'll leave the stove on in the morning when I start out. And the window over your bed cracked just enough to give you some air. I'll leave biscuits on the stove and a pot of beans, and the rest of the canned milk. Sleep all you can and I'll see you when I get home at sundown. Don't go outside in those thin clothes."

"Where you going?"

"Out with the sheep. They're ready to leave the bedground at sunup and they'll graze a few miles from here tomorrow. Now, no more questions. Go to sleep."

She turned off the lamp and lay down on the straw-filled wool sacks, drawing the blankets and soogan over her. She listened for the dogs but heard nothing. Not a sound came from the sheep. The wind was dying down and she thought gratefully that perhaps tonight she would be able to sleep straight through. Jup or Juno would warn her if the coyotes came near, or if the sheep became restless and decided to look for higher ground, or if the lead sheep felt she hadn't had enough grass and set off to find more, with the rest of the flock following her.

She would think what to do with the boy tomorrow while she was out on the range. Right now she was tired and sunup was too few hours away.

FALSE START

Gil Rabin

The Puritans viewed childhood as a time of danger, when the soul was especially vulnerable to the devil's temptations, but that attitude was left behind in the last century. Many writers of this century have viewed childhood as a time of innocence, untroubled by important problems. This attitude underlies books like Henry Huggins. *Adults may enjoy such a view of childhood, but few children accept it as accurate.*

In the last decade more writers of juvenile fiction have been dealing with the realities of childhood, recognizing that many children suffer defeat, face serious problems, are confused, unhappy, or angry. The following selection is in direct contrast to Henry Huggins.

The emotions children feel when rejected by a parent are powerfully presented in this book. Richard's father cannot love. He is so defeated by his own sad childhood that he seldom responds warmly to his wife and son whose lives are filled with insecurity and anger. While Richard's hatred for his father seems justified to the reader, False Start *is not about hate but about* rachmones, *a Yiddish word for pity and compassion.*

This book will not be a classic, but it is an interesting example of the new honesty in children's literature. In an increasingly tense and insecure world, books like False Start *can bring understanding to many young readers, for very few children today live in worlds untouched by tension, hatred, and inconsistency.*

I ran up the steps three at a time; it was just perfect for my stride. Then the sole of my shoe flapped, and I missed a step. I banged my head right on the edge of the top step. For a minute I couldn't even move. I felt my head; a bump was beginning to stick out on the middle of my forehead.

Mom doesn't say anything stupid when something happens. She just goes ahead and does what has to be done no matter how much it hurts.

She took a knife and pressed it flat against the bruise. "Hold still! Where'd you hit your head?"

"On one of the steps. I was running up and my shoe got caught. It's torn. Take it eea-sy. It

feels like my whole head is going to crack wide open."

"It wasn't smart to run up the steps with a torn shoe."

"I know. Anyway I know now."

"And of course you won't do it again?"

"Mom? Are you trying to take my mind off what you're doing?"

"Only partly. I'm trying to take my mind off it. This thing's as big as a hen's egg. Please, Richard! Hold still. I must get the swelling down. Do you feel all right otherwise? Not dizzy or anything?"

"I feel funny."

"I'm not surprised. You look funny too. Put your sneakers on. We'll go see Mr. Spanier."

Mr. Spanier said, "You did the right thing, Mrs. Gould. A doctor couldn't have done more.

He'll be better in the morning. I'll give you some powders for the headache he's going to have. Give him one and get him to bed right away."

"Thank you," Mom said. "Come, Rich."

"I don't like those headache powders. They taste like . . . like . . ."

"I know," Mom said for me. "They taste ech-y. Do you like a headache better?" Mr. Spanier dug his hand into the jar and held out his fist.

"Red," I guessed.

He peeked at it. "Red it is," he said, and gave me the sourball. He's been doing that since I was a little kid.

"It's amazing how he always gets it right," Mom said.

Mr. Spanier shrugged. "Someday I'll get some green ones too, and then we'll see. Maybe you ought to take a headache powder too, Mrs. Gould. You look a little pale yourself."

"I'll be all right, Mr. Spanier. How much is that?"

"For the advice, nothing. Who knows if it's worth anything? For the sourball? Nobody has money for things like that anymore. The next time you really need something, I'll make up for it. Don't you worry, Mrs. Gould. Now go, take the boy home."

Pop said, "What happened to him?"

"He fell," Mom told him.

"That's because he's cock-eyed. He broke his glasses, didn't he? That's all I got to do is buy him new glasses every time."

"Don't raise your voice, Carl. All the neighbors will hear you. He fell because his shoes are torn. Because I didn't have money to fix them. That's why he fell. That's the only reason."

That was the first I knew I'd broken my glasses. I guess I'd been too upset to notice.

"I don't have any money," Pop said, glaring at Mom. "Where am I supposed to get money? I haven't worked for weeks."

"You have money for other things, Carl."

"What's that supposed to mean?" Pop yelled.

"Whatever you want it to mean."

"I know what you're getting at. I hear about it from you often enough, don't I? I come home and that's all you got to say. I'm sick and tired of it, you hear? So I take a drink once in a while. I

got a lot on my mind. Why don't you take that kid and get out of here if you don't like it?"

"You don't know what you're saying," Mom said.

"You don't want to go? All right. You stay. I'm going!" He slammed the door so hard it bounced.

"Do you think he'll come back?" I said.

"Of course he'll come back. Doesn't he always?"

"How would it be if he didn't?"

"We'd miss him."

"I don't mean that. I mean would we be all right?"

"Of course we would. We'd manage. But don't you worry. Your father will come back."

It was on the tip of my tongue to tell Mom that I didn't want him to come back, that I'd be the happiest person in the whole world if he didn't, even though I'd be a little bit scared. But I wouldn't be as scared without him as I was with him. If Mom said it first, I could tell her how I felt. But only if she said it first.

I tried to remember if Pop had always acted this way or if there had been a time when he didn't come home drunk and holler and scream and act like he was going to hit us.

"Was he ever . . . different?" I said.

Mom was taking down her hair, and she had a mouthful of hairpins. She took them out slowly, as if she was thinking about what I'd said. "He would drink once in a while, not every day the way he does now. He never got really drunk. I thought he would stop after we were married. And he had a steady job. I don't know, Richard. I don't know if he was different or if I was different. Or maybe if things were just different. Anyhow, it's not the drink. A lot of people drink and they're all right. But your father shouldn't!"

I tried to touch the knob on my head, but it was too tender. I sat up in the bathroom, reading until Mom got suspicious and chased me out. "For you the three R's are reading, running, and wrecking glasses," Mom said. "Go to bed!"

Mom thinks wrecking begins with r. It's hard to believe, but Mom can't read. Not even her name. She told me once how it was in Europe when she was little. There was just her and her brother and my grandfather and grandmother.

They lived in this little town, and every once in a while the soldiers would come riding in on their horses and kill some Jews. They killed my grandfather and Mom's brother when Mom was just a little girl, not even as old as I am now, so Mom had to help out in the house while my grandmother kept the farm going so they could eat. Mom couldn't go to school, not even for one day in her whole life. When she came to this country after her mother died, she was still just a kid. She lived with her uncle, but she had to go to work and help support herself and her uncle's family. Then she got married, and she had me.

Most of the time it didn't matter particularly. But once when my teacher gave her a letter to read, I was so ashamed I wanted to die right on the spot. Then I was even more ashamed that I had been ashamed, knowing why it was that Mom had never learned to read and write.

Mom had fiddled around in her pocketbook. "I left my glasses at home," Mom said. "I'll take the letter, and I'll read it at home. Richard can bring it to school tomorrow."

I looked at Mom. She kind of pursed her lips to show me she knew she was doing something wrong. But I didn't care. I was glad! That teacher would have thought there was something wrong with Mom if she knew she couldn't read. Mom could learn quicker than anybody if she had the chance.

Pop could read a little and write his name, but not much more. He had gone to school at night for about a year right after he came here. He did it so he could become a citizen. One time he said to me, "If I had your education, I could read blueprints. I'd have been a foreman long ago."

I didn't say anything. But I didn't believe him. I bet a foreman had to know more than just how to read blueprints. If he acted with the men the same way he did with Mom and me—fighting with them and calling them names—he would never be foreman. He just didn't act like somebody who could be a foreman.

I was half asleep when I heard somebody knock on the door. I pulled up the covers and turned my back so Pop would think I was sleeping.

Mom whispered, "Carl? Is that you?"

I couldn't hear too clearly, but I could tell it wasn't Pop's voice. Then I remembered the man who came to the house earlier, and I thought maybe it was him.

Mom said, "Jack?" like she wasn't sure.

"Open up, Amy," Cousin Jack said. "I have a friend with me."

"Wait just a minute," Mom said.

"You don't have to put up your hair for my friend," Jack said. How did he know that's what Mom was doing?

Mom opened the door, and then she laughed when she saw what was in the hall. A big ball of black fur almost knocked her down and skidded across the floor and crashed into the kitchen table. I was out of bed and into that furry thing before I knew what I was doing. I grabbed the wrong end first. Then I found his head and I wrestled with him and he licked my face with his big tongue. I wondered if Jack had brought him for me. But I was afraid to even think it; I might jinx it if he was going to do it.

"Say hello to Cousin Jack," Mom said.

"Who needs me," Jack said, "with Snowflake here? What a stringbean Rich is now! Look at him. Tall and skinny like a deer."

"He runs like he is an animal," Mom said. "You should see him. All the kids in the neighborhood come to watch him race. Some of the men even bet money."

Mom had never said anything before about my running. I never thought she paid any attention to it.

"You must be hungry, Jack. When was the last time you ate?" Mom said.

"When was the last time I was here?" Jack said.

"I wish I could believe that," Mom said. "You probably go to the best restaurants. Sit down. I've got some herring. And I'll scramble some eggs. It won't take but a minute."

"Don't rush, Amy. I've waited almost a year; I can wait for a few more minutes."

Mom broke the eggs with no fooling around: One crack each and they were in the bowl. I got back in bed and called Snowflake. He came over and put his head down next to me like he'd been doing it all his life. Every once in a while he stuck out his tongue and licked my face again.

"Where's Carl?" Jack said.

"He had to go out to see somebody," Mom

said. But she didn't look at Jack when she said it.

"No change?" Jack said.

Now Mom looked right at him. "No. No change."

"What's eating him?"

Mom put the plate down in front of Jack. "He's terribly . . . unhappy. Being a husband and a father doesn't seem to come naturally to him. Maybe because he never had any kind of home life himself. He doesn't remember much about his father, and you know what his mother was. I don't know, Jack. You ask me, and I don't know how to answer. He can't find work regularly. You know how it is being a bricklayer. When the job is done he has to wait, sometimes for months, before he can get another one. But not all brick-layers are as angry as he is. And they don't all drink the way he does. Everybody has it hard today. But everybody doesn't act the way he does. Nothing satisfies him; nothing gives him joy. It's like he's still a little boy, hurt and angry that his mother ran off and left him and his sister. And he's mad because his father died. Maybe if he had had either a father or a mother, he would be different. He's . . . he's not happy. And we're not happy. All I really know is that it's no good the way it is."

Jack kind of nodded his head toward me, and Mom said, "No, Jack. How can I keep anything from him when he sleeps in the kitchen? He sees everything that goes on. I can't hide a thing from him. Not with the three of us living in these two rooms."

Jack ate the eggs like he was really hungry. He took a drink of coffee; then he lit a cigarette. He blew the smoke out toward me in a big ring and winked. I'd known Jack all my life, and I couldn't remember once when he wasn't kind. Mom was looking at me too. "Snowflake's so beautiful, Jack. Where did you get him?" she said.

"I don't know," Jack said. "My fighter Bummy was training somewhere out West. Near Denver I think. One day Snowflake showed up. Maybe he just likes fighters."

I hadn't really thought Snowflake was for me. Pop wouldn't have let me have him even if Jack could give him to me.

"Bummy's really coming along, Amy. You re-member the last time we were in town when I said I didn't know if he'd ever make it? He was always strong as a bull, but he wasn't willing to train hard. I think he learned his lesson after his first few fights. He lost only one decision on the road. He's fighting a semifinal at the Coliseum in a couple of weeks. That's how come I'm back. If he wins this one, he should get a title shot next winter."

"And you like it?" Mom asked, surprised. "The fighting. And the blood?"

"Come on, Amy. It's not that bad, A good fighter doesn't get hurt often. What's not to like? We travel; we stay at hotels. Maybe not the best, but not bad either. You'd be surprised, Amy, but there's a lot of excitement in it, an awful lot of excitement. When he climbs through those ropes, it's like I'm getting in there with him. It really gets to me."

Jack never complains about things the way Pop does. He's really great.

I was watching Jack as he talked to Mom. His suit really fit him like it had been made only for him, and it looked like he had never even worn it until just now. He was wearing black shoes, and even though they weren't brand new, they had a shine. He was shining all over. He made our house feel like a castle. I felt safe when he was with us, as though nothing bad could ever happen.

"Is Carl working now?" Jack said.

"No. A lot of the new office buildings are using other materials, not brick. Let's stop this talk, Jack. I don't want to tell you all our troubles."

Jack said, "Do you have a little more coffee?"

"I'm sorry," Mom said. "I should have offered. I'll heat it up."

They talked, but not about anything interest-ing, and then Jack stood up to leave. "You'll say hello to Carl for me?"

"He'll be so disappointed, Jack. Stay where you are, please. I think I know where he is. He'd want to see you, even if it's only for a minute. It's just down the street. I'll run and get him."

"I'll see him next time. There's no need for—"

"Nonsense," Mom said. "I'd never hear the end of it."

Mom had her coat halfway on, and she was opening the door before Jack could say anything else.

He sat down next to me on my cot. "Shove over," he said. "Now, bring me up to date."

"What do you want to know?"

"What do you want to tell me? That's what I want to know."

"Well. . . I go to school. . ."

"Not now you don't. It's summertime. Anyway, when you do go, do you just go or are you learning something?"

"I'm learning."

"What?"

"I don't know. Things."

I thought he was going to say what things. But instead he said, "Fair enough. What else do you do? What did you do to your head?"

"I fell."

"Hurts, huh"

"It's not too bad."

"Did you cry?"

"No."

"You never cry, do you?"

"No. Sissies cry."

"Those who have to cry the most never cry."

"What does that mean?"

"It means . . . what's the harm in crying when you've got a good reason? And don't tell me sissies cry, or I'll belt you."

"Do you cry?"

"All the time."

"You're kidding!"

"No I'm not. Who told you only sissies cry?"

"Everybody knows that."

He just said, "Oh?" Then he said, "It's really not true."

I said, "Oh?" trying to sound just like him. He laughed, and I laughed too.

Even when Pop was in the best mood ever in his whole life, he never asked me anything that had to do with me.

Mom came in, and her eyes looked like she couldn't close them if she tried. Pop was right behind her. When I saw how he was acting, I knew why Mom looked like she did. I could smell his breath clear across the room. Snowflake snorted as though he'd gotten a whiff too.

Pop and Jack shook hands. "Hello, stranger," Pop said.

"I'll make you some coffee, Carl," Mom said.

"Don't make me any coffee!" Pop said, starting to get mad just from that. "How about a drink, Jack?" he said.

He stumbled, and he would have fallen if Jack hadn't reached out quickly for him. Pop shook his hand off. "Let's sit down and talk, Carl," Jack said. "We have a lot of catching up to do."

Mom said, "Carl, Jack really ought to go. He's been driving for days. You'll see him next time. I knew you'd want to say hello to him."

Pop looked at Mom the same way he looks at me. Jack noticed it because he said, "Amy's right, Carl. I'll be back soon. I'm going to be in the city for a while. We'll have plenty of chance to talk."

Jack started to get up and Pop stopped him by putting his hand on his arm. "Sit down," he ordered. "This is still my house. Not hers. Tell me about Bummy."

Jack looked at Mom, and she kind of nodded. "He's good, Carl," Jack said. "He's very good. Maybe the best around, next to the champ. It is late, Carl. What do you say we let this go for now?"

Pop had one eye closed, and he squinted at Jack out of the other one. I was keeping very still so Pop would think I was asleep. I rested one hand on top of Snowflake as though it had fallen down on top of his head. Pop acted like Jack hadn't said a word. "You remember when we went to the market with the old man, Jack, and the wolves came after us? We couldn't have been more than . . . what? Six? Seven, maybe? You remember what we did, Jack?"

I must have heard Pop tell that story a hundred times. Jack nodded; then he said, "Sure I remember, Carl. You don't forget something like that."

Pop didn't hear a word Jack said. He just went on. "The wolves were coming through the snow, and my father busted open one of the crates of chickens we were taking to the market. You remember what I said, Jack? I told him, 'Pop! Don't give them the chickens!' The old man looked like a wild man. He was scared. But not me. I was never afraid of anything. I could beat up every kid in the village, no matter how big they were. You remember, Jack?"

Jack didn't answer, but Pop didn't notice. "I had guts even then," he said. "I threw myself across those crates, and the old man couldn't get at them until he rapped me over the head. He gave them every one of those chickens. Every last one. And by the time we got rid of those wolves and got to the market, he had nothing to sell. You remember what a winter that was, Jack? We almost starved."

"I remember, Carl," Jack said.

"He shouldn't have given them the chickens."

"They'd have killed the horses. And us too."

"He should have fought them off."

"With what? His bare hands? And he had the two of us to worry about. Don't forget that. He couldn't do anything else. I thank God he had sense enough to give them the chickens. We'd never have made it except for that."

Pop's head had dropped to the table. Mom said, "Go now, Jack. You'll get little enough sleep as it is."

Jack whistled, so low I almost didn't hear it. But Snowflake was on his feet in a second and jumping up on him. "Take it easy, boy," Jack said. He gave Mom a kiss on the cheek. He waved to me, and it was better than if he'd kissed me or shook my hand. It was like we were friends, not relatives. Then he was gone. I felt the floor where Snowflake had been. It was still warm. I tried to swallow. If I could have a dog, even if he wasn't as great as Snowflake, I wouldn't want the other things I wanted anymore. I wouldn't even think about the baseball glove and the roller skates and the bike. Until tonight a bike had been the thing I'd wanted most.

Without opening his eyes Pop said, "Give me something to eat."

I closed my eyes and turned over, but I couldn't sleep. I heard Mom put some dishes on the table, and then she went into the bedroom. Pop ate for a while; then he was quiet. I knew he'd be sitting and looking at me with that look in his eyes that told me how much he hated me. I thought about why he hated me. I knew I wasn't the kind of kid he wanted for a son. But that wasn't a good enough reason. It had to be something else. Something more, something I didn't know about. Maybe it was because he didn't like anything I did. Like when the man came around and I didn't find out who he was. I was always doing things like that, and Pop always got sore. Every time I broke my glasses, even when I couldn't help it, you'd think I was the only kid in the world who ever broke his glasses. You'd think I had put them on the sidewalk and jumped up and down on them.

I pressed my eyes and I saw colors and designs even better than in a kaleidoscope. There were colors I'd never even seen before. They must have come from somewhere inside my head that knew things I didn't know myself. I pressed my eyes until all the colors suddenly went black.

I thought Pop had gone to bed, but he hadn't. I heard him push his chair back. I turned my head so I could see him, and I opened one eye just a crack. He picked up my glasses and looked at them for a long time. He was swaying, and I could smell the whiskey on his breath. Then he put them down and he said, "Lousy kid."

I wanted to stand up and hit him. I wanted to hit him so hard I would kill him. If I was bigger, I would have done it. I never thought I could be a murderer. But if I was as big as him, I would have done it.

He was muttering something, and even through the roaring in my ears, I heard him. "It's almost a day's pay."

MINE FOR KEEPS

Jean Little

The handicapped are a sizable minority group yet, because disabled children are often kept at home or educated in institutions, many people have no understanding of them. Some children thoughtlessly tease or taunt those who seem "different." Books that show the special problems of the handicapped as well as their similarities to the reader can develop in children the essential human trait of empathy.

Sal Copeland has cerebral palsy. For five years she has lived at the Allendale School for Handicapped Children, coming home only twice a year. Mine for Keeps is the story of her adjustment to noninstitutional life. She must attend public school, where she is the only student with braces and crutches but, more important, she must prove to herself that she can succeed even with a handicap.

Mine for Keeps is a well-written book that reveals, through action and dialogue, just how difficult it is for a handicapped person to do simple things and how embarrasing it can be to be different. The book also shows that the handicapped have the same needs, hopes, and reactions that all people have. Too many books that deal with handicaps emphasize information to the detriment of plot and character development. These books have the tone of a lecture. Mine for Keeps avoids this danger by seldom talking about cerebral palsy. Instead it shows what cerebral palsy can be like through Sal's fears, experiences, and actions.

5   TOO MANY FACES

"Mother, wait!" Sal whispered urgently.

Mother, who had taken a step closer to the classroom door, stopped. She looked down at Sal understandingly.

"Honey, Mr. Mackenzie is expecting us and it's getting late. Let's get it over with," she said firmly.

She put her hand on Sal's shoulder, urging her forward with a gentle push. Sal, already in a panic, did her best to back away. At that moment the door flew open. A girl came shooting through it and collided head-on with Sally. Sal clutched wildly at thin air. Mother grabbed her from behind. The crutches skidded across the hall. And the girl went down on both knees at Sally's feet, with a look of intense astonishment on her face.

"Oh my!" she gasped.

She scrambled up, her cheeks as red as poppies.

"You're Sally Copeland!" she cried. "Oh, I'm sorry. . . . Your crutches!"

She dived after them while Mother got Sal balanced. Then, as Sally was getting her crutches

adjusted, she ordered off four or five children who had gathered to see what was going on. At last, with Sal standing straight again and the children dispersed, the girl relaxed. She smiled widely.

"I'm Libby Reeves," she introduced herself, her voice still a bit breathless.

Sal smiled back. She could not have helped it. Libby's smile, as anyone could tell you, was something special. So was the rest of her. Her short, curly hair was a flaming, carroty red. Her face was splattered with freckles. Her eyes were as green as grass. Her glasses, which had been knocked askew and now perched crookedly on her upturned nose, had been mended in three places. And she was the thinnest person that Sally had ever seen. Sal herself had been called "skinny," but Libby was nothing short of spidery, with long pipe-cleaner legs stretching down beneath the hem of her skirt and equally long bony arms which she kept waving about while she talked.

A nudge from Mother warned Sal not to stare, but Libby must have been used to it for she talked steadily on.

"Mr. Mackenzie said you'd start today and I was all ready to greet you but I didn't mean to give you such a knockdown welcome. Buddy was chasing me and I never thought someone would be standing right outside the door like that. My mother always says I act first and think second. I didn't hurt you did I?"

"No, I'm fine." Sal's voice was rusty with shyness.

"Good. Oh, here's Mr. Mackenzie now. This is Sally Copeland, sir."

Mr. Mackenzie was tall with broad shoulders and a dark, kind face. As she shook hands with him, Sal stood straighter and felt braver.

"Libby, will you show Sal where to hang her coat, and then bring her to the classroom?" he asked.

Mother and he walked off together, talking, and Libby led the way to a row of lockers built into the wall.

"This will be yours," she said, opening the last one. "Elsje's and mine is down two."

Sal propped herself against the wall and began working her way out of her coat. Libby watched her uncertainly.

"Do you need any help?" she ventured at last.

"No," Sal answered, thankful there was just one, easy button, "I do it better sitting down but it's okay. Who's Elsje?"

"Elsje Jansen. She's my best friend. She's from Holland. Her family only came to Canada a little over a year ago but you should hear her speak English! She's really smart!"

Sal stayed balanced with one hand while she hung up her coat with the other. She kept her head down.

"Does she have a brother named Piet?"

"How did you know?" Libby said in surprise.

"Oh, my brother said something about a Piet Jansen going to this school," Sal answered vaguely.

It was no use thinking any more about being Libby's friend. Libby had just said herself that Piet's sister was her "best friend." Sally got herself balanced again on her crutches. A bit of the rhyme Kent had chanted about Piet sang inside her head.

Piet, Piet
Fat as a beet . . .

"Here comes your mother."

Sal straightened, gripping the crosspieces of her crutches tightly. Mother reached the two girls and looked down into Sally's eyes. Sal was sure that she saw Scarey Sarey looking back at her, but she only gave Sal's shoulder a little squeeze and said:

"Behave yourself, Sarah Jane, we'll be waiting to hear all about it at lunch. 'By for now."

"Good-by."

It came out so faintly that Sal herself could scarcely hear it. Mother turned, walked briskly down the hall and vanished through a door at the far end. Sal did not move. Perhaps, she thought, if she just stayed absolutely still she would be safe.

Then Libby said "Come on," in a matter-of-face voice, and Sal found herself following the other girl across the hall to the classroom door.

Libby in the lead, they went through the door and into the room itself. "Scarey Sarey" was everywhere, shouting at Sal to turn and run before it was too late, but she kept going like a small machine, her eyes glued to the middle of Libby's back, her braces and crutches clanking and thumping with every step she took. She had thought, for a moment, that just standing still in the hall would keep her safe. Now she was sure that the one thing she had to do was to go on looking at Libby. She must not make the mistake of raising her eyes, even for a split second . . .

"Here's your seat," Libby said, turning—and Sal looked up.

She was face to face with a roomful of strange children. After the first glance, some of them looked away uneasily, but many stared back at her, their eyes bright with curiosity. Sal did not stop to think that she had stared at Libby like this only a few minutes before. Too many faces, too many . . . she thought dizzily.

"Sally?"

Libby's smile, even though it was a little puzzled, acted like a lucky piece. Sal's eyes found it and everything that had been going wrong suddenly was right again.

"Thanks," she said.

Awkwardly, she turned herself sideways in the aisle. Libby backed up, out of the way of her crutches. Then, with an unexpected thud and a small feeling of victory, Sal took her seat.

For the next few minutes, she was too busy to notice whether anyone was staring at her or not. She had to get her crutches stowed out of the way, and then undo the kneelocks on her braces and get turned around so that her feet were under the desk instead of sticking out blocking the aisle. The lock on the left brace jammed. Sally tugged at it angrily. Her fingers, stiff with tension and damp with perspiration, slipped on the smooth steel. She wiped her palm on her skirt, gave one more tug, and the lock clicked open. Her knees bent. She swung her feet under her desk and sighed thankfully.

Never before had she noticed how much room she took up or how much noise she made, doing this simple thing. Never before had it seemed to take such a long time to get it done. But then, this was the first time she had ever done it in a schoolroom where others weren't doing it too.

Libby's whisper cut through her thoughts.

"Hey, Sally, look. Here comes Elsje."

Sally looked. She saw a girl cross the front of the room, come down the aisle and slide into a chair near her own. Elsje was small, but sturdy, with square shoulders and a straight back. Her hair hung nearly to her waist in glossy braids, so neatly braided you might have thought that Miss Jonas had arranged that hair, Sal thought admiringly. Under a navy-blue jumper, Elsje wore a white blouse with long sleeves and a round collar. The collar made her look young. Yet there was something in her face that made Sal feel that Elsje was more grown-up than she was.

Libby had been scribbling busily on a piece of paper. Now she smiled at Sal and passed the note to Elsje. Piet's sister pulled absent-mindedly on one of her braids as she read what her friend had written.

It's about me, Sal thought—It's something about me!

Elsje finished reading. She folded the scrap of paper and shoved it out of sight into her desk. Then she lifted her head and looked at Sal. Sal stared back. Elsje looked as though she were facing up to a dragon in her path, instead of just another girl. Sal had no idea what was wrong, but the feeling in Elsje's eyes burned so fiercely that she drew back in spite of herself. At that, Elsje's expression changed. Her eyelids dropped for an instant. When they rose again, the glance she gave Sal was cold and hard. All the fire of a moment before was gone. Yet when Sal turned quickly away, she found that she could not make her hands stop shaking for a minute.

Don't be crazy! she told herself. She doesn't know you. You're just letting yourself be Scarey Sarey again!

Then she forced herself to look at the other girl once more. Elsje had turned away, but on her lap her hands were knotted together so tightly the knuckles were white. She was sitting stiffly, her shoulders strained back. Her face looked set as though she had managed to turn her own bones and skin into a mask to hide what was happening in her heart. It had not been Scarey Sarey after all.

Clang!

A bell rang suddenly and every child in the room, except Sal, stood up. Sally stared wildly at the empty desks all around her and at the forest of plaid skirts, blue jeans, jumpers and slacks that had risen on every side. What was happening? Then they began to sing "God Save the Queen." She still did not know what to do. By the time she again got her braces locked, her crutches in place and herself standing, it would be finished and they would all sit down and leave her—the only child on her feet. She stayed where she was.

All through the "Queen" . . . All through the Lord's Prayer! She tried to sing and pray with them, but she couldn't. Then she just tried to look as though she didn't care. A smile, real enough to fool anybody, was more than she could manage.

Amen, the children around her murmured, and the class sat down.

"Boys and girls," Mr. Mackenzie said, when the rustling stopped, "I'd like you to meet the new member of our class, Sally Copeland."

Sal was pretending she was not there. She had not been sitting there through the opening exercises. She had never looked at Elsje. She had not even heard of Piet. She looked through Mr. Mackenzie instead of at him and she said inside herself *I am invisible,* but it didn't work.

"Sally, I'm sorry," the teacher said, his voice warm with amusement and sympathy. "We should have prepared you for 'God Save the Queen.' You must have wondered what on earth was happening when everybody jumped up like that. It won't be half as exciting coming to school tomorrow."

The children around Sal laughed. She sat very still trying not to hear that word "tomorrow." Mr. Mackenzie glanced at her and then went on easily:

"I'd introduce you to everybody, but you'd be more muddled at the finish than you are right now. There are a few rascals, however, about whom somebody should warn you. Randy, for instance. If Randy offers to help you with your spelling, Sal, be polite, but say NO!"

The boys and girls laughed again as though they were used to his teasing and liked it. Sal smiled too. The boy Mr. Mackenzie was talking about had stuck his nose in the air and was pretending to be deeply hurt about the whole thing.

"Libby is an expert on how to have fun—even in school," the teacher went on. "And Elsje? Why, she is learning to speak English so well I have to study at night secretly so that she won't catch me making a mistake and have me fired!"

Stealing a look at Elsje, Sal could hardly believe this was the same girl. She actually dimpled as she protested, "No, no. I shall never be so good as that. Never!"

After that, it seemed that Sally's troubles were over. First the children wrote stories. When she had finished, Sal scowled down at hers for a moment. Some of the letters were thin, some fat, some almost too cramped to read, some sprawling. And the lines all went uphill instead of straight across the page. Then she read it over and her face cleared. Sal had always had fun writing stories. Mr. Mackenzie would understand that it was hard for her to handle a pencil easily.

She was through early and Libby brought her a library book to read. Sal sat beaming at the book. That must mean that Libby didn't care what Elsje thought.

They did spelling. The words were new to everybody. As they finished, Sal caught sight of the clock and realized with amazement that over an hour of the morning had gone.

It's all right, she thought joyfully. I'll be home soon.

And then they had the mental arithmetic test!

INCREDIBLE JOURNEY

Sheila Burnford

Fictional animals are often given human characteristics, emotions, and reactions. Some are really disguised as people; they talk, wear clothes, and have homes quite similar to those of humans. Others may not be so completely personified, but their actions are interpreted through human behavior. These treatments of animals appeal to children, who not only give their pets names but also make up lives and ascribe human motivations to their behavior. When an author does the same, it is not realism, but a delightful fantasy may be the result.

Not all authors personify animals; some write adventure stories in which animals are treated realistically. The Incredible Journey is an excellent example of this type of literature. Sheila Burnford has not personified her main characters: a Siamese cat, an old English bull terrier, and a young Labrador retriever. To keep them true to their animal natures, she was careful to use no personification. The treatment of these animals makes an interesting comparison with that in The Wind in the Willows in Chapter 11, Fantasy.

The three animals trek across northwestern Ontario, guided by instinct, to their home. The journey is complicated by the terrier's age and the labrador's training not to eat the game he catches. The animals grow weaker but never cease their efforts to reach home.

There was a slight mist when John Longridge rose early the following morning, having fought a losing battle for the middle of the bed with his uninvited bedfellow. He shaved and dressed quickly, watching the mist roll back over the fields and the early morning sun break through. It would be a perfect fall day, an Indian summer day, warm and mellow. Downstairs he found the animals waiting patiently by the door for their early morning run. He let them out, then cooked and ate his solitary breakfast. He was out in the driveway, loading up his car when the dogs and cat returned from the fields. He fetched some biscuits for them and they lay by the wall of the house in the early sun, watching him. He threw the last item into the back of the car, thankful that he had already packed the guns and hunting equipment before the Labrador had seen them, then walked over and patted the heads of his audience, one by one.

"Be good," he said. "Mrs. Oakes will be here soon. Good-by, Luath," he said to the Labrador, "I wish I could have taken you with me, but there wouldn't be room in the canoe for three of us." He put his hand under the young dog's soft muzzle. The golden-brown eyes looked steadily into his, and then the dog did an unexpected thing: he lifted his right paw and placed it in the man's hand. Longridge had seen him do this many a time to his own master and he was curiously touched and affected by the trust it conveyed, almost wishing he did not have to leave immediately just after the dog had shown his first responsive gesture.

He looked at his watch and realized he was already late. He had no worries about leaving the animals alone outside, as they had never attempted to stray beyond the large garden and the adjacent fields; and they could return inside the house if they wished, for the kitchen door was the kind that closed slowly on a spring. All that

he had to do was shoot the inside bolt while the door was open, and after that it did not close properly and could be pushed open from the outside. They looked contented enough, too—the cat was washing methodically behind his ears—the old dog sat on his haunches, panting after his run, his long pink tongue lolling out of his grinning mouth; and the Labrador lay quietly by his side.

Longridge started the car and waved to them out of the window as he drove slowly down the drive, feeling rather foolish as he did so. "What do I expect them to do in return?" he asked himself with a smile. "Wave back? Or shout 'Good-by?' The trouble is I've lived too long alone with them and I'm becoming far too attached to them."

The car turned around the bend at the end of the long tree-lined drive and the animals heard the sound of the engine receding in the distance. The cat transferred his attention to a hind leg; the old dog stopped panting and lay down; the young dog remained stretched out, only his eyes moving and an occasional twitch of his nose.

Twenty minutes passed by and no move was made; then suddenly the young dog rose, stretched himself, and stood looking intently down the drive. He remained like this for several minutes, while the cat watched closely, one leg still pointing upwards; then slowly the Labrador walked down the driveway and stood at the curve, looking back as though inviting the others to come. The old dog rose too, now, somewhat stiffly, and followed. Together they turned the corner, out of sight.

The cat remained utterly still for a full minute, blue eyes blazing in the dark mask. Then, with a curious hesitating run, he set off in pursuit. The dogs were waiting by the gate when he turned the corner, the old dog peering wistfully back, as though he hoped to see his friend Mrs. Oakes materialize with a juicy bone; but when the Labrador started up the road he followed. The cat still paused by the gate, one paw lifted delicately in the air—undecided, questioning, hesitant; until suddenly, some inner decision reached, he followed the dogs. Presently all three disappeared from sight down the dusty road, trotting briskly and with purpose.

About an hour later Mrs. Oakes walked up the driveway from her cottage, carrying a string bag with her working shoes and apron, and a little parcel of tidbits for the animals. Her placid, gentle face wore a rather disappointed look, because the dogs usually spied her long before she got to the house and would rush to greet her.

"I expect Mr. Longridge left them shut inside the house if he was leaving early," she consoled herself. But when she pushed open the kitchen door and walked inside, everything seemed very silent and still. She stood at the foot of the stairs and called them, but there was no answering patter of running feet, only the steady tick-tock of the old clock in the hallway. She walked through the silent house and out into the front garden and stood there calling with a puzzled frown.

"Oh, well," she spoke her thoughts aloud to the empty, sunny garden, "perhaps they've gone up to the school. . . . It's a funny thing, though," she continued, sitting on a kitchen chair a few minutes later and tying her shoelaces, "that Puss isn't here—he's usually sitting on the window sill at this time of the day. Oh, well, he's probably out hunting—I've never known a cat like that for hunting, doesn't seem natural somehow!"

She washed and put away the few dishes, then took her cleaning materials into the sitting room. There her eye was caught by a sparkle on the floor by the desk, and she found the glass paperweight, and after that the remaining sheet of the note on the desk. She read it through to where it said: "I will be taking the dogs (and Tao too of course!) . . .", then looked for the remainder. "That's odd," she thought, "now where would he take them? That cat must have knocked the paperweight off last night—the rest of the note must be somewhere in the room."

She searched the room but it was not until she was emptying an ash tray into the fireplace that she noticed the charred curl of paper in the hearth. She bent down and picked it up carefully, for it was obviously very brittle, but even then

most of it crumbled away and she was left with a fragment which bore the initials J. R. L.

"Now, isn't that the queerest thing," she said to the fireplace, rubbing vigorously at the black marks on the tile. "He must mean he's taking them all to Heron Lake with him. But why would he suddenly do that, after all the arrangements we made? He never said a word about it on the telephone—but wait a minute, I remember now —he was just going to say something about them when the line went dead; perhaps he was just going to tell me."

While Mrs. Oakes was amazed that Longridge would take the animals on his vacation, it did not occur to her to be astonished that a cat should go along too, for she was aware that the cat loved the car and always went with the dogs when Longridge drove them anywhere or took them farther afield for walks. Like many Siamese cats, he was as obedient and as trained to go on walks as most dogs, and would always return to a whistle.

Mrs. Oakes swept and dusted and talked to the house, locked it and returned home to her cottage. She would have been horrified to the depths of her kindly, well-ordered soul if she had known the truth. Far from sitting sedately in the back of a car traveling north with John Longridge, as she so fondly visualized, the animals were by now many miles away on a deserted country road that ran westward.

They had kept a fairly steady pace for the first hour or so, falling into an order which was not to vary for many miles or days; the Labrador ran always by the left shoulder of the old dog, for the bull terrier was very nearly blind in the left eye, and they jogged along fairly steadily together— the bull terrier with his odd, rolling, sailorlike gait, and the Labrador in a slow lope. Some ten yards behind came the cat, whose attention was frequently distracted, when he would stop for a few minutes and then catch up again. But, in between these halts, he ran swiftly and steadily, his long slim body and tail low to the ground.

When it was obvious that the old dog was flagging, the Labrador turned off the quiet, graveled road and into the shade of a pinewood beside a clear, fast-running creek. The old dog drank deeply, standing up to his chest in the cold water; the cat picked his way delicately to the edge of an over-hanging rock. Afterwards they rested in the deep pine needles under the trees, the terrier panting heavily with his eyes half closed, and the cat busy with his eternal washing. They lay there for nearly an hour, until the sun struck through the branches above them. The young dog rose and stretched, then walked towards the road. The old dog rose too, stiff-legged, his head low. He walked toward the waiting Labrador, limping slightly and wagging his tail at the cat, who suddenly danced into a patch of sunlight, struck at a drifting leaf, then ran straight at the dogs, swerving at the last moment, and as suddenly sitting down again.

They trotted steadily on, all that afternoon—mostly traveling on the grassy verge at the side of the quiet country road; sometimes in the low over-grown ditch that ran alongside, if the acute hearing of the young dog warned them of an approaching car.

By the time the afternoon sun lay in long, barred shadows across the road, the cat was still traveling in smooth, swift bursts, and the young dog was comparatively fresh. But the old dog was very weary, and his pace had dropped to a limping walk. They turned off the road into the bush at the side, and walked slowly through a clearing in the trees, pushing their way through the tangled undergrowth at the far end. They came out upon a small open place where a giant spruce had crashed to the ground and left a hollow where the roots had been, filled now with drifted dry leaves and spruce needles.

The late afternoon sun slanted through the branches overhead, and it looked invitingly snug and secure. The old dog stood for a minute, his heavy head hanging, and his tired body swaying slightly, then lay down on his side in the hollow. The cat, after a good deal of wary observation, made a little hollow among the spruce needles and curled around in it, purring softly. The young dog disappeared into the undergrowth and reappeared presently, his smooth coat dripping water, to lie down a little way apart from the others.

The old dog continued to pant exhaustedly for a long time, one hind leg shaking badly, until his eyes closed at last, the labored breaths came further and further apart, and he was sleeping—still, save for an occasional long shudder.

Later on, when darkness fell, the young dog moved over and stretched out closely at his side and the cat stalked over to lie between his paws; and so, warmed and comforted by their closeness, the old dog slept, momentarily unconscious of his aching, tired body or his hunger.

In the nearby hills a timber wolf howled mournfully; owls called and answered and glided silently by with great outspread wings; and there were faint whispers of movement and small rustling noises around all through the night. Once an eerie wail like a baby's crying woke the old dog and brought him shivering and whining to his feet; but it was only a porcupine, who scrambled noisily and clumsily down a nearby tree trunk and waddled away, still crying softly. When he lay down again the cat was gone from his side—another small night hunter slipping through the unquiet shadows that froze to stillness at his passing.

The young dog slept in fitful, uneasy starts, his muscles twitching, constantly lifting his head and growling softly. Once he sprang to his feet with a full-throated roar which brought a sudden splash in the distance, then silence—and who knows what else unknown, unseen or unheard passed through his mind to disturb him further? Only one thing was clear and certain—that at all costs he was going home, home to his own beloved master. Home lay to the west, his instinct told him; but he could not leave the other two—so somehow he must take them with him, all the way.

3

In the cold hour before dawn, the bull terrier woke, then staggered painfully to his feet. He was trembling with cold and was extremely hungry and thirsty. He walked stiffly in the direction of the pool nearby, passing on his way the cat, who was crouched over something held between his paws. The terrier heard a crunching sound as the cat's jaws moved, and, wagging his tail in interest, moved over to investigate. The cat regarded him distantly, then stalked away, leaving the carcass; but to the terrier it was a disappointing mess of feathers only. He drank long and deeply at the pool and on his return tried the feathers again, for he was ravenous; but they stuck in his gullet and he retched them out. He nibbled at some stalks of grass, then, delicately, his lips rolled back over his teeth, picked a few overripe raspberries from a low bush. He had always liked to eat domestic raspberries this way, and although the taste was reassuringly familiar, it did nothing to appease his hunger. He was pleased to see the young dog appear presently; he wagged his tail and licked the other's face, then followed resignedly when a move was made towards the direction of the road. They were followed a few moments later by the cat, who was still licking his lips after his feathery breakfast.

In the gray light of dawn the trio continued down the side of the road until they reached a point where it took a right-angled turn. Here they hesitated before a disused logging trail that led westward from the side of the road, its entrance almost concealed by overhanging branches. The leader lifted his head and appeared almost as though he were searching for the scent of something, some reassurance; and apparently he found it, for he led his companions up the trail between the overhanging trees. The going here was softer; the middle was overgrown with grass and the ruts on either side were full of dead leaves. The close-growing trees which almost met overhead would afford more shade when the sun rose higher. These were all considerations that the old dog needed, for he had been tired today even before he started, and his pace was already considerably slower.

Both dogs were very hungry and watched enviously when the cat caught and killed a chipmunk while they were resting by a stream in the middle of the day. But when the old dog advanced with a hopeful wag of his tail, the cat, growling, retreated into the bushes with his prey. Puzzled and disappointed, the terrier sat listening to the crunching sounds inside the bushes, saliva running from his mouth.

A few minutes later the cat emerged and sat down, daintily cleaning his whiskers. The old dog licked the black Siamese face with his panting tongue and was affectionately patted on the nose in return. Restless with hunger, he wandered up the banks of the creek, investigating every rock and hollow, pushing his hopeful nose through tunnels of withered sedge and into the yielding earth of molehills. Sadly he lay down by an unre-warding blueberry bush, drew his paws down tightly over his blackened face, then licked the dirt off them.

The young dog, too, was hungry; but he would have to be on the verge of starvation before the barriers of deep-rooted Labrador heredity would be broken down. For generations his ancestors had been bred to retrieve without harming, and there was nothing of the hunter in his make-up; as yet, any killing was abhorrent to him. He drank deeply at the stream and urged his companions on.

The trail ran high over the crest of this hilly, wooded country, and the surrounding countryside below was filled with an overwhelming beauty of color; the reds and vermilions of the occasional maples; pale birch, and yellow poplar, and here and there the scarlet clusters of mountain ash berries against a rich dark-green background of spruce and pine and cedar.

Several times they passed log ramps built into the side of the hill, picking their way across the deep ruts left by the timber sleighs below; and sometimes they passed derelict buildings in rank, overgrown clearings, old stables for the bush horses and living quarters for the men who had worked there a generation ago. The windows were broken and sagging and weeds were growing up between the floorboards, and even one old rusted cookstove had fireweed springing from the firebox. The animals, strangely enough, did not like these evidences of human occupation and skirted them as far as possible, hair raised along their backs.

Late in the afternoon the old dog's pace had slowed down to a stumbling walk, and it seemed as if only sheer determination were keeping him on his feet at all. He was dizzy and swaying, and his heart was pounding. The cat must have sensed this general failing, for he now walked steadily beside the dogs, very close to his tottering old friend, and uttered plaintive worried bleats. Finally, the old dog came to a standstill by a deep rut half-filled with muddy water. He stood there as if he had not even the strength to step around it; his head sagged, and his whole body was trembling. Then, as he tried to lap the water, his legs seemed to crumple under him and he collapsed, half in and half out of the rut. His eyes were closed, and his body moved only to the long, shallow, shuddering breaths that came at widening intervals. Soon he lay completely limp and still. The young dog became frantic now: he whined, as he stretched at the edge of the rut, then nudged and pushed with his nose, doing everything in .his power to rouse the huddled, unresponsive body. Again and again he barked, and the cat growled softly and continuously, walking back and forth and rubbing his whole length against the dirty, muddied head. There was no response to their attention. The old dog lay unconscious and remote.

The two animals grew silent, and sat by his side, disturbed and uneasy; until at last they turned and left him, neither looking back—the Labrador disappearing into the bushes where the crack of broken branches marked his progress farther and farther away; the cat stalking a partridge which had appeared at the side of the trail some hundred yards away and was pecking unconcernedly at the sandy dirt. But at the shrill warning of a squirrel, it flew off across the trail with a sudden whirr into the trees, while the cat was still some distance away. Undaunted, still licking his lips in anticipation, the cat continued around a bend in the trail in search of another, and was lost to sight.

The shadows lengthened across the deserted track, and the evening wind sighed down it to sweep a flurry of whispering leaves across the rut, their brown brittleness light as a benison as they drifted across the unheeding white form. The curious squirrel peered in bright-eyed wonder from a nearby tree, clucking softly to itself. A shrew ran halfway across, paused and ran back; and there was a soft sound of wings as a whisky-jack landed and swayed to and fro on a birch branch, tilting his head to one side as he looked down and called to his mate to come and join him. The wind died away—a sudden hush descended.

Suddenly, there was a sound of a heavy body pushing through the underbrush, accompanied by a sharp cracking of branches, and the spell was broken. Chattering shrilly in alarm and excitement, the squirrel ran up the trunk of the tree and the whisky-jacks flew off. Now onto the trail on all fours scampered a half-grown bear cub, round furry ears pricked and small deep-set eyes alight with curiosity in the sharp little face as he beheld the old dog. There was a grunting snuffling sound in the bush behind the cub: his mother was investigating a rotten tree stump. The cub stood for a moment and then hesitantly advanced toward the rut where the terrier lay. He sniffed around, wrinkling his facile nose at the unfamiliar smell, then reached out a long curved black paw and tapped the white head. For a moment the mists of unconsciousness cleared and the old dog opened his eyes, aware of danger. The cub sprang back in alarm and watched from a safe distance. Seeing that there was no further movement, he loped back and cuffed again with his paw, this time harder, and watched for response. Only enough strength was left in the old dog for a valiant baring of his teeth. He snarled faintly with pain and hatred when his shoulder was raked by the wicked claws of the excited cub, and made an attempt to struggle to his feet. The smell of the drawn blood excited the cub further; he straddled the dog's body and started to play with the long white tail, nibbling at the end like a child with a new toy. But there was no response: all conscious effort drained, the old dog no longer felt any pain or indignity. He lay as though asleep, his eyes veiled and unseeing, his lip still curled in a snarl.

Around the bend in the trail, dragging a large dead partridge by the wing, came the cat. The wing sprang back softly from his mouth as he gazed transfixed at the scene before him. In one split second a terrible transformation took place; his blue eyes glittered hugely and evilly in the black masked face, and every hair on the wheat-colored body stood upright so that he appeared twice his real size; even the chocolate-colored tail puffed up as it switched from side to side. He crouched low to the ground, tensed and ready, and uttered a high, ear-splitting scream; and, as the startled cub turned, the cat sprang.

He landed on the back of the dark furred neck, clinging with his monkeylike hind legs while he raked his claws across the cub's eyes. Again and again he raked with the terrible talons, hissing and spitting in murderous devilry until the cub was screaming in pain and fear, blinded with blood, making ineffectual brushing movements with his paws to dislodge the unseen horror on his back. His screams were answered by a thunderour roar as the huge black she-bear crashed through the bushes and rushed to the cub. She swiped at the clinging cat with a tremendous paw; but the cat was too quick for her and with a hiss of fury leaped to the ground and disappeared behind a tree. The unfortunate cub's head received the full force of the blow and he was sent spinning across the track into the bushes. In a blind, frustrated rage, maddened by the cries of her cub, the mother turned for something on which to vent her fury, and saw the still figure of the old dog. Even as she lumbered snarling towards him the cat distracted her attention with a sudden leap to the side of the track. The bear halted, then reared up to full height for attack, red eyes glinting savagely, neck upstretched and head weaving from side to side in a menacing, snakelike way. The cat uttered another banshee scream and stepped forward with a stiff-legged, sideways movement, his squinting, terrible eyes fixed on his enormous adversary. Something like fear or indecision crept into the bear's eyes as the cat advanced; she shuffled back a step with lowered head. Slow, deliberate, purposeful, the cat came on—again the bear retreated, bewildered by the tactics of this terrible small animal, distraught by her cub's whimpering, slowly falling back before the relentless inch-by-inch advance. Now the cat stopped and crouched low, lashing his tail from side to side—the bear stopped too, shifting her weight uneasily before the spring that must follow, longing to decamp but afraid to turn her back. A sudden crackle of undergrowth turned the huge animal into a statue, rigid with apprehension—and when a great dog sprang out of the bush and stood beside the cat, teeth bared and snarling, every hair on his russet back and ruff erect, she dropped to all fours, turned swiftly and fled towards her cub. There was a last growl of desperate bravado from the bush and a whimpering cry; then the sounds of the bears' escape receded in the distance. Finally all was quiet again; the curious squirrel leaped from his ringside seat and scrambled farther down the trunk of the tree.

The cat shrank back to his normal size. His eyes regained their usual cool, detached look. He shook each paw distastefully in turn, glanced briefly at the limp, muddied bundle by his feet, blood oozing from four deep parallel gashes on the shoulder, then turned and sauntered slowly down the track towards his partridge.

The young dog nosed his friend all over, his lips wrinkling at the rank bear smell, then attempted to stanch the wounds with his rough tongue. He scratched fresh leaves over the bloodstained ones then barked by the old dog's head; but there was no response, and at last he lay down panting on the grass. His eyes were uneasy and watchful, the hairs still stood upright in a ridge on his back, and from time to time he whined in perplexity. He watched the cat drag a large gray bird almost up to the nose of the unconscious dog, then slowly and deliberately begin to tear at the bird's flesh. He growled softly, but the cat ignored him and continued his tearing and eating. Presently, the enticing smell of raw, warm meat filtered through into the old dog's senses. He opened one eye and gave an appreciative sniff. The effect was galvanizing: his muddied half-chewed tail stirred and he raised his shoulders, then his forelegs, with a convulsive effort, like an old work horse getting up after a fall.

He was a pitiful sight—the half of his body that had lain in the rut was black and soaking, while the other was streaked and stained with blood. He looked like some grotesque harlequin. He trembled violently and uncontrollably throughout the length of his body, but in the sunken depths of the slanted black-currant eyes there was a faint gleam of interest—which increased as he pushed his nose into the still-warm bundle of soft gray feathers. This time there was no growling rebuff over the prey: instead, the cat sat down a few yards away, studiedly aloof and indifferent, then painstakingly washed down the length of his tail. When the end twitched he pinned it down with a paw.

The old dog ate, crunching the bones ravenously with his blunt teeth. Even as his companions watched him, a miraculous strength slowly seeped back into his body. He dozed for a while, a feather hanging from his mouth, then woke again to finish the last morsel. By nightfall he was able to walk over to the soft grass at the side of the track, where he lay down and blinked happily at his companions, wagging his pitiful tail. The Labrador lay down beside him, and licked the wounded shoulder.

An hour or two later the purring cat joined them, carelessly dropping another succulent morsel by his old friend's nose. This was a deer mouse, a little creature with big eyes and long hind legs like a miniature kangaroo. It was swallowed with a satisfying gulp, and soon the old dog slept.

But the cat purring against his chest and the young dog curled at his back were wakeful and alert most of the remaining night; neither moved from his side.

A POCKETFUL OF CRICKET

Rebecca Caudill

A Pocketful of Cricket, *a book for young children, deals with the loneliness and shyness of a small country boy. Until he finds Cricket, Jay has no one to play with. By having Jay wander through the fields and describing natural objects through his eyes, Miss Caudill effectively reveals his aloneness.*

All children, even those who live in cities and have many playmates, know loneliness; all children have felt shy in new surroundings; all children have been a little insecure the first day of school. Reading about Jay can help them accept these feelings as normal emotions.

This boy, Jay, lived with his father and his mother in an old farmhouse in a hollow. He was six years old.

All around his house Jay could see hills. He could see hills when he stood whittling in the kitchen doorway. He could see hills when he swung on the gate in front of his house. When he climbed into the apple tree beside his house, he could see hills.

Woods covered most of the hills. Corn grew on some of them. On a far green hill, farther than Jay could see, cows ate grass in a pasture.

Every afternoon, in spring and summer and fall, Jay went to the pasture to drive the cows home.

On this afternoon, late in August, he set out before sundown, eating the slice of buttered bread his mother had given him.

He walked along the lane on the side of a hill. The dust under his feet felt soft and warm. He

spread his toes and watched the dust squirt between them.

After he had walked forward for a while, he turned around and walked backward for a while. As he walked, he looked at his footprints in the dust.

Queen of the meadow grew on the hillside below the lane. The great pinkish crowns nodded on tall stalks.

A gray spider slept in a web between two of the stalks.

A yellow butterfly sucked nectar from one of the pink flowers. Jay stood and watched it fan its wings—open and shut, open and shut.

A hickory tree grew beside the lane. Its branches cast a dark pool of shade on the hillside. Nuts grew among its leaves.

With a stick Jay knocked a nut from a low branch.

He picked up the nut and smelled the tight green hull that enclosed it. The smell tingled in his nose like the smell of the first frost.

Jay put the nut in his pocket.

A creek flowed across the lane at the bottom of the hill.

Jay waded into the creek.

The clear water rippling against his ankles cooled his feet. It washed them clean of dust.

Jay wiggled his toes in the smooth brown gravel on the bottom of the creek.

He picked up a small flat rock lying in the water. He turned it over. On its underside was the print of a fern.

Jay put the rock in his pocket.

When Jay waded out of the creek he stood for a minute on the bank.

He watched a crayfish scuttling backward among the rocks.

He watched minnows darting about in the water.

At his feet he saw a gray goose feather. He picked it up, smoothed it with his fingers, and put it in his pocket.

A rail fence zigzagged between the creek and a cornfield.

As Jay walked toward the fence he heard a scratchy noise. He saw a gray lizard slithering along the middle rail.

He stopped. He stood very still and watched.

The lizard slithered away, out of sight.

Jay climbed the fence. He sat on the top rail.

He heard the wind rustling in the ripening corn.

He heard bugs and beetles ticking.

He heard a cicada fiddling high notes in the August heat.

He heard an owl hooting in the dusky woods.

On the hill beyond the cornfield he heard a cow bawling.

Jay climbed down from the fence and walked between two rows of corn.

In the dirt he saw an Indian arrowhead, turned up by a plow. He picked it up, brushed the dirt from it, and put it in his pocket.

A woolly brown caterpillar looped fast along a corn blade.

"Why are you hurrying, Caterpillar?" Jay asked.

Beans had been planted with the corn. The vines climbed the tall cornstalks.

Jay picked a bean pod. With his thumb nail he pried it open.

He shelled the beans into his hand. They were white, striped with red speckles. The stripes on every bean were different from the stripes on every other bean.

In Jay's hand the beans felt cool—like morning.

Jay put the beans in his pocket.

At the far end of the cornfield Jay climbed over the rail fence into the pasture.

The cows looked up from their grazing.

Jay walked past the cows. He climbed up the steep pasture hill. The cows went back to their grazing.

An old apple tree stood at the top of the hill. The russet apples that grew on one side of the tree were sweet. The red apples that grew on the other side of the tree were sour.

Jay picked a russet apple with one hand, and a red apple with the other. He took a bite from one apple, then a bite from the other—sweet and sour, sweet and sour.

As he ate, he looked off into the hollow below him. It was long and narrow. A road ran the length of it. At the end of the road stood a white schoolhouse.

Jay looked a long time at the schoolhouse. Then he turned and walked slowly down the hill toward the cows.

The cows looked up once more from their grazing. They switched their tails and started home. Nodding their heads and switching their tails, they walked, one behind another, along the cow path beside the fence.

Jay walked behind them.

Beside the cow path a cricket jumped.

Jay watched the cricket crawl underneath a stone.

Quietly he lifted an edge of the stone.

Quickly he cupped his hand over the cricket.

He gathered the cricket in both hands. Carrying it gently, he hurried after the cows.

Across the creek he waded.

Along the lane he trudged in the dust.

Into the barn he drove the cows. His father was waiting to milk them.

"What took you so long?" asked Jay's father.

"Nothing," said Jay.

Jay hurried to the house.

"What's that in your hands?" asked Jay's mother.

"Cricket," said Jay.

"What are you going to do with him?" asked Jay's mother.

"Keep him," said Jay.

"What will you do with him when you go to school?" asked Jay's mother.

"How many days till I go to school?" asked Jay.

"Five," said Jay's mother. "Next Monday you'll begin."

"Cricket will stay in my room and wait for me," said Jay.

"You'll need a cage to keep him in," said Jay's mother.

She opened a kitchen drawer and took from it a tea strainer. She tucked the handle of the strainer into Jay's pocket.

Off Jay hurried to his room.

He laid the strainer upside down on his table and put Cricket inside.

He brought Cricket water in a bottle cap.

He brought Cricket a piece of lettuce leaf, a thin slice of cucumber, and a slice of banana the size of a nickel.

Cricket sat inside the tea strainer. Jay sat on his bed beside the table and watched.

Cricket sat and Jay sat.

Cricket did not drink the water.

He did not eat the lettuce, nor the cucumber, nor the banana.

"Jay, come to supper!" called Jay's mother.

Jay lay on his bed beside the table, watched Cricket.

"Jay!"

After supper Jay hurried back to Cricket.

Some of the lettuce leaf was gone, Jay thought.

A nibble had been nibbled off the cucumber, he thought.

He sat on his bed beside the table and looked at Cricket.

"Do you like your new home, Cricket?" he asked.

Cricket sat and Jay sat.

The light in the room grew dim.

Night came.

Jay pulled the table closer to his bed. He got into bed and fell asleep.

A noise waked him. "Chee! Chee!"

Cricket was fiddling. Cricket was fiddling loud and clear. "Chee! Chee! Chee!"

Jay sat up in bed and listened.

"You do like your new home, don't you, Cricket?" he asked.

"Chee! Chee! Chee!" fiddled Cricket.

Jay reached under his pillow and found his flashlight.

He turned the flashlight on. The fiddling stopped.

Jay turned the flashlight off and put it under his pillow.

He lay down again. In the dark he waited, listening . . . listening.

"Chee! Chee! Chee!" fiddled Cricket.

The next day Jay made Cricket a cage out of a piece of wire screen. It was bigger than the tea strainer.

Every morning Jay brought Cricket fresh pieces of lettuce and cucumber and banana. He put fresh water in the bottle cap.

Every afternoon Jay shut the door of his room, turned Cricket out of his cage, and played with him.

Cricket jumped about the room. Jay jumped after him.

Cricket crawled up the curtain at Jay's window. He jumped to the door of Jay's closet.

"Don't let Cricket in that closet," warned Jay's mother. "He might eat your new sweater. Then what would you wear to school?"

Every night, when Jay got into bed and the dark room grew still, Cricket fiddled.

"Chee! Chee! Chee!" And "Chee! Chee! Chee!"

Monday came.

Jay was ready for school early.

He said good-bye to Cricket. He looked at Cricket a long time.

"You'd better be going now," said Jay's mother. "You mustn't be late for the bus your very first day of school."

Jay said good-bye to his mother. He said good-bye again to Cricket. He started down the road.

When he had gone a few steps he turned and

hurried back. He went into his room. He stood looking at Cricket.

"Jay!" called his mother.

Quickly Jay emptied his pocket. He piled on the table an Indian arrowhead, hickory nuts, buckeyes, and beans.

"Jay!"

Into his pocket Jay tucked Cricket. Away he ran down the road.

At the mailbox Jay waited.

Along came the yellow school bus. It stopped, and the driver opened the door. Jay climbed in. He sat down beside a window in the front of the bus.

The bus was filled with boys and girls. A few of them, like Jay, were going to school for the first time. Most of them were big boys and girls. They talked and laughed.

"Chee! Chee!"

Inside Jay's dark pocket Cricket began fiddling.

The talking stopped. Everybody listened.

"Chee! Chee! Chee!" fiddled Cricket.

Jay cupped his hand against his pocket to quiet Cricket.

"Maybe somebody's taking a cricket to Teacher," said a big boy.

Everybody on the bus laughed—everybody but Jay. He cupped his hand harder against his pocket.

"Chee! Chee! Chee!" fiddled Cricket.

"Maybe Towhead down there in front has that cricket," said a big boy in the back of the bus.

Everybody on the bus looked at Jay.

Jay crowded against the window. He pressed his hand hard against his pocket. He looked straight ahead.

"Chee! Chee! Chee!" fiddled Cricket.

"I'd like to see Teacher when that cricket starts singing in school," said a big boy.

Everybody on the bus laughed very loud—everybody but Jay.

When the bus reached the schoolhouse it stopped.

Jay waited until all the other boys and girls had got off. Then, pressing his hand against his pocket, he too climbed off.

He stood wondering where to go.

The driver smiled at him. "You belong in that room just inside the front door," he said to Jay. "Good luck with your cricket!" he added.

Jay looked at the big boys and girls in the schoolyard. They were calling to one another. They were laughing and talking.

Jay kept close to the fence as he made his way around them.

He found his room.

He found Teacher inside the room.

He told her his name.

He sat at the desk she pointed out to him.

All around him sat other boys and girls. They were all his size.

Jay kept his hand pressed over his pocket. He sat still and waited.

A bell rang.

Teacher began talking to the children. The children listened. The room was very quiet.

"Chee!" fiddled Cricket.

Jay pressed his hand against his pocket to quiet Cricket.

"Chee! Chee! Chee!" fiddled Cricket.

The children turned in their seats. They giggled.

Teacher stopped talking. She looked about the room.

"Does someone have a cricket in this room?" she asked.

No one answered.

Teacher began talking again.

"Chee! Chee!" fiddled Cricket.

Teacher left the front of the room. She walked up and down between the rows of desks. As she walked, she talked to the children. As she talked, she listened.

She reached Jay's desk.

"Chee! Chee!" fiddled Cricket.

"Jay," Teacher asked, "do you have that cricket?"

Jay swallowed hard. He nodded his head.

"You'd better put it outside," said Teacher. "It's disturbing the class."

Jay sat very still. He looked at his desk. He pressed his hand hard against his pocket. He felt Cricket squirming.

"Jay," said Teacher, "put the cricket outside."

Still Jay sat. Still he looked at his desk.

"Jay," said Teacher, "aren't you going to put the cricket outside?"

Jay shook his head.

"Why not?" asked Teacher.

"I couldn't find him again," said Jay.

"Put him outside anyway," said Teacher. She waited.

Jay swallowed hard. He glanced up at Teacher. Then he looked at his desk again.

"You could find another cricket, couldn't you?" asked Teacher.

Jay shook his head. "It wouldn't be this one," he said.

"Chee! Chee!" fiddled Cricket.

Jay looked up at Teacher.

"Jay," said Teacher, "is this cricket your friend?"

Jay nodded his head.

"I see," said Teacher.

Teacher walked slowly to the front of the room.

"Boys and girls," she said, "every day in the first grade we have what we call 'Show and Tell.' Anyone who has something special may bring to to school to show the class and tell about it. This morning Jay has brought a cricket to class. It is something special. It is his friend. Jay, will you come to the front of the room and show the boys and girls your cricket? You can put him under this glass," she said.

She turned a water glass upside down on her desk.

Jay walked to the front of the room.

He took Cricket from his pocket.

He put Cricket under the upside-down glass.

"Tell the class about your cricket, Jay," said Teacher. "How did you catch him?"

Jay told the class how he had caught Cricket in the cow pasture.

The boys and girls asked Jay many questions.

"How long have you had Cricket?"

"What does he eat?"

"Where does he sleep?"

"How high can he jump?"

"Can he do tricks?"

Jay answered all their questions.

"What makes him sing?" asked a girl.

"He doesn't sing," said Jay. "He fiddles with his wings."

"Tell him to fiddle now," said all the boys and girls.

"He likes to fiddle in the dark," explained Jay. "That's why he was fiddling in my pocket. It's dark in there."

"Does Cricket fiddle especially for you sometimes?" asked Teacher.

"Every night," said Jay.

"You may put Cricket back in your pocket now, Jay," said Teacher. "If he fiddles, he won't disturb us. When you have something else special, bring it for 'Show and Tell.'"

"What are you going to bring next, Jay?" asked a boy.

Jay thought of the stone with the print of a fern on one side. He thought of the gray goose feather. He thought of the Indian arrowhead.

He thought of the hickory nut, and of the smell of it that tingled in his nose like the smell of the first frost.

He thought of the beans.

He thought of the cicada fiddling high notes in the August heat.

He thought of the russet apples and the red apples growing on the same tree—sweet and sour, sweet and sour.

He thought again of the beans—white, striped with red speckles, and, in his hand, cool, like morning.

"Beans," he said.

Related Reading

References for Adults

Arbuthnot, May Hill. *Children and Books*, 3d ed. Glenview, Ill.: Scott, Foresman, 1964.

Baker, Augusta. *Books about Negro Life for Children*. New York: New York Public Library, 1963. A discussion of criteria for evaluation as well as an annotated bibliography.

Berry, Erick, and Herbert Best. *Writing for Children.* Illustrated by Erick Berry. Miami: University of Miami, 1964.

Eakin, Mary K., compiler. *Good Books for Children,* 3d ed. Chicago: University of Chicago Press, 1966. This book contains 407 pages of annotations of the best children's books reviewed in the *Bulletin of The Center for Childrens Books,* 1950 to 1965.

Egoff, Sheila. *The Republic of Childhood: A Critical Guide to Canadian Children's Literature in English.* New York, London: Oxford, 1967. A very knowledgeable Canadian children's librarian discusses the important children's books of her country, fiction and nonfiction, especially those published between 1950 and 1965.

Egoff, Sheila, G. T. Stubbs, and L. F. Ashley, eds. *Only Connect: Readings on Children's Literature.* New York, London: Oxford, 1969. Forty articles, most written in the sixties, that should be familiar to all those interested in children's literature. An excellent source book.

Forster, E. M. *Aspects of the Novel.* New York: Harcourt, 1927. An excellent discussion of the elements of fiction.

Haviland, Virginia. *Children's Literature: A Guide to Reference Sources.* Prepared under the direction of Virginia Haviland, Head of the Library of Congress Children's Book Section. Washington D.C.: Library of Congress, 1966. An extremely useful annotated bibliography of books, pamphlets, and articles on children's literature.

Hazard, Paul. *Books, Children and Men.* Boston: Horn Book, 1947. This discussion of children's books, with its emphasis on presenting literature of quality to children, has become a classic in its field.

Huck, Charlotte S., and Doris Young Kuhn. *Children's Literature in the Elementary School,* 2d ed. New York: Holt, Rinehart and Winston, 1968. Several excellent and very helpful chapters on children's fiction.

Lucas, F. L. *Style: An Entertaining Guide to Recognizing and Writing Good English Prose.* New York: Collier Books, 1962.

Smith, Lillian H. *The Unreluctant Years; A Critical Approach to Children's Literature.* Chicago: American Library Association, 1953. A fine book that examines the question of excellence in children's literature. Very helpful for the teacher or librarian interested in developing critical judgment.

Domestic and Realistic Fiction for Children

Alcott, Louisa May. *Little Women.* New York: Crowell. Illustrated by Barbara Cooney. The text was first published in 1868. A discussion of and an excerpt from this book can be found in this chapter. (Grades 5–9)

Brown, Margaret Wise. *The Dead Bird.* Illustrated by Remy Charlip. New York: Scott, 1958. A simple picture book about a group of children who while playing find a dead bird which they bury. Soon they are playing again. (Preschool–grade 1)

Burch, Robert. *Queenie Peavy.* Illustrated by Jerry Lazare. New York: Viking, 1966. A very believable portrayal of a thirteen-year-old girl with a chip on her shoulder because her father is in jail and her mother works long hours. However, Queenie's strength of character helps her mature. (Grades 5–7)

————. *Skinny.* Illustrated by Don Sibley. New York: Viking, 1964. A discussion of and an excerpt from this book can be found in this chapter. (Grades 4–7)

Burnford, Sheila. *The Incredible Journey.* Illustrated by Carl Burger. Boston: Little, Brown, 1961. A discussion of and an excerpt from this book can be found in this chapter. (Grades 6–9)

Burton, Virginia Lee, author-illustrator. *The Little House.* Boston: Houghton Mifflin, 1942. As the years pass, the town reaches toward the little farm house in the country. Eventually it is surrounded by the busy city. After even more years someone moves the house into the country and it is among the hills and farms once more. Awarded the 1943 Caldecott Medal. (Grades K–2)

Campbell, Hope. *Why Not Join the Giraffes?* New York: Norton, 1968. A teenager rebels against the freedom and nonconformity of her family and longs for conventional parents. (Grades 6–9)

Caudill, Rebecca. *A Pocketful of Cricket.* Illustrated by Evaline Ness. New York: Holt, 1964. A discussion of and an excerpt from this book can be found in this chapter. (Grades K–3)

Dickens, Charles. *A Christmas Carol.* Illustrated by Philip Reed. New York: Atheneum, 1966. Dicken's classic is still enjoyed by older elementary school children. It is a wise teacher who reads this aloud that distracted week before Christmas when the class is too excited to do long division. This story holds their attention. (Grades 5–up)

Enright, Elizabeth, author–illustrator. *The Four-Story Mistake.* New York: Holt, 1942. Elizabeth Enright is a popular writer of domestic fiction; she creates warm family relationships and resourceful children. (Grades 4–6) Some of her other books are:

————. *Gone-Away Lake.* Illustrated by Beth and Joe Krush. New York: Harcourt, 1957. (Grades 4–6)

————. *Return to Gone-Away Lake.* Illustrated by Beth and Joe Krush. New York: Harcourt, 1961. (Grades 4–6)

————. *The Saturdays.* Illustrated by the author. New York: Rinehart, 1941. (Grades 4–6)

————.*Thimble Summer.* Illustrated by the author. New York: Rinehart, 1938. Awarded the 1939 Newbery Medal. (Grades 4–6)

Ets, Marie Hall, author-illustrator. *Gilberto and the Wind.* New York: Viking, 1963. A picture story about a young boy's relationship with the wind. (Grades K–1)

Fitzhugh, Louise, author-illustrator. *Harriet the Spy.* New York: Harper & Row, 1964. A discussion of and an excerpt from this book can be found in Chapter 8, American Minorities. (Grades 4–6)

————. *The Long Secret.* New York: Harper & Row, 1965. A sequel to *Harriet the Spy.* (Grades 4–6)

Garfield, James B. *Follow My Leader.* New York: Viking, 1957. Blinded by a firecracker thrown by a teammate, Jimmy must learn to adjust to sightlessness and learn the skills necessary for him to live independently. An interesting story, but occasionally marred by the author's telling about the problems of the sightless rather than showing them through plot and character interaction. (Grades 4–7)

George, Jean, author-illustrator. *My Side of the Mountain.* New York: Dutton, 1959. A teenage New York City boy decides to run away and live alone in the Catskills mountainous farm country. This book is more a description of how to survive in the wilderness than a novel. (Grades 4–7)

Hader, Berta and Elmer, authors-illustrators. *The Big Snow.* New York: Macmillan, 1948. A plotless picture book about a little old man and woman who put out food for the animals and birds all winter. Awarded the 1949 Caldecott Medal. (Grades K–3)

Henry, Marguerite. *Misty of Chincoteague.* Illustrated by Wesley Dennis. Skokie, Ill.: Rand McNally, 1947. Marguerite Henry's horse stories are very popular with elementary school readers, especially girls. Some of her other books are: *Sea Star: Orphan of Chincoteague,* 1949; *Stormy, Misty's Foal,* 1963. (Grades 4–7)

Keats, Ezra Jack, author-illustrator. *The Snowy Day.* New York: Viking, 1962. An excellent picture book story about a young boy's enjoyment of the snow. Awarded the 1963 Caldecott Award. (Preschool–grade 1)

————. *Whistle for Willie.* New York: Viking, 1964. A picture book about a little boy who wants to whistle like the bigger boys. (Preschool–grade 1)

Konigsburg, E. L., author-illustrator. *About the B'nai Bagels.* New York: Atheneum, 1969. A discussion of and an excerpt from this book can be found in Chapter 8, American Minorities. (Grades 4–6)

————.*From the Mixed-up Files of Mrs. Basil E. Frankweiler.* New York, Atheneum, 1967. A very original story about two precocious children who run away from home, stay one week in the Metropolitan Museum of Art, and become intrigued with the history of one of its works of art. Awarded the 1968 Newbery Medal. (Grades 5–9)

————. *Jennifer, Hecate, Macbeth, William McKinley, and Me, Elizabeth.* New York: Atheneum, 1967. Two lonely fifth-graders, Elizabeth and Jennifer, become good friends in an interesting book with well-developed characters. Jennifer claims to be a master witch and, although Elizabeth is not quite certain it is true, she becomes Jenifer's apprentice in witchcraft. (Grades 4–6)

Little, Jean. *Home from Far.* Illustrated by Jerry Lazare. Boston: Little, Brown, 1965. Sensitive portrayal of the problems faced by an eleven-year-old boy who must adjust to a new foster family and those of the daughter of that family whose twin brother has recently died in an automobile accident. (Grades 4–7)

————. *Mine for Keeps.* Illustrated by Lewis Parker. Boston: Little, Brown, 1962. A discussion of and an excerpt from this book can be found in this chapter. (Grades 4–6)

MacDonald, Golden, pseud. (Margaret Wise Brown). *The Little Island.* Illustrated by Leonard Weisgard. New York: Doubleday, 1946. Illustrated with lovely paintings which, together with the text, build an appreciation of beauty and nature. (Preschool–grade 2)

McCloskey, Robert, author-illustrator. *Blueberries for Sal.* New York: Viking, 1948. An amusing picture-storybook about a little girl and a baby bear who follow each other's mothers while picking berries. (Preschool–grade 2)

————. *Lentil.* New York: Viking, 1940. An amusing picture book story of a young boy who saves the day. (Grades 1–3)

————. *One Morning in Maine.* New York: Viking, 1952. A sequel to *Blueberries for Sal,* three years later. (Preschool–grade 2)

————. *Time of Wonder.* New York: Viking, 1957. A beautiful picture book about the beauties of nature and the pleasures of spending the summer on a Maine island. Awarded the 1958 Caldecott Award. (Grades 2–5)

Miles, Miska. *The Fox and the Fire.* Illustrated by John Schoenherr. Boston: Little, Brown, 1966.

Powerful, realistic picture-book story about a fox caught in a forest fire. (Grades K–3)

Ness, Evaline, author-illustrator. *Sam, Bangs & Moonshine*. New York: Holt, 1966. Sam, Samantha, a motherless girl, liked to talk "moonshine" —her mother was not dead, she was a mermaid, her cat Bangs talked to her, her pets included a baby kangaroo and a lion (both imaginary). This imagining worried her father, but it was not until it almost caused her friend's death that Sam learned the dangers of "moonshine." An interesting book, but one whose message implies that imagination is not only dangerous but bad. Awarded the 1967 Caldecott Medal. (Preschool–grade 3)

Neville, Emily Cheney. *The Seventeenth Street Gang*. Illustrated by Emily McCully. New York: Harper & Row, 1966. A group of defiantly independent children from relatively well-to-do New York homes conspire against the "flots"—their name for those they don't like. Their taunting of the new boy almost leads to tragedy. (Grades 4–6)

Newbery, Clare Turlay, author-illustrator. *April's Kittens*. New York: Harper & Row, 1940.

———. *Mittens*. New York Harper & Row, 1936. Picture-story books about children and the cats they love. (Preschool–grade 2)

Rand, Ann and Paul. *I Know a Lot of Things*. Illustrated by Paul Rand. New York: Harcourt, 1956. A book to help young children notice the beauty of nature. Stylized illustrations make an effective picture book for the very young. (Preschool–grade 1)

Raskin, Ellen. *Nothing Ever Happens on My Block*. New York: Atheneum, 1967. An amusing picture book in which a bored boy complains how dull his neighborhood is, while behind him a house burns, robbers sneak past, etc. (Grades K–2)

Sachs, Marilyn. *Veronica Ganz*. Illustrated by Louis Glanzman. New York: Doubleday, 1968. Veronica, a domineering bully who resents being a girl, meets a boy she cannot defeat and learns more socially acceptable behavior. A lively, nondidactic story. (Grades 4–6)

———. *Peter and Veronica*. Illustrated by Louis Glanzman. New York: Doubleday, 1969. A sequel to *Veronica Ganz*. (Grades 4–7)

Snyder, Zilpha Keatley. *The Egypt Game*. Illustrated by Alton Raible. New York: Atheneum, 1967. Five middle-class children, from varied racial backgrounds find an abandoned fenced yard in which to play. There they create "Egypt," with altars to Isis and Set. When a child is murdered in the neighborhood, their parents restrict them to their homes. Drawn back to the seemingly safe hideout,

they attract the attacker's attention. (Grades 4–6)

Stolz, Mary. *The Bully of Barkham Street*. Illustrated by Leonard Shortall. New York: Harper & Row, 1963. (Grades 4–6)

———. *A Dog on Barkham Street*. Illustrated by Leonard Shortall. New York: Harper & Row, 1960. Two books that deal with the same characters. In the second novel Edward desperately wants a dog and to solve his problems with "Fatso" Martin, the neighborhood bully. In *The Bully of Barkham Street* many of the same incidents are shown from Martin's point of view, and the reader learns he is both insecure and misunderstood. (Grades 4–6)

———. *The Noonday Friends*. Illustrated by Louis S. Glanzman. New York: Harper & Row, 1963. Two girls from poor families have too many responsibilities to permit them to play together after school. Their need for friendship is convincingly shown. (Grades 4–6)

Tresselt, Alvin. *Hi, Mr. Robin*. Illustrated by Roger Duvoisin. New York: Lothrop, 1950. A little boy longs for spring. Tresselt writes simple picture books filled with love of natural beauty. (Preschool–grade 1) Others by the same author and for the same age group are:

———. *Hide and Seek Fog*. Illustrated by Roger Duvoisin. New York: Lothrop, 1965.

———. *Rain Drop Splash*. Illustrated by Leonard Weisgard. New York: Lothrop, 1946.

———. *Sun Up*. Illustrated by Roger Duvoisin. New York: Lothrop, 1949.

———. *A Thousand Lights and Fireflies*. Illustrated by John Moodle. New York: Parents Institute, 1965.

———. *Wake Up, City!* Illustrated by Roger Duvoisin. New York: Lothrop, 1957.

———. *Wake Up, Farm!* Illustrated by Roger Duvoisin. New York: Lothrop, 1955.

———. *White Snow, Bright Snow*. Illustrated by Roger Duvoisin. New York: Lothrop, 1947. Awarded the 1948 Caldecott Award.

Twain, Mark, pseud. (Samuel Langhorne Clemens). *The Adventures of Huckleberry Finn*. New York: Harper & Row, 1884.

———. *The Adventures of Tom Sawyer*. New York: Harper & Row, 1876. A discussion of and an excerpt from this book appear in this chapter.

Udry, Janice May. *The Moon Jumpers*. Illustrated by Maurice Sendak. New York: Harper & Row, 1959. A dreamy picture book about four children who dance and play in the moonlight before bed. (Grades K–3)

Ward, Lynd, author-illustrator. *Nic of the Woods*.

Boston: Houghton Mifflin, 1965. The picture-book adventures of a boy and his dog who spend summer vacation in the woods. (Grades 1–3)

Wier, Ester. *The Loner*. Illustrated by Cristine Price. New York: McKay, 1963. A discussion of and an excerpt from this book can be found in this chapter. (Grades 5–7)

————. *The Barrel*. Illustrated by Carl Kidwell. New York: McKay, 1966. The adjustment of a sensitive boy to the Florida swamp wilderness is well portrayed. (Grades 5–7)

Zemach, Margot, adapter-illustrator. *Mommy, Buy Me a China Doll*. Chicago: Follett, 1966. A picture-book adaptation of an Ozark children's song. A little girl begs for a china doll that her parents cannot afford. Humorous situations occur as she tries to find an object for trade. (Preschool–grade 3)

Zion, Gene. *Do You Know What I'll Do?* Illustrated by Garth Williams. New York: Harper & Row, 1958. A simple picture book about the seasons. (Preschool–grade 1)

————. *Over and Over*. Illustrated by Garth Williams. New York: Harper & Row, 1951. Picture-story treatment of a progression through the year, highlighting the holidays. (Preschool–grade 1)

————. *The Sky Was Blue*. Illustrated by Garth Williams. New York: Harper & Row, 1963. A young girl looks through the photograph album and learns about life in the past. A picture book. Grades K–2)

Chapter 8
American Minorities

From *Indian Festivals* by Paul Showers, illustration by Lorence Bjorklund; copyright © 1969 by Lorence Bjorklund. Thomas Y. Crowell Company, Inc., publishers.

America is a land of tract housing and mass production, a land where conformity often seems a way of life; yet America is also a land developed by strong individuals, a country that believes in and often honors the unique man. But the man who is too "different"—one whose culture, dress, speech, religion, or color places him apart from others—is often distrusted or misunderstood.

For many American children the first and perhaps only contact with people whose cultural or racial backgrounds are different from their own will come from literature. Because of this, good literature has great potential to help children understand people of other racial, social, economic, or religious groups as individuals. Literature can break down stereotypes by helping children recognize the similarities of all men and by showing the value of each group's uniqueness.

To do this, it is essential that books about minority groups create rounded characters, because stereotypes dehumanize rather than individualize. Categorizing a group by a few adjectives, such as "a dumb Swede," "the lazy, ignorant Negro," "the sly Jew," "the vicious savage," or even "the pious, gentle Quaker," makes it unnecessary for the reader to think of or accept a character as an individual, as a human being. Stereotypes lead to an oversimplification of thought and judgment. And this leads to unconscious prejudice.

Poor books about any minority group show them as totally different from all other Americans *or* show them as completely the same except for a few superficial traits. Every person has the same desires and needs, but the member of a minority group has additional problems and pressures unknown to those of the majority. His life is in many ways quite different because of prejudice and distrust. This difference needs to be shown in literature about minority groups if other people are to understand what their lives are like. Another difference of minority life is that some groups have cultures quite different from that of most Americans. Some of their basic outlooks on life are quite different and so seem "strange."

Cultural behavior and attitudes are tied to emotions, for every group tends to believe its ways are "right" and all other ways "wrong." When two groups live by different values or philosophies, misunderstanding is quite likely to occur. Even something as simple as a love of bright colors has made it difficult for Puerto Ricans to find jobs in New York City; they do not look "right" to employers. *The Girl from Puerto Rico* shows this difference. While most Americans prize competition, it is nonexistent in Pueblo and Seminole life. This cultural difference is illustrated in this excerpt from *The Winners* by Ester Wier.

"Race you 'round the pond," he challenged, "through the trees and back here." Because he admired his friend, there was nothing in the world he would have liked more than proving himself as good or even better than Johnny Cloud at something. What a lift that would give him!

The Indian sprang into action and Scrub leaped up and started along the bank toward the pond. He had shorter legs than Johnny but he was fast and he gained the lead as they were entering the buttonwoods. Looking over his shoulder to see how far ahead he was, he didn't see the log lying in his path and pitched forward, face down, onto the moss floor of the small forest. It knocked the wind out of him and when he could breathe again, he raised his head to see if his friend was back at the clearing yet. Johnny was right beside him.

"Why didn't you keep goin'?" he asked, indignant, wanting no special favors from anyone. He knew he would have raced on if Johnny had been the one to fall.

"What for?" the Indian asked.

"To win, that's what for."

"Why?"

It seemed to Scrub that sometimes Johnny Cloud could act dumber than anyone he'd ever known. "Cause it ain't fair to run and not to try to win. You . . . well, you just got to!"

Johnny shrugged. "I think it's better if you help me, I help you. That way we both win."

When they got back to where Cap was, Scrub said disgustedly, "He don't know nothin' 'bout racin'. He don't even try to be first."

Cap nodded. "Seminoles and Miccosukees don't compete. They believe in everyone helping everyone else, with no one trying to be best. They race for exercise, not to win."[1]

RACIAL MINORITIES

Almost all Americans are descendents of immigrants, yet the non-European immigrants and the native Indians have faced discrimination by those of European ancestry. In the 1960s minority groups, notably the Negroes, Indians and the Mexican-American field workers, began to demand equality. They focused attention on their plight, and some people belonging to the majority began to work for tolerance and acceptance of all racial groups.

Children need help to see that all people are similar; too often they are aware only of surface differences. Books that show how Americans of many racial groups live and think can, if written with subtlety and sensitivity, give children insights they might never otherwise receive. Examples of well-written books about Japanese-Americans, Puerto Ricans in New York City, American Indians, and Negroes are included in the following section.

The largest body of American minority literature deals with Negroes. Until recently Negro fictional characters usually were shown only in menial positions as servants and unskilled laborers, never as skilled workers or professionals, and the tone of these books was often patronizing. Today however, Negroes are shown in all walks of life and with strengths and weaknesses recognizable in all people.

[1] Reprinted by permission of David McKay Company, Inc., from *The Winners* by Ester Wier. Copyright © 1967 by Ester Wier.

Hopefully, this new type of literature will help eliminate prejudice. But regardless of the advances made by Negroes, prejudice is still a strong force in their lives. Books that end with all their problems solved and everyone accepting and liking members of minority groups not only are unrealistic but also dishonest.

The following section contains several selections for comparison. *Little Brown Koko* illustrates how bigotry has been fostered through children's literature. *Call Me Charley* and *Bright April* show how prejudice began to be dealt with in books for youngsters. They can be compared with each other and *Mary Jane*, a more recent book that concerns the integration of a school district.

RELIGIOUS MINORITIES

Since America has no state church, all religions are respected and permitted. Yet many groups in America have known religious intolerance. Hopefully this will be lessened as other people gain an understanding of their traditions and beliefs. Well-written literature about children who belong to these religious groups can help develop the understandings that will build greater respect and tolerance. Two examples of such literature are included in the following selections. *Plain Girl* is about the Amish, a small group that has been and still is troubled by the government. *About the B'nai Bagels* shows contemporary Jewish life.

ECONOMIC MINORITIES

An economic minority little written about is that of the rich. While children in such homes are not materially deprived, they too can have problems caused by their parents' economic status. *Harriet the Spy* is a book about a rich child whose security is shaken when her nurse leaves to get married.

Although the majority of Americans are prosperous, there is a sizable minority that lacks enough money for necessities. Many are migrant workers who follow the crops, others are poor share croppers who never accumulate enough to buy their own land. These are the forgotten people; no town or city wants the responsibility of caring for those who pay no taxes. They have little opportunity to vote, are protected by few laws, are helped by almost no relief agencies. Locked in poverty, they have almost no escape. Books for children that are sympathetic toward these people are beginning to be written. Hopefully they will help the new generations of middle-class American children grow up without prejudice.

Didactic writers preach about the evil of prejudice, good writers show the cruelty of it by involving the reader, making him care about the characters. Through the reader's empathy with them he begins to realize vicariously something of what it is like to be a part of a minority group in America.

THE MOVED-OUTERS

Florence Crannell Means

No matter how well members of a minority group seem to be accepted, it is difficult for them to feel truly secure, for they know that in times of national stress fear can change tolerance into repression. This occurred during World War II when American fear of a Japanese invasion of the west coast led to the internment of thousands of Japanese Americans. Since it has happened here, no one should expect American minority literature to ignore the tension of insecurity.

The following selection accurately portrays this experience in America's history. All over the west similar internments occurred. Although the Japanese Americans were released after the war, emotional scars must still remain among this minority.

MOVED OUT

Even when evacuation day came, Sue Ohara's eyes were dry. She would not have confessed to anyone how much easier it was to be stoic when she learned that the Ito family would be going to the same Assembly Center. And the hurry and rush of getting ready made the young Oharas forget, most of the time, that this was— for nobody knew how long—Last Day.

The last night Sue spent with Emily, and the girls talked till the small hours. Kim stayed with Jim Boyd, and Mrs. Ohara with the Clemonses. Then, after early breakfast, the Oharas met at their deserted house, where the car was packed and waiting in the locked garage.

With the house empty and the yard stripped of its choicest foliage and flowers, it was not so hard to say good-bye to home. Still, Sue did run upstairs for a last look through her bedroom window. The palms and pepper trees seemed woven with girlhood dreams. And she did stand and gaze a moment at the chubby heart and the S. O. on the front walk. The cement of the new sidewalk had happened to be still wet, that day ten years ago when the twelve-year-old Jiro had come to their house with his father. He had carved the design deep, smiling at her through his thick lashes. The young Oharas did not know why he did not come to the house again, nor his father. They did not know why Mr. Ito was always too polite, and Father cool and stiff; nor whether their unfriendliness stemmed from that very day.

The hour of departure had been set for eight-thirty, and Cordova was just getting to work when the Oharas reached the town hall where they had been directed to meet. From farms, market gardens, fruit ranches, all around Cordova, the Japanese had gathered. A line of cars were drawn up at the curb, all but the Itos' big Buick and the Oharas' Dodge, dingy workaday ones. The people who were going in buses sat on their bags and suitcases or drooped patiently above them.

It seemed like some strange going-away party, all blurred and distorted by Sue's excitement. She politely thanked Mrs. Clemons and the other church women, who were pouring hot coffee and passing puffy sugared doughnuts; but she hardly knew that she was eating and drinking. Still munching doughnuts, she and Emily drifted over to the Ito car and talked to Tomi, wedged into the back seat between her mother and younger sister, and to Jiro, behind the wheel.

"Look, Sue," Emily cried, tugging at her arm, "the gang——"

Sue hung back, saying "You come, too, Tomi. And Jiro. It's kids from school."

Jiro shook his head. "It's your crowd, Susie. And Tomi's in too much of a funk. I can't convince her but what we're going to be dumped in a camp and left to starve."

"Oh, Tomi, for goodness' sake! Well, we'll be seeing you." She laughed protestingly, but Tomi's face was almost as white and frightened as it had been on Pearl Harbor Day.

And then Sue forgot Tomi as the dozen boys and girls swarmed around her, and around Kim. Gloria was there and among the rest were Peter Lucca and Elsa Schonberg, who didn't have to be pulled up by the roots and dropped on new soil whether or not.

Now it was more than ever like a going-away party, with "train-letters," boxes of candy, a basket of goodies, a boutonnière—with everyone talking at once, with girls laughing artificially and boys pushing each other around.

Then the M.P.'s began to load people into the buses, and a tight, awkward silence seized the group of schoolmates. The evacuees climbed quietly into the waiting vehicles, some with a heavy weariness, some stolidly, some with determined smiles. There was no outcry until one old woman pushed aside the hands helping her aboard, turned wildly toward Cordova, and uttered a sobbing, gulping cry.

She had a single glimpse of the old face, furrowed deep as a dried peach, the corded throat working convulsively. Then the two hands, like bundles of sticks, came up to hide that naked grief, and the woman's friends lifted her into the bus.

"She thinks she'll never see her home again. Likely she's been coming here to market since she was young," Emily quavered, the tears running.

"Guess the clock's struck, Sis," Kim said loudly, heartily—and the young people moved in a mass toward the car.

Hands thrust out to shake hers—and Emily's wet face against her own—boys slapping Kim's back till he staggered——

The gang breaking down in the middle of "He's a jolly good fellow." Mrs. Clemons starting "God be with you til we meet again." Pitching it too high. Mr. Clemons pitching it too low. The church people joining in, waveringly, voices thick with grief.

Just as the buses rumbled into motion and the song ended, a kindergartener leaned out of the window of a bus and piped to his teacher, "See you in the morning, Mis' Jones!" just as he had done every day.

At that, all the determined smiles of church women and schoolgirls melted into weeping, and the boys ran alongside the Ohara car hiding their emotion with pointless jokes: "Don't take any wooden nickels!" "Write once in a while if you haven't too many dates!"

From the Ito car Jiro looked back and waved. His head was high and his eyes lost themselves behind his thick lashes. He seemed to signal, "Adventure, Sue! Pioneers, remember!"

The caravan gained speed, and Sue screwed around to watch the throng at the town hall until the turn of a corner hid them from sight. Then she fixed her gaze on Cordova till they passed its limits and sped out along the highway. Heading the procession, bringing up the rear, weaving through it, keeping back other traffic, were the dusty jeeps, and the young M.P.'s in them shouted friendly directions, joked with the evacuee children, grinned or looked sympathetically sober. Sue's heart swelled with gratitude toward them.

"Since we've got to go, I'm sort of glad we're

going to Santa Anita," said Sue, trying to lift Kim's dejection.

Kim only growled.

"All these years I've wanted to see the races there," Sue went on, vivaciously, "and never dreamed I'd be living there some day. Swankiest race-track——"

"Oh, dry up," Kim begged with brotherly courtesy.

The ride was short. Within two hours the entourage slowed up, and Sue, peering out, could see that the buses were turning in at the Santa Anita entrance. Jiro grinned back at her, flipping a hand in mock awe at the tall, many-windowed façade, the lofty palms, the fountain. They had arrived.

Private cars were left at the entrance, where they would be cared for and sold for the owners. Sue saw Kim's hand linger on the wheel of their Dodge in a furtive caress. He had done his first driving in that car, and he would not see it again.

The Oharas lugged their bags inside and left them on tables where inspectors were opening the luggage. Behind the Ito family they filed past the doctor at the entrance, showing him their throats and their hands and then pushing on along the graveled walk.

"Barracks 15, Apartments A-2 and A-3, that's where we're assigned," said Jiro. "What about you folks?"

"Barracks 15, Apartment B-2," Kim read from the page of instructions that had just been handed to his mother.

Sue felt herself flushing with pleasure. Jiro would be their neighbor, no matter how frosty Mother was looking about it. Jiro would be their neighbor, so it didn't matter much that there were only one or two familiar faces among those peering from stable doors and windows to watch the newcomers.

"And here we are," said Jiro, striding ahead to throw open the Oharas' door. "Welcome home!"

"Gosh," said Kim, momentarily forgetting his gloom, "must have been a prince of a horse to rate this. Reckon it was Whirlaway or Seabiscuit?"

"A horse's stall as big as my kitchen!" cried Mrs. Ohara.

"Doesn't smell like your kitchen," said Sue.

The individual exercise yard had been walled up to make another room; an asphalt floor had been put in; the walls had been whitewashed; but the odor remained.

"Smells?" asked Jiro, from the half-door of the next stall. "I can't smell anything. Too used to it, maybe." Grinning, he gestured toward the small hallway between the stalls. "This was where they forked in the hay. The former inmates just stuck their heads through these halfdoors and got their grub. Service, what?"

"You make me hungry," Sue said. "And we don't have long to wait. Look: this sheet says 'Breakfast six-thirty, dinner eleven-thirty, supper four-thirty.' Good grief!"

Kim said, "At Alcatraz they wake the prisoners even earlier."

Surely they said cots and mattresses would be supplied," Mother said anxiously, looking around the complete emptiness of the twenty-by-ten feet.

"Yes," said Sue; "and it isn't going to be so bad. In New York it's all the style to turn old barns into swanky houses. We'll be in fashion. But when will they let us have our bags?" she demanded of Jiro, as if he should know everything.

"Want to go see if they're ready?" he asked.

He and Kim, Tomi and Sue, walked back along the streets of stalls and stood watching the M.P.'s opening bundles and bags.

"Gosh," said Kim, "can't they take our word for it that we haven't any contraband?"

Without speaking, Jiro pointed at the cameras, the radios, the one or two knives the M.P.'s had tossed aside.

"Remember the Kimuras, Kim," said Sue, adopting Jiro's easy attitude. "Trouble is, they think we're all tricky, and we think we're all woolly white lambs. Really, we're like any other bunch of folks. Lookit! Another camera!"

When they got back to their quarters with their exonerated luggage, they found that three cots had been delivered to the Oharas. When Mother and Sue had made them up with white sheets and the army blankets, even those cots gave the stalls a feeling of home.

"Almost dinnertime!" Jiro called, just as Sue plumped her pillow into place. "And a fellow told me we'd have a plenty long wait if we weren't on time."

A tremendous bang and clatter put a period to his words. "Gong of the Blue Mess," he added.

The Oharas and the Itos were soon part of the queue winding toward the mess-hall door. A kitchen boy whanged his battered dishpan a few more times, flourished his stick and vanished into the kitchen.

"Cowboy style, I take it," said Jiro.

Inside the hall, the Itos and Oharas were engulfed in warm heavy food odors and the din of forks, spoons, tins. Presently they were balancing heaped plates and hunting a place at the tables. As they came to a vacant place, Mrs. Ohara hesitated outside the long backless bench.

Sue giggled. "Turn sidewise," she instructed, taking her mother's dishes. "Put one foot over, like this. Now sit astraddle, so, and lift over your other foot. You don't have to blush so, Mom. Everybody's doing it. But it would be easier in slacks."

The scraping of dishes at the end of the hall drowned conversation, but Sue was too engrossed in the endless file of diners to talk. Young people called to each other as they made their way down the crowded aisles between tables, fathers and mothers kept their children under their wings, older Japanese bowed rhythmically to acquaintances, or shuffled along blank-faced and silent. Sue looked more than she ate, but Kim emptied his plate and stood in line for a second helping, coming home an hour after the others, because it had taken forty-five minutes to get to the serving table again.

The afternoon passed. There were letters to write. There were the first inoculations to take. There was the evening meal at half-past four.

For a while after supper the young people walked to and fro before their stalls. Here, withdrawn from the barbed wire which fenced the camp, and with other people walking, talking, laughing around them, the place did not feel abnormal. The difference showed itself when twilight thickened and the searchlights began to flash. Up and down the streets, across roofs, in at windows, played the hard white light. It swept across Sue's and Tomi's faces as they loitered before the Ohara door. Tomi ducked her head, shutting her eyes and mewing like a drenched kitten, and even Sue felt as if she were drowning in that bright relentless flood.

"This is like prison," Sue thought desperately. "Like the searchlights wheeling ceaselessly round Alcatraz——"

Even without the lights, that first night would have been wakeful. The legs of the cots had sunk into the soft asphalt so that the beds tilted and wabbled. It was late before the day's heavy heat began to lift from the Ohara apartment; and in the row of stalls behind it where windows were fewer, babies whimpered and wailed till midnight. The partitions were thin, and Sue could hear Kiku Ito ask for a drink; could hear his mother say that no one had remembered to bring water from the hydrant several doors away. Twice an hour the neighbor on the Oharas' right wakened them with a magnificent sneeze; and from the stall that back up against theirs came another set of coughs, laughs, squeakings of restless cots.

"My grief!" Sue muttered. "I suppose all those other people can hear us breathing, too. Likely they heard me ask Mom what became of my p.j.'s."

From the wall to the right a chuckling little-boy voice inquired, 'Well, what did become of 'em, kid?'

Sue flounced on her cot, making a face of violent protest, and the little boy snickered. Kim, from the corner which he had curtained with a sheet, make his voice deep and inquired, "What's-this-what's-this, young people?"

Sue dozed at length, rousing with a start whenever a searchlight lashed in at the window. Toward morning her slumber deepened into profound sleep, so that when she wakened she pushed hard against the unfamiliar hammocky sag of her cot, refusing to open her eyes, though daylight shone through her lids.

The noise bewildered her: thudding feet, shrieking beds, slamming doors, crying of children. She could hear the clamor of birds, the rattle of palm leaves. She could smell spicy fragrances. Yes, but battling those aromas was the unmistakable edge of horse odor. And on Sue's nose a fly settled and bit viciously. Her eyes popped open and she stared up into the bare rafters, where more flies buzzed and circled. Her gaze flew to the windows, round the board walls.

At a pushed-out knothole she caught the glint—the blue glint—of an eye. Jerking the sheet up to her chin she called indignantly, "Kim! Look at that knothole!"

Before Kim could respond, the eye vanished, to the accompaniment of a loud smack and an aggrieved "Ouch! I only wanted to see what the kids looked like."

Sue leaped from bed, snatched an envelope out of her suitcase, licked the flap, whacked it on the wall so that it hung over the hole. "My grief!" she protested.

So the first day began.

* * *

VALLEY FORGE

Saturday morning. The day before Easter. Sue and Kim sat on the floor with their biology note books, inking in the drawings they had sketched at home in the Cordova lab. The only other place to work was the big room at the grandstand, but its tables were always crowded, its clamor deafening.

Tomi sat on a cot, sighing and turning the pages of a textbook. Mother had the electric iron attached to the light cord that swung from the rafters, and was pressing lengths of flowered scarlet calico. She had ripped up Sue's broomstick skirt to make appliquéd designs on unbleached muslin she had bought for curtains and bedspreads: already a community store was going full blast in camp. Jiro was sociably sandpapering his pine wardrobe, just beyond the half-door. The common wood, repeatedly rubbed down and shellacked, acquired a lovely glow, and even its brown streaks and knots became decorative. Beyond Jiro Sue could see his twelve-year-old sister Mitsu sitting in a corner with string stretched across her slender hands, making an intricate cat's-cradle for Kiku, who crouched between her knees.

"No, I don't see how we can stand Easter," Sue said once more, and splashed a drop of ink on a carefully drawn cell.

Before the subject could be taken up again, Tommy Filkins stuck his head in the door. "Callers for the 'Haras," he announced, his blue eyes darting into every corner.

Sue jumped up, smoothing her hair with both hands and leaving the blot to dry. Kim came to his feet as eagerly. Mrs. Ohara's fingers shook as she disconnected the iron.

"Couldn't be Dad," Sue reminded her. "Nor Tad nor Amy."

Nevertheless, they walked so hurriedly across the camp that they arrived breathless at the rear entrance. Callers!

Many people clustered along the barbed wire, sitting or standing, talking across the prickly barrier. All on the inside were Japanese, but those on the outside were a mixed assemblage. There were Caucasians—evacuation had added this word to its everyday vocabulary—Negroes, Chinese, and even Japanese. For now, on April 24, evacuation was only half-completed.

Sue's eyes raced from group to group. "Oh," she cried, her voice catching, "the Clemonses—and the Andrewses——"

"And Jim Boyd, the nut," Kim finished.

They clasped hands across the wire. Sue and Emily kissed. Everyone struggled for words and then talked all at once.

"We brought a cake—and cookies and junk——"

"But some guy took 'em——"

"Marian couldn't come. The Easter sales at the shop are marvelous——"

"Almost everything you transplanted in our yard is growing like mad."

"The kids in English class sent an Easter basket, but the guard took that, too. If they don't shell out, just let us know!" Jim flexed a threatening arm.

"We'll get the things," they assured him. Of course they would. Everything was fine. Sue's face felt stretched with its smiles. This was next to being home again.

The young people dropped to the ground to talk more comfortably, listening betweenwhiles to scraps of conversation from their elders on the one side, from a visiting group on the other. The Clemonses could have come in—ministers were allowed entrance; but they would stay outside with the Andrewses today. Tomorrow they would visit the Ohara stall, for tomorrow Mr. Clemons was to have part in the Easter service. And now, what was there that Mrs. Ohara would like him to bring her from town?

Some of the visitors on the other side were

Chinese. Even the old grandmother had come, in black coat and trousers and with a funny black bandeau across the bald spot on her brow. Evidently they were keeping their Japanese friends' dog for them; the little black cocker flew under the wire, long ears flapping, feet as big as if he were wearing fur galoshes. He climbed into his young master's arms, frantically licking the tears that ran down the boy's face. Looking at him, Sue felt old and sad and wise; and Emily reached through the fence and patted her hand sympathetically.

Sue smiled at her and changed the subject: "The preacher's asking Mom what she wants. Know what I'd like?"

Emily shook her gleaming head.

"A hamburger!" Sue gestured across the street.

Emily and Jim twisted to look. Directly opposite the race-trace entrance, beyond the highway with its stream of traffic, stood a Drive-In stand.

"That's easy," said Jim, on his feet with the words. "I'll be back in a smack with a sack."

She put out a detaining hand. "No, I didn't mean that, I want to get it myself. I want to saunter in, free as air, and sit down at the fountain like a princess, and eat two hamburgers, with onions and dill and mustard and ketchup and potato chips."

Jim cast a quick look around him. "That's easy, too. Look, kids, with all these other Japanese on the outside, how would anybody notice you weren't visitors, yourselves? All you have to do is roll under when the guards aren't looking."

They gaped at him.

"Shucks, Kim, you roll under enough barbed wire when we go fishing," Jim exclaimed. "Just make sure there's no guard watching——"

Kim's Adam's apple bobbed up and down above his plaid collar. Sue's head whirled. Emily babbled, "Oh, do you THINK it's SAFE——?" even while she was grabbing the strand of wire and holding it high as Jim was doing.

They were wriggling under. They were sitting up, hearts pounding, outside the fence, furtively brushing dust from themselves. They were sauntering between Emily and Jim toward the strip of highway and its whizzing cars.

"Kimio! Sumiko!" Mrs. Ohara's shocked voice

stabbed them. Two or three cars were roaring toward them, and Sue felt as if she were standing poised on the brink for minutes.

But she managed to turn and wave her hand, "See you again soon, Mrs. Ohara!" she called. Her voice was strained and her body stiff from trying to be natural, and she could feel eyes boring into her from all directions.

"All clear!" Jim said, and they darted across.

By the time their first order was filled, Sue's heart had stopped shaking her. They ate two hamburgers apiece, though prices were outrageous; and they had double-decker cones; and finally they sauntered back to camp, with cones for their elders held before them like flags of truce. They formed a knot before Mrs. Ohara, and by the time the cones had been distributed, Kim and Sue were inside the fence again.

"My grief!" Sue murmured, sitting up and brushing herself, while her stomach settled. "I'd never had believed I could be so thankful to be on this side. Like a mouse safe in its own hole."

Mrs. Ohara was scolding softly, and the faces of the adult visitors were variously amused, sympathetic, dubious, disapproving.

"Might—less innocent people," Mr. Clemons wondered aloud, "do the same thing—and keep going? Keep going?"

"There's roll-call, sir," Kim put in quickly. "Three times a day—and almost time for it now."

So they said their good-byes, watched until their friends drove away, and loitered back toward their quarters. Later that night they investigated the gifts that had come from Cordova and passed inspection.

"I'm sure the cake is Mrs. Andrews's special chocolate angelfood," Sue said devoutly. "Emily put on the letters, though. Emily can't draw a straight line with a ruler."

The inscription, HAPPY EASTER TO THE OHARAS, wavered in violet letters across the piled white frosting.

"Mrs. Andrews's own special icing," Sue went on, running her tongue hungrily round her lips. Then she bent to look closer. "Funny," she said. "I never saw any of her icing that was pockmarked like that—little bits of holes all over it."

"They use long needles," cheerfully observed Jiro, who had been invited in to share the goodies.

The others stared at him.

"You mean they—searched—our CAKE?" Kim asked.

"Now, Bud, be realistic," Sue said soothingly. "If any of the bunch is dangerous—and it's likely there've been dangerous ones, though most of them are in detention camps now—but if there's any chance, wouldn't the Government be silly not to make sure no contraband is smuggled in? Though it does seem funny when they let us visit through the barbed wire."

"Really dangerous guys wouldn't risk passing things in the open like that," Jiro guessed. "Or maybe the Intelligence is just getting into swing——"

"Well, you needn't cut any of the old cake for me," Kim growled. "I've lost my appetite."

Mrs. Ohara went on serenely, counting noses and taking expert measure of the tall cake, and then drawing a free-hand design of her own which made a many-petaled flower and reduced the confection to equal slices. And presently Kim was eating his share, with lemonade as cold as water from the tap two doors away would make it. The camp was soon to go on Army A rations, but as yet it was on B rations, and butterless, and meals were drab. The high, light cake, its delicate brown surmounted by drifted sweetness, was luscious after the dull tastes and textures with which their plates had been piled.

Easter eggs, both the genuine kind, dyed, and chocolate ones trimmed with crimped white sugar ribbons and flowing script, "Love to Sue," "Kisses to Kim"; an Easter lily plant for Mother and an azalea for Sue, cookies, fudge, and panocha from the church choir.

"Maybe it isn't such a horrible Easter after all," said Sue, when lights went out at ten and they groped their way to bed.

"As if a cake could make Easter!" Kim said loftily.

But for Sue the next day did make Easter.

The Oharas dressed carefully, glad that they had brought some good clothes, together with the work clothes mentioned in the instructions. When they came to the great grandstand it was evident that most of Santa Anita had done likewise. Thousands of people were assembled there, and they were as smart, as well-groomed, as any city church congregation.

The choir had been practicing under a noted Japanese director, and now the music swelled out gloriously on the soft spring air. Palms rustled, birds sang, the San Gabriel Mountains rose in beauty. Mr. Clemons offered prayer that was strong and tender, and the speaker of the day, a man known across the continent, lifted the hearts of the people.

As they walked home, Sue said haltingly, "I don't know that I ever felt more Easterish."

Even Kim's face was relaxed from its tight brooding. "Remember it was just before Easter, two years ago, that I had my appendix out. That was the Easter that meant most to me. Up to now."

Sue thought, "It's the pain, the sorrow, that make Easter. There's no real Easter without the Cross."

Kim's mind must have been working along like lines, for he said: "I suppose good things are worth suffering for. I mean things like democracy. They don't come cheap. Maybe this—You know what I want to name our stall? Know what I wish you'd letter over it, instead of your kiddish fooling? 'Valley Forge.'"

Sue's thoughts stumbled momentarily and then fell in step with his. "Valley Forge," she assented, BECAUSE ALL THIS WOULD BE DIGNIFIED, MADE BEARABLE, IF WE COULD REMEMBER TO THINK OF IT SO: AS SUFFERING FOR OUR COUNTRY. FOR AMERICA.

THE SPIDER PLANT

Yetta Speevack

Written for third and fourth graders, this book just touches on the prob-
lems Puerto Ricans face in New York City. Poor housing, low income, and
prejudice are a part of The Spider Plant, *yet in this book serious problems*
are easily solved. The reader is left with impressions that prejudice is easily
erased and that Puerto Ricans really live fairly well in New York City.

In contrast to this book, the next selection, The Girl from Puerto Rico, *is*
about the more usual position of Puerto Ricans new to New York. Written
for older children, it shows the effects social and economic restrictions have on
people.

As they walked down the street, she said, "Do the people in New York always walk so fast?"

"It only seems so in the beginning. You'll get used to it." Papá looked down and smiled at her, but she knew he understood.

"Aren't there any trees?" Carmen went on, looking up and down Eighth Avenue.

"As soon as we're settled, we'll pack a big lunch and take the bus to Central Park for a picnic. There you'll see some beautiful trees," Papá promised.

Carmen looked up to see if he was teasing. But he wasn't. What a strange place this was. Never before had it been necessary to ride to see a tree. Was it possible to come to like such a place? Carmen wasn't sure.

Papá soon stopped in front of the big, five-story, faded brick building on 27th Street. They had to carry their baskets up three flights of stairs. On every floor there was a long hall with apartment doors on either side. Their apartment was in the back, at the end of the long hall.

Papá put his key in the hole and opened the door. Carmen looked in eagerly. But there wasn't much to see. Inside, everything was small and dark. Was this where they were going to live? Carmen could not believe it. Mamá and Pedro looked disappointed, too.

Papá must have noticed, for he said, "Rents are high and apartments are scarce. I looked everywhere, and this was the best I could find. It's not much, but it's something."

After depositing their baskets in the already cluttered living room, Papá showed them the kitchen, which had a sink, stove, and refrigerator. Opening the refrigerator, he showed Mamá that it was full of food. Mamá was surprised to see that all the food was familiar, all things she was used to in Puerto Rico.

"There is a *bodega* just down the street," said Papá. "There you will find all the things you need to cook the good meals you like to make. And I will be glad to eat them." The whole family laughed, and everyone felt better.

"Of course it would be better if the kitchen were big enough to hold a table and chairs so we wouldn't have to eat all our meals in the living room," Papá went on. "But I'm hungry enough for your cooking, Mamá, that I could eat it anywhere."

Carmen looked around at the small kitchen. How different it was from the big kitchen in Puerto Rico. There they had cooked, eaten, sewn, done their homework, and even slept. Carmen wondered if Papá remembered how often she had run in and out of the kitchen door there, which led to the little garden. This kitchen didn't even *have* a door, let alone a garden outside. But no one else said anything, so Carmen kept still, too.

Then Papá showed Carmen where she would sleep. She was luckier than Pedro. She had a room to herself, although it was tiny and the family had to pass through it to get to the living room. It was in the living room that Pedro would sleep, on a studio bed.

Mamá looked around, took off her kerchief, put on an old dress, and began to unpack and put things away. But the place seemed to close in on Carmen long before the unpacking was finished. Everything was so tight and dark she felt she couldn't bear it.

Finally Papá saw how restless she was and suggested that she go downstairs and wait on the stoop of the house. As soon as the rest had finished unpacking, he said, they would join her and go for a walk to see the neighborhood.

"Thank you, Papá," said Carmen. With a sigh of relief, she ran downstairs to the street, where she watched people hurrying by. They talked as they passed, but she couldn't understand a word. Pedro and she had studied English in the schools of Puerto Rico, but the words she heard now didn't sound the same. People spoke so fast.

New York was a dark and lonely place. Of that Carmen was sure. Her friends were all miles and miles away. And even the streets here were strange. Nothing was like the streets and houses, and especially the little garden, that she had known. If only she could run under a palm tree and look up at its great high fronds. *Everything* was better in Puerto Rico.

Carmen looked up, as if the tree were there. But all she really saw were big dirty buildings. Even the sky looked different.

"Hi, do you live here?"

The voice caught Carmen unawares. She looked down startled. In front of her was a girl about her own age, with dark curly hair. The English words were strange, though, and Carmen could not reply, so she just smiled. To her relief, the girl asked in Spanish:

"*Vives aquí?*"

This time Carmen answered, "*Sí.*"

"I live in the house next to yours," said the girl pointing to the brownstone house next door. "I'm twelve, and my name is Iris. What's yours?"

"I'm Carmen Santos. This is my first day in New York. I'm twelve, too."

"Then you'll be going to my school," Iris said with delight. "We can go together. I'll wait for you, and you wait for me."

"Good," Carmen said. "Will we be in the same class?"

"I hope so," said Iris. "Want me to show you the school?"

Carmen wanted to go. But what would Papá say if he came down and she was gone. "Is it far?" she asked.

The girl shook her head, so Carmen nodded and the two of them walked over to Ninth Avenue. When they got to the school, Carmen exclaimed, "*Que linda!* It's beautiful, and it's so big, too. It's almost as long as the whole block!"

"It's new," said Iris proudly. "We have a big gym and an auditorium with a real stage, and curtains that draw when we have plays in the assembly."

Carmen looked around, as she and Iris started back. The houses were the same, dirty and ugly, and the streets were the same, too, just as bare and dark. But she had a new friend and a new school. Maybe everything about New York was not bad.

THE NEW HOME

School was going to be exciting. Carmen felt it even more on Monday when she went inside. The halls were wide. And one glass-enclosed bulletin board had a display of dolls from all over the world. Carmen had never seen such a thing before. The monitor, taking her from the office to her classroom, had to pull her away.

He led her to a room with six wide windows that went up to the ceiling. Green plants lined the window sills. They were the first thing Carmen saw. It must be that her new teacher loved plants. That was a good sign. Carmen was getting used to New York streets, but she still missed the pineapple palms and the flowers of Puerto Rico.

Tearing her eyes from the plants, she looked around the room. To her delight, there was Iris, who smiled and nodded as the teacher came over to greet Carmen. The teacher was tall and blond and had a welcoming smile.

"I'm Miss Hall," she said. "*Bienvenido*."

Delighted to hear the teacher speak Spanish, Carmen answered, "*Gracias*. I'm Carmen Santos."

"*No hablo mucho español, pero estudio ahora español. Yo te ayudo inglés, y tu me enseñas español. Sí?*"

Carmen smiled at the strange way the teacher said her Spanish words. This teacher was going to be nice.

And the teacher was nice. She helped Carmen get acquainted with all the strange new things she had to learn and with words she did not understand. In a few weeks it seemed as if she had been in the school for a long time.

The children in this school, Carmen soon discovered, all had jobs, and these were changed every week. Some children liked to wash the boards because they could jump up and down to reach the top; others liked to go on errands; and some liked to dust the collection of shells on a shelf in the bookcase because they could hold the shells to their ears and listen for the sound of the ocean. When the teacher asked, "Who will take care of the plants?", Carmen always put up her hand. She sometimes got the job. And that was what she liked best of all at the school.

Everything was fine except for one thing. In Puerto Rico, everyone in school had been her friend. But here, that was not true. Or at least it did not seem so. With Iris as a friend, Carmen had quickly gotten acquainted with the other girls who were Puerto Ricans, because they all spoke Spanish. And with them Carmen had fun. They were like the girls she had always known. But the other girls sometimes laughed when she said things, and Carmen knew they were laughing at her. Iris said not to mind them, but Carmen did. It did not feel good to be laughed at.

One day Miss Hall asked Carmen if she knew a poem that the class had been memorizing.

"I know it to my little finger," Carmen said.

The class laughed, and Carmen looked at them confused and unhappy. She did not know what she had done. But she must have said something funny to them. And suddenly she was very angry.

"I can't help it," she said in a mixture of Spanish and English. "I may not know English as well as you, but I'm trying. And it's not nice of you to laugh."

"Carmen, Carmen," said Miss Hall. "Don't be angry. We weren't really laughing at you. We say, 'I know it by heart' in English, and in Spanish you say 'I know it to my little finger.' To us, what you said sounds funny. Just as I am sure some of the things we say sound funny to you. Someday, you will laugh at your mistakes, too. We are all your friends here. And we want to help you. So don't be angry with us."

Carmen was embarrassed. She had not meant to say what she did. But after school that day some of the girls whom she did not know well came up and offered to help her with English. "Thank you," Carmen said. "It's nice of you to offer. I'm sure you can help me when I make funny mistakes."

That night she told Mamá and Papá and Pedro what had happened. "She is right," said Papá. "And Americans do say funny things, too. When I first went to work, it was very hard for me to understand all that was said to me. Often I heard one man say to people who came in, 'Gerarahee.' I didn't know what he was saying."

"What was he saying, Papá?" asked Carmen. "I never heard that word either."

Papá laughed. "Finally I asked one of the other Puerto Ricans who had been there longer than I He laughed when I asked and said it had puzzled him, too; but finally he found out that the man was really saying four words: 'Get out of here.'"

The whole family laughed. And Carmen glanced at Pedro. She did not know whether he was having the same trouble as she was. Pedro, of course, did not talk about his troubles. From the look on his face, she suspected that he was. She knew he did not have as many friends as she did. But he did have a job on Saturdays, and sometimes in the afternoons, at Mr. Rocano's fish store. He helped Mr. Rocano clean the big fish tanks. What a smelly job! But Pedro seemed to like it. He talked about nothing but fish.

No one in the Santos family was really surprised then, when one day, a few weeks after Carmen's English problem had been settled, Pedro came home with some fish. In fact, everyone had been expecting it. But no one but Pedro had realized that he would also bring a big fish tank, a thermometer for the tank, fish food, and a light to keep the fish warm. He had bought them all with the money he was making.

"I should think you'd get enough fish at Mr. Rocano's," Carmen said. But Pedro didn't answer. He just put the tank on the floor of the living room and got everything all set up. Carmen had to admit to herself that the fish were pretty, like bright moving flowers. Of course, she didn't tell that to Pedro.

Pedro loved his fish; every day after that when he came home from school, he went right to his fish tank. He talked to his fish as if they understood him. Once when he thought no one was at home, Carmen heard him say softly, "Hello, Little Snapper. You're a pretty good swimmer.

"Don't hide behind the reef, pretty Squirrel Fish.

"Eat some food, Black Striper!"

Pedro never talked like that to her, and Carmen decided he loved his fish better than his family. But in a way she understood. It was nice to have a pet—something to take care of. It made her homesick for Puerto Rico to think of it; there she had had a garden to care for, and that had been almost like a pet.

For Pedro's birthday, late in November, Papá bought a special little table to hold the tank. Papá was pleased that Pedro had a job he liked and that he seemed to be happy in New York; and this was his way of saying so.

Papá, himself, was happy too, now that he had his family with him. And so was Mamá. She was happy mostly because her family was happy, Carmen thought. For many times Mamá talked of the good days in Puerto Rico. She remembered the flowers and picnics at the beach and the garden where they often sat in the evening.

Mamá did not get out as much as the rest of the family. She did not have as many chances to make new friends. She did know Mrs. Morales next door, though. Carmen liked it when Mrs. Morales came in with her baby, María. Sometimes she even let Carmen take care of María when she went to the store. The Morales apartment was much like the one the Santos family had, and often Mrs. Morales mentioned how dark it was. Not at all like Puerto Rico.

"Do you really like this dark apartment, Mamá?" Carmen asked one day, when Mamá was talking about doing a little more painting.

"It is dark," said Mamá. "And both Papá and I would like something better. But as long as we must stay here, the love we have for each other will make it bright." And Mamá, Carmen decided, was doing more than her share to help make it so. She had worked hard to make it look as nice as possible. And every day she cooked the good dinners that they all, and especially Papá, liked so well.

When Papá came in from work, he always called out, "*Buenas noches*, Good evening," or "Hello, hello everybody," or "What smells so good? Does the good smell come from his house?" or "I'm hungry. What's for supper today?"

When they sat down at the table, Papá always got them all to talking. "How's school?" he would ask Carmen and Pedro.

One day Pedro told about some of the boys in his class who were always disturbing everyone. "In Puerto Rico, they would be put out of school," Pedro said.

"They are very foolish," Papá said. "Today everyone needs a good education. If I had been to school longer, I could get a better job and then perhaps we could live in a better place. In Puerto Rico when I was growing up it was not possible for everyone to go to school as long as he wanted. But here it is. People who do not take advantage of this are foolish." He shook his head as if he did not understand such boys. Then he turned to Carmen. "How's your class, Carmen? Do the children listen to your teacher?"

"My teacher says my class would win a medal if they gave one for the most talking."

"And you, Carmen, what do you do?" he went on.

"I would help win the medal," she answered. Everyone, even Papá, laughed.

Ever since the night Carmen had come home from school with her story about the children laughing, Papá had also had English lessons at the dinner table. He especially liked to tease Mamá about her funny mistakes. Somehow the talk about the medal reminded Carmen of a story her mother had told about buying socks for Pedro in a store where only English was spoken.

"Mamá," she said, "tell about buying the socks for Pedro."

With some coaxing, Mamá agreed. "I said,"

she explained, "my boy, she need size 10." Mamá always said *she* for *he*.

"It's *he*, Mamá, *he* for Pedro," Carmen said again, laughing. But the next time she spoke, Mamá got mixed up and said *she* again. When they laughed at her, she laughed as loudly as they did.

Carmen still had some problems with saying things and hearing things right. But not nearly as many as she had had at first. The girls who had promised to help her, had, and Iris and the other Puerto Rican girls had tried harder to help her, too. By early winter, Carmen had even more friends, and there was a surprising number of things to do in New York City, she found.

In the late fall, while it was still warm, she played hopscotch with the girls on the sidewalk or at the edge of the street. They played jump rope on the sidewalk, too, and sometimes jacks. And they played with their dolls on the high front steps of Iris' house. Once in a while, they went walking and looked in the store windows, playing a wishing game as they went, each one picking the one thing in each window she would like best to have. But most of all, Carmen liked an exciting game of tag on the wide front steps of the big post office. Of course, the men sometimes chased them off, but that only added to the fun. When Carmen wrote to her friends in Puerto Rico, which was not as often as she had thought it would be, the things she was doing sounded exciting even to her.

THE GIRL FROM PUERTO RICO

Hila Colman

This selection is included for comparison with the previous passage from The Spider Plant. *In* The Girl from Puerto Rico, *Hila Colman shows several sides to life in New York. Some Puerto Ricans enjoy city life while others, like Felicidad, can never adjust to the prejudice they encounter and so save their money to return home.*

Hila Colman attempts to give an accurate portrayal of Puerto Rican life in New York, and she often succeeds. As happens in too many books about minority groups, however, she occasionally becomes didactic to make her point. And at other times she slips into sentimentality. These two weaknesses and the lack of character development makes The Girl from Puerto Rico *less successful literature than* The Spider Plant. *Yet Hilda Colman's picture of minority life is more realistic than that drawn by Yetta Speevac.*

"I'm taking Willy to school this morning," she announced in the kitchen to her mother and to Mrs. Esteves. "And then I'm going to look for a job."

Mrs. Marquez had a resigned look on her face. "God wills it," she said. "But how is Willy going to come home? He'll get killed crossing the streets."

"Danny'll bring him home. Don't worry."

"A fine thing for Willy to have to be taken care of by someone like Danny!"

Felicidad wanted to scold her mother, but she held her tongue. Her mother's eyes looked so sad and bewildered that Felicidad knelt down beside her and hugged her instead. Her mother used to be gay and full of fun, like Mrs. Esteves, and Felicidad couldn't help worrying about her. Perhaps she and Carlos had pushed too much upon her. She hadn't even recovered from the shock of her husband's death when they moved her up north, but then they had thought hopefully that the change would do her good.

But Felicidad couldn't stay depressed long, especially today. It was too exciting to think of going out by herself to find a wonderful job! Then she'd have money, and she could cheer her mother up. The salaries she'd read in the paper sounded like a lot of money just for waiting on tables. Soon they'd go up to Radio City, and then she would take her mother down to the wonderful store on Fourteenth Street, and maybe she'd buy a television set!

Felicidad dressed herself in the new clothes they had bought on her first day in New York—a slim, mustard-colored wool skirt and a bright-red jersey. Her mother had fussed about the colors, saying they were far too bright, and also about the skirt's being much too tight, but Felicidad had noticed other girls in the store wearing things just like that, and more than anything in the world she wanted to look like the girls in the States. She had never seen so many clothes to choose from in her life. In the store they had visited there were racks and racks of dresses, and the store itself seemed to be blocks long. Back home in Barranquitas they had sometimes ordered from a mail-order catalogue, but most of the time Felicidad had made her own clothes or bought something ready-made at the little store on the plaza.

Her ankles wobbled in her high heels, and Mrs. Esteves laughed at the way she walked. "You'd better be careful. I don't know how you'll get on a bus, with that tight skirt and those high heels!"

"She looks like a girl of twenty-one or twenty-two," Mrs. Marquez remarked critically, "not like a proper, nice young girl."

"That's good. That'll make it easier for me to get a job," Felicidad answered good-naturedly. "I want to look older."

"Don't talk to anybody—no strangers at all," Mrs. Marquez warned her again before she and Willy left. "Do you think you can find your way back here all right?" she asked anxiously.

"Yes, don't worry. I'll be fine," Felicidad kissed her mother and Mrs. Esteves good-by.

Mrs. Esteves handed her a piece of paper with their address carefully printed on it. "Here. Take this. And if you get lost, just ask a policeman—a man in a blue uniform. You know what a policeman looks like?"

"Yes, yes." Felicidad was anxious to be off, and she followed Willy down the steps. She would have liked to run down quickly the way he did, but she did have to walk carefully in the high heels and the tight skirt. Before she stepped out into the cold, she buttoned up her jacket and tied a purple silk scarf around her head.

If she lived in New York a million years she would never get used to the cold. Each time she stepped out of the house it hit her anew. This morning it seemed worse than ever, but perhaps she had not been out this early before. The cold was bitter, and the wind wrapped itself cruelly around her legs. Perhaps her mother had been right about Felicidad's buying a long coat. The whole lower half of her *was* freezing! But there was nothing she could do about it now.

Determinedly she grasped Willy's hand. "Stay right with me," she told him. Her heart was fluttering as they crossed the wide avenue. The way the cars darted around corners without any warning, you could get hit in a second! She and Willy ran until they reached the other side.

Willy already knew where the school was and led Felicidad to it. Her heart fell when she saw it. It was not what she had imagined. It looked like a prison, not a bit like a school. The big, drab, colorless building, with iron grates across its dirty windows, had cement all around it. There was no grass to play on—no place to play at all. It was a forbidding and frightening place to have to enter. She held on tighter than ever to Willy's hand, her heart hammering. She wondered if he was as scared as she was. At least she didn't have to stay —but to leave Willy in this place! A look at his white face filled her with pity, and for a wild moment she thought maybe it would be better not to have him go to school at all. But maybe it would be better inside; maybe it would be prettier and friendlier. . . .

If anything, the inside was worse than the outside. There were soiled, battleship-gray corridors and closed doors. Through a little pane of glass in the doors you could see the classrooms, with everyone sitting stiffly in his seat, two children to a seat, and so crowded on top of each other that you wondered how they could even write. And the classrooms were as drab and colorless as the rest of the building, with the monotonous voices of tired-looking women droning away in front of the children.

Felicidad thought of the pink stucco building where she and Willy had gone to school back home. Hibiscus flowers grew outside the building —you could reach out the windows and touch them or look out at the trees and the blue sky. And young, jolly Mrs. Martinez, who waddled a little when she walked, had filled her classroom with all kinds of growing things—plants and tiny toads and lizards. Colored pictures of all kinds were stuck around the walls. Mrs. Martinez loved color. She came to school wearing the brightest dresses imaginable, and you felt happy just coming into her classroom.

Felicidad didn't know where to go in this huge building, and she and Willy stood in the corridor awkwardly, until finally Felicidad got up the courage to knock on one of the closed doors. A teacher's voice called out, telling them to come in.

Felicidad went in, holding Willy's hand, and shyly announced in Spanish that she wanted to come to school. The whole class burst out laughing. Felicidad's face turned a fiery red, and she wished the floor would open up and close over her. There was a sick smile on her lips, and she felt even worse when the teacher rapped sharply on her desk with a ruler and scolded the class for laughing.

She then ordered a very dark, small Puerto Rican boy in the front row to take them somewhere. He got up willingly, and once they were outside the room, Felicidad asked him in Spanish where they were going. He explained he had to take them to the principal's office and that the principal would send Willy to the right classroom. He also offered the information that this teacher was the worst one in the school and that the principal was a man and wasn't half bad. At least *he* could speak a little Spanish, but the classes were all in English, and they were a pain in the neck. Half the time, he said, he didn't know what was going on, but he didn't care, because he didn't like school anyway.

The boy took them to the door of the principal's office and left them standing there while he went back to his classroom. Felicidad pulled down her skirt, adjusted the scarf on her head, and holding Willy's hand firmly in her own, knocked on the door timidly. A man's voice told them to come in.

Mr. Adams really was nice. He had a friendly smile, and he asked them to sit down. He spoke Spanish quite well for a Continental, Felicidad thought, and he asked Willy a few questions about how old he was and what class he had been in back home and what he had been studying.

Then he said he'd put him in the sixth grade. While it might be a little young for him, he said, it would be better and easier for him until he learned more English.

Willy said he didn't care what class he was put into, but Felicidad felt worried when Mr. Adams explained that Willy would be in school only in the mornings, because they had double sessions.

"But what will he do all afternoon?" Felicidad asked. "We thought he'd be in school all day until three o'clock, the way he is at home."

Mr. Adams shook his head sadly. "That's what we'd like to do, but we don't have enough schools for all the children. So some come in the afternoon and some in the morning."

Felicidad thought it very odd that a country as rich as the United States didn't have enough schools. In her little island there were schools everywhere, and the rooms weren't crowded and dreary the way they were here. But she was much too polite and shy to say anything.

She felt sad as she left Willy at the door of the classroom. "I hope you find Danny to come home with. Remember, he promised to wait for you right outside. Take care. And Willy, no fighting."

He looked much too scared to do anything, and with a heavy heart, she finally left him.

Outside, the cold and the wind had not abated. Felicidad walked as quickly as she could in her high heels and tight skirt. She stayed close to the buildings, hoping they would protect her from the wind, and waited in the doorway of a drugstore for a bus that would take her uptown to the first place on her list for a job.

She showed the bus driver the address and, in her faltering English, asked him please to let her know where to get off. He answered her in rapid English, which she didn't understand, and the bus stopped so abruptly that she almost fell into a strange man's lap. She didn't know what to do, until fortunately, a Puerto Rican man told her in Spanish that she was on the wrong bus. He told her to get off and walk over two blocks. Without even trying to get her fare back, she got off the bus as soon as it stopped, and trudged in the cold once more.

At last she found herself on the right bus, and she got off at Madison Avenue and Forty-sixth Street, a neighborhood that was very different from the part of New York she had seen so far. Here there were mostly big buildings and beautiful shops and very grand-looking fur coats on the women who walked by.

Felicidad pulled her scarf tighter under her chin. She stopped in a doorway to powder her nose, although her mother had often told her this was something a lady never did in public. But she didn't care. She wanted to be sure she looked all right before she went to see about the job.

At the self-service elevator she stopped, because she was afraid to go in alone. She felt shy about asking a man for help, so she waited until a young girl came along. Then she showed her the clipping she'd torn from the newspaper. It clearly said, *Seventeenth floor.* Luckily the girl understood what she wanted, and she got into the elevator with her and pushed the button. Up they went. Felicidad had never been in an elevator before, and her heart was in her mouth until it stopped. She was glad to get out and wondered how she would ever get down again, but she'd worry about that later. First, the job.

She walked into a waiting room that was filled with girls and women. Were they all after the same job? A very pretty blond woman sat at a desk in the middle of the room and coolly handed Felicidad a number. She motioned to her to sit down and wait.

Felicidad felt as if all eyes were on her. As she sat on a deep, low chair, her skirt slithered up over her knees, and she frantically tried to pull it down. Self-consciously, she undid the scarf around her head. The other girls were either bareheaded or had on hats. Timidly, she kept her eyes down, but every once in a while she glanced swiftly around the room to see if there were any other Puerto Rican girls she could possibly talk to. But none of the girls looked Spanish, and

English was all that was being spoken. She wished she knew how to smoke. She envied the girls who were puffing on one cigarette after another.

There was no restaurant in sight way up here, and it seemed odd to be looking for a job as a waitress in a place like this. Carefully, she read the ad from the newspaper over again, and she realized this must be an office for a chain of restaurants. Good. That meant more jobs.

She sat for an hour and a half before her number was called, and when her turn finally came, she was so sleepy she came to with a start. The girls who were still waiting laughed when she suddenly jumped up, and Felicidad blushed a fiery red.

Nervously she followed the girl who had come for her, down a long corridor and then into a large, cheerful room. Here an older woman sat at a desk and greeted her with a fixed smile. "Good morning. Sit down." In her hand she had a card that Felicidad had filled out in the waiting room. "I see you worked at an inn in Puerto Rico. You Puerto Rican?" the woman asked.

Felicidad nodded her head. "Yes," she said in English.

"I'm so sorry, but the jobs are all taken."

Felicidad looked up and caught the woman's blue eyes looking at her. She knew instantly that the woman was lying. She didn't know how she knew, but she did.

"I speak some English, and I know how to wait good." Felicidad said.

"I'm sorry. The jobs are all filled up." She dismissed Felicidad with a curt nod. Felicidad walked back down the corridor and saw all the other girls still waiting to be interviewed. She had sat there for an hour and a half, and the whole thing had taken less than a minute!

Flushing with shame, anger, and humiliation, Felicidad went through the waiting room hurriedly and back to the elevators. There was no one else waiting for an elevator, but she couldn't bear to wait until another girl came out, and she was terrified to get into one of those things alone. She might press the wrong button. Heaven alone knew what might happen! Desperately, she looked for the stairs and saw a door with a little red light over it. Felicidad opened it and gratefully welcomed the flight of stairs.

Seventeen . . . sixteen . . . fifteen. . . . It was a

nightmare walking down all those floors. She thought she'd never come to the end of them, never! She was only thankful that she didn't have to face another human being on the way. When at last she reached the bottom she sat down on the steps, ready to weep. The image of that woman's cold blue eyes kept glaring at her, and she heard her sweet, polite voice. "I'm sorry. The jobs are all taken. . . ."

Felicidad took her scarf out of her bag, combed out her hair, and put it up again, wrapped in the scarf. She powdered her face and retouched her mouth with lipstick. There were five more places to go—she couldn't give up yet. Surely there'd be a job for her somewhere.

But one after another, the excuses came. She didn't have enough experience, or she was too young, or the jobs were already taken. But in her heart, Felcidad knew in each place that they didn't want her because she was a *puertorriqueña*. Otherwise, why were all the other girls waiting? They were just as young as she. They couldn't have that much experience. If the jobs were really filled they'd send them all home. And the way the people looked at her—apologetic, pretending to be truly sorry! But all the while, their eyes were saying, "You poor little fool! Don't you know we don't hire Puerto Ricans around here? We want our own, and you're not one of us."

You're not one of us! But I'm an American too, Felicidad thought fiercely. I don't want to be Puerto Rican, I want to be *American*. And I'm going to speak and look and think exactly like you—you wait and see!

It was the end of the day, and she got on an over-crowded bus to go back home. She was downhearted and discouraged, but c;omething in her was very, very angry, too. She'd show them. She wouldn't *let* them treat her this way! She elbowed and pushed her way through the crowded bus. All these girls and men and women coming home from jobs! She didn't care if she stepped on that fat woman's foot—served her right for having it there. And with a total, illogical fierceness she hated the whole busload of people. She hated them all.

She got off the bus at Twenty-third Street and faced the long, windy blocks across town toward home. As she turned down Ninth Avenue, a little sign in the dirty window of a dingy lunchroom

caught her eye. It was in Spanish. "*Yo necesito una muchacha que trabaje*." Waitress needed. She knew without looking up at the name over the door that it was a Puerto Rican restaurant. Well, they'd have a job for her here.

With a sigh of resignation, she went in and spoke to the owner. He was no cleaner than his store—a small, dark man, with a carefully tended mustache and most of him covered by a soiled white apron. She took Margarita's advice and lied about her age, saying she was over eighteen. He hired her right away and told her to come to work the following day at twelve noon. The salary he mentioned was less than half that offered by the clean, beautiful places uptown, and the hours were longer. The place smelled of stale food, but it was familiar Puerto Rican food, and the customers spoke only Spanish, so that part of it was a relief.

"O.K.," Felicidad said. "I'll be here," she added in Spanish.

She was tired, and she walked home slowly. How do you become a New Yorker? she wondered. How do you learn English? How do you learn new ways if you must all huddle together in your own little corners?

Perhaps Fernando was right. Perhaps they would be better off staying home on their own little island, sticking to their own ways, even if they were old-fashioned. As always, when she thought of Fernando, her heart filled with a great longing to see him and to be at home. He and home were part of each other, and she wondered if the sun was shining brightly today and if Fernando was even now out in the fields with his machete and what tune he would be whistling. Neither one of them was much at letter writing, so the letters were few and far between.

But Fernando is stubborn, she thought. He'll never know what the rest of the world looks like. We're here, and I *did* get a job, and Carlos *is* making money, and Willy *is* going to an American school. . . .

Willy! Remembering Willy, she hurried her steps, worrying about whether he had got home all right. She'd completely forgotten about him and his first day of school.

She was exhausted, but she went up the stairs quickly and walked into the kitchen. This was the only living room the apartment had, and everyone stayed there, except when it was time to sleep. Immediately, from her mother's face, she knew something unpleasant had happened. Willy was sitting and staring out the window, while her mother walked about the kitchen, nervously picking up a speck of dirt here and there and putting it down again. Mrs. Esteves was preparing rice and beans for supper, although Margarita, Carlos, and Mr. Esteves never got home until late, because they had to work through dinnertime at the hotel.

"Where were you all day? I was worried sick about you," her mother said accusingly.

"I told you I was going out to look for a job," Felicidad said.

"Did you get one?" her mother asked her sharply.

"Yes." Felicidad drew herself up proudly. The look of disbelief on her mother's face hurt her as much as anything that had happened all day. So her mother thought she couldn't get a job! "And a good one too," she added, lying calmly. No one would ever know what she had suffered this day, and she was suddenly determined also that her mother would never know she was working at a cheap, greasy Puerto Rican restaurant. She'd make up more details later, when she had a chance to think, and if her mother asked her, she'd tell her she was working for a beautiful New York restaurant uptown.

"That's very good," Mrs. Esteves said cheerfully. "It's O.K."

"What's the matter with you, Willy? How was school?" His face was so woebegone Felicidad almost didn't want to hear his answer. She couldn't bear any more unpleasantness this day.

And Willy's story was not a happy one. His mother answered for him. "He lost his new coat," she said, and her eyes were tragic. "His brand-new coat. He hung it up in the coatroom, and it's gone. What kind of a city is this? They steal a little boy's brand-new coat! The teacher said she couldn't do anything. . . . You children haven't been to Mass—that's the trouble. That's why everything is no good."

"But who would steal your coat, Willy?" Felicidad asked in consternation. "What a terrible thing to do!"

"What do they care!" Mrs. Esteves said bitterly. "A Puerto Rican kid doesn't need a coat! They'll steal anything from him they can get. And then they say he makes the trouble. Willy, you'll have to learn how to take care of yourself up here. Don't be afraid to fight if you have to."

Mrs. Marquez was shocked by this advice. "No, you mustn't fight, Willy. Someone will stab you with a knife. But don't put your coat down anyplace. Just hold on to it. Keep it with you—on your seat by your desk."

"Ma, I haven't got any coat now. And if I get one, I gotta put it in the coatroom. The teacher says so." He shrugged his shoulders. "What can I do?"

"Felicidad will go to school with you tomorrow and see if she can find the coat," Mrs. Marquez ordered.

Felicidad was too tired to argue. But her mother didn't understand any part of it. She didn't know what it really meant to be living up here. Felicidad wondered idly if she'd ever find out. Her mother throught it was all Willy's fault, and if she knew the kind of job Felicidad had taken, she'd say that was Felicidad's own fault too, that she was forgetting to keep her head high. Wearily, she set the table for their supper. But it wasn't their fault, not hers or Willy's.

It was the fault of all the other people in the city. They were making the mistake. They were doing the hating. And she hated them in return.

With an uncontrollable feeling of contempt, she took the bag of garbage Mrs. Esteves had asked her to put outside, and she threw it out the window. She watched it land gently all over the sidewalk, and for an instant it made her heart feel quiet and strong. But when she realized what a foolish, mean thing she'd done, she went into the bedroom, closed the door behind her, and shed the tears she had been holding back all day.

QUIET BOY

Lela and Rufus Waltrip

The Waltrips have written a sensitive story about the loneliness of being part of two cultures and so not completely belonging to either. Quiet Boy, Chee, studies at a white man's school during the week but spends each weekend helping his mother care for their family. He would prefer to remain at home, but his father, who was killed in World War II, had wished him to be educated.

Because his father is dead, Quiet Boy has more responsibility than most twelve-year-olds. He must choose from each culture what will best help his family. Such choices are not easy because they have emotional overtones. While his mother and grandfather are secure in their belief in "the Navaho way," Quiet Boy has secret questions and doubts. Athough in no way does he reject his heritage, being forced to choose makes him fear he is being disloyal to his people.

Thousands of Indian children face Quiet Boy's dilemma today. This well-written book can help non-Indian children understand a seldom recognized problem of minority life.

The late evening sun was sinking behind the red cliffs of Arizona's Canyon de Chelly when the school bus drew up at the Navajo Trading Post. It was Friday, five days since Sunday.

"Hurry up there. Let's get going!" shouted the Indian boys and girls as they pushed and shoved, pouring out of the long yellow school bus stopped beside the highway.

Quiet Boy sat still and waited. He always waited. He was always the last one off and last one on. He said nothing.

"Come on, sheep's tail—Quiet One," called Pepe, son of Many Goats. "Let's have a game of marbles before your mother comes for you."

Quiet Boy grinned good-naturedly. He knew Pepe's nickname for him was with good intent. Chee was his real Indian name—Chee, son of Ditsa Toddy. He got up then and followed the others to the front. He fondled the marbles in his

blue-jeans pocket. There was one thing he could do best—win at marbles. He took out the small black agate and looked at it. It held magic for him. He was sure of it. Soon he would prove this. He would carry home a pocket full of these magic gems, that is, if Nespah didn't come for him too soon. And she would not, for his mother had much to do at the hogan at the end of the week.

The slanting rays of the setting sun glinted on the smooth, polished black agate in his hand. Quiet Boy would almost as soon have lost his turquoise-studded belt as that black-agate taw. And the turquoise in the wide silver concho belt had been left him by his father, Ditsa Toddy. It was said to be worth upward of a hundred dollars. He had made the concho belt himself. From the true bright silver he had hammered it, guided by the experienced hand of Grandfather. In the silver buckle he had put the turquoise shaped like a Thunderbird, for the Thunderbird was a good omen.

"The blue stone will ward off danger and sickness," Nespah had told him, when he had finished the belt.

Quiet Boy had wondered about his mother's teaching. Why had not the blue stone kept his father from danger? Why had he not come back from the white man's war across the seas, since the turquoise was on his dog chain around his neck? He wanted so much to know, to understand. But all Nespah could say was, "That is what we have been taught. It is the Navajo way."

But that was not enough. Quiet Boy wished to know more. Was his mind tricking him? Would the government school teach him these things? He was in the seventh grade now and he had learned many things already but he had not learned this.

"Black Chiddi, Black Chiddi!" someone cried, and all the boys ran at once to an old black automobile that had driven up beside the Trading Post.

There was great excitement connected with that rattling, rusty, black car. The driver, Black Chiddi, as he had become known, was a teller of tales. True or untrue, the tales were fascinating.

Quiet Boy put the agate in his pocket and ran to catch up with the others.

"And you, sheep's tail, what did you learn at the school today?" Black Chiddi pointed a long crooked finger at Quiet Boy as he came up. "Did you learn how to shear a sheep? Did you learn to weave a Navajo blanket better than your grandmother?"

"E-e-e-e-!" shouted Tall Boy in delight, and a yell went up from the group as they slapped their sides in laughter.

Quiet Boy's ears turned a reddish-purple like the tall cliffs of Canyon de Chelly. His friends could call him sheep's tail, yes, but Black Chiddi —He started to speak but caught himself in true Navajo fashion. "Hold your tongue," Grandfather always said. "It is well to teach what we think is right but not with angry words or with force of blows."

He thrust his hands deep into his pockets. He could not look up. The black agate seemed to turn over in his clenched fist. He was plainly confused. Black Chiddi turned to the others then with a satisfied air.

"Did you learn how the great Kit Carson and his soldiers drove the Navajos out of their own land that had been theirs for centuries? Did they show you a movie of the white men burning the hogans of the Dineh, the people, destroying our flocks and our horses?"

"We had the best horses in the land!" Tall Boy shouted.

"And the best horsemen!" Pepe cried.

"And the best—" other voices began and broke off as all eyes turned toward the Trading Post.

"What's going on here?" Jack Burns, nephew of the trader, came to the edge of the group. He put his arms across the shoulders of Quiet Boy and Pepe and peered over at Black Chiddi sitting there in the black car with the ragged top down.

Abruptly, Black Chiddi decided he had said enough. He turned on the ignition switch, stepped on the gas, and pulled away. The boys fell back with sly glances and moved off as the car roared toward the highway.

"*Yo hoi*! Until next time!" some of them shouted after him in Navajo and in English.

"Another one of his wild stories," Pepe told Jack as they walked back to the Trading Post. "He is always talking about Black Horse of long ago, and how he came to blows with the white man over the schools."

"True or untrue," Quiet Boy added, shrugging indifferently, glad to be rid of the man. He had never liked the trouble-maker and now he did not like him at all.

"Maybe so true," Tall Boy said.

"Let's go!" Pepe ran forward a little, squatting to make a round circle in the dry earth with his fingers.

"Play?" Quiet Boy looked at Jack as he took the marbles from his jeans pockets.

"Sure," said Jack, squatting beside the circle.

Then Quiet Boy saw it. His mother's green-covered wagon topped the hill and rolled leisurely down the long flat road toward the Trading Post. On the seat beside her sat his younger brother, eight-year-old Atchee. He could see the head of his younger sister, Ti-wi, bob up and down in the back of the wagon as it bounced over the rough road. Gogo, the sheep dog, trotted behind with tongue out, seeing everything, saying nothing, very much like Quiet Boy.

"Later," Quiet Boy called to the boys. Putting the marbles back into his pocket, he ran out to meet his family.

Nespah, smiling, stopped the wagon to let him in. But before the ponies were drawn up, while the wagon was still rolling, Quiet Boy grasped the side boards, put one foot on the brake beam and threw himself over. His family was smiling. How glad they were to see him and he to see them!

"You are too big already," Ti-wi said laughing.

"You do look as though you had grown in these five days," Nespah said.

Standing straight and tall in the wagon behind the spring seat, arms folded on his chest, Chee, son of Ditsa Toddy, rode on down to the Trading Post. He gave Gogo a pat on the head, and they all went into the store to do their weekly trading.

Over her shoulder, Nespah carried the orange-and-purple rug that she had just finished. Ti-wi, who was only ten, two years younger than Quiet Boy, carried another rug, similar only smaller. Atchee took in the silver-and-turquoise bracelet he had fashioned by hand with the help of his grandfather.

Quiet Boy gazed proudly at the weaving and at the silversmith work. If the trader thought it was good, he would pay them well for it, for he had proved to be an honest man and his tongue was straight. The boy drew himself up to his full height, tall for twelve years, and went forward to meet the trader. He had been there many times before but always his mother had taken the lead. Now he was almost a man. Hadn't he been going to government school for two months? Wasn't he in the seventh grade?

"You are a big boy now," Nespah had told him only five days ago. "You have learned to read and write. You speak the English well. It is time to take your father's place."

This had been a great responsibility for so small a boy. But Grandfather was old. No one knew how old. And so he, Quiet Boy, would have to do it.

"What is to be done, is to be done," Nespah always said. "Many words won't change things."

Often before he had hung back. He had followed his family, but from today he was the leader. He remembered his mother's trust. He eyed the trader arranging some canned goods on the shelves and went slowly back to meet him.

"Want something, son?" The trader's voice startled him even though he had been waiting for him to speak.

"My—my family," the boy stammered an gestured toward them. "They have come to trade."

"Yes," the trader said, and went to help them.

Quiet Boy sighed with relief. He leaned shyly on the counter and watched as the trader examined the rugs and the bracelet and put out canned goods, dress material, sugar or "sweet salt," and flour for them to take out to the wagon.

Quiet Boy dawdled, inspecting the new electrical equipment on the shelves. It was truly bewitching. Grandfather called the radio a "witch box" and wanted no part of it. But someday, Quiet Boy was sure, they would have one. It seemed such a useful thing. Many Navajos owned them. That is, they owned those that worked with batteries. It was this kind that Quiet Boy wanted.

The sun was dropping out of sight behind the red cliffs when they came out of the Trading Post. The boys had all disappeared. Only a few Navajo men stood or squatted here and there in little groups and talked.

Nespah held her full skirts just so as she climbed to the wagon seat, and sat to the left side. Always before she had sat on the right side next to the brake handle. She had driven the team of ponies and managed the brake when they went down long steep hills. Today she handed the reins to Quiet Boy who sat on the right. Quiet Boy knew what to do. He put his feet on the high front endgate, slapped the ponies with the reins, clucked his tongue and there were off. Back up the long, flat, bumpy road they went toward home.

Ti-wi and Atchee plied him with many questions in Navajo. "What did you learn at the school?" Ti-wi could hardly wait to find out. At first Boy was reluctant to talk. He was thinking of Black Chddi and of Tall Boy.

"What did you learn in school?" Black Chiddi had asked. "Did they show you a movie of the white men burning the hogans of the Dineh?"

The sound of the man's words rang in his ears. He shifted in the seat, slapped the ponies with the reins again. He would forget Black Chiddi.

"There were the English words," he told Ti-wi and Atchee.

"What English words?" Ti-wi interrupted.

Quiet Boy knew how impatient she was to learn about the white man's ways. Perhaps next month or the next, she, too, could start school. It all depended on the sheep, how well they turned out at the market. It depended, too, on the *Yei-bi-chai*, the strong medicine of the Mountain Chant which lasted for nine days. It depended on how well the evil influences had been driven out —how well the gods were appeased.

"Home," he told her in his native tongue. "Home is the English word, like our mother's hogan. It is a place to eat, and to sleep—and to be happy."

"O'o, yes." Ti-wi laughed aloud, her eyes dancing. "It is true. Our hogan is a happy one."

"Happy, yes, except for one—" Quiet Boy hesitated, the English lesson forgotten. He was talking too much.

"One?" Ti-wi stood up in the green-covered wagon. She held on to the seat in front of her. She relished every moment of this, every word spoken. "Except for one?" she asked again in Navajo.

Quiet Boy waited for the thoughts to go away. But they did not go. Six black eyes were upon him. He could feel them in the evening dusk. He sat very still and looked straight ahead, straight up the road. The sound of a plane hummed high in the sky and died out. A tumbleweed danced grotesquely across the road and waited for them to pass. The walls of the canyon shone blood red in the last rays of the afternoon sun. Like battlements of the ancient gods, like great strongholds, they stood there mysterious and beckoning, waiting.

"Our father," he finally spoke out. "A hogan needs one." And the silence was broken.

"O'o, yes," Ti-wi answered.

"O'o, yes," Atchee repeated.

"Ugh." Nespah shifted her weight on the spring seat. "That is true. But what is, is. That is done. We must look to the future. You are here. The hogan now has a man." She had spoken the words again.

Something quivered around Quiet Boy's heart like a taut bowstring. He was proud, yes, but he was lonely, always lonely and afraid. He didn't know why pains stabbed him. He didn't know why he should be confused about the Navajo ways and the ways of his white brothers. If he could only make up his mind to follow one trail or the other! Disturbed he was, all over again, by Black Chiddi.

But he must be brave. No one must know he was afraid. He sat a little straighter on the seat. He clucked his tongue to the ponies. Sheep's tail —or—man? His mind was made up. He would never be the sheep's tail again, that is, if he could help it.

The family began to plan for the week-end trip to the mesa to gather the small piñon nuts that fell out of the cones of the piñon pines. They would go early this year, very early, before the small black nuts were all gone. If he picked many nuts perhaps he could buy a witch box, a radio!

Then it was dark. They had only the stars to guide them, the stars and the instinct of the ponies. The little ponies could find the way home in the darkest night.

"Just give them the reins," Grandfather had told him once.

Grandfather was old but he knew many things. Quiet Boy loosened the reins in his hands. The long leather lines fell slack along the backs of the ponies and up over the wagon front. The ponies plodded steadily, surely, along the dark road. Their small hoofs clicked on the hard ground. Occasionally sparks flew from the rocks struck by the horses' hoofs and Quiet Boy wondered if this was a good omen. Were the gods on his side?

When it was time to turn off the big road onto the dim trail that led up to the hogan, the ponies turned off. Nespah nodded on the seat beside Quiet Boy, confident, sure of his ability to take them home. The young ones slept on blankets in the back. Not until they drew up at the hogan did anyone stir.

"Grandfather has made a light for us," Ti-wi whispered as they reached the door of their hogan. Through the cracks between the logs they could see it, and through the openings beside the door that faced the east, and through the one small window beside the door where shone the gold star.

"Ssh!" Nespah cautioned.

But the old man did not wake when they raised the rug that covered the door opening and went inside. He lay on his sheepskin at one side of the large, mud-plastered room.

"He is old and tired." Nespah shook her head as she went about preparing a meal for her hungry brood.

When Quiet Boy had put the ponies in the coral he joined his family around the center fireplace. His eyes took in the hogan at one glance. There was the sewing machine of which his mother was very proud. And there the "gold" bedstead with the soft mattress for his mother and Ti-wi. It had been a gift from his father. And a real table with chairs. There was an empty place between the bed and the machine. It would be a good place for a radio, if every they had one. And there was his father's workbench with all the tools the silversmith would use, the hammers, the sandstone molds, the bellows, the ladle for heating the silver, files and sandpaper.

Soon the steaming meal was ready. The mutton stew and the store-bought bread tasted good, and Quiet Boy caught himself dipping into the bowl oftener than he really should.

Ti-wi flashed him a smile when he noticed that she was aware of this.

"The food at the government school was never so good," Quiet Boy told them, and saw his mother's face light up. She, too, had been to the school for a little while. She had tasted the food there, and thought it good.

"What is the food like at the school?" Ti-wi finally asked.

"There are many kinds," he told her.

"Like what?" she queried.

"They have milk and vegetables," he answered her. "There are eggs and cheese, and fresh raw things—carrots and lettuce. Jack says that is rabbit food." Quiet Boy grinned.

"I would like some rabbit food." Ti-wi laughed.

"We must sleep now," Nespah told them. "Tomorrow is the piñon hunt."

Sheepskins were unrolled and spread out around the wall of the log hogan for the boys. Quiet Boy took off his shoes and blue jeans and folded them to one side as he had been taught to do at school. But before he blew out the small kerosene lamp, he held it high above his head and studied the picture that had hung on the wall so long. Quiet Boy had been only five when it was first put up. The Marine, the third from the left in the picture, was his father, Ditsa Toddy. A lump filled the boy's throat as he blew out the light and lay down on his sheepskin bed.

LITTLE BROWN KOKO

Blanche Seale Hunt

Little Brown Koko, *published in 1940, is an example of the worst kind of stereotyping. An excerpt is presented here to show how the Negro has been portrayed in the recent past. In the post-depression period Negroes were still unable to find work; their future looked, and indeed in retrospect was, bleak. They lived on farms or in ghettoes in extreme poverty.*

The literature and the films of the forties, including some of the very popular Shirley Temple movies, portrayed Negroes as childish, stupid, undependable, and lazy. Such caricatures taught intolerance and encouraged white children to fear and mock people different from themselves. Compare this selection with the following examples of literature about Negroes.

Once there was a little brown boy named Little Brown Koko. He was the shortest, fattest little Negro you could ever imagine. He had the blackest, little woolly head and great, big, round eyes, and he was the prettiest brown color, just like a bar of chocolate candy. Little Koko's Mammy thought him the most beautiful little boy in the whole wide world. Oh, he was a beautiful little brown boy, all right, but he had one bad habit. He was greedy. Why, compared with Little Brown Koko, a pig should be called a well-mannered gentleman.

One day Little Brown Koko's nice, good, ole, big, fat, black Mammy made a big seven-layer cake with seven layers of good, thick, sweet, brown chocolate frosting.

*   *   *

"Li'l Brown Koko, you-all run over to yore Aunt Sally's an' fetch me this here cup full o' sugar. An' mind you hurry, now! Then I'll bake my li'l' boy some sugar cookies when he gits back." And Little Brown Koko's nice, good, ole, big, fat, black Mammy tied on a clean white apron. Then she took down a big blue bowl from the cupboard and got out her big wooden spoon and three eggs.

Now, Little Brown Koko liked sugar cookies. Indeed he did! So he just crammed his little straw hat on one side of his little, black, woolly head, picked up the cup, and whistled for Shoog.

But Shoog didn't come. Little Brown Koko whistled again. Still Shoog didn't come. So Little Brown Koko started out without him. Of course, he wanted Shoog to go with him, all right, but, you see, he was in a hurry for those sugar cookies. And Little Brown Koko knew good and well that his Mammy couldn't bake 'em until he fetched the sugar.

He hurried down the little path just as fast as his short, fat, brown legs would carry him. His Mammy had told him to hurry, and that's *exactly* what he was doing. Only once, when he crawled through the pasture fence, he hurried a little *too* fast and left part of his little red rompers behind—hanging on an ole barb.

From *Stories of Little Brown Koko* by Blanche Seale Hunt. Illustrated by Dorothy Wagstaff. Published by American Colortype Co., © 1940.

Little Brown Koko was skipping along just as happy as you please and thinking how good those sugar cookies would taste when his Mammy got 'em baked, when—

"Gobble-gobble-gobble! gobble-gobble-gobble! gobble-gobble-gobble!" And there was an ole turkey gobbler coming *right* at him with its tail spread out in a big fan and its long red tassels bobbing up and down every step.

And, land sakes! maybe you think Little Brown Koko wasn't scared 'most out of his little red rompers—at least what was left of 'em, 'cause he had left most of 'em hanging on that ole barbed-wire.

Poor Little Brown Koko! He just stood there and shook from the hole in the top of his little ole straw hat clear down to the very tips of his little, fat, brown toes. Yes, sir! he most certainly did. He shook so hard that his pretty, little, white teeth chattered. And his poor little heart just jumped 'way up in his mouth and fell *smack*, clear down into his little round pooched-out tummy.

And all the time that ole turkey gobbler just kept coming closer, and closer, and closer. And he kept gobbling louder, and louder, and louder, and *louder*.

Pretty soon he was so close that Little Brown Koko could see his mean little ole eyes just blinkin' like *everything*.

Little Brown Koko was so scared he didn't know what in the world to do—except just stand there and shake all over.

He would have run away, I guess, but he was more afraid to have the ole turkey gobbler behind him than he was to have it in front of him.

All at once Little Brown Koko happened to think about the teacup in his little, fat, brown hand, and he just up and threw it *right* at that ole turkey gobbler. Yes, sir! he most certainly did. But the teacup didn't hit that ole turkey gobbler a bit more than anything. No, sir! it just hit an ole rock and broke smack-dab into *three pieces*.

Oh, my! Little Brown Koko was in for it now, sure, for that ole turkey gobbler was angrier than ever. And by this time it was right up *at* him, too.

Poor Little Brown Koko just shut his big round eyes up tight and held his breath, for he knew that ole turkey gobbler was ready to jump right on him.

Then the most surprising thing happened!

"Bow-wow-wow! Bow-wow-wow! Bow-wow-wow! Bow-wow-wow!" barked a little dog almost right under Little Brown Koko's little, flat, brown nose.

Little Brown Koko opened his big, round eyes up wide and just stood there with his little, red mouth hanging open. And, no wonder! For Shoog *had* followed him, after all, and was right there chasing that ole turkey gobbler away from his little master.

Then what do you think Little Brown Koko did? Why, he took to his little, fat, brown heels and never stopped running until he reached a tree. Then he skinned up it quick'n *scat* and just sat up there and made faces at that ole turkey gobbler until Shoog chased it *clear* out of sight.

At last Shoog came trotting back, and Little Brown Koko skinned down the tree and hugged him tight and told him what a good little puppy-dog he was.

Then he said, "Oh, well! Mammy won't be mad 'cause I broke her teacup when I tell her why. An' she can bake us some 'lasses cookies. They's mos' nigh as good as sugar ones, nohow, hain't they, Shoog?"

CALL ME CHARLEY

Jesse Jackson

Published in 1945, just five years after Little Brown Koko, Call me Charley *was one of the first books to show racial prejudice in action, to show how it can hurt. The book deals with Charley's struggle, as the first Negro in his new school, to become accepted by the boys and teachers. The characters' attitudes and personalities are well drawn so neither they nor the story become unbelievable. An interesting study of stereotypes and round characters can be made by comparing* Call Me Charley, Little Brown Koko, *and* Bright April.

Tom, a white boy, and Charley work together to win a contest. Their design wins them each a summer pass to the swimming pool, but when the judges see Charley they ask him to wait for the pool manager, who wants to talk to him.

"Move on, Sambo," George said and turned to Tom.

"My name is Charles. Charles Moss," the boy said. He carefully laid the rolled paper in the side of his paper sack and took out another paper. Tom, still holding his breath, beckoned the boy to his side.

"Go on, Sambo," George said. He clenched his hands into fists.

Rag came off the porch, yawning. He went over to Charles and put his nose against him. The dog sniffed the boy's feet and legs thoroughly. Satisfied, the dog walked slowly over to Tom and reported his findings by touching Tom's neck with his nose. Rag stood watching Tom for orders.

"Now," Tom exclaimed. "I knew I could do it." He gulped a full breath.

George looked from Tom to Charles. His gray eyes were slits. He picked up a stick. "Tom, let's show Sambo."

"My name is Charles," the boy repeated. "Sometimes I'm called Charley. Nobody calls me Sambo and gets away with it." He dropped the paper he was rolling and moved closer to George. George swung back with the stick.

"Don't you guys know I just broke my record?" Tom said, and he stood up and brushed the seat of his trousers. "I just held my breath for two full minutes. That's better than one of the lifeguards did at camp this summer." Charley and George stared at one another like Bantam roosters.

"We don't allow niggers around here. Do we, Tom?" George said. Tom reached down to Rag and petted the dog's head. Charley lowered his eyes and his lips moved as if he were going to say something and had changed his mind.

The sun banked downward to the southwest and the air was so quiet the painted leaves could be heard as they fell to the pavement. Rag got up and yawned. He moved to the shade of a small maple tree near by. The screen door opened as Charley lifted his bag to his shoulder. Hannah came out.

"George Reed! George Reed, you take that kind of talk across the street where it belongs. Mrs. Hamilton don't have none of that trashy talk over here."

Tom remembered what his mother told him about the paper. He said, "Say, Charley, I want to show you where to put the paper. Rag will get it if you throw it on the porch. Come on." Tom took Charley to the side of the porch where there was a little nook to place the paper in. "Rag can't get in here and it won't get wet if it rains," Tom said. George remained standing a few feet from the curbstone in the street. Hannah came down the steps and got the paper. She glared at George. "It's gettin' so," she grumbled as she entered the house, "this new trash in the neighborhood is gettin' worse and worse each day."

*   *   *

Tom, Charley, and George sat watching the band pack their instruments. Most of the people were leaving.

"Come on, Charley, I'll show you the locker rooms and where to get a pair of trunks," Tom said.

"I've got to wait for the manager," Charley said.

"Aw, I forgot. I just didn't want to get in the water last."

"Come on, Tom, if you're going," George said. Some other boys had joined them and were waiting with George.

Just then the manager approached them. "May I see the pass I gave you?" he asked Charley.

"Sure," Charley said.

The manager took the pass, put it in his pocket and handed Charley a ten-dollar bill instead.

"Sorry, boy, but here is what that pass is worth. We don't allow Negroes to swim here, Sambo." He pointed to the big sign over the pool. "Sorry, but that's the pool's policy."

Charley swallowed hard and stared at the money in his hand. Then he saw the pool and the way the water showed the clouds overhead. He couldn't say anything.

"But we were all going swimming," Tom said. "We—" But the manager had already turned away.

Charley's shoulders sank as if the whole world had suddenly fallen on them. Then George was the first to speak. "See, I told you, Mr. Engineer. You didn't believe me when I told you that you were going to fall hard."

Charley turned and walked slowly to the gate.

"Wait for me!" Tom shouted after him.

"Aw, Tom," George said, "there you go spoiling everything. You can't go now. There are just enough of us for a game of polo."

One of the boys with George asked: "Why didn't Charley speak up and tell the manager that he was entitled to the pass?"

Another boy said: "Gee, he won the prize. He should have told the manager."

"It isn't fair," Tom said.

"He got ten dollars. That's what the pass was worth," George said.

"Maybe if he had spoken up, the manager would have let him keep the pass and stay for a swim."

"Aw, how could he? You know how the manager is."

"He won a prize with me," Tom said, "and he's entitled to stay and swim like the rest of us."

"You know how it is, Tom," George said. "They don't want any Negroes around here."

"Oh, can it. That doesn't make sense," Tom said.

"Come on. Let's go swimming. They'll be chasing us all out of here pretty soon."

"Yes. We can't spend all day talking about that guy."

The boys moved toward the locker room. Tom started to the exit.

"Come on, Tom," George said.

"I promised to ride Charley home."

"Let him walk. Somebody will pick him up."

"No, I promised. He rode me over. It's my turn now."

"O. K. O. K. If you want to spoil everything. Go ahead, I don't care."

Outside the gate Tom caught up with Charley.

"It's my turn to pedal you home," he said.

"Ain't you going swimming?"

"Aw, if we hurry I can come back. That is, I might come back."

They got on the bicycle. "Sure beats me," Charley said slowly.

"Me, too."

"Can't make head or tail of it." Charley shook his head.

"And that guy called you Sambo, didn't he?"

"He did."

"That wasn't right. I'm going to see what Dad says about it. He'll be mad."

"I am mad myself," Charley said.

"Maybe you should have gotten mad back at the pool and told the manager something instead of taking the money."

"It all happened so quick. I didn't have time to think of giving him the money back or asking him to let me stay."

The road back to the boys' homes was uphill and quite steep in parts. Perspiration gathered on Tom's face as he pedaled the bicycle with Charley sitting on the crossbar. Tom was out of breath when they came to the abandoned quarry. Charley said, "We ought to get off and walk."

"No," said Tom. "It isn't far now. I can make it."

"All right."

"Now I wish I had stayed at the pool and had a swim. If you had talked up maybe the manager would have let you stay. Why didn't you, Charley?"

"I told you the whole thing surprised me. I didn't know he was going to keep the pass when I gave it to him."

"I think you were just scared." Tom gripped the handlebars and pressed down on the pedals. The chain broke and the boys fell with the bicycle. When they recovered from the surprise of the fall, and got up, Tom said, "That settles the old bike for a few days."

They picked it up and Charley got an old newspaper from the roadside to wrap around the greasy chain. Tom pushed the bicycle and Charley carried the chain. They had reached the quarry now and sat down in the tall grass to rest.

"Might just as well have gone swimming here this morning for all the good it did us to go to the pool," Charley said.

"That's an idea!" Tom said. "Let's go swimming down there." They noticed a sign: "No Trespassing."

"Maybe we better not go in," Charley said.

"It won't hurt to look around," Tom answered.

The weeds came up to their shoulders. They listened to the bull frogs calling from the pool in the pit of the quarry.

"Any snakes around here?" Charley asked, as they climbed down.

"Oh, there might be a few rattlers. Just little ones abut eight feet long. But they won't bother us."

"*What?*"

Tom knelt down in the grass. Charley stopped. "What did you say, Tom? Tom!"

Tom stood up. "I thought I heard a rattler."

"Wish I had a stick," Charley said.

Tom laughed. "Don't you see I'm kidding?"

The boys had come to the clearing where the pool was. They looked down on the motionless water.

"Sure is awful quiet," Charley said. "Why, you can't even see the road from here or hear a car pass."

"That's all the better. We don't want anyone to find out about this." Tom sat down on the steep bank overlooking the pool. There was a diving board nearby.

Charley threw some stones into the water.

"Got to find out how deep the water is," he said.

"How can you tell?"

"By the sound of the splash. If it's a deep place, the stone don't make much sound." He tossed a stone near the diving board.

"It's good and deep there," Tom said.

"Yes? Where's the shallow part?"

Tom pointed to the opposite side. "Over there is where the small kids used to swim." Tom started to take off his clothes. "Ain't you coming in?" he asked.

"Sure. What you think I came here for?"

"Well, let's get started. It's almost lunch time now."

"It is. I can tell time from my stomach." Charley began to undress.

Tom went to the diving board and jumped up and down on it. Charley watched him, his eyes growing bigger each time Tom jumped up and did not go off. "I got to test it," Tom said. Then he jumped into the air and did a jack knife. When he came to the surface he shook his head once and began swimming lazily in a circle.

"Come on in, Charley. It's wonderful."

Charley walked to the end of the diving board and looked down. The water was dark green. Anxiously he looked toward the shallow part of the pool.

"Jump!" Tom shouted. Charley jumped.

It was part dive and part fall. The water hurt his eyes. He came up the first time, and then he sank. He struggled once more to the surface, then sank again.

"What's the matter?" Tom shouted as he swam over to Charley as quickly as he could. "Can't you swim?" He got hold of Charley's arm.

Charley grabbed him around the neck. The two boys sank. Before his head went under the water Tom took a deep breath. Then he struggled to free himself from Charley's grasp and held on to him until they reached the bottom. Then Tom slipped his left arm across Charley's chest and held him firmly as he pushed up from the bottom with all his strength. His lungs hurt.

The boys shot to the surface. Tom started swimming with one arm toward the shallow end of the pool, holding Charley with the other one. When he felt ground under his feet, Tom let go

of Charley. Charley crawled on his hands and knees until he was out of the water. Then he fell to the ground. Tom sank down panting.

Charley lay on his back now. His chest rose and fell. When he had recovered a little, he sat up and looked at Tom.

"I'm awful sorry, Tom. I thought I was a goner."

"Can't you swim, Charley?"

"A little bit."

"I told you it was deep near the diving board."

"I tried to dive toward the shallow part."

Tom got up and walked over to his clothes. Charley followed him. Without a word the two got dressed. Then they walked back to the road where they had left the bicycle. Tom took the bicycle and the broken chain. He walked off.

"I'll carry the chain or push the bike," Charley said, following him.

"No."

"What's the matter, Tom? I told you I was sorry."

"It isn't that."

"Well, what is it?"

"Nothing."

"It must be something."

Tom did not answer.

"Why don't you tell me what it is, Tom?"

"I certainly have been a fool, believing you. Letting you spoil a lot of fun I might have had with the other fellows."

"I can swim a little, Tom. You saved my life. I don't want you to be mad at me."

"If you had said you couldn't swim it wouldn't have been so bad. But no, you don't open your mouth. It's just like the school play. You won't talk to Miss King, to tell her you want a part in the play. You wouldn't tell the manager at the swimming pool that you wanted to stay. No, you're scared. I'm going home, now."

"Well, Tom—"

"That isn't the only thing. You got me in trouble at home, too, when you let that tiger burn. Pop is going to close the workshop for a couple of days. All because of you. He said it might have caused a fire. I get the blame for something you did."

"I'll tell him I did it."

"No. You won't have to. I don't want anything

to do with you. George is sore at me. He thinks I've let him go for you."

"George just doesn't like me."

"That's it. I tried to give you an even break and what do you do for me?"

The boys had reached the park now. The Cunningham home lay east of it and Tom's home was to the north. "What do you do for me?" Tom repeated. "Why, you go and try to get yourself drowned so everybody would blame me for taking you into that quarry. You are a swell pal!" Tom turned to go. "I'm through, Charley. I don't want to have anything to do with you."

Tom went off pushing the bicycle. Charley watched him but Tom did not look back.

Slowly Charley walked home. His head hurt and his lungs burned. His mother was standing in front of the Cunningham house, waiting for him. Charley took the ten-dollar bill out of his pocket and looked at it. When he came to his mother he gave the money to her.

"Hi, Mom," he said, avoiding her eyes. "Here's some money to keep for me."

"Where on earth have you been, Son? Come into the garage."

Charley did not answer.

"You have worried me clear out of my mind today. Where have you been? All the rest of the children who went to the swimming pool are home. You've been into something."

Charley did not answer.

"What's the matter with you, Charley?"

Charley stood looking at his mother.

"Tell me, boy. What's gotten into you?"

"Tom won't have anything to do with me any more, and they wouldn't let me in the swimming pool. Manager gave me ten dollars for the pass I won. Then he went swimming in the quarry."

"What did you do to Tom? Why is he mad at you?"

"He's just through with me, that's all. He thinks I'm scared. They won't let me in the school play. George never did like me. I'm not going back to that school again. I guess Pop knew they didn't want colored folks around here. Pop told me."

"Hush that talk, boy. Come in the kitchen for something to eat and tell me all about it. You'll change your mind after you finish eating."

"No, I won't go back to school. Nobody wants me."

Charley ran up the steps to his room. His mother followed him. He was looking forlornly out his window at the hollyhocks in the yard.

"Charley, you got to go to school. What will Doctor Cunningham say?"

"I made good grades and I studied hard for the school play and I won that prize, but they don't want me. I won't go back."

"But Charley, you got to get some education. You want to be an engineer when you grow up, don't you?"

"I don't know, Mom. What's the use?"

BRIGHT APRIL

Marguerite De Angeli

Bright April is another of the first books to show racial prejudice. April is an intelligent but sheltered Negro girl who is just learning that life may impose cruel limits and that prejudice exists. Miss De Angeli writes with sensitivity and with such subtlety that many children will completely miss her references to the injustices April's brother and sister must accept.

In comparison to books such as Mary Jane, *which show racial prejudice more realistically,* Bright April's *ending seems too pat to be believable. While fiction should offer hope, it should not make bigotry seem to be a slight problem, easily solved.*

Flicker drove up just as April came back all out of breath. There was a seat for her next to Mrs. Cole, who introduced her to the other girls in the car and to the grown-up young ladies she didn't know.

"This is April Bright," she said, "only sometimes we turn her name around and call her 'Bright April.'"

"It has begun," April thought to herself. "And it will last till night. It will be fun all the time we are going, and while we are there, and all the way home."

They were soon beyond Germantown and going over the city-line road to meet the other car beyond. Through the park, across the bridge, up the hill and down again, past beautiful homes, past the old Lancaster Road, and on to the road where the Conestoga wagons used to travel many years ago. Flicker told them about it as they went.

"And the pony express went out this road too, April. Remember telling us about it?" Mrs. Cole added.

The other car hailed them at the main road, then went on ahead to show the way. It seemed a long way to April, who had never been so far from home, but it was only about twenty miles after all. They turned off onto a side road after a few miles, then went up over hills and on down into valleys through woods that grew on both sides of the road, past deep green pastures where horses were grazing, and where the meadow rose steeply to a crown of woodland. The fields seemed to fold one into another, and sometimes it seemed to April as if the rounded hills rose and fell like a great breast. "Maybe that's what it means when they say "Mother Nature," she thought.

The girls sang as they rode, and sometimes April joined in, but there was so much to see, she liked better to just look and listen.

Deep Meadow Farm lay to the right of the road after they made the next turn. It nestled just below the small village where they stopped to inquire the way, and where there was a post office.

Before getting out of the car one of the leaders reminded the girls, "These nice people are not in

From *Bright April* by Marguerite de Angeli. Copyright 1946 by Marguerite de Angeli. Reprinted by permission of Doubleday & Company, Inc.

scouting, but they like to do things for others. We must show them how well behaved all Brownie Scouts are. Remember, no gates must be left open on a farm, and no doors left unlatched where animals could go astray." And Mrs. Cole whispered to April, "We must show them what a fine troop *we* have. Remember, D.Y.B.!"

The other car had already arrived, and the girls stood about laughing and talking like old friends, though they had only met an hour or so before. Griz, one of the leaders, introduced each girl and leader to the others and then, putting her arm around a child near her, said:

"This little girl is Phyllis Merchant. She is visiting my neighbor, and though she isn't a Brownie, I know you will make her welcome. Perhaps she will like us so much that she will help start a Brownie Scout troop when she goes back home. Phyllis lives way out in the country and has no brothers or sisters, so we must show her what good sisters Brownies can be."

Phyllis smiled and turned her blue eyes on one girl after another. But when they fell on April the smile began to fade. She drew her brows together in a slight frown and glanced away. April felt again that unpleasant thud inside. But Mrs. Cole said Quickly:

"Come, Mrs. Green is there waiting for us." She took April's hand, and they went through the white gate where Mrs. Green met them. She was a pretty lady and so pleasant that April soon forgot the look Phyllis had given her and only remembered the secret letters Mrs. Cole had whispered, "D.Y.B."

Leaving sweaters and coats on the wide porch, they all followed Mrs. Green to the big barn to see the animals. It stood on the rise of the hill so that it was on two levels. It was built of stone and very old, though it was freshly painted and in good condition.

"This is what they call a 'bank barn,'" Mrs. Green told them as they walked up the slope. "You see, the ground is filled in up to the large door so that the hay wagons can drive right into the barn."

She opened the big high doors, and the girls walked in to the warm sweet dark where the haylofts were. They were nearly empty now, for the haying season hadn't begun. Shafts of sunlight sifted through cracks near the roof and showed motes dancing. April could hear pigeons cooing in the loft and the squeaking "swish" of their wings as they rose into flight.

She wished she might climb the ladders that were built to the wall and look into the loft, but didn't dare ask if she might, till Mrs. Green spoke of it. Then they all took turns going up. It was higher than it looked, and April was glad to get down again!

They went from one part of the barn to another, up ladders and down around narrow winding steps, through low stone passageways and empty stalls. One large room was filled with discarded furniture. One was filled with bales of hay. Then they stepped up into a room that smelled like fresh bread. The ceiling was low and hung with white-dusted cobwebs. The walls were silvery and the floor was rubbed white and smooth with the floury powder that sifted through grain bags stored there.

"Be careful!" cautioned Mrs. Green as they came into the room, and April gasped as she looked out through the door that opened into the air!

They seemed to be far, far off the ground, for through that open door the whole countryside lay unfolded to view. They had come to an upper level of the barn and were at the back where the ground level was much lower than at the front. It seemed as if they could see for miles! But when April looked cautiously down below, there were the cows in the barnyard, just being let out after milking.

When Mrs. Green led them down more twisting stairs to the floor of the lower barn, they could look out over a half-door into the yard where the cows stood. April had never been so close to a cow before in her life! She could have reached out and touched Molly's nose, but she didn't.

Flicker came and stood next to her. "See the barn swallows!" she said. "And there are the nests."

She showed April the little basket-shaped nests of clay clinging to the sides of the beams extending out over the doorway. Sharp-tailed swallows darted about the barnyard, and April even saw one leaving the nest!

"They are eating their supper," said Flicker. "See how they catch the gnats and flies on the wing?" They made little mewing cries as they dipped and soared. "There's another bird for your list, April."

In another part of the barn they saw the horses: two large work horses with tremendous broad backs, and one for Mrs. Green to ride. He was a beautiful bright chestnut that Mrs. Green called "Red." There were pigs in still another section of the barn, and right near was the pen where a little new calf lay. He was so new that he was still trembly on his legs.

Mrs. Cole said, "He looks like every other baby thing, doesn't he?" April could see what she meant. He *did* look just like a baby, any baby, Sophie's kitten, Mrs. Cole's puppy, or even Edith's little brother, Danny.

Mrs. Green had set the table out on the lawn where it looked over the meadow and away off to the blue hills beyond. The air was as warm as summer, and now that the wind had died, it began to be very close, so the fire that burned in the outdoor fireplace was uncomfortably warm. One of the leaders helped Mrs. Green to cook the kabobs she had already prepared. The table looked inviting with its colorful paper cover and napkins, its stone crock filled with tulips and iris and a great bowl of green salad. While the cooking was being done, the girls played tag or pushed one another in the swing that hung from the walnut tree. April sat on the porch and played with the kittens. There was a whole basketful. There were nine of them, all different, with the mother cat who sat near the door with her tail slowly moving back and forth on the floor and her ears cocked forward, as if she were not too sure that her children were safe.

When it was time to go to the table, April was the last to find a seat.

"Here, child, sit here!" called Mrs. Green as April hesitated, not being sure where to go.

She went to the table, and just as she stepped over the long bench to sit down, the little girl sitting in the next place turned around. It was Phyllis! She looked at April and started to get up.

"I'm not going to sit there next to—" She got no further, for there was Mrs. Green who had followed April to help her find her seat.

Mrs. Green did as Mrs. Cole had done once before, clapped her hands over Phyllis's thoughtless mouth, and at the same time helped her to rise, then led her away into the house, where Griz quickly followed. Mrs. Cole was near at hand too. She gently led April down the hill out of sight of the others, who were so busy chattering they hadn't heard what Phyllis said.

"Dear child," she said as they walked together, "remember D.Y.B. It means allowing for the thoughtlessness of others as well as trying to be thoughtful yourself. It means being forgiving because someone else doesn't know what she is saying."

Mrs. Cole smoothed April's hair as she talked and with her quiet voice and gentle way helped April to swallow the lump in her throat and to feel sorry for Phyllis when Mrs. Cole told her that she had no mother.

"Now," said Mrs. Cole at last, "will you promise to try to forget that Phyllis didn't want to sit near you? Will you show her what a Brownie is like? Come on, now, up with the corners of your mouth! Remember, it's your birthday!"

Phyllis wasn't very friendly to April during the meal, but one of the leaders sat between them, and April was able to enjoy the kabobs which she had never eaten before. They were long skewers filled with alternate pieces of meat, tomato, and onion, broiled over the open fire. Everyone made April feel as if it were a birthday party just for her. They sang the birthday song, and there was even a cake Mrs. Green had made and put ten candles on. April cut it first. She was happy.

The sky began to cloud, and a chill wind blew before they had finished eating, but Mrs. Green said:

"It's April, don't forget. What if we do have a shower? It won't last long. We'll gather things up and go into the house. Then we can have a sing in front of the fireplace."

What fun it was! The fireplace was large, and there was room on the floor for all the girls. The leaders knew the Scout songs and, by the time they sang the second verse, most of the Brownies could sing them, too. They scarcely heard the deep roll of thunder that was followed by a sudden spatter of rain against the windows. The walls were thick and stout, and April felt safe and secure with such warm friends about, for one of the girls, Margaret, sat close by and put her arm around her. Even Phyllis began to move near her

as they sat on the floor. She looked curiously into April's face for a moment, then timidly touched her hand with a finger tip.

Suddenly Flicker said, "I believe the storm is getting worse. Listen!" There was a flash of lightning and a roar of wind and rain, followed by a crash of thunder.

"You can't go home in this!" Mrs. Green exclaimed. "you'll have to stay all night!"

"Sixteen people stay all night! Where would you put us?" laughed Flicker. "Nonsense! We will wait awhile till the storm lessens, then we can go."

Mr. Green brought in popcorn and long-handled poppers to use over the bed of coals left from the fire. April thought it a wonderful lark to be caught away from home in the storm, but Phyllis whimpered, "I wish it would stop. I wish we could go home. I wish the thunder would stop." She crept closer to April.

The storm went on and on. Mr. Green went out to see if there was any sign of its stopping, but reported that the road was a rushing torrent and the wind was very strong.

"It wouldn't be safe to start home in this," he said. "We can find enough beds and cots and blankets for all of you. You'll have to stay."

At first it seemed out of the question, but as Mr. Green helped Griz do the telephoning to let the girls' parents know they were safe, and Mrs. Green and Mrs. Cole and Flicker found bedding in the enormous closet upstairs, it didn't look so impossible after all. The house was much too large for two people anyway, Mr. Green said, and hadn't seen enough of overnight crowding!

Mrs. Green helped the girls to get ready for bed and put April into the same room as Phyllis and two of the other girls. There was a double bed and a couch in the room and a folding cot. Two of the girls got themselves ready and into the big bed first, leaving the couch over by the window for Phyllis, where Flicker helped her to get comfortable.

The cot was for April. Mrs. Cole tucked her in and whispered, "You *did* remember to live up to the secret sign didn't you? You are a brave girl. Did you have a nice birthday?"

"Oh, yes," whispered April, "wonderful!"

"I know now that when you leave our troop to 'fly up' to the next group, you will still remember

D.Y.B. Don't forget! *Always* D.Y.B.!" Mrs. Cole kissed April good night, put out the light, and closed the door.

The storm howled and beat upon the window panes. The lightning flashed and filled the room with brightness, and the rolling thunder shook the roof.

Jane and Betty, the two girls in the big bed, giggled and whispered and made nonsensical noises at every flash of lightning.

Phyllis began to whimper again, and April was going to call out to her that everything was all right, but remembering Phyllis's look, she just lay still and wondered if they missed her at home.

She could hear the floor boards squeak as someone moved about in the hall, and lowered voices coming from the next room.

For a long time there was a dim light under the door, but it finally went out.

Jane and Betty suddenly were quiet, and April knew they were asleep.

It was still raining very hard, and though the lightning was not as severe, it still flashed at short intervals.

April could hear Phyllis moving about on the couch. She heard her sigh. She thought how lonely Phyllis must be with no mother. She felt sorry for her and wanted to go and comfort her. But when she remembered how Phyllis had refused to sit beside her at the table, she just couldn't, so she set her lips together and turned over, pulling the covers over her ears.

The delicate smell of lavender coming from the smooth sheets, the light warmth of the blanket were comforting. April fell asleep.

Some time later April felt herself gently but firmly pushed over to the edge of the cot. She half awoke as two little arms crept about her. Then came a whisper, "It's me—Phyllis. I'm cold, and I'm *so* lonesome. Can't I stay here with you?" April was awake now.

"Of course," she answered, hugging Phyllis close.

Phyllis was quiet for a moment, then said hesitantly, "You know, at first I didn't like you. I never knew anyone just like you before. But Flicker told me about you and how nice you are. She told how much you know about birds and trees, too, and she says you like to read books. So do I. I read all the time, even when I'm drying dishes. I prop the book up on the shelf against the salt box. I like fairy stories best. Do you?"

She didn't wait for April to answer, but went on as if she couldn't wait to get it all out at once: "When I touched your hand that time, I felt how nice and smooth it was. I saw that your dress was just as fresh and clean as mine, too." She stopped for a moment, then went on, "I like you now." She breathed a deep sigh and went sound asleep!

April sighed too. What a wonderful birthday it had been!

When she woke in the morning, April couldn't think where she was.

There was no sound of cars going over pavements, no trolly screeching around corners, no lumbering truck shaking the house as it passed. Instead, there were chickens muttering to themselves, cows mooing, the faraway barking of a dog, and, just as at home, birds singing.

Then she remembered. It was not Chris who lay beside her, but Phyllis, her new-found friend.

The storm was over and bright sunshine filled the new-washed world.

It was fun dressing with four girls in the room. Phyllis stayed close to April as she dressed, and they chattered as if their whole lives depended on their getting acquainted in the short time they would be together. A whole new world seemed to open for April as Phyllis told her about her home and the small town where she went to school.

"And I'll write to you," Phyllis went on, "and you can write to me, and we can tell each other what we are reading and everything. I'll try reading some of those books you told me about; those that seem real and tell about different ways people live."

"Yes," agreed April, "and I'll try reading fairy tales too. And you can tell me about the Brownie Scout troop you're going to join, and I can tell you about the real Girl Scout troop I'm going to 'fly up' to, and—"

"Yes," Phyllis began again, not even waiting for April to stop. "I know my daddy would like me to be a Brownie if I can learn all those things about setting the table and making things and being thoughtful. But tell me, what does D.Y.B. mean?"

"That's a secret," said April. "I can't tell that. But if you join a Brownie troop, you'll find out!"

Just then Chris called up the stairs for the girls to stop talking and hurry down. Phyllis was ready first so she ran on ahead while April finished smoothing her hair. April thought to herself about "D.Y.B." and how remembering those secret letters had helped her. They had made it easier for her to have a good time at the supper party, even when Phyllis was unfriendly; easier to be nice to Phyllis when she needed comfort in the night. And by remembering them she had made Phyllis her friend; Phyllis who had no mother, no sister like Chris, and no brothers like Ken and Tom. It paid to DO YOUR BEST!

It was fun having breakfast in the big farm kitchen, for Mrs. Green insisted that they eat before they went home. Phyllis chose the seat on one side of April and on the other side sat Margaret, who had put her arm around April the night before. The table was stretched to its full length, and there was room for everybody.

"I promised all your mothers that you would be home early this morning," said Flicker, "so we must start soon."

Phyllis and April said good-by to each other with renewed promises to write. Then came the ride home through the fresh cold air, and the singing.

"Oh," thought April, "it's all much better than I thought it *could* be, and it's lasting longer too. Besides, I have a new friend!"

It was still early when they reached home, and April had time before church to tell Mamma all about it. She began by telling how Phyllis had first looked at her; how Phyllis wouldn't sit next her at the table, and then how at last, the lonely little girl had crept into bed with her.

"You see, Mamma," April exclaimed, "she didn't know the truth about me at all. She didn't know at first that my skin is just like hers, only a different color, and she didn't know what good care you take to keep my clothes nice and clean, and she didn't know how I like to read just as she does! I guess if she had known the truth about me, she would have liked me at first!" April laughed in sheer joy at remembering her new friend.

"Yes," agreed Mamma soberly. "Yes, that is just it, exactly. She didn't know the truth. We must know *the truth* always, even when it hurts. The Bible says, 'Ye shall know the TRUTH, and the truth shall make you free!'"

MARY JANE

Dorothy Sterling

Mary Jane's family is highly educated, and she wants to enter the all-white junior high school because it offers classes that will help her in college. That her family is quite worried surprises her, for she sees no danger in being one of the first Negroes to integrate a southern school.

This well-written chapter not only shows but builds in the reader the tension felt by the townspeople who feared change and by the black children who were unwelcome. In writing about racial bias, Miss Sterling tries to report rather than to editorialize. She avoids didacticism and lets her plot and characterization arouse the reader's empathy.

HEADS UP, EYES FRONT

Mr. Jackson and Fred arrived at the Douglases' while Mary Jane was still eating break-fast. Tall Mr. Jackson making polite talk with Daddy while she spooned up her cereal, and Fred looking stiff and uncomfortable in a new suit and freshly shined shoes. Mary Jane almost wanted to giggle, to tell them all that it wouldn't hurt a bit. But she couldn't, because there was a lump in her throat, as if her tonsils had grown back.

Mamma had little frown lines on her forehead as she smoothed the lapels of Mary Jane's new blazer and straightened the bow on her pony tail and asked if she'd remembered to take a handkerchief.

"Now you be good and don't fret your teachers," she said. "Hear?"

It was the same thing she said every year on the first day of school. The same thing she used to tell Lou Ellen and James when they were little. Only people who knew Mamma well, like Mary Jane and Daddy, could have said there was anything different about her good-by kiss that showed this wasn't any ordinary first school day.

She stood on the porch, waving to them as they drove off. Mary Jane watched her through the back window of the car until she was only a blur. Fred, who had grown about a mile over the summer, was talking about basketball. He talked goals and fouls and dribbles steadily until Daddy parked the car across the street from school. Then Fred stopped—right in the middle of a sentence.

Mary Jane looked out to see what had made Fred stop talking. The fluttery feeling traveled from her stomach to her chest to her throat, and she clutched her schoolbag with a perspiring hand.

"Man!" Fred whistled through his teeth.

Because across the street, in front of Wilson, there was a row of green and white police cars. And behind the cars there were millions of people. Men and women and children sitting on the low stone wall, swarming over the big lawn and crowding the broad limestone steps. Men and women and children shouting and talking until Daddy and Mr. Jackson and Fred and Mary Jane got out of the car, then putting their voices together for a thundering "Boo-o-o!"

For a moment Mary Jane thought about Curly following her to school and how frightened he'd be by the noise. Then she stopped thinking about anything at all. With Daddy and Mr. Jackson on the outside and Fred and Mary Jane in the middle like a sandwich, the four of them marched across the street.

On the school sidewalk, two policemen joined them. The policemen went first, clearing a path through the crowd, leading the way. It was as if they were marching in a parade.

Heads up. Eyes front. One-two-three-four.

Only instead of drums to keep time to there were screams.

A man, angry. "Go back to Africa!"

Mary Jane turned her head, trying to see who it was. What did he mean?"

A woman, high-pitched—could it have been a woman? "Pull her black curls out!"

Mary Jane's scalp tingled as if someone were tugging at it. Automatically her hand jerked up toward her forehead, toward the little fluff she'd combed so carefully at her new dressing table that morning. Then Daddy caught her hand, squeezing it in his own.

Heads up. Eyes front. Eyes on the broad blue backs of the policemen.

They were on the steps now, the white steps that led to the open school door. The crowd, not people, but a crazy Thing of faces and open mouths, was behind them, roaring in their ears. The Thing moved closer, closer, until it seemed as if it were about to pounce. Mary Jane stifled a scream, and one of the policemen turned and shouted.

"Stand still. Move back."

The Thing stood still, stepped back, turned into people again. In a way, that was worse, because the people were yelling at *her*, at Mary Jane Douglas, beloved daughter of Mamma and Daddy, baby sister of Lou Ellen and James. Mary Jane, who'd never had anything bad happen to her in her life, except to her tonsils, and even then the doctor didn't mean to hurt. They couldn't be screaming at her—but they were.

Daddy squeezed her hand again. Heads up. Eyes front. They were on the landing now, close to the door. A group of boys were chanting, for all the world as if they were at a football game:

"Two-four-six-eight
We ain't gonna integrate."

Two-four-six-eight. The four of them marched through the door and all the way down the corridor to the principal's office keeping time to the rhythm of the chant.

While they waited to meet Mrs. Davis, Daddy

let go of her hand to give her a quick little hug. She looked up at him, her eyes round, black, startled. He looked down at her, straightening the bow on her pony tail, not neatly the way Mamma would do, but clumsily, like Dad. Mary Jane put down her schoolbag and straightened it all over again, as if fixing her bow was the most important thing in the whole world just then.

"Boy, that was rough," Fred whispered. "Look at my hand." When he held out his hand, it was trembling.

"Are you all right?" Daddy asked anxiously. "Should I take you home?"

Mary Jane shook her head. After the noise outside it was so quiet in the corridor that her ears buzzed. It was hard to speak around the lump in her throat. "I'm all right," she gulped. "You can go now."

But Daddy stayed until Mrs. Davis said "Hello" to all of them and introduced them to the other Negro children, three boys and a girl, who were entering the upper grades. When the warning bell rang, Daddy kissed her good-by and Mr. Jackson kissed Fred, who looked embarrassed but pleased just the same. After that it was definitely time for parents to leave and school to begin.

"Junior High Assembly," Mrs. Davis explained as she led them along winding corridors to the auditorium. "This is where you'll get your assignments to your home rooms."

In the big auditorium Mary Jane and Fred sat alone. Alone in the midst of a room full of boys and girls. Alone, as if they were on a desert island in the middle of the ocean.

Mrs. Davis gave a welcoming speech, saying how glad she was to greet all the new people and that she hoped everyone had had a restful summer so that they could buckle down to some good hard work this term. It was a nice speech. Mary Jane had heard Mrs. Buckley give one like it at Dunbar every fall.

After Mrs. Davis' talk, another teacher stood up to read the home-room assignments. She called boys and girls up to the front of the room, one after the other, to get their cards

The A's, the B's, the C's. Fred looked down sympathetically as the teacher began on the D's. For a moment Mary Jane thought he was going to pat her hand. Only then he remembered that he was a boy and she was a girl and that patting hands just wasn't done, in school or out, first day or last, when you were twelve.

"Mary Jane Douglas." She shivered a little, even though she was still wearing her blazer. Slowly she stood up and walked down the aisle to the front of the room. Head up. Eyes front.

The room was so quiet that she could hear her own footsteps tapping on the floor, her new loafers with the good-luck pennies in them. Until, from somewhere behind her, there was a muffled chorus:

> "We don't want her
> You can have her.
> She's too black for me."

Mary Jane flushed, faltered, kept on walking. Her cheeks were burning as Mrs. Davis jumped up from her seat on the stage and sternly rapped for order.

"Disgraceful . . . no more of that . . . rude . . . won't permit . . ."

Words. Words that Mary Jane scarcely heard as she took her assignment card and walked back to her seat. Head up, eyes front, not listening, not seeing anything. Not even reading the card until Fred came back with his and they compared them. He was in home room 127, she in room 124. Her home-room teacher was Miss Rousseau, the card said.

After all the assignments had been given out and the junior high had pledged allegiance and sung "Oh, say can you see," the boys and girls shuffled through the auditorium doors to the crisscross of corridors beyond. Everyone seemed to know where to go except Fred and Mary Jane. They stood there looking uncertainly at each other, when something surprising happened. At least Mary Jane *thought* it happened. Puzzling over it later, she wasn't sure that it hadn't been a dream.

A girl came up to them, a little girl with bright red cheeks and pale blond hair, and said that she was sorry about the crowd outside. "Can I help you find your way?" she asked. "My sister used to go here, so I know where the rooms are, sort of. It's awfully confusing if you don't."

Instead of answering, they showed her their cards. She led them up a flight of stairs and down a hall to their home rooms. Then she disappeared without even saying "Good-by."

Room 124 was pleasant and sunny, with high windows and movable desks and a green blackboard behind the teacher's chair. Not much different from the classrooms at Dunbar except for the color of the blackboard, and the desks which were brand-new.

Even Miss Rousseau looked like the Dunbar teachers. Ageless, the way teachers always seemed to be, not exactly pretty, but not ugly either. Like the Dunbar teachers, except that Miss Rousseau's skin was fair instead of brown and she talked with a funny sort of accent. She rolled her *r*'s and did things with her *th*'s in a way that Mary Jane had never heard before.

"Good morning." She smiled as Mary Jane hesitated in the doorway, not sure of what to do next.

A bell rang and Miss Rousseau started to assign seats. Alphabetical order again, which put Douglas in the second row, with a window on one side and a girl named Duncan on the other.

Only the girl named Duncan didn't sit down. Instead she marched up to the teacher's desk and loudly announced, "My mother said I wasn't to sit by *her*."

Miss Rousseau lifted her eyebrows. "In my class," she answered, "pupils sit where they are assigned." Calmly she continued to read out the names.

The girl named Duncan started to leave the room, then thought better of it. Without looking at Mary Jane, she slid her desk over until it was almost touching the one at her right. It stayed there until Miss Rousseau finished with her seating list.

"Now, Darlene." The teacher's voice was calm. "You can put your desk back in place."

Mumbling under her breath, Darlene obeyed. Through the entire period, however, she kept her head turned toward the door. If she *had* to sit next to Mary Jane, at least she wasn't going to look at her. For a crazy moment Mary Jane felt like giggling. Darlene was going to have an awful stiff neck by the end of the term.

The next minutes were busy ones. Miss Rousseau gave out schedule cards and locker numbers and explained about periods and bells and lunch and gym and not being late and bringing a note

to the nurse if you were sick. Then the whole class trooped out to the hall to find their lockers and practice their combinations.

The combinations worked like the locks on safes. Two turns to the right. Stop at 27. One turn to the left. Stop at 14. Then right again until the lock clicked open when you reached 7. Mary Jane twirled and stopped and twirled and stopped until she knew her combination by heart. After she hung up her blazer on the hook inside the locker she went back to her home room.

There was another bell and still another, and regular classes began. Today was only a half day, so classes meant learning your teachers' names and getting your seat and your books. For first period Mary Jane stayed right where she was, alongside Darlene, because their class was French and Miss Rousseau taught it.

Miss Rousseau not only taught French, she *was* French, she told the class. Which explained the funny accent. At any other time Mary Jane, who had never met a person before who didn't come from North Carolina or Kentucky or Tennessee, would have been interested in someone from Paris, France, who said "ze" when she meant "the". But not today when her head ached and the back of her neck felt sore and she couldn't swallow the lump in her throat no matter how hard she tried.

After French and more bells came English and more bells, then Arithmetic, History, and Science. Only History was called Social Studies now, and Arithmetic was Math. All of the classrooms looked like her home room, except Science, which had tables instead of desks and a sink in the back of the room, and Social Studies, which had Fred.

Mary Jane had never realized before how much she liked Fred until she saw his friendly, dark face when she entered the Social Studies room. While people were still finding their seats, he leaned forward to whisper in her ear.

"Already I've been kicked in the shins and had my books knocked out of my arm. Score, Wilson two, Jackson nothing. This keeps up, I'll get a complex or something. I'll begin to think they don't like me," he chuckled.

"Who did it?" Mary Jane's lips framed the words as the teacher called the class to order.

Fred shrugged his shoulders, the smile gone from his face. "Seems like all of them."

Mary Jane chewed her underlip as she copied the homework assignment from the board. "Columbus Finds a New World, pages 3–11." The next bell would mean Science, and then school would be over for the day. The bell after the next one would mean going outside to face that howling, hating crowd. Maybe, she thought, they wouldn't be there. Maybe they had forgotten and gone away. But after she'd taken her blazer from her locker and found Fred and then Daddy in the noisy vestibule, she knew that the crowd was still outside, still waiting.

Down the steps and across the lawn she walked, with the policemen leading and the voices screaming. Mean, hate-filled voices screeching in her ears. She blinked at the white light from a photographer's flash gun. She ducked when a stick glanced off her shoulder. But she wasn't what you'd really call hurt. She was still putting one foot in front of the other and squeezing Daddy's hand and trying not to listen to the roar of the crowd.

One-two-three-four, and they had crossed the street. One-two-three-four, and they were in the car. With the doors closed and the windows rolled up to shut out the noise.

It was the end of Mary Jane's first day in junior high.

PLAIN GIRL

Virginia Sorenson

Esther is one of the Plain People; she is Amish. The authorities force her parents to send her to the public school where she will be the only Amish student. Her parents are concerned because her older brother has left his home and his Amish way of life after graduating from the school.

Esther is at first timid but finds a friend, Mary, who wears a pink dress and is as different from Esther as anyone can be. This makes Esther wonder if it is right to play with Mary and to like someone who is not Amish.

Never in all her life had Esther dreaded anything so much as telling Mary she could not play again. Father left her at the schoolhouse early, before even the teacher came, for he had work to do. Father was always on time for everything, or else ahead of time. He knew a saying, "One who wastes Time wastes Life itself."

Esther sat alone on the very step where she and Mary could no longer play. The sky was full of plunging gray clouds. Maybe it would rain. Maybe nobody would be able to go outside today. Then she could wait and tell Mary tomorrow.

The school bus was coming. It was bright orange, very beautiful on the brown road between

the green and yellow trees. It was pleasant to watch the big door swing open and the children come out one by one. They looked gay. Every one had a different color; you couldn't know which color would come out next. One was blue and one was red. A yellow sweater. Then a green cap! One boy had no cap, but his hair was exactly the color of a robin's breast. If she had *that*, Esther thought, how cheerful it would be, better than if she could have a bright scarf and mittens —for nobody could object to colored hair. Objecting to a bright beautiful color that grew out of you and belonged to you would be foolish. It would be as foolish as objecting to colored flowers, or carrots. Or cardinals. Or beetles. Or berries. Or to sunshine itself.

Mary came out of the bus. At the same moment the sun came out of the clouds, and Mary was shining as she ran. "Esther, if it rains she lets us play jacks on the floor!" she said. She had been thinking about it too. Esther felt a sudden wave of happiness. Mary had been thinging about playing again, just as she had herself. As naturally as could be, Mary took hold of her hand and they went into the schoolhouse together. It did not even occur to Esther to tell Mary that she couldn't play. After all, there was plenty of time.

In writing class, Mary turned and slipped another note onto Esther's desk. She did it so quickly that Esther hardly saw the motion. But there was the note, neatly folded, with *Esther* printed on it in letters nearly an inch high.

What would it say this time? She had started to unfold it before she remembered about the preaching the day before and how strong she had meant to be. Her fingers trembled. *But Mary was sweet*, she thought. Nobody could deny it who saw her at her desk with her head lowered over her work, clean and neat and pretty with her hair shining and tied with a pink ribbon. Like the fountain, Mary could not possibly be bitter too. Maybe that was what the Bible meant!

Of course. Why hadn't she thought of it before? Firmly, she unfolded Mary's note.

Dear Friend Esther:

Why don't you write a letter to me?

Your friend,
Mary.

Esther sat as still as she had ever sat in church. Why didn't she? She had learned from the beginning that when one received a kindness, a kindness should be given in return as soon as possible. Mother said that all the time, and Father too.

Well, then—She tore a sheet of paper from her notebook and began to make letters carefully. They didn't look as good as Mary's, no matter how carefully she made them. She reached into her desk and brought out Mary's first note. Then she began on a fresh sheet:

Dear Friend Mary:

I like you too. I think your pink dress is pretty. And your hair is cute. Your friend,

Esther.

She folded it very small and neat. Then she had an idea. She reached down and pulled a dark purple thread out of her dress. She was glad her dress was purple today and not black. With the thread she tied a neat little bow, so the letter looked like a package. She dropped it over Mary's shoulder, onto her desk. Her heart was beating hard as it had in the Meeting; she felt it thumping against the desk as she leaned forward. Now it was done, she thought.

Mary turned with a quick smile. She liked the package with its little bow. And then Esther watched as she opened it, hardly breathing. What would she say? But writing class ended before anything could be said. It was time for recess, and the sun had decided to shine, after all.

How could she say, "I can't play with you again." It was not possible. Mary took her hand as the line moved forward. Esther could not have taken away her hand any more than she could draw a sword from a stone. In two minutes they were on the step, bouncing the ball, gathering up the jacks, bouncing and gathering. "Good! Good!" Mary said whenever Esther did not miss. When the ball dropped or rolled away or when one of the jacks escaped, Mary never squealed with pleasure the way most of the girls always did. Instead, she would say, "Too bad! They were scattered too far that time." Or even, "The ball went crooked; it bounced on that crack in the step."

All afternoon Esther felt happy and lighthearted and gay. She ate her lunch in a huge circle of girls, under a tree. Nobody laughed in an unkind way. She did not look down all the time, but up and around to see what everybody was doing.

As the children went out to the orange bus again, Esther saw Father coming far down the road. Mary stopped beside her, by the step. "See you tomorrow!" she said.

Would Father notice? No, Esther thought, relieved, he was still too far away.

"Good-by," she said quickly, and sat down on the step.

But Mary did not go just then. The children were filing onto the bus. She had plenty of time. "Once I was in a play," Mary said, and sat down on the step too. "I took the part of a Pilgrim—it was a Thanksgiving play—and I had a dress just like yours."

"A dress like *mine?*" It seemed strange to think of Mary in such a dress.

"I love wearing long dresses," Mary said. "And those darling little high shoes—with laces. And bonnets that tie under the chin."

Father was coming very close now.

"You'll miss getting on the bus," Esther said.

Mary stood up. "If you'd like," she said quickly, "some day at recess—when I wear my pink—we can go out to the girls' place and *change*. Just for the rest of the day."

She didn't wait for an answer, but had to run. Somebody was calling her. It was lucky she hadn't waited, either, because Esther was completely without words to say. Change? She looked down at her dress and the tips of her black shoes. She hardly saw or heard the bus go roaring away. When she looked up again, Father was driving out of the cloud of dust it left behind it, looking very angry. She saw him glance back at the roaring thing that made such an ugliness out of a good road.

At first Esther did not speak, beyond her greeting. She was thinking about what Mary had said. If only she could tell Father and he would understand!

"And how is it going at school?" he asked kindly, at last.

"Very well."

"Do you read in the books yet?"

"Mostly in one book."

"And you write the letters?"

Her heart bounced like the little red ball. How did he *know?* But then she realized what it was he meant. He did not mean letters to Mary, but the letters A and B and C and all the rest.

"Yes," she said, relieved. "All of the alphabet now."

He drove along in silence awhile. The horse went clip-clop-clop, clip-clop-clop, a sound Esther loved.

'It's too bad you are the only one of the Plain children at the school just now," Father said. "It isn't easy to be alone there. But next year there will be the Yoder child, and the year after, several others."

She looked up at him gratefully. Perhaps he

did know, after all, exactly how hard it was. He had said, "*It isn't* easy . . ." She thought, "I'll ask him. It'll be all right to ask him now." But she didn't know exactly what to ask, or how. She swallowed twice and then began slowly, looking straight ahead down the road. "I've been wondering since I came to school—"

He did not look at her either. He gazed at the rump of the horse going from side to side. "Yes, Esther?" he asked.

"I've been wondering why— Well—" Her voice stopped as on the edge of a cold pool and then plunged: "Why is it that people must wear different clothes?" She would like it if she had been able to ask the question the way Dan did, how buttons might harm a man's soul. But this was good enough to begin with. She knew her question was well understood.

"You have been wondering why *we* wear different clothes, Esther?" he asked.

"Yes," she said.

He did not answer until he had turned the buggy into their own farm and the horse had stopped by the barn. He did not offer to get out of the buggy, but sat still for a while. Esther sat still beside him, looking at the horse and at her hands in her lap and at the toes of her shoes.

"It is not only *wearing*," he said at last. "It is *who we are*. It is what we believe." He said it with his strongest look; she knew the look was there even before she raised her eyes to his face. It was the look he had when he swung an ax over his head, or when he carried a big stone. It was stronger than the look he read the Bible with.

"We are Plain People," he said, "and so we wear plain clothes. There are not very many in the world now who live as it was intended in the beginning." She knew he believed every word and was proud because he believed them.

"But why—" She paused, to be sure of what she meant to say. She looked up, puzzled, to ask it, with Mary in her thoughts. "Who are *they*, then? The others? They wear different clothes nearly every day." Inside herself she was asking, "Who is Mary?"

His voice was still strong, but heavy too, like something boiled too thick. "They don't know who they are!" he said. "They are something different every day! They are anything and everything, those people. They are like beans in a hat. They are nothing and nobody!"

Now he seemed very angry and it was almost as if she had shouted "Daniel! Daniel! Who is Daniel?" Or even "Who is Dan?" He got down and began to unharness the horse with impatient hands. Esther saw Mother coming from the house to welcome her.

All evening she thought about what Father had said. It sounded sensible and true. Each living thing had its special color, and this never varied among its kind except sometimes for the seasons. You were Red Squirrel, or you were Gray Squirrel. If Red you were quarrelsome and your meat was not sweet and good and you drove Gray out of the trees and robbed him of his nuts. If you were a mouse instead you had another gray, smooth and flat, and a different tail without fuzz on it. If you were a woodcock you had still another gray, but had a bill for bug-digging added onto the front of you and eyes that never blinked for fear of missing something important. Or dangerous.

Every one "after its own kind" as the Bible said God made them right at first.

But when she thought once more about herself, something was wrong again. Something was different with all those creatures and with people. Not until the middle of the night did she see what the difference was. She woke suddenly with it quite clear in her mind. People were not different, like squirrels and mice and woodcocks. Underneath their clothes they were all the same. She blushed to be thinking about such a thing, but it was true. So the difference was that *people made who they were with their wearing.* For people, wearing this and that didn't come naturally at all, like fur and pinfeathers. They decided for themselves who they would be. Even Adam and Eve had decided, had they not?

Father and Mother had decided. That was

what he had meant. Plain People, with nothing fancy or bright to distract them. Dan had not made up his mind to be Plain, and when they tried to make it up for him, he went away.

And she herself. She must decide too. Sometime, not very long away, she must decide. Her mind swung to and fro, to and fro. Here were Father and Mother and so many good kind ones who cared about everything she thought and did. But here was Mary, smiling on the other side. And curiously enough, beside Mary stood Dan, tall and handsome as she remembered him.

She sat straight up in bed. Had Dan fallen in love, then? With somebody away, not Sarah? With somebody he could walk with in the town, and speak with even before he turned his light into her window? The thought made such a great shivering that she drew the covers tight under her chin. *With somebody in a pink dress?*

Now she recalled the row of small pink buttons down the back of Mary's dress.

If only she could see Dan now! Dan is the one to tell, she thought. I could ask Dan every question and he would answer. She was filled with loneliness for him. How far away had he gone? If she searched and asked questions, could she find him? He had not taken his buggy or his horse, so he could not have gone very far.

Shivering, she slipped out of bed and said her prayers all over again, from the beginning. But one prayer was different now. Usually she said, "Help Dan to be all right wherever he is, and help him to come home." Now she said, "Help me to find Dan. Help me to see him soon."

Back under the covers, she went instantly to sleep. Whenever she made a good prayer she felt peaceful afterward. Every prayer she had ever made for a good and necessary thing had always been answered. In her sleep she did not even stir or dream.

ABOUT THE B'NAI BAGELS

E. L. Konigsburg

Books written in the first person often prevent the reader from identifying with the narrator. Precocious, perceptive fictional children can, if not carefully developed, become annoying or unbelievable. Yet Konigsburg avoids both weaknesses. He even makes the seemingly stereotyped "Jewish mother" come alive in a believable, warm, and humorous portrayal.

This book keeps a careful balance between humor and prejudice. Most of the book is about Mark's loss of his best friend and his need to become a good ball player. Yet bigotry is such a factor in Jewish life that to ignore it would be to create a dishonest book. Konigsburg carefully shows its presence in Mark's life but balances it by showing truly human relationships between Mark, Simon, Sylvester, and Cookie.

Playgirl finally broke up the game. *Playgirl* being the magazine that Franklin P. Botts carried under his arm when he arrived and stood waiting by the fence. The kids crowded around him, and he collected a nickel from each of them. I didn't have any money with me; you're not supposed to take money to synagogue on Sabbath. I stretched my head to see if I could get a peek at the fold-out center picture. I knew what she wasn't wearing, but I couldn't get close enough to see anything important. I guess Cookie didn't have any money either.

She told me, "Botts went to camp. Overnight camp. Some rich relative, an aunt or something, sent him. When he came back, he taught us four dirty songs and started buying *Playgirl*. His Little League coach benched him four games last year, one for each song. And this year that coach didn't bother to pick up his option. But Botts doesn't care as long as he gets his price. He always charges admission. Some of the kids buy so many looks that they could have bought the magazine in the first place, but I guess they're always afraid to bring it into the house."

"Oh, I'd take a look if I had the money. But you can't take money to synagogue on Sabbath.

Synagogue!" I yelled. "What time is it?" No answer. "What time is it? Somebody, what time is it? Somebody? Anybody?"

"Botts yelled back, "It's five after eleven." He had a watch.

"Oh, boy. Oh, boy," I muttered as I grabbed my jacket off the fence. The prongs tore the lining a little. "Oh, boy," I said again as I began to make a dash for it. I had meant to ask the time when I arrived so that I could gauge how long the return trip would take, but I had gotten involved and forgot all about it.

Cookie ran after me carrying my shoes. "What's the matter?" she called, "you turn into a pumpkin or something at five after eleven?"

Botts laughed. "No, a bagel!" Everyone else laughed, too, although I'd bet that half of them didn't know what a bagel was.

"His ma's the manager of our team, the B'nai Bagels," he said, laughing. Getting up from the center of his group, he yelled to me, "What does B'NAI mean, anyway?"

I answered, walking backwards so they could hear me, but so that I wouldn't lose more time getting home. "SONS OF. It means SONS OF in Hebrew."

"Then we're all Sons of Bagels?" one of the twins asked, smiling to his brother.

Cookie was still running alongside me; she kept tossing the hair out of her eyes. "What's a bagel?"

"What I'll turn into in about ten minutes." I turned around and began running sincerely.

I arrived home before the mail and stashed my shoes and mitt in the shrubbery in front of the house to retrieve later. Aunt Thelma's car was in the driveway. I don't know why she even has a convertible because she doesn't like her hair to blow. She must like to put the top down to air out the upholstery.

They were having coffee at the kitchen table when I walked in. The dining room table was covered rim to rim with the records of last season's games: Mom's homework.

"How were services?" Mom asked.

"The usual," I answered. I glanced up at the light fixture before hurrying upstairs to hang up my jacket before the lining got discovered.

"Why," Aunt Thelma asked as I got to the stairs, "do you allow that boy to wear tennis shoes to Sabbath services?"

I was grateful that I was upstairs and out of sight.

"Allow? I don't allow," Mother answered. "He just wore them. Better that he should wear sneakers to synagogue on Saturday morning, Thelma, than that he shouldn't go at all. I'm sure the dear Lord wouldn't care if he walked unshoed."

"Unshod," Aunt Thelma corrected.

"Shod? I thought horses get shod."

"Shod is the past tense of shoe," Aunt Thelma informed.

"I'm sure the dear Lord wouldn't care if he walked in BAREFOOTED," Mother said.

Aunt Thelma sniffed.

I rejoined the family downstairs just as Dad walked in. He started taking off his tie the minute he crossed the threshold. He always did. Dad didn't have office hours on Saturday; it just seemed that way. He always had to catch up. I guess homework is a way of life for some people. Only they call book bags briefcases when they get older. Truth was, my dad really likes books. He would rather read about a baseball game than see one. That's a fact. He read the sports page as thoroughly as the international news, but I never saw him throw a ball or watch a game on TV. He

wandered toward the dining room table as he was loosening his tie.

"What's all this, Bessie?" he asked.

Mother called back from the kitchen. "Last year's Little League records, Sam. I thought they would help, but they're not too much use. There are so many new players this year."

Dad began looking over the records, and Aunt Thelma emerged from the kitchen holding her saucer chest high in the palm of one hand and her coffee cup with the thumb and forefinger of the other; her head would dart down now and then, and she'd sip from the cup in a motion that looked like a duck straining water.

Besides books, my Dad's good at concentrating.

Aunt Thelma sipped again and said, "Hello, Samuel." Aunt Thelma was the only person who called my father SAMUEL and my mother BESS. Even Spencer called Mother BESSIE, and he wasn't supposed to.

Dad's head darted up. "Oh, hi, Thelma. How is Ben?"

"Ben has a head cold."

Mother erupted from the kitchen before Dad had a chance to answer. "Men with such a little bit of hair should wear hats."

"What do you mean?" Aunt Thelma asked. "It's been at least seventy-five degrees out for the past week. Why should Ben wear a hat?"

"Because," Mother continued, "your Ben is practically—you should excuse the expression—practically bald. And when he perspires, his scalp gets wet and then the slightest breeze and he's holding open house for viruses."

"Science has found that there is no relationship between getting a chill and getting a cold."

"That's what science has found out for this week, Thelma, but wait five minutes. They'll find out what our mother always said. That men who are absolutely bald like Ben should wear hats."

Aunt Thelma sniffed.

Dad continued glancing over the records. He did it very fast, numbers sort of being his business. "It seems that the total in the errors column is extraordinarily high," he said.

"Well, after all," Mother said, "This is Little League. We're not the L.A. Dodgers, you know. Or even the New York Mets."

"Now, Bessie, don't get offended. I'm just

doing an account analysis. My recommendation to you is to win by cutting down on the errors. Concentrate on your defense for the first part of the season. It doesn't appear that the other teams have such great batters. And at the beginning of the season, most of the hits were made on errors. Practically every run the Elks Club team made against the B'nai B'rith was a home run. That means a lot of monkey business in the outfield. Errors. My advice to you, Bessie, is to cut your losses by tightening up on defense. Follow that up with batting."

Mother gave Dad a big kiss. "Sam, you are a genius."

"I know, Bessie, I know," Dad answered, looking at Aunt Thelma from under his eyebrows. He was pleased about himself and embarrassed about Aunt Thelma. When Mom was happy with someone, her enthusiasm was awful. You can't avoid it or even help catching it.

"You see, Thelma, my Sam not only has something ON his head: hair, but something IN his head: brains."

"My Ben is no slouch in the brains department, either," Aunt Thelma answered.

"That's true," Mother said, "Ben IS bright even if he's as bald as a baby's backside."

Aunt Thelma took long enough to set her cup and saucer on top of last year's records before she marched out of the house.

Mother looked at Dad and said, "What ever did I say wrong, Sam?"

Dad shook his head at Mother and ran after Aunt Thelma, who couldn't get her car out of our driveway because ours was blocking hers. Dad brought her back.

"I demand an apology," she hissed at Mother.

"O.K. An apology. I'm sorry that Ben is bald."

Aunt Thelma threw up her arms and began marching out of the house again. Dad caught her by the shoulders and turned her around. The two sisters faced each other and glared. The air between them growled.

And Aunt Thelma charged, "Good grief, Bess! I want you to be sorry for hurting my feelings, not for Ben's being bald."

"Did I hurt your feelings? I didn't realize."

"You didn't realize because you didn't care.

All you care about is having a winning team. Ever since you've become manager, that's all you care about. Is that more important than hurting people's feelings?"

"What you don't realize," Mother said, "is what will be hurt if we don't have a winning team."

"Don't be ridiculous. Nothing will be hurt. One of the values of Little League is to teach the boys to win and lose gracefully."

"Except how can a team learn to win and lose gracefully when all they do is lose? Then they lose something else, too. Their fight they lose; that's where the hurt comes in. Their spirit gets hurt. I saw it in my own Mark here. At the end of last season he never felt it mattered whether his team even showed up at the ball park. They forgot how to care. I want to do something much harder than teaching them how to win and lose gracefully. I want to teach them to care. I want they should feel rotten when they lose."

"You want them to feel rotten?" Aunt Thelma repeated.

Mother nodded. "Rotten but not hopeless."

"If you take Samuel's advice, you're going to make them specialists. Offense. Defense. Sounds like platoons in professional football. And you can't tell me that's good for Little League."

"Strategy that is. Training. Discipline. They need that to make caring count. It would be mean to make them care, and then not give them the training to make caring count."

Aunt Thelma sucked in her breath and added, "I'm not convinced that . . ."

I interrupted Aunt Thelma in a voice that belonged out-of-doors, "You can't accuse my mother of being interested only in winning. That's not true, and I can prove it in two words. Just two words!"

Aunt Thelma, Mother and Dad all focused on me. I backed up to the wall in the el, swallowed, and whispered, "Sidney Polsky."

Dad laughed. "The case for the defense rests." The sisters laughed, too, and it was a good thing. It turned out that we needed Aunt Thelma on our side. And I was surprised at how quickly I had come to my mother's defense, even though I didn't approve of her language. (I would have bet that Mrs. Jacobs never even THOUGHT that anyone was as bald as a baby's backside.) It seems I had no trouble with my mother, the mother; it was my mother, the manager, who gave me headaches and doubts.

* * *

In some silent way practices at the Projects had promoted me from a C— to a B+ and sometimes an A— player. I think that regular practices with the team had helped in an out-loud way, but they had probably helped the other kids more. To the world we were known as the B'nai B'rith team, but to us we were the B'nai Bagels.

My mother was something of a comical genius on the practice field. She could nag those kids in such a way that they thought that it was fun. One of Mother's big manias was to have each kid lengthen his stride. "C'mon," she'd yell, "stretch those legs. Three steps take less time than four; two take less than three. C'mon you guys, take a giant step." The Bagels would tease her and say, "May I?" And Mother would play it straight and answer, "Of course."

Another of her specialties was fielding. "Back up your man!" "Call your balls! Call your balls!" And then Sonefield would say, "Matzo balls!" and someone else would yell "Ding dong balls!" but they would be catching like crazy as they did it.

If Mother was the comical captain, Spencer was the tough drill sergeant, and, strangely enough, the kids loved that, too. We practiced twice a week and after each session you could feel your muscles loosen and your nerves tighten. Our fielding became like some complicated dance number, the timing was so good. Spencer's having been catcher on his Little League Championship Team helped, too. He remembered how he felt AT FIRST; that kind of remembering is unusual in older brothers, especially when they are as old as Spencer. But he remembered how heavy the catcher's equipment felt, and how you wished that you could sight the ball from behind the plate as well as you can when it is coming toward you in the outfield. And he remembered what a nervous-maker it was to have that bat swinging in front of your eyes. Right in front. And how that made the ball even harder to sight. So what Spencer did was to train a catcher for us. He trained Hersch, who took it very well.

Spencer also made us practice bunting even though it quickly become obvious that Barry was the only kid who could pick a spot to lay down a bunt and beat it out. It should have happened to some nicer guy because Barry resented bunting the way I resent having to wear rubbers when I don't really believe it will rain and would like to take my chances with shoes. Barry always thought he could get a big hit.

Spencer's proclamation that everyone should walk to the playing field cut down on the number of parents who came. Mrs. Polsky came with Mrs. LaRosa, though. Sidney and Louis walked, and their mothers drove alongside in the Polsky's VW. They had to drive so slowly that the car never got out of first gear and their coming was announced by the erg-erg-erg sound getting louder and louder. Barry's mother also came to all the practices; she watched her son as if he were Macy's Thanksgiving Day Parade. The whole parade. Did you ever get the feeling about a guy that everything he does is rehearsed? Like the way Barry walked. I got the feeling that he had watched baseball movies and practiced that loose-jointed kind of saunter. Maybe a baseball uniform just makes you look that way. Maybe I even looked that ways as I left the field. I wouldn't mind if I did.

Long before our first game came along, everyone on our team was in love with my mother. They called her Mother Bagel, and they called Spencer Brother Bagel. They preferred Mother to Brother, which wasn't exactly one of the Great Decisions of the Western World. But it does show that they had quite forgotten that she is a woman.

Simon and Sylvester, who are Catholic and who used to cross themselves before each time at bat, began tipping their hats to the Big Light Fixture in the sky. It wasn't that Mother did anything to convert them, it's just that kids have a way of imitating people they like. That's how Si and Syl probably began crossing themselves in the first place; they saw some ball player doing it on TV. Everyone including mother was having great trouble telling which was where on the field. They each had a number: Simon was Number 5, and Sylvester was Number 4, but Mother always had to check her list to see which number belonged to which. She finally brought a red handkerchief and made Simon wear it in his back pocket, but it was always falling out, and Mother couldn't remember whether she had assigned the handkerchief to Simon or to Sylvester. And sometimes for fun Sylvester would pick it up and wear it. Mother ended up addressing either or both of them as Twin. All she knew was that they were terrific.

Of all the kids who loved my mother, Sidney Polsky loved her best. Mother had been the first to call a spade a spade and fat, fat. Maybe Sidney didn't know that he was fat because no one had ever told him that before; his mother had banned the word from the entire language. I can see her now, changing all her recipes to "fry the potatoes in Crisco plump." After Sidney realized that what he was was fat, he began to lose weight, and Mother congratulated him after each pound he lost. The polite thing to do would have been to ignore his losing weight because you were supposed to have ignored that he was fat in the first place. But Sidney reported to Mother each pound his lost, and Mother reported to the team, and we all cheered. I mentioned how Mother's enthusiasm was a hard thing to be up against.

The kids loved it, and it made them love Sidney. He was looking better on the ball field, too. Partly because of Spencer's coaching, partly because of Mother's enthusiasm, and partly because of his mother's hiring a baseball tutor for him.

* * *

Even after the season officially began, I continued going to the Projects on Saturdays. After those first two times, I went in the afternoons. Every Saturday, and usually on Sunday, too, even if I wasn't buying *Playgirl*. I went until the incident with Botts. There was something about handling a ball there at the Projects that was like magic. The ball would come to me: in my mitt if I was fielding or square onto my bat if I was batting. At Little League I was like a watched kettle; I got hot, but I never got up enough steam to boil. I was better than average. Better enough than average to be in the starting lineup even though Mother and Spencer never worked with me at home, the way I had thought they would. And I no longer wanted them to. When I played at the Projects, I wasn't anybody's pupil or somebody's brother or someone's son. I was myself,

and I liked that. I felt guilty for sometimes preferring the Projects to the Bagels.

The thing with Botts happened late in June, more than three-quarters of the way through our season. Cookie had made a habit of walking me part of the way home. Every time she would ask me to bring back my good jacket, the one whose lining I had ripped. Finally, one Saturday I remembered, and I brought it in a brown paper bag. And that was the last Saturday I went to the Projects.

Who would ever have taken Cookie's walking me part way home seriously? Certainly not me. Cookie was like a puppy or a mascot or something. After the first week I mostly forgot that she was a girl. Except when she smiled. One time I had asked the kid with the beginnings of a beard why it was that everyone listened to Cookie. (He really ought to have started shaving. He didn't look kempt.) He explained that there were seven Riveras; six of them were boys. Cookie had to do a lot around the house. She was a little bit spoiled, being the only girl, but only a little bit; being that she worked so hard around the house, I guess she deserved it.

On the Saturday it happened with Botts I had gotten into the game right away. Botts had been waiting and my arrival made an even number. Our teams were not full count, and the guys in the outfield had to cover a lot of ground. Which they did. I dropped one fly ball, but since it didn't break a window or anything, the only comment was STUPID and GREASY-FINGERS. At first I tried to say something in my own defense, but they didn't care; they just wanted to pitch the next ball, and we all had to concentrate on that. It was great not having an audience.

Then Fortune came down and called time out.

Just like that.

And everyone took time out.

Just like that.

"I want to see Mark Bagel," she said.

I walked over to her. "There was already an even number when I got here."

"I'm not playing today, anyway," she answered. "I came down to fix your jacket. Did you bring it in that bag I saw you carrying in?"

"Oh, yeah. Almost forgot. Just a minute, you guys," I called as I ran to get the bag.

Simon, who was due up at bat, got impatient. "Really, Cookie," he said, "Why do we all have to take time out while you woo with Mark?"

He shouldn't have said that. Sylvester began singing, "Woo woo woo-ooo-ooo."

And that was all it took for the others to pipe in.

"Go along and play," I yelled. "I'll be up for my time at bats."

Cookie pulled a needle and thread out of her pocket. The right color. And I had worn it only those first times; she had remembered the color. The jacket had been a present from Aunt Thelma: navy blue with silver buttons and a scarlet lining. The best I had ever had.

Cookie sewed invisibly. You could hardly see where it had been ripped. "Where do you learn to sew?" I asked.

"Guess I was just born to it. Mother works in a girdle factory. She sews the elastic across the tops."

"Oh," I said. "Must be interesting work."

"I don't know why you'd think that. It's a job."

"Well, there are all those different sizes and all," I stammered.

"That's nothing. The big ones need big elastic and the small ones need small elastic. It's that simple." She handed me my jacket.

"Say, thanks. Thanks a lot. You sure have a talent for sewing."

"I am also excellent at drawing and arithmetic. I speak Spanish as excellent as I do English. I make marshmallow fudge, and I can hold my breath to a count of eighty-five—if you count fast."

She turned and started back upstairs.

"Cookie!" I yelled.

"Your time at bat, Setzer. C'mon, let's make it count."

"Just a minute, you guys." And I began to run after Cookie, yelling, "I brought you something."

The whole gang heard me. Which wasn't very hard because I didn't exactly whisper. You don't whisper when you're trying to get a guy's attention out in the open air. Or a girl's.

Cookie stopped and turned around and smiled. Her smile sort of dawns on her face; it starts as a small streak and then lights up everything. It's like announcing daybreak. Even if her mouth is too big.

I dug my hand into the bag and took out what I had brought. Cookie held out her hand, and something about the way she did it made me slip it onto her forefinger.

"A bagel," I explained. "It's to eat."

She looked up at me and still looking at me began to nibble around the edge as she held it on her forefinger.

"It's delicious," she said.

"It's delicious-er with cream cheese," I said.

I should have noticed how quiet the whole gang had been. That would have given me a good idea that they were watching us. But I guess I was so interested in Cookie's reaction to the bagel and that smile and all that I didn't pay any real attention. Until they began that chanting again. "Woo woo wooo-ooo-ooo." They kept it up.

"Cut it out, you guys," I said.

They kept it up.

Botts broke out of the rhythm by calling out, "Is that why you never buy a look at my magazine? Because you've got a girl of your own?"

"Don't be silly," I said. "I don't have a girl. I have my own copy."

"I'll just bet," he smirked.

"I do, too. I'll bring it. I'll show you."

"I'm going to tell you something, Setzer. And I'm going to tell you good. You better never bring that magazine around here. You hear me?"

"I hear you," I said. "I imagine that the kids up on Crescent Hill can hear you. Now, you hear me. Quit calling Cookie my girl. She just did me a favor."

"Yeah, a favor," he said. "Is that why you slipped a bagel over her finger? . . . AND WITH THIS BAGEL I DO THEE WED . . ."

"Cut that out," I yelled. By this time Botts and I were kind of separated from the rest of the gang. Cookie walked up to Botts and stretched her neck so that she was practically nose to nose with him. She said, "Botts, you drop this subject. Drop it right now. Because if you don't, I'm going to tell your mother and your aunt what you do with your money. And what you do with your time. I know, and I'll tell."

"You wouldn't dare."

"I would."

"They won't believe you."

"They will," she said softly and calmly. We knew, as Botts must have known, that she would dare tell, and that they would believe.

Botts blinked his eyes fast; his shoulders and chin dropped. The whole gang saw it, Botts backing down. Cookie shouldn't have done that even if she did it for me, and even if she did it to a louse like Franklin P. Botts.

He turned on me. "You just better never bring that magazine around here, Setzer. You cut in on my territory, and I'll liquidate you."

When a guy isn't on TV and he uses a word like LIQUIDATE to another guy, he comes off pretty silly.

I laughed.

Botts socked me.

I'm not great at hand-to-hand combat, so I was slow winding up. Simon pulled on Botts, and I felt Sylvester pinning my arms back.

"Break it up. Break it up," they yelled together.

Botts, with his arms pinned back and his neck stretched out, yelled again, "Wattcha gonna do, Setzer? Tell your mother and have me kicked off the team?"

"That's what you deserve," I said. "But I'm no squealer. I won't tell." The B'nai Bagels certainly deserved better than him, I thought. If my mother had not been manager, I probably would have told on him, but I couldn't. He knew that.

"Go ahead and tell," he teased. "See if I care."

"I'm not going to tell. You just quit poking fun at other people like Cookie."

"Why ya so worried about Cookie? Cookie IS your girl. Woo woo wooo..."

I freed one arm and landed it in Botts' stomach. It didn't have much punch, though, so much of the muscle having been wasted in freeing it from Sylvester.

Simon spoke up. "Now you're even. Let's finish the game. You're at bat, Setzer." He let Botts go after saying that.

And Sylvester added, "Hey, Cookie, how about your not calling times-out any more?"

Cookie sniffed the air. "O.K., I won't call times-out when it's times-out for supper, either."

"You know what Syl means," Simon scolded.

"O.K.," Cookie said. She looked at me and said, "Thanks for the bagel, Mark." She looked at Botts and said something in Spanish. I would write what she said, but I don't know Spanish, and I've already included enough foreign words like HAFTORAH.

Botts didn't understand Spanish either. Cookie looked up at Botts and smiled and said, "O.K.?" That smile!

Botts softened. "O.K.," he answered.

Cookie walked toward their building.

"What did she say?" Botts asked. No one answered. "What did that mean?"

"Skip it," Sylvester said.

"C'mon now, you guys, what does that mean?"

The big kid said, "Cookie told you that..."

Simon interrupted, "Let's play ball."

"I wanna hear," Botts urged. "What did she say?"

The kid with the beard continued, "She said, 'If brains were Holy Water, you wouldn't have enough to baptize a mosquito.'"

Simon and Sylvester poked the ground with their toes. The big kid laughed, and so did I. That Cookie was a clever guy.

Botts looked from the big kid to me and then squinted his eyes and said, "Watch it, Jew Boy. Watch who you're laughing at."

And that's the way it happened. That's the way it is with kids like Botts. The feeling is always there. Like bacteria, just waiting for conditions to get dark enough to grow into a disease.

I picked up my jacket and went home.

ROOSEVELT GRADY

Louisa R. Shotwell

Thousands of Americans are trapped in poverty by their need to follow the crops. The only possible way to escape is education, yet few cities, north or south, east or west, are eager or even willing to permit migrant children to attend their schools. At the time of this writing, most of the housing provided by farmers for harvesters is inadequate, and few middle-class Americans are aware of conditions of migrant workers. Remnants of Puritan disdain for the poor are apparent in the contemporary attitude that there must be something "wrong" with these people or they would not be poor.

The problems of migrant workers are well presented by Miss Shotwell. Through Roosevelt's longings for a home and a chance to learn "putting into" in school, she shows both the migrant workers' lives and their hopes.

PUTTING INTO

Roosevelt bunched his sweater underneath him to soften the jouncing floor of the moving truck. He leaned his head back against his mother's arm. If the air got any chillier, he'd have to take his sweater out from under him and put it on to keep warm, but it wasn't quite that cold. Not yet.

Along with three other families, the Gradys rode in the back of the truck. All but Papa, who sat up front to spell Cap Jackson. Cap was the regular driver and he was the crew leader, too. He owned the truck and in it he carried the people to places where crops were ready for picking.

"We're heading for beans and cucumbers," Cap Jackson said.

Roosevelt's mother sat straight up on the flat side of the family suitcase. It was made of metal and it was slippery, so she had her feet planted wide apart and flat on the floor to brace herself. On her lap she held Princess Anne, sleeping.

Between Mamma's feet lay Sister. She was seven years old and dainty, with dimples. Her smile, Papa always said, could charm a snake out of a tree.

"Honest, could it?" Roosevelt asked him once.

"Well, I tell you, Roosevelt," Papa said, "the first time we find a snake in a tree, we'll get Sister to smile at him and we'll see what happens." So far they hadn't found a tree with a snake in it.

On the other side of Mamma slumped Matthew, who was only five and chubby. Matthew had a lame foot, but that didn't keep him from enjoying life. He was great on making jokes, and he didn't miss a thing.

The truck had a canvas roof. The roof sloped up on each side to a peak like the top of a barn, and it kept you from seeing the sky. Anyway, it was dark outside. It was the middle of the night, but the truck kept right on going.

Between sleeping and waking, Roosevelt thought about putting into. He thought about that special thing he wanted to know. The question kept running around his head the way a mosquito teases you in the dark.

This was his question: When you put something into something else and it doesn't come out even, what do you do with what's left over?

What happened yesterday was exactly what had happened at the school where he'd first heard about putting into. The teacher came to where it seemed she must explain it the very next day. And then what? That time it wasn't beans that ran out. It was celery, but it didn't matter what the crop was. If it ran out, it ran out, and that was the end. The whole family packed up and piled into Cap Jackson's sputtery old truck and away they went to find a place where onions or tomatoes or some old thing was coming along ready to harvest. And same as yesterday, Roosevelt never got back to school to hear what the teacher had to say.

Some places there wouldn't be any school at all. Or else there'd be a school and the bean-picker boys and girls didn't get to go to it. The school would be for residents, and bean-picker families weren't residents. They didn't belong.

Once there was a school and it was closed when they got there. It was closed because the crop was ripe. A crop vacation, folks called this, and everybody picked, young ones and grown-ups and old people. Everybody except, of course, Princess Anne. Over in Louisiana she sat by herself in a fruit crate at the end of the strawberry rows and sucked her thumb, cute as a bug.

Roosevelt rubbed his eyes, leaned his head against Mamma's knee, and tried hard to go to sleep. He'd almost made it when buzz went that old mosquito again, nagging at him about putting into. Like 3 into 17. You can't say 17's got six 3's in it, because six 3's need 18. So the answer has to be five 3's. But that's only 15. So what do you do with the poor little 2 that gets left over?

Roosevelt liked to have things come out even. He liked to have a place to put every piece of whatever it was he had. He liked to pick all the ripe beans quick and clean off one plant and then move along that row to the next. He liked to fill his basket just full enough so it was even across the top. If one bean stuck up in the air, he'd pull it out and make a little hole among the other beans and poke it carefully down in. He liked to make a pan of corn bread and cut it into exactly enough squares to make one piece for everybody in the family. Except Princess Anne. Her teeth hadn't come through far enough yet to chew anything crusty. Sometimes Mamma would break off a little of her piece of corn bread and dunk it in her coffee to soften it. Then she gave that to Princess Anne.

Bouncing along through the dark, Roosevelt got to thinking some more about numbers. Take

nine. Right now nine was an important number in his life. He was nine years old. His birthday was the ninth day of September, and if you began to count the months with January one and February two and so on, what did September turn out to be? Why, nine!

To be perfectly sure, he whispered the months over to himself, counting on his fingers. Sure enough, nine came out to be September.

How many different schools had he been to in his lifetime? He counted to himself. Six, seven, eight . . . and nine. There was that nine again. Different schools, that is. If you counted twice the schools he'd been to and then gone back to, they made thirteen, but Roosevelt didn't want to count that way. He didn't like the number thirteen. Papa said thirteen was unlucky. Mamma said she didn't believe in lucky or unlucky, but there was no use tempting fate.

"What's tempting fate?" Roosevelt asked her.

"It means trying to outsmart the devil," Mamma said. "And he's really smart. You're best off to stay clean away from thirteen this and thirteen that. You can just as easy make it twelve or fourteen and not take any chances."

One day a while back, Roosevelt had asked Papa about putting into and the poor little left-over number. He had laughed and said: "Just throw it away."

But Roosevelt couldn't feel right doing that. What would become of it?

Another day he had asked Mamma. She said: "Save it till you need it."

"What do you do with it," Roosevelt wanted to know, "while you're waiting to need it?"

Mamma didn't laugh nearly so often as Papa did, but she laughed that time.

"Put it in your pocket," she said, "and go fetch me a bucket of water."

THE SECRET

The truck jerked to a stop, and the motor coughed and went still. From the driver's seat, Cap Jackson called out:

"Anybody want a drink? There's a spring here at the edge of the woods."

The people stirred. Cap came around and let down the tailgate and put up the ladder. Roosevelt experimented with a swallow and his mouth felt dry, so he clambered down. The stars were bright. The air was cold and it had a piney smell, clean and fresh. He waited his turn in line in front of a pipe with water bubbling out of it. In the starlight the pipe looked rusty. The men had to stoop over to reach it, but it was exactly the right height for Roosevelt. He didn't have to bend down or stand on his toes, either one.

When his turn came, the water was cool and he took a big gulp, but it didn't taste good. Not good at all. It tasted like a bad egg.

"Sulphur water," said one of the men.

Roosevelt spit his mouthful out on the ground. He shivered. When he climbed back into the truck, he put his sweater on and sat right flat down on the boards.

As the motor wheezed and the truck began to move, Sister and Matthew both woke up and wiggled. Roosevelt was glad they'd waked up. He felt like having company.

"Talk to us, Mamma," said Matthew. "Tell us a story."

"Hush," said Mamma. "Other folks want to go to sleep."

"Talk to us soft-like," begged Matthew. "Whisper to us about . . . you know . . ."

Roosevelt knew what was coming. Matthew always asked for the same story. It was Roosevelt's favorite story, too.

". . . about the olden days. And the dog run."

All right," said Mamma. "Lean close and I'll tell it to you short. Then you go to sleep."

And she did. She didn't make it too short either. About the little house in the cotton field in Georgia, how it sat up on stilts and was a house in two parts like, with this comfortable sitting-out place in between and a roof over the whole thing. The sitting-out place was the dog run, and it had a rocking chair like President Kennedy's.

The Gradys had a dog there too, a hound, sort of. Named Nellie. She had short tan hair and floppy ears and brown eyes. Her eyes were wistful.

"What's wistful?" Matthew demanded.

"Wistful is you want something and you don't know what," said Mamma.

They had chickens, too, and two big pigs and a litter of little pigs. And a goat. And growing out back they had sweet potatoes and collards and mustard greens.

Roosevlt moved his tongue around to see if he could make himself remember the taste of a sweet potato. He couldn't.

Now it was Sister's turn. Was she still awake? She was.

"Take us back to your wedding day, Mamma," she said. "Tell us about your white dress and what Papa said."

"There was this magnolia tree," said Mamma, "right outside the Pink Lily Baptist Church. And it was brim full of waxy white blossoms. I wore a shiny white dress with a green sash and long streamers and I had a veil, all cloudy, made of net. Your papa told me I was almost the prettiest thing in the whole county."

"'*Almost* the prettiest? Why *almost*?' I said, kind of sniffy and jealous."

"Jealous," said Sister. "Tell us what's jealous."

"Jealous is you're scared somebody you like likes somebody else better than you," Mamma explained. "Now don't interrupt me any more. And your papa said, 'You or that magnolia tree. I can't make up my mind which one is prettier. But I'll pick you.' So off we went to live in the little house in the cotton field."

"Now tell us why we left the little house in the cotton field," insisted Matthew. "Why did we go away and leave our dog Nellie and the little pigs and the dog run all behind us?"

"Why we left? Why, honey, the machines came along. The tractors got bigger and bigger and they did more and more of the work the people used to do. Mr. Wilson let us stay on a while and your papa got some work in the sawmill six miles off. But pretty soon Mr. Wilson plain had to tear down our house to plant more cotton. So that's when we went on the season, looking for work wherever we could find it."

She stopped a minute. When she went on, her voice sounded different. Angry, almost.

"Some folks say now they've even got a machine that knows how to pick cotton. A big red monster. With fingers."

Sister sighed, a long whishy sigh that meant

she was on her way to sleep again. Roosevelt waited. When Matthew breathed so even it seemed certain he must be asleep too, Roosevelt sat up close to Mamma's ear.

"Now let's you and me talk about our secret," he whispered.

"Hush," said Mamma.

"Please," said Roosevelt.

Mamma didn't say anything right away, and Roosevelt sat stiff and still. Then she spoke, not whispering but still so low he could hardly hear. She said just what he knew she'd say.

"Someday we'll find ourselves a house in a place where there's work for your papa every one of all twelve months in the year. Maybe the house won't have a dog run, but it'll sure enough be a home. And you and Sister and Matthew will go to school, the same school right along, day in,

day out, fall and winter and right on to the end of spring."

"And Princess Anne?" asked Roosevelt.

"Princess Anne, too, soon as she's big enough. You'll all go right along with the children that belong. Because we'll be in a place where we'll all belong. We'll be right out of this bean-picking rat race and we'll stay put."

"How will we find this place?" asked Roosevelt anxiously, even though he'd asked this before and knew what the answer would be.

"I don't know how," said Mamma, "but we'll know it when we see it. There'll be something about it so we'll know it. And don't you forget. This is our secret."

"It's our secret," said Roosevelt, and he dropped his head in the crook of Mamma's elbow and fell sound asleep.

THE WINNERS

Ester Wier

Although this book is about Scrub's journey from self-shame to self-respect after Ernie, Joe, and Buck have robbed and demoralized him, this chapter is the most powerful presentation in children's literature of the treatment of migrant workers. Please see the introduction to Roosevelt Grady, *the previous selection, for information pertinent to this economic group.*

Ester Wier is an exceptionally fine writer. Her style is always suited to the mood of the plot and the character's personalities.

"Why'd you have to go and call me Scrub?" the boy asked his father. "You know what it means? Puny and mean and second-rate and pitiful. That's what."

Big Will raised his great shaggy head and looked at his son in amazement. "Who said so? It don't mean none of them things to me."

Scrub struck his chin out, stubbornly. "Teacher did, that's who. Some of them smarty kids from town said it meant a runt steer so I asked her if

From *The Winners* by Ester Wier. Copyright © 1967 by Ester Wier. Reprinted by permission of David McKay Company, Inc.

they was right and she read out of the dict'nary what it means."

Big Will, a giant of a man, looked down at his work-hardened hands where dirt from a hundred vegetable fields had sifted deep into cracks at his knuckles. "Pity you wasn't able to have no say when name choosin' time came 'round. Your ma was all set to call you Wee Willie. She knowed some story 'bout a boy with that name."

The boy's face twisted in horror. "Wee Willie? That'd been even worse'n Scrub."

Still rubbing absent-mindedly at the soil-imbedded skin, his father shrugged. "Well, you got a good whole name, Wilford Roscoe Nolan." He bent his head to one side and said it over several times as if it brought back pleasant memories. "Even got a touch of class to it. Your ma figgered it out, changed Will to Wilford and tacked on the Roscoe after she heard it somewheres." He sighed. "No kid likes the name his folks give him. 'Specially girls. They always think up somethin' fancy they'd rather be called."

"Well, I ain't no girl," Scrub said impatiently, "and I don't want nothin' fancy. All I said was it ain't so good bein' saddled with somethin' that means puny and misserble. Besides, how'll it sound when I grow up tall like you?"

A smile came slowly over Big Will's face, softening the harsh features. "Guess I wasn't thinkin' of you big and tall thirteen years ago when you was born. You know what I was thinkin'? That you wasn't no bigger'n a flea. Brought to mind scrub palms and pines and palmettos back home in Florida." He looked thoughtful. "'Course if you really ain't happy 'bout it, we could still take to callin' you Wee Willie or Wilford."

Scrub backed water fast. Shrugging, he said, "Well, since I'm used to it, I'll just keep it for a while, till I grow up big. Then I'll see."

The two of them were sitting on the edge of cots in the wooden shanty they shared temporarily with two brothers working in the same crop fields. It was Saturday night and since tomorrow wasn't a work day, Big Will was allowing himself the luxury of resting before fixing dinner. He had spent from sunup to sundown in the carrot fields, helping to bring in the winter harvest, and for the first time in two years, Scrub wasn't working beside him. This season the boy had been going to school "regular," ever since September.

Scrub was short for his age, pole skinny, tough, and strong. His eyes were a light blue and his yellow-white hair grew long and ragged on his neck, the way Big Will's black hair did. For his age he was undersized so that his name was a good description of his general appearance. Walking all over the country with Will, stoop-bending over crops while picking them, shinnying up trees to pluck fruit, had built up his muscles and made him lean and wiry.

He should have been farther ahead in his education but there wasn't always a school near the migrant camps that had been home to him all his life. When there was, Big Will made him go. When there wasn't or when they were closed for a crop vacation, he worked. Even Scrub knew crop vacations were a trick towns used to avoid taking the children of migrant workers into its public schools as pupils, having to support them with local taxes. In most areas it was against the law to hire anyone under sixteen to work in the fields while school was in session so the crop vacation was the best way to get around that.

By now Scrub hadn't much left to believe in, except Big Will. He had seen the "washcloth armies" come into the pickers' camps, talking big about how much they wanted to help, all they intended to do. They would line up the children and give them a good clean-up with soap and water. Then they would go away and never come back. Other do-gooders came on Sundays with prayer and talk about all men being brothers, but when a migrant woman tried taking them at their word in one of the towns and herded the camp children to church, everyone in the pews nearby got up and moved away as the group sat down.

His bitterest memory lingered from his early childhood. Big Will could be tough when he had to be but that night there had been a look on his father's face that frightened Scrub, a look of helplessness and defeat, as the town doctor said, "You think I'm crazy enough to come to that camp and treat your wife? Why, I'd lose every patient I have if it got around I'd treated one of you people. We take care of our own here, not strangers. Don't we have enough to put up with from you pickers, all the filth and disease and crime you bring into our community?" As young as he'd been then, Scrub remembered the slam of the door and the turn of the lock, and the feeling it left him with, as though the world lay on the other side, warm and safe and comfortable. On his side and Big Will's and his dying mother's, there was only cold and hunger and misery.

"How much more schoolin' you got here, boy?" Big Will asked him now. "Ain't it gittin' time for one part to let up and the next start?"

Scrub knew he meant semesters. Big Will had never gone to school so he didn't always know the right name for things. He was about to answer when the bare electric bulb hanging by a cord from the center of the ceiling was turned on, its light shining down on the hop sack curtains strung on wire, dividing the room. The make-shift barrier, sewn double-deep, cleared the floor by some ten inches or so. He could see legs and feet close to the other side of the burlap wall.

"You there, Will?" a sharp voice called out. It belonged to one of the brothers, the one called Ernie Joe. He and Buck had lived in the shanty with Big Will and Scrub for the past two weeks, ever since they'd drifted into camp looking for work to provide them with cash enough to enable them to move on.

Right from the start Ernie Joe had made it plain he and his brother only did crop work when they'd had a run of bad luck. "We're first rate grease monkeys," he boasted. "We can fix any motor so's it'll hum like a top. We move 'round the country pickin' up jobs 'stead of doin' steady work in one place. That way we got plenty time for huntin'. If there's one thing Buck and I'd rather do than anythin' else, it's hunt." Scrub remembered how after he'd said that, he'd put a make-believe rifle to his shoulder and yelled, "Zing! zing! zing! Got that big ole bear right in the gut!"

Big Will grunted a reply.

"You decided yet? Me'n Buck is gonna start 'bout a week from now."

"Not yet," Big Will said. "Gotta be sure I'm doin' the right thing."

Scrub listened, puzzled. Apparently something was up. His father hadn't said anything to him about it and that was unusual. Now that he thought about it, he realized it was about time to move on to the next job. He'd been forgetting how short the early vegetable harvest was, being busy at school all day. Spring was at hand and it sent the migrants spreading to the north and west to pick the cotton and later vegetable and fruit crops as they ripened. Like a tide, the workers flowed across the land to pluck the riches of irrigated fields, to live the underprivileged and overworked lives of those who were welcome only when their hands and backs were needed to do the tiring stoop labor in the fields or the reach labor in the orchards.

A flicker of anticipation crossed the boy's face. He was never sorry to leave school. All another interruption in his studies meant to him was that now he could be with Big Will all the time in-stead of just evenings and Sundays. That the total of his classroom hours, like fish strung together on the line, made up a mighty sparse and disappointing catch, worried him not at all.

When his father turned his attention back to him, Scrub said, "It won't be more'n a week 'fore the first half of school's done. Why?"

"'Cause I talked to a crew leader today who's lookin' for workers to fill out his crew. He's a good 'un, promises to git his workers wherever they're goin' in his truck, git 'em a place to live, look after 'em, pay 'em, and find work to keep 'em busy all year if they sign his contract. Since I ain't got no wheels of my own, it sounds good to me."

"Where'll we go first?" the boy asked. "Arizona?" They often went there from Texas.

Big Will began rubbing his knees now, his big hands moving back and forth over the faded and worn denim trousers. All day, as Scrub knew, he crawled along the rows between the carrot plants, scraping his knees against the earth, straining his muscles, torturing his back. When his knees got to hurting too much, he'd stand up, bending over to pick till he couldn't abide that any longer, then down he'd go to his knees again. Up and down he bobbed from early morning to twilight.

He didn't look at his son as he said. "Not 'us' this time, Scrub. This feller'll only take workers. Ain't got room for kids on his truck. Says he can't make transportin' a crew pay 'less he gits a cut out of every passenger's wages."

Scrub's eyes narrowed and he stuck his chin out belligerently. Rough as Big Will could be when faced with trouble, he had never lifted his hand to his son nor tried to cow him into knuckling under, even seeming to take place in the boy's spirit. "You wasn't figgerin' on leavin' me, was you? I go where you go and if that's the way it is with this here crew leader, I work too. I can always git schoolin' later on. We could save our wages and next winter mebbe we could take it kinda easy down 'round Loosiana, fishin' and restin'."

Still Big Will didn't look at him, only shook his head and kept his eyes fixed on his aching legs. "Already talked to the feller 'bout that. I tole him what a good worker you was but he won't take on no one under sixteen. Some places he could git away with a kid workin', others he could go to jail for signin' one on his crew." His eyes shifted now to the nails on the wall which took the place of a closet for the two of them. On these hung all the clothes they possessed, and he said softly as though to himself, "Good thing I got a little put by. It'll git you clothes you won't be 'shamed of, leastwise."

Scrub was bewildered. It wasn't like his father to do things behind his back, to make plans without talking them over with him first. "What I need clothes for? What you got in mind?"

Big Will's brow was furrowed by his heavy thinking. "I been turnin' it over in my mind all day," he admitted. "I figger to take this here job 'cause it means sure and steady work for the rest of the year. Good money too. What I'm aimin' for is gittin' my own wheels by next year so's you'n I can go wherever the work's good and there's schools handy. You'd like that, wouldn't you?"

Scrub thought it over, then slowly nodded. "Okay," he said, but he looked at Big Will accusingly. "You got somethin' all planned for me while you go off with that crew, ain't you?"

The big man rose painfully, pausing to limber up one leg, then the other while holding onto the edge of the rusted cot. "Sure am lookin' to git to a hot place," he said. "Want to just bake in the sun and git rid of all these here aches I got inside. It'd even be a pleasure reach-pickin' for a while. Anythin' just as long as it ain't stoopin'."

This was something new too. Big Will never complained and Scrub looked at his father harder, listened harder, hoping to find out what accounted for all these changes. He had an idea his father was putting off telling him because it was something he knew his son wouldn't like.

When there wasn't any more stretching and limbering to do, Will sat down again. "Ernie Joe and Buck is goin' to Florida," he began and the boy knew that at last he was going to tell him. "They're fixin' to do some fishin' this summer and wait 'round for the sugar cane harvest in the fall. Said they'd give you a ride with 'em if I was to pay for your eats and some towards the gas." He looked at Scrub and now there seemed to be a kind of worry on his face as he said, "You could stay with 'em for the summer if you wanted, then in the fall you could go to your Aunt Lena's up near De Land. Since Fred died, she ain't got no

one and she'd likely be glad to have you for comp'ny and to help 'round. You could go to school regular that way." He waited a minute, apparently expecting Scrub to object, but the boy remained silent so he went on. "I'd come git you soon as I git my wheels."

Scrub's eyebrows had shot up at the mention of his aunt's name. Now he spoke slowly, determined not to let on to his father the awful emptiness he felt inside at the thought of being parted from him for a whole year. "I ain't gonna let her keep me, then tell me all the time how much I'm costin' her. Ain't I heard you say over and over she's like that?"

Big Will looked relieved. "Glad you got that kind of pride, son," he said, "but you got nothin' to worry 'bout. I'm plannin' to send her some money I got saved up and it'll take care of you till I come.

In a last desperate effort to keep the two of them together, the boy implored, "Can't you come too? Couldn't you git work in Florida same as you could in Arizona or California?"

Big Will shook his head patiently. "Like I told you, I got a chance at a real good year with this feller. You know I ain't been doin' us no favors free-wheelin'."

Scrub knew free-wheeling—the practice of arriving at a camp without a job or housing already arranged for, taking a chance on getting both—was a risky and poor way of living but still he felt he had to put up a fight. "I sure don't think he can be so much if he won't take kids with him," he said scornfully. "And I'll bet he works you right down to the bone."

"I won't mind," Big Will said, "if I git some wheels out of it."

Scrub tried a different approach. "Guess the reason you're worried 'bout clothes for me is 'cause Aunt Lena's gonna make me git all dressed up everyday and go off to school lookin' like I was headin' for church. Take a bath everday too. And she'll call me Wilford 'cause I bet she was the one put Ma up to namin' me that." An awful thought struck him and he said hoarsely, "Or Roscoe." That prospect overwhelmed him and he sat with his hands clasped tightly together, a look of terrible anguish on his face.

"Son," Big Will said, "it ain't no use us talkin' anymore 'bout it. I got plans for you to go on to higher school so you won't have to spend your life grubbin' 'round on your hands and knees in the dirt the way I been doin' all my life."

Scrub started to say something but Big Will cut him short. "Don't tell me I been wrong 'bout you all this time. I figgered you got the starch to do whatever you got to do. Looks like this is your chance to find out if I'm right 'cause it's when a man's on his own that he finds out what he's made of. Always figgered you was able to handle things good, that you was a real tough little nut, hard to crack." He smiled when he said this and Scrub's heart almost burst with pride.

He looked at his pa and saw the mouth that usually twisted up at the corners naturally now seemed to have to force a smile, that the usual gleam in the eyes was faded so that now they looked set and dull. Instead of carrying on in his usual humorous, half-teasing way, Big Will most

of the time recently seemed tired and worn out and discouraged. Suddenly Scrub remembered the night at the doctor's door and wondered if again he was seeing defeat in his father's face.

What scared him most was that Big Will didn't seem to want to meet his eyes and kept looking everywhere else but into them. Mebbe, he told himself, he feels as bad as I do 'bout this and he's 'fraid of me seein' it. Mebbe I better make it easy for him and stop arguin'.

Looking toward the burlap curtains, Scrub saw the dirt-streaked bare feet of one of the brothers and wondered if he had been standing there close all the time, listening. Swallowing hard, he shrugged and said with a show of toughness, "Okay, okay. You tell Ernie Joe 'n' Buck I can be ready to start any old time they are and the sooner we git goin' out of here, the better I'm gonna like it."

COTTON IN MY SACK

Lois Lenski

Miss Lenski has written many books on economic and regional groups. Before writing each book she goes to the area and lives and learns to know the people. In Cotton in My Sack *she realistically shows how a family's spending habits trap them in poverty. Since she is writing for children and believes they need a happy ending, her book ends with the family's learning to budget their money to have a better life. But the transformation is gradual and believable.*

Miss Lenski uses regional dialects in her books to add authenticity. She handles the dialect with skill, never making it difficult for children to read or understand.

SATURDAY IN TOWN

Oh, it's Saturday—beautiful Saturday! The minute she woke up, Joanda felt happy all over. Saturday was the most wonderful day of the week because the whole family went to town. Town was a magic place on Saturday, because all the people had money to spend.

After Daddy's cotton was picked, the Hutleys had started picking for J. T. Burgess, and were paid off in cash every night. On Saturday, they went to town to spend the money.

Right after breakfast they climbed into the truck. Mama and Daddy took Lolly in the cab with them. The other four children stood up in the back. It was a five-mile ride to town. The sun was already hot and the wind blew their hair in the breeze. They rode along the dirt road to the crossroad, then took the smooth highway.

When they got to town it was like a parade, so many cars and trucks going down Main Street. Cars in front and in back of them. Cars parked on both sides. The children leaned over the high board sides of the truck. They could see everything—the cars, the people, the stores. But the crowds on the sidewalks did not notice them at all.

Daddy always parked in the same place, in an empty lot back of the Beehive store. They got out and Daddy gave Mama a ten-dollar bill. The children had the money they had earned for picking cotton. Ricky had a dollar, Joanda had her $3.45 and the older children had more because they were faster pickers. Mavis and Joanda had their money in bright red purses they had bought the week before. The boys carried theirs in their pockets.

The Hutleys did what they always did. First they walked down the street and just looked. There was so much to see. All the show-windows were full of tempting things to buy, and many stores had things set out on the sidewalks.

So often when they came to town, they had no money in their pockets at all. Now, in cotton-picking time, it was different. They had money and anything could happen. All the things they saw took on a shining glory because they were within their reach—rings, gold watches, bracelets, jewelry, anything. Joanda walked on wings, looking hard. *I can have that, I can have that*, she kept saying to herself. *I can have all these things if I want them.* She had never known happiness like this.

They paused in front of Atkins' furniture store.

"I'd like a couch like that," said Mama softly. "If I paid something down on it, it wouldn't take but about three or four months, I don't guess."

But she did not go in. The most fun was thinking what you *might* buy, even if you didn't.

The Hutleys saw the one-armed hot tamale man. He had a high yellow box, with the words HOT TAMALES on it, set on a three-wheeled cart. The cart held a fire to keep the tamales hot. The tamales were made of groundup peppered pork and cornmeal. They had been wrapped in cornshucks and steamed.

"Want a tamale?" asked Daddy.

"No, they're too hot," said Ricky. "I had one once and it burned my tongue."

The Hutleys walked on. Suddenly they heard music and Lolly began to clap her hands. They stopped and listened. A man and a woman came shuffling along sideways in front of Carter's drug store. The man had a guitar strapped across his shoulder, with a tin cup on the end. He began to strum the guitar and to sing in a hollow voice:

> "Now we are aged and gray, Maggie,
>   The trials of life are nearly done . . ."

"The man's blind," whispered Mama.

"But the woman can see," said Joanda. "She leads him and takes care of him."

"Pretty bad shape they're in," said Mama, shaking her head.

"Always somebody worse off than we are," said Daddy.

"*We* got money!" whispered Ricky.

Mama looked at Daddy and then they all put some money in the man's cup. Joanda gave one of her dimes.

"God bless you," said the blind man.

The Hutleys came to the Star Movie Theater, but it had not opened yet. The picture was called *Six Shootin' Sheriff*. They studied the scenes in the glass cases.

"I'm comin' back and see this," said Steve.

"So'm I," said Mavis. "It's got outlaws in it."

A man had a popcorn stand at the theater entrance. The popping corn sent out an inviting fragrance. Daddy said, "Let's have some popcorn." So he bought seven sacks, one for each, and they stood and ate it.

Lolly squatted on the sidewalk and dipped her fat hands into her sack. Ricky perched on a sack of potatoes in front of the grocery next door to eat his. Steve and Mavis took theirs and walked on. Ricky ate his up first and Daddy bought him a second sack. When that was gone, Daddy gave him half of his.

"How long can you keep this up, Ricky?" he asked.

"Till I starve to death!" answered the boy.

Daddy and Mama laughed. Suddenly Lolly began to sputter.

"Take that popcorn away from the baby before she chokes," said Mama.

Joanda took Lolly's sack away and gave her Ricky's empty one. Lolly threw it down and began to howl. She snatched her own bag from Ricky, dropped it and scattered the popcorn all over the sidewalk. A fresh wind blew it in all directions. Lolly ran to chase the rolling kernels.

"Don't let her eat 'em, they're nasty," said Mama.

Joanda picked Lolly up. They walked on down the street.

"You're fixin' to git some new duds, ain't you, Neva?" asked Daddy.

"Sure thing," said Mama.

They went to the Beehive for clothes. Dresses and suits hung across in front of the store, flapping in the wind. A table of True Blue shoes stood outside. People could choose what they wanted before they went in. Mavis and Steve were waiting at the entrance.

"I ain't seen a soul I know," complained Mavis. She had a towel bandage round her neck which made her hold her head to one side. "Nobody's in town but us."

"You'll see everybody in Mississippi County, Arkansas, before the day's over," laughed Daddy. "Well, I reckon I'll just mosey along."

"Dave," said Mama, "you won't . . ."

"Don't you worry, Neva," said Daddy.

"We'll wait for you at the Goodwill," said Mama, "when we git through our tradin'." As Daddy walked away, Mama looked after him anxiously.

Ricky pulled on Mama's sleeve. "Buy me a buggy bicycle, Mama."

"I just bought you one two weeks ago," said Mama.

"Joanda won't let me ride on it," said Ricky. "She's mean."

"Yes she will," said Mama. "It's too little for her."

"Buy me a tractor then . . ."

They went into the Beehive and they all got new clothes, the girls each a cotton dress and sweater, the boys overalls, shirts and caps. When they came out they had bulky packages under their arms. They stopped at Hank's hot-dog stand and bought hot-dogs and cold drinks.

They came to the Goodwill, a big brick store that covered half a block. It said GOODWILL FOR EVERYBODY across the top. Here, everything was sold—groceries, dry goods, notions, hardware, seeds and farm machinery. It was a common meeting place for the country people. A radio on a chair outside the store door blared hillbilly music. Mama and the children stopped to listen.

Then they went in. Mama looked around and saw the Suttons, Jed and Maggie, at the blanket counter. It had a sign that said: *Use our Lay Away Plan 50¢ Down on Any Blanket.* Maggie carried a stove pipe with an elbow, and Jed had a coal bucket hanging on his arm.

"Buyin' you some blankets?" asked Mama.

"Yes *ma'm,*" said Jed, "gittin' ready for winter."

Mama laughed. "Oh, winter's a long time off. How's your cotton?"

"As sorry a crop as I ever saw in my life," said Maggie. "I'm sick and sore all over, couldn't sleep but two hours last night. My fingers are plumb stiff from pickin' cotton, but I can't sit still in the house till it's done picked. We lack three bales of gittin' ours out."

"We got part of ours out," said Mama. "We been pickin' for J. T. while we're waitin' for the rest of ours to open up."

Maggie began to talk about her ills. "I told the Lord if He'd save me, I'd never fool with doctors no more."

Mama sighed sympathetically. "I wisht I had faith like that . . ."

Just then the Burgesses, who were the Hutley's nearest neighbors, came up. There were J. T. and Mrs., who was always called "Aunt Lessie," and all four children. The boys, Bug and T. W., nicknamed Tightwad, took Steve off between them to go to the moving-picture show. Mavis went away with the twins, Arlene and Jolene. J. T. talked awhile, then went off with Jed Sutton. That left the women alone with the younger children.

"Got through your tradin'?" asked Mrs. Burgess.

"Law, no, I ain't begun," said Mama, "but my money's gone."

Joanda held Lolly up and Mrs. Burgess said: "Ain't she a sight!"

"She's proud to see you, Aunt Lessie," said Joanda.

"Sech curls. She sure favors you, Neva," said Mrs. Burgess.

"Face dirty and the day just half over," laughed Mama.

"Some folks' cotton ain't but six inches tall," began Mrs. Sutton. "It's the least I ever seen. Last year it was high as my head—I could hide myself in it."

"Not enough rain this summer," said Mama.

"In summer when we need it, it don't rain," said Mrs. Burgess. "In fall, time to pick cotton, it goes to rain."

The store was filled with family groups, some buying, others visiting. Mexicans and Negroes city and country people filled the aisles. Joanda put Lolly down on the floor. The baby began to run around the store, between and under the counters, bumping into strangers, tumbling down and getting up again. Joanda followed, laughing.

Ricky came up, his mouth full of candy. Lolly snatched a lollipop out of his hand and ran off with it. Ricky chased, but could not catch her. She went running out the street door.

Suddenly, fear clutched at Joanda's heart. Lolly was running into danger. The streets and sidewalks were more crowded than ever. Joanda hurried out to find her. Beside the door stood a man, with a box on his left arm, selling shoestrings and chewing gum.

"Did you see a little girl with red hair come out the door jest now?" asked Joanda.

The man pointed: "Way down yonder she goes like a streak of lightnin'."

Joanda dashed through the crowd and found her little sister almost at the curb. She picked her up and brought her back to the store. She saw Ricky beside the candy counter, sucking a lollipop. "How many lollipops you had?" she asked.

"Six," said Ricky. "Jest gonna git me some more."

He paid his money, took the candy and went over to the toy counter. There he bought a balloon and began to blow it up. It was a long, thin one with a snake head on the end. He blew it at his sister.

"You jest better not blow that horrid thing at me," said Joanda, "or I'll bust it." Anger flitted across her thin face. "You know I hate snakes."

Ricky kept on shoving the balloon closer and closer. Joanda put the baby down and snatched at the balloon. Ricky dodged and jerked away. The balloon suddenly popped like a pistol and fell to the floor in bits.

Everybody turned to look. Joanda and Ricky smiled at each other, but Lolly began to cry. The clerk said. "She's cryin' for a purty."

"I'll git you a play-purty, Lolly," said Joanda, "if you'll hush up. What you want—a bunny or a dolly? A colorin' book? Peanuts?"

Lolly pointed to everything she saw. Sometimes Joanda said, "No, you can't have that," but more often she made the purchase. Soon Joanda's arms were filled with packages.

"You buyin' her all them things?" asked Ricky.

"She has to have somethin'," said Joanda. "Nobody else buys her a thing. Each thing I show her, she cries for it. I tell her she's not gonna git it, but she *makes* me buy it. I spend more on her than on me."

"Lolly can't color no colorin' book," said Ricky. "She can't even hold a pencil."

"I can color it for her, can't I?" said Joanda hotly.

"Oh, you jest want it for yourself!" said Ricky. "Why don't you buy one for *me?*"

"Go buy a little ole coloring book for yourself if you want one!" snapped Joanda. "If you ain't spent all your money on stuff to eat and I s'pose you have!"

She looked around and saw Lolly running away again. "*She's takin' off!*" Joanda rushed to her mother, dumped her packages and ran out. "*Which way? Which way did she go?*"

But the shoestring man hadn't seen her and didn't know which way she went. Joanda looked at the cars and trucks and shuddered. What if Lolly got run over? She would die if anything happened to Lolly, she loved her so much.

Ever since Lolly was born, Joanda had taken care of her. Always, Joanda was the one who could quiet her. Joanda knew that Lolly liked her better than anybody in the family. *She's crazy about me, because I like her so much. She won't let me git three inches away from her. Every time she cries the least bit I pick her up....*

And now Lolly was gone and it was all Joanda's fault. She should have kept tight hold of her hand. Lolly was only two, though most people took her for three. She was still a baby who needed looking after. Joanda ran so hard she didn't look where she was going. Before she knew it, she bumped headlong into some one coming the other way. *Oh dear, it's one of them stuck-up people—a woman with a hat on,* she thought. She drew back quickly.

"Little girl, why don't you look where you are going, if you're in such a hurry?" said the woman sharply. Then she saw who it was. "Why, Joanda, it's *you.* I'm surprised."

Joanda recognized her. It was Mrs. Shands, the wife of Big Charley, Daddy's boss-man.

"*Yes ma'm,*" she gasped. "I . . . er . . . Lolly . . ." but she could not take time to explain, so on she went

Breathless, Joanda searched. She ran up and down the block, she crossed the street and went up and down the other side. She came back and went round the entire block. She went in the Goodwill store, looked under the counters, and through the aisles. She asked Mama and Mrs. Burgess, who were standing at the lunch counter, drinking coffee. Mama said, "Go find her." Joanda asked strange people, but no one knew or cared. *I'll have to ask a cop soon . . . that's the cop out in the middle of the street. I know, 'cause cops have guns,* and she was terrified at the thought. She knew she could never get up that much courage, even to save her beloved Lolly.

She stopped suddenly. She was trembling all over and breathing hard. The tears came in a flood, she could not hold them back. She buried her face in her hands.

"That you, Nannie?" She heard a man's voice. "What's the matter?"

Joanda looked up. It was J. T. Burgess and he was smiling as if nothing could possibly be wrong.

"*Lolly's lost! Lolly's lost and I don't know which way to go!* cried Joanda. She let go my hand and took off . . ."

"She's not at the Goodwill?" asked J. T. quietly.

"I went back and looked," said Joanda. "Mama and Aunt Lessie said she wasn't there. They told me to go hunt."

"There's only one other place she knows to go. Let's have a look."

J. T. led Joanda to the Beehive and down the alley at the side. They went to Daddy's truck, and there in the bed, on a pile of tow sacks lay Lolly, sound asleep.

"She came to a safe place—the little tyke," said J. T., laughing. "I told you we'd find her. Now, see you don't lose her again."

Lolly woke up and Joanda took her in her arms. She held her tightly as if she would never let her go again. With a thankful heart, she carried her back to the store. Mrs. Burgess had gone away and Mama was still waiting for Daddy to come. Mama had been standing all this time. There were no chairs at the store.

Lolly grew sleepy again and too heavy to hold. Joanda sat down on one of the lower shelves of the men's coat counter. She made a bed for the baby on the pile of coats and leaned against them to rest. Ricky curled up beside her with his head in her lap and fell asleep. After a while, Mavis and Steve came back, full of excitement over the show.

"*Six Shootin' Sheriff* was wonderful," said Mavis. "At first I couldn't tell who was the outlaw and who was goin' to ketch who . . ."

"It was clear as daylight," said Steve. "They had a bunch of cattlemen and some wicked guys that did some rustlin'. I knew jest what was goin' to happen and it did."

"Got any money left?" asked Mama in a dull voice.

"No," said Mavis and Steve.

"Did you buy anything to take home?" asked Mama.

"No," they said. "You kept our clothes packages, didn't you?"

"Yes," said Mama. "You had anything to eat?"

"Hot-dogs and ice cream and cold drinks . . . and candy and . . ."

"You seen Daddy anywhere?"

"No," they said.

"I don't know where all the money went," said Mama sadly. "We had plenty when we started out. We shoulda bought our winter groceries first thing. I wanted Daddy to git some last week, but he didn't and now . . ."

The crowd in the store had thinned out. It was supper time, but the store would be open until nine. Suddenly darkness fell and with the going of the sun, the glamour of the bright day faded.

"Let's go to the truck and wait for Daddy," said Mama. "We can't buy no supper because we've spent all our money. If Daddy has any left . . ." but she knew he wouldn't.

Mama carried Lolly to the truck. The three little ones curled up on the front seat, leaned against Mama and fell asleep. Mavis and Steve sat on the back and dangled their legs over. They talked on and on about the show.

After a long time, men's voices were heard and Joanda woke up. She looked out the cab window and saw two men helping a limp figure along. She heard J. T.'s voice and it comforted her.

"Here's Dave, Neva," said J. T. "He couldn't make it himself, so we brought him. Got some sacks in the truck?"

"Yes," said Mama. The men helped Daddy in.

"I'll drive you folks home," said J. T. "Lessie took our kids home a good while ago."

"I sure do thank you," said Mama. The truck started with a clatter.

Beautiful Saturday . . . all its magic was gone, but Joanda was too tired to notice. She dozed off to sleep again.

HARRIET THE SPY

Louise Fitzhugh

The poor are not the only economic minority in America. While the rich belong to a minority group most Americans would like to join, life is not always easy for children of this class. Their schools may be exclusive, their homes expensive, but they are too often brought up by servants and ignored by their parents.

Louise Fitzhugh shows what can happen to a highly intelligent, unusual child raised in such a situation. Harriet's parents love her but are too involved in their own lives to give her much time. Her nurse, Ole Golly, is a highly literate, intelligent woman who, while firm with Harriet, teaches her to observe and learn as much about life as possible. To do this Harriet spies on others. This is not a childish game but a serious daily routine in which she spies in the most antisocial meaning of the word. She records her observations of the people on her "route" and her opinions of her schoolmates in a notebook which she carries everywhere.

Harriet's life, while unique, is stable until Ole Golly leaves to be married. Without Ole Golly, Harriet becomes less sure of herself; she has no one to talk to, no one to understand what she really feels. And so Harriet begins to feel "terribly evil" and that "something terrible" will happen to her. In the following selection, it does.

Harriet is ostracized for a long while and her classmates are extremely cruel in their punishment. Yet in time she gains her revenge. In the end Ole Golly writes Harriet and tells her she must lie—she must apologize even though she is not sorry for what was written in the notebook. That a child's book should advocate lying shocked many adults. And yet . . . are unrepentant apologies so uncommon among adults?

That day, after school, everyone felt in a good mood because the weather was suddenly gay and soft like spring. They hung around outside, the whole class together, which was something they never did. Sport said suddenly, "Hey, why don't we go to the park and play tag?"

Harriet was late for her spying, but she thought she would just play one game and then leave. They all seemed to think this was a smashing idea, so everyone filed across the street.

The kind of tag they played wasn't very complicated; in fact Harriet thought it was rather silly. The object seemed to be to run around in circles and get very tired, then whoever was "it" tried to knock everyone else's books out of their arms. They played and played. Beth Ellen was eliminated at once, having no strength. Sport was the best. He managed to knock down everyone's books except Rachel Hennessey's and Harriet's.

He ran round and round then, very fast. Suddenly he knocked a few of Harriet's things off her arms, then Rachel tried to tease him away, and Harriet started to run like crazy. Soon she was running and running as fast as she could in the direction of the mayor's house. Rachel was right after her and Sport was close behind.

They ran and ran along the river. Then they were on the grass and Sport fell down. It wasn't any fun with him not chasing, so Rachel and Harriet waited until he got up. Then he was very quick and got them.

All of Rachel's books were on the ground, and some of Harriet's. They began to pick them up to go back and join the others.

Suddenly Harriet screeched in horror, "Where is my notebook?" They all began looking around, but they couldn't find it anywhere. Harriet suddenly remembered that some things had been knocked down before they ran away from the others. She began to run back toward them. She ran and ran, yelling like a banshee the whole way.

When she got back to where they had started she saw the whole class—Beth Ellen, Pinky Whitehead, Carrie Andrews, Marion Hawthorne, Laura Peters, and The Boy with the Purple Socks

—all sitting around a bench while Janie Gibbs read to them from the notebook.

Harriet descended upon them with a scream that was supposed to frighten Janie so much she would drop the book. But Janie didn't frighten easily. She just stopped reading and looked up calmly. The others looked up too. She looked at all their eyes and suddenly Harriet M. Welsch was afraid.

They just looked and looked, and their eyes were the meanest eyes she had ever seen. They formed a little knot and wouldn't let her near them. Rachel and Sport came up then. Marion Hawthorne said fiercely, "Rachel, come over here." Rachel walked over to her, and after Marion had whispered in her ear, got the same mean look.

Janie said, "Sport, come over here."

"Whadaya mean?" said Sport.

"I have something to tell you," Janie said in a very pointed way.

Sport walked over and Harriet's heart went into her sneakers. "FINKS!" Harriet felt rather hysterical. She didn't know what that word meant, but since her father said it all the time, she knew it was bad.

Janie passed the notebook to Sport and Rachel, never taking her eyes off Harriet as she did so. "Sport, you're on page thirty-four; Rachel, you're on fifteen," she said quietly.

Sport read his and burst into tears. "Read it aloud, Sport," said Janie harshly.

"I can't." Sport hid his face.

The book was passed back to Janie. Janie read the passage in a solemn voice.

SOMETIMES I CAN'T STAND SPORT. WITH HIS WORRYING ALL THE TIME AND FUSSING OVER HIS FATHER, SOMETIMES HE'S LIKE A LITTLE OLD WOMAN.

Sport turned his back on Harriet, but even from his back Harriet could see that he was crying. "That's not *fair*," she screamed. "There're some nice things about Sport in there."

Everyone got very still. Janie spoke very quietly. "Harriet, go over there on that bench until we decide what we're going to do to you."

Harriet went over and sat down. She couldn't hear them. They began to discuss something rapidly with many gestures. Sport kept his back turned and Janie never took her eyes off Harriet, no matter who was talking.

Harriet thought suddenly, I don't have to sit here. And she got up and marched off in as dignified a way as possible under the circumstances. They were so busy they didn't even seem to notice her.

At home, eating her cake and milk, Harriet reviewed her position. It was terrible. She decided that she had never been in a worse position. She then decided she wasn't going to think about it anymore. She went to bed in the middle of the afternoon and didn't get up until the next morning.

Her mother thought she was sick and said to her father, "Maybe we ought to call the doctor."

"Finks, all of them," said her father. Then they went away and Harriet went to sleep.

In the park all the children sat around and read things aloud. These are some of the things they read: NOTES ON WHAT CARRIE ANDREWS THINKS OF MARION HAWTHORNE

IS ROTTEN IN MATH
HAS FUNNY KNEES
IS A PIG

Then:

IF MARION HAWTHORNE DOESN'T WATCH OUT SHE'S GOING TO GROW UP INTO A LADY HITLER.

Janie Gibbs smothered a laugh at that one but not at the next one:

WHO DOES JANIE GIBBS THINK SHE'S KIDDING? DOES SHE REALLY THINK SHE COULD EVER BE A SCIENTIST?

Janie looked as though she had been struck. Sport looked at her sympathetically. They looked at each other, in fact, in a long, meaningful way.

Janie read on:

WHAT TO DO ABOUT PINKY WHITEHEAD
  1. TURN THE HOSE ON HIM.
  2. PINCH HIS EARS UNTIL HE SCREAMS.
  3. TEAR HIS PANTS OFF AND LAUGH AT HIM.

Pinky felt like running. He looked around nervously, but Harriet was nowhere to be seen.

There was something about everyone.

MAYBE BETH ELLEN DOESN'T HAVE ANY PARENTS. I ASKED HER HER MOTHER'S NAME AND SHE COULDN'T REMEMBER. SHE SAID SHE HAD ONLY SEEN HER ONCE AND SHE DIDN'T REMEMBER IT VERY WELL. SHE WEARS STRANGE THINGS LIKE ORANGE SWEATERS AND A BIG BLACK CAR COMES FOR HER ONCE A WEEK AND SHE GOES SOMEPLACE ELSE.

Beth Ellen rolled her big eyes and said nothing. She never said anything, so this wasn't unusual.

THE REASON SPORT DRESSES SO FUNNY IS THAT HIS FATHER WON'T BUY HIM ANTHING TO WEAR BECAUSE HIS MOTHER HAS ALL THE MONEY.

Sport turned his back again.

TODAY A NEW BOY ARRIVED. HE IS SO DULL NO ONE CAN REMEMBER HIS NAME SO I HAVE NAMED HIM THE BOY WITH THE PURPLE SOCKS. IMAGINE. WHERE WOULD HE EVER FIND PURPLE SOCKS?

The Boy with the Purple Socks looked down at his purple socks and smiled.

Everyone looked at the sock boy. Carrie spoke up. She had a rather grating voice. "What *IS* your name?" even though by now they all knew perfectly well.

"Peter," he said shyly.

"Why *do* you wear purple socks?" asked Janie.

Peter smiled shyly, looked at his socks, then said, "Once, at the circus, my mother lost me. She said, after that, if I had on purple socks, she could always find me."

"Hmmmmm," said Janie.

Gathering courage from this, Peter spoke again. "She *wanted* to make it a whole purple suit, but I rebelled."

"I don't blame you," said Janie.

Peter bobbed his head and grinned. They all grinned back at him because he had a tooth missing and looked rather funny, but also he wasn't a bad sort, so they all began to like him a little bit.

They read on:

MISS ELSON HAS A WART BEHIND HER ELBOW.

This was fairly boring so they skipped ahead.

I ONCE SAW MISS ELSON WHEN SHE DIDN'T SEE ME AND SHE WAS PICKING HER NOSE.

That was better, but still they wanted to read about themselves.

CARRIE ANDREWS' MOTHER HAS THE BIGGEST FRONT I EVER SAW.

There was a great deal of tension in the group after this last item. Then Sport gave a big horse-laugh, and Pinky Whitehead's ears turned bright red. Janie smiled a fierce and frightening smile at Carrie Andrews, who looked as though she wanted to dive under the bench.

WHEN I GROW UP I'M GOING TO FIND OUT EVERY-THING ABOUT EVERYBODY AND PUT IT ALL IN A BOOK. THE BOOK IS GOING TO BE CALLED SECRETS BY HARRIET M. WELSCH. I WILL ALSO HAVE PHOTO-GRAPHS IN IT AND MAYBE SOME MEDICAL CHARTS IF I CAN GET THEM.

Rachel stood up, "I have to go home. Is there anything about me?"
They flipped through until they found her name.

I DON'T KNOW EXACTLY IF I LIKE RACHEL OR WHETHER IT IS JUST THAT I LIKE GOING TO HER HOUSE BECAUSE HER MOTHER MAKES HOMEMADE CAKE. IF I HAD A CLUB I'M NOT SURE I WOULD HAVE RACHEL IN IT.

"Thank you," Rachel said politely and left for home.
Laura Peters left too after the last item:

IF LAURA PETERS DOESN'T STOP SMILING AT ME IN THAT WISHY-WASHY WAY I'M GOING TO GIVE HER A GOOD KICK.

The next morning when Harriet arrived at school no one spoke to her. They didn't even look at her. It was exactly as though no one at all had walked into the room. Harriet sat down and felt like a lump. She looked at everyone's desk, but there was no sign of the notebook. She looked at every face and on every face was a plan, and on each face was the same plan. They had

organization. I'm going to get it, she thought grimly.
That was not the worst of it. The worst was that even though she knew she shouldn't, she had stopped by the stationery store on the way to school and had bought another notebook. She had tried not to write in it, but she was such a creature of habit that even now she found herself taking it out of the pocket of her jumper, and furthermore, the next minute she was scratching in a whole series of things.

THEY ARE OUT TO GET ME. THE WHOLE ROOM IS FILLED WITH MEAN EYES. I WON'T GET THROUGH THE DAY. I MIGHT THROW UP MY TOMATO SAND-WICH. EVEN SPORT AND JANIE. WHAT DID I SAY ABOUT JANIE? I DON'T REMEMBER. NEVER MIND. THEY MAY THINK I AM A WEAKLING BUT A SPY IS TRAINED FOR THIS KIND OF FIGHT. I AM READY FOR THEM.

She went on scratching until Miss Elson cleared her throat, signifying she had entered the room. Then everyone stood up as they always did, bowed, said, "Good morning, Miss Elson," and sat back down. It was the custom at this moment for everyone to punch each other. Harriet looked around for someone to do some poking with, but they all sat stony-faced as though they had never poked anyone in their whole lives.
It made Harriet feel better to try and quote like Ole Golly, so she wrote:

THE SINS OF THE FATHERS

That was all she knew from the Bible besides the shortest verse: "Jesus wept."
Class began and all was forgotten in the joy of writing Harriet M. Welsch at the top of the page.
Halfway through the class Harriet saw a tiny piece of paper float to the floor on her right. Ah'ha, she thought, the chickens; they are making up already. She reached down to get the note. A hand flew past her nose and she realized that the note had been retrieved in a neat backhand by Janie who sat to the right of her.
Well, she thought, so it wasn't for me, that's all. She looked at Carrie, who had sent the note, and Carrie looked carefully away without even giggling.

Harriet wrote in her notebook:

CARRIE ANDREWS HAS AN UGLY PIMPLE RIGHT NEXT
TO HER NOSE.

Feeling better, she attacked her homework
with renewed zeal. She was getting hungry. Soon
she would have her tomato sandwich. She looked
up at Miss Elson who was looking at Marion
Hawthorne who was scratching her knee. As Harriet looked back at her work she suddenly saw a
glint of white sticking out of Janie's jumper
pocket. It was the note! Perhaps she could just
reach over ever so quietly and pull back very
quickly. She *had* to see.

She watched her own arm moving very quietly
over, inch by inch. Was Carrie Andrews watching?
No. Another inch. Another. *There!!* She had it.
Janie obviously hadn't felt a thing. Now to read!
She looked at Miss Elson but she seemed to be in
a dream. She unfolded the tiny piece of paper
and read:

Harriet M. Welsch smells. Don't you think so?

Oh, no! Did she really smell? What of? Bad,
obviously. Must be very bad. She held up her
hand and got excused from class. She went into
the bathroom and smelled herself all over, but
she couldn't smell anything bad. Then she
washed her hands and face. She was going to
leave, then she went back and washed her feet
just in case. Nothing smelled. What were they
talking about? Anyway, now, just to be sure, they
would smell of soap.

When she got back to her desk, she noticed a
little piece of paper next to where her foot would
ordinarily be when she sat down. Ah, this will
explain it, she thought. She made a swift move, as
though falling, and retrieved the note without
Miss Elson seeing. She unrolled it eagerly and
read:

*There is nothing that makes me sicker than
watching Harriett M. Welsch eat a tomato sandwich.*
                                             Pinky Whitehead

The note must have misfired. Pinky sat to the
right and it was addressed to Sport, who sat on
her left.

What was sickening about a tomato sandwich?
Harriet felt the taste in her mouth. Were they
crazy? It was the best taste in the world. Her
mouth watered at the memory of the mayonnaise.
It was an experience, as Mrs. Welsch was always
saying. How could it make anyone sick? Pinky
Whitehead was what could make you sick. Those
stick legs and the way his neck seemed to swivel
up and down away from his body. She wrote in
her notebook:

THERE IS NO REST FOR THE WEARY.

As she looked up she saw Marion Hawthorne
turn swiftly in her direction. Then suddenly she
was looking full at Marion Hawthorne's tongue
out at her, and a terribly ugly face around the
tongue, with eyes all screwed up and pulled down
by two fingers so that the whole thing looked as
though Marion Hawthorne were going to be
carted away to the hospital. Harriet glanced
quickly at Miss Elson. Miss Elson was dreaming
out the window. Harriet wrote quickly:

HOW UNLIKE MARION HAWTHORNE. I DIDN'T THINK
SHE EVER DID ANYTHING BAD.

Then she heard the giggles. She looked up.
Everyone had caught the look. Everyone was gig-
gling and laughing with Marion, even Sport and
Janie. Miss Elson turned around and every face
went blank, everybody bent again over the desks.
Harriet wrote quietly.

PERHAPS I CAN TALK TO MY MOTHER ABOUT
CHANGING SCHOOLS. I HAVE THE FEELING THIS
MORNING THAT EVERYONE IN THIS SCHOOL IS IN-
SANE. I MIGHT POSSIBLY BRING A HAM SANDWICH
TOMORROW BUT I HAVE TO THINK ABOUT IT.

The lunch bell rang. Everyone jumped as
though they had one body and pushed out the
door. Harriet jumped too, but for some reason or
other three people bumped into her as she did. It
was so fast she didn't even see who it was, but the
way they did it she was pushed so far back that
she was the last one out the door. They all ran
ahead, had gotten their lunchboxes, and were outside by the time she got to the cloakroom. It's
true that she was detained because she had to

make a note of the fact that Miss Elson went to the science room to talk to Miss Maynard, which had never happened before in the history of the school.

When she picked up her lunch the bag felt very light. She reached inside and there was only crumpled paper. They had taken her tomato sandwich. They had *taken* her tomato sandwich. Someone had *taken* it. She couldn't get over it. This was completely against the rules of the school. No one was supposed to steal your tomato sandwich. She had been coming to this school since she was four—let's see, that made seven years—and in all those seven years no one had ever taken her tomato sandwich. Not even during those six months when she had brought pickle sandwiches with mustard. No one had even asked for so much as a bite. Sometimes Beth Ellen passed around olives because no one else had olives and they were very chic, but that was the extent of the sharing. And now here it was noon and she had nothing to eat.

She was aghast. What could she do? It would be ridiculous to go around asking "Has anyone seen a tomato sandwich?" They were sure to laugh. She would go to Miss Elson. No, then she would be a ratter, a squealer, a stoolie. Well, she couldn't starve. She went to the telephone and asked to use it because she had forgotten her lunch. She called and the cook told her to come home, that she would make another tomato sandwich in the meantime.

Harriet left, went home, ate her tomato sandwich, and took to her bed for another day. She had to think. Her mother was playing bridge downtown. She pretended to be sick enough so the cook didn't yell at her and yet not sick enough for the cook to call her mother. She had to think.

As she lay there in the half gloom she looked out over the trees in the park. For a while she watched a bird, then an old man who walked like a drunk. Inside she felt herself thinking "Everybody hates me, everybody hates me."

At first she didn't listen to it and then she heard what she was feeling. She said it several times to hear it better. Then she reached nervously for her notebook and wrote in big, block letters, the way she used to write when she was little.

EVERYBODY HATES ME.

Related Reading

Books for Children

ECONOMIC MINORITIES

Estes, Elinor. *The Hundred Dresses*. Illustrated by Louis Slobodkin. New York: Harcourt, 1944. A moving story of a little girl who always wore the same dress but, when teased and taunted by her school classmates, claimed to have one hundred others at home. (Grades 2–4)

Fitzhugh, Louise, author-illustrator. *Harriet the Spy*. New York: Harper & Row, 1964. A discussion of and an excerpt from this book can be found in this chapter. (Grades 4–6)

————. *The Long Secret*. New York: Harper & Row, 1965. A sequel to *Harriet the Spy*. (Grades 4–6)

Gates, Doris. *Blue Willow*. Illustrated by Paul Lantz. New York: Viking, 1940. A story about migrant farm workers and their longing for a secure home. Not as well written as *Roosevelt Grady* by Louisa R. Shotwell, but still moving to many young girls. (Grades 4–6)

Lenski, Lois, author-illustrator. *Coal Camp Girl*. Philadelphia: Lippincott, 1959. Interesting books about regional minorities by an author who researches her information by going to live with the people about whom she intends to write. Other books are: *Corn Farm Boy*, 1954;

————. *Cotton in My Sack*, 1949 (A discussion of and an excerpt from this book can be found in this chapter); *Judy's Journey*, 1947; *Prairie School*, 1951; *Shoo-Fly Girl*, 1963; *Strawberry Girl*, 1945; *Texas Tomboy*, 1950 (Grades 4–6)

Rabin, Gil. *False Start*. New York: Harper & Row, 1969. A discussion of and an excerpt from this book can be found in this chapter. (Grades 4–9)

Wier, Ester. *The Winners*. New York: McKay, 1969. A discussion of and an excerpt from this book can be found in this chapter. (Grades 5–7)

Zemach, Margot, adapter-illustrator. *Mommy, Buy Me a China Doll*. Chicago: Follett, 1966. A picture book adaptation of an Ozark children's song. A little girl begs for a china doll that her parents cannot afford. Humorous situations occur as she tries to find an object for trade. (Preschool–grade 3)

RACIAL MINORITIES

Armstrong, William H. *Sounder*. Illustrated by James Barkley. New York: Harper, 1969. Although it is a powerful story of grief and endurance, *Sounder* is also an unfortunate example of the stereotyping all whites as stupid bullies; there are no decent white characters in *Sounder*. Such stereotyping does no service to children, black or white, nor to their literature; it is a step back into the past. (Grades 5–up)

Armer, Laura Adams. *Waterless Mountain*. Illustrated by Sidney Armer and Laura Adams Armer. New York: Longmans, 1931. The traditional customs and tribal beliefs of the Navaho are revealed through the life and thoughts of Younger Brother. Awarded the 1932 Newbery Medal. (Grades 5–7)

Behrens, June. *Soo Ling Finds a Way*. Illustrated by Taro Yashima. San Carlos, Calif.: Golden Gate Junior Books, 1965. When a laundromat opens across the street, Grandfather's laundry is threatened. Little Soo Ling's resourcefulness, however, prevents its closure. (Grades K–2)

Bontemps, Arna. *Lonesome Boy*. Illustrated by Feliks Topolski. Boston: Houghton Mifflin, 1955. A mood story about a young New Orleans Negro boy and his love for his trumpet and jazz. (Grades 5–up)

Bulla, Clyde Robert. *Indian Hill*. Illustrated by James J. Spanfeller. New York: Crowell, 1963. A story about a young Navajo boy's adjustment to life in the city. (Grades 2–5)

Carlson, Natalie Savage. *The Empty Schoolhouse*. Illustrated by John Kaufmann. New York: Harper & Row, 1965. This book shows the conflicts that occur when a Louisiana parochial school is integrated. Although the ending is oversimplified, Lullah's personality, her courage and confusion, makes an interesting story. (Grades 3–5)

De Angeli, Marguerite, author-illustrator. *Bright April*. New York: Doubleday, 1946. A discussion of and an excerpt from this book can be found in this chapter. (Grades 3–5)

Hill, Elizabeth Starr. *Evan's Corner*. Illustrated by Nancy Grossman. New York: Holt, 1967. A picture book dealing with a young Negro boy's desire for a place of his very own, almost an impossibility in a small Harlem apartment. An understanding mother provides Evan with a corner that is only for him. However, his enjoyment is not as great as he had expected. Both Evan and the reader develop new insights into pleasure. (Grades K–3)

Hunter, Kristin. *Soul Brothers and Sister Lou*. New York: Scribner, 1968. An interesting story about a group of northern ghetto Negro teen-agers who have no place to gather. Many different Negro attitudes are illustrated through the characters. In time, the teen-agers attain success as a singing group. Unlike most books for teen-agers, this is not the expected happy ending, for Lou discovers that success is not as pleasant as she had expected. It brings anxiety and uncertainty because those on the top must always work to stay there. (Grades 6–10)

Jackson, Jesse. *Call Me Charley*. Illustrated by Doris Spiegel. New York: Harper & Row, 1945. A discussion of and an excerpt from this book can be found in this chapter. (Grades 4–7)

Justus, May. *New Boy in School*. Illustrated by Joan Balfour Payne. New York: Hastongs House, 1963. A young Negro boy's adjustment to an all-white classroom. (Grades 2–4)

Keats, Ezra Jack, author-illustrator. *Goggles!* New York: Macmillan, 1969. Peter finds a pair of motorcycle goggles and has to flee a gang of boys who want to take them away from him. (Grades K–2)

————. *Peter's Chair*. New York: Harper, 1967. Peter's jealousy of his baby sister who was sleeping in *his* crib and was going to use *his* high chair! Shows Peter's adjustment to sharing. While not as successful as *The Snowy Day*, still, a charming book. (Grades K–3)

————. *The Snowy Day*. New York: Viking, 1962. An excellent picture book story about a young Negro boy's enjoyment of a beautiful snowy day. Awarded the 1963 Caldecott Award. (Preschool–grade 1)

————. *Whistle for Willie*. New York: Viking, 1964. A picture book about a little boy who wanted to whistle like the bigger boys. (Preschool–grade 1)

Krumgold, Joseph. *. . . And Now Miguel*. Illustrated by Jean Charlot. New York: Crowell, 1953. A sensitive story about a young boy growing from childhood to adulthood. Based on a documentary film about New Mexican sheepherders written and directed by the author. Awarded the 1954 Newbery Medal. (Grades 5–7)

Means, Florence. *The Moved-Outers*. Illustrated by Helen Blair. Boston: Houghton Mifflin, 1945. A discussion of and an excerpt from this book can be found in this chapter. (Grades 6–12)

Politi, Leo, author-illustrator. *Juanita*. New York: Scribner, 1948. The life and customs of one group of Mexican-Americans is shown in this happy picture book about a little girl who lives in Olvera Street, Los Angeles. (Grades K–2)

Shotwell, Louisa. *Roosevelt Grady*. Illustrated by Peter Burchard. Cleveland: World Publishing, 1963. A discussion of and an excerpt from this book can be found in this chapter. (Grades 5–7)

Speevack, Yetta. *The Spider Plant*. Illustrated by Wendy Watson. New York: Atheneum, 1965. A discussion of and an excerpt from this book can be found in this chapter. (Grades 4–6)

Sterling, Dorothy. *Mary Jane*. Illustrated by Ernest Crichlow. New York: Doubleday, 1959. A discussion of and an excerpt from this book can be found in this chapter. (Grades 5–7)

Waltrip, Lela and Rufus. *Quiet Boy*. Illustrated by Theresa Kalab Smith. New York: McKay, 1961. A discussion of and an excerpt from this book can be found in this chapter. (Grades 4–6)

Weik, Mary Hays. *The Jazz Man*. Illustrated by Ann Grifalconi. New York: Atheneum, 1966. A young Negro boy, abandoned by his mother and left for long periods by his father, listens to the jazz player across the court from his Harlem apartment. (Grades 3–5)

Yashima, Taro, pseud. (Jun Iwamatsu), author-illustrator. *Umbrella*. New York: Viking, 1958. The picture story of a Japanese-American preschool girl who longs to use her new umbrella. (Preschool–grade 2)

RELIGIOUS MINORITIES

Cone, Molly. *A Promise Is a Promise*. Illustrated by John Gretzer. Boston: Houghton Mifflin, 1964. A story of contemporary Jewish life that does not avoid the problem of religious bias. Since there are relatively few books on this subject, *A Promise Is a Promise* will be interesting to many children; however, the main character seems more petulant than honestly confused about her religion. (Grades 4–6)

De Angeli, Marguerite, author-illustrator. *Thee Hannah!* New York: Doubleday, 1949. An interesting book about a lively Quaker girl's growing understanding of her religion. When an escaping slave approaches her for help because of her dress, Hannah learns to appreciate her gray garb and not to long for the brighter clothes of her friends. (Grades 3–5)

Milhous, Katherine, author-illustrator. *Appolonia's Valentine*. New York: Scribner, 1954. A young Pennsylvania Dutch girl earns money to buy paints so she can make a Valentine to send to her pen-pal in Brittany. (Grades 2–5)

————. *The Egg Tree*. New York: Scribner, 1950. A charming picture book about the Easter customs of the Pennsylvania Dutch. The illustrations include many traditional designs. Awarded the 1951 Caldecott Medal. (Grades K–4)

Neville, Emily. *Berries Goodman*. New York: Harper & Row, 1965. A meeting with Sidney Fine after six years brings back to Berries Goodman memories of their friendship when they were both nine years old, a friendship broken by the prejudice of their neighbors in Olcott Corners, a suburb of New York City. In flashbacks Berries recreates the pleasures they shared together and the destructiveness of bigotry. A subtle, nondidactic novel that will interest older children. (Grades 6–10)

Sachs, Marilyn. *Peter and Veronica*. Illustrated by Louis Glanzman. New York: Doubleday, 1969. In this sequel to *Veronica Ganz*, Peter insists on inviting Veronica to his Bar Mitzvah, a decision that creates unhappiness in his home. When Veronica does not come, it almost destroys their friendship. Serious problems are deftly handled in a light manner that avoids any hint of didacticism. (Grades 4–7)

Sorensen, Virginia. *Plain Girl*. Illustrated by Charles Geer. New York: Harcourt, 1955. A discussion of and an excerpt from this book can be found in this chapter. (Grades 4–6)

Taylor, Sydney. *All-of-a-Kind Family*. Illustrated by Helen John. Chicago: Follett, 1951. Warm stories about five Jewish girls who live on New York City's East side before World War I. While they are not rich, they are well loved and know no prejudice. Episodic plots but good characterization. Other books in the series are: *All-of-a-Kind Family Uptown*, 1958 (illustrated by Mary Stevens); *More All-of-a-Kind Family*, 1954 (illustrated by Mary Stevens). (Grades 4–6)

Chapter 9
Other
Countries

Reprinted with permission of The Macmillan Company from *Call It Courage* by Armstrong Sperry. Copyright 1940 by Armstrong Sperry, renewed 1968 by Armstrong Sperry.

Psychologists say that everyone has the same basic needs: to love and to be loved, to trust and be trusted, to belong, to be physically secure, to have status, to have self-respect and autonomy. These universal drives are emphasized in most children's books about foreign lands. The reader is able to feel empathy for fictional characters whose hopes and fears are similar to those he has felt. Many books show children in other countries searching for security, trying to make mature decisions, attempting to overcome fear or gain respect. These desires are familiar to all children and so involve them in the lives of Polynesian, African, and Chinese children

In children's literature these universal needs receive more attention than do cultural differences. Yet by seeing differences as well as similarities, young readers can learn to respect other traditions, attitudes, and beliefs. In addition to sharing the universal needs, each group has significant cultural differences. Not all peoples have the same attitudes toward life and about "proper" behavior. North Americans and northern Europeans believe sitting still without doing anything is wasting time; most organize their recreation as strictly as they do their work. In contrast, Asians believe idleness is as essential as hard physical and mental work. North Americans and Europeans believe men are calm and practical while women are emotional and impractical. Just the opposite is true of the Persians, who leave practicality to women; men are sensitive and emotional. North Americans place great importance on promptness, while South Americans consider forty-five or sixty minutes late to be punctual.

Each culture believes its social, religious, and political patterns are not only "right" but also the *only* logical ways to behave and believe. This cer tainty prevents them from viewing other peoples with clear understanding. Such understanding is increasingly important as more people travel abroad and as more countries have close dealings with each other. Anthropologists claim that much of the current distrust between nations would be minimized if cultural differences were recognized by diplomats and politicians.

Children's books, of course, cannot influence these men, but well-written, perceptive novels about other countries may help develop the cultural tolerance a steadily shrinking world demands. Books that show children interacting with their country's cultural demands, restrictions, and physical environment may give American youngsters an understanding of other ways of life. Because fiction has the interest-holding devices of plot and character, well-written fiction often gives a greater sense of reality and a clearer picture than do many social studies and nonfiction books.

Novels about other countries should be evaluated by the same criteria of plot, character, theme, and style that are discussed in the introduction to fiction. In addition to these, the most important element of this genre is authenticity. Two important weaknesses to watch for are superficiality and the use of old-fashioned stereotypes: Hawaii as a land of grass huts uninfluenced by modern life or Holland as a pastoral country with many windmills, wooden shoes, and tulips, for example. The opposite weakness is apparent when life in the foreign country seems to be identical with the reader's own. Usually the authors of these books know nothing of the country about which they are writing but place their characters in a foreign setting to make the story seem more interesting.

577

The best books have a balance between the recognizable and the foreign. While the problems faced by the main characters may be quite different from those North American children encounter because of the cultural differences, their hopes and fears are those of all people, universal and recognizable.

THE HINDOO GIRL SEEKING JESUS

From the Religious Tract Society (n.d.)

In Victorian children's literature people of other cultures and races are shown either as inferior to the English or as objects of missionary activity. There is seldom any attempt to accurately portray the customs of Asians or Africans so as to give nineteenth-century children an understanding of other cultures. These stories lack reality and seem highly didactic. But many Victorian children and the working class supported missions to convert the "heathens" and were moved by tracts like The Hindoo Girl Seeking Jesus *and* The African Monitor Girl. *This cultural context should be recognized.*

A Hindoo girl was playing before the door of her father's house. Some wicked men came that way and, taking her in their arms, ran away with her to a distant place, where they sold her as a slave.

An Indian lady, who bought the girl, soon loved her as her own child. She had her dressed in fine clothes and many jewels. Everything was done to make her happy, and to lead her to forget the home of her early days.

Time passed away. As the girl grew in years, she felt that she was a sinner. She did not know what made her so feel. All she knew was, that she was a sinner, and could not tell how sin was to be forgiven.

When she spoke to the lady about it, she got no comfort, for the lady had never heard of the only way in which a sinner can find peace.

'Oh,' she cried, 'I shall die in my sins.'

One day she was sitting full of sorrow, when a Hindoo begger came to the door. He told her that he had come from a place where many of the people were called Christians, for they believed in a holy one, named Jesus Christ, who could save from sin.

'Oh, show me the way to this place and to these people,' she said.

'Why, that I will do,' replied the man. 'If you go to a village some miles away, you will find a Hindoo, who has become one of these Christians. He was once a rich native, but he has given up all his worldly goods that he may follow Christ. He will tell you what you should do!'

A few days after this time, the Hindoo girl was on her way to the village; and as she went along, she asked those she met if they could tell her where the man lived who led the people to Jesus. Some mocked, and others scolded, saying she should not forsake the gods of her country.

At last she thought she must give up the search. She was in a strange part of the country, and was tired and worn out with her journey. When, just then she met a Hindoo, and once more she asked, 'Can you tell me the way to the man who knows Jesus Christ?' To her great joy, she found that he knew what she meant, and he pointed out the road to the teacher's house.

When she came to the door, as soon as she saw the teacher, she cried, 'I want you to take me to Jesus, who takes away sin. Oh, take me to him *now*; I want him to remove sin from my heart.'

The Christian native heard her tell of her sorrow, and how she had gone about in search of peace without finding it.

The pious teacher then spoke to her of the Son of God, who was once on earth, and who invited sinners to come to him that they might be saved.

As the Hindoo maiden heard these good words, hope came into her mind. She saw that Jesus was the only Saviour, and in him she could find rest for her soul.

After staying some days at the mission-house, she returned home.

We can tell no more about this young Hindoo. If she yet lives, we hope she knows more of Jesus, and loves him better than when she first went forth to seek him.

This true story is given to show that there is no peace to be found until a sinner believes in Jesus Christ.

THE AFRICAN MONITOR GIRL

From the Religious Tract Society (*n.d.*)

A ship was on the sea, not far from the shores of Africa. It was not full of sugar, cotton, oil or anything of the kind. It was crowded with black men, women, and children, who had been stolen from their homes, and were now being carried to a distant land, there to be sold as slaves. These poor people were cruelly used; they were bound with chains to the decks, and very little food was given them to eat.

But an English ship came that way, and seized the slave vessel. The iron chains were then taken off their limbs, and the poor blacks were carried to a place in West Africa, called Free Town. There they soon found happy homes, and Christian teachers.

Among those who were thus saved from slavery were a black man and his wife, with their little girl. They settled in a spot where they could hear about the Lord Jesus Christ, and their child was sent to a school. The teachers gave her the name of Charlotte Bell. It is thought she was so called after the name of some lady in England, who paid the money for her support.

"The African Monitor Girl," reprinted by permission of The World Publishing Company and Arthur Barker Ltd. from *Little Wide Awake, an Anthology from Victorian Children's Books and Periodicals in the Collection of Anne and Fernand G. Renier.* Copyright © 1967 by Leonard de Vries for this selection.

Many of the black children are quick in learning; but it was not so with Charlotte. At first she could not learn at all, but she tried very much, and that was the right way. It is the right way for *you*, young friend.

After some time, Charlotte got on very nicely with her lessons.

Four or five years passed away, and she had so much improved in learning that she was made a monitor, and used to assist in teaching some of her little dark-faced companions.

But her time for labour was short. Some have only a short day of labour; and this should teach us all to do what we ought to do without delay. At the age of fifteen, Charlotte was taken ill, when a missionary went to see her.

Charlotte told him that, while lying at home, she had seen more of her sinful state before God than she had seen before, and had sought Jesus her Saviour with all her heart. 'Oh, yes,' she said, 'it is good for me that I have been brought low. I have learned to know God: I have learned to love Jesus.'

As she lay in the poor hut from week to week, she was always found with the Bible on her bed, and she told all who came to see her how glad she was that she had been taught to read it.

Although very weak, and in much pain, a murmur was not heard from her lips: she was always grateful for every little kindness done for her. Her great delight was in reading the Scriptures and in prayer.

The day before Charlotte Bell died, she called her mother and said, 'When I am gone, you must not be sorry: nobody must cry. I do not want you to put on a black dress for me; you should all have white, because I am going to a happy place.' The next morning, before the sun shone into the little window of her hut, she wished her father to pray for her. She then spoke aloud the hymn, which begins--

'How did my heart rejoice to hear
    My friends devoutly say,
In Zion let us all appear,
    And keep the solemn day!'

Charlotte now lay very quiet, and in a few hours she died.

When the people took her body to the grave, the girls and boys of the school walked after the coffin, and wept as they saw it laid in the ground.

We should do what we can to help those who carry the gospel to other lands. Had it not been for kind Christian teachers, Charlotte Bell would have died a poor heathen girl.

HANS BRINKER, OR THE SILVER SKATES

Mary Mapes Dodge

Dutch life in the middle of the nineteenth century is said to be accurately portrayed in this American children's classic, but today's children should understand that the Netherlands has changed considerably and is now a highly industrialized, modern country. The basic story about Hans and Gretel with its mystery is exciting and suspenseful, and the cheerfulness and fortitude of the two children are touching. But the book's long historical passages are dull and show how literature was used by last century writers to teach through fictional stories and characters. Two main purposes of Hans Brinker were to give American children information about another country and to teach them behavior and manners—the "proper" attitude and relationship of the rich toward the poor, for example. Today's youngsters skip over these sections and remember only the dramatic story of Hans and his family.

On a bright December morning long ago, two thinly clad children were kneeling upon the bank of a frozen canal in Holland.

The sun had not yet appeared, but the gray sky was parted near the horizon, and its edges shone crimson with the coming day. Most of the good Hollanders were enjoying a placid morning nap; even Mynheer von Stoppelnoze, that worthy old Dutchman, was still slumbering "in beautiful repose."

Now and then some peasant woman, poising a well-filled basket upon her head, came skimming over the glassy surface of the canal; or a lusty boy, skating to his day's work in the town, cast a good-natured grimace toward the shivering pair as he flew along.

Meanwhile, with many a vigorous puff and pull, the brother and sister, for such they were, seemed to be fastening something upon their feet —not skates, certainly, but clumsy pieces of wood narrowed and smoothed at their lower edge, and pierced with holes, through which were threaded strings of rawhide.

These queer-looking affairs had been made by

the boy Hans. His mother was a poor peasant woman, too poor to even think of such a thing as buying skates for her little ones. Rough as these were, they had afforded the children many a happy hour upon the ice; and now as with cold, red fingers our young Hollanders tugged at the strings—their solemn faces bending closely over their knees—no vision of impossible iron runners came to dull the satisfaction glowing within.

In a moment the boy arose, and with a pompous swing of the arms, and a careless "come on, Gretel," glided easily across the canal.

"Ah, Hans," called his sister plaintively, "this foot is not well yet. The strings hurt me on last Market day; and now I cannot bear them tied in the same place."

"Tie them higher up, then," answered Hans, as without looking at her he performed a wonderful cat's cradle step on the ice.

"How can I? The string is too short."

Giving vent to a good-natured Dutch whistle, the English of which was that girls were troublesome creatures, he steered towards her.

"You are foolish to wear such shoes, Gretel, when you have a stout leather pair. Your klompen[1] would be better than these."

"Why, Hans! Do you forget? The father threw my beautiful new shoes in the fire. Before I knew what he had done they were all curled up in the midst of the burning peat. I can skate with these, but not with my wooden ones.—Be careful now—"

Hans had taken a string from his pocket. Humming a tune, as he knelt beside her, he proceeded to fasten Gretel's skate with all the force of his strong young arm.

"Oh! oh!" she cried, in real pain.

With an impatient jerk Hans unwound the string. He would have cast it upon the ground, in true big-brother style, had he not just then spied a tear trickling down his sister's cheek.

"I'll fix it—never fear," he said with sudden tenderness, "but we must be quick; the mother will need us soon."

Then he glanced inquiringly about him, first at the ground, next at some bare willow branches above his head, and finally at the sky now gorgeous with streaks of blue, crimson, and gold.

[1] Wooden shoes.

Finding nothing in any of these localities to meet his need, his eye suddenly brightened as, with the air of a fellow who knew what he was about, he took off his cap and, removing the tattered lining, adjusted it in a smooth pad over the top of Gretel's worn-out shoe.

"Now," he cried triumphantly, at the same time arranging the strings as briskly as his benumbed fingers would allow, "can you bear some pulling?"

Gretel drew up her lips as if to say "hurt away," but made no further response.

In another moment they were laughing together, as hand in hand they flew along the canal, never thinking whether the ice would bear or not, for in Holland ice is generally an all-winter affair. It settles itself upon the water in a determined kind of way and, so far from growing thin and uncertain every time the sun is a little severe upon it, it gathers its forces day by day and flashes defiance to every beam.

Presently, squeak! squeak! sounded something beneath Hans' feet. Next his strokes grew shorter, ending ofttimes with a jerk, and finally he lay sprawling upon the ice, kicking against the air with many a fantastic flourish.

"Ha! Ha!" laughed Gretel, "that was a fine tumble!" But a tender heart was beating under her coarse blue jacket, and even as she laughed, she came, with a graceful sweep, close to her prostrate brother.

"Are you hurt, Hans? oh, you are laughing! catch me now"—and she darted away shivering no longer, but with cheeks all aglow, and eyes sparkling with fun.

Hans sprang to his feet and started in brisk pursuit, but it was no easy thing to catch Gretel. Before she had traveled very far her skates, too, began to squeak.

Believing that discretion was the better part of valor she turned suddenly and skated into her pursuer's arms.

"Ha! ha! I've caught you!" cried Hans.

"Ha! ha! I caught *you*," she retorted, struggling to free herself.

Just then a clear, quick voice was heard calling "Hans! Gretel!"

"It's the mother," said Hans, looking solemn in an instant.

By this time the canal was gilded with sunlight. The pure morning air was very delightful, and skaters were gradually increasing in numbers. It was hard to obey the summons. But Gretel and Hans were good children; without a thought of yielding to the temptation to linger, they pulled off their skates leaving half the knots still tied. Hans, with his great square shoulders and bushy yellow hair, towered high above his blue-eyed little sister as they trudged homeward. He was fifteen years old and Gretel was only twelve. He was a solid, hearty-looking boy, with honest eyes and a brow that seemed to bear a sign "goodness within" just as the little Dutch zomerhuis[2] wears a motto over its portal. Gretel was lithe and quick; her eyes had a dancing light in them, and while you looked at her cheek the color paled and deepened just as it does upon a bed of pink and white blossoms when the wind is blowing.

As soon as the children turned from the canal they could see their parents' cottage. Their mother's tall form, arrayed in jacket and petticoat and close-fitting cap, stood, like a picture, in the crooked frame of the doorway. Had the cottage been a mile away, it would still have seemed near. In that flat country every object stands out plainly in the distance; the chickens show as distinctly as the windmills. Indeed, were it not for the dykes and the high banks of the canals, one could stand almost anywhere in middle Holland without seeing a mound or a ridge between the eye and the "jumping-off place."

None had better cause to know the nature of these same dykes than Dame Brinker and the panting youngsters now running at her call. But before stating *why*, let me ask you to take a rocking-chair trip with me to that far country where you may see, perhaps for the first time, some curious things that Hans and Gretel saw every day.

HOLLAND

Holland is one of the queerest countries under the sun. It should be called Odd-land or Contrary-land, for in nearly everything it is different from other parts of the world. In the first place, a large portion of the country is lower than the level of the sea. Great dykes or bulwarks have

been erected, at a heavy cost of money and labor, to keep the ocean where it belongs. On certain parts of the coast it sometimes leans with all its weight against the land, and it is as much as the poor country can do to stand the pressure. Sometimes the dykes give way, or spring a leak, and the most disastrous results ensue. They are high and wide, and the tops of some of them are covered with buildings and trees. They have even fine public roads upon them, from which horses may look down upon wayside cottages. Often the keels of floating ships are higher than the roofs of the dwellings. The stork clattering to her young on the house-peak may feel that her nest is lifted far out of danger, but the croaking frog in neighboring bulrushes is nearer the stars than she. Water bugs dart backward and forward above the heads of the chimney swallows; and willow trees seem drooping with shame, because they cannot reach as high as the reeds near by.

Ditches, canals, ponds, rivers, and lakes are everywhere to be seen. High, but not dry, they shine in the sunlight, catching nearly all the bustle and the business, quite scorning the tame fields stretching damply beside them. One is tempted to ask, "which is Holland—the shores or the water?" The very verdure that should be confined to the land has made a mistake and settled upon the fishponds. In fact, the entire country is a kind of saturated sponge or, as the English poet, Butler, called it,

"A land that rides at anchor, and is moor'd,
    In which they do not live, but go aboard."

Persons are born, live, and die, and even have their gardens on canal boats. Farmhouses, with roofs like great slouched hats pulled over their eyes, stand on wooden legs with a tucked-up sort of air, as if to say "we intend to keep dry if we can." Even the horses wear a wide stool on each hoof to lift them out of the mire. In short, the landscape everywhere suggests a paradise for ducks. It is a glorious country in summer for bare-footed girls and boys. Such wadings! Such mimic ship-sailing! Such rowing, fishing, and swimming! Only think of a chain of puddles where one can launch chip boats all day long, and never make a return trip! But enough. A full recital would set all young America rushing in a body toward the Zuider Zee.

2 Summerhouse.

Dutch cities seem at first sight to be a bewildering jungle of houses, bridges, churches, and ships sprouting into masts, steeples, and trees. In some cities vessels are hitched like horses to their owners' door-posts and receive their freight from the upper windows. Mothers scream to Lodewyk and Kassy not to swing on the garden gate for fear they may be drowned! Water roads are more frequent there than common roads and railways; water fences in the form of lazy green ditches enclose pleasure ground, polder, and garden.

Sometimes fine green hedges are seen; but wooden fences such as we have in America are rarely met with in Holland. As for stone fences, a Dutchman would lift his hands with astonishment at the very idea. There is no stone there excepting those great masses of rock that have been brought from other lands to strengthen and protect the coast. All the small stones or pebbles, if there ever were any, seem to be imprisoned in pavements or quite melted away. Boys with strong, quick arms may grow from pinafores to full beards without ever finding one to start the water rings or set the rabbits flying. The water roads are nothing less than canals intersecting the country in every direction. These are of all sizes, from the great North Holland Ship Canal, which is the wonder of the world, to those which a boy can leap. Water omnibuses, called *trekschuiten*,[3] constantly ply up and down these roads for the conveyance of passengers; and water drays, called *pakschuyten*,[3] are used for carrying fuel and merchandise. Instead of green country lanes, green canals stretch from field to barn and from barn to garden; and the farms, or *polders* as they are termed, are merely great lakes pumped dry. Some of the busiest streets are water, while many of the country roads are paved with brick. The city boats with their rounded sterns, gilded prows, and gaily painted sides are unlike any others under the sun; and a Dutch wagon with its funny little crooked pole is a perfect mystery of mysteries.

[3] Canal boats. Some of the first named are over thirty feet long. They look like green houses lodged on barges, and are drawn by horses walking along the bank of the canal. The trekschuiten are divided into two compartments, first and second class, and when not too crowded the passengers make themselves quite at home in them; the men smoke, the women knit or sew, while children play upon the small outer deck. Many of the canal boats have white, yellow, or chocolate-colored sails. This last color is caused by a preparation of tan which is put on to preserve them.

"One thing is clear," cries Master Brightside, "the inhabitants need never be thirsty." But no, Odd-land is true to itself still. Notwithstanding the sea pushing to get in, and the lakes struggling to get out, and the overflowing canals, rivers, and ditches in many districts there is no water fit to swallow; our poor Hollanders must go dry, or drink wine and beer, or send far into the inland to Utrecht and other favored localities for that precious fluid older than Adam yet young as the morning dew. Sometimes, indeed, the inhabitants can swallow a shower when they are provided with any means of catching it; but generally they are like the Albatross-haunted sailors in Coleridge's famous poem of "The Ancient Mariner"—they see

> "Water, water everywhere,
> Nor any drop to drink!"

Great flapping windmills all over the country make it look as if flocks of huge sea birds were just settling upon it. Everywhere one sees the funniest trees, bobbed into fantastical shapes, with their trunks painted a dazzling white, yellow, or red. Horses are often yoked three abreast. Men, women, and children go clattering about in wooden shoes with loose heels; peasant girls who cannot get beaux for love, hire them for money to escort them to the Kermis;[4] and husbands and wives lovingly *harness* themselves side by side on the bank of the canal and drag their *pakschuyts* to market.

Another peculiar feature of Holland is the *dune* or sand hill. These are numerous along certain portions of the coast. Before they were sown with coarse reed-grass and other plants, to hold them down, they used to send great storms of sand over the inland. So, to add to the oddities, farmers sometimes dig down under the surface to find their soil, and on windy days *dry* showers (of sand) often fall upon fields that have grown wet under a week of sunshine.

In short, almost the only familiar thing we Yankees can meet with in Holland is a harvest song which is quite popular there, though no linguist could translate it. Even then we must shut our eyes and listen only to the tune which I leave you to guess.

[4] Fair.

"Yanker didee, dudel down
Didee dudel lawnter;
Yankee viver, voover, vown,
Botermelk und Tawnter!"

On the other hand, many of the oddities of Holland serve only to prove the thrift and perseverance of the people. There is not a richer, or more carefully tilled garden spot in the whole world than this leaky, springy little country. There is not a braver, more heroic race than its quiet, passive-looking inhabitants. Few nations have equaled it in important discoveries and inventions; none has excelled it in commerce, navigation, learning, and science—or set as noble examples in the promotion of education and public charities; and none in proportion to its extent has expended more money and labor upon public works.

Holland has its shining annals of noble and illustrious men and women; its grand, historic records of patience, resistance, and victory; its religious freedom, its enlightened enterprise, its art, its music, and its literature. It has truly been called "the battle field of Europe," as truly may we consider it the asylum of the world, for the oppressed of every nation have there found shelter and encouragement. If we Americans, who after all are homeopathic preparations of Holland stock, can laugh at the Dutch, and call them human beavers, and hint that their country may float off any day at high tide, we can also feel proud, and say they have proved themselves heroes, and that their country will *not* float off while there is a Dutchman left to grapple it.

There are said to be at least ninety-nine hundred large windmills in Holland, with sails ranging from eighty to one hundred and twenty feet long. They are employed in sawing timber, beating hemp, grinding, and many other kinds of work; but their principal use is for pumping water from the lowlands into the canals, and for guarding against the inland freshets that so often deluge the country. Their yearly cost is said to be nearly ten millions of dollars. The large ones are of great power. Their huge, circular tower, rising sometimes from the midst of factory buildings, is surmounted with a smaller one tapering into a cap-like roof. This upper tower is encircled at its base with a balcony, high above which juts the axis turned by its four prodigious, ladder-backed sails.

Many of the windmills are primitive affairs, seeming sadly in need of Yankee "improvements"; but some of the new ones are admirable. They are so constructed that, by some ingenious contrivance, they present their fans, or wings, to the wind in precisely the right direction to work with the requisite power. In other words, the miller may take a nap and feel quite sure that his mill will study the wind, and make the most of it, until he wakens. Should there be but a slight current of air, every sail will spread itself to catch the faintest breath; but if a heavy "blow" should come, they will shrink at its touch, like great mimosa leaves, and only give it half a chance to move them.

One of the old prisons of Amsterdam, called the Rasphouse, because the thieves and vagrants who were confined there were employed in rasping logwood, had a cell for the punishment of lazy prisoners. In one corner of this cell was a pump, and in another an opening through which a steady stream of water was admitted. The prisoner could take his choice, either to stand still and be drowned, or to work for dear life at the pump and keep the flood down until his jailer chose to relieve him. Now it seems to me that, throughout Holland, Nature has introduced this little diversion on a grand scale. The Dutch have always been forced to pump for their very existence and probably must continue to do so to the end of time.

Every year millions of dollars are spent in repairing dykes and regulating water levels. If these important duties were neglected the country would be uninhabitable. Already, dreadful consequences, as I have said, have followed the bursting of these dykes. Hundreds of villages and towns have from time to time been buried beneath the rush of waters, and nearly a million of persons have been destroyed. One of the most fearful inundations ever known occurred in the autumn of the year 1570. Twenty-eight terrible floods had before that time overwhelmed portions of Holland, but this was the most terrible of all. The unhappy country had long been suffering under Spanish tyranny; now, it seemed, the crowning point was given to its troubles. When we read Motley's history of the "Rise of the

Dutch Republic" we learn to revere the brave people who have endured, suffered, and dared so much.

Mr. Motley in his thrilling account of the great inundation tells us how a long continued and violent gale had been sweeping the Atlantic waters into the North Sea, piling them against the coasts of the Dutch provinces; how the dykes, tasked beyond their strength, burst in all directions; how even the Hand-boss, a bulwark formed of oaken piles, braced with iron, moored with heavy anchors, and secured by gravel and granite, was snapped to pieces like pack thread; how fishing boats and bulky vessels floating up into the country became entangled among the trees, or beat in the roofs and walls of dwellings, and how at last all Friesland was converted into an angry sea. "Multitudes of men, women, children, of horses, oxen, sheep, and every domestic animal were struggling in the waves in every direction. Every boat and every article which could serve as a boat were eagerly seized upon. Every house was inundated, even the graveyards gave up their dead. The living infant in his cradle, and the long-buried corpse in his coffin, floated side by side. The ancient flood seemed about to be renewed. Everywhere, upon the tops of trees, upon the steeples of churches, human beings were clustered, praying to God for mercy and to their fellowmen for assistance. As the storm at last was subsiding, boats began to ply in every direction, saving those who were struggling in the water, picking fugitives from roofs and tree tops, and collecting the bodies of those already drowned." No less than one hundred thousand human beings had perished in a few hours. Thousands upon thousands of dumb creatures lay dead upon the waters; and the damage done to property of every description was beyond calculation.

Robles, the Spanish governor, was foremost in noble efforts to save life and lessen the horrors of the catastrophe. He had formerly been hated by the Dutch because of his Spanish or Portuguese blood, but by his goodness and activity in their hour of disaster he won all hearts to gratitude. He soon introduced an improved method of constructing the dykes, and passed a law that they should in future be kept up by the owners of the soil. There were fewer heavy floods from this time, though within less than three hundred years six fearful inundations swept over the land.

In the spring there is always great danger of inland freshets, especially in times of thaw, because the rivers, choked with blocks of ice, overflow before they can discharge their rapidly rising waters into the ocean. Added to this, the sea chafing and pressing against the dykes, it is no wonder that Holland is often in a state of alarm. The greatest care is taken to prevent accidents. Engineers and workmen are stationed all along in threatened places and a close watch is kept up night and day. When a general signal of danger is given, the inhabitants all rush to the rescue, eager to combine against their common foe. As everywhere else straw is supposed to be of all things the most helpless in the water, of course in Holland it must be rendered the mainstay against a rushing tide. Huge straw mats are pressed against the embankments, fortified with clay and heavy stone, and, once adjusted, the ocean dashes against them in vain.

Raff Brinker, the father of Gretel and Hans, had for years been employed upon the dykes. It was at the time of a threatened inundation, when in the midst of a terrible storm, in darkness and sleet, the men were laboring at a weak spot near the Veermyk sluice, that he fell from scaffolding, and was taken home insensible. From that hour he never worked again; though he lived on, mind and memory were gone.

Gretel could not remember him otherwise than as the strange, silent man, whose eyes followed her vacantly whichever way she turned; but Hans had recollections of a hearty, cheerful-voiced father who was never tired of bearing him upon his shoulder, and whose careless song still seemed echoing near when he lay awake at night and listened.

THE SILVER SKATES

Dame Brinker earned a scanty support for her family by raising vegetables, spinning, and knitting. Once she had worked on board the barges plying up and down the canal, and had occasionally been harnessed with other women to the towing rope of a *pakschuyt* plying between Broek and Amsterdam. But when Hans had grown strong and large he had insisted upon doing all such drudgery in her place. Besides, her husband had become so very helpless of late that he required her constant care. Although not having as much intelligence as a little child, he was yet strong of arm and very hearty, and Dame Brinker had sometimes great trouble in controlling him.

"Ah! children, he was so good and steady," she would sometimes say, "and as wise as a lawyer. Even the Burgomaster would stop to ask him a question, and now alack! he don't know his wife and little ones. You remember the father, Hans, when he was himself—a great brave man—don't you?"

"Yes, indeed, mother, he knew everything, and could do anything under the sun—and how he would sing! why, you used to laugh and say it was enough to set the windmills dancing."

"So I did. Bless me! how the boy remembers! Gretel, child, take that knitting needle from your father, quick; he'll get it in his eyes maybe; and put the shoe on him. His poor feet are like ice half the time, but I can't keep 'em covered all I can do—" and then half wailing, half humming, Dame Brinker would sit down, and fill the low cottage with the whirr of her spinning wheel.

Nearly all the outdoor work, as well as the household labor, was performed by Hans and Gretel. At certain seasons of the year the children went out day after day to gather peat, which they would stow away in square, bricklike pieces for fuel. At other times, when home-work permitted, Hans rode the towing horses on the canals, earning a few *stivers*[5] a day; and Gretel tended geese for the neighboring farmers.

Hans was clever at carving in wood, and both he and Gretel were good gardeners. Gretel could sing and sew and run on great, high, home-made stilts better than any girl for miles around. She could learn a ballad in five minutes, and find, in its season, any weed or flower you could name; but she dreaded books, and often the very sight of the figuring-board in the old schoolhouse would set her eyes swimming. Hans, on the contrary, was slow and steady. The harder the task, whether in study or daily labor, the better he liked it. Boys who sneered at him out of school, on account of his patched clothes and scant

leather breeches, were forced to yield him the post of honor in nearly every class. It was not long before he was the only youngster in the school who had not stood at least *once* in the corner of horrors, where hung a dreaded whip, and over it this motto:

"Leer, leer! jou luigaart, of dit endje touw zal je leren!"[6]

It was only in winter that Gretel and Hans could be spared to attend school; and for the past month they had been kept at home because their mother needed their services. Raff Brinker required constant attention, and there was black bread to be made, and the house to be kept clean, and stockings and other things to be knitted and sold in the market place.

While they were busily assisting their mother on this cold December morning, a merry troop of girls and boys came skimming down the canal. There were fine skaters among them and, as the bright medley of costumes flitted by, it looked from a distance as though the ice had suddenly thawed and some gay tulip-bed were floating along on the current.

There was the rich burgomaster's daughter, Hilda van Gleck, with her costly furs and loose-fitting velvet sacque; and nearby a pretty peasant girl, Annie Bouman, jauntily attired in a coarse scarlet jacket and a blue skirt just short enough to display the gray homespun hose to advantage. Then there was the proud Rychie Korbes, whose father, Mynheer van Korbes, was one of the leading men of Amsterdam; and, flocking closely around her, Carl Schummel, Peter and Ludwig[7] van Holp, Jacob Poot, and a very small boy rejoicing in the tremendous name of Voostenwalbert Schimmelpenninck. There were nearly twenty other boys and girls in the party, and one and all seemed full of excitement and frolic.

Up and down the canal within the space of a half mile they skated, exerting their racing powers to the utmost. Often the swiftest among them was seen to dodge from under the very nose of some pompous law-giver or doctor, who with

---

[5] A stiver is worth about two cents of our money.

[6] (Learn! learn! you idler, or this rope's end shall teach you.)
[7] Ludwig, Gretel and Carl were named after German friends. The Dutch form would be Lodewyk, Grietje, and Karel.

folded arms was skating leisurely toward the town; or a chain of girls would suddenly break at the approach of a fat old burgomaster who, with gold-headed cane poised in air, was puffing his way to Amsterdam. Equipped in skates wonderful to behold, from their superb strappings and dazzling runners curving over the instep and topped with gilt balls, he would open his fat eyes a little if one of the maidens chanced to drop him a courtesy, but would not dare to bow in return for fear of losing his balance.

Not only pleasure-seekers and stately men of note were upon the canal. There were work-people, with weary eyes, hastening to their shops and factories; market-women with loads upon their heads; peddlers bending with their packs; bargemen with shaggy hair and bleared faces, jostling roughly on their way; kind-eyed clergymen speeding perhaps to the bedside of the dying; and, after awhile, groups of children with satchels slung over their shoulders, whizzing past towards the distant school. One and all wore skates excepting, indeed, a muffled-up farmer whose queer cart bumped along on the margin of the canal.

Before long our merry boys and girls were almost lost in the confusion of bright colors, the ceaseless motion, and the gleaming of skates flashing back the sunlight. We might have known no more of them had not the whole party suddenly come to a standstill and, grouping themselves out of the way of the passers-by, all talked at once to a pretty little maiden, whom they had drawn from the tide of people flowing toward the town.

"Oh, Katrinka!" they cried, in a breath, "have you heard of it? The race—we want you to join!"

"What race?" asked Katrinka, laughing—"Don't all talk at once, please, I can't understand."

Every one panted and looked at Rychie Korbes, who was their acknowledged spokeswoman.

"Why," said Rychie, "we are to have a grand skating match on the twentieth, on Mevrouw[8] van Gleck's birthday. It's all Hilda's work. They are going to give a splendid prize to the best skater."

[8] Mrs. or Madame (pronounced Meffrow).

"Yes," chimed in a half a dozen voices, "a beautiful pair of silver skates—perfectly magnificent! with, oh! such straps and silver bells and buckles!"

"*Who* said they had bells?" put in the small voice of the boy with the big name.

"*I* say so, Master Voost," replied Rychie.

"So they have,——" "No, I'm sure they haven't——" "*Oh*, how can you say so?——" "it's an arrow——" "and Mynheer van Korbes told *my* mother they had bells——" came from sundry of the excited group; but Mynheer Voostenwalbert Schimmelpenninck essayed to settle the matter with a decisive—

"Well, you don't any of you know a single thing about it; they haven't a sign of a bell on them, they—"

"Oh! oh!" and the chorus of conflicting opinion broke forth again.

"The girls' pair are to have bells," interposed Hilda, quietly, "but there is to be another pair for the boys with an arrow engraved upon the sides."

"*There!* I told you so!" cried nearly all the youngsters in a breath.

Katrinka looked at them with bewildered eyes.

"Who is to try?" she asked.

"All of us," answered Rychie. "It will be such fun! And you must, too, Katrinka. But it's school time now, we will talk it all over at noon. Oh! you will join of course."

Katrinka, without replying, made a graceful pirouette, and laughing out a coquettish—"Don't you hear the last bell? Catch me!"—darted off toward the schoolhouse, standing half a mile away, on the canal.

All started, pell-mell, at this challenge, but they tried in vain to catch the bright-eyed, laughing creature who, with golden hair streaming in the sunlight, cast back many a sparkling glance of triumph as she floated onward.

Beautiful Katrinka! Flushed with youth and health, all life and mirth and motion, what wonder thine image, ever floating in advance, sped through one boy's dreams that night! What wonder that it seemed his darkest hour when, years afterward, thy presence floated away from him forever.

HANS AND GRETEL
FIND A FRIEND

At noon our young friends poured forth from the schoolhouse intent upon having an hour's practising upon the canal.

They had skated but a few moments when Carl Schummel said mockingly to Hilda:

"There's a pretty pair just coming upon the ice! The little rag-pickers! Their skates must have been a present from the king direct."

"They are patient creatures," said Hilda, gently. "It must have been hard to learn to skate upon such queer affairs. They are very poor peasants, you see. The boy has probably made the skates himself."

Carl was somewhat abashed.

"Patient they may be, but, as for skating, they start off pretty well only to finish with a jerk. They could move well to your new *staccato* piece I think."

Hilda laughed pleasantly and left him. After joining a small detachment of the races, and sailing past every one of them, she halted beside Gretel who, with eager eyes, had been watching the sport.

"What is your name, little girl?"

"Gretel, my lady," answered the child, somewhat awed by Hilda's rank, though they were nearly of the same age, "and my brother is called Hans."

"Hans is a stout fellow," said Hilda, cheerily, "and seems to have a warm stove somewhere within him, but *you* look cold. You should wear more clothing, little one."

Gretel, who had nothing else to wear, tried to laugh as she answered:

"I am not so very little. I am past twelve years old."

"Oh, I beg your pardon. You see I am nearly fourteen, and so large of my age that other girls seem small to me, but that is nothing. Perhaps you will shoot up far above me yet; not unless you dress more warmly, though—shivering girls never grow."

Hans flushed as he saw tears rising in Gretel's eyes.

"My sister has not complained of the cold; but this is bitter weather they say—" and he looked sadly upon Gretel.

"It is nothing," said Gretel. "I am often warm—too warm when I am skating. You are good jufvrouw[9] to think of it."

"No, no," answered Hilda, quite angry at herself. "I am careless, cruel; but I meant no harm. I wanted to ask you—I mean—if—" and here Hilda, coming to the point of her errand, faltered before the poorly clad but noble-looking children she wished to serve.

"What is it, young lady?" exclaimed Hans eagerly. "If there is any service I can do? any——"

"Oh! no, no," laughed Hilda, shaking off her embarrassment, "I only wished to speak to you about the grand race. Why do you not join it? You both can skate well, and the ranks are free. Any one may enter for the prize."

Gretel looked wistfully at Hans, who tugging at his cap, answered respectfully:

"Ah, jufvrouw, even if we could enter, we could skate only a few strokes with the rest. Our skates are hard wood you see," holding up the sole of his foot, "but they soon become damp, and then they stick and trip us."

Gretel's eyes twinkled with fun as she thought of Hans' mishap in the morning, but she blushed as she faltered out timidly:

"Oh no, we can't join; but may we be there, my lady, on the great day to look on?"

"Certainly," answered Hilda, looking kindly into the two earnest faces, and wishing from her heart that she had not spent so much of her monthly allowance for lace and finery. She had but eight kwartjes[10] left, and they would buy but one pair of skates, at the furthest.

Looking down with a sigh at the two pair of feet so very different in size, she asked:

"Which of you is the better skater?"

"Gretel," replied Hans, promptly.

"Hans," answered Gretel, in the same breath. Hilda smiled.

"I cannot buy you each a pair of skates, or even one good pair; but here are eight kwartjes. Decide between you which stands the best chance of winning the race, and buy the skates accordingly. I wish I had enough to buy better ones—

[9] Miss—Young lady (pronounced yuffrow). In studied or polite address it would be jongvrowe (pronounced youngfrow).
[10] A kwartje is a small silver coin worth one-quarter of a guilder, or ten cents in American currency.

good-bye!" and, with a nod and a smile, Hilda, after handing the money to the electrified Hans, glided swiftly away to rejoin her companions.

"Jufvrouw! jufvrouw van Gleck!" called Hans in a loud tone, stumbling after her as well as he could, for one of his skate strings was untied.

Hilda turned, and with one hand raised to shield her eyes from the sun, seemed to him to be floating through the air, nearer and nearer.

"We cannot take this money;" panted Hans, "though we know your goodness in giving it."

"Why not indeed?" asked Hilda, flushing.

"Because," replied Hans, bowing like a clown, but looking with the eye of a prince at the queenly girl, "we have not earned it."

Hilda was quick-witted. She had noticed a pretty wooden chain upon Gretel's neck,—

"Carve me a chain, Hans, like the one your sister wears."

"That I will, lady, with all my heart, we have whitewood in the house, fine as ivory; you shall have one tomorrow," and Hans hastily tried to return the money.

"No, no," said Hilda, decidedly. "That sum will be but a poor price for the chain," and off she darted, outstripping the fleetest among the skaters.

Hans sent a long, bewildered gaze after her; it was useless he felt to make any further resistance.

"It is right," he muttered, half to himself, half to his faithful shadow, Gretel, "I must work hard every minute, and sit up half the night if the mother will let me burn a candle; but the chain shall be finished. We may keep the money, Gretel."

"What a good little lady!" cried Gretel clapping her hands with delight, "oh! Hans, was it for nothing the stork settled on our roof last summer? Do you remember how the mother said it would bring us luck, and how she cried when Janzoon Kolp shot him? And she said it would bring him trouble. But the luck has come to us at last! Now, Hans, if mother sends us to town tomorrow you can buy the skates in the market place."

Hands shook his head. "The young lady would have given us the money to buy skates; but if I *earn* it, Gretel, it shall be spent for wool. You must have a warm jacket."

"Oh!" cried Gretel, in real dismay, "not buy the skates! Why I am not often cold! Mother says the blood runs up and down in poor children's veins humming 'I must keep 'em warm! I must keep 'em warm.'"

"Oh, Hans," she continued with something like a sob, "don't say you won't buy the skates, it makes me feel just like crying—besides, I want to be cold—I mean I'm real, awful warm—so now!"

Hans looked up hurriedly. He had a true Dutch horror of tears, or emotion of any kind, and, most of all, he dreaded to see his sister's blue eyes overflowing.

"Now mind," cried Gretel, seeing her advantage, "I'll feel awful if you give up the skates. *I* don't want them. I'm not such a stingy as that; but I want *you* to have them, and then when I get bigger they'll do for me—oh-h—count the pieces, Hans. Did ever you see so many!"

Hans turned the money thoughtfully in his palm. Never in all his life had he longed so intensely for a pair of skates, for he had known of the race and had, boy-like, fairly ached for a chance to test his powers with the other children. He felt confident that with a good pair of steel runners, he could readily distance most of the boys on the canal. Then, too, Gretel's argument was so plausible. On the other hand, he knew that she, with her strong but lithe little frame, needed but a week's practice on good runners, to make her a better skater than Rychie Korbes or even Katrinka Flack. As soon as this last thought flashed upon him his resolve was made. If Gretel would not have the jacket, she should have the skates.

"No, Gretel," he answered at last, "I can wait. Some day I may have money enough saved to buy a fine pair. You shall have these."

Gretel's eyes sparkled; but in another instant she insisted, rather faintly:

"The young lady gave the money to *you*, Hans. I'd be real bad to take it."

Hans shook his head, resolutely, as he trudged on, causing his sister to half skip and half walk in her effort to keep beside him; by this time they had taken off their wooden "rockers," and were hastening home to tell their mother the good news.

"Oh! *I* know!" cried Gretel, in a sprightly tone. "You can do this. You can get a pair a little too small for you, and too big for me, and we can take turns and use them. Won't that be fine?" and Gretel clapped her hands again.

Poor Hans! This was a strong temptation, but he pushed it away from him, brave-hearted fellow that he was.

"Nonsense, Gretel. You could never get on with a big pair. You stumbled about with these, like a blind chicken, before I curved off the ends. No, you must have a pair to fit exactly, and you must practice every chance you can get, until the 20th comes. My little Gretel shall win the silver skates."

Gretel could not help laughing with delight at the very idea.

"Hans! Gretel!" called out a familiar voice.

"Coming, mother!" and they hastened toward the cottage, Hans still shaking the pieces of silver in his hand.

On the following day, there was not a prouder nor a happier boy in all Holland than Hans Brinker as he watched his sister, with many a dexterous sweep, flying in and out among the skaters who at sundown thronged the canal. A warm jacket had been given her by the kind-hearted Hilda, and the burst-out shoes had been cobbled into decency by Dame Brinker. As the little creature darted backward and forward, flushed with enjoyment, and quite unconscious of the many wondering glances bent upon her, she felt that the shining runners beneath her feet had suddenly turned earth into Fairyland, while "Hans, dear, good Hans!" echoed itself over and over again in her grateful heart.

"By den donder!" exclaimed Peter van Holp to Carl Schummel, "but that little one in the red jacket and patched petticoat skates well. Gunst! she has toes on her heels, and eyes in the back of her head! See her! It will be a joke if she gets in the race and beats Katrinka Flack, after all."

"Hush! not so loud!" returned Carl, rather sneeringly. "That little lady in rags is the special pet of Hilda van Gleck. Those shining skates are her gift, if I make no mistake."

"So! so!" exclaimed Peter, with a radiant smile, for Hilda was his best friend. "She has been at her good work there, too!" And Mynheer van Holp, after cutting a double 8 on the ice, to say nothing of a huge P, then a jump, and an H, glided onward until he found himself beside Hilda.

Hand in hand, they skated together, laughingly at first, then staidly talking in a low tone.

Strange to say, Peter van Holp soon arrived at a sudden conviction that his little sister needed a wooden chain just like Hilda's.

Two days afterward, on St. Nicholas' Eve, Hans, having burned three candle-ends, and cut his thumb into the bargain, stood on the market-place at Amsterdam, buying another pair of skates.

HEIDI

Johanna Spyri

As a child Johanna Spyri lived near Zurich, Switzerland, and spent one summer on the Alps recovering her health. In writing Heidi, her best novel, Mrs. Spyri drew from her acquaintance with the mountains and the people who lived there.

Unlike most authors of her day, she did not try to preach to or "improve" her readers. This is one reason why Heidi is much more popular with children today than Hans Brinker. Heidi is also far better written. The characterizations of Heidi and the Grandfather are masterfully drawn, and the book's continued popularity probably rests on how real they seem to the reader.

Although Heidi *was written in 1880 for German children, in translation it was one of the first good books about another country available for nineteenth-century American children. While Switzerland has changed since then, the story Johanna Spyri tells interests young girls today as much as it did when it first appeared.*

PART ONE—HER YEARS OF LEARNING

1. *Up to the Alm-Uncle*

From the pleasant village of Mayenfeld a path leads through green fields, richly covered with trees, to the foot of the mountain, which from this side majestically overhangs the valley. Where the path grows steeper, and goes straight up to the Alps, the perfume of sweet mountain plants welcomes the traveler.

Along this steep mountain path a sturdy, wholesome girl climbed one clear, sunny morning in June, leading by the hand a child whose cheeks flamed as if an inner fire glowed through her sunburned skin. And little wonder, for the child was as bundled up on this sunny June morning as if she were to be protected from a bitter frost. She could be scarcely more than five years old; but it was impossible to judge her size or shape, for she had on two, if not three, dresses, one on top of the other. And over all, wound around and around, was a long red woolen scarf.

The lumpy figure, with its heavy hobnailed mountain shoes, toiled, hot and weary, up the steep hillside. After an hour's climb from the valley, the two girls reached the hamlet of Dörfli, halfway up the Alm Mountain. Here they were greeted from almost every doorway and along the street, for the older girl had now reached her home town. However, without once stopping, she answered all questions and greetings as she swung along, until they reached the end of the hamlet, where only a few scattered cottages stood. Here someone called from a doorway: "Wait a minute, Dete, I will go with you if you are going farther." As Dete stood still, the child pulled loose and sat down on the ground.

"Are you tired, Heidi?" asked her companion.

"No, but I'm hot," replied the child.

"We are almost there. Try to hold out a little while longer. Take big steps, and in an hour we'll be there," Dete promised. A large, kindly woman came from a doorway to join the pair. The little girl fell in behind the two women who were deep in conversation about Dörfli people.

"Now, where are you taking the child, Dete?" asked the newcomer. "She's your sister's child, isn't she—the little orphan?"

"Yes, she is," said Dete. "I am taking her up to her grandfather's. She'll have to stay with him."

"What! Leave this child with the Alm-Uncle? You're out of your head, Dete. How can you even think of such a thing? He'll soon set you straight!"

"No, no, Barbel. He is her grandfather, and he has to do his share. I've looked after Heidi up to this time, and now I have a chance at a job that I can't pass up because of this child. Her grandfather simply has to take over."

"Yes, if he were like other people, Dete," rejoined Barbel anxiously. "But you know how he is. What's he going to do with a child? Such a young one, too! It won't work. But where are you planning to go?"

"To Frankfort," explained Dete, "where I've been offered a really good place. The family was at the Baths last summer. I took care of their rooms in the hotel, and looked after their comfort so well that they wanted to take me back with them then. Now they have come again, they still want me, and I mean to accept this time."

"I wouldn't want to be that child," said Barbel, shaking her head. "No one knows how he lives up there. He has nothing to do with anybody, year in year out. He never sets foot in church. And when he comes down here once a year, with that heavy stick of his, everyone is afraid of him and keeps out of his way. With his bushy gray eyebrows, and his frightful beard, he looks so like a wild man that people hope they won't meet him alone."

"Just the same," insisted Dete, "he is the grandfather, and he has to take care of the child. He won't hurt her. Anyhow, I'm through."

"I certainly would like to know," Barbel speculated, "what that old man has on his conscience. He always looks around so suspiciously, and he lives all alone up there on the Alm, hiding like a hermit. People say all sorts of queer things about him, but you must know the truth from your sister. Don't you, Dete?"

"Yes, but I'm not telling because if he ever thought I had said anything, I'd get what-for!"

But Barbel had long wanted to know why the Alm-Uncle had lived alone on the mountain top; and why people spoke so cautiously about him, as if they could not say anything favorable, and would not speak against him. Neither did Barbel know why everybody in Dorfli called the old man Alm-Uncle. He could not be the real uncle of all the inhabitants; but as they always called him so, she did, too.

Because Barbel had been married only a short time, and had come from the village of Prattigau after her wedding, she did not yet know all the ins and outs of life in Dorfli, nor the peculiarities of the people there or in the region. Her good friend Dete, however, had been born in Dorfli, and had lived there until her mother's death; then she had gone to Ragatz Bad, to work in the big hotel as chambermaid, at very good pay.

The very morning Dete had come with the child from Ragatz; a friend had given them a ride in his hay cart as far as Mayenfeld. Barbel longed to learn a little more. She laid her hand confidentially on her friend's arm, saying: "Dete, you can tell me the real truth about the Alm-Uncle. I don't believe half that people here say. Do tell me. What's wrong with the old man? And has everyone always been afraid of him? Has he always seemed to hate his fellow beings as he does now?"

"Whether he has always been like this, I can't say, since I'm just twenty-six years old, and he is at least seventy. So don't ask me to tell you how he was when he was young. If I could only be sure that what I tell you wouldn't be spread around in Prattigau, I might give you an earful. My mother and he both came from Domleschg."

"Oh, Dete!" replied Barbel, reproachfully, "what do you mean? We aren't all blabber-mouths in Prattigau, after all. I can keep a secret,

if necessary. So go on and tell me, do. You won't be sorry."

"Well, I will. But mind you keep your word," Dete warned. She looked back, to see if the child were near enough to overhear what they said, but Heidi was nowhere in sight. She had ceased following some time earlier, but they had been too busy talking to notice her absence. Dete stopped, and looked about in every direction. The path made one or two curves, but yet the eye could follow it almost down to Dorfli. There was no one visible for its whole length.

"I see her now!" exclaimed Barbel. "Down there, don't you see her?" and she pointed to a spot quite distant from the mountain path. "She is climbing up the cliff with Peter, the goatherd, and his flock. I wonder why he is so late today? It is lucky for us, for you can go on with your story while he looks after the child."

"Peter won't need to put himself out much, looking after her," said Dete. "She uses her own eyes, and sees everything that goes on. I have found that out, and it's good that she is bright. The old man never will be able to provide much for her. All he has are his two goats and the Alm-hut."

"Did he ever have more?" asked Barbel.

"Oh, my, yes!" replied Dete emphatically. "He used to have the very best farm in Domleschg. He was the eldest son, and had only one brother, who was quiet and steady. But Alm-Uncle was a playboy and ran around with bad company. He gambled away every bit of his property, and when they found out, his father and then his mother died of mortification. His brother had nothing, of course, and he moved away somewhere, out of humiliation. And since Alm-Uncle had nothing left but a bad name, *he* disappeared. At first, no one knew where he had gone, but after a while the word went around that he had joined the army, and gone to Naples. Then nobody heard anything for twelve years or more. All at once he showed up in Domleschg, with a half-grown boy, and tried to get his kinfolks to take them in. When he found every door closed against him, he became embittered and swore he would never set foot in Domleschg again. So he came to Dorfli. He lived here with his boy, maybe he still had a little money, because he gave Tobias, his son, a trade. Tobias was a nice fellow, a carpenter, and well liked by everyone in Dorfli. But nobody trusted the old man. People said that he had deserted from Naples, got in a brawl, and killed someone. But anyhow we recognized the relationship, because my great-grandmother and his mother were ·sisters; so we called him Uncle. Since we are related to everybody in Dorfli, on our father's side, gradually everybody called him Uncle; and when he moved on the Alm, everyone called him Alm-Uncle."

"But what happened to Tobias?" said Barbel, eagerly.

"Wait, I am coming to that. I can't tell you everything at once.

"Tobias went to learn his trade in Mels, and when he finished he returned to Dorfli, and married my sister, Adelheid, whom he had always liked. They got along fine, but, two years later, as Tobias was helping build a house, a beam fell on him and killed him. The shock, and sorrow, gave Adelheid a fever from which she never recovered. Strong and hearty as she had been, she went into a coma, so that you could not tell if she were waking or asleep. Two months after Tobias's death we buried Adelheid.

"Everybody talked about the sad fate of this couple, and they said that it was a judgment on the Uncle for his godless life. Our pastor, appealing to his conscience, told him that he should come to church, but he just glowered and spoke to no one. Finally everyone avoided him. Next we heard, he had gone up to the Alm. Never coming down, he lived withdrawn from God and man.

"When Mother and I took Adelheid's little girl, Heidi, to live with us, she was a year old. Then, after Mother died, I decided to go to the Baths to work; I boarded Heidi at old Ursel's in Pfafferserdorf. I was able to stay at the Baths all winter, for there was plenty of sewing and mending for me to do. As I told you, the family I worked for last year came back from Frankfort early this spring, and they still want to take me back with them. I am going, day after tomorrow, and it's a fine job, believe me."

"And you'll leave that child up there with the old man? I can't understand what you are thinking of, Dete," Barbel shook her head reproachfully.

"What do you mean?" snapped Dete. "I've done my share for the child, and what else can I do? I can't drag along a five-year-old to Frankfort with me. Now where are you going, Barbel? Here we are already halfway up the Alm."

"I've reached the place I want," said Barbel. "I have to speak to the mother of Peter, the goatherd. She spins for me in the winter. So good-bye, Dete! Good luck to you!"

Dete shook hands with her companion. She stood watching Barbel go toward the small dark brown cottage which stood a little way off the main path. Built in a sheltered hollow, halfway up the Alm, the house was so ramshackle and weatherbeaten that—exposed to the fierce mountain winds—it seemed a dangerous dwelling.

Indeed, it looked as if it might be swept down into the valley at any time. Here lived Peter, the eleven-year-old boy whose business it was to drive the goats from Dorfli, every morning, up on the Alm, to let them crop the short, succulent bushes that grew there. In the evening he led his nimble-footed herd down into Dorfli again and gave a shrill whistle on his fingers as a signal to the owners to come to the little square and get their goats. Usually, little boys and girls came for the animals, for such gentle creatures could do them no harm. All summer long, this was the only time of day when Peter was with young companions. All the rest of the time he spent alone with his goats.

To be sure, he had the company of his mother and his blind grandmother; but he left the hut early in the morning, and returned late from Dorfli. Because he wanted to play with the children as long as possible, he spent only enough time at home to swallow his bread and milk.

His father, who also had been called goat-Peter, had been killed while felling trees the year before. His mother, whose name was Brigitte, was always spoken of as goat-Peterin, or goat-Peter's mother, and "Grandmother" was what everybody, far and near, called his blind grandmother.

Dete stood waiting for a full ten minutes, looking in every direction for the children and the goats, who again were nowhere to be seen. Then, impatiently, she climbed still higher to get a better view of the valley, searching in every direction.

In the meantime, the children had gone a roundabout way. Peter knew of many spots where there were all sorts of fine bushes and herbs for his goats to nibble. To reach these, he wandered from one place to another with his flock. At first Heidi laboriously climbed after him. Encumbered by her heavy wraps, she was obliged to exert all her little strength just to keep going.

She said nothing, however, but studied first Peter, who, with his bare feet and light trousers, sprang here and there without the least trouble; and then the goats, with their thin, slender legs, climbing still more easily over bushes and stones, and even up the precipices. Suddenly Heidi sat down and pulled off her shoes and stockings. Up again, she threw off the thick woolen scarf; then, unfastening the buttons on her top dress, she flung it away, and began undoing the next one. To avoid carrying the clothes, Dete had put on all the child's Sunday things over her everyday garments. In a twinkling Heidi tore off her everyday dress too, and stood in her petticoat, delightedly stretching her bare arms out of the short sleeves of her little undershirt into the cooling wind.

Then she folded all her clothes into a neat pile and scrambled after the goats to Peter.

Peter had not noticed what the child was doing while she stayed behind, but when she came up beside him in her new costume he grinned. Then as he looked back and saw the little heap of clothes, his grin broadened, but he said nothing.

Now that Heidi felt herself so free and comfortable, she began to talk to the boy, and he had to answer all sorts of questions. How many goats had he? Where was he taking them, and what did he do when he reached his destination? At last, however, the children and the goats reached the hut, and Aunt Dete caught sight of them.

As soon as she saw her niece, she shouted, "Whatever have you been doing, Heidi? What have you done with your two dresses? And the shawl? And the new shoes that I bought you for the mountain? Where are the new stockings I knitted for you myself? Are they all gone? What have you done with them all?"

Heidi pointed down the mountainside. "There," she said.

Dete looked. Down below she saw something —and on the top of it was a spot of red. Was that the scarf?

"You mischievous girl!" cried Dete. "Why have you taken your clothes off? What does it mean?"

"I don't need them," Heidi replied, and did not look the least bit sorry for what she had done.

"Oh, you thoughtless child!" Dete scolded. "Who is to go for them now? It will take at least a half-hour. Peter, do run down and fetch them for me. Well, don't stand there staring, as if you were nailed to the earth."

"I am late already," Peter replied, not stirring from the spot, and with his hands in his pockets, just as he'd stood when Dete's cries had first reached him.

"Come now, you shall have something nice for your trouble," Dete coaxed. "Do you see this?" She showed him a shining new coin.

Instantly he ran down the mountain, taking the shortest way, and reached the clothes in great strides. He scooped them up, and was back again so quickly that Dete had to praise him and give him the promised coin without delay. Peter thrust it deep into his pocket, his face beaming with pleasure, for a treasure like this rarely fell to his lot.

"You can carry the things for us up to Alm-Uncle's. You are going that way, I believe," said Dete, while she applied herself to climbing the path that rose steeply behind the goatherd's hut. He followed her willingly, carrying the bundle under his left arm, while he swung his rod with his right.

Heidi and the goats leaped about joyfully in every direction.

Thus the small procession at last reached the summit of the Alm, after three-quarters of an hour's climbing. There stood the old uncle's hut, exposed to all the winds of heaven, but taking advantage of every ray of sunlight, and commanding a most beautiful view of the valley.

Behind the hut grew three very old pine trees, with long, thick branches. Then the mountain rose up and up to the old gray rocks, first over slopes covered with succulent herbs, then through thickly strewn boulders. At last came the bald, steep cliffs.

On the side of his hut overlooking the valley, Alm-Uncle had put a bench. Here he sat now. His pipe was in his mouth and his hands rested on his knees as he watched the children, the goats, and Aunt Dete clambering up the slope.

Heidi reached the summit first, and went directly to the old man. Stretching out her hand, she said, "Good evening, Grandfather."

"Well! And what does this mean?" answered the Alm-Uncle, his voice harsh. However, he gave his hand to the small girl and looked at her with a steady piercing gaze from under great bushy eyebrows.

Heidi returned his look with equal steadiness. What a strange-looking man, was this grandfather of hers, with his long beard, and his gray eyebrows growing together in the middle. She had never seen anyone like him.

Meanwhile, Peter and Dete came to stand beside Heidi, Peter staying on to see what would happen.

"Good day, Uncle," said Dete. "I have brought you Tobias and Adelheid's child, whom you have not seen since she was only a year old."

"And what is this child to do with me?" demanded the old man. "You there!" he gestured to Peter, "move along with your goats. You are late! Take mine with you."

Peter jumped to obey. No one argued with Alm-Uncle.

"The child is to stay here with you," Dete began in a firm voice, "I have done my duty by her for four years. It is your turn now."

"Indeed!" roared the old man, his eyes flashing, "and if she starts to cry and whimper for you, what am I to do then?"

"That is your affair," Dete said. "No one told me what to do with her when she was thrust upon me—a year-old mite. What with my mother and myself to look after, I had my hands full already. Now I must go my way, and you are Heidi's next of kin. If you don't want to keep her, do what you please with her. Whatever happens to her is your business now."

For all her blustering, Dete's conscience was not easy, and she was working herself up into a temper, saying much more than she really meant. At her last words, Alm-Uncle stood up. He looked at her so strangely that she retreated a couple of steps.

"Go right on back where you came from," he shouted, "and don't come around any more."

Dete wasted no time. "Good-bye then—and to you, too, Heidi," she said, and ran down the mountainside without stopping, until she reached Dorfli. In Dorfli, people called to her and tried to

stop her, for they all were curious to know what had become of the child. They knew Dete well, and they knew whose child Heidi was, too. "Where is the little girl? What have you done with the young one, Dete?" they called from doors and windows.

"Up there with the Alm-Uncle," she shouted back impatiently, without stopping.

But she was not comfortable about the situation. Everybody seemed too shocked. "How could you do it?" "The poor, poor little thing! How could you leave that helpless child up there?" All through the town horrified voices pursued her. "The poor tot!" "Poor motherless soul."

Dete raced on, and soon was beyond the reach of their voices. But her mind was troubled, for her mother, as she lay dying, had entrusted this grandchild, Heidi, to Dete. She tried to still her conscience by telling herself that she could do more for the child once she was in her fine new job. Nevertheless, she was glad to get away as quickly as possible from the questions and reproaches of her old friends.

2. At the Grandfather's

When Dete had left them, the old man sat down on his bench once more. Blowing great clouds of smoke from his pipe, he stared silently at the ground.

Heidi looked about her curiously. Discovering the goat shed, she peeped in, but it was empty, so she went on with her investigations. Finally she ran behind the hut to look at the great old pines.

The wind seemed to sing through the branches. Heidi stood listening, enchanted. But when the wind grew still, she went back to her grandfather. He sat as she had left him. Planting herself directly in front of the old man, she put her small hands behind her back and stared at him.

After a few moments he raised his head. "What do you want?" he asked.

"I want to see what you have there, in the hut," said Heidi.

"Well then, take up your things and come with me," her grandfather said, rising from the bench.

"I don't want them any more," the child said.

The old man turned to inspect his small granddaughter. Her black eyes were dancing with expectation.

"She's bright enough," he murmured to himself. To her he said, "Why don't you want them, child?"

"Because I want to go about like the goats," said Heidi, "to run as they do."

"And so you shall," replied her grandfather. "Bring your things in, anyway, and we will put them away." She picked up the bundle of her clothes and followed him into the one large room which was the entire hut.

The bed was in one corner; in another a big kettle hung over the hearth. There was also a table and a chair. In the wall was a door. This the grandfather opened to show a large closet. There he hung his clothes. On the shelves were shirts, stockings, handkerchiefs, cups, plates, saucers, and glasses. Above him the smoked meat, cheese and a round loaf of bread were set within easy reach. While he held the door open, Heidi stepped up with her bundle of clothes, which she stuffed in behind her grandfather's things, as far out of sight as possible. Then she turned and looked carefully about the room.

"Where shall I sleep, Grandfather?"

"Wherever you wish," he answered.

Pleased, Heidi ran about the room, inspecting every corner, to find the place that would suit her. Near her grandfather's bed stood a ladder which led into the hayloft. Heidi climbed right up and found the loft heaped with fresh, sweet-smelling hay. From a round hole in the rafters she found she could look far down into the valley.

"I'll sleep here!" she cried. "It's beautiful. Do come up, Grandfather, and see how beautiful it is here."

"That I know," he answered from below.

"I shall make my bed here," Heidi said, working busily away, "but you must bring me a sheet. There must be a sheet on my bed."

"Well, now," replied her grandfather. Going to the closet, he searched about, and finally pulled out from under his shirts a long, coarse linen cloth. It might serve as a sheet.

He mounted the ladder with it, and found the hay piled neatly into the shape of a small bed with the head purposely high, so that from it one could look straight through the round open window.

"That is well done," said the old man. "Now we'll put on the sheet, but first—" He took up great armfuls of hay, piling the bed up until it was twice as thick as Heidi had made it. Now she would not feel the hard floor through the hay. "Bring on the sheet," he directed Heidi.

She seized the sheet, but the linen was heavy —and that, of course, was good, for the hay could not get through such thickness. They both spread this sheet over the hay, and Heidi busily tucked it under. Now the bed looked neat and trim, and Heidi stood back to study it thoughtfully. "We have forgotten something, Grandfather," she said at last.

"What is that?"

"A coverlet! When one goes to bed, one must have a coverlet."

"But I have none," he said.

"Oh—well, that's all right," Heidi shrugged. "I'll just get more hay instead." She ran to fetch it, but her grandfather stopped her.

"Wait," he said. He went down the ladder, and over to his bed. Climbing up once more, he placed a heavy linen sack on the floor. "Isn't this better than hay?" he asked.

Heidi tugged at the sack, but she could not manage the heavy stuff. However, with the grandfather's help, it was soon properly arranged, and then the bed looked so nice that Heidi stood entranced.

"It's a perfect bed!" she said. "I wish it were night and bedtime already."

"We might have something to eat first," he suggested. "What do you think?"

Heidi had been so interested in her bed that she had forgotten everything else. Now she suddenly felt very hungry, for she'd eaten nothing since breakfast. And then she'd had only a piece of bread and a little weak coffee. Not much preparation for a long journey. Now she replied heartily to her grandfather's question, "Yes, I think we should."

"Let's go down then," the old man said, and followed her on the ladder.

At the fireplace, he moved the big kettle aside and hung a smaller one in its place on the chain. Then he seated himself on the three-legged stool and blew the fire until there was a good blaze.

Soon the kettle began to boil. Now he held a long iron fork over the fire, with a big piece of cheese speared upon it. This he turned slowly around and around until it became golden yellow.

Heidi watched him, fascinated. Suddenly she had an idea and she ran to the closet, then back again to the table many times. When her grandfather brought the pot, and the toasted cheese on the fork to the table, the round loaf, two plates, and two knives, were already there, all neatly arranged. Heidi had noticed everything in the closet and she knew exactly what was needed for the meal.

"Now this is nice, that you can think of things yourself," the old man said, putting the cheese upon the bread. "But there is still something lacking."

The pot was steaming so invitingly, Heidi knew what was wanted, and dashed to the closet again. She found only one mug, but two glasses stood back of it. She soon returned with a glass and the mug.

"Very good. You are helpful. Now, where will you sit?" Grandfather asked, for he occupied the only high stool himself. Like an arrow Heidi sped back to the fireplace and returned with the little three-legged stool.

Grandfather nodded. "Now you have a seat," he said, "even though it is rather low. However, you would be too short, even on mine, to reach the table; still, you must have something to eat, so begin."

He rose, filled the mug with milk and set it upon the high stool. This he drew up to Heidi so that she had a table to herself. Seating himself on the corner of the table, Grandfather began to eat his dinner also.

Heidi seized the mug and drank and drank without stopping once. All the thirst of her journey seemed to come up at once. Then she drew a long breath and set down her mug.

"Is the milk good?" asked her grandfather.

"I never drank such good milk," Heidi said.

"You must have more, then," he said, filling the mug to the top. Heidi was now eating her bread, spread thickly with the hot cheese. It was soft as butter from the heat, and tasted delicious. She looked perfectly happy.

When they had finished, the old man went out to the goats' shed to put things to rights there. Heidi watched him carefully. First he swept everything up with the broom; then he strewed fresh straw about for the animals to sleep upon. Next he went to the woodpile near by and cut heavy round sticks of the right size and a board to the right shape. He bored holes in it, fitted the sticks in, and it suddenly became a stool like his own, only higher. Heidi was speechless with wonder.

"Do you know what this is, Heidi?" he asked.

"It must be my stool, because it's so high. How fast you made it!" she exclaimed.

"She knows what she sees," the old man said to himself, as he moved around the hut, driving in a nail here, making something fast there, going with his hammer and nails and pieces of wood from one place to another, constantly finding something to do, or to mend. Heidi followed his every step, watched everything that he did with complete attention, for everything that happened interested her.

Evening came at last. The wind sighed through the old trees. As it blew harder, the branches swayed back and forth. Heidi felt the sounds not only in her ears, but in her heart, and she was so happy that she ran out under the pines and leaped about for sheer joy.

Her grandfather stood in the doorway and watched the child.

Suddenly a shrill whistle sounded. Heidi stood still, and the old man stepped out. Down the mountain streamed the goats, one after the other, with Peter in their midst.

With a shout Heidi rushed into the flock, to greet her old friends of the morning.

Reaching the hut, all the animals stopped, and from out of the herd came two beautiful slender goats, one white and one brown. They went to the old man and licked his hands, for he held a small quantity of salt for them every evening as a welcome when they came home. Peter moved on with his flock. Heidi stroked Grandfather's goats gently; one, then the other. Next she ran to the other side, and did the same, delighted with the charming creatures.

"Are they both ours, Grandfather? Will they go into our shed? Will they always stay with us?"

Heidi's questions rushed out in her excitement, with Grandfather scarcely given a chance to answer.

"Yes, child. Yes, yes." When the goats had licked up all the salt, Grandfather said, "Fetch me your little mug and some bread."

Heidi obeyed, and Grandfather first milked the goats into the mug, and then cut bits of bread and dropped them in.

"Now eat your supper, and go to bed," he said. "Dete left another bundle for you with your night clothes and other things. You'll find them in the closet. I must care for the goats now. So sleep soundly."

"Good night, Grandfather!" Heidi shouted after him, as he vanished with the goats. "What are their names, Grandfather?"

"The white one is Schwänli, the other Bärli," he called back.

"Good night, Schwänli! Good night, Bärli!" shouted Heidi at the top of her voice.

With the goats gone, she sat down on the bench to eat her bread and milk, but the wind grew so strong that it almost blew her off her seat.

She ate as fast as she could, went into the cottage, and climbed up to her bed. She no sooner stretched out than she was fast asleep, and she slept all night as comfortably as a princess in a palace.

Before it was quite dark, the old man also went to bed, for he got up by sunrise, which came very early in summer on the mountain. During the night the wind blew so hard that the whole hut shook, and all the beams creaked. The wind roared and moaned in the big chimney; and in the old pine tree it broke some branches off as if in anger.

It awakened the old man and he rose, thinking, "The little one will be afraid."

He climbed the ladder, and went softly into Heidi's loft. The moon was shining brightly through the round hole in the roof, and the beams fell on Heidi's bed. The child slept peacefully, her cheeks rosy, one round arm under her head. Her little face beamed with contentment. Grandfather stood long, gazing at the sleeping child, until clouds obscured the moon. Then he turned and went down the ladder.

LITTLE BLACK SAMBO

Helen Bannerman

In 1889 Helen Bannerman brought her children from India to be educated in Scotland. On her lonely return trip she wrote this story to send back to them. While long considered a classic, beloved by generations of white children, Little Black Sambo *reveals the patronizing attitude held by nineteenth-century Englishmen toward the Indian native and shows what English children were unconsciously taught about a nonwhite culture.*

Today, most readers of Little Black Sambo, *unaware that it is set in India, assume that the characters are Negroes. When this occurs the attitudes created by the book are less than positive. Certainly the fact that the term "Sambo" has been used to express contempt should help parents and teachers understand why Negroes resent this book. Modern Indians would also feel insulted by the tone of* Little Black Sambo.

The story's popularity among those of European descent is in large measure due to Mrs. Bannerman's use of folktale conventions such as cumulative repetition, rapidity of action, and escape from danger.

Once upon a time there was a little black boy, and his name was Little Black Sambo.

And his Mother was called Black Mumbo.

And his Father was called Black Jumbo.

And Black Mumbo made him a beautiful little Red Coat, and a pair of beautiful little Blue Trousers.

And Black Jumbo went to the Bazaar, and bought him a beautiful Green Umbrella, and a lovely little Pair of Purple Shoes with Crimson Soles and Crimson Linings.

And then wasn't Little Black Sambo grand?

So he put on all his Fine Clothes, and went out for a walk in the Jungle. And by and by he met a Tiger. And the Tiger said to him, "Little Black Sambo, I'm going to eat you up!" And Little Black Sambo said, "Oh! Please Mr. Tiger, don't eat me up, and I'll give you my beautiful little Red Coat." So the Tiger said, "Very well, I won't eat you this time, but you must give me your beautiful little Red Coat." So the Tiger got poor Little Black Sambo's beautiful little Red Coat, and went away saying, "Now I'm the grandest Tiger in the Jungle."

And Little Black Sambo went on, and by and by he met another Tiger, and it said to him, "Little Black Sambo, I'm going to eat you up!" And Little Black Sambo said, "Oh! Please Mr. Tiger, don't eat me up, and I'll give you my beautiful little Blue Trousers." So the Tiger said, "Very well, I won't eat you this time, but you must give me your beautiful little Blue Trousers." So the Tiger got poor Little Black Sambo's beautiful little Blue Trousers, and went away saying, "Now I'm the grandest Tiger in the Jungle."

And Little Black Sambo went on and by and by he met another Tiger, and it said to him, "Little Black Sambo, I'm going to eat you up!" And Little Black Sambo said, "Oh! Please Mr. Tiger, don't eat me up, and I'll give you my beautiful little Purple Shoes with Crimson Soles and Crimson Linings."

But the Tiger said, "What use would your shoes be to me? I've got four feet, and you've got only two; you haven't got enough shoes for me."

Little Black Sambo by Helen Bannerman. Published by J. B. Lippincott Company and reprinted in its entirety with their permission.

But Little Black Sambo said, "You could wear them on your ears."

"So I could," said the Tiger: "that's a very good idea. Give them to me, and I won't eat you this time."

So the Tiger got poor Little Black Sambo's beautiful little Purple Shoes with Crimson Soles and Crimson Linings, and went away saying, "Now I'm the grandest Tiger in the Jungle."

And by and by Little Black Sambo met another Tiger, and it said to him, "Little Black Sambo, I'm going to eat you up!" and Little Black Sambo said, "Oh! Please Mr. Tiger, don't eat me up, and I'll give you my beautiful Green Umbrella." But the Tiger said, "How can I carry an umbrella, when I need all my paws for walking with?"

"You could tie a knot on your tail and carry it that way," said Little Black Sambo. "So I could," said the Tiger. "Give it to me, and I won't eat you this time." So he got poor Little Black Sambo's beautiful Green Umbrella, and went away saying, "Now I'm the grandest Tiger in the Jungle."

And poor Little Black Sambo went away crying, because the cruel Tigers had taken all his fine clothes.

Presently he heard a horrible noise that sounded like "Gr-r-r-r-rrrrrrr," and it got louder and louder. "Oh! dear!" said Little Black Sambo, "there are all the Tigers coming back to eat me up! What shall I do?" So he ran quickly to a palm tree, and peeped round it to see what the matter was.

And there he saw all the Tigers fighting, and disputing which of them was the grandest. And at last they all got so angry that they jumped up and took off all the fine clothes, and began to tear each other with their claws, and bite each other with their great big white teeth.

And they came, rolling and tumbling right to the foot of the very tree where Little Black Sambo was hiding, but he jumped quickly in behind the umbrella. And the Tigers all caught hold of each other's tails, as they wrangled and scrambled, and so they found themselves in a ring round the tree.

Then, when the Tigers were very wee and very far away, Little Black Sambo jumped up, and called out, "Oh! Tigers! why have you taken off all your nice clothes? Don't you want them any more?" But the Tigers only answered, "Gr-r-rrrrr!"

Then Little Black Sambo said, "If you want them, say so, or I'll take them away." But the Tigers would not let go of each other's tails, and so they could only say "Gr-r-r-r-rrrrrrr!"

So Little Black Sambo put on all his fine clothes again and walked off.

And the Tigers were very, very angry, but still they would not let go of each other's tails. And they were so angry that they ran round the tree, trying to eat each other up, and they ran faster and faster, till they were whirling round so fast that you couldn't see their legs at all.

And they still ran faster and faster and faster, till they all just melted away, and there was nothing left but a great big pool of melted butter (or "ghi," as it is called in India) round the foot of the tree.

Now Black Jumbo was just coming home from his work, with a great big brass pot in his arms, and when he saw what was left of all the Tigers he said, "Oh! what lovely melted butter! I'll take that home to Black Mumbo for her to cook with."

So he put it all into the great big brass pot, and took it home to Black Mumbo to cook with.

When Black Mumbo saw the melted butter, wasn't she pleased! "Now," said she, "we'll all have pancakes for supper!"

So she got flour and eggs and milk and sugar and butter, and she made a huge big plate of most lovely pancakes. And she fried them in the melted butter which the Tigers had made, and they were just as yellow and brown as little Tigers.

And then they all sat down to supper. And Black Mumbo ate Twenty-seven pancakes, and Black Jumbo ate Fifty-five, but Little Black Sambo ate a Hundred and Sixty-nine, because he was so hungry.

THE FAMILY UNDER THE BRIDGE

Natalie Savage Carlson

The Family under the Bridge *is a delightful book for primary children. Set among the poor people of Paris, it shows the gradual transformation of an irascible old tramp after he meets a homeless family. He resists the civilizing effect they have on him, but in the end he capitulates and becomes a "family man."*

Mrs. Carlson's books have engrossing plots and well-developed characters. She catches up her reader and carries him into the world she so ably creates.

Once there was an old hobo named Armand who wouldn't have lived anywhere but in Paris. So that is where he lived.

Everything that he owned could be pushed around in an old baby buggy without any hood, so he had no worries about rents or burglars. All the ragged clothing he owned was on his back, so

he didn't need to bother with trunks or dry-cleaners.

It was easy for him to move from one hidey-hole to another so that is what he was doing one late morning in December. It was a cold day with the gray sky hanging on the very chimney pots of Paris. But Armand did not mind because he had a tickly feeling that something new and exciting was going to happen to him today.

He hummed a gay tune to himself as he

pushed his buggy through the flower market at the side of Notre Dame cathedral. The flowers reminded him that someday it would be spring even though it wasn't bad winter yet.

There were pots of fragile hyacinths and tulips crowded together on planks in front of the stalls. There were pink carnations and oleanders in great tin pails. Most of all there were bouquets of red-beaded holly, clumps of white-pearled mistletoe and little green fir trees because it would soon be Christmas.

Armand's keen eye caught sight of a pile of broken branches and wilted flowers swept away from one stall. "Anabel" was the name written over the stall, and Armand touched his black beret to the stocky woman whose blue work apron hung below her wooly coat.

"By your leave and in gratitude for your generosity, madame," he said to the woman who was surely Anabel. He piled the broken branches on top of his belongings in the baby buggy. Then he fastidiously picked a sprig of dried holly from the litter and pulled it through his torn buttonhole. He wanted to look his best for whatever gay adventure was waiting for him this day.

The woman who must have been Anabel only frowned at Armand as he trundled his buggy toward the Rue de Corse. Past the ancient buildings he shuffled, his buggy headed for the far branch of the Seine River.

But as he entered the square in front of Notre Dame, a hand grasped his arm from behind.

"Your fortune, monsieur," wheedled a musical voice. "You will meet with adventure today."

Armand let go of the handle of the buggy and whirled around to face a gypsy woman in a short fur coat and full, flowered skirt.

He gave her a gap-toothed smile. "You, Mireli," he greeted her. "Your people are back in Paris for the winter?"

The gypsy woman's dark face beamed under the blue scarf. "Doesn't one always spend the winters in Paris?" she asked, as if she were a woman of fashion. "But have you taken to the streets so early?"

Armand shrugged his shoulders under the long overcoat that almost reached to his ankles. "It's back under the bridge for me," he answered. "I've had enough of the crowded corners and tight alleys in the Place Maubert. And I'm tired of

sorting rags for that junk dealer. I'm ready for that adventure you're promising me."

Mireli could understand. "That courtyard we rent seems like a cage after the freedom of the long, winding roads," she said, "but the men have found plenty of work for the winter. A city with as many restaurants as Paris has more than enough pots and pans to be mended. Of course the children can talk of nothing but the fields and woods of spring."

"I can't abide children," grumped Armand. "Starlings they are. Witless, twittering, little pests."

Mireli shook her finger at him. "You think you don't like children," she said, "but it is only that you are afraid of them. You're afraid the sly little things will steal your heart if they find out you have one."

Armand grunted and took the handle of the buggy again. Mireli waved him away, swaying on bare feet squeezed into tarnished silver sandals. "If you change your mind about the bridge, you can come to live with us," she invited. "We're beyond the Halles—where they're tearing down the buildings near the old Court of Miracles."

Armand tramped under the black, leafless trees and around the cathedral by the riverside without even giving it a glance.

In the green park behind the flying buttresses, some street urchins were loitering. Two of them played at dueling while a third smaller one watched, munching a red apple. The swordsmen, holding out imaginary swords, circled each other. Closer and closer came the clenched fists, then the boys forgot their imaginary swords and began punching each other.

They stopped their play as Armand went by. "Look at the funny old tramp!" one cried to his playmates.

Armand looked around because he wanted to see the funny old tramp too. It must be that droll Louis with his tall black hat and baggy pants. Then he realized that he was the funny old tramp.

"Keep a civil tongue in your head, starling," he ordered. He fingered the holly in his lapel. "If you don't, I'll tell my friend Father Christmas about your rude manners. Then you'll get nothing but a bunch of sticks like these on my buggy."

The boys looked at him with awe. Father

Christmas is the Santa Claus of France. He rides down from the north on his little gray donkey and leaves presents for good children.

The small boy held out his half-eaten apple. "Are you hungry, monsieur?" he asked. "Would you like the rest of this apple?"

But the biggest boy mockingly punched the air with his fist. "Pouf!" he scoffed. "There's no Father Chistmas. He's just make-believe."

"If you doubt my word," said Armand with dignity, "just take a look in the Louvre store. You'll find him on the mezzanine floor."

He grinned like one of the roguish gargoyles on the cathedral. There really was a Father Christmas and it was his friend Camille, who felt the urge to work when the weather turned cold.

"I believe you, monsieur," said the boy with the apple. "I saw Father Christmas outside the store yesterday. He was eating hot chestnuts on the street."

Armand hunched his shoulders and quickly walked toward the bridge. Mireli was right. These starlings would steal your heart if you didn't keep it well hidden. And he wanted nothing to do with children. They meant homes and responsibility and regular work—all the things he had turned his back on so long ago. And he was looking for adventure.

Down a few blocks was the bridge under which he lived when the weather wasn't too raw. And plenty of company he had during the summer with all the homeless of Paris staking their claims to this space or that.

"But first I must have dinner," he told himself, looking up at the restaurant across the street. He licked his thumb and held it up. "The wind is just right," he decided.

So he parked his buggy beside the low wall and settled himself in the breeze that came from the restaurant. He pulled all the kitchen smells deep into his lungs. "Ah, steak broiled over charcoal," he gloated. "And the sauce is just right. But they scorched the potatoes."

For two hours Armand sat on the curb enjoying the food smells because that is the length of time a Frenchman allows himself for lunch in the middle of the day.

Then he daintily wiped his whiskered lips with his cuff and rose to his knobby shoes. "And just

keep the change, waiter," he said generously, although there wasn't a white-uniformed waiter in sight. "You'll need it for Christmas."

He started down the steps that dropped from the street to the quay beside the Seine. He bounced the back wheels of the buggy down each step. "I am really quite stuffed," he told himself, "but I wish I had taken that apple. It would have been the right dessert after such a rich sauce."

Down the quay he pushed the buggy toward the bridge tunnel that ran along the shore. On the cobbled quay a man was washing his car with the free Seine water. A woman in a fur coat was airing her French poodle. A long barge, sleek as a black seal, slid through the river. It was like coming home after a long absence, thought Armand. And anything exciting could happen under a Paris bridge.

As he neared the tunnel, his eyes widened with surprise and anger. A gray canvas was propped over the niche that had always been his own. And a market pushcart was parked by the pillar.

He raced his buggy across the cobblestones toward the arch. When he arrived there, he reached up and angrily tore down the canvas with one swoop of his arm. Then he jumped back in surprise and horror.

"Oh, là, là!" he cried. "Starlings! A nest full of them!"

Because three startled children snuggled into a worn quilt looked up at him with eyes as surprised as his own. The little girl and the boy cowered deeper into the quilt. But the older girl quickly jumped to her feet. She had direct blue eyes and they matched her determined chin and snubbed nose and bright red hair.

"You can't take us away," she cried, clenching her fists. "We're going to stay together because we're a family, and families have to stick together. That's what mama says."

As Armand glared at the children, a shaggy dog that should have been white came bounding across the quay. It protectively jumped between the tramp and the children, barking fiercely at Armand. The hobo quickly manuevered his buggy between himself and the dog.

"If that beast bites me," he cried, "I'll sue you for ten thousand francs."

The girl called the dog to her. "Here, Jojo!

Come, Jojo! He won't take us away. He's only an old tramp."

The dog stopped barking and sniffed at the wheels of Armand's baby buggy.

The man was insulted. "I'll have you know that I'm not just any old tramp," he said. And he wasn't. "I'm not friendless, and I could be a workingman right now if I wanted. But where are your parents and who are you hiding from? The police?"

He studied the children closely. Redheads they were, all of them, and their clothes had the mismatched, ill-fitting look of poverty.

The older girl's eyes burned a deep blue. "Our landlady put us out because we don't have enough money to pay for the room since papa died," she explained. "So mama brought us here because we haven't any home now. And she told us to hide behind the canvas so nobody could see us, or they'd take us away from her and put us in a home for poor children. But we're a family, so we want to stay together. I'm Suzy and they're Paul and Evelyne."

The boy swaggered a little. "If I was bigger, I'd find a new place for us to live," he boasted.

"It looks to me like you've already found a new place," said Armand, "and it's my old place. You've put me out of my home just like that landlady did to you."

Suzy was apologetic. She moved the pushcart over and measured Armand with one eye closed. Then she carefully drew a long rectangle on the concrete with a piece of soft coal.

"That's your room," she said. "You can live with us." On second thought, she scrawled a small checkered square at the foot of the rectangle. "There's a window," she said gravely, "so you can look out and see the river."

Armand grumbled to himself and pulled his coat tighter across his chest as if to hide his heart. Oh, this starling was a dangerous one. He'd better move on. Paris was full of bridges the way the Seine meandered through it. No trouble finding another one. But as he started away, the girl ran over and clutched him by his torn sleeve.

"Please stay," she begged. "We'll pretend you're our grandfather."

Armand snorted. "Little one," he said, "next to a millionaire, a grandfather is the last thing I hope to be." But even as he grumbled, he began unpacking his belongings.

He stacked the branches and twigs, and made a pile of the dead leaves he had gathered. He pulled out a dirty canvas and a rusty iron hook. He set a blackened can with a handle near the leaves. He sorted some bent spoons and knives. Last of all, he pulled out an old shoe with a hole in the sole.

"Might come across its mate one of these days," he explained to the children. "And it fits me just right."

The children wanted to help him. Oh, these starlings were clever. They knew how to get around an old man. Lucky he wasn't their grandfather. But he laid his canvas over the rectangle Suzy had made for him.

He started a fire with the branches and dead leaves. Then he hung a big can over the fire. Into it he dropped scraps of food he unwrapped from pieces of newspaper.

"In the good old days of Paris," he told the children, "they used to ring bells in the market places at the close of day so the tramps would know they were welcome to gather up the leftovers. But no more. Nowadays we have to look after ourselves."

They watched him eating his food. Even the dog that should have been white watched each morsel that went into his mouth and drooled on the concrete. Armand wriggled uneasily. "What's the matter?" he asked gruffly. "Haven't you ever seen anybody eat before?" They said nothing in reply, but four pairs of eyes followed each move of his tin spoon. "I suppose you're hungry," he growled. "Starlings always have to be eating. Get your tinware."

Suzy pulled some stained, cracked bowls and twisted spoons from the pushcart. Armand carefully divided the food, even counting in the dog.

It was dark by the time the children's mother joined them. The lights of Paris were floating in the river, but the only light in the tunnel flickered from a tiny fire Armand had made. He could not see the woman's face well, but he felt the edge of her tongue.

"What are you doing here?" she demanded of the hobo.

Armand was angered. "And I might ask you the same, madame," he retorted. "You have taken my piece of the bridge."

"The bridges don't belong to anybody," said the woman. "They're the only free shelter in Paris."

Suzy tried to make peace. "He's a nice, friendly old tramp, mama," she explained, "and he's going to live with us."

"I'm not a friendly old tramp," said Armand indignantly. "I'm a mean, cranky old tramp, and I hate children and dogs and women."

"Then if you hate us," said Paul, "why did you give us some of your food?"

"Because I'm a stupid old tramp," replied Armand. "Because I'm a stupid, soft-hearted old tramp." Oh, Là, Là! There it was. He had let slip that he really had a heart. Now this homeless family would surely be after that too.

The mother was displeased to hear that the children had accepted the hobo's food. "We are not beggars," she reminded them. "I have a steady job at the laundry, and that is more than he can say."

She went to work warming a pan of soup and breaking a long loaf of bread that she had brought with her. Armand sat in the rectangle marked by Suzy and thought that this woman's trouble was pride, and that pride and life under the bridge weren't going to work out well together.

By the dying light of the fire, the woman went back and forth to her pushcart, pulling out moth-eaten blankets and making bedplaces on the concrete. Just overhead the automobiles roared, lights garlanded the bridge and people walking along the higher quay laughed lightly. But it could have been a million miles away from the little group under the bridge.

"You ought to put the starlings in some charity home until you find a place of your own, madame," suggested Armand, after the childen had dropped off to sleep. "This life is not for them. Now, you wouldn't want them to end up like me, would you?"

"Families should stick together through the lean times as well as the fat," replied the woman. "And I have hopes. I'm going to see my sister-in-law soon. She may know of a place for us out in Clichy."

Armand stretched out his canvas without bothering about any covering. He was used to the cold. He never felt it any more. But he was sure these children would feel it. As he lay on the hard concrete an uneasy thought worried him, like a mouse gnawing at his shoestring. Now that he had befriended these starlings, his life would never again be completely his own.

TWENTY AND TEN

Claire Huchet Bishop
(Told by Janet Joly)

World War II ended long ago, yet its impact on the twentieth century was so great it seems essential that contemporary generations of children understand some of its reality. Children tend to glamorize war, to think of it as a time of bravery and excitement. Twenty and Ten *shows not only what this war was like for French youngsters, but also dramatically reveals the effect war has on children. European children were separated from their families and sent to the country for safety. There were many DP's, displaced people without homes. Jews were hunted and killed—even children—and a few people all over Europe risked their lives to save them from the Nazis.*

After the ten Jewish children arrive, Sister Gabriel is detained in the vil-

lage by the Nazis. In her absence other German soldiers come to search the school. The Jewish children are hidden and the French youngsters, afraid they will inadvertently reveal their existence, refuse to speak to the Germans. Their situation becomes rather tense in this well-written book for middle-graders.

It all started when we were playing at The Flight into Egypt. Make-believe. It was in the schoolyard, at recess time, right after the Christmas vacation, beginning of the year 1944.

I have to write all about it now, lest I forget later on, the way most grownups do forget the very important things, such as not talking about a treasure or not asking what one is thinking about. If I write now all I remember about "it," perhaps when I am old, let us say twenty, somebody may find these pages and make a book. But that is a very long way off: I am only thirteen, and I was eleven when "it" happened.

My name is Janet. There were also George and Philip and Henry and Denise and Louis and many others. Twenty in all. And we were all fifth-graders except Louis, who was only four years old but was allowed to be with us because he was Denise's little brother. And this was permitted because the war was on and France was occupied, and the children were herded all together where it was safest for them to be. In our town the boys' school and the girls' school were combined and each grade was sent somewhere in the country. We, the fifth-graders, boys and girls, were given that lovely old house on the top of a mountain. It was called Beauvallon, Beautiful Valley, because we could see the valley for miles and miles from up there, and it was very beautiful.

Anyway, we were all up there, the fifth-graders and Louis, and Sister Gabriel was with us, and we were very happy because we just loved her. She was young and gay and quick. She never walked, she flew.

Now, as I was saying at the very beginning, we were playing at The Flight into Egypt. I was Mary, and George was Joseph, and Louis was the little one.

The other boys and girls asked, "And who are we going to be?"

From *Twenty and Ten* by Claire Huchet Bishop, as told by Janet Joly. Copyright 1952 by Claire Huchet Bishop and William Pene du Bois. Reprinted by permission of The Viking Press, Inc.

I said, "The Egyptians, of course. Can't you see? The three of us, Joseph, the little one, and myself, we are DP's, refugees, Jewish refugees. We have fled into Egypt."

"Why?" asked Denise.

"Because King Herod wanted to kill the little one. Don't you remember? Sister Gabriel told us all about it," I said proudly.

"What do we Egyptians do?" asked Philip.

Then it was that Henry said flatly, "We sell."

"Sell?" I cried.

"Well, what do you think?" went on Henry. "Jewish refugees have got to eat, just like the others, don't they?"

I didn't know what to say because I didn't want to make Henry angry. He is so very good at make-believe games. Also, it was really because of him that I was Mary. Joseph, I mean George, said he did not want a fair Mary. He said it was all wrong, since Mary was dark. And I was furious, because I knew all the time he said that because he prefers Denise, who is dark. So I said Mary was a blond, and the proof was that I had seen a picture of her made by a man called Memling, and she did have blond hair in that picture.

Then Henry stepped in and said, "George is right, and Janet is right too, because sometimes Mary is dark and sometimes she is fair. Mary can be French, Spanish, Russian, Negro, Indian, Chinese, anything, anything at all."

Denise said, "How do you know?"

And Henry said, "I know." And that was that, because Henry is very, very clever. Then he added that since we had had a dark Mary for the Nativity (Denise), we could have a fair one for The Flight into Egypt, and I could be Mary. (Henry does like me.)

"Don't you think it is only just?" asked Henry grandly.

George nodded; he could hardly do anything else.

So I was Mary, and I didn't want to make Henry mad. When he suggested that the Egyptians had to sell to the Holy Family because refugees have got to eat, I had to think very fast for an answer.

"Henry is right," I said cautiously. "All refugees have got to eat. My idea was that we—the little one, Joseph, and myself—we would make the journey first." I pointed to the whole playground. "Then when we get to Egypt, you Egyptians give us everything: the baker bread, the butcher meat, the housewives diapers for the little one—"

"Phew," interrupted Henry, "that's no fun. What is the matter with Joseph anyway?" he asked, turning toward Joseph-George and getting right into the game as he knew so well how to do. "Can't you pay for the stuff, Mr. Joseph?"

" 'Course," said Joseph. "I can work. I am a carpenter."

"Look, fellow," said Henry, "already there are not enough jobs to go around in this village."

"Henry!" I stamped my foot, I was almost cross. "Henry, you cannot talk to Joseph that way, to *Joseph*!"

"Be quiet," ordered Henry. "Are we playing or not?"

"Yes, of course. I guess I'm just stupid. Go ahead. Only," I added, "don't make it too long, because Louis, I mean Jesus, is awfully heavy in my arms. I think that all you Egyptians could at least offer me a chair."

Philip made the gesture of pushing a chair toward me, and I thanked him.

"All right," said Henry, "Now we men can talk this over. Mr. Joseph, what about your ration cards?"

"We don't have any." answered Joseph.

"That's bad," mused Henry, stroking an imaginary beard.

"But, as I told you," retorted Joseph, "I can work."

"Not so fast, not so fast," admonished Henry. "I already told you: work is no good. And now you have no ration cards."

"We've got to eat," went on Joseph doggedly.

"Sure, sure," said Henry. Then he dropped his voice. "But you have got money, haven't you?"

"Henry!" wailed Denise. (She was very sentimental.)

"Don't butt in," snapped Henry. "I know what I'm saying. That Mr. Joseph is trying to get work

away from us Egyptians. And he has no ration cards. And he pretends he has no money, but he is double-crossing us, because, as a matter of fact, he is rich."

We all said, "Oh!" We were petrified. (That means turned into stones.) And Louis, I mean Jesus, in my arms, started to cry. Then I was really cross and I shrieked, "See what you have done! Now the little one is crying. You are horrid, Henry, horrid! Everyone knows that the Holy Family was very poor!"

"Is that so?" queried Henry as cool as could be. "Well, what about that myrrh, frankincense, and gold the Wise Men brought them? That's worth a lot. What about it, Mr. Joseph?"

Everybody was quiet, quiet. We were just holding our breath and waiting for Joseph-George's answer. But it did not come. Joseph-George only looked crestfallen. So I had to speak up.

"Dear Joseph," I said tenderly, "you are so unpractical. Just as when we went up to Bethlehem for the census and you had made no hotel reservation in advance. Now, what do you think happened to the Wise Men's gifts? All gone, of course. How could we have taken that long journey and come this far without paying our way through? I have handed over our treasures right and left. And now I have nothing: not a bit of myrrh, not a grain of frankincense, not a mite of gold. See—hold the little one a minute please—"

Then I turned my pockets inside out, and I shook my dress, and I cried, "Look, Egyptians! Nothing! Nothing!"

"It's a trick!" announced Henry.

I hardly knew what happened next, it happened so fast. Joseph-George put down the little one quickly, glaring at me, of all people, with blazing eyes. Then he marched toward Henry with closed fists, muttering, "Unpractical! A trick! Money! Ration cards! Work! I'll show you!"

And suddenly we were all fighting like cats and dogs, some of us on George's side and others on Henry's but soon we did not know which was which. It was a regular free-for-all, the boys pummeling one another and the girls pulling one another's hair.

The soft white wings of Sister Gabriel's headdress flapped hurriedly across the yard.

"There, there, children!" she called. "Shame

on you! No, I don't want to hear about a thing. Think of you getting into a fight when I was just coming to tell you—"

"What? What?" we cried eagerly, crowding around her.

"You will see. In the classroom. Quick. Now you shake hands with one another and file in on tiptoe."

We did. In the classroom a young man sat on a chair. He looked very tired. He was not shaved. His clothes were covered with dust. We slipped noiselessly to our benches and waited in dead silence until Sister Gabriel made a sign with her head for the young man to speak.

When he opened his mouth his voice had a croak, as it does when one has not slept. "Boys and girls," he said, "I have to speak to you just as if you were adults. You know that the Germans occupy France. You know also about the refugees and the DP's?" We nodded. "Now, do you know that there are people who not only are refugees and DP's but have absolutely no place to go, because if the Nazis find them they will kill them?"

A shiver ran through the class.

"Do you know who those people are?" asked the young man.

You could have heard a pin drop, and we were amazed when we saw George raising his hand. He got up and said, "The Jews."

We had no idea what he was talking about, but the young man looked very startled and asked, "How did you know?"

George became very excited and shrieked, "Because there was Herod, and the Egyptians, and I was Joseph, and—"

He was all red and confused and he dropped to his seat and hid his head in his arms. We almost burst out laughing, but we did not dare because the young man was very serious and sad. To our surprise he said, "That boy is right. It is the same story—always—throughout the centuries. This time Herod's soldiers are the Nazis. That's all."

He waited a little while, then he asked quietly, "Boys and girls, do you know what happened when Jesus' family was hunted by Herod's soldiers?"

We all sang out at once, "They fled into Egypt."

"Yes," said the young man, "and they remained hidden there, did they not? Now, once more, Jesus' family is hunted and will be killed if we do not hide them. Will you, boys and girls, help? Will you take with you, here, and hide, ten Jewish boys and girls whose fathers and mothers are dead already?"

Of course we all cried, "Yes! Yes!" We were absolutely thrilled. This was not make-believe any more. It was the real thing.

Sister Gabriel spoke up, "I did not expect less from you boys and girls. But you must understand what this means. The Nazis are looking for those children. If we take them we must never let on that they are here. Never. Even if we are questioned. We can never betray them, no matter what the Nazis do to us. Do you understand?"

Well, of course! Had we not played at being the Egyptians? By then, anyway, we could hardly wait to see the new children. And we were delighted when the young man turned to Sister Gabriel and said, "They are hiding in the woods now. We have walked all night. May I bring them in?"

Sister Gabriel nodded.

The young man went over to her; he took her hand and touched his forehead with it, bowing at the same time, and he said, "You know that *you* can be shot for this?"

Sister Gabriel smiled quietly. "Bring them in quickly," she said. "They must be so tired."

THE ARK

Margot Benary-Isbert

After cataclysmic events people seem to need to work through the past, to give it order and try to understand what has happened. Life in post-World War II Germany was chaotic for many homeless people. Written by a German for German children, The Ark *realistically recreates this period.*

Enough time has passed since America fought Germany so that now Americans can feel sympathy for the homeless refugees of that war.

Mrs. Benary-Isbert has produced a number of well-written books for children. Some continue the lives of this family; Rowan Farm *is an interesting sequel to this book.*

THE HOUSE IN PARSLEY STREET

The wind swept around the corners and chased clouds of dust out of the ruins of bombed houses. The cold, clinging darkness of the October evening dropped down upon the strange city from a leaden sky. The streets were deserted. Nobody was out who could possibly help it.

Nevertheless, the little band of people who were walking toward the center of the town was in high spirits. The two girls, Margret and Andrea, walked ahead, chatting gaily with one another. Behind them came their small, dark-haired mother, holding Joey's hand and trying to answer his endless questions. "Will we have a stove, too, Mummy? Will there be other kids there to play with? And if I have to begin school, can I just stay out if I don't like it?"

"You'll like it well enough," his mother said. "It's about time a big boy like you learned to read and write, now you're going on seven. You want to, don't you?"

"I'm not sure," Joey said dubiously. "After all, Tom Thumb never went to school, and he was smarter than the man-eater."

Margret, who was holding the slip of paper

from the Housing Office, crossed the street and the others followed her. " 'Down the street by the station,' the man said, 'as far as the square with the trees.' You see, there are the trees. 'Then the first street to the right and the second to the left.' "

"Parsley Street Number 13," Andrea cried, dancing a little jig, as though the address alone contained wonderful and mysterious possibilities.

"Parsley Street sounds nice, doesn't it, Joey," Mother said.

"It sounds green and good to eat. Tell me a story about it."

"Wait a while, we'll be there soon."

Since noon they had stood around in the big, cold gymnasium where the refugees were being assigned quarters. The mothers with little babies had to be taken care of first, of course. But finally their turn had come. After nine months of moving from place to place, from refugee camp to refugee camp, they would now be getting something that could be called a home. Not their own apartment, of course; the cities of West Germany were so crowded that they could not hope for anything like that. But at least they would have their own room. In fact two! Two rooms all to themselves—it was almost too good to be true. Rooms without a crowd of other people, of squabbling women and crying children. How wonderful it will be to be by ourselves, Margret thought, sighing to herself. What would Parsley Street and the house itself be like? The various barracks where they had stayed had always been full of such bad smells. There had been only a small space for each family, and people had to keep potatoes and their supply of firewood under the cots, and hang what few clothes they had on a string above the tattered straw mattress.

"Where are we going now?" the children had asked each time they and their belongings were loaded into a cattle car. No one had known. "Somewhere," had always been the answer.

At home, in Father's book case, there had been a book about the wanderings of Ulysses. Ulysses, too, had wandered about the world for many years after a war before he finally found his way back home. The *Odyssey* had been one of Margret's favorite books. She used to read it over and over with her brother Christian, and they had acted out the parts. Then they had wanted to have wonderful adventures like Ulysses. But now Margret herself had become almost a Ulysses, traveling homeless through the world, and it was not nearly so marvelous as she had imagined. "In fact it has been horrible," she said with a shudder, speaking more to herself than to her sister Andrea who trudged cheerfully along at her side —a slender little girl with her mother's dark hair and her father's blue eyes. She wasn't ten yet— ages younger than Margret, who would soon be all of fourteen.

"Why do you call it horrible?" Andrea asked. "It's been lots of fun—going to so many different places and having so many train rides and so many other children to play with. Joey has always loved it."

Margret nodded. Of course, the younger children had enjoyed it. They hardly remembered what a decent, orderly life was like. They didn't even notice how terribly thin Mother had become, or how much grey there was in her hair. What would Father say about the way Mummy looked when he came back from Russia? "Take good care of your Mummy for me," he had told the three older children when he had had to leave them. That was three years ago now. Margret's thoughts kept returning to this, and she gave her mother a look of deep concern. "You've gotten so terribly thin," she said. "There's hardly anything left of you."

"There's still plenty of me here, don't worry," Mother said, and for a moment little sparks of gold danced in her eyes—the way they used to whenever Father teased her. "I can keep going for quite a while yet, my big girl. I have to, until you learn to sew on the buttons for your brother and sister. Look, there's another one coming off Joey's jacket."

Margret's forehead wrinkled in a frown. "I'd just like to know one time when something isn't coming off Joey," she said. Being a big sister was just about the worst thing that could happen to a person. As if it weren't hard enough already being a girl. Nobody asked Matthias to sew on buttons. On the other hand, of course, he had to split wood and pull the little cart which held the family's baggage—and sometimes even Joey on top of the baggage.

"See if you can read that street sign across the street, Margret," Mother said. "There's just enough light from that window. It can't be much further."

"If it is much further I'm going to cry," Joey threatened. "I'm hungry and I'm cold."

"Cry!" Andrea exclaimed. "What a baby!"

"This is Capuchin Street," Margret called from across the way. "The man at the gym said it's one block after Capuchin Street."

"Look at the slip again."

"Number Thirteen Parsley Street. Mrs. Verduz, the widow of Chief Municipal Secretary Verduz. He must have been something very important, Mother."

"Now you must make a good impression, children," Mother said, and she examined her flock with a worried expression. Her family looked rather wild and ill-kempt, and the wildest looking of them all, big Matthias, was not here yet. It was impossible to take care of clothes that were being worn all the time. During their brief stay with relatives in Hamburg there had been a chance for all of them to rest up and get clean—but all traces of that visit had long since vanished. Hamburg had been full of occupation troops and it had been impossible to get a permit to stay there. Mother had worn out the precious soles of her shoes going from one official to the next, but in vain. They had been assigned to Hesse and to Hesse they had to go; there was no help for it.

Mother sighed. "It's a good thing Matthias

won't be coming with the cart for a while," she said reflectively. "I'm glad I won't have to introduce our whole horde at once to the poor landlady. We'll go down better a spoonful at a time. I feel sorry for her already."

"I don't," Andrea said firmly. "She ought to be glad. We're a very nice family, I think."

"I wish you wouldn't tell her so right off, Andrea," Mother said. "Perhaps she'll notice it herself."

And then they were in it—Parsley Street, a little lane like something out of a picture book. Almost all the houses were undamaged. They were pressed right up against one another as if they had given each other support through the perils of war. Most of them were half-timber houses, with wide flat surfaces of mortar between the dark old beams. In the yellow lamplight from the many windows the family saw that a large number of the beams were carved or painted in bright colors. Beneath the steep gables the attic windows looked out like peering eyes. The doors were painted brown or green, and the hardware on them was shiny brass.

"It must be that one," Margret said. "The skinny little one that looks sort of crooked. Yes, see, there it is: Number Thirteen."

The little house really looked as if it were hunchbacked. It leaned its left shoulder against the house next to it as though it were tottering and feeble from old age. On the great beam that supported the first floor was painted the date 1683, and in intricate lettering was a motto which could not be read in the dim light.

"An historical house," Andrea exclaimed, her eyes sparkling. "Just think of how many things must have happened in it in almost three hundred years. Maybe even a murder," she added hopefully. "Probably there's a ghost. I'd like to see a real ghost."

"I don't like ghosts," Joey said perversely.

"Anyway, Andrea will find out about everything that has ever happened in the house before we've been here three days," Margaret said knowingly.

"Let me ring," Joey cried when he saw the gleaming brass bell pull. He pulled it. Inside a little bell tinkled. Then for a while nothing happened. What if nobody were home and they had to stand out in the street and wait? Joey was so

overtired he would certainly start to cry. Even the older girls were shivering with cold, and all of them were hungry. The icy wind seemed to reach through their clothes right into their bones.

"Ring again, Joey," Mother said.

Maybe it's an enchanted house and you have to do everything three times, Margret thought. Three was her number, her own secret, magic number; it banished the bad and brought all good things. She had three stars of her own, the stars of Orion's belt. Those stars had stood above the Polish camp where her mother had had to work when she was separated from the children. Matthias had been sent elsewhere, to a men's camp, and for a long time they did not know what was happening to him. Joey and the two girls had been sent to live with a peasant family near the Polish camp. There the girls had had to work hard, but otherwise conditions were pretty decent. And on winter nights the three stars had shone down upon Margret steadfastly. After three months Mother had finally come back to them. Not all those in the camp returned. Many had been buried on the heath. Mother's face was grey and her hair had turned grey, and the gloss had gone out of it. But she was alive, she was back with them, and as if by a miracle Matthias, too, found his way back to them—because the good stars had watched over them.

But where had the stars been before that on the May night when Margret's twin brother Christian was shot, and with him their Great Dane who had leaped at the first of the men who came rushing into the house? Those two, Christian and the dog, Cosi, had been closer to Margret than anyone else, her companions from babyhood. And now she was alone. She never mentioned their names, never spoke of the days when all of them had been together.

"Three times!" she thought, and she rang the bell again.

Immediately they heard a door creaking and footsteps coming downstairs. Margret's heart pounded. If only Mrs. Verduz would be friendly. "Be nice," she murmured as if she were saying a spell. "Please be nice, be nice."

"What's that, Margret?" her mother asked.

"Nothing. You see, someone is opening the door."

The door opened just a tiny crack, hardly big

enough for a mouse to slip through. "What do you want?" asked a voice which was just as thin as the crack of the door.

"Good evening," Mother said.

"Good evening," the children's three voices echoed.

"We were sent here, we're to live in your house," Mother explained.

The door opened a few inches more. A tall thin woman stuck her head out and stared at the group. "Is that so?" she said. "You are to live here? Is it possible?"

The light from the hallway fell upon her thin figure. She was wearing a grey dress with a ruche of black lace down the front. She seemed to have stepped right out of great-grandmother's photograph album. An odd-looking pair of glasses hung from a silk ribbon pinned to her dress. These glasses, their mother later explained, were called pince-nez, meaning pinch-the-nose. The lady set them on her nose so that she could see better.

"Good Heavens!" she exclaimed. "Four persons! What are those people at the Housing Office thinking of. I was promised a childless couple. It must be an error."

"No, here it is written down," Margret said, showing her slip of paper. "Here, you see, is the name: Mrs. Verduz. You are Mrs. Verduz, aren't you? And the rooms have been under requisition for a long time."

"No, no, no," the lady cried, raising her hands imploringly. "This is impossible. Four persons! Why, I have only two beds."

"Five persons," Mother said. The grey old lady might as well be told all the dreadful truth at once. "My oldest boy is coming along later on. I'm very sorry we have to invade you at night this way, but there's nothing to be done about it now. The children have been standing around all day; they're tired and frozen, and where else could we go for the night? There's no one left in the gymnasium by this time, and the barracks are already filled up with new people."

"Well, since that's how things stand I suppose you can come in for the night," Mrs. Verduz said unwillingly. "Tomorrow I shall have to go down to the Housing Office right away and explain the mistake."

They climbed the steep staircase. Along the walls hung pictures and devout mottoes in hand-

some carved frames. On the landing stood two large tubs in which green plants were growing. A big black cat slipped silently between them.

"What a beautiful cat," Margret cried softly. "Andrea, look at the wonderful cat."

She crouched down on a step and coaxed the cat to come to her. Its amber eyes blinked at her; then, with head stretched forward, it cautiously approached and graciously permitted Margret to scratch it behind the ears.

"That's Caliph," the lady said without turning. "He never lets strangers touch him."

"All animals let Margret touch them," Andrea said. Mrs. Verduz turned her head and her eyebrows shot up, half in surprise, half in pleasure. For a moment she looked quite human.

On the ground floor there were two doors, on the second floor three. The third floor was the attic, and here also there were three doors. Mrs. Verduz opened the one opposite the stairs and silently pointed to a spacious room filled with an odd assortment of furniture. It had two windows overlooking Parsley Street, and Andrea rushed over to look out. There was real glass in them, and each had a pair of faded curtains. In one corner stood a drum stove. In the brass lamp, which had once been a kerosene lamp, there was actually an electric bulb! Mrs. Verduz switched on this lamp as they entered. On both sides of the room the wall sloped sharply down, following the line of the roof.

"How lovely," Andrea said impulsively. Margret glanced reprovingly at her. But what was wrong with saying that the room was attractive, with its big, grey-and-red figured sofa, carved chairs and other old-fashioned things?

Mrs. Verduz raised her glasses to her nose again and studied Andrea with a pleased air. "The bedroom adjoins," she said in an almost kindly tone. "Yes, it is a very fine apartment, but there are only two beds; it won't do for five persons."

The bedroom was narrow. Two beds stood against the long wall, and beneath the small window was a stand which held an enamel washbasin. In one corner were a small table and two chairs.

"We could put one of the beds in the living room," Mother said—and Margret realized that Mother hoped to be able to stay here. "The sofa can be moved in here for Matthias, one bed for the two girls, and the other in the big room for Joey and me. That would do it."

"But I want to sleep with Matthias," Joey said.

"You can later, but this winter I want you sleeping in the warm room so that you won't get any more sore throats."

Downstairs the bell rang. "That's Matthias," Andrea cried, and went clattering down the steps. She could have done it less noisily, because the banisters were perfect for sliding down without a sound. But Andrea had not quite dared to slide because Mother had said they must make a good impression.

"Quiet, Andrea!" Margret called after her—but the warning was already too late. Andrea did not see Mrs. Verduz's face or she would have realized why her sister had called out.

"I'm so sensitive about noise after all the bombings." Mrs. Verduz said. "That is one reason I cannot endure children in the house. I suppose you have your linen with you, Mrs. . . . what was your name again?"

"Lechow," Mother said. "No, no linen, unfortunately . . ."

Mrs. Verduz shook her head in silent disapproval. Not only was her house being filled up with strangers to whom she had to entrust all this good furniture, but on top of it all she would have to let them use her bed linen too.

"We have one wool blanket each," Margret said hastily. "We can get along without sheets. We did in camp."

"Sleep without sheets!" Mrs. Verduz said with a frown. "Not in my house. What would happen to my good mattresses?" With a sigh she went across to the spare attic room. She could be heard rattling keys. Margret winked at her mother and whispered, "Sheets, Mummy! And featherbeds, too—see them all folded up? We won't leave here, no matter how disagreeable she is. And besides the cat is so nice." She bent down and stroked Caliph, who purred and rubbed against her ankles. Obviously it was a case of mutual love at first sight.

Mrs. Verduz returned with a bundle of linen in her arms—snowy white sheets and bright-colored coverlets. The linen smelled rather musty, as though it had not been used for many years.

Matthias was coming up the stairs with Andrea. Between the two of them they were carrying one of the two sacks which contained the family's precious possessions—the wool blankets, some underwear and the one spare set of clothing each owned. Their bread and the rest of their provisions were distributed among their rucksacks. Now they would be getting regular food ration cards, just like the people who belonged here.

Matthias had tucked his precious violin case under his arm and parked the cart in the small courtyard back of the house. Matthias always got the hang of places quickly.

"This is my oldest boy, Matthias," Mother said, and Matthias removed the cap from his blond shock of hair and made a bit of a bow. Margret felt proud of him. Not that she personally placed much importance on fine manners. But if the grey lady didn't let them stay—no, she couldn't bear to think of that! Manners were a small price to pay, if only they could stay.

"Oh, the dirt all these children will track in," Mrs. Verduz wailed, and her face twisted up as though she had a toothache.

"We can always take our shoes off downstairs," Margret suggested.

"And I can sweep the stairs on Saturdays," Andrea said. "I won't mind that a bit."

"Yes," Mrs. Verduz said. "I really cannot be expected to clean up after other people. My maid has just up and left me again. There's no depending on people any more."

"The girls will be glad to help with the work," Mother said.

"That would be fine," Mrs. Verduz replied. The prospect evidently pleased her (She'll keep us, she'll keep us, Margret rejoiced.) "Yes, I certainly could use a little help in the house. And perhaps the big boy could split some wood now and then and bring it in."

Margret gave Matthias a suggestive poke with her elbow. "I'll do that," he said, nodding. "And me too," Joey promised. "I can split wood and carry it in too—I'm almost seven."

"Well, then, you may as well get settled for the night," the grey lady said, with gracious condescension. "We'll see what tomorrow brings. Good night. Come, Caliph!"

As soon as she had gone Andrea took a hop, skip and jump. "It's fine here, I like it," she exclaimed happily, and dropped down on the sofa to test the springs.

"Be careful of the furniture," Mother warned her. "What do you say, Margret?"

"She's a witch," Margret said darkly.

Mother shook her head. "Just imagine what *we* would have said if an utter stranger with four wild-looking children were suddenly quartered on us and we had to give them our own bed linen besides."

"Why, Mummy!" both girls exclaimed together, and Margret added, "You would probably have said, 'How nice of you to drop in.' And you would at least have offered a good hot drink to people as frozen as we are."

Silently, Matthias unpacked their provisions. He could never see why other people talked so much.

"Eat quickly, children," Mother said. "I'm looking forward so much to sleeping in a real bed again that I can hardly wait. Do you girls still remember how to make a bed?"

"We'll learn again," Andrea said. "I used to do the crib for the Polish woman. But the big beds were never made up as long as we were there, and we slept in the hay, thank Heaven."

"Tomorrow I'll go to the Economic Office about wood and potatoes," Matthias said. "When we have something to run the stove with, it will be nice and comfortable here."

Margret was sure it would be comfortable. Mother would have made a tent in the desert pleasant to live in.

"Then can we stay here?" Joey asked. "And will Father be able to find us?"

"Of course he'll find us," Mother assured him. "We left a trail of pebbles behind us, like Hansel and Gretel."

"Oh, tell me the story, Mummy." While listening, Joey chewed away at a thick slice of bread spread with fake liverwurst.

"You know that we wrote our names down everywhere, wherever we passed. In the camps and in the homes of the relatives in Berlin and Hamburg. And we left our names at the Red Cross and at the railroad stations. All Father has to do is to track us down. And now we'll write letters to all those places again and give our new address, 13 Parsley Street. But go get some water now, children, so we can wash up. I saw the faucet right outside in the hall, to the left of the stairs."

"Wash up?" Andrea and Joey said slowly, and Joey suddenly remembered that he was terribly tired.

"It's really too cold here to wash," Margret said.

Matthias, who was to sleep on the sofa, had already undressed and slipped under the blanket. "Good night," he said.

The others went to the bedroom, and while Mother helped a sleepy Joey to undress, the two girls skillfully made the beds.

"Do you think she'll keep us?" Margret asked as she slipped under the featherbed. "Don't you think she has to? There's nothing she can do about an order from the Housing Office."

"Everything will turn out all right," Mother said. "Isn't it good to be lying in a bed again?"

Andrea pressed close against Margret. The bedding was uncomfortably clammy, but gradually she began to feel warmer. "Being a refugee is very nice after all," she murmured, her teeth chattering.

"Nice?" Margret asked.

"Yes, you know there's something new every day. I've always wanted to live in an old house like this. And at home we were never allowed to sleep together and I'd freeze to death if I had to sleep alone tonight."

"Joey is asleep already," Mother called out. "Good night. We have a lot to do tomorrow." She shifted about once or twice, as though savoring the pleasure of stretching out in a real bed. Then there was no further sound. Andrea, too, fell asleep instantly. Like a warm little animal, she snuggled up to her sister, breathing softly. Margret alone remained awake, conscious of the calm, healthy, warm little body of her sister. What a happy creature Andrea was, carrying her house on her back like a snail, feeling at home wherever she was. I will never feel at home anywhere again, Margret thought.

Home—that meant the old orchard under the expanse of clear sky in Pomerania, the white house on the outskirts of the town, Father's roses on the edge of the terrace where the family took their breakfast on warm summer days. Cosi would lie in the sun and drink in its warmth. And there was Christian, too. But all this, this strange city with its ruined streets, this old, old house with its steep stairway, this grey old woman who disliked their coming—this could never be home, could it?

Outside came the cries of the owls—many of them had nested in the ruins. Hoo, hoohoohoo, they cried, and it seemed to Margret that the city itself was wailing a complaint against the grey army of refugees who had descended upon it, and who had to be found room for. Suddenly Margret felt afraid. She was tempted to call to her mother as she used to when she was a small child, whenever something frightened her. But no, of course it would not do to wake Mother up. Mother was so tired, and Margret would not even have been able to say what she was afraid of. She listened to the silence of the sleeping house. Outside something rattled. A floorboard creaked. From the times she had spent in her grandparents' farmhouse in Silesia Margret knew that old houses often began to speak at night. Perhaps Caliph the cat was stalking about. What a beautiful animal he was, and how friendly he had been to her right away. Perhaps things were really not so bad. What was it the grey lady had said? He doesn't let strangers touch him! Margret smiled at this, and smiling, she fell asleep.

CALL IT COURAGE

Armstrong Sperry

Armstrong Sperry effectively reveals the cultural beliefs of these island people, their high regard for courage and their disgust for cowardice, and their attitudes toward the sea. While the hero belongs to an unfamiliar culture, Mr. Sperry makes his fear and shame understandable to twentieth-century American children. There is an excellent blend of cultural differences and universal human needs in Call It Courage. *And the style of this gripping adventure story is especially suited to evoke mood and to involve the reader. This book was the 1941 Newbery Award winner.*

Mafatu, son of a Polynesian chief, fears the sea, but because he longs to bring honor to his father and gain his respect, Mafatu struggles to conquer terror.

FLIGHT

It happened many years ago, before the traders and missionaries first came into the South Seas, while the Polynesians were still great in numbers and fierce of heart. But even today the people of Hikueru sing this story in their chants and tell it over the evening fires. It is the story of Mafatu, the Boy Who Was Afraid.

From *Call it Courage* by Armstrong Sperry. Copyright 1940 by Armstrong Sperry, renewed 1968 by Armstrong Sperry. Reprinted with permission of The Macmillan Company.

They worshiped courage, those early Polynesians. The spirit which had urged them across the Pacific in their sailing canoes, before the dawn of recorded history, not knowing where they were going nor caring what their fate might be, still sang its song of danger in their blood. There was only courage. A man who was afraid—what place had he in their midst? And the boy Mafatu—son of Tavana Nui, the Great Chief of Hikueru—always had been afraid. So the people drove him forth. Not by violence, but by indifference.

Mafatu went out alone to face the thing he feared the most. And the people of Hikueru still sing his story in their chants and tell it over the evening fires.

It was the sea that Mafatu feared. He had been surrounded by it ever since he was born. The thunder of it filled his ears; the crash of it upon the reef, the mutter of it at sunset, the threat and fury of its storms—on every hand, wherever he turned—the sea.

He could not remember when the fear of it first had taken hold of him. Perhaps it was during the great hurricane which swept Hikueru when he was a child of three. Even now, twelve years later, Mafatu could remember that terrible morning. His mother had taken him out to the barrier-reef to search for sea urchins in the reef pools. There were other canoes scattered at wide intervals along the reef. With late afternoon the other fishermen began to turn back. They shouted warnings to Mafatu's mother. It was the season of hurricane and the people of Hikueru were nervous and ill at ease, charged, it seemed, with an almost animal awareness of impending storm.

But when at last Mafatu's mother turned back toward shore, a swift current had set in around the shoulder of the reef-passage: a meeting of tides that swept like a millrace out into the open sea. It seized the frail craft in its swift race. Despite all the woman's skill, the canoe was carried on the crest of the churning tide, through the reef-passage, into the outer ocean.

Mafatu would never forget the sound of his mother's despairing cry. He didn't know then what it meant; but he felt that something was terribly wrong, and he set up a loud wailing. Night closed down upon them, swift as a frigate's wing, darkening the known world. The wind of the open ocean rushed in at them, screaming. Waves lifted and struck at one another, their crests hissing with spray. The poles of the outrigger were torn from their thwarts. The woman sprang forward to seize her child as the canoe capsized. The little boy gasped when the cold water struck him. He clung to his mother's neck. Moana, the Sea God, was reaching up for them, seeking to draw them down to his dark heart. . . .

Off the tip of Hikueru, the uninhabited islet of Tekoto lay shrouded in darkness. It was scarcely more than a ledge of coral, almost awash. The swift current bore directly down upon the islet.

Dawn found the woman still clinging to the *purau* pole and the little boy with his arms locked about his mother's neck. The grim light revealed sharks circling, circling. . . . Little Mafatu buried his head against his mother's cold neck. He was filled with terror. He even forgot the thirst that burned his throat. But the palms of Tekoto beckoned with their promise of life, and the woman fought on.

When at last they were cast up on the pinnacle of coral, Mafatu's mother crawled ashore with scarcely enough strength left to pull her child beyond reach of the sea's hungry fingers. The little boy was too weak even to cry. At hand lay a cracked coconut; the woman managed to press the cool, sustaining meat to her child's lips before she died.

Sometimes now, in the hush of night, when the moon was full and its light lay in silver bands across the pandanus mats, and all the village was sleeping, Mafatu awoke and sat upright. The sea muttered its eternal threat to the reef. The sea. . . . And a terrible trembling seized the boy's limbs, while a cold sweat broke out on his forehead. Mafatu seemed to see again the faces of the fishermen who had found the dead mother and her whimpering child. These pictures still colored his dreams. And so it was that he shuddered when the mighty seas, gathering far out, hurled themselves at the barrier-reef of Hikueru and the whole island quivered under the assault.

Perhaps that was the beginning of it. Mafatu, the boy who had been christened Stout Heart by his proud father, was afraid of the sea. What manner of fisherman would he grow up to be? How would he ever lead the men in battle against warriors of other islands? Mafatu's father heard the whispers, and the man grew silent and grim.

The older people were not unkind to the boy, for they believed that it was all the fault of the *tupapau*—the ghost-spirit which possesses every child at birth. But the girls laughed at him, and the boys failed to include him in their games. And the voice of the reef seemed pitched for his ears alone; it seemed to say: "You cheated me once, Mafatu, but someday, someday I will claim you!"

Mafatu's stepmother knew small sympathy for

him, and his stepbrothers treated him with open scorn.

"Listen," they would mock. "Moana, the Sea God, thunders on the reef. He is angry with us all because Mafatu is afraid!"

The boy learned to turn these jibes aside, but his father's silence shamed him. He tried with all his might to overcome his terror of the sea. Sometimes, steeling himself against it, he went with Tavana Nui and his stepbrothers out beyond the reef to fish. Out there, where the glassy swells of the ocean lifted and dropped the small canoe, pictures crowded into the boy's mind, setting his scalp atingle: pictures of himself, a babe, clinging to his mother's back . . . sharks cruising. . . . And so overcome would he be at the remembrance of that time that he would drop his spear overboard, or let the line go slack at the wrong moment and lose the fish.

It was obvious to everyone that Mafatu was useless upon the sea. He would never earn his proper place in the tribe. Stout Heart—how bitter the name must taste upon his father's lips!

So, finally, he was not allowed to fare forth with the fishermen. He brought ill luck. He had to stay at home making spears and nets, twisting coir—the husk of the coconut—into stout shark-line for other boys to use. He became very skillful at these pursuits, but he hated them. His heart was like a stone in his breast.

A nondescript yellow dog named Uri was Mafatu's inseparable companion—Uri with his thin coat which showed his ribs, and his eyes so puzzled and true. He followed the boy wherever he went. Their only other friend was Kivi, an albatross. The boy had once found the bird on his lonely wanderings. One of Kivi's feet was smaller than the other. Perhaps because it was different from its kind, the older birds were heckling and pestering the fledgling. Something about that small bird trying to fight off its more powerful fellows touched the boy's heart. He picked it up and carried it home—caught fish for it in the shallows of the lagoon. The bird followed Mafatu and Uri about, limping on its one good leg. At length, when the young albatross learned to fly, it began to find its own food. In the air it achieved perfection, floating serenely against the sky while Mafatu followed its effortless flight with envious

eyes. If only he, too, could escape to some world far removed from Hikueru!

Now, once more, it was the beginning of the season of storms. Men scanned the skies anxiously, watching for the dreaded signs which might spell the destruction of their world. Soon the great bonitos would be swimming beyond the reef—hundreds, thousands of them—for they came each year at this time with the unfailing regularity of the tides. They were held to be the special property of young boys, since it was by killing them that a youth learned to kill the swordfishes and tiger-sharks, progressing from one stage to a higher. Every boy in the village sharpened his spear, tested the shaft, honed his shark knife. Every boy, that is, except Mafatu.

Kana stopped one afternoon to watch Mafatu at work on his nets. Of all the youths of his own age, Kana alone had been friendly. Sometimes he even stayed behind when the others were fishing to help the boy with his work.

"The bonitos have begun to run, Mafatu," Kana said quietly.

"Yes," the other returned, then fell silent. His fingers faltered as they flew among the sennit fibers of the net he was making.

"My father brought back word from the reef today," Kana went on. "Already there are many bonitos out there. Tomorrow we boys will go after them. That's our job. It will be fun, eh?"

Mafatu's knuckles whitened. His ears pounded with the swift fury of the sea. . . .

"That will be fun, won't it?" Kana insisted, watching Mafatu closely. But the boy made no answer. Kana started to speak; he stopped, turned impatiently, and walked away. Mafatu wanted to cry out after him: "Wait, Kana! I'll go! I'll try—" But the words would not come. Kana had gone. Tomorrow he and all the other boys would be taking their canoes out beyond the reef. They would return at sunset, loaded down with bonitos, their faces happy, their shouts filling the dusk. Their fathers would say: "See what a fine fisherman is my son! He will be a Chief one of these days." Only Tavana Nui would be silent. *His* son had not gone.

That night a new moon rose above the edge of the sea, silvering the land with a bloom of magic. Wandering along the outer beach with Uri, Mafatu heard laughing voices and drew hastily into the black shadow of a pandanus. A group of boys were pulling their canoes above high watermark, and laying their plans for the morrow. Their voices were shrill with eagerness.

"Tomorrow at daybreak . . ." one was saying.

"There'll be Timi and Tapu and Viri . . ."

"Aué!" another voice broke in. "It's work for us all. How else will we become fishermen and warriors? How else will we feed our families and keep the tribe alive?"

"True! Hikueru is too poor. There are only the fish from the sea. A man must be fearless to provide food. We will all go—every one of us!"

Mafatu, standing tense in the shadows, heard a scornful laugh. His heart contracted. "Not all of us will go," he heard Kana scoff. "Not Mafatu!"

"Ha! He is afraid."

"He makes good spears," offered Viri generously.

"Ho! That is woman's work. Mafatu is afraid of the sea. *He* will never be a warrior." Kana laughed again, and the scorn of his voice was like a spear thrust through Mafatu's heart. "Aiá!" Kana was saying. "I have tried to be friendly with him. But he is good only for making spears. Mafatu is a coward."

The boys disappeared down the moonlit beach. Their laughter floated back on the night air. Mafatu stood quite still. Kana had spoken; he had voiced, once for all, the feeling of the tribe. Mafatu—Stout Heart—was a coward. He was the Boy Who Was Afraid.

His hands were damp and cold. His nails dug into his palms. Suddenly a fierce resentment stormed through him. He knew in that instant what he must do: he must prove his courage to himself, and to the others, or he could no longer live in their midst. He must face Moana, the Sea God—face him and conquer him. He must.

The boy stood there taut as a drawn arrow awaiting its release. Off to the south somewhere there were other islands. . . . He drew a deep breath. If he could win his way to a distant island, he could make a place for himself among strangers. And he would never return to Hikueru until he should have proven himself! He would

come back with his head high-held in pride, and he would hear his father say: "Here is my son Stout Heart. A brave name for a brave boy.". . . Standing there with clenched fists, Mafatu knew a smarting on his eyelids and shut his eyes tight, and sank his teeth into his lower lip.

Far off in the *himené* house the Old Ones were singing. Their voices filled the night with rich sound. They sang of long voyages in open canoes, of hunger and thirst and battle. They sang the deeds of heroes. The hair on the boy's damp forehead stirred; the long-drawn mutter of the reef sounded its note of warning in his ears. At his side, Uri touched his master's hand with a cold nose. Mafatu pulled the dog close.

"We're going away, Uri," he whispered fiercely. "Off to the south there are other islands.". . .

The outrigger canoes lay drawn up on the beach like long slim fish. Silent as a shadow, the boy crossed the sand. His heart was hammering in his throat. Into the nearest canoe he flung half a dozen green drinking nuts, his fish spear. He gave his *pareu* a brave hitch. Then he picked up a paddle and called to Uri. The dog leaped into the bow. There was only Kivi—Mafatu would miss his albatross. He scanned the dark sky for sight of the bird, then gave it up and turned away.

The lagoon was as untroubled as a mirror. Upon its black face the stars lay tracks of fire. The boy shoved off and climbed into the stern. Noiselessly he propelled the canoe forward, sending it half a length ahead with each thrust of his paddle. As he drew nearer to the barrier-reef, the thunder of the surf increased. The old familiar dread of it struck at his stomach's pit, and made him falter in his paddling. The voices of the Old Ones were fainter and fainter now.

The reef thunder mounted: a long-drawn, hushed yet mighty sound that seemed to have its being not in the air above but in the very sea beneath. Out beyond lurked a terrifying world of water and wind. Out there there lay everything most to be feared. The boy's hands tightened on his paddle. Behind him lay safety, security from the sea. What matter if they jeered? For a second he almost turned back. Then he heard Kana's voice once more saying: "Mafatu is a coward."

The canoe entered the race formed by the

ebbing tide. It caught up the small craft in its churn, swept it forward like a chip on a millrace. No turning back now. . . .

The boy was aware of a sudden whir and fury in the sky above, a beat of mighty wings. Startled, he glanced upward. There was Kivi, his albatross. Mafatu's heart lifted. The bird circled slowly in the moonlight, its wings edged with silver. It hovered for a moment just over the bow of the canoe, then it rose easily, lightly in its effortless flight. Out through the passage in the reef. Out into the open ocean.

Mafatu gripped the steering paddle and followed.

MEETING WITH A STRANGER

Duane Bradley

A young Ethiopian boy is caught between his tribe's traditions and new ways of raising sheep. He needs the modern techniques but fears the American stranger may try to destroy the African world Teffera belongs to. The plot of Meeting with a Stranger *revolves around Teffera's test of the American's intent.*

This chapter was chosen to illustrate how dialogue can move a story, how it can reveal the characters' positions, fears, and hopes without long, dull, explanatory passages.

The next day there was a feeling of excitement in the house and the courtyard around it. Teffera's mother and the servant girl were busy cooking; his father paced restlessly up and down, talking to Bekele. Teffera tried to be everywhere at once so he could be helpful, and still hear what was being said.

His grandfather was coming—that much he knew, and his heart leaped high. Surely there was not a more wonderful man, except for his father, in all of Ethiopia! Tall and straight and handsome, made more dignified and impressive by his sixty years, the courage that had made him a mighty hunter in his youth could be seen in every glance of his dark eyes.

He would know a way to defeat the ferangi, and perhaps even the right medicine to cure the eyes of Teffera's father. Then all would be well again, and Teffera could forget his worries.

The beating of drums and the deep pleasant sounds of men's voices came to his ears. He rushed to the gate of the courtyard. Sure enough, it was his grandfather, the great Kagnazmatch Abraham Kidane. Sitting proudly erect in his silver-mounted saddle, his spotless white shemma gleaming under his brilliantly embroidered blue cape, his eyes flashing and his face smiling with joy, he was every inch a king among ordinary men, and those men the proudest people on earth.

Teffera ran to greet him and bowed low to the ground. Then he stood quietly to one side until it was time for him to be noticed.

The women of the household brought out food and drink, and there was much loving, happy talk, as there is with people who do not see each other often but feel very close. In the afternoon, the men of the family sat down together, and it was clear that weighty matters were to be discussed. To his amazement, Teffera heard his own name called.

"You will join us, Teffera. Soon you will be a

man, and what concerns the family concerns you," his grandfather said.

When they were seated, Kagnazmatch Abraham turned to his son, Teffera's father. "And how are your eyes, my son?"

Paulos faced him squarely, his own face as strong and as brave as his father's, but torn with trouble and sorrow. "I cannot lie to you. Every evening I have put the leaves the wogesha gave me on them, and every morning they are no better."

Kagnazmatch Abraham nodded slowly. "And if they are no better, my son, are they worse?"

The words seemed bitter on Paulos's tongue. "Every day they are worse," he said. "At first it was as if the sun was hiding behind a thin cloud, but each day the cloud gets darker, and now it is almost as if the night is upon me."

"And what do you plan to do?"

Paulos shook his head in despair. "I do not know. With the help of Teffera and my household, we are able to keep the farm going. I have thought that Teffera is almost a man and will soon be able to take my place. Bekele tells me that is wrong."

"And what is it that you say, Bekele?"

Bekele leaned forward, his eyes shining. "I say that misfortune can be outwitted. It is one thing to be brave and to bear troubles patiently, but sometimes that is the fool's way. The wise man finds a new path when the old one is washed away."

He stood up, so carried away with his ideas that he could not sit still. "For many years I have tried to tell Paulos that a new day has come to our country. Teffera should be a part of that new day, and not live buried in the past. I say that he should come to live with me in the town and go to a school. He will be taught many things, and when he is finished he can get a job in the town and make a home for his parents.

"What kind of job would that be?"

"It could be many different things. He could work in an office or teach school or choose what he liked."

Kagnazmatch Abraham's eyes flashed like lightning in a summer storm. "And in these jobs," he asked abruptly, "would he work with the ferangis?"

Bekele bowed his head before his father's gaze.

"Perhaps," he admitted. "Many Ethiopians do."

"Reeds bend in the wind," said his father, "but not trees. Is it good that some of our people are following ferangi ways? Is it not true that the townsmen are forgetting our history and what we are, and trying to be like foreigners?" His voice softened. "Do not fear to speak to me honestly and freely, Bekele. I am no fool, and I know that things are changing in our country. We who are alive today cannot live yesterday over again. But this must not keep us from using our wisdom to solve our problems."

Bekele made a sudden gesture toward Teffera. "Come here," he said, and drew the boy close to his grandfather. "Take off your shemma and shirt," he ordered.

Teffera did as he was told, uncertain what was going to happen.

Bekele put his hands on the boy's shoulders and turned him carefully around. "Look at him closely, father, and see how strong and well he is. When I took him into town he was cut in many places, and his bones were broken. If the wogesha had tried to heal him, Teffera would be crippled and weak. In the new hospital they knew what to do, and you can hardly tell that he was ever injured."

He released Teffera and motioned for him to put his clothes on.

"I love Ethiopia as much as any man, and I want what is best for her. For thousands of years we have lived on top of our high mountains, considering the rest of the world nothing but a stretch of sand. When the ferangi came, they brought us trouble. Perhaps our memories are too long, and we forget that they also brought us other things.

"Now they tell us that the world is changing. Are we so proud that we cannot believe them? Paulos has chosen to stay here with his land where he can live as our people have always lived. I chose to go to the town and learn what I could of the new wisdom. When Teffera was hurt, it was not the old ways that saved him, but the new. If he stays on the farm he can learn to take the place of Paulos, but why should he tie himself to the past?"

Kagnazmatch Abraham turned to Paulos. "And what do you say to this?"

Paulos shook his head. "I do not like following

blindly in the way of the ferangis. It is said that one must eat fish with care. If we try to go ahead too rapidly, we will be swallowing the fish whole, taking the bones with the meat."

Kagnazmatch Abraham put his hands over his eyes for a minute and was silent. "We must remember that our country is beloved of God," he said. "For many centuries all the people of the world called it God's land, and they spoke truly. But because this is true, we must not think that other people are not worthwhile. Since God made them, He must love them, too."

Paulos spoke softly. "But I do not trust them," he said. "I have heard of terrible things they are doing, even now."

"I know. I have heard such stories." Kagnazmatch Abraham looked again at Teffera. "Were they kind to you in the place where they made you well? Did anyone hurt or frighten you?"

All that Teffera could remember was bad, but he wanted to be truthful. No one had spoken harshly to him, no one had hurt him except when they bound his arms and shoulders tightly and stuck needles in him. His uncle had said those things were to make him well. There was no doubt that he was well, and that he had been injured very badly in the accident.

"I did not like it," he said, "but they were not cruel to me."

Kagnazmatch Abraham looked Bekele squarely in the eyes. "Can they do great things in these hospitals? Can they cure ills that our wogesha cannot?"

"Oh, yes. There is no doubt of that."

"And could they cure such a thing as this?" He pointed at the eyes of Paulos, and the room was silent with the shock of what he had said.

Bekele thought a long time before he spoke.

"Yes, father, I believe they could. Perhaps not in the hospital in my town, but certainly in the bigger one in Addis Ababa. I have heard that they almost perform miracles there."

Kagnazmatch Abraham nodded his head.

"It would be a dangerous thing to put oneself in the hands of the ferangis, and no one could tell what might happen. Perhaps they are good as Bekele says, and perhaps they are wicked, as Paulos thinks. Whatever they are, they might cure your eyes for reasons of their own, Paulos. What do you think?"

Teffera could feel that his father was looking at him, and he dared not meet his eyes. At last Paulos spoke.

"A man who cannot see is only half a man. For the last few months Teffera has had most of the care of the sheep, and things are so bad that Bekele wants to take him away from the farm forever. I will go to the hospital in Addis Ababa, but if I do, Teffera must stay here and be a man in my place while I am gone."

Bekele went quickly to his brother and clasped both of his hands in his.

"You are a brave man, Paulos. You will not regret what you are doing. Teffera will stay here on the farm and care for it, and I will help him."

"But there is one thing," Paulos said clearly. "If I put myself in the hands of the ferangis, it does not mean that I trust in them, or believe in them, or will follow their ways. If they give me back my sight, it will be as if I went into the wild jungle and killed a lion, and brought his skin back with me. I will take what I can get from the ferangis, but I will not become one of them."

THE HOUSE OF SIXTY FATHERS

Meindert DeJong

It is difficult to select one passage from Meindert DeJong's many excellent books for children. The following selection is from a gripping adventure story about pre-communist China during World War II.

Tien Pao and his family flee upriver ahead of the invading Japanese army. After they reach safety and Tien Pao's parents search for work, the boy ferries an American flier across the river to earn money for food. The next day while his parents are working and Tien Pao is sleeping, water buffaloes jostle their sampan home. It, Tien Pao, his ducks, and pig float down river.

When he is finally able to land, Tien Pao is far within Japanese occupied territory. He and the pig, his only contact with home, begin the dangerous trek back to safety.

They weren't hills, they weren't mountains; but, hills or mountains, all that mattered to Tien Pao and the little pig that trudged beside him was that they were terribly hard to climb. The going down among the rocks and brush was almost as hard as the going up. The early dawn when Tien Pao had shoved the dishpan with the ducklings back into the river seemed far away and long ago. The rain was falling steadily again, but though Tien Pao had traveled long, his own village had not loomed up again out of the rain gloom. For that one thing the exhausted Tien Pao felt dumbly grateful. He hoped he had gone far around it.

It must be afternoon. Tien Pao still clutched the bowl of watery rice, but he did not dare stop to eat. He was hungry, he was exhausted, but he did not dare to stop to rest. There were paths in the little mountains, but Tien Pao did not dare to use them. Coolies came down those paths, and farmers. Once from his height among the rocks Tien Pao had even seen a Japanese soldier hurrying down a distant path. And once he had seen a woman like his mother. Even her walk had been like his mother's walk—tall, straight, and willow-slim. His heart pounding, Tien Pao had watched her, and everything in him had wanted him to run down to her, to tell her what had happened to him, and to ask her what to do. But he'd kept his distance, he'd kept himself hidden while he watched her out of sight.

He still did not trust himself to go among his own people. He did not know whether it would be safe in this country that the Japanese had taken over. Perhaps the Japanese soldier would have paid no more attention to him than he had

to the other Chinese that he had passed on the path, but Tien Pao didn't know.

In the late afternoon Tien Pao suddenly could go no farther. He broke into a cold sweat, his legs trembled under him, he was nauseated with hunger. He had reached the top of a round, grassy hill. There were a few sheltering bushes, and he crawled behind them. He had to eat, had to rest. He dug his hand into the rice bowl and gulped a choking, big mouthful. Glory-of-the-Republic began tearing at the grass. Tien Pao dug his hand into the bowl again, stuffed his mouth full. Again his hand went to the bowl. He pulled it back. There was only a good handful of rice left in the bottom of the bowl. He mustn't touch it, mustn't eat it—he mustn't keep looking at it! It had to be saved for one more meal.

He heard voices. He peered through the bushes. A group of boys and girls were coming up the hill with baskets on their backs and grass knives in their hands. They came slowly and weakly—like old people. They even looked like old people! The skin was drawn like old paper over their cheekbones. The children stopped halfway up the hill, cut grass with their hooked knives. Those children put their baskets down, and began sawing at the sparse grass! They stuffed whole handfuls into their mouths before they put as much as a blade of grass into their baskets. Then one little boy began to eat mud!

Tien Pao looked on, horrified. The mud-eating boy was the smallest of the lot. He kept away from the others, as if he were ashamed. He dragged himself around behind his bloated, huge stomach. His sticks of legs looked silly under that big stomach. And now the little boy scooped up a handful of dirt again and brought it to his mouth. His sister saw it, and scolded him in a tired old way. The other children looked up, but did not seem to care. The little fellow hung his head. He slowly opened his hand and let the mud dribble out of it. He looked at his empty, dirty hand and began to cry.

Tien Pao looked on—sickened. His glance went from the skeleton boy with the bloated stomach to the sturdy little pig beside him. Suddenly he was desperately afraid. Glory-of-the-Republic was food! He was in danger from these starving people. If those children down the hill saw the little pig, they would fall on him and tear him to pieces. They'd drink his warm blood.

The little shamed boy who had eaten the dirt had thrown himself down and lay, face hidden in his arm, sobbing. The other children had gone out of sight around the side of the hill. Tien Pao could stand it no longer. He took Glory-of-the-Republic by the rope and stole toward the crying boy. Without a sound he set the rice bowl on the ground close to the little fellow's head. When he'd at last look up from his hungry, shamed crying—he'd see food!

Tien Pao started to steal away, but ten paces beyond the little boy he broke into a hard run. He had to run even though these starved, weak children couldn't possibly catch him and Glory-of-the-Republic. He and the pig raced down the hill and up and over the next one. Tien Pao wasn't weary any more, he wasn't hungry. He wanted to rush on and on, over this rocky hill and the next, far from this country and the evil the Japanese had brought to it.

Glory-of-the-Republic could not stand the pace, or did he like it. He began dragging on the end of the rope, and he tried to grab mouthfuls of grass in passing. Tien Pao would not let him. He did not dare stop for anything now. For now he remembered other things. All this rainy day he had not seen one little black goat. Always before the little black goats had capered in the mountains. He had not seen a single ox in a field, a pig in a yard, nor a water buffalo in a single rice paddy below the mountains. There hadn't even been one lean dog on any mountain path, or around the mud huts among the paddies. It could only mean that the Japanese had taken everything from the people, and the hungry people had eaten the dogs.

But if the Japanese had taken everything, he wasn't safe in these hills with a pig! The thought stopped Tien Pao in his tracks. He wasn't safe in daylight! He'd merely been lucky so far this dark rainy day, but the Japanese had but to get one glimpse of him with a pig, and they'd know he wasn't from this wasted land. Here were no pigs! Tien Pao stared desperately around him from the tall rock on which he was standing. He did not know what to do. He wanted to rush away from this horrible country, but it would be dangerous to take another step in daylight—sooner or later he and his pig would be seen.

Glory-of-the-Republic rooted about while Tien Pao stood hesitating. The little pig snorted and dug. Leaves rustled at Tien Pao's feet, pebbles rattled. He became so noisy, it finally aroused Tien Pao's attention. He looked down. Right at his feet Glory-of-the Republic had shoved himself under a rock ledge. He'd almost disappeared, only his curly excited tail still showed. Under the ledge was a little cave. The little pig had found a cave! Suddenly Tien Pao knew what to do—hide in little caves by day, and travel by night!

He dropped to hands and knees beside the rooting pig, helped him dig out the collected leaves and debris until the cave was big enough. After a long look all around to see that no one had observed them, Tien Pao squirmed into the opening with Glory-of-the-Republic. It was a narrow little hole, but Tien Pao reached out and scraped all the leaves back into the entrance. When the cave's opening was completely closed with leaves, Tien Pao and his pig stretched out behind them to wait for the coming of night.

It was a horrible, tense feeling, lying in a hole in a rock in the daytime, waiting and listening. But the little cave was high, and far from any path. Gradually, as not a single sound penetrated the wall of leaves, Tien Pao began to feel safer. No one was near. No one had passed the mouth of the cave. Tien Pao eased his tense, rain-soaked body.

Gradually a little warm light began filtering through the leaves. The cave was becoming snug, warm almost. But warmth—light! That meant the sun! The sun must have come out. After all the days the rain at last had stopped. Outside, the sun was shining.

The comfort of the sun warmth, the stillness, the waiting brought a new sick gnawing. All in a moment Tien Pao went sick with longing for his mother and his father and the baby sister. The desperation grew so strong Tien Pao had to fight to keep from bursting through the leaves and start running home—impossible as it was. The homesickness gnawed at his insides like a huge, relentless rat. He mustn't cry—crying made a noise. He mustn't—he wasn't a baby! Suddenly Tien Pao shoved his face hard against the little pig's side to stifle his sobs. In the muffled cave behind the leaves, his face pressed against the sleeping pig, Tien Pao had to let go, had to cry himself out. And then he slept. And while he slept, night fell.

It was deep, dark night when Tien Pao awoke. He cautiously pushed away some of the leaves and peered out of the cave. The mountains lay in black silence. Tien Pao listened long. Then to his ears came a slight sound, and the blood started pounding in his ears. He clung to his pig. Something was coming in the dark, came running— running straight toward him and the cave. Tien Pao's heart stood still. Long, frozen moments later he began to realize that the soft running round was the sound of the river. Why, of course, below the mountains ran the river! And then Tien Pao could manage a hollow little laugh at himself. He laughed at himself again, a little louder. It somehow made him feel bolder.

Now that he knew what it was, the running sound of the river actually made him feel safer. It was the river. Somehow in running wildly away from the children on the grassy hill, he had blundered back to the river. The sound of the river was good. It was a guide. He must never go away from the sound of the river, Tien Pao decided. Since he'd have to travel by night, the river's sound would have to lead him home. Oh, the sound of the river was good! The river had taken him away, the river would take him back—back to Hengyang and his mother and his father and the baby sister. Tien Pao mumbled a little prayer to the river god. The good river god! "Bring me home. Bring me safely home."

As if he could still reach home that night, Tien Pao grabbed the rope, pushed himself out of the cave, and pulled the unwilling, sleep-warm pig out after him. Together they started out through the little black mountains.

Five nights later Tien Pao and Glory-of-the-Republic were still in the little river mountains. The going was painfully slow. Tien Pao forced himself up still another steep mountain path. His knees buckled under him. He had the little pig slung over his shoulder, but it was too much, he was too weak with hunger. But he had to carry Glory-of-the-Republic. The little pig was not made to climb mountains. The sharp rocks cut his feet, grinding gravel dug between his narrow, cloven hoofs. His feet were bleeding.

Tien Pao felt his way up the path. He pulled himself up by the jutting rock wall that loomed over him. His fingers touched a bunch of grass, he tore it up by the roots and brought it to his mouth. The gritty grass under his teeth nauseated him. He gave it to the little pig on his shoulder. At least Glory-of-the-Republic could eat grass. He could eat, but he couldn't walk. Soon, Tien Pao knew, he himself would not be able to walk any more. The hunger gnawed too fiercely. It burned and gnawed all night long, every slow step of the back-breaking way. It never let up, it only dulled when, stupefied with exhaustion, he slept in some little cave.

Halfway up the steep path Tien Pao had to set the pig down. Enormous ballooning black spots came swimming before his eyes. He backed away until he felt a rock, he leaned against it. Cold, clammy sweat stood out on him. He pulled his eyes wide with his fingers to make the awful lilting spots go away. Still they ballooned before his eyes, darker than the night—an evil dark. They were everywhere. They were above him and before him, huge, threatening, closing in on him.

It must be hunger. It was only hunger. It was only that he was weak and dizzy from hunger. That's what made the spots. There wasn't really anything else. Tien Pao shook his head to clear it, but fear clamped his heart. He wasn't alone. They were still there—things on the path! Spirits? Were these the evil spirits of the mountains he'd often heard about in his village? The old people kept talking about them and their horror. How they hid in caves, oozed out of rocks. Now they were coming for him!

They had waited until he was weak, but now they were everywhere. Leering down at him from all the rocks! Lilting, lifting, reaching out. Tien Pao tried to shake away the terror. They weren't real! It was only because he was so weak and hungry. They kept coming. Tien Pao tore his eyes away from the coming horror, looked down. The little pig wasn't beside him! Glory-of-the-Republic was gone. Without a sound they'd gotten Glory-of-the-Republic!

With a cry of terror Tien Pao broke and ran. He ran with the mad strength of terror, blindly, headlong down the mountain. The evil came right on behind him—rattling rocks, sharp crunching gravel rolled at his heels. Tien Pao threw himself ahead of the rattling sounds. He could hear panting. It kept coming—at his heels.

Tien Pao could not keep up his headlong speed down the mountain. He tripped, he hurtled into space, with a great, scary splash he was flung headlong into water. Gasping with the shock, Tien Pao struggled to a sitting position in the muddy water. But water—mud! Then this was a rice paddy. But then he was out of the mountains. Then he was safe from the terrible spirits of the mountains. A rice paddy! Tien Pao almost lay back in it as if it were a bed, so great was his relief. He breathed deep.

All of a sudden something nudged Tien Pao's arm. Tien Pao reared up out of the water. It was Glory-of-the-Republic! They hadn't got Glory-of-the-Republic! Why, it must have been the little pig that had come bowling on behind him in his wild flight down the mountain. That was why the gravel had rattled—that was the panting. Foolish with relief, Tien Pao sat back in the water and pulled the little pig into his lap. Why, all the time it had been his own wonderful pig—not spirits!

Glory-of-the-Republic was far more interested in the muddy paddy than in being gratefully petted. He squirmed free, and grunting happily he wallowed up to his nostrils in the oozy mud. Tien Pao fondly watched him, and watching the pig gave Tien Pao a good, useful idea.

It was easy to sit here in the rice paddy below the mountain spirits. But he had to go back up into the mountains. This was a rice paddy, and rice paddies meant that people were near. Tien Pao could dimly see the shadowy wall of a village compound looming up beyond the misty paddies. Japanese soldiers might be quartered right behind that wall. He had to go up. Maybe there weren't spirits in the mountains. Maybe it was only his hunger that made him see things that weren't there, but Tien Pao couldn't convince himself.

He quailed at the thought of going up into the mountains.

There was only one thing to do—do what Glory-of-the-Republic had done, wallow in the mud, disguise himself with mud and try to fool the mountain spirits so they wouldn't recognize him as the same weak, exhausted boy when he climbed back among them. Tien Pao brought up mud from the bottom of the paddy and plastered his face with the oozy, syrupy, reeking stuff. He rolled himself in it. With bluish, vile mud dripping from him Tien Pao stood up and studied the little pig critically. He was encouraged. The thick mud must fool the spirits! Why, Glory-of-the-Republic looked like nothing but a mud ball with four mud legs. If his own plaster of mud was as good, the mountain spirits wouldn't think he was human; they'd never recognize him as the same scared, weak, hungry boy. The mud was thick enough, but it was still a thin hope. Still, he had to go up.

Quaking with fear, Tien Pao began the long ascent. But as he climbed, he realized he was weaker than ever after his mad, headlong dash, and he was terrified. There they were again, darker than the rock darkness—swelling, lilting, lifting. Waiting for him on the upward path, reaching down for him.

It was hunger. There wasn't anything in the darkness.

"It's hunger," Tien Pao yelled up into the mountains. The rocks echoed it back. From far above him his distorted voice came mocking back as if something were laughing at him. "It's only hunger," Tien Pao whispered to the little pig. "That's all. There's nothing. There really is nothing."

He kept whispering it to the little pig, as if the little pig had to be convinced, as if the pig were scared. It did not help, he could not force himself to take another upward step. He stood sick with fear, listening, watching. And then he suddenly realized it—he was also lost. He was lost! In his wild dash down the mountainside he had lost the guiding sound of the river. The river was gone. Instead there was a new sound. There it was again—a rumbling in the valley far beyond the rice paddies and the cluster of dim houses. Tien Pao tried to puzzle out the distant sound, but in the evil, brooding silence right around him his mind was too numb with fear to think. He eyed the looming mountain again. Oh, if only he did not have to go up!

The next moment Tien Pao forgot the rumbling in the valley. A sleeping cuckoo called in a muffled, dreamy voice among the rocks right above him. Glory-of-the-Republic was rustling in the loose gravel, snuffling out a cave where he could find leaves to eat. The friendly, homely sounds reassured Tien Pao.

Again the muffled cuckoo called, but now it was higher in the mountains. Tien Pao pulled Glory-of-the-Republic out of the little cave. With the friendly cuckoo calling above him as if leading him on, Tien Pao thought he dared to go up. It took all his strength to lift Glory-of-the-Republic to his shoulder, but they had to go up now or he'd never dare. Tien Pao took one step up the steep path, and then he pitched forward. Glory-of-the-Republic hurtled off his shoulder to the rocky path. The little pig uttered a short, piercing scream, and was still.

The sharp squeal of the pig roused Tien Pao from his momentary faint. There lay Glory-of-the-Republic across the path, his four legs stretched out stiff and straight. Dead! Oh, not dead! Tien Pao crawled on hands and knees to his little pig. He blindly felt for the cave where Glory-of-the-Republic had been rooting. He pulled himself and the silent pig inside. "Oh, not dead, not dead!"

Tien Pao kept praying but he could not force himself to make sure whether the little pig was dead or just stunned. He could not let himself think about the nights ahead without the little pig. To go on alone in the dark through the evil blackness in the silent, brooding mountains—he couldn't do it! Tien Pao kept frantically stuffing the mouth of the cave with leaves to keep himself from thinking. He hardly noticed that the leaves were wet and soggy. Dumbly, hopelessly, he kept building a wall of leaves.

Behind him in the cave there was a muffled sound. Tien Pao whirled. There stood Glory-of-the-Republic—on his four feet! He wasn't dead—he was eating leaves! Tien Pao grabbed him and babbled words into the little pig's twitching ear. He almost crushed him. Glory-of-the-Republic grunted and wriggled free and hurried back to his meal of leaves.

Tien Pao could hardly do it, but he had to stop the little pig. These leaves were so wet, they packed down so tightly, he had to keep every leaf for the little wall he had built up in the mouth of the cave. Tien Pao pulled four handfuls from the inside of the wall of leaves. "There—but that's all you can have."

He sat listening almost wistfully to the little pig gobbling leaves. Suddenly he pulled a handful out of the little wall. He sniffed at the wet handful. Maybe leaves tasted better than grass. He closed his eyes and shoved some into his mouth. He smacked his lips loudly to make himself believe the soggy, musty mess tasted good. He swallowed them. They were bitter as gall, but at once they helped. For a moment his fierce hunger left him. He opened his eyes. His eyes had cleared! The spots were gone—the ballooning, lilting spots had gone away. Tien Pao grabbed another handful of leaves.

Almost at the same moment that his hunger gnawings were stilled, Tien Pao became unbearably weary and sleepy. He couldn't force his eyes to stay open. He still tried to plaster some wet leaves on Glory-of-the-Republic's head where he thought it must be sore from the fall, but the little pig promptly shook them off and ate them. Tien Pao stared hard at the little pig, and in a sleepy, heavy way he pondered that the leaves might do Glory-of-the-Republic even more good from the inside than from the outside. Before he had finished the ponderous thought, he was sound asleep. He did not hear the cuckoo call.

Related Reading

Books for Children

AFRICA

Bradley, Duane. *Meeting with a Stranger*. Illustrated by E. Harper Johnson. Philadelphia: Lippincott, 1964. A selection from this book appears in this chapter. (Grades 4–6)

Economakis, Olga. *Oasis of the Stars*. Illustrated by Blair Lent. New York: Coward-McCann, 1965. A picture book about the life of a nomadic desert family. The stylized illustrations add to the story. (Grades K–2)

Mirsky, Reba Paeff. *Thirty-one Brothers and Sisters*. Illustrated by Mary Stevens. New York: Hastings, 1957. The daily routine and adventures of an intelligent daughter of an African chieftan. (Grades 4–6)

————.*Seven Grandmothers*. Illustrated by W. T. Mars. Chicago: Follett, 1955. A sequel to *Thirty-one Brothers and Sisters*. (Grades 4–6)

Schatz, Letta. *Bola and the Oba's Drummers*. Illustrated by Tom Feelings. New York: McGraw-Hill, 1967. Bola, a young African farm boy, longs to become a Royal Drummer for the Oba. The details about daily life add richness to this interesting story. (Grades 3–6)

ASIA

Buck, Pearl S. *The Big Wave*. Illustrated with prints by Hiroshige and Hokusai. New York: Day, 1948. A sensitive portrayal of grief and maturity. A young Japanese boy's family is killed by a tidal wave. (Grades 4–7)

DeJong, Meindert. *The House of Sixty Fathers*. Illustrated by Maurice Sendak. New York: Harper & Row, 1956. A discussion of and an excerpt from this book can be found in this chapter. (Grades 5–7)

Handforth, Thomas, author-illustrator. *Mei Li*. New York: Doubleday, 1938. A picture book about a little Chinese girl who goes to the fair. Awarded the 1939 Caldecott Medal. (Grades 1–3)

Matsuno, Masako. *A Pair of Red Clogs*. Illustrated by Kazue Mizamura. Cleveland: World Publishing, 1960. A poignant picture story about a young girl in Japan. (Grades K–2)

Yashima, Taro, pseud. (Jun Iwamatsu), author-illustrator. *Crow Boy*. New York: Viking, 1955. A moving picture story about a "different" country boy who attends the Japanese school. (Grades 2–4)

Yashima, Taro and Mitsu, authors-illustrators. *Plenty to Watch*. New York: Viking, 1954. Simple picture book presentation of Japanese everyday life as it was when the authors were young. (Grades K–3)

EUROPE

Benary-Isbert, Margot. *The Ark*. Translated from the German by Clara and Richard Winston. New York: Harcourt, 1953. An excerpt from and a discussion of this book can be found in this chapter. (Grades 5–7)

————.*Castle on the Border*. New York: Harcourt, 1956. Some familar characters from the other two books appear in this novel about post-World War II Germany. A group of young people have developed a theater group in an old castle. (Grades 5–7)

————.*Rowan Farm*. New York: Harcourt, 1954. A sequel to *The Ark*. (Grades 5–7)

Bishop, Claire Huchet. *Twenty and Ten*. As told by Janet Joly. Illustrated by William Pène de Bois. New York: Viking, 1952. A discussion of and a selection from this book can be found in this chapter. (Grades 5–7)

Bonzon, Paul-Jacques. *The Orphans of Simitra*. Translated from the French by Thelma Niklaus. Illustrated by Simon Jeruchim. New York: Chilton, 1962. Porphyra and Mina, two Greek children orphaned by a violent earthquake, are sent to a foster family in Holland. Although very kindly treated, Mina cannot adjust to the gray climate and runs away. Porphyra sets out in search of her. (Grades 5–7)

Brown, Marcia, author-illustrator. *Felice*. New York: Scribner, 1958. A well-written, lushly illustrated story of a homeless cat in Venice. (Grades K–2)

————. *Tamarindo*. New York: Scribner, 1960.

The adventures of four Italian boys who set out to recover a lost donkey and lose their clothes to goats. (Grades K–2)

Butler, Suzanne. *Starlight in Tourrone*. Illustrated by Rita Fava Fegiz. Boston: Little, Brown, 1965. The traditional Christmas march to bring gifts to the Baby and His Mother had lapsed after World War II. A group of children attempt to revive the custom, but fail until an almost miraculous appearance of an unknown mother and her babe. A warm, moving story that reveals Christmas customs from another land. (Grades 2–4)

Carlson, Natalie Savage. *A Brother for the Orphelines*. Illustrated by Garth Williams. New York: Harper & Row, 1959. Others in this popular series about a group of contented French orphans who do not want to be adopted are: *The Happy Orpheline*, 1957; *The Orphelines in the Encanhted Castle* (illustrated by Adriana Saviozzi), 1964; *A Pet for the Orphelines* (illustrated by Fermin Rocker), 1962. (Grades K–3)

————. *The Family under the Bridge*. Illustrated by Garth Williams. New York: Harper & Row, 1958. A discussion of and an excerpt from this book can be found in this chapter. (Grades 2–4)

Day, Véronique. *Landslide!* Translated from the French by Margaret Morgan. Illustrated by Margot Tomes. New York: Coward-McCann, 1963. For twelve days five French children are trapped inside an isolated mountain cottage by a landslide that has entirely covered the house. A gripping story of bravery and resourcefulness. (Grades 5–7)

DeJong, Meindert. *Far out the Long Canal*. Illustrated by Nancy Grossman. New York: Harper & Row, 1964. Nine-year-old Moonta must learn to skate long after all the other children know how. DeJong's books about Dutch life are well written and interesting. (Grades 4–6)

————. *Shadrach*. Illustrated by Maurice Sendak. New York: Harper & Row, 1963. Another sensitive story about a Dutch boy. (Grades 1–4)

————. *The Wheel on the School*. Illustrated by Maurice Sendak. New York: Harper & Row, 1954. One of DeJong's most popular books. Awarded the 1955 Newbery Medal. Six Dutch school children decide to make their town roofs so attractive that the storks will again come back for part of the year. (Grades 3–6)

Francoise, pseud. (Francoise Seignobost). *Jeanne-Marie Series*. New York: Scribner. *The Big Rain*, 1961. A picture story book about a French farm family caught in a flood. Other books about the same girl are: *Jeanne-Marie at the Fair*, 1959; *Jeanne-Marie Counts her Sheep*, 1957; *Jeanne-Marie in Gay Paris*, 1956; *Noel for Jeanne-Marie*, 1953; *Springtime for Jeanne-Marie*, 1953; *What Time Is It, Jeanne-Marie?*, 1963. (Preschool–grade 2)

Holm, Anne. *North to Freedom*. Translated from the Danish by L. W. Kingsland. New York: Harcourt, 1965. Helped to escape from the Communist prison camp in which he was brought up, David is told only to go north to Denmark to find his mother. A long odyssey toward freedom. A powerful, often moving book, but the emphasis on David's thoughts rather than actions may prevent some children from finishing it. (Grades 5–8)

Ish-Kishor, Sulamith. *A Boy of Old Prague*. Illustrated by Ben Shahn. New York: Pantheon, 1963. Jewish ghetto life in mid-sixteenth-century Bohemia is powerfully revealed. (Grades 5–7)

Oleson, Claire. *For Pepita—An Orange Tree*. Illustrated by Margot Tomes. Garden City, N.Y.: Doubleday, 1967. A picture book about a young Spanish girl who wants an orange tree for her seventh birthday. (Grades 1–3)

Spyri, Johanna. *Heidi*. New York: Macmillan. First published in 1880. A discussion of and an excerpt from this book can be found in this chapter. (Grades 4–6)

Wojciechowska, Maia. *Shadow of a Bull*. Illustrated by Alvin Smith. New York: Atheneum, 1964. The son of Spain's greatest bullfighter has no wish to follow his dead father's career; however, many kind friends are counting on him to bring glory to his village. This is a sensitive account of a boy's uncertainty and developing courage. Awarded the 1965 Newbery Medal. (Grades 4–8)

INDIA

Arora, Shirley. *What Then Raman?* Illustrated by Hans Guggenheim. Chicago: Follett, 1960. Set in India. Raman, the first boy in the village to learn to read, finds books so interesting he withdraws from his hill culture. A "Merkin" lady asks him what he will do with his knowledge. Eventually Raman learns he must share it with others. (Grades 5–7)

Rankin, Louise. *Daughter of the Mountain*. Illustrated by Kurt Wiese. New York: Viking, 1948. A Tibetan girl searches for her lost dog, eventually reaching the coast of India. Written by an author who knows the country and its people. (Grades 4–7)

Sommerfelt, Aimée. *The Road to Agra*. Illustrated by Ulf Aas. New York: Criterion, 1961. A thirteen-year-old boy takes his sister across much of modern India to a hospital for an operation to save her eyesight. (Grades 5–7)

————. *The White Bungalow*. Translated by Evelyn Ramsden. Illustrated by Ulf Aas. New York: Criterion books, 1963. A sequel to *The Road to Agra*. (Grades 5–7)

SCANDINAVIA

Lindgren, Astrid. *Springtime in Noisy Village*. Illustrated by Ilon Wikland. New York: Viking, 1965. A picture book story about the everyday adventures of seven Swedish country children. (Grades K–2)

McSwigan, Marie. *Snow Treasure*. Illustrated by Mary Reardon. New York: Dutton, 1942. When the Nazis occupy Norway, a group of Norwegian children helped smuggle blocks of gold out of the country by fastening them onto their sleds and sleighing through the German lines. Based on a true incident, the book is an interesting adventure story. (Grades 4–6)

Sorensen, Virginia. *Lotte's Locket*. Illustrated by Fermin Rocker. New York: Harcourt, 1964. Lotte's reactions to her widowed mother's remarriage to an American and the necessity of leaving her home in Denmark are convincingly portrayed. (Grades 4–6)

OTHER AREAS

Otley, Reginald. *Boy Alone*. Illustrated by Clyde Pearson. New York: Harcourt, 1966. The first book of a moving trilogy about an orphan working as a "wood-and-water-joey" on a large Australian cattle ranch. Although the ranch people are kind the boy is lonely. *Boy Alone* is the best of the three novels but they all hold the reader's attention. (Grades 4–7) The others are:

————. *Rain Comes to Yamboorah*. Illustrated by Robert Hales. New York: Harcourt, 1968. (Grades 4–7)

————. *The Roan Colt*. Illustrated by David Parry. New York: Harcourt, 1967. (Grades 4–7)

Rugh, Belle Dorman. *Crystal Mountain*. Illustrated by Ernest H. Shepard. Boston: Houghton Mifflin, 1955. Four American boys and an English girl become involved in a mystery in the Lebanon mountain country. (Grades 4–7)

Sperry, Armstrong. *Call It Courage*. New York: Macmillan, 1941. A discussion of and an excerpt from this book appear in this chapter. Awarded the 1941 Newbery Medal. (Grades 5–7)

Chapter 10
Historical Fiction

From *The Perilous Road*, by William O. Steele, illustrated by Paul Galdone, © 1958 by William O. Steele. Reprinted by permission of Harcourt Brace Jovanovich, Inc.

Historical fiction is very popular with children because they enjoy reading about people whose lives, long ago, were so different from their own. For young children historical fiction like *The Bears of Hemlock Mountain* and *The Little House in the Big Woods* are often little more than an interesting story about children who lived in a past era. The important historical events of the time are secondary to the daily experiences a child might have and to some of the more common problems and dangers encountered by his family. Older children, however, enjoy books in which the main characters, usually children, are involved with the historical events and heroes of the day, for example, *The Perilous Road* and *The Matchlock Gun*. But they are still more interested in the main character's problems than the historical events. As children mature they are ready for historical fiction in which the important events and the forces at work are made clear in fictional form, as in *Johnny Tremain* and *Killer-of-Death*.

Regardless of the complexity of the novel, historical fiction must be authentic. The writer of good historical fiction is one who has researched the period thoroughly. He has learned not only how the people lived, dressed, and talked, but he also knows what they thought and believed. Historical fiction, like fantasy, must create a world so real the reader becomes a part of it.

The best writers of the third type of historical fiction develop their plots around those political or social forces at work that make the period exciting. Rosemary Sutcliff does this in her books about early English history. Each novel deals with two cultures in conflict for the possession of England: British and Roman, Romanized British and Saxon, Saxon and Norman. These conflicts create the action that is so necessary in children's historical fiction.

In contrast, poor writers superimpose a few historical details and archaic idioms on a plot that has nothing to do with the conditions of a specific time. This superficial approach can not give their books the sense of historical reality that Rosemary Sutcliff's novels have. They do not bring to life former cultures or give insights to man's past.

HAKON OF ROGEN'S SAGA

Erik Christian Haugaard

Hakon's father, who has kidnapped an earl's daughter for his second wife, is killed when the earl sends a host to take revenge. Too young to rule, Hakon becomes the ward of Sigurd, his unscrupulous uncle. In an attempt to gain control of the island for himself and his son, Sigurd shames and torments

Hakon. Only a few slaves and free men remain faithful and help Hakon regain his birthright.

Haugaard's recreation of a past culture is well done. He tells of the pre-Christian Norsemen's philosophy, moral code, and religion in this novel and its sequel, A Slave's Tale. Without didacticism, the author shows through Hakon's life how Christianity slowly began to influence Norsemen's behavior.

"Your dog, your horse, your friends, and you, yourself: all shall die. Eternally live only your deeds and man's judgment over them." This was the credo of the Vikings—the lonely heroes ever watched by the future, ever composing their own sagas. From manhood unto death, they were players upon a public stage that stretched from the northern tip of Norway west to Greenland, east to Nizhni-Novgorod, and south to Constantinople, which they called Mikkelgard.

They were not a nation; Norway had more kings than all of the countries of Europe have today. They were a group of poets who, according to their own taste and ability, were composing epic poems out of their lives.

Their gods fitted them: Odin and Thor, father and son, Gods of Battle and Brutality. Freya, the Goddess of Love; and Frig, who guarded the apples from which the gods ate to keep their youth eternally. The Vikings had many gods, for their poems were long and well written. Loki, the God of Evil: the God of the Broken Promise, whose symbol was the fire; and Balder, the God of Goodness, who, swordless, was to inherit the world, when all the other gods had died.

They were not romantic heroes, for the romantic hero is but a dream—a paper doll cut with a pair of embroidery scissors. They were intensely alive; their minds and bodies were linked together, as Achilles' and Hector's were.

In *Hakon of Rogen's Saga*, I have attempted to tell the story of a boy who lived at the end of the Viking period. It was not written for "youth," in the sense that I have blunted my pen before I started. I abhor those writers who have not the skill to keep the attention of adults, and therefore think themselves equipped to write for children. I

have done my best, and I leave you to be my critic.

* * *

Spring passed and summer came. On Grass Island the eggs hatched, and the gulls were busy filling their young ones' stomachs with fish. When at Midsummer, Magnus Thorsen and his men had not yet arrived, we grew lighthearted; and the young men pretended to be sorry that they would get no chance to prove their courage.

But unfortunately for many of them, their courage would be tested that summer, and many a jestful lip would scream its death cry before it had learned to form the words of love. One evening, as we sat at table, a young man pushed the door to the hall open with such force that the door banged against the wall.

We all turned to look at him, while he stood in the doorway trying to catch his breath. His head was wet with sweat, and his face white, for he had run all the way from the south of the island.

"They are coming!"

Oh, he needn't have said it. We all knew his message before it was spoken.

"One ship?" My father's hand held a bone upon which, a moment before, he had been gnawing; now it was poised halfway between the table and his mouth, as he waited for an answer.

"Three ships."

My father dropped the bone. It fell clattering, first onto the table, then to the floor, where it was immediately grasped by a dog's jaws.

If I had not known, I could have guessed how serious this news was by the way my father slumped together in his seat. For a moment he looked like an old man. "Are they big ships?" he almost whispered.

"There are at least a hundred men in each."

In the silence the words, although they had

not been spoken loudly, sounded like the noise of thunder. We had, at most, seventy men of weapon-bearing age on the island: four swords to one would be our lot.

My father stood up. "Victories are given by the gods!"

No one looked at him, but an old man whispered, "And defeat is the gift of your enemies."

"Bring out some mead, and let each man drink to our victory!" The mead was brought and the drinking horns filled. Then my father spoke this verse:

> "A man's name
> Never dies,
> Eternal fame
> In courage lies."

Lifting his horn toward the sky, he shouted, "To the gods! To victory!"

The men regained their spirit and the blood that Magnus' men soon would spill surged through their veins, shouting life and courage.

All the old men, women, and children were sent to our fortress. They were to drive along with them two cows and a herd of sheep. These, and the five pigs which had already been transported to the plateau, and some dried fish were to be our food supply.

The wind blew from the north, and Magnus' ships could not use their sails; therefore, their progress against the waves was slow. We would have all night to prepare ourselves for their attack. Our fortress was strong, and our desperation made us cunning and resourceful.

I was sent on horseback to summon my uncle and his men to come to our aid. There were only three horses on Rogen—two that belonged to my father and a stallion that was the property of my uncle. I rode the small mare. She was a pretty animal: brownish black in color and of a docile temperament. I felt very grown-up, being the bearer of such a message. I was thinking of putting it into verse, as was the custom of the adults when they spoke of matters of importance.

When I entered my uncle's hall, I found him and his men still at table.

"They have come!"

I had expected these words to have the effect of a sudden wind that springs up on a calm day, and in a moment whips the sea white. But my uncle did not even glance at me. He continued gnawing on the rib of a pig, as if I had spoken about the arrival of a school of fish.

"My father has sent me to ask you to come!"

My uncle only smiled.

"You will come?" I believe that I knew the answer before I had asked the question.

My uncle laughed, and told me to remember these lines of verse, so I could repeat them to my father:

> "No mouse grows fat
> That fights
> A hungry cat.
> Nor will night
> Become day,
> Because a fool
> Will have his way."

Anger filled me as suddenly as a pitcher is filled in a deep well; and as the water spills over the pitcher's rim, so did my anger. "An ill-made verse, like soggy wood, will kindle no fire. Go tell him yourself, if you dare!"

Some of the men laughed and my uncle's face darkened with rage. "A pup that barks when the sun rises will whine before it sets."

I turned from my uncle, and looked from one to the other of his men. "Will no one come?"

They avoided my eyes, and none of them rose. Then, in anger, I spoke my first lines of verse:

> "Sigurd will hide,
> Swordless his side,
> Coward his name,
> Infamy his fame."

As I walked out of the hall, three men got up to follow me: Harold the Bowbender, who had been with my father on his every trip to Tronhjem, and his two sons.

"Hakon!" Harold called after me, as I got up on my horse. "Wait and we will come with you."

I was pleased, for they were the best warriors in my uncle's village; but I could not wait for them, because I had to hasten to my father to tell him the news of Sigurd's treachery. Harold and his sons promised to come as soon as they had gathered their weapons. I dug my heels into the sides of the mare and galloped homeward.

Along the way I met two old men who were taking the remainder of the sheep and cows south, to the Mountain of the Sun. I told them of my uncle's betrayal, and they decided to drive the animals across the island, and then south, in order to bypass his hall.

I admitted that I did not think well of the whole idea. Surely our enemies would find the animals. Would it not be better to slaughter them and throw them into the sea?

"And what would we eat this winter?" one of the old men said. And I am certain he added in his mind, You little fool.

I did not argue with them.

The animals struggled up a steep hill, protesting wildly, not understanding why they could not follow their usual paths. I knew every one of these animals by name. Could I really have killed them and dumped their bodies into the sea? I rode on. In the distance I heard the bleating of the sheep—a sound of home, of comfort, of peace.

When I arrived back at the hall, I could see that my father had given up hope of giving battle there. The inside of the hall was stripped of everything valuable; it appeared as if it had been raided. The floor was littered with worn-out skins and clothing, and no fire was burning in the hearth.

I was told that my father was down at the harbor. Twenty men—among them my father— were pulling the big boat up on land. When they saw me, they paused in their work. "What news do you bring, Hakon?"

I looked down at my feet, trying to think of a way to phrase my news. "He is not coming," I blurted.

For the second time that day my father looked to me as if he were an old man. He muttered a verse, but he did not look at us. Instead he gazed at the sky, as if he were speaking to the gods:

> "Loki's gift:
> Envy and greed;
> Sand to sift,
> Snakes to breed."

Then—as at the table when he had heard of the approach of Magnus' ships—he straightened his back, as if his worries were burdens that he could throw off like a sack.

"Let the ship be!" he ordered.

"Aren't we going to burn it?" one of the young men asked in surprise.

"If we win, we shall sail in it again. If not, it will not matter. Let no man call Olaf Sigurdson mean or ungenerous, even to his enemies." My father smiled, a small bitter smile, and walked back to the hall. The men and I followed him, but none dared walk beside him.

The last things were packed and carried up to our fortress; and yet, my father tarried. I think he wanted to say goodbye. I believe he knew that he would never return. He didn't seem to be aware that I had stayed behind with him. He walked about the hall, his eyes searching and yet blind. For a moment, he stood at the hearth and scuffed the dead ashes; then, as though an idea had occurred to him, he walked to the door, only to stand there, looking back into the hall. Slowly he turned and walked outside. The stillness of the hall shouted in my ears and I fled.

From the doorway I could see my father. He was making his way, slowly, down to the ship. I followed him hesitantly, like a dog that is not sure whether or not it ought to have a bad conscience.

He walked around the boat. He stood by the prow, his hand caressing the wood. Though his eyes were gazing out over the sea, he called to me. I walked up to him, both flattered and frightened.

"I had hoped one day to sail with you." A forlorn smile curved his lips: a smile without gaiety.

"We will win, Father!" I was not a man yet, and lived still in a world where the brave killed giants without difficulty.

"I sacrificed our last bull to Odin, while you were gone." Then he sighed and paused. "I think the gods have died. I know that it is said that this would not happen before the end of the world; but maybe the new god that the King believes in has killed them." Then, he spoke this verse:

> "Thor's hammer will fall
> And Odin grow blind,
> Deserted Freya's Hall
> And tearless the wind."

We both stood motionless for a long time—or what seemed to me a long time. Suddenly we heard, from far away, the voices of men and the noise of oars in the water. We returned to the hall. From there, we could see out over Grass Island to the sea beyond it. The three ships were beautiful, and so calm was the water near the island that their reflection was almost as real as they were.

"There are more than three hundred men," he said softly. "Come, my son, let us go to our men."

The compliment my father paid me by saying "our men" made my feet light and my heart easy; for death is a shadow that the eyes of a child cannot see.

* * *

At dawn—while we were still sleeping—the day after the enemy had left, my uncle and his men came. They were all armed, and my uncle was on horseback. Sigurd Sigurdson flung open the door with such force that it banged against the wall, awakening all of us.

With sleep-matted eyes we stared at him. He was wearing his finest clothes and his right hand rested on his sword hilt. "Awake and dress yourselves," he cried, assuming what he must have thought to be a masterful pose.

"You are late, Sigurd," one of my father's old comrades spoke from his bench. "We are tired from work. We have earned a bit of sleep. Go sing your song somewhere else."

My uncle had little courage but much pride. He drew his sword and walked over to Bjorn, who was lying motionless on his bench, as if he intended to return to sleep. "Get up, Bjorn."

Bjorn smiled and said, "I think I hear a fly buzzing, a carrion fly."

"I warned you!" screamed my uncle, his face contorted with anger. Then swiftly, before anyone could stop him, he thrust his sword through Bjorn.

"Brave man," Bjorn muttered; then sighing, he spoke his last words, "Now I shall sleep." Blood flowed from his mouth, and his body twisted and fell with a dull thud from his bench to the floor.

Rogen that had first been ruled by my father's justice, and later by my stepmother's love, now

would know how it felt to be ruled by the sword. Like many weak people's, my uncle's cruelty was dictated by his fears. Ruled by fear himself, he could not conceive that man could be governed by love and respect. Several of the men in the hall gladly would have killed him, but behind him stood his men with swords drawn.

We were a sad-looking group that stood outside the hall in the yellow light of the early autumn morning. My uncle climbed back upon his horse, feeling no doubt that he could impress us more, speaking from that position.

"My brother harvested the crop that grows from the seeds of folly. The gods have meant people to be ruled, and have given them kings and earls and chieftains to obey. My brother thought himself mightier than Magnus Thorsen and paid the price of disobedience, as Bjorn has just paid it."

Some men mumbled something about not being slaves, but none dared to speak aloud.

"I am now the ruler of Rogen, and those who serve me well shall be fittingly rewarded. And so"—here my uncle laughed—"shall those who serve me ill."

To our surprise, two of Sigurd's men now entered the hall and came back with the body of Bjorn.

"For those who disobey me, there will be shame, and their death shall be like the death of an animal." Turning to his men he ordered, "Go, throw his body into the sea, and let the fishes eat it."

I thought the murder of Bjorn a shameful deed, but his last resting place not an unfit one for a hero.

Each of us had to swear allegiance to Sigurd. When my turn came, my uncle said, "I need not the word of a child. I shall be in your father's stead, and I shall teach you humility. Go among the women, and give me that sword."

I would have rushed at him, but Harold the Bowbender took my sword from me, and whispered in my ear, "The wind cannot break a blade of grass, but it can fell an oak."

I believe that my uncle was disappointed when I did not attack him; for if I had, he could have killed me in self-defense, and no one could ever have disputed his right to my father's property.

My uncle decided to make his home in my

father's house. His own he gave to Eirik the Fox, one of his companions: a lying, deceitful man who knew well that his power depended upon my uncle's goodwill. The men whom my uncle suspected of not being loyal to him were divided between the two houses. Two of my father's old friends disappeared shortly afterwards; my uncle claimed that they had been drowned while fishing, but others thought that they had been murdered. With their death the last hope of an open revolt was gone. Backs were bent under the whip of the despot, the weak taking pleasure in it, the strong growing sullen and dull.

Rark and little Helga reappeared. They had been hiding in a cave in the Mountain of the Sun. But Rark, whom my father even before he made him a freeman had treated almost as if he were one, now learned the wages of slavery. All heavy work fell on him, and curses and kicks were his only rewards. The man who lives in the present and has no plans for the future will sink in his own misery, but there are those who will ever invent hope when only despair is present. I knew that Rark was planning his escape, although he did not speak of it, fearing—no doubt—that although my ears were old enough for his secrets my tongue might not be.

Also I learned to work, woman's work: lighting and tending the fires, scrubbing pots, turning the spit the meat was roasted on. My bow and arrows were taken from me, as my sword had been; even the little knife my father had given me the summer I was six, I was not allowed to keep. My uncle wanted me to appear like a slave to the other men. The clothes I wore were the meanest rags, my sleeping place, among the children. With many of the men he succeeded. Some of them took a pleasure in ordering me—their former chieftain's son—to do the work of a slave. The drink of a slave is bitter water; but from that, too, there is a lesson to be learned. Those who abuse slaves have themselves slaves' souls. They are so foolish that they cannot see the difference between the respect given by a freeman to another freeman and the fawning flattery of a slave. They fill their purses with pebbles and think themselves rich. Foolborn, they strut around like geese in the farmyard, who think their fate will be better than that of the hens.

Little Helga suffered even more than I did

from my father's defeat. Used to kindness from my father, and love from her mother, Gunhild, she was doubly robbed. Helga was given to Eirik the Fox to be his slave. Although my uncle was mean, his ambitions were too great for him to spend much of his time tyrannizing a child; but Eirik the Fox was not above such pettiness.

How did Helga bear his mistreatment? She never cried, even when he beat her, but her face grew older, and it was strange to see this little child with the face of an old woman.

All this I was told by the other children, for I saw Helga only once during that first winter after my father's death. My uncle suspected me of plotting against him and did not allow me to walk far from the hall. The one time I did meet Helga was on a wet, dismal fall day. We were both gathering brushwood on the side of Thor's Mountain.

When I saw how thin she had grown, tears came into my eyes; and when she saw my rags, she wept. "Oh, Hakon, Father Olaf has left us!"

I touched her dirty, matted hair (Eirik had taken her comb from her, and he did not even allow her to wash). "Little Helga . . . little sister, I shall take care of you."

She shook her head and looked down at the ground; and at that moment, the idea that had been so vague in my mind became a certainty.

"We shall run away!" I exclaimed, and pointed out toward the sea. "We shall sail away. We will steal a boat next summer—you, Rark, and me."

When I mentioned Rark's name, a little smile flew over her face; and in that moment it became a child's face again. "They will be expecting me soon, and if I haven't gathered enough wood, Eirik will beat me."

I took all my wood and gave it to her. The heavy bundle on her back made her look like a dwarf, like one of the ones that lives in the mountains. "I will die if you leave without me," she whispered earnestly.

"I shall never leave alone. I swear it!"

She took a few steps. Then she turned around to stare at me. Without another word, a moment later, she was running down the mountainside.

Now I had no wood for myself, and probably would be scolded and made to appear the fool by

Sigurd's wife, who was now mistress of my father's hall. But all concern about my own situation had vanished from my mind. I decided that instead of gathering wood, I would climb to the top of the mountain to visit my father's grave.

The wind blew a fierce dance on the plateau. I ran into the storehouse, but it was roofless now and gave little protection. My father's grave had been covered with big boulders. I kneeled by its side, and my blue lips murmured, "I shall avenge you, Father." It was not Magnus Thorsen that I was thinking about when I spoke of vengeance, but my Uncle Sigurd.

A gull screamed near my head. It startled me and I thought that it might be one of Odin's ravens, until I saw its white wings. I glanced up into the cloud-filled sky and spoke loudly: "By Odin, by Thor, I shall avenge myself!"

The winds blew my words out over the sea, and no one heard them; but then, most words spoken to the gods are merely conversations we hold with ourselves.

The day after my visit to my father's grave, I was feverish, and by night I was unconscious. I shivered with cold, though my body was burning like fire under the bearskin that covered me. Had it not been for Rark, I would have died before the Midwinter Feast. He fed me when my hand was too helpless to hold a bowl, and sat by my side during the long nights, when the fever brought monsters to my dreams.

Winter came late that year. It arrived at the time of the Midwinter Feast and, like a hungry guest, it did not like to depart. We learned that year that the bark of trees could be eaten, and there was no animal—no matter how small— that was not hunted. We grew gaunt and our bellies swelled, and the least bit of work made us tired. Seven people died that winter, and we were hardly able to dig their graves. How I survived, who had been sick all fall, must have been by the grace of the gods.

Rark had fed me seaweed, which the others had refused to eat. But I think there must have been magic in it, for, in spring when so many were sick, Rark and I were not. Maybe this is the food of the God of Fishes. Some say that there is a god who has a castle on the bottom of the sea

—so far down that the light of the sun doesn't reach it.

* * *

I was surprised and suspicious when my uncle, who had taken all my weapons from me, gave me back my bow and quiver of arrows and suggested that I should go hunting. Still, the pleasure of a day away from the hall was too attractive to be spurned, and I set out for the Mountain of the Sun, hoping that I might see little Helga along the way. I did not go directly to the other hall (the one which used to be my uncle's home), because I had no wish to meet Eirik the Fox— between us no love was lost. But in my search for Helga I passed very near the outer buildings, which surrounded the hall. Helga was nowhere to be seen, but a man who was busy mending a fence greeted me by my name, Hakon Olafson, and I took this to be a good omen. It was a sign of respect, for Sigurd and his men never called me anything but Hakon the Orphan.

To be alone in nature, to be an animal among other animals, to feel the sun baking on your back and smell the earth and the grass. I forgot the past and had no thought for the future. I was the first man on earth, ageless as the gods.

I wanted to find the cave that Rark and Helga had hidden in when they had been hunted by Ulv Erikson. Rark had described it to me. It was located halfway up the southwestern slope of the Mountain of the Sun. Its entrance was narrow, almost blocked by a large boulder. Near the boulder grew two small birch trees.

There are many boulders and many birch trees on the Mountain of the Sun, and it was late, when I finally found the cave. The dark opening was so narrow that I had to squeeze myself through, but once inside, the cave was huge—as big as my father's hall, if not bigger.

The light was very dim, but near the entrance, under some branches, I found a bow and some arrows and a sword. Rark had told me that he had hidden these weapons in the cave. The sword was a fine one. It had belonged to Thorkild the Mute, who had been killed by Ulv Erikson.

A cave attracts and repels you at the same time. It is an opening into the unknown: into a sunless and moonless world, where you might meet your most bitter dreams.

There are often deep holes in the floor of a

cave. I had no fire, and I did not dare to explore it without light.

On my way home I hunted for hares, but my luck was not with me. By the foot of the Mountain of the Sun, I hid among some bushes, hoping that the hares would be tempted by the good grazing in front of my hiding place.

No hares came. It was growing late. The shadow of the mountain stretched out over the valley, and the evening breeze was chilly. I stood up, and at that moment, I realized that I was not the only hunter on the Mountain of the Sun that day. An arrow sang past my ear. I threw myself upon the ground, expecting a second arrow to follow the first, but none came. I looked towards the mountain, for the arrow had come from behind, but I could see no one. I leaped over the bushes and threw myself down along the other side of them, so that I would be protected from the view of my hunter. For, that I was the hare for whom that arrow had been intended, I did not doubt. A little less than an arrow's shot above me, a pile of boulders made a perfect shelter for a hunter. I put an arrow in my bow and pointed it in that direction.

How long I lay clutching the bent bow, I do not know, but my hands began to tremble. Finally, when the ache in my arms became unbearable, I turned my gaze away from the boulders and, to my amazement, saw the hunter.

It was Eirik the Fox. He had retreated from the boulders by following a dried out riverbed. He was now below me. He must have thought that I had fled, when I jumped over the bushes, for he was walking confidently, making no effort to conceal himself.

Not far away I found the arrow that had missed me. The arrow told me nothing; it could have been anyone's arrow. I put it in my quiver—that arrow that had destroyed my childhood world. I looked at my shadow—the only companion that I dared trust—and laughed.

On the way back, a thousand plans occurred to me, but none satisfied me. When I entered the hall I found my uncle seated at the table with Eirik. They both looked up and Eirik scowled.

"Well, Hakon, how many hares do you bring us?" My uncle's voice was jovial, but his face stern.

"None . . . I saw a fox though. If it had been within arrow's shot I would have killed it."

Neither my uncle nor Eirik responded. I placed my weapons at my sleeping place; then, taking Eirik's arrow from the quiver, I walked back to the table. "I found an arrow: an ill-made arrow, a crooked arrow, an arrow like the one Loki killed the God Balder with." I threw the arrow down in front of them, and kept my glance on Eirik's face.

"Where did you find it?" my uncle asked.

"It came flying like a bird—like a crow."

My uncle took the arrow into his hands and, breaking it in two, he said, "Yes, it is an ill-made arrow." He rose and flung the broken arrow into the fire and watched it burn. "And you are an ill-natured boy."

At my uncle's words, a shiver passed through me and I knew that I had been a vain fool. We were not alone in the hall. Sigurd's wife, Signe, a stupid woman who worshipped her husband as a dog its master, was stirring the soup kettle, which hung over the hearth.

"Pack your things," my uncle ordered. "You are to go with Eirik and stay at his house."

"So long as my father's house stands, I need not work for strangers."

In a few quick strides, my uncle crossed that part of the hall that separated us. His arm was lifted and his hand clenched.

I knew what was to come, but I did not stir. The fifth time my uncle hit me, I fell to the ground and a loud scream opened my tightly closed lips. Blood ran from my nose and mouth. It tasted salty, like the waters of the sea. Twice my uncle kicked me, then my memory stopped. My last thought was, "Now I die."

I did not die. Some of the men had come when they heard my screams and this saved me. My side ached and my nose swelled to almost double its normal size; but in a few days I was up and around again.

If I breathed deeply, it felt as though a knife were being stuck in my side, and I could lift nothing. My uncle acted as if I didn't exist, and I knew that he was making plans for my murder. I was too weak to attempt to escape; besides, there was my promise to little Helga. All I could do to save myself was to keep close to the hall and to other people.

Seven days after my beating, my aunt told me to go to Thor's Mountain to gather wood. I went to my sleeping place to get my bow and arrows, but she took them from me saying, "I told you to gather wood, not to hunt."

I thought of appealing to her, but she was not clever enough to respect the rights of any but the strong. Besides, the thought of what her sons would inherit, if I were killed, made her a willing accomplice to my murder, though I doubt if she herself could have delivered the death blow.

As I looked at Thor's Mountain from the yard in front of the hall, it struck me as being as good a place as any to die. I was so tired, so weak. The yard was empty, for all men had been sent out to fish. I looked about me and whispered, "I shall never see this again." Here I had played when a child. A cat came out of one of the storehouses, blinked its eyes at the sun, and sat down to wash itself. Tears of self-pity formed in my eyes and rolled down my cheeks. It is hard to die, especially when you are only thirteen years old.

As I passed one of the haystacks, a pebble hit me on my shoulder. I turned and there was Rark. He beckoned me to come. I ran to obey him, my heart beating with new-found hope at the sight of his face.

"Your uncle and Eirik the Fox, with three of his men, are on Thor's Mountain. They are going to kill you."

I nodded wearily.

"Go to the cave."

Again I nodded.

Rark took me by the shoulders and shook me gently. "Hakon, are you a child that a beating can break you?"

I could not explain to him that it was not the beating, for, to be perfectly truthful, I did not know what had broken my spirit.

"I have a plan. I shall come to you soon. Be brave, little Hakon."

My uncle's blows had not made me weep, but Rark's kindness did. When he called me "little Hakon," the tears came running like a spring rain. Rark let me cry, holding me close to him without speaking.

When my tears had finally stopped, I felt much better, and Rark laughed. "Will you go to the cave?"

"Yes," I answered firmly and, turning my face defiantly toward Thor's Mountain, I decided that it was too early to hunt for my grave.

"You will need a fire and some skins. Stay here by the haystack, until I come back."

I sat down on the ground at a spot where the haystack would protect me from view, both from the hall and the mountain. The spirit of life, which so mysteriously had been drained from me, came back now like a tide. The idea of living alone in a cave in the Mountain of the Sun appealed to me. It seemed to be the pleasantest house a boy of thirteen could have.

When Rark returned, he had with him a bearskin and a clay pot, filled with embers and ashes. From one ear of the pot to the other, he had tied a piece of rope, so that I could carry it without burning my hands.

"Now run, Hakon. But don't build too large a fire."

I threw the bearskin over my back and picked up the pot. When I turned to say goodbye to Rark, he had disappeared. I took the path which followed the sea until I was near Eirik's hall, then I crossed the island, thinking it better to approach the mountain from the more deserted, western shore.

It was almost midnight when I came to the cave. The sun had disappeared under the horizon, but a strong red glow burned over the dark sea. I entered my cave and built a fire. The flames' flickering light illuminated the cave's high loft. It was a huge cave and even now, at Midsummer, very cold. I wrapped myself in the bearskin and fell asleep. I dreamed about my father and Thora; but my father had Rark's features, and Thora's face was tear stained.

THE LANTERN BEARERS

Rosemary Sutcliff

Rosemary Sutcliff is one of the best writers of historical fiction for children and young adults. Her books are not only accurate and well written but also exciting. She is a master in recreating a past time through believable characters and action.

The Lantern Bearers is the third of Rosemary Sutcliff's trilogy about Roman Britain, following The Eagle of the Ninth and The Silver Branch. In The Lantern Bearers the last of the Roman auxiliaries are withdrawn from Britain to help defend Rome, and Britain is left with no defence from the Sea Wolves, the Saxon raiders. Aquila, a Britain-born Roman and a Legion officer, cannot bring himself to desert his home and so remains behind. Immediately after he returns to his home, the Sea Wolves attack, kill his father, and take his sister captive. As a sadistic jest, they leave Aquila tied to a tree to be devoured by wolves.

THE WOLVES OF THE SEA

The posting stations were still in existence, but to use them without a military permit cost money, and Aquila had never been one to save his pay, so it was upward of a week later when he came at last up the track from the ford, on an evening of soft mizzle rain. He saw the light in the atrium window and made for it, brushing the chill, spattering drops from the low branches of the damson tree as he mounted the terrace steps. He crossed the terrace and opened the atrium door, and stood leaning against the doorpost, feeling like a very weary ghost.

Margarita, who would have been baying her head off at a stranger's footfall before he was half-way up the valley, had risen, stretching and yawning her pleasure, and came padding across the tiled floor to greet him, with her tail swinging behind her. For an instant he saw the familiar scene caught into perfect stillness in the candle light as though it were caught in amber; his father and Demetrius with the chess board between

From *The Lantern Bearers*. © Rosemary Sutcliff, 1959. Used by permission of Henry Z. Walck, Inc., publishers, and Oxford University Press.

them—they often played chess in the evenings, on a board with faint ridges between the ivory and ebony squares; Flavia sitting on the wolfskin rug before the low fire, burnishing the old cavalry sword that she had taken down, as she often did, from its place above the hearth. Only the look on their faces, turned towards the door, was not familiar; the blank, startled, incredulous look, as though he were indeed a ghost that had come back to them mired with the white chalky mud of his journeying.

Then his father said, frowning, 'Is that you, Aquila?'

'Yes, Father.'

'I thought that the last of the Eagles had flown from Britain.'

There was a little silence. Then Aquila said, 'I have deserted the Eagles.'

He pushed off from the door post, and came in, closing the door behind him against the rain that was dark on the shoulders of his leather tunic. Old Margarita was rubbing her head against his thigh, and he put down a hand to fondle her, without being aware that he did so. He was standing before his silent father now. Demetrius would not judge him, he knew: Demetrius judged no man but himself; and Flavia would care for nothing but that he had come home. But with his father it would be another matter. 'I belong to Britain,' he heard himself saying; not trying to defend himself, simply telling his father what had happened. 'More and more, all those three days, I found that I belonged to Britain. And in the end—I let the galleys sail without me.'

For a long moment his father still sat silent, with the chesspiece he had been holding when Aquila entered still in his hand. His face, turned full on Aquila, was stern and uncompromising. 'Not an easy choice,' he said at last.

'Not an easy choice,' Aquila agreed, and his voice sounded hoarse in his own ears.

His father set down the chess-piece with careful precision.

'Nothing, nothing, Aquila, excuses deserting the Eagles. But since it seems to me very probable that in your place I should have done the same as you have done, I can scarcely pass judgement on you.'

'No, sir,' Aquila said, staring straight before him. 'Thank you, sir.'

Old Demetrius smiled a little under his long upper lip, and shifted his own piece on the board.

And Flavia, who had sat ever since he appeared in the doorway, as though caught in some witch's spell of stillness, flung aside the naked sword and sprang up, and came running to set her hands on his shoulders. 'Oh, Aquila, I'm so glad, glad, glad that you did let them sail without you! I thought I should have died when your letter came . . . Does Gwyna know you are here?

'Not yet,' Aquila said.

'I'll go and tell her, and we'll bring you some food—much, much food. You look so hungry. You look—' She broke off, her eyes searching his face. 'Oh, my dear, you said that I had grown up in a year, but you have grown up in twelve days.'

She put her arms round his neck, and held him fiercely close, her cheek pressed against his; then ran from the room calling, 'Gwyna! Gwyna! Aquila's home again! He has come back to us after all, and we must feed him!'

Behind her, Aquila crossed to the fire that burned British fashion on a raised hearth, at the end of the room, and held his hands to it, for he was cold with the rain. Standing there, he said to his father, only half in question, 'No word out of Gaul?'

'I imagine the withdrawal of our last troops is all the word out of Gaul that we shall ever receive,' his father said. He turned in his chair to follow the direction of Aquila's voice. 'Rome has cut her losses, where the province of Britain is concerned, and what the future holds for the province, or for any of us, God knows. Whatever it is, I am glad that you will be sharing it with us, Aquila.'

Two evenings after Aquila's homecoming, they had a fire again, not so much for warmth as to fight the cheerlessness of the summer gale beating against the walls; and with dinner over and the candles lit—you couldn't get oil for the lamps any more—the atrium had taken on its winter aspect, the sense of safety and shelter within firelit walls, and the storm shut out, that belongs to winter time. Aquila had drawn a stool to the side of the hearth, and Flavia had settled herself on the rug beside him, leaning against his knee while she combed and combed her hair. The chessboard had not been brought out tonight, and instead Demetrius, with a scroll spread before him on the table, where the candlelight fell brightest, was reading to their father from The Odyssey.

' "For two days and two nights we lay there, making no way and eating our hearts out with despair and the unceasing labour. But on the third morning bright-haired Dawn gave us clear daylight; wherefore up went our masts and white shining sails . . . Indeed that time I all but came unscathed to my Fatherland, only for the swell and sea currents and a north wind which united against me as I worked round Cape Malcia and drove me wide to Cythera." '

Aquila heard the familiar sentences above the beating of the wind, and realized for the first time that Demetrius had a beautiful voice. His gaze wandered about the room that he had known all his life, brushing over the small household shrine with the sign of the Fish painted on the wall above it, the couches with their coverings of deerskins and gay native rugs, his father's sword hanging above the hearth, the pretty tumble of women's gear—Flavia had never in her life put anything away. His gaze lingered on his father's face, alert and listening in the firelight, his hand with the great dolphin ring fondling Margarita's head on his knee; on Demetrius's grey and gentle features bent over his scroll. Demetrius had been a slave until their father had brought him to be their tutor, and given him his freedom; and when he was no longer needed as a tutor, he had stayed to be Flavian's steward and his eyes. Demetrius was a stoic, a man to whom life was a discipline to be endured with dignity and death a darkness to be met without flinching. Maybe that was what he had taught himself in his slave days, to make them bearable. It came to Aquila suddenly how terrible it must be to be a stoic: but he did not believe that Demetrius was really like that; he loved ideas and people too much. His gaze dropped to Flavia, combing her hair in the firelight that made a glow all round her. She was looking up at him through the dark, flying strands as she flung it this way and that, sweeping the comb through it. And as she combed, she was humming, so softly that the sound would not reach her father or Demetrius at all; a dark, thin, sweet humming that Aquila could barely catch above the voices of the summer storm.

He bent down towards her, his arm across his knee. 'What are you nooning?'

She glimmered with laughter. 'Perhaps I make a singing magic. What would you say if I told you that I combed my hair—just like this—and made a singing magic, on the evening that the galleys sailed, to call you home again?'

He looked at her with unexpected soberness. 'I don't know. But I do not think that I should ever feel quite the same about you again.'

Flavia stopped combing. 'No,' she said, 'I knew that you would not. That is why I did not do it, though I longed to—you can't know how I longed to—because I knew that if I did, and it worked, I should have to tell you. I don't know why, but I should have to tell you, and I couldn't bear that you should not feel the same about me again.'

'Do you know,' Aquila said, 'I don't think I could, either.'

A few weeks ago he would not have dreamed of saying that to Flavia; he would scarcely have thought it to himself. But now it was different; now, when the present moment mattered so much, because there mightn't be anything to come after.

The wind that was roaring up the valley fell away into a long trough of quiet, and in the hush, faint and far off and infinitely sad, rose the hunting cry of a wolf. Aquila cocked up his head, listening. It wasn't often that you heard the wolves in the summer, they were a winter sound; and hearing the long-drawn howl between gust and gust of the storm, he grew freshly aware of the warmth and shelter of the firelit atrium.

Demetrius checked in his reading, to listen also; and Margarita bristled, growling deep in her throat without raising her head from her lord's knee.

'The Forest Wolves call to their brothers of the Sea,' Flavian said, grimly.

Aquila looked at him quickly, knowing that in the past few days there had been several raids on farms nearer the coast. He had seen the distant glare of one such burning farmstead as he followed the downs homeward. It was for that reason that the farm-hands all slept in the house now.

The wind swooped back. Demetrius took up his reading once more at the place where he had broken off, and the group around the fire settled again. But Margarita continued growling, her ears pricked forward, her coat rising a little. She prowled to the door and back, turned round three times after her own tail, and collapsed at her lord's feet, but almost at once she was up again, still growling.

'Hush now. Have you never heard the wolf kind before?' her lord said, and she licked his thumb and sat down again, but still with raised, uneasy head. A few moments later, Bran the sheepdog barked from the farm-hand's quarters, and she sprang up, baying, was silent a moment to listen, then broke out baying again.

'I wonder if it is the Wolves,' Aquila said, half-rising as he spoke, his hand going to his sword.

And almost in the same instant a wild cry broke through the storm, and a babble of shouting rose in the night outside.

'Name of Light! What is that?'

Aquila didn't know which of them had asked

it, but the answer was in all their minds. They were all on their feet now, Demetrius rolling up his precious scroll as the door burst open, letting in a great swoop of wind to drive the smoke billowing from the hearth and set the candle-flames streaming, and Finn the shepherd appeared on the wings of the storm, wild-eyed and panting.

'It is the Saxons! They are all about us! I blundered into them when I went to see to the sheep.' The others were crowding in after him, old Kuno and the farm-hands, all with their weapons, for in these days men were never far from their weapons; little, shrivelled, valiant Gwyna with a long knife from the kitchen, the other women all with what they had been able to catch up. At least there were no children, Aquila thought, only Regan's baby, that was so young it would know nothing . . .

Flavian was quickly and surely issuing his orders; he must have been prepared so long for this to happen, known so exactly what it would be like when it did. The dogs had ceased their baying, and crouched snarling with laid-back ears. Aquila had crossed in two strides to the open doorway. No point in closing it; better to die fighting than be burned in a trap. He called back over his shoulder as red fire sprang up in the farmyard below and he glimpsed the flanged helmets against the uprush of flame.

'They're questing through the out-houses, firing them as they close in. They're driving off the cattle. Lord God! There must be two score of them at least!'

'So. At all events we have a space to breathe until they finish with the byres,' his father said.

Despite the wind, despite the shouting and lowing outside and the red glare that was beginning to beat up from below the terrace, there was a sense of quietness in the long atrium, where the farm-hands with their hastily-snatched-up weapons stood to their appointed places. Aquila supposed that it was the knowing without any doubt that one was going to die, but he thought also it was something that flowed from his father standing in their midst, a kind of strength that was like confidence. Demetrius carefully returned his scroll to the open scroll chest, closed the lid, and, reaching up, took down a long, slender dagger from among the beautiful weapons on the wall.

In the leaping, storm-driven light his face was as grey and gentle as ever.

'I think I expressed to you my gratitude for my freedom at the time,' he said to Flavian, testing the blade. 'I have never spoken of it again. I should like now to thank you for the years that I have been a free man, and—I find on reflection —an extremely happy one.'

'Nay, man, there is no debt that you have not paid; and no time for thanks, on either side, between you and me. Will somebody bring me my sword?'

Aquila, who had turned away from the door, leapt to take it down. He drew it from the worn sheath, and casting the sheath aside, set the weapon naked in his father's outstretched hand.

'There it is, sir.'

His father's strong fingers closed round the grip, and there was a faint smile on his mouth. 'So—it is a long time, but the feel is still familiar . . . They will not know that I am blind. It doesn't show, Aquila?'

'No, sir,' Aquila said, looking for what he knew was the last time into his father's thin, scarred face. 'It doesn't show.'

The shouting was drawing nearer, sounding from all round them now. Flavian crossed with a sure step to the shrine at the far end of the atrium, and laid his naked sword for an instant before the little shielded light that burned quite steadily in the flower-shaped alter lamp.

'Lord, receive us into Thy Kingdom,' he said, and took up his sword again, and turned towards the open door.

Aquila also was standing with drawn sword, his arm round Flavia. She felt light and hard and braced in the curve of it. 'Try not to be afraid,' he said.

'I don't think I am,' she returned. 'Not really afraid. It—doesn't seem real, does it?'

No, it didn't seem real. It didn't seem real even when the shouting and the tumult burst upward into a new savagery and the first Saxon came leaping up the terrace steps to meet the resolute figure of the master of the house, standing with drawn sword in the doorway.

After that, for a while, Aquila knew only a red chaos; a great splurge of shouting in his ears and the snarling of the hounds and the ring and clash of weapons; and Flavia with a high, fierce cry snatching the dagger from his belt as he sprang into the doorway beside his father. The flare of firebrands was in his eyes, and the flash of the fire on leaping saex blades. There seemed flame everywhere, ragged, wind-blown flame, and the bull's-horned and boar-crested warriors thrusting in on them out of the rolling smoke. The rafters were alight now over their head, the flames running along them in bright waves before the wind, and the atrium was full of smoke that tore at the defenders' lungs, choking and blinding them. But there were fewer defenders now; only seven where there had been nine, only six—old Kuno was down, Finn too, and Demetrius. A blazing shutter gave way, and a Saxon sprang in yelling through the high window-hole; and now they were beset from behind as well as before. A man in a great flanged helmet, with the golden torc of a chieftain about his neck, made for Flavian with war-axe up-swung for a blow that there could have been no turning even if the man at whom it was aimed had been able to see it coming. Aquila saw his father fall, and with Flavia fighting like a young fury beside him, hurled himself forward against the leaping saex blades to make a last rallying point of his body.

'To me! To me! Close up!'

Through the red haze that beat before his eyes he saw a snarling face with eyes that seemed all blue fire, and wild yellow hair streaming from beneath the great flanged helmet; he drove the point of his sword in over the golden torc, and saw the man drop his axe in mid-swing and stagger back, clutching at his throat with blood spurting between his fingers; and laughed, knowing that at least his father was avenged.

He did not feel the blow that fell glancing on his own temple and brought him down like a poled ox. He only knew that he had leapt forward in time—how much time he didn't know—and everything seemed to be over, and he was still alive, which bothered him because the two things didn't fit. He was being dragged to his feet, which seemed odd too, for he did not remember being on the ground, dazed and half blind with the blood running into his eyes. And then he heard Flavia shrieking his name, 'Aquila! Aquila!' and wrenched round in his captors' grasp to see her carried past, struggling like a wild cat, over the

shoulder of a laughing, fair-haired giant. He tried to spring towards her, dragging his captors with him, but they were all about him, his arms were wrenched behind his back, and he was flung to his knees, struggling until his heart seemed like to burst and blood pounded like a hammer in his temples. For a moment the world darkened and swam in a red haze about him; Flavia's shrieks died as though somebody had stifled them with a hand over her mouth.

Somehow, fighting still, he found himself thrust to a halt with his arms twisted at his back, before a huge man who stood at the head of the familiar terrace steps under the scorched and shrivelled skeleton of the damson tree. The glare of the wind-driven fire that seemed all about them played on his helmet and yellow hair and beard, and made shifting fishscale jinks of light on the byrnie he wore. And his face, Aquila saw, was the face of the man he had killed for his father's death. But there was no gold torc round this man's neck, and no red hole above it, and therefore it could not be the same.

He stood with arms folded on his breast, staring at Aquila under down-drawn golden brows. Something sparkled green on one great hand, and Aquila, ceasing to struggle now, gasping and spent, knew that it was his father's ring.

'Aye,' the huge Saxon said after a long scrutiny, 'it is the man who slew my brother.'

Through the beating in his head, Aquila understood the meaning of the guttural words, for he had not served a year with Lower Rhenus troops without learning something of the Saxon tongue. He dragged up his head, trying to shake the blood out of his eyes. 'Your brother, who slew my father on the threshold of his own house!'

'So! And he speaks our tongue,' the huge Saxon said, and he smiled, as a wolf smiles. 'Vengeance for a kinsman is sweet. I also, Wiermund of the White Horse, I find it sweet,' and with a slow deliberateness he drew the stained saex from his belt, fondling it, dandling it in his big hands . . .

Aquila waited, his eyes on the Saxon's face. He heard the roar of the flames, and the cattle lowing as they were rounded up, and under it the quietness, the dreadful quietness, full of only the wind. And even the wind was dying now. He was aware of the bodies that lay crumpled and grotesque in the doorway; even Margarita lying dead at her lord's feet, where she must have crawled to him in her last moment. He did not feel very much about them, because he knew that in a few moments he would have joined them. Flavia was the only one he felt anything about—Flavia.

Wiermund of the White Horse had already raised his saex for the death-blow when, far off, above the hoarse moaning of the gale-torn woods, rose a cry that Aquila had heard once already that night: the cry of a hunting wolf, answered by another from away over towards the flank of the downs.

Wiermund checked, listening. Then he lowered his blade, and the smile broadened and broadened on his face until it was a snarl. 'Aiee, the wolf kind smell blood,' he said. 'Soon they will come following their noses.' He seemed to consider a moment, still fingering his saex blade. Then, abruptly, he drove it back into the sheath. 'Take him out to the wood-shore and bind him to a tree.'

The warriors about him looked quickly at each other, and then uncertainly at their leader.

'Alive?' someone said.

'Alive until the wolf kind come,' said the dead Chieftain's brother simply; and a growl of agreement, a grim breath of laughter ran from one to another of the war band. 'Aye, leave him to the wolves! He slew Wiergyls our Chieftain!—They call the wolves our brothers, let the wolves avenge their kin!'

They half thrust, half dragged him down the terrace steps skirting the blazing farmyard, and away up to the tongue of the woods above the old vine terraces, where he had stood with Flavia looking down on their home so short a time ago. At the last moment he began to struggle again, wildly, desperately. It was one thing to brace oneself for the quick dispatch of the saex blade, but quite another to stand unresisting to be tied to a tree for living wolf-bait. His body revolted at the prospect and went on struggling without anything to do with his will. But all his strength seemed to have gone from him, and he was powerless in their hands as a half-drowned pup. They stripped him naked; someone brought a partly charred wagon-rope from the blazing shed, and with the sound part of it they lashed his hands behind his back and bound him to the trunk of a young beech tree. Then they drew off and stood about him, very merry.

He forced up his head against the intolerable weight that seemed to bear it down, and saw their shapes dark against the glare of the blazing farmstead.

'So, bide there with a good fire to warm you until the wolf kind come,' said the man who had been the Chieftain's brother, and he called off his warriors like a hunter calling off his hounds. Aquila did not see them go, only he realized suddenly, through the swimming confusion in his head, that he was alone.

Only the wind swept up the valley, and below the wind he heard the silence. The fires below were sinking; and there would be no more fires in the valley where the hearth fire had burned for so many generations of men; and the silence and the desolation washed up to Aquila like the waves of a dark sea, engulfing him. Swirling nightmare pictures washed to and fro on the darkness of it, so that he saw over and over again the last stand in the atrium doorway, and his father's death, so that he saw over and over again the hideous vision of Flavia struggling in the hands of the barbarians that set him writhing and tearing at his bonds like a mad thing until the blood ran where the ropes bit into him.

He must have lost consciousness at last, because suddenly the grey dawn was all about him, and the gale quite died away. The wolf kind had not come. Maybe there were too many of their human brothers hunting these hills; for he heard the mutter of voices, and the first thing he saw when his eyes opened on a swimming world were a pair of feet in clumsy raw-hide shoes, and the lower rim of a Saxon buckler. Men were standing round him again, but he realized dimly that though they were Saxons, they were not last night's band, but a new raiding party that had come questing out of the woods to find that others had been before them.

'Nay then, why should you meddle with another man's kill?' someone was protesting in a deep growl of exasperation.

And somebody else was hacking at his bonds with a saex blade, waying through shut teeth, 'Because I have a mind to him, that's why.'

The last strands parted, and Aquila swayed forward. He struggled to keep upright before these new tormentors, but his numbed legs gave under him and he crumpled to the ground, his wrists still bound behind him. The man who had cut him from the tree straddled over him hacking at his remaining bonds, and as the last strands of those also parted, he rolled over and saw, frowning upward through the throbbing in his head, that it was a lad younger than himself, a mere stripling in ring-mail byrnie, with a skin that was clear red and white like a girl's under the golden fuzz of his beard.

'Get some water from the stream,' said the stripling to the world in general; and it seemed that somebody must have brought it in his helmet, for suddenly the iron rim was jolting against Aquila's shut teeth. Someone dashed the cold water into his face, and as he gasped, a wave of it went down his throat, making him choke and splutter, yet dragging him back to life whether he would or no. As his head cleared, he realized that there were about a score of men standing round him, with laden ponies in their midst. Clearly they had had better luck with their raiding in other places than they had in this one.

'What Thormod the son of Thrand should want with another's leavings is a thing beyond my understanding,' said the voice that he had heard before; and Aquila saw now that it belonged to a bull-necked individual with red hair sprouting out of his nose and ears. 'If you would carry home a slave at the summer's end, let it be one of your own taking.'

The boy he had called Thormod stood over Aquila still, the red of his face spreading over the white from the gold collar he wore to the roots of his yellow hair, though he was yet half-laughing. 'Ran the Mother of Storms fly away with you, Cynegils! Must you be for ever telling me what I should do and what I should not do? He has a dolphin on his shoulder, and often Bruni my grandsire has told me how in his seafaring days he

knew always when he saw a dolphin that his luck would be good, wherefore he took the dolphin for his lucky sign. And therefore I've a mind to take this other man's leavings for a gift to my grandsire that I reckon will catch at his fancy more than a jewelled cup or a little silver god.'

'As for the dolphin, it is but painted on and will surely wash off,' somebody said, bending to peer more closely at Aquila as he half-lay in their midst.

'Nay, it is pricked in after the manner of the patterns that the Painted People wear. I have seen their envoys.' The boy Thormod spat on his hand and rubbed it to and fro over the tattooing on Aquila's shoulder, then held up his hand triumphantly. 'See, it does not wash off!'

Somebody laughed. 'Let the boy take his findings; it is his first raiding summer.'

'Also I am Sister's Son to Hunfirth the Chieftain,' said the boy.

A tall man with eyes that were very blue in a square, brown face reached out an arm heavy with bracelets of copper wire and shining blue glass, and caught him a lazy buffet on the side of the head. 'Not so loud, my young cockerel. No man's word counts more than another's in my ship, saving only my own. Nevertheless, we've room for another rower since Ulf was killed, and you shall take him—and be responsible for him —if you've a mind to.'

And so, still half dazed, Aquila was jerked to his feet, and his hands twisted again behind his back and strapped there. And when the little band of Saxon raiders turned seaward, climbing the long slope of the downs, they carried Aquila stumbling in their midst.

Behind him the valley was left to its silence, and nothing moved save the last faint smoke that still curled up from the blackened ruins of his home.

THE SHIELD RING

Rosemary Sutcliff

The Shield Ring, another of Rosemary Sutcliff's excellent historical novels about England's past, dramatically portrays the last days of Saxon freedom in northeastern England. The Normans, having subdued the south, are attempting to bring to heel the remaining Saxon strongholds in the north. The struggle is bitter. Even though the most that can be gained is a little more time of freedom before their eventual defeat, the Saxons fight on.

The thing happened with the appalling swiftness of a hawk swooping out of a quiet sky, on a day in late spring, when Frytha was not quite five.

She had been out about the sheep with Grim, who had been her father's shepherd in the old days before Norman William laid waste the North in payment for the massacre of his York garrison, and was now hind, ploughman and everything else as well; and they had made a wide cast through Garside Wood on the way home, to visit a flycatcher's nest that Grim had found for her. Five speckled eggs the nest had in it, faintly and wonderfully blue. Now they were on their way home in earnest; little black hairy Grim and Frytha with her kirtle kilted to her bare brier-scratched knees and her honey-brown hair full of twigs, hand in hand, in companionable silence, for Grim discouraged chatter in the woods; it drove things away, he said. And just ahead of them, Vigi the big black sheepdog, looking round every few moments to make sure that they were following. Vigi was as silent in the woods as his master, and never chased squirrels or ran yelping on the scent of the fallow deer, as more foolish dogs did.

They were late, for there had not really been time for such a roundabout way home. The last sunlight had flickered out among the tree-tops

long since and as they came up the long slope toward the crest of the ridge, the day was fading fast and the woods growing shadowy about them. 'I shall ketch it from thy mother, bringing thee home at owlhoot,' Grim said, grinning down at Frytha through the tangle of black hair that almost covered his face.

Frytha gave something between a gasp and a giggle by way of reply, for the slope was steep just there and full of pitfalls. She had an uneasy feeling on the edge of her mind that she also would ketch it from her mother, but most of her was still taken up with the flycatcher's nest, and in her heart she knew that a possible smacking was no more than a fair price to pay for the round perfection of the moss-lined nest and the magic of those five eggs; so tiny, and so blue under the darkness of the ivy leaves.

They were almost at the top of the ridge now, and the white tip of Vigi's tail waving plume-wise just in front of her was beginning to take on a faint shine of its own, as white flowers shine in the twilight. She climbed on, and on, her legs growing tired under her—and then all at once she knew that something, somewhere, was wrong.

All about her, the wood was uneasy. The little rustlings and flutterings of the woodland creatures had died away as though there were a storm coming. Vigi seemed to catch the strange unease at the same moment. He stopped in his tracks, his muzzle raised, the white star of his tail tip quivering downward. And when Frytha reached out to touch his back, she felt his coat rise under her

From *The Shield Ring* by Rosemary Sutcliff. Used by permission of Henry Z. Walck, Inc., publishers, and Oxford University Press.

palm, and snatched her hand away as though something had stung her.

'Grim!' She was suddenly frightened, too, as Vigi began to stalk forward on stiff legs. 'Grim, I don't like it!'

Grim said nothing, but his hand tightened over hers until it hurt her, and she had the feeling that his hairs were rising in the same way as Vigi's.

A distant confused sound of shouting came dipping toward them over the crest of the wooded ridge.

And then they were on the crest, among the crack-willow and whitehorn of the woodshore, staring down the long curve of ploughland and summer fallow toward the home steading.

There were many men down there, a dark flicker of men all round the house-place and among the byres, and a saffron flicker of torches, and in the instant that they checked there on the woodshore, something like a flower—a rose—of flame sprang out on the house-place roof, and spread and blurred, sending out wriggling threads of brightness through the dark thatch.

Next instand Grim had a hand on Vigi's collar, and the other round Frytha, scooping her up, sweeping both of them back into the shelter of the trees. 'Bide you here' he said, setting her down among arching brambles between the roots of an ancient may tree, 'and bide you still, until I come again.' And to Vigi he said 'Keep!' as he did when he wanted him to hold a clump of sheep together. Then he was gone, slipping along the woodshore like a shadow, toward the place where the curving wind-break ran down toward the rick-garth.

Vigi lay down in front of Frytha, nose on paws, watching her with an unwinking gaze, as he would have watched a clump of sheep left in his charge, unmoving so long as they did not move. Frytha made no attempt to move. She sat where Grim had set her down, like a young hare frozen in the grass when a hawk hovers over, staring down through the brambles and tall-growing things of the woodshore. She saw the torches jigging to and fro; she saw the threads of fire spread and run together, until suddenly a sheet of flame leapt into the dusk, roaring up from the dry thatch. She heard cattle lowing and the frightened neighing of a horse, and saw the dark shapes of her father's kine against the fire, as men drove

them past toward the Lancaster road; and the shouting seemed to rise higher with the flames. The flames were pale and bright in the dusk. That was the thing that Frytha remembered ever afterward: the pale bright flame of burning thatch.

Behind her, Garside Wood began uneasily to make its night-time noises; bats flittered needle-squeaking overhead among the branches of the may tree, and the owls were crying, answering each other from tree to tree, and still Frytha sat frozen, waiting for Grim to come back. She was not afraid; she seemed to have gone through fear and come out the other side in a place where it was black and very cold. It seemed a long, long time that she waited, a whole night—many nights. And yet the dusk had not deepened to full dark when there was the faintest rustle among last year's leaves, and the ghost of a whine from Vigi, and Grim was crouching beside her breathing hard as though he had been running.

It seemed to Frytha that the shouting was coming nearer, but she could not see what was happening, because now Grim was between her and the open land. But she saw the sheet of flame leap higher yet, rimming the bramble leaves with fire behind the dark bulk of his head and shoulders as he looked back. 'That is thy home burning,' he said in a grating voice that did not sound like Grim at all. 'That is the Normans' work, and never thee forget it!'

Then he caught her up, and began to run again, deeper and deeper into the wood. Once or twice he checked to listen, cranning his chin over one shoulder or the other, and Frytha, clinging to him without quite knowing why, could feel the life-thing in his chest, where he was holding her tight against it, thud-thud-thud, very fast, like the hoof-beats of a stampeding horse, somehow more frightening than the torchlight and the shouting behind them. And then at last there was no more torchlight and no more shouting; only the night sounds of the woodland, when Grim stopped to listen. Only the bark of a dog fox in the distance, and the little night wind among the trees.

After that there was a time that always seemed to Frytha, looking back on it, to be a kind of cloud in which things came and went half seen and no more real than the things one dreams just before waking up. She thought that they went a long way, she and Grim and Vigi. There were days and nights in the cloud, and sometimes she walked until her legs gave out, but most often Grim carried her on his back or on his shoulder. Grim was very kind to her in this way, and spread his ragged cloak over her in the night time, when she lay curled against Vigi for warmth. But there did not seem to be any warmth in Vigi, no warmth anywhere. Sometimes there were things to eat—once Vigi caught a hare, and Grim cooked it in a fire that he lit from the little fire-stones he always carried with him; and once they robbed a hen's nest that they found in a ruined garth, and sucked the warm eggs. And Frytha ate whatever Grim gave her to eat, and lay down and got up, and walked or climbed on to his back to be carried, just as he told her; and never thought to ask, or even wonder, where they were going, because she never really understood that they were going anywhere, only that the world had fallen to pieces and that it was very cold among the ruins.

Then there began to be mountains; grey and dun and purple mountains with mist hanging among their high corries, that towered above the tangle of forest and marsh and great sky-reflecting lakes; mountains so high that the upward rush of them made her want to crawl under something and hide. There were men, too, though which came first, the men or the mountains, she never knew; but clearly they belonged to each other. And after the men came there was more food— flat cakes of barley bread that looked as hard as millstones; but when Grim broke a piece off one and gave it to her, it was soft and sweet under the hard crust as bread newly baked. Once there was a steading at the foot of a great sweep of moor, and warm milk in a little birchwood bowl, and a woman who was kind. Frytha thought that the woman would have had them stay, but Grim would not; and they pressed on again, and the men with them—but whether they were the same men she did not know.

The mountains began to come down all around them; either that or they were climbing up into the mountains, further and further up until the world of men was left behind and they came into another world that belonged to the great singing wind of the emptiness. And then they came down out of the emptiness, down and

down and down, and there was a grey lake shore in the twilight, and little wavelets lapping on it.

And at last, when she had fallen half asleep in Grim's arms, bursting on her unawares out of the gathering dusk, there was a great hall full of fire-light and torchlight and hounds and men and a roar of voices.

With Vigi at his heel, Grim carried her straight in, thrusting through the thronging men and hounds, toward a golden giant who turned in the High Seat, midway up the hall, to watch them coming; and bent and set her down on the giant's knee.

The giant put out an arm on which there were great golden rings twisted like serpents above the elbow, and crooked it about her lest she roll straight off again; and his eyes under their thick golden brows went thrusting from her to Grim and back. 'God's greeting to you, Stranger,' he said, in a voice that matched his huge size. 'What wind is it blows you and the bairn up here into Butharsdale?'

'A wind from Normandy, Jarl Buthar,' Grim said harshly.

'So, What roused the wind this time? Deer-stealing?'

'Some hungry fool robbed and slew a knight on the Lancaster road, half a moon since, and for that the whole countryside must pay wyrgeld in blood and burning. It is in my heart that my master knew who the robber was, and would not give him up. For that also there must be payment.'

A ragged muttering rose from the men along the walls, who had fallen silent to listen.

'The North has paid over much wyrgeld in blood and burning for Duke William's York garrison twenty summers ago,' said Jarl Buthar, as though half to himself. 'And so you fled up here to the mountains.'

'Aye, as many a one has done before.'

The Jarl nodded, pulling with his free hand at his golden beard. 'Aye, many and many a one; and none that was not heartily welcome.' He looked down at Frytha. 'Is the bairn yours?'

'Nay, I was her father's man, and his father's before him, in the days when the farm was rich before the wasting of the North, with as many serfs on the land as there are fingers on my two hands. Of late years there's been none but me.'

Frytha heard their voices going to and fro above her, but the words had no meaning. Just for a moment, as the light and the roar of voices broke over her, she had thought that she was going to wake up, and find herself in her own corner behind the bolster in the great box bed at home. But she had not woken up, and she was not in her own corner; she was in a place such as she had never seen before; a long firelit hall that must surely be greater than the great church at Lancaster where her father had taken her last Christmastide. Rooftrees rose out of the firelight into the dark beyond the drifting peat-reek overhead, like trees in the aisles of a forest and everywhere there were men, crowding the benches along the shadowy walls, lounging with their legs outstretched among the hounds on the fern-deep floor, with the firelight flickering on their weapons and in their eyes. Her gaze scurried to and fro among them, searching frantically for faces that she knew, but they were all strange to her save Grim standing with a hand on Vigi's collar; Grim and Vigi were part of the bad dream in which she was trapped, so that they could not help her now.

And then her darting, terrified gaze found another giant, sitting close at the golden giant's feet; a grey giant, this one, with nothing golden about him save the firelight on the strings of the harp he held on his knee. His mane of hair was striped and brindled grey and dark, with a great white wing in it so that it seemed to grin like a badger's striped mask in the firelight' and long yellow teeth showed in the grey tangle of his beard as he smiled up at her, so that his face might have been the most frightening of all the faces there, but it made Frytha think of Bran, her father's old brindled wolfhound, who she had loved, and somehow that made it a thing to cling to.

'. . . I crept in under their noses for a closer look,' Grim was saying, 'but there wasn't naught to do but bring the bairn away.'

And suddenly the faces were closing in on Frytha, all eyes and teeth, and terrible because they were strange. She sat rigidly upright on the Jarl's knee, like a small proud figure carved in stone; but her wide terrified eyes were fixed on the grey giant's face like a cry for help. The grey giant laid down his harp and rose to his feet with a harsh

exclamation. She did not hear what he said, nor what the golden giant answered, but strong arms caught her and swung her up, up and away out of the confusion and the terrible crowding faces.

Food was being brought for Grim and the mountain men who had come with him, and room and welcome made for them on the benches, as the grey giant carried Frytha high against his shoulder up the Jarl's Hearth Hall, and thrusting open a door at the end of it, into a place beyond.

Here there was softer, clearer light from a lamp, and women were gathered round the central hearth, combing and braiding their hair as Frytha's mother had used to do when she made ready for bed; and one of them, who was tall like a spear, with a cloud of pale hair round her head, rose from a cushioned bench as they entered, and came quickly through the rest, saying 'Why, what is this that you bring us, Haethcyn?'

'A girl-bairn,' said the grey giant, 'a small, very spent girl-bairn, with a long road and a burned home behind her, my Lady Tordis. A shepherd-has just brought her in from beyond Lancaster.'

'Her father?'

'Nay, you must ask of the Normans concerning her father, and all her kin,' the grey giant said meaningly.

The other women were exclaiming softly and bitterly as they crowded round. The one who was like a spear said: 'Give her to me,' and held out her arms. 'Signy, do you bring milk and warm it.'

* * *

'Ah, poor bairn, she's as light as a half-fledged tit.' She asked no more questions. She had seen many fugitives from the outer world here in this Norse settlement of the Cumberland Fells, but she sat down again beside the hearth, and held Frytha close on her lap, and called her by the soft cradle names that Frytha's mother had used.

Frytha sat as still and straight on the woman's knee as she had done on the Jarl's, not hearing the cradle names, and looked about her. The light of the low-set lamp scarcely reached to the walls, and the gloom seemed to move and deepen among the great carved kists and the furry animal darkness of bear and wolf skins piled upon the low benches; and there was something tall and skeleton-gaunt against the gable wall that might be a loom in the daytime, but was not quite a loom now, and a thing that glimmered pale behind the half open door of the huge box as though something were crouching there.

The women had gathered about the fire again, and Frytha's gaze scurried to and fro among them, searching as she had searched among the faces in the hall. They looked back at her kindly, but they were not her mother; and the grey giant had gone, and taken safety with him; and she had lost even Grim now. A very old woman sat by the fire spinning; her hair was like rough silver in the lamplight, but her brows were black as feathers from a raven's wing, and under them she peered at Frytha, half smiling, through the faint fronds of the peat smoke.

'That is Unna. She will be very kind to you,' said the woman like a spear, seeing whom Frytha was looking at. 'She was my nurse when I was smaller than you are now, and she was very kind to me.'

The girl called Signy had come back from somewhere, with a pipkin of milk, and as she stooped to set it over the fire, her shadow leapt up and swallowed half the chamber, as though she had spread dark wings. Panic began to whimper up in Frytha, tightening in her chest so that it was hard to breathe; but the woman held her closer, and whispered, 'Na Na, you must not be afraid, Tita, there is nothing here to be afraid of. Soon you shall have some warm milk, and then you will sleep. You shall have a little straw pillow, and a dappled deerskin to keep you warm; and in the morning when you wake, the shadows will be gone—all gone, you will see.'

But she could not reach Frytha through the nightmare.

And then there was a faint rustling somewhere in the far shadows, like an animal gathering itself to spring; and with a little gasp, Frytha wrenched herself round to face it. Something was humping and upheaving in the darkness of a closet that yawned blackly in the far wall. One of the women laughed half in exasperation, but Frytha never heard her. She was watching the humping and upheaving in a fascinated horror that left no room for anything else.

But the thing that shook itself clear of the shadows and the dark piled skins was neither wolf nor ghost, but a boy. He stood in the closet doorway, shaking the black hair from his face, and stared at her. Frytha stared back. He was a year or two older than she was, a very dark boy—dark as Grim—with a long cleft chin, and eyes as tawny-pale as peat water and bright as a wild animal's. And something in his ruthlessly interested stare came piercing through the nightmare, and reached Frytha in the cold place where she was, so that all at once she drew a long breath, and let it go out softly, like a sigh.

'I heard things happening,' said the boy. 'What does the girl-bairn here?'

'You should be asleep,' one of the women began. 'The wolf out of the North Star will come and eat you if—'

But the woman like a spear said very quietly: 'No, Margrit, wait,' and her hold on Frytha grew lighter.

The boy completely ignored the interruption. 'Why does she look like that?' he demanded. 'Has somebody hurt her?'

'Somebody has hurt her, yes,' said the woman like a spear, and her touch on Frytha grew as light as a leaf.

Without knowing it, Frytha slid off her lap, and stood wavering a little with sheer weariness, then moved forward. At the same instant, the boy moved forward also. They squatted down in the rushes, and stared at each other, tense and wary, like two small wild things, each unsure whether the other is friend or enemy, or perhaps both; while the women watched, and from the great hall beyond the door came the sound of voices and harp music to fill the silence.

The girl Signy was making a soft nest of rugs on one of the sleeping-benches; and when that was done, she brought a little bowl of blue earthenware, and poured the warm milk into it, and brought a piece of bannock thick with butter, and gave them to Frytha.

For the first time the boy's eyes moved. He looked at the bannock, and put both hands over his stomach. 'I am hungry, too,' he said.

The old woman Unna gave a cackle of laughter. 'Never think to feed one puppy and fast another in the same basket.'

So Signy laughed too, and brought more buttered bannock and gave it to the boy, who took it without again turning his gaze from Frytha's face, and began to chew.

Frytha tried to eat her own bannock, but she was not hungry; and now that she was no longer afraid, she was growing desperately sleepy. Someone was coaxing her at least to drink the milk, and she managed to obey. Everything was turning hazy, and the warm milk seemed to make it hazier still; but even through the waves of sleep, she saw the pale bright eyes of the boy staring at her; and she stared back over the tilting rim of the bowl.

Then the voices were saying something about going to sleep, and somebody stooped over her as though to pick her up. But the boy swallowed his last mouthful of bannock with a gulp, and reaching out, caught hold of the tattered hem of her kirtle. 'Na, Na,' he said. 'She must come in-by with me'; and then, speaking to Frytha herself for the first time, 'Come you.'

And wavering to her feet, unquestioningly, Frytha came, followed by the cackling laughter of the old woman by the fire. 'He is the Lordly One! The Lordly One! "Come you," says he, like as it might be the King of Norway!'

It was warm and dark under the skins in the closet, and Frytha and the boy burrowed together like a pair of puppies. She was too far gone in sleep to hear the women moving in the Bower, or the sea-surge of voices in the great hall where the men still sat; but she felt and heard when the boy rolled over against her shoulder, and whispered 'What is you name?'

'Frytha.'

'My name is Bjorn the Bear, and my father's name was Bjorn the Bear, but mostly people call me "Bear-cub" yet awhile,' said the boy, and flung an arm over her neck. 'I shall call you Fryth, but nobody else must. And nobody shall hurt you again, excepting me.'

And then the quiet and kindly waves of sleep broke over her.

THE MATCHLOCK GUN

Walter D. Edmonds

The Matchlock Gun is based on a true experience that happened to the Van Alstyne family in 1756. This well-written historical picture book will interest children in the primary grades as well as older students. The plot is exciting and the characters are believable. The Matchlock Gun was awarded the Newbery Medal in 1942.

Notice how Edmonds develops tension and fear both in the story and in the reader. Compare the reader's reactions to Indians in this book and in Killer of Death, *an excerpt from which is included in this chapter.*

When Indians begin raiding Dutch settlers, Edward's father, Teunis, shows his son how to fire the old matchlock gun and then goes to help prevent the Indians from entering the Hudson Valley. The Indians, slipping by the guards, attack Edward's family.

INDIAN FIRES

John Mynderse rode down after lunch, carrying his musket in his hands, balancing it on

the withers of his bright bay horse. He called for Gertrude to come out, and she closed the door behind her so that the children, looking through the window, could not hear what was said. The sun was warmer now and the wind was dying down and the bay horse rested his hip while Mynderse talked down to their mother. She tilted her face up at him, looking young and small and worried.

"Teunis says to tell you everything is all right. But the French Indians are burning the upper settlements. People have been killed. They have sent a company from Albany to the Flats. The company will stop them all right, Gertrude."

"What are you doing?"

"Teunis wanted to let you know, that is all. I am riding over to Van Epps' and to my own place. But Teunis thinks maybe you had better go over to the big house." Mynderse looked down at her. "He won't get back tonight either, probably."

"Tell him not to worry about us. We are fine." He looked away from her as she squared her shoulders. "Tell me, does he want anything?"

Mynderse shook his head. "Yes, I forgot. He wants his schnapps in the wood flask."

"All right," she said. "Doesn't he want any food? Bread?"

"He didn't say, but he could use food. There are quite a lot of us."

"Just a minute." She flew into the house to get the schnapps. "Get the big loaf of bread, Trudy. And you get the ham, the big one at the end, Edward."

In a moment they had the food ready for Mynderse. He put the flask over his shoulder and the loaf in his bag and took the ham in his arm. "Just like my baby," he said, grinning at the children, and they laughed soberly.

They watched him clop away up the road, leaving deep tracks in the mud, and Edward said, "Mynderse does not ride like Father. He is like a flour sack sitting on a horse."

"You must not say such things about Mynderse. He is very kind."

Trudy clapped her hands and said, "The Indians don't wear breeches!" She sang it. "The Indians don't wear breeches. Oh, the Indians don't wear breeches," till she was hushed up and was sullen and went around muttering something. Edward finally asked her what she said, and she answered in a deep voice, "Bergom op Zoom!"

He looked up at the Spanish Gun at once. It seemed like a cannon with the afternoon light shining through the window along the whole length of it. He thought they need not be afraid with that in the house.

Gertrude said, "Let us go out for a little walk."

"Where to?"

"Oh, just for some air. And then we can get in the cows."

They went out, and to please Trudy, Mama allowed her to wear the old shawl, so that she looked like a comical dwarf woman with fat legs. The children chattered all the way along and Gertrude had no trouble in leading them up the knoll beyond the garden. It was quite a high rise of ground. From the top of it one could see out clear into the north and east.

The sun was half way down and the west wind, though it was much milder, was like a stream against their cheeks. The children saw the smoke as soon as Gertrude did. It was a leaning cloud, far in the north. They could see it plain against the pale horizon.

"Is it far away?" the children asked.

"Yes." Gertrude was straining her eyes. She tried to imagine where it came from. She thought it was much nearer than the north settlements. Near the Flats, she thought, since it showed so distinctly.

"Is it a big fire, Mama?"

"Yes, I think so."

"I want to see it!" said Trudy. "I want."

"It is too far. It is time to be getting back to the house."

Edward was silent. They walked down together with the wind cold in their faces and saw the cows by the creek.

"Come," cried Gertrude, "we must get them in."

"I'll get them," said Edward.

"No, we'll all get them. Hurry."

Trudy ran, waving a stick and screeching, "Bergom op Zoom!" but Edward kept waching his mother. He knew now that she was afraid.

"Are the Indians near?"

"Not very." She made her voice sound calm. Luckily the cows were eager to be brought in. They fastened them and went into the house. Then Trudy was sent to wash her face and Gertrude called Edward.

She looked pale and serious.

"I think the Indians are quite near, Edward. You must not go out any more."

"Why don't we go over to Grandmother's?"

"It is better here." She thought of an excuse. "If Papa comes back, he would want to find us at home, Edward."

LOADING THE GUN

She had thought out her course while getting the cows. It was better to stay. Their place was away from the main road, and raiders would be more likely to know and see the brick house. She knew that she could not help the grandmother, who would not want her help in any case, and she thought only of the best way to keep the children safe. To stay seemed the best way to her. Trudy's shouting had given her an idea for defending the house, for it seemed to her that if the Indians came they would not arrive as far as this except in small groups.

"Edward, I want you to be a brave boy and do everything I tell you."

"Yes, Mama."

"Would you be afraid to fire Great-Grandfather's gun?"

Edward looked up at the Spanish matchlock, all the great length of it, and said with a white, excited face, "No, Mama. But I can't hold it."

"I can fix that," she said. "But you must do exactly what I say."

She went over to the fireplace and mounted a stool and took down the huge gun. It was beginning to grow dusky in the Kill Valley already, and the kitchen had turned gray and shadowy. She lit a candle.

"Fetch the big powder horn."

She had no idea how much powder to put into the gun, but she doubled what seemed to her a musket charge. She wadded it down with a piece of writing paper, standing at the end of the barrel and pushing the rod, because of the length of the gun.

"It hasn't any bullets," Edward said.

"See if there are some with Papa's mold."

Edward found two. They rolled down the barrel with a faint rattling sound. Gertrude was not satisfied. She leaned the gun on a chair and told Edward not to let Trudy touch it. Trudy came in at that moment and as soon as she saw the gun she stopped dead. For once she was speechless.

Gertrude rummaged, finding some horseshoe nails and some small pebbles and two brass buttons. She rammed them all down and wadded them hard. Then she got Teunis's axe and chopped out a corner of the blind of the window at the left of the stoop door.

With Edward helping, she dragged the table to the window and then lifted the gun onto it, and with all her flatirons propped the gun so that it pointed to the missing corner of the blind, straight out onto the steps of the stoop. She bolted the blinds then, not only of that window but of the other windows also, and dropped the bar over the shed door.

She had become very silent in doing these things, and so had the children watching her. Edward trembled a little when she drew a stool up to the table and told him to get onto it. Then she primed the gun and set the candle beside it.

Seeing the whole thing complete, Trudy suddenly said with great acuteness, in a loud voice, "Bergom op Zoom!"

"Hush," said Gertrude. "Trudy, you must not talk. You must play on Mama's and Papa's bed." She made a doll out of a handkerchief and got a large lump of maple sugar and some of the silver spoons and put them and Trudy together on the bed, leaving the door open so that she would not be frightened. The little girl settled down in delight on the big bed and held her doll up so she could see, and whispered, "Bergom op Zoom," very softly.

EDWARD'S ORDERS

Gertrude went back to her son, thinking how young he was to have so much to do. "Edward, you must listen to me."

"Yes, Mama."

"I am going outside to look for Indians. If they come, I shall call your name, ATEOORD! Loud as I can. Then you must touch the candle to this place."

"Yes, Mama," he said eagerly.

"You must not do it before."

"No, Mama."

"You must not touch anything until I call your name. If I call Teunis, or Mynderse, or Uncle Sylvanus, you must not touch anything. But when I call ATEOORD, then what will you do?"

Edward reached for the candle.

"No, NO! You must not touch anything."

"I wasn't going to," he said in a low, indignant voice. He moved his hand through the gesture of touching the priming. She leaned down from behind and put her arms around him and kissed him.

"Good, brave boy."

He sat rigidly still. He looked small and white and dark-eyed. There was a hole in the knee of his stocking—she had meant to mend it that day.

"What do you do?" she asked again.

He repeated her instructions carefully and accurately.

"You are a smart boy," she said. "Do you know, even Papa has never fired that Spanish Gun?"

"Yes, I know." His voice shook a little. "Will it make an awful noise, Mama?"

"Yes, it will scare the Indians, and Papa will be so proud."

"Where are you going?"

"Just outside, Edward, to watch for the Indians."

"Not far?"

"No, I'll be near. Remember, you must not even move from the stool."

"No, Mama."

She looked at him once, then at Trudy; then, making her face serene as she could, she took up her shawl and a basket and went out of the house, closing the door upon them.

INDIANS ON THE FARM

She had taken the basket to pick beans into. The pods remaining were worthless, but she wanted to have an excuse to stay out. Any raider coming must not be made suspicious. She had thought of picking the bean pods because she had noticed them early that morning. It had seemed to her as if the whole day had been made of pieces that had fitted together suddenly when silly little Trudy began screeching "Bergom op Zoom" after the cows.

Now, walking up to the garden patch, across the wind, she wondered whether she had not been acting hysterically. She had put Edward

under a strain that no boy only ten years old ought to have. She had left him frightened, cold, with his resolution to be brave. She seemed to see him sitting there by the table at the end of the monstrous gun, listening and listening. But she knew that she could have done nothing else, unless she took them to Widow Van Alsyne's. As for that, she could still persuade herself that she had been right in considering her own house the safer place.

Twilight had stretched across to the Helderbergs when she came among the bean vines. She began picking pods into her basket, slowly, one at a time, fumbling with her hands in the cold wind, and watching the woods unceasingly. It would soon be too dark to be able to see the woods. There was only a pale light to show the rolling tops of the hills. There was no light at all to the north now, and the night was a visible blackness in the sky.

So that Edward might not feel too deserted, now and then she sang, her voice carrying away from her lips along the wind. She hoped he could hear her.

> "Trip a trop a troenje;
> De varken en de boenjen."

> "Up and down on a little throne;
> The pigs are in the beans."

The wind seemed to be falling still lower with the failing light. Now and then she could hear the water running in the Hunger Kill below.

The widow's was a brick house, stout as a fort. As she thought of it, Gertrude turned in that direction and saw a rise of flames through the branches. She had been right, then. Van Alstyne's was afire. The wind was dying and the flames sprang high. Silence had come into their own little valley. She understood suddenly that the Indians had got by. They were in the Helderbergs. Where Teunis and his men could be she did not know. It was too late for him to help her now. But if she had been right all the way through, maybe she would not need him, after all. Maybe the Indians would not come along the Hunger Kill to find their house.

It was then that she saw the Indians.

THE WITCH OF BLACKBIRD POND

Elizabeth Speare

Mrs. Speare successfully reveals the Puritan culture, one that played an important role in America's history and in the development of American character. When historical fiction accurately recreates a former time in addition to telling an interesting story, it best fulfills its potential to help men understand their past.

Kit, an orphan, has been pampered by her wealthy grandfather in Barbados. When he dies his overseer absconds with his money and Kit is left penniless. She takes passage for Connecticut to live with Aunt Rachel, her mother's sister. Connecticut, however, is quite different from Barbados, and impulsive, gay Kit has difficulty adjusting to the stern Puritan life.

The Puritans, forgetful of the religious persecution that forced them to America, are intolerant of all other religions. Kit is caught up in a witch hunt for Hannah, an old Quaker who is forced to live on the edge of the meadows. After Hannah escapes the mob, Kit herself is accused of being a witch and is brought to trial by the angry townspeople.

Five days after John Holbrook's departure Judith fell ill. Her mother, inclined at first to attribute her complaints to moping, took a second look at her flushed cheeks and put her to bed. Within two more days alarm had spread to every corner of Wethersfield. Sixteen children and young people were stricken with the mysterious fever, and none of the familiar remedies seemed to be of any benefit. For days Judith tossed on the cot they had spread for her in front of the hearth, burning with fever, fretful with pain, and often too delirious to recognize the three women who hovered about her. A young surgeon was summoned from Hartford to bleed her, and a nauseous brew of ground roasted toads was forced between her cracked lips, to no avail. The fever simply had to run its course.

On the fourth day Kit felt chilly and lightheaded, and by twilight she was thankful to sink down on the mat they dragged to the fireside near her cousin. Her bout with the malady was short, however. Her wiry young body, nourished by Barbados fruits and sunshine, had an elastic vitality, and she was back on her feet while Judith was still barely sitting up to sip her gruel. Dressing rather shakily, Kit was compelled to ask Mercy's assistance with the buttons down her back, and was shocked when her older cousin suddenly bent double in a violent fit of coughing. Kit whirled round on her.

"How long have you been coughing like that?" she demanded. "Let me feel your hand! Aunt Rachel, for heaven's sakes, get Mercy to bed quick! Here she's trying to wait on us!"

Tears of weakness and protest ran down Mercy's cheeks as Rachel stooped to take off her oldest daughter's shoes. Kit heated the warming pan to take the chill off Mercy's bed in the corner, and Mercy buried her face in the pillows as though it were a shame past bearing that she should cause so much trouble.

Mercy was seriously ill. Twice the young doctor rode out from Hartford to bleed her. The third time he stood looking soberly down at her. "I dare not bleed her further," he said helplessly.

Rachel raised timid eyes to her husband. "Matthew—do you think—that perhaps Gershom Bulkeley might know something to help her? He is so skilled."

Matthew's lips tightened. "I have said that man does not come into my house," he reminded her. "We will hear no more about it."

Rachel, already worn from the long vigil with Judith, was near the breaking point. Matthew, after working in the fields all day, forced his wife against her will to get some rest while he sat by his daughter's bedside at night. Judith watched helplessly, still too weak even to comb her own hair. The meals fell to Kit, and she did the best she could with them, measuring out the corn meal, stirring up the pudding, spooning it into a bag to boil, and cursing the clumsiness that she had never taken the pains to overcome. She built up the fire, heated kettles of water for the washing, so that Mercy might have fresh linen under her restless body. She fetched water, and strained a special gruel for Judith, and spread her uncle's wet clothes to dry before the fire. At night she dozed off, exhausted, and woke with a start sure that something was left undone.

Mercy lay on some remote borderline between sleeping and waking. Nothing could rouse her, and every breath was such a painful struggle that the slow rasp of it filled the whole house. Fear seeped in at the corner of the room. The family dared not speak above a whisper, though certainly Mercy was beyond hearing. On the fourth morning of Mercy's illness Matthew did not go to work at all, but sat heavily at the table, turning the pages of the Bible, searching in vain for some hope to cling to, or shut himself in the company room where they heard his heavy tread back and forth, back and forth, the length of the room. Toward noontime he took down his coat from the peg. "I am going out for a time," he said hoarsely.

He had one sleeve in the coat when a knock sounded at the door, and as he drew back the bolt a man's voice grated harshly through the silent room.

"Let me in, man. I've something to say."

Matthew Wood stepped back from door, and the Reverend Bulkeley loomed on the kitchen threshold.

"Matthew," he said, "you're a stubborn mule and a rebel. But this is no time for politics. Time was your Mercy was like my own daughter. Let me see her, Matthew. Let me do what I can, with God's help, to save her."

Matthew's voice was almost a sob. "Come in, Gershom," he choked. "God bless you! I was coming to fetch you."

Dr. Bulkeley's solid presence brought to them all new hope. "I have a theory," he told them. "I've read something like it, and 'twill do no harm to try. Cook me some onions in a kettle."

For four long hours Kit labored at Dr. Bulkeley's bidding. She sliced onions, blinking her eyes against the stinging tears. She kept the fire blazing under the iron kettle. When the onions were cooked to just the right softness, Dr. Bulkeley piled them in a mass on a linen napkin and applied the blistering poultice to Mercy's chest. As soon as the poultice cooled a new one must be ready.

Late in the afternoon the doctor rose to his feet. "There are others I must tend to," he muttered. "Keep her warm. I'll be back before midnight."

Kit busied herself to prepare a meal which none of them could eat. With fingers so heavy from fatigue and fear that she could scarcely force them to move, she cleared the table and put away the untouched food. She wondered if ever again she would escape from the sound of that dreadful breathing. Her own lungs ached with every sighing breath that Mercy drew.

Then without warning a new fear came rushing in upon her. From without the house there was an approaching sound of stamping feet and murmuring voices, gathering volume in the roadway outside. There was a crashing knock on the outer door. The three women's eyes met in consternation. Matthew Wood reached the door in one stride and flung it open.

"How dare you?" he demanded in low-voiced anger. "Know you not there is illness here?"

"Aye, we know right enough," a voice replied. "There's illness everywhere. We need your help to put a stop to it."

"What do you want?"

"We want you to come along with us. We're going for the witch."

"Get away from my house at once," ordered Matthew.

"You'll listen to us first," shouted another voice, "if you know what's good for your daughter."

"Keep your voices down, then, and be quick," warned Matthew. "I've no time to listen to foolishness."

"Is it foolishness that there's scarce a house in this town but has a sick child in it? You'd do well to heed what we say, Matthew Wood. John Wetherell's boy died today. That makes three dead, and it's the witch's doing!"

"Whose doing? What are you driving at, man?"

"The Quaker woman's. Down by Blackbird Pond. She's been a curse on this town for years with her witchcraft!"

The voices sounded hysterical. "We should have run her out long ago."

"Time and again she's been seen consorting with the devil down in that meadow!"

"Now she's put a curse on our children. God knows how many more will be dead before morning!"

"This is nonsense," scoffed Matthew Wood impatiently.

"There's no old woman, and no witchcraft either could bring on a plague like this."

"What is it then?" shrilled a woman's voice.

Matthew passed a hand over his forehead. "The will of God"— he began helplessly.

"The curse of God, you mean." another voice screamed. "His judgment on us for harboring an infidel and a Quaker."

"You'd better come with us, Matthew. Your own daughter's like to die. You can't deny it."

"I'll have naught to do with it," said Matthew firmly. "I'll hold with no witch hunt."

"You'd better hold with it!" the woman's voice shrilled suddenly. "You'd better look to the witch in your own household!"

"Ask that high and mighty niece of yours where she spends her time!" another woman shouted from the darkness. "Ask her what she knows about your Mercy's sickness!"

The weariness dropped suddenly from Matthew Wood. With his shoulders thrown back he seemed to tower in the doorway.

"Begone from my house!" he roared, his caution drowned in anger. "How dare you speak the name of a good, God-fearing girl? Any man who slanders one of my family has me to reckon with!"

There was a silence. "No harm meant," a man's voice said uneasily. "'Tis only woman's talk."

"If you won't come there's plenty more who will," said another. "What are we wasting our time for?"

The voices receded down the pathway, rising again in the darkness beyond. Matthew bolted the door and turned back to the dumfounded women.

"Did they wake her?" he asked dully.

"No," sighed Rachel. "Even that could not disturb her, poor child."

For a moment there was no sound but that tortured breathing. Kit had risen to her feet and stood clinging to the table's edge. Now the new fear that was stifling her broke from her lips in an anguished whisper.

"What will they do to her?"

Her aunt looked up in alarm. Matthew's black brows drew together darkly. "What concern is that of yours?"

"I know her!" she cried. "She's just a poor helpless old woman! Oh, please tell me! Will they harm her?"

"This is Connecticut," answered Matthew sternly. "They will abide by the law. They will bring her to trial, I suppose. If she can prove herself innocent she is safe enough."

"But what will they do with her now—tonight —before the trial?"

"How do I know? Leave off your questions, girl. Is there not trouble enough in our own house tonight?" He lowered himself into a chair and sunk his head in his hands.

"Go and get some sleep, Kit," urged Rachel, dreading any more disturbance. "We may need you later on."

Kit stared from one to the other, half frantic with helplessness. They were not going to do anything. Unable to stop herself she burst into tears and ran from the room.

Upstairs, in her own room, she stood leaning against the door, trying to collect her wits. She would have to get to Hannah. No matter what happened, she could not stay here and leave Hannah to face that mob alone. If she could get there in time to warn her—that was as far as she could see just now.

She snatched her cloak from the peg and, carrying her leather boots in her hand, crept down the stairs. She dared not try to unbolt the great front door but instead tiptoed cautiously through the cold company room into the back chamber and let herself out the shed door into the garden. She could hear shouts in the distance, and slipping hurriedly into her boots she fled along the roadway.

In Meeting House Square she leaned against a tree for an instant to get her bearing. The crowd was gathering, a good twenty men and boys and a few women, carrying flaring pine tourches. In the hoarse shouting and the heedless screaming of the women there was a mounting violence, and a terror she had never known before closed over Kit's mind like a fog.

For a moment her knees sagged and she caught at the tree for support. Then her mind cleared again, and skirting the square, darting from tree to tree like a savage, she made her way down Broad Street and out onto South Road.

She had never before seen the Meadows by moon light. They lay serene and still, wrapped in thin veils of drifting mist. She found the path easily, passed the dark clump of willows, and saw ahead the deep shining pool that was Blackbird Pond and a faint reddish glow that must be Hannah's window.

Hannah's door was not even bolted. Inside, by the still-flickering embers of the hearth, Hannah sat nodding in her chair, fast asleep. Kit touched the woman's shoulder gently.

"Hannah dear," she said, struggling to control her panting breath. "Wake up! 'Tis Kit. You've got to come with me, quickly."

"What is it?" Hannah jerked instantly awake. "Is it a flood?"

"Don't talk, Hannah. Just get into this cloak. Where are your shoes? Here, hold out your foot, quick! Now—"

There was not a moment to spare. As they stepped into the darkness the clamor of voices struck against them. The torches looked very near.

"Not that way! Down the path to the river!"

In the shelter of the dark bushes Hannah faltered, clutching Kit's arm. She could not be budged. "Kit! Why are those people coming?"

"Hush! Hannah, dear, please—"

"I know that sound. I've heard it before. They're coming for the Quakers."

"No, Hannah, come—I"

"Shame on thee, Kit. Thee knows a Quaker does not run away. Thomas will take care of us."

Desperately Kit shook the old woman's shoulders. "Oh, Hannah! What shall I do with you?" Of all times for Hannah to turn vague!

But Hannah's brief resolution suddenly gave way, and all at once she clung to Kit, sobbing like a child.

"Don't let them take me again," she pleaded. "Where is Thomas? I can't face it again without Thomas."

This time Kit succeeded in half dragging the sobbing woman through the underbrush. They made a terrible rustling and snapping of twigs as they went, but the noise behind them was still louder. The crowd had reached the cottage now. There was a crashing, as though the furniture were being hurled to splinters against the walls.

"She was here! The fire is still burning!"

"Look behind the woodpile. She can't have got far."

"There's the cat!" screeched a woman in terror. "Look out!"

There was a shot, then two more.

"It got away. Disappeared into thin air."

"There's no bullet could kill that cat."

"Here's the goats. Get rid of them too!"

"Hold on there! I'll take the goats. Witched or no, goats is worth twenty shillings apiece."

"Scotch the witch out!"

"Fire the house! Give us a light to search by!"

Desperately the two women pushed on, over a marshy bog that dragged at their feet, through a cornfield where the neglected shocks hid their scurrying figures, past a brambly tangle, to the shelter of the poplar trees and the broad moonlit stretch of the river. There they had to halt, crouching against a fallen log.

Behind them a flare of light, redder than the moonlight, lit up the meadows. There was a hissing and crackling.

"My house!" cried out Hannah, so heedlessly that Kit clapped a hand over her mouth. "Our own house that Thomas built!" With the tears running down her own cheeks, Kit flung both arms around the trembling woman, and together they huddled against the log and watched till the red glow lessened and died away.

For a long time the thrashing in the woods continued. Once voices came very close, and the search party went thwacking through the cornfield. Two men came out on the beach, not twenty feet from where they hid.

"Could she swim the river, think you?"

"Not likely. No use going on like this all night, Jem. I've had enough. There's another day coming." The men climbed back up the river bank.

When the voices died away it was very still. Serenity flowed back over the meadows. The veil of mist was again unbroken. After a long time, Kit dared to stretch her aching muscles. It was bitterly cold and damp here by the river's edge. She drew Hannah's slight figure closer against her, like a child's and presently the woman's shuddering ceased, and Hannah drifted into the shallow napping of the very old.

There was no such escape for Kit. Her first surge of relief soon died away, and her thoughts, numbed by the sheer terror of pursuit, began to stir again in hopeless circles. What chance did they have when morning came? Should she rouse Hannah now and push on down the river? But where could they go? Hannah was exhausted; all her strength seemed to have died with the dying flames of her house. She could take Hannah home with her, where at least there would be warm clothes and hot food. But her uncle was a selectman. It would be his bounden duty to turn Hannah over to the law. And once they had her locked up in jail, what then? What use would a trial be with no one to speak in her defence but a foolish girl who was suspected of being a witch herself? Hannah could not even be trusted to answer the questioning straight. Like as not her mind would wander and she would talk about her Thomas.

Yet as the long hours wore away Kit could find no better solution. Whatever might happen, Hannah needed immediate care. Even the jail would be better than this unprotected place. As the first gray light slanted along the river, Kit made up her mind. They would not risk the main roads. They would pick their way along the shore of the

river and cut through the meadows back to her uncle's house.

Then, unbelievably, out of the mist came the miracle. First two points of mast, then sails, transparent and wraithlike in the fog, then, as Kit strained her eyes, the looming hull, the prow, and the curved tail of a fish. The *Dolphin!* Glory be to heaven! The most beautiful sight in the world! The *Dolphin,* moving down toward Wright's Island on a steady breeze.

Kit leaped to her feet. "Hannah! Wake up! Look—look there" Her stiff lips could scarcely babble. She flung her arms into the air, waving wildly. She could hear a man's voice across the water, but the fog rolled tantalizingly between her and the ship. She tore off her petticoat and waved it hysterically. But she dared not shout, and if she could not attract their notice the *Dolphin* would sail past down the river and their chance would be gone.

Kicking off her shoes, Kit waded into the water, plunged in and struck out toward the ship. It was a very short swim, but she had overdrawn her strength for days past. She was panting when the black hull loomed over her head, and at first she could barely raise her voice above the wash of the ship. She drew a careful breath and tried again.

There was a cry above her and a sound of running feet. "Ahoy All hands! Man overboard!"

"Tis a woman!"

"Hold on there, ma'am, we're coming!"

She heard shouted orders; a thumping and creaking of ropes. Then the life boat swung out over her head and lowered with a smack into the water. Nat and the redheaded sailor were inside, and she had never before been so happy to see anyone.

"I knew it," groaned the redheaded one, as she clung, gasping, to the side of the boat.

"Kit! What kind of a game is this?"

"Hannah—she's in terrible trouble, Nat. They burned her house. Please—can you take her on the *Dolphin?*"

They dragged her over the side of the boat. "Where is she?" Nat demanded. "Tell the captain to heave to!" he yelled up toward the deck. "We're going ashore."

"There," pointed Kit, "by that pile of logs. We've been there all night. I didn't know what to do, and when I saw the ship—" All at once she was sobbing and babbling like a three-year-old, about the witch hunt, and the chase through the cornfield, and the man who had come so close. Nat's hands closed over hers hard and steady.

" 'Tis all right, Kit," he said, over and over. "We'll take you both on and get you some dry clothes. Just hold on a few minutes more till we get Hannah." The boat scraped the shore.

Still dazed, Hannah accepted the miracle and the prospect of a journey like a docile child. Then after two shaky steps she turned obstinate. She would not set foot in the boat without her cat.

"I can't go off without her," she insisted. "I just can't and thee ought to know that Nat. She'd just grieve her heart out with no home to go to and me gone off on a ship."

"Then I'll get her," said Nat. "You wait here, and keep quiet, both of you."

Kit was outraged. If she had been Nat she would have picked Hannah up and carried her off in the boat with no more nonsense. As he strode up the bank, she scrambled after him through the wet underbrush. "You're crazy, Nat!" She protested, her teeth chattering with cold. "No cat is worth it. You've got to get her out of here. If you could have heard those people—"

"If she's set on that cat she's going to have it. They've taken everything else." Nat stood in the midst of the charred cinders that had been the little house. "Damn them!" he choked. "Curse all of them" He kicked a smoldering log viciously.

They searched the trampled garden and presently they heard a cautious miaow. The yellow cat inched warily from beneath a pumpkin vine. She did not take to the idea of capture. They had to stalk her, one on each side of the garden, and Nat finally dived full length under a bush, dragged the cat out, and wrapped it tightly in his own shirt. Back at the shore Hannah received the writhing bundle with joy and climbed obediently into the rowboat.

"Where are we going, Nat?" she asked trustfully.

"I'm taking you to Saybrook for a visit with my grandmother. You'll be good company for her, Hannah. Come on Kit. Father will go on without us."

"I'm not going, Nat. All I wanted was to see Hannah safe."

Nat straightened up. "I think you'd better, Kit," he said quietly. " 'Till this thing blows over, at least. This is our last trip before winter. We'll find a place for you in Saybrook and bring you back first trip next spring."

Kit shook her head.

"Or you can go on the West Indies with us."

Barbados! The tears sprang to her eyes. "I can't, Nat. I have to stay here."

The concern in his eyes hardened to awareness. "Of course," he said courteously. "I forgot. You're going to be married."

" 'Tis Mercy," she stammered. "She's terribly ill. I couldn't go, I just couldn't, not knowing—"

Nat looked intently at her, and took one step nearer. The blue eyes were very close. "Kit—"

"Ahoy, there!" There was a bellow from the *Dolphin*. "What's keeping you?"

"Nat, quick! They'll hear the shouting!"

Nat jumped into the boat. "You'll be all right? You need to get warm—"

"I'll go home now. Only hurry—"

She stood watching as the boat pulled away from the sand. Halfway to the ship Nat turned to stare back at her. Then he raised an arm silently. Kit raised her own arm to wave back, and then she turned and started back along the shore. She dared not wait to see them reach the *Dolphin*. In another moment she would lose every shred of common sense and pride and fling herself into the water after the rowboat and plead with them not to leave her behind.

Though it was long past daybreak now, her luck still held. She met no one in the north field. Once she dodged behind a brushpile as the town herder came by with some cows to pasture. She reached the house without further danger. The shed door was still unbolted, and she let herself in and crept noiselessly through the house. She heard the murmur of voices, and as she reached the hallway the door to the kitchen opened.

"Is that you, Kit?" Aunt Rachel peered at her. "We decided to let you sleep, poor child. Dr. Bulkeley has been here all night. Praise God—he says the fever is broken!"

In her joy and weariness, Aunt Rachel did not even notice the sodden dress and hair under Kit's woolen cloak.

JOHNNY TREMAIN

Esther Forbes

After writing a number of adult historical fiction novels, Esther Forbes decided to study one period in depth. The result of this was the biography Paul Revere and the World He Lived In, *which not only has been highly praised for its authenticity but was awarded the Pulitzer Prize for American history.*

As she wrote Paul Revere, *Miss Forbes became interested in the role played by the young Boston apprentices who, although now nameless and unrecorded in history books, must have played a significant role in America's war for independence. When she heard on December 7, 1941, that Pearl Harbor had been bombed, Miss Forbes made the decision to write a novel for both children and adults about the many youngsters who actually fight their country's wars. From this decision and her previous research came* Johnny Tremain, A Novel for Old and Young.

No better book has been written for children about the Revolutionary War. The characterization is exceptionally good, Johnny growing and changing throughout the novel. For a hero his actions are not always admirable, but they are always believable. The historical characters—James Otis, Sam Adams, Paul Revere, John Hancock—come to life as real people and are not the stock figures they so often seem in history books. The characterization, plot, and theme are all closely interrelated in this fine novel. The reader is carried along by a dramatic story, but he also gains insight into human behavior and the causes of the American Revolution.

The book begins with Johnny powerful in his capability as a gifted apprentice silversmith. Because his skill and industry really support his master's family, he gains extra privileges and becomes proud. His arrogance naturally creates hostility in the other less gifted apprentices.

THE PRIDE OF YOUR POWER

The week wore on, each day as hot as the one before, for it was July. Every day after dinner Mr. Lapham took a long nap under his basket snoring as gently as he did everything else. Johnny would let him sleep for an hour, then wake him up, scold him, and get him to work. His work was beautiful. The body of the sugar

basin was quickly completed and he began repousséing on it the rich garlands of fruit with the same skill he had had forty years before.

Johnny's own work did not satisfy him as well. He had exactly enlarged the handle in his wax model. Mrs. Lapham and the girls, even Mr. Lapham, said it was fine, and he could go ahead and cast it in silver. It was only Johnny himself who was dissatisfied.

Friday evening, when the light was failing and work over, Johnny took the silver pitcher and his own wax model and left the shop. He was in Fish Street, in a minute stopping outside the silver shop of Paul Revere. He didn't dare knock, but he knew that any moment now the silversmith would be closing his shop, leaving for his dwelling in near-by North Square. He was so prosperous a smith that he did not live and work in the same place.

So at last he saw Mr. Revere, a stocky, ruddy man, with fine, dark eyes, shutting his shop, taking out his key preparing to lock up.

'Good evening, Mr. Revere.' The man smiled with a quick flash of white teeth. He had a quick smile and a quick face and body.

'Good evening, Johnny Tremain.' The boy had long admired Mr. Revere as the best craftsman in Boston. He had no idea Mr. Revere knew his name. He did not know all the master silversmiths had an eye on him.

'Mr. Revere, I'd like to talk with you.'

'Man to man,' Mr. Revere agreed, opening his shop door, motioning Johnny to follow him.

Johnny's eyes flew about the shop, taking in the fine anvils, the hood upon the annealing furnace, the neat nests of crucibles. It was just such a shop he would himself have when he was man-grown. Not much like Mr. Lapham's.

Although Paul Revere was as busy a man as there was in all Boston, he took everything so easily in his stride (doing the one thing after another) that he never seemed rushed, so now, because an apprentice stopped him on the street and said he wanted to talk to him, he appeared to have all the time in the world.

'Sir,' said Johnny, 'it's a matter of handles.' He took the silver pitcher out of the cloth he had wrapped it in and his own wax model and explained Mr. Hancock's order.

'So you want to talk to me as a silversmith to silversmith, do you?' He had Johnny's wax model in his hands—delicate hands to go with such heavy wrists. 'What does your master say of your work?'

'Mr. Lapham won't even look at it much. But he says it's good enough and I can go ahead and cast tomorrow. I've *got* to cast tomorrow because it's Saturday and we can't work Sunday, and it must be done Monday at seven. Although my master thinks it's all right, I'm not sure . . .'

'He is wrong and you are right. Look, you've just copied the handle on the pitcher too slavishly —just enlarged it. Don't you see that your

winged woman looks coarse in comparison? I'd have the figures the same size on both pieces—fill in with a scroll. Then, too, your curve is wrong. The basin is so much bigger you cannot use the same curve. Yours looks hunched up and awkward. It's all a matter of proportion.' He took up a piece of paper and a pencil and drew off what he meant with one sure sweep of his hand. 'I'd use a curve more like that—see? This is what I meant when I said I'd add a scroll or two below the figure of the winged woman—not just enlarge her so she looks like a Boston fishwife in comparison to the angel on the pitcher. See?'

'I see.'

The man looked at him a little curiously.

'There was a time,' he said, 'when your own master could have shown you that.'

'Mr. Lapham is . . . well . . . he's feeble.'

'Not doing very much work these days?'

'Not what *you'd* call much.' Johnny felt on the defensive. 'Not much fine hollow ware. Plenty of buckles, spoons, and such.'

'How many boys?'

'Three of us, sir.'

'I'd hardly think he'd need three. Now, if he wants to cut down, you tell him from me that I'll buy your unexpired time. I think between us we could make some fine things—you and I.'

The boy flushed. To think the great Paul Revere wanted him!

'Tell your master I'll pay a bit more than is usual for you. Don't let him shunt one of those other boys off on me.'

He stood up. It was time for Johnny to go.

'I couldn't leave the Laphams, sir,' he said as he thanked Mr. Revere. 'If it wasn't for me, nothing would ever get done. They'd just about starve.'

'I see. You're right, of course. But if the old gentleman dies or you ever want a new master, remember my offer. So . . .' and he turned to shake hands; 'may we meet again.'

By Saturday noon, Johnny, following Mr. Revere's advice and his curve, had got the model of the handle exactly right. He could tell with his eyes closed. It felt perfect. He rapidly made a duplicate, for when the molten silver was poured in on the wax, it would melt and float away, so he made a model for each handle.

Now, no matter how long it took him (and if

all went well it should not be too long), he must get his handles cast, cleaned, and soldered to the basin itself which Mr. Lapham had made. Of course, on Sunday the shop would be locked up all day, the furnace cold. Mr. Lapham would as always escort his household, dressed in Sunday best, to the Cockerel Church and after that back for a cold dinner. Whether they went again or not to afternoon meeting, the master left for each to decide. He himself always went. Madge and Dorcas usually entertained their beaux. Mrs. Lapham slept. Cilla would take Isannah out along the little beach. Johnny, Dove, and Dusty were apt to steal off for a swim, although Mr. Lapham had no idea of it. He thought they sat quietly at home and that Johnny read the Bible out loud to them.

So Sunday was out. But if he got up at three or four Monday morning, he would have time to clean his work before he took it over to Mr. Hancock at seven.

After Saturday dinner, Mr. Lapham as usual prepared for a snooze, stretched out in the one armchair in the shop, with his basket over his head to keep off the flies. Perhaps Johnny's tyranny during the week had irritated the old gentleman—who never believed it made the least difference to anyone when anything was finished.

'Dove, Dusty,' Johnny was yelling, 'build up the furnace, fetch in charcoal. Hi! you lazy, good-for-nothing dish-mops.'

Dove ran out to the coal house. There was a queer, pleased look on his face when he returned.

'Charcoal all gone, Master Johnny.'

'Gone!'

'Yep. I haven't said anything because you always like to take charge of things like that 'round here.'

'Get a basket! Quick! Run to Mr. Hamblin over on Long Wharf. Try Mrs. Hitchbourn down on Hitchbourn's Wharf. You've got to get charcoal. Hurry!'

Dove did not hurry. It was getting on toward sunset when at last he came back, pushing his big basket on a wheelbarrow.

It was the worst-looking charcoal Johnny had ever seen.

'This isn't what we silversmiths use. This is fourth-rate stuff—fit for iron-maybe. You know that, Dove.'

'Naw. Not me. I don't know anything—see? You're always telling me.'

'I want willow charcoal.'

'You never said so.'

'I'll go myself, but this delay means we'll be working in lamplight and up to midnight. You are the stupidest animal God ever made—if He made you, which I doubt. Why your mother didn't drown you when you were a pup, I can't imagine. Come Lord's day and I have a spare moment, I'm going to give you such a hiding for your infernal low-down skulking tricks, you'll be . . .'

The basket over Mr. Lapham's head moved. He laid it down.

'Boys,' he said mildly, 'you quarrel all the time.'

Johnny, in angry mouthfuls, told him what he thought about Dove and the charcoal, and threw in a cutting remark about Dusty.

The old master said, 'Dove, I want to speak to Johnny alone.' And then, 'Johnny I don't want you to be always riding them boys so hard. Dove tries, but he's stupid. Ain't his fault, is it? If God had wanted him bright He would have made him that way. We're all poor worms. You're getting above yourself—like I tried to point out to you.' God is going to send you a dire punishment for your pride.'

'Yes, sir.'

'One trouble with you is you haven't been up against any boys as good as yourself—or better, maybe. Because you're the best young one in this shop—or on Hancock's Wharf—you think you're the best one in the world.'

Johnny was so anxious to be on with the work —tediously delayed by Dove's tricks—he hardly listened.

'And, boy, don't you go get all fretted up over what's after all nothing but an order for silver. It's sinful to let yourself go so over mundane things. Now I want you to set quietly and memorize them verses I had you read about pride. Work's over for the day.'

'*What?*'

'Yep. It always was the old-fashioned way to start Lord's Day at sunset on Saturday and I've decided to re-establish the habit in my house.'

'Mr. Lapham, we've *got* to work this evening. We've promised Mr. Hancock.'

'I doubt God cares even a little bit whether Mr. Hancock has any silver. It's better to break faith with him, isn't it, than with the Lord?'

Johnny was tired. His head was ringing. His hands shook a little. He walked out of the shop, slamming the door after him, and stormed into the kitchen. He knew Mrs. Lapham did not take much stock in her father-in-law's pious ways. She and all four girls were in the kitchen. Madge was frying corn meal, Dorcas wringing out a cheese-cloth. Cilla was setting the table, and Isannah playing with the cat.

Mrs. Lapham looked at him. 'Boy, have you seen a ghost?'

Johnny sat and told his story. He was beyond his customary abusive eloquence.

The girls stared at him with piteous open mouths. Mrs. Lapham's jaw set grimly.

'Dorcas, *shut the door*. Don't let your grandpa hear. Johnny—how many more work-hours will you need?'

'Seven—maybe. I can get two Monday morning.'

'You shall have them. Sabbath or no Sabbath, that sugar basin is going to be done on time. I'm not letting any old-fashioned, fussy notions upset the best order we've had for ten years. And if Mr. Hancock is pleased, he may come again and again. I can't have my poor, fatherless girls starve just to please Grandpa. Listen now to me.'

Sunday afternoon Mr. Lapham was not only going to the second service, as usual, but there was to be a meeting of the deacons, a cold supper afterward, and a prayer service at the pastor's. 'That's where you get them five hours, Johnny—tomorrow afternoon.'

Johnny knew that working on the Sabbath was against the law as well as against all his religious training. He might very well go to the stocks or to Hell for it, but when Mrs. Lapham said, 'Darest to, Johnny?' he said, 'I darest.'

'Not a word to the old gentleman, mind.'

'Not a word.'

'Girls, if you so much as peep . . .'

'Oh, no, Ma.'

Dove and Dusty were to be bribed into service by the promise of delivering the basin to Mr. Hancock when done. He always gave money to boys who brought things to the house.

Mrs. Lapham was breathing hard, but she had the matter well in hand. It was settled.

'Isannah,' she said quietly, 'you call Grandpa and the boys in to supper. Cilla, run down cellar and fetch cold ale.'

Her mouth and the folds about it, even her nose and eyes, were like iron.

3

Sunday afternoon and the work went forward with never a hitch. Even Dove and Dusty were good and obedient, although Dove was half-threatening to tell 'old Grandpa' when he got home. Johnny did not care what his master might say—only, please God, the basin were done and Mr. Hancock come again and again with his rich orders. If Mr. Lapham was angry, he could sell Johnny's time to Paul Revere.

The four girls, still dressed in their pretty go-to-meeting frocks, watched him with fascinated, admiring eyes. Their mother sent them out-of-doors. Did the smoke from the furnace show from the wharf? From Fish Street? Did they hear any comments?

Having found for himself the proper willow charcoal, Johnny went quickly ahead with his casting. He set his two wax models in wet sand. The furnace was piping hot. His hands were very sure. He was confident he could do the work, yet inside he was keyed up and jumpy.

Mrs. Lapham fussed about him and he ordered her to do simple things.

'Not the draft yet, Mrs. Lapham . . . now get to work with the bellows.'

Once he even told her to 'look sharp,' and she took it with a humble 'Yes, Johnny.'

'Now fetch me the crucible.'

She turned to Dove. 'Which one does he want, boy?'

'I'll get her down.'

Dove went to the shelves where the crucibles for melting silver were kept. Johnny did not see Dove standing on a stool, reaching far back and carefully taking out a cracked crucible. Dusty saw him and giggled. He knew the crack in it was so small it was hard even to see. It might stand the heat of the furnace, but the chances were that it would not. That was why Mr. Lapham had put it so far back. Both he and Dove thought it would just about serve Johnny Tremain right—after the

insufferable way he had been bossing everybody
—if the crucible gave way and the hot silver did
spill all over the top of the furnace. It would
certainly make Johnny look like a fool, after all
his fussing.

Johnny took the cracked crucible in his trusting hands, put in it silver ingots, set it on top of
the furnace.

Cilla flew in. 'Ma, there's a man looking at our
chimney.'

'How's he dressed?'

'Seafaring man.'

'No seafaring man ever objected to a little Sab-
bath-breaking. But mind if you see any deacons
or constables.'

The work went on.

Issannah sat with the cat in her lap. 'Johnny's
going to Hell,' she said firmly. Johnny himself
thought this was possible.

He called to Mrs. Lapham to 'look sharp' and
put the old silver turnip watch where he could see
it. The silver must be run at a certain speed and
be allowed to cool for just so long.

Mrs. Lapham was so slavishly eager to help
him, he almost felt fond of her. He did not
notice Dusty and Dove snickering in a corner.

Some of the beeswax he had used for his models had been left too near the furnace. It had
melted and run over the floor. Johnny had been
taught to clean up as he went along, but today he
was in too much of a hurry to bother.

'Johnny,' cried Mrs. Lapham, 'isn't it time to
pour? Look, the silver is melted and begun to
wink.' It was true.

He moved forward delicately, his right hand
outstretched. The crucible began to settle—col-
lapse, the silver was running over the top of the
furnace like spilled milk. Johnny jumped toward
it, his right hand still outstretched. Something
happened, he never knew exactly what. His feet
went out from under him. His hand came down
on the top of the furnace.

The burn was so terrible he at first felt no
pain, but stood stupidly looking at his hand. For
one second, before the metal cooled, the inside of
his right hand, from wrist to fingertips, was
coated with solid silver. He looked at the back of
his hand. It was as always. Then he smelled
burned flesh. The room blackened and tipped
around him. He heard a roaring in his ears.

When he came to, he was stretched out upon
the floor. Dorcas was trying to pour brandy down
his throat. Mrs. Lapham had plunged the burned
hand into a panful of flour and was yelling at
Madge to hurry with her bread poultice.

He saw Cilla's face. It was literally green. 'Ma,'
she said, licking her white lips, 'shall I run for
Doctor Warren?'

'No—no . . . oh, wait, I've got to think. I don't
want any of them doctors to know we was breaking Sabbath Day. And we don't need no doctor
for just a burn. Cilla, you run down the wharf
and you fetch that old midwife, Gran' Hopper.
These old women know better than any doctor
how to cure things like this. Johnny, how you
feel?'

'All right.'

'Hurt yet?'

'Not yet.'

He knew it would later.

4

Johnny lay in the 'birth and death room.' This
was hardly more than a closet with a tiny window
off the kitchen, used for storage except in times
of sickness. His hand had been done up in a
linseed poultice. The smell of the linseed was
stifling, and now, on the second day, the pain had
really begun. His arm throbbed to the shoulder.
Gran' Hopper was in the kitchen, talking to Mrs.
Lapham.

'Mind you keep that poultice wet. Just leave it
wrapped up and wet it now and then with lime
water. There's more luck than anything else in
things like this is. If it don't come along good, I'll
make a charm.'

Not many years before, Gran' Hopper would
have been hanged for a witch. She had the traditional venerable years, the toothless cackle, the
mustache. Nor was she above resorting to charms.
But she had had vast experience. No doctor in
Boston knew more than she about midwifery and
children's diseases. So far she had done as well as
any of them, except for one thing. The hand had
been allowed to draw together—turn in on itself.
It was less painful than if it had been held out
flat.

By the fourth day ulceration had set in. This
was considered Nature's way of healing an injury.
Gran' Hopper gave him laudanum and more lau-

danum. There followed drowsy days and nights that ran together, a ceaseless roaring in the ears. There was nothing left of him but the pain and the drug.

The fever abated and with it the doses of the drug. Johnny had not once looked at his hand since he had stood before the furnace and seen it lined with silver. Gran' Hopper said on the next day she would unwrap it and see, as she cheerfully put it, 'what was left.'

Thus far the pain and the drug and the fever had dulled his mind. He had not thought about the future, for of what use to anyone was a cripple-handed silversmith? But that night Gran' Hopper's words haunted him. Next day she would see 'what was left.'

He was utterly unprepared for the sight of his hand when finally it was unwrapped and lay in the midwife's aproned lap. Mrs. Lapham, Madge, Dorcas, all had crowded into the little birth and death room. Cilla and Isannah were in the kitchen, too frightened to go near him.

'My!' said Madge, "isn't that funny-looking? The top part, Johnny, looks all right, although a little narrow, but, Johnny, your thumb and palm have grown together.'

This was true. He bent and twisted his fingers. He could not get the thumb to meet the forefinger. Such a hand was completely useless. For the first time he faced the fact that his hand was crippled.

'Oh, let me *see!*' Dorcas was leaning over him. She gave her most elegant little screech of horror, just like a great lady who has seen a mouse.

'My!' said Mrs. Lapham, 'that's worse than anything I had imagined. Now isn't that a shame! Bright boy like Johnny just ruined. No more good than a horse with sprung knees.'

Johnny did not stay to hear more. That morning he had dressed (with Mrs. Lapham's competent help) for the first time. He got up, stood facing them stiffly, his bad hand jammed into his breeches pocket.

'I'm going out,' he said thickly.

Cilla and Isannah sat close together in a frightened huddle, staring at him, not daring to speak. He said rudely, 'You should have come in too—and seen the fun.'

Cilla gaped at him, tried to say something, but only swallowed.

'You two—sitting there—looking like a couple of fishes.'

He slammed the front door after him. He had always been bad about slamming doors. In the fresh air he felt better. He pretended not to hear Mrs. Lapham calling him from a window to come right back. All Fish Street could hear when Mrs. Lapham called. He paid no heed.

He walked all over Boston, his hand thrust deep in his breeches pocket. Instinctively he wanted to tire himself out (which was easy in his weakened condition) so he could not think.

When he came back, there was something queer about the silence of the kitchen. No one reproved him because he had disobeyed Mrs. Lapham. He knew they had been talking about him.

Cilla, for one of the first times in her life, tried to be polite to him.

'Oh, Johnny,' she whispered, 'I'm sorrier than I was ever sorry before.'

Isannah said, 'Is it true, like Ma says, you'll be only good for picking rags?'

Cilla turned on Isannah. 'You're crazy! Johnny isn't going to pick rags . . . But oh, Johnny, it's so awful and I'm so sorry and . . .'

Johnny's face was crimson. 'Will you stop talking about it!'

Isannah went on—'Madge says it looks awful . . .'

'If either of you girls,' he stormed, 'ever mention that I've even got a hand, I'll . . . I'll . . . just get on a ship and never come back. I'm not going to have you mucking about with your infernal cry-baby "Oh how dreadfuls." '

So he went to the shop.

He saw with anger that Dove was sitting at his bench, daring to use his tools. He had not been in the shop for a month. Of course it should be expected that Dove would use his bench—for a little while—just until he was back at himself.

Mr. Lapham had looked up from his work, blinked gently, shook his head and sighed. Dusty was making a terrific din in one corner.

Johnny stood and watched Dove's clumsy work as long as he could in silence. At last he burst out.

'Dove, don't hold your crimping iron like that . . .'

Dove leaned back. His fat, white face grinned up at him with exaggerated innocence.

'Thank you, Master Johnny. I know I'm not as good as you are. Won't you please to show me just how I should hold my crimping iron?'

Johnny walked out of the shop by the door leading to the wharf. He'd never show anybody again how to hold a crimping iron. If you can't do, you had best shut up. He started to slam the door, thought better of it. If you can't do, you'd best not slam doors.

So he strolled the length of the wharf. There was a big ship in from Jamaica. He idly watched porters rolling barrels of molasses out of its hold. A sailor was trying to sell an old lady a parrot. He saw John Hancock standing in a group of men. The sugar basin had never been delivered. When Mr. Lapham had discovered the evil that had gone on in his absence and the terrible punishment God had meted out to Johnny Tremain, he had ordered the whole thing melted down and he himself had gone over to Mr. Hancock, returned the cream pitcher, and merely said he had found it impossible to make a sugar basin. No explanation.

The boy was accustomed to working from eight to twelve, sometimes fourteen hours in a day. He had no holidays, no Saturday afternoons. He had often imagined to himself the pleasure it would be just to stroll once down Hancock's Wharf, as he was strolling now. Nothing to do. His hands in his pockets. Other boys—friends of his—would look up from their work, envy his idleness. Here and there he did see a familiar face. He believed every one of them was talking about his burn—pitying him. There was not a boy on the wharf Johnny did not know. He had made friends with some and enemies of others, and had played or fought with all of them. He saw Saul and Dicer packing salt herrings in a tub; Andy, his leather thimble strapped to his palm, sewing a sail; Tom Drinker (the local bully) coopering a barrel. This was Johnny's world, but now he walked through it an alien. They knew what had happened. They did not envy Johnny's idleness. He saw one nudge another. They were whispering about him—daring to pity him. Dicer's master, the herring-pickler, yelled some kind remark to him, but Johnny did not answer. Seemingly in one month he had become a

stranger, an outcast on Hancock's Wharf. He was maimed and they were whole.

* * *

[*Compare this passage from* Johnny Tremain *with the following passage from* John Treegate's Musket *by Leonard Wibberley. The two passages deal with the same scene and are told from the same point of view—a young boy observing the Boston rebel leaders. Compare the differences in the two characterizations of Otis. Since Miss Forbes' knowledge about the Revolutionary period is highly regarded and she has often been praised for her authenticity, it is likely her characterization is accurate. Also notice how exciting Miss Forbes makes the meeting and how the famous men appear.*]

Sam and John Adams were standing and the other members were crowding about them, shaking hands with them, wishing them success at the Continental Congress in Philadelphia. They were starting the next day. Everyone was ready to give them advice whom to see, what to say, or to prophesy the outcome of this Congress. Paul Revere and Joseph Warren were apart a little, making plans for that spy system which was needed badly. They called Johnny to them, but he could hear one of the men standing about the two Adamses saying, 'But there must be some hope we can still patch up our differences with England. Sir, you will work for peace?'

Sam Adams said nothing for a moment. He trusted these men about him as he trusted no one else in the world.

'No. That time is past. I will work for war: the complete freedom of these colonies from any European power. We can have that freedom only by fighting for it. God grant we fight soon. For ten years we've tried this and we've tried that. We've tried to placate them and they to placate us. Gentlemen, you know it has not worked. I will not work for peace. "Peace, peace—and there is no peace." But I will, in Philadelphia, play a cautious part—not throw all my cards on the table—oh, no. But nevertheless I will work for but one thing. War—bloody and terrible death and destruction. But out of it shall come such a country as was never seen on this earth before. We will fight . . .'

There was a heavy footstep across the floor of the shop below. Rab leaped to the ladder's head.

'James Otis,' he reported to the men standing about Adams.

'Well,' said Sam Adams, a little crossly, 'no one needs stay and listen to *him*. He shot his bolt years ago. Still talking about the natural rights of man—and the glories of the British Empire! You and I, John, had as well go home and get a good night's sleep before leaving at dawn tomorrow.'

Otis pulled his bulk up the ladder. If no one was glad to see him, at least no one was so discourteous as to leave. Mr. Otis was immediately shown every honor, given a comfortable armchair and a tankard of punch. Seemingly he was not in a talkative mood tonight. The broad, ruddy, good-natured face turned left and right, nodding casually to his friends, taking it for granted that he was still a great man among them, instead of a milestone they all believed they had passed years before.

He sniffed at his punch and sipped a little.

'Sammy,' he said to Sam Adams, 'my coming interrupted something you were saying . . . "We will fight," you had got that far.'

'Why, yes. That's no secret.'

'For what will we fight?'

'To free Boston from these infernal redcoats and . . .'

'No,' said Otis. 'Boy, give me more punch. That's not enough reason for going into a war. Did any occupied city ever have better treatment than we've had from the British? Has one rebellious newspaper been stopped—one treasonable speech? Where are the firing squads, the jails jammed with political prisoners? What about the gallows for you, Sam Adams, and you, John Hancock? It has never been set up. I hate those infernal British troops spread all over my town as much as you do. Can't move these days without stepping on a soldier. But we are not going off into a civil war merely to get them out of Boston. Why are we going to fight? Why, why?'

There was an embarrassed silence. Sam Adams was the acknowledged ringleader. It was for him to speak now.

'We will fight for the rights of Americans. England cannot take our money away by taxes.'

'No, no. For something more important than the pocketbooks of our American citizens.'

Rab said, 'For the rights of Englishmen—everywhere.'

'Why stop with Englishmen?' Otis was warming up. He had a wide mouth, crooked and generous. He settled back in his chair and then he began to talk. It was such talk as Johnny had never heard before. The words surged up through the big body, flowed out of the broad mouth. He never raised his voice, and he went on and on. Sometimes Johnny felt so intoxicated by the mere sound of the words that he hardly followed the sense. That soft, low voice flowed over him: submerged him.

. . . For men and women and children all over the world,' he said. 'You were right, you tall, dark boy, for even as we shoot down the British soldiers we are fighting for rights such as they will be enjoying a hundred years from now.

'. . . There shall be no more tyranny. A handful of men cannot seize power over thousands. A man shall choose who it is shall rule over him.

'. . . The peasants of France, the serfs of Russia. Hardly more than animals now. But because we fight, they shall see freedom like a new sun rising in the west. Those natural rights God has given to every man, no matter how humble . . .' He smiled suddenly and said . . . 'or crazy,' and took a good pull at his tankard.

'. . . The battle we win over the worst in England shall benefit the best in England. How well are they over there represented when it comes to taxes? Not very well. It will be better for them when we have won this war.

'Will French peasants go on forever pulling off their caps and saying "Oui, Monsieur," when the gold coaches run down their children? They will not. Italy. And all those German states. Are they nothing but soldiers? Will no one show them the rights of good citizens? So we hold up our torch —and do not forget it was lighted upon the fires of England—and we will set it as a new sun to lighten a world . . .'

Sam Adams, anxious to get that good night's sleep before starting next day for Philadelphia, was smiling slightly, nodding his gray head, seeming to agree. He was bored. It does not matter, he was thinking, what James Otis says these days—sane or crazy.

Joseph Warren's fair, responsive face was aflame. The torch Otis had been talking about seemed reflected in his eyes.

'We are lucky men,' he murmured, 'for we have a cause worth dying for. This honor is not given to every generation.'

'Boy,' said Otis to Johnny, 'fill my tankard.'

It was not until he had drained it and wiped his mouth on the back of his hand that he spoke again. All sat silently waiting for him. He had, and not for the first time, cast a spell upon them.

'They say,' he began again, 'my wits left me after I got hit on the head by that customs official. That's what you think, eh, Mr. Sam Adams?'

'Oh, no, no, indeed, Mr. Otis.'

'Some of us will give our wits,' he said, 'some of us all our property. Heh, John Hancock, did you hear that? *Property*—that hurts, eh? To give one's silver wine-coolers, one's coach and four, and the gold buttons off one's sprigged satin waistcoats?'

Hancock looked him straight in the face and Johnny had never before liked him so well.

'I am ready,' he said. 'I can get along without all that.'

'You, Paul Revere, you'll give up that silver-craft you love. God made you to make silver, not war.'

Revere smiled. 'There's a time for the casting of silver and a time for the casting of cannon. If that's not in the Bible, it should be.'

'Doctor Warren, you've a young family. You know quite well, if you get killed they may literally starve.'

Warren said, 'I've thought of all that long ago.'

'And you, John Adams. You've built up a very nice little law practice, stealing away my clients, I notice. Ah, well, so it goes. Each shall give according to his own abilities, and some—' he turned directly to Rab—'some will give their lives. All the years of their maturity. All the children they never live to have. The serenity of old age. To die so young is more than merely dying; it is to lose so large a part of life.'

Rab was looking straight at Otis. His arms were folded across his chest. His head flung back

a little. His lips parted as though he would speak, but he did not.

'Even you, my old friend—my old enemy? How shall I call you, Sam Adams? Even you will give the best you have—a genius for politics. Oh, go to Philadelphia! Pull all the wool, pull all the strings and all the wires. Yes, go, go! And God go with you. We need you, Sam. We must fight this war. You'll play your part—but what it is really about . . . you'll never know.'

James Otis was on his feet, his head close against the rafters that cut down into the attic, making it the shape of a tent. Otis put out his arms.

'It is all so much simpler than you think,' he said. He lifted his hands and pushed against the rafters.

'We give all we have, lives, property, safety, skills . . . we fight, we die, for a simple thing. Only that a man can stand up.'

With a curt nod, he was gone.

Johnny was standing close to Rab. It had frightened him when Mr. Otis had said, 'Some will give their lives,' and looked straight at Rab. Die so that 'a man can stand up.'

Once more Sam Adams had the center of attention. He was again buttoning up his coat, preparing to leave, but first he turned to Revere.

'Now *he* is gone, we can talk a moment about that spy system you think you can organize in Boston.'

Paul Revere, like his friend, Joseph Warren, was still slightly under the spell of James Otis.

'I had not thought about it that way before,' he said, not answering Sam Adams's words. 'You know my father had to fly France because of the tyranny over there. He was only a child. But now, in a way, I'm fighting for that child . . . that no frightened lost child ever is sent out a refugee from his own country because of race or religion.' Then he pulled himself together and answered Sam Adams's remarks about the spy system.

That night, when the boys were both in bed, Johnny heard Rab, usually a heavy sleeper, turning and turning.

'Johnny,' he said at last, 'are you awake?'

'Yes.'

'What was it he said?'

'That a man can stand up.'

Rab sighed and stopped turning. In a few moments he was asleep. As often had happened before, it was the younger boy who lay wide-eyed in the darkness.

'That a man can stand up.'

He'd never forget Otis with his hands pushed up against the cramping rafters over his head.

'That a man can stand up'—as simple as that.

And the strange new sun rising in the west. A sun that was to illumine a world to come.

JOHN TREEGATE'S MUSKET

Leonard Wibberley

Compare the following passage with the preceding selection from Johnny Tremain *by Esther Forbes. Mr. Wibberley's scene is so dull his hero becomes drowsy, and his characters appear stick-like.*

Sam Adams opened the proceedings and, after thanking the gentlemen for meeting with him at such short notice, gave them the news of his visit to Governor Hutchinson, the decision to move all the soldiers to Castle William in the harbor, and the further decision that the eight men and their captain must stand trial for murder.

These tidings were hardly news to the men in the room, but they were receiving them officially from Adams who, for all his untidiness, was certainly the leader of the group.

"And now, gentlemen," he said, "we must consider the significance of this event and what is to be done in respect to the future. The significance is plain. The soldiery can no longer be tolerated in Boston or anywhere in these colonies. They must be got rid of—completely. All must, as I see it, unite in a demand that they be removed to England."

"Why are you so harsh against these Redcoats, Sam?" asked Dr. Warren. "Do not recite to me the list of the various hardships they have imposed on the city, culminating in this frightful butchery. I know them all. What is your deeper reason?"

"A simple and basic one, sir," said Sam Adams. "The soldiers are here to enforce compliance by the people of Boston to laws which the people of Boston have had no hand in making. We are, sir, to put it plainly, ruled by the musket. We have no vote in the passing of laws. If we protest against them, it will be at the peril of being shot. And that, sir, is Tryanny. No other name will serve."

He spoke quietly but with an intensity of feeling which left a deep impression on the gentlemen around the table, and even Peter found himself stirred.

"Is it not possible that they are here only temporarily in any case," said Dr. Warren, "and that they will be withdrawn when matters are more settled?"

"Withdrawn!" cried Adams. "And for how long, sir? Until some other incident such as the Stamp Act, or the abominable taxations of that blackguard Townshend, are reimposed upon these colonies by the parliament in Westminster? And then what will happen?

"We will protest, will we not, as we have a right to protest as free men. And what will follow?

"Why more ships of war in Boston harbor, more Redcoats landed on the Long Wharf and quartered in Faneuil Hall and the Old State House. And more massacres in the streets of Boston.

"What the rulers in London are doing is not only depriving us of representation, of the right to vote. They are also depriving us of the right to protest.

"A more unnatural state of affairs the world has never seen, sir."

There was a grunt from the end of the table where the big man Sullivan was seated. Peter leaned forward on his stool and caught a glimpse of the Irishman's head appearing out of the shadows into the candlelight. He sat so tall at the table that the candles lit only the underparts of his face so that his forehead was in shadow, but his cheeks, chin and nose were brightly lit and the effect was almost frightening.

"I will beg leave to differ with you, Mr. Adams," said Mr. Sullivan. "For in the country of my father, Ireland, which I call the fourteenth Atlantic colony, matters are in a worse pass than here. There a man may not own a horse over the value of five pounds, he may not own a weapon with which to defend himself, nor buy or sell property for profit, nor school his children as he will, nor meet in groups of more than five.

"And all this enforced at the point of the musket, for the nation is teeming with Redcoats. You see the Irish arrive here daily as refugees from their own country. They are a testimony of what tyranny is, when fully enforced."

"But that is a matter of the control of the rebellious and obnoxious Papists," said Mr. Otis.

"Papists be damned!" roared Sullivan, pounding the table with a huge fist and his face glowing red like a coal in a fire. "The freedom of a man is not something to be given or withheld on the basis of his worship. You are not to have one law for the Papists and one law for the Protestants. Men are men, sir—Irish, English or Hottentot. Papist, Episcopalian or Plymouth Brother. God alone may judge of the state of men's lives and their immortal souls. Repress one group and you have at a later time an excuse for repressing another. Liberty is not divisible, sir. It is the common heritage and birth right of all men."

"I had not intended to offend," said Mr. Otis.

"I take no offense," said Sullivan. "But if it is right to garrison Londonderry, then it is equally right to garrison Boston. What protest we make here must be not for Boston alone, but for every city in every colony under the control of Britain. And I will make so bold as to add every city and every people who find themselves oppressed in any part of the world."

"Ah," said Sam Adams. "Now we get nearer to the nub of the matter. For it is not the liberties of the people of New York and of Philadelphia and of Charleston, and of every city and town and settlement in these colonies. And these people in these cities and places must be made to see that.

"They must not come to think, as they may readily be made to think by their various governors and king's agents, that it is only because we in Boston are rebellious and stiff-necked that we are garrisoned with troops. All must be made to see that our cause is theirs and their cause ours— that the soldiers in Boston deny them the right of protest as they deny us."

Dr. Warren smiled gently and nodded his neatly wigged head. "I suppose you have a plan as always, Sam?" he said.

"I do," said Adams. "It is a simple one. We must see to it that news of everything that takes place in Boston is fully and accurately known all over the colonies. We must see to it that anything that occurs elsewhere is fully and accurately known here."

Sullivan snorted. "You will do nothing with newspapers," he said. "They are too readily suppressed or bought with the King's gold."

"I don't propose a newspaper," said Adams. "I propose what we might term a Committee of Correspondence. Several gentlemen in this city will undertake to write letters giving the story of our troubles, which will be printed and circulated throughout the colonies. Gentlemen in other cities—New York, Philadelphia and so on—will do likewise. Thus there will be a free and ready flow of information throughout these colonies. And the governors will not be able either to suppress the writing of these letters, nor bribe the authors to cease writing them."

"And what about the acts of sedition and libel?" asked Mr. Warren.

"A skillful letter writer may slip through these without trouble," said Adams. "You do not have to use your own name in any case. A pen name will suit admirably."

"And who will see to the distribution of these letters?" Otis asked.

"I will," replied Adams. "Give them to me and, with the aid of Mr. Revere, I will get them around. And I will write to my friends in Philadelphia, New York and elsewhere and ask them to join in the plan. We have already, Mr. Revere and I, made a start on this plan for spreading our news to all the people of these colonies. Do you have your sketch with you, Mr. Revere?"

Up to this point, the silversmith had not taken any part in the discussion. He now reached inside his frock coat and took out a roll of paper which he smoothed open on the table, to reveal a colored sketch of the troops firing into the Boston crowd. The men around the table stood up to look at it and grunted their approval.

"Mr. Revere is to engrave this upon a copper plate, and send as many copies as he can around the colonies," said Adams.

"It is a spirited rendering of the scene," said Otis.

"I have never seen a better piece of work," said Sullivan.

Revere gave an elaborate shrug and then smiled at them in the candlelight.

"I do not deceive myself that this is art, gentlemen," he said, "but I will hazard that this drawing will have a bigger effect upon the world than many a painting by a far more eminent man."

The meeting had convened at Mr. Adams' house at seven that evening and it was still going strong at nine o'clock when Mr. Fielding glanced at his watch. The room was stuffy and hot and Peter, worn out by the excitements of the day, had dozed off on the little stool in the corner.

THE BEARS ON HEMLOCK MOUNTAIN

Alice Dalgliesh

The Bears on Hemlock Mountain *is a well-written book for kindergarten, first- and second-grade children. They become caught up in the suspense of the story and Jonathan's fear that there* might *be bears on Hemlock Mountain. Many youngsters use the book as a springboard for a discussion of their own hidden fears. When well handled by a tactful adult, such a discussion is very healthy.*

Jonathan, nearly eight years old, is sent over a big hill called Hemlock Mountain to borrow an iron pot from his Aunt Emma for his mother to prepare a dinner for twenty aunts, uncles, and cousins. Although Jonathan has told his Uncle James, who is only fourteen and Jonathan's good friend, that he would rather see a bear than "anything in the world," when he is sent alone over the mountain he worries that he may encounter one. His mother says, "Stuff and nonsense." All the way to his Aunt Emma's house Jonathan repeats the refrain, "There are no bears on Hemlock Mountain." At home his mother repeats it, too, as she cuts out cookies. This musical refrain not only adds an attractive verbal pattern that children enjoy chanting with the reader of the book but also builds the story's suspense.

AUNT EMMA'S HOUSE

When Jonathan began to think about spring and about bears, it made him feel the need to hurry.

So he went on, very quickly. Down here on the other side of Hemlock Mountain the sun was even warmer. Drip, drip, drip, went the trees. Jonathan's boots no longer went crunch on the snow. They sank into it, and he made bigger footprints than before.

Soon he was at his Aunt Emma's house. By the gate some hungry birds were hopping about on the snow. Jonathan felt in his pockets. Yes, there were a few crumbs. So he threw them to the birds and went round to the back door.

Jonathan lifted the brass knocker and let it fall. How loud it sounded! But it was a cozy, comfortable sound, not a lonely one. Jonathan had come over Hemlock Mountain and here he was, safe at his aunt's house! He began to feel big and noble and brave. Jonathan seemed to grow an inch taller as he stood waiting for his aunt to open the door.

Footsteps came hurrying through the kitchen. The door opened and there was his Aunt Emma. She was wearing a big white apron, and Jonathan hoped she had been cooking. By now he was very, very hungry.

"Mercy sakes, Jonathan!" said his Aunt Emma. "What are you doing here this snowy day? Come in!"

Jonathan went in, but first he shook the snow carefully off his boots. Aunt Emma was a good housekeeper. Then he went into the kitchen. A big fire was burning, and the kitchen was pleasant and warm. The air was full of a good smell. Jonathan sniffed—M-m-m-cookies!

It was quite hard to be polite. But Jonathan sat down in the rocker and tried not to look hungry. He had quite forgotten about the cookies eaten on the way.

"Well," said his Aunt Emma, "what brings you here?"

"I came to see you, Aunt," said Jonathan, full of politeness and hunger. The big black cat came and rubbed against his legs. Jonathan stroked her.

"Tush!" said his aunt. "You can't tell me that you came all the way over Hemlock Mountain just for a visit?" Then she looked at him sharply.

"Jonathan! *Did you come all alone over Hemlock Mountain?*"

"Yes," said Jonathan. "Why?"

"Because—" said his aunt.

"Because what?" asked Jonathan.

"Because, nothing." But Jonathan knew she was thinking about BEARS.

The cat arched her back and purred. Jonathan thought he had been polite long enough. So he allowed himself to give just a small sniff.

Sniff, sniff, "Smells good in here!" said Jonathan.

Sniff!

"Mercy's sake," said his aunt. "You must be hungry coming all the way over the Mountain. Would you like a cookie?"

"Please. Thank you," said Jonathan hoping he did not sound too eager. Hoping, too, that it would not be just *one* cookie.

He need not have worried. His aunt brought a plate with a whole pile of crisp crunchy cookies. She put them on the table beside him. Then she brought a mug and a big blue pitcher of milk.

Mm-m-m! The cookies were good! Not as good as his mother's perhaps, but *good*, just the same.

Jonathan rocked and munched on cookies. He drank milk. He rocked and munched and drank. The clock on the kitchen shelf did its best to tell him that time was passing.

"Tick-tock, tick-tock, time to go, tick-tock."

But Jonathan rocked and ate and did not hear it.

"Tick-tock, tick-tock."

The fire was warm and Jonathan was most awfully full. He stopped rocking and slowly, slowly, slowly, his eyes closed. Jonathan was asleep!

Mercy's sakes! thought his aunt. *I wonder what the boy wanted? But it would be a shame to wake him* . . . So she let him sleep.

THERE MAY BE BEARS

Time went on. Jonathan slept. The sun went lower in the sky.

"Tick-tock!" said the clock. "Time to go!" But Jonathan went on sleeping.

The big black cat had also been sleeping by the fire. Now she got up, stretched, and came to rub against Jonathan's legs.

As she rubbed she purred, a loud rumble of a purr. And then, at last, Jonathan awoke!

At first he did not know where he was. Then he remembered.

"Oh!" he said. "It is late and Ma said I must be home before dark."

"There is still time, if you hurry," said his aunt. She wondered if Jonathan had come there just to eat her cookies. Why should he when his mother made such good cookies of her own. It was quite a puzzle.

Jonathan put on his muffler and his coat and his boots.

"Goodbye Aunt Emma," he said politely.

"Goodbye Jonathan. Do not waste time going over the mountain."

"Why not?"

"Because . . ."

"Because what?"

"Oh, just because . . ."

Jonathan was quite sure she was thinking about bears. But he was brave, and off he went toward Hemlock Mountain.

Jonathan had gone quite a way before it suddenly came to him. He stood still in the snow, feeling very cross with himself. You and I know what he had forgotten.

THE BIG IRON POT!

There was nothing for poor Jonathan to do but to turn and go back.

How silly I am, he said to himself. How silly I am!

In a short time he was back at his Aunt Emma's house. Once more he lifted the brass knocker. Aunt Emma came to the door.

"Jonathan! Did you forget something?"

"I forgot what I came for," Jonathan said truthfully. "Mom sent me to ask for the loan of your big iron pot. After the christening all the aunts and uncles and cousins are coming to supper."

"And as I am one of them, I'll be glad to lend you my big iron pot," said Aunt Emma. She went into the kitchen and came back with the big iron pot. It was very large. Now Jonathan did not feel as if he had grown at least an inch. He felt like a very small boy.

"Do you think you can carry it?"

"Indeed I can," said Jonathan, trying to feel big and brave again. He took the pot by the handle and started off toward Hemlock Mountain.

When he was out of sight his aunt began to worry.

"He is not very big," she told the black cat. "And it is growing dark."

"Purr-rr-rr," said the black cat. "Purr-rr-rr."

"Oh, don't tell *me*," said Jonathan's aunt with crossness in her voice.

"YOU KNOW
THERE MAY BE BEARS
ON HEMLOCK MOUNTAIN!"

Watch Out, Jonathan!

Jonathan and the big iron pot were going up the side of Hemlock Mountain.

Now it was really beginning to be dark. Jonathan knew he should hurry, but the iron pot was heavy. Jonathan's steps were heavy and slow. This time he was stepping in the big foot-prints he had made coming down.

It was really and truly dark. The tall trees were dark. The woods were dark and scary.

"Crack!" a branch broke in the woods. It was as loud as a pistol shot.

"Woo-ooh. Woo-ooh!" That was an owl, but it was a most lonely sound.

Jonathan began to think about bears. And to keep up his courage he said, in time to his own slow steps:

THERE . . . ARE . . . NO . . . BEARS
ON . . . HEMLOCK . . . MOUNTAIN
NO BEARS . . . NO . . . BEARS . . . AT . . . ALL.

He was tired and out of breath. So he rested for a minute, then he went on saying:

THERE . . . ARE . . . NO . . . BEARS . . .
ON . . . HEMLOCK . . . MOUNTAIN.
NO BEARS . . .

Watch out, Jonathan. WATCH OUT! What was that, among the trees, right on top of the mountain? Two, big, dark . . . what could they be?

They moved slowly . . . slowly . . . but they were coming nearer . . . and nearer . . . and nearer . . .

Jonathan had to think quickly. There was only one thing to be done. Jonathan did it. He put the big iron pot upside down on the snow. Then he dug out a place and crawled under it.

The pot was like a safe house. Jonathan dug out another little place in the snow so that he could breathe.

Then he waited.

PAWS ON THE SNOW

Crunch! Crunch! Crunch. It was the sound of big, heavy paws on the snow.

The bears were coming!

Crunch! Crunch! Crunch Nearer and nearer and nearer . . .

Jonathan's hair stood up straight on his head. He thought about a lot of things. He thought of his mother and father and the gray stone farmhouse. Had they missed him? Would they come to look for him? He thought about the bears and wondered how they knew it was spring.

Crunch! Crunch! Crunch! Nearer and nearer . . . Jonathan made foolish words to the sound just to keep up his courage:

THERE . . . ARE . . . NO . . . BEARS
ON . . . HEMLOCK . . . MOUNTAIN
NO BEARS . . . AT . . . ALL . . .

But the sound had stopped. The bears were *right beside the big iron pot.*

Jonathan could hear them breathing.

And he was all alone on Hemlock Mountain.

Suddenly, above the breathing of the bears, Jonathan heard a noise.

It was a twittering and a chattering. The twittering was the soft, comfortable noise that birds make before they go to sleep.

And then Jonathan knew that the trees were full of birds and squirrels. He was not alone on Hemlock Mountain.

Perhaps the bears knew this, too. Perhaps they had not quite waked up from their long winter nap. They sat there by the big iron pot. They waited and waited. But they did not try to dig under it.

Inside the iron pot it was dark. Jonathan was far from comfortable. Outside he could hear the bears going sniff, sniff, sniff, sniff. Poor Jonathan!

Oh, he said to himself. *Why did I wait so long at Aunt Emma's? Why did I eat so many cookies? Why did I go to sleep?* There did not seem to be any answer to these questions, so he stopped asking them.

The birds kept up their twittering and the squirrels kept up their chattering.

Sniff, sniff went the bears. One began scraping at the snow around the iron pot.

Poor Jonathan!

Then the birds stopped twittering and the squirrels stopped chattering. The bears stopped sniffing and listened. What was that?

Crunch! Crunch! Crunch!

Away off in the distance there was the sound of boots on the snow. Someone was coming up Hemlock Mountain!

It was very still. The only sound was the crunch of boots. And at last Jonathan heard it. His father's voice!

"Hello-o-o-oh, Jon-a-than!"

"Hello-o-o-h, Pa!"

Jonathan's voice did not sound very loud under the iron pot. Would his father hear it?

Again his father's voice came, nearer and louder.

"HELLO-O-O-OH, JON-A-THAN!"

"HELLO-O-O-OH, PA!"

The bears had had enough of this. They went lumbering off into the woods. And the crunch of boots on the snow came nearer and nearer . . .

THERE ARE BEARS

Jonathan pushed back the big iron pot and stood up.

There were no bears. But up the path came his father, carrying his gun. And with him were Jonathan's Uncle James and his Uncle Samuel, his Uncle John and his Uncle Peter. Jonathan had never in all his life been so glad to see the uncles.

"Jonathan!" said his father, "what a fright you have given us! Where have you been all this time."

"Coming over Hemlock Mountain," said Jonathan in a small voice. And he ran right into his father's arms.

"Well," said his father, when he had finished hugging Jonathan. "What is this?" He was looking at the big iron pot. "And why is it upside down?"

"Bears," said Jonathan.

"THERE
are
BEARS ON HEMLOCK MOUNTAIN."

Jonathan's father looked at the bear tracks in the snow. His uncles looked at them, too.

"So!" they said. "So-o-o!"

And the uncles went off into the woods with their guns.

"You and I must go home, Jonathan," said his father. "Your mother is worrying herself sick. You have been a mighty long time coming over Hemlock Mountain."

"Yes, Pop," said Jonathan, and he hung his head.

"But what kept you so long?" asked his father. They were going down the mountain, now, and Jonathan's father was carrying the big iron pot.

"Well," said Jonathan. "First I ate cookies, then I drank milk, then I slept . . ."

"H'm," said his father. "It is not the way to do when you are sent on an errand. But I guess you have learned that by this time."

It was very still on Hemlock Mountain.

There was only the crunch, crunch of boots on the snow. A squirrel scampered to a tree. He sat looking at Jonathan and his father, his paws on his heart.

"I know what I know!" he seemed to say.

Crack! What was that? A shot in the woods! Or a branch snapping? The squirrel, frightened, scampered higher up in the tree.

"Oh!" said Jonathan.

"Something tells me," his father said. "Something tells me we shall have bear steak for dinner!"

They kept on down the mountain. The birds twittered in the trees.

"We know what we know."

"The birds and the squirrels and the rabbits helped me," Jonathan said. "They are my friends."

"How could they help you?" asked his father. "They are so little."

"Well" . . . said Jonathan. But now they were near the great stone farmhouse and there was no time to explain.

The firelight shone through the open door. It made a warm, golden path on the snow. And in the doorway was Jonathan's mother.

"Oh, Johnny!" she said, as she hugged him. "How glad I am that you are safely home!"

As for Jonathan, all he said in a rather out-of-breath way was:

"THERE . . . *are* . . . BEARS
  ON . . . HEMLOCK . . .
    MOUNTAIN,
THERE . . .
  ARE . . .
    BEARS!"

Then he took the iron pot from his father and set it down in the middle of the floor. Now his voice was proud.

"I brought it," he said. "All the way over Hemlock Mountain. And here it is!"

THE LITTLE HOUSE IN THE BIG WOODS

Laura Ingalls Wilder

Unlike most children's books, Little House in the Big Woods *has no central plot. It is one of those rare novels that is successful even though it does not follow the general rules. A very popular book with second and third graders, it is read and reread by many pre-teen girls.*

The first in a series of seven books written by Mrs. Wilder about her childhood, Little House in the Big Woods *is set in Wisconsin in 1872. Readers learn a great deal about pioneer life: how headcheese and butter were made, how meat was preserved, how much fun roasting a pig's tail was and how good it tasted, how bullets were made and rifles loaded. So many homey details are given in a charming style that the reader, young or old, experiences delighted interest. The book's lack of plot is no handicap because the many anecdotes about frontier life are engrossing. The characters have so much personality, are so rounded, that they remain in the mind as quiet friends long after the book has been read.*

Few series are as well developed as that written by Mrs. Wilder. As Laura and Mary grow up, the style of the books becomes increasingly mature. This series does not hold reading skills back by being all written on the same level, instead by its high interest it leads the reader on and keeps pace with her maturity.

CHRISTMAS

Christmas was coming.

The little log house was almost buried in snow. Great drifts were banked against the walls and windows, and in the morning when Pa opened the door, there was a wall of snow as high as Laura's head. Pa took the shovel and shoveled it away, and then he shoveled a path to the barn, where the horses and the cows were snug and warm in their stalls.

The days were clear and bright. Laura and Mary stood on chairs by the window and looked out across the glittering snow at the glittering trees. Snow was piled all along their bare, dark branches, and it sparkled in the sunshine. Icicles hung from the eaves of the house to the snow banks, great icicles as large as the top as Laura's arm. They were like glass and full of sharp lights.

Pa's breath hung in the air like smoke, when he came along the path from the barn. He breathed it out in clouds and it froze in white frost on his mustache and beard.

When he came in, stamping the snow from his boots, and caught Laura up in a bear's hug against his cold, big coat, his mustache was beaded with little drops of melting frost.

Every night he was busy, working on a large piece of board and two small pieces. He whittled them with his knife, he rubbed them with sandpaper and with the palm of his hand, until when Laura touched them they felt soft and smooth as silk.

Then with his sharp jack-knife he worked at them, cutting the edges of the large one into little peaks and towers, with a large star carved on the very tallest point. He cut little holes through the

wood. He cut the holes in shapes of windows, and little stars, and crescent moons, and circles. All around them he carved tiny leaves, and flowers, and birds.

One of the little boards he shaped in a lovely curve, and around its edges he carved leaves and flowers and stars, and through it he cut crescent moons and curlicues.

Around the edges of the smallest board he carved a tiny flowering vine.

He made the tiniest shavings, cutting very slowly and carefully, making whatever he thought would be pretty.

At last he had the pieces finished and one night he fitted them together. When this was done, the large piece was a beautifully carved back for a smooth little shelf across its middle. The large star was at the very top of it. The curved piece supported the shelf underneath, and it was carved beautifully, too. And the little vine ran around the edge of the shelf.

Pa had made this bracket for a Christmas present for Ma. He hung it carefully against the log wall between the windows, and Ma stood her little china woman on the shelf.

The little china woman had a china bonnet on her head, and china curls hung against her china neck. Her china dress was laced across in front, and she wore a pale pink china apron and little gilt china shoes. She was beautiful, standing on the shelf with flowers and leaves and birds and moons carved all around her, and the large star at the very top.

Ma was busy all day long, cooking good things for Christmas. She baked salt-rising bread and rye'n'Injun bread, and Swedish crackers, and a huge pan of baked beans, with salt pork and molasses. She baked vinegar pies and dried-apple pies, and filled a big jar with cookies, and she let Laura and Mary lick the cake spoon.

One morning she boiled molasses and sugar together until they made a thick syrup, and Pa brought in two pans of clean, white snow from outdoors. Laura and Mary each had a pan, and Pa and Ma showed them how to pour the dark syrup in little streams on to the snow.

They made circles, and curlicues, and squiggledy things, and these hardened at once and were candy. Laura and Mary might eat one piece each, but the rest was saved for Christmas Day.

All this was done because Aunt Eliza and Uncle Peter and the cousins, Peter and Alice and Ella, were coming to spend Christmas.

The day before Christmas they came. Laura and Mary heard the gay ringing of sleigh bells, growing louder every moment, and then the big bobsled came out of the woods and drove up to the gate. Aunt Eliza and Uncle Peter and the cousins were in it, all covered up, under blankets and robes and buffalo skins.

They were wrapped up in so many coats and mufflers and veils and shawls that they looked like big, shapeless bundles.

When they all came in, the little house was full and running over. Black Susan ran out and hid in the barn, but Jack leaped in circles through the snow, barking as though he would never stop. Now there were cousins to play with!

As soon as Aunt Eliza had unwrapped them, Peter and Alice and Ella and Laura and Mary began to run and shout. At last Aunt Eliza told them to be quiet. Then Alice said:

"I'll tell you what let's do. Let's make pictures."

Alice said they must go outdoors to do it, and Ma thought it was too cold for Laura to play outdoors. But when she saw how disappointed Laura was, she said she might go, after all, for a little while. She put on Laura's coat and mittens and the warm cape with the hood, and wrapped a muffler around her neck, and let her go.

Laura had never had so much fun. All morning she played outdoors in the snow with Alice and Ella and Peter and Mary, making pictures. The way they did it was this:

Each one by herself climbed up on a stump, and then all at once, holding their arms out wide, they fell off the stumps into the soft, deep snow. They fell flat on their faces. Then they tried to get up without spoiling the marks they made when they fell. If they did it well, there in the snow were five holes, shaped almost exactly like

four little girls and a boy, arms and legs and all. They called these their pictures.

They played so hard all day that when night came they were too excited to sleep. But they must sleep, or Santa Claus would not come. So they hung their stockings by the fireplace, and said their prayers, and went to bed—Alice and Ella and Mary and Laura all in one big bed on the floor.

Peter had the trundle bed. Aunt Eliza and Uncle Peter were going to sleep in the big bed, and another bed was made on the attic floor for Pa and Ma. The buffalo robes and all the blankets had been brought in from Uncle Peter's sled, so there were enough covers for everybody.

Pa and Ma and Aunt Eliza and Uncle Peter sat by the fire, talking. And just as Laura was drifting off to sleep, she heard Uncle Peter say:

"Eliza had a narrow squeak the other day, when I was away at Lake City. You know Prince, that big dog of mine?"

Laura was wide awake at once. She always liked to hear about dogs. She lay still as a mouse, and looked at the fire-light flickering on the long walls, and listened to Uncle Peter.

"Well," Uncle Peter said, "early in the morning Eliza started to the spring to get a pail of water, and Prince was following her. She got to the edge of the ravine, where the path goes down to the spring, and all of a sudden Prince set his teeth in the back of her skirt and pulled.

"You know what a big dog he is. Eliza scolded him, but he wouldn't let go, and he's so big and strong she couldn't get away from him. He kept backing and pulling, till he tore a piece out of her skirt."

"It was my blue print," Aunt Eliza said to Ma.

"Dear me!" Ma said.

"He tore a big piece right out of the back of it," Aunt Eliza said. "I was so mad I could have whipped him for it. But he growled at me."

"Prince growled at you?" Pa said.

"Yes," said Aunt Eliza.

"So then she started on again toward the spring," Uncle Peter went on. "But Prince jumped into the path ahead of her and snarled at her. He paid no attention to her talking and scolding. He just kept on showing his teeth and snarling, and when she tried to get past him he kept in front of her and snapped at her. That scared her."

"I should think it would!" Ma said.

"He was so savage, I thought he was going to bite me," said Aunt Eliza. "I believe he would have."

"I never heard of such a thing!" said Ma. "What on earth did you do?"

"I turned right around and ran into the house where the children were, and slammed the door," Aunt Eliza answered.

"Of course Prince was savage with strangers," said Uncle Peter. "But he was always so kind to Eliza and the children I felt perfectly safe to leave them with him. Eliza couldn't understand it at all.

"After she got into the house he kept pacing around it and growling. Every time she started to open the door he jumped at her and snarled."

"Had he gone mad?" said Ma.

"That's what I thought," Aunt Eliza said. "I didn't know what to do. There I was, shut up in the house with the children, and not daring to go out. And we didn't have any water. I couldn't even get any snow to melt. Every time I opened the door so much as a crack, Prince acted like he would tear me to pieces."

"How long did this on on?" Pa asked.

"All day, till late in the afternoon," Aunt Eliza said. "Peter had taken the gun, or I would have shot him."

"Along late in the afternoon," Uncle Peter said, "he got quiet, and lay down in front of the door. Eliza thought he was asleep, and she made up her mind to try to slip past him and get to the spring for some water.

"So she opened the door very quietly, but of course he woke up right away. When he saw she had the water pail in her hand, he got up and walked ahead of her to the spring, just the same as usual. And there, all around the spring in the snow, were the fresh tracks of a panther."

"The tracks were as big as my hand," said Aunt Eliza.

"Yes," Uncle Peter said, "he was a big fellow. His tracks were the biggest I ever saw. He would have got Eliza sure, if Prince had let her go to the spring in the morning. I saw the tracks. He had been lying up in that big oak over the spring, waiting for some animal to come there for water.

Undoubtedly he would have dropped down on her.

"Night was coming on, when she saw the tracks, and she didn't waste any time getting back to the house with her pail of water. Prince followed close behind her, looking back into the ravine now and then."

"I took him into the house with me," Aunt Eliza said, "and we all stayed inside, till Peter came home."

"Did you get him?" Pa asked Uncle Peter.

"No," Uncle Peter said. "I took my gun and hunted all around the place, but I couldn't find him. I saw some more of his tracks. He'd gone on north, farther into the Big Woods."

Alice and Ella and Mary were all wide awake now, and Laura put her head under the covers and whispered to Alice, "My! weren't you scared?"

Alice whispered back that she was scared, but Ella was scareder. And Ella whispered that she wasn't, either, any such thing.

"Well, anyway, you made more fuss about being thirsty," Alice whispered.

They lay there whispering about it till Ma said: "Charles, those children never will get to sleep unless you play for them." So Pa got his fiddle.

The room was still and warm and full of firelight. Ma's shadow, and Aunt Eliza's and Uncle Peter's were big and quivering on the walls in the flickering firelight, and Pa's fiddle sang merrily to itself.

It sang "Money Musk," and "The Red Heifer," "The Devil's Dream," and "Arkansas Traveler." And Laura went to sleep while Pa and the fiddle were both softly singing:

"My darling Nelly Gray, they have taken you away,
And I'll never see my darling any more. . . ."

In the morning they all woke up almost at the same moment. They looked at their stockings, and something was in them. Santa Claus had been there. Alice and Ella and Laura in their red flannel nightgowns and Peter in his red flannel nightshirt, all ran shouting to see what he had brought.

In each stocking there was a pair of bright red

mittens, and there was a long, flat stick of red-and-white-striped peppermint candy, all beautifully notched along each side.

They were all so happy they could hardly speak at first. They just looked with shining eyes at those lovely Christmas presents. But Laura was happiest of all. Laura had a rag doll.

She was a beautiful doll. She had a face of white cloth with black button eyes. A black pencil had made her eyebrows, and her cheeks and her mouth were red with the ink made from pokeberries. Her hair was black yarn that had been knit and raveled, so that it was curly.

She had little red flannel stockings and little black cloth gaiters for shoes, and her dress was pretty pink and blue calico.

She was so beautiful that Laura could not say a word. She just held her tight and forgot everything else. She did not know that everyone was looking at her, till Aunt Eliza said:

"Did you ever see such big eyes!"

The other girls were not jealous because Laura had mittens, and candy, *and* a doll, because Laura was the littlest girl, except Baby Carrie and Aunt Eliza's little baby, Dolly Varden. The babies were too small for dolls. They were so small they did not even know about Santa Claus. They just put their fingers in their mouths and wriggled because of all the excitement.

Laura sat down on the edge of the bed and held her doll. She loved her red mittens and she loved the candy, but she loved her doll best of all. She named her Charlotte.

Then they all looked at each other's mittens, and tried on their own, and Peter bit a large piece out of his stick of candy, but Alice and Ella and Mary and Laura licked theirs, to make it last longer.

"Well, well!" Uncle Peter said. "Isn't there even one stocking with nothing but a switch in it? My, my, have you all been such good children?"

But they didn't believe that Santa Claus could, really, have given any of them nothing but a switch. That happened to some children, but it couldn't happen to them. It was so hard to be good all the time, every day, for a whole year.

"You mustn't tease the children, Peter," Aunt Eliza said.

Ma said, "Laura, aren't you going to let the other girls hold your doll?" She meant, "Little girls must not be so selfish."

So Laura let Mary take the beautiful doll, and then Alice held her a minute, and then Ella. They smoothed the pretty dress and admired the red flannel stockings and the gaiters, and the curly woolen hair. But Laura was glad when at last Charlotte was safe in her arms again.

Pa and Uncle Peter had each a pair of new, warm mittens, knit in little squares of red and white. Ma and Aunt Eliza had made them.

Aunt Eliza had brought Ma a large red apple stuck full of cloves. How good it smelled! And it would not spoil, for so many cloves would keep it sound and sweet.

Ma gave Aunt Eliza a little needle-book she had made, with bits of silk for covers and soft white flannel leaves into which to stick the needles. The flannel would keep the needles from rusting.

They all admired Ma's beautiful bracket, and Aunt Eliza said that Uncle Peter had made one for her—of course, with different carving.

Santa Claus had not given them anything at all. Santa Claus did not give grown people presents, but that was not because they had not been good. Pa and Ma were good. It was because they were grown up, and grown people must give each other presents.

Then all the presents must be laid away for a little while. Peter went out with Pa and Uncle Peter to do the chores, and Alice and Ella helped Aunt Eliza make the beds, and Laura and Mary set the table, while Ma got breakfast.

For breakfast there were pancakes, and Ma made a pancake man for each one of the children. Ma called each one in turn to bring her plate, and each could stand by the stove and watch, while with the spoonful of batter Ma put on the arms and the legs and the head. It was exciting to watch her turn the whole little man over, quickly and carefully, on a hot griddle. When it was done, she put it smoking hot on the plate.

Peter ate the head of his man, right away. But Alice and Ella and Mary and Laura ate theirs slowly in little bits, first the arms and legs and then the middle, saving the head for the last.

Today the weather was so cold that they could not play outdoors, but there were the new mittens to admire, and the candy to lick. And they all sat on the floor together and looked at the pictures in the Bible, and the pictures of all kinds of animals and birds in Pa's big green book. Laura kept Charlotte in her arms the whole time.

Then there was the Christmas dinner. Alice and Ella and Peter and Mary and Laura did not say a word at table, for they knew that children should be seen and not heard. But they did not need to ask for second helpings. Ma and Aunt Eliza kept their plates full and let them eat all the good things they could hold.

"Christmas comes but once a year," said Aunt Eliza.

Dinner was early, because Aunt Eliza, Uncle Peter and the cousins had such a long way to go.

"Best the horses can do," Uncle Peter said, "we'll hardly make it home before dark."

So as soon as they had eaten dinner, Uncle Peter and Pa went to put the horses to the sled, while Ma and Aunt Eliza wrapped up the cousins.

They pulled heavy woolen stockings over the woolen stockings and the shoes they were already wearing. They put on mittens and coats and warm hoods and shawls, and wrapped mufflers around their necks and thick woolen veils over their faces. Ma slipped piping hot baked potatoes into their pockets to keep their fingers warm, and Aunt Eliza's flatirons were hot on the stove, ready to put at their feet in the sled. The blankets and the quilts and the buffalo robes were warmed, too.

So they all got into the big bobsled, cosy and warm, and Pa tucked the last robe well in around them.

"Good-by! Good-by!" they called, and off they went, the horses trotting gaily and the sleigh bells ringing.

In just a little while the merry sound of the bells was gone, and Christmas was over. But what a happy Christmas it had been!

ISLAND OF THE BLUE DOLPHINS

Scott O'Dell

The Aleuts who have come to the Island of the Blue Dolphins to hunt otters kill most of the men of Karana's tribe. The tribespeople send a messenger to the mainland asking for a boat to help them leave their isolated island off the California coast.

Scott O'Dell has never surpassed this, his first book. Through skillful use of language he creates a strong mood of isolation and loneliness in this story of a girl left behind when her tribe emigrates from their island.

We took nothing with us when we thought we would have to flee, so there was much excitement as we packed our baskets. Nanko strode up and down outside the houses, urging us to hurry.

"The wind grows strong," he shouted. "The ship will leave you."

I filled two baskets with the things I wished to take. Three fine needles of whalebone, an awl for making holes, a good stone knife for scraping hides, two cooking pots, and a small box made from a shell with many earrings in it.

Ulape had two boxes of earrings, for she was vainer than I, and when she put them into her baskets, she drew a thin mark with blue clay across her nose and cheekbones. The mark meant that she was unmarried.

"The ship leaves," shouted Nanko.

"If it goes," Ulape shouted back, "it will come again after the storm."

My sister was in love with Nanko, but she laughed at him.

"Other men will come to the island," she said. "They will be far more handsome and brave than those who leave."

"You are all women of such ugliness that they will be afraid and soon go away."

The wind blew in fierce gusts as we left the village, stinging our faces with sand. Ramo hopped along far in front with one of our baskets, but before long he ran back to say that he had forgotten his fishing spear. Nanko was standing on the cliff motioning us to hurry, so I refused to let him go back for it.

The ship was anchored outside the cove and Nanko said that it could not come closer to the shore because of the high waves. They were beating against the rocks with the sound of thunder. The shore as far as I could see was rimmed with foam.

Two boats were pulled up on the beach. Beside them stood four white men and as we came down the trail, one of the men beckoned us to walk faster. He spoke to us in a language which we could not understand.

The men of our tribe, except Nanko and Chief Matasaip, were already on the ship. My brother Ramo was there too, Nanko said. He had run on ahead after I had told him that he could not go back to the village for his spear. Nanko said that he had jumped into the first boat that left the cove.

Matasaip divided the women into two groups. Then the boats were pushed into the water, and while they bobbed about we scrambled into them as best we could.

The cove was partly sheltered from the wind, but as soon as we went through the passage between the rocks and into the sea, great waves struck us. There was much confusion. Spray flew, the white men shouted at each other. The boat pitched so wildly that in one breath you could see the ship and in the next breath it had gone. Yet we came to it at last and somehow were able to climb onto the deck.

The ship was large, many times the size of our biggest canoes. It had two tall masts and between them stood a young man with blue eyes and a black beard. He was the chieftain of the white men, for he began to shout orders which they quickly obeyed. Sails rose on the tall masts and two of the men began to pull on the rope that held the anchor.

I called to my brother, knowing that he was very curious and therefore would be in the way of the men who were working. The wind drowned my voice and he did not answer. The deck was so crowded that it was hard to move, but I went from one end of it to the other, calling his name. Still there was no answer. No one had seen him.

At last I found Nanko.

I was overcome with fear. "Where is my brother?" I cried.

He repeated what he had told me on the beach but as he spoke Ulape who stood beside him pointed toward the island. I looked out across the deck and the sea. There, running along the cliff, the fishing spear held over his head, was Ramo.

The sails had filled and the ship was now moving slowly away. Everyone was looking toward the cliff, even the white men. I ran to one of them and pointed, but he shook his head and turned from me. The ship began to move faster. Against my will, I screamed.

Chief Matasaip grasped my arm.

"We cannot wait for Ramo," he said. "If we do, the ship will be driven on the rocks."

"We must!" I shouted. "We must!"

"The ship will come back for him on another day," Matasaip said. "He will be safe. There is food for him to eat and water to drink and places to sleep."

"No," I cried.

Matasaip's face was like stone. He was not listening. I cried out once more, but my voice was lost in the howling wind. People gathered around me, saying again what Matasaip had said, yet I was not comforted by their words.

Ramo had disappeared from the cliff and I knew that he was now running along the trail that led to the beach.

The ship began to circle the kelp bed and I thought surely that it was going to return to the shore. I held my breath, waiting. Then slowly its direction changed. It pointed toward the east. At that moment I walked across the deck and, though many hands tried to hold me back, I flung myself into the sea.

A wave passed over my head and I went down and down until I thought I would never behold the day again. The ship was far away when I rose. Only the sails showed through the spray. I was still clutching the basket that held all of my things, but it was very heavy and I realized that I could not swim with it in my arms. Letting it sink, I started off toward the shore.

I could barely see the two rocks that guarded the entrance to Coral Cove, but I was not fearful. Many times I had swum farther than this, although not in a storm.

I kept thinking over and over as I swam how I would punish Ramo when I reached the shore, yet when I felt the sand under my feet and saw him standing at the edge of the waves, holding his fishing spear and looking so forlorn, I forgot all those things I planned to do. Instead I fell to my knees and put my arms around him.

The ship had disappeared.

"When will it come back?" Ramo asked. There were tears in his eyes.

"Soon," I said.

The only thing that made me angry was that my beautiful skirt of yucca fibers, which I had worked on so long and carefully, was ruined.

The wind blew strong as we climbed the trail, covering the mesa with sand that sifted around our legs and shut out the sky. Since it was not possible to find our way back, we took shelter among some rocks. We stayed there until night fell. Then the wind lessened and the moon came out and by its light we reached the village.

The huts looked like ghosts in the cold light. As we neared them I heard a strange sound like that of running feet. I thought that it was a sound made by the wind, but when we came closer I saw dozens of wild dogs scurrying around through the huts. They ran from us, snarling as they went.

The pack must have slunk into the village soon after we left, for it had gorged itself upon the abalone we had not taken. It had gone everywhere searching out food, and Ramo and I had to look hard to find enough for our supper. While we ate beside a small fire I could hear the dogs on the hill not far away, and through the night their howls came to me on the wind. But when the sun rose and I went out of the hut, the pack trotted off toward its lair which was at the north side of the island, in a large cave.

That day we spent gathering food. The wind blew and the waves crashed against the shore so that we could not go out on the rocks. I gathered gull eggs on the cliff and Ramo speared a string of small fish in one of the tide pools. He brought them home, walking proudly with the string over his back. He felt that in this way he had made up for the trouble he had caused.

With the seeds I had gathered in a ravine, we had a plentiful meal, although I had to cook it on a flat rock. My bowls were at the bottom of the sea.

The wild dogs came again that night. Drawn by the scent of fish, they sat on the hill, barking and growling at each other. I could see the light from the fire shining in their eyes. At dawn they left.

The ocean was calm on this day and we were able to hunt abalone among the rocks. From seaweed we wove a rough basket which we filled before the sun was overhead. On the way home, carrying the abalone between us, Ramo and I stopped on the cliff. The air was clear and we could look far out to sea in the direction the ship had gone.

"Will it come back today?" Ramo asked.

"It may," I answered him, though I did not think so. "More likely it will come after many suns, for the country where it has gone is far off."

Ramo looked up at me. His black eyes shone.

"I do not care if the ship never comes," he said.

"Why do you say this?" I asked him.

Ramo thought, making a hole in the earth with the point of his spear.

"Why?" I asked again.

"Because I like it here with you," he said. "It is more fun than when the others were here. Tomorrow I am going to where the canoes are hidden and bring one back to Coral Cove. We will use it to fish in and to go looking around the island."

"They are too heavy for you to put into the water."

"You will see."

Ramo threw out his chest. Around his neck was a string of sea-elephant teeth which someone had left behind. It was much too large for him and the teeth were broken, but they rattled as he thrust the spear down between us.

"You forget that I am the son of Chowig," he said.

"I do not forget," I answered. "But you are a small son. Someday you will be tall and strong and then you will be able to handle a big canoe.

"I am the son of Chowig," he said again, and as he spoke his eyes suddenly grew large. "I am his son and since he is dead I have taken his place. I am now Chief of Ghalas-at. All my wishes must be obeyed."

"But first you must become a man. As is the custom, therefore, I will have to whip you with a switch of nettles and then tie you to a red-ant hill."

Ramo grew pale. He had seen the rites of manhood given in our tribe and remembered them. Quickly I said, "Since there are no men to give the rites, perhaps you will not have to undergo the nettles and the ants, Chief Ramo."

"I do not know if this name suits me," he said, smiling. He tossed his spear at a passing gull. "I will think of something better."

I watched him stride off to get the spear, a little boy with thin arms and legs like sticks, wearing a big string of sea-elephant teeth. Now that he had become Chief of Ghalas-at, I would have even more trouble with him, but I wanted to run after him and take him in my arms.

"I have thought of a name," he said when he came back.

"What is it?" I asked solemnly.

"I am Chief Tanyositlopai."

"That is a very long name and hard to say."

"You will soon learn," Chief Tanyositlopai said.

I had no thought of letting Chief Tanyositlopai go along to the place where the canoes were hidden, but the next morning when I awoke I found that Ramo was not in the hut. He was not outside either, and I knew then that he had gotten up in the dark and left by himself.

I was frightened. I thought of all that might befall him. He had climbed down the kelp rope once before, but he would have trouble pushing even the smallest of the canoes off the rocks. And if he did get one afloat without hurting himself, would he be able to paddle around the sandspit where the tides ran fast?

Thinking of these dangers, I started off to overtake him.

I had not gone far along the trail before I began to wonder if I should not let him go to the cliff by himself. There was no way of telling when the ship would come back for us. Until it did, we were alone upon the island. Ramo therefore would have to become a man sooner than if we were not alone, since I would need his help in many ways.

Suddenly I turned around and took the trail toward Coral Cove. If Ramo could put the canoe in the water and get through the tides that raced around the sandspit, he would reach the harbor when the sun was tall in the sky. I would be waiting on the beach, for what was the fun of a voyage if no one were there to greet him?

I put Ramo out of my mind as I searched the rocks for mussels. I thought of the food we would need to gather and how best to protect it from the wild dogs when we were not in the village. I thought also of the ship. I tried to remember what Matasaip had said to me. For the first time I began to wonder if the ship would ever return. I wondered about this as I pried the shells off the rocks, and I would stop and look fearfully at the empty sea that stretched away farther than my eyes could reach.

The sun moved higher. There was no sign of Ramo. I began to feel uneasy. The basket was filled and I carried it up to the mesa.

From here I looked down on the harbor and farther on along the coast to the spit that thrust out like a fishhook into the ocean. I could see the small waves sliding up the sand and beyond them a curving line of foam where the currents raced.

I waited on the mesa until the sun was overhead. Then I hurried back to the village, hoping that Ramo might have come back while I was gone. The hut was empty.

Quickly I dug a hole for the shellfish, rolled a heavy stone over the opening to protect them from the wild dogs, and started off toward the south part of the island.

Two trails led there, one on each side of a long sand dune. Ramo was not on the trail I was traveling and, thinking that he might be coming back out of sight along the other one, I called to him as I ran. I heard no answer. But I did hear, far off, the barking of dogs.

The barking grew louder as I came closer to the cliff. It would die away and after a short silence start up again. The sound came from the opposite side of the dunes, and leaving the trail I climbed upward through the sand to its top.

A short distance beyond the dune, near the cliff, I saw the pack of wild dogs. There were many of them and they were moving around in a circle.

In the middle of the circle was Ramo. He was lying on his back, and had a deep wound in his throat. He lay very still.

When I picked him up I knew that he was dead. There were other wounds on his body from the teeth of the wild dogs. He had been dead a long time and from his footsteps on the earth I could see that he had never reached the cliff.

Two dogs lay on the ground not far from him, and in the side of one of them was his broken spear.

I carried Ramo back to the village, reaching it when the sun was far down. The dogs followed me all the way, but when I had laid him down in the hut, and came out with a club in my hand, they trotted off to a low hill. A big gray dog with long curling hair and yellow eyes was their leader and he went last.

It was growing dark, but I followed them up the hill. Slowly they retreated in front of me, not making a sound. I followed them across two hills and a small valley to a third hill whose face was a ledge of rock. At one end of the ledge was a cave. One by one the dogs went into it.

The mouth of the cave was too wide and high to fill with rocks. I gathered brush and made a fire, thinking that I would push it back into the cave. Through the night I would feed it and push it farther and farther back. But there was not enough brush for this.

When the moon rose I left the cave and went off through the valley and over the three hills to my home.

All night I sat there with the body of my brother and did not sleep. I vowed that someday I would go back and kill the wild dogs in the cave. I would kill all of them. I thought of how I would do it, but mostly I thought of Ramo, my brother.

KILLER-OF-DEATH

Betty Baker

One of the tragedies of America has been the ruthless appropriation of Indian land. Even those who were sympathetic enough to believe Indians had a right to some land were able to do little to prevent the continuation of more and more dispossession.

Most books about frontier life portray Indians as vicious savages who, through trickery or cruelty, attempt to destroy innocent settlers. Both in reality and in western movies the cavalry eventually won and the defeated were considered the villains. But there is now a growing body of historical fiction for children that reveals what it was like to be an Indian threatened by an undefeatable force. The following selection is a well-written example of this type of book. Compare the reader's reactions to Indians in The Matchlock Gun *and in* Killer-of-Death *to understand how authors control their readers' attitudes.*

The Continental Divide, that rocky ridge from which all rivers flow east on one side and west on the other, hugs the western border of New Mexico. Tight against the Divide on the east flows the Rio Grande and beyond that stretches the dreaded White Sands. On the west the Divide falls away into the hilly, canyoned desert of Arizona. This was Apache country, Mimbreño Apache.

In the mid-1800's it was also disputed country. The border between Mexico and the United States was somewhere in the southern portion of the territories of Arizona and New Mexico. Just where no one was quite sure. Maybe someplace south of Tucson, maybe north of that town. The Mexicans pursued the raiding Apaches as far north as they could follow the trail. Wherever they turned back became the boundary for them. The Americans, busy with their mines in the northern mountains of Arizona, didn't worry about who owned the desert to the south. There was nothing there of importance.

Then plans began to take shape for a railroad that would stretch from coast to coast. The best route was through the southern portions of Arizona and New Mexico. The boundary must be settled once and for all.

The United States proposed the present border and offered to pay Mexico for any land she claimed north of it. This was the Gadsden Purchase. The Mexican government agreed to the purchase, but only after the United States promised to keep the Apaches north of the border and prevent raids on Sonora and Chihuahua. It seemed a simple task for the Army, but Easterners had no idea of the rugged vastness of the country or the nature of the Indians who lived in it.

In 1851 a survey party, followed by the Army, finally began to trace the border as we know it today. But other progress was slow. Two years passed before Congress at last approved the Gadsden Purchase, and in the meantime the Apaches had continued their raids. Angry and desperate, Mexico enforced her terrible Project of War, the payment of gold for Apache scalps.

Injustices followed misunderstandings until

hatred consumed all hearts, "Mexicano," "white-eye" and those of "the People." There was no peace until the Mimbreños and other Apaches were placed on the reservation in the White Mountains of Arizona in 1876. Even then Geronimo and his followers raced back and forth across the border, taking refuge from the Mexican Army by crossing into Arizona and escaping the Americans by crossing into the mountains of Mexico. But in 1886 Geronimo also surrendered.

Today some Mimbreños still live in the White Mountains of Arizona. The rest are on the Mescalero Apache Reservation in New Mexico, where they can gaze west across the glittering White Sands to the mountains their ancestors once roamed. If they have time, that is. For the Mescalero Reservation boasts ranches, lumber camps, a sawmill, a famous fire-fighting team, hunting, fishing, camping, skiing, a restaurant, a service station . . . and beauty. The prosperous reservation is a cool haven of spectacular pine-covered mountains tucked unexpectedly between two deserts. This now is the land of the People.

* * *

I was born too late. Growing to manhood in the time of my grandfather's father would have made the heart sing. The country and all it contained belonged to the People. One's days passed in hunting, with an occasional raid against the Papago to relieve them of the burden of storing their harvest. Even better to have been born in my father's time, when easy raids against the Mexicanos supplied all the blankets, cookpots, horses and guns one needed. But if one is born to see what I have seen, it is better not to be born at all. For when the medicine woman strapped me to my cradleboard, sprinkled the sacred hoddentin and offered me to the Four Directions, the white-eyes were sneaking past the Cheyenne and creeping into our mountains.

I knew nothing of this until later. My early childhood was unclouded. I toddled after my elder brother and imitated his every act. Thus, sooner than most I received my first bow and arrow.

I was not yet sure of my aim when the season of Many Leaves came round. We moved into the dry country so the women could harvest the mescal. I followed my brother on his hunting trips, eager to bring in my share of rabbits for the cookfire. On the last of these hunts I led the way through an arroyo. My brother trod close on my heels, alert to my every mistake. My passage disturbed the sleeping rattlesnake, but when it struck, my brother took the poison.

He was the only child of my father's first wife. She tore her hair and gashed her legs until I wished that I had been the one following. To ease her sorrow my father joined a raid and captured a young Mexicano boy. The woman ceased her mourning. The boy was adopted by the People, and I found myself the elder brother, the one who must teach and lead.

The boy did well. Sooner than most he buried his memories and learned our tongue. None had a keener eye for a trail, and his skill with a bow soon exceeded mine. Only in two ways did he differ from the People. His eyes were blue, and when there was a race to be run or a message to be carried, he would mysteriously vanish. Many were the times I found him sleeping under the drooping branches of a mesquite or curled in the shade of a cliff. Lazy Legs I called him, and the name clung like the two-horned thorns.

It was in my twelfth harvest that I first became aware that things were changing. Word came that three bands of white-eyes, larger than any that had come before, were camped in our mountains. The news disturbed my father and the other second chiefs. They talked long of what had happened to the buffalo-hunting tribes when the white-eyes moved among them. As for me, I worried only that exciting things might happen before I was ready to serve my warrior apprenticeship.

I trained harder than ever, running far into the desert and keeping my hand from dipping too often in my mother's cookpot. But the talk of war came to nothing.

The one the Mexicanos called Juan José gave word to leave the white-eyes in peace. Juan José was our great chief, so old that all those who knew his true name had joined the spirits. Everyone knows that with age comes wisdom, so his order was obeyed. But that order said nothing of the white-eyes' stock. When Ghost Face laid his chill over our canyons, more than one mule found its way into the cookpots.

Two harvests passed. The grumbling of the warriors grew louder. My father led more and more raids against the Mexicanos, but the white-eyes were like a forbidden pot of stew set before a starving man. I drove myself harder, determined to be ready when the time came.

The night was far gone. From where we camped outside the village we could hear the laughter and chanting of the dances fade and stop. My father had ordered us to wait while he went with the shaman to see Juan José. So we waited, our heads cloudy with sleep, until he returned.

"The chief will listen to nothing now," he said. "We must wait. The feast is tomorrow."

The women smiled. Lazy Legs licked his lips.

"I will not go," I said. "Not with this shame upon my name."

My brother gasped. The women began to chatter, but my father silenced them.

"That is best. Until Juan José has spoken, it is better for you to stay away from the People."

"But the feast," said my mother.

"We will go. I wish to see this trader. One can tell much of a man by the manner in which he gives."

"I will bring you food," whispered my brother. "And if there are knives among the gifts, I will get you one."

"It does not matter," I told him.

But as I sat alone sharpening my knife the next day, I thought of his promise. We had eaten little the night before, and hunger twisted my stomach. When a twig snapped on the trail from the village, I looked up eagerly.

"I am glad you came, brother."

With a laugh the shaman's son stepped into the clearing. I rose slowly, the newly sharpened knife in my hand. He drew his from the top of his moccasin and stepped forward, crouching low.

I told him, "I do not want to fight you now."

"You do not want to fight me ever. Or anyone else." He took another step. "Your blood runs like water at the thought of fighting. You are rabbit-hearted, like your friends the Mexicanos."

"That's not true."

"It is. You treat the enemy like your brother."

That was true. But how did he know of Red Sash and the Papago girl? Then, with his next words, I knew that was not what he meant.

"You eat with him, hunt with him, pretend he is one of the People."

"Lazy Legs is my brother!"

"He's an enemy. When I finish with you, I will kill him. But not as quickly. I will hang him head down over a fire as we do with the enemy. I will laugh at his screams . . ."

I leaped, knife slashing. He side-stepped. I shot past, stumbled and fell. Grinning, he came at me, the knife ready. I raised myself to one knee and waited. When he lunged, he would be off balance. I dared not move too soon or wait too long. Sweat broke out.

He ran, but it seemed days passed before he reached me. His arm swept down and then up toward my belly. I grabbed the wrist. Weight on one knee, I swung my other leg hard against his. He went down and rolled on his back. Jumping like a frog, I landed with both knees low on his belly. His breath whooshed from his mouth. He lay gasping, his open mouth working.

I raised my knife. Surely now my need was great. Where was the strength my father had said would come? Kneeling over Gian-nah-tah, I knew I could not plunge the knife into that great bear chest. His arms strained my grip. I would not be able to hold him much longer.

Why was he after blood? Because he knew Juan José would decide against him? Because he hated me or wanted to be chief? He twisted under me. I rolled away and sprang to my feet. Again we circled. He lunged. I stepped easily away.

"You could have killed me," he said. "But you are weaker than a woman. You haven't the strength of a rabbit. You are good for nothing but warming a blanket by the fire."

I dove at him, slashing blindly. He dodged past me and laughed.

"That is more like it. Now we shall have a fight."

Suddenly I understood. Gian-nah-tah had no reason for this fight, except that I was easily angered. Also, I was still weak and the shaman's son was one of those who would always worry and

tear at the weak. He was one of those who lived only for fighting. He would not hunt but raid, make war and torture prisoners. In time of peace his presence would make the camp uneasy. He would beat his wife, seek insults where there were none. Anything for a fight, just as he had stung me twice to an angry attack. I straightened and threw my knife on the ground.

"Pick it up," he snarled.

I shook my head. "I will not fight."

"You'll fight!" He came close, swishing the knife at my body, my face and drawing blood on my upper arm. I stared into the trees and did not flinch. If I did not put an end to it now, there would be no stopping Gian-nah-tah's insults until one of us was dead. Killed for no reason except to satisfy his hunger for fighting.

He walked backward, staring at me in bewilderment. He waved the knife and threatened, "This time I will not stop. Pick up your knife."

A small brown figure tumbled from the bushes and ran between us.

"Get away, Little One," I shouted.

She ran to me, holding something in both hands. A gun. One of those worn in the belt. It was new and it was loaded. A shadow fell over it. Gian-nah-tah hissed, staring at the gun in my hand.

"Where did you get this?" He grabbed her shoulders and shook her. "Where did you get it?"

"She can't talk."

"She must. Our people left their guns in their wickiups. The Mexicanos were to leave theirs in the town."

"Perhaps the guns are to be given as gifts."

He laughed bitterly. "The Mexicanos give us guns?"

I knelt beside my sister. "Listen to me, Little One. Were there guns with the gifts?"

She nodded and held up one finger.

"One gun with the gifts?" Another nod. "This gun?"

She shook her head. I looked at Gian-nah-tah, but he did not understand either. I tried again.

"There was only one gun with the gifts?"

She nodded and stretched her arms wide. Her mouth worked and her first words squeezed out. "Big, big gun."

I still did not understand. But Gian-nah-tah

knelt beside me and traced a picture in the ground with his knife.

"Is this the gun?" When she nodded, he hissed again. "A soldier's gun. The kind they pull with mules."

I pointed to the gun in my hand. "Are there more of these?"

She nodded and walked about pointing to one spot and then another. Under the blankets, the saddles, the bushes. Guns must be everywhere at the feast. Gian-nah-tah and I stood and stared at each other.

"They have hidden guns," I said. "It is a trap."

"Now it will be our trap." He grabbed the gun from my hand and looked to see if it was loaded.

I pulled my father's gun and ammunition from his blanket and ran after Gian-nah-tah. The big gun thundered. Screams filled the air. Then gunfire. A lot of gunfire—and our people had no guns.

We threw ourselves behind the rise of ground near the Mexicano town and looked down at the feast. Men, women and children littered the ground like limp bundles of old clothes. Near us, in the closed-in place with horses, stood the white-eye Johnson, smiling as he watched the Mexicanos shoot down the crawling wounded.

Gian-nah-tah gripped my arm. "Our chief!"

Juan José ran among the horses. We heard his high cracked voice plead with Johnson to stop the slaughter. With our own ears we heard him call the white-eye friend. And as he said it, the trader Johnson took a gun from his belt and shot our chief through the head. I raised the rifle, but horses moved between it and the trader. I swung round and shot a Mexicano who was raising a hatchet over a woman's head. I had seven shots. Gian-nah-tah had five. When they were gone, I beat my fists against the ground.

"Like shooting rabbits," said Gian-nah-tah. "Just as if they were shooting rabbits."

With his words I remembered the night Lazy Legs and I had slaughtered the rabbits in their sacred dance. I laid my head on my arms and cried. The Little One crept up to me, whimpering. I held her close, not seeing her for my tears. Then I touched Gian-nah-tah's arm.

"Some must have escaped. We must find them."

He nodded and pointed to the mountain behind us. "Up on that cliff is a cave once used by the Ancient Ones. Send all you find up there."

I began to crawl away, but his hand seized my foot. I looked back and saw that he also had wept.

"Take care," he said softly. "We can do nothing to help the ones down there. It is better for us to live and take vengeance. Two warriors can kill a great many enemies."

Tugging Little One after me, I moved off to search the rocks and woods for those who lived.

Juan José's village had been our largest. Two small camps had joined it for the feast. When I counted those huddled in the cave, I found there were only enough to make one village, and not a large one. Many were wounded, for the big gun had been loaded with small bullets, nails, bits of glass and pieces of metal. I walked among them, seeking those I knew. Of my family, only the Little One was there. I stopped by the shaman's son. He stared straight ahead, even when I laid my hand on his shoulder. I at least had the Little One. Gian-nah-tah was alone.

A stone rattled on the mountainside. The huge form of Mangas Colorado filled the entrance of the cave. In his arms, as one might carry a child, was the body of my father. Gently Mangas placed him on the dry earth of the cave. I knelt beside him. His eyes opened and looked into mine. His lips moved. A gourd of water was pressed to my hand. I lifted my father's head and helped him drink. He lay back and, after a moment, spoke slowly.

"My gun . . . Do not bury the gun with me . . . You will need . . . ." He raised his hand as if reaching for me. "My son."

"I have already used your gun." Suddenly I realized that I had killed two Mexicanos. When the need had been truly great, my strength had come.

My father smiled. From his torn flesh I pulled all the nails and glass I could find, but there was no medicine man to chant and hold back the evil spirits. When the first rays of the sun lit the top of the cave, my father closed his eyes and went away.

I mourned, and my grief struck spark to the flame of vengeance. A flame that blazed from foot to head, lashing the heart and mind to blind fury when we crept back to the feast and saw what the Mexicanos had done. We could not believe it. Soundlessly we crept about the scene of the massacre. Every body had been scalped, even to the smallest baby.

I found my family together. The women had thrown themselves across my brother, but they had not saved him. They also had been scalped.

Gian-nah-tah paused beside me. "They scalped even their own." He turned his head and spat.

"He was of the People," I said.

"Not to them. They could see he was their own."

I gazed at the unseeing blue eyes and the face that had laughed so often. It was true. The Mexicanos had known and had scalped him just the same. Together we buried them, along with the bodies of the shaman, his wife, the small still form of Shy Maiden, her father and many others. We stood long over the grave of Shy Maiden. When we turned away, we were no longer enemies.

The Mexicanos kept to their town. The men went heavily armed, and no children or women walked the streets. Ey, they had reason to fear! We made our way far into the mountains, moving like a huge turtle in our shell of grief. When our new camp was made, the women and children and old ones safe, then we would cry for vengeance.

The wickiups were built and food collected, but silence hung heavy over the camp. Families were broken. All gathered to eat at one fire. Then we sat together far into the night, stomachs full and hearts empty. It was on such a night that Broken Nose returned from the town of Tucson. He carried a big paper with him. He unrolled it and held it to the light, but Juan José was gone and no one could read the marks.

"I know what they say," said Broken Nose. "I crouched by the wall where it hung and listened to the Mexicanos and the white-eyes read and laugh."

We stared at the big black marks and, as he told us their meaning, it seemed as if we could read them.

> $100 FOR APACHE SCALPS
> THE GOVERNMENT OF MEXICO
> WILL PAY $100 FOR THE SCALP OF
> A MALE APACHE
> $50 FOR THE SCALP OF A SQUAW
> $25 FOR THE SCALP OF A CHILD

"Everyone in Tucson is talking of it," said Broken Nose. "The men say they will soon be rich on Apache scalps. The trader Johnson was paid well for his scalps."

"He took them to Tucson?" asked Mangas.

"No, Apache scalps must be taken south of the magic line."

"Apache!" shouted Gian-nah-tah. "How can they call us enemy? They are the enemy."

Broken Nose raised his hand. "There is more. I came through our camp to lead the old ones here. They have gone away. Their scalps are in Mexico."

Apache scalps. It was then we became Apache. Truly, we were the enemy, for no man was our friend.

Mangas led us. In his great mind he carried a plan. We followed it without question. In the dark of night we rode round the town of the traitors and far into the plain below. There we separated. I went with Mangas. We watched the trails Juan José had protected. Every wagon, every horseman, every Mexicano, every dog that moved along the trails was destroyed. Day after day our war cries rang. Blood darkened the sand. Smoke billowed in the sky and the buzzards gathered. Still we raided and waited. Nothing had gone into the town. No machinery, no food, no ammunition. Soon the Mexicanos must come out or starve. They crept forth at last, the murderers who feasted on Apache scalps.

I do not lie. Over three hundred Mexicano men and women and children began the journey from the town to their cities below the magic line. One by one we cut them down. From every hill, every rock, every cactus came arrows and bullets. They ran, but we were there to meet them. They fired, but they could not see us. Day by day their number lessened. On your fingers and toes you could count the ones who survived, and those we let through to carry the word. To tell the scalpers how the Apache took revenge.

There was peace in our mountains after that. The price of scalps was not great enough for a man to risk death by fire. I took a wife, a girl from another village, and we had a daughter. We lived the old way and were happy. But the time of peace was short. White-eyes found the Mexicano town and began to dig the copper. They did not ask us for permission, as the Mexicanos had done. They just came, strong and fearless in their walk and talk.

We held council. Gian-nah-tah spoke for war. But Mangas had a plan he wished to try. The same plan he had spoken to my father long ago. Mangas went to each of the white-eyes and told them where much gold could be found, for the white-eyes pursue gold as coyotes chase rabbits. It was true, and he would have led them there, for the place was deep in the Navajo country. But the white-eyes suspected a trap. I understand why they would think so. Why did they not attack us? Or arm themselves and wait? Never will I understand why they did the terrible thing. It was without reason.

They seized our chief, bound him to a tree and beat him until life was nearly gone. Mangas was a big man to fill with hatred. For every blow they struck, one hundred white-eyes would die.

When his wounds were healed, Mangas received a message from Cochise, our cousin in the Chiricahuas. The white-eyes had slain his brother. Cochise had declared war on the white-eyes. The blue-coated soldiers were marching to the Chiricahua Mountains.

"We will go," said Mangas. "It does not matter where we kill white-eyes, just so long as we wipe them from the land."

It was the only time our People joined with others to make war. The soldiers brought up big guns, many times larger than the one at the Johnson massacre. Our people were defeated. From then on, no war party numbered more than thirty. Sometimes six or seven. That is true, no matter what the white-eyes say. But it was in this first battle that my cousin's dream showed true.

Fourteen of us were with Mangas. We had cut one soldier off from the rest. Gian-nah-tah shot his horse from under him, and we circled, closing in. The soldier rolled behind the horse and fired one shot. Mangas slumped in his saddle. I yelled to Gian-nah-tah. Riding beside our chief, we supported him until out of danger. Then we lowered him to the ground.

"He will leave us," said Gian-nah-tah.

"No." Who would lead us? There was no one worthy. No one with my cousin's great heart and mind.

"Nothing can save him," said a warrior. "Look at his face. He has gone away."

I frowned, for it reminded me of something, somewhere. Leaping to my feet, I ordered them to put Mangas on a horse. They thought me crazy until I explained my plan. In the dark of night we rode into the Mexicano town and found their medicine man.

"Take out the bullet," I told him. "If our chief lives, we will leave in peace. If you do not save him, every person in this town will die."

It took a long time. The people of the town gathered in their church and prayed to their God. We sat watching the shaman's nervous hands and prayed to Usen. We rode out the next night, leaving the town as we had found it. The leader of our people had been slain. I had returned him to life. My cousin's dream had been true, and Mangas Colorado lived to kindle a blaze of vengeance that Cochise, Victorio and others kept burning.

Season after season we rode and killed and plundered. No longer could the women gather harvests. No longer was there time for hunting. We fled from canyon to canyon, ever searching for safety, ever raiding, ever killing, ever fleeing. All the time my first son grew to manhood the blanket burned with the hot flames of hatred. When it was finished, it was as my father had said. There was nothing left but ashes. For a proud free people, ashes are bitter food.

THE PERILOUS ROAD

William O. Steele

Most books about war are clearly partisan. (See The Matchlock Gun *and* Killer-of-Death.*) The Perilous Road is unusual in its objectivity, an especially valuable attitude when dealing with as emotionally charged a subject as the Civil War.*

Mr. Steele shows there were good men fighting on both sides in the Civil War. Chad, the hero of The Perilous Road, *is a young southern boy who judges too simply; he sees events and people, as do most children, only as good and bad, right and wrong. He believes the South is right and that all northern soldiers are inhuman. His parents disappoint Chad because they refuse to make such simple judgments. When his brother's moral sense makes him join the northern army, Chad is angry. As the story progresses he matures enough to understand that life is never as simple as it seems to a child.*

Chris stood watching the soldiers stuff flitches of bacon and middling meat and handfuls of turnips into their saddlebags. He could hardly believe it. He hadn't reckoned the Yankees would ever find their way to his cabin, stuck 'way back in the woods such a long piece from Anderson Road. But there they were, stealing all the Brabsons' food, even loading up his pappy's onliest horse with bags of corn and strings of shucky beans.

Anger swelled up inside his chest so hot and big he couldn't breathe, spread through his body till he thought he'd bust wide open. He hated those blue-coated soldiers so bad all he could think about was hate—hate and how fine it would be to shoot one of the Yankees, to see him lie still in the clearing. He flung aside his squirrels and swung his rifle up.

Silas grabbed him quick. "Whatever ails you, boy?" he grunted.

Chris jerked away and put his rifle to his shoulder. He would shoot one of those scabby-faced, sow-colored Yankees or die trying.

But Silas was after him like a snake. "Quit

that!" he snarled. He knocked the gun aside and dug his fingers in the boy's shoulders.

Chris jerked and twisted, trying to squirm away. He kicked angrily at Silas's legs and jabbed at his stomach with his elbow, but the man's fingers squeezed all the harder.

"Leave go, Silas!" Chris panted. "They ain't after your meal and your horse and your seed corn!"

He went right on struggling, and Silas shook him hard, well-nigh snapping his head off his body. It brought him up short, and he stopped still. Silas dragged him along the trail away from the clearing.

"You oughta be bored for the simples!" Silas growled at him. "You shoot now and you're just as liable to kill your own ma as one of them blue boys. And if'n you was to hit one of the Yanks, I reckon them others would kill your folks just to get even. And come after you and kill you too, like as not. Them's cavalry, and they don't think twice about running them fancy swords right through poor folks like you and me."

Chris wasn't listening. He was remembering all the hot back-breaking hours he'd spent planting and hoeing and working those beans and turnips and corn. And now it had all come to naught. Oh, the Brabsons would be hungry this winter, for a fact. It was all he could do to keep from crying, thinking about it.

And it was mortal hard to stand here and see Federal soldiers stealing and not lift a hand to prevent it. What was the matter with the world, that half its people could be so cruel and hateful? It wasn't right.

He gripped his rifle tight with both hands. It was more than human flesh could bear.

"Don't you act up again," Silas warned him. "You do and I swear I'll swat you a master blow."

Chris looked up at him, his eyes filled with fury. "I can't stand letting them get away with all that meanness," he blurted out.

"Hush," Silas said softly. "Don't I know how you feel? And I know a way we can get back at them devils."

Chris felt his heart give a triumphant lurch under his ribs. He was ready for anything.

Silas glanced toward the clearing. Through the trees Chris could see two of the soldiers mounting their horses. Mr. Brabson stood off to one side, talking with an officer.

"Come along," Silas urged. "They're a-fixing to leave." He stuffed his squirrels into a bush and jogged off down the trail, and the boy followed.

For some time they ran silently through the woods. They startled a deer, and it rose out of the laurel, sun-red in the black leaves. Pine trees stretched up overhead tall as the wind. And everywhere were square blocks of dark hemlocks. Chris felt strange and light-headed. It didn't seem real. The Yankees hadn't really been to his house. None of this was true.

Chris got a stitch in his side and stopped. He wiped his face with his sleeve. It was a powerful hot day to be running at a pace like this. Silas stopped too. But he didn't have any stitch, Chris could tell. He was hardly breathing deep. Silas was hickory-tough.

"You know Iron Creek Holler?" Silas asked. "The place where your brother Jethro's horse throwed him that time? Well, that's the spot I figured we could ambush these rascals. You get on one side and me on the other. We can get in a couple of shots apiece."

Chris pictured the spot in his mind, how the trail ran beside the creek to the head of the hollow. It was the finest kind of place for an ambush. "You reckon they'll give chase?"

"Naw, I don't reckon so," answered Silas. "They'll be scared to. Just that little handful by themselves up here in the woods. They ain't much for fighting less'n they got a heap of captains and generals around to tell 'em what to do. They'll just hope to get back to camp with all that plunder. They won't fight back."

He paused. "If'n they do, run for the bluffs. That's rough country, and they won't follow far." He looked hard at Chris and asked, "You ain't scared, be you?"

"You know I ain't scared one bit," Chris retorted quickly. "I'd do anything to get even with them lowdown critters."

A horse snorted and a man yelled at it. Chris jumped. The Yankees had almost caught up with them. He and Silas would have to burn up the ground. They set out running again, across a gorge, through an oak woods, and at last reached the hollow where the hills on each side crowded close to the trail.

But the soldiers were right behind them, had come on at a trot.

"Quick," panted Silas. "They're mighty nigh on us. Hide in that dog-hobble bush up there."

Chris scrambled up the slope. It was steep and slick with dead leaves. He slid and slipped and finally had to drop down on his hands and knees, pulling himself up by roots and saplings.

When at last he pushed down into the thick leaves of the dog-hobble, the soldiers had reached the hollow. He could hear the squeak of leather and the jingle of spurs above his thumping heart. He was panting so, he'd never be able to steady his rifle. Oh, if Silas just wouldn't shoot yet, give him a chance to get set.

There was the sharp sound of iron hoofs on rock. Chris sat up and peered out. The soldiers were on the trail right beneath him. He tried to bring his rifle up through the hobble, ease it to his shoulder as quick and quiet as possible.

Silas's shot rang out, and Chris all but cried, for he'd not get even one shot at the blue-coats now. The cock of his gun was caught under a twig. He yanked at it angrily, rising up out of the bushes to give it a tug. There was a heap of noise and confusion on the trail, shouts and yells and whinnies, but he didn't take time to see what was happening. He jerked his rifle loose and pulled the leaves from under the cock.

He brought his rifle up, unsteady as he was, trying to brace one foot against a rock. For a minute he couldn't make out a thing on the trail. Suddenly a horse reared right below him, and the rider beat at it with his fist, shouting and cursing. Before Chris could fire, the horse and soldier charged off.

The officer was pointing straight at him, screaming, "Get 'em! Get 'em! Up yonder in the bushes."

There was another shot, but Chris didn't know whether it was Silas again or one of the Yanks shooting at him. His foot was sliding off the rock, but there was no time to worry about that. His rifle was wobbling all over the place. Quickly he pulled the trigger, and the gun roared in the hollow. He fell backwards into the bushes, not knowing whether he'd hit anything or not. A horse screamed, and the officer kept on shouting.

Chris grabbed the dog-hobble and pulled himself over on his knees. Digging his toes into the soft earth, he struggled up the rest of the slope. They were already coming after him. He could hear the heavy breathing of the horses.

"They won't make it up that hillside," he told himself. "It's like trying to climb a peeled slippery elm."

But he was wrong. He hadn't more than reached the top before the horses came up a little to the right of the way he'd made it. "They must of found a draw or something," he thought. "I made sure horses couldn't get up there."

He ran then, for a fact. He wasn't a coward, but he'd heard a heap of tales about cavalrymen, and all of them were fierce. Silas had been right about those swords.

But Silas had been wrong about the rough country discouraging the Yankees. Chris was the one who was getting discouraged. He ran over rocks and down gullies and through laurel tangles, but he couldn't seen to shake off the horsemen. He was tired to the bone, and a great fiery pain throbbed in his side. But he wouldn't give up.

He stumbled and fell to his knees. Gulping air, he crouched there a minute, trying to think. What in creation was he going to do? He glanced around, feeling like a cornered rat. He could hide in some laurel slick, but he misdoubted they'd be hard put to find him. He could climb a tree but not these big old trees with their lowest limbs out of reach over his head.

He heard his pursuers coming, and he got up and trotted off along the edge of the mountain, his feet stumbling over every root and rock. He couldn't keep up this running. He'd been going hard since sunup this morning, and he was plumb beat out.

He staggered wearily on through the bushes and around boulders and finally came out onto the flat top of a bluff. He knew he'd have to give up. He'd run his last bit; he couldn't take another step. With trembling hands Chris loaded his rifle. He would fight for his life, get in one shot anyway before he was run down and hacked to pieces.

Then he saw the great crack at the side of the bluff, a place where the rock had split apart. He ran over to it and looked down. There were enough cracks and grab-holds for him to climb down. He could hide there out of sight of the soldiers. He'd have to be mighty quick though.

There was a long drop to the bottom of the split and the wickedest-looking rocks in all creation right under him. It gave him a queer, clutching feeling in his stomach, and he drew back.

"But I ain't got no choice," he told himself. "It's my onliest chance."

Quickly he hid his rifle among the bushes, covering it with dead leaves. Then he dropped to the edge and squirmed over, holding on to a little twisty pine. His toes found a crack in the rock, and he let go the pine tree and dropped from sight. He grabbed a rough knob and lowered himself still farther down the cliff.

He heard the soldiers coming then. The horses' iron shoes clanged on the rock. He cowered in his hiding place. They were almost on top of him. They'd see him sure if he didn't edge down a little more. He shifted his body and crouched a little, reaching for a handhold.

But he reached too far. For a minute he clung to the wall, and then his feet slipped off the tiny ledge below him. He was falling!

Chris clawed frantically at the cliff, scrabbling about for a foothold, grabbing at any crack, anything at all. His body slithered down the rough surface. He was as good as killed, headed straight down for those jagged rocks. He'd end up a heap of broken bones and bleeding meat, too dead to skin.

His hands raked over the ledge he'd been standing on, and he grasped it desperately. The weight of his body almost jerked his fingers loose, but there he hung with his face pressed against the rock. Chris shut his eyes tight. He knew in reason he couldn't hold on here long.

He almost cried out. He had to shut his jaws tight so he wouldn't yell and grind his teeth together to keep himself from begging the soldiers to pull him up. He was scared of dying but not so scared that he'd ask help of a Yankee. Never!

"I'd sooner ask a rattlesnake," he thought, and he thought, and he gripped the rock edge for all he was worth.

Over his head one of the soldiers spoke. Chris could hardly hear what he said, the horses were making such a racket, pawing at the rock and snorting around.

"He's gone. Got away from us slick as a snake going down a hole."

The other soldier laughed. "I expect these mountain folks know holes around here even the snakes don't know about," he answered. "You know, I wouldn't mind living here myself. I've never in my life seen a finer sight than this view."

"Go away, go away, go away," Chris prayed silently. His fingers were getting numb. "Don't let them bluecoats be here when I drop. Make 'em go away."

"View!" the first man grunted scornfully. "There ain't no view fine enough to make me want to live in this Godforsaken country. Why, the folks around here are ignorant as skinned mules. Give me flat country where people have got some sense."

He wheeled his horse and rode off. After a moment the other soldier went after him.

"Come back!" cried Chris. "Oh, come back and pull me up. It's all your fault I'm a-hanging here about to die."

But he didn't cry it aloud. He only said it inside his head. He wouldn't ask these Yankee soldiers for so much as a crumb of help. He couldn't think of words wicked and vile enough to say about them. For a minute he hated them

so much he forgot about his hands hurting, forgot he was hanging on a cliff high above Sequatchie Valley.

They were gone. There wasn't even the echo of a hoofbeat, only the wind sighing along the bluff's edge. He was alone with only a few minutes left to live. His hands ached like they'd been frostbitten, and his arms were about to pull out of the joints. Sweat ran down his face and neck.

His fingers slipped a mite on the edge. Hard as he tried, he couldn't make them keep their grip. Oh, he knew how this kind of thing happened! No matter how hard a body tried, he got so tired his muscles wouldn't do what he told them to. In a spell now his hands would give way, would lose their hold in spite of all his efforts. He would fall then.

He wished he'd been able to say good-by proper to his mammy. He loved his mammy. He wished he'd been able to see her just one more time, to tell her . . .

Somebody was coming!

He could hear somebody singing and hear footsteps on the bluff. He was going to be saved, but he'd have to holler. Even if it was a Yankee, Chris knew he'd never in this world keep himself from yelling this time.

He opened his mouth to shout, and no sound came out—not so much as a squeak. The footsteps were closer and the singing louder. Whoever it was would go on by and never know that under his feet Chris Brabson hung by his fingertips in the direst kind of peril. He swallowed and worked his tongue around inside his mouth.

> "Come all ye fair damsels, take warning from
>   me.
> Never place your affections on a green willow
>   tree;
> For the leaves they will wither like flowers in
>   the spring
> While the waters are a-gliding and the nightingales
>   sing."

He could hear the song plain now. He knew that voice. Jethro! It was his brother Jethro singing a tune!

"Jethro!" Chris cried. This time he did it, but his voice was hoarse and not near loud enough to carry above his brother's singing.

Jethro hit a low note and paused in his song. Chris filled his lungs with air and shrieked, "Jethro, help!" Oh, his brother had better hurry. He closed his eyes and tried to put all his strength into his fingers to make them hold on a little longer.

"Chris!" breathed Jethro's voice from overhead.

Chris opened his eyes then and looked up. When he saw his brother leaning down to him, he went limp as a rag. He almost let go and dropped, with help not four feet away from him.

Jethro must have seen he was in a bad way, for he didn't waste time asking questions, just climbed down the crack and grabbed Chris and hoisted him up safe to the top of the bluff.

Chris lay there, curled up like a drowned grub worm. He couldn't say a word, and his arms stretched out before him like two dead sticks, no good to him whatsoever. He was scratched from running through the bushes, and his bare toes had been scraped and rubbed raw where he'd tried to find a toe hold in the cliff. And he reckoned he'd never get both feet off the ground again without remembering how he'd felt there on the cliffside, alone and helpless, with nothing to stand on but a heap of empty air. He shuddered all over and sat up.

Jethro rubbed his hands and arms with quick strokes till they didn't ache so bad. Chris was breathing easier now.

"Here," Jethro said, handing over his hat. "I got these here pawpaws for Sallie Jean. But you look like you need 'em the worse way."

The pawpaws were sweet and juicy. They tasted wonderful to Chris's dry mouth and throat. No wonder Sallie Jean liked them so well. Right after she and Jethro were married, she'd planted a heap of pawpaw seeds near where they were building their cabin, Chris remembered. But he didn't reckon the trees were old enough to bear fruit yet. He ate three, spitting the flat brown seeds out over the mountainside.

"Now tell me how in the nation you come to be in a predicament like that?" Jethro asked.

The boy's eyes grew dark with anger. "Did you know the Yankees had been to our house?" he asked. "They done stole everything, all our food and old Codger and the chairs and table and beds, like as not. They aim to starve us to death."

"I reckon you'll make out," said Jethro briefly.

"But that don't tell how come you to be hanging over the edge of Walden's Ridge that-a-way. The Yankees never put you there."

"I reckon they did just that," Chris answered sulkily. "Leastways it was their fault I was there. Me and Silas was out squirrel-hunting. And when we come home, we seen the Yanks at the cabin, going off with the turnips and corn and meat." He stopped and gritted his teeth. Every time he thought about it he got mad all over again.

"Go on," urged Jethro.

"Well, me and Silas cut out across the woods to Iron Creek Holler and laid wait for 'em," said Chris. "Oh, it was the finest kind of place for an ambush, Jethro. But I didn't have time to get hid good, and when Silas fired, they seen me and come after me. I run, but I couldn't shake 'em. They chased me out on the bluff here, and I aimed to make a stand and fight. And then I seen that crack. I figured I could hide in it. But I slipped getting down in it, and if you hadn't come along, I reckon the buzzards would be picking me up about now."

"I reckon they would at that," said Jethro slowly. "And you wouldn't have deserved no better, falling in with one of Silas's wild schemes."

Chris was surprised. "I never figured you'd talk that way about Silas," he interrupted. "Silas is a good hunter. I reckon he's the best hunter anywhere in these parts. I think a heap of him."

Jethro gave him a look. "I reckon Silas is a mighty fine hunter," he agreed. "But that's all there is to him. He's a fly-by-night. He always likes to have something to be against. Right now he's against the Federals, but he don't rightly take it serious. It's just somebody to take his meanness out on."

Chris sprang up. "You'd ought to be ashamed, Jethro Brabson!" he yelled. "Silas was taking up for your mammy and pappy and brother and sister that the Yankees was a-stealing from. Maybe you didn't break your back over that corn and them turnips. But I did. Maybe you didn't see how proud Mammy was over that smoked side meat she had saved back. But I did. And I wasn't feared to try to shoot the blue-backed mud puppies that stole it, nor Silas neither."

Jethro looked at his brother soberly. "Chris, maybe you didn't know it, but this country's at war. Them soldier boys has got to get food somehow. They can't raise it. If they didn't take it, the Rebels would. Folks on Walden's Ridge won't starve. They may go without, but they won't starve."

"I'd a heap rather the Rebs had it," said Chris. He went over·and pulled his rifle out from under the laurel bushes.

Jethro grinned. "So you aimed to stand and fight," he repeated. "Just you against the United States Cavalry."

"I'd have killed one of 'em anyway," Chris muttered fiercely.

"Where was the Yanks when you was hanging off the bluff?" asked Jethro. "How come they didn't pull you up?"

"They was right here," burst out Chris. "Ain't I told you I was hiding from them. Did you think I was going to holler out and let 'em know where I was? It ain't easy to die falling off a bluff, but I misdoubt it's any easier to get cut up by them swords."

Jethro's blue eyes widened. "You mean you was hanging there, with nothing between you and breaking your fool neck, all the time the Federals was looking for you? And you never hollered out?" He laughed a little. "I never heared the like."

"I don't care," the boy said defiantly. "I hate them Yankees. I'd rather die than take help from them."

Jethro was silent a minute, studying his brother. "Well, that's too bad," he said finally, "for you just did."

Chris stared. "What do you mean?" he asked. "What?"

Jethro picked up the hat full of pawpaws. "I mean I'm on the Union side," he told him quickly. "I aim to join the Federal Army."

Chris went on staring. For a minute he had again that dizzy, light-headed feeling that nothing was real. And then he turned and ran blindly off into the woods.

THE TOTEM CASTS A SHADOW

Margaret Bell

A story's sense of realism can be destroyed by sentimentality. This affected emotionalism can be seen in the following passage from a book about pioneer life in Alaska.

It is this type of literature, pretending to be realistic, that creates false expectations of life. Girls who moon over passages such as these may never be satisfied with the real life behavior of their boyfriends or husbands.

Another weakness of this novel is the patronizing attitude toward the Indians. Florence's brother has married a native girl, not out of love but out of a sense of obligation for her warning of danger. His parents are indignant. Feeling the "shame" yet loving her brother, Florence writes Beldon Craig, her fiance, for comfort. When there is no answer from him she begins to believe he has rejected her because of the "disgrace." He finally comes and she runs from the house in embarrassment . . .

Nowhere was there a sign of human life. No smoke rose to indicate a neighbor's house, and

out across the lonely bay no craft rode; only the sea gull soared in the rain-swept air above the sea. Florence stopped walking and stood looking out across the water.

Doubts began to assail her now that the excitement of her escape had died away. Suppose nothing happened. Suppose the afternoon should wear on and Beldon failed to come. Suppose Pa had talked to Captain Craig and Beldon and they had decided merely to wait for her to come back. She would have to return before dark. Wet and tired, she would have to go back and face Pa, and everything would be worse than it had been before. Oh, what could a girl do? What could a girl do for herself alone? It would be so humiliating, so undignified, to stay here and get soaking wet and then go trailing back.

Uncertain whether to go on or go back, she stood like a waif lost in the enormous indifference of the wilderness around her. Beldon and Pa and Gregory all pulled her heart in different directions and now she began to wonder if any of them really cared which way she went.

There was a rush of sound behind her and she turned with a start. Donny came racing along the beach, his curly ears flapping and his tongue out. He ran up to her, licked her hands, and immediately dashed back in the direction from which he had come. Florence turned and looked back toward Our Point. She saw Beldon Craig coming out of the drooping cedars onto the band of snow above the beach. He paused there and stood looking toward her with the white snow behind him. Without any warning, tears fell from her eyes and mingled with the rain on her face. Beldon started walking toward her and she toward him.

As they drew closer to each other she could see that he was not smiling; his face was grave and full of concern. Donny ran back and forth between the two, but they had eyes only for each other. Without words they met and Beldon took her hands in his and drew her to him. He took her in his arms and they stood in the rain clinging to each other and it seemed to Florence that her spirit had found haven at last. Beneath the comfort that Beldon's embrace brought to her, she felt a deep joy that this could be so, that it could be so without words. Anything they would say would be apart from this. The rain was on their lips when they kissed. It was her first kiss, tender and full of longing. When she drew away from him, they looked at each other, their eyes declaring their love. She saw that the mist stood on his fair hair in tiny droplets and that in the blue of his eyes there was tenderness and wonder.

He knelt down on the wet shale and took her hands and leaned his face against them. She sank down beside him, pressing her cheek against his hair. Brokenly she tried to tell him how she needed him, how when no letter came she had doubted his love, thinking that he, like Pa, had found Gregory's action intolerable.

"Oh, my darling," Beldon said, "I came the moment I read your letter. We sailed out that very afternoon, and we should have been here days ago but for the head winds. I couldn't write. I had to come. We'll find Gregory. When we have our own home we'll see him."

Kneeling there in the rain, they found the loyalties of their hearts and the truth in them, and they recognized each other's honor. Florence thought her heart would break for the faith she had not kept.

"I am not worthy of such love," she whispered. "Oh, Beldon, I thought I knew what love is—but I have never known it until now!"

"Hush," he said, drawing her up to her feet. "Without you I couldn't even exist."

Arm in arm, they walked slowly back to Our Point. They talked seriously of many things, of their coming marriage and their future home, and of Gregory and Pa. Heedless of the rain, they paused often to stand enchanted in their mutual devotion.

Florence was full of wonder at this further discovery of love. She knew now that Beldon would fly to the ends of the earth to save her one moment's anguish. All that he did was faultless; all that he said was true.

As they came out from under the trees Beldon swept her up in his arms and carried her through the deep snow to the beach. He set her on her feet and they stood holding hands, breathless and laughing.

Related Reading

References for Adults

"Dimensions in Time; a Critical View of Historical Fiction for Children," by Carolyn Horovitz. *The Horn Book Magazine*, vol. 38, pp. 255–267. Also in *Horn Book Reflections*, ed. by Elinor Whitney Field. Boston: Horn Book, 1969.

"On Writing Historical Fiction," by Jean Fritz. *The Horn Book Magazine*, vol. 43, pp. 565–570.

"Only the Best," by Carolyn Horovitz. *Newbery and Caldecott Medal Books: 1956–1965*, ed. by Lee Kingman. Boston: Horn Book, 1965.

"Realism in Children's Literature," by Elizabeth Enright. *The Horn Book Magazine*, vol. 43, pp. 165–170.

"The Writing of Historical Novels," by Hester Burton. *The Horn Book Magazine*, vol. 45, pp. 271–277.

Books for Children

AMERICA

Baker, Betty. *Killer-of-Death*. Illustrated by John Kaufmann. New York: Harper & Row, 1963. A discussion of and an excerpt from this book can be found in this chapter. (Grades 5–9)

————. *Walk the World's Rim*. New York: Harper & Row, 1965. The story of a sixteenth-century Indian boy's experiences with Spanish explorers. (Grades 5–7)

Beatty, Patricia. *The Nickel-Plated Beauty*. Illustrated by Liz Dauber. New York: Morrow, 1964. Family life in the coast lands of the Washington Territory in the late 1880s. (Grades 4–7)

Bulla, Clyde Robert. *Down the Mississippi*. Illustrated by Peter Burchard. New York: Crowell, 1954. Mississippi river life in the 1850s. (Grades 2–5) This author has written a number of books for the young reader that have strong enough plot and character developments to appeal to older children with reading problems. Other titles by Bulla are:

————. *John Billington, Friend of Squanto*. Illustrated by Peter Burchard. New York: Crowell, 1956. The difficult first year of the Pilgrim settlement at Plymouth Harbor. (Grades 2–5)

————. *Riding the Pony Express*. Illustrated by Grace Paull. New York: Crowell, 1948. Set in the West in 1860s. A boy saves the mail. (Grades 2–5)

Caudill, Rebecca. *Barrie & Daughter*. Illustrated by Berkeley Williams, Jr., New York: Viking, 1943.

Excellent characterizations and strong plot combine in a story about a family's fight against injustice. Mountain life in the early 1900s. (Grades 5–9) Other historical fiction books by this author are:

————. *The Far-off Land*. Illustrated by Brinton Turkle. New York: Viking, 1964. (Grades 5–9)

————. *Tree of Freedom*. Illustrated by Dorothy Morse. New York: Viking, 1949. (Grades 5–9)

Credle, Ellis, author-illustrator. *Down, Down the Mountain*. New York: Nelson, 1961. Two Blue Ridge Mountain children, who have never had shoes, raise turnips to trade for them. A picture book with warmth and charm. (Grades K–2)

Dalgliesh, Alice. *The Bears on Hemlock Mountain*. Illustrated by Helen Sewell. New York: Scribner, 1952. A discussion of and an excerpt from this book can be found in this chapter. (Grades K–3)

————. *The Courage of Sarah Noble*. Illustrated by Leonard Weisgard. New York: Scribner, 1954. An excellent historical fiction novel for younger readers. (Grades 2–4)

De Angeli, Marguerite, author-illustrator. *Elin's Amerika*. New York: Doubleday, 1941. The experiences of a Swedish emigrant family that settled on the Delaware River in 1643. (Grades 4–6)

————. *Skippack School: Being the Story of Eli Shrawder and of One Christopher Dock, Schoolmaster about the Year 1750*. New York: Doubleday, 1961. (Grades 4–6)

————. *Thee, Hannah!* New York: Doubleday,

1940. An interesting book about a lively Quaker girl's growing understanding of her religion. When an escaping slave approaches her for help because of her dress, Hannah learns to appreciate her gray garb and to not long for the brighter clothes of her friends. (Grades 3–5)

Edmonds, Walter D. *The Matchlock Gun*. Illustrated by Paul Lantz. New York: Dodd, 1941. An excellent historical fiction picture book. Awarded the 1942 Newbery Medal. A discussion of and an excerpt from this novel can be found in this chapter. (Grades 2–4) Other historical fiction books by this author are:

————· *Two Logs Crossing*. Illustrated by Tibor Gergely. New York: Dodd, 1943. (Grades 3–5)

————· *Wilderness Clearing*. Illustrated by John de Martelly. New York: Dodd, 1945. (Grades 3–5)

Field, Rachel. *Calico Bush*. Illustrated by Allen Lewis. New York: Macmillan, 1946. Marguerite Ledoux, a French bound-servant, goes with the Sargent family to Indian-troubled Maine in 1743. (Grades 4–6)

Fleischman, Sid. *By the Great Horn Spoon!* Illustrated by Erick von Schmidt. Boston: Little, Brown, 1963. Humorous historical fiction about a young boy and his aunt's butler who stow away on a ship bound for the California gold fields. (Grades 4–7)

————· *Mr. Mysterious and Company*. Illustrated by Eric von Schmidt. Boston: Little, Brown, 1962. Another amusing historical novel set in the 1880s. (Grades 3–5)

Forbes, Esther. *Johnny Tremain*. Illustrated by Lynd Ward. Boston: Houghton Mifflin, 1943. A discussion of and an excerpt from this excellent book can be found in this chapter. Awarded the 1944 Newbery Medal. (Grades 6–9)

Henry, Marguerite. *Justin Morgan Had a Horse*. Illustrated by Wesley Dennis. Skokie, Ill.: Rand McNally, 1954. The story of a work horse who became the first of the "Morgans." (Grades 3–6)

Hunt, Ruth. *Across Five Aprils*. Chicago: Follett, 1964. A well-written book about the Civil War for older children. A family's peaceful life is shaken when sons enlist on both sides of America's conflict. (Grades 6–9)

Meigs, Cornelia. *The Covered Bridge*. Illustrated by Marguerite de Angeli. New York: Macmillan, 1936. Vermont farm life in 1788. (Grades 3–5)

————· *The Willow Whistle*. Illustrated by E. Boyd Smith. New York: Macmillan, 1931. Friendship between two midwestern pioneer children and the Indians. (Grades 3–5)

————· *Wind in the Chimney*. Illustrated by Louise Mansfield. New York: Macmillan, 1934. The story of an English widow and her children who emigrate to America ten years after the American Revolution. (Grades 3–5)

Morrow, Honore Willsie. *On to Oregon!*. Illustrated by Edward Shenton. New York: Morrow, 1946. The dramatic story of a family's journey to the Oregon Territory. When both parents die, the children are to be sent back east to relatives. Instead they decide to travel west on their own. Based on the true experiences of the Sager family. What makes this story especially poignant is that all but one of the children were killed in the Whitman massacre several years later. (Grades 5–9)

O'Dell, Scott. *The Dark Canoe*. Illustrated by Milton Johnson. Boston: Houghton Mifflin, 1968. Sixteen-year-old Nathan goes with his brothers Jeremy and Caleb to Magdalena Bay in Baja California to find the *Amy Foster*, a sunken ship whose wreck had cost Caleb his captaincy. Caleb attempts to recover the ship's log and so discover if he had been responsible for the shipwreck. (Grades 6–9)

————· *Island of the Blue Dolphins*. Boston: Houghton Mifflin, 1960. A discussion of and an excerpt from this book can be found in this chapter. Awarded the 1961 Newbery Medal. (Grades 5–9)

Speare, Elizabeth George. *Calico Captive*. Illustrated by W. T. Mars. Boston: Houghton Mifflin, 1957. The story of a girl carried off by the Indians in the French-Indian wars. (Grades 4–6)

————· *The Witch of Blackbird Pond*. Boston: Houghton Mifflin, 1958. A discussion of and an excerpt from this well-written novel can be found in this chapter. Awarded the 1959 Newbery Medal. (Grades 5–9)

Steele, William O. *Flaming Arrows*. Illustrated by Paul Galdone. New York: Harcourt, 1957. Although in some of Steele's historical fiction sympathy is evoked for the Indian's point of view, this novel powerfully reveals the fear of pioneers living in Indian territory. The story takes place in a fort surrounded by attacking Indians. (Grades 4–6) Some of the other historical fiction novels by this author are:

————· *The Perilous Road*. Illustrated by Paul Galdone, New York: Harcourt, 1958. A discussion of and an excerpt from this well-written book can be found in this chapter. (Grades 4–7)

————· *Wayah of the Real People*. Illustrated by Isa Barnett. Colonial Williamsburg. New York: distributed by Holt, 1964. A sympathetic presentation of a Cherokee Indian boy's years at the Brafferton School for Indians at colonial Williamsburg. (Grades 5–7)

————. *Wilderness Journey*. Illustrated by Paul Galdone. New York: Harcourt, 1953. (Grades 4–7)

————. *Winter Danger*. Illustrated by Paul Galdone. New York: Harcourt, 1954. (Grades 4–6)

————.*The Year of the Bloody Sevens*. Illustrated by Charles Beck. New York: Harcourt, 1963. (Grades 4–6)

Turkle, Brinton, author-illustrator, *Thy Friend, Obadiah*. New York: Viking, 1969. A picture book about a young boy's annoyance at the seagull who follows him everywhere. In time he learns to like its friendship. Awarded the 1969 Childrens Spring Festival award. (Grades K–3)

Wilder, Laura Ingalls. *By the Shores of Silver Lake*. Illustrated by Garth Williams. New York: Harper & Row, 1953, first published 1939. (Grades 5–7) All of Mrs. Wilder's books, except *Farmer Boy*, described her life as a pioneer child. Unlike most books in a series, these excellently written autobiographical novels progress from a simple style appropriate for primary children to the more complex style appropriate for older readers. Thus, the books keep pace with the child's progress in reading as well as with the progress of the central figure's life, from childhood to marriage.

————.*Farmer Boy*. Illustrated by Garth Williams. New York: Harper & Row, 1953, first published 1933. The everyday farm life of young Almanzo Wilder in 1868. (Grades 3–5)

———— *Little House in the Big Woods*. Illustrated by Garth Williams. New York: Harper & Row, 1953, first published 1932. The first in the series about Laura Ingalls' childhood. A discussion of and an excerpt from this book can be found in this chapter. (Grades 2–4) Other books in the series are:

————.*Little House on the Prairie*. Illustrated by Garth Williams. New York: Harper & Row, 1953, first published 1935. A sequel to *Little House in the Big Woods*. (Grades 3–5)

————. *The Long Winter*. Illustrated by Garth Williams. New York: Harper & Row, 1953, first published 1940. A sequel to *By the Shores of Silver Lake*. (Grades 4–6)

————. *On the Banks of Plum Creek*. Illustrated by Garth Williams. New York: Harper & Row, 1953, first published 1937. A sequel to *Little House on the Prairie*. (Grades 4–6)

————.*These Happy Golden Years*. Illustrated by Garth Williams. New York: Harper & Row, 1953, first published 1943. The sequel to *The Long Winter*. (Grades 6–8)

EUROPE AND SCANDINAVIA

Bulla, Clyde Robert. *Viking Adventure*. Illustrated by Douglas Gorsline. New York: Crowell, 1963. Well-written book about a young boy's adventures on a voyage to Wineland. (Grades 2–5)

Haugaard, Erik Christian. *Hakon of Rogen's Saga*. Illustrated by Leo and Diane Dillon. Boston: Houghton Mifflin, 1963. A discussion of and an excerpt from this book can be found in this chapter. (Grades 5–8)

————.*A Slave's Tale*. Illustrated by Leo and Diane Dillon. Boston: Houghton Mifflin, 1965. Sequel to *Hakon of Rogen's Saga*. A tragic tale of honor and treachery in which Hakon frees his slave Rark and attempts to return him to his family and estate in Brittany. (Grades 6–9)

Ish-Kishor, Sulamith. *A Boy of Old Prague*. Illustrated by Ben Shahn. New York: Pantheon, 1963. Jewish ghetto life in mid-sixteenth century Bohemia is powerfully revealed. (Grades 5–7)

Kelly, Eric P. *The Trumpeter of Krakow*. Illustrated by Angela Pruzynska. New York: Macmillan, 1928. A great deal of historical information but little character development and rather stilted dialogue. Awarded the 1929 Newbery Medal. Grades 4–6)

O'Dell, Scott. *The King's Fifth*. Maps and decorations by Samuel Bryant. Boston: Houghton, 1966. While Estéban de Sandoval is held in jail awaiting trial for withholding the King of Spain's share of treasure, he writes down the events that lead him to this predicment. The characterizations are not especially good, many of the personages are symbols of evil rather than rounded individuals, but the setting and the time are well depicted. This is not as well written as the author's *Island of the Blue Dolphins*. (Grades 6–10)

Polland, Madeleine. *The White Twilight*. Illustrated by Alan Cober. New York: Holt, Rinehart and Winston 1962. Hanne, the insecure daughter of a brillant architect, joins her father at Elsinore, Denmark, where he is building the castle of Kronborg for King Frederick II. There she becomes involved with the "son" of a nobleman whose real father is the pirate who steals from the King. An interesting story which does not romanticize the renegade father. (Grades 5–9)

Pyle, Howard, author-illustrator. *Otto of the Silver Hand*. New York: Scribner, 1888. An example of historical fiction used to preach to the reader about the horrors of barbarism. (Grades 3–6)

Treece, Henry. *The Road to Miklagard*. Illustrated by Christine Price. New York: Criterion, 1957. A sequel to *Viking's Dawn*. (Grades 5–8)

————. *Viking's Dawn*. Illustrated by Christine Price. New York: Criterion, 1956. The first in an interesting trilogy of Viking sea adventures set in the eighth century. (Grades 5–8)

————. *Viking's Sunset*. Illustrated by Christine Price. New York: Criterion, 1961. The last in the trilogy. (Grades 5–8)

Winterfeld, Henry. *Detectives in Togas*. Translated from the German by Richard and Clara Winston. Illustrated by Charlotte Kleinert. New York: Harcourt, 1956. Someone wrote "Caius is a dumbbell" on the wall of the temple of Minerva, and when Rufus is imprisoned for this desecration his schoolmates attempt to prove his innocence. An interesting mystery set in ancient Rome. All is convincing except for the villain's long, detailed confession to the boys. (Grades 4–7)

GREAT BRITAIN

Bulla, Clyde Robert. *The Sword in the Tree*. Illustrated by Paul Galdone. New York: Crowell, 1956. A young nobleman's son, driven from his inheritance by a wicked uncle, goes to Camelot for aid. (Grades 2–5)

De Angeli, Marguerite, author-illustrator. *The Door in the Wall*. New York: Doubleday, 1949. Robin, a nobleman's son, left crippled as the result of a long illness, looses all hope of being a knight and a source of pride for his father. With the help of a kindly friar and his own strong will, Robin learns to read, write, swim, and play the lute; all of which help him rescue a beseiged castle. Awarded the 1950 Newbery Medal. (Grades 4–6)

Harnett, Cynthis, author-illustrator. *Caxton's Challenge*. Cleveland, Ohio: World, 1960. The adventures of an apprentice to the great fifteenth-century English printer. (Grades 4–7)

Henry, Marguerite. *King of the Wind*. Illustrated by Wesley Dennis. Skokie, Ill.: Rand McNally, 1948. A horse story based on historical fact about the Godolphin Arabian, ancestor of Man-o-War. Winner of the 1949 Newbery Medal. (Grades 4–6)

Hodges, Walter C., author-illustrator. *The Marsh King*. New York: Coward, 1967. Only one English ruler has ever been called the Great: Alfred, the ninth-century king whose endurance and cleverness prevented the Viking invaders from gaining total domination of the island. Hodges' novel dramatically recreates that struggle and Alfred's life in the marshes where he hid his forces and from which he emerged to fight the Vikings. A companion novel is *The Namesake* by the same author. (Grades 5–8)

Picard, Barbara Leonie. *Lost John*. Illustrated by Charles Keeping. New York: Criterion, 1963. The son of an English baron is robbed and beaten as he seeks revenge on his father's murderer. Later captured by Sir Ralf the Red, John becomes the robber knight's squire. Only after he has grown to love his new leader does John discover that Sir Ralf is the man who killed his father. An interesting story with convincing characterizations. (Grades 5–9)

Polland, Madeleine. *Children of the Red King*. Illustrated by Annette Macarthur-Anslow. New York: Holt, Rinehart and Winston, 1959. The thirteenth-century Irish-Norman conflict is revealed through the experiences of two children of the Irish king. Sutcliff's *The Shield Ring* portrays two worlds in conflict more dramatically than this novel by Polland. (Grades 4–8)

————. *The Town across the Water*. Illustrated by Esta Nesbitt. New York: Holt, Rinehart and Winston, 1961. The plight of sixteenth-century Irish fisherfolk is shown in this story of two brave children. (Grades 4–7)

————. *Queen without Crown*. Illustrated by Herbert Danska. New York: Holt, Rinehart and Winston, 1965. In the sixteenth century England controlled most of Ireland, but many rebellious leaders refused to pay homage to Queen Elizabeth. One such rebel was Grainne O'Malley, a pirate queen. Her decision to "offer" her services to the English queen are tied to her relationship with Patraick O'Flaherty, a young boy she rescued from the English soldiers. (Grades 5–9)

Sutcliff, Rosemary. *Dawn Wind*. Illustrated by Charles Keeping. New York: Walck, 1962. A moving story set in sixth-century England by one of the best and most accurate writers of historical fiction for young people. (Grades 6–up)

————. *The Eagle of the Ninth*. Illustrated by C. Walter Hodges. New York: Walck, 1954. The dramatic tale of a young legionnaire who goes into enemy territory to recover the lost eagle of the Ninth Legion. Second-century Britain. (Grades 6–up)

————. *The Lantern Bearers*. Illustrated by Charles Keeping. New York: Walck, 1959. When the last Roman Legion leaves Briton to its fate, one Legionnaire remains behind and becomes caught up in the Viking invasions. (Grades 6–up)

————. *The Mark of the Horse Lord.* New York: Walck, 1965. A remarkable story of the development of Phaedrus, a former slave and gladiator in Roman Britain, into the Horse Lord of the Dalriadain. Although his rank was achieved through a plot, and he only impersonated the prince of the Dalriadain, when tested all his loyalties were with the people he led and he proved his right to leadership. Second-century Scotland. (Grades 6–up)

————. *The Outcast.* Illustrated by Richard Kennedy. New York: Walck, 1955. The experiences of a young boy outcast by both the Romans and the Britons. (Grades 6–up)

————. *The Shield Ring.* Illustrated by C. Walter Hodges. New York: Walck, 1957. The powerful story of the resistance of a small group of Saxons in the north of England against the conquering Normans. Set in the eleventh century. (Grades 6–up)

————. *The Silver Branch.* New York: Walck, 1958. A tale of intrigue set in the last days of Roman Britain. One of Sutcliff's best. (Grades 6–up)

————. *Warrior Scarlet.* Illustrated by Charles Keeping. New York: Walck, 1958. Life in England's Bronze Age. (Grades 6–up)

Chapter II
Fantasy

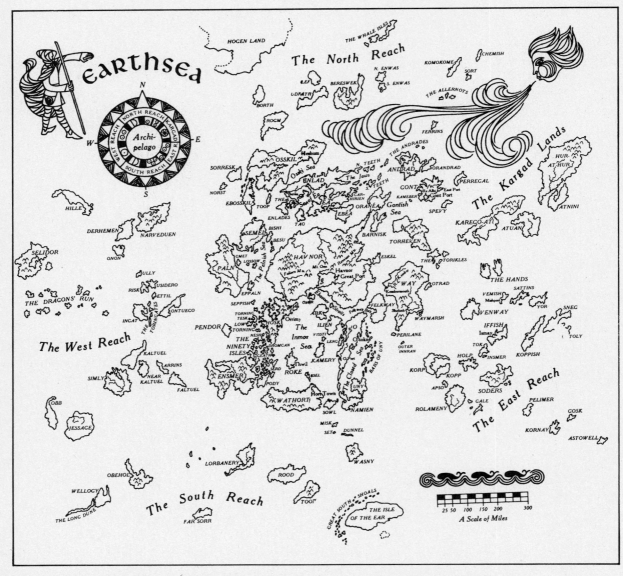

From *A Wizard of Earthsea* by Ursula K. Le Guin, illustrated by Ruth Robbins. Copyright 1968 by Ursula K. Le Guin, prose; art, Ruth Robbins. Reprinted by permission of Parnassus Press.

Fantasy demands more from the reader than realistic fiction does. It demands a willingness to accept an unknown world and its laws of nature. Fantasy cannot be successfully read without Coleridge's "willing suspension of disbelief." Many readers refuse to accept this condition and so reject the genre. Some people believe fantasy conveys a false impression of life. Children, however, easily recognize that giants, dragons, and magic do not exist in their own world. More likely to create a false impression of life is the wish-fulfillment literature portraying highly improbable success stories: the shy girl becoming a Broadway star, the humiliated boy scoring the winning run. Such literature is called realistic, but it encourages daydreaming and emotions varying from wistful regret to bitterness that the reader has not had such success. The readers of well-written fantasy, however, intuitively gain encouragement about human capabilities. Good fantasy, regardless of how unique the world or the characters, deals with human hopes and fears without catering to man's desire to escape the human condition.

Fantasy makes extra demands on the author as well as on the reader. To be successful, plot, characterization, and the fantastic must be carefully balanced. When reading realistic fiction the reader can draw upon his own experiences to understand and enter into the story. Often his knowledge of the author's subject—school, family life, pets—helps him suspend his disbelief and identify with the characters and the situation. But the author of fantasy must carefully build a world that is unique and believable. The best fantasy, such as J. R. R. Tolkein's books, C. S. Lewis' Narnia series, Yrsula Le Guin's *A Wizard of Earthsea* and Kenneth Grahame's *The Wind in the Willows*, builds a world that surprises the reader only at first. Lovers of fantasy easily accept the fact that the laws and conditions of the fantasy world do not exist in their own lives but are true and believable in the fictional world of the well-written book. One of the pleasures of good fantasy is that it creates a world so real readers can be a part of it for a time. That is why sequels and fantasy series are so popular; children enjoy the sense of returning to a group of people, in another world, who are their friends.

This illusion of reality so essential to the success of fantasy is created in several ways. A nonrealistic situation, such as animals that live and act in many ways like people, can be introduced immediately and seriously with no attempt at persuasion. The author establishes the reality of the situation by giving the reader no time for doubt. Grahame begins *The Wind in the Willows* in this way.

The Mole had been working very hard all the morning, spring-cleaning his little home. First with brooms, then with dusters; then on ladders and steps and chairs, with a brush and a pail of whitewash; till he had dust in his throat and eyes, and splashes of whitewash all over his black fur, and an aching back and weary arms. Spring was moving in the air above and in the earth below and around him, penetrating even his dark and lowly little house with its spirit of divine discontent and longing. It was small wonder, then, that he suddenly flung down his brush on the floor, said 'Bother!' and 'O blow!' and also 'Hang spring-cleaning!' and bolted out of the house without even waiting to put on his coat. Something up above was calling him imperiously, and he made for the steep little tunnel which answered in his case to the gravelled carriage-drive owned by animals whose residences are nearer to the sun and air. So he scraped and scratched and scrabbled and scrooged, and then he scrooged again and scrabbled and scratched and scraped, working busily with his little paws and muttering to himself, 'Up we go! Up we go!' till at last, pop! his snout came out into the sunlight, and he found himself rolling in the warm grass of a great meadow.

'This is fine!' he said to himself. 'This is better than whitewashing!'[1]

If Grahame had begun with an amused detachment or appeared, even for a few sentences, to apologize or had shown any doubt at the idea of a mole whitewashing his home, he would have allowed the reader to become detached and doubtful too. Had this occurred the illusion of reality would not have developed.

Notice how Charles Kingsley in his moralistic fantasy of the last century, *The Water Babies*, labors to convince his reader that water babies exist and then destroys his arguments in the last paragraph.

A water-baby? You never heard of a water-baby. Perhaps not. That is the very reason why this story was written. There are a great many things in the world which you never heard of; and a great many more which nobody ever heard of; and a great many things, too, which nobody will ever hear of, at least until the coming of the Cocqcigrues, when man shall be the measure of all things.

"But there are no such things as water-babies."

How do you know that? Have you been there to see? And if you had been there to see, and had seen none, that would not prove that there were none. If Mr. Garth does not find a fox in Eversley Wood—as folks sometimes fear he never will—that does not prove that there are no such things as foxes. And as is Eversley Wood to all the woods in England, so are the waters we know to all the waters in the world. And no one has a right to say that no water-babies exist, till they have seen no water-babies existing; which is quite a different thing, mind, from not seeing water-babies; and a thing which nobody ever did, or perhaps ever will do.

"But surely if there were water-babies, somebody would have caught one at least?"

Well. How do you know that somebody has not? . . . .

On and on it goes for many pages until Kingsley tells us he has been teasing.

And meanwhile, my dear little man, till you know a great deal more about nature than Pro-

fessor Owen and Professor Huxley, put together, don't tell me about what cannot be, or fancy that anything is too wonderful to be true. "We are fearfully and wonderfully made," said old David; and so we are and so is everything around us, down to the very deal table. Yes; much more fearfully and wonderfully made, already, is the table, as it stands now, nothing but a piece of dead wood, than if, as foxes say, and geese believe, spirits could make it dance, or talk to you by rapping on it.

Am I in earnest? Oh dear no. Don't you know that this is a fairy tale, and all fun and pretense; and that you are not to believe one word of it, even if it is true?

This is nothing but inexcusable patronizing.

In contrast to Kingsley, Mary Norton in *The Borrowers* uses detail to create an illusion of reality. She skillfully blends objects from the everyday world with the extraordinary by adding detail to detail in a logical and appropriate way to show that such small people actually could borrow and adapt human's possessions and so live a very comfortable life under the kitchen floor. By using recognizable objects that form a part of children's everyday life, a strong sense of probability is developed while the sense of the fantastic is heightened.

Ursula Le Guin in *A Wizard of Earthsea* creates a world so real that for many of her readers the experiences are their own. She uses maps and references to past history and records to give her story authenticity, but it is Mrs. Le Guin's skill in characterization that makes the book memorable. Whether fantasy's creations are animals, wizards, or people, they must have human qualities: hopes, fears, and problems that the reader can recognize and identify with. No matter how fantastic the fantasy world is, if the characters are distinct individuals, it will be believable.

Mrs. Le Guin also has a compelling plot with much action and suspense in her allegory of the struggle between good and evil. Fantasy is not always this serious but it does need a story strong enough to carry the reader along; it cannot rely solely on fanciful or extraordinary elements to hold the attention.

There are three types of fantasy. One is represented in this anthology by *The Wind in the Willows*, *Wizard of Earthsea*, Hans Christian Anderson's literary folktales, and several other selec-

[1] Reprinted with the permission of Charles Scribner's Sons from *The Wind in the Willows* by Kenneth Grahame.

tions. In addition to their fantastic elements, they have strong themes and deal with man's basic concerns. Children are not always consciously aware of this, but they can sense there is something beneath the surface story.

The second type of fantasy is more light-hearted. *Mary Poppins* and "Eeyore's Birthday" are two good examples. The intent behind them is to entertain, to bring pleasure. While the more serious aspects of life are seldom hinted at in this category, when well written they make delightful reading.

A third type of fantasy is the arrangement of a group of manufactured, fantastic incidents into book form. It lacks originality of character development and usually is plotless. This unsuccessful category is represented in this anthology with the chapter from *Mr. Pudgins* by Ruth Christoffer Carlsen. In this book a number of incidents involving magical occurrences are narrated in a series of unrelated episodes. Their only connection is that Mr. Pudgins, a magical babysitter, and the same three children participate in each. Too many fantasies like this are written for children on the assumption that if the story has magic or supernatural creatures children will love it. This patronizing attitude underestimates children.

Fortunately there are excellent fantasies with originality of conception and believable characters. In the following section excerpts from children's books have been selected to facilitate comparisons of well-written and less successful fantasy. Examples from the last century are also included for comparison with more recent works.

ALICE'S ADVENTURES IN WONDERLAND

Lewis Carroll

Alice's Adventures in Wonderland *and* Through the Looking Glass *are two classic fantasies from the Victorian period. The first adventures were originally told by Charles Lutwidge Dodgson—an Oxford Don and mathematician—to Dean Liddell's three daughters, Alice, Edith, and Rhoda. They were so enthusiastic they made him promise to write the story for them.*

Satire and parody of moralistic children's literature are seen in many of the verses in these books. Dodgson also satirizes contemporary theories of education. These most children and adults of today will miss. Some children are even repelled by the nightmarish quality of the books. In The Annotated Alice, *Martin Gardner says that the Alice books are still popular only because adults enjoy them so much. But there are some children who will be delighted by Alice's adventures and reactions to her experiences. She is able to adjust to the inexplicable and survive in the difficult world into which she has dropped, and she is always aware that it is an unnatural world.*

Alice, bored with sitting next to her sister on the bank, follows a white rabbit into a hole where she falls into a well. She falls very slowly and is not hurt when she lands. Following the rabbit down a passage, she finds herself alone in a hall with the only way out a door much smaller than herself. In her attempts to get out of the hall, she drinks a liquid and grows small enough to go through the door but finds she has left the key on the table that is now high above her head. She then eats a cake and suddenly grows nine feet high. In her misery Alice cries huge tears. As she fans herself she shrinks and shrinks until she is only two feet tall. Her foot slips and Alice finds herself in the pool of tears along with many animals and birds.

A CAUCUS-RACE AND A LONG TALE

They were indeed a queer-looking party that assembled on the bank—the birds with draggled feathers, the animals with their fur clinging close to them, and all dripping wet, cross, and uncomfortable.

The first question of course was, how to get dry again: they had a consultation about this, and after a few minutes it seemed quite natural to Alice to find herself talking familiarly with them, as if she had known them all her life. Indeed, she had quite a long argument with the Lory, who at last turned sulky, and would only say, "I am older than you, and must know better." And this Alice would not allow, without knowing how old it was, and as the Lory positively refused to tell its age, there was no more to be said.

At last the Mouse, who seemed to be a person of some authority among them, called out, "Sit down, all of you, and listen to me! *I'll* soon make you dry enough!" They all sat down at once, in a large ring, with the Mouse in the middle. Alice kept her eyes anxiously fixed on it, for she felt sure she would catch a bad cold if she did not get dry very soon.

"Ahem!" said the Mouse with an important air. "Are you all ready? This is the driest thing I know. Silence all round, if you please! 'William the Conqueror, whose cause was favoured by the Pope, was soon submitted to by the English, who wanted leaders, and had been of late much accustomed to usurpation and conquest. Edwin and Morcar, the Earls of Mercia and Northumbria—'"

"Ugh!" said the Lory, with a shiver.

"I beg your pardon?" said the Mouse, frowning, but very politely. "Did you speak?"

"Not I!" said the Lory, hastily.

"I thought you did," said the Mouse. "I proceed. Edwin and Morcar, the Earls of Mercia and Northumbria, declared for him; and even Stigand, the patriotic Archbishop of Canterbury, found it advisable—'"

"Found *what*?" said the Duck.

"Found *it*," the Mouse replied rather crossly; "of course you know what 'it' means."

"I know what 'it' means well enough, when *I* find a thing," said the Duck: "it's generally a frog or a worm. The question is, what did the Archbishop find?"

The Mouse did not notice this question, but hurriedly went on, "'—found it advisable to go with Edgar Atheling to meet William and offer him the crown. William's conduct at first was moderate. But the insolence of his Normans—' How are you getting on now, my dear?" it continued, turning to Alice as it spoke.

"As wet as ever," said Alice in a melancholy tone: "it doesn't seem to dry me at all."

"In that case," said the Dodo solemnly, rising to its feet, "I move that the meeting adjourn, for the immediate adoption of more energetic remedies—"

"Speak English!" said the Eaglet. "I don't know the meaning of half those long words, and what's more, I don't believe you do either!" And the Eaglet bent down its head to hide a smile: some of the other birds tittered audibly.

"What I was going to say," said the Dodo in an offended tone, "was, that the best thing to get us dry would be a Caucus race."

"What *is* a Caucus-race?" said Alice; not that she much wanted to know, but the Dodo had paused as if it thought that *somebody* ought to speak, and no one else seemed inclined to say anything.

"Why," said the Dodo, "the best way to explain it is to do it." (And as you might like to try the thing yourself, some winter day, I will tell you how the Dodo managed it.)

First it marked out a race-course, in a sort of circle ("the exact shape doesn't matter," it said), and then all the party were placed along the course, here and there. There was no "One, two, three, and away!" but they began running when they liked, and left off when they liked, so that it was not easy to know when the race was over. However, when they had been running half-an-hour or so, and were quite dry again, the Dodo suddenly called out, "The race is over!" and they all crowded round it, panting, and asking, "But who has won?"

This question the Dodo could not answer without a great deal of thought, and it stood for a long time with one finger pressed upon its forehead (the position in which you usually see Shakespeare, in the pictures of him), while the rest waited in silence. At last the Dodo said, "*Everybody* has won, and all must have prizes."

"But who is to give the prizes?" quite a chorus of voices asked.

"Why, *she*, of course," said the Dodo, pointing to Alice with one finger; and the whole party at once crowded round her, calling out in a confused way:

"Prizes! Prizes!"

Alice had no idea what to do, and in despair she put her hand into her pocket, and pulled out a box of comfits (luckily the salt water had not got into it), and handed them round as prizes. There was exactly one a-piece, all round.

"But she must have a prize herself, you know," said the Mouse.

"Of course," the Dodo replied very gravely. "What else have you got in your pocket?" he went on, turning to Alice.

"Only a thimble," said Alice sadly.

"Hand it over here," said the Dodo.

Then they all crowded round her once more, while the Dodo solemnly presented the thimble, saying, "We beg your acceptance of this elegant thimble"; and, when it had finished this short speech, they all cheered.

Alice thought the whole thing very absurd, but they all looked so grave that she did not dare to laugh; and as she could not think of anything to say, she simply bowed, and took the thimble, looking as solemn as she could.

The next thing was to eat the comfits: this caused some noise and confusion, as the large birds complained that they could not taste theirs, and the small ones choked and had to be patted on the back. However it was over at last, and they sat down again in a ring, and begged the Mouse to tell them something more.

"You promised to tell me your history, you know," said Alice, "and why it is you hate—C and D," she added in a whisper, half afraid that it would be offended again.

"Mine is a long and sad tale!" said the Mouse, turning to Alice, and sighing.

"It *is* a long tail, certainly," said Alice, looking down with wonder at the Mouse's tail; "but why do you call it sad?" And she kept on puzzling about it while the Mouse was speaking, so that her idea of the tale was something like this:—

> "Fury said to
>   a mouse, That
>   he met in the
>   house, 'Let
>   us both go
>   to law: *I*
>   will prose-
>   cute *you* —
>   Come, I'll
>   take no de-
>   nial; We
>   must have
>   a trial:
>   For really
>   this morn-
>   ing I've
> nothing
> to do.'
> Said the
>   mouse to
>   the cur,
>   'Such a
>   trial, dear
>   sir, With
>   no jury
>   or judge,
>   would
>   be wast-
>   ing our
>   breath.'
>   'I'll be
>   judge,
>   I'll be
>   jury,'
>   said
>   cun-
>   ning
>   old
>   Fury:
>   'I'll
>   try
>   the
>   whole
>   cause,
>   and
>   con-
>   demn
>   you to
>   death.'"

"You are not attending!" said the Mouse to Alice, severely. "What are you thinking of?"

"I beg your pardon," said Alice very humbly: "you had got to the fifth bend, I think?"

"I had *not!*" cried the Mouse, sharply and very angrily.

"A knot!" said Alice, always ready to make herself useful and looking anxiously about her. "Oh, do let me help to undo it!"

"I shall do nothing of the sort," said the Mouse, getting up and walking away. "You insult me by talking such nonsense!"

"I didn't mean it!" pleaded poor Alice. "But you're so easily offended, you know!"

The Mouse only growled in reply.

"Please come back and finish your story!" Alice called after it. And the others all joined in chorus, "Yes, please do!" But the Mouse only shook its head impatiently, and walked a little quicker.

"What a pity it wouldn't stay!" sighed the Lory, as soon as it was quite out of sight. And an old Crab took the opportunity of saying to her daughter, "Ah, my dear! Let this be a lesson to you never to lose *your* temper!"

"Hold you tongue, Ma!" said the young Crab, a little snappishly. "You're enough to try the patience of an oyster!"

"I wish I had our Dinah here, I know I do!" said Alice aloud, addressing nobody in particular. "*She'd* soon fetch it back!"

"And who is Dinah, if I might venture to ask the question?" said the Lory.

Alice replied eagerly, for she was always ready to talk about her pet. "Dinah's our cat. And she's such a capital one for catching mice, you can't think! And oh, I wish you could see her after the birds! Why, she'll eat a little bird as soon as look at it!"

This speech caused a remarkable sensation among the party. Some of the birds hurried off at once. One old Magpie began wrapping itself up very carefully, remarking, "I really must be getting home; the night-air doesn't suit my throat!" and a Canary called out in a trembling voice to its children, "Come away, my dears! It's high time you were all in bed!" On various pretexts they all moved off, and Alice was soon left alone.

"I wish I hadn't mentioned Dinah!" she said to herself in a melancholy tone. "Nobody seems to like her, down here, and I'm sure she's the best cat in the world! Oh, my dear Dinah! I wonder if I shall ever see you any more!" And here poor Alice began to cry again, for she felt very lonely and low-spirited. In a little while, however, she again heard a little pattering of footsteps in the distance, and she looked up eagerly, half hoping that the Mouse had changed his mind, and was coming back to finish his story.

THE RABBIT SENDS IN A LITTLE BILL

It was the White Rabbit, trotting slowly back again, and looking anxiously about as it went, as if it had lost something; and she heard it muttering to itself, "The Duchess! The Duchess! Oh my dear paws! Oh my fur and whiskers! She'll get me executed, as sure as ferrets are ferrets! Where *can* I have dropped them, I wonder!" Alice guessed in a moment that it was looking for the fan and the pair of white kid gloves, and she very good-naturedly began hunting about for them, but they were nowhere to be seen—everything seemed to have changed since her swim in the pool, and the great hall, with the glass table and the little door, had vanished completely.

Very soon the Rabbit noticed Alice, as she went hunting about, and called out to her in an angry tone, "Why, Mary Ann, what *are* you doing out here? Run home this moment, and fetch me a pair of gloves and a fan! Quick, now!" And Alice was so much frightened that she ran off at once in the direction it pointed to, without trying to explain the mistake that it had made.

"He took me for his housemaid," she said to herself as she ran. "Hòw surprised he'll be when he finds out who I am! But I'd better take him his fan and gloves—that is, if I can find them." As she said this, she came upon a neat little house, on the door of which was a bright brass plate with the name "W. Rabbit" engraved upon it. She went in without knocking, and hurried upstairs, in great fear lest she should meet the real Mary Ann, and be turned out of the house before she had found the fan and gloves.

"How queer it seems," Alice said to herself, "to be running errands for a rabbit! I suppose Dinah'll be sending me on errands next!" And she began fancying the sort of thing that would happen: " 'Miss Alice! Come here directly, and get ready for your walk!' 'Coming in a minute, nurse! But I've got to watch this mouse-hole till Dinah comes back, and see that the mouse doesn't get out.' Only I don't think," Alice went on, "that they'd let Dinah stop in the house if it began ordering people about like that!"

By this time she had found her way into a tidy little room with a table in the window, and on it (as she had hoped) a fan and two or three pairs of tiny white kid gloves: she took up the fan and a pair of the gloves, and was just going to leave the room, when her eye fell upon a little bottle that stood near the looking-glass. There was no label this time with the words "DRINK ME," but nevertheless she uncorked it and put it to her lips. "I know *something* interesting is sure to happen," she said to herself, "whenever I eat or drink anything; so I'll just see what this bottle does. I do hope it'll make me grow large again, for really I'm quite tired of being such a tiny little thing!"

It did so indeed, and much sooner than she had expected: before she had drunk half the bottle, she found her head pressing against the ceiling, and had to stoop to save her neck from being broken. She hastily put down the bottle, saying to herself, "That's quite enough—I hope I shan't grow any more—As it is, I can't get out at the door—I do wish I hadn't drunk quite so much!"

Alas! It was too late to wish that! She went on growing and growing, and very soon had to kneel down on the floor: in another minute there was not even room for this, and she tried the effect of lying down, with one elbow against the door, and the other arm curled round her head. Still she went on growing, and, as a last resource, she put one arm out of the window, and one foot up the chimney, and said to herself, "Now I can do no more, whatever happens. What *will* become of me?"

Luckily for Alice, the little magic bottle had now had its full effect, and she grew no larger: still it was very uncomfortable, and, as there seemed to be no sort of chance of her ever getting out of the room again, no wonder she felt unhappy.

"It was much pleasanter at home," thought poor Alice, "when one wasn't always growing larger and smaller, and being ordered about by mice and rabbits. I almost wish I hadn't gone down that rabbit-hole—and yet—and yet—it's rather curious, you know, this sort of life! I do wonder what *can* have happened to me! When I used to read fairy tales, I fancied that kind of thing never happened, and now here I am in the middle of one! There ought to be a book written about me, that there ought! And when I grow up, I'll write one—but I'm grown up now," she added in a sorrowful tone: "at least there's no more room to grow up *here*."

"But then," thought Alice, "shall I *never* get any older than I am now? That'll be a comfort, one way—never to be an old woman—but then

—always to have lessons to learn! Oh, I shouldn't like *that*!"

"Oh, you foolish Alice!" she answered herself. "How can you learn lessons in here? Why, there's hardly room for you, and no room at all for any lesson-books!"

And so she went on, taking first one side and then the other, and making quite a conversation of it altogether, but after a few minutes she heard a voice outside, and stopped to listen.

"Mary Ann! Mary Ann!" said the voice. "Fetch me my gloves this moment!" Then came a little pattering of feet on the stairs. Alice knew it was the Rabbit coming to look for her, and she trembled till she shook the house, quite forgetting that she was now about a thousand times as large as the Rabbit, and had no reason to be afraid of it.

Presently the Rabbit came up to the door, and tried to open it; but, as the door opened inwards, and Alice's elbow was pressed hard against it, that attempt proved a failure. Alice heard it say to itself, "Then I'll go round and get in at the window."

"*That* you won't!" thought Alice, and, after waiting till she fancied she heard the Rabbit just under the window, she suddenly spread out her hand, and made a snatch in the air. She did not get hold of anything, but she heard a little shriek and a fall, and a crash of broken glass, from which she concluded that it was just possible it had fallen into a cucumber-frame, or something of the sort.

Next came an angry voice—the Rabbit's— "Pat! Pat! Where are you?" And then a voice she had never heard before, "Sure then I'm here! Digging for apples, yer honour!"

"Digging for apples, indeed!" said the Rabbit angrily. "Here! Come and help me out of *this*!" (Sounds of more broken glass.)

"Now tell me, Pat, what's that in the window?"

"Sure, it's an arm, yer honour!" (He pronounced it "arrum.")

"An arm, you goose! Who ever saw one that size? Why, it fills the whole window!"

"Sure, it does, yer honour: but it's an arm for all that."

"Well, it's got no business there, at any rate: go and take it away!"

There was a long silence after this, and Alice could only hear whispers now and then, such as, "Sure, I don't like it, yer honour, at all at all!" "Do as I tell you, you coward!" and at last she spread out her hand again and made another snatch in the air. This time there were *two* little shrieks, and more sounds of broken glass. "What a number of cucumber-frames there must be!" thought Alice. "I wonder what they'll do next! As for pulling me out of the window, I only wish they *could!* I'm sure *I* don't want to stay in here any longer!"

She waited for some time without hearing anything more: at last came a rumbling of little cart-wheels, and the sound of a good many voices all talking together: she made out the words, "Where's the other ladder?—Why, I hadn't to bring but one: Bill's got the other—Bill! Fetch it here, lad!—Here, put 'em up at this corner—No, tie 'em together first—they don't reach half high enough yet—Oh, they'll do well enough. Don't be particular—Here, Bill! Catch hold of this rope —Will the roof bear?—Mind that loose slate— Oh, it's coming down! Heads below!" (a loud crash)—"Now, who did that?—It was Bill, I fancy—Who's to go down the chimney?—Nay, *I* shan't! *You* do it!—That I won't then!—Bill's got to go down—Here, Bill! The master says you've got to go down the chimney!"

"Oh, so Bill's got to come down the chimney, has he?" said Alice to herself. "Why, they seem to put everything upon Bill! I wouldn't be in Bill's place for a good deal: this fireplace is narrow, to be sure, but I *think* I can kick a little!"

She drew her foot as far down the chimney as she could, and waited till she heard a little animal (she couldn't guess of what sort it was) scratching and scrambling about in the chimney close above her: then, saying to herself, "This is Bill," she gave one sharp kick and waited to see what would happen next. The first thing she heard was a general chorus of "There goes Bill!"—then the Rabbit's voice alone: "Catch him, you by the hedge!"—then silence, and then another confusion of voices—"Hold up his head—Brandy now —Don't choke him—How was it, old fellow? What happened to you? Tell us all about it!"

Last came a little feeble squeaking voice ("That's Bill," thought Alice.) "Well, I hardly know—No more, thank ye, I'm better now—but I'm a deal too flustered to tell you—all I know is, something comes at me like a Jack-in-the-box, and up I goes like a sky-rocket!"

"So you did, old fellow!" said the others.

"We must burn the house down!" said the Rabbit's voice, and Alice called out as loud as she could:

"If you do, I'll set Dinah at you!"

There was a dead silence instantly, and Alice thought to herself, "I wonder what they *will* do next! If they had any sense, they'd take the roof off." After a minute or two they began moving about again, and Alice heard the Rabbit say, "A barrowful will do, to begin with."

"A barrowful of *what?*" thought Alice. But she had not long to doubt; for the next moment a shower of little pebbles came rattling in at the window, and some of them hit her in the face. "I'll put a stop of this," she said to herself and shouted out: "You'd better not do that again!" which produced another dead silence.

Alice noticed with some surprise that the pebbles were all turning into little cakes as they lay on the floor, and a bright idea came into her head.

"If I eat one of these cakes," she thought, "it's sure to make some change in my size: and as it can't possibly make me larger, it must make me smaller, I suppose."

So she swallowed one of the cakes, and was delighted to find that she began shrinking directly. As soon as she was small enough to get through the door, she ran out of the house, and found quite a crowd of little animals and birds waiting outside. The poor little Lizard, Bill, was in the middle, being held up by two guinea-pigs, who were giving it something out of a bottle. They all made a rush at Alice the moment she appeared, but she ran off as hard as she could, and soon found herself safe in a thick wood.

"The first thing I've got to do," said Alice to herself, as she wandered about in the wood, "is to grow to my right size again; and the second thing is to find my way into that lovely garden. I think that will be the best plan."

It sounded an excellent plan, no doubt, and very neatly and simply arranged; the only difficulty was, that she had not the smallest idea how to set about it; and while she was peering about anxiously among the trees, a little sharp bark just over her head made her look up in a great hurry.

An enormous puppy was looking down at her with large round eyes, and feebly stretching out one paw, trying to touch her. "Poor little thing!" said Alice in a coaxing tone, and she tried hard to whistle to it, but she was terribly frightened all the time at the thought that it might be hungry, in which case it would be very likely to eat her up in spite of all her coaxing.

Hardly knowing what she did, she picked up a little bit of stick, and held it out to the puppy; whereupon the puppy jumped into the air off all its feet at once, with a yelp of delight, and rushed at the stick, and made believe to worry it; then Alice dodged behind a great thistle, to keep herself from being run over, and, the moment she appeared on the other side, the puppy made another rush at the stick, and tumbled head over heels in its hurry to get hold of it; then Alice, thinking it was very like having a game of play with a cart-horse, and expecting every moment to be trampled under its feet, ran round the thistle again; then the puppy began a series of short charges at the stick, running a very little way forwards each time and a long way back, and barking hoarsely all the while, till at last it sat down a good way off, panting, with its tongue hanging out of its mouth, and its great eyes half shut.

This seemed to Alice a good opportunity for making her escape, so she set off at once, and ran till she was quite tired and out of breath, and till the puppy's bark sounded quite faint in the distance. "And yet what a dear little puppy it was!" said Alice, as she leant against a buttercup to rest herself, and fanned herself with one of the leaves. "I should have liked teaching it tricks very much, if—if I'd only been the right size to do it! Oh dear! I'd nearly forgotten that I've got to grow up again! Let me see—how *is* it to be managed? I suppose I ought to eat or drink something or other; but the great question is, what?"

The great question certainly was, what? Alice looked all round her at the flowers and the blades of grass, but she could not see anything that looked like the right thing to eat or drink under the circumstances. There was a large mushroom growing near her, about the same height as herself; and when she had looked under it, and on both sides of it, and behind it, it occurred to her that she might as well look and see what was on the top of it.

She stretched herself up on tiptoe, and peeped over the edge of the mushroom, and her eyes immediately met those of a large blue caterpillar, that was sitting on the top with its arms folded, quietly smoking a long hookah, and taking not the smallest notice of her or of anything else.

THE WATER BABIES

Charles Kingsley

The Water Babies *was published only two years before Lewis Carroll's* Alice in Wonderland *and the two fantasies make an interesting contrast. Kingsley, of the old school, was primarily interested in teaching his reader through fiction, while Carroll, in his forerunner of modern children's literature, was primarily interested in entertaining his audience.*

Kingsley does not trust his reader to discover the many lessons, but addresses him directly. This may have been an accepted technique of writing in the last century, but today's young readers resent or ignore it. While Alice in Wonderland *is now considered a classic,* The Water Babies *is interesting only in the study of the development of children's literature. More informa-*

tion on and passages from this book are given in the introduction to this chapter.

Tom is an abused chimney sweep whose story as told in the first chapter arouses the reader's sympathy and interest. After becoming lost in an elaborate chimney, he blunders into a room and so frightens the occupant that the entire estate is upset. They chase Tom over the fields and hills until they lose his trail. Tom eventually finds a lovely valley where he painlessly passes from this life into that of the "water babies'."

"He prayeth well who loveth well,
Both man and bird and beast;
He prayeth best who loveth best,
All things both great and small:
For the dear God who loveth us,
He made and loveth all."

—*Coleridge*

Tom was now quite amphibious. You do not know what that means? You had better, then, as the nearest Government pupil-teacher, who may possibly answer you smartly enough thus—

"Amphibious. Adjective, derived from two Greek words, *amphi*, a fish, and *bios*, a beast. An animal supposed by our ignorant ancestors to be compounded of a fish and a beast; which therefore, like the hippopotamus, can't live on the land, and dies in the water."

However that may be, Tom was amphibious; and what is better still, he was clean. For the first time in his life, he felt how comfortable it was to have nothing on him but himself. But he only enjoyed it: he did not know it, or think about it; just as you enjoy life and health, and yet never think about being alive and healthy: and may it be long before you have to think about it!

He did not remember having ever been dirty. Indeed, he did not remember any of his old troubles, being tired, or hungry, or beaten, or sent up dark chimneys. Since that sweet sleep, he had forgotten all about his master, and Harthover Place, and the little white girl, and in a word, all that had happened to him when he lived before; and what was best of all, he had forgotten all the bad words which he had learned from Grimes and the rude boys with whom he used to play.

That is not strange: for you know, when you came into this world, and became a land-baby, you remembered nothing. So why should he, when he became a water-baby?

Then have you lived before?

My dear child, who can tell? One can only tell that, by remembering something which happened where we lived before; and as we remember nothing, we know nothing about it; and no book, and no man, can ever tell us certainly.

There was a wise man once, a very wise man, and a very good man, who wrote a poem about the feelings which some children have about having lived before; and this is what he said—

"Our birth is but a sleep and a forgetting;
The soul that rises with us, our life's star,
Hath elsewhere had its setting,
And cometh from afar:
Not in entire forgetfulness,
And not in utter nakedness,
But trailing clouds of glory, do we come
From God, who is our home."

There, you can know no more than that. But if I was you, I would believe that. For then the great fairy Science, who is likely to be queen of all the fairies for many a year to come, can only do you good, and never do you harm; and instead of fancying, with some people, that your body makes your soul as if a steam engine could make its own coke; or, with some other people, that your soul has nothing to do with your body, but is only stuck into it like a pin into a pincushion, to fall out with the first shake;—you will believe the one true,

orthodox,	realistic,
rational,	inductive,
philosophical,	deductive,
logical,	seductive,
irrefragable,	productive,
nominalistic,	salutary,
	comfortable,

and on-all-accounts-to-be-received

doctrine of this wonderful fairy-tale; which is, that your soul makes your body, just as a snail makes his shell. For the rest, it is enough for us to be sure that whether or not we lived before, we shall live again; though not, I hope, as poor little heathen Tom did. For he went downward into the water: but we, I hope, shall go upward to a very different place.

But Tom was very happy in the water. He had been sadly overworked in the land-world; and so now, to make up for that, he had nothing but holidays in the water-world for a long, long time to come. He had nothing to do but enjoy himself, and look at all the pretty things which are to be seen in the cool clear water-world, where the sun is never too hot, and frost is never too cold.

And what did he live on? Water-cresses, perhaps; or perhaps water-gruel, and water-milk: too many land-babies do so likewise. But we do not know what one-tenth of the water-things eat; so we are not answerable for the water-babies.

Sometimes he went along the smooth gravel water-ways, looking at the crickets which ran in and out among the stones, as rabbits do on land; or he climbed over the ledges of rock, and saw the sand-pipes hanging in thousands, with every one of them a pretty little head and legs peeping out; or he went into a still corner, and watched the caddises eating dead sticks as greedily as you would eat plum-pudding, and building their houses with silk and glue. Very fanciful ladies they were; none of them would keep to the same materials for a day. One would begin with some pebbles; then she would stick on a piece of green weed; then she found a shell, and stuck it on too; and the poor shell was alive, and did not like at all being taken to build houses with: but the caddis did not let him have any voice in the matter, being rude and selfish, as vain people are apt to be; then she stuck on a piece of rotten wood, then a very smart pink stone, till she was patched all over like an Irishman's coat.

Then she found a straw, five times as long as herself, and said, "Hurrah! my sister has a tail, and I'll have one too"; and she stuck it on her back, and marched about with it quite proud, though it was very inconvenient indeed. And, at that, tails became all the fashion among the caddisbaits in that pool, as they were at the end of the Long Pond last May, and they all toddled about with long straws sticking out behind, getting between each other's legs, and tumbling over each other, and looking so ridiculous, that Tom laughed at them till he cried, as we did. But they were quite right, you know; for people must always follow the fashion, even if it be spoon-bonnets.

Then sometimes he came to a deep still reach; and there he saw the water-forests. They would have looked to you only little weeds; but Tom, you must remember, was so little that everything looked a hundred times as big to him as it does to you, just as things do to a minnow, who sees and catches the little water-creatures which you can only see in a microscope.

And in the water-forest he saw the water-monkeys and water-squirrels (they had all six legs, though; everything almost has six legs in the water, except efts and water-babies); and nimbly enough they ran among the branches. There were water-flowers there, too, in thousands; and Tom tried to pick them: but as soon as he touched them, they drew themselves in and turned into knots of jelly; and Tom saw that they were all alive—bells, and stars, and wheels, and flowers, of all beautiful shapes and colors; and all alive and busy, just as Tom was. So now he found that there was a great deal more in the world than he had fancied at first sight.

There was one wonderful little fellow, too, who peeped out of the top of a house built of round bricks. He had two big wheels, and one little one, all over teeth, spinning round and round like the wheels in a thrashing machine; and Tom stood and stared at him, to see what he was going to make with his machinery. And what do you think he was doing? Brick-making. With his two big wheels he swept together all the mud which floated in the water: all that was nice in it he put into his stomach and ate; and all the mud he put into his little wheel on his breast, which really was a round hole set with teeth; and there he spun it into a neat hard round brick; and then he took it and stuck it on the top of his house-wall, and set to work to make another. Now was not he a clever little fellow?

Tom thought so: but when he wanted to talk to him, the brick-maker was much too busy and proud of his work to take notice of him.

Now you must know that all the things under

the water talk: only not such a language as ours; but such as horses, and dogs, and cows, and birds talk to each other; and Tom soon learned to understand them and talk to them; so that he might have had very pleasant company if he had only been a good boy. But I am sorry to say, he was too like some other little boys, very fond of hunting and tormenting creatures for mere sport. Some people say that boys cannot help it; that it is nature, and only a proof that we are all originally descended from beasts of prey. But whether it is nature or not, little boys can help it, and must help it. For if they have naughty, low, mischievous tricks in their nature, as monkeys have, that is no reason why they should give way to those tricks like monkeys, who know no better. And therefore they must not torment dumb creatures; for if they do, a certain old lady who is coming will surely give them exactly what they deserve.

But Tom did not know that; and he pecked and howked the poor water things about sadly, till they were all afraid of him, and got out of his way, or crept into their shells; so he had no one to speak to or play with.

The water-fairies, of course, were very sorry to see him so unhappy, and longed to take him, and tell him how naughty he was, and teach him to be good, and to play and romp with him too: but they had been forbidden to do that. Tom had to learn his lesson for himself by sound and sharp experience, as many another foolish person has to do, though there may be many a kind heart yearning over them all the while, and longing to teach them what they can only teach themselves.

At last one day he found a caddis, and wanted it to peep out of its house: but its house-door was shut. He had never seen a caddis with a house-door before: so what must he do, the meddlesome little fellow, but pull it open, to see what the poor lady was doing inside. What a shame! How should you like to have any one breaking your bedroom-door in, to see how you looked when you were in bed? So Tom broke to pieces the door, which was the prettiest little grating of silk, stuck all over with shining bits of crystal; and when he looked in, the caddis poked out her head, and it had turned into just the shape of a bird's. But when Tom spoke to her she could not answer; for her mouth and face were tight tied up

in a new nightcap of neat pink skin. However, if she didn't answer, all the other caddises did; for they held up hands and shrieked like the cats in Struwelpeter: "Oh, you nasty, horrid boys; there you are at it again! And she had just laid herself up for a fortnight's sleep, and then she would have come out with such beautiful wings, and flown about, and laid such lots of eggs: and now you have broken her door, and she can't mend it because her mouth is tied up for a fortnight, and she will die. Who sent you here to worry us out of our lives?"

So Tom swam away. He was very much ashamed of himself, and felt all the naughtier; as little boys do when they have done wrong, and won't say so.

Then he came to a pool full of little trout, and began tormenting them, and trying to catch them: but they slipped through his fingers, and jumped clean out of water in their fright. But Tom chased them, he came close to a great dark hover under an alder root, and out floushed a huge old brown trout ten times as big as he was, and ran right against him, and knocked all the breath out of his body; and I don't know which was the more frightened of the two.

Then he went on sulky and lonely, as he deserved to be; and under a bank he saw a very ugly dirty creature sitting, about half as big as himself; which had six legs, and a big stomach, and a most ridiculous head with two great eyes and a face just like a donkey's.

"Oh," said Tom, "you are an ugly fellow to be sure!" and he began making faces at him; and put his nose close to him, and hallooed at him, like a very rude boy.

When, hey presto! all the thing's donkey-face came off in a moment, and out popped a long arm with a pair of pincers at the end of it, and caught Tom by the nose. It did not hurt him much; but it held him quite tight.

"Yah, ah! Oh, let me go!" cried Tom.

"Then let me go," said the creature. "I want to be quiet. I want to split."

Tom promised to let him alone, and he let go. "Why do you want to split?" said Tom.

"Because my brothers and sisters have all split, and turned into beautiful creatures with wings; and I want to split too. Don't speak to me. I am sure I shall split. I will split!"

Tom stood still, and watched him. And he swelled himself, and puffed, and stretched himself out stiff, and at last—crack, puff, bang—he opened all down his back, and then up to the top of his head.

And out of his inside came the most slender, elegant, soft creature, as soft and smooth as Tom: but very pale and weak, like a little child who has been ill a long time in a dark room. It moved its legs very feebly; and looked about half ashamed, like a girl when she goes for the first time into a ballroom; and then it began walking slowly up a grass stem to the top of the water.

Tom was so astonished that he never said a word: but he stared with all his eyes. And he went up to the top of the water too, and peeped out to see what would happen.

And as the creature sat in the warm bright sun, a wonderful change came over it. It grew strong and firm; the most lovely colors began to show on its body, blue and yellow and black, spots and bars and rings; out of its back rose four great wings of bright brown gauze; and its eyes grew so large that they filled all its head, and shone like ten thousand diamonds.

"Oh, you beautiful creature!" said Tom; and he put out his hand to catch it.

But the thing whirled up into the air, and hung poised on its wings a moment, and then settled down again by Tom quite fearless.

"No!" it said, "you cannot catch me. I am a dragon-fly now, the king of all the flies; and I shall dance in the sunshine, and hawk over the river, and catch gnats, and have a beautiful wife like myself. I know what I shall do. Hurrah!" And he flew away into the air and began catching gnats.

"Oh! come back, come back," cried Tom, "you beautiful creature. I have no one to play with, and I am so lonely here. If you will but come back I will never try to catch you."

"I don't care whether you do or not," said the dragon-fly; "for you can't. But when I have had my dinner, and looked a little about this pretty place, I will come back; and have a little chat about all I have seen in my travels. Why, what a huge tree this is! and what huge leaves on it!"

It was only a big dock: but you know the dragon-fly had never seen any but little water-trees: stalwart, and milfoil, and water-crowfoot, and such like; so it did look very big to him. Besides, he was very shortsighted, as all dragon-flies are; and never could see a yard before his nose; any more than a great many other folks, who are not half as handsome as he.

The dragon-fly did come back, and chatted away with Tom. He was a little conceited about his fine colors and his large wings; but you know, he had been a poor dirty ugly creature all his life before; so there were great excuses for him. He was very fond of talking about all the wonderful things he saw in the trees and meadows; and Tom liked to listen to him, for he had forgotten all about them. So in a little while they became great friends.

And I am very glad to say, that Tom learned such a lesson that day, that he did not torment creatures for a long time after. And then the caddises grew quite tame, and used to tell him strange stories about the way they built their houses, and changed their skins, and turned at last into winged flies; till Tom began to long to change his skin, and have wings like them some day.

THE WORLD OF POOH: Eeyore's Birthday

A. A. Milne

The Pooh stories have delighted many children since 1926, but there are signs that the present generation of children is not interested in them. This need not be, for when they are read aloud well, with Eeyore's whining indi-

cated by a rising and falling voice much like a donkey's hee-haw, children are able to catch the humor they may miss in silent reading.

Everyone, even a child, knows someone like Eeyore: the whiner, the complainer, the martyr. He is the type of person who demands attention by prefacing his constant complaints with, "It doesn't matter, I'm not important . . . sniff, sniff."

Eeyore, the old grey Donkey, stood by the side of the stream, and looked at himself in the water.

"Pathetic," he said. "That's what it is. Pathetic."

He turned and walked slowly down the stream for twenty yards, splashed across it, and walked slowly back on the other side. Then he looked at himself in the water again.

"As I thought," he said. "No better from *this* side. But nobody minds. Nobody cares. Pathetic, that's what it is."

There was a crackling noise in the bracken behind him, and out came Pooh.

"Good morning, Eeyore," said Pooh.

"Good morning, Pooh Bear," said Eeyore gloomily. "If it *is* a good morning," he said. "Which I doubt," said he.

"Why, what's the matter?"

"Nothing, Pooh Bear, nothing. We can't all, and some of us don't. That's all there is to it."

"Can't all *what*?" said Pooh, rubbing his nose.

"Gaiety. Song-and-dance. Here we go round the mulberry bush."

"Oh!" said Pooh. He thought for a long time, and then asked, "What mulberry bush is that?"

"Bon-hommy," went on Eeyore gloomily. "French word meaning bonhommy," he explained. "I'm not complaining, but There It Is."

Pooh sat down on a large stone, and tried to think this out. It sounded to him like a riddle, and he was never much good at riddles, being a Bear of Very Little Brain. So he sang *Cottleston Pie* instead:

From the book *Winnie-the-Pooh* by A. A. Milne, with decorations by E. H. Shepard. Copyright 1926 by E. P. Dutton & Co., Inc. Renewal copyright 1954 by A. A. Milne. Published by E. P. Dutton & Co., Inc., and reprinted with their permission.

Cottleston, Cottleston, Cottleston Pie,
A fly can't bird, but a bird can fly.
Ask me a riddle and I reply:
"Cottleston, Cottleston, Cottleston Pie."

That was the first verse. When he had finished it, Eeyore didn't actually say that he didn't like it, so Pooh very kindly sang the second verse to him:

Cottleston, Cottleston, Cottleston Pie,
A fish can't whistle and neither can I.
Ask me a riddle and I reply:
"Cottleston, Cottleston, Cottleston Pie,"

Eeyore still said nothing at all, so Pooh hummed the third verse quietly to himself:

Cottleston, Cottleston, Cottleston Pie,
Why does a chicken, I don't know why.
Ask me a riddle and I reply:
"Cottleston, Cottleston, Cottleston Pie,"

"That's right," said Eeyore. "Sing. Umty-tiddly, Umty-too. Here we go gathering Nuts and May. Enjoy yourself."

"I am," said Pooh.

"Some can," said Eeyore.

"Why, what's the matter?"

"*Is* anything the matter?"

"You seem so sad, Eeyore."

"Sad? Why should I be sad? It's my birthday. The happiest day of the year."

"Your birthday?" said Pooh in great surprise.

"Of course it is. Can't you see? Look at all the presents I have had." He waved a foot from side to side. "Look at the birthday cake. Candles and pink sugar."

Pooh looked—first to the right and then to the left.

"Presents?" said Pooh. "Birthday cake?" said Pooh. "*Where*?"

"Can't you see them?"

"No," said Pooh.

"Neither can I," said Eeyore. "Joke," he explained. "Ha ha!"

Pooh scratched his head, being a little puzzled by all this.

"But is it really your birthday?" he asked.

"It is."

"Oh! Well, many happy returns of the day, Eeyore."

"And many happy returns to you, Pooh Bear."

"But it isn't *my* birthday."

"No, it's mine."

"But you said 'Many happy returns'—"

"Well, why not? You don't always want to be miserable on my birthday, do you?"

"Oh, I see," said Pooh.

"It's bad enough," said Eeyore, almost breaking down, "being miserable myself, what with no presents and no cake and no candles, and no proper notice taken of me at all, but if everybody else is going to be miserable too——"

This was too much for Pooh. "Stay there!" he called to Eeyore, as he turned and hurried back home as quick as he could; for he felt that he must get poor Eeyore a present of *some* sort at once, and he could always think of a proper one afterwards.

Outside his house he found Piglet, jumping up and down trying to reach the knocker.

"Hallo, Piglet," he said.

"Hallo, Pooh," said Piglet.

"What are *you* trying to do?"

"I was trying to reach the knocker," said Piglet. "I just came around——"

"Let me do it for you," said Pooh kindly. So he reached up and knocked at the door. "I have just seen Eeyore," he began, "and poor Eeyore is in a Very Sad Condition, because it's his birthday, and nobody has taken any notice of it, and he's very Gloomy—you know what Eeyore is—and there he was, and—What a long time whoever lives here is answering this door." And he knocked again.

"But Pooh," said Piglet, "it's your own house!"

"Oh!" said Pooh. "So it is," he said. "Well, let's go in."

So in they went. The first thing Pooh did was to go to the cupboard to see if he had quite a small jar of honey left; and he had, so he took it down.

"I'm giving this to Eeyore," he explained, "as a present. What are *you* going to give?"

"Couldn't I give it too?" said Piglet. "From both of us?"

"No," said Pooh. "That would *not* be a good plan."

"All right, then I'll give him a balloon. I've got one left from my party. I'll go and get it now, shall I?"

"That Piglet, is a *very* good idea. It is just what Eeyore wants to cheer him up. Nobody can be uncheered with a balloon."

So off Piglet trotted; and in the other direction went Pooh, with his jar of honey.

It was a warm day, and he had a long way to go. He hadn't gone more than half-way when a sort of funny feeling began to creep all over him. It began at the tip of his nose and trickled all through him and out at the soles of his feet. It was just as if somebody inside him were saying, "Now then, Pooh, time for a little something."

"Dear, dear," said Pooh, "I didn't know it was as late as that." So he sat down and took the top off his jar of honey. "Lucky I brought this with me," he thought. "Many a bear going out on a warm day like this would never have thought of bringing a little something with him." And he began to eat.

"Now let me see," he thought, as he took his last lick of the inside of the jar, "where was I going? Ah, yes, Eeyore." He got up suddenly.

And then, suddenly, he remembered. He had eaten Eeyore's birthday present!

"*Bother!*" said Pooh. "What *shall* I do? I *must* give him *something*."

For a little while he couldn't think of anything. Then he thought: "Well, it's a very nice pot, even if there's no honey in it, and if I washed it clean, and got somebody to write 'A *Happy Birthday*' on it, Eeyore could keep things in it, which might be Useful." So, as he was just passing the Hundred Acre Wood, he went inside to call on Owl, who lived there.

"Good Morning, Owl," he said.

"Good Morning, Pooh," said Owl.

"Many happy returns of Eeyore's birthday," said Pooh.

"Oh, is that what it is?"

"What are you giving him, Owl?"

"What are *you* giving him, Pooh?"

"I'm giving him a Useful Pot to Keep Things In, and I wanted to ask you——"

"Is this it?" said Owl, taking it out of Pooh's paw.

"Yes, and I wanted to ask you——"

"Somebody has been keeping honey in it," said Owl.

"You can keep *anything* in it," said Pooh earnestly. "It's Very Useful like that. And I wanted to ask you——"

"You ought to write 'A HAPPY BIRTHDAY' on it."

"*That* was what I wanted to ask you," said Pooh. "Because my spelling is Wobbly. It's good spelling but it Wobbles, and the letters get in the wrong places. Would *you* write 'A Happy Birthday' on it for me?"

"It's a nice pot," said Owl, looking at it all round. "Couldn't I give it too? From both of us?"

"No," said Pooh. "That would *not* be a good plan. Now I'll just wash it first, and then you can write on it."

Well, he washed the pot out, and dried it, while Owl licked the end of his pencil, and wondered how to spell "birthday."

"Can you read, Pooh?" he asked, a little anxiously.

"There's a notice about knocking and ringing outside my door, which Christopher Robin wrote. Could you read it?"

"Christopher Robin told me what it said, and *then* I could."

"Well, I'll tell you what *this* says, and then you'll be able to."

So Owl wrote . . . and this is what he wrote:

HIPY PAPY BTHUTHDTH THUTHDA

BTHUTHDY

Pooh looked on admiringly.

"I'm just saying 'A Happy Birthday,'" said Owl carelessly.

"It's a nice long one," said Pooh, very much impressed by it.

"Well, *actually*, of course, I'm saying 'A Very Happy Birthday with love from Pooh.' Naturally it takes a good deal of pencil to say a long thing like that."

"Oh, I see," said Pooh.

While all this was happening, Piglet had gone back to his own house to get Eeyore's balloon. He held it very tightly against himself, so that it shouldn't blow away, and he ran as fast as he could so as to get to Eeyore before Pooh did; for he thought that he would like to be the first one to give a present, just as if he had thought of it without being told by anybody. And running along, and thinking how pleased Eeyore would be, he didn't look where he was going . . . and suddenly he put his foot in a rabbit hole, and fell down flat on his face.

BANG!!!???***!!!

Piglet lay there, wondering what had happened. At first he thought that the whole world had blown up; and then he thought that perhaps only the Forest part of it had; and then he thought that perhaps only *he* had, and he was now alone in the moon or somewhere, and would never see Christopher Robin or Pooh or Eeyore again. And then he thought, "Well, even if I'm in the moon, I needn't be face downwards all the time," so he got cautiously up and looked about him.

He was still in the Forest!

"Well, that's funny," he thought. "I wonder what that bang was. I couldn't have made such a noise just falling down. And where's my balloon? And what's that small piece of damp rag doing?"

It was the balloon!

"Oh, dear!" said Piglet. "Oh, dear, oh, dearie, dearie, dear! Well, it's too late now. I can't go back, and I haven't another balloon, and perhaps Eeyore doesn't *like* balloons so *very* much."

So he trotted on, rather sadly now, and down he came to the side of the stream where Eeyore was, and called out to him.

"Good morning, Eeyore," shouted Piglet.

"Good morning, Little Piglet," said Eeyore. "If it *is* a good morning," he said. "Which I doubt," said he. "Not that it matters," he said.

"Many happy returns of the day," said Piglet, having not got closer.

Eeyore stopped looking at himself in the stream, and turned to stare at Piglet.

"Just say that again," he said.

"Many hap——"

"Wait a moment."

Balancing on three legs, he began to bring his

fourth leg up to his ear. "I did this yesterday," he explained, as he fell down for the third time. "It's quite easy. It's so as I can hear better. . . . There, that's done it! Now then, what were you saying?" He pushed his ear forward with his hoof.

"Many happy returns of the day," said Piglet again.

"Meaning me?"

"Of course, Eeyore."

"My birthday?"

"Yes."

"Me having a real birthday?"

"Yes, Eeyore, and I've brought you a present."

Eeyore took down his right hoof from his right ear, turned round, and with great difficulty put up his left hoof.

"I must have that in the other ear," he said. "Now then."

"A present," said Piglet very loudly.

"Meaning me again?"

"Yes."

"My birthday still?"

"Of course, Eeyore."

"Me going on having a real birthday?"

"Yes, Eeyore, and I brought you a balloon."

"*Balloon*?" said Eeyore. "You did say balloon? One of those big coloured things you blow up? Gaiety, song-and-dance, here we are and there we are?"

"Yes, but I'm afraid—I'm very sorry, Eeyore—but when I was running along to bring it you, I fell down."

"Dear, dear, how unlucky! You ran too fast, I expect. You didn't hurt yourself, Little Piglet?"

"No, but I—I—oh, Eeyore, I burst the balloon!"

There was a very long silence.

"My balloon?" said Eeyore at last.

Piglet nodded.

"My birthday balloon?"

"Yes, Eeyore," said Piglet sniffing a little. "Here it is. With—with many happy returns of the day." And he gave Eeyore the small piece of damp rag.

"Is this it?" said Eeyore, a little surprised.

Piglet nodded.

"My present?"

Piglet nodded again.

"The balloon?"

"Yes."

"Thank you, Piglet," said Eeyore. "You don't mind my asking," he went on, "but what colour was this balloon when it—when it *was* a balloon?"

"Red."

"I just wondered. . . . Red," he murmered to himself. "My favourite colour. . . . How big was it?"

"About as big as me."

"I just wondered. . . . About as big as Piglet," he said to himself sadly. "My favourite size. Well, well."

Piglet felt very miserable, and didn't know what to say. He was still opening his mouth to begin something, and then deciding that it wasn't any good saying *that*, when he heard a shout from the other side of the river, and there was Pooh.

"Many happy returns of the day," called out Pooh, forgetting that he had said it already.

"Thank you, Pooh, I'm having them," said Eeyore gloomily.

"I've brought you a little present," said Pooh excitedly.

"I've had it," said Eeyore.

Pooh had now splashed across the stream to Eeyore, and Piglet was sitting a little way off, his head in his paws, snuffling to himself.

"It's a Useful Pot," said Pooh. "Here it is. And it's got 'A Very Happy Birthday with love from Pooh' written on it. That's what all that writing is. And it's for putting things in. There!"

When Eeyore saw the pot, he became quite excited.

"Why!" he said. "I believe my Balloon will just go into that Pot!"

"Oh, no, Eeyore," said Pooh. "Balloons are much too big to go into Pots. What you do with a balloon is, you hold the balloon——"

"Not mine," said Eeyore proudly. "Look, Piglet!" And as Piglet looked sorrowfully round, Eeyore picked the balloon up with his teeth, and placed it carefully in the pot; picked it out and put it on the ground; and then picked it up again and put it carefully back.

"So it does!" said Pooh. "It goes in!"

"So it does!" said Piglet. "And it comes out!"

"Doesn't it?" said Eeyore. "It goes in and out like anything."

"I'm very glad," said Piglet happily, "that I thought of giving you a Useful Pot to put things in."

"I'm very glad," said Piglet happily, "that I thought of giving you Something to put in a Useful Pot."

But Eeyore wasn't listening. He was taking the balloon out, and putting it back again, as happy as could be. . . .

"And didn't *I* give him anything?" said Christopher Robin sadly.

"Of course you did," I said. "You gave him—don't you remember—a little—a little——"

"I gave him a box of paints to paint things with."

"That was it."

"Why didn't I give it to him in the morning?"

"You were so busy getting his party ready for him. He had a cake with icing on the top, and three candles, and his name in pink sugar, and——"

"Yes, *I* remember," said Christopher Robin.

THE WIND IN THE WILLOWS

Kenneth Grahame

The Wind in the Willows is one of the most beautifully written of all children's books. Grahame's exceptional characterization and use of language, which is always perfectly fitted to each scene's mood and action, has never been surpassed.

The Wind in the Willows is considered a children's classic, but it is loved more by adults than by contemporary children. While young readers enjoy Toad's wild adventures and his boisterous personality, they often skim over the other chapters in their interest to follow Toad and so miss much of Grahame's poetic use of language, sensitive character portrayal, and descriptive ability. However, if the perceptive adult chooses the right time to introduce it, there are some mature elementary school children who will enjoy reading all of The Wind in the Willows.

In the first chapter, Mole, caught up by spring, flings his paint brush aside and rushes up to the out-of-doors. He meets Rat who, after they enjoy a river jaunt, invites him to stay at his home so he can enjoy the river's pleasures. A few days later they visit Toad.

"Ratty," said the Mole suddenly, one bright summer morning, "if you please, I want to ask you a favour."

The Rat was sitting on the river bank, singing a little song. He had just composed it himself, so he was very taken up with it, and would not pay proper attention to Mole or anything else. Since early morning he had been swimming in the river in company with his friends the ducks. And when the ducks stood on their heads suddenly, as ducks will, he would dive down and tickle their necks just under where their chins would be if ducks had chins, till they were forced to come to the surface again in a hurry, spluttering and angry and shaking their feathers at him, for it is impossible to say quite *all* you feel when your head is under water. At last they implored him to go away and attend to his own affairs and leave them to mind theirs. So the Rat went away, and sat on the river bank in the sun, and made up a song about them, which he called

Ducks' Ditty

All along the backwater,
Through the rushes tall,
Ducks are a-dabbling,
Up tails all!

Ducks' tails, drakes' tails,
Yellow feet a-quiver,
Yellow bills all out of sight
Busy in the river!

Slushy green undergrowth
Where the roach swim—
Here we keep our larder,
Cool and full and dim.

Every one for what he likes!
We like to be
Heads down, tails up,
Dabbling free!

High in the blue above
Swifts whirl and call—
We are down a-dabbling
Up tails all!

"I don't know that I think so *very* much of that little song, Rat," observed the Mole cautiously. He was no poet himself and didn't care who knew it; and he had a candid nature.

"Nor don't the ducks neither," replied the Rat cheerfully. "They say, '*Why* can't fellows be allowed to do what they like *when* they like and *as* they like, instead of other fellows sitting on banks and watching them all the time and making remarks, and poetry and things about them? What *nonsense* it all is!' That's what the ducks say."

"So it is, so it is," said the Mole, with great heartiness.

"No, it isn't!" cried the Rat indignantly.

"Well then, it isn't, it isn't," replied the Mole soothingly. "But what I wanted to ask you was, won't you take me to call on Mr. Toad? I've heard so much about him, and I do so want to make his acquaintance."

"Why, certainly," said the good-natured Rat, jumping to his feet and dismissing poetry from his mind for the day. "Get the boat out, and we'll paddle up there at once. It's never the wrong time to call on Toad. Early or late he's always the same fellow. Always good-tempered, always glad to see you, always sorry when you go!"

"He must be a very nice animal," observed the Mole, as he got into the boat and took the sculls, while the Rat settled himself comfortably in the stern.

"He is indeed the best of animals," replied Rat. "So simple, so good-natured, and so affectionate. Perhaps he's not very clever—we can't all be geniuses; and it may be that he is both boastful and conceited. But he has got some great qualities, has Toady." Rounding a bend in the river, they came in sight of a handsome, dignified old house of mellowed red brick, with well-kept lawns reaching down to the water's edge.

"There's Toad Hall," said the Rat; "and that creek on the left, where the notice-board says, 'Private. No landing allowed,' leads to his boathouse, where we'll leave the boat. The stables are over there to the right. That's the banqueting-hall you're looking at now—very old, that is. Toad is rather rich, you know, and this is really one of the nicest houses in these parts, though we never admit as much to Toad."

They glided up the creek, and the Mole shipped his sculls as they passed into the shadow of a large boat-house. Here they saw many handsome boats, slung from the cross-beams or hauled up on a slip, but none in the water; and the place had an unused and deserted air.

The Rat looked around him. "I understand," said he. "Boating is played out. He's tired of it, and done with it. I wonder what new fad he has taken up now? Come along and let's look him up. We shall hear all about it quite soon enough."

They disembarked, and strolled across the gay flower-decked lawns in search of Toad, whom they presently happened upon resting in a wicker garden-chair, with a preoccupied expression of face, and a large map spread out on his knees.

"Hooray!" he cried, jumping up on seeing them, "this is splendid!" He shook the paws of both of them warmly, never waiting for an introduction to the Mole. "How *kind* of you!" he went on, dancing round them. "I was just going to send a boat down the river for you, Ratty, with strict orders that you were to be fetched up here at once, whatever you were doing. I want you badly—both of you. Now what will you take? Come inside and have something! You don't know how lucky it is, your turning up just now!"

"Let's sit quiet a bit, Toady!" said the Rat, throwing himself into an easy chair, while the Mole took another by the side of him and made some civil remark about Toad's "delightful residence."

"Finest house on the whole river," cried Toad boisterously. "Or anywhere else, for that matter," he could not help adding.

Here the Rat nudged the Mole. Unfortunately the Toad saw him do it, and turned very red. There was a moment's painful silence. Then Toad burst out laughing. "All right, Ratty," he said. "It's only my way, you know. And it's not such a very bad house, is it? You know you rather like it yourself. Now, look here. Let's be sensible. You are the very animals I wanted. You've got to help me. It's most important!"

"It's about your rowing, I suppose," said the Rat, with an innocent air. "You're getting on fairly well, though you splash a good bit still. With a great deal of patience, and any quantity of coaching, you may—"

"O, pooh! boating!" interrupted the Toad, in great disgust. "Silly boyish amusement. I've given that up *long* ago. Sheer waste of time, that's what it is. It makes me downright sorry to see you fellows, who ought to know better, spending all your energies in that aimless manner. No, I've discovered the real thing, the only genuine occupation for a lifetime. I propose to devote the remainder of mine to it, and can only regret the wasted years that lie behind me, squandered in trivialities. Come with me, dear Ratty, and your amiable friend also, if he will be so very good, just as far as the stable-yard, and you shall see what you shall see!"

He led the way to the stable-yard accordingly, the Rat following with a most mistrustful expression; and there, drawn out of the coach-house into the open, they saw a gipsy caravan, shining with newness, painted a canary-yellow picked out with green, and red wheels.

"There you are!" cried the Toad, straddling and expanding himself. "There's real life for you, embodied in that little cart. The open road, the dusty highway, the heath, the common, the hedgerows, the rolling downs! Camps, villages, towns, cities! Here to-day, up and off to somewhere else to-morrow! Travel, change, interest, excitement! The whole world before you, and a horizon that's always changing! And mind, this is the very finest cart of its sort that was ever built, without any

exception. Come inside and look at the arrangements. Planned 'em all myself, I did!"

The Mole was tremendously interested and excited, and followed him eagerly up the steps and into the interior of the caravan. The Rat only snorted and thrust his hands deep into his pockets, remaining where he was.

It was indeed very compact and comfortable. Little sleeping-bunks—a little table that folded up against the wall—a cooking-stove, lockers, bookshelves, a bird-cage with a bird in it; and pots, pans, jugs and kettles of every size and variety.

"All complete!" said the Toad triumphantly, pulling open a locker. "You see—biscuits, potted lobster, sardines—everything you can possibly want. Soda-water here—baccy there—letter-paper, bacon, jam, cards and dominoes—you'll find," he continued, as they descended the steps again, "you'll find that nothing whatever has been forgotten, when we make our start this afternoon."

"I beg your pardon," said the Rat slowly, as he chewed a straw, "but did I overhear you say something about 'we' and 'start' and 'this *afternoon*'?"

"Now, you dear good old Ratty," said Toad imploringly, "don't begin talking in that stiff and sniffy sort of way, because you know you've *got* to come. I can't possibly manage without you, so please consider it settled, and don't argue—it's the one thing I can't stand. You surely don't mean to stick to your dull fusty old river all your life, and just live in a hole in a bank, and *boat*? I want to show you the world! I'm going to make an *animal* of you, my boy!"

"I don't care," said the Rat doggedly. "I'm not coming, and that's flat. And I *am* going to stick to my old river, *and* live in a hole, *and* boat, as I've always done. And what's more, Mole's going to stick to me and do as I do, aren't you, Mole?"

"Of course I am," said the Mole loyally. "I'll always stick to you, Rat, and what you say is to be—has got to be. All the same, it sounds as if it might have been—well, rather fun, you know!" he added wistfully. Poor Mole! The Life Adventurous was so new a thing to him, and so thrilling; and this fresh aspect of it was so tempting; and he had fallen in love at first sight with the canary-coloured cart and all its little fitments.

The Rat saw what was passing in his mind, and wavered. He hated disappointing people, and he was fond of the Mole, and would do almost anything to oblige him. Toad was watching both of them closely.

"Come along in and have some lunch," he said diplomatically, "and we'll talk it over. We needn't decide anything in a hurry. Of course, *I* don't really care. I only want to give pleasure to you fellows. 'Live for others!' That's my motto in life."

During luncheon—which was excellent, of course, as everything at Toad Hall always was—the Toad simply let himself go. Disregarding the Rat, he proceeded to play upon the inexperienced Mole as on a harp. Naturally a voluble animal, and always mastered by his imagination, he painted the prospects of the trip and the joys of the open life and the roadside in such glowing colours that the Mole could hardly sit in his chair for excitement. Somehow it soon seemed taken for granted by all three that the trip was a settled thing; and the Rat, though still unconvinced in his mind, allowed his good-nature to override his personal objections. He could not bear to disappoint his two friends, who were already deep in schemes and anticipations, planning out each day's separate occupation for several weeks ahead.

When they were quite ready, the now triumphant Toad led his companions to the paddock and set them to capture the old grey horse, who, without having been consulted, and to his own extreme annoyance, had been told off by Toad for the dustiest job in this dusty expedition. He frankly preferred the paddock, and took a deal of catching. Meantime Toad packed the lockers still tighter with necessaries, and hung nose-bags, nets of onions, bundles of hay, and baskets from the bottom of the cart. At last the horse was caught and harnessed, and they set off, all talking at once, each animal either trudging by the side of the cart or sitting on the shaft, as the humour took him. It was a golden afternoon. The smell of the dust they kicked up was rich and satisfying; out of thick orchards on either side the road, birds called and whistled to them cheerily; good-natured wayfarers, passing them, gave them "Good day," or stopped to say nice things about their beautiful cart; and rabbits, sitting at their front doors in the hedgerows, held up their fore paws, and said, "O my! O my! O my!"

Late in the evening, tired and happy and miles from home, they drew up on a remote common far from habitations, turned the horse loose to graze, and ate their simple supper sitting on the grass by the side of the cart. Toad talked big about all he was going to do in the days to come, while stars grew fuller and larger all around them, and a yellow moon, appearing suddenly and silently from nowhere in particular, came to keep them company and listen to their talk. At last they turned into their little bunks in the cart; and Toad, kicking out his legs, sleepily said, "Well, good night, you fellows! This is the real life for a gentleman! Talk about your old river!"

"*I don't* talk about my river," replied the patient Rat. "You *know* I don't, Toad. But I *think* about it," he added pathetically, in a lower tone: "I think about it—all the time!"

The Mole reached out from under his blanket, felt for the Rat's paw in the darkness, and gave it a squeeze. "I'll do whatever you like, Ratty," he whispered. "Shall we run away to-morrow morning, quite early—*very* early—and go back to our dear old hole on the river?"

"No, no, we'll see it out," whispered back the Rat. "Thanks awfully, but I ought to stick by Toad till this trip is ended. It wouldn't be safe for him to be left to himself. It won't take very long. His fads never do. Good night!"

The end was indeed nearer than even the Rat suspected.

After so much open air and excitement the Toad slept very soundly, and no amount of shaking could rouse him out of bed next morning. So the Mole and Rat turned to, quietly and manfully, and while the Rat saw to the horse, and lit a fire, and cleaned last night's cups and platters and got things ready for breakfast, the Mole trudged off to the nearest village, a long way off, for milk and eggs and various necessaries the Toad had, of course, forgotten to provide. The hard work had all been done, and the two animals were resting, thoroughly exhausted, by the time Toad appeared on the scene, fresh and gay, remarking what a pleasant easy life it was they were all leading now, after the cares and worries and fatigues of housekeeping at home.

They had a pleasant ramble that day over

grassy downs and along narrow by-lanes, and camped, as before, on a common, only this time the two guests took care that Toad should do his fair share of work. In consequence, when the time came for starting next morning, Toad was by no means so rapturous about the simplicity of the primitive life, and indeed attempted to resume his place in his bunk, whence he was hauled by force. Their way lay, as before, across country by narrow lanes, and it was not till the afternoon that they came out on the high road, their first high road; and there disaster, fleet and unforeseen, sprang out on them—disaster momentous indeed to their expedition, but simply overwhelming in its effect on the after-career of Toad.

They were strolling along the high road easily, the Mole by the horse's head, talking to him, since the horse had complained that he was being frightfully left out of it, and nobody considered him in the least; the Toad and the Water Rat walking behind the cart talking together—at least Toad was talking, and Rat was saying at intervals, "Yes, precisely; and what did *you* say to *him*?"—and thinking all the time of something very different, when far behind them they heard a faint warning hum, like the drone of a distant bee. Glancing back, they saw a small cloud of dust, with a dark centre of energy, advancing on them at incredible speed, while from out the dust a faint "Poop-poop!" wailed like an uneasy animal in pain. Hardly regarding it, they turned to resume their conversation, when in an instant (as it seemed) the peaceful scene was changed, and with a blast of wind and a whirl of sound that made them jump for the nearest ditch, it was on them! The "Poop-poop" rang with a brazen shout in their ears, they had a moment's glimpse of an interior of glittering plate-glass and rich morocco, and the magnificent motor-car, immense, breath-snatching, passionate, with its pilot tense and hugging his wheel, possessed all earth and air for the fraction of a second, flung an enveloping cloud of dust that blinded and enwrapped them utterly, and then dwindled to a speck in the far distance, changed back into a droning bee once more.

The old grey horse, dreaming, as he plodded along, of his quiet paddock, in a new raw situation such as this simply abandoned himself to his natural emotions. Rearing, plunging, backing steadily, in spite of all the Mole's efforts at his head, and all the Mole's lively language directed at his better feelings, he drove the cart backwards towards the deep ditch at the side of the road. It wavered an instant—then there was a heart-rending crash—and the canary-coloured cart, their pride and their joy, lay on its side in the ditch, an irredeemable wreck.

The Rat danced up and down in the road, simply transported with passion. "You villains!" he shouted, shaking both fists. "You scoundrels, you highwaymen, you—you—road-hogs! —I'll have the law on you! I'll report you! I'll take you through all the Courts!" His home-sickness had quite slipped away from him, and for the moment he was the skipper of the canary-coloured vessel driven on a shoal by the reckless jockeying of rival mariners, and he was trying to recollect all the fine and biting things he used to say to masters of steam-launches when their wash, as they drove too near the bank, used to flood his parlour carpet at home.

Toad sat straight down in the middle of the dusty road, his legs stretched out before him, and stared fixedly in the direction of the disappearing motor-car. He breathed short, his face wore a placid, satisfied expression, and at intervals he faintly murmured "Poop-poop!"

The Mole was busy trying to quiet the horse, which he succeeded in doing after a time. Then he went to look at the cart, on its side in the ditch. It was indeed a sorry sight. Panels and windows smashed, axles hopelessly bent, one wheel off, sardine-tins scattered over the wide world, and the bird in the bird-cage sobbing pitifully and calling to be let out.

The Rat came to help him, but their united efforts were not sufficient to right the cart. "Hi! Toad!" they cried. "Come and bear a hand, can't you!"

The Toad never answered a word, or budged from his seat in the road; so they went to see what was the matter with him. They found him in a sort of trance, a happy smile on his face, his eyes still fixed on the dusty wake of their destroyer. At intervals he was still heard to murmur "Poop-poop!"

The Rat shook him by the shoulder. "Are you coming to help us, Toad?" he demanded sternly.

"Glorious, stirring sight!" murmured Toad, never offering to move. "The poetry of motion! The *real* way to travel! The *only* way to travel! Here to-day—in next week to-morrow! Villages skipped, towns and cities jumped—always somebody else's horizon! O bliss! O poop-poop! O my! O my!"

"O *stop* being an ass, Toad!" cried the Mole despairingly.

"And to think I never *knew!*" went on the Toad in a dreamy monotone. "All those wasted years that lie behind me, I never knew, never even *dreamt!* But *now*—but now that I know, now that I fully realize! O what a flowery track lies spread before me, henceforth! What dust-clouds shall spring up behind me as I speed on my reckless way! What carts I shall fling carelessly into the ditch in the wake of my magnificent onset! Horrid little carts—common carts—canary-coloured carts!"

"What are we to do with him?" asked the Mole of the Water Rat.

"Nothing at all," replied the Rat firmly. "Because there is really nothing to be done. You see, I know him from of old. He is now possessed. He has got a new craze, and it always takes him that way, in its first stage. He'll continue like that for days now, like an animal walking in a happy dream, quite useless for all practical purposes. Never mind him. Let's go and see what there is to be done about the cart."

A careful inspection showed them that, even if they succeeded in righting it by themselves, the cart would travel no longer. The axles were in a hopeless state, and the missing wheel was shattered into pieces.

The Rat knotted the horse's reins over his back and took him by the head, carrying the bird-cage and its hysterical occupant in the other hand. "Come on!" he said grimly to the Mole. "It's five or six miles to the nearest town, and we shall just have to walk it. The sooner we make a start the better."

"But what about Toad?" asked the Mole anxiously, as they set off together. "We can't leave him here, sitting in the middle of the road by himself, in the distracted state he's in! It's not safe. Supposing another Thing were to come along?"

"O, *bother* Toad," said the Rat savagely; "I've done with him!"

They had not proceeded very far on their way, however, when there was a pattering of feet behind them, and Toad caught them up and thrust a paw inside the elbow of each of them; still breathing short and staring into vacancy.

"Now, look here, Toad!" said the Rat sharply; "as soon as we get to the town, you'll have to go straight to the police-station, and see if they know anything about that motor-car and who it belongs to, and lodge a complaint against it. And then you'll have to go to a blacksmith's or wheelwright's and arrange for the cart to be fetched and mended and put to rights. It'll take time, but it's not quite a hopeless smash. Meanwhile, the Mole and I will go to an Inn and find comfortable rooms where we can stay till the cart's ready, and till your nerves have recovered from their shock."

"Police-station! Complaint!" murmured Toad dreamily. "Me *complain* of that beautiful, that heavenly vision that has been vouchsafed me! *Mend the cart!* I've done with carts forever. I never want to see the cart, or to hear of it, again. O, Ratty! You can't think how obliged I am to you for consenting to come on this trip! I wouldn't have gone without you, and then I might never have seen that—that swan, that sunbeam, that thunderbolt! I might never have heard that entrancing sound, or smelt that bewitching smell! I owe it all to you, my best of friends!"

The Rat turned from him in despair. "You see what it is?" he said to the Mole, addressing him across Toad's head: "He's quite hopeless. I give it up—when we get to the town we'll go to the railway-station, and with luck we may pick up a train there that'll get us back to River Bank to-night. And if ever you catch me going a-pleasuring with this provoking animal again!"—He snorted, and during the rest of that weary trudge addressed his remarks exclusively to Mole.

On reaching the town they went straight to the station and deposited Toad in the second-class waiting-room, giving a porter twopence to keep a strict eye on him. They then left the horse at an inn stable, and gave what directions they could about the cart and its contents. Eventually, a slow train having landed them at a station not very far from Toad Hall, they escorted the spell-bound, sleep-walking Toad to his door, put him inside it, and instructed his housekeeper to feed him, undress him, and put him to bed. Then they got out their boat from the boat-house, sculled down the river home, and at a very late hour sat down to supper in their own cosy riverside parlour, to the Rat's great joy and contentment.

The following evening the Mole, who had risen late and taken things very easy all day, was sitting on the bank fishing, when the Rat, who had been looking up his friends and gossiping, came strolling along to find him. "Heard the news?" he said. "There's nothing else being talked about, all along the river bank. Toad went up to Town by an early train this morning. And he has ordered a large and very expensive motor-car."

THE TALE OF PETER RABBIT

Beatrix Potter

Like The Wind in the Willows *by Kenneth Grahame,* The Tale of Peter Rabbit *began as a letter to a small child. Both little boys loved their letters which later developed into children's classics.*

It now seems strange that when Miss Potter attempted to publish her short illustrated story it was refused at least six times. Only by paying for a private edition, which cost £11, was she able to see her story in print. In 1900 she showed a copy of this book to F. Warne & Co. who published the first color edition in 1901. A number of other small books followed Peter Rabbit: The Tale of Benjamin Bunny, The Tale of Jemima Puddle-Duck, The Tale of Tom Kitten, The Tale of Squirrel Nutkin, The Tailor of Gloucester, *and* The Tale of Mrs. Tiggy-Winkle. *Although these never achieved the popularity of* The Tale of Peter Rabbit, *preschool children have enjoyed the gentle humor and suspenseful stories.*

Once upon a time there were four little Rabbits, and their names were—

Flopsy,
Mopsy,
Cotton-tail,
and Peter.

They lived with their Mother in a sandbank, underneath the root of a very big fir-tree.

"Now, my dears," said old Mrs. Rabbit one morning, "you may go into the fields or down the lane, but don't go into Mr. McGregor's garden: your Father had an accident there; he was put in a pie by Mrs. McGregor. Now run along, and don't get into mischief; I am going out."

Tale of Peter Rabbit by Beatrix Potter. Reprinted by permission of Frederick Warne & Co., Ltd., publishers.

Then old Mrs. Rabbit took a basket and her umbrella, and went through the wood to the baker's. She bought a loaf of brown bread and five currant buns.

Flopsy, Mopsy, and Cotton-tail, who were good little bunnies, went down the lane to gather blackberries; but Peter who was very naughty, ran straight away to Mr. McGregor's garden, and squeezed under the gate!

First he ate some lettuces and some French beans; and then he ate some radishes; and then, feeling rather sick, he went to look for some parsley.

But round the end of a cucumber frame, whom should he meet but Mr. McGregor!

Mr. McGregor was on his hands and knees

planting out young cabbages, but he jumped up and ran after Peter, waving a rake and calling out, "Stop thief!"

Peter was most dreadfully frightened; he rushed all over the garden, for he had forgotten the way back to the gate.

He lost one of his shoes among the cabbages, and the other shoe amongst the potatoes.

After losing them, he ran on four legs and went faster, so that I think he might have got away altogether if he had not unfortunately run into a gooseberry net, and got caught by the large buttons on his jacket. It was a blue jacket with brass buttons, quite new.

Peter gave himself up for lost, and shed big tears; but his sobs were overheard by some friendly sparrows, who flew to him in great excitement, and implored him to exert himself.

Mr. McGregor came up with a sieve, which he intended to pop upon the top of Peter; but Peter wriggled out just in time, leaving his jacket behind him. And rushed into the toolshed, and jumped into a can. It would have been a beautiful thing to hide in, if it had not had so much water in it.

Mr. McGregor was quite sure that Peter was somewhere in the toolshed, perhaps hidden underneath a flower-pot. He began to turn them over carefully, looking under each.

Presently Peter sneezed—"Kertyschoo!" Mr. McGregor was after him in no time, and tried to put his foot upon Peter, who jumped out of the window, upsetting three plants. The window was too small for Mr. McGregor and he was tired of running after Peter. He went back to his work.

Peter sat down to rest; he was out of breath and trembling with fright, and he had not the least idea which way to go. Also he was very damp with sitting in that can.

After a time he began to wander about, going lippity—lippity—not very fast, and looking all around.

He found a door in a wall; but it was locked, and there was no room for a fat little rabbit to squeeze underneath.

An old mouse was running in and out over the stone door-step, carrying peas and beans to her family in the wood. Peter asked her the way to the gate, but she had such a large pea in her mouth that she could not answer. She only shook her head at him. Peter began to cry.

Then he tried to find his way straight across the garden, but he became more and more puzzled. Presently, he came to a pond where Mr. McGregor filled his water-cans. A white cat was staring at some goldfish; she sat very, very still, but now and then the tip of her tail twitched as if it were alive. Peter thought it best to go away without speaking to her; he had heard about cats from his cousin, little Benjamin Bunny.

He went back towards the toolshed, but suddenly, quite close to him, he heard the noise of a hoe—scr-r-ritch, scratch, scratch, scritch. Peter scuttered underneath the bushes. But presently, as nothing happened, he came out, and climbed upon a wheelbarrow, and peeped over. The first thing he saw was Mr. McGregor hoeing onions. His back was turned toward Peter, and beyond him was the gate!

Peter got down very quietly off the wheelbarrow, and started running as fast as he could go, along a straight walk behind some black-currant bushes.

Mr. McGregor caught sight of him at the corner, but Peter did not care. He slipped underneath the gate, and was safe at last in the wood outside the garden.

Mr. McGregor hung up the little jacket and the shoes for a scare-crow to frighten the blackbirds.

Peter never stopped running or looked behind him till he got home to the big fir-tree.

He was so tired that he flopped down upon the nice soft sand on the floor of the rabbit hole, and shut his eyes. His mother was busy cooking; she wondered what he had done with his clothes. It was the second little jacket and pair of shoes that Peter had lost in a fortnight!

I am sorry to say that Peter was not very well during the evening.

His mother put him to bed, and made some camomile tea; and she gave a dose of it to Peter!

"One table-spoonful to be taken at bedtime."

But Flopsy, Mopsy, and Cotton-tail had bread and milk and blackberries for supper.

YERTLE THE TURTLE

Dr. Seuss (*Theodor S. Geisel*)

That Dr. Seuss has a great talent for writing fantasy is revealed by Yertle the Turtle, *but not all of his writing is up to this standard.* Green Eggs and Ham *lacks the thought, care, and originality of* Yertle the Turtle, *which retains its freshness even after many readings while* Green Eggs and Ham *soon bores most children. Its repetitiveness lacks the linguistic charm of the cumulative tales whose style it imitates. The "problem" is so slight that few readers care if he eats the eggs and ham or not. The language and story are little better than the primer style Dr. Seuss was trying to improve.*

The language and style of Yertle the Turtle, *on the other hand, delight children from kindergarten age on; it has even been used in high school discussions of dictatorship and democracy. The underlying message surely should not be explained to young children, but some elementary school classes may enjoy talking about Yertle and Mack.*

On the far-away Island of Sala-ma-Sond,
Yertle the Turtle was king of the pond.
A nice little pond. It was clean. It was neat.
The water was warm. There was plenty to eat.
The turtles had everything turtles might need.
And they were all happy. Quite happy indeed.
They *were* . . . until Yertle, the king of them all,
Decided the kingdom he ruled was too small.
"I'm ruler," said Yertle, "of all that I see.
But I don't see *enough*. That's the trouble with
  me.
With this stone for a throne, I look down on my
  pond
But I cannot look down on the places beyond.
This throne that I sit on is too, too low down.
It ought to be *higher!*" he said with a frown.
"If I could sit high, how much greater I'd be!
What a king! I'd be ruler of all I could see!"
So Yertle, the Turtle King, lifted his hand
And Yertle, the Turtle King, gave a command.
He ordered nine turtles to swim to his stone
And, using these turtles, he built a *new* throne.

He made each turtle stand on another one's back
And he piled them all up in a nine-turtle stack.
And then Yertle climbed up. He sat down on the
  pile.
What a wonderful view! He could see 'most a
  mile!
"All mine!" Yertle cried. "Oh, the things I now
  rule!
I'm king of a cow! And I'm king of a mule!
I'm king of a house! And, what's more, beyond
  that,
I'm king of a blueberry bush and a cat!
I'm Yertle the Turtle! Oh, marvelous me!
For I am the ruler of all that I see!"
And all through that morning, he sat there up
  high
Saying over and over, "A great king am I!"
Until 'long about noon. Then he heard a faint
  sigh.
"What's *that?*" snapped the king
And he looked down the stack.
And he saw, at the bottom, a turtle named Mack.
Just a part of his throne. And this plain little
  turtle
Looked up and he said, "Beg your pardon, King
  Yertle.

"I've pains in my back and my shoulders and knees.

How long must we stand here, Your Majesty, please?"

"SILENCE!" the King of the Turtles barked back

"I'm king, and you're only a turtle named Mack."

"You stay in your place while I sit here and rule.

I'm king of a cow! And I'm king of a mule!

I'm king of a house! And a bush! And a cat!

But that isn't all. I'll do better than *that*!

My throne shall be *higher*!" his royal voice thundered,

"So pile up more turtles! I want 'bout two hundred!"

"Turtles! More turtles!" he bellowed and brayed.

And the turtles 'way down in the pond were afraid.

They trembled. They shook. But they came. They obeyed.

From all over the pond, they came swiming by dozens.

Whole families of turtles, with uncles and cousins.

And all of them stepped on the head of poor Mack.

One after another, they climbed up the stack.

THEN Yertle the Turtle was perched up so high,

He could see forty miles from his throne in the sky!

"Hooray!" shouted Yertle. "I'm king of the trees!

I'm king of the birds! And I'm king of the bees!

I'm king of the butterflies! King of the air!

Ah, me! What a throne! What a wonderful chair!

I'm Yertle the Turtle! Oh, marvelous me

For I am the ruler of all that I see!"

Then again, from below, in the great heavy stack,

Came a groan from that plain little turtle named Mack.

"Your Majesty, please . . . I don't like to complain,

But down here below, we are feeling great pain.

I know, up on top you are seeing great sights,

But down at the bottom we, too, should have rights.

We turtles can't stand it. Our shells will all crack!

Besides we need food. We are starving!" groaned Mack.

"You hush up your mouth!" howled the mighty King Yertle.

"You've no right to talk to the world's highest turtle.

I rule from the clouds! Over land! Over sea!

There's nothing, no, NOTHING, that's higher than me!"

But, while he was shouting, he saw with surprise

That the moon of the evening was starting to rise

Up over his head in the darkening skies.

"What's THAT?" snorted Yertle. "Say, what IS that thing

That dares to be higher than Yertle the King?

I shall not allow it! I'll go higher still!

I'll build my throne higher! I can and I will!

I'll call some more turtles. I'll stack 'em to heaven!

I need 'bout five thousand, six hundred and seven!"

But, as Yertle, the Turtle King, lifted his hand

And started to order and give the command,

That plain little turtle below in the stack,

That plain little turtle whose name was just Mack,

Decided he'd taken enough. And he had,

And that plain little lad got a little bit mad

And that plain little Mack did a plain little thing.

He Burped!

And his burp shook the throne of the king!

And Yertle the Turtle, the king of the trees,

The king of the air and the birds and the bees,

The king of a house and a cow and a mule . . .

Well, *that* was the end of the Turtle King's rule!

For Yertle, the King of all Sala-ma-Sond,

Fell off his high throne and fell *Plunk*! in the pond!

And today the great Yertle, that Marvelous he,

Is King of the Mud. That is all he can see.

And the turtles, of course . . . all the turtles are free

As turtles and, maybe, all creatures should be.

GREEN EGGS AND HAM

Dr. Seuss (Theodor S. Geisel)

Please see the introduction to Yertle the Turtle, *the previous tale, for a comparison of these two stories. Although* Green Eggs and Ham *lacks the imagination and skill of the previous piece, it is included in this anthology for comparative purposes and as an example of less satisfactory fantasy for young children. It is important to remember that no matter how famous and excellent a writer may be, each work should be evaluated individually.*

That Sam-I-am! That Sam-I-am! I do not like that Sam-I-am!

Do you like green eggs and ham?

I do not like them, Sam-I-am. I do not like green eggs and ham.

Would you like them here or there?

I would not like them here or there. I would not like them anywhere. I do not like green eggs and ham. I do not like them, Sam-I-am.

Would you like them in a house? Would you like them with a mouse?

I do not like them in a house. I do not like them with a mouse. I do not like them here or there. I do not like them anywhere. I do not like green eggs and ham. I do not like them, Sam-I-am.

Would you eat them in a box? Would you eat them with a fox?

Not in a box. Not with a fox. Not in a house. Not with a mouse. I would not eat them here or there. I would not eat them anywhere. I would not eat green eggs and ham. I do not like them, Sam-I-am.

Would you? Could you? In a car? Eat them! Eat them! Here they are.

I would not, could not, in a car.

You may like them. You will see. You may like them in a tree!

I would not, could not in a tree. Not in a car! You let me be.

I do not like them in a box. I do not like them with a fox. I do not like them in a house. I do not like them with a mouse. I do not like them here or there. I do not like them anywhere. I do not like green eggs and ham. I do not like them, Sam-I-am.

A train! A train! A train! A train! Could you, would you, on a train?

Not on a train! Not in a tree! Not in a car! Sam! Let me be!

I would not, could not, in a box. I could not, would not, with a fox. I will not eat them with a mouse. I will not eat them in a house. I will not eat them here or there. I will not eat them anywhere. I do not eat green eggs and ham. I do not like them, Sam-I-am.

Say! In the dark? Here in the dark! Would you, could you, in the dark?

I would not, could not, in the dark.

Would you, could you, in the rain?

I would not, could not, in the rain. Not in the dark. Not on a train. Not in a car. Not in a tree. I do not like them, Sam, you see. Not in a house. Not in a box. Not with a mouse. Not with a fox. I will not eat them here or there. I do not like them anywhere!

You do not like green eggs and ham?

I do not like them, Sam-I-am.

Could you, would you, with a goat?

I would not, could not, with a goat!

Would you, could you, on a boat?

I could not, would not, on a boat. I will not, will not, with a goat. I will not eat them in the rain. I will not eat them on a train! Not in the dark! Not in a tree! Not in a car! You let me be! I do not like them in a box. I do not like them with a fox. I will not eat them in a house. I do not like them with a mouse. I do not like them here or there. I do not like them ANYWHERE!

I do not like green eggs and ham!

I do not like them, Sam-I-am.

You do not like them. So you say. Try them!

Try them! And you may. Try them and you may, I say.

Sam! If you will let me be, I will try them. You will see.

Say! I like green eggs and ham! I do! I like them, Sam-I-am! And I would eat them in a boat. And I would eat them with a goat . . . And I will eat them in the rain. And in the dark. And on a train. And in a car. And in a tree. They are so good, so good, you see!

So I will eat them in a box. And I will eat them with a fox. And I will eat them in a house. And I will eat them with a mouse. And I will eat them here and there. Say! I will eat them ANY-WHERE! I do so like green eggs and ham! Thank you! Thank you, Sam-I-am!

MILLIONS OF CATS

Wanda Gág

The delightful, melodic refrain "Cats here, cats there, Cats and Kittens every-where, Hundreds of Cats, Thousands of Cats, Millions and billions and tril-lions of cats" has given this story great popularity among adults as well as children. Wanda Gág's softly curving black and white illustrations gracefully complement the text and make Millions of Cats *one of the great American picture books. An illustration from this book is reproduced in Chapter 2,* Illustrations in Children's Literature.

Once upon a time there was a very old man and a very old woman. They lived in a nice clean house which had flowers all around it, except where the door was. But they couldn't be happy because they were so very lonely.

"If we only had a cat!" sighed the very old woman.

"A cat?" asked the very old man.

"Yes, a sweet little fluffy cat," said the very old woman.

"I will get you a cat, my dear," said the very old man.

And he set out over the hills to look for one.

He climbed over the sunny hills. He trudged through the cool valleys. He walked a long, long time and at last he came to a hill which was quite covered with cats.

Cats here, cats there, Cats and Kittens
everywhere,
Hundreds of cats,
Thousands of cats,
Millions and billions and trillions of cats.

"Oh," cried the old man joyfully, "Now I can choose the prettiest cat and take it home with me!" So he chose one. It was white.

But just as he was about to leave, he saw another one all black and white and it seemed just as pretty as the first. So he took this one also. But then he saw a fuzzy grey kitten way over here which was every bit as pretty as the others so he took it too.

And now he saw one way down in a corner which he thought too lovely to leave so he took this too.

And just then, over here, the very old man found a kitten which was black and very beautiful.

"It would be a shame to leave that one," said the very old man. So he took it.

And now, over there he saw a cat which had brown and yellow stripes like a baby tiger.

"I simply must take it!" cried the very old man, and he did.

So it happened that every time the very old man looked up, he saw another cat which was so pretty he could not bear to leave it, and before he knew it, he had chosen them all.

And so he went back over the sunny hills and down through the cool valleys, to show all his pretty kittens to the very old woman.

It was very funny to see those hundreds and thousands and millions and billions and trillions of cats following him.

They came to a pond.

"Mew, mew! We are thirsty!" cried the
> Hundreds of cats,
> Thousands of cats,
Millions and billions and trillions of cats.

"Well, here is a great deal of water," said the very old man.

Each cat took a sip of water, and the pond was gone!

"Mew, mew! Now we are hungry!" said the
> Hundreds of cats,
> Thousands of cats,
Millions and billions and trillions of cats.

"There is much grass on the hills," said the very old man.

Each cat ate a mouthful of grass and not a blade was left!

Pretty soon the very old woman saw them coming.

"My dear!" she cried, "What are you doing? I asked for one little cat, and what do I see?—

> "Cats here, cats there, Cats and kittens
> everywhere,
> Hundreds of cats,
> Thousands of cats,
Millions and billions and trillions of cats.

"But we can never feed them all," said the very old woman, "they will eat us out of house and home."

"I never thought of that," said the very old man, "What shall we do?"

The very old woman thought for a while and then she said, "I know! We will let the cats decide which one we should keep."

"Oh yes," said the very old man, and he called to the cats, "which one of you is the prettiest?"

"I am!"

"I am!"

"No, I am the prettiest!" "I am!"

"No, I am! I am! I am!" cried hundreds and thousands and millions and billions and trillions of voices, for each cat thought itself the prettiest.

And they began to quarrel.

They bit and scratched and clawed each other and made such a great noise that the very old man and the very old woman ran into the house as fast as they could. They did not like such quarreling. But after a while the noise stopped and the very old man and the very old woman peeped out of the window to see what had happened. They could not see a single cat!

"I think they must have eaten each other all up," said the very old woman, "It's too bad!"

"But look!" said the very old man, and he pointed to a bunch of high grass. In it sat one little frightened kitten. They went out and picked it up. It was thin and scraggly.

"Poor little kitty," said the very old woman.

"Dear little kitty," said the very old man, "how does it happen that you were not eaten up with all those hundreds and thousands and millions and billions and trillions of cats?"

"Oh, I'm just a very homely little cat," said the kitten. "So when you asked who was the prettiest, I didn't say anything. So nobody bothered about me."

They took the kitten into the house, where the very old woman gave it a warm bath and brushed its fur until it was soft and shiny.

Every day they gave it plenty of milk—and soon it grew nice and plump.

"And it is a very pretty cat, after all!" said the very old woman.

"It is the most beautiful cat in the whole world," said the very old man.

"I ought to know, for I've seen—
    Hundreds of cats,
    Thousands of cats,

Millions and billions and trillions of cats—
and not one was as pretty as this one."

THE HUCKABUCK FAMILY & HOW THEY RAISED POPCORN IN NEBRASKA & QUIT & CAME BACK

Carl Sandburg

Carl Sandburg is known primarily as a poet, yet in Rootabaga Stories *he demonstrates his ability with prose as well as poetry. His enjoyment of sounds and play with words is reminiscent of Rudyard Kipling's style. Both writers not only give their readers pleasure but also seem to have had fun writing their stories.*

The following tale is delightful when read aloud. Fourth-grade and older students, no matter how bored with reading groups, will practice diligently to read "The Huckabuck Family . . ." aloud with the proper rhythm and ease. They enjoy sharing their own pleasure with their classmates whose delighted chuckles make the effort worthwhile.

Jonas Jonas Huckabuck was a farmer in Nebraska with a wife, Mama Mama Huckabuck, and a daughter, Pony Pony Huckabuck.

"Your father gave you two names the same in front," people had said to him.

And he answered, "Yes, two names are easier to remember. If you call me by my first name Jonas and I don't hear you then when you call me by my second name Jonas maybe I will.

"And," he went on, "I call my pony-face girl Pony Pony because if she doesn't hear me the first time she always does the second."

And so they lived on a farm where they raised pop corn, these three, Jonas Jonas Huckabuck, his wife Mama Mama Huckabuck, and their pony-face daughter, Pony Pony Huckabuck.

After they harvested the crop one year they had the barns, the cribs, the sheds, the shacks, and all the cracks and corners of the farm, all filled with pop corn.

"We came out to Nebraska to raise pop corn," said Jonas Jonas, "and I guess we got nearly enough pop corn this year for the pop corn poppers in these United States."

And this was the year Pony Pony was going to bake her first squash pie all by herself. In one corner of the corn crib, all covered over with pop corn, she had a secret, a big round squash, a fat yellow squash, a rich squash all spotted with spots of gold.

She carried the squash into the kitchen, took a long sharp shining knife, and then she cut the squash in the middle till she had two big half squashes. And inside just like outside it was rich yellow spotted with spots of gold.

And there was a shine of silver. And Pony Pony wondered why silver should be in a squash. She picked and plunged with her fingers till she pulled it out.

"It's a buckle," she said, "a silver buckle, a Chinese silver slipper buckle."

She ran with it to her father and said, "Look what I found when I cut open the golden yellow squash spotted with gold spots—it is a Chinese silver slipper buckle."

"It means our luck is going to change, and we don't know whether it will be good luck or bad luck," said Jonas Jonas to his daughter, Pony Pony Huckabuck.

Then she ran with it to her mother and said, "Look what I found when I cut open the yellow squash spotted with spots of gold—it is a Chinese silver slipper buckle."

"It means our luck is going to change, and we don't know whether it will be good luck or bad luck," said Mama Mama Huckabuck.

And that night a fire started in the barns, crib, sheds, shacks, cracks, and corners, where the pop corn harvest was kept. In the morning the ground all around the farm house and the barn was covered with white pop corn so it looked like a heavy fall of snow.

All the next day the fire kept on and the pop corn popped till it was up to the shoulders of Pony Pony when she tried to walk from the house to the barn. And that night in all the barns, cribs, sheds, shacks, cracks and corners of the farm, the pop corn went on popping.

In the morning when Jonas Jonas Huckabuck looked out of the upstairs window he saw the pop corn popping and coming higher and higher. It was nearly up to the window. Before evening and dark of that day, Jonas Jonas Huckabuck, and his wife Mama Mama Huckabuck, and their daughter Pony Pony Huckabuck, all went away from the farm saying, "We came to Nebraska to raise pop corn, but this is too much. We will not come back till the wind blows away the pop corn. We will not come back till we get a sign and a signal."

They went to Oskaloosa, Iowa. And the next year Pony Pony Huckabuck was very proud because when she stood on the sidewalks in the street she could see her father sitting high on the seat of a coal wagon, driving two big spanking horses hitched with shining brass harness in front of the coal wagon. And though Pony Pony and Jonas Jonas were proud all that year, there never came a sign, a signal.

The next year again was a proud year, exactly as proud a year as they spent in Oskaloosa. They went to Paducah, Kentucky; to Defiance, Ohio; Peoria, Illinois; Indianapolis, Indiana; Walla Walla, Washington. And in all these places Pony Pony Huckabuck saw her father, Jonas Jonas

Huckabuck, standing in rubber boots deep down in a ditch with a shining steel shovel shoveling yellow clay and black mud from down in the ditch high and high up over his shoulders. And though it was a proud year they got no sign, no signal.

The next year came. It was the proudest of all. This was the year Jonas Jonas Huckabuck and his family lived in Elgin, Illinois, and Jonas Jonas was watchman in a watch factory watching the watches.

"I know where you have been," Mama Mama Huckabuck would say of an evening to Pony Pony Huckabuck. "You have been down to the watch factory watching your father watch the watches."

"Yes," said Pony Pony. "Yes, and this evening when I was watching father watch the watches in the watch factory, I looked over my left shoulder and I saw a policeman with a star and brass buttons and he was watching me to see if I was watching father watch the watches in the watch factory."

It was a proud year. Pony Pony saved her money. Thanksgiving came. Pony Pony said, "I am going to get a squash to make a squash pie." She hunted from one grocery to another; she kept her eyes on the farm wagons coming into Elgin with squashes.

She found what she wanted, the yellow squash spotted with gold spots. She took it home, cut it open, and saw the inside was like the outside, all rich yellow spotted with gold spots.

There was a shine like silver. She picked and plunged with her fingers and pulled and pulled till at last she pulled out the shine of silver.

"It's a sign; it is a signal," she said. "It is a buckle, a slipper buckle, a Chinese silver slipper buckle. It is the mate to the other buckle. Our luck is going to change. Yoo hoo! Yoo hoo!"

She told her father and mother about the buckle. They went back to the farm in Nebraska. The wind by this time had been blowing and blowing for three years, and all the pop corn was blown away.

"Now we are going to be farmers again," said Jonas Jonas Huckabuck to Mama Mama Huckabuck and to Pony Pony Huckabuck. "And we are going to raise cabbages, beets and turnips; we are going to raise squash, rutabaga, pumpkins and peppers for pickling. We are going to raise wheat, oats, barley, rye. We are going to raise corn such as Indian corn and Kaffir corn—but we are *not* going to raise any pop corn for the pop corn poppers to be popping."

And the pony-face daughter, Pony Pony Huckabuck, was proud because she had on new black slippers, and around her ankles, holding the slippers on the left foot and the right foot, she had two buckles, silver buckles, Chinese silver slipper buckles. They were mates.

Sometimes on Thanksgiving Day and Christmas and New Year's, she tells her friends to be careful when they open a squash.

"Squashes make your luck change good to bad and bad to good," says Pony Pony.

MARY POPPINS

P. L. Travers

Episodic stories, in which each chapter is an unrelated incident and in which there is no unified plot, are generally less successful than those books with organic plots in which each event relates to an overall unity. However, two excellent exceptions are The Wind in the Willows *and* Mary Poppins. *These books demonstrate that exceptional writers can successfully defy some of the "rules" of writing and still produce excellent novels.*

Mary Poppins' personality is so skillfully drawn that her strength carries this book and the entire series. A vain, angular woman, who tolerates no sentimentality or argument, she is one of the unique and memorable characters in children's literature. P. L. Travers' writing skill is revealed in her ability to create a rounded, believable character who despite her no-nonsense attitude, is warm and likeable.

Excellent character development and its many interesting episodes separate this book from one like Mr. Pudgins. *While he, too, is a magical babysitter, his personality is not strongly developed and the book's incidents are too similar to each other to retain interest. A comparison of these two books and* The Wind in the Willows *would be of value in a study of fantasy.*

"Are you quite sure he will be at home?" said Jane, as they got off the Bus, she and Michael and Mary Poppins.

"Would my Uncle ask me to bring you to tea if he intended to go out, I'd like to know?" said Mary Poppins, who was evidently very offended by the question. She was wearing her blue coat with the silver buttons and the blue hat to match, and on the days when she wore these it was the easiest thing in the world to offend her.

All three of them were on the way to pay a visit to Mary Poppins's uncle, Mr. Wigg, and Jane and Michael had looked forward to the trip for so long that they were more than half afraid that Mr. Wigg might not be in, after all.

"Why is he called Mr. Wigg—does he wear one?" asked Michael, hurrying along beside Mary Poppins.

"He is called Mr. Wigg because Mr. Wigg is his name. And he doesn't wear one. He is bald," said Mary Poppins. "And if I have any more questions we will just go Back Home." And she sniffed her usual sniff of displeasure.

Jane and Michael looked at each other and frowned. And the frown meant: "Don't let's ask her anything else or we'll never get there."

Mary Poppins put her hat straight at the Tobacconist's Shop at the corner. It had been one of those curious windows where there seem to be three of you instead of one, so that if you look long enough at them you begin to feel you are not yourself but a whole crowd of somebody else. Mary Poppins sighed with pleasure, however, when she saw three of herself, each wearing a blue coat with silver buttons and a blue hat to match. She thought it was such a lovely sight that she wished there had been a dozen of her or even thirty. The more Mary Poppins the better.

"Come along," she said sternly, as though they had kept *her* waiting. Then they turned the corner and pulled the bell of Number Three, Robertson Road. Jane and Michael could hear it faintly echoing from a long way away and they knew that in one minute, or two at the most, they would be having tea with Mary Poppins's uncle, Mr. Wigg, for the first time ever.

"If he's in, of course," Jane said to Michael in a whisper.

At that moment the door flew open and a thin, watery-looking lady appeared.

"Is he in?" said Michael quickly.

"I'll thank you," said Mary Poppins, giving him a terrible glance, "to let *me* do the talking."

"How do you do, Mrs. Wigg," said Jane politely.

"Mrs. Wigg!" said the thin lady, in a voice even thinner than herself. "How dare you call me Mrs. Wigg? No, Thank you! I'm plain Miss Persimmon *and* proud of it. Mrs. Wigg indeed!" She seemed to be quite upset, and they thought Mr. Wigg must be a very odd person if Miss Persimmon was so glad not to be Mrs. Wigg.

"Straight up and first door on the landing," said Miss Persimmon, and she went hurrying away down the passage saying: "Mrs. Wigg indeed!" to herself in a high, thin, outraged voice.

Jane and Michael followed Mary Poppins upstairs. Mary Poppins knocked at the door.

"Come in! Come in! And welcome!" called a loud, cheery voice from inside. Jane's heart was pitter-pattering with excitement.

"He *is* in!" she signalled to Michael with a look.

Mary Poppins opened the door and pushed them in front of her. A large cheerful room lay before them. At one end of it a fire was burning brightly and in the centre stood an enormous table laid for tea—four cups and saucers, piles of bread and butter, crumpets, coconut cakes and a large plum cake with pink icing.

"Well, this is indeed a Pleasure," a huge voice greeted them, and Jane and Michael looked round for its owner. He was nowhere to be seen. The room appeared to be quite empty. Then they heard Mary Poppins saying crossly:

"Oh, Uncle Albert—not *again*? It's not your birthday, is it?"

And as she spoke she looked up at the ceiling. Jane and Michael looked up too and to their surprise saw a round, fat, bald man who was hanging in the air without holding on to anything. Indeed, he appeared to be *sitting* on the air, for his legs were crossed and he had just put down the newspaper which he had been reading when they came in.

"My dear," said Mr. Wigg, smiling down at the children, and looking apologetically at Mary Poppins, "I'm very sorry, but I'm afraid it *is* my birthday."

"Tch, tch, tch!" said Mary Poppins.

"I only remembered last night and there was no time then to send you a postcard asking you to come another day. Very distressing, isn't it?" he said, looking down at Jane and Michael.

"I can see you're rather surprised," said Mr. Wigg. And, indeed, their mouths were so wide open with astonishment that Mr. Wigg, if he had been a little smaller, might almost have fallen into one of them.

"I'd better explain, I think," Mr. Wigg went on calmly. "You see, it's this way. I'm a cheerful sort of man and very disposed to laughter. You wouldn't believe, either of you, the number of things that strike me as being funny. I can laugh at pretty nearly everything, I can."

And with that Mr. Wigg began to bob up and down, shaking with laughter at the thought of his own cheerfulness.

"Uncle Albert!" said Mary Poppins, and Mr. Wigg stopped with a jerk.

"Oh, beg pardon, my dear. Where was I? Oh,

yes. Well, the funny thing about me is—all right, Mary, I won't laugh if I can help it!—that whenever my birthday falls on a Friday, well, it's all up with me. Absolutely U.P.," said Mr. Wigg.

"But why—?" began Jane.

"But how—?" began Michael.

"Well, you see, if I laugh on that particular day I become so filled with Laughing Gas that I simply can't keep on the ground. Even if I smile it happens. The first funny thought, and I'm up like a balloon. And until I can think of something serious I can't get down again." Mr. Wigg began to chuckle at that, but he caught sight of Mary Poppins's face and stopped the chuckle, and continued:

"It's awkward, of course, but not unpleasant. Never happens to either of you, I suppose?"

Jane and Michael shook their heads.

"No, I thought not. It seems to be my own special habit. Once, after I'd been to the Circus the night before, I laughed so much that—would you believe it?—I was up here for a whole twelve hours, and couldn't get down till the last stroke of midnight. Then, of course, I came down with a flop because it was Saturday and not my birthday any more. It's rather odd, isn't it? Not to say funny?

"And now here it is Friday again and my birthday, and you two and Mary P. to visit me. Oh, Lordy, Lordy, don't make me laugh, I beg of you—" But although Jane and Michael had done nothing very amusing, except to stare at him in astonishment, Mr. Wigg began to laugh again loudly, and as he laughed he went bouncing and bobbing about in the air, with the newspaper rattling in his hand and his spectacles half on and half off his nose.

He looked so comic, floundering in the air like a great human bubble, clutching at the ceiling sometimes and sometimes at the gas-bracket as he passed it, that Jane and Michael, though they were trying hard to be polite, just couldn't help doing what they did. They laughed. *And* they laughed. They shut their mouths tight to prevent the laughter escaping, but that didn't do any good. And presently they were rolling over and over on the floor, squealing and shrieking with laughter.

"Really!" said Mary Poppins. "Really, *such* behaviour!"

"I can't help it, I can't help it!" shrieked Michael as he rolled into the fender. "It's so terribly funny. Oh, Jane, *isn't* it funny?"

Jane did not reply, for a curious thing was happening to her. As she laughed she felt herself growing lighter and lighter, just as though she were being pumped full of air. It was a curious and delicious feeling and it made her want to laugh all the more. And then suddenly, with a bouncing bound she felt herself jumping through the air. Michael, to his astonishment, saw her go soaring up through the room. With a little bump her head touched the ceiling and then she went bouncing along it till she reached Mr. Wigg.

"Well!" said Mr. Wigg, looking very surprised indeed. "Don't tell me it's *your* birthday, too?" Jane shook her head.

"It's not? Then this Laughing Gas must be catching! Hi—whoa there, look out for the mantelpiece!" This was to Michael, who had suddenly risen from the floor and was swooping through the air, roaring with laughter, and just grazing the china ornaments on the mantelpiece as he passed. He landed with a bounce right on Mr. Wigg's knee.

"How do you do," said Mr. Wigg, heartily shaking Michael by the hand. "I call this really friendly of you—bless my soul, I do! To come up to me since I couldn't come down to you—eh?" And then he and Michael looked at each other and flung back their heads and simply howled with laughter.

"I say," said Mr. Wigg to Jane, as he wiped his eyes. "You'll be thinking I have the worst manners in the world. You're standing and you ought to be sitting—a nice young lady like you. I'm afraid I can't offer you a chair up here, but I think you'll find the air quite comfortable to sit on. I do."

Jane tried it and found she could sit down quite comfortably on the air. She took off her hat and laid it down beside her and it hung there in space without any support at all.

"That's right," said Mr. Wigg. Then he turned and looked down at Mary Poppins.

"Well, Mary, we're fixed. And now I can enquire about *you*, my dear. I must say, I am very glad to welcome you and my two young friends here today—why, Mary, you're frowning. I'm afraid you don't approve of—er—all this."

He waved his hand at Jane and Michael, and said hurriedly:

"I apologise, Mary, my dear. But you know how it is with me. Still, I must say I never thought my two young friends here would catch it, really I didn't, Mary! I suppose I should have asked them for another day or tried to think of something sad or something—"

"Well, I must say," said Mary Poppins primly, "that I have never in my life seen such a sight. And at your age, Uncle—"

"Mary Poppins, Mary Poppins, do come up!" interrupted Michael. "Think of something funny and you'll find it's quite easy."

"Ah, now do, Mary!" said Mr. Wigg persuasively.

"We're lonely up here without you!" said Jane, and held out her arms towards Mary Poppins. "Do think of something funny."

"Ah, *she* doesn't need to," said Mr. Wigg sighing. "She can come up if she wants to, even without laughing—and she knows it." And he looked mysteriously and secretly at Mary Poppins as she stood down there on the hearth-rug.

"Well," said Mary Poppins, "it's all very silly and undignified, but, since you're all up there and don't seem able to get down, I suppose I'd better come up, too."

With that, to the surprise of Jane and Michael, she put her hands down at her sides and without a laugh, without even the faintest glimmer of a smile, she shot up through the air and sat down beside Jane.

"How many times, I should like to know," she said snappily, "have I told you to take off your coat when you come into a hot room?" And she unbuttoned Jane's coat and laid it neatly on the air beside the the hat.

"That's right, Mary, that's right," said Mr. Wigg contentedly, as he leant down and put his spectacles on the mantelpiece. "Now we're all comfortable—"

"There's comfort *and* comfort," sniffed Mary Poppins.

"And we can have tea," Mr. Wigg went on, apparently not noticing her remark. And then a startled look came over his face.

"My goodness!" he said. "How dreadful! I've just realised—that table's down there and we're up here. What *are* we going to do? We're here

and it's there. It's an awful tragedy—awful! But oh, it's terribly comic!" And he hid his face in his handkerchief and laughed loudly into it. Jane and Michael, though they did not want to miss the crumpets and the cakes, couldn't help laughing too, because Mr. Wigg's mirth was so infectious.

Mr. Wigg dried his eyes.

"There's only one thing for it," he said. "We must think of something serious. Something sad, very sad. And then we shall be able to get down. Now—one, two, three! Something *very* sad, mind you!"

And they thought and thought, with their chins on their hands.

Michael thought of school, and that one day he would have to go there. But even that seemed funny today and he had to laugh.

Jane thought: "I shall be grown up in another fourteen years!" but that didn't sound sad at all but quite nice and rather funny. She could not help smiling at the thought of herself grown up, with long skirts and a hand-bag.

"There was my poor old Aunt Emily," thought Mr. Wigg out loud. "She was run over by an omnibus. Sad. Very sad. Unbearably sad. Poor Aunt Emily. But they saved her umbrella. That was funny, wasn't it?" And before he knew where he was, he was heaving and trembling and bursting with laughter at the thought of Aunt Emily's umbrella.

"It's no good," he said, blowing his nose. "I give it up. And my young friends here seem to be no better at sadness than I am. Mary, can't *you* do something? We want our tea."

To this day Jane and Michael cannot be sure of what happened then. All they know for certain is that as soon as Mr. Wigg had appealed to Mary Poppins, the table below began to wriggle on its legs. Presently it was swaying dangerously, and then with a rattle of china and with cakes lurching off their plates on to the cloth, the table came soaring through the room, gave one graceful turn, and landed beside them so that Mr. Wigg was at its head.

"Good girl!" said Mr. Wigg, smiling proudly upon her. "I knew you'd fix something. Now, will you take the foot of the table and pour out, Mary? And the guests on either side of me. That's the idea," he said, as Michael ran bobbing through the air and sat down on Mr. Wigg's right. Jane was at his left hand. There they were, all together, up in their air and the table between them. Not a single piece of bread-and-butter or a lump of sugar had been left behind.

Mr. Wigg smiled contentedly.

"It is usual, I think, to begin with bread-and-butter," he said to Jane and Michael, "but as it's my birthday we will begin the wrong way—which I always think is the *right* way—with the Cake!"

And he cut a large slice for everybody.

"More tea?" he said to Jane. But before she had time to reply there was a quick, sharp knock at the door.

"Come in!" called Mr. Wigg.

The door opened, and there stood Miss Persimmon with a Jug of hot water on a tray.

"I thought, Mr. Wigg," she began, looking searchingly round the room, "you'd be wanting some more hot—Well, I never! I simply *never!*" she said, as she caught sight of them all seated on the air round the table. "Such goings on I never did see. In all my born days I never saw such. I'm sure, Mr. Wigg, I always knew *you* were a bit odd. But I've closed my eyes to it—being as how you paid your rent regular. But such behaviour as this—having tea in the air with your guests—Mr. Wigg, sir, I'm astonished at you! It's that undignified, and for a gentleman of your age—I never did—"

"But perhaps you will, Miss Persimmon!" said Michael.

"Will what?" said Miss Persimmon haughtily.

"Catch the Laughing Gas, as we did," said Michael.

Miss Persimmon flung back her head scornfully.

"I hope, young man," she retorted, "I have more respect for myself than to go bouncing about in the air like a rubber ball on the end of a bat. I'll stay on my own feet, thank you, or my name's not Amy Persimmon, and—oh dear, oh *dear*, my goodness, oh DEAR—what *is* the matter? I can't walk, I'm going, I—oh, help, HELP!"

For Miss Persimmon, quite against her will, was off the ground and was stumbling through the air, rolling from side to side like a very thin barrel, balancing the tray in her hand. She was

almost weeping with distress as she arrived at the table and put down her jug of hot water.

"Thank you," said Mary Poppins in a calm, very polite voice.

Then Miss Persimmon turned and went wafting down again, murmuring as she went: "So undignified—and me a well-behaved, steady-going woman. I must see a doctor—"

When she touched the floor she ran hurriedly out of the room, wringing her hands, and not giving a single glance backwards.

"So undignified!" they heard her moaning as she shut the door behind her.

"Her name can't be Amy Persimmon, because she *didn't* stay on her own feet!" whispered Jane to Michael.

But Mr. Wigg was looking at Mary Poppins —a curious look, half-amused, half-accusing.

"Mary, Mary, you shouldn't—bless my soul, you shouldn't, Mary. The poor old body will never get over it. But, oh, my Goodness, didn't she look funny waddling through the air—my Gracious Goodness, but didn't she?"

And he and Jane and Michael were off again, rolling about the air, clutching their sides and gasping with laughter at the thought of how funny Miss Persimmon had looked.

"Oh dear!" said Michael. "Don't make me laugh any more. I can't stand it! I shall break!"

"Oh, oh, oh," cried Jane, as she gasped for breath, with her hand over her heart. "Oh, my Gracious, Glorious, Galumphing Goodness!" roared Mr. Wigg, dabbing his eyes with the tail of his coat because he couldn't find his handkerchief.

"IT IS TIME TO GO HOME." Mary Poppins's voice sounded above the roars of laughter like a trumpet.

And suddenly with a rush, Jane and Michael and Mr. Wigg came down. They landed on the floor with a huge bump, all together. The thought that they would have to go home was the first sad thought of the afternoon, and the moment it was in their minds the Laughing Gas went out of them.

Jane and Michael sighed as they watched Mary Poppins come slowly down the air, carrying Jane's coat and hat.

Mr. Wigg sighed, too. A great, long, heavy sigh.

"Well, isn't that a pity?" he said soberly. "It's

very sad that you've got to go home. I never enjoyed an afternoon so much—did you?"

"Never," said Michael sadly, feeling how dull it was to be down on the earth again with no Laughing Gas inside him.

"Never, never," said Jane, as she stood on tip-toe and kissed Mr. Wigg's withered-apple cheeks. "Never, never, never, never . . . !"

They sat on either side of Mary Poppins going home in the Bus. They were both very quiet, thinking over the lovely afternoon. Presently Michael said sleepily to Mary Poppins:

"How often does your Uncle get like that?"

"Like what?" said Mary Poppins sharply, as though Michael had deliberately said something to offend her.

"Well—all bouncy and boundy and laughing and going up in the air."

"Up in the air?" Mary Poppins's voice was high and angry. "What do you mean, pray, up in the air?"

Jane tried to explain.

"Michael means—is your Uncle often full of Laughing Gas, and does he often go rolling and bobbing about on the ceiling when—"

"Rolling and bobbing! The idea! Rolling and bobbing on the ceiling! I'm ashamed of you for suggesting such a thing!" Mary Poppins was obviously *very* offended.

"But he did!" said Michael. "We saw him."

"What, roll and bob? How dare you! I'll have you know that my uncle is a sober, honest, hard-working man, and you'll be kind enough to speak of him respectfully. And don't bite your Bus Ticket! Roll and bob, indeed—the idea!"

Michael and Jane looked across Mary Poppins at each other. They said nothing, for they had learnt that it was better not to argue with Mary Poppins, no matter how odd anything seemed.

But the look that passed between them said: "Is it true or isn't it? About Mr. Wigg. Is Mary Poppins right or are we?"

But there was nobody to give them the right answer.

The Bus roared on, wildly lurching and bounding.

Mary Poppins sat between them, offended and silent, and presently, because they were very tired, they crept closer to her and leant up against her sides and fell asleep, still wondering. . . .

WALT DISNEY'S MARY POPPINS

Adapted by Annie North Bedford

Here the same incident from Mary Poppins *has been adapted. Compare the two for style, development of interest, and Mary Poppins' personality.*

Good books really should not be adapted. If the language is beyond a child's reading level it is better to read it aloud to him than to destroy its uniqueness, as so often happens in adaptations. Reading a poorly written version that differs markedly from the author's originality, intent, and style cannot create a lasting respect for the book. One can only hope that the readers of Walt Disney's *nonliterature will discover the true* Mary Poppins.

Taking Jane and Michael by the hand, Mary Poppins started off the way Andrew had come. And in no more than a moment or two she was rapping at the door of a small, quaint house.

It was Bert who opened the door. "How is he?" Mary Poppins asked. "Never seen him like this," said Bert soberly, "and that's the truth." He pushed the door wide open. Jane and Michael peeked in.

A large, cheerful room lay before them. In the center stood a table laid for tea. "Bless-bless my soul," said a voice rich with chuckles. "Is that Mary Poppins? I'm delighted to see you."

The voice came from above. They looked up, and there in the air sat Mary Poppins' Uncle Albert, chuckling merrily.

"You have just got to stop laughing, Uncle Albert," said Mary Poppins sternly. "I know, my dear, but I do enjoy it so," said Uncle Albert. Here the chuckles bubbled out so that he bobbed against the ceiling. "And the moment I start—hee hee—it's all up with me."

He looked so comic that Jane and Michael, though they were trying hard to be polite, just couldn't help doing what they did. They began to chuckle.

By now Bert was rolling about, shaking with laughter. Soon he rose from the floor and was bobbing about beside Uncle Albert. At the sight of him, Jane and Michael found themselves simply filled with laughter, too. They grew lighter and lighter until their heads bumped the ceiling! Only Mary Poppins remained firmly on the ground.

"You're the silliest things I've ever seen," said Mary Poppins severely from below, "or my name isn't Mary Poppins."

"Speaking of names," said Bert, "I know a man with a wooden leg named Smith . . ."

"Really?" chuckled Uncle Albert. "What's the name of his other leg?" And they all roared with laughter, bouncing in the air.

"Now then, Jane, Michael! It's time for tea," said Mary Poppins.

"Won't you pour out, Mary Poppins?" asked Uncle Albert.

At that the tea table came soaring through the air and Mary Poppins rose sedately to sit near the tea pot.

"I'm having such a good time, my dear," said Uncle Albert as they laughed their way through tea. "I wish you could all stay up here with me always."

"We'll jolly well have to," grinned Michael. "There's no way to get down."

"Well, to be honest," said Uncle Albert, "there is a way. Think of something sad and down you go."

"Time to go home." Mary Poppins' voice sounded like a trumpet above all the laughter in the room.

And at that saddest thought of all, down they all came with a bump.

MR. PUDGINS

Ruth Christoffer Carlsen

Both Mary Poppins *by P. L. Travers and* Mr. Pudgins *have magical, unpredictable babysitters and episodic plots. But* Mary Poppins *is becoming a classic children's fantasy while* Mr. Pudgins *is less and less read. The difference between the two fantasies results largely from the authors' abilities at characterization. Because* Mary Poppins *is a singularly unique and rounded character, her personality unifies the many episodes into a complete book.* Mr. Pudgins' *character however, is undeveloped; he never becomes more than a benign, roly-poly old gentleman with fantastic powers. After reading several incidents in* Mr. Pudgins, *a sameness becomes apparent because the author relied too heavily on the impossible and did not have enough concern for plot or character development. A comparison of* Mary Poppins *and* Mr. Pudgins *in their entirety will reveal a great deal about how fantasy operates.*

MR. PUDGINS TURNS PLUMBER

Boy, this was a hot day even for July. I felt sorry for Dad, off being the rear end of a horse. His club was putting on a show and supper for the kids in the Crippled Children's Hospital, and that's the part Dad drew. Mother kept saying she thought a man of his intelligence at least ought to have been the front part, but Dad said he could be funnier where he was. I wished I could see him. Mother had to help serve the supper.

We were lucky, though, because Mr. Pudgins was staying with us, and you could never tell what might happen. I decided to build a stand to sell lemonade. I'd do a big business on a day like this. About the time I began pounding the board across the two orange crates, Janey and Pete came in from the back yard. They were a mess. I guess they had turned the hose into the garden and then dug in the mud. Mr. Pudgins took one look at them and said, "Bathtub for you two. Forward march."

And they marched, but right away the trouble began. I could hear the fuss in the bathroom. The cold water wouldn't run.

"Where's a wrench?" asked Mr. Pudgins, sticking his head out of the door and calling to me.

"You'd better call a plumber. Mother's written his name down on that little book on the telephone stand."

"Nonsense!" he answered. "I can handle this myself. Where's a wrench?"

I showed him where the wrench was, and he clumped down into the basement. Awful noises—banging, clanging, whooshing noises came out of the basement. Then Mr. Pudgins came upstairs looking very satisfied. "I guess that fixed it," he said, rubbing his hands together. "Is it all right, Janey?" he called.

We could hear the water running and excited squeals from the bathroom. "All's well," said Mr. Pudgins and sat down to smoke his pipe. "Might as well let them play awhile and cool off."

I had just finished the sign that said "Cold Drink 5¢" when I heard Mr. Pudgins say in a

horrified voice, "For goodness sakes!" I ran into the house. Something was up.

When I saw Janey and Pete, I just stared. They were a pale purple all over—hair, cheeks, stomach, legs. Back and forth they paraded, as if they had a fancy costume on.

"What happened to them?" I gasped.

"I was wondering the same thing myself," said Mr. Pudgins. He got up, and we followed him to the bathroom. The tub was filled with some purple stuff.

"What's in that tub?" said Mr. Pudgins sternly.

"I don't know," said Janey. "It just whooshed right out of the faucet."

"Good to drink, too," said Petey.

I turned on the tap, and a purple liquid gushed out. I stuck my finger in the stuff and tasted it. "Ummmmm. It is good—grape pop."

Mr. Pudgins tried a bit and smiled. "Not bad at all."

"I'm going to run that into pitchers and sell it just like that. Boy, what luck! Try the washbowl, Janey."

And she did. Out came, not purple stuff, but orange. And that tasted like orange pop. In fact, it was orange pop. I almost knocked Petey down running to the kitchen. There the cold-water faucet ran lime pop. "Down to the basement, kids," I yelled. And we tore downstairs. Janey turned on the faucet in the washtub and out gushed a brown drink.

Pete tasted it and grinned. "Root beer," he yelled. "This is my place. I'm going to drink here."

"Everybody get a pitcher and fill it with a different pop," I shouted. "Watch our business grow." And away we tore. But Mr. Pudgins caught Petey and Jane, and made them put on sunsuits. They really attracted people. Everyone who walked by our house wanted to know how the youngsters got purple. So while we told them about the faucets in our house, they drank lots of glasses of root beer, orange pop, limeade, and grape pop. Business was wonderful.

Even some of the mothers came to buy our drinks by the quart. By then, though, Janey and Pete had disappeared, so the parents didn't get to see their new color. Dinner was certainly different, too. The potatoes had been boiled in orange pop, and they had a very different flavor. For a change, Mr. Pudgins had cooked the carrots in the limeade, and our lettuce had been washed in the grape pop. Only the meat looked perfectly normal.

"Yummmm," said Petey. "I like these potatoes." He hadn't eaten any potatoes for months, but he just dived into those orange-colored ones.

"And I like the grape-pop salad," said Janey. "Lettuce and grape pop is delicious."

"Say, even these limeade carrots are good. I bet nobody in town is having a dinner like this," I said.

"I daresay you are absolutely right," said Mr. Pudgins, eating quietly and quickly. "Would you like some more root beer?" asked Mr. Pudgins. We had decided to have root beer as our drink, since there was no cold water. And to finish our meal we had cookies and popsicles, any flavor we wanted. We had made them from our pop. Oh, that was the best meal we had ever had. When it was over, though, Mr. Pudgins looked very thoughtful. "Now," he said, "I must go down to the basement and see just what I did wrong."

"Oh no, Mr. Pudgins," begged Janey, "please don't make the faucets run water. We like it this way."

"I want my root beer," wailed Petey. He looked ready to cry. We all felt pretty sad.

"There are a lot of milk bottles in the kitchen," said Mr. Pudgins. "Why don't you each fill two bottles with your favorite kind of drink and put them in the refrigerator. That should be enough for a long while."

It was pretty hard for me to decide on my favorite flavors. But not for Pete. He clumped right downstairs and got two quarts of root beer. Janey decided on one grape pop and one orange. I finally took a quart of limeade and one of grape pop. Gosh, that stuff was good! Then from the basement came an awful banging and clanging. The pipes rattled. They gurgled. Then it was quiet. I ran to the faucet in the kitchen and turned it on. Nothing but water. The bathtub faucet? Nothing but water. Only the washbowl seemed to run a little orange now and then.

Mr. Pudgins insisted that Petey and Jane have a bath and get the purple off of them. They didn't want to at first, but when they thought about it, they knew that Mom would be mad if she found they had been bathing in grape pop.

The house was all quiet when Mother and Dad came home. After Mr. Pudgins had left, I heard them in the kitchen. "My heavens, Jack, look at all the pop in the refrigerator. Bottles and bottles of the stuff."

"Good heavens!" came Dad's voice. "Where did it come from?"

"I suppose Johnny had a sale. I guess it can't hurt them," said Mother. I smiled to myself in the dark. Wouldn't they be surprised if they knew the truth, though? Then from the bathroom came Mother's voice again. "Jack, I've told you over and over to call that plumber. He's just got to check the rust in the pipes. The cold water is colored with orange."

I wanted to tell her it was really orange pop, but I was too sleepy. I decided to wait until morning. And in the morning I decided she wouldn't believe me. Sometimes after that the neighbors kidded Mother about letting her youngsters take a bath in grape pop, but she only laughed. She knew that they really hadn't.

A WIZARD OF EARTHSEA

Ursula K. Le Guin

A Wizard of Earthsea is exceptionally well written. Ursula Le Guin effectively uses cadence and language that complement her serious fantasy. From the first few pages the reader is aware that he has entered another world. The believability of that world's concerns and its social and philosophical laws never falters. The reader is left with the hope that there will be more novels of Ged's experiences.

The ending may confuse the reader unable to sense the allegorical nature of the conflict between Ged and the "thing" he calls forth. However, the mature child who enjoys fantasy could ask for nothing more: a believable world, an interesting, rounded main character, exciting and suspenseful action, and a valid theme.

At all these studies Ged was apt, and within a month was bettering lads who had been a year at Roke before him. Especially the tricks of illusion came to him so easily that it seemed he had been born knowing them and needed only to be reminded. The Master Hand was a gentle and light-hearted old man, who had endless delight in the wit and beauty of the crafts he taught; Ged soon felt no awe of him, but asked him for this spell and that spell, and always the Master smiled and showed him what he wanted. But one day, having it in mind to put Jasper to shame at last, Ged said to the Master Hand in the Court of Seeming, "Sir, all these charms are much the same; knowing one, you know them all. And as soon as the spell-weaving ceases, the illusion vanishes. Now if I make a pebble into a diamond—" and he did so with a word and a flick of his wrist— "what must I do to make that diamond remain diamond? How is the changing-spell locked, and made to last?"

The Master Hand looked at the jewel that glittered on Ged's palm, bright as the prize of a dragon's hoard. The old Master murmured one word, "Tolk," and there lay the pebble, no jewel but a rough grey bit of rock. The Master took it and held it out on his own hand. "This is a rock; tolk in the True Speech," he said, looking mildly up at Ged now. "A bit of the stone of which Roke Isle is made, a little bit of the dry land on which men live. It is itself. It is part of the world. By the Illusion-Change you can make it look like a diamond—or a flower or a fly or an eye or a flame—" The rock flickered from shape to shape as he named them, and returned to rock. "But that is mere seeming. Illusion fools the beholder's senses; it makes him see and hear and feel that

the thing is changed. But it does not change the thing. To change this rock into a jewel, you must change its true name. And to do that, my son, even to so small a scrap of the world, is to change the world. It can be done. Indeed it can be done. It is the art of the Master Changer, and you will learn it, when you are ready to learn it. But you must not change one thing, one pebble, one grain of sand, until you know what good and evil will follow on that act. The world is in balance, in Equilibrium. A wizard's power of Changing and of Summoning can shake the balance of the world. It is dangerous, that power. It is most perilous. It must follow knowledge, and serve need. To light a candle is to cast a shadow. . . ."

He looked down at the pebble again. "A rock is a good thing, too, you know," he said, speaking less gravely. "If the Isles of Earthsea were all made of diamond, we'd lead a hard life here. Enjoy illusions, lad, and let the rocks be rocks." He smiled, but Ged left dissatisfied. Press a mage for his secrets and he would always talk, like Ogion, about balance, and danger, and the dark. But surely a wizard, one who had gone past these childish tricks of illusion to the true arts of Summoning and Change, was powerful enough to do what he pleased, and balance the world as seemed best to him, and drive back darkness with his own light.

In the corridor he met Jasper, who, since Ged's accomplishments began to be praised about the School, spoke to him in a way that seemed more friendly, but was more scoffing. "You look gloomy, Sparrowhawk," he said now, "did your juggling-charms go wrong?"

Seeking as always to put himself on equal footing with Jasper, Ged answered the question ignoring its ironic tone. "I'm sick of juggling," he said, "sick of these illusion-tricks, fit only to amuse idle lords in their castles and Domains. The only true magic they've taught me yet on Roke is making werelight, and some weatherworking. The rest is mere foolery."

"Even foolery is dangerous," said Jasper, "in the hands of a fool."

At that Ged turned as if he had been slapped, and took a step towards Jasper; but the older boy smiled as if he had not intended any insult, nodded his head in his stiff, graceful way, and went on.

Standing there with rage in his heart, looking after Jasper, Ged swore to himself to outdo his rival, and not in some mere illusion-match but in a test of power. He would prove himself, and humiliate Jasper. He would not let the fellow stand there looking down at him, graceful, disdainful, hateful.

Ged did not stop to think why Jasper might hate him. He only knew why he hated Jasper. The other prentices had soon learned they could seldom match themselves against Ged either in sport or in earnest, and they said of him, some in praise and some in spite, "He's a wizard born, he'll never let you beat him." Jasper alone neither praised him nor avoided him, but simply looked down at him, smiling slightly. And therefore Jasper stood alone as his rival, who must be put to shame.

He did not see, or would not see, that in this rivalry, which he clung to and fostered as part of his own pride, there was anything of the danger, the darkness, of which the Master Hand had mildly warned him.

When he was not moved by pure rage, he knew very well that he was as yet no match for Jasper, or any of the older boys, and so he kept at his work and went on as usual. At the end of summer the work was slackened somewhat, so there was more time for sport: spell-boat races down in the harbor, feats of illusion in the courts of the Great House, and in the long evenings, in the groves, wild games of hide-and-seek where hiders and seeker were both invisible and only voices moved laughing and calling among the trees, following and dodging the quick, faint werelights. Then as autumn came they set to their tasks afresh, practising new magic. So Ged's first months at Roke went by fast, full of passions and wonders.

* * *

THE LOOSING OF THE SHADOW

That spring Ged saw little of either Vetch or Jasper, for they being sorcerers studied now with the Master Patterner in the secrecy of the Immanent Grove, where no prentice might set foot. Ged stayed in the Great House, working with the Masters at all the skills practised by sorcerers, those who work magic but carry no staff: windbringing, weatherworking, finding and binding, and the arts of spellsmiths and spellwrights, tellers, chanters, healalls and herbalists. At night alone in his sleeping-cell, a little ball of werelight burning above the book in place of lamp or candle, he studied the Further Runes and the Runes of Éa, which are used in the Great Spells. All these crafts came easy to him, and it was rumored among the students that this Master or that had said that the Gontish lad was the quickest student that had ever been at Roke, and tales grew up concerning the otak, which was said to be a disguised spirit who whispered wisdom in Ged's ear, and it was even said that the Archmage's raven had hailed Ged at his arrival as "Archmage to be." Whether or not they believed such stories, and whether or not they liked Ged, most of his companions admired him, and were eager to follow him when the rare wild mood came over him and he joined them to lead their games on the lengthening evenings of spring. But for the most part he was all work and pride and temper, and held himself apart. Among them all, Vetch being absent, he had no friend, and never knew he wanted one.

He was fifteen, very young to learn any of the High Arts of wizard or mage, those who carry the staff; but he was so quick to learn all the arts of illusion that the Master Changer, himself a young man, soon began to teach him apart from the others, and to tell him about the true Spells of Shaping. He explained how, if a thing is really to be changed into another thing, it must be renamed for as long as the spell lasts, and he told how this affects the names and natures of things surrounding the transformed thing. He spoke of the perils of changing, above all when the wizard transforms his own shape and thus is liable to be caught in his own spell. Little by little, drawn on by the boy's sureness of understanding, the young

Master began to do more than merely tell him of these mysteries. He taught him first one and then another of the Great Spells of Change, and he gave him the Book of Shaping to study. This he did without knowledge of the Archmage, and unwisely, yet he meant no harm.

Ged worked also with the Master Summoner now, but that Master was a stern man, aged and hardened by the deep and somber wizardry he taught. He dealt with no illusion, only true magic, the summoning of such energies as light, and heat, and the force that draws the magnet, and those forces men perceive as weight, form, color, sound: real powers, drawn from the immense fathomless energies of the universe, which no man's spells or uses could exhaust or unbalance. The weatherworker's and seamaster's calling upon wind and water were crafts already known to his pupils, but it was he who showed them why the true wizard uses such spells only at need, since to summon up such earthly forces is to change the earth of which they are a part. "Rain on Roke may be drouth in Osskil," he said, "and a calm in the East Reach may be storm and ruin in the West, unless you know what you are about."

As for the calling of real things and living people, and the raising up of spirits of the dead, and the invocations of the Unseen, those spells which are the height of the Summoner's art and the mage's power, those he scarcely spoke of to them. Once or twice Ged tried to lead him to talk a little of such mysteries, but the Master was silent, looking at him long and grimly, till Ged grew uneasy and said no more.

Sometimes indeed he was uneasy working even such lesser spells as the Summoner taught him. There were certain runes on certain pages of the Lore-Book that seemed familiar to him, though he did not remember in what book he had ever seen them before. There were certain phrases that must be said in spells of Summoning that he did not like to say. They made him think, for an instant, of shadows in a dark room, of a shut door and shadows reaching out to him from the corner by the door. Hastily he put such thoughts or memories aside and went on. These moments of fear and darkness, he said to himself, were the shadows merely of his ignorance. The more he learned, the less he would have to fear, until

finally in his full power as Wizard he need fear nothing in the world, nothing at all.

In the second month of that summer all the school gathered again at the Great House to celebrate the Moon's Night and the Long Dance, which that year fell together as one festival of two nights, which happens but once in fifty-two years. All the first night, the shortest night of full moon of the year, flutes played out in the fields, and the narrow streets of Thwil were full of drums and torches, and the sounding of singing went out over the moonlit waters of Roke Bay. As the sun rose next morning the Chanters of Roke began to sing the long DEED OF ERRETH-AKBE, which tells how the white Towers of Havnor were built, and of Erreth-Akbe's journeys from the Old Island, Éa, through all the Archipelago and the Reaches, until at last in the uttermost West Reach on the edge of the Open Sea he met the dragon Orm; and his bones in shattered armor lie among the dragon's bones on the shore of lonely Selidor, but his sword set atop the highest tower of Havnor still burns red in the sunset above the Inmost Sea. When the chant was finished the Long Dance began. Townsfolk and Masters and students and farmers all together, men and women, danced in the warm dust and dusk down all the roads of Roke to the sea-beaches, to the beat of drums and drone of pipes and flutes. Straight out into the sea they danced, under the moon one night past full, and the music was lost in the breakers' sound. As the east grew light they came back up the beaches and the roads, the drums silent and only the flutes playing soft and shrill. So it was done on every island of the Archipelago that night: one dance, one music binding together the sea-divided lands.

When the Long Dance was over most people slept the day away, and gathered again at evening to eat and drink. There was a group of young fellows, prentices and sorcerers, who had brought their supper out from the refectory to hold private feast in a courtyard of the Great House: Vetch, Jasper, and Ged were there, and six or seven others, and some young lads released briefly from the Isolate Tower, for this festival had brought even Kurremkarmerruk out. They were all eating and laughing and playing such tricks out of pure frolic as might be the marvel of a king's court. One boy had lighted the court with a hundred stars of werelight, colored like jewels, that swung in a slow netted procession between them and the real stars; and a pair of boys were playing bowls with balls of green flame and bowling-pins that leaped and hopped away as the ball came near; and all the while Vetch sat cross-legged, eating roast chicken, up in mid-air. One of the younger boys tried to pull him down to earth, but Vetch merely drifted up a little higher, out of reach, and sat calmly smiling on the air. Now and then he tossed away a chicken bone, which turned to an owl and flew hooting among the netted star-lights. Ged shot breadcrumb arrows after the owls and brought them down, and when they touched the ground there they lay, bone and crumb, all illusion gone. Ged also tried to join Vetch up in the middle of the air, but lacking the key of the spell he had to flap his arms to keep aloft, and they were all laughing at his flights and flaps and bumps. He kept up his foolishness for the laughter's sake, laughing with them, for after those two long nights of dance and moonlight and music and magery he was in a fey and wild mood, ready for whatever might come.

He came lightly down on his feet just beside Jasper at last, and Jasper, who never laughed aloud, moved away saying, "The Sparrowhawk that can't fly . . ."

"Is jasper a precious stone?" Ged returned, grinning. "O Jewel among sorcerers, O Gem of Havnor, sparkle for us!"

The lad that had set the lights dancing sent one down to dance and glitter about Jasper's head. Not quite as cool as usual, frowning, Jasper brushed the light away and snuffed it out with one gesture. "I am sick of boys and noise and foolishness," he said.

"You're getting middle-aged, lad," Vetch remarked from above.

"If silence and gloom is what you want," put in one of the younger boys, "you could always try the Tower."

Ged said to him, "What is it you want, then, Jasper?"

"I want the company of my equals," Jasper said. "Come on, Vetch. Leave the prentices to their toys."

Ged turned to face Jasper. "What do sorcerers have that prentices lack?" he enquired. His voice was quiet, but all the other boys suddenly fell

still, for in his tone as in Jasper's the spite between them now sounded plain and clear as steel coming out of a sheath.

"Power," Jasper said.

"I'll match your power act for act."

"You challenge me?"

"I challenge you."

Vetch had dropped down to the ground, and now he came between them, grim of face. "Duels in sorcery are forbidden to us, and well you know it. Let this cease!"

Both Ged and Jasper stood silent, for it was true they knew the law of Roke, and they also knew that Vetch was moved by love, and themselves by hate. Yet their anger was balked, not cooled. Presently, moving a little aside as if to be heard by Vetch alone, Jasper spoke, with his cool smile: "I think you'd better remind your goatherd friend again of the law that protects him. He looks sulky. I wonder, did he really think I'd accept a challenge from him? a fellow who smells of goats, a prentice who doesn't know the First Change?"

"Jasper," said Ged, "what do you know of what I know?"

For an instant, with no word spoken that any heard, Ged vanished from their sight, and where he had stood a great falcon hovered, opening its hooked beak to scream: for one instant, and then Ged stood again in the flickering torchlight, his dark gaze on Jasper.

Jasper had taken a step backward, in astonishment; but now he shrugged and said one word: "Illusion."

The others muttered. Vetch said, "That was not illusion. It was true change. And enough. Jasper, listen—"

"Enough to prove that he sneaked a look in the Book of Shaping behind the Master's back: what then? Go on, Goatherd. I like this trap you're building for yourself. The more you try to prove yourself my equal, the more you show yourself for what you are."

At that, Vetch turned from Jasper, and said very softly to Ged, "Sparrowhawk, will you be a man and drop this now—come with me—"

Ged looked at his friend and smiled, but all he said was, "Keep Hoeg for me a little while, will you?" He put into Vetch's hands the little otak, which as usual had been riding on his shoulder, its great bright eyes always on its master.

"Now," Ged said to Jasper, quietly as before, "what are you going to do to prove yourself my superior, Jasper?"

"I don't have to do anything, Goatherd. Yet I will. I will give you a chance—an opportunity. Envy eats you like a worm in an apple. Let's let out the worm. Once by Roke Knoll you boasted that Gontish wizards don't play games. Come to Roke Knoll now and show us what it is they do instead. And afterward, maybe I will show you a little sorcery."

"Yes, I should like to see that," Ged answered. The younger boys, used to seeing his black temper break out at the least hint of slight or insult, watched him in wonder at his coolness now. Vetch watched him not in wonder, but with growing fear. He tried to intervene again, but Jasper said, "Come, keep out of this, Vetch. What will you do with the chance I give you, Goatherd? Will you show us an illusion, a fireball, a charm to cure goats with the mange?"

"What would you like me to do, Jasper?"

The older lad shrugged. "Summon up a spirit from the dead, for all I care!"

"I will."

"You will not." Jasper looked straight at him, rage suddenly flaming out over his disdain. "You will not. You cannot. You brag and brag—"

"By my name, I will do it!"

They all stood utterly motionless for a moment.

Breaking away from Vetch who would have held him back by main force, Ged strode out of the courtyard, not looking back. The dancing werelights overhead died out, sinking down. Jasper hesitated a second, then followed after Ged. And the rest came straggling behind, in silence, curious and afraid.

The slopes of Roke Knoll went up dark into the darkness of summer night before moonrise. The presence of that hill where many wonders had been worked was heavy, like a weight in the air about them. As they came onto the hillside they thought of how the roots of it were deep, deeper than the sea, reaching down even to the old, blind, secret fires at the world's core. They stopped on the east slope. Stars hung over the

black grass above them on the hill's crest. No wind blew.

Ged went a few paces up the slope away from the others and turning said in a clear voice, "Jasper! Whose spirit shall I call?"

"Call whom you like. None will listen to you." Jasper's voice shook a little, with anger perhaps. Ged answered him softly, mockingly, "Are you afraid?"

He did not even listen for Jasper's reply, if he made one. He no longer cared about Jasper. Now that they stood on Roke Knoll, hate and rage were gone, replaced by utter certainty. He need envy no one. He knew that his power, this night, on this dark enchanted ground, was greater than it had ever been, filling him till he trembled with the sense of strength barely kept in check. He knew now that Jasper was far beneath him, had been sent perhaps only to bring him here tonight, no rival but a mere servant of Ged's destiny. Under his feet he felt the hillroots going down and down into the dark, and over his head he saw the dry, far fires of the stars. Between, all things were his to order, to command. He stood at the center of the world.

"Don't be afraid," he said, smiling. "I'll call a woman's spirit. You need not fear a woman. Elfarran I will call, the fair lady of the DEED OF ENLAD."

"She died a thousand years ago, her bones lie afar under the Sea of Éa, and maybe there never was such a woman."

"Do years and distances matter to the dead? Do the Songs lie?" Ged said with the same gentle mockery, and then saying, "Watch the air between my hands," he turned away from the others and stood still.

In a great slow gesture he stretched out his arms, the gesture of welcome that opens an invocation. He began to speak.

He had read the runes of this Spell of Summoning in Ogion's book, two years and more ago, and never since had seen them. In darkness he had read them then. Now in this darkness it was as if he read them again on the page open before him in the night. But now he understood what he read, speaking it aloud word after word, and he saw the markings of how the spell must be woven with the sound of the voice and the motion of body and hand.

The other boys stood watching, not speaking, not moving unless they shivered a little: for the great spell was beginning to work. Ged's voice was soft still, but changed, with a deep singing in it, and the words he spoke were not known to them. He fell silent. Suddenly the wind rose roaring in the grass. Ged dropped to his knees and called out aloud. Then he fell forward as if to embrace earth with his outstretched arms, and when he rose he held something dark in his straining hands and arms, something so heavy that he shook with effort getting to his feet. The hot wind whined in the black tossing grasses on the hill. If the stars shone now none saw them.

The words of the enchantment hissed and mumbled on Ged's lips, and then he cried out aloud and clearly, "Elfarran!"

Again he cried the name, "Elfarran!"

And the third time, "Elfarran!"

The shapeless mass of darkness he had lifted split apart. It sundered, and a pale spindle of light gleamed between his opened arms, a faint oval reaching from the ground up to height of his raised hands. In the oval of light for a moment there moved a form, a human shape: a tall woman looking back over her shoulder. Her face was beautiful, and sorrowful, and full of fear.

Only for a moment did the spirit glimmer there. Then the sallow oval between Ged's arms grew bright. It widened and spread, a rent in the darkness of the earth and night, a ripping open of the fabric of the world. Through it blazed a terrible brightness. And through that bright misshapen breach clambered something like a clot of black shadow, quick and hideous, and it leaped straight out at Ged's face.

Staggering back under the weight of the thing, Ged gave a short, hoarse scream. The little otak watching from Vetch's shoulder, the animal that had no voice, screamed aloud also and leaped as if to attack.

Ged fell, struggling and writhing, while the bright rip in the world's darkness above him widened and stretched. The boys that watched fled, and Jasper bent down to the ground hiding his eyes from the terrible light. Vetch alone ran forward to his friend. So only he saw the lump of shadow that clung to Ged, tearing at his flesh. It was like a black beast, the size of a young child, though it seemed to swell and shrink; and it had

no head or face, only the four taloned paws with which it gripped and tore. Vetch sobbed with horror, yet he put out his hands to try to pull the thing away from Ged. Before he touched it, he was bound still, unable to move.

The intolerable brightness faded, and slowly the torn edges of the world closed together. Nearby a voice was speaking as softly as a tree whispers or a fountain plays.

Starlight began to shine again, and the grasses of the hillside were whitened with the light of the moon just rising. The night was healed. Restored and steady lay the balance of light and dark. The shadow-beast was gone. Ged lay sprawled on his back, his arms flung out as if they yet kept the wide gesture of welcome and invocation. His face was blackened with blood and there were great black stains on his shirt. The little otak cowered by his shoulder, quivering. And above him stood an old man whose cloak glimmered pale in the moonrise: the Archmage Nemmerle.

The end of Nemmerle's staff hovered silvery above Ged's breast. Once gently it touched him over the heart, once on the lips, while Nemmerle whispered. Ged stirred, and his lips parted gasping for breath. Then the old Archmage lifted the staff, and set it to earth, and leaned heavily on it with bowed head, as if he had scarcely strength to stand.

Vetch found himself free to move. Looking around, he saw that already others were there, the Masters Summoner and Changer. An act of great wizardry is not worked without arousing such men, and they had ways of coming very swiftly when need called, though none had been so swift as the Archmage. They now sent for help, and some who came went with the Archmage, while others, Vetch among them, carried Ged to the chambers of the Master Herbal.

All night long the Summoner stayed on Roke Knoll, keeping watch. Nothing stirred there on the hillside where the stuff of the world had been torn open. No shadow came crawling through moonlight seeking the rent through which it might clamber back into its own domain. It had fled from Nemmerle, and from the mighty spellwalls that surround and protect Roke Island, but it was in the world now. In the world, somewhere, it hid. If Ged had died that night it might have tried to find the doorway he had opened, and follow him into death's realm, or slip back into whatever place it had come from; for this the Summoner waited on Roke Knoll. But Ged lived.

They had laid him abed in the healing-chamber, and the Master Herbal tended the wounds he had on his face and throat and shoulder. They were deep, ragged, and evil wounds. The black blood in them would not stanch, welling out even under the charms and the cobweb-wrapped perriot leaves laid upon them. Ged lay blind and dumb in fever like a stick in a slow fire, and there was no spell to cool what burned him.

THE GAMMAGE CUP

Carol Kendall

The Gammage Cup is a well-written fantasy that subtly deals with individual differences, social ostracism, and noncomformity. These problems are not imposed on the book but logically grow out of a dramatic story and believable characters, so the reader never feels the author is trying to teach or preach.

Nine- and ten-year-old children enjoy The Gammage Cup, *and even junior high students read it with interest because of its relevance to their own lives. In* The Whisper of Glocken *Miss Kendall continues the adventures of these people.*

In the long far off
Of the land Outside
Brave Minnipins lived
And some of them died.

Lost are their treasures, buried deep.

Till the Dry Time came
And the world was sand—
Then Minnipins fled
To a wetter land.

Lost are their treasures; in the ground they sleep.

And nobody knew
That the Minnipins went
To the land of the River,
Where they live content.

Lost are their treasures, and the secret they keep.
　　　　　　　—Gummy, *Scribbles*

(Collected Works)

It was quite untrue that the Minnipins, or Small Ones, were a lost people, for *they* knew exactly where they were. They dwelt along the banks of the Watercress River in the Land Between the Mountains, where they fished and tended their famous water-cress beds and grew their own peculiar reeds, which could be milled into flour or used for thatching or pulped into paper or woven into cloaks of moth-wing softness.

It was a snug and secure valley, completely surrounded by unclimbable mountains, so perfectly made for stay-at-home, peace-loving Minnipins that it was no wonder they were to be found there. There were twelve villages in all, starting with Watersplash at the very head of the valley where the freshets foamed down the cliffs of old Snowdrift Mountain, and ending with Water Gap, where the waters of the river roared through the very heart of the craggy mountain known as Frostbite.

It was through this tunnel in Frostbite (according to legend) that the only remaining Minnipins on earth had traveled, under their leader Gammage, to reach the green valley in those old far-off days of the great Dry Time. The river was a mere muddy trickle then, like all the rivers of the land. It was said (by Walter the Earl, who made a study of such things from a few old moldy parchments in his possession) that the Minnipins were running for their lives from a savage band known as Mushrooms, or the Hairless Ones, when they entered the long tunnel, yanking their two-wheeled carts after them. They were only saved from being spitted and roasted for the Mushrooms' dinner by a miraculous rain, which filled the river bed after they had come through the tunnel and washed out their pursuers. Once the river closed the underground passage, there was no way in or out of the Land Between the Mountains, except for high-flying birds—and Fooley the Balloonist, of course. But Fooley came along some time later, and Fooley was special.

One of the twelve villages was Slipper-on-the-Water, which got its name (so the legend went on) when those first Minnipins paddled their rudely made boats up the Watercress to explore their new valley. It was at this spot that Gammage lost his left slipper overboard. For three days and three nights it floated on the water in the selfsame spot, never moving with the current. Clearly, this was a symbol not to be ignored. So it was that ten of the Minnipins never got to the head of the valley at all. They stayed at Slipper-on-the-Water, building their cottages of river clay and reed thatch, establishing their water-cress beds, and raising their small families. But before Gammage and the others traveled on to found other villages along the Watercress, each of the ten drank deeply from the precious Cup of Wisdom that Gammage carried wrapped in silk and slung over his shoulder.

So much and no more was known of the far past, for no real records had been kept during the early ages. At least, none had ever been discovered, though Walter the Earl was convinced that they existed. His several fragments of ancient parchment hinted, he said (nobody else could decipher the old writing), of treasures buried in the village, possibly in his own garden. His cottage had the oldest foundation of any in Slipper-on-the-Water and was believed to have been the first meetinghouse in the village. So Walter the Earl dug up his garden and probed at the walls of

his house in search of ancient scrolls and treasure, and occasionally buttonholed folk to talk about Historical Facts, while more sensible Minnipins worked at their practical jobs and, when they thought of Walter the Earl at all, considered him a dry old bore.

Now, in this year of Gammage 880, though Slipper-on-the-Water had the usual river-clay cottages with reed thatch, lived in by the usual Minnipins and Minnipin children, it was by no means an ordinary village.

For one thing, there were those few villagers known as the Periods. Periods were special—everyone agreed to that. Not only did they have a special way of spelling their names, but they wore a special air of dignity, and, of course, they held most of the village offices. It had been this way in Slipper-on-the-Water ever since the time of Fooley the Balloonist, for the Periods were the descendants of Fooley, and that explained everything as far as the villagers were concerned.

It was just four hundred and forty years ago that Fooley, afterward known as Fooley the Magnificent or The Great Fooley, had sailed away over the cliffs of Snowdrift in a balloon of reed silk and woven willow, the first, last, and only balloon ever constructed in the Land Between the Mountains. Even more miraculous to ground-loving Minnipins, he had sailed back just one hundred and twenty-nine days later, bringing with him a case full of curiosities from the Land Beyond the Mountains. But as though to underline the moral that Minnipins were meant to stay at home, the balloon contraption had burst when he landed, scattering its contents, including Fooley, over several Minnipin acres of ground. When Fooley was picked up, he had no recollection of what he had seen in the Land Beyond the Mountains. If it hadn't been for the curiosities and the queer book he had filled with notes, Fooley would in time have become a misty legend, and Slipper-on-the-Water only number ten of the twelve very ordinary Minnipin villages spread along the banks of the Watercress.

But as it was, the Periods, descendants of that long-ago adventurer, were special. Though Minnipins in general never strayed far from their homes (always excepting the mayors of the villages, who once a year made the long trip to Watersplash for the Big Meeting), the fame of these descendants had gone up and down the valley. Periods were like that.

But it wasn't only the Periods who made Slipper-on-the-Water different. There were three Minnipins in the village who were usually referred to by their neighbors as "Oh, Them." "They" were not considered respectable; They were a law among themselves; They lived alone instead of marrying and raising families, as normal Minnipins did; worst of all, They flaunted cloaks of such an outlandish hue that it was shaming to be seen talking to them. Furthermore, the "Oh, Thems" didn't properly work at anything: Walter the Earl spent his time digging holes in the ground in his ridiculous search for hidden treasure; Curley Green was usually to be seen sitting on her stool in a corner of the market place, blobbing pictures onto stretched reed-paper, and Gummy—well, Gummy was bone-idle.

Gummy was never seen doing anything but wearing a dreamy look along with his sun-colored cloak and peaked hat. He disappeared for hours at a time in his tiny boat, but where he went and what he did nobody knew, though there were rumors aplenty. Only two things were surely known about Gummy: he was overfond of childish pranks, and he made rhymes. Not proper poems, such as the one brought back by Fooley, now hanging in the museum, but scribbles—nonsense rhymes about rain and birds and flowers and the wind, and they bubbled out of him as water bubbles from a spring.

Then, of course, there was Muggles. Muggles couldn't be called one of "Them," exactly, but she wasn't just an ordinary villager, either. While it was true that she dutifully wore the Minnipin green cloak and brown-weave dress, it cannot be denied that upon occasion she tied up her middle with a vivid orange sash.

Besides being the caretaker of the Fooley curiosities in the museum, she was a candymaker, which was a good steady sort of thing to be, but on the other hand she distressed the tidy Minnipin housewives by keeping her house in a deplorable muddle. She was a collector of odds and ends and bits and pieces (another good trait), but they overflowed her tiny cottage until it was next to impossible to step inside, and that was disgraceful. There had been complaints, of course, and

only last year the mayor himself had begged her to tidy up, like a good Minnipin. Ever anxious to please, Muggles had tried hard, but the more she put away, the less able was she to find anything. Gradually, the articles she had neatly folded into cupboards slipped back into their old places on the floor, closets disgorged their precise piles of oddments, and drawers leaked their contents, until once more Muggles knew exactly where everything was.

So Muggles was something of a trial to Slipper-on-the-Water, but it was agreed that there was no real harm in her. She was always ready to oblige, always in a good humor, and if she was a little simple-minded, why, she could hardly be blamed for that. Being simple-minded never interfered with her candy recipes or the job she had been given at the museum.

The museum! Muggles awoke with the panicky feeling that she had overslept. She shot out of bed like a surfacing trout and then stood blinking in the chill half-light of her little room. *How very odd,* she thought in her sleep-fogged mind. *How very odd that it is still so dark. What can have happened to the sun?* Groping her way to the window, which overlooked the market place, she peered anxiously through the slatted reed shade. There had been rain during the night, for the cobblestones gleamed wet in the dim flare of the reed-light still burning fitfully in the center of the market place. But why was the sun so late in appearing, today of all days, when the mayor was coming home from the Big Meeting? Still convinced that she had overslept, Muggles stood winking and blinking at the deserted cobblestones. Where had everybody got to? Why wasn't the square full of green-cloaked figures hustling and bustling about to make ready for the mayor's return?

Then with a sigh of relief she saw a line of golden fire on top of the Sunset Mountains in the west. Why, the sun must be just rising—only there was something wrong about that, too, wasn't there? Suddenly she heard the pat-pat of soft woven slippers on the cobblestones of the square. Rubbing her blurred eyes, she made out the figure of Gummy, one of Them. He was coming from the Street Going to the River, and stumbling across the market place as though he had just got off a dizzy-swing at the fun fair. His yellow cloak drooped from his shoulders, and his peaked hat looked wilted. In the middle of the market place he stopped and stared up at the orange fire on the mountains for several moments before he staggered on. Muggles watched him going toward his own shabby cottage. Then he stopped again and veered to the right. A moment later he had gone into Walter the Earl's house.

Muggles blinked and stared and blinked again. Odder and odder. The reed-light continued to flicker, casting its weird shadows over the cottages around the square and the four public buildings in the center.

The door through which Gummy had gone opened once more, and he came out, this time accompanied by Walter the Earl, his gold-embroidered cloak slung around his shoulders. They both looked up at the Sunset Mountains—but now the fire had disappeared! While Muggles was pondering this further oddity, Gummy and Walter the Earl moved back toward Walter the Earl's house where they spent some minutes inspecting the mounds of earth in the garden. Finally, Gummy trudged off to his cottage, and Walter the Earl picked up a spade and plunged it into the ground in a spot close up to the house itself. And still the reed-light flickered eerily over the wet cobblestones of the empty market place. . . .

Muggles stumbled back to her bed, struggling to make sense out of this very queer morning. It was not until her feet grew toasty warm under the comforter that the explanation occurred to her. *What a ninny I am*, she thought with a drowsy laugh. *It's not the sun that's late, it's me that's early. I was having a dream. I might have known when I saw the sun rising in the west that it was a dream. But what a queer dream to have, and it seemed so real.*

Yawning mightily, she snuggled deeper into her feather bed and let sleep creep back into her body.

* * *

[*Muggles was not having a dream; the fire over the mountains is the first sign that a great danger threatens the Minnipins. The treasure Walter the Earl has been searching for suddenly is found along with more parchment records. These play an important role in combating the ancient enemy. The Periods, however, do not believe there is danger and are angry with Muggles, Walter the Earl, Curley Green, and Gummy.*

—M.A.N.]

When she left the museum at last, Etc. had already performed the ritual of striking fire to the reed-light. Muggles hurried past it on the far side to escape its fumes. The market place was empty except for herself and—

A sodden, muddy figure staggered from the Street Going to the River into the square. He wavered a few steps farther and then, with a little cry, fell into a heap and did not rise.

"Gummy!" Muggles flew across the cobblestones to the huddle of yellow cloak. "Gummy, is it really you?"

He gave a groan and rolled over to stare glassily at the burning reed.

"Etc. lit a little light," he mumbled.

> *"Etc. lit a little light,*
> *And now we've got it every night.*
> *It may burn orange as new quince jelly,*
> *But let's admit it's rather smelly!"*

"Hush," said Muggles, looking fearfully over her shoulder. "What happened to you? Where have you been?"

Gummy's eyes flickered shut and then open again. "Fell overboard. Coming home from mountains. Almost . . . didn't make it. . . . Been . . . keeping watch . . . last two nights. . . ."

"Did you— What did you—Gummy!" She gave him a little shake as his eyes began to close again.

"Pocket . . . right-hand pocket."

Quickly, Muggles searched first one pocket, then the other. "No, there's nothing. Gummy! What was it?"

Gummy gave a groan. "Must have fallen out . . . in the river. Just a . . . half-burned twig . . ."

"Half-burned twig?" cried Muggles. "But what—?"

"It . . . it blew off the mountain."

She stared at him.

"Brought it home to prove to Co. Doesn't matter. . . . Wouldn't believe . . . anyway . . ."

Muggles half pulled, half carried Gummy inside her house.

After she had wrapped him in her comforter

and given him some soup and two cups of strong hot tea, he promptly fell asleep, curled up on her bed.

Muggles stood looking down at his white drawn face for a few minutes. *Not altogether undependable after all*, she thought. *It just depends on what you're depending on.*

> Curley had a little door,
> Its color was bright scarlet.
> It blazoned forth both night and day,
> By sun and moon and starlet.
> Till one dark night. . . .
>
> —Wm., *Uncompleted Poem*

It was fully dark now except for Etc.'s reed-light. Muggles blew out the candle and huddled before her fire where she could keep watch on the distant Sunset Mountains through the window.

Like fish being handed from a fishing boat and counted, her worries flopped one by one into her mind: Curley Green's scarlet door . . . the mutterings against Walter the Earl . . . Co.'s visit to the museum . . . the secret of the treasures in the vault . . . the words of the Seventeenth Earl—"It is my belief that such a one will appear when he is needed for the safety of his people." And underneath all these nagging, torturing worries lay the biggest one of all, that she hardly dared look at—the fires on the mountains. Fires on the mountains! Things—people—out there spying down upon the valley. Trying to get in. Gummy said they couldn't come over the Sunset Mountains, but how could he be sure? They had got up the other side, hadn't they? And even if they couldn't come over the cliffs at that place, who was to say there weren't other spots, farther up the valley, open to them? Muggles shuddered.

A small, secret, furtive sound on the still night air brought her upright. Who would be in the market place at this hour? Forcing herself to stand up, she went to her door and softly opened it. There were no lights visible in any of the cottages, and the reed-light in the center of the market place had settled down to a soft glow, but there was enough illumination to make out a cloaked figure hurrying across the square. Muggles's eyes widened. It was certainly Geo., and he was carrying something. She stood and watched to see what he was about, while her wonderment

changed to indignation. When Geo. at last returned across the market place, Muggles quietly closed her door and leaned against it, thinking hard. Then, her lips set in a determined line, she lit the candle and stole across the room to extract the things she needed from various heaps and piles. When all was in readiness, she swung her door open and set to work.

At last she was finished, and she stepped back with a pleased smile. It was even more glorious than she had expected. She put her materials carefully away where they belonged, and sat down before the fire again. And though she was trembling a bit at her daring, the corners of her mouth curved into a satisfied smile.

> When something happens, something else always happens.
> —Muggles, *Maxims*

When the sun got up the next morning, Thatch had already placed his ladder against Fooley Hall and climbed up on the roof to start work. With his bundle of dried reeds on his back, he crawled along, whistling softly around the clove of garlic he always sucked as a remedy against chills, and counting in his head the number of gold pieces he would have by the end of the week.

When he reached the chimney, he stood up to survey the roofs still to be done in the new scalloped fringe—one goldbit for each. It was an encouraging sight, and Thatch's heart swelled with happiness. Roofs to the north of him, roofs to the west of him, roofs to the. . . . Perplexed, Thatch turned back to scan the houses on the west side of the market place. What was different about them this morning? What—? He clutched the chimney in astonishment.

Curley Green's door was as green as the greenest door on the square!

"*Well!*" said Thatch, shifting the garlic from one cheek to the other. He swept his gaze round the market place, at the rows of shining white houses and uniform green doors. Then he clutched the chimney again, his eyes almost popping out of his head. Across the square from Curley Green's door glowed a splotch of bright color. Thatch blinked and blinked again. It was Muggles's house, and her door was painted a vivid orange!

"*Well!*" said Thatch, and gaped so broadly that his garlic fell out and rolled down the roof unheeded.

Other folk had more to say when they discovered the changes wrought during the night. Small groups clustered together on the cobbles to whisper and glance sidelong at the two doors, broke up, and reclustered to whisper some more. Somebody—no one knew who—started a rumor going that Geo. the Official Village Painter knew more about Curley Green's painted door than Curley Green herself. When this news circulated itself among the clusters, there was a sound like a gobble of fish snapping at green flies.

Reedy, the basketmaker's wife, was indignant. "Right or wrong," said she, "it's Curley Green's door, and Geo. has no business meddling with it behind her back."

Bun, the baker's wife, was more cautious. "But Geo. being a Period. . . . Now, if it was somebody ordinary, like Dingle or Spill or Thatch, that did the painting, we should know at once it was wrong, but with Geo. being a Period . . . well, there's a difference, Reedy."

"That's right. There's a difference," Wove the Weaver agreed.

"Periods know what is right and what is wrong," said Dingle the Miller solemnly. "It has always been that way. Don't the Periods hold the high offices because of their wisdom?"

"Yes, yes!" everybody agreed.

The question settled, the clusters began to break up, but just then there was a new diversion. The door of Gummy's house opened, and Gummy stepped outside.

Instantly, every eye was riveted on him.

He set a pail down on his doorstone. With a carefree air, he produced a brush, dabbled it in the pail, cocked his head from side to side, and then, raising the dripping brush, he applied a broad stroke of yellow paint to his door.

On the west side of the square Walter the Earl stepped out on his doorstone and methodically began to paint his own door bright blue.

The tense silence of the watching villagers broke into a concerted gasp.

"How do they dare!" cried Bun.

"The Periods will never stand for it!"

"Stand for what?" demanded Scot., the town clerk's wife. She and Eng., followed by Wm. and Geo., pushed their way through the excited cluster. "If it's poor simple Muggles and her door, you needn't concern yourselves. . . ."

For answer, Fin Longtooth pointed first at Gummy's house, then at Walter the Earl's.

"Why, those—" Geo. started forward, his face aflame.

Wm. held on to him. "Ltd. said no more fuss," he warned.

"But they're cheating us of the Gammage Cup with every stroke!" Eng. cried shrilly.

The ordinary villagers, jolted by this new thought, began to grumble in indignation.

"Shouldn't be allowed, then," Fin Longtooth declared. "Now I remember when there was a bit of trouble over cutting down a family tree. . . ."

"Of course, it's *their* doors," Reedy pointed out.

"But it's *our* village!" cried Bun.

"They shouldn't be allowed to spoil our village!"

Geo. suddenly turned and made off for the mayor's house.

Ignoring his audience, Gummy covered the last bit of his door with paint and stepped back to admire the effect. Then he took his pail and brush and himself inside. Walter the Earl had already disappeared behind his bright blue door.

Unaware of these happenings, Muggles was just getting up. The night's vigil had been long and unrewarding, for there were no fires to be seen on the mountains, and at dawn she had fished an old comforter from the under-the-table heap and made a cozy bed by the fire.

When she woke up, Gummy had gone, leaving on her table a scribble.

> "*For picking me up*
> *And taking me in,*
> *For cheating the mice*
> *Of nibbling my chin*—
> THANKS!
>
> "*For the use of your bed*
> *And the soup and the tea,*
> *May you never regret*
> *What you've done for me.*
> THANKS!"

"I hope I won't," Muggles murmured. She made herself a pot of water-cress tea and three fish cakes and after restoring the old comforter to its proper place and otherwise making her house neat and tidy, she ventured forth. The brightness of her door as she swung it open made her wince. It was *very* orange by daylight. Still, nobody seemed to be bothering his head about it. She struck straight across the market place toward the museum.

A lot of villagers were clustered round the the lamppost where Geo. was putting up a hastily lettered sign. Muggles paused on the fringe of the crowd to read it.

Notis
First Spring Meeting
After Tee—Important

With three sharp raps of his tap hammer, Geo. nailed the notice securely to the post.

"And now," he crowed, stepping back, "we'll see about *Them!*"

> You never can tell
> From a Minnipin's hide
> What color he is
> Down deep inside.
>
> —Gummy, *Scribbles*
> (Collected Works)

There was no loitering over tea in Slipper-on-the-Water that afternoon. Fish cakes and water-cress were downed in a hurry, dishes washed even more hurriedly, and then, snatching up their stools, the villagers made their way to the market place to talk in whispering groups until time for the meeting to begin.

Only Muggles remained inside her house. In one hand she held her ordinary brown sash, in the other, her orange. She would have to decide very soon. . . .

There was a stir in the market place, and then the buzz of voices hushed. Ltd. had just emerged from the mayor's house and was walking in stately slowness across to the meetinghouse.

The brown or the orange . . . ?

Muggles peered out her window at the slowly moving throng following Ltd. Like a patch of sunset sky, Curley Green's scarlet cloak flamed at the doorway of the meetinghouse beside Mingy's patched green, and then was swallowed up. Muggles dropped one of the sashes on the floor and hurried out into the market place.

When Curley Green and Mingy slipped into the gloom of Fooley Hall, they placed their stools neatly in line with the others already there, and went up to the table to receive steaming mugs of water-cress punch and biscuits. But when they went back to their places, the stools which had been beside theirs had pointedly been removed, while the row behind was filling up rapidly.

"Good," said Mingy, not looking at Curley Green. "Plenty of elbowroom. Hate being crowded. Folks crunching biscuits in your ear so you can't hear your own crunches."

Curley Green looked troubled. "Don't sit with me, Mingy," she said in a whisper.

"Sit where I please," Mingy snapped, and folded his arms.

Gummy and Walter the Earl threaded their way through the press of villagers a moment later and plumped their stools down beside Curley Green in the almost empty row.

"Good of you to save us a space," said Walter the Earl sardonically.

Muggles arrived breathless, her hastily tied orange sash askew. "Mind if I sit here?" she asked, putting her stool down next to Mingy. "Have a pepmint, do." And she passed a crumpled bag of sweets down the line.

Mingy took one with a scowl. "Why don't you be sensible and sit somewhere else?"

"Because this is where I belong," said Muggles with simple dignity.

In a few moments Fooley Hall was full and everybody had been helped to steaming mugs of punch and biscuits. But instead of the usual gay chatter of voices, a curious silence descended, broken only by a nervous whisper here and there.

There was no need to rap the wall for order, but Ltd. rapped anyway. The last whisper stopped abruptly.

"Good folk," said the mayor, "we have plans to make for receiving the three judges when they come. They may arrive any day now."

There was clapping of hands, and Ltd. smiled round at his audience. "Free paint has already been distributed to everybody, and I want to thank you for the promptness with which you have painted your cottages."

The clapping was more sporadic this time. Veiled glances were aimed in the direction of the sixth row of stools where gold and scarlet, yellow and orange intermingled, and there was an uneasy rattle of the money box.

"You have seen the excellent work already done by Thatch. He will continue until every roof in Slipper-on-the-Water has a scalloped fringe. All roofing will be paid for out of the money box."

Loud and prolonged applause greeted this statement. Mingy scowled and stood up.

"Then I must warn the assembled company that this raid on the money box will leave the village poor for the rest of the year!"

Co. leaped to his feet. "I should like to ask our money keeper just what he proposes to do with the village wealth. Stack it up in big piles and put it in the museum for everybody to look at?"

Mingy's face turned red. "I propose to spend it sensibly," he retorted. "Not on fancying up the village to win prizes. What good will scalloped roofs do if the dock suddenly caves in when the judges arrive? And then there's the sick fund. We need a sick fund to take care of folk when they have bad luck or can't work. What will the judges think if they see some of our villagers starving themselves for lack of a gold piece?"

A murmur of approval started up, but it was quickly quelled by Wm. "As to that," he cried, "I am *sick* of hearing about Mingy's *sick* fund! It's pure foolishness, as I can show in one moment. Is there anybody here who is starving to death?"

There were mutters of "No" and "Of course not," although Spill the Candlemaker and a few others stirred uncomfortably on their stools. Spill's candles were more costly to make than Etc.'s reed-lights, and he was feeling the pinch.

Bros. popped up to speak. "It's clear enough that Mingy doesn't *want* us to win the Gammage Cup—along with several others!" He darted a venomous look at the outcast row. "I say, let's get on with the meeting for the sake of the rest of us who do!"

"Very well," said Ltd. "The meeting is thrown open for suggestions as to what more may be done to our village that will help us to win the Gammage Cup."

Geo. sprang up. "Green doors!" he burst out. "Everybody should have a green door. It spoils the appearance of the village if folk are going to paint their doors any old color they please."

"And green cloaks!" his wife Eng. cried. "Proper, decent Minnipin green cloaks for everybody so we'll not feel ashamed!"

"Ahum, yes," said Ltd., "the matter of color. . . ." He stroked his beard with nervous fingers. "I am going to make an appeal to certain members of our village." He fixed the row of gold and scarlet, yellow and orange, with a stern eye. "Now, then . . . there seems to be a difference of opinion about what color is proper to a Minnipin's door and a Minnipin's cloak."

"Don't forget Walter the Earl's sword!" cried Co.

"And the candy warriors Muggles made!" cried Scot.

"And what they're saying about the family tree!" This was from Geo. and Wm. together.

Ltd. held up his hand for silence. "We won't go into that for the moment. The question right now is: shall we all have green doors and green cloaks, which are traditional with Minnipins, or . . . Walter the Earl, do you wish to address the meeting?"

Walter the Earl kept his hands folded over his ashplant and pushed himself to his feet.

"I painted my door blue because I objected to *someone's* sneaking out at night and painting Curley Green's door without her consent or knowledge. I wear my gold-embroidered cloak because it suits me. My family was a family of warriors, and in the old days, long before they came to this valley, they wore the gold with pride. History—*fact* history, not Fool history—"

Co. gave an excited shout. "There! You see, he's insulting Fooley!"

"Fooley's name was properly The Fool while he lived," said Walter the Earl coldly. "I see no reason for changing it now."

There were cries of indignation over the hall. Several Periods jumped to their feet with fierce shouts. Ltd. banged hard on the wall.

"Gummy?"

With a flowing motion Gummy stood up.

"When the sun is shining on the trees,
Dappling the green with golden ease,
And spring is bursting in every part,
I must wear yellow o'er my heart."

He made a deep bow and sat down again. There was a heavy silence.

"Curley Green?" said Ltd. with a sigh.

She got up slowly and looked about at all the familiar faces in the hall. "I'm sorry," she said softly, "I'm sorry that my door seems to have started all this trouble. I hadn't realized that it was so offensive to everybody. I even thought, but I suppose this is silly, that there were some folk who enjoyed looking at my door. . . ."

Thatch suddenly straightened himself. "Well . . ." he began, but then his tongue got tangled up with the garlic clove in his mouth, and before he could get it popped back into his cheek, his voice was drowned out.

"Not likely," snorted Eng.

"An eyesore to the whole village," said Geo.

"Poor excuse!"

"More impudence!"

Ltd. made banging sounds and nodded to Muggles, who turned white and then pink with embarrassment as she wobbled to her feet.

"I don't know much about things," she faltered, "but—well, it seems to me—" She stopped short and looked round for rescue, but there was nobody to help her out. Then she caught Curley Green's eye, and Curley Green smiled at her.

"What I mean is," she went on, "well, I don't think it's doors or cloaks or . . . or orange sashes. It's *us*. What I mean is, it's no matter what color we paint our doors or what kind of clothes we wear, we're . . . well, we're those colors inside us. Instead of being green inside, you see, like other folk. So I don't think maybe it would do any good if we just changed our outside color. We would still be . . . be orange or scarlet inside, and, well, we would do orange and scarlet things all the time, and everybody would still—"

"Really!" said Eng. "She *is* simple!"

"Yes, I know," Muggles agreed. "Everybody always says so. But what I really want to say is, wouldn't it be cheating if we changed our outsides just for the judges? I mean, it doesn't seem quite fair, does it?" She tried to think of something more to explain, but her brain was already dizzy from its exertion. She sat down.

"Good sense," Mingy said suddenly. "Most sense I've heard today. Me, I like green. Good sensible color. Doesn't show dirt. Don't have to wash it to pieces, waste soap and water. How would I like it if somebody came along and said I had to wear yellow now? Wouldn't do it. Don't know what color I am inside. Don't think I'm green, though. Probably a good sensible brown. Doesn't show the dirt. But whatever color it is, I'm not going to change it for all the judges in the Land Between the Mountains."

Villagers exchanged bewildered glances. One or two shuffled their feet as though they would rise and speak, but each waited for the other, and by that time the official village painter had the floor.

"I've never heard so much nonsense!" Geo. sputtered. "Ridiculous! All this chatter about folk being green inside, or orange, or scarlet—ridiculous, I say!"

"We've put up with them long enough!" Wm. cried. "Them and their blobs and scribbles and history. They—"

"They teach our children bad things!" interrupted Scot.

"And only yesterday," said Geo., "Co. caught them *tampering* with the museum!"

"Tampering with the *museum!*" somebody said in a shocked voice.

"That's right!" Geo. said triumphantly. "They will do anything. Anything!" He dropped his voice almost to a whisper. "Good folk, you know what happens to a gobble of fish when a lamprey enters the river. Unless it is found and cast out, the fish disappear, one by one." He paused, and everybody hung breathless on his words. "It is plain to see that we now have five lampreys in our village. Every minute that these lampreys spend with us from now on is a minute of *danger!*"

"Lampreys!" Fin Longtooth gasped, and turned white.

"Lampreys!" echoed the villagers, and those sitting near that row of bright color cringed away from it.

The town clerk now rose to his feet and faced the assemblage. "Am I right in thinking that all of you want the Gammage Cup to come to Slipper-on-the-Water?"

"Yes!" the villagers shouted with one accord.

"And am I right in believing that you trust the Periods, your own Periods in your own village, to do all they can to get it for you?"

"*Yes!*"

"Then," Co. intoned, "we must take action against these troublemakers, these . . . these *destroyers*." He paused for a deep breath. "They must be *outlawed*!"

For a second there was silence in the hall. Then came a horrified sucking-in of breath from the assembly. Not to live in a village securely surrounded by neighbors—a Minnipin could hardly even imagine such a thing. No one had ever before been outlawed. It was the worst of all punishments, written down in the law books but never used.

The dreadful word went whispering around the hall . . . outlawed . . . *outlawed*. . . .

Ltd. rapped for order; he looked unhappy. "Now, my good people, we must think very carefully—"

"That won't be necessary!" Walter the Earl stood up, straight and proud in his gold-embroidered cloak. "We have no wish to set Minnipins at odds with their consciences. Nor do we intend to stand in the way of their winning the Gammage Cup. We are not lampreys, but neither are we flies to be swallowed by trout. And so tomorrow morning we shall take leave of this village to settle elsewhere. In short, *we* are outlawing Slipper-on-the-Water."

Walter the Earl turned, and without a backward glance stalked from the meetinghouse. Curley Green and Gummy followed close behind him. For a moment Muggles and Mingy looked at each other, and then, in the awful waiting silence, they too rose and walked out.

The money box remained behind on Mingy's stool.

THE BORROWERS

Mary Norton

Borrowers, people only a few inches tall, derive their name from their occupation of borrowing from "human beans," whose only use, they are convinced, is to provide the Borrowers with objects. Mary Norton has made them very real with well-developed personalities: Homily is an anxious mother with a strong drive for material affluence, Pod is a capable but aging provider, and Arriety is a curious, self-confident child. The illusion of reality is developed through the multitude of details about their daily life and home beneath the kitchen floor. The following selection shows how Miss Norton does this.

Miss Norton's strength of characterization and use of detail overcome her unusual way of beginning a fantasy. Her narrator, an old lady reminiscing about her childhood, is uncertain if the story she tells is true. Yet the doubt is inconclusive because there is always an object or event that is unexplainable unless such people do exist. The popularity of the Borrower series with middle graders indicates that the narrator's doubts are not shared by children.

Being seen by a human being is the most serious thing that can happen to a Borrower. Arrietty, however, is curious enough to talk to a lonely human boy. The Borrowers, the first book in this series, shows what happens to her family's life because of their friendship.

Arrietty wandered through the open door into the sitting room. Ah, the fire had been lighted and the room looked bright and cozy. Homily was proud of her sitting room: the walls had been papered with scraps of old letters out of wastepaper baskets, and Homily had arranged the handwriting sideways in vertical stripes which ran from floor to ceiling. On the walls, repeated in various colors, hung several portraits of Queen Victoria as a girl; these were postage stamps borrowed by Pod some years ago from the stamp box on the desk in the morning room. There was a lacquer trinket box, padded inside and with the lid open, which they used as a settle; and that useful stand-by—a chest of drawers made of match boxes. There was a round table with a red velvet cloth, which Pod had made from the wooden bottom of a pill box supported on the carved pedestal of a knight from the chess set. (This had caused a great deal of trouble upstairs when Aunt Sophy's eldest son, on a flying midweek visit, had invited the vicar for "a game after dinner." Rosa Pickhatchet, who was housemaid at the time, gave in her notice. After she had left other things were found to be missing, and no one was engaged in her place. From that time onwards Mrs. Driver ruled supreme.) The knight itself—its bust, so to speak—stood on a column in the corner, where it looked very fine, and lent that air to the room which only statuary can give.

Beside the fire, in a tilted wooden bookcase, stood Arrietty's library. This was a set of those miniature volumes, which the Victorians loved to print, but which to Arrietty seemed the size of very large church Bibles. There was Bryce's *Tom Thumb Gazetteer of the World*, including the last census; Bryce's *Tom Thumb Dictionary*, with short explanations of scientific, philosophical, literary, and technical terms. Bryce's *Tom Thumb Edition of the Comedies of William Shakespeare*, including a foreword on the author; another book, whose pages were all blank, called *Memoranda*; and, last but not least, Arrietty's favorite Bryce's *Tom Thumb Diary and Proverb Book*, with a saying for each day of the year and, as a preface,

From *The Borrowers* by Mary Norton, illustrated by Beth and Joe Krush, copyright, 1952, 1953, by Mary Norton. Reprinted by permission of Harcourt Brace Jovanovich, Inc.

the life story of a little man called General Tom Thumb, who married a girl called Mercy Lavinia Bump. There was an engraving of their carriage and pair, with little horses—the size of mice. Arrietty was not a stupid girl. She knew that horses could not be as small as mice, but she did not realize that Tom Thumb, nearly two feet high, would seem a giant to a Borrower.

Arrietty had learned to read from these books, and to write by leaning sideways and copying out the writings on the walls. In spite of this, she did not always keep her diary, although on most days she would take the book out for the sake of the saying which sometimes would comfort her. Today it said: "You may go farther and fare worse," and, underneath: "Order of the Garter, institute 1348." She carried the book to the fire and sat down with her feet on the hob.

"What are you doing, Arrietty?" called Homily from the kitchen.

"Writing diary."

"Oh," exclaimed Homily shortly.

"What did you want?" asked Arrietty. She felt quite safe; Homily liked her to write; Homily encouraged any form of culture. Homily herself, poor ignorant creature could not even say the alphabet. "Nothing. Nothing," said Homily crossly, banging away with the pan lids; "it'll do later."

Arrietty took out her pencil. It was a small white pencil, with a piece of silk cord attached, which had come off a dance program, but, even so, in Arrietty's hand it looked like a rolling-pin.

"Arrietty!" called Homily again from the kitchen.

"Yes?"

"Put a little something on the fire, will you?"

Arrietty braced her muscles and heaved the book off her knees, and stood it upright on the floor. They kept the fuel, assorted slack and crumbled candle grease, in a pewter mustardpot, and shoveled it out with the spoon. Arrietty trickled only a few grains, tilting the mustard spoon, not to spoil the blaze. Then she stood there basking in the warmth. It was a charming fireplace, made by Arrietty's grandfather, with a cogwheel from the stables, part of an old cider-press. The spokes of the cogwheel stood out in starry rays, and the fire itself nestled in the center. Above there was a chimney-piece made from a small brass funnel, inverted. This, at one time, belonged to an oil lamp which matched it, and which stood, in the old days, on the hall table upstairs. An arrangement of pipes, from the spout of the funnel, carried the fumes into the kitchen flues above. The fire was laid with match-sticks and fed with assorted slack and, as it burned up, the iron would become hot, and Homily would simmer soup on the spokes in a silver thimble, and Arrietty would broil nuts. How cozy those winter evenings could be. Arrietty, her great book on her knees, sometimes reading aloud; Pod at his last (he was a shoemaker, and made button-shoes out of kid gloves—now, alas, only for his family); and Homily, quiet at last, with her knitting.

Homily knitted their jerseys and stockings on black-headed pins, and, sometimes, on darning needles. A great reel of silk or cotton would stand, table high, beside her chair, and sometimes, if she pulled too sharply, the reel would tip up and roll away out of the open door into the dusty passage beyond, and Arrietty would be sent after it, to rewind it carefully as she rolled it back.

The floor of the sitting room was carpeted with deep red blotting paper, which was warm and cozy, and soaked up the spills. Homily would renew it at intervals when it became available upstairs, but since Aunt Sophy had taken to her bed Mrs. Driver seldom thought of blotting paper unless, suddenly, there were guests. Homily like things which saved washing because drying was difficult under the floor; water they had in plenty, hot and cold, thanks to Pod's father who had tapped the pipes from the kitchen boiler. They bathed in a small tureen, which once had held *pâté de foie gras*. When you had wiped out your bath you were supposed to put the lid back, to stop people putting things in it. The soap, too, a great cake of it, hung on a nail in the scullery, and they scraped pieces off. Homily liked coal tar, but Pod and Arrietty preferred sandalwood.

* * *

Sighing, Arrietty put away her diary and went into the kitchen. She took the onion ring from Homily, and slung it lightly round her shoulders, while she foraged for a piece of razor blade. "Really, Arrietty," exclaimed Homily, "Not on

your clean jersey! Do you want to smell like a bitbucket? Here, take the scissor—"

Arrietty stepped through the onion ring as though it were a child's hoop, and began to chop it into segments.

"Your father's late," muttered Homily again, "and it's my fault, as you might say. Oh dear, oh dear, I wish I hadn't—"

"Hadn't what?" asked Arrietty, her eyes watering. She sniffed loudly and longed to rub her nose on her sleeve.

Homily pushed back a thin lock of hair with a worried hand. She stared at Arrietty absently. "It's that tea cup you broke," she said.

"But that was days ago—" began Arrietty, blinking her eyelids, and she sniffed again.

"I know. I know. It's not you. It's me. It's not the breaking that matters, it's what I said to your father."

"What did you say to him?"

"Well, I just said—there's the rest of the service, I said—up there, where it always was, in the corner cupboard in the schoolroom."

"I don't see anything bad in that," said Arrietty as, one by one, she dropped the pieces of onion into the soup.

"But it's a high cupboard," exclaimed Homily. "You have to get up by the curtain. And your father at his age—" She sat down suddenly on a metal-topped champagne cork. "Oh, Arrietty, I wish I'd never mentioned it!"

"Don't worry," said Arrietty, "Papa knows what he can do." She pulled a rubber scent-bottle cork out of the hole in the hot-water pipe and let a trickle of scalding drops fall into the tin lid of an aspirin bottle. She added cold and began to wash her hands.

"Maybe," said Homily. "But I went on about it so. What's a tea cup! Your Uncle Hendreary never drank a thing that wasn't out of a common acorn cup, and he's lived to a ripe old age and had the strength to emigrate. My mother's family never had nothing but a little bone thimble which they shared around. But it's once you've *had* a tea cup, if you see what I mean. . . ."

"Yes," said Arrietty, drying her hands on a roller towel made out of surgical bandage.

"It's that curtain," cried Homily. "He can't climb a curtain at his age—not by the bobbles!"

"With his pin he could," said Arrietty.

"His pin! I led him into that one too! Take a hat pin, I told him, and tie a bit of name-tape to the head, and pull yourself upstairs. It was to borrow the emerald watch from Her bedroom for me to time the cooking." Homily's voice began to tremble. "Your mother's a wicked woman, Arrietty. Wicked and selfish, that's what she is!"

"You know what?" exclaimed Arrietty suddenly.

Homily brushed away a tear. "No," she said wanly, "what?"

"I could climb a curtain."

Homily rose up. "Arrietty, you dare stand there in cold blood and say a thing like that!"

"But I could! I could! I could borrow! I know I could!"

"Oh!" gasped Homily. "Oh, you wicked heathen girl! How can you speak so!" and she crumpled up again on the cork stool. "So it's come to this!" she said.

"Now, Mother, please," begged Arrietty, "now, don't take on!"

"But don't you see, Arrietty . . ." gasped Homily; she stared down at the table at loss for words and then, at last, she raised a haggard face. "My poor child," she said, "don't speak like that of borrowing. You don't know—and, thank goodness, you never will know"—she dropped her voice to a fearful whisper—"what it's like upstairs. . . ."

Arrietty was silent. "What is it like?" she asked after a moment.

Homily wiped her face on her apron and smoothed back her hair. "Your Uncle Hendreary," she began, "Eggletina's father—" and then she paused. "Listen!" she said. "What's that?"

Echoing on the wood was a faint vibration—the sound of a distant click. "Your father!" exclaimed Homily. "Oh, look at me! Where's the comb?"

They had a comb: a little, silver, eighteenth-century eyebrow comb from the cabinet in the drawing room upstairs. Homily ran it through her hair and rinsed her poor red eyes and, when Pod came in, she was smiling and smoothing down her apron.

Pod came in slowly, his sack on his back; he leaned his hat pin, with its dangling name-tape, against the wall and, on the middle of the kitchen table, he placed a doll's tea cup; it was the size of a mixing bowl.

"Why, Pod—" began Homily.

"Got the saucer too," he said. He swung down the sack and untied the neck. "Here you are," he said, drawing out the saucer. "Matches it."

He had a round, currant-bunny sort of face; tonight it looked flabby.

"Oh, Pod," said Homily, "you do look queer. Are you all right?"

Pod sat down. "I'm fair enough," he said.

"You went up the curtain," said Homily. "Oh, Pod, you shouldn't have. It's shaken you—"

Pod made a strange face, his eyes swiveled round toward Arrietty. Homily stared at him, her mouth open, and then she turned. "Come along, Arrietty," she said briskly, "you pop off to bed, now, like a good girl, and I'll bring you some supper."

"Oh," said Arrietty, "can't I see the rest of the borrowings?"

"Your father's got nothing now. Only food. Off you pop to bed. You've seen the cup and saucer."

Arrietty went into the sitting room to put away her diary, and took some time fixing her candle on the upturned drawing pin which served as a holder.

"Whatever are you doing?" grumbled Homily. "Give it here. There, that's the way. Now off to bed and fold your clothes, mind."

"Good night, Papa," said Arrietty, kissing his flat white cheek.

"Careful of the light," he said mechanically, and watched her with his round eyes until she had closed the door.

"Now, Pod," said Homily, when they were alone, "tell me. What's the matter?"

Pod looked at her blankly. "I been 'seen,'" he said.

Homily put out a groping hand for the edge of the table; she grasped it and lowered herself slowly on to the stool. "Oh, Pod," she said.

There was silence between them. Pod stared at Homily and Homily stared at the table. After a while she raised her white face. "Badly?" she asked.

Pod moved restlessly. "I don't know about

badly. I been 'seen.' Ain't that bad enough?"

"No one," said Homily slowly, "hasn't never been 'seen' since Uncle Hendreary and he was the first they say for forty-five years." A thought struck her and she gripped the table. "It's no good, Pod, I won't emigrate!"

"No one's asked you to," said Pod.

"To go and live like Hendreary and Lupy in a badger's set! The other side of the world, that's where they say it is—all among the earthworms."

"It's two fields away, above the spinney," said Pod.

"Nuts, that's what they eat. And berries. I wouldn't wonder if they don't eat mice—"

"You've eaten mice yourself," Pod reminded her.

"All draughts and fresh air and the children growing up wild. Think of Arrietty!" said Homily. "Think of the way she's been brought up. An only child. She'd catch her death. It's different for Hendreary."

"Why?" asked Pod. "He's got four."

"That's why," explained Homily. "When you've got four, they're brought up rough. But never mind that now. . . . Who saw you?"

"A boy," said Pod.

"A what?" exclaimed Homily, staring.

"A boy." Pod sketched out a rough shape in the air with his hands. "You know, a boy."

"But there isn't—I mean, what sort of a boy?"

"I don't know what you mean 'what sort of a boy.' A boy in a night-shirt. A boy. You know what a boy is, don't you?"

"Yes," said Homily, "I know what a boy is. But there hasn't been a boy, not in this house, these twenty years."

"Well," said Pod, "there's one here now."

"Homily stared at him in silence, and Pod met her eyes. "Where did he see you?" asked Homily at last.

"In the schoolroom."

"Oh," said Homily, "when you was getting the cup?"

"Yes," said Pod.

"Haven't you got eyes?" asked Homily. "Couldn't you have looked first?"

"There's never nobody in the schoolroom. And what's more," he went on, "there wasn't today."

"Then where was he?"

"In bed. In the night-nursery or whatever it's called. That's where he was. Sitting up in bed. With the doors open."

"Well, you could have looked in the nursery."

"How could I—halfway up the curtain!"

"Is that where you was?"

"Yes."

"With the cup?"

"Yes. I couldn't get up or down."

"Oh, Pod," wailed Homily, "I should never have let you go. Not at your age!"

"Now, look here," said Pod, "don't mistake me. I got up all right. Got up like a bird, as you might say, bobbles or no bobbles. But"—he leaned toward her—"afterwards—with the cup in me hand, if you see what I mean. . . ." He picked it up off the table. "You see, it's heavy like. You can hold it by the handle, like this . . . but it drops or droops, as you might say. You should take a cup like this in your two hands. A bit of cheese off a shelf, or an apple—well, I drop that . . . give it a push and it falls and I climbs down in me own time and picks it up. But with a cup—you see what I mean? And coming down, you got to watch your feet. And, as I say, some of the bobbles was missing. You didn't know what you could hold on to, not safely. . . ."

"Oh, Pod," said Homily, her eyes full of tears, "what did you do?"

"Well," said Pod, sitting back again, "he took the cup."

"What do you mean?" exclaimed Homily, aghast.

Pod avoided her eyes. "Well, he'd been sitting up in bed there watching me. I'd been on that curtain a good ten minutes, because the hall clock had just struck the quarter—"

"But how do you mean—'he took the cup'?"

"Well, he'd got out of bed and there he was standing, looking up. 'I'll take the cup,' he said."

"Oh!" gasped Homily, her eyes staring, "and you give it him?"

"He took it," said Pod, "ever so gentle. And then, when I was down, he give it me." Homily put her face in her hands. "Now don't take on," said Pod uneasily.

"He might have caught you," shuddered Homily in a stifled voice.

"Yes," said Pod, "but he just give me the cup. 'Here you are,' he said."

Homily raised her face. "What are we going to do?" she asked.

Pod sighed. "Well, there isn't nothing we can do. Except—"

"Oh, no," exclaimed Homily, "not that. Not emigrate. Not that, Pod, now I've got the house so nice and a clock and all."

"We could take the clock," said Pod.

"And Arrietty? What about her? She's not like those cousins. She can *read*, Pod, and sew a treat—"

"He don't know where we live," said Pod.

"But they look," exclaimed Homily. "Remember Hendreary! They got the cat and—"

"Now, now," said Pod, "don't bring up the past."

"But you've got to think of it! They got the cat and—"

"Yes," said Pod, "but Eggletina was different."

"How different? She was Arriety's age."

"Well, they hadn't told her, you see. That's where they went wrong. They tried to make her believe that there wasn't nothing but was under the floor. They never told her about Mrs. Driver or Crampfurl. Least of all about cats."

"There wasn't any cat," Homily pointed out, "not till Hendreary was 'seen.'"

"Well, there was, then," said Pod. "You got to tell them, that's what I say, or they try to find out for themselves."

"Pod," said Homily solemnly, "we haven't told Arrietty."

"Oh, she knows," said Pod; he moved uncomfortably. "She's got her grating."

"She doesn't know about Eggletina. She doesn't know about being 'seen.'"

"Well," said Pod, "we'll tell her. We always said we would. There's no hurry."

Homily stood up. "Pod," she said, "we're going to tell her now."

THE FORGOTTEN DOOR

Alexander Key

Some people have suggested that science fiction is the fantasy of today. If this is true it seems strange there is so little good science fiction for children. Many writers use this genre to philosophize or moralize, much like the Victorian writers, unfortunately, for it seems to reflect a belief that fantasy can be justified only when it teaches.

Except for three adults and two children, the people in The Forgotten Door *are vicious and selfish, they steal and lie, they and their governments are deceptive and uninterested in human rights. Such a point of view is surely a great over-simplification of contemporary life. The book ends with a total rejection of this world for another world where men are wiser and better.*

In spite of the above mentioned negative attitude, The Forgotten Door *is one of the best written works of science fiction for children and young adults. Its fantasy and tension are both well developed.*

Jon's fall from his world to ours through a forgotten door makes him unable to remember where he has come from. Because he is different and has amazing powers, his life and the lives of the family that takes him in are threatened.

It happened so quickly, so unexpectedly, that Little Jon's cry was almost instantly cut short as the blackness closed over him. No one knew the hole was there. It hadn't been there the day before, and in the twilight no one had noticed it.

At the moment it happened, the first shooting stars were crossing the sky—they were beginning to stream across like strings of jewels flung from another planet—and everyone was watching them. The smaller children were exclaiming in delight, while the older ones stood silent and enthralled. Here on the hill, where the valley people often came to watch the glittering night unfold, you could see the whole magic sweep around you, and you felt close to everything in the heavens. Other people, you knew, were standing on other hills on other worlds, watching even as you watched.

Little Jon, whose eyes were quicker than most, should have seen the hole, but all his attention was on the stars. Small for his age, he had moved away from the rest for a better view, and as he stepped backward, there was suddenly nothing under his feet.

It was astonishing at that moment to find himself falling swiftly into the hill at a spot where he had walked safely all his life. But in the brief seconds before the blackness swallowed him, he realized what must have happened: there had been a cave-in over the old Door—the Door that led to another place, the one that had been closed so long.

He cried out and tried to break his fall in the way he had been taught, but the effort came an instant too late. His head struck something, and darkness swirled over him.

Long later, when Little Jon was able to sit up, he had no idea where he was or what had happened. Memory had fled, and he ached all over. He would have been shivering with cold, but his thick jacket and trousers and heavy, woven boots kept him warm.

He seemed to be in a narrow cleft of broken rock. There were mossy stones around him, and just ahead he could make out a bed of ferns where water trickled from a spring. He was still

too dazed to be frightened, but now he realized he was thirsty, terribly so. He crawled painfully forward and lay with his face in the water while he drank.

The coldness of the water startled him at first, but it was wonderfully sweet and satisfying. He bathed his face and hands in it, then sat up at last and looked around again.

Where was he? How did he get here? He pondered these questions, but no answers came. He felt as if he had fallen. Only—where could he have fallen *from?* The rocky walls met overhead, sloping outward into a tangle of leafy branches.

There was another question his mind carefully tiptoed around, because it was more upsetting than the others. Whenever he approached it, it caused a dull aching in his forehead. Finally, however, he gave his head a small shake and faced it squarely.

Who am I?

He didn't know. He simply didn't know, and it made everything terribly wrong.

All at once, trembling, he got to his feet and fled limping toward a shaft of sunlight ahead. Thick shrubs barred his way. He fought blindly through them, tripped, and fell sprawling. Fortunately he missed the boulders on either side, and landed in a soft bed of old leaves under a tree. He scrambled up in panic, started to run again, then stopped himself just in time.

This wasn't the sort of country where you could run. There were steep ledges here, and below them the ground sloped sharply downward for a great distance. All of it was covered with a wild tangle of forest. Little Jon rubbed his eyes and looked around him with growing wonder and fright.

Nothing here was familiar. He was *sure* of that. He had never seen trees quite like the ones around him. Many of the smaller trees were in bloom, covered with showers of white blossoms —these were *almost* familiar, as were the ferns and lichens on the rocks. But there was a difference. But what the difference was, he was unable to tell.

Carefully he worked down to an open area below the ledge, and stood listening. The *sounds* were familiar, and hearing them made him feel a bit better. Birdsong, the gurgling of hidden springs, the faint clatter and fuss of a rushing stream somewhere. And there were the hesitant steps of wild creatures that came pleasantly to his sharp ears. Without quite realizing his ability, which was as natural as breathing, his mind reached toward them and found nothing strange in them—except that they were afraid. Afraid of him!

"Don't be afraid," he told them, so softly that his lips barely moved. "I'd *never* hurt you."

After a minute, two of the creatures—they were a doe and her fawn—moved hesitantly down the slope and stood looking at him curiously. Little Jon held out his hands, and presently the doe came close and nuzzled his cheek with her cold nose.

"Where am I?" he asked her plaintively. "Can you tell me?"

The doe couldn't answer, and all he could gather was that she was hungry, and that food could be found in the valley below.

"Lead the way," he told her. "I'll follow."

The doe and the fawn started down through the tangle. Little Jon went scrambling and limping behind them. Walking was difficult, for both his knees were badly bruised and one ankle pained with every step. Soon, however, they reached a winding game trail and the going was much easier. Even so, it was hard to keep up with the doe, and several times in the next hour he had to beg her to stop and wait for him.

It did not seem at all strange to be following her. Her presence was very comforting and kept the unanswered questions from troubling him.

As they wound down near the bottom of the slope, the trees thinned and they passed through an open gate. Ahead he could see bright sunlight on a small greening field. Around a corner of the field ran a clattering stream—a stream different from the one he had heard earlier.

At the sight of the field Little Jon caught his breath. Fields and cultivated things were familiar. There would be people near. Soon he would meet them and find out about himself.

The doe paused at the edge of the field, sniffing the air currents. Little Jon could feel her uneasiness, though he could not understand it. He sniffed too, but all he could smell were the pleasant scents of fresh earth and blossoms, and the richness of the forest behind them. He was disappointed that he couldn't make out the scent of humans near, but maybe this was because the air was flowing down from the mountain, away from him.

As the doe stepped daintily into the field and began to nibble the young plants, Little Jon unconsciously did what he should have done earlier. His mind reached out, searching hopefully. He had no thought of danger. The sudden discovery that there *was* danger was so shocking that he could only spring forward with a strangled cry as he tried to tell the doe to run.

The doe whirled instantly and leaped, just as the sharp report of a rifle shattered the peace of the morning.

Little Jon had never heard a rifle shot before, but he was aware of the hot slash of pain across the doe's flank, and he could see the weapon in the hands of the man who rose from his hiding place at the edge of the stream. He was a lean man in overalls, with one shoulder higher than the other. The harsh features under the cap showed surprise and disbelief as he stared at Little Jon. Then the thin mouth twisted in fury.

"Devil take you!" the man roared, striding forward. "You ruint my aim! What you doin' in my field?"

Little Jon could make nothing of the words. The language was strange, but the hate-driven thoughts behind it were clear enough. For a moment he stood incredulous, his mind trying to fight through the shock of what had happened. Surely the man approaching was a being like himself. But why the intent to kill another creature? Why the sudden hate? How could anyone ever, ever . . .

The anger that rose in him was a new thing. It was something he had never experienced before, at least in this measure. His small hands balled into fists and he trembled. But just as quickly, he realized that he couldn't quench hate with hate, and that now there was danger to himself. He turned abruptly and fled.

"Stop!" the man bellowed, close behind him. "I know you—you're one o' them Cherokees from over the ridge! I'll teach you to come meddlin' in my land!"

Little Jon tried to lighten his feet and put distance between himself and his pursuer. Ordinarily he might have managed it in spite of his pains, but he knew nothing of barbed-wire fences. The rusty wires were hidden by the shrubbery until he was almost on them. When he attempted to slide through them, the barbs caught his jacket. The tough material refused to tear. In another second he was squirming in the man's firm grasp.

The man dragged him roughly back to the field, then turned at the sound of an approaching motor. Presently a small farm truck whirled around the bend of the creek and stopped close by. A large woman, wearing faded overalls, got out and waddled over to them. She had a fleshy face, with small, shrewd eyes as hard and round as creek pebbles.

Little Jon had never seen a woman like her. Though he was repelled by her, she drew his attention far more than the truck, which was equally strange.

"I declare!" she muttered, staring. "What you got there, Gilby?"

"Not what I was aimin' at," the man growled. "The thievin' varmint spoiled my shot."

"Just as well, I reckon, or he'd tell. Whose kid is he?"

"Dunno, Emma. Figured 'im for a Cherokee, but—"

"Pshaw, *he* ain't no Indian," she interrupted, peering closer.

"Got black hair like one, near long as a girl's. Could be half an' half."

"H'mp! Look at them *clothes!* Seems more foreignlike. Gypsy, maybe. Where you from, boy?"

Little Jon clenched his teeth and looked stonily back at her. Though her speech was strange, the rising questions and ugly thoughts in her mind were easily understood. She was a person to be avoided, and he wouldn't have answered her even if he had known how.

"Cat got your tongue?" she snapped. "Well, I reckon I can loosen it." Abruptly she slapped him, hard.

He knew the slap was coming, and he managed in time to go limp and roll his head. As he did so, the man unclenched his hand to get a better grip on him. Immediately Little Jon twisted free and ran.

This time he was able to lighten his feet, and went over the fence in a bound. He heard gasps

of astonishment behind him, then shouts, and the man's pursuing footsteps. Presently these sounds faded, and the forest was quiet.

Little Jon ran on until he was nearly exhausted. He would have followed the doe and the fawn, but they had gone over a ridge where the way was too steep for his throbbing ankle.

Finally he huddled by a fallen log, removed one boot, and rubbed his swollen ankle while he gained his breath. Tears rolled down his cheeks. He missed the doe terribly. She was his only friend in all this strangeness.

Suddenly he dug his knuckles into his eyes, drew on his boot, and struggled to his feet. He couldn't stay here all day. It solved nothing. He had to keep moving, searching. . . .

Resolutely he began limping around the curve of the slope, taking the easiest course. Somewhere there must be other people—people unlike those behind him. But when he found them he would have to be careful. Very careful.

He heard the soft slither of the snake ahead before he saw it, even before it rattled its deadly warning. Its sudden rattle astonished him. He stared at it with more curiosity than fear. What a strange creature, legless and covered with scales, and with a rattle on the end of its tail! It seemed he had heard of such things, vaguely, just as he had heard of the odd kind of vehicle the woman had driven. But where?

Troubled, he limped carefully around the snake. With the thought that there might be other dangers here, dangers he knew nothing about, he drew a small knife from his belt and cut a staff from the shrubbery. The knife felt so much a part of him that he hardly questioned it till he had finished using it. It was only a tool—it seemed that someone had given it to him long ago—but he couldn't remember any more about it.

The staff made walking easier for a while, and he trudged painfully on, stopping at times to rest or to drink from one of the many springs. The sun, which he could glimpse only at intervals through the trees, began to sink behind him. He was very hungry, and his eyes searched continually for food. There ought to be berries. He had noticed some earlier, growing near the barbed-wire fence where the man had caught him.

Edible things, he decided finally, must grow in the open places, lower down.

Warily, slowly, he began to angle toward the valley. He reached the bottom of the slope much sooner than he had expected, only to discover that the valley had vanished. Another slope rose immediately ahead. In sudden alarm he realized he could no longer see the sun. With every step the gloom was deepening. The forest had chilled, and for the first time he saw the gray mist creeping down from above.

The gloom, the chill, and the creeping mist in this strange and bewildering land, together with his growing hunger and lameness, were almost too much. A sob broke from his lips, and he began to tremble with a black dread. He couldn't go much farther. What would he do when darkness came?

Then, like a glow of warmth in the chill, he felt the comforting knowledge of wild creatures near. They were friendly, but timid. He was on the point of calling to them when he heard the distant sound of a motor.

He stiffened, his hands clenched tightly on his staff. Memory of the angry man and the ugly woman rose like a warning. He shook off the thought of them. He *had* to go on. It was the only way . . .

Abruptly he began plunging toward the sound, following the narrow gully that curved away on his right.

A half hour later he broke through a tangle of evergreens and stared in amazement at the scene ahead.

He was on the edge of a steep bank that dropped down to a winding gravel road. Beyond the road a broad valley opened. The valley was ringed by wave on wave of blue and purple mountains that rose to the clouds. The valley was in shadow, but he could make out the farms with their little white houses, and see animals grazing in the pastures.

The motor he had heard earlier had passed, but a second one was approaching. Instantly his mind went out to it, exploring. There were several people in the vehicle, and they were very different from the ones he had met—but not different in a way that mattered. As the machine swung into sight, he allowed himself only a curious glimpse of its bright newness, before he cowered back into the tangle.

The shadows deepened in the valley, and began to creep over the distant mountains. Three more vehicles passed, and once a man on a horse went by. The horse sensed his presence and whinnied. Little Jon liked the horse, but he fought down the urge to call to it, for the man filled him with uneasiness.

It was nearly dark when he heard the final motor. This time, aware of the friendliness of its occupants—and something beyond friendliness —he did not hesitate. It was a small truck, and as it swung around the bend in the road, he slid quickly down the bank to meet it.

THE CITY UNDER GROUND

Suzanne Martel

This book's initial situation is interesting. The characters live in a city far beneath the earth's surface, built by their ancestors when the earth had become uninhabitable through man's violence. For centuries these people have known nothing but peace; violence is inconceivable and their scientific advances have been remarkable. Unknown to them the atmosphere has become habitable and men now live above ground in primitive societies. With this beginning it seems impossible not to write a good book about the meeting of two such dissimilar groups.

Yet the only strength of The City under Ground *is suspense. There is no character development nor any sense of style. The number of cliches is unusually great and perhaps may be the result of the translator's carelessness rather than the author's indifference to good standards of writing.*

The first scene illustrates the poor quality of dialogue in this novel. Bernard's responses sound exactly like those of the Chief, and their reference to "a soldier reconnoitering" is jarring in a book that stresses the people's belief in peace. There is too much distance from the pain of a broken leg and the terror of being lost in an alien world for the second scene to seem believable. Certainly this is not how two frightened boys would talk. The author or the translator could have used a more staccato cadence to convey pain and fear, and if the boys had responded to their situation with less nonchalance the scene would have been more believable. Throughout this book the characters seem to be stick figures moved through the action, mouthing cliches.

"Bernard! What are you doing here at the Power Center? I thought you were in bed with an injured hand."

"Oh no, Chief, I'm better now. I've just come from the doctor's. He put my hand under the curative-ray machine, and now there's nothing left but a pink scar."

"And aren't you enjoying a holiday with your friends?"

"Well, no, Chief. I can't take a holiday when our work isn't finished."

"You're right about that. We've been talking about it all night."

"I thought maybe I could still be useful . . . we have to know what's hidden behind that patch soldered in the pipe."

"We've thought of that, son. We're looking for a way of clearing up the mystery. Your father is with the experts right now, trying to find a way of seeing things from a long distance."

"But—what about *me?* Can't I go back into the conduits?"

"We've agreed that you've already done more than we should expect of a youngster."

"But Chief, you trusted me with the job. Father always says that when you start a job, you ought to finish it."

"Your father himself wouldn't want you to go back into the conduits, Bernard."

"I'm sure he wouldn't stop me from finishing my work!"

"Maybe you're right. After all, you get your courage from your father. You're quite sure you wouldn't be afraid?"

"Oh, I'll be afraid all right!"

"Then why do you want to go in again? It's very important for me to know."

"I don't quite know how to explain it, Chief. . . . When I was crawling through the conduits, I said to myself, in fun, that I was a soldier reconnoitering . . ."

"Go on."

"Well, a soldier doesn't run away the day before the battle."

"You don't want to be merely a soldier on parade, eh, Bernard? I'm going to accept your offer. If your father consents, you will return with the tools, and tell us what there is behind that soldering in the northwest conduit."

"That's fine, Chief. What time shall I come?"

"Be here at ten o'clock. And, confidentially, I was hoping you'd offer what I couldn't ask of you. Let me shake your hand, Bernard—you haven't disappointed me."

"So long, Chief. See you this afternoon. I've just time for a swim with Eric."

* * *

Before leaving, he remembered Luke's cry; his brother had lost his mask and broken his leg, and there would be unknown dangers. So Paul began to prepare systematically for the expedition.

He put the meal pill left over from supper into his pocket. He would sneak a mask from the reserves left at every terminus—an unpardonable crime in the city, where thieving was unknown. He went into his father's night-cubicle, opened the medicine chest and took out bandages, disinfectants, and an automatic syringe filled with anesthetic liquid, and put them into his emergency kit. Then he took the coverlet from his bed. Vague ideas of first aid reminded him that a person in a state of shock needed warmth. Finally, he put in his speleology tunic.

His ice-ax clattered to the ground and he picked it up; the long arm, ending in a pointed iron hammer, would make a reassuring weapon. Ready for battle like the warriors of old, the young knight dashed to the terminus where Eric was waiting.

Crouched face to face where the opening widened, the two boys illuminated each other with their rays, as Eric and Luke had done before in the same spot. "You can't make any mistake when you leave here," Eric told Paul. "But I don't know where Luke went when he got to the outer world. He only showed me the opening of the tunnel, and we never spoke about it again."

"Thanks, Eric. Get back to your dwelling before the curfew—you've only just time. If I don't get back by tomorrow, warn my father at the laboratory. I won't give you away, and nobody will ever know you've crossed the boundary. Your little expedition was illegal, you know!"

"Will you get into much trouble if they catch you?"

"It doesn't matter. My crimes can't be counted any more," Paul said bitterly. And Eric burned with admiration for his hero.

"I'm leaving! Here's your poem—it's a give-away, Eric. You'd better destroy it." Paul nodded his ray-helmeted head in farewell and started off into the passage, his coverlet slung over his shoulder and his ice-ax in his hand.

The cool air of the night struck him in the face. The distant stars made him dizzy. Spurred by the same confidence that Luke had felt that

afternoon, Paul was quite sure that he would easily find his brother. One of his prehistoric heroes was Long Knife, the woodsman from whom the forest held no secrets, described by the ancient author, James Fenimore Cooper. Paul told himself that even if he couldn't read the book of nature easily, he could at least spell it out. He would follow Luke's traces—broken branches, trodden grass, footprints in the sand.

He was prepared for anything, except this immense black vault which, somewhere in its interior, hid his desperate young brother.

Perplexed, he stopped unsteadily on the rocks. He had an inspiration. Perhaps Luke was conscious again? Synchronizing his watch-radio, he called for a long time. At last the bracelet crackled. Joyful, he heard Luke's voice, much nearer this time, but shaken and weak.

"Paul—help!"

"I'm coming, Luke. Don't be afraid, I'm on my way. I'm at the entrance to the outer world. Tell me how to get to you."

"I'm deep in the forest. I walked for hours."

"In what direction? Don't waste time—talk fast."

"Go down the mountainside."

There was silence for a time, interrupted only by Paul's exclamations and the clatter of stones cascading. . . . Silence again . . . then—"I'm at the bottom. What now?"

"Come into the forest and turn to the right as far as the path that goes south."

With a sound of breaking branches, Paul served his apprenticeship to walking on the earth. In spite of the seriousness of the situation, Luke could not help smiling when he heard the familiar litany which his brother muttered during his difficult advance.

"By a thousand motors! By all the caves of Surréal! These branches are a nuisance!"

Suddenly there was silence as Paul emerged on the beaten track. After the rugged trail through the underwood it looked as smooth as the moving sidewalks of the city.

Now he could advance more quickly. His clumsy course was punctuated with headlong falls and he soon realized that, on a trip like this, his motto should be "Slowly but surely." One disabled boy in the family was quite enough. While he stumbled along, he chatted with Luke, knowing him to be frightened and in pain, all alone in the dark night.

Mocking laughter broke out on his left, and was echoed by the same kind of laughter on the right.

"Do you hear that?" Luke asked, trembling.

"It's only owls," Paul reassured him, feeling certain that they were wolves.

"Oh, good—I was afraid they might be wolves." Luke was confident now, trusting in his elder brother's knowledge.

To distract him, Paul asked Luke how he had discovered the outer world and learned to his astonishment about the rescue mission on which Luke had set out.

"It's much farther than I thought," Luke said, crestfallen. "And then the night fell."

"And you, too!"

Luke chuckled faintly. "Fortunately I didn't lose my ray helmet. I would have died of fear in the dark."

"What about your mask?"

"First I thought I'd suffocate. But I found I could breathe quite well—fresh air smells good, you know. Paul, do you think the air could have become pure after such a long time?"

"Right now anything seems possible," grumbled Paul, who felt as if the whole forest was alive around him, and didn't like the feeling at all.

Reassured by the sound of his own voice and by his brother's closeness, Luke forgot his pain as they talked. "Fortunately, the Upsilon-ray box isn't broken," he said. "They'll be able to use it in Laurania."

"If we ever get there," said his brother, who was finding the journey endless. "In the name of the Prime Mover, where *are* you, Luke?" he cried. "You must have gone to the ends of the earth."

The answer was a terrified whisper. "Paul, there's an enormous beast in the tree over my head. I can see its eyes gleaming in my light ray. It looks like a huge cat."

Paul dashed forward, sending caution to the winds. He gasped out instructions to his brother. "Keep your light focused on it. . . . Don't take your eyes off it for a second. Have . . . you . . . any . . . weapon?"

"I have a stone in my hand. Oh Paul, *hurry!*"

Fear either paralyzes or lends wings. Paul ran as he had never run before—but he was running headlong into danger.

"I hear you, Paul! I hear the branches breaking. I'm at the bottom of a slope—don't fall."

Between the leaves, the rescuer saw a wavering light. He plunged on, though the pine branches scratched him painfully.

"Don't move, Luke. Whatever you do, don't move! I can see you now."

Out of breath, Paul reached the top of the slope. What he saw froze him with horror. The frail figure of Luke, in his white tunic, was only ten feet away. Seated with his back against his haversack, one leg twisted under him, the boy was staring fixedly overhead at the branch of a tree. A huge puma, dazzled by the light, was climbing cautiously along the branch. Reassured by the boy's stillness, it suddenly decided to conquer its fear of the light, and stretched its muscles to leap. Its tail thrashed the air, its head sank into its shoulders.

The puma made a spring; at the same moment Paul leaped toward it and they collided in mid-air. Hit on the side by this unexpected projectile, the startled beast made a half turn in the air, and came down two feet from Luke.

Winded by the collision, Paul rolled a little farther along the ground, losing his helmet, but not letting go of his ice-ax. He snatched off his mask so that he could see more clearly, and saw the wild beast getting ready to leap at its new prey.

Trained for defense by many hours of robot-balloon, Paul got up on one knee, clutching his inadequate weapon in both hands.

When the puma was ready to leap, Paul was prepared for him. The animal's huge shadow seemed to blot out the sky. Paul smelled its fetid breath and heard its deep growl. Hurling himself to one side, he struck blindly at the enemy with all his force. The violence of the blow tore the weapon out of his hands.

For the second time, the puma rolled over to one side, and Paul to the other. This time Paul was disarmed, but at least their fall had taken them away from Luke.

Groping around, the boy tried to find a stone

with which he could carry on the desperate struggle. Gasping for breath, he peered into the darkness, trying to detect his enemy's movements. But the puma did not budge. Even its growling had stopped. Scarcely daring to believe it, Paul scrambled to his feet, and his eyes, growing accustomed to the darkness saw the animal's lifeless body.

He rushed over to Luke. Overcome by terror and pain, the boy had fainted. Paul took off Luke's helmet and put it on his own head, so that he could approach his victim safely. By a heaven-sent chance, which the young hunter would remember with shivers of anguish for the rest of his life, his ice-ax had struck at the very heart of the mountain lion.

Paul found his own helmet and put Luke's back on his head. Then he climbed to the top of the slope, where he had left the emergency kit and the coverlet.

Quickly he attended to the injured boy. He gave him a sedative injection with the hypodermic syringe. Then as well as he could, he straightened Luke's broken leg and tied it firmly to a straight branch that served as an improvised splint.

He wrapped his younger brother tenderly in the torn coverlet. Then he put the black box, the cause of all Luke's trouble, under a jutting rock.

"We'll come back and look for it later," he told himself.

Hoisting his brother on his shoulders, Paul made use of the techniques which he had learned during his rescuing course, and tried to find the most comfortable way to carry the injured boy. For a moment he thought of putting their masks on again, but he gave up that idea. Now that they had discovered the open air, they might as well trust it.

Slowly, taking care not to jolt his precious burden, the rescuer continued his journey to Laurania. He wondered how he would be received. Would the friendship of a girl be enough to overcome the superstitions of a primitive people? Would they welcome two boys from the world below the ground?

The rising dawn tinted the sky pink. Before his incredulous eyes, the sun rose, causing the sky to blaze with magnificent colors. Soon Paul was crossing cultivated fields.

He was so tired that he felt as if he were carrying the world on his back. At last he spotted a high palisade, made of stones and tree trunks, which hid the village. Smoke was rising from the chimneys. Dogs barked, and birds sang in the green trees.

Related Reading

Books for Children

Aiken, Joan. *Nightbirds on Nantucket*. Illustrated by Robin Jacques. New York: Doubleday, 1969. A girl who sleeps for ten months, a pink whale, cruel adults, brave children, and mystery all add up to a fantasy in the style of nineteenth-century Gothic novels. Great fun for those children who like a little of the tongue-in-cheek with their suspense. (Grades 4–8)

————. *The Wolves of Willoughby Chase*. Illustrated by Pat Marriott. New York: Doubleday, 1968. Another tongue-in-cheek melodrama in the style of nineteenth-century novels about cruel adults and brave, resourceful children. A great deal of gripping suspense. (Grades 4–8)

Alexander, Lloyd. *The Book of Three*. New York: Holt, Rinehart and Winston, 1964. The first book in a series about Taran, assistant pig keeper for the good wizard Dallben. Taran attempts to find his identity and in the search helps in the struggle against the evil Lord of Annuvin. In the end it is because of Taran's efforts that Annuvin is destroyed. For some readers there are too many parallels with Tolkien's *Lord of the Rings*, but Alexander's characterization is better than that in

Tolkien's trilogy. However, Tolkien creates a more memorable world and a more powerful conflict between the forces of good and evil. For children too young for Tolkien, Alexander's series is an enjoyable introduction to this type of serious fantasy. Other books in the series are: *The Black Cauldron*, 1965; *The Castle of Llyr*, 1966. *The High King*, 1968 (The last of the series. Awarded the 1969 Newbery Medal); *Taran Wanderer*, 1967. (Grades 4–6)

————.*Coll and His White Pig*. New York: Holt, Rinehart and Winston, 1965. A picture book introduction to the land of Prydain for children too young to read the series about Taran. Coll rescues Hen Wen from the Lord of the Land of Death. (Grades 1–3)

Ardizzone, Edward, author-illustrator. *Little Tim and the Brave Sea Captain*. New York: Walck, 1955. A well-written story for primary children about a young boy who stows away and has to work his passage. He and the captain are the last to leave the ship when it sinks, and Tim returns home a hero. Other books in the series are: *Tim All Alone*, 1957; *Tim in Danger*, 1953; *Tim to the Rescue*, 1949. (Preschool–grade 2)

Atwater, Richard and Florence. *Mr. Popper's Penguins*. Illustrated by Robert Lawson. Boston: Little, Brown, 1938. When Mr. Popper receives a penguin from Antarctica, his family's life is changed. A humorous book still loved by children. (Grades 3–5)

Baum, L. Frank. *The Wonderful Wizard of Oz*. Illustrated by W. W. Denslow. Chicago: Reilly & Lee, 1956, 1900. A classic that still delights children. (Grades 3–6)

Bontemps, Arna, and Jack Conroy. *The Fast Sooner Hound*. Illustrated by Virginia Lee Burton. Boston: Houghton, 1942. Amusing tale of a dog who would sooner run than eat. (Grades 3–6)

Boston, L. M. *The Children of Green Knowe*. Illustrated by Peter Boston. New York: Harcourt, 1955. An intriguing fantasy set in a lovely old English estate owned by an elderly woman. Her lonely grandson meets children from the past. (Grades 4–7)

————. *An Enemy at Green Knowe*. Illustrated by Peter Boston. New York: Harcourt, 1964. A suspenseful story in which witchcraft threatens the peace and security of Green Knowe. (Grades 4–7)

————.*The River at Green Knowe*. Illustrated by Peter Boston. New York: Harcourt, 1959. Two elderly women and three displaced children inhabit Green Knowe in this book which is not as good as the first two. (Grades 4–7)

————.*A Stranger at Green Knowe*. Illustrated by Peter Boston. New York: Harcourt, 1961. A gorilla, escaped from a zoo, is harbored in the thicket at Green Knowe by Ping, a sensitive Chinese refugee boy. (Grades 4–7)

————. *The Treasure of Green Knowe*. Illustrated by Peter Boston. New York: Harcourt, 1958. A sequel to *The Children of Green Knowe*. (Grades 4–7)

Bradbury, Ray. *S is for Space*. New York: Doubleday, 1966. Sixteen science fiction short stories that grip the reader's interest. (Grades 7–up)

Brooke, L. Leslie, author-illustrator. *Johnny Crow's Garden*. New York: Warne, 1903, first published. A charmingly illustrated picture book that still delights today's children. Other books in the series are: *Johnny Crow's New Garden*, 1963, 1935; *Johnny Crow's Party*, 1907, first published. (Preschool–grade 2)

Bulla, Clyde Robert. *The Moon Singer*. Illustrated by Trina Schart Hyman. New York: Crowell, 1969. A sensitively written and beautifully illustrated story about a young boy who is at first scorned and then honored for his singing. Perhaps Bulla's best book. An illustration from this picture book is found in the color insert in Chapter 2. Older children will have even more enjoyment than younger readers. (Grades 3–6)

Burton, Virginia Lee, author-illustrator. *Mike Mulligan and His Steam Shovel*. Boston: Houghton, 1939. Mary Ann, Mike's steam shovel, faces obsolescence; only when they succeed in one last challenge can they settle down. (Grades K–2)

Carroll, Lewis, pseud. (Charles Dodgson). *Alice's Adventures in Wonderland and Through the Looking Glass*. Illustrated by John Tenniel. New York: Macmillan, 1963. First published separately in 1865 and 1872. A discussion of and an excerpt from *Alice's Adventures in Wonderland* can be found in this chapter (Grades 5–9)

Caudill, Rebecca. *A Pocketful of Cricket*. Illustrated by Evaline Ness. New York: Holt, Rinehart and Winston, 1964. A discussion of and an excerpt from this picture book can be found in this chapter (Grades K–2)

De Brunhoff, Jean, author-illustrator. *The Story of Babar*. Translated from the French by Merle S. Haas. New York: Random, 1960, 1933. The story of a little elephant who goes to town where it is clothed and housed by a rich Old Lady who likes elephants. (Preschool–grade 2)

Dennis, Wesley. *Flip*. New York: Viking, 1941. A horse story for the youngest readers. (Grades K–1)

————. *Flip and the Cows*. New York: Viking, 1942. A sequel to *Flip*. (Grades K–1)

De Regniers, Beatrice Schenk. *May I Bring a Friend?* Illustrated by Beni Montresor. New York: Atheneum, 1964. An amusing picture story of the antics of unusual "friends" brought to visit the king and queen. (Grades K–2)

Du Bois, William Pène, author-illustrator. *Twenty-One Ballons*. New York: Viking, 1947. The exciting adventures of Professor Sherman who set off to cross the ocean in a balloon but spent three weeks on a remarkable island which blew up almost without time for him and the inhabitants to escape. Awarded the 1948 Newbery Medal. (Grades 2–6)

Duvoisin, Roger, author-illustrator. *Petunia*. New York: Knopf, 1950. An amusing picture book about a goose. Some other animal fantasies by Duvoisin are: *Lonely Veronica*, 1963; *Veronica*, 1961; *Veronica's Smile*, 1964. (Preschool–grades 2)

Ets, Marie Hall, author-illustrator. *Mr. Penny's Race Horse*. New York: Viking, 1956. An amusing picture story of how Mr. Penny's animals conspire to help him win prizes at the fair. (Grades 1–3)

Fatio, Louise. *The Happy Lion*. Illustrated by Roger Duvoisin. New York: McGraw-Hill, 1954. A picture book about a lion in a French zoo who decides to visit all his friends among the townspeople. Other books in the series are: *The Happy Lion and the Bear*, 1964; *The Happy Lion in Africa*, 1955; *The Happy Lion Roars*, 1957; *The Happy Lion's Quest*, 1961; *The Three Happy Lions*, 1959. (Grades 1–3)

Gág, Wanda, author-illustrator. *Millions of Cats*. New York: Coward-McCann, 1928. A discussion of this book and its entire text can be found in this chapter. A picture from it is reproduced in Chapter 2, Illustrated Books. (Preschool–grade 4)

Grahame, Kenneth. *The Reluctant Dragon*. Illustrated by E. H. Shepard. New York: Holiday, 1953, 1938. A boy helps a dragon who wants to be left in peace and a St. George who does not really want to kill the dragon save face. (Grades 3–5)

————. *The Wind in the Willows*. Illustrated by E. H. Shepard. New York: Scribner, first published 1908. A discussion of and an excerpt from this book can be found in this chapter. (Grades 5–9)

Gramatky, Hardie, author-illustrator. *Little Toot*. New York: Putnam, 1939. A picture book about a small tugboat who proves his worth by rescuing an ocean liner. (Grades K–2)

Green, Alexander. *Scarlet Sails*. Translated from the Russian by Thomas P. Whitney. Illustrated by Esta Nesbitt. New York: Scribners, 1967. A poor girl is told a prince will one day come for her in a ship with scarlet sails. The villagers mock her for this; and yet, by the miracles of love and kindness the prophecy is fulfilled. A well-translated, beautiful story that belongs both to the realm of fantasy and the world of reality. (Grades 5–9)

Jarrell, Randall. *The Animal Family*. Illustrated by Maurice Sendak. New York: Pantheon, 1965. A lonely hunter rescues a mermaid and together they live happily, yet both have a longing for something besides themselves. A bear cub and a lynx kitten help ease their yearning somewhat, but not until a young shipwrecked boy is found is the family really complete. A beautiful, gentle story; one with great charm. Beautifully illustrated. (Grade 5–up)

Johnson, Crockett, author-illustrator. *Harold and the Purple Crayon*. New York: Harper & Row, 1955. Imaginative picture book. Harold's crayon can draw him into and out of anything. Other books in the series are: *Harold's Circus*, 1959; *Harold's Fairy Tale*, 1956; *Harold's Trip to the Sky*, 1957. (Preschool–grade 2)

Keats, Ezra Jack, author-illustrator. *Jennie's Hat*. New York: Harper & Row, 1966. With the birds' help, Jennie's plain hat is transformed into the most elaborately beautiful hat of all. A charming picture book. (Grades K–2)

Kendall, Carol. *The Gammage Cup*. Illustrated by Erik Blegvad. New York: Harcourt, 1959. A discussion of and an excerpt from this book can be found in this chapter. (Grades 4–6)

————. *The Whisper of Glocken*. Illustrated by Imero Gobbato. New York: Harcourt, 1965. When the Watercress River begins flowing backwards, the Minnipin villages are threatened. Five new heroes must go outside the valley to discover and remove the cause of the flooding. (Grades 4–6)

Key, Alexander. *The Forgotten Door*. Philadelphia: Westminster, 1965. A discussion of and an excerpt from this book can be found in this chapter. (Grades 4–9)

Kipling, Rudyard. *The Elephant's Child*. Illustrated by Feodor Rojankovsky. New York: Garden City Books, 1942. Picture book treatments of three of Kiplings most popular tales. Others are: *How the Camel Got His Hump*, 1942; *How the Leopard Got His Spots*, 1942. (Grades 3–6)

————. *Just-So Stories*. Illustrated by Nicolas. New York: Doubleday, 1952. Ever popular tales. (Grades 3–6)

Lagerlöf, Selma. *The Wonderful Adventures of Nils.* Translated from the Swedish by Velma Swanston Howard. Illustrated by H. Baumhauer. New York: Pantheon, 1947. An abridgment of the two-volume Swedish classic originally published in 1907 and 1911. Nils, transformed to only a few inches in height, travels on a grey goose all over Sweden. Much of Swedish history and folklore is revealed in this beautiful and interesting novel. (Grades 4–7)

Langstaff, John, reteller. *Frog Went A-Courting.* Illustrated by Feodor Rojankovsky. New York: Harcourt, 1955. Picture-book treatment of a nonsensical old Scottish ballad. Awarded the 1956 Caldecott Medal. (Grades K–2)

Lawson, Robert, author-illustrator. *Ben and Me: A New and Astonishing Life of Benjamin Franklin, As Written by His Good Mouse Amos; Lately Discovered, Edited & Illustrated by Robert Lawson.* Boston: Little, Brown, 1939. An amusing account of how a mouse helped Benjamin Franklin achieve success. (Grades 2–5)

————. *Mr. Revere and I . . . . .* Boston: Little, Brown, 1953. Another amusing biography of a famous American, told by his horse. (Grades 2–5)

Lawson, Robert, author-illustrator. *Rabbit Hill.* New York: Viking, 1945. With a new family moving into the Big House, all the wild animals were anxious about their attitudes toward gardening and animals. A fine fantasy with good characterization. (Grades 3–6)

————. *Robbut, a Tale of Tails.* New York: Viking, 1948. An amusing story about a rabbit discontented with his tail. The moral does not spoil the reader's enjoyment. (Grades 1–4)

————. *The Tough Winter.* New York: Viking, A sequel to *Rabbit Hill.* (Grades 3–6)

Leaf, Monro, *The Story of Ferdinand.* Illustrated by Robert Lawson. New York: Viking, 1936. The amusing story of a peace-loving bull who did not want to hurt bull fighters. (Grades K–3)

Le Guin, Ursula K. *A Wizard of Earthsea.* Illustrated by Ruth Robbins. Berkely, Calif.: Parnassus Press, 1968. A discussion of and excerpts from this book can be found in this chapter (Grades 6–9)

Lewis, C. S. *The Horse and His Boy.* Illustrated by Pauline Baynes. New York: Macmillan, 1962. Known as the Chronicles of Narnia by their many admirers, these books deal with the conflict between the forces of good and the forces of evil.

Four children find their way into another world and become involved with the lives of its peoples. Other books in this series are: *The Last Battle,* 1964; *The Lion, the Witch, and the Wardrobe,* 1961; *The Magician's Nephew,* 1964; *Prince Caspian, The Return to Narnia,* 1964; *The Silver Chair,* 1962; *The Voyage of the "Dawn Trader,"* 1962. The order in which the books should be read is: *The Lion, The Witch and the Wardrobe, Prince Caspian . . . , The Voyage of the Dawn Trader, The Silver Chair, The Horse and His Boy, The Magician's Nephew, The Last Battle.* (Grades 4–7)

Lindgren, Astrid, adapter. *The Tomten and the Fox.* From a poem by Karl-Erik Forsslund. Illustrated by Harald Wiberg. New York: Coward-McCann, 1961. The Tomten is a protector of Swedish farms. The peace of Christmas night and a snow covered farm are shown in this exceptionally beautiful picture book. (Grades 1–4)

Lionni, Leo, author-illustrator. *Inch by Inch.* New York: Obolensky, 1959. A simple picture book about an inchworm who cleverly avoids being eaten by the birds. (Preschool–grade 1)

————. *Little Blue and Little Yellow.* New York: Obolensky, 1959. (Grades K–2)

————. *Swimmy.* New York: Pantheon, 1963. These last two picture books have overtones of subtle social commentary. (Grades K–1)

Lobel, Anita, author-illustrator. *The Troll Music.* New York: Harper & Row, 1966. A picture book about a group of bewitched musicians whose music sounds like animal noises. They attempt to placate the troll whose spell has them in its power. (Grades K–3)

MacGregor, Ellen. *Miss Pickerell and the Geiger Counter.* Illustrated by Paul Galdone. New York: McGraw-Hill, 1953. Science fiction and adventure stories for younger children. Other books in the series are: *Miss Pickerell Goes to Mars,* 1951; *Miss Pickerell Goes to the Arctic,* 1954; *Miss Pickerell Goes Undersea,* 1953. (Grades 2–4)

McCloskey, Robert, author-illustrator. *Burt Dow, Deep-Water Man.* New York: Viking, 1963. A delightful fantasy about the encounter of a sea man and his leaky boat with a school of whales. (Grades 1–3)

————. *Make Way for Ducklings.* New York: Viking, 1941. An interesting picture book about a pair of ducks who hatch their eggs in a Boston park. Awarded the 1942 Caldecott Medal. (Grades K–3)

McKenzie, Ellen Kindt. *Taash and the Jesters.* New York: Holt, Rinehart and Winston, 1968. Taash rescues a baby from witches and then attempts to return him to his parents, the king and queen. An engrossing fantasy of the struggle between the forces of good and evil. (Grades 5–8)

Milne, A. A. *The House at Pooh Corner.* Illustrated by Ernest H. Shepard. New York: Dutton, 1928. A sequel to *Winnie the Pooh.*

————·*Winnie the Pooh.* Illustrated by Ernest H. Shepard. New York: Dutton, 1926. A discussion of and an excerpt from this book can be found in this chapter. (Grades 1–4)

Norton, Andre. *Key out of Time.* Cleveland: World Publishing, 1963. Andre Norton is one of the most popular writers of science fiction for children and adolescents. Some of her other titles are:

————·*Moon of Three Rings.* New York: Viking, 1966.

————· *Night of Masks.* New York: Harcourt, 1964.

————·*Steel Magic.* Illustrated by Robin Jacques. Cleveland: World Publishing, 1965.

Norton, Mary. *Bed-Knob and Broomstick.* Illustrated by Erik Blegvad. New York: Harcourt, 1957. A story of magic in which the Wilson children have many adventures. (Grades 3–5)

————. *The Borrowers.* Illustrated by Beth and Joe Krush. New York: Harcourt, 1953. A discussion of and an excerpt from this book can be found in this chapter. Other books in this popular series are: *The Borrowers Afield,* 1955; *The Borrowers Afloat,* 1959; *The Borrowers Aloft,* 1961. (Grades 3–6)

Parish, Peggy. *Amelia Bedelia and the Surprise Shower.* Illustrated by Fritz Siebel. New York: Harper & Row, 1966. An I Can Read picture book for first graders that portrays colloquialisms literally. The title comes from the incident when Amelia Bedelia and a friend turn the hose on a group of women at a party. A good motivation for discussions of colloquialisms; useful for older children who are also puzzled by them. (Grades K–3)

Payne, Emmy. *Katy No-Pocket.* Illustrated by H. A. Rey. Boston: Houghton Mifflin, 1944. An amusing picture book about a kangaroo who had no pocket in which to carry her son. (Grades K–2)

Potter, Beatrix, author-illustrator. *The Tailor of Gloucester.* New York: Warne, 1902. A Christmas story. (Preschool–grades 2)

————·*The Tale of Benjamin Bunny.* New York: Warne, 1904, first published. A sequel to *Peter Rabbit.* (Preschool–grade 2)

————· *The Tale of Jemima Puddle-Duck.* New York: Warne, 1908, first published. A humorous

story of a duck who is determined to hatch her eggs. (Preschool–grade 2)

————·*The Tale of Mrs. Tittlemouse.* New York: Warne, 1910, first published. An amusing story about a very tidy woodmouse. (Preschool–grade 2)

————. *The Tale of Peter Rabbit.* New York: 1903, first published. Still a classic young children love. A discussion and the entire text of this book can be found in this chapter. (Preschool–grade 2)

————. *The Tale of Squirrel Nutkin.* New York: Warne, 1903, first published. Nutkin asks many riddles of Mr. Brown. (Preschool–grade 2)

————. *The Tale of Tom Kitten.* New York: Warne, 1907, first published. Three kittens undo their mother's meticulous grooming of them. (Preschool–grade 2)

————. *The Tale of Two Bad Mice.* New York: Warne, 1904, first published. A story of two mischievous mice. (Preschool–grade 2)

Sandburg, Carl. *Rootabaga Stories.* Illustrated by Maud and Miska Petersham. New York: Harcourt, 1922. A selection from this book, "The Huckabuck Family and How They Raised Popcorn in Nebraska and Quit and Came Back," can be found in this chapter. (Grades 4–8)

Selden, George. *The Cricket in Times Square.* Illustrated by Garth Williams. New York: Farrar, Straus, 1960. A country cricket, Chester, unintentionally gets left in the Times Square subway station. He becomes the pet of Mario, whose father has the newsstand. Amazing things occur before Chester can return to the country. (Grades 3–6)

Sendak, Maurice, author-illustrator. *Higglety, Pigglety, Pop! Or, There Must Be More to Life.* New York: Harper & Row, 1967. A humorous picture book, beautifully illustrated with engravings, that will delight older children and adults. Adapted from an old nursery rhyme. (Grades 4–up)

————· *The Nutshell Library.* New York: Harper & Row, 1962. Four amusing picture books popular with young children: *Alligators All Around, Pierre, One Was Johnny,* and *Chicken Soup with Rice.* (Preschool–grade 2)

————· *Where the Wild Things Are.* New York: Harper & Row, 1963. A naughty little boy is sent supperless to bed. In his room he sails away to where the "wild things" live and is made king of all wild things. An excellent picture book, especially enjoyed by boys. Awarded the 1964 Caldecott Medal. (Preschool–grade 2)

Seuss, Dr., pseud. (Theodor Seuss Geisel), author-illustrator. *And To Think that I Saw It on Mulberry Street.* New York: Vanguard, 1937. A nonsense story told in verse. A small boy's imagination transforms a plain horse and wagon into an elaborate parade. (Grades K–3)

————. *The 500 Hats of Bartholomew Cubbins.* New York: Vanguard, 1938. A young peasant boy removes his hat as the king rides by, only to find he still has a hat on his head. Again and again he removes hats, each time angering the king more and more. (Grades 1–3)

————. *Horton Hatches an Egg.* New York: Random House, 1940. (Grades K–3)

————. *Yertle the Turtle, and Other Stories.* New York: Random House, 1958. A discussion of this story and its entire text can be found in this chapter. (Grade K–up)

Sharp, Margery. *Miss Bianca.* Illustrated by Garth Williams. Boston: Little, Brown, 1962. Miss Bianca, a small, sophisticated mouse, leads an expedition to rescue a young girl held captive by the cruel Grand Duchess in the Diamond Palace. An engrossing plot and a delightful fantasy. (Grades 3–5). Others in the series are:

————. *Miss Bianca in the Salt Mines.* Illustrated by Garth Williams. Boston: Little, Brown, 1966. Miss Bianca and Bernard brave great obstacles and dangers to rescue Teddy, age eight, from the Salt Mines. (Grades 3–5)

————. *The Rescuers.* Illustrated by Garth Williams. Boston: Little, Brown, 1959. The first in the series in which Miss Bianca's Aid Society (of mice) sets out to rescue a Norwegian poet held in the Black Castle. (Grades 3–5)

————. *The Turret.* Illustrated by Garth Williams. Boston: Little, Brown, 1963. Miss Bianca almost singlehandedly rescues a reformed jailer held prisoner by the wicked Grand Duchess. (Grades 3–5)

Slobodkin, Louis. *The Space Ship Returns to the Apple Tree.* New York: Macmillan, 1958; *The Space Ship Under the Apple Tree,* 1952. Entertaining science fiction. (Grades 2–4)

Thurber, James. *The Great Quillow.* Illustrated by Doris Lee. New York: Harcourt, 1944. When a giant comes to prey on the town, Quillow, the short toymaker, cleverly thinks of a plan to make the giant leave. (Grade 3–up)

————. *Many Moons.* Illustrated by Louis Slobodkin. New York: Harcourt, 1943. A spoiled princess demands the moon and the court must get it for her. (Grades 4–5)

Tolkien, J. R. R. *The Hobbit.* Boston: Houghton Mifflin, 1938. An engrossing adventure–fantasy; very popular. (Grade 7–up)

————. *The Fellowship of the Ring.* Boston: Houghton, Mifflin, 1954; *The Return of the King,* 1956; *The Two Towers,* 1955. These three books form a continuous trilogy in which the power and danger of the ring found in *The Hobbit* are revealed. Tension and suspense are the main qualities of these books, and they are so strong they prevent the casual reader from realizing there is little characterization. (Grade 7–up)

Travers, Pamela L. *Mary Poppins.* Illustrated by Mary Shepard. New York: Harcourt, 1934. *Mary Poppins Comes Back,* 1935; *Mary Poppins in the Park,* 1952; *Mary Poppins Opens the Door.* (Illustrated by Mary Shepard and Agnes Sims), 1943. A very popular series about a vain but appealing English Nanny. A discussion of and an excerpt from *Mary Poppins* can be found in this chapter. (Grades 3–6)

Waber, Bernard, author-illustrator. *An Anteater Named Arthur.* New York: Houghton Mifflin, 1967. Arthur, an anteater, is very like many little boys: stubborn, loving, forgetful, lovable, funny, finicky. His story is told with comments on children's behavior in an humorous nondidactic way. (Grades K–3)

————. *Lyle, Lyle, Crocodile.* New York: Houghton Mifflin, 1965; *Rich Cat, Poor Cat,* 1963; *You Look Ridiculous Said the Rhinoceros to the Hippopotamus,* 1966. Humorous picture books about animals who act and talk like people. (Grades K–2)

Ward, Lynd, author-illustrator. *The Biggest Bear.* Boston: Houghton Mifflin, 1952. A young boy raises a bear cub that grows and grows. A humorous picture book. (Grades K–3)

Zemach, Harve. *The Judge: An Untrue Tale.* Illustrated by Margot Zemach. New York: Farrar, 1969. An original verse story written in the style of a cumulative folktale. Amusing; will delight both elementary children and adults. (Grades K–3)

Zolotow, Charlotte, *Mr. Rabbit and the Lovely Present.* Illustrated by Maurice Sendak. New York: Harper & Row, 1962. With Mr. Rabbit's help a little girl searches for the perfect present for her mother. An entertaining picture book. (Preschool–grade 2)

Part IV

INFORMATIONAL BOOKS

Many older elementary school children prefer informational books, biographies and nonfiction works, to novels. They are eager to read every book available in the library that deals with their individual area of interest. Such readers often need guidance to find the books most appropriate for their reading abilities and most helpful in providing accurate information. Even those children who prefer fiction should experience the different type of pleasure to be gained from informational books.

The field of informational literature has expanded greatly in the last twenty years. Unfortunately many books have been written quickly with too little attention to accuracy or quality. In the following section the elements and types of biography and nonfiction written specifically for children are discussed in the introductory essays.

The biography section includes excerpts from books written for young readers as well as for older elementary and junior high school students.

The major emphasis is on American figures, with two representatives from minority groups. Two other selections deal with Europeans.

The nonfiction excerpts begin with several short pieces from seventeenth- and eighteenth-century books for children. These not only provide a historical perspective, but are also entertaining in their own right. Even contemporary children will enjoy reading these selections. The other excerpts in this chapter were chosen to illustrate the many types of children's nonfiction discussed in the introductory essay.

Both the biography and nonfiction chapters include a few examples of poorly developed books to facilitate comparisons between the well written and the mediocre. Since many informational books are poorly written, it is important that criteria of evaluation be established. Children can gain varied insights as well as factual knowledge from this type of literature, but they need many experiences with the best the field can offer.

Chapter 12

Biography

From *Benjamin West and His Cat Grimalkin* by Marguerite Henry and Wesley Dennis, copyright, 1947, by The Bobbs-Merrill Company, Inc., reprinted by permission of the publishers.

Because many children appear to be more interested in men of action than men of ideas, biographies written for young readers are usually about those who have lived dramatic lives. Children are drawn to this genre by the knowledge that it is based on truth, but they still insist on a gripping story.

Although many biographies have been produced for young readers in the last fifty years, no other type of children's literature has so many poorly written books. Some are no more than mediocre reworkings of old material in which new historical findings are not included. Others are rather dull lists of facts. This occurs when biographers are unable to select from their many carefully collected details those that will best create a unified picture of the subject. Louisa May Alcott, the central figure of *Invincible Louisa*, by Cornelia Meigs, is obscured by multitudinous details meant to reveal her personality. Another cause of dullness is the author who prefers telling about the subject rather than using action and dialogue to reveal the personality and recreate the life. This happens in *Invincible Louisa*, a chapter of which appears in the following section.

A more serious weakness occurs when an author becomes so involved in his subject's importance that he relies more on insistence and direct editorializing than on revealing his information in narrative form. A selection from *Lone Journey* by Jeanette Eaton is reprinted to illustrate the ineffectiveness of this approach. Better arranged and conceived biographies, such as *America's Ethan Allen* by Stewart Holbrook and Lynd Ward and *America's Mark Twain* by May McNeer, clearly show the significance of those details that are included. Both books incorporate facts into dramatized scenes of both public and private experiences to create a feeling of reality and to give the reader an understanding of the central figure's personality and motivations.

Because children respond best to a narrative style, biographers who write for them usually must create dialogue, thoughts, and scenes. Responsible writers do not invent these, but use the ideas found through careful research of letters, diaries, other writings, and speeches. Such material can create the sense of immediacy so essential in books for children.

Biographies written for juveniles differ from those written for adults in several ways. Much more fictionalizing is present in biographies for children, and the documentation essential in adult biographies is still rare in children's books. Also, while adults expect to read about the central character's weaknesses as well as his strengths, his failures as well as his successes, biographies for children traditionally have stressed the positive aspects of the life and minimized the failures. The tragedies and scandalous events, no matter how significant, have been glossed over or entirely ignored as being inappropriate for children.

Change has been occurring, however. In his biography for young children Ronald Syme did not exclude Vasco da Gama's arrogance and foolish behavior. *Hero of Trafalgar* is another example of this move toward a more complete presentation. In addition to the great victories, A. B. C. Whipple also shows the cruelty of eighteenth-century British naval life. And he not only reveals Lord Nelson's heroic qualities of leadership but also includes the fact that he deserted his wife to live with Lady Hamilton.

These two biographies are part of the trend toward greater honesty in children's literature that gained momentum in the 1960s. This movement is based on the knowledge that children today see many sad and tragic events on television and even in their own neighborhoods. If they are going to be able to accept the reality of literature and if books are to help them handle the reality of their own lives, then the literature they read should not create false expectations. Modern biographies that show how people with recognizable human faults have made remarkable achievements can give children realistic hopes for their own potential.

For comparative purposes, examples of well-written and poorly written biographies are included in the following collection. Individual introductions go into greater detail about their strengths and weaknesses. The selections also have been chosen to permit a cross-cultural approach. Biographies about a religious man, a military hero, an Indian, a Portugese explorer, and other significant figures have been included.

AMERICA'S ETHAN ALLEN

Stewart Holbrook
Lynd Ward

Ethan Allen played an important role in the movement toward America's freedom. In 1775 he led eighty-three of his Green Mountain Boys across Lake Champlain. They captured Fort Ticonderoga and Fort Crown Point from the British and opened an invasion route to Canada. This victory, less than a month after the battles at Lexington and Concord, cheered the delegates of the Second Continental Congress.

As the following excerpt from America's Ethan Allen *reveals, previous to the Revolution Ethan Allen was instrumental in defending the rights of small farmers against large absentee landowners. Allen was representative of the Yankee spirit of independence that has characterized many New Englanders.*

The biography by Stewart Holbrook and Lynd Ward presents the issues behind Allen's struggle more clearly than any of the other biographies written about him for children. Through dramatic recreation the authors show the significance of the Green Mountain Boys' fight against New York.

Selling out his iron business, Ethan looked around for something to do. He wanted to get away, he said, to do something new, something different than he had been doing. There was a lot of talk going around about the wild region north of Connecticut colony. Not much was known of it other than that the governor of New Hampshire was selling land very cheaply up there. The region was generally known as the New Hampshire Grants.

Only a few brave souls had seen this distant

northern country. It was said to be full of game and fish, now becoming scarce in Connecticut. Its forests, so Ethan heard, were of wonderful pine, and its steep hills were so well covered with timber they were called Green Mountains. It sounded to Ethan like a good country.

Always a man of quick action, Ethan called brothers Heman and Levi into conference. "I am going up and look over the New Hampshire Grants," he said.

"What's the idea?" asked Heman.

"I think it might be a good place, maybe, to start a new colony."

"What's the matter with Connecticut?"

"Oh, the people are becoming too thick. These settlements are too close together. I want room."

"I hear it's pretty cold up there on the Grants," put in Levi.

"Well, it's winter right now," said Ethan. "A good time to find out how cold it is."

"Think you can find your way around?"

"Find my way around?" Ethan exploded. "Why I could find my way clean to Canada, if I was to go there."

Taking a hunting knife, a gun, a powder horn, with flint and steel, and a pocketful of dried venison, Ethan strapped on his snowshoes and said good-bye to his brothers and his wife and child.

"Mary," he told his wife, "I think that is good country up on the Grants. Maybe I will find a place for us to settle on the frontier."

"I don't know whether I'd like to be so far from home."

"You wait and see. We can have land for almost nothing up there."

Ethan Allen had become one of the best woodsmen in America. Now he traveled a hundred miles into the deep pine forest, making camp at night under a windfall of branches, cooking game that he shot, noting the streams and the hills, the fine pines and spruces, the groves of great maples, and the ridges of fine beech. He was enchanted with this great wilderness, with its hush, broken only by the melancholy cry of the owl, and the howls of wolves and bobcats.

For many days he traveled without seeing a human being or a house. And then a fierce blizzard came on suddenly. His clothes were damp. Knowing that he might well freeze to death if he stopped moving, and unable to find any natural shelter from the storm, Ethan marked out a path in a circle and walked it all night. Long before morning his powerful body became woefully tired, and he staggered and even fell a few times. Each time, however, he managed to get to his feet.

The storm let up about daylight. Ethan had survived. Now that he could see, he found a spot under some thick pines where the snow had not penetrated. Digging with his hands he scooped together a mass of dry pine needles. With his knife he cut dead branches from trees, and soon he had a brisk fire going, hot enough to thaw out his clothes and to warm his dried venison. In later years he told how he had never been quite so near death as that night in the blizzard.

Yet he had fallen in love with this new, untouched region, and by the time he was home again in Connecticut, he knew that he wanted to move to the Grants.

Ethan Allen could hardly have known what a violent place the New Hampshire Grants were soon to become. When he first saw the country, it was all silent except for the calls of the wild birds and animals and the sighing of wind in the pines.

It was soon going to be changed from solitude to a storm of troubles by the King of England, who did not know very much about his colonies in America. For one thing, he had permitted the governor of New Hampshire to sell land west of the Connecticut River. For another, he had permitted the governor of New York to sell land eastward from the Hudson to the Connecticut River.

Many Connecticut men, including friends of Ethan Allen, had bought lands on the Grants from New Hampshire. Other men, in New York, had bought the same lands from their governor.

Everyone knows that two men cannot each own the same piece of ground. By the time Ethan had returned from his winter trip, a number of Connecticut men were worried. They had bought New Hampshire land on the Grants. Some had already moved to settle there. Others were planning to do so. But now they were told by the governor of New York that their lands had been sold elsewhere, especially in large tracts to New York land speculators—people who bought and sold land to make money not to live on.

Not long after his trip through the Grants, a group of Connecticut men called on him.

"Ethan," said the spokesman, "you know what is going on about our lands up there?"

"I think I do. They have been sold two ways."

"That's it. We men here paid cash for our lands to Governor Wentworth of New Hampshire. Now New York claims we have no right to them."

"It is a case, gentlemen, of speculation by the wealthy men of New York."

"They themselves are not going to live on the Grants."

"Not they," growled Ethan. "They will not even see the lands they claim to have bought."

"We know that. But what can we do to hold the lands we have paid for?"

"Sirs, you can fight for them."

"But the courts are slow."

"Hang the courts! I mean fight, FIGHT—unless you are sheep."

There was silence for a moment, then Ethan, his brow darkening, his eyes squinting, spoke again.

"Gentlemen," he fairly roared, "you can't defend your titles until you get busy. The Yorkers are up there right now!"

There was more talk, and the group went away with plans to meet soon again, well satisfied that they had found a staunch man in rugged young Ethan Allen.

The next meeting was held one day in March, 1770, in a tavern at Canaan, Connecticut. Ethan was there by invitation. The group agreed for each man to pay a sum of money into a fund to be used to defend their land titles against the Yorkers. Ethan was to act for the group. He was to use the courts, they instructed him, or, if the courts failed to act, any other method that seemed best.

Calling for his horse immediately, Ethan mounted in front of the tavern. "My friends," he cried in tones that shook the window panes, "I am on my way to Portsmouth to talk to Governor Wentworth. If he can do nothing to help us, I shall act. . . ." Waving his hat, he slapped his steed and away he galloped on the trail northward, while the Connecticut men cheered.

At Portsmouth Ethan got copies of the deeds to the lands sold on the Grants by New Hampshire. He also bought a tract for himself. While riding back to Connecticut, he learned that the governor of New York had just issued a proclamation ordering all New Hampshire settlers on the Grants to give up their lands and leave, or be ejected (thrown out) by the New York officers. By now some thirty or more Connecticut families had actually settled on the Grants. They had made clearings for their fields. Gardens were growing. Fences had been put up. Cabins and barns had been built.

Ethan hired the best lawyer he could find in Connecticut and rode fast to Albany, in New York, where the hearings for ejectment were to be held. The judges, all New York men, quickly decided in favor of the New York claimants. Ethan was more than disappointed. He was very angry. Then one of the Yorkers came to him.

"Mr. Allen," said he, "if you will aid the New York cause, we shall be glad to give you, free, a large parcel of land on the grants."

"Sir," Ethan spoke indignantly, "I represent the genuine settlers, the poor people who are living there. I want none of *your* land."

"Mr. Allen," the Yorker spoke very sternly, "you should be advised that your people already on the Grants will do well to deal with *us*. We Yorkers are the rightful landlords. We have might on our side and you know that might often makes right."

Ethan was getting hot under the collar, but he held his temper well. "Sir," he replied, just as sternly as the other, "the gods of the hills are not the gods of the valleys."

The Yorker did not understand. "What do you mean?" he asked.

"Come with me to the Grants," answered Ethan, "and what I mean will become clear." It was obviously some sort of threat. Ethan followed it up. "Our country people on the Grants," said he, "do not understand your complicated and unfair city laws. But they do understand they have paid for the lands they are living on."

"They are mistaken."

"Perhaps, sir, you Yorkers are mistaken. Do you think that a man who has cut his home out of the savage woods, who has made corn grow among the stumps is to be driven off by words?"

With that, Ethan Allen mounted his horse and rode back to the Grants to the new village of Bennington. On the way he thought over the problem. These Yorkers were simply owners of huge grants of land which they meant to sell. Not one of them planned to settle on the land they claimed. It was quite different with Ethan's group of small farmers. More were already coming to the Grants to add to the thirty pioneer families.

On arriving at Bennington Ethan was met by the settlers in the new tavern built by Landlord Stephen Fay. It was called "The Catamount," and to show that Landlord Fay was on the side of the settlers headed by Ethan Allen, a stuffed catamount, or mountain lion, crouched on a pole outside the door. The animal's mouth was open in a snarl with its glittering teeth showing in the direction of New York.

Ethan was delighted with the big cat. "Show your teeth!" he shouted as he drove up. "Show your teeth and snarl! By the gods of the hills I swear that Yorkers shall not steal our lands by the trickery of courts!"

The settlers gathered around the tall young man whose voice could carry almost a full mile. "Boys," he shouted, "boys, we've got to organize a regiment of fighting men if we are going to hold our lands."

Landlord Fay spoke up. "Do you think they will try to put us out by force?"

"By force?" shouted Ethan. "By force? Of course they will. They will drive us off like so many wolves—if we don't protect ourselves."

"Well, why don't we protect ourselves?" It was Peleg Sunderland who spoke, a tough old Indian fighter, a man who knew the woods and the rivers, who liked bear meat for breakfast.

"Yes, let's have an army," put in Levi Allen now come to live on the Grants. His huge brother Ethan looked over the men present, his wild eyes flashing with the idea of a backwoods army. "Come," he rumbled, "let us get busy."

Then and there, in the Catamount Tavern, Ethan Allen formed a company of fighting men, a small army whose soldiers all swore they would be ready to meet at a moment's notice to defend the farms of all New Hampshire settlers.

Ethan Allen was elected colonel. His chief officer was his cousin, Seth Warner. Among the rank and file were brothers Levi and Ira, and the seasoned old Indian fighter, Peleg Sunderland.

Yorker spies in Bennington quickly got word to the governor of New York, reporting that Allen had raised a company of men and was drilling them. The governor boiled over. He swore that he would drive those bad men into the Green Mountains.

Ethan, always quick to sense the value of good publicity, was elated. "Men," he cried, "the

Yorker governor has named us. We are the 'Green Mountain Boys'!"

But the governor was not fooling. Soon on his order came Yorker Sheriff Ten Eyck and a posse of three hundred men, all armed, to evict a settler named Breakenridge. Word of his coming was brought on ahead by a New Hampshire man, and young Jonas Fay, son of the Catamount landlord, sent runners speeding to the scattered farms.

"A wolf hunt, a wolf hunt!" shouted the runners. "A wolf hunt at the Breakenridge place."

This was all the news that was needed. Young men in buckskin took down their long guns from over fireplaces, and quickly gathered near the Breakenridge farm, all unknown to the Yorker sheriff and his crew. The Green Mountain Boys signaled each other by imitating bird calls, and presently had taken places where they could cover the farm with their guns.

When Sheriff Ten Eyck and his three hundred men moved into the Breakenridge clearing, they saw that the cabin was well barricaded and the log walls pierced with mean-looking loopholes, each just large enough for a gun barrel.

In the Breakenridge field were forty men with guns across their arms. This reception did not look very encouraging to the sheriff, but he marched on until he came to the edge of the field. Here he was stopped by seven of the waiting men.

"Out of my way!" roared the sheriff. "I am here to enforce the laws of the colony of New York."

"The laws of New York do not apply in the Green Mountains," growled one of the seven.

"Go back to New York where you belong," said another.

But after a brief discussion the sheriff was permitted to advance to a spot near the house, where Farmer Breakenridge came out to meet him. The sheriff read the order of eviction.

"That paper means nothing to me," said the resolute farmer. "I am under protection of the town of Bennington and her Green Mountain Boys. He waved his hand toward the armed men in the field, who stood silent and sinister and ready. Breakenridge waved his hand again, and the sheriff noted something he had not seen before: the heads and guns of what looked to be another hundred or more men, peering down from the top of a ridge above the field.

It was a tough spot, but the sheriff was equal to it. He returned to his army and gave orders to advance. But the men did not have the spirit needed to move under the guns of those half-hidden men on the ridge. They started to fall away, first in two's and three's, then by the dozen. But the brave sheriff and some twenty men walked toward the cabin.

"Open the door or I'll batter it down!" he shouted.

It was a tense moment. Just then the sheriff heard what sounded like an order given in the woods on the ridge, followed by clicking noises. In one glance the Yorker saw that the forty men in the field had leveled their guns at him, while another hundred guns were trained from the ridge. Sheriff Ten Eyck knew when he was beaten. Letting go a loud curse, he and his remaining crew turned and went away.

The Green Mountain Boys had won their first battle without a shot.

LONE JOURNEY: The Life of Roger Williams

Jeanette Eaton

For fourteen chapters Lone Journey *is a satisfactory although not an exceptional biography; it has enough dramatized passages to prevent the information from becoming boring. While it never rises to excellence, it is only in the last chapter that it becomes overtly didactic. Jeanette Eaton, like many writers, refuses or is unable to allow plot and characterization to reveal her subject's importance and contributions. Subtlety is put aside for sermonizing that should be unnecessary; it only reveals the author's feeling that she has not "made her point" clearly enough. In well-written biography, the reader learns the subject's value through the interaction of characterization and the events of his life.*

The following excerpt, the final chapter of Lone Journey, *is given as an example of didactic literature. Miss Eaton here abandons narrative form to lecture her reader, who is already convinced of the greatness of Roger Williams. Such a lecture is ineffective and even destroys the reader's enjoyment of the previous fourteen chapters.*

Americans are just beginning to realize what Roger Williams did for us. Without him, the New World would not have been new, for he brought to it an irresistible passion for freedom which started us on our way.

He won the great battle for religious freedom. To do so he had to strive on both sides of the

ocean. In America he founded a state based on liberty of conscience. In England his written and spoken words made minds tingle with the electricity of brave ideas. In a rush of healthy shame persecution was outlawed. Colonies began to be started in a more liberal spirit and slowly the belief spread that religion and government should be separate. For this reason the United States never had a national church and all faiths have been welcomed here.

The second contribution of this pioneer was to

create the first truly democratic government. Theories pointing that way had been growing in popularity. But Williams stated them with breath-taking courage:

> "Governmental agencies have not the least inch of civil power but what is measured out to them from the free consent of the whole."

Then he put the principle into practice and proved that a government which was the instrument of the people would actually work.

By sheer genius he devised a sound and flexible plan for a self-ruled society. He made citizens of his colony the envy of all who lived under the thumb of theocracies, royal governors, and arbitrary proprietors. The moment the Thirteen States declared independence of England, each of them adopted some form of democratic organization. Naturally the Constitutional Convention framed a similar plan for the nation.

Political power and liberty of thought as possessions of the people were novelties three hundred years ago. True, ever since the Reformation thinkers of the Western World had been discussing such possibilities. But Williams was the first to outline the *rights of man*. He did so in his pamphlets and in the preamble to the original constitution of Rhode Island. Never before on earth had these rights been embodied in an actual government.

Loyalty to this tradition met its great test in 1788. When the citizens of the state were presented the Constitution in that year, they refused to accept it until Congress had passed the Bill of Rights. Theirs was a powerful influence for the protection of our whole people.

As long as Roger Williams lived—and he lived to be an old man—he himself *was* the spirit of liberty in America. With unflagging energy, patience, and love of all living creatures, he worked to realize his dream of fellowship. Because he created a practical government of the people, organized a system of courts, and wrote a just penal code; because, after having done so, he could train men to use these tools, he proved himself one of the greatest statesmen who ever lived.

The power of this leader was not cut off by death. He belongs to our present and our future. The man who called himself a Seeker opened up new vistas to the religious impulse. He showed narrow-minded fanatics of all time that the important factor in a man's life is direct contact with the Spiritual World. Belonging to a church is no substitute for applying the principles of religion to life itself.

Roger Williams' life illustrates what has to be done if religion is to come true on earth. How to apply it to all relationships, all tasks and duties, is made very clear by this man's activities. They throw light on the most gripping problems of the immediate future.

Foremost among them is race prejudice. What is race prejudice? It is an unreasoning and unloving attitude toward a whole group of people born into the world as members of a certain race. Prejudice against a race is based on a feeling of superiority.

Roger Williams saw it operating in New England against the Indians. Englishmen considered them inferior. Certainly in education, opportunity, and the kind of social experience we call civilization, the natives were no match for the immigrants. But white superiority expressed itself by taking every possible advantage of the redskins. Land was stolen from them—hundreds of acres at a clip. Traders exchanged worthless gewgaws for valuable furs. Continual sale of liquor to the tribes undermined their morale in a single generation. Colonial officials really preferred military expeditions to arbitration when trouble with a tribe arose, for it gave them a chance to seize more land and power.

While superiority was thus at work, John Eliot of Massachusetts was translating the Bible into the Indian language and was boasting of converting savages to Christianity. Churchmen in London and New England alike were very proud of this work. It was a beautiful screen for the wickedness of English and Dutch officials in their policy toward the natives.

Like a white silhouette on a black page, the attitude of Roger Williams towards the Indians stands out in contrast to that of other leaders.

To him, superior endowment and worldly advantage came by Heaven's Grace. They carried an obligation to love and understand all who were less fortunate. To fulfill that obligation brings humility. For the moment one begins to love and understand others, their own superior virtues appear. Roger's *Key into the Language of America* gave Englishmen for the first time some notion of the admirable traits of the Indians.

"I could never discern that excess of scandalous sins amongst them which Europe aboundeth with. Drunkenness and gluttony generally they knew not what sinnes they be; and although they have not so much to restrain them both in respect of a knowledge of God, and the laws of men, as the English have, yet a man shall never hear of such amongst them as robberies, murthers, adulteries, etc., as amongst the English."

Of their hospitality, Williams said:

"Whomsoever cometh in when they are eating, they offer them to eat of that which they have, though but little enough prepared for themselves. . . . Many a time and at all times in the night, as I have fallen in travel upon their houses, when nothing hath been ready, have themselves and their wives risen to prepare me some refreshing. It is a strange truth that a man shall generally find more free entertainment and refreshing amongst these Barbarians than amongst thousands that call themselves Christians."

He admired the strength and cleverness of the Indians. He said they were "joyful in travel" and inventive about household tools and decorations. To him, their tribal family life had much beauty of affection and of custom. He watched their games, their ceremonies and conferences. Affection without tinge of sentimentality led him to fair judgment of this people. He judged them just as he did Englishmen. Some were tricky, some had an unfailing sense of honor.

After learning much about their religion, which included thirty-seven gods, he came to the conclusion that converting Indians to Christianity was possible in only one way. It wasn't by baptism or ritual or Sabbath laws or teaching prayers by rote. Only if a white man himself practiced his beliefs with passionate conviction could he make any impression upon a savage. So long as the English and Dutch failed to apply to Indians the love, mercy, and justice taught by their religion, talk of conversion was hypocrisy and illusion.

To do as you would be done by—that was Roger's simple rule. Because he never ceased to follow it, he was the trusted friend of all the tribes. He returned their hospitality, sold them useful articles only, paid in wampum or services for land, and at all times told them the truth. In order to prevent destructive wars he traveled hundreds of miles, risked his life, argued and planned.

All these things he did because he really cared for the good of native Americans. He hoped that somehow the two races might learn to share life together in the wilderness. How little he felt the superiority of the white man appears in this quaint verse from *Key into the Language of America:*

"When Indians hear the horrid filth
    Of Irish, Englishmen
The horrids oaths and murders hate
    Thus say the Indians then:
"We wear no clothes, have many gods
    And yet our sins are less.
You are barbarians, pagans wild,
    Your land's the wilderness.
"Oft have I heard the Indians say
    These English will deceive us.
Of all that's ours, our lands and lives,
    in the end they will bereave us."

Every word and act of Roger Williams in dealing with the Indians should be studied by Americans today. In this land are many nationalities, many races. All of us have to learn to live and work together. With humor, patience, and mutual respect we, too, may hope that all the races on this continent can some day share life here on equal terms. Williams showed us the way. He knew that good and bad persons can be found in every race. His example shows that it is the duty of every individual to work actively against racial prejudice wherever it blazes out.

To Roger Williams, Jews were people of an ancient religion, not a separate race. When the question of admitting Jews to Rhode Island came up, it seemed to him no different from the question of welcoming Quakers. And there could be but one answer to it. Either one believed in the *principle* of liberty of conscience or one didn't. Believers had to apply the principle to all people everywhere.

Williams hated backward ideas and selfishness wherever he found them. He saw no difference between the trickery of Uncas, the Mohegan, and that of the notable members of the Massachusetts General Court, who tried by forgery to steal Narragansett territory. An individual must be judged, not by race or color, but by what he himself is—that was his rule. It holds good today.

Another reason why Roger Williams belongs to our day and to the future is very different in character. It concerns the problems of wealth and trade. They loom before the whole world—enormous, confused, unsolved. In Roger's primitive society no such complexities appeared. But they were foreshadowed. Now, as then, human thought about money-making enterprises is the important factor in progress. And the founder of the colony which came to be called Rhode Island offered such far-reaching suggestions that we haven't yet grown up to them.

First of all, modern business has become tangled up with government. Many men believe this is one of the main causes of war. The workers and the farmers, the artists and the scientists around the globe do not wish to fight one another. But when powerful groups, representing invested capital, succeed in getting special favors from a government, that nation is soon involved in a struggle for territory, for oil fields, airports, mines, and plantations in the far corners of the earth.

Compared to this mighty clash of interests in modern times, the colonial issues in the 17th Century seem no more intense than a chess game. Yet they offer in miniature a clear picture of the unholy alliance between government and private power.

In Connecticut and Massachusetts the government was composed of landowners, capitalists, and industrial magnates of fishing, shipping, and lumber interests. They wanted to dominate the entire Narragansett Bay region. With no warrant from the people they governed, these officials used every possible means to that end. Rhode Island out-maneuvered them, thanks to its leader. But their policy finally brought about King Philip's War. That was the bitterest cup ever pressed to the lips of the one true friend of the Indians. Tribal power was then destroyed and the English could expand at will.

Roger Williams judged New England politics for what they were. In his philosophy there was no imperialism. Certainly he was sure the state ought not to go into business. He rejoiced when Plymouth gave up its attempt to own and operate enterprises as a communal effort. Nothing like

that was ever tried in Providence Plantations. There men were free to use talent, invention, and energy for the creation of wealth—*provided the common welfare was preserved!*

An instance of what this safeguard meant is Roger's action when he was president of the Colony in 1655. Through his influence the Assembly then passed measures to control the liquor trade. Chief among these was a law prohibiting a dealer from selling more than half a pint of liquor to an Indian. Drunken savages were a source of grave peril to the community.

The main duties of the government to its people, as Williams framed them, were positive. First on the list was defense of citizens. Even the original handful of settlers took turns as guards to prevent fires and keep off human and animal marauders. Later the central government was empowered to settle quarrels at home and abroad by arbitration. If that means failed, the militia was ready to act. Threat of riots among headstrong townfolk or of invasion by the Dutch or by hostile Indians was met by the armed guard.

In the primitive annals of the Colony we also find a hint of modern provision for social security. In 1650 Williams made an eloquent plea to the Assembly for an allowance to an orphaned girl, "distracted" because a penniless condition was forcing her into a miserable marriage.

An instrument for common, equal rights—that was what government should be, according to this statesman. If today, governments the world over were devoted only to the equal rights of their people, there would be far less danger of bureaucracy and of the lobbying for special privilege which leads to war.

Since the dawn of time the most basic of all privilege is private ownership of land. Land, of course, is in a class by itself. Men do not invent it as they invent machines. Age-old processes of nature created the forests, the fertile fields, and all the buried treasures of coal, metals, minerals, and oil. Who ought to possess this gift of nature on which civilization depends?

Roger Williams never stated that land should be commonly owned. But we do know that he believed it ought to be shared. He set the example by practically giving away huge tracts of territory ceded to him by the Narragansetts. As long as he lived he made it possible, by standing off the opposition of certain mean-minded townsmen, for newcomers to get land in Providence, and he insisted on grants of twenty-five acres to poor men. These also had, by Rogers's insistence, a right in public pasture meadows. When he bought Prudence Island from old Canonicus, he shared it with John Winthrop for the purpose of raising goats.

All his transactions show a powerful conviction that man's right to land depends on *use*. Private ownership worked no ill so long as it meant merely the erection of homes, mills, trading stations, and the development of farms. But in that untamed wilderness soon appeared the disease which has undermined our economy—land speculation. This accounts in large part today for bankrupt cities, poor housing, high rents, and unfair distribution of wealth. Buy land and hold it idle until increase of population or some other change makes it very desirable; then sell or rent it for huge sums—that is the practice which imperils economic health.

In Providence Plantations a group of ambitious men started such operations soon after they arrived. It was the more disheartening to the founder of the Colony because when he accepted these individuals as residents of the town, all but one was penniless. For years Roger battled with this evil. He knew it as the greatest enemy to the success of his experiment in democracy. To John Winthrop he wrote:

"I fear the common Trinities of the world, (Profit, Preferment, Pleasure) will here be the tri omnia, as in all the world beside . . ."

How can the deeply rooted maladies of speculation and private ownership in land be overcome? Not easily. Any people determined on a cure must find a genius to devise a method of relief and then be ready for long, resolute effort. Yet what is impossible? Three hundred years ago one man's unique combination of statecraft and devotion to his fellows achieved a democracy for the first time. In proving that a great conviction can be practically demonstrated, Williams held up a light which might today flood the darkest corners of the world.

That conviction was the very one which inspired the great slogan of the French Revolution. Williams tried to apply in a living way the same threefold principle—liberty of thought and worship, equality in the political sphere and—what about fraternity? At least he had the courage to raise that still unanswered question—how can a feeling of brotherhood modify the tigerish competition in business and industry without smothering individual enterprise?

How strange it is that only lately we have begun to take the measure of such a leader! It is partly his own fault. Roger Williams had a kind of modesty we hardly understand in this day of glaring publicity. Like the architect of the Parthenon and the sculptors of the marvelous figures on the cathedral of Chartres, this man was only interested in results. He wanted to strip religion of hate and prejudice and ignorance. His aim was to build a free society. What did he care about personal credit? Future fame meant nothing to him.

There was another reason why we haven't known him. Nobody living in America during his lifetime had the ability to appreciate him. His enemies called him "divinely mad," said he was a "firebrand" and a "windmill blown about by crazy ideas."

Even those who loved him couldn't estimate what he accomplished. They handed down a radiant tradition of his friendship with the Indians and of his readiness to protect the persecuted. But they couldn't recognize his genius.

That was natural. There is nothing startlingly dramatic about the slow work of molding a new world. What he wanted was to teach men to take responsibility for a healthy social life. Therefore, when he held office, made speeches, wrote pamphlets, and created a constitution, it was only in order to advance an idea or push forward other leaders. When the enterprise began to go, few remembered how it started. But today we are becoming keenly conscious of the meaning of America. Young and old grope through modern material success to find the clean, daylit spaces where the seeds of liberty were planted. Hard at work there, all by himself, we have discovered the founder of Rhode Island.

American history offers no more thrilling episode than the lone journey of Roger Williams. He set forth on a dangerous path into the unknown. It led to freedom for mankind. He didn't reach the goal, but he never faltered. And he blazed the trail!

CHIEF JOSEPH OF THE NEZ PERCÉS

Shannon Garst

There are few biographies of Indian leaders. Fortunately there is this well-written one which brings to life an extraordinary man. All children should read the book. White children will gain a greater and more balanced understanding of history; Indian children should gain pride in the greatness of a remarkable leader.

The Nez Percés fought only when, as the men crossed the mountains to hunt buffalo, they were attacked by the Blackfeet. Otherwise they lived in peace with their Indian and white neighbors. Chief Joseph's father was receptive to the American missionaries, Whitman and Spalding, and Joseph himself was baptized and schooled by the Spaldings. Even so, the time came when the Nez Percés were driven from their land.

After a few young men killed white settlers, Chief Joseph, knowing the Territorial Government would take revenge, began leading his people to the safety of Canada. Engaged by American troops, settlers, and warriors of the enemy Crow tribe, this man of peace demonstrated great tactical brillance. He held large forces at bay and outwitted the army's trained strategists for three months. The few remaining Nez Percés were defeated at last by the army's cannon only thirty miles from Canada.

THE BIG COUNCIL

The snows came and locked the Wallam-wat-kim band within a narrow world. It was pleasant though. Joseph enjoyed tracking game through the silent forests. He whooped with joy when he skimmed down an icy hill on an elk hide which he folded back over his feet. There were mock battles from behind fortresses of snow. The best of all were the gatherings—which he was now old enough to attend—in the long, five-fire lodge where the dances and ceremonies were held and where the old men told stories of long ago. Joseph could listen by the hour.

One day the herald went through the village calling, "Hear now, my people. Lay everything aside, for tonight we will have the dance of the Guardian Spirit."

From *Chief Joseph of the Nez Percés* by Shannon Garst. Reprinted by permission of Julian Messner, A Division of Simon & Schuster, Inc., copyright 1953 by Shannon Garst.

Joseph's heart beat fast when he heard this cry. Tonight he would get up before all of his people of the village and perform the dance of his Guardian Spirit. The exact message and vision of his Sacred Vigil must forever remain locked in his heart; but tonight he could show through the dance what the message had been, and he could at last tell that the Tah-mah-ne-wes had given him a fine Indian name.

He went without supper and purified himself in the sweat bath before he put on his ceremonial garb of jacket, breechcloth, fringed leggings and moccasins, all of white deerskin beautifully embroidered by Arenoth. On his chest, forehead, and cheeks he painted yellow dots to represent thunder. He placed a roach of porcupine quills in his hair from his forehead to the nape of his neck. He braided his hair with strips of otter skin and onto his moccasins he hung tinkling bells his father had got from the white men. Then he was ready.

His father preceded him, and Arenoth and Joseph followed at his heels, as they went to the long ceremonial lodge. It was the most important time of his life and when they entered all eyes turned toward him.

He took his place sitting cross-legged in the circle, and men started to beat the drums. One after another who had been given a vision in a Sacred Vigil during the summer or fall got up and began a dance in imitation of the animal or bird which had become his Wyakin, or Guardian Spirit. Finally the dancer ceased his prancing and shuffling and stood singing his Spirit song. After he had sung it two or three times, those in the circle joined in the song; and others who had had a successful Vigil joined him in a repetition of his dance. Those who had not been given a vision were not allowed to dance, although they could join in the singing.

Finally Joseph stood up and, while shuffling his feet, went through a pantomime with his hands and arms—intended to show the approach of a man with a bundle extended in his hands, which he gave to Joseph. Then a wild waving of arms indicated the opening of the heavens in lightning streaks and the crash of thunder.

Ceasing his wild gestures, he shuffled quietly and sang:

> "Thunder rolls out over the mountain;
> From the mountain rolls the thunder;
>   The hills shoot thunder from them;
>   See thunder rolling from the mountain;
> From the mountain rolls the thunder;
> Thunder rolls out over the mountain."

Then his feet were still and he said, "The Tah-mah-ne-wes did give me a name and a Wyakin. Hin-mut-too-yah-lat-kekht—Thunder Rolling over the Mountains—is my name. Thunder is my Wyakin."

His voice sounded thin and young to him, but at his words a murmur rose from the circle of spectators. "Thunder Rolling over the Mountains!" He heard the name repeated from mouth to mouth in tones of amazement and awe. Joseph had been given one of the strong forces of nature as a Wyakin. It was an omen of great portent. This was much better than being given an animal or bird as a Guardian Spirit. Having the thunder as his Wyakin meant that Joseph was certainly chosen by the Spirit Father for greatness among We People.

Joseph pretended not to notice the effect of his announcement. He went on shuffling and singing and others joined him. Never had his heart been so filled with gladness. Power seemed to fill him until it was as though he could accomplish anything he willed. Now he had a fine name. He had stepped over the dividing line between boyhood and young manhood.

The white men would always call him Joseph and many among his own people still clung to the name which had become familiar to them; but always in his own heart he knew that he was Hin-mut-too-yah-lat-kekht—Thunder Rolling over the Mountains—a name much too long and important-sounding for everyday use, but one which distinguished him above the common rank and file of Nez Percés. Never again would he feel inferior and insignificant before Gray Wolf, who had not even been granted a vision. Neither would he ever swell up with conceit, how always within him would lie the strength of knowledge of his own worth because of his strong Wyakin.

Every day now he went for a time alone into the forest to send out his thoughts in nearness to the Spirit Chief. He realized that one of the secrets of his father's strong hold over his people was his ability to speak well, and he knew that orators were held in esteem by the Nez Percés. Sometimes he, Hin-mut-too-yah-lat-kekht, became vexed with himself for his halting way of talking in the mock councils held by the boys. His rival, Gray Wolf, had a loud voice and he liked the sound of it, and it was his ability to talk which still gave him a strong following.

Now that the Tah-mah-ne-wes had given Joseph evidence that he was destined for leadership, he deliberately set out to practice oratory. He talked earnestly to the birds and animals of the forest, and when he spoke even the chipmunks hushed their scolding. In time, speaking became easier and he knew that he was doing better and better.

Now Joseph, as befitted the oldest son of the chief, often sat with the old men in council and he well knew the worry that was in his father's mind over the steady stream of white men which each summer came into the country. Not that the settlers bothered the Nez Percés. They were bound for land farther south; but if such swarms of them kept coming, they would need more and more room—more land. Already there had been trouble between the whites and the Walla Wallas and Cayuses. Tu-eka-kas had had to exert all of his skill to keep his headstrong young men from mixing in the trouble, for the other tribes were constantly trying to get the Nez Percés to join them in driving the whites from their country.

"Our people have never harmed a white man," Tu-eka-kas' strong voice rang out in the councils. "Let us avoid trouble. We are happy in our own land. We will make it plain that we will not allow the whites to take our country from us— but we will not seek trouble."

Tu-eka-kas was, however, not averse to allowing his braves to profit from the emigrants. The ford of the Grande Ronde River was about fifteen miles west of the Wallowa Valley, and it became a regular practice for the Nez Percés to gather there with their fine horses and trade for the emigrants' worn out livestock and guns and ammunition. Joseph himself now had a good herd of Appaloosas and he derived keen enjoyment from horse trading with settlers. Thus he gained a fine rifle, ammunition, and a good knife—articles he had long desired.

The Nez Percés had no liking for the heavy work animals of the emigrants; however, they allowed these animals to graze on their rich pasturelands and by the next summer they were rested and plump and ready for trading again.

Now Arenoth was proud of her iron kettles and pans, but Joseph still preferred the baskets and pottery shaped with her own hands. Food cooked in these vessels seemed to him to have a better flavor than when cooked in the iron things of the white men.

The Nez Percés now owned many cattle and some sheep through trade with the emigrants. These were turned loose to graze and to breed and increase. The Indians, though, had little use for them as food, much preferring the wild game which was still plentiful in the mountains of their homeland.

Joseph was proud of his father's horse herd. He owned over a thousand head, according to the white man's count, and they were the finest Appaloosas in the country. Both Indians and white men came from many miles to trade for them and Tu-eka-kas was becoming richer in white men's goods as well as in horses.

Joseph, whose keenness of mind had been developing as fast as his tall lean body, was well aware that his father's idea of the white men had changed.

"Once you welcomed the white men to our country," Joseph said one day as they talked by the campfire. "Now you hold them in contempt."

Tu-eka-kas puffed thoughtfully on his pipe. "Once I thought the white men were good—that they would teach us the best things of their civilization. Some whites are good. But most of them are selfish. They seek to trick us, believing us stupid. They do not speak with the straight tongue. Their greed for the thing called money makes them dishonest."

One day a white man in a blue coat rode into the Wallowa village. He was followed by a Cayuse Indian called Tom, who had been educated in the white man's school. Tom acted as interpreter, since he could speak English as well as the Indian tongue.

Joseph had been swimming in the lake when he saw the white man ride to his father's lodge and dismount. He quickly tied his breechcloth around his waist and ran to see what was about to take place.

The white man and the Indian called Tom were seated in the lodge facing Tu-eka-kas, who was lighting the ceremonial pipe. He offered it to the six directions—the sky, the earth, and east, west, north, and south—then puffed solemnly for a few moments before handing it to his guests. Joseph sank onto a grass mat and smoked when it came his turn.

"My name is James Doty," the white man said through the interpreter. "I have come from the white chief Governor Stevens, who invites you to meet for a big powwow with him at Walla Walla. All of the Northwest tribes will be there —the Cayuse, the Klickitat, the Yakima. There will be many presents. The governor wishes to make a treaty so that there will be peace forever between the white and the red people."

"The Nez Percés have always been at peace

with the white men," Tu-eka-kas said with dignity.

"Governor Stevens knows that," James Doty agreed. "It is to avoid trouble in the future that the big council will be held."

"I will be there with my people," Tu-eka-kas promised.

"You will let me go with you?" Joseph cried eagerly after the white messenger had left.

His father looked at him and nodded. "I want you by my side," he said. "I am an old man. Someday you will step into my moccasins and wear my chief's war bonnet. I fear that troubled days are ahead for my people. You must learn to deal with the white men."

Alokut was to go, too. Joseph was fifteen, his brother about a year younger; but now they were nearly the same height and taller than their father, who stood over six feet. Joseph was powerful of build; Alokut was slimmer; otherwise they looked alike and derived enjoyment from the fact that one was often mistaken for the other.

Joseph spent hours getting Thunderbird ready for the journey. He brushed him thoroughly; then he braided dyed rawhide strips in his mane and tail, and on his red and white spotted rumps he drew zigzag lightning streaks and yellow dots representing thunder—the same symbols which would decorate his own cheeks and chest—the signs which depicted his name, Thunder Rolling over the Mountains.

He put on his best fringed leggings, his quill-embroidered sleeveless jacket; his big knife in its beaded sheath was fastened to his belt. He took his painted shield and his finest bow and arrows.

Proudly he rode out ahead of the long column beside his father, still handsome and strong of face although he was now an old man whose sight was growing dim. Many people told Joseph that he looked like his father, but he was sure that he was not so fine-looking.

Always, in his handsome war bonnet and his beautiful deerskin clothing, Tu-eka-kas was a magnificent figure. Both Joseph and Alokut, riding on each side, were very proud to be his sons.

When they were at the top of a hill Joseph turned and looked back at the procession. The braves in their flowing headdresses and finest trappings made a colorful sight in the bright sunlight.

Strips of otter skin or dyed rawhide were twined in their braids. Feathers and fur streamed from lances.

The women and girls, too, were dressed in their finest white robes and wore their bright, close-fitting basket hats, which reminded Joseph of the shape of the small cooking pans of the white men turned upside down.

The squaws rode on horses with saddles with high pommels and led the horses which carried the camp equipment. Farther back, boys drove the spare ponies. For hours the procession rode through the silent, fragrant forest trails, then down a steep ravine toward the Snake River. Before they came to the meeting place the men and women stopped beside the river to whiten their deerskin garments and remove any spots with clay.

When the many tribes gathered, their white tepees stretched for miles along the Mill Creek in the lovely Walla Walla Valley about six miles from the ill-fated Whitman mission. This was the usual council ground of the various tribes.

One by one the other tribes came in—the Cayuses, Yakimas, Walla Wallas, and Umatillas.

When all had arrived—about five thousand by the white man's count—it was time for the ceremony to commence. Tu-eka-kas' people spent hours decking themselves out in the best feathers and war bonnets and paint, and in painting their horses and braiding ornaments in mane and tail.

Joseph was ready to burst with pride that he was to be allowed to ride at the head of the splendid cavalcade of naked warriors gaudy with bright paint and carrying shields, lances, and guns. When all were ready, Tu-eka-kas raised his hand in signal and the party thundered across the prairie to where the governor's party stood waiting. Two abreast they galloped until they were almost upon the governor and his bluecoats.

Joseph could scarcely suppress a grin at the dismayed expression upon the faces of the white men.

The warriors wheeled their horses and galloped away—only to return, clashing shields, beating tomtoms, and singing warrior songs. Then they formed a circle and galloped about and came on with wild war whoops, as though charging.

It was all a good show and obviously the white

men were impressed, to such an extent that some of them were on the point of running—if there had been any place to run.

Then the chiefs dismounted and went forward to meet the governors with solemn dignity. The discussions went on for several days, but Joseph and the boys his age were not very interested. As was usual at such gatherings, it was a time of feasting, dancing, and visiting and a time of making new friends and of renewing acquaintance with old ones.

Squaws bent over their fires and their ever-bubbling stewpots. The air was savory with cooking food, and eating went on at all hours. Children darted about from camp to camp. Dogs barked unceasingly. Drums boomed. Old men smoked and talked of hunts and fighting and of how much better things were before the white men came.

Joseph joined the numerous races on Thunderbird and won nearly every time. There was no horse anywhere like his.

Now Joseph stood head and shoulders above the other boys of his age and he could not help being aware of the glances which followed him whenever he walked or rode through the camps. He knew that there was envy in the glances of some of the boys who were ambitious for leadership. And he knew that there was admiration in the shy glances of some of the maidens, although it was against native custom for the boys and girls to speak to each other.

Joseph sat beside his father in many of the pow-wows, although he grew tired of the endless arguments. Governor Stevens said that there were many white people in the Northwest country and that many more would come. He wanted the land marked out so that the Indians and white men would be separated—that it was necessary to do this if peace were to be maintained. He told the Indians that the Great White Father in Washington had set apart some of the land for them and that they must go there and stay.

Tu-eka-kas rose and his presence seemed to fill the council tent as he said, "I will not have anything to do with such a plan. I am a free man. I and my people wish to remain free."

Reverend Spalding stepped up and plucked at his arm. "Come now," he said impatiently as though speaking to an exasperating child. "Don't be stubborn. You must sign the treaty as the others have."

Tu-eka-kas pushed him away and cried in a forceful manner, "Why do you ask me to sign away my country? It is your business to talk to us about spirit matters, and not to talk to us about parting with our land."

"You must sign," Governor Stevens insisted.

"I will not sign your paper," Tu-eka-kas replied. "You go where you please. So do I. You are not a child. I am not a child. I can think for myself. No man can think for me. I will not give up my land to any man. My people would have no home. Take away your paper. I will not touch it with my hand."

He stalked from the council tent with Joseph at his heels. However, most of the other chiefs did sign the white paper, for which they were given many fine presents.

"Do not take the white man's money or his presents," Tu-eka-kas told his people. "If you do, someday they will say that we sold the land. That we will never do."

"That we will never do!" The words echoed in Joseph's heart. "The land is our own. We will never sell it."

INVINCIBLE LOUISA

Cornelia Meigs

This book is only in part a biography of Louisa May Alcott; much of it is a sympathetic defense of her father, Bronson Alcott, an impecunious philosopher of great charm.

Although Invincible Louisa *won the Newbery Award in 1934, many better biographies for children have since been written. The mature reader with a deep affection for Louisa May Alcott will enjoy the book's mood and will appreciate its careful information. But most children might become restless with the excessive detail about Germantown and Boston, and other background detail. Few will understand or care about the biographer's sentimental discussions of Bronson Alcott's philosophy and educational theories.*

The book is written in a detached style because Miss Meigs unfortunately preferred to tell about Louisa's life in slow, careful, and at times tedious detail. Since she seldom recreated a scene through action and dialogue, only rarely does the book come to life. One of the few moments when this occurs ends the following selection from Invincible Louisa.

Because this anthology of children's literature has a comparative approach, examples of less successful works, such as Invincible Louisa, *are contrasted with the best writing for young people.*

DAMASK ROSES

The highroad which stretches from within the State of Pennsylvania down to the Delaware River becomes, as it nears Philadelphia, the main street of Germantown. It was a well-traveled road long before the Revolution; but even so late as the year 1832 it was still unimproved, and often so deep in mud that—so the residents of Germantown said—it was necessary to saddle a horse to get from one side of it to the other. Not all of its roughness and its wet, however, could interfere with the joyful stride of a triumphant young father who tramped the difficult mile, on a cold November day, from his house to the big dwelling at Wyck, home of his dearest friends. Nothing could stay Bronson Alcott as he hurried, breathless, to the Haines house, as he burst in at the door to tell the great news. He had a new daughter, a lusty, lively, altogether remarkable daughter, and he had come to take all the Haines children over to see the new baby. Back they all went with him, trooping along the highway, buzzing with talk and questions, all seven of the small Haineses. They stood, presently, in an awed, respectful circle around the small, red, but extremely sound and vigorous baby, who, so it was settled even then, was to be called Louisa May Alcott.

It was, therefore, not upon New England, but upon the snow-wrapped Pennsylvania countryside,

that Louisa looked out at her first vision of the world. Low rounded hills, groups of white-powdered pine trees, winding valleys where a black line showed how the water ran, and where smooth, glittering slopes stretched up to patches of woodland—all these were before her eyes and her brisk young mother's as they sat at the tall window and looked abroad upon the whiteness of Louisa's first winter. It was not the deep-drifted, biting Massachusetts winter which Louisa was to know so well later, but a gentle, soft coldness, with the grass always green in the sheltered places, and with the snow slopes broken by upthrusting laurel bushes and clumps of honeysuckle which never lost their summer leaves.

At a certain hour a door would open, somewhere, and the two at the window would hear a burst of children's voices and laughter. School was over for the day, Bronson Alcott's school, and the small pupils were going home. They would troop past down the walk—plump little German girls with fat, flaxen braids, little Quaker boys in roundabout jackets, who leaped and frolicked and threw snowballs as they all went chattering out of sight. Enlivened by the sight of all this energy, Louisa would jump and wriggle and plunge in her mother's arms, anxious to get down, and very different from her quiet older sister Anna, who was playing so decorously on the hearth rug. Abba Alcott, her mother, would take one last look at the broad garden, at the long cedar fence heaped and decorated with white, beautiful as only snow and cedar can be. Then she would turn to light the lamp; for Bronson would be coming in, now that school was ended for the day. Abba had written home to New England that the place where they were living was a "Little Paradise." It looked more like Paradise than ever, that winter, since there had begun to arise the unhappy possibility that they must leave it soon.

Two years they had lived in the pleasant, square, farmhouse-like dwelling where Bronson Alcott carried on his teaching. It was a time of great happiness, peace and security, those first two years of the Alcotts' married life. Happiness was to continue, sometimes interrupted in strange ways; but peace and security were not to come again for a very long time. When they were achieved, they were to be won for them by Louisa, by Louisa battling against overwhelming odds for half her life, bound never to be conquered, even though every circumstance seemed to be against them all. No one could have any knowledge of that now, least of all Louisa herself, the enterprising small person rolling and tumbling at this moment with Anna before the fire, both of them turning about to cry out in high, baby delight as the door of the room opened and their father came in.

It had been a great adventure for Abba May, after a quiet, staid girlhood, to marry, rather on a sudden, this tall Bronson Alcott, with his visionary blue eyes, his blond hair, and his finely chiseled, thin, handsome countenance. Certain people had looked dubious and had hinted that the young man was "not very practical," and that he would never "make his way." In all the fire of her enthusiasm, Abba May put aside such warnings. She had been engaged to a distant cousin, an affair which had ended unhappily and had deeply hurt her. Then she had met this man, who was visiting her brother; she had been taken with him as instantaneously as he had been taken with her, and she had discovered that this was the real love of which the other had been an empty imitation. She understood Bronson Alcott; she knew that he needed somebody to take care of him as he furthered his great ideas. Joyfully she undertook to be that person, and she continued to be, unquestioning and ungrudging in the outpouring of her strength, until a time came when she taught Louisa to care for him in her place.

A strange, interesting, rather marvelous figure

was Bronson Alcott. He was a student, a scholar, and most of all a teacher, to the last depths of his nature. Yet in preparation for these things he had had only the slightest and most irregular of educations, beginning in the farmhouse at Spindle Hill, Wolcott, Connecticut, where he was born, and stretching out over strange roads to come to its end. He used to tell his children how his mother had taught him to write on the kitchen floor. The wide boards were kept covered with clean white sand in those early days, which was swept away at intervals to give place to a new supply. Just before the floor was to be scrubbed, Bronson would be allowed to write in the sand, making the great staggering letters of a little boy just faltering into learning. A—B—cat—dog—patience—fortitude . . . he moved from the little words to the big ones, and presently could read and write. That was as far as his mother could take him, but she was as determined as he that his education should go forward. The rocky ridges of his father's farm were not harder than Bronson's stubborn purpose to learn and to learn in the right way.

The boy's father lacked the money to give his son schooling, and further lacked, totally, the inclination to believe in such a necessity. Work was what put a person forward in the world, so he believed, hard work with feet and hands and back. The boy learned to work on the farm, but he was always nursing a greater ambition. As the years passed, it became evident that the college education for which he longed was completely out of the question. Therefore he set out to seek what he needed in another way. He was eighteen years old when he started, on foot, to travel to Virginia and find himself a place to teach; to teach and to study. He had heard that young men of New England were more or less in demand as instructors or tutors in the South. He could see no means of getting there except by walking.

A kindly ship captain gave him a lift, by water, from New Haven to Norfolk, on the understanding that Bronson should repay the passage money as soon as he found work. So anxious was the boy to be rid of the debt that he did not take time to look for a school and closed with the first employment which offered—service with a tinsmith in Norfolk. Part of his duty was to go about the town selling the cups and kettles and pans made by the man who had hired him. He unexpectedly found himself to be a good salesman and rather liked his new pursuit. He repaid Captain Sperry at once and then set out from Norfolk into the country to look for a school.

He found the search most disheartening. Not only were schools scarce and very few of them without a schoolmaster, but the very nature of them was not what he had expected. Rude cabins with chinks in the walls, set at the edge of waste forest land where razor-backed hogs ran wild: such were, for the most part, the institutions of learning which he came across. Long-legged, shock-headed boys looked dully up from their slates to stare with sullen hostility at the newcomer from Connecticut. The committeemen who had in charge the hiring of teachers seemed little more receptive. After many miles of tramping, Bronson decided that there was no chance of teaching and returned to Norfolk to his former employer in the tin trade. That worthy man, seeing that he had found a successful salesman, sent him, this time, into the country to dispose of more of his wares. So well did Bronson carry out his mission that presently he decided to follow this combination of travel and selling on his own account.

"I mean to make peddling in Virginia as respectable as any other trade," he declared stoutly in a letter to his father. He made it something not merely respectable but alluring. In those days of bad roads and small transportation, the big plantations, far from even the small resources of the village shops, depended on traveling peddlers to renew their supplies of buttons and thread, of ribbons and tin plates and tortoiseshell combs.

It was also true that life in the country could be very monotonous, so that any person from the outside world, bringing news and opinions as well as material wares, was very welcome. It was surprising to see this upstanding, blue-eyed youth from Connecticut, with his neat clothes and quiet manners, come to the door, attended by a flock of small colored children and the miscellaneous gathering of hound and mastiff dogs which were supposed to guard the gates against strangers. The mistress of the house would be called and would fall into conversation with the young man. The young ladies would flutter in the background and

presently slip forward to look at ribbons and combs and to have a word with him also.

Bronson had a charm beyond the mere possession of good manners, which seemed to capture everyone. Presently the master would come out of his office, from amongst his guns and fishing rods and dog-eared plantation books, and ask whether the pack contained razors or tobacco. He, too, would fall into conversation with Bronson, which always ended by his being invited to dinner, to pass the night, to spend several days. After the girls had their evening of talk with him, finding him an interesting, responsive person who could tell them much of what they wanted to know about what was going forward in Norfolk or Richmond, they would retire, and Bronson and his host would sit late in the library, talking and talking of the great questions of the day.

Young as he was, the boy was wise enough not to discuss slavery; but there were politics and commerce, the exiled Napoleon imprisoned on St. Helena, the recent invention by Fulton of a boat which would run by steam, a world of matters to review as the hours passed. Bronson Alcott was always a singularly good talker, a stimulating talker, who seemed to make other people have better thoughts than they ever had in their own company. The invitation to stay, if accepted, led to his spending long hours in those libraries, rich with the treasures of three generations, which were enchanted ground to him, for never before had he been within reach of a real supply of books of this sort. History, philosophy, poetry— he plunged deep into them all, trying to absorb as much as was humanly possible before he shouldered his pack and went on again. After this feast of learning, he had what is another priceless necessity—long, quiet hours in which to think over and appraise what he had read. He tramped the roads alone, sat under the hedgerows and ate his solitary lunch, exchanged brief greetings with the travelers he passed, but always went on thinking, thinking. Very few are the courses in education which allow time to think; but this education of Bronson's was complete, even to that final need.

He saw the big, pillared plantation houses, the squat, white-washed cabins which housed the slaves, he saw the teams of mules go by, jingling with bells, the driver riding the "nigh leader," and guiding the whole four or six with a single rein. He saw the wide cotton fields and the Negroes working and singing, warmed, if it were chilly, by a huge fire of stumps around which they would gather between the rounds of "toting baskets" on their heads up to the cotton shed. He made money and prospered, then grew extravagant and spent the whole proceeds of a single season on new clothes in which to go home. He set out again, prospered once more, and finally fell very ill with fever and ague and was nursed back to thin, weak-kneed life by some hospitable Quakers in Norfolk. His strict New England belief had been shocked by the lack of religious interest amongst the planters; it was comforted and satisfied by the quiet righteousness of the Quakers. He came home at last, penniless, but so full of memories and experience that the four years amply repaid all of the toil which he had put into them.

When he was a small boy, only newly master of reading, someone had lent him a copy of *Pilgrim's Progress*. The book fired his spirit and imagination in a way beyond the power of words to describe. He loved it with intense devotion all of his life, and made it a fundamental part of his children's education. He once said that the sort of life which would satisfy him completely was to walk through the world all of his days, stopping to have conversations with people by the way. It was just such a life as he had in these years. He received much, but it is very certain that he gave much also, and that the thoughts and ideas he left behind him lived long amongst all of those whom he met.

Although he had not been able to find any teaching to do, except now and then a few weeks of carrying on a writing school in one or another of the larger towns, he came back from his wanderings knowing that he must be a schoolmaster. He understood people, most of all he understood children; he must teach them. He became an instructor in a district school in Cheshire. There he met the Reverend Samuel May, and through him his sister Abba May, who presently, as has been said, very willingly and happily became Abba May Alcott. He left the Cheshire school and began teaching in Boston, where his new ideas came, finally, to the notice of Reuben Haines, of Germantown.

Schools were not everywhere so rude and rough as those which Bronson had seen in the South, but they were in many places very little better. The able Mr. Haines, enterprising member of the Quaker community outside Philadelphia, who was interested in stock breeding and stars and horticulture and the science of the weather, was also greatly interested in education. It was his plan to start a series of schools in his town, to support them from his own funds, and to offer children of all ages the stuff which their growing minds really needed. He journeyed to Boston, saw this young schoolmaster of whom people were beginning to talk, and decided that here was the man to give what children wanted. He was right.

Thus it came about that Bronson and Abba Alcott, newly married, came to Germantown to live under the strong protection of Reuben Haines. All their lives the members of this haphazard family were singularly lucky in friends, in people who appreciated and loved them and would do anything in the world for them. Reuben Haines was one of the first and perhaps one of the most interesting of all these kindly spirits. Although Bronson Alcott was unfortunate in never being understood by the many, he was singularly blessed by being understood by the distinished few.

A tall man, with a thin, thoughtful face, ruddy skin, deep-set, affectionate eyes and a broad, gentle mouth, such was Reuben Haines. His Quaker plainness of speech and thought, his sturdy directness of high purpose, made him an ideal person with whom to work. Under his patronage the school opened in the "Little Paradise" of Pine Place, the house he had bought for Bronson Alcott. All the Quakers of the community liked Bronson's gentle methods; the Germans liked his thoroughness; the children loved him. It was a cruel mischance for all concerned that the dearly loved Reuben Haines died not long after the founding of the school. Yet in spite of that, Abba and Bronson Alcott had two years at Germantown, the first, at least, being one of untroubled and prosperous serenity. Here Anna, the eldest child, was born three months after their arrival. And here, on November 29 in the year 1832, Louisa also joined them.

It is, of course, practically impossible that

Louisa could have remembered anything of what went on in Germantown, but, as is always the case, what she really recollected became inseparably joined to what she heard from other people, so that the memory of these early years always seemed to be hers. The heavy sorrow which hung over her family during her early babyhood was the loss of Reuben Haines, who had died before she was born. The depth of personal bereavement concealed from the eyes of Abba and Bronson for a little while the fact that with his going the school could no longer continue. They struggled forward bravely, but without his management the experiment was impossible. It was this anxiety, slowly growing greater, which weighed down that courageous young mother during the months in which lively young Louisa learned to creep, to walk, and then to run.

The friendship with the Haines family, celebrated almost on Louisa's actual birthday by the impromptu reception of all the small Haineses in the Pine Place nursery, was to continue even though the head of the household was gone. The big house a mile away, on the beautiful old farm of Wyck, old even in that day, was still a place of stimulating and happy intercourse for the two families. The pair of mothers exchanged advice on their many perplexities, gentle Jane Haines struggling with the effort to care for seven children who had no father, Abba Alcott in doubt as to what to do with an unquenchable baby, who never would stay where she was put and who, as soon as she could really walk, loved nothing so much as to run away. Wyck, however, was a place from which even enterprising Louisa never sought to depart. The farm, with its ducks and pigs and heavy, gentle-eyed cows, was a joy to her, for from the beginning she loved animals and living things. The garden in summer, with its tall rows of damask roses, its magnolia trees, its neat round beds with borders of stiff, spriggy box, was such a region as not many young persons have for the practice of their first attempts at walking. Louisa, fat and agile and overflowing with chuckles, had many a glorious hour in that beautiful garden at Wyck.

The family in that plain, stately house, the cheery Haines household, meant more to the Alcotts, more to the memory which they were to carry away from Germantown, than could any of the charms of the farm and garden. There is something in Quaker family life that is not matched anywhere else. Because in those times Quakers were cut off from the more usual outside pleasures of living—from music, which had no place in the Quaker scheme of things; from dancing and theaters and gaiety of the social sort—something very different developed within those big, lively households. The amusement was all from within, a common spirit of delight in small things, of family jokes and understandings of complete comradeship between parents and children. The utter simplicity, almost bareness of living, did away with the cares and complications which luxuries bring with them. There was comfort in the Haines house—warm fires, good food, spotless cleanliness—but there was never the smallest pretense of anything more.

The deep, square windows had no curtains, but through them the sunshine came flooding in upon the painted floors. The "great room" of the house was merely a hallway, with broad glass doors at each end, and with a glimpse of the peonies and larkspur of the garden massed beyond. Here, only a very few years before, Lafayette had received the worthies of Germantown, the throng of people pouring in at one of the great doors, and out at the other into the garden. Here Audubon had come to give drawing lessons to the eldest Haines daughter; here had come Rembrandt Peale, one of the greatest of American painters, to make a portrait of Reuben Haines, who had befriended him when he was struggling and unknown. And here, most of all, were the unruffled peace and the genuine happiness of living, of a household devoted and gay, high-spirited and happy, even in the face of sorrow. It seems as though the Alcotts' own family life always carried with it the indelible stamp of that earliest friendship. They also always seemed to possess that contentment with simple things, that knowledge of what was the best in living, with which the household of Wyck was so peculiarly blessed.

By the second summer in which Louisa played amongst the ducks and roses she was a strong and energetic little girl, scarcely a baby any more. Her eyes were bright and observant, her voice resounding, her will strong. Her mother's busy hands were busier than ever, with this lively person to care for. The household at Pine Place held board-ing-school scholars as well as the little Alcotts; and there were no servants now, for the school was in desperate straits for money. Without the backing of Reuben Haines, the criticism which always attends a new venture became greater and greater, and the number of scholars shrank daily. Still, the enterprise went forward, no one admit-ting, aloud, that it might end in failure. Louisa's very energy and unquenchable restlessness were a distraction for her mother's anxious mind. It was a constant task merely to watch over her and see that she came to no harm.

The two little girls, at least, were very happy as those last spring months at Germantown went by. There were walks along the wooded Wissahickon River, and the Schuylkill, where the wild flowers grew so thickly on the steep slopes, and where the scattering row of great Tory mansions crowned the hill. There was beautiful country everywhere about tidy, well-kept Germantown, with fields blue with violets, with gray-trunked beech trees in the woods and Mayflowers creeping through the brown leaves. There were full, singing streams which ran under arched stone bridges; there were birds everywhere.

Anna and Louisa could not know how, all those days, their father and mother were so sorely missing that good friend Reuben Haines, missing his generosity, his far vision, and his patient good sense in those small practical matters of which Bronson had little knowledge. It required more than a gift for teaching, at that time, to keep alive an undertaking of the nature of Bronson's school. It needed money from some other source than the small fees which could be paid by the pupils. It needed, also, the confidence and peace of mind which comes from a consciousness of security. None of these things did Abba and Bronson have. They did wonderfully well to bat-tle forward as long as they did. The school grew smaller and smaller; it finally came to an end and a great plan dwindled into nothingness.

There was a brief session in Philadelphia at another school which also failed to prosper. Then, suddenly, there was a momentous decision and a great bustle of packing. Without in the least knowing, or caring, how it came about, Louisa found herself on board a steamer, journeying down the broad Delaware River and out into the bay, on the way to Boston. It was summer, the shores were green. The old stone farmhouses and cottages showed between the trees, with drifts of bright color in the gardens to remind the travelers for the last time of the warm, sweet rose garden of Wyck. They were leaving behind some very good friends, some very happy memories as they sailed away, full of hope for new things.

Not long after the voyage began, Louisa disap-peared completely and was not recovered until a thorough search of the whole boat had been made. She was in the engine room, a wonderful place for smells, for glimpses of enormous glow-ing fires, of shiny surfaces and of great steel shafts going back and forth as though by magic. She was covered with coal dust and black grease when discovered, but she had spent an hour of com-plete happiness. Her mother saw that no such excursions into the lower regions happened again, and must have breathed a sigh of relief when the boat came steaming up Boston Harbor.

The city in which Louisa was born was broad and low. This new city was upon a hill, with its spires and pointed roofs and the dome of the State House high above her against the blue of the sky. The steamer puffed and churned the water, backed and roared as it came into its berth. Louisa and her family had arrived at their second abiding place.

She was to learn to know that tall hill very well, although from a different aspect. Bronson Alcott proceeded at once to open a new school in the Masonic Temple, where the plain, large room was as full of sunlight as of beautiful things. He had for assistant Miss Elizabeth Peabody, who later was to do so much to make the beginnings of kindergarten teaching in America. She was a young woman then, still learning, learning very much from Bronson Alcott. Anna was old enough to be a pupil at the school, and during the long autumn mornings while she and her father were absent, Abba would walk with Louisa from their house on Front Street over to the Common.

Here Louisa played upon the grass, made friends with the passers-by, or, plumping down to rest, would sit looking up at the tall elms with their high trunks and enormously long branches, so different from the round, leafy beeches of the woods at her birthplace. The tall, elderly houses of Beacon Hill looked down upon her out of their many-paned windows, where the blue and purple glass was a sign of exceedingly aristocratic old age. Along Beacon Street there toiled by, on the rough pavement, an endless procession of market carts, of creaking wagons, and those shiny, low-hung carriages which a little later were to be named victorias. In them sat beautiful ladies, overflowing the seats with billowing skirts and carrying the most minute of parasols to protect their complexions from the sun. Sellers of fruit, of pies, of strawberries went by, calling their street cries to attract custom. A scissors grinder would move slowly along, his grindstone on his back, his jingling bell in his hand, ringing as he walked. Now and then the town crier would stride past, ringing his bigger, deeper bell and proclaiming some piece of news small or great—the dropping of a purse, a warning against pickpockets, the tidings of President Jackson's newest proclamation. It was all wonderful and exciting to the little girl, so extraordinarily different from the still, rose-bowered garden in Germantown, and the view over green, rolling hills.

There was one day when her mother was busy, perhaps away for an hour or two, teaching at Bronson's school, where she had taken charge of the music. Small Louisa set out to see something of Boston on her own account. It is the general experience of newcomers to Boston to begin by losing themselves. Louisa was no exception. She wandered from one narrow street to another, light-heartedly ignoring the fact that she must remember how to come home again. She played with some very ragged children, to their great delight and her own. She caressed passing alley cats; she smiled gaily at strangers; she rambled here and there, and finally grew very weary. Some other child would have fallen into panic on finding that she wanted to go home and that she did not know the way. Louisa merely sat down in an entry to rest herself, and there fell comfortably asleep with her head on the shoulder of a big, friendly dog. It was twilight when she awoke, but even that did not seem to dismay her. Not far away a great booming voice was coming through the dusk, and a bell was ringing. The town crier was proclaiming: "Lost, a little girl in a pink dress and green morocco shoes!"

Of whom could he be talking, Louisa wondered as she heard him go through the recital, and then had a sudden inkling of the truth. This magnificent officer of the City of Boston was talking about her. Not in the least overcome, she lifted her small voice and called through the evening darkness: "That's me."

AMERICA'S MARK TWAIN

May McNeer

The author carefully selected those incidents from Samuel Clemens' life which illustrated her theme: how a writer may draw from his past to enrich his works of fiction. Cornelia Meigs had much the same theme in her book about Louisa May Alcott. Yet Miss Meigs was unable to be selective and so the relationship between the author's life and work—so important in both Louisa May Alcott and Mark Twain's writings—is almost lost in the meticulous detail present in Invincible Louisa. *Miss McNeer, in contrast to Miss Meigs, chose to dramatize her biography, letting action and dialogue reveal Twain's life and character. Mark Twain is always alive for the reader, while Louisa May Alcott never really becomes known. These two books provide interesting comparisons of style and character revelation.*

America's Mark Twain is distinctive for the way in which periods of Twain's life are followed by short summaries of his books. The reader not only learns about a unique personality but also becomes stimulated to read Twain's works.

Sammy was sent to school at the age of four and a half. His teachers were two dignified ladies, Mrs. Horr and her spinster daughter, who taught the younger children of Hannibal in a small log cabin. On his second day Sammy disobeyed his teacher. Mrs. Horr sternly told him to go out and pick a switch for his own punishment. Sammy found several bushes bearing switches, but couldn't bring himself to break one off. Across the way a cooper's shop was puncturing the pleasant spring day with the noise of planing that sent long shavings into the dusty street. Sammy returned to Mrs. Horr with a curled shaving in hand, and solemnly presented it for a switch. The outraged teacher not only sent out for one that would sting Sammy's unfortunate legs but also reported his impudence to his mother.

As "Little Sam" became "Sammy" and "Sammy" grew old enough to be called "Sam," the devilish twinkle in his innocent face came more frequently. His schooldays, though filled with troubles, were not without fun. Sam scarcely ever came to school without bringing a pinch bug in a box, to set loose in a quiet moment, or persuading John Briggs to put a verse on the blackboard—a verse about "Cross Mr. Cross"— or doing some other devilment. But it was the thought of Saturday that dominated Sam's life. Sometimes he played hooky because he couldn't wait for the end of the week.

Sam had a brother, Henry, who was two years younger than he. Henry was handsome and good, whereas Sam was only handsome—when dressed for Sunday School. Sam was strong and was no longer expected to die young, especially since it was generally believed that only the good die young. Henry, on the other hand, was a great help to his mother. He took delight in helping her keep tabs on Sam. When Jane sent Sam off to Mr. Cross's school of a morning she sewed his shirt at the collar so that she could tell whether he had played hooky to go swimming with Tom Blankenship, son of the town drunkard. And when she nodded in satisfaction at suppertime, seeing that it was still sewed, who but Henry would sing out, "Ma, didn't you sew Sam's shirt with white thread? It's fastened with black now."

For that favor Sam threw clods of mud at Henry, and his opinion of Mother's good boy didn't rise into respect until Henry retaliated by pelting him back with stones.

Mrs. Clemens' punishments came in the form of work. On a Saturday morning just made for fishing in a "borrowed" rowboat and for the company of tattered Tom Blankenship, Sam had to whitewash the fence. To add insult to injury Sam's best friends—John Briggs, Will and Sam Bowen, and others—passed by, fishing rods trailing over shoulders. One morning gazing mournfully down at a large pail of whitewash, Sam had a flash of genius. He would make his friends believe that whitewashing a fence was a privilege. When they began to ask permission, he was so reluctant to give up the brush, that they gave him their valuables in order to be allowed to whitewash—old doorknobs, apple cores, frogs, and a box of worms, among other things.

When Jane Clemens came out to check on his progress, she found Sam gone, and, stretching out before her eyes a long freshly whitewashed fence. She shook her head. "How that boy could paint so fast beats me. It just beats me to here and gone!"

Although Sam grew to be as tough as a ranging colt, his mother seemed quite unaware that his health had improved. She was still in the habit of forcing all sorts of medicine into him, from sulphur and molasses to a black noxious fluid simply called "Pain-killer." One day Sam gave a dose of Pain-killer to the favorite of all his mother's nineteen cats. When she reproached him for causing the poor animal to climb the walls in a frenzy, Sam said, in his funny, slow way, that he was only doing Peter good. If that stuff was good for a boy why wasn't it good for a cat?

Sam Clemens' inventiveness brought him many friends. The boys of Hannibal were constantly forming themselves into bands of various kinds, and Sam was the leader of every band. He was the Avenger of the Spanish Main, the chief Knight of the Round Table, Robin himself in the Band of Merry Men, and Blackbeard the Pirate. These rousing gangs operated in the woods on Holliday's Hill, sometimes with the added pleasure of Tom Blankenship's company.

More often, though, Tom went fishing, and condescended, as was the way of a great man, to take along Sam and John and Will. Tom knew the best holes where the biggest catfish could be caught. He knew the place to hunt for turtle eggs on the islands, and he taught the other boys to smoke corncob pipes and swear. Tom Blankenship was the envy of Sam and all of his friends. He slept in a hogshead barrel, and was nothing but a "ruin of rags," as Sam said, but nobody told him what to do, or how to do it. He didn't have to go to school to Mr. Cross, or to the Presbyterian Sunday School in a clean shirt, after a painful scrubbing behind the ears.

Tom's hogshead was in a broken-down barn just behind Sam's house. On many an evening when his shrill catcall came to Sam's ears, Sam would wait until Henry was asleep and slide down the porch roof to go off with Tom. They would visit the cemetery, carrying a dead cat to cure warts, or dig for a treasure supposedly buried near the village by the hideous Murrel gang of robbers some years before.

Though Sam felt that wielding a paintbrush on a fence was more hard work than he should be asked to do, he was only too glad to make the dirt fly when Tom told him to dig for treasure under a pawpaw tree—while Tom sat nearby, comfortably smoking his pipe. At dawn, having found no golden horde of stolen coins, Sam staggered home exhausted, yet when the next whistle came, out he scrambled to dig in another place that Tom allowed was sure to be the right one.

Sam was a great one for what he called a joke, and one time his joke came close to tragedy. The boys enjoyed rolling stones down steep Holliday's Hill in front of a wagon, or a rider, who might be passing along the road below. The game was to scare the passer-by without getting caught by the patrol, whose duty it was to maintain order in town and on the road and to keep the slaves within bounds. One Sunday Sam, Will, and John picked out a huge boulder to roll. They worked and sweated and dug in turns, intending to send it crashing down, though not too close to anyone. Somebody miscalculated.

"Look out! She's a-rolling!"

John leaped from the hole, and the boulder roared and crashed down the hill. At that moment a Negro man had the bad luck to be driving past the spot. As his frightened eyes turned upward the stone bounced completely over his wagon without touching it, and landed on the other side.

That was the last time Sam ever rolled a stone. He and his friends hid from the patrol. And that evening when a resounding thunderstorm swept in over the river, to rip the heavens with bolt after bolt of lightning, Sam pulled covers over his head in bed and made a promise to lead a better life.

Sam had been told, time and again, that he would be struck by lightning if he didn't behave better. Wasn't that solemn warning given all of the worshipers in the Presbyterian Church attended, though reluctantly, by young Sam? Every time a storm broke Sam turned pale and thought that the bolt was directed at him. His remorse lasted until next morning. When the sun shone forgivingly and no fury remained in the heavens, Sam decided that it would do no harm to play hooky and go with Tom to explore the caves again.

The miles of cave passages winding through the cliffs overlooking the river never lost their scary fascination. Sam was once lost in the caves after a picnic, along with his little sweetheart, Laura Hawkins, and the terror that he felt when he caught a glimpse of a murderer known as Injun Joe gave him nightmares for months.

Sam saw other things that gave him nightmares too. In a village on the frontier life was fun, but it could be suddenly frightening. Although Hannibal was part of the South, and some of its people owned a few household and farm slaves, it did not have a plantation society. Immigrants going into the West came continuously through the town, and it did not have the settled life of the South before the war. Sight of death was not unusual, even for children. Once Sam saw his quiet father, not naturally a violent man, stop a street fight by hitting one of the men with a stone cutter's mallet.

And when he was a young child Sam had seen a man shot down in cold blood on the plank sidewalks of Hannibal. So he was used to violence, and he learned to hate it early. One night he came home from a forbidden trip a little way downriver in a rowboat "borrowed" for the occasion. Sam's conscience was not exactly hurting him, but he thought that maybe he would do well to remain away from his mother's watchful eye until morning, when there would be no time to talk to him. So Sam went to his father's office and crawled in through a window. He curled up on a horsehair sofa and went to sleep.

After a time he awakened, strangely uneasy. His eyes opened to see a shaft of moonlight touching a figure stretched out on the floor. Sam sat up and took a better look. It was the body of a man murdered that day on the street, put here until the undertaker could come for him. Sam could see a bullet hole in his head. He described afterwards how he went out of the place. "I do not say that I went in a hurry, but I simply went out of the window, and I carried the sash with me. I did not need the window sash, but it was easier to take it than to leave it, and so I took it. I was not scared, but I was considerably agitated."

Sam's friends in town included the Negroes, both slaves and freedmen. To him slavery was just a fact, like the flowing river and the town— like the one-room jail, where he and Tom Blankenship took matches and food to pass through the barred window to a tramp—like gunfights in the street—like the school and the church and the caves. This was Hannibal, Missouri, before the Civil War. This was Sam's world. Yet there were things about it that he didn't like even as a child, and they made him wonder how such things could come to be.

Sam saw slaves chained together being taken down the river for sale. This was the way it was. He once saw his just and kind father whip Jenny, their slave girl, because she had been impudent to her mistress. Mrs. Clemens, who had great sympa-

thy for the troubles of slaves, accepted the fact of slavery, and it was she who had asked her husband to punish Jenny. Later, when Jenny was sold because the family hadn't the income to keep her and needed the money that she would bring, they hired a little slave boy named Sandy to help with the chores a few hours a week. Sandy had a habit of singing the same song over and over, much to everybody's annoyance. Once Sam asked his mother to make Sandy stop singing —it was awful to hear it so much. Jane Clemens replied sadly, "Sandy is far from his family, and will never see them again. When he sings it shows maybe he is not remembering. When he stops I can't bear it."

As Sam grew he became a fine judge of his mother's moods, and expert in circumventing her wrath. She believed that she could always detect his circumventions—but he had a rather low opinion of her skill. Yet his admiration for her courage and character knew no bounds. Once he watched her deliberately stand before a terrified girl, whose wild, drunken father was threatening her with a knife. Jane Clemens gave the man a tongue lashing that caused him to drop his weapon and go away in silence.

"Sam," he could often hear his mother call, "Sam!" No answer. "What's gone with that boy, I wonder? You, sam!"

He could hear her, for he was hiding nearby, but he made it a rule never to show himself until that "You, sam!" came ringing out. Then he went in a hurry. That meant business.

The Adventures of Tom Sawyer are the boy adventures of Sam Clemens, although the story is imaginary. Most of the names are different, and somehow the story changed into fiction, for Mark Twain combined the adventures of his friends with his own, and so wove his plot into a pattern of interest and excitement. Cardiff Hill was really Holliday's Hill, and Sam Clemens became Tom Sawyer. Tom Blankenship, that hero of his boyhood, turned into Huckleberry Finn. Between the covers of this book Sam put his memories of the caves, his friends, his sweethearts, his sister, and brother Henry, Injun Joe, the village of Hannibal, and the great wide-spreading river. And Jane Clemens is there too, for she is the Aunt Polly of *The Adventures of Tom Sawyer*.

* * *

A PREVIEW OF THE ADVENTURES OF TOM SAWYER

Spring had come to St. Petersburg, Missouri, bringing a smile to even the grimmest winter face. Yet Tom Sawyer was downhearted. His Aunt Polly had caught him playing hookey from school the day before, and so today he must whitewash the fence. It was Saturday morning, just right for fishing or watching a steamboat edge in to the river landing. And then, "at this dark and hopeless moment an inspiration burst upon him." Tom's inspirations were not only original, they were successful too, and hilariously funny as well.

There was a newcomer in town. She was Becky Thatcher, whose golden braids and blue eyes were the envy of girls and the admiration of boys. Which boy would she notice? Tom Sawyer put on a campaign to achieve that honor, which he felt would be well deserved. Forthcoming events placed an awful strain on him, yet he was ready to prove his devotion at all times, even if he died doing it.

Aunt Polly told Tom not to play with Huckleberry Finn because he wasn't respectable. But, since Huck was the only boy who could live as he pleased, and knew more exciting things than all the other boys put together, Tom became Huck's friend. He even went with Huck to the graveyard to learn how to cure warts. Instead, the boys were cured of going to the graveyard, for that night they were the only witnesses to a horrible murder. Now Tom and Huck had a dangerous secret to keep, and trying to keep it scared them nearly to death.

A time came when life at home, in school, and in Sunday school wasn't worth shucks to Tom Sawyer. He felt that he was blamed for everything bad that happened in the town. So Tom persuaded Huck and Joe Harper to run away with him to a big wooded island. For a while they led a wonderful life. Then things began to happen, and it was up to Tom to think of some fancy escapades and schemes to solve their problems. That wasn't too difficult for the most ingenious boy on the Mississippi, and the results were surprising.

The sleepy town of St. Petersburg was shaken awake by the murder trial of old Muff Potter, who could remember nothing of that night in the graveyard. Tom and Huck knew who the murderer was, but they were afraid to break their vow of secrecy. Finally Tom realized that he had to stand up and tell the truth. That made him a hero all right, but he couldn't find much glory in it, for he knew that the murderer was still at large.

Of all the events of the year Tom and his friends looked forward most to a big summer picnic near a vast and mysterious cave. The party always ended with an exploration of some of the cave passages. Tom and Becky, wandering deeper and deeper, and farther and farther from the others, became lost. It took all of Tom's courage to face the dangers in the cave, and to try to rescue Becky. People thought well of him because of the way he did both. And they thought so much of Huck Finn, too, that a kind widow took him into her home to live.

* * *

WHEN IN DOUBT—DO IT!

Sam had tried hard to persuade his mother to let him leave school. He left the reading to Henry, and if he wanted to know anything from a book he just asked his brother. From the age of eleven on Sam had various odd jobs that brought in some small financial help to the family.

John Marshall Clemens was suddenly taken ill with pneumonia and lived only a short time afterwards. He left his wife and children without means of support, dazed with grief and shock. Sam, sensitive and impulsive, loving and rebellious at the same time, was crushed by remembrance of his own constant careless disobedience of his father's wishes. Orion came home from St. Louis, where he was working as a typesetter on a newspaper, and the family considered ways of survival.

Orion could send home a part of his small wages. Pamela could teach piano and guitar, and Jane Clemens could take a few boarders. What about Sam?

A year later Jane and Orion decided that Sam must become a printer's apprentice. A Mr. Ament had just come to Hannibal and had bought the equipment of the defunct *Gazette*, the newspaper of the Democratic Party of the town, and set up his *Missouri Courier*. He agreed to take Sam to work, pay him with board and room, and to give him two suits of clothes a year.

At first Sam was the errand boy and printer's devil, carrying out these jobs outside school hours. Then it was discovered that he learned quickly, so he was taught the printing trade, and Sam's wish to leave school was granted when he was thirteen or fourteen years old. There was one other apprentice, as well as a journeyman printer living in the print shop, and the three had fine times together. Sam was the smallest, the other apprentice was a giant of a boy. Ament gave them his own cast-off clothing. Sam was swallowed up in them, and had to set type standing on a box with his sleeves and trousers turned up "to his ears," as he put it, while the other boy could scarcely sit down for fear that he would split his skin-tight breeches.

Cigars were cheap, and all Hannibal boys learned to smoke at about the age of nine or so. Sam had a strong cigar or a corncob pipe hanging from the corner of his mouth as he worked. He put it down when he wanted to sing a comic song, and he was always ready to lay it aside, assume that innocent look, and play a joke on somebody.

Since he usually finished about three in the afternoon, there was still time for adventures on Holliday's Hill, in the cave, the creek, and on the river. But for all the jokes, and the free roaming life with his friends after work, Sam was leading a hard life now. Mr. Ament gave him mighty little to eat. The boys had to sleep on quilts on the floor of the printing office but they felt that they had a right to steal down cellar at night, bring up apples, onions, and potatoes and cook them on the office heating stove.

A year after his apprenticeship began Sam was the standby of the newspaper office. He became a first-class typesetter. He worked well, and he read all of the copy that came into the office, since nobody forced him to do it. He could run the job-press and sing at the same time. He delivered the papers. He made no money, but by the time he was fifteen he was acting as subeditor. He still enlivened any place where he happened to be.

One fine summer's day Sam, looking out of the window, had to make a split-second decision. Would he eat the luscious ripe piece of watermelon in his hand, or would he drop it on the unsuspecting head of his brother Henry, who was walking past the print shop? Sam never hesitated at a crucial time like that. His motto was "When in doubt—do it!" He did. The sight of his brother crowned with watermelon was sufficient compensation for its loss to Sam.

Sam was on hand for every excitement. When the circus came to Hannibal he was there, and he sat in the front row at the minstrel show. Sam went to see the hypnotist perform, and volunteered as a subject. He gave the crowd a wild performance and afterwards said that it was all an act on his part, although his mother and Orion always insisted that Sam was really hypnotized. He carried Laura Hawkins' skates when a winter crowd went to the frozen river, and he gallantly held her basket of lunch at the summer picnics.

One day Sam was hungry and feeling miserable. He was a boy of rapidly shifting moods, and his troubles were many. He was going home from the newspaper office. A strong wind blew through his thin jacket. He bent his head into the blast, and suddenly saw a sheet of paper tossed at his feet. Sam picked it up and read it as he walked. It was a page torn from a book. No book had ever really interested Sam. This page was from the story of Joan of Arc. It caught his wild imagination, and his ready sympathy and compassion. He read it over and over. Then he went around borrowing all of the books that he could find, and plunged deep into the world of reading. Joan of Arc became his favorite story. From this discovery there grew an enormous interest in all history, in all of the activity of mankind, and this interest was to remain with him for the rest of his life. To everybody's amazement, Sam began to thirst for knowledge. He even talked John Briggs and several other boys into joining him in a small class that he persuaded a German shoemaker to teach. Since the shoemaker knew little English this was not too hopeful a pursuit; yet it was here that Sam began to learn German, a language he later spoke well.

Everybody liked Sam, although he sometimes made them uncomfortably aware that they were ridiculous. He was strangely full of contradictions, rude and yet often considerate, rough, and often gentle, funny and sometimes very serious. He loved animals, particularly cats. Like his mother he felt at home with cats, and always had a favorite among them, a cat that invariably sat on a chair beside him when he had dinner at home. Sam could play pranks, and he could hate a bully, too. Any injustice sent him into a raging, fighting fury, and so did cheating.

When Orion returned to Hannibal and got a loan that enabled him to buy one of the newspapers in the village, the Hannibal *Journal*, Sam went to work for him. Henry, two years younger, was put to learning typesetting after school. Sam moved back home. At this time he believed that his future was to become journeyman printer, roaming about from one newspaper to another. He thought that such a life would be full of adventure and fun. Now, however, he was only fifteen and must stay at home to help Orion for a while.

A country boy named Jim Wolfe, green and bashful, came to room with Sam and learn the trade. One night Pamela gave a candy-pulling party. The boys were not invited, for they were too young, and so went up to bed. As they dropped off to sleep a fearful caterwauling began on the sloping roof outside the window. These sounds were mixed with laughter and conversation from the party, where at that moment pans of candy were placed to cool in the arbor built against the shed roof.

Jim Wolfe grew enraged at the cat fight, and muttered, "I'd like to knock those cats' heads together."

"Why don't you?" asked Sam. "You're scared to. I dare you!"

Jim got out of bed, pulled some knit stockings on his legs, and crawled out of the window into the snow. The roof sloped gently, and Jim had little trouble advancing on the cats, although it was very cold out there, and he in his nightshirt and stockings! Just as he got halfway down his feet struck a patch of ice and flew out from under him. The cats screeched and ran for cover. Sam, head out of window, howled for joy as he saw Jim go crashing through the snow-covered arbor right down into the party guests and their pans of molasses candy!

The next day while he was eating gingerbread with the baker's son, Sam regaled him with "Jim Wolfe and the Tom Cats" and sent the boy off into peals of laughter. This was the first funny story that Sam Clemens ever told, and he went home pleased with himself. He had tasted the pleasure of realizing that he was a born storyteller.

THE STORY OF HELEN KELLER

Lorena A. Hickok

Children respond to few biographies with more interest than to those of Helen Keller. Her struggle to overcome the greatest of all handicaps seems to move youngsters deeply. It is valuable for children to know of Helen Keller and Miss Sullivan because they represent and reveal two of the most important facets of the human spirit: the will to know and to escape limitations, and the desire to love, to reach out in help.

There are many biographies about Miss Keller's life; this is one which can be read by children in the upper elementary school and read aloud to those in the early grades. Because The Story of Helen Keller *has a good balance between information and drama, it would be an excellent introduction to biography for young children.*

HELEN HAS A TANTRUM

Before she could be taught anything else, Helen would have to learn obedience. The Stranger realized this from the start.

Partly because Helen's parents were sorry for her and partly because they did not know how to go about it, they had never really tried to make her mind. The result was that whenever Helen could not have her own way she would fly into a rage, and nobody could manage her.

"But I'm strong, too, young lady," The Stranger thought. "And I can be just as stubborn as you are."

Their first real battle came at the breakfast table a couple of mornings after The Stranger arrived.

Helen's table manners were very bad. She did not even know how to eat with a spoon. Instead of sitting in her place and eating from her own plate, she was allowed to run around the table, grabbing from other people's plates whatever smelled good to her.

When she was very small, people had thought this was amusing. It was like feeding a puppy at the table. Now that she was almost seven, her parents had grown used to it. When she snatched food from their plates they would go on talking as if nothing out of the ordinary was happening.

But this morning Helen made a sudden dive at The Stranger's plate and started to grab a handful of scrambled eggs. The Stranger pushed her greasy little hand away. And when Helen tried again, she slapped her.

Helen threw herself on the floor, kicking and screaming with rage.

While Mr. and Mrs. Keller looked on in horrified silence, The Stranger pulled the child up off the floor, shook her, and set her down, hard, on her chair. Helen squirmed and kicked, but The Stranger's hands held her in a firm grip.

"Don't worry—it's just a tantrum!" The Stranger panted as she noted the expression on the faces of Helen's parents.

She finally managed to get a spoon into Helen's hand. Holding it firmly there, she showed her how to scoop up the scrambled eggs onto the

From *The Story of Helen Keller* by Lorena A. Hickok. Copyright © 1958 by Lorena A. Hickok. Published by Grosset & Dunlap, Inc.

spoon. Then she tried to guide it up to Helen's mouth. But Helen angrily jerked her hand away and threw the spoon on the floor.

Without a word The Stranger dragged Helen off the chair. Firmly holding onto her hand, she guided it to the spoon and made her pick it up. Then she set her down hard on the chair again.

Helen was now crying. She could not understand why this was being done. It had never happened to her before.

Captain Keller threw down his napkin and got up from the table.

"I've had all of this I can stand," he growled, and he went stamping out of the room. Helen's mother followed him.

The Stranger went over and locked the door behind them. Then she returned to her breakfast, although every mouthful choked her.

"We've got to have this battle sometime," she told herself. "It might as well be now."

Helen began to pinch her. And each time she did it The Stranger slapped her.

Next Helen slid down off her chair and felt her way around the table. But there was no one at her mother's place nor her father's.

Quietly now, because she was puzzled, she found her way back to The Stranger. She did not try to grab anything this time. But placing her hand on The Stranger's wrist, she felt it being raised and lowered. The Stranger was eating.

Again The Stranger placed the spoon in Helen's hand and guided it up to her mouth. And this time Helen let her do it. Being very hungry, she finished her breakfast without any more bursts of temper.

As soon as she had finished, Helen jerked off the napkin that had been tied around her neck and threw it on the floor. Then she slid off her chair and ran over to the door.

Discovering that she could not open it, she flew into another rage, pounding on the door. The Stranger came over, but she did not open the door.

Instead, she firmly led the howling, kicking Helen back to the table and forced her to pick up the napkin off the floor. She started to show her how to fold it. But Helen threw the napkin on the floor again and herself on top of it.

This time, instead of pulling her up, The

Stranger let her alone and went on with her own breakfast—even harder to eat now, because it was stone cold.

Helen could not understand this. And because she couldn't she was even more angry. She tried several times to jerk The Stranger's chair out from under her. That was impossible, so she broke into a violent fit of sobbing. Everything was going wrong this morning! But *why?*

"I hate you! I hate you! I hate you!" she kept crying inside herself. "Why are you doing this to me?"

And The Stranger, looking down at her, was saying softly, "Poor little girl! I'm not happy about this either. But you've got to learn to mind me. Otherwise I can't do anything for you."

The morning wore on. Again and again Helen ran to the door, found it locked, and threw herself on the floor kicking and howling with rage.

"I'll just have to let you wear yourself out," The Stranger sighed.

Again and again she tried to make Helen pick up the napkin, but Helen fought her off.

Helen's father left for his office. "I have a good notion to send that Yankee woman back to Boston," he snapped as he went out the door.

Helen's mother hurried upstairs, to the room farthest away from the dining room, so she could not hear the noise.

Martha Washington's mother was beginning to wonder if she would ever be able to get into the dining room to clear away the dirty dishes and set the table for lunch.

Finally Helen's anger left her, and she lay on the floor quiet, her tear-stained face cradled in her arms.

Gently The Stranger bent over her and stroked her tumbled curls. Then she placed the napkin in Helen's hand once more and lifted her up to the table.

Without any struggle, Helen let The Stranger guide her hands. They folded the napkin and laid it on the table. Then The Stranger led her over to the door and opened it.

A very much subdued little girl wandered out onto the porch and on into the sunny garden.

The Stranger, starting wearily up the stairs, met Mrs. Keller on the landing.

"She finished her breakfast and folded her napkin," The Stranger said. But there was no triumph in her voice.

Back in her own room, she threw herself on the bed and cried herself to sleep.

THE WORD GAME

The battle of the Breakfast Table was the longest and one of the most violent of Helen's tussles with The Stranger. But it was by no means the last one.

After living with the Kellers for a week, Miss Sullivan decided that she could not help Helen unless she could take her away from her parents for a while. In order to make the child mind she was often forced to punish her, and Helen's parents constantly interfered. Especially her father, who could not bear to see his little girl cry.

Helen very quickly sensed the fact that her parents were on her side. And she would run to them every time The Stranger tried to discipline her.

The Stranger and Mrs. Keller were talking about this as they sat on the porch watching Helen at play in the garden.

"We can't help interfering," Mrs. Keller said. "We feel so sorry for the poor little thing."

The Stranger's reply was quick and urgent.

"Helen doesn't need your pity," she said. "She needs your help!"

"But what can we do?" Mrs. Keller sighed.

"I have an idea that might work," The Stranger answered, "if only you can persuade Captain Keller to agree to it. If I had Helen alone with me for a while, I think I could teach her to obey me. But now she can run to you every time I try to make her mind.

"I want her to learn to trust me and like me, as well as to obey. But this is impossible so long as she looks upon me as an outsider who makes her do things you don't make her do."

Mrs. Keller nodded.

"We own a cottage, about a quarter of a mile from here," she said. "You must have noticed it when you were out walking. It's tiny, but could be made comfortable. Perhaps you and Helen could stay there awhile."

"Just the thing!" The Stranger agreed. And Mrs. Keller promised to speak to her husband about the matter that evening.

At first Captain Keller did not think much of the idea. "Helen will be homesick," he predicted. "Poor little thing! Being away from us might even make her ill!" But his wife was so anxious to try Miss Sullivan's plan that at last he reluctantly agreed.

The following afternoon Helen was taken for a drive, which she loved. But this time she did not return home. Instead, she found herself in an unfamiliar place, alone with The Stranger.

She accepted it quietly at first. "They'll come and get me," she told herself. They always had before.

When bedtime came, however, this hope vanished. Helen was used to sleeping in her own small bed, alone. It was bad enough to have to get into this wide, unfamiliar bed. But when The Stranger started to get in with her, Helen rebelled.

"No! No! No!" she cried fiercely inside herself. "I won't have you close to me! I won't! I won't! I hate you! Go away!"

She hurled herself out of the bed, and it took The Stranger two hours to get her back. Finally, Helen fell asleep from sheer exhaustion, as close to the edge of the bed as she could get. The Stranger wearily crawled in on the other side.

"Perhaps they should have brought her own bed down here," The Stranger thought. "But it might have confused her. She's got to learn to accept changes. Dear God, help me to make it easy for her!"

In the days that followed Helen was so busy that she began to forget a little, her dislike of The Stranger. There were so many interesting things to do!

First The Stranger gave her some beads and a string. The beads were of different shapes and sizes. Some were made of wood, some of glass.

Helen's sensitive little fingers very quickly learned to string the beads and to sort them out into piles. The Stranger started a more complicated string for her—so many beads from one pile, so many from another. Helen learned to do that too with surprising ease.

"This is fun!" she told herself. And for the first time since they had been alone, The Stranger saw her smile.

The next game was harder. And because it was harder, it was more interesting. The Stranger gave her a ball of yarn and a crochet hook. Holding Helen's hands in her own, she showed her how to loop the yarn in and out, over and under the hook, making a chain.

Helen was fascinated. But she made many mistakes at first. Forgetting that she didn't like The Stranger, she went back to her again and again to find out what was wrong.

"I *can* do this!" she kept telling herself. "I'll *do* it!"

She kept at it until one day she had made a chain that stretched almost all the way across the room. She smiled with pleasure when The Stranger rewarded her with a piece of cake. And she did not jerk away when she felt The Stranger's hand patting her shoulder approvingly.

But most interesting of all was the game they played with their hands. Helen had no way of knowing, of course, but The Stranger actually was teaching her the Manual Alphabet.

The Manual Alphabet, which is shown on page 159, is a sign language. It was developed many years ago so that deaf and dumb people can talk with their hands.

As you see when you examine it, each position of the fingers means a different letter.

Learning to talk with the Manual Alphabet is not too difficult if you can see. You simply spell out the words with your fingers. In fact, it can be fun—a secret language!

But since Helen could not see, the only way she could learn the Manual Alphabet was for someone to make the letters in her hand. With her fingers she could learn the different positions, each one a letter. Then with her own fingers she could make the letters.

This would have been a very slow, tedious, almost hopeless task, had not Helen's mind been so quick. Far from being feeble-minded, as some of her elders had suspected, she was an exceptionally bright child. And she had a remarkable memory. In a few days she learned how to make almost every letter in the Manual Alphabet. She was not learning them, however, as separate letters in order: A, B, C, and so on. Instead, she learned them grouped together in words.

She learned how to make new words every day. For instance, C–A–K–E. W–A–T–E–R. C–U–P. H–E–L–E–N. P–A–P–A. M–A–M–A. B–A–B–Y.

But so far, these words had no meaning for her at all. It was just a game.

"I'm pretty good at it," she would think. "It's fun!"

And The Stranger, patiently going over the same words with her day after day, would look at her and think:

"Some day these words will unlock the door to your prison, little Helen. I don't know when or how. But they will. They *must!*"

Every morning on his way to the office Helen's father would stand outside, looking in the window to see how she was getting along. Helen, of course, did not know he was there.

"How quiet she is!" he often exclaimed as he watched her contentedly playing with her beads or her crochet hook. "She's not like the same child at all!"

One morning he brought Helen's dog Belle into the cottage. Helen greeted the dog with a little cry of delight and a big hug. Then she sat down on the floor, picked up one of Belle's paws, and began to move her claws about, this way and that.

"What on earth is she doing to the dog?" her father asked as he and The Stranger both stared. Suddenly The Stranger, watching Helen's fingers, smiled broadly.

"Look—she's teaching the dog to spell!" she said. "She's trying to get her to spell *DOLL!*"

But Captain Keller shook his head in discouragement.

"What's the good of it?" he demanded. "She doesn't know the meaning of the word. It's just a game."

The Stranger's expression was pleading, as she said quietly, "She'll learn the meaning. Give her a little more time—just a little more time."

W—A—T—E—R

The day had got off to a bad start. It was April 5th, just two days over a month since The Stranger had come to be Helen's teacher.

Because Captain Keller had insisted on it, Helen and The Stranger had moved out of the cottage. He wanted his little girl at home. Now he and Helen's mother were learning the Manual Alphabet. But Captain Keller wasn't trying very hard.

"What's the use?" he kept saying.

"You're going to need it," The Stranger told him. "Sooner or later—and I believe it will be before very long—Helen will know the meaning of words. And then you can talk to her, with your fingers in her hand."

Helen was now much quieter and better behaved than she had been. Everybody noticed it. She did not have so many tantrums. And when she did have one it did not last very long.

But sometimes, as on this April morning, she would wake up feeling out of sorts and cross. For one thing, she was getting bored with the word game.

"I know all that," she would think impatiently. "Why don't we play something else?"

All the morning The Stranger had been spelling two words into Helen's hand, W–A–T–E–R, and C–U–P. She would spell C–U–P and give her a cup to hold. Then she would pour a little water into the cup, dip Helen's fingers into it, and wait hopefully for Helen to spell back, W–A–T–E–R.

But Helen, not understanding, would spell C–U–P.

"What is it you want?" she kept thinking. "I'd do it if I knew. But I don't know. Can't you see I'm trying?"

"Poor child, you're getting tired," The Stranger said as Helen jerked her hand away and nearly upset the cup. "Let's rest awhile. Here!"

And she handed her the new doll she had brought her from Boston. Helen played with the doll awhile, but she was thinking of the word game.

"What do you want?" she kept saying to herself. "Why can't I do it? I try and try!"

Presently The Stranger started in on the word game again. C–U–P. W–A–T–E–R. But Helen kept getting more and more mixed up and irritable. Finally she seized her doll and dashed it to the floor. Its head broke in half a dozen pieces.

With grim satisfaction she followed with her hands The Stranger's motions as she swept up the broken pieces.

"I don't care!" Helen told herself fiercely. "I don't care the least little bit! Why don't you leave me alone?"

She gave a little sigh of relief when The

Stranger brought her hat to her. They were going outdoors. No more of that stupid game.

Although Helen did not know it, The Stranger carried the cup in her hand as they walked down the path toward the pump house.

Helen raised her head and sniffed with pleasure. That sweet smell! Although she didn't know the word for it, it was honeysuckle. She reached out her hand and touched the vine lovingly as they passed.

Someone was pumping water. The Stranger led Helen to the pump, placed the cup in her hand again, and held it under the spout.

Helen's first impulse was to throw the cup away. But she liked the sensation as the cool water flowed down over her hand into the cup. So she held it there, smiling a little.

The Stranger took hold of her other hand and began to spell the word again. W–A–T–E–R. Slowly at first. Then faster. Over and over again.

Suddenly Helen dropped the cup. She stood absolutely still, rigid, hardly breathing. Inside her mind, a new thought spun round and round:

"W–A–T–E–R! W–A–T–E–R! This lovely, cool stuff. W–A–T–E–R?"

Wildly she groped for The Stranger's hand. Her trembling little fingers began, W–A–T–? She had not finished when she felt The Stranger's pat of approval on her shoulder. She was right! That was it!

For the first time in her life Helen Keller had "talked" with another human being!

The Stranger's eyes were wet as she cried:

"Helen, you've got it! You've *got* it!"

Helen could not hear her. But that did not matter. For now another idea came flashing into her mind.

If that stuff was W–A–T–E–R, what about the other games they played with their hands?

She reached down and touched the ground, then turned eagerly to The Stranger. Her heart pounding like a little hammer, she felt The Stranger's fingers moving in her hand.

Several times The Stranger's fingers spelled the word, Helen intently following every movement. Then she spelled it back. G–R–O–U–N–D. She had it fixed in her memory now. She would not forget.

Now she must find out about more things. Fast! She ran about, touching everything she could reach. The Stranger's fingers told her: V–I–N–E, P–U–M–P, T–R–E–L–L–I–S.

Helen bumped into the nurse, who was coming into the pump house carrying Helen's baby sister, Mildred, whom she still thought of as "It." She touched "It" and ran back to The Stranger. B–A–B–Y! It had been spelled into her hand many, many times. Now it had meaning. Little Mildred was no longer just a thing called "It."

Suddenly Helen stood still, thinking hard. Then she reached out toward The Stranger.

Although she could not put it into words, as you or I would, her hand grasping The Stranger's hand asked a question:

"Who are you?"

And into her eager little palm the word came back: T–E–A–C–H–E–R.

In that warm, glowing moment all the hostility Helen had felt toward The Stranger melted away. For no longer was she a stranger. She was Teacher.

T–E–A–C–H–E–R! To Helen Keller, the most important word she would ever learn. And to Anne Sullivan, the most beautiful.

BENJAMIN WEST AND HIS CAT GRIMALKIN

Marguerite Henry

Marguerite Henry's biography of America's first famous painter is a well-written fictionalized, dramatic account. Yet it is a part of the school of thought that limits biography for children to the subject's childhood. More recent biographies deal with their subjects' mature achievements. However, Miss Henry's book presents an enjoyable introduction to biography for younger children.

After studying in America, under the patronage of James Hamilton of Pennsylvania, Benjamin West was able to study abroad when William Allen, a Philadelphia merchant, sent him to Italy. Benjamin West, the first colonial painter to achieve distinction, later became an expatriate and settled in England, as Miss Henry explains in her foreword.

This is the story of the Quaker lad, Benjamin West, and his cat, Grimalkin, who lived in the wilds of America when Pennsylvania was still a province, and the Indians were saying, "Itah! Good be to you!"

Because Quakers thought that pictures were needless, Benjamin never saw a picture; that is, not until he grew up to be seven years old and painted one himself.

Some people say it was the Delaware Indians who helped Benjamin to fame and fortune. Some say it was an artist and seaman by the name of William Williams. And some insist that it was Uncle Phineas Pennington, a merchant of Philadelphia.

But if Benjamin himself could have settled the question, he would probably have said:

"Why, it was Grimalkin, my glossy black cat with the uncommonly long tail!"

As for Grimalkin, he would have pricked his ears forward with pleasure and purred in agreement. For while HE did not go to London to visit the Queen, he helped send Benjamin there to visit the King. And it wasn't long before Benjamin West was Court Painter to King George III and had a fine studio right in his palace.

When artists in America heard about Benjamin's good fortune, they came knocking at his door. There were John Copley, Charles Wilson Peale, Gilbert Stuart, John Trumbull, Thomas Sully and more besides. Benjamin West helped them all because he remembered when he was a boy and needed help.

Today Benjamin West is remembered because he was the father of American painting; and many like to think of him as the only American

ever to become President of the Royal Academy of England. But I like to remember him as a boy who wanted so very much to paint that he dug his colors out of the earth and made his brushes from his cat's tail.

* * *

"What would thee say to my taking Benjamin to Philadelphia for a fortnight?"

Benjamin held his breath until his chest hurt. His eyes darted like arrows from Papa's face to Mamma's, then to Master Snevely's. He was unmindful of everyone else in the room.

Papa stroked his beard, thinking of all the reasons why Benjamin should not go. "School. Chores," he said. "Chores. School."

"What does THEE think?" he asked of the schoolmaster.

Benjamin shuddered.

"The boy" said Master Snevely, shaking his head gravely, "is not so quick in his sums as I would have him, but of late he has been diligent. He has cut enough goose-quill pens to last out my days as a master. A journey may teach him the importance of sums. I am favorable to the plan."

Benjamin's eyes opened wide in astonishment.

"Mamma?" questioned Papa.

"I want to say 'yes,' " said Mamma, smoothing her apron. "And I want to say 'no.' A whole day's journey from home is a long way for our little wren."

Papa flinched. Pet names annoyed him. Little wren indeed! He turned to Uncle Phineas.

"Mamma is right," he said. "The answer is 'yes.' Take him along, Phineas. He may forget his notions about painting. Make a merchant of him. Aye, make a merchant of him."

Suddenly Benjamin's happiness faded. What of Grimalkin? A trip without Grimalkin would be only half a trip.

"Papa," Benjamin questioned as they stood side by side at the wash bench next morning, "could I take—"

"As touching Grimalkin," Papa interrupted, "do not worry. I will caution Mamma and the girls to see to his happiness."

Breakfast had no flavor that morning. No matter how much milk Benjamin poured over his porridge, it seemed to lodge in his throat. He was glad when the meal was over and he could slip out of doors. He watched the travelers load their wagons and set off together in a long pack train. As they turned out of the yard, Benjamin ran alongside the driver. "Should thee someday see a lad of the name of Jacob Ditzler . . ." he said breathlessly and then stopped in embarrassment.

The driver slowed down.

"And what if we do?" he said, not unkindly.

"Please . . . please to tell him that Grimalkin is well and I am going to Philadelphia this day."

The man nodded gravely, and the women and children stared after Benjamin, making him feel quite important.

He strode back toward the courtyard where Uncle Phineas was strapping their knapsacks to his big pacer's saddle, while all of the family looked on.

Benjamin felt a gentle hand on his shoulder. It was Mamma holding out an old black coat that once had belonged to brother Samuel.

"The north wind blows raw and sharp for autumn," she said anxiously. "Samuel's coat worn over thy own coat will help to keep thee warm."

Benjamin frowned. He did not want to go to Philadelphia wearing two coats! And just when he was about to explain how warm he was, he swallowed his words. He looked at Samuel's coat as if he had never really seen it before. His eyes brightened. How big and roomy is Samuel's coat! he said to himself. Why, it would hold . . . a cat . . . extremely well.

He took the coat with a polite thank-you, then ran toward the inn, slipping his arms into the sleeves as he ran. "I just now remembered something in my room," he explained.

He looked back over his shoulder and smiled to see Grimalkin bounding after him.

A few moments later he stood breathless at the upping block.

"I declare!" exclaimed Papa. "Thee looks as stuffed as a pudding bag in Samuel's coat."

Benjamin laughed nervously. Grimalkin was a strong, active cat. He was not used to being buttoned inside a coat, and every time he squirmed he either tickled Benjamin's ribs or sent his claws into Benjamin's flesh. To cover the wriggling motions about his waist, Benjamin folded his arms and scratched himself lightly, trying his best to quiet Grimalkin.

"Phineas," said Papa, "Mamma and I have made out a list of things we are needing."

Benjamin suddenly looked down in horror. Grimalkin's pink nose peeked out of a buttonhole which he had left open as a porthole.

He glanced around quickly to see if anyone had noticed, but everyone was listening to Papa.

Why was it, Benjamin asked himself, that home always looked so good just when he was about to leave it! He had felt the very same way on his first day of school, and on the first day he rode to Miller Clinkenbeard's.

Mamma mistook Benjamin's searching glance for quite another reason.

"I must confess—" she shook her head— "it seems strange that Grimalkin is not here to say good-by to thee. It is not like him."

Papa stood thoughtful a moment. "A gopher, likely," he mused. "Grimalkin ever was fond of an early morning hunt."

At sound of his name Grimalkin tried to squeeze out of the little porthole.

Quick as a flash Benjamin clapped his hand over his stomach.

"Is thee ailing, little wren?" asked Mamma.

"No, Mamma!" replied Benjamin, his face reddening. "I am fine!"

"He appears feverish to me," said Sarah. "And from the way he is scratching he may be breaking out with the measles."

"The prospect of adventure always brings blood to the traveler's face," replied Uncle Phineas as he mounted and gave a hand to Benjamin. "Is thee comfortable perched behind me?"

"Oh, yes!" exclaimed Benjamin in a panic, for Grimalkin was now exploring the back of Samuel's coat and mewing faintly.

"Let us be off," he begged in a voice loud enough to drown out Grimalkin's cries.

Uncle Phineas' horse pawed the ground in agreement.

"Easy there," cried Uncle Phineas, and the big pacer swung out of the courtyard while the family shouted words that Benjamin could not hear.

Benjamin's right hand and forearm were fastened securely about Uncle Phineas' belt. With his left hand he now unbuttoned four more buttons of Samuel's coat. He could feel Grimalkin scrabbling around for an exit. He could see Grimalkin's head peer out like an opossum from its mother's pouch.

Benjamin heaved a great sign of relief. They were safely off at last! Now they could both enjoy the sights and the smells of autumn.

"Stroke Grimalkin for me," chuckled Uncle Phineas.

"How's thee know?" gasped Benjamin.

"Because," laughed Uncle Phineas, "I saw a black tail wave from between the flaps of thy coat as I helped thee mount. I knew thee could not possibly have sprouted a tail so quickly."

* * *

By midday Benjamin was tired and discouraged. He shared a piece of journeycake with Grimalkin. Then they both curled up in the shelter of a long wooden shed and dozed in the sun.

Just as they were falling into a deep sleep, they woke with a start. Steeple bells were clanging. Guns were saluting. And from all the red houses up and down the hillsides people came running.

"What is it?" asked Benjamin of a lad who almost stumbled over Benjamin's feet.

The boy was running so fast he could not stop. "The ANTELOPE PACKET," he called over his shoulder. "She's almost ready to dock."

Benjamin scooped Grimalkin into his arms and raced in the direction of Winn Street.

"Uncle! Uncle!" he cried as he burst into Uncle Phineas' shop. "The city has come alive. I need a paintbox!"

A slow smile spread over Uncle Phineas' face. He reached far back on a shelf and produced a clean canvas and a paintbox exactly like the one he had sent Benjamin. The bells were still clanging. The guns were still saluting as Benjamin set up his canvas on the banks of the Delaware. Grimalkin patted and sniffed the cakes of paint. Then he settled down at Benjamin's feet and blinked up as if to say, "This seems almost like home. Now I can take a real snooze."

Sailors from Spain and Portugal, from New England and old England, from the West Indies and the Azores gathered about Benjamin. Few spoke the same language. But they all understood the picture that took shape before their eyes. A shining river going out to sea. Men fishing on the banks. A ship in the harbor. And a white cow eying the water.

Perhaps Benjamin would not have painted so easily had he seen the scarlet chariot of Samuel Shoemaker draw up behind him.

Samuel Shoemaker was known throughout the colonies as a big merchant. If Uncle Phineas had five boxes of salt in his warehouse, Samuel Shoemaker had twenty and five. If Uncle Phineas had ten rolls, each, of calico and cambric, Samuel Shoemaker had ten times ten, and silks and velvets besides.

After handing the reins to a slave, Samuel Shoemaker threaded his way through the crowd of sailors and tapped Benjamin on the shoulder with his gold-headed cane.

Benjamin looked around in surprise. He had never seen a man quite like this before. His face was as plain as a salt box, but his wig and his clothes were wonderful to behold. His wig was tied to resemble pigeons' wings at the sides. And he wore a purple waistcoat with a cascade of white ruffles that reminded Benjamin of the waterfall in Grevling's picture.

"Lad, who are you?" asked Samuel Shoemaker, his eyes on the canvas rather than on Benjamin.

"Why, I am Benjamin West, son of John West," replied Benjamin in a voice so like Papa's that Benjamin scarcely knew it for his own. "I come from Door-Latch Inn, in the Township of Springfield, in the County of Chester."

The man threw back his head and laughed so vigorously that the powder from his wig rose like a white fog. "Egad!" he whistled. "You must be Penington's nephew. I am Samuel Shoemaker."

"Thee knows my Uncle Phineas?" asked Benjamin.

"La, yes! Here is the proof."

And right there on the banks of the Delaware with all the sailors tapping their feet to the tune, the great Samuel Shoemaker recited:

"I eat my peas with honey,
   I've done it all my life.
It makes the peas taste funny,
   But it keeps them on my knife."

When the foot-tapping and the laughter died away, Mr. Shoemaker said: "I have just ordered a picture from the artist William Williams. I am on my way to his lodgings now and should be glad of your company."

"But I—I have a cat——"

Mr. Shoemaker looked down at Grimalkin, who was now sniffing his shoe buckles.

"A mannerly cat is welcome anywhere," he nodded.

"Why, that is what Mamma says. Her very words!" smiled Benjamin as he handed Mr. Shoemaker his paintbox.

Carrying his picture very carefully in one arm and Grimalkin in the other, Benjamin climbed into the chariot while the sailors thumped one another on the back and grinned at his good fortune.

William Williams was a little cricket of a man who had gone to sea in his youth. He lived in a small studio with hardly any furniture. But to Benjamin it was the most beautiful room he had ever seen. Canvases lined the walls. And from them pink flamingo birds and ships' captains and parrots and white-wigged ladies and gentlemen looked down with a superior air. It was almost as if they could smell the turnips and cabbages cooking in the rooms below. To Benjamin, however, no room had ever smelled more exciting. He sifted out the familiar cooking odors and breathed in the good smell of paints and oils.

Mr. Shoemaker seemed in a hurry to leave. He introduced Benjamin and Grimalkin, asked when his picture would be delivered, then turned to go. "I'll leave you two artists alone," he said with a wink. "You'll have much to talk about."

But when the door was closed Benjamin seemed to be struck dumb. He wanted to ask a million questions. Yet he could think of more.

At last William Williams thought of a question. "What books," said he, "have you read?"

"Why, I've read the Bible. I've read about John and Thomas and Samuel and Joseph. My brothers were named for them."

"I mean books on the art of painting," said Mr. Williams with a slow smile.

"Oh," gulped Benjamin in surprise. "Are there books on painting?"

For answer Mr. Williams reached up on his chimney shelf and took down two sizable volumes. They were bound in brown leather that had the nice look of an old saddle.

There was a kind of worship in the way Mr. Williams held them. "These two authors are Richardson and Dufresnoy. They were my teachers," he said as he looked down at Benjamin. "Now they can be yours, too." And he laid the books in Benjamin's hands.

Just then Grimalkin began to mew hungrily.

"Yo-ho!" laughed Mr. Williams. "Here is a cat that wants his dinner. Now it so happens that a lady who is sitting for her portrait just brought me a whortleberry pie and a crock of fresh milk. I'll heat the pie to make it juicy and toothsome. Meanwhile we can speak about your picture."

Benjamin had eaten nothing but dry journey-cake since breakfast. His mouth watered at the thought of hot whortleberry pie, but no sooner had Mr. Williams left the room than his appetite was gone. He wished he could hide the picture. A hundred doubts began pricking at his mind. Were the colors too bright? Did the cow stand out too sharply?

He had about decided to snatch up his picture and his cat and run down the flight of stairs when Mr. Williams returned with the pie and a basin of milk for Grimalkin. All the while that he set the milk on the floor and placed the pie in the warming oven at the side of the chimney, he had one eye on Benjamin's picture.

Benjamin stole a sly glance at his face. It was as blank as a wig rest. He listened for some word of criticism. None came. Instead, Mr. Williams reached for the tongs hanging at the side of the mantel, took a live ember from the fire, then slowly lighted his pipe.

And just when Benjamin could bear the silence no longer Mr. Williams spoke. Even then Benjamin could not tell how he felt, for all he said was, "Will you leave your picture with me, lad? I want to show it to Dr. Smith of the Academy."

"Can't see that thee has changed much," said Papa when Benjamin and Grimalkin returned from Philadelphia.

"Except," said Papa, stroking his beard thoughtfully, "thee and Grimalkin be thinner while thy knapsack appears heavier."

"Yes, Papa. It is filled with presents—a parcel of thread for Mary, bone buttons for Sarah, a comb for Hannah and buckles for Elizabeth."

"Mere trifles," snorted Papa. "What gives it the bulk?"

"A johnnycake pan for Mamma, and . . .'

"And what?"

"Two books," replied Benjamin as he placed them in Papa's hand. "For thee—and me," he added in a weak voice.

Papa looked over the books, trying to make out their titles.

"My spectacles are on the candle shelf," he said. "Take the books inside. They will bear looking into."

That night Benjamin went to sleep to the pleasantest of sounds. Overhead, the small patter of rain on the cedar shingles. Below, Papa's voice reading aloud from Richardson's book on the art of painting. Benjamin strained his ears. He could not make out the words, but the tune was good. For when Papa's voice began to rise and fall and boom and quake, he was mightily pleased. Even Grimalkin could tell that. He burrowed deep in under the quilts and purred in his loud rumbly fashion, as he always did when Papa and The Family were at peace.

As the news of Benjamin's trip spread, neighbors made all manner of excuses to visit Door-Latch Inn. They wanted to hear about the great Samuel Shoemaker. Mrs. Tomkins came down from the hills to borrow some live coals. The fire on her hearth had gone out, she said. However, she seemed in no hurry to get back home with her pot of glowing embers. She sat down on the settle while her eyes scoured the inn for a glimpse of Benjamin.

A spry-legged old man came ten miles to borrow duck eggs. "The creek on my place over-flowed," he said. "Washed all my duck eggs downstream. Come to borry a few of yours, and maybe sit down a spell."

Only Mr. Wayne, a gentleman of Springfield, made no excuses. He dropped in one evening, purposely to watch Benjamin at work.

"By my life!" he exclaimed to Papa. "Your son's pictures are very acceptable. I should like to have one or two on my own mantel shelf. Then, when winter closes in, I could regard green trees and flowers. It would be like special windows opening onto spring."

Benjamin's heart sang. Never before had anyone WANTED his pictures. Quickly he slipped down from his stool and opened the pine dresser. He selected three landscapes and three portraits, including his very favorite—that of Grimalkin.

"If it please thee, I should like to give these to Mr. Wayne," he said, handing the pictures to Papa.

Papa nodded. He seemed glad to get them out of the house.

The next morning when Benjamin was on his way to school, Mr. Wayne, on his black stallion, galloped up beside him. He leaped to the ground and led his horse along the road.

"My wife prizes the pictures," he smiled, as he fell into step with Benjamin. "Especially that of Grimalkin. She is overfond of cats, you know. 'Vastly pretty!' she exclaims every time she chances to look at it. I myself half expect the creature to miaow—he looks so lifelike. Mind my words, Benjamin, we shall soon be sending sitters to you for their portraits."

All this while Mr. Wayne had been jingling some coins in his pocket. Now he pulled out a whole handful of them and began counting. "One—two—three—four—five—six. Six dollars," he said, as he piled the money into a neat little stack. Then he reached for Benjamin's hand and placed the money inside it.

"Mrs. Wayne and I wish to buy the pictures," he said. "And we hope a dollar apiece will please you."

"A dollar apiece!" repeated Benjamin. "Oh, Mr. Wayne . . . !" Then his throat filled and could say no more.

All day long the words sang themselves over in Benjamin's heart. "Vastly pretty." "We wish to buy the pictures." "Vastly pretty." "We wish to buy the pictures." And in his pocket the six dollars kept a jingly tune to the words.

Now that Benjamin and Grimalkin were back home, it was almost as if they had never been gone.

Winter was closing in, and Benjamin had to take his place with Papa and his brothers. He dug turnips, piled them in a neat mound, and covered them with warm straw and earth. He husked corn. He gathered cattails for bed stuffing. He stacked swamp grass for the cows and bullocks. He helped yard the cattle.

Grimalkin was quite as busy as the rest of the family. Field mice were trying to find winter quarters at Door-Latch Inn, and there were days on end when he had to catch his sleep with one eye open.

The days wore into weeks. Weeks wore into months. But no word came from William Williams, or from Uncle Phineas either.

"Does thee suppose we dreamed that trip to Philadelphia?" whispered Benjamin to Grimalkin one long winter evening.

At that precise moment the door opened and in came a horseman. He pulled a letter from his boot and flourished it over his head. "For John West, Innkeeper," he announced as his eyes, unaccustomed to the firelight, tried to single out Mr. West.

Papa rose stiffly. He accepted the letter without even glancing at it. But Benjamin could see his hands tremble as he slipped it into his pocket.

"Thomas," he said, "see to the gentleman's horse.

"Hannah, be so good as to brew a cup of tea.

"Thee, Benjamin, carry warm water and fresh linen up to the front bedchamber."

Papa was first of all an innkeeper. Not until he had made certain that the rider and his horse were comfortable did he take the letter out of his pocket. Then he lighted a candle, clamped the candlestick over the back of his chair, put on his spectacles, and unfolded the fine white paper.

His fingers began drumming on the table board. The drumming grew louder as he read, louder even than the household noises: Mamma

at her spinning wheel, the girls making click-clack noises with their knitting needles, Benjamin and the boys whittling treenails, Grimalkin playing with a wooden spool. Finally the spinning wheel stopped. The knitting needles lay idle in the girls' laps. The boys put their jackknives down. Even Grimalkin stopped his play.

"I feared it," said Papa, his face white.

"What is it?" asked Mamma in alarm.

"It is about Benjamin," Papa replied. "The letter comes from the Reverend Dr. Smith of the Academy of Philadelphia."

Benjamin's hands tightened around a handful of treenails until they dug into his flesh.

"Read it out," suggested Mamma.

Papa cleared his throat, then read very slowly.

"For
John West, Esquire
Door-Latch Inn
near Springfield
in Chester County

"Dear Sr John West—I have this day seen a painting done by your son, Benjamin. It is a lively piece of work, and holds a promise for the future.

"I am desirous of schooling the lad in history. History needs painters. The printed word is sometimes cold. Pictures can set words on fire.

"As touching on the matter of money, I am of the belief that Benjamin can earn his keep and his schooling by painting miniatures.

"I hope you will approve my recommendation.

"I am,
"Yours most truly,
Provost, The Academy
William Smith
Philadelphia"

Papa turned away from the fire and fixed his eyes on Benjamin. Something of the fire was left in his stare.

"I thought thee would outgrow painting," he said. "I thought it a childhood pastime like blindman's buff or puss-in-the-corner. I held great hopes for thee, lad. I never dreamed thee would become a painter of images."

"Then I can go?" asked Benjamin breathlessly.

"It is not for me to decide."

"For Mamma?"

"No. It is not a matter for Mamma to decide. It is for God. I will lay the whole matter before

Him at the meetinghouse next First Day." In silence he raked ashes over the fire for the night and with a heavy step went upstairs to bed.

After his footsteps had died away, Grimalkin wrapped himself about Benjamin's boots and looked up questioningly.

"Don't forget ME in thy plans," he seemed to say.

CARRY ON, MR. BOWDITCH

Jean Lee Latham

Nat Bowditch, an exceptionally intelligent boy, should have attended Harvard. But his father's ship had gone aground April 19, 1775. This loss combined with the war impoverished the family. Even after peace was declared the family's fortunes did not improve. Instead of attending Harvard, Nat was indentured as a bookkeeper for nine years. Yet he continued his studies—teaching himself Latin so he could learn more about astronomy. At twenty-one, finally released from his indenture, Nat was offered his first position aboard ship.

Nathaniel Bowditch was a mathematical genius. With little formal education he corrected Moore's Navigation, charts used by European and American sailors. Many shipwrecks had been caused by its mathematical errors. Bowditch's New American Practical Navigator made sailing much safer.

While children's heroes are often men of action, Nathaniel Bowditch was a man of ideas whose accomplishments were those of the mind. Yet his story is one of courage; it shows how a refusal to be becalmed can lead a man to success. Jean Lee Latham, recognizing children's interest in action, uses dialogue and drama effectively to sustain the reader's interest. This book deservedly won the 1956 Newbery Award.

DOWN TO THE SEA

"Nathaniel," said Mr. Derby, "Captain Prince is commanding a ship of mine—the *Henry*—on a voyage to Bourbon. He agrees with me that you'd make an excellent clerk."

Just like that! Not a word about the trouble with Gibaut! Nat tried to sound as cool and collected as Mr. Derby. "I'd like to ship as clerk under Captain Prince, sir."

"Clerk—and second mate," Prince growled. "I never carry idlers on my ship! Between ports, a clerk isn't worth the hardtack to keep him alive." He turned to Mr. Derby. "Anything else, sir?"

Mr. Derby leaned back and matched his finger tips. "Just this, Captain Prince—which I tell all my masters—every time they sail. When you're off soundings, you're on your own. I've given you suggestions for trading when you reach Bourbon. But when you get there, you may find my suggestions aren't worth the paper they're written on. You'll use your own judgment. There are only two things I expressly forbid. You'll never break a law of any port you enter. And you'll never—NEVER enter into slave trade." He leaned forward, gripping the arms of his chair. "I'd rather lose any ship I own than to have it become a slaver! There is no excuse that I'd accept. Even if a slaver attacked you, overpowered you, and ordered you to carry a cargo of slaves—even that would be no excuse! You'd go down fighting—but you wouldn't turn a Derby ship into a slaver!"

Before Nat realized what he was doing, he clapped his hands. "Good for you!" Captain Prince stared at him. He felt his face get hot.

A frosty twinkle touched Mr. Derby's eyes. "I'm glad we agree, Nathaniel." He stood. "Well, gentlemen, I believe that is all."

Captain Prince and Nat left the office together. Prince clapped his hand on Nat's shoulder. "Glad you're sailing with me, Nat."

Nat explained about his venture. "It's a pretty sizable bit of cargo, sir. I invested nearly all the money I have in it—almost a hundred and thirty-five dollars."

"A hundred and . . ." Prince chuckled. "Don't worry, Nat. There's plenty of room for your venture. A hundred and thirty-five dollars . . ." Still chuckling, he waved good-by and strode off.

Nat didn't see the captain again until the raw January morning when the *Henry* was ready to sail. He was waiting on deck with the rest of the crew when he saw Captain Prince striding along the wharf. Nat grinned to himself, thinking of Prince's laughter. "He must really shake the timbers of a ship!"

Captain Prince came on board, grim-jawed, frowning. His black eyes whipped a glance over the deck, seeing everything, looking at no one. Nat gulped. Something must be wrong. Had Prince had a quarrel with Mr. Derby, too?

Captain Prince spoke to Mr. Collins, his first mate—a tall, rangy man with a lean face and cool gray eyes. Soon came the hoarse cry, "All hands! Up anchor!" All around him, men leaped to their duties, spreading sails, bracing the yards. Men walked round the capstan, leaning on the bars, heaving the anchor. Then, "Anchor's aweigh!" And the *Henry* was moving out to sea.

That evening in the middle of the dog watch, Captain Prince took his departure from Cape Ann. Navigation, Nat thought, was like surveying, all right. In surveying you started from a known point and ran your lines by compass. In navigation, you took your departure from a known point, too, and steered your course by compass. But there the likeness ended.

Taking sights wouldn't be the same. In survey-ing, the earth was firm beneath your telescope. You could take all the time you wanted to check and recheck a sight. If you thought you had made a mistake, you could go back and do it over again. Here at sea, nothing would ever hold quite still. When you shot the sun at noon you'd have one instant to get it and get it right.

And measuring your distances wouldn't be the same either. In surveying, your chainmen could measure your distances for you. Here on the open sea, you'd measure your distance by checking your speed, and multiplying that by how long you had sailed that fast. "Many a man," Sam Smith had said, "sails halfway around the world by log, lead, and lookout." The log checked the speed, the lookout warned of dangers they could see, and the lead warned of dangers beneath the surface of the water—sudden shoals and reefs where they might go aground. He really knew a good bit about a ship, Nat thought, even though this was his first voyage.

Mr. Collins called all hands on deck to be divided into watches.

I know what the watches are, too, Nat thought. A watch is four hours: eight to mid-night, midnight to four, and four to eight in the morning; then eight till noon, and noon till four. Then the next watch is the dog watch; it's di-vided into two watches; four to six and six to eight. Dividing the dog watch that way switches the hours of the watches for the next twenty-four, so that the same men don't stand two watches every night.

Mr. Collins was calling a man's name. The fellow nodded and moved to the larboard rail. Nat was thinking: I know about bells, too. One bell sounds the first half hour, and so on until . . . Yes, I know a good bit about a ship. I know the—

Mr. Collins said, "Your choice, Mr. Bowditch. A man for your starboard watch."

Nat gulped and his brains began to spin. He had known he would stand watch, but he hadn't realized he'd command a watch. With his thoughts still in a whirl he said, "Chad Jensen."

Old Chad said, "Aye, aye sir!" and moved to the starboard side. Mr. Collins chose again. It was Nat's turn once more. "Dan Keeler."

He felt Mr. Collins' surprise. He was surprised at himself. Why had he chosen Dan Keeler? Dan was a troublemaker who'd been spread-eagled for twelve lashes many times.

Dan Keeler slewed a sidelong stare at Nat. "Aye, aye, sir," he rumbled. His glance seemed to say, You lubberly little runt!

When the crew had been divided into watches, Captain Prince came topside and stood on the quarter-deck, staring down at the men. He was still in a temper, Nat thought. Funny, what anger could do to a man. He looked ten years older than he had that day in Derby's office.

The captain began to speak. His words bit like the lash of a whip. It did not take him long to tell the men what he expected of them, and what would happen if they did not obey on the double. He finished, wheeled, and strode below.

They heaved the log and set the course. Eight bells.

Mr. Collins said, "Lay below the larboard watch!"

And Nat stood on the deck of the *Henry*, in command of the first watch. With a hollow feeling where his stomach should have been he stared miserably about him. Old Chad Jensen was taking the first trick at the wheel. Thank goodness he knew someone. He went over and stood at Chad's shoulder, watching the compass in the glow on the binnacle light. Good old Chad. He'd known him ever since his first days at the chandlery, when he used to drop in between voyages and spin yarns with Sam Smith.

Nat said, "You steer a straight course, Chad."

Chad's eyes did not move. His gaze was fixed on the compass. "Aye, aye, sir. Thank you, Mr. Bowditch."

The hollow feeling hit Nat's stomach again. Was he going to spend months—maybe a year —with men who acted as though they had never seen him before? He paced the deck and then stared miserably over the rail.

"Mr. Bowditch." Captain Prince was standing by him.

"Aye, aye, sir!"

"In any emergency, call me. Remember, a captain always sleeps with one ear cocked." He wheeled and went below again.

His voice was still grim. He seemed to be speaking from the other side of a gulf that Nat could never cross. But Nat felt comforted.

At eight bells, when Mr. Collins relieved him, Nat stumbled below, surprised to find he was utterly exhausted. What had he done? Nothing. Just stayed on the alert, watching for emergencies. He threw himself into his bunk with his clothes on. "I know what that is, too," he muttered, "when you tumble in with your clothes on. You turn in ALL STANDING. Yes, I know a lot, I do!"

It seemed to him he had scarcely dozed off when confusion topside wakened him. He heard feet thudding across the deck, and men shouting. Someone banged on a hatch and bellowed, "All hands on deck!"

Nat stumbled topside. As he emerged from the hatchway, the wind almost took him off his feet. The *Henry* was rolling heavily, shipping water with every roll.

The rest of that night, and for six days and nights that followed, Nat found out what men meant by the Roaring Forties of the North Atlantic. Numb with weariness, he lived in wet clothes and ate cold food. It was bad enough on deck; it was worse below deck. The hatchways had to be closed, and below deck the air grew so foul that the very lanterns burned dim. Whenever Nat had to go below, the stench grabbed at his throat and turned his stomach. Why, he wondered, had he ever wanted to come to sea? Why did any man choose this life?

It was all right maybe for a man who became a captain—but what about men like Keeler and Jensen—who'd spent their lives on the fo'c'sle? Why would they live like this for salt beef, hardtack, and twelve dollars a month?

The sixth night, just before midnight, Nat went on deck for his watch. The storm had ended; the sky glittered with stars. Nat caught his breath and stared. No man, he thought, had ever seen stars until he had seen them from a ship in mid-ocean.

The next morning, just after seven bells of the forenoon watch, Captain Prince came on deck with his sextant, ready to shoot the sun. "Have you ever used a sextant, Mr. Bowditch?"

"Not at sea, sir. But I have one."

"Then get it."

"Aye, aye, sir!" Nat hurried below for his sextant and slate. If he could just do this smartly and well, maybe Prince wouldn't be so grim. He hurried topside, fumbled his sextant out of its case, and dropped the case. He flushed, and didn't pick it up. He leveled the sextant to catch the horizon, and started to bring the sun into focus.

Captain Prince drawled, "Don't you think you'll need a shade, Mr. Bowditch?"

Nat felt his ears burn. He fumbled the red glass into place. When the sun reached its zenith and stood still the fractional moment, Nat took his reading. He checked in the almanac. His slate pencil streaked through his figuring. Captain Prince stood watching him.

When Nat had finished, he said, "Hmmm. You are quick at figures, Mr. Bowditch. Well, we've got our latitude, all right. The longitude— that's something else again. I wish chronometers weren't so infernally expensive."

Nat said, "How about a lunar, sir? Won't that give you your longitude?"

Prince shrugged. "Once in a blue moon you can get one, but by the time you've worked out all your computations, it's about two days later. You may find out where you were, but you'll never know where you are."

"I don't think the mathematics would take quite that long, sir," Nat said. "I'd like to try taking a lunar, first chance we have."

Prince shrugged again. "Go ahead. Be handy to know our longitude. If we could be sure." He didn't sound as though he thought much of the idea.

Nat checked his nautical almanac closely, hunting for the first night the moon promised to be in a good position for a lunar. That night he went on deck before the time for his watch, with his sextant.

Little Johnny, the cabin boy, joined him. "Mr. Bowditch, sir, would you tell me what you're going to do?"

"Of course, Johnny. I'm trying to find out a little more about where we are. We know our latitude—how far north of the equator we are. The trick is to find our longitude—how far east or west we are."

"East or west of where?" Johnny asked; then, hastily, "Sir?"

"That's a good question, Johnny. First, we have to pick a north-south line to be east or west of. And since we used to belong to England, we use the same line that the English use—the north-south line through London. We call it the meridian of London."

"But how can we even figure how far west of London we are—when we're here—and London is away off somewhere else?"

"We have to figure that by time," Nat told him.

Johnny stared. "Time? Mr. Bowditch, sir, is that a joke?"

"No, Johnny. Every twenty-four hours, the earth turns around once. So the sun seems to be rising somewhere, every hour—even every minute. When it's sunrise in London, we know it's sunset halfway around the world. And, a fourth of the way around the world, it's midnight. If we had one of those fine ship's clocks called chronometers, we could use it to tell how far from London we are. We'd keep it set to London time. In the morning, when we checked our sunrise, we'd look at the clock and see what time it was in London, and we could figure how far from London we were, because we know how many miles the earth turns every hour."

"But we don't have one of those—uh—uh— special clocks, do we?"

"No, Johnny. So I'm going to check our position by the moon. You see, we know by the nautical almanac exactly where the moon will be —every hour, every minute, every second. And we know where a great many of the brightest stars will be. So, if we can catch the moon as it crosses in front of a certain star—we call it 'occulting' the star—we can figure how far away from London we are when we see it happen."

"That sounds easier," Johnny declared.

Nat grinned. "Most people don't think so. There's quite a little figuring to do. But the big problem is to catch the moon crossing in front of a star that is bright enough for us to still see the star when it's that close to the moon. There ought to be some better way to work a lunar— but we don't have it—yet."

Johnny stared at Nat's sextant and sighed. "I wish some time I could look through a sextant."

"You can," Nat said. "The moon's going to be bright enough tonight for us to catch the horizon. I'll teach you to check Polaris—the North Star."

The next night, when Nat came topside before his watch, Keeler approached him. "Mr. Bowditch, sir, is it true that you let Johnny look through your sextant? Or was the little lubber lying to us?"

"He did try his hand with the sextant. Would you like to?"

"Me?" Keeler gulped. "You mean—ME?"

"Why not?"

"But—but—nothing, sir."

That night Keeler had his turn at hearing about the moon and trying to check the angle of Polaris.

Then one evening during the dog watch, before the stars were visible, Nat leveled his sextant to catch the horizon. Johnny was at his elbow.

"Mr. Bowditch, sir, what are you doing now?"

"I'm sighting a star."

Johnny turned a puzzled glance to Nat. "But there aren't any stars."

"Yes, there are, Johnny. There are always stars. We just can't see them until it's dark enough for them to show. When you want to get an angle on a star, and we don't have bright moonlight, the problem is to get the horizon when it's light enough to see it, and to get the star when it's dark enough to see it. So I'm starting to check the star while I can still see the horizon. And I'm watching where I know the star will be when I can see it."

The men gathered round to listen. From that night on, the dog watch was Nat's busy time. Even Herbie, the huge Negro cook, wanted to hear Mr. Bowditch talk about the stars.

"Daggone," Herbie said, "it kind of picks a fellow up to think about the stars. Kind of makes you forget about soaking the salt beef till it's fitten to eat, and about smelling the bilge water." He shook his head and grinned, "Just think of me learning things! Me!"

"Of course you can learn," Nat told him. "Every one of you can learn."

But teaching them wasn't so easy. Time and again Nat explained something in the simplest words he could think of—only to see a blank look on the man's face. Time and again he wanted to shout, "Can't you see? Can't you understand anything?" But he always remembered

Elizabeth Boardman and the parallel rulers. He always remembered how she said, "Your brain— it's too fast. So you stumble on other people's dumbness—like a chair in the dark. And you want to kick something."

He would bite back his impatience. Slowly, carefully, he'd explain again—and again. At last he'd see the man's eyes brighten. He'd hear the happy, "Oh, yes! Simple, isn't it?" Nat would grin. "Yes—simple."

When he got back to his cabin, he would write down the explanation that had finally made sense to a man. Just so I won't forget it, if I ever have to explain that again! he told himself. After three weeks, he had quite a stack of notes. He was making a new notebook, he realized; a very different sort of notebook. All his other notebooks just said enough to explain things to him. But this notebook said everything he had to say to explain things to other men—to the men who sailed before the mast.

Weeks passed. Nat saw much more of the fo'c'sle and the cabin boy than he did of the captain, first mate, and their passenger. Captain Prince, Mr. Collins, and Monsieur Bonnefoy dined together. The second mate dined alone, after they had eaten. Nat didn't mind. At first he read at the table. But after he started teaching the men, he spent all his time at mess answering Johnny's questions. It helped—to explain things to Johnny. After he'd made Johnny understand, Nat didn't have to go over things so many times to make the men in the fo'c'sle understand.

One day Captain Prince called Nat to his cabin. The captain's grimness had not relaxed. "Tell me, Mr. Bowditch, just what are you trying to do with the men during the dog watch?"

"Teach them what they want to know, sir."

Captain Prince cocked an eyebrow. "And can learn?"

"They finally get it, sir," Nat told him, "if I just find the right way to explain it."

"But, Mr. Bowditch, why are you doing it?"

Nat was silent for a moment. "Maybe, sir, it's because I want to pay a debt I owe to the men who helped me; men like Sam Smith and Dr. Bentley and Dr. Prince and Nathan Read. Maybe that's why. Or maybe it's just because of the men. We have good men before the mast, Captain

Prince. Every man of them could be a first mate —if he knew navigation."

Captain Prince muttered something under his breath. "An odd business!" he said. "But I've never had less trouble with a crew. Carry on, Mr. Bowditch."

"Aye, aye, sir."

Someone tapped on the door, and Monsieur Bonnefoy entered, smiling. "I have a confession to make, Captain Prince. I was eavesdropping through the skylight. Not by intention. I just happened to be there, and could not help hearing. Monsieur Bowditch—he has the magnificent spirit! It is worthy of the French Revolution! Liberty! Equality! Fraternity!"

Captain Prince roared, "What do you mean —the French Revolution? Who started this business of rebelling against kings? We did! We started it in 1775! It took you French until 1789 to get around to it!" Then, for he first time since the *Henry* had sailed, Nat saw a twinkle in Prince's eyes.

Monsieur Bonnefoy apologized. He was so embarrassed and he talked so fast that he started talking French. Without thinking, Nat answered him in French.

Bonnefoy beamed. "Monsieur! You speak French! Why didn't you tell me?"

"I—I—guess I just didn't think of it."

Captain Prince roared again. "So you didn't think of it? And here I've been expecting all along I'd have to have an interpreter in Bourbon! Have you any more tricks up your sleeve, Mr. Bowditch?"

"No, sir, I—I—don't think so, sir."

"No more languages?"

"Just—just—Latin, sir. I learned that to read Newton's *Principia*."

Prince mimicked him. "JUST LATIN: TO READ *Principia*. And you still think it's worth your time to teach those poor devils in the fo'c'sle?"

"Yes, sir, I do!" Nat snapped.

Captain Prince gave him a long, hard stare. "Carry on, Mr. Bowditch. That's all."

Almost three months out of Salem, the *Henry* reached the Cape of Good Hope, and ran into more bad weather. For three days and nights they fought head winds, trying to make their easting. Again the men lived in wet clothes and ate cold food, and turned to all standing, because they knew they'd be called out again soon by the bellow, "All hands on deck!"

"I wonder who named this the Cape of Good Hope?" Nat said.

Prince growled, "The Portygee explorers named it right—Cape TEMPESTUOSO—the Cape of Storms. But I guess their king didn't like the sound of that. After all, he was interested in trade with the east. So he changed it to Cape of Good Hope."

Nat said, "I suppose Hope fits—in a way. You can always HOPE you'll get around it."

"DOUBLE IT, Mr. Bowditch!" Prince roared. "You don't GET AROUND a cape! You DOUBLE IT! You—you—lubber!"

"Aye, aye, sir." Nat smiled to himself. He knew just how Prince felt. It was a relief to know he wasn't the only man who ever stumbled on someone's dumbness—like a chair in the dark— and wanted to kick something.

One night early in May Nat got a good lunar observation and worked out their longitude. He went to Prince's cabin. "According to my figures, sir, we're sixty-one miles east of our dead reckoning."

Captain Prince shook his head. "We couldn't have overrun our reckoning that much!"

"If my figures are right, sir, at our present speed, we'll sight Bourbon on the eighth."

Prince drawled, "So, Mr. Bowditch? I wouldn't put on my go-ashore clothes if I were you."

It was during Nat's watch early the morning of the eighth when he heard the lookout's singsong, "Land, ho-o-o-o-o!"

Captain Prince came on deck. He said, "Hmmmm . . ." He rubbed his chin and swept Nat with a sidelong glance. "I believe you can work a lunar, Mr. Bowditch."

"Of course," Nat said. "It's a simple matter of mathematics, sir."

Captain Prince said, "Hmmmm" again and returned to his cabin.

Nat stared across the water until the rugged peaks of Bourbon loomed on the horizon. Bourbon—where they'd sell their cargo for double its cost—or lose their shirts. For the first time in months, Nat thought of his venture. What would happen to his cargo of shoes in Bourbon? Would he win—or lose? He watched the ragged outline take shape in the mist. Bourbon . . .

HERO OF TRAFALGAR: The Story of Lord Nelson

A. B. C. Whipple

Horatio Nelson, 1758–1805, played a significant role in preventing Napoleon's expansionist drives from destroying England's empire. When he discovered the French fleet anchored in Aboukir Bay, east of Alexandria, Egypt, ready to fire point-blank on the English ships as they sailed in front of them, Nelson's daring strategy of sailing between the ships and the shore allowed his fleet to destroy all but four of the French ships. This was the most decisive victory of modern warfare up to that time and won Nelson great fame and honors. He was made Baron Nelson of the Nile and Burnham Thorpe by the grateful English government.

Later Nelson's daring destroyed much of the Danish fleet and prevented the powerful Scandinavian navy from joining forces with France. For this victory he was made Viscount Nelson. In 1805 he prevented the French and Spanish fleets from meeting for an intended attack on England.

Lord Nelson suffered greatly for these victories. He lost the sight of his right eye leading his soldiers in a land attack on Calvi in Corsica in 1795, his right arm had to be amputated after a battle at Santa Cruz, and he received a head wound in the fight at Aboukir Bay that caused intense pain for several years.

Yet none of these injuries made Nelson less daring. In the great sea battle off Cape Trafalgar in 1805, Nelson refused to stay below decks. While directing the English fleet from the quarterdeck of his command ship, Nelson was shot by a soldier on the French ship Redoubtable. *He died October 21, 1805.*

Lord Nelson is still honored in Trafalgar Square, London, by a column with an eighteen-foot statue of the admiral.

Whipple's biography of Nelson, written for children, is unusual for its honesty in revealing the brutality of the British navy in the seventeenth and eighteenth centuries. Another unusual feature is the inclusion of Nelson's love affair with Lady Hamilton. Hero of Trafalgar *is an interesting biography of a man whose strong will overcame physical weakness and drove him to become the hero he wanted to be. The importance of Lord Nelson's victories over Napoleon's powerful navy cannot be overestimated in the history of Europe.*

"I WILL BE A HERO"

Horatio Nelson's uncle was a gruff old sea dog. When he finally came aboard the *Raisonable* he had little time to devote to his nephew. The ship was made ready. All hands were assigned to their watches. Sails were broken out. The men marched around the capstan and chanted as the anchor chain came clanking up through the hawsehole. *The Raisonable* began to move slowly. She picked up speed, as her sails filled with wind, and moved out past *Sheerness* and into the English Channel. Young Horatio

Nelson was already too busy to spend any time looking back on the England he was leaving, at twelve years of age, to start his career.

The English Channel can be one of the roughest bodies of water in the world. The *Raisonable* was not long out of the harbor before she started rolling, pitching and shuddering as she plunged into the head-on seas. As a midshipman, Horatio was crowded into a tiny cabin area with so many others that there was barely room to swing a hammock. On the first windy night many of the other new boys were seasick. So was Nelson. The ship was battened down, with every opening closed to keep out the flying spray. As everyone grew sicker, the air itself became nauseating.

Through the ship's thick sides could be heard the pounding of the sea, the crash of the waves and the howling of the wind. Inside the cabin there was the moaning and the retching of seasick sailors. Young Horatio Nelson learned what it took to be a sailor on that first stormy night at sea.

In the next few days and weeks he learned a great deal more. He learned his way about the floating world of his warship. He learned how hard it was to climb out on a wet yardarm high over the roaring sea on a stormy night. He learned how the British navy recruited and treated its men. He learned how the men sometimes rebelled, and what happened to them when they did. Above all, he learned to be a naval officer in the finest tradition of the best navy in the world.

The ship on which young Horatio sailed had been captured from the French twelve years earlier. That was why she carried the French name of *Raisonable*. To a boy going to sea for the first time she was a huge ship, with masts so high they made him dizzy and sails that seemed to cover the sky. She carried row on row of big guns along her sides—sixty-four of them, almost enough for a boy to lose count. Yet the big ship always seemed crowded below. In the quarters Horatio Nelson shared with other young midshipmen there was space only for his hammock and scarcely any room for stowing his gear. But he was far better off than the seamen in the lower decks. Down below the waterline, there were no portholes and the only light came from lanterns even in the middle of the day. The men quart-ered there were so crowded that they could lie in their hammocks and not even swing to the roll of the ship, so closely were they packed.

In fact, a warship in those days did not have enough room for the entire crew to sling hammocks at any time. The crew was divided into watches, with half the men working while the other half rested or slept. And it was while on watch that Horatio Nelson learned to be a sailor in the British Navy.

Much of his work was done aloft, on yardarms higher than a housetop. From the deck he was forced to climb up the rigging until the sailors below looked like midgets. There he could stand on a tiny platform until he got used to the fact that he was swinging far out over the water with every roll of the ship. Then he had to crawl out along the yardarm, hanging on as he tried to keep from missing the footrope and falling while the ship plunged under him. At first, like all new hands, he tried to work with one arm, using the other to hang on for dear life, as he furled sail. But soon an officer was shouting at him, or swinging a knotted rope at him to make him work with both hands.

Sometimes, when the breeze was light and the ship ran along on an even keel, it was pleasant to stand on the footrope and lean over the yardarm, looking down at the blue sea swishing by and daydreaming as the wind sang softly in the rigging. But then there were nights when all was black and the gale screamed and the sails thundered and the ship plunged so that the masts seemed to keep going right on over into the water. On nights like this Horatio Nelson had to work harder and faster than ever. If he did not, the ship might sink in to storm, taking all hands down with her.

Often the footropes and hards were covered with ice. If a sailor's fingers, numb and cold, fumbled and let go, he could pitch from the swaying footrope into the empty blackness below. If the ship were at that moment swinging out over the sea, he would drop like a cannonball and sink so deep that he could not hold his breath long enough to struggle back to the surface. Even if he did, there was little chance that the ship could come about and find him in the dark, stormy waters. His cries would not be heard above the shrieking of the storm.

But the sailor who fell into the sea and drowned died a less painful death than the one who plunged onto the deck. A fall like this was enough to break nearly every bone in a man's body, and the ship's surgeon could do little but try to comfort him through his hours of agony until he died. It was a very lucky sailor who happened to fall into a sail. If his comrades worked fast, they could haul him back onto the footrope, still alive but scared within an inch of his life.

Sometimes it was just as dangerous on deck. In a pitching sea one of the huge guns could break loose from the ropes that held it to the gun port at the ship's side. Each gun weighed hundreds of pounds and was set on wheels so it could be rolled back and forth at its port. When one broke loose and slewed around, the iron monster could roll the length or width of the deck, crushing anything in its way. The only way to stop it was to get a long iron bar under the gun and heave it over on its side. Only a brave man would try that on a slippery, rolling deck.

When the weather grew rough and cold, there was always the chance of being struck by a shipmate falling from above. And when the seas rose higher and the ship plunged her bow under the towering waves, the hissing green water poured aboard and swept the length of the deck. Any sailor who was not ready to grab hold of something could be picked up like a cork in this boarding sea and carried over the rail.

There were plenty of men aboard Horatio Nelson's ship who had not joined up willingly. If the navy had waited for volunteers, it would never have been able to complete a crew for any of its warships. In those days a man could be walking the streets of a port town like Chatham or Liverpool one minute and, the next thing he knew, wake up in a hammock aboard a ship—after being knocked unconscious and kidnapped by a "press gang." These press gangs were roving bands authorized to capture men for service as sailors.

A man was not safe even if he were serving aboard a merchant ship. The ship could be boarded by a navy press gang, and the sailors from the merchant vessel could be hustled aboard a warship putting out to sea. There was no law against this in England, except the one that stated that press gangs could board only the ships returning home and had to leave enough sailors aboard to work the merchant ship into port.

About half of a warship's crew was made up of men who had been caught like this and forced into the navy. Others had been "drafted" by the officials of their towns, who had been ordered to provide men for the navy. Often the local officials sent beggars, thieves, pickpockets and juvenile delinquents whom they were happy to be rid of. When these men came aboard, one sailor wrote: "Stand clear! Every finger was fairly a fishhook; neither chest nor bed nor blanket nor bag escaped their sleight-of-hand thievery."

It was a rough and rebellious crew that manned most ships of the British navy in those days. And the officers used rough methods to keep them working. The seaman's "on watch" usually started with the shriek of the boatswain's whistle and the bellow of the mate: "All hands ahoy!" and "Up all hammocks ahoy!" Every man moved fast; if he did not, the mate "started" him with the flick of a knotted rope's end. When the work was not dangerous, it was long and dreary: scrubbing decks, tarring ropes, painting the ship's sides, shifting sail to make the most of every slant of wind.

For their labor the men were paid what amounted to a few dollars a month. And they did not receive that until they were released, sometimes after years of service. The food was often spoiled and there was usually not enough of it. Many of the officers believed that the only thing that could make good seamen was the harshest form of discipline. Any sailor who moved too slowly or grumbled over the work or the food was "corrected" by the whistling end of the knotted rope or the heavy end of a marlinespike. There were even navy regulations against swearing. An ordinary seaman caught using profanity was forced to wear a heavy wooden collar and pace up and down the deck until he was ready to drop. One captain added two 32-pound shots to the collar and nearly broke the man's neck.

If a sailor made the mistake of talking back to a superior or falling asleep on watch, he received far sterner punishment. Taken below and chained, he was given a length of rope and ordered to make his own cat-o'-nine-tails. Then he was taken on deck, because in the crowded quarters below decks there was "not enough room to swing a cat." On deck the sailor was stripped to the waist. His wrists were tied and hoisted. Then he was lashed with the cat he had made, until his back was a bloody pulp. The bleeding back was doused with salt water, partly to add to the punishment but mostly to clean the wounds. Aboard British naval ships in the days when Horatio Nelson went to sea, this was an almost everyday occurence.

Often the men rebelled, in hidden ways and in the dark of the night. An officer would fall down a companionway because someone had left a bucket on the steps. A marlinespike would drop from aloft and knock an unpopular mate unconscious. A 32-pound cannonball could roll the length of the deck, thundering down on an officer and crushing him against the rail if he did not jump quickly out of its path. Rarely were the seamen who tried such tricks of revenge found out. Woe to them when they were.

Some sailors who could not take the abuse and punishment tried to desert. It was not easy. Whenever a naval ship was in port or near land, a marine sentry was constantly on duty, patrolling the special "marine walk" to watch for any attempted desertion. If a man did get away, he was hunted down by the navy. If he was caught, his punishment was far worse than he had had before. A "run man" was taken back to his ship and sometimes "flogged through the fleet." As an example to others who might be planning to jump ship, he was taken in a boat and flogged before every vessel in the fleet. His punishment was usually halted before he died, and he was put back to work as soon as he could walk again.

With conditions like these—press gangs kidnaping the worst water-front riffraff and naval officers trying to beat them into submission—it was no wonder that there was sometimes open mutiny. In fact, the year 1797 was known in England as "the year of mutinies." That was the year when an entire British fleet mutinied at the great naval base at Spithead. The sailors refused to work the ships. Seizing the vessels, they sent the officers ashore. Not until the Admiralty agreed to raise their pay, improve their living conditions and even obtain the king's pardon for every mutineer, did the seamen allow the officers to return and assume command of the fleet.

This was the British navy that Horatio Nelson joined at the age of twelve. It was a navy in which few sailors wanted to serve, a navy for which crews had to be provided by press gangs. It was a navy that still underpaid and mistreated its men. And yet it was the greatest navy in the world. It was the navy that beat France, the navy that captured or sank all but one ship in the American navy in the Revolutionary War. It was the navy that made England a great power. It was the navy that kept Napoleon from conquering most of the world.

How could England's sailors be so poorly treated, so rebellious and such good sailors and fighters all at the same time? One good reason was Englishmen like Horatio Nelson. Like Nelson, the English sailors were great patriots. Every man was more than ready to die for his country. None could think of greater glory than bravery in battle for England. Even during the famous mutiny at Spithead, which happened while England was at war with France, the mutinous sailors announced that if the French fleet should put to sea, the mutiny would be postponed.

A more important reason was that the British navy was the first in the world to train its officers professionally instead of simply letting a wealthy or titled man, with no experience or training purchase his officer's commission. British naval officers, schooled by harsh discipline, were proud of their competence. And this competence was recognized by their subordinates.

Most of the officers saw to it that discipline was maintained but with fairness to all, and these officers won the affection as well as the respect of their men. The commander in chief of the British navy at the time of the mutiny at Spithead was Lord Richard Howe. He was a tough old admiral, but he had always seen to it that everyone was treated fairly aboard his own ship. The sailors called him "Black Dick." This was, sailor fashion, their term of endearment. And when the Commander in Chief helped negotiate a settlement of their mutiny against the Admiralty, the sailors paraded Black Dick on their shoulders about the streets of Portsmouth as they celebrated their victory against the officers.

These were the years when a man's station in life was important, to the lower classes as well as the upper classes. The British seaman was brought up to respect what he called "his betters." In the British navy of that day a minister's son was a "gentleman" and therefore born to be an officer. He may have been poor, as Nelson was, but he expected to be an officer and a gentleman whether rich or poor. If another Norfolk boy who was a shoemaker's son joined the navy at the same time as Horatio Nelson, he expected to be a seaman, and never an officer. This was a simple fact of life accepted by all. The seaman's station aboard a warship was forward, while "his betters," the officers, were stationed aft.

So twelve-year-old Horatio Nelson was rated a midshipman, an officer candidate. With the other young gentlemen he was stationed in the gun room instead of the midshipmen's cockpit. The cockpit was on the orlop, or lowest, deck—below the ship's waterline. It was the home of the older midshipmen, who were not gentlemen and would probably not rise any higher in rank. The cockpit was famous for the rowdy and raucous life the older midshipmen lived. It was not considered a proper place for a boy not yet in his teens who was on his way to becoming an officer. Instead, the gentlemen midshipmen were quartered with the gunner on the gun deck, where portholes let in some light and where the air—and the company—were cleaner. The gunner, who commanded the men manning the ship's guns, had no more chance than the older midshipmen of rising higher in rank. But he was already of higher rank than they. And most gunners were good, steady men who could be counted on to be firm and fair and good teachers to the young gentlemen learning their way about the ship.

* * *

He did have some time for his loved ones at Merton. These were no longer Lady Nelson and his stepson. They were Lady Emma Hamilton and her daughter Horatia, who was Nelson's goddaughter. Seven years earlier, in Naples, Nelson had stayed with Sir William and Lady Hamilton after the Battle of the Nile. Lady Hamilton had treated his head injury and nursed him back to health. Sir William Hamilton was then Britain's Ambassador to Naples, and both he and his wife became fond of Nelson. They returned to England with him. Nelson found that his many years at sea had drawn him away from his wife. He and Lady Nelson tried to pick up their marriage where it had broken off, but without success.

Nelson moved out of his home and into that of the Hamiltons, who welcomed him. And just before Nelson went off to watch the French fleet off Toulon, Sir William Hamilton died, with Lady Hamilton cradling him in her arms and Nelson holding his hand. Now Lady Hamilton kept house at Merton. She was Nelson's age, and she and Nelson were in love. The Admiral was just as fond of his goddaughter Horatia. Many of his friends and relatives criticized him for leaving his wife, and Nelson himself must have felt twinges of conscience over it. But he never returned to his wife and his rightful home.

VASCO DA GAMA: Sailor toward the Sunrise

Ronald Syme

In this biography for younger elementary school children, Ronald Syme reveals da Gama's weakness as well as his strength. Readers of fiction have long expected rounded characters who have both faults and virtues, yet until recently few biographers have drawn realistic pictures of their subjects. Usually only the man's accomplishments have been shown. Mr. Syme's honesty helps show children that even famous men have several sides to their character.

"Friend Vasco da Gama!" King John exclaimed. "I know you as one of the best sea captains of Portugal. There will be a fine expedition for you to lead before very long, for I have decided to send ships to India."

King John did not live to see his expedition sail from Lisbon. He died a few months after he had chosen Vasco da Gama as commander. But John's cousin, Manuel, who then became king, went ahead with the idea. He found the money for the voyage and ordered the ships to be built. Manuel asked Bartholomew Diaz to advise Gama on the building of these ships.

"We've had the wrong idea in the past," Diaz told Gama. "Our ships' decks curve too much, and those high wooden castles we've been building at bow and stern are all wrong. They're useful for defense when an enemy boards the ship, but they create too much weight. When you hit those wild seas around the Cape of Good Hope, you should have level decks and not too much weight above the water line. Low-built ships with deep hulls are what you'll need.

"And here's something else, friend Vasco. For the past seventy-five years our ships have always steered along the African coast when they voyaged south. Winds and currents are against them all the way. I found that out for myself when I got far south. So I advise you, my good friend, to steer well out into the Atlantic until you reach twenty degrees south of the equator. Then swing eastward, and I've an idea—it's just an idea, mind you—that you'll go tearing in toward the Cape of Good Hope with a singing breeze to tighten your sails. It's what I'd do if King John —God rest his soul—had chosen me as leader instead of you.

"One more thing. Watch your men for mutiny. If my own hadn't rebelled I might have reached India seven years ago. But the men would sail no farther, and I gave way to them. Maybe that's why our present king—may his reign be happy and prosperous—didn't choose for me to go with you."

Three little ships arose on the wooden slipways beside Lisbon's wide Tagus River. All of them were three-masters. There was the *Sao Gabriel*,

From *Vasco da Gama: Sailor toward the Sunrise* by Ronald Syme. Reprinted by permission of William Morrow and Company, Inc. Copyright © 1959 by Ronald Syme.

the flagship, which weighed about 240 tons; the *Sao Rafael*, about 200 tons; and the *Sao Maria*, about 150 tons. A fourth vessel, the *Berrio*, was bought from a Portuguese sea captain. She was a two-masted little vessel of 100 tons, fitted with triangular fore-and-aft sails, like those of a modern yacht.

Veteran seamen scratched their heads and wondered greatly when they looked at the three new ships. They were reasonably high at bow and stern, but their decks were strangely level. Foremasts and mainmasts carried square sails, but the mizzenmasts—those nearest the stern—were fitted with triangular sails. On each mast was a lofty crow's-nest for lookouts. The decks were fitted with clumsy iron guns, and a good deal of space was occupied by heavy boats.

"Flatter-bottomed than most and fitted with those new-fangled watertight compartments," muttered the seamen. "They're queer-looking vessels, but Captain Diaz designed them and Captain da Gama approved of the design. Between them there isn't much they don't know about seamanship. Even so, no vessels like those yonder have ever yet sailed out of Portugal."

The completed vessels were moored beside the wharves of Lisbon. Into their holds were swung barrels of salt beef and pork; barrels of wine; cases of lentils, sardines, plums, onions, honey; bags of salt and sugar; and casks of brandy. There were other barrels containing gunpowder, and coils of flax rope, spare anchors, sails, steel breastplates, crossbows, and bundles of clothing. The voyage might last three years, and Gama had no intention of running short of supplies.

There was only one important item which Gama apparently overlooked—or perhaps did not bother to include. He took no supplies of costly presents for the native princes he might meet during the journey. Gama was accustomed to dealing with the simple Negroes of west Africa. He had a rather superior attitude toward colored races, and he believed any kind of trash was good enough for them, as long as it was made in Europe. This mistake was to cause endless trouble.

While the vessels were being loaded and the hatches fastened down, Gama went searching for crews to man his vessels. He chose his older brother, Paulo, to be captain of the 200-ton *Sao*

Rafael. Paulo was a lean, gentle-voiced man with a generous heart. Behind his polite manners and soft voice, however, there dwelt a fierce temper and unlimited courage. In addition, he was a first-class seaman.

One by one, men came forward. They were already scared at the thought of the coming voyage into strange and unknown seas. Apart from the gentlemen who volunteered merely for the sake of adventure, there were some strange characters. Martin Affonso, seaman, had lived for years among the Negro tribes of west Africa and spoke their queer, clicking language. Joao Nunes, sailmaker, had wandered through Arabia and spoke Hebrew and Arabic. Pero Aguilar, clerk, was an ugly little man and handy with a knife. Some said he was a fugitive from Spain. Fernao Martins spoke Arabic but was careful not to reveal how and where he had learned that language. Juan de Acaray, quartermaster, was a Spaniard and a deadly shot with a crossbow.

Gama also enlisted twelve convicts who had been condemned to long imprisonment or death. During the voyage they were to be put ashore, if necessary, to search for food and water, to look for signs of treachery among the natives, and to make friends with tribes who appeared hostile. Provided these men behaved themselves—and lived long enough—they were to receive a pardon for their crimes. Altogether, Vasco da Gama collected about 150 men for his ships.

On July 8, 1497, the four vessels moved a mile or two downstream from the city of Lisbon. They anchored in a reach where the river ran wide and deep. Cool orchards and bright gardens covered the banks. On the summit of the low hills, windmills spun briskly in a warm breeze. The sun was bright in a cloudless summer sky, and the blue surface of the Tagus River was covered with sparkling wavelets.

The four vessels looked trim and efficient. Gay flags and pennons were flying from the masts; the freshly-painted hulls glistened in the sunlight. On each white sail was painted a large red cross. The officers and the gentlemen on deck were wearing new cloaks and uniforms, and the ships glowed with their bright colors.

A great crowd had gathered on the grassy banks to say farewell to the men who now came ashore for the last time. Highborn ladies with scarlet flowers in their black hair stood next to handsome peasant women who wore colored silk scarves knotted loosely round their shoulders. Shepherds, cowherds, and farmers, in homespun clothing, gazed with wonder—and perhaps with envy, too—at the splendid little vessels and the brown-skinned sailors in their red tasseled caps. There were dark-skinned gypsy girls; gray-haired, wrinkled seamen who had sailed in the vessels sent out by Prince Henry the Navigator forty years earlier; and pale-faced priests in garments of black.

Watching this bright yet sorrowful scene—for many in the crowd were weeping—was Vasco da Gama. He was leaning on the poop rail of the *Sao Gabriel*, a thickset, heavy-shouldered, strong-jawed man, thirty-seven years old. Sailors on the deck below cast inquisitive glances up at him. They noticed his dark, watchful eyes, his powerful arms, and the hard line of his mouth.

"Not a man to rouse to anger," muttered a seaman. "I've heard stories about what he's like in a temper. A devil spitting fire, so they say!"

"Aye," murmured another, "but he's surely the best man to lead us to this distant land of India. He's never lost a ship in all his years at sea, or known a mutiny either. He'll give justice to those who obey his orders, whatever he may do to the others."

The seamen were right. Years spent in the slave trade of west Africa had turned Captain Vasco da Gama into a hard and sometimes ruthless man. Nothing and no one were allowed to stand in his way. While the crowd on shore wept as they embraced their departing husbands, fathers, and sons, Gama's bearded face remained grim and without emotion. The greatest voyage of his life was about to begin. The king of Portugal had entrusted the expedition to him. Success meant wealth for the country; failure would bring disgrace on the family name of Gama. There must be no mistakes on this voyage, and no rebellious crews to threaten mutiny because of fear.

The breeze was coming from the east. It would carry the ships down the river and into the Atlantic Ocean. Gama issued the order for trumpets to sound. The seamen rowed back aboard their vessels. Then, as the sound of weeping rose more loudly from the shore, anchors began to rise from the river mud. The white sails with the bright red crosses swelled outward from the masts. One by one, the *Sao Gabriel* leading, the little fleet began to glide down the Tagus River. The long and dangerous voyage to India had begun. This was to be the greatest day in Portugal's history.

Past low shores of sandbanks the ships steered down the west African coast. In those days ships were not fitted with water tanks below deck. Fresh water had to be carried in barrels, and there was never enough of it for a long voyage. Gama swung his ships to an anchorage in the Cape Verde Islands, where the casks were refilled. Sailors chopped great quantities of wood for the cooking stoves aboard their ships, and gathered all the fresh food they could find.

Far south of the Cape Verde Islands, Gama gave a surprising order to his officers. "Steer southwest," he commanded. "We are leaving the coast. There'll be many thousands of miles of open sea for us to cover before we sight land again."

Outward to the great Atlantic swung the heavy little ships. Day after day there was only the ocean around them, where great-winged albatrosses swung and dipped between the gray, hissing wave tops. The southeast trade wind blew steadily on the port quarter. Progress was slow, but not as slow as it would have been had the vessels kept to the coast on their southward run.

At twenty degrees south of the equator, Gama, following the suggestion Bartholomew Diaz had made, altered course again. "South-southeast," he ordered. "We'll swing in to the coast."

Now a westerly wind filled the great white sails and sent the four ships pounding along to far-off Africa. August went by, and then September.

"We'll sight land in three weeks' time," said Gama, and he was right. On November 1, 1497, the three ships came tearing into St. Helena Bay, about 150 miles north of the Cape of Good Hope.

Gama had done his navigation with a sandglass and a primitive compass. His only chart was the rough one drawn by Diaz, and he used a clumsy astrolabe instead of the modern sextant to find his latitudes. It is no wonder that his navigation is still described by seafarers today as one of the finest pieces of pure navigation ever accom-

plished. The course he steered was used ever afterward by sailing ships bound for South Africa.

Around the Cape of Good Hope went Gama with his ships. They called at lonely bays inhabited by Negro tribes, where they bought fat oxen in exchange for pewter bracelets or little copper bells, and refilled the empty water casks. Portuguese seamen ate porridge like millet and roast chicken from wooden platters in mud-walled village huts. Good-natured Negroes helped them roll the water barrels down to the boats, and afterwards sang and danced to the thin piping of native flutes.

Exploring Portuguese seamen in those days used to erect stone pillars at easily noticed places along the coast. These PADRAOS, as they were called, served as guides for other ships. Each PADRAO was a circular stone column, topped by a square block of stone, upon which stood a heavy little stone cross, fixed in place with lead. On December 16, 1497, Gama left behind the last PADRAO erected by Bartholomew Diaz. His ships had reached water never seen before by any European sailor.

As the vessels crept northward up the coast of east Africa, an illness called scurvy made its terrifying appearance among the men. The disease was caused by the lack of certain vitamins found in fresh fruits and vegetables, which were almost entirely absent from a seaman's diet. Men's gums turned black, and their teeth fell out. Their legs and arms swelled most painfully, and their flesh rotted. They grew weaker day by day. Some of them died in their bunks, loudly cursing the day they had signed on for this voyage or weeping sadly for the sweet countryside of Portugal they would never see again.

With their crews of sick and dying men, the four ships found their way into the wide, low-lying harbor of Mozambique. The surrounding hillsides were covered with green jungle, where monkeys and bright-feathered parrots chattered and squawked from dawn to sunset. On the foreshore stood white-walled houses with dome-topped windows, heavy carved doors, and verandas with iron latticework.

Mozambique was an Arab town. Fierce Arab warriors, sweeping down from the north, had settled there centuries before. Their descendants had built fine houses and established trading stores. They had bought African ivory, gold, and slaves, which they exported to India in exchange for spices, carpets, and rare silks. These Arabs had grown prosperous from their trade across the Indian Ocean. Their nation was hostile to all Christian races, so it was scarcely surprising that the Arabs in Mozambique were suspicious of the Portuguese.

Lean-faced, light-skinned men, wearing silken turbans and flowing robes of white cotton, gazed warily at the oncoming ships. The ruler of Mozambique came aboard the *Sao Gabriel* as soon as the flagship dropped anchor. He arrived in a fine large canoe, reclining on silken cushions placed on the carpet-covered deck. He was a dark, handsome man, wearing a short velvet jacket, a long blue cloak, and baggy white trousers secured tightly at his ankles. A blue silk sash encircled his waist, and from it protruded the silver-mounted handle of a dagger.

Gama sent for Fernao Martins, the man who spoke Arabic. "We are sailing onward to India," Gama told the Arab ruler through his interpreter. "I ask you to find for us a good pilot who knows the course to steer across the Indian Ocean."

"The matter might be arranged," the Arab said politely.

He paused and looked around in an expectant manner. Fernao Martins explained to Gama that on such occasions it was customary to give the prince a present. The Arab was awaiting his gift.

Gama presented his wealthy and finely dressed Arab with a cheap red cloak, a few felt hats, a couple of shoddy linen shirts, and some coral-bead necklaces! These poor gifts put an end to any possibility of friendship between the Portuguese and the people of Mozambique. The Arab abruptly returned to the shore. Gama, realizing that trouble might start, hastily bought fresh coconuts, melons, and cucumbers from the boats which clustered round his ships. Once again he sent a party of men ashore to refill the water barrels.

Arabs attacked the seamen rolling the barrels up the beach to a nearby spring. Confronted by the angry, shouting warriors, the Portuguese retreated hastily and rowed back to their ships.

"We must have water," Gama said angrily. "Send the boats tomorrow and arm them with bombards. These Moors must be made to understand that we are now the masters here."

A fight started on the beach the following morning. The Arabs came down to the water's edge, waving swords and barbed stabbing spears. Three bombards fired, one after the other. These portable guns were noisy and inefficient weapons, but there was no defense against their half-pound iron shot. Many Arabs dropped on the beach, and the rest fled into the jungle. Sweating Portuguese seamen hastily trundled the refilled water barrels back to the waiting boats.

Gama had reached Mozambique on March 2, 1498. His ships remained there until March 31, for northerly winds and ocean currents prevented them from leaving. He spent the entire month squabbling and skirmishing with the Arab population. The Arabs were difficult people, it was true, but Gama's violent temper was to blame for much of the trouble. He was proud and obstinate, and he was a dangerous man to deal with. When his ships finally sailed from Mozambique, he opened fire on the town with falconets and rabinets. These were light deck guns made of brass, and their one-pound shot probably caused little serious damage to the houses ashore. Yet this final action of Gama's earned for the Portuguese the undying hatred of the Arab population of east Africa. Good seaman though he was, Gama—like most Portuguese—had no idea about how to make friends with native races.

Related Reading

References for Adults

Arbuthnot, May Hill. *Children and Books*, 3d ed. Glenview, Ill.: Scott, Foresman, 1964. Chapter 17 discusses biography for children.

Beatty, John and Patricia. "Watch Your Language— You're Writing for Young People!" *The Horn Book Magazine*, vol. 41 (February 1965), pp. 34–40.

Miller, Bertha Mahony, and Elinor Whitney Field. *Newbery Medal Books: 1922–1955*. Boston: Horn Book, 1955. See the acceptance speech of Elizabeth Janet Gray for her 1943 award-winning book *Adam of the Road*.

Sprague, Rosemary. "Biography: The Other Face of the Coin." *The Horn Book Magazine*, vol. 42 (June 1966), pp. 282–289.

Books for Children

Aliki, pseud. (Aliki Brandenberg). *George and the Cherry Tree*. New York: Dial, 1964. Aliki's biographies are written with a controlled vocabulary for beginning readers. While her style is simple, she avoids stilted sentence patterns. Other biographies by this author are: *The Story of Johnny Appleseed*, 1963; *The Story of William Penn*, 1964; *The Weed Is a Flower, The Life of George Washington Carver*, 1965. (Grades 1–3)

d'Aulaire, Ingri and Edgar, authors-illustrators. *Abraham Lincoln*, rev. ed. New York: Doubleday, 1957. A brief biography that covers most of Lincoln's life but excludes his assassination. Awarded the 1940 Caldecott Medal. Other biographies by the d'Aulaires are: *Benjamin Franklin*, 1950; *Buffalo Bill*, 1952; *Columbus*, 1955; *George Washington*, 1936; *Leif, the Lucky*, 1951; *Pocahontas*, 1949. (Grades 2–4)

Braymer, Marjorie. *The Walls of Windy Troy*. New York: Harcourt, 1960. An interesting biography of Heinrich Schliemann, the man who found the site of Troy. (Grades 5–9)

Bulla, Clyde Robert. *John Billington, Friend of Squanto*. Illustrated by Peter Burchard. New York: Crowell, 1956. Fictional account based on historical facts of the Pilgrims' first year in America. (Grades 2–4)

Campion, Nardi Reeder. *Patrick Henry, Firebrand of the Revolution*. Illustrated by Victor Mays. Boston: Little, Brown, 1961. An enjoyable biography of a man whose role in the events leading up to the Revolutionary War should be better known. (Grades 5–7)

Dalgliesh, Alice. *The Columbus Story*. Illustrated by Leo Politi. New York: Scribner, 1955. An interesting book that presents the highlights of Columbus' life. (Grades 2–5)

———. *Ride on the Wind*. Illustrated by Georges Schreiber. From *The Spirit of St. Louis* by Charles A. Lindbergh. New York: Scribner, 1956. (Grades 4–7)

Daugherty, James, author-illustrator. *Abraham Lincoln*. New York: Viking, 1943. A comprehensive biography; well illustrated. (Grades 6–10)

———. *Daniel Boone*. New York: Viking, 1939. (Grades 5–9)

———. *Marcus and Narcissa Whitman, Pioneers of Oregon*. New York: Viking, 1953. (Grades 5–9)

———. *Poor Richard*. New York: Viking, 1941. Biography of Benjamin Franklin. (Grades 5–9)

De Treviño, Elizabeth Borton. *I, Juan de Pareja*. New York: Farrar, 1965. The biography of a Negro slave who became Velazquez's assistant. The portrait of Juan sold in 1970 for more than three million dollars. This book effectively recreates the world of King Philip's court in the early seventeenth century. (Grade 8–up)

Epstein, Sam and Beryl. *George Washington Carver: Negro Scientist*. Illustrated by William Moyers. Champaign, Ill.: Garrard, 1960. One of Garrard's Discovery Books, biographies for primary grade children. Although complexities are ignored, the reader realizes George Washington Carver's excitement about learning. (Grades 2–4)

Foster, Genevieve. *Abraham Lincoln, an Initial Biography*. New York: Scribner, 1950. An interesting and accurate account of the major events of Lincoln's life. Other biographies by the same author are: *Abraham Lincoln's World*, 1944; *Andrew Jackson, an Initial Biography*, 1951; *George Wash-*

ington, *an Initial Biography*, 1949; *George Washington's World*, 1941; *Theodore Roosevelt, an Initial Biography*, 1954. (Grades 4–6)

Garst, Shannon. *Chief Joseph of the Nez Percés*. New York: Messner, 1953. A discussion of and an excerpt from this book can be found in this chapter. (Grades 6–9)

Hays, Wilma Pitchford. *Abe Lincoln's Birthday*. Illustrated by Peter Burchard. New York: Coward-McCann, 1961. The events of Abe's twelfth birthday make a simple story for primary children. (Grades 2–3)

Henry, Marguerite, and Wesley Dennis. *Benjamin West and His Cat Grimalkin*. New York: Bobbs-Merrill, 1947. A discussion of and an excerpt from this book can be found in this chapter. (Grades 3–5)

Hickok, Lorena A. *The Story of Helen Keller*. Illustrated by Jo Polseno. New York: Grosset, 1948. A discussion of and an excerpt from this book can be found in this chapter. (Grades 4–6)

Holbrook, Stewart. *America's Ethan Allen*. Illustrations by Lynd Ward. Boston: Houghton Mifflin, 1949. A discussion of and an excerpt from this book can be found in this chapter. (Grades 4–7)

Judson, Clara Ingram. *Abraham Lincoln*. Illustrated by Polly Jackson. Chicago: Follett, 1961. Deals with Lincoln's boyhood through his years as president. Other biographies by this author are: *Abraham Lincoln, Friend of the People* (Illustrated by Robert Frankenberg), 1950; *Andrew Carnegie* (Illustrated by Steele Savage), 1964; *Andrew Jackson, Frontier Statesman* (Illustrated by Lorence F. Bjorklund), 1954; *Christopher Columbus* (Illustrated by Polly Jackson), 1960; *George Washington* (Illustrated by Polly Jackson), 1961; *George Washington, Leader of the People* (Illustrated by Robert Frankenberg), 1951; *Mr. Justice Holmes* (Illustrated by Robert Todd), 1956; *Theodore Roosevelt, Fighting Patriot* (Illustrated by Lorence F. Bjorklund), 1953; *Thomas Jefferson, Champion of the People* (Illustrated by Robert Frankenberg), 1952. (Grades 3–5)

Keating, Bern. *Zebulon Pike: Young America's Frontier Scout*. New York: Putnam, 1965. An objective biography that reveals Pike's achievements and some of his shortcomings (Grades 6–9)

Latham, Jean Lee. *Carry On, Mr. Bowditch*. Illustrated by John O'Hara Cosgrave II. Boston: Houghton Mifflin, 1955. A discussion of and an excerpt from this book can be found in this chapter. (Grades 5–9)

————. *Far Voyager: The Story of James Cook*. Maps by Karl W. Stuecklen. New York: Harper, 1970. Cook's amazing rise from the son of a day laborer to a naval officer is dramatically presented by Miss Latham, who goes beyond the surface events of his life and shows him as a complex individual. (Grades 5–9)

————. *Medals for Morse*. Illustrated by Douglas Gorsline. New York: Aladdin, 1954. (Grades 4–7)

————. *Retreat to Glory, the Story of Sam Houston*. New York: Harper & Row, 1965. (Grades 5–9)

————. *Trail Blazer of the Seas*. Illustrated by Victor Mays. Boston: Houghton Mifflin, 1956. Biography of Matthew Fontaine Maury, founder of the Naval Academy. (Grades 5–9)

————. *Young Man in a Hurry, the Story of Cyrus W. Field*. Illustrated by Victor Mays. New York: Harper & Row, 1958. (Grades 4–7)

Lawrence, Jacob, author-illustrator. *Harriet and the Promised Land*. New York: Simon & Schuster, 1968. A powerfully illustrated biography of Harriet Tubman for young readers, written in verse with echoes of the folk ballad and the Negro spiritual. (Grades 1–5)

Lawson, Robert, author-illustrator. *Ben and Me: A New and Astonishing Life of Benjamin Franklin, as written by His Good Mouse Amos; Lately Discovered, Edited & Illustrated by Robert Lawson*. Boston: Little, Brown, 1939. An amusing account of how a mouse helped Benjamin Franklin achieve success. (Grades 2–5)

————. *Mr. Revere and I. . . .* Boston, Little, Brown, 1953. An amusing biography of a famous American told by his horse. (Grades 2–5)

McNeer, May Younge. *America's Abraham Lincoln*. Illustrated by Lynd Ward. Boston: Houghton Mifflin, 1957. An excellent biography with authentic dialogue. (Grades 5–7)

————. *America's Mark Twain*. Illustrated by Lynd Ward. Boston: Houghton Mifflin, 1962. A discussion of and an excerpt from this book can be found in this chapter. (Grades 4–7) Other biographies by May Younge McNeer are:

————. *Armed with Courage*. Illustrated by Lynd Ward. New York: Abingdon, 1957. Biographies of Florence Nightingale, Father Damien, George Washington Carver, Jane Addams, Wilfred Grenfell, Mahatma Gandhi, and Albert Schweitzer. (Grades 5–7)

————. *John Wesley*. Illustrated by Lynd Ward. New York: Abingdon, 1951. (Grades 5–7)

————. *Martin Luther*. Illustrated by Lynd Ward. New York: Abingdon, 1953. (Grades 5–7)

Mirsky, Jeanette. *Balboa: Discoverer of the Pacific*. Illustrated by Hans Guggenheim. New York:

Harper & Row, 1964. History and biography are well blended in this authentic book about Balboa. Helpful supplementary materials are included. (Grades 5–9)

Mirsky, Reba Paeff. *Beethoven*. Chicago: Follett, 1957. Beethoven's struggles against poverty, illness, and deafness are emphasized. Other biographies by this author are: *Brahms* (Illustrated by W. T. Mars), 1966; *Haydn* (Illustrated by W. T. Mars), 1963; *Johann Sebastian Bach* (Illustrated by Steele Savage), 1965; *Mozart* (Illustrated by W. T. Mars), 1960. (Grades 5–7)

North, Sterling. *George Washington, Frontier Colonel*. Illustrated by Lee Ames. New York: Random House, 1957. A partial biography; only the early years of Washington's life are shown. (Grades 5–7)

Peare, Catherine Owens. *The Helen Keller Story*. New York: Crowell, 1959. An interesting and authentic biography. Helen Keller's life particularly interests middle graders. (Grades 4–6)

_____. *Mary McLeod Buthune*. New York: Vanguard, 1951. A fine biography about a Negro leader. (Grades 4–6)

Petry, Ann. *Harriet Tubman: Conductor on the Underground Railroad*. New York: Crowell, 1955. The dramatic story of a Negro woman who escaped from slavery and then returned to the South again and again to lead other slaves to freedom. A more interesting biography than Dorothy Sterling's *Freedom Train, the Story of Harriet Tubman*. (Grades 7–9)

Ripley, Elizabeth. *Botticelli*. Philadelphia: Lippincott, 1960. Elizabeth Ripley's interesting biographies explore the relationship between artists' lives and their work. Illustrated with black and white photographs of the artists' works. Others are:

_____. *Goya*. New York: Walck, 1956. (Grades 6–12)

_____. *Leonardo da Vinci*. New York: Walck, 1952. (Grades 6–12)

_____. *Michelangelo*. New York: Walck, 1953. (Grades 6–12)

_____. *Rembrandt*. New York: Walck, 1955. (Grades 6–12)

_____. *Rodin*. Philadelphia: Lippincott, 1966. (Grades 6–12)

_____. *Rubens*. New York: Walck, 1957. (Grades 6–12)

_____. *Titian, a Biography*. Philadelphia: Lippincott, 1962. (Grades 6–12)

_____. *Vincent Van Gogh*. New York: Walck, 1954. (Grades 6–12)

_____. *Winslow Homer, a Biography*. Philadelphia: Lippincott, 1963. (Grades 6–12)

Singer, Isaac Bashevis. *A Day of Pleasure: Stories of a Boy Growing up in Warsaw*. Photographs by Roman Vishniac. New York: Farrar, 1969. The poignant memories of a poor rabbi's son growing up in Poland just before World War I. Fourteen of the brief stories are adapted from Singer's *In My Father's Court*. (Grades 7–up)

Sterling, Dorothy. *Captain of the Planter*. Illustrated by Ernest Crichlow. New York: Doubleday, 1958. The story of Robert Smalls, a Negro pilot, who took the steamer *Planter* to the Northern troops. He later became a Congressman. (Grades 6–10)

_____. *Freedom Train, the Story of Harriet Tubman*. Illustrated by Ernest Crichlow. New York: Doubleday, 1954. A biography of an amazing Negro woman who not only escaped from slavery but returned to the South again and again to lead other slaves north. (Grades 5–10)

_____. *Lucretia Mott, Gentle Warrior*. New York: Doubleday, 1964. Active in the nineteenth-century abolitionist and women's rights movement. (Grades 6–12)

Sterling, Dorothy, and Benjamin Quarles. *Lift Every Voice*. Illustrated by Ernest Crichlow. New York: Doubleday, 1965. Four short biographies of Booker T. Washington, W. E. B. DuBois, Mary Church Serrell, and James Weldon Johnson. (Grades 5–12)

Swift, Hildegarde Hoyt. *The Edge of April: A Biography of John Burroughs*. Illustrated by Lynd Ward. New York: Morrow, 1957.

_____. *From the Eagle's Wing*. Illustrated by Lynd Ward. New York: Morrow, 1962. A biography of John Muir, the father of America's national park system. (Grades 4–7)

Syme, Ronald. *African Traveler, the Story of Mary Kingsley*. Illustrated by Jacqueline Tomes. New York: Morrow, 1962. Mary Kingsley traveled through much of West Africa for the British Museum. This is the story of her experiences. (Grades 5–7) Other biographies by this author are:

_____. *Balboa, Finder of the Pacific*. Illustrated by William Stobbs. New York: Morrow, 1956. (Grades 4–6)

_____. *Cortes of Mexico*. Illustrated by William Stobbs. New York: Morrow, 1951. (Grades 4–6)

_____. *John Smith of Virginia*. Illustrated by William Stobbs. New York: Morrow, 1951. (Grades 4–6)

_____. *Vasco da Gama, Sailor toward the Sunrise*. Illustrated by William Stobbs. New York: Morrow, 1959. An excerpt from and a discussion of this book can be found in this chapter. (Grades 4–6)

Whipple, A. B. C. *Hero of Trafalgar, the Story of Lord Nelson*. New York: Random House, 1963. A discussion of and an excerpt from this book can be found in this chapter. (Grades 6–9)

Yates, Elizabeth. *Amos Fortune, Free Man*. Illustrated by Nora S. Unwin. New York: Dutton, 1950. A well-written biography. (Grades 6–9)

Ziner, Feenie. *Dark Pilgrim, the Story of Squanto*. Philadelphia: Chilton, 1965. A carefully researched biography with notes to distinguish between fact and conjecture. (Grades 6–9)

Chapter 13
Nonfiction

2—Driver's box and front boot, leather sides.   5—Panel opening, fitted with sliding glass window.
3—Candle lamp, one on each side.   6—Door window, fitted with sliding glass window.
4—Leather curtains, roll-down, damask-lined.   7—Metal reenforcement braces, three on each side.

Reprinted with permission of The Macmillan Company from *Overland Stage* by Glen Dines.
© Harry G. Dines 1962.

Early children's literature was primarily informational. Books not only instructed children in their proper relationship with God but also gave them lessons in manners and behavior befitting their social rank. There were titles such as *How the Good Wijf Taughte Hir Dougtir, The Boke of Curtasye,* and *Lessons of Wyesdome for all Manner Children.*

The first illustrated informational book was *Orbis Sensualium Pictus* or *The World in Pictures,* written by John Amos Comenius. Published in Nuremberg in 1657, it was soon translated into English and remained in print until 1777. This last English edition was reprinted in America in 1812. Comenius's purpose was to make learning facts about the world and Latin vocabulary easier and more interesting through the use of pictures. A page from this book is reproduced on page 20.

Informational literature continued to stress behavior and religion through the nineteenth century. But as the English and American middle classes grew, more parents wanted books that would teach their children facts about the natural world. Rousseau's followers produced nonfiction to help parents capitalize on children's interests to further their education.

The eighteenth and nineteenth centuries saw a rapid increase in European colonization and scientific discovery. These developments produced material for both adult and children's informational books. Rising literacy created additional readers, and the expansion of newspapers helped interest the people in nonfiction.

Today informational literature is still an important part of children's reading. In place of the former exclusively religious and social instruction, books now deal with subjects such as biology, botany, chemistry, zoology, astronomy, mathematics, and other sciences. Also covered are history, anthropology, ethics, philosophy, different cultures, and other areas dealing with man. In many books the categories are not strictly separated: a book may deal with man and his relationship to an area of science; for example, the influence of a scientific discovery on human life.

Some nonfiction is presented in picture book form. Written for young children, preschoolers and first and second graders, many books have only a word or two under each picture. The pictures vary both in type and quality. The best illustrations extend the "reader's" knowledge by revealing aspects of the animal or object pictured that the child might not have been aware of. Because young children are explorers of the everyday world, most of these books deal with common experiences: pets, buildings, vehicles, leaves, trees, flowers, and shops. Rather than captions, some picture books have explanatory texts to elaborate on the information in the illustrations. One such book is *Travelers All.* Its text is reprinted in the following section, but without its pictures the information is incomplete.

Another type of nonfiction, the illustrated book, also relies on pictures to convey information and to supplement its text. These books are written for older elementary school children and contain much more detail and abstract concepts than do the picture books. Each page of text is often faced by a page of supplementary illustrations and captions. The text, captions, and pictures must all be read to gain the book's full information. The pictures should never be mere decoration, for they are meant to clarify and supplement the text. The following selection from

Overland Stage, an excellent example of this type of nonfiction, includes only the text, for unfortunately it was impossible to reprint all the pictures and their captions.

A third category of informational literature imbeds the factual detail into a story. The reader follows the adventures of a child walking through the woods looking at birds or hears kind old Captain Bob explain about his shell collection.

A problem of story books of knowledge is that some try to teach children about wild animals and nature through anthropomorphism. By giving animals human traits, emotions, and motives, the authors hope to relate new information to children's previous knowledge. Instead, anthropomorphism tends to distort facts and mislead children. The excerpt from *When the Root Children Wake Up* is an example of this approach. Scientists have found that animals, regardless of how nonscientists may interpret their actions, do not react or perceive as do humans. The combination of fact and fantasy in informational books is seldom successful. Children read nonfiction for information, and facts are more easily understood when presented realistically and directly.

In factual books, as the term is used in this discussion, the emphasis is on information about a particular subject. These books make little attempt to relate the facts to scientific or humanistic concepts. Such a book on dinosaurs would give a great deal of information about each type but would not emphasize the relationship between the dinosaurs' physical characteristics and their environment.

The best science books do not present facts only, for with the rapid expansion of knowledge, those facts may be modified by the time the child enters high school or college. Concept books try to show the relationships that underlie physical and social occurrences. This type of nonfiction can help children draw conclusions and understand abstractions and interrelationships. This type of informational literature is represented in the following section by selections from *You and Relativity, Spring Comes to the Ocean,* and *Free Men Must Stand.*

To be successful, information needs to be presented in a way that will interest children. Clara Ingram Judson in her *St. Lawrence Seaway* has dramatized the struggle between man and nature in the centuries-long effort to build a continuous navigational seaway from the Great Lakes to the Atlantic Ocean. She wisely minimized the statistics and lists of details that would have been beyond the grasp of her audience. *Orbiting Stations,* however, is less interesting because the author, Irwin Stambler, lost sight of his audience, fourth through seventh graders. Only the very knowledgeable and highly motivated child will willingly read the endless details presented in an unappealing style. The information in factual books needs to be carefully selected and arranged to create a comprehensible, interesting, unified whole.

When a science book from any of the previous categories has activities for children, that book may also be classified as a participation book. Many simply present the facts necessary to build a model airplane or to do simple experiments. Other participation books go beyond the practical steps and teach scientific methods: to observe carefully, to be interested in cause and effect, to see relationships, and to draw conclusions. A book that teaches these abilities through participation can make children excited about scientific inquiry and discovery. *You and Relativity* and *Science on the Shore and Banks,* both represented in the following section, are participation books.

Because children tend to believe that everything they read in books is true, adults need to be certain they read only accurate nonfiction when they are young. As children mature they should, of course, learn to evaluate what they read and to check for accuracy. Unfortunately, not all the facts in children's informational books have been verified. Many publishers exploit current interests by producing quickly written, superficial books about new historical or scientific discoveries. A number of authors distort the truth through oversimplification. A theory may inaccurately be presented as accepted fact, and only one side of a topic still under investigation or in dispute may be given without the necessary balance of the other theories. Adults also need to watch for out-of-date information. Scientific knowledge is expanding so rapidly that books for children may be out-of-date in a relatively short time. Books about other cultures and nations also need to be checked for contemporary accuracy.

Some authors of nonfiction are experts in the

subject, others are professional writers who, hopefully, have done careful research. But the author of children's books also needs to know the abilities and limits of his intended audience. A great deal that is understood by adults must be explained to children. Yet too much background detail may seem boring or patronizing. Oversimplification, on the other hand, can create distortions. The author must carefully find the balance between too many and too few details. Specialized terminology can confuse children. While their vocabulary limitations should be considered by the author, essential terms can be included if explained in the context, as "centrifugal force" is clarified in *You and Relativity*.

In addition to accuracy and appropriate coverage, a good style is essential. Awkward sentences, whether short and choppy or long and overinvolved, hinder meaning and make the book more difficult to read. The space-buff may struggle through *Orbiting Stations* with its dull style, but most children will put it down unfinished. The rough rhythm and syntactic oversimplification of *O Canada!* are inappropriate for the children who will read it in the third, fourth, and fifth grades. No matter how much valuable information a book contains, if it is not a pleasure to read it will not be as useful as the author intended it to be. Good writers match sentence length and rhythm to their mood and meaning. They also employ concrete images and figures of speech to clarify the unknown.

Since most adults are not expert in many fields, help is needed in evaluating informational books. *Horn Book Magazine* has monthly reviews but they usually discuss books for older readers. Other professional journals have occasional sections devoted to informational literature, but it is not always apparent that the reviewers are knowledgeable about the books' subjects. The *AAA Scientific Book List for Children*, which was published in 1963 by the American Association for the Advancement of Science, lists over nine hundred titles. However, while still useful, some of the books are now out-of-date. An excellent aid is *Natural History*'s annual list of the best science books for children, published each November, with critical reviews written by qualified specialists. *The Bulletin of the Center for Children's Books* also has specialists review the books.

Children have wide interests about nature, man, and the past. They are born into an unknown world that is so large they can personally experience only a small part of its wonders. Through well-written and accurate informational books, their understanding, their perspective, and their world are widened.

The nonfiction materials presented here include works from early children's literature for historical comparison. Critical comparisons can also be made, for examples of well-written informational books are contrasted with excerpts from less successful works.

The following three selections, the first published in 1767, the second in 1762, and the third in 1788, provide interesting examples of how children's literature has been used in past centuries.

A PRETTY BOOK OF PICTURES . . .

Anonymous

From *A Pretty Book of Pictures for Little Masters and Misses: or, Tommy Trip's History of Beasts and Birds. With a familiar description of each in verse and prose. To which is prefixed The History of Little Tom himself, of his dog Jouler, and of Woglog the great Giant.* Ninth Edition. London: Printed for J. Newbery, in St. Paul's Churchyard. MDCCLXVII.

Of The Lion and Jackal.
The Lion is commonly called the king of beasts. . . . The report of his being afraid of the crowing

of a cock is found by experience to be entirely false. The Jackal is frequently called the lion's provider. It is said that when he seizes his prey, by his cries he gives notice to the lion, at whose sight he retires and when he has gone returns to eat what his master the lion has left.

* * *

The Fox is remarkable for his craft and subtilty. When he is troubled with fleas he is said to take a piece of wool in his mouth and going by slow steps into a river, the fleas, leaping by degrees to avoid the water, assemble in the wool; after staying for a moment with only his nose above stream, he lets it go and is immediately quit of his troublesome companions.

Of The Porcupine.
This creature shoots his pointed quills,
    And beasts destroys and men;
But more the rav'nous lawyer kills
    With his half-quill the pen.

Of The Bison or Wild Ox.
The bison though neither
    Engaging nor young,
Like a flatt'rer can lick
    You to death with his tongue.

The bison's tongue is long, hard and as rough as a file; with this alone he is said to be able to draw a man to him and by only licking wound him to death. He smells like a musk cat; but though his flesh is in summer very fat it is too strong to be eaten.

Of The Crocodile.
The crocodile with false perfidious tears,
    Draws the unwary trav'ler nigh,
Who by compassion warm'd no danger fears
    But ah! th' unhappy wretch must die.

Of The Hawk and Kite.
The Hawk and Kite, both birds of prey
    Will kill and bear your fowls away,
And since your foes you cannot shun,
    Then cock your eye—and cock your gun.

THE POLITE ACADEMY FOR YOUNG LADIES AND GENTLEMEN

Anonymous

From *The Polite Academy for Young Ladies and Gentlemen*. London: R. Baldwin. 1762.

Of Behaviour
Before you speak make a Bow or Curtesy, and when you have received your Answer make another.

Be careful how you speak to those who have not spoke to you.

Nothing shows the difference between a young Gentleman and a vulgar Boy so much as the Behaviour in eating.

Never touch your Meat with your Fingers.

Pick your Bones clean and leave them on your plate; they must not be thrown down.

Seldom blow your Nose and use your Handkerchief for that Purpose, making as little noise as you can.

Never spit in a Room.

Never sing or whistle in Company: these are the idle tricks of vulgar children.

Take care not to make Faces nor Wink.

Keep your Hands quiet, and use no antick Motions.

Never laugh immoderately at a Story told by another Person. Never laugh at all what you tell yourself.

Never talk about any Thing but what you know.

Directions for Young Ladies to attain a Genteel Carriage.
To Make a Curtesy.
Hold yourself properly and easily upright.

Raise your Head with a free Air, not with a stiff Formality.

Let your Shoulders fall back with an easy Air.

Let your Arms fall easy to your Waist, and keep them straight to your sides, not putting them backwards or forwards.

Lay your Hands across and do not raise them too high, nor let them fall too low.

Let the Hollow or inside of your Hands be turned towards you.

Let your Fingers be a little open.

Bend your Wrists a little.

Turn with an easy Air towards the Person you are to compliment.

Step a little Sideways with either Foot.

Join the other to it.

Turn your Eyes a little downward.

Being thus placed bend softly and gradually into a curtesy.

Rise gently from it; and lift up your Eyes as you draw up your Head.

RULES FOR BEHAVIOUR AT TABLE

Anonymous

From *The Honours of the Table, or Rules for Behaviour during Meals. For the Use of Young People.* London: Printed for the Author at the Literary Press, No. 14 Red Lion Street, Clerkenwell. 1788.

Of all the graceful accomplishments, and of every branch of polite education, it has been long admitted, that a gentleman and lady never show themselves to more advantage than in acquitting themselves well in the honours of their table; that is to say, in serving their guests and treating their friends agreeable to their rank and situation in life.

When dinner is announced, the mistress of the house requests the lady first in rank, in company, to shew the way to the rest, and walk first into the room where the table is served; she then asks the second in precedence to follow, and after all the ladies are passed, she brings up the rear herself. The master of the house does the same with the gentlemen. Among persons of real distinction, this marshalling of the company is unnecessary, every women and every man present knows his rank and precedence, and takes the lead, without any direction from the mistress or the master.

When they enter the dining-room, each takes his place in the same order; the mistress of the table sits at the upper end, those of superior rank next her, right and left, those next in rank following, then the gentlemen, and the master at the lower-end; and nothing is considered as a greater mark of ill-breeding, than for a person to interrupt this order, or seat himself higher than he ought. Custom, however, has lately introduced a new mode of seating. A gentleman and a lady sitting alternately round the table, and this, for the better convenience of a lady's being attended to, and served by the gentleman next her. But notwithstanding this promiscuous seating, the ladies, whether above or below, are to be served in order, according to their rank or age, and after them the gentlemen in the same manner.

When there are several dishes at table, the mistress of the house carves that which is before her, and desires her husband, or the person at the bottom of the table, to carve the joint or bird, before *him*.

Where there are not two courses, but one course and a remove, that is, a dish to be brought up, when one is taken away; the mistress or person who presides, should acquaint her company with what is to come; or if the whole is put on the table at once, should tell her friends, that "they see their dinner"; but they should be told what wine or other liquors is on the side board. Sometimes a cold joint of meat, or a salad, is placed on the sideboard. In this case, it should be announced to the company.

As it is unseemly in ladies to call for wine, the gentlemen present should ask them in turn, whether it is agreeable to drink a glass of wine. ("Mrs.——, will you do me the honour to drink a glass of wine with me?") and what kind of wine present they prefer, and call for two glasses of such wine, accordingly. Each then waits till the other is served, when they bow to each other and drink.

If you dislike what you have, leave it; but on no account, by smelling to, or examining it, charge your friend with putting unwholesome provisions before you.

To be well received, you must always be circumspect at table, where it is exceedingly rude to scratch any part of your body, to spit, or blow your nose (if you can't avoid it, turn your head), to eat greedily, to lean your elbows on the table, to sit too far from it, to pick your teeth before the dishes are removed, or leave the table before grace is said.

OVERLAND STAGE

Glen Dines

As gold and land drew men to the west, a need arose for rapid transportation. Before the Overland Stage, people could cross the continent only in wagon trains, by boat around the Horn, or by boat to Panama, which they crossed by mule train, and then again by boat to San Francisco. All of these journeys were slow and hazardous. Such routes, while somewhat convenient for those bound for California, were less satisfactory for people who wished to go to inland areas.

The Overland Stage, which traveled day and night by numerous exchanges of teams, allowed a rapid transit for gold, mail, and passengers. Its nineteen-day journey from Kansas to California now seems slow, but in contrast to the other methods of travel, which took six to twelve months, it then seemed quick indeed. In Roughing It Mark Twain describes the speed of his first trip west by Overland Stage with the enthusiasm used by people today to describe the speed of supersonic jets.

The following selection contains only half the information presented in this factual picture book. Many more facts are given in the captions accompanying the numerous illustrations, as can be seen in the picture reproduced at the beginning of this chapter. The pictures themselves add to the informational quality of the Overland Stage *by revealing in a nonverbal fashion much about western life.*

This book is written in a rapidly paced style appropriate to its subject. It conveys a great deal of information in but a few pages, yet never appears superficial, as do so many short books of nonfiction.

The United States of the 1860's was strong, youthful and vigorous, a restless giant with arms outstretched from sea to sea. Americans were moving west where land was free and mountains glittered with silver and gold. They went by foot, horseback and wagon, following roads that traced the trails of mountain men and Indians. They crossed a wilderness and spanned a nation. But their way was long and slow. Something faster than lumbering wagons or fleet-but-far-sailing clip-per ships was needed to carry the mail. For a brief moment in history the West echoed the pounding hooves of the Pony Express. Then humming strands of copper dulled thunder. But even the lightning-fast telegraph could not carry a letter to Denver, a doctor to Salt Lake City, or a shipment of gold bullion to San Francisco. Wires alone could not link the arms of this giant.

From the east came the answer—born of New England skill and named after the New Hampshire town in which they were built—the famous Concord overland stagecoaches.

Big for the job, they weighed over a ton, stood

From *Overland Stage* by Glen Dines. Reprinted with permission of The Macmillan Company. © Harry G. Dines 1962.

8 feet tall and left a track 5½ feet wide. Yet each coach was handmade of the finest wood. Each piece, from the tiniest cleat to one of the massive 7-foot perches, was fashioned and fitted and finished with patient craftsmanship. The graceful bass-wood panels were steamed and curved to fit stout ash frames. The planks were hewn of clearest pine and birch. The wheels, with hubs of specially seasoned elm, were rimmed with hardest hickory and spoked with tough oak. The best parts of 14 selected steer hides went into the boots and thorough braces. Where extra strength was needed, wood was strapped with iron and bolted through. Nearly every stagecoach that rumbled overland in the '60's was a ruggedly handsome Mail Coach or a lighter, canvas-topped "Mud Wagon," built by Abbot, Downing of Concord, New Hampshire.

The overland coaches were painted as carefully as they were built. Bold, manly colors were used —vermilion, yellow, red and black. Their sides were decorated with handsome gilt scrolls. Colorful pictures were painted on each door, the work of skilled artists, these paintings were mostly landscapes with no two alike. Well known landmarks were also popular and sometimes there were portraits of famous people. The panels, wheels and ironwork were skillfully striped and even the unseen parts of the undercarriage were decorated.

The name of the company ordering the coach was usually lettered above the windows. U.S. Mail or U.S.M. often appeared at the tops of the doors. Sometimes a driver's name was lettered on the side of the box and the coach itself christened with a name like *Argosy*, *Western Monarch* or *Prairie Queen*. The entire coach was coated with tough, glass-smooth varnish after the decoration was completed.

But the Concords were not all glitter and gilt. They were also plain tough. An example was the famous "Deadwood Stage," shown throughout the world in Buffalo Bill Cody's Wild West Show. This Concord Mail Coach, built in 1868 and shipped to California by clipper, was first used in the Sierra Nevadas, then in the Rockies and finally on the route between Cheyenne, Wyoming and Deadwood in the jagged Black Hills of South Dakota. After some 27 years of rough mountain roads, the running gear of this battered old veteran was still in good order.

One of the reasons for this toughness was the thorough brace slings—the "springs" of the Concords. These many-layered leather "hammocks" gave a swinging forward and backward motion which helped both coach and team over the roughest of frontier roads.

On the frontier, where a common kitchen chair was often a rarity, the leather-covered, well padded seats of a Mail Coach were sheer luxury. A standard nine-passenger coach had two high-backed seats facing each other and a "jump" seat (1) with a wide, leather band (2) as back rest. Both ends of this narrow bench folded up and inward. Topside, many of the coaches were equipped to seat 8 more passengers; three in the "dickey" seat (3), three in the deck seat (4), and two squeezed beside the driver in the messenger's seat (5). Sometimes passengers even slept on the top deck, after spreading hay and blankets and tying themselves securely.

The kingly Concords were sometimes matched by the horses that pulled them. Teams were often paired for color and handsomely tapered; smallest in the lead, largest and darkest near the wheels.

Stage horses, however, were selected for work, not show. Sorrels, bays, brindles, grays, they varied from gamy western stock to big 1500-pound Kentucky-bred trotters.

New horses were usually carefully trained, making their first runs beside veterans who knew their jobs and the road almost as well as the driver. With good care they worked their 10 to 20 miles day after day, year after year. A sorrel in California made his run every day for 15 years— nearly a quarter million miles! And, possibly, he did his work in a harness of J. R. Hill and Company of Concord or Main and Winchester of San Francisco, famous makers of rugged, lightweight, "fast hitch" stage harness.

Tuesday, 7:52 A.M., sometime in the mid-1860's. Shimmering in the Kansas sun, a scarlet red Concord stands before the Overland Stage depot in Atchison. Departure time in eight minutes. As the last of the luggage is loaded into the rear boot, a late arriving passenger scurries across the dusty street. He might be a young mining engineer, a salesman or a lawyer. Whatever his work, his name is on the passenger list, destination Placerville, and he has paid the $325.00 fare in full.

Because of the 25-pound limit on luggage, he is wearing an extra pair of trousers and shirt. For small comfort and safety, the pockets of his overcoat are stuffed with socks, a woolen scarf, several cans of sardines, some hardtack, a water bottle, a bar of soap, toilet articles and 20 rounds of ammunition for his Sharps carbine.

The road to be traveled is the famous Central Overland route, stretching 1913 miles across half a continent. It is made up of three divisions: the Eastern from Atchison to Denver, the Mountain from Denver to Salt Lake City and the Western from Salt Lake to Placerville. Each of these divisions is divided into 200-mile sections with relay points, or stations, every 10 or 15 miles. There are 153 stations on the entire route.

It is a mountain road for the most part, spanning the massive Rockies, the Wasatch, the rib-like ranges of the Great Basin and the granite-capped Sierra Nevadas of California. For more than 1300 miles it never dips lower than one mile above sea level as it winds through the breeding grounds of blizzards, cloudbursts, scourging sandstorms and the fickle mountain creeks that can change into raging rivers overnight.

Yet storms pass and a stream can be bridged, but the swift and deadly Plains Indians, like the Sioux and Cheyenne, the Arapaho and Ute, must be either outfought or outrun. And the Overland road cuts through the very heartland of these warrior tribes.

Still, there is a schedule to make, and at exactly 8:00 o'clock the big red Concord rolls out across the Kansas prairie bound for Placerville, 19 days away—with luck.

The road is dry and there's a nip in the morning air. Between stations the teams are "let out." Flashing into Lancaster, Kennekuk and Kickapoo, the lurching Concord fills the prairie with the thunder of hooves, the pop and snap of harness, the jangly clink of brass and steel. From above come the shouts of the driver. "Hy-yi! G'lang! Up thar, Dutch! Go you, Red!"

A passenger riding beside the driver clutches the railing. Inside the drumming coach, trunks and mail sacks toss and tumble to the throb of the thudding wheels.

2nd Day. The scarlet coach rumbles west from the Big Sandy and into the beautiful valley of the Little Blue. Topside, the driver is captain, crew and compass all in one. His strong, swift hands play the lines, "talking" to each horse—holding one, taking in another, letting out a third. A true reinsman, he does not "drive" the loosely coupled teams but helps them work together. His only tools are the brake and the "pop" of his lightweight, silver-ferruled whip. But to make his 40-mile drive on schedule, west one day, east the other, rain or shine, winter and summer, the driver must know his horses and every dip and bend in the road. And each driver has his own tricks: many use no breeching, some cross the inside traces, others carry a pocketful of pebbles to encourage lazy "doggers."

Some drivers are close-mouthed; others jolly. Some wear fancy buckskin; others plain homespun. But whether he answers to Mr. Bishop, "Pop" Wright or "One-eyed Tom," the lordly driver is "Knight of the Road," king to all passengers and the envy of lowly stock tenders and stableboys—and sometimes the section boss himself.

3rd Day. Skirting the south bank of the broad and twisting Platte River, the stage flashes past a long train of lumbering freight wagons. The air is thick with dust. The "bullwhackers' " whips crack like pistol shots. West from Ft. Kearny it's uphill all the way to Denver, 400 miles of water grade. Some of the finest stock is strung along this division—horses, as well as big five-mule "spike" teams that pull the stage through the worst stretches of heavy sand.

West to Ft. Kearny the gently rolling prairie gives way to sand hills, twisting gullies and the thin, clumpy grass of the high plains. For miles at a stretch the roadside is pocked with the rimmed holes of yip-yapping prairie dogs. The stage rocks across ancient buffalo trails cut in the valley floor. A few shaggy forms are spotted on the rim of a distant bluff but the driver can remember when great herds sometimes blocked the road.

A column of U.S. Cavalry jogs into view, men and horses streaked with sweat. Two saddles are empty. Both driver and passengers look to their guns as the road ahead curves out of sight among steep sand bluffs.

West of Ft. Kearny the frontier begins.

The driver spots them first—three young braves on horseback standing in the road ahead. They motion him to stop. He answers with a quick snap of the whip. The team breaks into a gallop. Arrows buzz angrily as the Indians charge forward, then swerve. More arrows hiss to the crack of pistols.

"War party!" someone shouts.

The driver shakes his head. "Not this time. These lads are jist playin' Injin tag." Nevertheless he keeps the team at a smart pace as they pound across the flat, sage plains that border the South Platte.

7th Day. The passengers are strangely silent as the stage rocks north out of Denver. There are reports of Indian trouble along the line—not like last year when stations and ranches on whole sections were attacked and burned or abandoned—but bad enough with several stations attacked, horses stolen and a stock tender killed.

The driver reins in before a lonely "swing" station and glances nervously about as the fresh team is hitched. Tiny, one-room cabins like these, with two or three men to guard a dozen or more horses, are favorite targets for raiding Indians.

But many "swing" station stock tenders are wanted by the law and glad to exchange the rugged, dangerous life of an isolated stage station for that of a prison cell. To this rough, scraggly-bearded crew a Saturday night "bath" means draping blankets and underwear across a nearby ant hill so that the ants can feast on the lice and bedbugs.

"Leastwise," they explain, "you can see an ant."

8th Day. At high noon a cluster of stone and log buildings comes as a welcome sight. It is the end of this driver's run and a famous stopping place because his wife is one of the best cooks west of Denver. Almost before the stage stops rolling, the passengers are crowding into the small kitchen-dining room of the sod-roofed station house.

After a delicious dinner of antelope steaks, freshly baked bread, pickles, apple pie and ever-present coffee—well worth the $2.00 price—several passengers hurry down to the nearby creek for a quick "bath," despite the pesky "buffalo flies" and mosquitoes. Others wander about the well kept ranch that includes a hayfield, a barn, several sheds and a blacksmith and carriage repair shop. The station house boasts two "overnight" sleeping rooms with real feather beds. A far cry

from the bigger home stations on the route, but better than most.

Meanwhile a new coach is brought up and its axles greased. After the luggage and mail sacks are transferred and a fresh team is hitched, the passengers and new driver climb aboard and the stage rocks westward once again. It lurches through huge, trenchlike Bridger Pass and out into the butte-studded Bitter Creek country.

9th Day. In the bleak sage desert west of Green River, the "Cherokee Trail" short cut—begun some 300 miles to the east—comes to an end. The stage swings south along the Black Fork to bump and sway once again in the ruts of the famous old Oregon Trail. And, once again, the poles of the transcontinental telegraph flick past the coach windows.

Old Fort Bridger, an oasis of cottonwood and willow, is cluttered with the wagons of a huge eastbound freight train. To the south the jagged peaks of the Unita Mountains loom darkly against a predawn sky.

Just before the stage pulls out, an iron-bound treasure box is hoisted into the front boot and a company messenger swings up beside the driver. Stagecoach robberies are common on the branch lines to the north and in ore-rich Nevada and California and there are reports of some buffalo-hunters-turned-outlaw lurking in the hills near Muddy Creek. However, the veteran driver is not too worried.

Few main-line stages have ever been robbed "on the road." The passengers are usually well armed and the guards know their business.

On the morning of the tenth day the stage thunders into red-rimmed Echo Canyon, pathway through the Wasatch for the Mormon pioneers and many California-bound emigrants. In lush Weber River Valley the route hooks south past Kimball's Junction on the westernmost section of Ben Holladay's Overland Stage Line. In neat, bustling Salt Lake City the "through" passengers board a Concord of the Overland Mail Company and grate westward across an ancient, salt-crusted lake bed. Handling the lines is an old-timer who drove a Celerity Wagon on the Southern Overland route. This was the famous Butterfield Line that carried the mail from St. Louis through El Paso and into southern California until the outbreak of the Civil War.

13th Day. Hour after hour the stage grinds across a gigantic washboard of sage flats and scrub-stubbed mountain ranges. In the basins the wheels cut deeply, churning up itchy alkali grit that cakes on driver, passengers and sweat-lathered horses alike. In the mountains the burn of dust gives way to spine-jarring thuds as the stage pounds and plunges through narrow rock-strewn passes.

It is a big land—harsh and unyielding—yet vastly beautiful.

On the sixteenth day the stage carries a special passenger—the Division Superintendent himself —once a driver, now chief of a small army of section bosses, clerks, bookkeepers, drivers, blacksmiths, harness makers, farriers, carpenters, wainwrights, stationmasters and stock tenders who keep the coaches rolling.

Also in his charge are twenty to thirty teamsters, whose lumbering freight wagons supply the stations. For the more than 550 horses on this division alone, some seven tons of feed are needed every day—nearly three thousand tons a year. And at a few stations every buckle, bean and drop of water must be hauled in by wagon.

Choking in the dust of a "washoe" blowing down from the Sierras, the driver reins up in "rip-roarin'," silver-rich Carson City on the afternoon of the seventeenth day.

A stage of the Pioneer Line carries the passengers and mail south to Genoa, then west through rugged Daggett Pass and into California.

Here, in California, western staging was born. Hard on the heels of the first gold strike in '49, stagecoaches began rolling regularly through the Mother Lode country. By 1853, when much of the mail carried west from the Mississippi went by mule wagon, handsome Concords, brought "'round the horn" in Clippers, were rumbling over the 1500-mile route of the California Stage Company. In 1857, when Denver was just starting to grow, a Concord of the famous Pioneer Stage Company made the first stagecoach crossing over the towering Sierras.

It is fitting that a coach of this proud line—to many the best west of the Missouri—should tick off the last few miles of the overland route. It skirts the south tip of Lake Tahoe, struggles over 7000-foot Echo Summit, thunders down the narrow canyon of the South Fork of the American River and stops at last, on the nineteenth day, before the ornate Cary House in Placerville.

Out of the California Overland Mail Act of 1857 and Chorpenning and Hockaday's struggling Central Overland came the Central Overland California and Pike's Peak Express, under the ownership of Russell, Majors and Waddell. This giant freighting concern also owned the fabulous Pony Express. When the ponies folded in 1861 so did their owners, and the C.O.C. and P.P.E. became Benjamin Holladay's Overland Stage Company. In the mid-'60's the overland route was the backbone of a 3000-mile stagecoach empire, which included the Western Stage Company, the Butterfield Overland Despatch, and the branch lines to Oregon, Idaho and Montana.

Late in 1866, famous Wells-Fargo and Company bought out Holladay, but the overland route was fast shrinking. In May, 1869, the transcontinental railroad was completed and the wheels of hickory that had bridged a nation gave way to stronger and faster wheels of steel.

FREE MEN MUST STAND: The American War of Independence

Eric Wollencott Barnes

In Free Men Must Stand *Eric Barnes does more than give facts; he reveals the attitudes and tensions that caused the War of Independence. The events leading to direct fighting are often presented in a narrative form, which not only holds the reader's interest but also complements the subject's inherent dramatic nature.*

*Although Barnes' sympathies obviously lie with the Americans, he is ob-
jective in his picture of the British. However, his attitude that the battle of
Breed's Hill and Bunker Hill "had been a magnificent spectacle—the fierce
fighting at the beach, the three advances of the scarlet lines into the death
trap on top of the hill, and to the left the whole of Charlestown in flames"
would be disputed by many readers of the 1970s. They would consider the
adjective "splendid" inappropriate to describe a "death trap" and the burning
of a town. This, however, is probably the only criticism that can be raised
against a fine book.*

*Young history buffs will find the book a careful study of the American
Revolution from the initial repressions that led the colonies to defy Parliament's power (1765) to General Washington's resignation as commander in
chief (1783). Mature elementary school readers and most junior high students will find the book not only accurate but exciting.*

". . . LET IT BEGIN HERE"

As 1774 moved into 1775 gloom settled
over British headquarters in Boston. General
Gage was now sending anxious pleas to London
for more troops. Since autumn, there had been
reports of rebel militia drilling on village greens
and wagons loaded with rebel supplies moving
along the roads. Now the reports were more frequent, and General Gage was beginning to lose
sleep. He was holding the fuse to a powder keg,
and he did not know at what moment some
flying spark would set it off.

It was all very well for Lord Dartmouth, the
British Secretary of State, to write that he should
arrest the ringleaders of the revolt and make a
show of power to impress the inexperienced colonists. How could he arrest men unless he could
find them, and what show of power could he
make with his 4,000 troops when three or four
times that number of colonial militia could be on
the march in a matter of hours?

All he could do was to render the militia harmless for the moment by seizing their guns and
ammunition. So far, his efforts in this line had
not been very successful. In September his soldiers had managed to capture some gunpowder
stored by the patriots at Cambridge. But similar
attempts at Salem and other towns had failed
because the Americans had gotten ahead of him,

and the supplies had vanished by the time the
redcoats arrived.

Now it was April, and he had just learned that
the rebels had collected a quantity of gunpowder,
flour, trenching tools, and other equipment at
Concord. He was also informed that the two most
conspicuous troublemakers of the province, John
Hancock and Samuel Adams, were hiding in Lexington, about to leave for Philadelphia to take
part in the Continental Congress. He saw the
chance to kill two birds with one blow, and he
decided to strike.

Preparations for a quick march to Concord
were made in all secrecy, but the British officers
had scarcely been alerted before the patriots knew
about it. As picked units of grenadiers and light
infantry began to assemble in the night of April
18, Dr. Joseph Warren, head of the Committee
of Safety in Boston, ordered Paul Revere and
William Dawes to carry the alarm to Concord.
Dawes made his way by Charlestown Neck, slipping past the guards posted on the road. Revere
waited in Boston until he learned that the redcoats were being ferried across the Charles River
and would start from Cambridge. After lighting
signal lanterns in the steeple of Old North
Church to convey the information to friends waiting on the other side of the river (Longfellow's
poem is inaccurate in this detail), Revere had
himself rowed across. Once ashore he jumped on
the horse that had been brought for him and
galloped for Lexington. He barely avoided capture when he ran into a group of British officers
near Medford, but he managed to cut across the

field and make his way by another road. He was in Lexington by midnight, in time to get Adams and Hancock out of bed and start them packing their belongings.

An hour later Dawes reached Lexington, and the two riders started for Concord. Presently they met another patriot, Dr. Samuel Prescott, and the three dashed along together. Half a mile beyond Lexington they came upon a British patrol. Dawes and Prescott dug in their spurs and got past, but Revere was caught. After an hour his captors, not knowing what to do with him, let him go. However, they prudently cut the girth of his saddle, so that Revere had to make his way back to Lexington on foot, leading his horse. He arrived just as Hancock and Adams were setting off. They made room for him in their chaise, and he drove with them to Burlington, thus ending his famous ride in some degree of comfort.

By four o'clock the marching redcoats had reached the outskirts of Lexington. It had not been a pleasant march. The weather was still bitterly cold, and the men were wet to the waist, having waded ashore from the boats and then crossed a mile of soggy marsh to reach the Concord road. They came on doggedly, apparently unconcerned by the lights in the houses and the sound of hoofbeats along the black lanes. Lt. Col. Francis Smith, commanding the 700-man column, did not anticipate serious trouble, but he had taken the precaution of placing an experienced officer, Major Pitcairn, as head of the advance unit.

Lexington had been astir since a little past midnight. At the first alert, Capt. John Parker called out his company of Minute Men. He had no orders and was not sure what he ought to do. About 130 men had assembled, and when they had waited for a couple of hours in the cold darkness Parker dismissed them with instructions to report back at the beating of a drum. All but forty or fifty went back home since they lived nearby. The others sought comfort in Buckman's Tavern, close to the green.

News that the British were at hand came suddenly at four A.M. The tattoo sounded. Alarm shots were fired. The Minute Men poured out of the tavern and the nearby houses. Half the men had no ammunition and hurried off to the meeting house where the town's supply was stored.

Only about sixty were lined up along the side of the green facing the highway as the redcoats appeared.

Major Pitcairn saw the rebels strung out ahead. He turned and ordered his men into line. The rear ranks moved up at the double, shouting as they came.

Captain Parker called to the Minute Men, "Stand your ground! Don't fire unless fired upon! But if they want to have a war, let it begin here!"

The British commander ordered his troops to halt. Then he shouted across the green, "Lay down your arms, you damned rebels, and disperse."

Some of Parker's men had already vanished. Parker hesitated for a few moments, then seeing that the situation was really hopeless he told the rest of the men to leave. They started off, taking their muskets with them.

Again Pitcairn shouted, "Lay down your arms!"

But muskets were not easily come by in the Colonies, and the rebels seemed reluctant to part with them, all the more so when a British officer cried furiously, "We will have them, damn you."

What happened next has never been certain. There was a flash of powder, and a shot rang out. Was it British or American? No one knows, probably because the man who fired it did not live long enough to tell. The shot was immediately followed by a command from a British officer—not Major Pitcairn, however—and a volley roared out. The first bullets went over the heads of the patriots. But a second volley, aimed lower, tore into the scattering Minute Men. Some of these turned and fired back. Captain Parker managed to get one shot before a British bullet hit him and he dropped to the ground. In fifteen minutes it was all over. Eight Americans lay dead on the ground, among them Captain Parker. Ten more were wounded and got away.

The Minute Men disappeared, brushed aside like flies, and the British column tramped on up the road to Concord, bayonets glinting in the early sunlight, fifes trilling, drums beating. This was the show of force Lord Dartmouth had recommended.

At Concord a larger patriot force had gathered.

A band of about 150 militia, the first to assemble, had taken a position on a ridge above the church. When it was reported that the approaching enemy outnumbered them three to one, the old men and boys who formed part of the village company were moved back. A group of Minute Men stayed where they were until Col. James Barrett, who had gone off to see about concealing the stores of powder and artillery, came back and ordered them up the slope on the other side of the bridge over the Concord River. Here they waited to see what the British would do.

The march from Boston had been long and wearisome. The British officers were ready for refreshment, which they found in Concord's two taverns. While they rested, the soldiers began to search the houses. What they found was not much—some barrels of flour, trenching tools, a couple of cannons, and 500 pounds of musket balls. Flour and musket balls were thrown into the mill pond. But they missed the gunpowder which was hidden under a huge pile of goose feathers in Colonel Barrett's attic. To give a show of warlike activity the troops set fire to a blacksmith shop and the courthouse, and then put out the fires themselves.

On the rise beyond the bridge the patriots stood and watched. The Concord Minute Men had now been joined by groups from Acton, Bedford, Lincoln, and other villages, who had answered the alarm. By this time there were perhaps 400 American troops in all. When they saw smoke rising from the town they started down the hill with two fifers in the middle playing "The White Cockade."

A British detachment had been sent to guard the bridge. They started to take up the planks as the rebel militia quickened its pace. Major Buttrick, leading the column, shouted to the redcoats to stop their work. The officer in charge seeing that the Americans meant business, called the men off the bridge and got them into line on the east bank of the river.

As the first rebels set foot on the bridge the British fired two or three random shots. One of the fifers fell. Then a volley struck the center of the column and Capt. Isaac Davis, head of the Acton Minute Men, dropped dead. Others were wounded before Major Buttick could give the order to return the fire. Three British soldiers were killed. Nine others, including four officers, were wounded. The redcoats started back at a run, until they met reinforcements. They got into line again and moved in good order back into the village.

The real fighting was about to begin. The Americans crossed the bridge, but went no farther. In an hour the British were heading back for Boston. They got as far as the outskirts of Lexington when a British flanking party, moving through the fields along the road, came on a group of Americans who had slipped down from Concord bridge and taken positions behind a stone wall. The British fired a volley in the air, merely as a sort of signal to clear the way. His Majesty's troops had performed their mission and meant to return peaceably to quarters.

This was not the Americans' idea. While the British were rummaging Concord, militia from Framingham, Woburn, Reading, and a dozen other towns and villages were pouring along the roads to Concord. As word spread that the British were heading back to Boston they made for the highway. By noon the road was lined on either side by men with muskets, strung out behind fences, crouching in thickets, lying on their bellies in the corn stubble. As the redcoats came on they were met by murderous bursts of fire that left gaping holes in the column. By the time they reached Lexington they were no longer in marching formation. Not until midafternoon, when they met a relief column sent out from Boston, was order restored.

After an hour's rest, the column started again with the Americans harrying it unmercifully. At Cambridge there was a mile and a half of continuous battle. The temper of the attackers had risen to fury pitch as the smoke of burning houses marked the passage of the redcoats. When they were not busy returning the rebel fire, the British destroyed whatever they could lay hands on. This was the traditional behavior of European troops moving through enemy country, but to the Americans such wanton destruction was barbarous. The British, for their part, considered the American sniping tactics wholly unfair. They were used to facing the enemy line to line. These rebels were invisible. Only bursts of flame from behind fences and trees, or from upper windows—and the sudden anguished cries of men toppling over in the ranks, told of their presence.

The slaughter did not cease until dusk had fallen and the remnants of the expedition reached the boats at Back Bay. When the final count was taken, the British were appalled at their losses: 73 men killed, 220 wounded or missing. American casualties totaled in all 94 men, few enough out of some 4,000 men involved.

News of the victory raced through the Colonies. Up and down the coast bells tolled wildly, fireworks were set off (causing almost as many casualties as the battle itself), and volunteers began flocking to recruiting offices.

Having pushed the British back into Boston, the Americans hoped to push them clear into the sea. But for the moment they were content to spread out and put the city under siege. Two days after the battle, the Massachusetts Provincial Congress met and voted to raise 13,600 troops. The other New England Colonies also acted. Connecticut promised to send 6,000 men, New Hampshire 2,000, and Rhode Island 1,500.

The Lexington-Concord engagement was a heavy blow to British prestige. It was inconceivable in London that highly trained professional soldiers should have been routed by a disorganized crowd of farmers and shopkeepers. But the men and officers who had marched back from Concord had the answer. The Americans knew little and cared less for military science. They fought out of pure rage at the sight of foreign troops marching through their countryside, seizing their belongings, burning their farms, and shooting men who simply tried to defend what was theirs.

One thing Gage managed to make the government at home understand. He had been outnumbered in this first clash three to one. If this situation continued, the quicker the British left the country the better. The King and his ministers were thoroughly aroused. A recruiting campaign for the American war was launched at once in England, and when this did not produce satisfactory results, the King set about hiring soldiers from his brother monarchs in Europe.

For the moment the war was at a standstill. Protected by redoubts and trenches on Charlestown Neck and by warships in the harbor, the British were safe, though scarcely happy as they settled down to a diet of salt meat and hardtack, for the besiegers had cut off all supplies of fresh food. The Americans, not yet organized into any kind of efficient fighting force, without artillery and ammunition for a major assault, could only sit and wait for something to happen.

Something did happen—far to the west, about three weeks after the battle of Concord. Two American columns, one led by dashing Benedict Arnold of Connecticut, the other Ethan Allen of New Hampshire, captured Fort Ticonderoga on Lake Champlain, the gateway from Canada to the lower Colonies. The raid netted forty prisoners, the entire British garrison, and sixty cannon—which would soon be put to good use.

Back in Boston General Gage was getting reinforcements. By June, 1,100 fresh troops had arrived, along with three generals. Sir William Howe, Sir Henry Clinton, and John Burgoyne had all won reputations in the Seven Years' War. Two of the generals, Howe and Burgoyne, were members of Parliament. Burgoyne, in addition, dabbled in playwriting and cut a great figure socially. For all his fine manners and gorgeous uniforms he was popular with his men who called him "Gentleman Johnny."

The new generals decided that something must be done at once to break the deadlock at Boston. Their first move was to issue a proclamation declaring the New England militia rebels and traitors, but offering pardon if they would disband and go home. The only effect this produced was to make the patriots dig more trenches and tighten their hold about the city. The British had no choice then but to attempt to break out. As a preliminary they decided to move on Dorchester Heights overlooking Boston from the south.

Like most of the British plans projected in great secrecy this soon reached the ears of the Americans who immediately took counter measures. During the night of June 16, 1775, 1,200 militia under Col. William Prescott slipped down onto Charlestown peninsula and began to build a redoubt and breastworks on Breed's Hill, with a second line of defense on Bunker Hill directly behind. If the British started a movement toward the south they would be in a strong position to launch an attack from the north.

Early in the morning of June 17 the lookout

on a British man-of-war anchored off Charlestown spotted the rebels furiously working with picks and shovels. The ship promptly opened fire and soon other British vessels joined in the bombardment. The British generals changed their minds about storming Dorchester Heights and turned to meet this new threat. After some debate it was decided to attack Breed's Hill directly, rather than attempt to take Bunker Hill first. There were as yet only sketchy defenses on Bunker Hill, and from its higher summit the British guns could shoot down on Breed's Hill. But once there the redcoats would be facing the Americans on two sides, a situation which an experienced commander like General Howe, who was in charge of the attack, would naturally avoid.

While the British embarked from Boston to cross to the peninsula the cannonading from the warships continued. Undaunted by bursting shells and the thud of cannonballs striking the soft earth, the Americans on Breed's Hill worked to complete the redoubt and breastworks. When Colonel Prescott saw the size of the British force heading across the water he sent a call to Gen. Artemus Ward, commander of the Massachusetts militia, to send reinforcements. As these were arriving Prescott saw that part of the British troops, which by now had landed, were moving along the beach to the east with the obvious intention of coming up behind the redoubt. Hastily Prescott ordered part of his force to form a line from the fortifications down to the water. The end of the line, on the beach itself, was held by a New Hampshire regiment under Col. John Stark.

It was Stark and his men behind a low wall of hastily piled up stones who threw the British attack out of gear. Howe counted on the force sent around by the beach to rush the American rear while the main assault was getting under way, thus cutting off the defenders of Breed's Hill from the rest of the Americans on Bunker Hill and farther up the peninsula. All that lay in the way was a straggling line of troops behind improvised defenses ending in a fragmentary stone wall on the beach. Since the beach offered a level footing for attack, the flanking force headed for the low stone wall thrown up by the New Hampshire troops. But when the Royal Welsh Fusiliers, leading the attack, started to deploy in front of Stark's men they met a blast of fire that sent them reeling back. Before the lines could reform, there was another thunderous roar of New Hampshire musketry that tore great bloody gaps in the advancing lines. At that the redcoats turned and fled, leaving ninety-six men dead on the beach.

Howe meanwhile had started his main force up the slope directly in front of the redoubt. The flank attack having failed, everything now depended on the assault uphill under the undivided fire from the American works. It was now three o'clock in the afternoon with a broiling sun overhead. The British, suffocating in their thick woolen uniforms, bowed down under heavy packs and their "Brown Bess" muskets, moved slowly up the hill.

The Americans in their trenches, already worn out from their night of hard digging, waited tensely for the attack by twice their number. The men had been told not to fire until they were ordered and then to aim at the white crossbelts of the officers. The patriots were short of ammunition, and every shot must count.

The redcoats came on stolidly, methodically, moving with drill-ground precision. At intervals they halted to fire a volley at the fresh-turned earth along the hilltop. But there was no answering fire until they had come near enough the entrenchments to lower their bayonets for a charge. Then a great sheet of flame leaped from the parapet. Privates and officers in the front ranks were down as though they had been clubbed. There were screams of pain and sudden wild confusion on the slope. Somehow the redcoats managed to re-form, but as they were loading to fire, another blast struck them. In panic the attackers broke and ploughed back down the hill.

Howe regrouped the men, brought in fresh troops, then started them back up the slope. The second ascent was worse than the first. Stumbling over the crumpled bodies of their comrades and blinded by sweat, the British struggled again toward the crest. Once more as they approached the point for a charge, the muskets above blazed out. Again they reeled and fell back.

"There was a moment," Howe reported later, "that I never faced before." Certainly his troops, many of them old campaigners, had never walked into such an inferno. Yet they rallied a third time to begin the climb. Again as they neared the American line they were struck by a hail of bullets. They came to a halt, wavered, then went on. This time there was no volley from the redoubt. Prescott's men had used the last of their ammunition. With bayonets fixed, British marines stormed over the parapet. The patriots met them with swinging muskets, and there was fierce bloody fighting in which the clang of steel and the cracking of skulls replaced the sound of gunfire.

The Americans began to fall back, their retreat covered by the line down to the beach which held to the last. On Bunker Hill where Connecticut Gen. Israel Putnam waited with the reserves there was a brief stand. But the redcoats now in full force were surging ahead. By five o'clock they had taken the whole of Charlestown peninsula, and the patriots were in tumultuous rout toward Cambridge. If Howe could have pushed his men they might have destroyed the disorganized, dog-weary Americans and crushed the whole New England army. But the victory had cost the British forty per cent of their men, and there was no margin for pursuit.

From steeples and housetops in Boston, people had watched the whole batttle. It had been a magnificent spectacle—the fierce fighting at the beach, the three advances of the scarlet lines into the death trap on top of the hill, and to the left the whole of Charlestown in flames. The British had set fire to the place at the beginning of the attack to smoke out Americans shooting from the windows of houses. It was a defensive measure, but to the patriots the burning of Charlestown was an act of wanton destruction—another detail to be chalked up to the ruthlessness of the invaders.

The British had broken out of Boston, but they had only gotten as far as Charlestown Neck and to venture beyond this—once the Americans had rested and regrouped at Cambridge—would have been to invite piecemeal destruction. So the redcoats were still bottled up, and for the moment the patriots were content to leave them that way.

OF COURAGE UNDAUNTED: Across the Continent with Lewis and Clark

James Daugherty

When Thomas Jefferson became president, he chose for his secretary young Meriwether Lewis. Both men had long wondered what lay beyond the Mississippi River, and even before the Louisiana Purchase was completed Jefferson decided to send west an expedition headed by Lewis. The purported reason was to expand "the external commerce of the United States," but in reality Lewis's job was to see if there was a continuous waterway across the continent—perhaps the Missouri and Columbia rivers met or were joined by other rivers. In addition, the economic value of the area west of the Louisiana Purchase was to be evaluated and natural resources described. The expedition was to travel to the edge of the continent, to the Pacific Ocean. This travel could be and later was used to support the American claim for western territory.

James Daugherty tells the story of this expedition in Of Courage Undaunted. *Often placed with the biographies, this book deals not with the personalities or lives of Lewis and Clark but rather with the courage and endurance of this heterogeneous group of American explorers. Their task was dangerous, their accomplishment remarkable. Daugherty's language is as powerful and evocative as his illustrations, and both reveal the men's strength against formidable odds in their successful mission.*

THE CORPS OF DISCOVERY

There was nothing that you would say was
    special about them.
They chawed tobacco and cussed and caterwauled
    that
they were double-jointed, fire-eating, leather-
    necked, half-horse
half-alligator men who could lick their weight in
    wildcats.
They were picked almost at random out of the
    Ohio Valley
of Virginia, Kentucky, Tennessee, or New England
    stock,
merely a sample fistful of what American
    democracy turns out,
as you might pick a handful of leaves and say,
    These are oak.

Any state in the Union can give you ten thousand
    such
at any time, or ten times ten thousand, if there
    is a call
to stand together in time of danger,
or hold the line on land, in the sea or air,
not without bragging and grousing and a sour
    kind of humor,
sometimes terribly scared but never
broken by fear, of courage undaunted.

Sweating and rank, coarse, muscular, lanky,
level-eyed, generous minded, free speaking,
    slangy—
you don't have to go far in any city or town to
    find them;
no farther than any street corner
or factory bench, farmyard, filling station, public
    high school.
As Lincoln said, "God must have loved them or
he would not have made so many."

* * *

THE BARGE

"A bas les perches," bawled the one-eyed Cruzatte from the stern deck where he stood at the tiller. The oarsmen facing aft lowered their long poles till they caught on the river bottom. Throwing their weight forward on the poles as one man, they pushed down the cleated catwalks along the gunwales of the boat. When the lead man reached the stern, Cruzatte shouted, "Levez les perches." The men lifted their poles and returned to the bow. The barge had pushed several lengths upstream. This routine was repeated with mechanical regularity hour after hour.

When the channel was too deep for the poles, twenty-two men manned the long oars and pulled the barge steadily against the current. Where it was possible to walk or scramble along the shore, the men towed her by a thousand-foot length of "cordelle" attached to the top of the mast. A guide rope, or bridle, fastened to the ring in the bow kept her from swinging sideways. In the bow a husky lookout or "bosseman" kept her clear of the banks with a long pole. When there was an obstacle on the bank, the cordelle was taken upstream and tied to a tree. The men on the boat then pulled the barge around the obstruction. This was called warping.

The shifting prairie wind was a pusher and booster that often puffed out the barge's big square sail and doubled her speed. Sometimes the wind put on a big show, with thunder and lightning and lashing rain that swooped out of a black cloud, roaring down from the northwest, bending the willows, lashing the water into great waves, and blowing blinding clouds of sand and spray down the river until they had to tie up under a lee shore until the storm was over.

The barge had ten-foot decks fore and aft. The forward cabin was for the captains and the after cabin was used as a sick bay and for the crew. Along the inside of the barge were lockers with doors that could be raised to make a rampart against attacks.

There were two small escort boats, or pirogues. The larger was known as the red pirogue and was manned by seven French voyageurs. The smaller was called the white pirogue, and had a crew of six soldiers. It was planned that the barge was to return from the winter camp on the upper river to St. Louis with specimens and reports for the President in Washington.

At night the men camped and cooked, ate and slept, ashore.

* * *

UP THE MISSOURI

The two tall captains in their army uniforms stood on the forward deck in the light rain. A gentle breeze filled the sail and the rhythmic strokes of the twenty-two oarsmen drove the barge steadily upstream against the stiff current. At last they were through with the farewell dinners and balls, the toasts and speeches, the cheering and bowing. Before them lay the shining path of the winding river calling to adventure. The Missouri was calling them across the mysterious prairies to the unknown mountains. Each day unfolded a new wild world in which the unexpected waited around each bend in the twisting river.

At the bow, Cruzatte the riverman with his one eye scoured the changing face of the waters, reading in the swirls and eddies the signs of snags, "sawyers," and sandbars lying in ambush just beneath the surface. The corps was divided into three "messes," commanded by Sergeants Ordway, Floyd, and Pryor. Drewyer and Colter hunted along the shores, bringing in bear, deer, beaver, and other game for the pot. Out of the river, the men yanked fat catfish. They camped at night on the low shores of willow-covered islands. The weary voyagers sniffed hungrily the fragrance of campfire supper at the end of each day's pull.

The captains took turns daily at walking along the shores. Clark would take Drewyer, Colter, Shannon, and York for company. Lewis liked to go alone through the wooded bottomlands or across the empty plains. After supper the captains sat on their bunks in the forecastle and wrote out the day's record, which they kept at the President's express order. Both were keen reporters, but it is hard to say which was the worst speller.

Lewis used the most words, recording what he thought, along with what he saw. Clark put down facts briefly. Together, day by day, they kept a detailed and vivid record of all they said and did.

After supper as the men sat gazing into the fire, Cruzatte would draw his fiddle from a leather bag and strike up a lively dance tune. In a moment hands were clapping and heels stomping in the antic capers of booted dancers. Suddenly York would leap into the center of the circle and dance down all comers with a grotesque buck and wing.

Through the night there were always two sentinels on guard. The mournful wolf-howls rose to the burning stars across the blackness of moving waters. As the men turned out in the gray dawn they sometimes shook a live rattlesnake from a blanket or pillow, where he had crept just to be warm and friendly. That helped to liven one up for the day's work.

The captains gave names to the rivers that poured prairie soil and sand into the Missouri and to the numberless long willow islands dreaming in its rolling torrent. On the Fourth of July they fired off the cannon with cheers and named the creek they were passing "Independence." They exchanged news with traders coming down from the Indian country on rafts. One of these was a Mr. Dorion who had lived among the Sioux for twenty years. He was engaged to return upriver as interpreter.

* * *

The river was still a mile wide, but definitely shallower with more and meaner sandbars. Beyond the river bluffs, the prairie was alive with vast herds of buffalo and elk and the swift and beautiful antelope. The river teemed with beaver, swans, geese, duck, and sometimes pelicans. A sandbar on which they were camped suddenly washed out from under them. They barely got the boats out from under the bank before it too caved in. The river was a tricky antagonist.

One evening three Indian boys swam out to the boats with word that two Sioux encampments were on the river just above them. They were sent back with presents of tobacco to the chiefs and an invitation to a council at the riverside.

There was great excitement in the Sioux camps over the news that the white men in their great winged canoe were coming up the river. Black Buffalo, the ranking chief, wished to trade with the white men. There would be presents and he was first in the receiving line. But the Partisan, also a powerful chief, wanted to stop the expedition. If his braves could carry out a surprise attack, there would be much loot and many scalps. The younger warriors were eager to follow him. But the ever-watchful enemy always kept their floating fortress in the middle of the river, safe from surprise attacks.

Sixty braves, magnificent in savage finery, came down to the council with the captains. Black Buffalo wore a white buffalo robe decorated with porcupine quills and headdress of eagle feathers. The Partisan was painted from head to foot in patterns of yellow and red and green. His leggings were trimmed with the scalps of his enemies and two fine skunk skins dragged from the heels of his beaded moccasins. He was a fierce and splendid image of terror out of a nightmare.

The captains were impressive in their uniforms with cocked hats and swords, though the soldiers were shabby in their worn deerskin shirts and leggings. But the bright flag in the wind and the perfect precision of their drill made a gallant show. Without Dorion, the interpreter, they could not understand each other's speeches, although the presents were accepted by the Indian chiefs with the usual pleasure and excitement. In the visiting back and forth from boat to shore, the Indians had been surly and insolent and a quarrel between Clark and the Partisan nearly came to blows, but Black Buffalo had intervened and kept the peace. The two chiefs had then come aboard for the night. Altogether it had been a tense and trying day. They called their camp that night "Bad-humoured Island."

Next day both sides were more friendly. The Sioux were preparing to celebrate a recent victory over their enemies, the Mahas, with a delicious dog feast and a ceremonial scalp dance. The shores were lined with excited squaws and children eager to see the white strangers. The captains went ashore and were carried triumphantly into the Indian camp on white buffalo robes. In the evening, they sat in the council circle with seventy solemn Indian warriors. Black Buffalo rose and pointed the ceremonial pipe to the heavens, to the earth, and to the four points of the compass.

He was addressing the Great Spirit, the Father of the Universe. The white men watched with awe the solemn rituals of the stone age. The pipe went around the circle. Black Buffalo made a long speech which the white men could not understand. The stewed dog was served from the kettles with horn spoons. The captains tasted it sparingly and looked hungrily at the great pile of jerked buffalo meat which the tribe had presented them. Wood was heaped on the fires and the center of the circle cleared for the dance.

Suddenly the drums rolled and the rattles sounded. The young braves began a chant, accented with shrill yells. On each side of the fire the squaws swayed and shuffled forward and back in two lines, carrying long poles from which hung fresh scalps. The rhythm of the drumbeat and the chanting bound the tribe together in a mystic union with their ancient gods of earth and wind and sky and filled their hearts with strength and joy. In the intervals a storyteller raised his voice and recited a tale out of the immemorial storehouse of tribal lore. A new dance began. The warriors stamped around the fire, bending to the earth and leaping up, and uttering high-pitched yells as they brandished their war clubs. Hour after hour, in the flickering light, fantastic figures were vignetted against the blue darkness in a weird pantomime. At last the weary white men politely excused themselves and went back to the boat.

* * *

MOSTLY ABOUT BEARS: MONTANA, MAY 14, 1805

Drewyer found eleven-inch footprints in the wet sand by the river. He was the undisputed king of the mountains and prairie. Every living thing that met him on the trail gave him wide and undisputed room. It was tribute to King Grizzly—the "white bear," as the Indians called him on account of his tawny-colored fur. When he stood on his hind legs, he towered eight to ten feet. On the end of each front paw were five long claws that ripped like knives when driven by a blow of his terrible arm.

Drewyer, Colter, and the Fields brothers had come upon him as he was looking for a beetree in the timber and brush along the river. At the moment he was lying in an open space and when he rose on his hind legs to inspect the strangers, two of the hunters fired into his massive bulk. With a guttural roar the monster charged. The two hunters did not just run—they flew for their lives toward the river and shoved off in the canoe. The other two, who had held their fire, now shot into the bear. He turned and charged after them as they made for the willows. Here they managed to hide, reload, and put several more bullets into him, but the great beast seemed indestructible. He charged after Reuben Fields and pressed so close that Fields jumped from a twenty-foot bank into the river, with the great brute hurtling through the air behind him. He was swimming for the canoe, with the bear just a few feet behind him, when his brother fired from the cliff and drilled a bullet directly through the bear's head. Still green and shaky with fright, the hunters dragged the huge carcass to the shore and stripped off the heavy pelt. Seven shots had passed through the vitals.

Later Captain Lewis barely escaped a pursuing grizzly by jumping into the Missouri. Taking to the river or the nearest tree because standard practice when you ran into a "white bear."

Once, one of the party stumbled on a grizzly concealed in the underbrush. His frightened horse had reared violently, thrown his rider, and dashed off. The man snatched up his rifle and cracked the bear over his sensitive nose. As the dazed monster rubbed his painful member with his paws, the hunter lit out for the nearest tree. White bears cannot climb trees, so Grizzly took up his post underneath to wait for the fruit to fall. All day long the hunter sat in the tree and reflected on a misspent life. At sundown the bear, possibly remembering that his wife expected him home for supper, ambled off. After a safe interval, the man came down, recovered his horse, and rode safely back to camp.

Through the night these monsters slunk about the camp hoping to raid the larder, but the faithful dog Scannon, growling and bristling, kept them from venturing within the radius of the firelight. Although the men often had to jump, run, or climb for life, no one was ever actually caught by a bear.

AN UPSET

The same day that the men met their first grizzly, a sudden squall hit the pirogue like a blow and laid the sail flat on the water, where she filled within an inch of her gunwales. Three of the men in the capsizing boat could not swim, and Sacajawea was there with her baby. In the boat were the instruments, papers, medicine, all that was vital to the expedition. As Cruzatte cut the sail loose, she slowly righted. Charbonneau had dropped the rudder and was calling on the saints. Sacajawea in the stern was quickly and coolly gathering in any valuable that was floating. The men were bailing frantically. On the distant shore, Lewis and Clark fired their guns and shouted orders, but nobody heard. "Grab that rudder or I'll shoot you," howled Cruzatte, furiously pointing his gun at Charbonneau.

The men now manned the oars and brought the boat safely to shore. Lewis remembered the adventure "with the utmost trepidation and horror." A bear hunt and a near-shipwreck, on May 14, marked the first anniversary of the start of the expedition.

THE MOUTH OF THE MARIA'S RIVER: JUNE 2, 1805

The river water was clearer now, and through the dry, clear air they caught distant glimpses of snow-capped mountains. The creeks and rivers teemed with the industrious beaver and on the highlands they could see herds of bighorn.

Suddenly, one night, the camp was roused by Scannon's barking and a terrific rushing about in the darkness. A buffalo bull had swum the river and blundered into one of the canoes. Mad with fright, he was charging about the camp among the sleeping men, barely missing trampling on their heads. Finally the bull rushed off into the darkness with Scannon snapping at his heels.

At the foot of a high cliff the men saw and smelled the rotting carcasses of a hundred buffalo. The herd had been driven over the precipice by the Indians, who had taken all the meat they could carry and left the rest to the wolves and bears.

Day by day, the men toiled at the tow rope,

wading waist deep in icy water. Their feet sank in mud, pulling off their moccasins, and their soles were cut as they scrambled over the rocky shores. The weary voyagers made camp on a point of land where the river forked into two almost equal channels. There was no signpost saying "This way to the Missouri."

The party must make a right choice if they were to reach the Pacific before winter. To the men, it was plain that the north fork was the right one. It was muddy and roiling and had the look and feel of the Missouri that they knew so well. Even Cruzatte the riverman was sure of it. The south fork was clear and deep, a mountain stream coming out of the West. The captains thought that this must be the main stream.

Just to make sure, each captain made an exploring trip up one of the forks. Lewis and six men went up the north fork. He came back after four days sure it was not the Missouri. This river went too far north. In the wind and the rain, he and some of the men had nearly slipped over a precipice. He named this stream Maria's River, after a girl in far-off Virginia.

When they got back, they found that Captain Clark had been anxiously awaiting them for two days. Clark had come back from his trip sure that the south branch was the true Missouri. Though the men were still certain the north fork was the Missouri, they were willing to follow wherever the captains led. Just to be safe, Lewis and some of the men went ahead up the south fork. If they found the great falls which the Indians had described to them, they would know they were on the Missouri and Lewis would send back word for the expedition to follow.

ST. LAWRENCE SEAWAY

Clara Ingram Judson

Mrs. Judson begins her history of the St. Lawrence Seaway with the formation of the Great Lakes in the glacial age. She ends it with the successful joint effort of Canada and the United States to make it possible for ocean-going ships to sail into the center of the continent. She shows the numerous pressures that caused the descendants of the European traders and settlers to reshape the river's course. To cover so long a period and to explain the work of so many men, great care was needed in the selection of illustrative incidents. The author successfully avoided superficiality and vagueness by recounting in detail some of the early attempts to control or change the waterways between the Great Lakes and Montreal. The balance between narrative action and factual information was well kept, and so the reader seldom becomes immersed in facts and dates.

DECADES OF CHANGE

Public enthusiasm for canals grew rapidly through the 1830's and 1840's. Canada built the

very useful Rideau Canal, linking several small lakes and rivers to make a waterway from Ottawa to Lake Ontario. The first Beauharnois Canal was opened in 1845; canals above and below Cornwall and the Galop Canal were opened at about the same time. By 1847 the state of Ohio had finished digging most of the 400 miles of canals planned; Indiana, Illinois, and other states were working hard to give their people the cheap water transport needed to get products to market.

Such transport had become a necessity, for during these same decades, thousands of Europeans migrated to North America, both to the United States and to Canada. Vast numbers of these people arrived with the idea of going west to settle; from New York, they went up the Hudson, on by the Erie Canal and then by sailing ships on the Great Lakes. Those who landed at Quebec or Montreal did not as yet have the smooth three-mile-an-hour transport the Erie Canal provided; canals along the St. Lawrence were not connected and were more useful for carrying cargo than people. A man named Alexander Sinclair wrote an account of his family's arrival in Montreal from Scotland and of their journey up the St. Lawrence River to Prescott. He was a boy of twelve then, but he never forgot the adventures and hardships of that trip. He wrote:

"The spring of 1831, my father sold the farm and everything except what we could take to America, which consisted of clothes, dishes and books. . . . On the first of May we went to Greenoch where we waited until an immigrant ship with room for us arrived. . . . The TAMERLINE set sail down the river and we bade goodby forever to all our kin and friends. . . . Most of the passengers were sick and on account of head winds we were seven weeks and two days crossing and coming to Quebec. The views along the river were beautiful and French farmers came to the ship to sell us vegetables.

"A large steamer came alongside and took passengers and their luggage for Montreal. From there we took barges or long boats to Prescott. Each barge or boat had six Frenchmen with pikes and oars to push or row the boat. It was then that I first saw oxen working. In coming up the rapids, they tied a long rope to the boat and hitched the oxen to the rope while the men with pikes kept the boat off the rocks. It took nearly two weeks between Montreal and Prescott."

During this long and dangerous journey passengers and crew slept on shore at night, rolled in blankets—if they had blankets with them. So many immigrants traveled this route that some farmers gave up farming for the more profitable work of dragging boats at the edge of the rapids.

At Prescott the travelers got a steamer for Toronto. Steamers of the early 1830's were very elegant, with a "parlour" and long rows of "couches" along the walls; passengers could rest if the trip was long. Compared with a blanket on a rock, this was luxury.

These were prosperous years in America; people were full of ambition and hope. Andrew Jackson, the first frontier president of the United States, was interested in the West, as George Washington and Thomas Jefferson had been before him. In the 1830's, even professional men and businessmen talked about going West, and some really went.

Young Cyrus McCormick, in the wheat state of Virginia, invented a reaping machine. He also originated an entirely new method of selling his machine; he was willing to deliver a reaper after a small down payment. A farmer then dared to plant several times the number of acres that could be reaped by hand and pay for his reaper when his crop was sold. McCormick's invention and his new way of selling enabled many a family to risk moving out to rich prairie land around and beyond the Great Lakes.

This movement of people required ships and houses—even small cabins needed lumber. Roads, such as they were, required cutting trees. Some areas made corduroy roads, logs laid at right angles to the direction of the road. These could be made quickly because the middle-sized trees used were plentiful and relatively easy to cut and handle; but travel on corduroy was rough and tiring. Other areas made plank roads of sawed lumber. Of course there were plenty of trees. Lower Michigan was believed to have more trees than could ever be used by man—fine hardwood south, good pine to the north of the lower peninsula. Wood was wasted recklessly. Good logs of hard timber were burned to clear a field.

"There's plenty," people said. "Plenty of everything in America!" All this was very well for settlers along Lake Huron, Lake Michigan, and the lower lakes. Land around and beyond Lake Superior was said to be good; the fishing there was profitable too. But the mile of rapids at Sault Ste. Marie was a barrier. Reapers and household goods, stoves, chests, and other general cargo could not be taken up the rapids in birchbark canoes. And how could crops be brought down?

These things, so unlike soft, compact furs, were difficult to portage, too, though a portage business had begun to develop.

In the year Michigan became a state, 1837, there was some talk and effort to build a canal along the south shore of the rapids and bypass its dangers; if some federal aid were granted, the work could be done. This hope was reasonable because the federal government was interested in "internal improvements" just then—canals, highways, railroads. But in congress, Henry Clay made an impassioned speech against spending money so far away. He ended with his famous sentence, "I would as soon think of building a canal on the moon!"

Michigan, her pride challenged, resolved to build the canal herself and open a waterway to her own northern shore. Portage people at Sault Ste. Marie objected, but plans were drawn, a contractor engaged, workmen hired, money paid out. Then an earnest officer, on duty at the fort at the Sault, discovered that Michigan's route for the canal cut through federal land by the fort. He used troops to halt the work.

There was a rumor that the contractor was glad to hurry away as he had bid too low. Anyway, he left, taking with him money he had been paid. Portage people smiled smugly. Fifteen years passed before people generally knew enough about northern Michigan and Lake Superior to listen to the idea of a waterway through to this greatest of freshwater lakes.

People in the United States and Canada in general had no interest in happenings at Sault Ste. Marie. The few who may have heard that the canal project was abandoned probably agreed with Henry Clay in thinking of the place as too remote to be important; there was none of the feeling of immediacy that had helped push through the Welland and other canals.

The Indians had long since learned to live with the rapids, as they had learned to navigate the Ottawa and the St. Lawrence rivers. Their skill and courage got the furs down and brought trade goods up on the return voyages. Few others ventured on the St. Marys River.

The villages by the rapids remained unchanged for years—half Indian, half American on the south shore; half Indian, half French in the little settlement on the north shore.

Then suddenly all that changed.

The era of prosperity ended in a deep depression. Men who had never been tempted to glowing tales of the West now thought of adventuring because they could not make a living where they were. Soon they and their families were on the move, by horse, mule, or ox teams. Others went by canal and lakes; still others walked, carrying what they could, saving their meager cash to buy land. The movement was opposite in direction from the Algonquin migration so long before, and it was vigorous and swift.

A second factor in the sudden change was the abrupt failure of the fur business. About 1840, fashion in Europe decreed that beaver hats were no longer stylish, and time was needed to develop other uses for the beautiful furs of North America. Bateaux piled with furs lined the docks of Montreal, Quebec, and other St. Lawrence port cities. As word drifted back up the lakes, fur-laden canoes no longer shot the rapids at Sault Ste. Marie during spring and summer, and far back into the wilderness there was hunger and disappointment and dismay.

A third cause of change—this a good one for the area—was the discovery, in the 1840's, of minerals on the shores of Lake Superior. The state of Michigan had appointed Dr. Douglass Houghton, a well-known young geologist, to explore the northern shore of upper Michigan. With a few helpers, Houghton sailed along near the shore of Lake Superior; he made five landings, each time staying for careful tests and studies. He sank the first salt well in the area, a forerunner of a great chemical industry. He found a little iron. And he confirmed the many Indian legends when he discovered copper on the Keweenaw Peninsula. This copper, in the purest form known, was lying on the ground, left by the retreating glaciers that had scooped out the lake basins.

Houghton's official report was cautious; he warned that moving even surface copper down to where industries were located would take considerable capital. But at that time men were not in a mood for caution. It was a time of adventure: men had courage, not caution. Scores hurried north expecting to wrest fortune from the ground with their bare hands. Most of them failed. Others, who waited to raise capital and who had the necessary knowledge, succeeded. Young Dr.

Houghton was drowned in a storm in Lake Superior; his wisdom might have helped many, for he was generous with his knowledge.

But as always, someone else took up needed work. William Burt was a deputy surveyor under Dr. Houghton; he had taught himself surveying as had many other Americans—George Washington and Andrew Jackson, for instance. Burt had an inventive mind; he had made the first attempt at a typewriter and had invented a solar compass which could determine location by sun, instead of magnetic force.

On a late summer day in 1844, Burt and his helpers were surveying in northern Michigan, a few miles from where the city of Marquette was built later. The day was cloudy, a disappointment because the solar compass could not be used. Suddenly the magnetic needle began to dance.

"You'll have to spread out, boys," Burt called, "and find out what makes the trouble." They found croppings of iron in several places.

"Hard luck," Burt said. "Maybe tomorrow the sun will shine and we can use the solar compass." He mentioned iron in his report, but the item was not noticed. No one was interested in iron.

Some time later Philo Everet of Jackson, Michigan, came north to search for silver which he had heard was on the peninsula. Word of discoveries traveled fast even without radio or television; often reports were exaggerated, but Everet cared enough to go and search for himself. At Sault Ste. Marie he hired an Indian guide and while buying supplies, chanced to hear of Burt's discovery.

"Can you show me where iron is?" he asked his guide.

"Yes, I can. But that black stuff is no good."

"Well, I'd like to see it, anyway," Everet answered.

He saw—and quickly went back to Jackson, formed a company, raised capital, and got that iron into use. Everet was one of the few who in that year saw a future for iron; he soon had a long trail of followers.

Getting iron out and moving it down nearer coal mines where it could be reduced to useful form, proved to be a major problem. As raw ore it was bulky. And Lake Superior was as remote from the other lakes as Lake Ontario once had been. Men were not thinking about a through water-

way; they simply wanted to get ore down. The one ship which had been built on Lake Superior was soon swamped with orders for transport. Barges, hurriedly built, were good enough in fine weather, but in a storm were apt to overturn—men and ore going to the bottom of a very deep, cold lake.

Then there was the problem of getting ore to a landing and then onto a ship or barge. Some companies dragged the ore to shore by cart in summer, by sled in winter. Ore itself was heavy and bulky. It could be melted into ingots at the mine or by the shore—but it could not be loaded into a birchbard canoe. And there was that mile at Sault Ste. Marie where iron must be carried or carted—a slow, expensive operation.

As the mining business grew, word of jobs spread and more families came north, increasing the congestion and confusion at the village by the rapids. A prosperous portage business grew fast. Men in the village lucky enough to have carts made "good money." Boys carried boxes or valises for a dime—that seemed like wealth. The village had never dreamed of such prosperity.

Seldon McKnight was the first villager to develop a real portage business. He not only had a cart, but also an old gray horse. The next year he risked getting several carts and horses and had more business than he could handle. So he built a railroad along the main street—now Portage Street—with wooden rails covered with iron strips to withstand the hard usage he expected. Small wooden carts, horse-drawn, moved through the village hauling iron ore, copper, and grain going down; machinery and general cargo going up. McKnight charged five cents a hundred pounds, with extra charge if cargo had to be put in his new warehouse to wait its turn for a ship. That warehouse was a good idea—and profitable, too.

McKnight's scheme for a railroad portage would not have suited the needs on the Niagara Peninsula a generation earlier—even if it had been thought of at that time. At the Niagara Peninsula the more than three-hundred-foot drop needed oxen to pull carts up or ease loads down. At the St. Marys rapids the fall was only twenty-one feet to the mile—a drop hardly noticed in a mile of village street. Yet the force of Lake Superior waters flowing down, the size and placement of rocks in the rapids, made the one mile an impossible barrier to transportation of the new cargoes.

Villagers were prosperous and happy as never before. Shippers and travelers fretted at delays and expense, but no one suggested a remedy except more portage, as confusion grew worse and piled-up cargoes mounted higher.

One unexpected result was the beginning of a lively tourist business; shippers and families en route must be housed and fed as they waited. And they had time to see the rare beauty of the rapids and the forests. Many wrote letters and sent them back by steamer to Detroit. One letter said: "You should come and see this place and 'shoot the rapids'—an adventurous sport that the Indians do well."

Some day, with this kind of publicity, Sault Ste. Marie would not seem as far away as the moon.

O CANADA!

Isabel Barclay

The following selection is included as an example of unsuccessful nonfiction. Both its style and its treatment of the subject are poorly handled. The writing is monotonous and rough, with too much dependence on short subject-predicate sentences, producing a tone of condescension. Sentences dealing with the same subject are often separated into several paragraphs instead of joined together into one. This cannot help the young child's growing intuitive understanding of writing conventions.

In addition to these weaknesses, the subject of this book is skimmed over rather than adequately covered. The reader's interest is aroused but never satisfied. Even young children will feel unsatisfied by the quick succession of unelaborated facts. O Canada illustrates a common weakness of children's nonfiction. Many authors are unable to narrow their subject sufficiently or are incapable of supplying enough supporting detail to give depth to the broad sweep. St. Lawrence Seaway by Clara Ingram Judson is a well-written example of how a very broad subject can be handled.

Once upon a time, long ago, nobody lived in Canada. There were animals and birds in the forests and on the plains and among the mountains. There were fish in the rivers and lakes and streams and in the seas, but there were no people.

For millions of years there were no people anywhere in North America. Then the first men came. They came across a strip of land that once made a pathway in the north between Asia and

America. They probably came to hunt the animals whose skins they used for clothes and whose flesh they used for food.

These people all came from Asia but they were not all alike nor did they all come at once. They kept coming in small numbers for thousands and thousands of years, and when they came they stayed.

Some of them settled along the Pacific coast.

Some wandered down the warm valleys behind the Rocky Mountains until they came to Mexico and South America.

Some settled on the edge of the prairies.

Others wandered first south and then north until they came to the eastern woodlands and the shores of the Atlantic Ocean.

There were still others who stayed in the arctic and learned to live by the frozen seas. There were the Eskimo, and their descendants are still there.

All these early people had different shades of brown skin and straight black hair and dark brown eyes, but they did not look alike, or speak the same language, or have the same customs. We call them *Indians* because of a mistake made nearly five hundred years ago. The first Europeans to reach America thought they had found India and so they called the people living there INDIANS and that is what they have been called ever since. The Eskimo and the Indians never had a name for themselves. They simply called themselves THE PEOPLE.

THE PEOPLE OF
THE ARCTIC

The Eskimo who lived in the arctic had pale brown skin, slanting eyes, and straight dark hair. They were not tall but they were very strong and great hunters. They hunted many animals, especially the seals and walrus that lived in the ocean and the polar bears and caribou that lived on the land.

During the winter, which in the arctic lasts half the year, the Eskimo lived in snow houses. These houses were made out of blocks of snow.

During the summer the Eskimo lived in tents made of animal skins.

In winter they travelled by dog sled or on foot.

In summer they went on foot or in their kayaks and umiaks. These are sealskin boats. The Eskimo made their boats from sealskin because trees do not grow in the arctic. The only wood the Eskimo had was the draftwood that floated down the rivers from places farther south where it was warm enough for trees to grow.

The Eskimo were Stone Age men. That is to say they lived without the discovery of metals and so most of their tools and weapons were made of stone. Even their arrowheads were pieces of chipped flint and their lamps were hollowed stones filled with seal or whale oil.

Like most Stone Age people the Eskimo lived in tribes. In each tribe were several families. The men and boys did the hunting and fishing. Hunting was hard and dangerous. Sometimes the Eskimo had to travel many miles before they found game.

The women cooked and sewed and cured the skins of the animals caught in the hunt.

This was done by scraping the skins with sharp stone scrapers and then stretching them on frames to dry. When they were dry, the women cut the skins with stone knives, then sewed the pieces together with bone needles and thread made of sinew.

The Eskimo believed in Good and Bad Spirits. The Good Spirits were the Spirits of their ancestors and the Bad Spirits the Beings who ruled the Earth and Air. The Eskimo made offerings to the Good Spirits and did their best to please the Bad Spirits, or else to frighten them away by shouting and cracking dog whips and making a great noise whenever they thought a Bad Spirit was about. But the Spirits of the Wind and the Sea and the Cold are not easily frightened and so the Eskimo had to learn to live with them as best they could.

The Eskimo were a friendly people. They did not waste their strength and skill fighting. It took all their strength and skill just to keep alive on the edge of the cold arctic seas.

THE PEOPLE OF THE
EASTERN WOODLANDS

The part of Canada that lies between the Great Lakes and the Atlantic Ocean is a land of woods and hills and lakes and rivers and streams. These are the Eastern Woodlands and here long ago lived the Woodland peoples. There were many different Woodland Indians.

The Boethuk lived in Newfoundland.

The Algonkians lived in Quebec and Labrador, and in what is now Nova Scotia and New Brunswick and Prince Edward Island and the north shore of the St. Lawrence River.

The Iroquois lived along the south shore of the St. Lawrence River and beside Lake Ontario and Lake Erie in parts of the country that now belong to the United States.

Other Algonkian people lived along the Ottawa River, while the Hurons lived in southern Ontario and round about Lake Huron, and the Cree lived among the lakes and woods that stretch from the west side of the Great Lakes to the Prairies.

Life was easier for the Woodland people than it was for the people of the arctic. In the parts of Canada where THEY lived, the sun shone all the year, the woods were filled with game and the lakes and rivers with fish.

Wild berries grew in the clearings and there were shellfish on the shore.

The Woodland Indians hunted moose and caribou and deer, and each tribe had its own hunting grounds.

All the Woodland people used skins to make their clothing, but not to make their dwellings. They lived in wigwams made of bark, or long houses that were built with slabs of bark and saplings.

They used bark to make canoes and baskets.

Some of the Woodland Indians painted their clothes and baskets with bright designs, or embroidered them with moose hair and porcupine quills. They made their dyes from plants and berries.

The Woodland Indians, like other people of the Stone Age, knew how to make fire but they did not know how to make wheels. When they travelled they had to carry their belongings on their backs or drag them over the snow on toboggans.

They used snowshoes to walk in the deep snow.

In summer travelling was easier because they could paddle along the lakes and rivers.

Birch bark canoes were made from the bark of the white birch tree. First the bark was cut from the tree in such a way that it came off all in one piece.

Then cedar branches were bent into the right shape and fastened to a frame.

The branches were covered with the birch bark and the bark and branches were lashed with roots and glued with gum from the evergreens.

These birch bark canoes were so light a man could carry one on his back. At the same time they were so strong a single canoe held many men.

When they made war, the Woodland Indians used bows and arrows, spears, and clubs. These weapons were made of wood and stone or bone. But mostly they were tipped with stone.

Many of the Woodland people depended on farming as well as on hunting and fishing for their food. The Iroquois were the best farmers. They lived in villages surrounded by high, spiked wooden fences. In each village there were a number of long houses. Several families lived in a long house. Each family had its own place and its own fire. The fires were built down the center of the long house and the smoke escaped through holes in the roof.

Outside the village walls were the fields where the Iroquois grew their crops. The women did all the work in the fields. They planted corn, beans, squash, pumpkins, and bright yellow sunflowers. Their tools were very simple. A hoe was made by fastening a sharp stone or clamshell to the end of a stick. They also used a pointed stick to dig holes for their seeds.

When the corn was ripe the women pounded it in a hollow log to make corn meal.

The Iroquois used hollow logs for all sorts of things. They even used them to make boats. They did not always have bark canoes like the Algonkians because very few birch trees grew in their part of the country. They often had hollow log boats, or dugouts, made from elm logs. They hollowed logs by burning them along one side and chipping out the burned wood.

The Woodland Indians made most of their clothes from deerskin. In summer the men wore only breechclouts and the women skirts. The children wore no clothes at all.

In winter the men and women and children wore deerskin skirts and leggings. They also had fur caps and mittens and fur-lined moccasins. When it was very, very cold they wrapped themselves in capes of beaver skin.

The mothers carried their papooses in cradleboards on their backs.

The Woodland Indians had exciting feasts and festivals. In the fall when the crops were ripe they had a Harvest Festival. There were other festivals in the winter and spring and summer. At these festivals everybody danced and sang and made long speeches and stuffed themselves with food.

All the people of the Eastern Woodlands believed in a Great Spirit. They said it was He who had made the world and all the people and animals in it. The Woodland Indians believed there were spirits in all things—in the trees and birds and fish and animals, as well as in themselves and in the wind and the rain.

SPRING COMES TO THE OCEAN

Jean Craighead George

Jean George has written many scientific books, some in collaboration with her husband, John. She is also the author of two popular books of juvenile fiction, My Side of the Mountain *and* Gull 737. *Both deal with aspects of nature: surviving alone in the woods for a long period and sea gull research. While the stories hold the reader, the primary interest comes from the presentation of scientific and practical information.*

In Spring Comes to the Ocean *Mrs. George reveals with great sensitivity the effects of spring on the ocean's inhabitants. She writes about the lives, dangers, and reproductive patterns of sea life from the gray whale to the sea worms. By showing the relationship between seasonal change and sea life,* Spring Comes to the Ocean *is far more valuable than books that simply give facts. Not only is Mrs. George accurate in this concept book, but her style is exceptionally suited to instill within children reverence for all living things.*

The first outward sign of spring in the ocean was a lazy drift of seaweed. The sargassum weed left the stillness of the winter sea and moved in rafts and floes northward in the Gulf Stream.

The sun was heating the waters, quickening the currents, and the weed simply told the sailors and seafaring biologist that a change had taken place, that spring had come to the ocean.

A hermit crab at the edge of the water on Florida's Key Largo, where the seasons are subtle and barely defined, felt the warming. He ran up the cool beach with just his feet sticking out of his gray and sea-worn conch shell. At a pile of seaweed he stopped and looked about.

He saw the brilliance that was the sun and the dark flatness that was ocean. Then he rotated his eyes on their stalks and saw the palm trees behind him. They were gray, for he could see no color,

and they were misty and vague because they were not important to his way of life.

However, he saw the beach. That was important! And he saw the shells splattered over it, for shells were the most necessary things in the world to this crab. In fact, on that cool January dawn, shells were so important that he saw them bigger than they really were. He climbed onto the seaweed. His thousand-faceted compound eyes saw a conch shell a thousand times. In his mind's eye, however, he saw only one shell, just as our two eyes bring but one picture to our brain. He ran toward the shell, for he was about to molt and grow bigger and he could not stay in his old house another day. He pinched the shell. A hard foot shot out and clamped his. The hermit crab turned away. The shell was occupied by another of his kind who would fight until death to keep his home.

The crab rushed to a board washed up by the sea. His ears did not exist as such; but he was infinitely sensitive to vibration of the air and sea, and so he was "listening" with every part of him for the sound of an empty shell. He walked around the board.

Suddenly, the sand in a cuplike cavity at the base of his feelers tilted the wrong way, and the hermit crab knew he was going downhill, not up. He did not want to go down. He turned until the sand ran the other way, then scooted on his eight hard, bristly feet up toward the edge of the palm forest where empty shells were often left by the birds.

As he came to fallen palm fronds he felt his outside coat loosen at his back. It would soon drop away, and he would have to shed it. And at that time he must have a shell.

Most of the other hermit crabs on the beach were not in his predicament. Those that were feeling their carapaces loosen were hanging onto empty shells. Some had carried them in their big left claws for weeks. So had this crab. But during the night a fisherman had dropped anchor on him and he had snapped into his shell in alarm. The anchor had rolled over beside him; but when the crab reached out to snatch his precious shell again, it was gone! Another hermit crab had snatched it and was toting it swiftly behind a coral fin. The hermit could not get it back.

There was little time to waste; he turned immediately to find another shell. By dawn he was still unsuccessful, and so he had come ashore for a last desperate search before the birds awoke.

Just as he was leaving the sea, the hermit crab took a deep draught of water, filling his mouth and wetting his gills so that he could travel on land. With the sea in his body he could stay ashore for several hours. The water bubbled and circulated around his mouth as he crawled over the brown leaves.

Beyond a seed pod of the royal palm he "felt" an empty shell. His need catapulted him over the pod, and down upon the hermit holding the shell. The other crab was smaller than he, and his grip on the shell was light, he held it at a distance. As the time to change shells draws near, the hermits clutch their new homes tighter, and hold them closer.

The first hermit slammed his pincer on the edge of a big conch, still pink and fresh. He pulled. The defending hermit pulled back.

They fought many minutes. Suddenly the top of the first crab's eyes saw sea gull wings. The birds had awakened. He snapped into his shell. The second one took advantage of the moment, grabbed his conch shell and ran. A gull saw him move and dropped from the sky. As the gull snatched the little runner in its hard beak, the crab let go of the shell. It tumbled and rolled into the palm fronds. The first hermit waited until the shadow of the bird was gone and then he thrust his head out. Where his opponent had been lifted into the air lay the empty shell.

He dashed to it, just as a third hermit scurried around the edge of the palm pod and reached for the conch. The first crab struck him a blow so hard that it echoed around the cupped walls of the pod. The third crab withdrew at the blow and the first snatched the shell. He ran with it into a pile of dried seaweed. Among the twisted leaves he found a dome-shaped room.

For a moment he rested. Then he came out of his shell, halfway, feeling a strange hermit-crab fear. He now had to shift shells, the most dangerous event in the life of a hermit. First he unhooked the muscle at the spiral end of his old shell. Then he pulled himself out and stood vulnerable, so naked that even a windblown grain of sand could kill him. His exposed belly was so delicate that a nodding grass blade could cut him in half. Nevertheless, he must change! He slashed his tail through the air and stuck it into the new shell. Backing carefully, he reached his tail down and around until he felt the last coil of the shell. Then he hooked onto it with a grip so strong that few could pull him out. When at last he had a firm hold, he contracted all his muscles and slammed himself deep into the shell. It was big and roomy. He relaxed.

By now the sea water in his mouth had begun to dry and he stuck out his feet to return to the ocean. He lifted the shell. It was heavier than the old one; but he was strong enough to carry it. He walked to the sea, leaving a trail like the marks of an eight-wheel cart.

The hermit felt the sea. He sank down into it and walked past the pile of dead coral toward a canyon cut by the tide, past the wooden pilings that held up the fishing pier, and drifted down through a school of yellow-and-black sergeant-major fish. He hit the bottom of the sea and crawled past the rock crab that lived in the crevass of the stones. He went to the edge of the mud flat where the seaweed grew and the water cucumbers lay quiet and unanimal-like in the slow water. He went under a tree of seaweed and there lifted his new shell.

He wiggled and moved, tensing all the muscles on his back and feet until he had pulled himself away from his old carapace. Then he leaned far out of his shell and his old coat floated into the sea. He pulled into his shell again, going deeper and deeper into the spirals, for he must rest until his new skeleton hardened.

The nights and days spun by. The hermit crab sat quietly, seeing and feeling nothing. One morning he felt hungry. He pushed up his shell. He was strong enough to lift it and taste the water. A thin thread of flavor enlivened his senses and he followed it until the came to the remains of a fish. He ate voraciously, stuffing the food into his many-parted mouth with his small claws. When he was comfortable, he released his grip on the ocean floor and rode a wave toward the beach. As he tumbled with it, he found he could not tell up from down, for there was no sand in his balancing organ, or statocyst, since molting his old coat. He was in a state of weightlessness. He blew out air until, tumbling in unknown directions, he struck bottom. There he thrust his feelers into the sand. As he did, minuscule grains of sand sifted into the little balancing cups, and he was all right again. The sand moved to tell him he was going up. He swam until he came to the swift current that swirled around the pier. Here he threw out his swimmerettes and stopped himself. Then he went down among the sea animals on the floor of the mud flat. The hermit crab wanted to be among these odd animals, for although his new house was splendid and colorful it was dangerous. It was much too conspicuous.

The hermit scurried among the sea anemones, strange tubular animals that look like round cups decorated on their edges with flowerlike tentacles. The tentacles hold poison darts that shoot into fish and paralyze them. When the fish are still, the tentacles slowly feed the fish to the tube mouth. The hermit crab wanted one of the sea anemones for protection. He tested three before he found the one he wanted. He took it firmly by its rubbery tube and slowly ran his claw up and down, up and down the animal.

It took many hours. Finally, this creature, which spends its life in one spot and cannot be removed alive from it by any man, gave in to the hermit crab. The anemone foot let go. When it was free the crab swiftly reached up and planted it on the top of his new shell. Again he stroked the tube creature, and its foot took firm hold of the crab's shell.

Sporting a yellow anemone, the crab moved among a colony of sponges. He planted several of these animals on the top of his too pink shell. Now he could walk the sea bottom safely. He looked like the rocks and reefs, not like a shining sea shell. In return for their protection, the crab carried these animals to new sources of food they would never reach by their own efforts.

Soon after being planted on the crab shell, the anemone stung a fish. The hermit reached up and took it for himself and the anemone, which had no sense of moral justice, did not care. It caught another a few minutes later, and fed not only itself, but the tiny lobsters that lived in the sponges.

One morning the hermit walked over to a female of his kind. Firmly he took her shell in his claw. He lifted her off the sand and carried her to the seaweed bed. There he put her down that she might eat some of the microscopic life that dwelt in the mud. But he did not let her go.

She was almost ready to molt. He could tell this by the way she behaved. She pulled at her muscles and kept in her shell. He held her until she had eaten, then he dragged her ashore to some pieces of a fish feed left by the sea gulls. She, too, was decorated with tiny sponges and red anemones, and as the crabs same out of the sea, their garden of animals closed water inside them. As the crabs ate they scrunched down to save water.

At twilight, the male hermit could feel tremblings within his mate's shell. This meant that she would soon toss her old carapace into the sea. Swiftly, he ran back to the ocean and, pushing with his swimming paddles, he carried the female to the base of the pier. In a hollow of sand made by the water as it moved around the piling, he waited for the female to shed her coat.

Presently she arched her body, lifted her shell and was free of her too small skeleton. But she did not snap back into her home. She waited; for now she was ready to mate. The male moved close to her and gently stuck his swimmerettes into pockets in her apron, as her belly is called. In an instant he had handed her the secret code for a million new hermit crabs. She would keep this code in her pockets until she was ready to use it. But not now.

Then the male hermit let go of the female and drifted away. She pulled into her shell to wait until her carapace hardened, and until she was ready to lay eggs. Then she would let them pass over the spermatozoa the male had just given her. They would be fertilized and she would hold them to her body until they were ready to hatch.

Such was the beginning of spring in the warming waters of Florida—a gentle exchange of shells and skeletons and life's mysterious genetic code.

WHEN THE ROOT CHILDREN WAKE UP

Helen Dean Fish

The following passage is included as an example of the anthromorphic-fantasy approach of informational literature. Rather than clarifying the progression of seasons for children, this book's "cuteness" can only distort and confuse a child's understanding of nature. Such an approach is patronizing in tone; it denies that young children are able to understand the concept of seasonal change and so must be talked down to. This selection can be contrasted with Spring Comes to the Ocean, *a simply written, yet accurate nonfiction book on the same subject.*

All winter long the trees are bare, the wind is cold and the fields are empty.

But very early in the Spring the Sun begins to grow warmer, the air softer and the sky bluer. And boys and girls grow happier though they cannot tell just why.

Down underground something is happening.

Something secret and wonderful.

The root children who have been sleeping soundly all winter are awakened by the Earth Mother. She comes with her candle and her little firefly helpers to tell them they must be up and at work for it will soon be Spring. They are very sleepy at first but soon begin to stretch and open their eyes and be glad that it is time to wake.

Wide awake at last, in their root house, the root children work busily on their new Spring dresses. Each chooses the color she loves best—violet, yellow, blue, white, orange or red—and with needle, thread and thimble, sews happily till her work is done.

Above them, in the little village by the sea, the children are learning carols to sing at Easter, and every day the sky and water are growing bluer.

The root children take their dresses to show to the good Earth Mother, where she sits comfortably with her tea and her knitting. Her busy ant helpers are about her. She is pleased when she sees how well each little root child has made her Spring dress.

It is time to be ready, for above them the ice on the little brook has melted and the water is slipping merrily over its pebbles. In the barns the sheep and lambs feel the Spring air and wish to be in the green fields again.

While the little root girls are sewing Spring

When the Root Children Wake Up by Helen Dean Fish. Published 1941 by J. B. Lippincott Company. Reprinted in its entirety by permission of the publishers. Illustrated by Sibylle V. Olfers.

dresses, the root boys are busy with their share in making ready for Spring. They wake up the sleeping insects—the beetles, grasshoppers, lady-bugs, crickets, bumble-bees, fireflies and June-bugs. They sponge them and brush them and paint their shells with bright Spring colors, while the fields over their heads are growing greener and the leaf-buds on the trees are swelling in the warm Spring air.

Then, when all is ready, Spring comes!

TRAVELERS ALL: The Story of How Plants Go Places

Irma Webber

This nonfiction book is an effective and well-written introduction to botany for young children in kindergarten and first grade. A great deal of information is given simply and clearly without any sense that the author felt she had to talk down to her readers. The style, however, is much less pleasing than Jean George's Spring Comes to the Ocean. *However, while it is typical of the short sentences of "easy books," the style of* Travelers All *is less choppy than most works written for this age group.*

The text is accompanied by effective illustrations which both clarify and supplement the words. Each plant seed mentioned is shown in simple pictures so the reader will be able to recognize it when he encounters it in nature.

Animals travel by air, by water and by land. Some run very fast. Some hop or jump along the ground. Others walk more slowly, or crawl still more slowly.

Do you know that plants are travelers, too? Most plants stay in the same spot from the time they begin to grow until they die. But the next season you find many of them growing in new places. How do they travel to their new homes?

Some plants travel by land.

The poppy has a seed pod which opens near the top. When the wind blows, the pod is tipped or shaken and the seeds fall to the ground. Right where they fall, some of these seeds will grow into new poppy plants.

The seeds of the wild oat can wiggle or jump along the ground. They have curly "tails" when they are dry. When it rains, their tails straighten out. Then the sun dries them, and they curl up

again. Each time the tails change shape, the seeds wiggle and jump a little way along the ground.

Strawberry plants send out runners along the ground. New plants grow out of these runners.

When plants travel this way, they do not go very far.

Heavy fruits like apples drop to the ground. Sometimes they stay right under the tree. Sometimes they bounce or roll away, and the seeds start to grow quite a distance from the tree.

Some plants are better suited for travel by water than by land.

The lotus is a kind of water lily. It grows in the shallow parts of lakes with its roots in the mud. Its seed pods have large air spaces that make them light enough to float. When the pods drop into the water, they often ferry their seeds clear across the lake.

Coconuts are sometimes water travelers. When coconut palms grow along the ocean shore, some of the nuts or seeds drop into the water. A thick fibrous husk covers the nut and is like a life belt that keeps it afloat. Sometimes coconuts make long stormy voyages across the ocean.

Many plants travel by air. Their seeds whirl, float, fly, or shoot through the air.

Violas are a kind of pansy. They shoot their seeds through the air. Their seed pods dry and shrink in the sun. This squeezes the seeds and shoots them out one by one.

The wind breaks off dry tumble-weeds close to the ground. Then it whirls them through the air or rolls them like balls across open fields. Tumble-weeds may travel for miles before they get caught on a fence or a tree. All along the way seeds fall from their hiding places between the stems and little spiny leaves.

Toadstools travel long distances by air. Instead of seeds, they have spores which are so small we cannot see them without a microscope. Hundreds of spores are formed on the under side of the umbrella-like part of a toadstool. These tiny spores are blown about by the wind like specks of dust.

Maple seeds have wings. They flutter in the wind and fly like gliders through the air. When the wind is strong, they fly quite far.

Milkweed seeds have silky parachutes that take them for long rides in the air. When their pods open, the seeds bail out and float on the wind.

Seeds also travel in other ways. Sometimes they are taken to new places by animals or people.

Squirrels carry away acorns, the seeds of the oak tree, and store them to eat later. They bury some of these acorns in the ground and forget them. The acorns that have been left in the ground sometimes grow into oak trees.

Birds like to eat cherries and many kinds of berries. They sometimes carry the seeds long distances.

Have you ever walked through the fields in the Fall? Then afterwards you picked burrs and seeds with sharp points or hooks from your clothes. Without meaning to, you were helping seeds to travel.

Every plant has its own way of traveling to reach new places. But people do not wait for plants to travel in these ways. We collect seeds and plant them where we want them to grow. People send seeds all over the world—by air, by sea and by land.

YOU AND RELATIVITY

Mary Lou Clark

The profound scientific concept of relativity has in this book been made understandable to children, a remarkable writing accomplishment. Hopefully older children will not be misled by the book's size and shape, which make it appear to have been written for young children. Because it ends with a mention of Einstein's Theory of Relativity, it is appropriate for older elementary and junior high school students who are able to work with abstract concepts. More such concept books are needed for today's sophisticated young readers.

What is up?
What is down?

That is easy you say. When I throw a ball into the air, it goes up; then it comes down. If I look at the sky, I look up. When I drop something, it falls down.

Now think about this. If several people want

to go to the third floor of a building, will they all go up? It depends on where they are when they start. Mr. X, who is on the first floor, will go up to get to the third floor. Mr. Y, who is on the sixth floor, must go down to get to the third floor. RELATIVE to the first floor, the third floor is up. The matter of up and down depends on where you are. It depends on your FRAME OF REFERENCE.

Let's try a thought experiment. A thought experiment is an experiment that you must think about only, because you can not really do it. Great scientists do a lot of thought experiments. They are fun. Doing a thought experiment is like playing make-believe.

Suppose you could make a hole right through the center of the earth and see the people on the other side. How would they look to you? To you they would be upside down. If the imaginary hole had a glass cover over it to stop the people from falling through, you would see the bottoms of their shoes as they walked across the glass. If they looked through the hole, you would be upside down to them. RELATIVE to you they are upside down. RELATIVE to them you are upside down. It depends on your frame of reference.

On our planet earth, down is toward the center of the earth. Up means away from the earth.

The earth's attraction for objects is called the FORCE OF GRAVITY. When an object is dropped, it is pulled to the earth by the force of gravity. Sometimes a force is created that is greater than the force of gravity.

To prove this put some water into a bucket and take it outdoors. Now swing the bucket rapidly in a vertical circle—a curved path circling the direction from your knees to your head and back to your knees. The water will remain in the bottom of the bucket as long as you keep swinging the bucket rapidly in a circle. In swinging the bucket a new force is created. This force is called CENTRIFUGAL FORCE. (We pronounce it sen-TRIF-yuh-guhl.)

As you swing the bucket centrifugal force becomes GREATER than the force of gravity. This forms a false force of gravity. The water pushes hard against the bottom of the bucket. The water stays in the bucket even when the bucket is upside down. When you stop swinging the bucket on its circular path, centrifugal force is halted and the force of gravity takes over. If you were to let go of the bucket while swinging it, the bucket would fly away tangent to the circle.

Pretend you are on a spaceship. It is shaped like a huge doughnut. As it whirls through space, a centrifugal force is reacted. The strong centrifugal force forms a gravity field. This false gravity field allows the people in the ship to use the outer rim of the ship as a floor. They can walk along the outer rim of the ship. Objects they drop fall to the "floor." While they are traveling in this ship, up becomes "toward the center" of the ship and down means "away from" the ship.

How does this compare to the meaning of up and down on planet earth?

Up and down are not the only directions that are relative. What do you think about left and right? Are they always the same to everybody? If you are not sure about the answers to these questions, do this experiment:

Stand face to face with another person. Now each of you move one step to the right. Did you both move in the same direction?

What happens if two people stand back-to-back and each one walks forward?

How are the directions north, east, south, and west relative depending on the frame of reference?

Forward, backward, inward, outward

Left or right—which place?

Relatively speaking

There's no up and down in space.

When Gulliver traveled to the land of Lilliput, he was a giant compared to those tiny people. If by some strange happening Gulliver became the same size as the Lilliputians, then what would be expected? Would Gulliver think he was smaller than he had been? Would there be a way for Gulliver to tell he was not his normal size?

This brings up another thought experiment. Suppose the same thing happened to you while you slept. During the night everything became smaller than it was when you went to sleep—you, your bed, your room, your house. This is not a case of the EAT ME cakes and DRINK ME potions of *Alice in Wonderland* that kept Alice changing her size RELATIVE TO HER SURROUNDINGS. Here is a situation in which EVERY SINGLE THING changes—from atoms and molecules to the earth and sun.

How, then, could you tell that a change had taken place? There is no possible way. Since

EVERYTHING has grown smaller, there is nothing to use as a comparison. Everything is in the same proportion as it was before. You could not tell that you were smaller.

You could not measure yourself because the yardsticks have become smaller. We measure objects by comparing them to something else. From this thought experiment, we conclude that size, too, is relative.

Time, also, is relative. There is no absolute time. One period of time is measured by comparing it with another period of time. A year on earth is 365 days. This is the length of time for the earth to make one revolution around the sun. One year on Mercury is equal to 88 earth days. One year on Uranus is about 84 earth years. What makes a day? A day on earth is the period of the earth's turning on its axis. It is divided into hours, minutes and seconds.

Does ten years seem like a long time to you? A geologist who measures the age of the earth by fossil stories, thinks of ten years as a very short time. To a small child even tomorrow seems a long way off. A year at your present age seems shorter than it did when you were five years old.

As your clock strikes noon, is it noon for everybody? When you have the season of winter, is everybody having winter? As long as we are on earth our clocks are set by earth time and corrections can be made for the time zones. In space, time has a different frame of reference. Think about this. If there were no motion would time mean anything to us? Time depends on motion.

We have discussed direction, size, and time, all of which are relative. None of these are absolute. Surely something in this world must be absolute. Are all things relative depending on the frame of reference?

In this strange world of relativity what are you ideas about motion? Is motion absolute or is it relative? How can we prove that a body is moving or standing still? We have seen that direction, size, and time require a standard of comparison. Does motion, also, need a standard of comparison?

To find the answers to these questions, ride in a car moving smoothly at a constant speed. Close your eyes. Unless the road is bumpy or your body is swayed around a curve, you cannot tell that you are moving. If the car had no windows and your eyes were open, you could not tell you were moving. The other people in the car would not appear to be moving. What would happen if you dropped an object? It would fall to the floor. This would be as normal as if you were sitting in a parked car. Unless you see the landscape passing by or are given clues by a bumpy or curving ride, you can not tell that you are in motion.

If you are riding in a smoothly running train and are traveling at 100 miles per hour and another train beside you is going at the same speed, it seems to you that you are standing still. If your train passes another train going 80 miles per hour in the opposite direction, your train seems to be going faster than 100 miles per hour. If you pass a train going 80 miles per hour in the same direction your train is going, then your train seems to be going slower than 100 miles per hour.

The train's speed of 100 miles per hour can be thought about in another way. Can you honestly say that 100 miles per hour is the true speed of the train? Why not?

The earth turns on its axis as it travels about 18 miles per second on its path around the sun. The sun itself hurtles through our galaxy, the Milky Way. The Milky Way moves through space relative to other galaxies. Add these to the train's speed of 100 miles per hour and you'll discover that you are traveling several thousand miles per hour!

Since it all depends on your frame of reference, we conclude that motion is relative. If you were in a spaceship and saw nothing passing by, you could not tell you were moving.

ORBITING STATIONS: Stopovers to Space Travel

Irwin Stambler

Nothing should be more gripping than space exploration. The world truly entered the space age when men first walked on the moon. Yet the astronauts' television reports of their space experiences are unsatisfactory, for they are able to speak only in scientific terms. Although objective scientific terminology is excellent for advancing technology, it lacks the precision that imagery and metaphor have to evoke a human response to the unknown.

It is exactly this inability to make the scientific understandable and interesting to laymen that has made Orbiting Stations *a dull book.*

THE TITAN III C

A prime consideration in any space program is the booster system. Engineers always like to use an available system if they can, and a careful review was made of the U.S. missile roster. At first it was decided to adapt a Titan Intercontinental Ballistic Missile to do the job. The Titan used storable liquid propellants (propellants that did not have to be supercooled to temperatures of —320 degrees F.) and had the highest takeoff thrust at the time. During early design stages, the Titan I missile was used as the basis for Dyna-Soar plans. On January 13, 1961, the Air Force announced it had decided to substitute the improved version of this missile, Titan II. Titan II had a first stage thrust of 430,000 pounds and a second stage thrust of 100,000 pounds.

But even Titan II left something to be desired. It just didn't have enough thrust to permit including all the systems in the spaceship that scientists and engineers wanted to put into it. Thus the Air Force decided to develop a brand new booster system to haul the Dyna-Soar into orbit. The system, though, would not be for Dyna-Soar alone, but would provide the U.S. with a new standardized space launch system. The new system would provide several million pounds of

thrust and could be used for a great many different space and satellite missions of the late 1960's and throughout the 1970's.

The new booster was designated the Titan III and the Air Force approved study plans for the system on August 20, 1962. Engineers at many companies worked for months on proposals for the new craft. Finally selected as the integration contractor was the same company responsible for building Titans I and II, the Denver Division of Martin-Marietta Corporation.

Heart of the new booster was the use of a breakthrough in solid rocket engines called segmented solids. During the late 1950's and early 1960's, propulsion engineers at many companies and research institutes had been looking for ways to make very large solid rockets possible. The drawback had been the tremendous weight of the solid fuel. For a liquid rocket, a huge, thin shell could be built into which the fuel could be transported by truck, railway car, or airplane from the factory to the pad.

But solid rockets must be made in one big piece. A solid rocket capable of delivering a half-million to a million pounds of thrust was possible. However, it would weigh so many tons, it would be impossible for the strongest crane to lift it or the most powerful truck or strongest railroad car to carry it. The answer, engineers decided, was to make the rocket in "segments." These segments would be small enough and light enough ("light" means able to be carried by available trucks or railroad cars—but a segment still weighs almost 50 tons) to be transported to the launch site. At the site, the segments could be attached together like the parts of an erector set. By 1962, scientists and engineers had brought the new idea to the point where 100-inch-diameter segmented rockets had been fired successfully in ground tests to give thrusts of over a half-million pounds.

It was decided to use a modified Titan II as the center section of a three-section booster. To this liquid fueled "core" would be strapped two huge solid propellant engines each able to provide over a million pounds of thrust. To achieve this thrust level with the proper booster height to mate with the core, the diameter of the engine was changed to 120 inches rather than the 100 of earlier tests. After a design competition, the company selected to build the solid fuel engines was United Technology Center of United Aircraft Corporation, Sunnyvale, California. Each huge solid booster would weigh over 250 tons and tower 75 feet into the air on the launch pad.

The core to which they were to be strapped was based on the Titan II ICBM, but with an added stage. The first stage of the core used a twin nozzle liquid propellant engine capable of delivering 430,000-pound thrust and a second stage twin nozzle engine rated at 100,000-pound thrust. On top of these, though, a new stage, called the Transtage, was added. The liquid propellant engines, including the Transtage, were provided to Martin-Marietta by Aerojet-General, Sacramento, California. For certain space missions, the solid boosters and the Titan II first stages had the job of propelling the Transtage and the payload towards a "parking orbit."

The parking orbit method was devised earlier in the space program to give scientists more leeway in launching spaceships out from earth. Without the parking orbit idea, there are only a few minutes to fire the payload towards its objective. This is a major handicap, for it is possible the craft may be in a relatively poor position for the final trajectory at that moment. The answer was to first put the payload and some kind of engine system into a preliminary orbit around the earth. This gave the scientists and engineers much more time to decide when to commit the spaceship to its final—or near final—course.

The Transtage was the engine system designed to provide Titan III with this parking orbit capability. To do this, the Transtage had to be able to fire more than once. After second stage burnout and separation, the Transtage would fire just long enough to propel itself and the payload into the orbit. It would then turn off, keeping enough fuel in its tanks to be restarted later on. Once the payload was in proper position, the Transtage would be started again to push the spacecraft into its desired course. For a deep space mission, the course might be outward towards the moon or distant planets. For a Dyna-Soar-type plane, the Transtage could move the craft into a reentry trajectory.

It can be seen that the Transtage has many uses. This reflects the whole idea in the Titan III of making one launch system vehicle that could be used for many different missions. For some satellite and space tests, the extra thrust of the solid boosters wasn't needed. Considering this, the Titan III was designed so the core alone could be used in such cases. The solid rockets only had to be added where more power was required. The fact that the solids were made in segments also meant that, if desired, fewer segments could be attached together. The Titan III design using the core only was designated the IIIA Vehicle. The complete three-section system was called the IIIC. The Titan IIIC with a typical unmanned space vehicle on top has a height of 120 feet. Depending on the mission, Titan III could launch payloads ranging from 5000 to 25,000 pounds into various earth orbits or on deep space journeys.

After reviewing the thousands of drawings and reports by engineers, the Department of Defense gave the green light for the Titan III research and development program to start on December 1, 1962. Up to this time, the Titan III only existed in plans and the minds of men. A tremendous new system such as this had to go through months of testing and slow buildup of production facilities, followed by a flight test program before it would be ready for operational use. The Department of Defense-Air Force program called for the research development phase to take 45 months from the starting date. By the middle of 1964, the parts for the first test vehicles would be completed.

Then, after weeks of rigorous ground testing, actual test launches would begin. The schedule called for five IIA and 12 IIIC test vehicles to be built and launched. The first IIIA launch was planned for late 1964, and the first IIIC by mid-1965. Some of these, it was known, would probably fail, but the failures would point out the "bugs" in the system and allow engineers and scientists to make corrections in following boosters. After 17 launches, all would finally be in order for the first operational Titan III to take to the air.

During these months, not only would the missiles themselves have to be developed and tested; many other things had to be done as well. Transportation methods had to be devised to carry the huge solid rocket segments to the launch site. Complete new ground electronic systems had to be designed, built and installed at Cape Kennedy and ground tracking stations. Some of this equipment had to automatically check out all the parts of a Titan III to make sure there was nothing wrong. Some of it gave ground stations the ability to either send signals to work the missile during launch and flight or to receive information from the booster and its payload.

Still another huge part of the jigsaw puzzle was the construction of a new Titan III assembly center and launch pad system at the Cape. This required building three artificial islands in the middle of the Banana River, which flows through the area. This launch site represents a new streamlined approach to the overall launch problem. The size of the parts called for special transportation-assembly methods. Thus not only were several huge assembly buildings needed, but a 4½-mile-long railroad system connecting these buildings to three new pads. (The pads are designated Complex 40, 41 and 42.)

One of the buildings, called the integration building, was designed for assembly of the core section and installation of the payload. To take care of the huge solid propellant segments, two barge docks were placed nearby. The solid segments would pass through the propellant inspection building where they would be carefully examined to make sure there were no minute cracks, swelling or other flaws in the solid "grain." (A solid propellant fuel in its final shape is called a grain.) Any of these flaws could result in im-

proper burning of the grain when it was ignited on launch. The segments, once okayed, then went to special solid segment storage bunkers. Here the air temperature and humidity has to be carefully controlled to prevent any damage to the grain.

Once the core and payload for a mission has been assembled and carefully examined by electronic check-out equipment, it is taken on its huge railroad car base to the next stopping point. The railroad carriage in this case is used all through the assembly and launch program. The Titan parts are built up on the car and when the IIIA missile is ready to fire, the car moves right onto the pad where it also serves as the launching base. After launch, the railroad car then is moved back to the assembly area for its next load. Thus the track system provides a great deal of flexibility for the launch program. It permits moving a missile onto the pad only when it's ready for launch. This eliminates tying up a pad for days or weeks because of problems in a launch vehicle. As a result, USAF estimated it could get over thirty launches per pad per year as against only nine or ten launches per year on current Atlas pads at the Cape.

The last paragraph didn't mention solid assembly. Again the rail system flexibility permits either going directly from the core assembly building to the launch site or going first through another building for attachment of the solids. This means one type of railroad car can be used to launch either a IIIA or IIIC system.

The solid assembly building is between the integration building and the launch sites. When a Titan IIIC vehicle is wanted, the proper number of 50-ton segments is carried into the assembly building. Here huge cranes can position each new segment on top of the lower one until the full five segments are together. The segments are fastened to each other by a series of metal pins inserted through a special mating joint on the top and bottom of the segments. When the solid booster is complete, the crane carries it onto the railroad car holding the core section. Then the solid rocket is bolted to the core at special attachment points.

When all the bolts have been fastened, all the electrical, hydraulic and other systems connected, electronic check-out equipment again makes sure everything is working as it should. If everything is "go", the Titan IIIC car moves out to the pad. The electronic check-out system on special vans of its own, goes right along with the car to the pad. Thus electronic signals can continue monitoring the "health" of the vehicle until a few minutes before launch.

SCIENCE ON THE SHORES AND BANKS

Elizabeth K. Cooper

Many science books present only facts. This book invites the reader to participate in scientific observations. In addition to the text, it has numerous drawings that add to and clarify the information. With this book plus a lake or stream, any observant child could learn a great deal about nature. Elizabeth Cooper's very practical and scientific approach is presented in a readable style that makes this an instructive and interesting book.

EXPLORING THE WATER'S EDGE

Wherever a body of water meets the land, you can discover a rich and exciting field for science. There is much to observe because you really have three separate worlds right there at arm's reach. First, you have the water world of plants and animals that cannot live except in the water. A fish will drown if you hold it too long in the air. It gets its oxygen from the water. Its body is beautifully formed for living and moving in its water environment. You have probably heard the saying, "As helpless as a fish out of water"—and that is helpless, indeed! Man and some other animals can learn to swim in water, but a fish cannot learn to swim in the air. Plants and animals that live in water have special features that enable them to thrive only in their native surroundings. There are plants without roots or leaves or flowers, living and drifting endlessly in the sea. There are animals that can regrow parts of their bodies that have been cut off and even, when cut into several pieces, grow each piece into a complete new body. There are animals that look and

From *Science on the Shores and Banks,* © 1960 by Elizabeth K. Cooper. Text and illustrations reprinted by permission of Harcourt Brace Jovanovich, Inc.

live like plants, and plants that are never green. There are animals that move on a single foot, and some that cannot move at all. Seaweed and pondweed and oysters and starfish and minnows and hydra are only a few of the living things that are perfectly at home in their water world.

The second life-area is on the bank or shore itself. It is the world of air and sun and dry land. This is the environment for flowers and trees and land birds and people and many other kinds of animals, large and small. The plants and animals of this air world cannot live long under water. You may be able to swim under water for a short time by holding your breath, but there is no way in which you, as a typical land animal, can live without getting oxygen from the air.

The third special area is the in-between world of air and water, the world of plants and animals that need both in order to live. There you will find insects that dive under water and insects that can walk on the surface without getting their feet wet. You can find the water boatman, which lives and feeds in the waters of ponds and quiet streams. But it must breathe air in order to live. Frogs and toads and other amphibians begin their lives as fishlike creatures, getting oxygen directly from the water. For the rest of their lives they are air breathers on the land or they dive into the water and come up every so often for a breath of air. There are many kinds of shore birds that depend upon water for food and upon the air world for everything else. They breathe air and fly through it and then paddle or float on the top of the water or even dive down below the surface to catch a seafood dinner. There are plants, too, like cattails and bulrushes, that need to have both water and air. Their roots grow in the mud deep below the water's surface, and their stems and blades and flowers extend up into the air and sunshine.

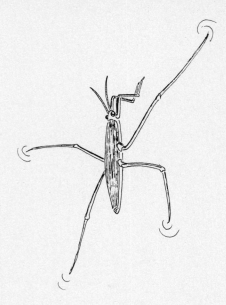

Water strider.

Water boatmen.

Wherever you go to explore the water's edge, there are enough science adventures to keep you busy for a week, a year, or for your entire life, depending on how much you want to find out about the interesting plants and animals along the shores and banks. There are things for a scientist to observe, explore, collect, and experiment with. Here's one way to begin.

First of all, just look around you. Practice sitting quietly until you can see the smallest motion near you. It may be some sand fleas tumbling out of a clump of damp seaweed and scurrying to bury themselves in the sand. Or, if you are beside a pond, it may be a water strider skating across the surface, his six slender legs ending in delicate feet that make dimples in the water as he moves. Or you may see a dragonfly with wings like cellophane hovering and darting above the reeds, or a crayfish under the water scooting backward to a safe place under some rocks.

Try to learn the art of listening, too. Close your eyes and find out what sounds there are around you and what each sound means. At first you may hear only the sound of the water itself. It may be the slow and regular breaking of waves against the shore. Or you may be hearing the bubbling and gurgling of a stream moving over the rocks, or perhaps the gentle lapping of a quiet lake against its banks. Suddenly you may hear a loud plop as a frog drops from an overhanging tree root into a pool. You may hear a double splash as a fish jumps out of the water and right back in again. Perhaps you can hear the faint buzzing of insects, or the flap-flap of wings and the cry of a sea bird as it dives suddenly toward the water. What special sounds can you hear, and how many of them can you identify?

Explore with your nose, too, for there are many unusual smells around the water's edge. There is the fresh, clean smell of wind blowing across a clear lake. Or the acid-sharp smell of wet willows and alder trees that grow beside a stream. There is the salty tang of the ocean, mingled at times with just a hint of the smell of dead fish. There are special smells wherever you are—the delicate smells of plant and animal life at the edge of the water, and the heavier smells of plant and animal death as the once living tissues softens, breaks apart, and is slowly intermingled with the water.

Now, for a close look, find a shallow place and put your face as close to the water as you can without actually touching it. You may be able to stretch out on a large rock, feet high and head low, and peer down into the water. Or lie on the bank of a stream with your head hanging over the water's edge. Or just wade in where the water is no more than two feet deep, bend over, and see what you can see. Try not to move. Do you see any moving creatures? Watch for swimming and diving insects, tiny fish, tadpoles, snails, turtles, crabs, and any other creatures that may live in these waters. Look also for the slippery, slimy algae growing on rocks and driftwood. You may discover some ribbon-like blades of eelgrass growing from a clump of roots in the mud, or the feathery strands of waterweed waving gently in the current. Or, at the edge of the sea, you may see several kinds of seaweed, perhaps a sheet of light green sea lettuce, a rope of floating brown sargassum, or a spray of rockweed, which is kept afloat by balloon-like air bladders. If it is a sunny day and the glare of the sun on the water begins to tire your eyes, try to make a shadow on the water. Then look through your own shadow and see what else you can discover. Strange plants, interesting insects, and amazing animals of many kinds—you should be able to discover some of them just by using your own powers of observation.

You may also find some interesting nonliving things to observe and collect and experiment with. Look for empty shells of different sizes, colors, and kinds. You may discover, too, some pieces of smooth driftwood, worn into graceful shapes or festooned with green algae or encrusted with shell-covered animals.

As you gaze down into this water world, think of it as an environment for living things. Plants and animals, water and rocks, and the light that filters down from the sun—all have effects upon each other. Among the animals, there is a ceaseless struggle to catch something to eat—and to avoid being caught and eaten. But nearly every living thing you see can provide food for some other living thing. Tiny tadpoles eat algae and other water plants; bigger tadpoles and large insects eat the little tadpoles; fish and frogs eat insects; and the smaller fish are eaten by the larger fish. Yet there are almost always enough of each kind of creature left to keep the waters well stocked. Nature has provided with great abundance in order that this eat-and-be-eaten life can continue. As you watch the struggle for existence in the water world, you will discover some interesting relationships among the creatures who live and die there.

After you have begun to look at and listen to and think about some of the things that are happening at the water's edge, perhaps you will want to explore further, using some of the methods and materials suggested in the next chapter. You can work alone or with friends, boys or girls of almost any age. You may find new interests and hobbies that will last for many years. And, who knows, you may even discover some special science field that is important enough to you to become your life's work. Whatever you find in your exploring at the water's edge, you are sure to have the fun of adventure and the thrill of discovery.

SCIENTIFIC EQUIPMENT AND METHODS

After you have spent some time just looking, listening, and sniffing at the water's edge, you will be ready to begin your scientific exploring. In order to work in a systematic and effective way, you will need to have the proper tools and equipment. Some of these things you may have at home or at school. Some you may be able to borrow or buy. Most of them, however, you can make or assemble from odds and ends found in the kitchen, the tool shed, and the rubbish barrel. Remember that these are only *suggestions* of things that may be useful to you. For your particular exploring projects, you will probably need only a few of the items listed here.

Equipment to Help You Observe
  Hand-lens magnifying glass for all careful observing
  Low-power microscope for observing life in drops of water
  A glass dish for looking down into the water

Tools for Collecting Specimens
  Garden trowel
  Putty knife

Large spading fork
Small hand fork or rake
Kitchen strainer, 4″ to 5″ across
Tin cans
Spoons
Nylon water net

Containers for Live Specimens
Small glass jars with screw tops, the kind used for peanut butter and mayonnaise
Metal or plastic window screening
Tank aquarium; fish globe; large wide-mouthed pickle jar, or other large glass containers
Glass-walled or wire-screen terrarium
Metal pail
Cake pan
Pie tins
Dishpan
Plastic jars and dishes

Materials for Making and Keeping Collections of Nonliving Things
Cardboard egg cartons
Cigar boxes with cardboard dividers
Glass or clear plastic pill bottles with caps
Sheets of heavy white paper for mounting seaweed and other water-plant specimens
Traylike cardboard boxes that hosiery comes in
Other shallow cardboard boxes

Materials for Recording Things
Notebook and pencil
Sketch pad and crayons or paints
Camera and film
Labels for permanent collections
Waterproof ink and pen for writing labels
Scotch tape
Scrapbook

Miscellaneous Supplies
Small stiff scrubbing brush
Sandpaper
Scissors
Pocket knife
Wire
Stapler
Old pots and pans
Old newspapers
Old cardboard boxes
Modeling clay
Plaster of Paris

Using some of the materials listed above, you can make some simple but useful tools and equipment. Here are a few ideas to get you started.

Make a scoop for water creatures by fastening an ordinary kitchen strainer to a long handle. For the handle, use a dowel rod, a broom handle, or a yardstick. Use wire or very strong twine to tie the short handle of the strainer to the long rod or stick. Another kind of scoop can be made from a small tin can. Punch holes with a large nail or an ice pick in the bottom of a frozen-juice can. Bend the top of the can backward and nail it to a long, flat handle. Use the tin-can scoop when you want to dredge up mud or sand from the bottom of a body of water.

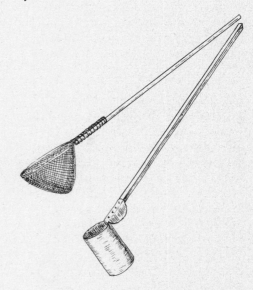

A handy net to use for dragging through the water can be made from a nylon stocking. Use a ladies' stocking, one that has no wide runs in it. Spread open the top and sew it around a wooden hoop, the kind sold in dime stores as embroidery hoops. Next, take two pieces of strong, heavy cord, each about a foot long. Poke four holes in the stocking right next to the hoop. Think of the hoop as the face of a clock, and punch the holes at twelve o'clock, three o'clock, six o'clock, and nine o'clock. Tie one end of one cord in the twelve-o'clock and the opposite end in the six-o'clock hole. Tie one end of the other card in the three-o'clock hole and the opposite end in the nine-o'clock hole. Then, hold up your net by the two loops of cord. Where the cords cross, tie them together with a long, strong cord. Use the long cord to hold or to tie to a boat when you drag your nylon net through the water.

Use glass jars of all sizes as containers for live water creatures. Make covers for the jars by bending pieces of wire or plastic window screening to fit over the open tops. Cheesecloth or mosquito netting can also be used to cover open jars. If cloth is used, you will have to tie it around the jar neck with a string or fasten it with a strong rubber band.

A large, beautiful, and inexpensive aquarium can be made from a five-gallon water bottle. This is the way to do it. Lay the bottle on its side. Make a hollow-square wooden frame for it to rest on. This can be made of four one-half-by-one-inch strips. This light frame will keep the bottle from rolling. If the bottle has a cork, pound the cork in tightly so that it is completely watertight. If it is a screw-cap bottle, make sure that the cap will not leak. You may wish to seal the cork or the cap by covering it with sealing wax. However, this is not necessary if you are sure that water cannot leak out.

Your next step is to go to a tombstone cutter and have one side of the bottle sandblasted off. This will cost very little, and the man who does the job will see to it that the cut edges of the bottle are sandblasted smooth. Your aquarium will then be ready to use. Large water bottles are

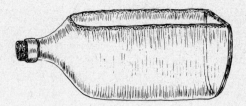

often made of lovely blue-green glass, which makes a very real-looking setting for underwater gardens.

Small aquariums can be made in any glass containers that are wide-mouthed. A container with a small opening does not allow enough oxygen to reach the water's surface. If you are trying to keep water specimens for any length of time, do not put them into a narrow-necked bowl or jar filled to the top with water. If you use such a vessel, fill it only to the widest part. This will leave a large area of surface water for the air to reach.

As you get on with your exploring, you will invent new uses for old materials. You will discover new ways of taking care of the particular collections and experiments that interest you most.

In order to work scientifically, you will want to use not only proper tools and equipment but also proper ways of working. Scientists usually follow definite steps when they are trying to find out about something. They use what is called a scientific method. Here is an outline of some steps you might like to follow in order to work in a scientific way.

FIRST, CHOOSE A PROBLEM. Think about what you want to discover. Decide on a question you want to have answered. You may have some questions like the following ones.

Are all worms alike?

Why do some starfish have one short arm?

How long does it take for a tadpole to grow into a frog?

Are dragonflies dangerous?

Can a crab live out of water?

SECOND, GATHER INFORMATION. Use as many ways as possible to collect information about the subject of your problem. Here are some ways in which you can get information.

Make observations

Collect samples or live specimens

Look at pictures

Go to see exhibits in museums

Read about things in books

Ask people who know something about the subject

THIRD, MAKE TESTS OR EXPERIMENTS.   Try to find answers to your questions by trying things out. Use measurements when you can. Experiment in ways like the following.

Measure how fast something grows

Try feeding different kinds of food to animals you are studying

Test a creature's senses with a flashlight, strong perfume on a wad of cotton, raw liver, and a bell

Try growing water plants in sunshine and in shade

Saw shells in half

FOURTH, KEEP RECORDINGS OF THINGS YOU SEE AND DO.   Try some of these different ways of recording your observations and experiments.

Keep a diary, listing the things you see and do on various days

Make black and white sketches, diagrams, and charts

Make colored drawings and water-color paintings from nature

Take photographs and keep them in an album

Cut out pictures and articles from magazines and newspapers and paste them in a scrapbook

FIFTH, DECIDE ON A POSSIBLE ANSWER TO YOUR ORIGINAL PROBLEM.   Your answer should be based on all the information you have gathered on the subject.

What did your observations show?

What did your experiments suggest?

What is the opinion of experts?

What do the books say?

Have you found any differences of opinion on the subject?

What is YOUR opinion?

Why?

SIXTH, CHECK AND RECHECK YOUR CONCLUSION BY MORE OBSERVATIONS, READING, AND EXPERIMENTING. It is important to realize that even after you have gone through all of these steps, the answers you discover may be true for only a certain time and under certain conditions. Scientists often remind us that there are few if any answers that are true for ever and ever. The earth and all that is in it, on it, and around it is continuously changing. As things change, and as more things are discovered, the answers to problems may change, too. Few questions have a single simple answer. While you are searching for answers, you will be making many discoveries. You will also be getting practical experience in using scientific methods.

INSECTS OF THE WATER WORLD

The first animal life you are likely to notice as you begin to explore is the flitting, darting, whirling, diving life of insects. Of all the water animals that are big enough for you to see, most of them are insects. You can find them in quiet ponds, in flowing streams, in roadside ditches, and in lakes that are edged with green rushes. Any body of fresh water with green plants growing in or around it will have many kinds of insects living among the leaves, stems, and roots.

As you look down into the water through a tangle of green plants, you will see a jungle in which strange animals live and die. Some of these animals seem frightening and ugly. Others look graceful and lovely. All of them are wonderfully formed for the jobs they have to do—hunt food, capture prey, escape enemies, find mates, lay eggs, and finally die and become part of the earth's crust.

As you watch several small creatures diving through the water or darting across the surface, you may wonder whether they are insects or some other kinds of water animals. It is not always easy to tell which are insects. Here are some clues to help you identify them.

First of all, water insects have the same general features as all insects. Every adult is a six-legged animal with a body that is in three parts. Its body has no bones but is protected by a hard coating or shell. Also, nearly every adult insect has two pairs of wings. And nearly every insect, no matter where it lives, passes through three or four separate stages during its lifetime.

The four-stage insects lay eggs that hatch into larvae, which are little wormlike creatures. The larvae eat and grow until they are ready for the third stage. Then they build themselves cocoons in which they rest quietly. In this stage they are called pupae. During the pupa stage, their bodies gradually change into adult forms. At the end of the pupa stage, the insects break out of their cocoons and are ready to fly off as winged adults.

The three-stage insects lay eggs, too. But their eggs hatch into nymphs or naiads, which are quite different from wormlike larvae. They are called nymphs or naiads after the water sprites in Greek and Roman myths. The baby water insects can breathe, eat, and grow under the water. In time, the nymphs or naiads climb out of their water world, split their skins, and emerge as winged, air-breathing insects. They are the adults that will return to the water when the time comes to mate and lay their eggs. Such insects grow from egg to nymph or naiad and to adult, while other insects change from egg to larva to pupa and then to adult. It is in the adult stage that insects are easily recognized, mainly by their six legs, three-part bodies, and two pairs of wings.

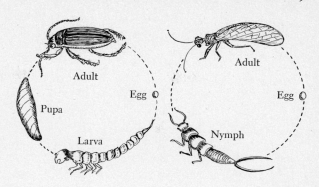

Left, Water beetle: A four-stage insect. *Right,* Stone fly: A three-stage insect.

How many different kinds of adult insects can you spot as you explore the water's edge? Watch for them flying among the water weeds on the shore, hiding in the blossoms of water lilies, hopping and crawling among the rocks, skating over the surface of the water, diving beneath the surface, and clinging to the underwater stems of plants. Watch a single insect for a long time and try to figure out what it is doing. Chances are that it is busy getting food to eat or oxygen to breathe.

Related Reading

References for Adults

ARTICLES

Adler, Irving. "On Writing Science Books for Children." *The Horn Book Magazine,* vol. 61 (October 1965). An explanation of the goals of a science writer.

Selsam, Millicent. "Nature Writing: Scientific and Nonscientific" in *Readings about Children's Literature,* Evelyn Rose Robinson, ed. New York: McKay, 1966. A discussion of the criteria for science books by a fine writer.

BOOKS

Huck, Charlotte S. and Doris Young Kuhn. *Children's Literature in the Elementary School.* 2d ed. New York: Holt, Rinehart and Winston, Inc., 1968. See the chapter on Informational Books.

Huus, Helen. *Children's Books To Enrich the Social Studies,* rev. ed. Washington, D.C.: National Council for the Social Studies, 1966. An annotated bibliography of fiction and nonfiction for children about history and contemporary life.

Smith, James Steel. *A Critical Approach to Children's Literature.* New York: McGraw-Hill, 1967. Chapter 11 is entitled "The Child and the Facts: Nonfiction for Children."

Smith, Lillian. *The Unreluctant Years.* Chicago: American Library Association, 1953. One chapter of this fine book is devoted to nonfiction.

BOOK LISTS AND REVIEWS

AAA Scientific Book List for Children. Published by the American Association for the Advancement of Science, 1963.

Reviews in *The Bulletin of the Center for Children's Books.*

Reviews in *The Horn Book Magazine.*

The annual list of the best science books for children published each November by *Natural History.*

Books for Children

CONCEPT BOOKS

Adler, Irving and Ruth. *Things That Spin.* New York: John Day, 1960. An activity book that can help children understand motion. (Grades 4–6)

_____. *Why? A Book of Reasons.* New York: John Day, 1961. Information about many topics is given in question and answer form. (Grades 4–6)

_____. *Why and How? A Second Book of Reasons.* New York: John Day, 1963. (Grades 4–6)

Black, Algernon. *The First Book of Ethics.* Illustrated by Rick Schreiter. New York: F. Watts, 1965. A beginning book on interpersonal behavior and personal standards. (Grade 4–up)

Bronowski, J., and Millicent Selsam. *Biography of an Atom.* Illustrated by Weimer Pursell. New York: Harper & Row, 1965. Interesting explanation of atoms, a concept children often have difficulty understanding. As further discoveries are made this book may need revising. (Grades 3–7)

Clark, Mary Lou. *You and Relativity.* Illustrated by Bill Sanders. Chicago: Childrens Press, 1965. A discussion of and an excerpt from this book can be found in this chapter. (Grade 4–up)

Froman, Robert. *Faster and Faster, a Book about Speed.* Illustrated by Arnold Spilka. New York: Viking, 1965. The concepts of speed and relativity are explained. (Grades 2–5)

Ravielli, Anthony. *The World Is Round.* New York: Viking, 1963. A concept book for children who are not able to really believe that the earth, which seems flat to them, is round. Also develops concepts about space and time. (Grades 3–5)

Schneider, Herman and Nina. *Follow the Sunset.* Illustrated by Lucille Corcos. New York: Doubleday, 1952. (Grades 1–4)

_____. *How Big Is Big? From Stars to Atoms,* rev. ed. Illustrated by Symeon Shimin. New York: W. R. Scott, 1950. The concepts of distance and size are explored. (Grades K–4)

Tresselt, Alvin. *How Far Is Far?* Illustrated by Ward

Brackett. New York: Parents Institute, 1964. The concept of distance is explored through illustrations and metaphors. (Grades K–3)

MAN

Anthropology and Archaeology

Friedman, Estell. *Man in the Making.* Illustrated by Frederic Marvin. New York: Putnam, 1960. Information about how anthropologists work and the contributions they have made. (Grades 5–9)

Mead, Margaret. *Anthropologists and What They Do.* New York: F. Watts, 1965. A description of anthropologists at work. (Grade 7–up)

_____. *People and Places.* Illustrated by W. T. Mars and Jan Fairservis. Cleveland: World Publishing, 1959. A description of the questions anthropologists ask and their methods of observing and recording. (Grade 7–up)

Perkins, Carol Morse. *The Shattered Skull.* New York: Atheneum, 1965. The investigation of the Leakey study of prehistoric man in Africa. (Grades 4–6)

Watts, Edith Whitney. *Archaeology, Exploring the Past.* New York: New York Graphic, 1965. The work of archaeologists is shown through a detailed description of the discovery and identification of a small pot. (Grade 9–up)

The Arts

Audsley, James. *The Book of Ballet.* Illustrated by Grace Golden, 2d rev. ed. New York: Warne, 1964. The history of ballet and biographies of some famous dancers. (Grade 5–up)

Glubok, Shirley. *The Art of Ancient Egypt.* Designed by Gerard Nook. New York: Atheneum, 1962. One of a series of books about art periods. Excellent photographs illustrate the texts. (Grades 3–8) Others in the series are:

_____. *The Art of Ancient Greece.* Designed by Oscar Krauss. New York: Atheneum, 1963. (Grades 3–8)

———. *The Art of the Eskimo.* Designed by Oscar Krauss. New York: Harper & Row, 1964. (Grades 2–6)

Goulden, Shirley. *The Royal Book of Ballet.* Illustrated by Maraja. Chicago: Follett, 1962. The plots of some popular ballets are retold. (Grade 5–up)

History

Asimov, Isaac. *Roman Republic.* Boston: Houghton Mifflin, 1966. (Grade 7–up)

———. *The Roman Empire.* Boston: Houghton Mifflin, 1967. Both of these readable books bring into focus the historical events up to the beginning of the sixth century. (Grades 8–11)

Barnes, Eric Wollencott. *Free Men Must Stand, the American War of Independence.* Illustrated by W. N. Wilson. New York: McGraw-Hill, 1962. A discussion of and an excerpt from this book can be found in this chapter. (Grade 7–up)

Berke, Ernest, author-illustrator. *The North American Indians.* New York: Doubleday, 1963. A beautifully illustrated book. (Grades 4–6)

Bleeker, Sonia. *The Apache Indians, Raiders of the Southwest.* Illustrated by Althea Karr. New York: Morrow, 1951. One of a series about past Indian life written in semifictionalized form by an anthropologist. (Grades 4–6) Other books in the series are: *The Cherokee, Indians of the Mountains* (Illustrated by Althea Karr), 1952; *The Chippewa Indians, Rice Gatherers of the Great Lakes* (Illustrated by Patricia Boodell), 1955; *The Crow Indians, Hunters of the Northern Plains* (Illustrated by Althea Karr), 1953; *Indians of the Longhouse, the Story of the Iroquois* (Illustrated by Althea Karr), 1950; *The Navajo* (Illustrated by Patricia Boodell), 1958.

Commager, Henry Steele. *The First Book of American History.* Illustrated by Leonard Everett Fisher. New York: F. Watts, 1957. An interesting survey of American history through World War II. (Grades 4–6)

Daugherty, James. *Of Courage Undaunted: Across the Continent with Lewis and Clark.* New York: Viking, 1951. A discussion of and excerpts from this book can be found in this chapter. (Grades 5–9)

Denny, Norman, and Josephine Filmer-Sankey. *The Bayeux Tapestry: The Story of the Norman Conquest: 1066.* New York: Atheneum, 1966. This nine-hundred-year-old tapestry shows the Norman view of the battle between Harold's forces and the Norman invaders of England. This book reproduces the tapestry with textual description of the events illustrated. (Grades 5–8)

Dines, Glen. *Overland Stage.* New York: Macmillan, 1961. A discussion of and an excerpt from this book can be found in this chapter. (Grades 4–6)

Dowd, David L. *The French Revolution.* New York: American Heritage, 1965. An interesting and authentic presentation of a dramatic event. (Grade 6–up)

Fisher, Leonard Everett. *The Hatters.* New York: F. Watts, 1965. One of a series of illustrated books about colonial trades. Others in the series are: *The Papermakers,* 1965; *The Wigmakers,* 1965. (Grade 4–up)

Foster, Genevieve. *Abraham Lincoln's World.* New York: Scribner, 1944. One of a series that presents an overview of the history and culture of the world during one man's lifetime. Other books in the series are: *Augustus Caesar's World,* 1947; *Birthdays of Freedom, Book One,* 1952; *Birthdays of Freedom, Book Two,* 1957; *George Washington's World,* 1941; *The World of Captain John Smith: 1580–1631,* 1959; *The World of Columbus and Sons,* 1965. (Grades 6–9)

Gringhuis, Dick. *The Big Dig, a Frontier Fort Comes to Life.* New York: Dial, 1962. A description of the excavation of the fort at Mackinac. (Grades 3–7)

Hodges, C. Walter, author-illustrator. *The Norman Conquest.* New York: Coward-McCann, 1966. The background for the Norman invasion and the Battle of Hastings is presented through text and dramatic full-color illustrations. (Grades 3–7)

Hoff, Rhoda. *Africa, Adventures in Eyewitness History.* New York: Walck, 1963. One of a series of books. The information comes from personal reports (diaries, letters, essays) by people who have lived or traveled in the country. Editorial comments add information. (Grade 3–up)

———. *America, Adventures in Eyewitness History.* New York: Walck, 1962. (Grade 7–up)

———. *Russia, Adventures in Eyewitness History.* New York: Walck, 1964. (Grades 7–9)

Johnson, Gerald White. *America Grows Up.* Illustrated by Leonard Everett Fisher. New York: Morrow, 1960. The second book in a trilogy. The first book covers the period from Columbus' discoveries to the Constitutional Convention of 1787, the second ends with the United States ready to enter World War I, and the last of the series covers the period from 1917 to the Eisenhower years. The other titles are: *America Is Born,* 1959; *America Moves Forward,* 1960. (Grade 7–up)

Judson, Clara Ingram. *St. Lawrence Seaway.* Illustrated by Lorence F. Bjorklund. Chicago: Follett, 1959. A discussion of and an excerpt from this book can be found in this chapter. (Grades 5–9)

Lester, Julius. *To Be a Slave.* Illustrated by Tom Feelings. New York: Dial, 1968. A powerful collection of reminiscences of Negro life, most of which were written by ex-slaves, illustrates the Negro experience in America from the early abductions in Africa through the Civil War and segregation. (Grades 7–12)

McGovern, Ann. . . . *If You Lived in Colonial Times.* Illustrated by Brinton Turkle. New York: Four Winds, 1964. Answers to questions that would be asked by primary grade children. (Grades 1–3)

Meltzer, Milton, editor. *In Their Own Words, a History of the American Negro, 1865–1966.* Three volumes. New York: Crowell, 1965. Excerpts from letters, books, court testimony, and speeches. Volume I covers 1619 to 1865; Volume II, 1865 to 1916; Volume III, 1916 to 1966. (Grade 7–up)

Meredith, Robert, and E. Brooks Smith. *Pilgrim Courage.* Illustrated by Leonard Everett Fisher. Boston: Little, Brown, 1962. Information from Governor Bradford's journal. (Grade 7–up) The following two books are also based on eyewitness accounts.

―――――. *The Quest of Columbus,* Illustrated by Leonard Everett Fisher. Boston: Little, Brown, 1966. (Grade 7–up)

―――――. *Riding with Coronado,* Illustrated by Leonard Everett Fisher. Boston: Little, Brown, 1964. (Grade 6–up)

Reeder, Red. *The Story of the Civil War.* Illustrated by Frederick Chapman. New York: Duell, Sloan, 1958. Colonel Reeder has written interesting and authentic books about two American wars. (Grade 9–up). The second one is *The Story of the War of 1812,* 1960.

Smith, E. Brooks, and Robert Meredith. *The Coming of the Pilgrims.* Illustrated by Leonard Everett Fisher. Boston: Little, Brown, 1964. An adaptation for younger children of *Pilgrim Courage* by the same authors. (Grades 1–3)

Tunis, Edwin, author-illustrator. *Shaw's Fortune: The Picture Story of a Colonial Plantation.* Cleveland: World Publishing, 1966. Mr. Tunis's books are well researched and attractive introductions to history for younger children. Other titles: *Colonial Living,* 1957; *Colonial Craftsmen,* 1965. (Grades 6–up)

The Human Body

Cohen, Robert. *The Color of Man.* Illustrated with photographs by Ken Heyman. New York: Random House, 1968. An explanation of the causes of different color of hair, skin and eyes. A genetic theory is presented first, followed by a discussion of the development of color prejudice. A valuable book for parents and teachers to read or give to children. (Grades 5–9)

Lerner, Marguerite Rush. *Who Do You Think You Are? The Story of Heredity.* Illustrated by Polly Bolian. Englewood Cliffs, N.J.: Prentice-Hall, 1963. An explanation for children of heredity's influence. (Grades 4–7)

Ravielli, Anthony. *Wonders of the Human Body.* New York: Viking, 1954. Text and illustrations develop an understanding of the body. (Grades 4–8)

Zim, Herbert. *What's Inside of Me?* Illustrated by Herschel Wartik. New York: Morrow, 1952. A discussion of human anatomy. (Grades 2–5)

―――――. *Your Heart and How It Works.* Illustrated by Gustav Schrotter. New York: Morrow, 1959. (Grades 2–5)

Human Societies

Evans, Eva Knox. *All About Us.* Illustrated by Vana Earle. New York: Capitol, 1957. A discussion of how culture influences behavior. (Grades 2–6)

Fisher, Dorothy Canfield. *A Fair World for All, the Meaning of the Declaration of Human Rights.* Illustrated by Jeanne Bendick. New York: McGraw-Hill, 1952. Each article of the Declaration of Human Rights is clearly explained by analogies to situations from everyday life. (Grade 5–up)

Johnson, Gerald. *The Congress.* Illustrated by Leonard Everett Fisher. New York: Morrow, 1963. Background information about an important element of American national government. (Grades 7–9)

Levine, David. *What Does a Congressman Do?* Photographs by Ira Mandelbaum. New York: Dodd, Mead, 1965. Information on America's governmental system. (Grades 4–6)

Showers, Paul. *Indian Festivals.* Illustrated by Lorence Bjorklund. New York: Crowell, 1969. An interesting explanation of the festivals of contemporary Indians. (Grades 2–6)

Thompson, Hildegard. *Geting To Know American Indians Today.* Illustrated by Shannon Stirnweiss. New York: Coward-McCann, 1965. A presentation of modern Navajo life. (Grades 3–5)

SCIENCE

Animals

Carthy, J. D. *Animals and Their Ways, the Science of Animal Behavior.* New York: Natural History, 1965. Inborn and learned behavior are discussed. (Grade 7–up)

Earle, Olive. *Mice at Home and Afield.* New York: Morrow, 1957. The life cycle of mice. (Grades 4–6)

George, John and Jean. *Masked Prowler, the Story of a Raccoon.* New York: Dutton, 1950. One of several books by the Georges about the life cycles of animals. Dramatic stories of their struggles for survival. Little anthropomorphism. (Grades 6–9) Similar books are:

————. *Vision, the Mink.* New York: Dutton, 1949. (Grades 6–9)

————. *Vulpes, the Red Fox.* New York: Dutton, 1948. (Grades 5–9)

Goudey, Alice E. *Here Come the Bears!* Illustrated by Garry MacKenzie. New York: Scribner, 1954. One of a series of books about the life cycle of animals. Other books are: *Here Come the Beavers!,* 1957; *Here Come the Seals!,* 1957. (Grades 1–5)

Mason, George F. *Animal Homes.* New York: Morrow, 1947. One of a series of books about animal life. Other books by the author are: *Animal Tools,* 1951; *Animal Tracks,* 1943; *Animal Weapons,* 1949. (Grades 4–6)

Pistorious, Anna. *What Dinosaur Is It?* Chicago: Follett, 1958. An identification book in question and answer form. (Grades 3–6)

Selsam, Millicent E. *Animals As Parents.* Illustrated by John Kaufmann. New York: Morrow, 1965. Facts are not isolated but arranged from the simple to the complex in parental behavior. (Grades 7–9)

————. *Benny's Animals and How He Put Them in Order.* Illustrated by Arnold Lobel. New York: Harper & Row, 1966. Classification of animals. (Grades K–3)

————. *The Courtship of Animals.* Illustrated by John Kaufmann. New York: Morrow, 1964. (Grades 7–9)

Zim, Herbert. *Golden Hamsters.* Illustrated by Herschel Wartik. New York: Morrow, 1951. The text provides general information while the illustrations and their captions provide more details. (Grades 4–6)

Birds

Darling, Louis, author-illustrator. *The Gull's Way.* New York: Morrow, 1965. Text, photographs, and pencil drawings complement each other in a detailed and fascinating report on the life patterns of herring gulls on a small island off the coast of Maine. (Grades 4–9)

Earle, Olive. *Robins in the Garden.* New York: Morrow, 1953. The life cycle of robins. (Grades 1–5)

————. *Swans of Willow Pond.* New York: Morrow, 1955. (Grades 1–5)

Kieran, John. *An Introduction to Birds.* New York: Doubleday, 1965. A guide for the young bird watcher. (Grades 5–9)

Peterson, Roger Tory. *How To Know the Birds,* 2d ed. Boston: Houghton Mifflin, 1957. Guide for middle-grade bird watchers. (Grades 3–5)

————. *The Junior Book of Birds.* Boston: Houghton Mifflin, 1939. (Grades 3–6)

Pistorious, Anna. *What Bird Is It?* Chicago: Follett, 1945. An identification book in question and answer form. (Grades 3–6)

Zim, Herbert. *Owls.* Illustrated by James Gordon Irving. New York: Morrow, 1950. A discussion of the habits and physical characteristics of the owls of North America. (Grades 3–6)

————, and Ira N. Gabrielson. *Birds: A Guide to the Most Familiar American Birds,* rev. ed. Illustrated by James Gordon Irving. New York: Golden Press, 1956. A useful guide for the person interested in birds. (Grade 6–up)

Books about Both Animal and Plant Life

Hogner, Dorothy Childs. *Conservation in America.* Illustrated by Nils Hogner. Philadelphia: Lippincott, 1958. A nondidactic presentation of the conflicting needs of nature and man in America. (Grades 7–9)

Reynolds, Christopher. *Small Creatures in My Garden.* New York: Farrar, Straus, 1965. A journal of the observations of an English writer. (Grades 3–6)

Russell, Selveig Paulson. *Saving Wildlife for Tomorrow.* Illustrated by Henry Lukes. Chicago: Melmont, 1960. The conflict of interests between man's needs and the needs of wildlife is shown. (Grades 3–8)

Sanger, Marjory Bartlett. *Cypress Country.* Illustrated by Christine Price. Cleveland: World Publishing, 1965. The sounds, colors, and activities of an entire day in a cypress swamp are dramatically presented in the text and pictures of this book. Excellent nature writing. (Grades 4–8)

Selsam, Millicent. *How To Be a Nature Detective.* Illustrated by Ezra Jack Keats. New York: Harper & Row, 1958. Observation skills are taught in this "easy" book. (Grades 1–5)

Zim, Herbert. *How Things Grow.* Illustrated by Gustav Schrotter. New York: Morrow, 1960. A brief presentation of growth patterns of plants, animals, and people. (Grades 2–5)

Books of Activities and Experiments

Cooper, Elizabeth. *Science on the Shores and Banks.* New York: Harcourt, 1960. A discussion of and an excerpt from this book can be found in this chapter. (Grades 5–7)

Freeman, Ira M., and Mae B. *Fun with Scientific Experiments.* New York: Random House, 1960. Over forty simple experiments that demonstrate scientific principles. Photographs and instructions are helpful. (Grades 4–7)

Leeming, Joseph. *The Real Book of Science Experiments.* Illustrated by Bette J. Davis. New York: Garden City Books, 1954. Experiments that demonstrate scientific principles. (Grades 4–6)

Milgrom, Harry. *Adventures with a String.* Illustrated by Tom Funk. New York: Dutton, 1965. Children who do the suggested experiments with string will develop greater skills in observing and making deductions. (Preschool–grade 2)

Podendorf, Illa. *101 Science Experiments.* Illustrated by Robert Borja. Chicago: Childrens Press, 1960. Varied experiments with plants, electricity, heat, water, sound, light, air, etc. (Grades 3–5)

————. *The True Book of More Science Experiments.* Illustrated by Chauncey Maltman. Chicago: Childrens Press, 1956. (Grades 1–3)

————. *The True Book of Science Experiments.* Illustrated by Mary Salem. Chicago: Childrens Press, 1954. (Grades 1–3)

————. *The True Book of Weather Experiments.* Illustrated by Felix Palm. Chicago: Childrens Press, 1961. (Grades K–4)

Selsam, Millicent, E. *Play with Plants.* Illustrated by James MacDonald. New York: Morrow, 1949. Through the "play" activities, the young reader learns to observe carefully. (Grades 4–9). Others in the series are: *Play with Seeds* (Illustrated by Helen Ludwig), 1957; *Play with Vines* (Illustrated by Fred Scherer), 1951.

Schneider, Herman and Nina. *Now Try This.* Illustrated by Bill Ballantine. New York: W. R. Scott, 1947. A book of experiments that leads the reader to discover scientific principles and methods. (Grades 4–8)

Schwartz, Julius. *It's Fun To Know Why.* Illustrated by Edwin Herron. New York: McGraw-Hill, 1952. Simple experiments, presented in a conversational style, that lead the reader to discover reasons for what happened. (Grades 4–6)

United Nations Educational, Scientific, and Cultural Organization. *UNESCO Source Book for Science Teaching: 700 Science Experiments for Everyone,* 2d ed. New York: UNESCO, 1962. Although written for science teachers, older elementary and junior high school students will find this book interesting. (Grades 6–12)

Wyler, Rose. *The First Book of Science Experiments.* Illustrated by Ida Scheib. New York: F. Watts, 1952. Safety and the scientific method are stressed. (Grades 4–6)

Wyler, Rose, and Eva-Lee Baird. *Science Teasers.* Illustrated by Jerry Robinson. New York: Harper & Row, 1966. An experiment book that can help develop independent thinking. (Grades 3–7)

Wyler, Rose, and Gerald Ames. *Prove It!* Illustrated by Tālivaldis Stubis. New York: Harper & Row, 1963. A science *I Can Read* book. Simple experiments for beginners. (Grades 1–3)

H_2O and Its Inhabitants

Archer, Sellers G. *Rain, Rivers and Reservoirs.* New York: Coward-McCann, 1963. The worldwide problems of conservation are shown. (Grades 6–8)

Buck, Margaret. *Along the Seashore.* New York: Abingdon, 1964. Both this and the following book describe plant and animal life found in these locations. (Grades 3–9). *In Ponds and Streams,* 1955.

Carlson, Carl Walter, and Bernice Wells Carlson. *Water Fit To Use.* Illustrated by Aline Hansens. New York: John Day, 1966. A discussion of one of the most serious problems facing modern man. (Grades 5–9)

Carson, Rachel Louise. *The Sea Around Us.* Adapted by Anne Terry White. New York: Golden Press, 1958. An adaptation of a fine book. (Grade 9–up)

Clarke, Arthur C. *The Challenge of the Sea.* Illustrated by Alex Schomburg. New York: Holt, Rinehart and Winston, Inc., 1960. Challenges such as navigating, exploring, harvesting, and using the seas resources are presented. (Grades 6–10)

Clemons, Elizabeth. *Tide Pools and Beaches.* Illustrated by Joe Gault. New York: Knopf, 1964. Coral, crabs, seaweed, shells, and starfish. Both scientific and common names are given. (Grades 3–6)

Cooper, Elizabeth. *Science on Shores and Banks.* New York: Harcourt, 1960. A discussion of and an excerpt from this activity book can be found in this chapter. (Grades 5–7)

George, Jean Craighead. *Spring Comes to the Ocean.* Illustrated by John Wilson. New York: Crowell, 1965. An excerpt from and a discussion of this book can be found in this chapter. (Grades 7–up)

Goudey, Alice. *Houses from the Sea.* Illustrated by

Adrienne Adams. New York: Scribner, 1959. A beautifully illustrated book about shells. (Grades 1–3)

Milne, Lorus and Margery. *The Crab That Crawled out of the Past*. Illustrated by Kenneth Gosner. New York: Atheneum, 1965. The behavior, physical appearance, and the evolution of crabs are described. (Grades 4–8)

Posell, Elsa. *The True Book of Whales and Other Sea Mammals*. Illustrated by Arthur Warheit. Chicago: Childrens Press, 1963. A brief book that gives most of the facts young children want to know. (Grades 1–4)

Selsam, Millicent. *Let's Get Turtles*. Illustrated by Arnold Lobel. New York: Harper & Row, 1965. An *I Can Read* book for young children. Observation and the scientific method are emphasized. (Grades K–3)

Sperry, Armstrong, author-illustrator. *Great River, Wide Land*. New York: Macmillan, 1967. Mr. Sperry describes the Rio Grande's geographic features, two thousand miles through mountains and desert; its history, from Indian times to the space age; and its economic and political significance. This is a well-written, dramatic work of nonfiction. (Grades 7–11)

Zim, Herbert S. *Sharks*. Illustrated by Stephen Howe. New York: Morrow, 1966. The text provides general information while the illustrations and their captions provide more details. (Grades 4–6)

Insects

Earle, Olive L. *Crickets*. New York: Morrow, 1956. The life cycle of crickets. (Grades 4–6)

Eeckhoudt, J. P. Vanden. *A Butterfly Is Born*. New York: Sterling, 1960. Excellent photographs with captions. (Grade 3–up)

Politi, Leo, author-illustrator. *The Butterflies Come*. New York: Scribners, 1957. Information about the Monarch butterflies in the Monterey Peninsula is given in story form in this picture book for young children. (Grades K–1)

Pistorious, Anna. *What Butterfly Is It?* Chicago: Follett, 1949. An identication book in question and answer form. (Grades 3–6)

Plants

Downer, Mary Louise. *The Flower*. Illustrated by Lucienne Bloch. New York: W. R. Scott, 1955. The development of seeds into plants. (Preschool–grade 1)

Grant, Madeleine P. *Wonder World of Microbes*. Illustrated by Clifford N. Geary. New York: McGraw-Hill, 1956. The continuity and development

of the discoveries of methods of microbe control are presented. (Grade 7–up)

Lerner, Sharon. *I Found a Leaf*. Minneapolis: Lerner, 1964. A guide for primary grade children, illustrated with crayon rubbings. (Grades K–2)

Pistorious, Anna. *What Tree Is It?* Chicago: Follett, 1955. An identification book in question and answer form. (Grades 3–6)

Selsam, Millicent E. *Birth of a Forest*. Illustrated by Barbara Wolff. New York: Harper & Row, 1964. The thousands-of-years process that changes a lake into a forest is shown. (Grades 4–6)

————. *Milkweed*. Photography by Jerome Wexler. New York: Morrow, 1967. The milkweed is explored through a clearly written text and photographs that magnify parts of the plant up to ten times their size. (Grades 4–6)

————. *Play with Plants*. Illustrated by James MacDonald. New York: Morrow, 1949. Through the "play" activities the young reader learns to observe carefully. (Grades 4–9) Others in the series are: *Play with Seeds* (Illustrated by Helen Ludwig), 1957; *Play with Vines* (Illustrated by Fred Scherer), 1951.

————. *See through the Jungle*. Illustrated by Winifred Lubell. New York: Harper & Row, 1957. (Grades 4–6)

Watts, May Theilgaard. *The Doubleday First Guide to Trees*. Illustrated by Michael Bevans. New York: Doubleday, 1964. A small sized, useful guide. (Grades K–5)

Webber, Irma E. *Bits That Grow Big*. New York: W. R. Scott, 1949. The development of seeds into plants. (Preschool–grade 1)

————. *Travellers All: The Story of How Plants Go Places*. New York: Scott, 1944. A discussion of and an excerpt from this book can be found in this chapter. (Grades 1–3)

The Solar System and Beyond

Branley, Franklyn M. *A Book of Mars for You*. Illustrated by Leonard Kessler. New York: Crowell, 1968. (Grades 3–6)

————. *A Book of the Milky Way Galaxy for You*. Illustrated by Leonard Kessler. New York: Crowell, 1965. (Grades 3–6)

————. *A Book of Stars for You*. Illustrated by Leonard Kessler. New York: Crowell, 1967. (Grades 1–4)

————. *A Book of Venus for You*. Illustrated by Leonard Kessler. New York: Crowell, 1969. (Grades 3–6)

————. *The Earth: Planet Number Three*. Illustrated by Helmut K. Wimmer. New York: Crowell, 1966. (Grade 7–up)

Fenton, Carroll Lane, and Mildred Adams. *Worlds in the Sky*, rev. ed. New York: John Day, 1963. (Grades 4–6)

Gallant, Roy A. *Exploring the Universe*, rev. ed. Illustrated by Lowell Hess. New York: Doubleday, 1968. (Grades 6–8)

Zim, Herbert S. *The Universe*. Illustrated by Gustav Schrotter. New York: Morrow, 1961. A survey of man's expanding knowledge and beliefs about the universe. (Grades 4–6)

————, and Robert H. Baker. *Stars: A Guide to the Constellations, Sun, Moon, Planets, and Other Features of the Heavens*. Illustrated by James Gordon Irving. New York: Golden Press, 1956. A helpful sky-watching guide for the beginner. (Grades 6–9)

Part V

POETRY

The poetry section of this anthology includes nursery rhymes, both traditional and modern adaptations; a thorough discussion of the elements of poetry to help develop the individual criteria for evaluation, necessary because so much trite and cloying verse is written for children; and a varied collection of poems children enjoy. As in the other parts of this anthology, examples from the literature of the eighteenth and nineteenth centuries are included for historical perspective.

In addition to contemporary poems for children, a section of poetry written by children is included. Many teachers encourage their students to write poetry, and there is no better motivation than reading poetry written by other children of their age. Poems written by adults are grouped under the following categories: Through the Seasons, Weather, Haiku, Holidays, Famous People, Animals, A Certain Mood, Personal Responses, Ballads and Songs, and Nonsense Poetry.

Preschool children delight in hearing and chanting poems. They, however, call them nursery rhymes and their favorite poet is Mother Goose. Since these rhymes form an excellent and charming introduction to poetry for the very young, as well as for kindergarten and first grade students, it seems inappropriate to separate them from the poetry enjoyed by older children. This is especially true when one considers how many of the respected and much discussed elements of poetry (rhyme, rhythm, alliteration, imagery, and so on) are to be found in nursery rhymes. Most parents, teachers, and librarians agree that every child should begin with Mother Goose rhymes.

The purpose of this section of the anthology is to stress the importance of poetry for children, to provide information useful in evaluating literary excellence in the genre, and to compile a collection of poems that neither patronizes nor bores children.

Chapter 14

Nursery Rhymes

From *National Nursery Rhymes* by J. B. Zwecker. Reprinted in *Illustrations of Children's Books, 1744–1945*, by Bertha E. Mahony et al., 1958. Courtesy of The Horn Book, Inc.

Nursery rhymes have long been a part of almost every culture's oral tradition. When young children have demanded entertainment, busy mothers have searched their memories for verses to sing or say to their children. Many rhymes came from the mother's own childhood, but others were adapted from contemporary songs, jests, and doggerel. Nursery rhymes are now considered the property of children, but few of them were originally meant exclusively for youngsters. Iona and Peter Opie in the introduction to their *Oxford Dictionary of Nursery Rhymes* explain the many ways in which adult literature and doggerel developed into nursery rhymes.

It can be safely stated that the overwhelming majority of nursery rhymes were not in the first place composed for children; in fact many are survivals of an adult code of joviality, and in their original wording were, by present standards, strikingly unsuitable for those of tender years. They are fragments of ballads or of folk songs ("One misty moisty morning" and "Old woman, old woman, shall we go a-shearing?"). They are remnants of ancient custom and ritual ("Ladybird, ladybird," and "We'll go to the wood"), and may hold the last echoes of long-forgotten evil (Where have you been all day?" and "London Bridge"). Some are memories of street cry and mummers' play ("Young lambs to sell! young lambs to sell!" and "On Christmas night I turned the spit"). One at least ("Jack Sprat") has long been proverbial. Others ("If wishes were horses," and "A man of words") are based on proverbs. One ("Matthew, Mark, Luke, and John") is a prayer of Popish days, another ("Go to bed, Tom") was a barrack room refrain. They have come out of taverns and mug houses. ("Nose, nose, jelly red nose" still flaunts the nature of its early environment.) They are the legacy of war and rebellion ("At the siege of Belle Isle" and "What is the rhyme for porringer?"). They have poked fun at religious practices ("Good morning, Father Francis") and laughed at the rulers of the day ("William and Mary, George and Anne"). They were the diversions of the scholarly, the erudite, and the wits (as Dr. Wallis on a "Twister," Dr. Johnson on a "Turnip seller," and Tom Brown on "Dr. Fell"). They were first made popular on the stage (Jack Cussans's "Robinson Crusoe") or in London streets (Jacob Beuler's "If I had a donkey"). They were rude jests (like "Little Robin Redbreast sat upon a rail"), or romantic lyrics of a decidedly free nature (as "Where are you going to, my pretty maid?"), which were carefully rewritten to suit the new discrimination at the turn of the last century. We can say almost without hesitation that, of those pieces which date from before 1800, the only true nursery rhymes (i.e. rhymes composed especially for the nursery) are the rhyming alphabets, the infant amusements (verses which accompany a game), and the lullabies. Even the riddles were in the first place designed for adult perplexity.[1]

Regardless of their origin, nursery rhymes have pleased generations of children. These verses should not be slighted in an increasingly sophisticated world; they contain many respected elements of poetry. Children enjoy their rhythm and rhyme, alliteration, onomatopoeia, and other sound patterns. Since young children are learning to handle the complexities of their language, they are delighted with and need to hear and say ear-pleasing word patterns. Nursery rhymes also introduce children to simple plots and character delineation. Rhymes that tell stories vary in complexity from "Solomon Grundy" to "The House

[1] Reprinted by permission of the Clarendon Press, Oxford, from *The Oxford Dictionary of Nursery Rhymes* edited by Iona and Peter Opie, 1951.

That Jack Built" and the personalities of Miss Muffet and Georgie Porgie are as interesting to youngsters as their stories. Children also enjoy the rhymes' humor which may be as innocent as "my son John" who "went to bed with his stockings on" or as seemingly cruel, to adults, as the crooked man who walked a crooked mile.

Nursery rhymes, or "melodies" as they are called in England, have long been associated with the name Mother Goose. Between 1760 and 1766 John Newbery, one of the first English publishers interested in children's books, published *Mother Goose's Melody: or Sonnets for the Cradle.* This small book included fifty-two nursery rhymes and sixteen songs "of that sweet Songster and Nurse of Wit and Humour, Master William Shakespeare." This book may have been edited by Oliver Goldsmith; he is thought to have written the preface and some of the facetious "Notes and Maxims, Historical, Philosophical and Critical." The importance of Newbery's *Mother Goose's Melody* is that it influenced most of the later books of nursery rhymes in England and America.

While many of the rhymes loved by today's children are from these old collections, some of the now traditional verses are remnants from the nineteenth century; for example, Jane Taylor's "Twinkle, Twinkle Little Star." Today's nursery rhymes, however, are not all from the past; children and mothers are still adapting old rhymes as well as creating new verses, riddles, and tongue-twisters, as can be seen in Carl Wither's modern collection, *A Rocket in My Pocket.*

Listening to children at play in any school yard or park will reveal that this genre of poetry is not dying but rather is a vital on-going force in the twentieth century. The Opies give examples of nursery rhymes being quoted not only in adult literature but also by twentieth-century English politicians as well as in advertising campaigns. During the 1960s popular songs were based on "Lavender's Blue" and "Parsley, Sage, Rosemary and Thyme."

For comparative purposes the following collection includes old rhymes, some now little known; contemporary, twentieth-century rhymes; and a few from foreign lands that are similar to those known by English and American children.

JOHN NEWBERY'S MOTHER GOOSE'S MELODY: or *Sonnets for Children*

1

Cock a doodle doo,
My Dame has lost her Shoe;
My Master's lost his Fiddle Stick,
And knows not what to do.

Cock a doodle doo,
What is my Dame to do?
Till Master finds his fiddling stick
She'll dance without her Shoe.

Cock a doodle doo,
My Dame has found her Shoe,
And Master's found his fiddling stick,
Sing doodle doodle doo.

Cock a doodle doo,
My Dame will dance with you,
While Master fiddles his fiddling stick,
For Dame and doodle doo.

The cock crows us up in the morning, that we may work for our bread, and not live upon charity or upon trust; *for he who lives upon charity shall be often affronted, and he that lives upon trust shall pay double.*

2

There was an old Woman
Lived under the Hill,
And if she's not gone
She lives there still.

This is a self-evident proposition which is the very essence of truth. *She lived under the hill, and if she's not gone, she lives there still.* Nobody will presume to contradict this. — Crausa.

3

Three wise men of Gotham
They went to Sea in a Bowl,
And if the Bowl had been stronger
My Song had been longer.

It is long enough. Never lament the loss of what is not worth having.

4

See saw, Margery Daw,
Jacky shall have a new Master;
Jacky must have but a penny a day,
Because he can work no faster.

It is a mean and scandulous practice in authors
to put notes to things that deserve no notice. —
Grotius.

5

A DIRGE

Little Betty Winckle she had a Pig,
It was a little Pig and not very big;
When he was alive he liv'd in Clover,
But now he's dead, and that's all over;
Johnny Winckle, he
Sat down and cry'd,
Betty Winckle she
Laid down and dy'd;
So there was an End of one, two, and three,
Johnny Winckle he,
Betty Winckle she,
And Piggy Wiggie.

A dirge is a song made for the dead; but
whether this was made for Betty Winckle or her
pig, is uncertain; no notice being taken of it by
Cambden, or any of the famous antiquarians.

6

There was an old Woman toss'd in a Blanket,
    Seventeen times as high as the Moon;
But where she was going no Mortal could tell,
    For under her arm she carried a Broom.
Old Woman, old Woman, old Woman, said I!
    Whither, ah whither, ah whither so high?
To sweep the cobwebs from the Sky,
    And I'll be with you by and by.

7

Who comes here?
    A Grenadier.
What do you want?
    A Pot of Beer.
Where is your Money?
    I've forgot.
    Get you gone
You drunken Sot.

8

Jack Sprat
Could eat no Fat,
His Wife could eat no Lean;
And so, betwixt them both,
They lick'd the platter clean.

9

High diddle, diddle,
The Cat and the Fiddle,
    The Cow jump'd over the Moon;
The little Dog laugh'd
To see such Craft,
    And the Dish ran away with the Spoon.

MISCELLANEOUS RHYMES

10

Thirty days hath September,
April, June, and November;
All the rest have thirty-one,
Excepting February alone,
And that has twenty-eight days clear
And twenty-nine in each leap year.

11

Cocks crow in the morn
    To tell us to rise,
And he who lies late
    Will never be wise;
For early to bed
    And early to rise,
Is the way to be healthy
    And wealthy and wise.

12

Monday's child is fair of face,
Tuesday's child is full of grace;
Wednesday's child is full of woe,
Thursday's child has far to go;
Friday's child is loving and giving,
Saturday's child works hard for its living;
But the child that is born on the Sabbath
    day
Is bonny and blithe, and good and gay.

"Monday's Child" from Andrew Lang, *The Nursery
Rhyme Book.*

13

Come, butter, come,
Come, butter, come!
Peter stands at the gate,
Waiting for a buttered cake;
Come, butter, come.
  (*for churning*)

14

Ride a cock horse
To Banbury Cross
To see a fair lady upon a white horse;
With rings on her fingers,
And bells on her toes,
She shall have music wherever she goes.

15

Mistress Mary, quite contrary,
 How does your garden grow?
With cockleshells, and silver bells,
 And pretty maids all in a row.

16

Jack be nimble,
 Jack be quick,
Jack jump over
 The candlestick.
Jump it lively,
 Jump it quick,
But don't knock over
 The candlestick.

17

Georgie, Porgie, pudding and pie,
Kissed the girls and made them cry;
When the boys came out to play,
Georgie Porgie ran away.

18

Higgledy, piggledy, my black hen,
She lays eggs for gentlemen;
Sometimes nine, sometimes ten;
Higgledy, piggledy, my black hen.

19

Come and see!
Come and see!
A black hen has laid
A white egg for me!

20

Little Robin Redbreast sat upon a tree,
Up went the Pussy cat, and down went he;
Down came the Pussy cat, away Robin ran,
Says little Robin Redbreast, "Catch me if you
 can."
Little Robin Redbreast jumped upon a wall,
Pussy cat jumped after him, and almost got a fall.
Little Robin Redbreast chirped and sang, and
 what did Pussy say?
Pussy cat said, "Mew," and Robin jumped away.

21

Pussy cat, pussy cat, where have you been?
I've been up to London to look at the queen.
Pussy cat, pussy cat, what did you there?
I frightened a little mouse under the chair.

22

Six little mice sat down to spin;
Pussy passed by and she peeped in.
What are you doing, my little men?
Weaving coats for gentlemen.
Shall I come in and cut off your threads?
No, no, Mistress Pussy, you'd bite off our
 heads.
Oh, no, I'll not; I'll help you to spin.
That may be so, but you don't come in.

23

Ladybird, ladybird,
Fly away home,
Your house is on fire
And your children all gone;

All except one
And that's little Ann
And she has crept under
The warming pan.

24

Lady bug, lady bug,
Fly away, do!
Fly to the mountain
To feed upon dew.

"Come and See!," and "Lady bug, lady bug," reprinted by permission of The World Publishing Company from *Chinese Mother Goose Rhymes*, selected and edited by Robert Wyndham. Special contents of this edition copyright © 1968 Robert Wyndham.

Feed upon dew
And when you are through,
Lady bug, lady bug,
Fly home again, do!

25
Baa, baa, black sheep,
　　Have you any wool?
"Yes, marry, have I,
　　Three bags full;
One for my master,
　　And one for my dame,
And one for the little boy
　　Who lives in the lane."

26
One misty moisty morning,
　　When cloudy was the weather,
I chanced to meet an old man,
　　Clothed all in leather.
He began to compliment
　　And I began to grin.
How do you do? And how do you do?
　　And how do you do again?

27
　　Rain, rain, go away,
　　　Come again another day;
　　Little Johnny wants to play.

28
Daffadowndilly
　　Has come up to town,
In a yellow petticoat
　　And a green gown.

29
　　Girls and boys, come out to play,
The moon doth shine as bright as day;
　　Leave your supper, and leave your sleep,
And come with your playfellows into the street.
　　Come with a whoop, come with a call,
Come with a good will or not at all.
　　Up the ladder and down the wall,
A half-penny roll will serve us all.
　　You find milk, and I'll find flour,
And we'll have a pudding in half an hour.

LULLABIES AND LYRICS

30
Bye, baby bunting,
Daddy's gone a-hunting,
To get a little rabbit skin
To wrap the baby bunting in.

31
Hush-a-bye baby, on the tree top,
When the wind blows the cradle will rock;
When the bough breaks the cradle will fall.
Down will come baby, cradle, and all.

32
Rock-a-bye, baby, thy cradle is green;
Father's a nobleman, mother's a queen;
And Betty's a lady, and wears a gold ring;
And Johnny's a drummer, and drums for the king.

33
Lavender's blue, diddle, diddle,
　　Lavender's green;
When I am king, diddle, diddle,
　　You shall be queen.
Call up your men, diddle, diddle,
　　Set them to work,
Some to the plough, diddle, diddle,
　　Some to the cart.
Some to make hay, diddle, diddle,
　　Some to thresh corn,
Whilst you and I, diddle, diddle,
　　Keep ourselves warm.

34
I saw a ship a-sailing,
　　A-sailing on the sea,
And oh! it was laden
　　With pretty things for thee!
There were raisins in the cabin,
　　And apples in the hold;
The sails were made of silk,
　　And the masts were made of gold.
The four-and-twenty sailors
　　That stood between the decks,
Were four-and-twenty white mice,
　　With chains about their necks.
The captain was a duck,
　　With a jacket on his back;
When the ship began to sail,
　　The captain cried, "Quack! quack!"

35
I had a little nut tree, nothing would it bear
But a silver nutmeg and a golden pear;
The king of Spain's daughter came to visit me,
And all because of my little nut tree.
I skipped over water, I danced over sea,
And all the birds in the air couldn't catch me.

36
I had a little pony,
    His name was Dapple-gray;
I lent him to a lady,
    To ride a mile away;
She whipped him, she slashed him,
    She rode him through the mire;
I would not lend my pony now
    For all the lady's hire.

37
Can you make a cambric shirt,
    Parsley, sage, rosemary, and thyme,
Without any seam or needlework?
    And you shall be a true lover of mine.

Can you wash it in yonder well,
    Parsley, sage, rosemary, and thyme,
Where never sprung water, nor rain ever fell?
    And you shall be a true lover of mine.

Can you dry it on yonder thorn,
    Parsley, sage, rosemary, and thyme,
Which never bore blossom since Adam was born?
    And you shall be a true lover of mine.

Now you've asked me questions three,
    Parsley, sage, rosemary, and thyme,
I hope you'll answer as many for me,
    And you shall be a true lover of mine.

Can you find me an acre of land,
    Parsley, sage, rosemary, and thyme,
Between the salt water and the sea sand?
    And you shall be a true lover of mine.

Can you plough it with a ram's horn,
    Parsley, sage, rosemary, and thyme,
And sow it all over with one pepper-corn?
    And you shall be a true lover of mine.

Can you reap it with a sickle of leather,
    Parsley, sage, rosemary, and thyme,
And bind it up with a peacock's feather?
    And you shall be a true lover of mine.

When you have done and finished your work,
    Parsley, sage, rosemary, and thyme,
Then come to me for your cambric shirt,
    And you shall be a true lover of mine.

MANY STORIES

38
Solomon Grundy
Born on a Monday,
Christened on Tuesday,
Married on Wednesday,
Took ill on Thursday,
Worse on Friday,
Died on Saturday,
Buried on Sunday;
This is the end
Of Solomon Grundy.

39
Hickory, dickory, dock,
The mouse ran up the clock.
    The clock struck one,
    The mouse ran down,
Hickory, dickory, dock.

40
Wee Willie Winkie runs through the town
Upstairs and downstairs, in his nightgown;
Rapping at the window, crying through the lock,
    "Are the children in their beds?
    Now it's eight o'clock."

41
Little Jack Horner
    Sat in a corner,
Eating his Christmas pie.
    He put in his thumb,
    And he pulled out a plum,
And said, "What a good boy am I!"

42
Little Bo-Peep has lost her sheep,
And can't tell where to find them;
Leave them alone, and they'll come home,
And bring their tails behind them.

Little Bo-Peep fell fast asleep,
And dreamt she heard them bleating;
But when she awoke, she found it a joke,
For still they all were fleeting.

Then up she took her little crook,
Determined for to find them;
She found them indeed, but it made her heart
    bleed,
For they'd left all their tails behind 'em!

It happened one day, as Bo-Peep did stray
Unto a meadow hard by—
There she espied their tails, side by side,
All hung on a tree to dry.

She heaved a sigh and wiped her eye,
And over the hillocks she raced;
And tried what she could, as a shepherdess should,
That each tail should be properly placed.

43
Little Boy Blue, come blow your horn,
The sheep's in the meadow, the cow's in the corn.
Where is the boy that looks after the sheep?
"He's under the haycock, fast asleep."
Will you wake him? "No, not I;
For if I do, he'll be sure to cry."

44
Jack and Jill went up the hill
    To fetch a pail of water.
Jack fell down and broke his crown
    And Jill came tumbling after.

Up Jack got and home he did trot
    As fast as he could caper.
He went to bed to mend his head
    In vinegar and brown paper.

45
Tom he was a piper's son,
He learned to play when he was young,
But all the tunes that he could play,
Was "Over the hills and far away."

Now Tom with his pipe made such a noise,
That he pleased both girls and boys,
And they stopped to hear him play
"Over the hills and far away."

Tom with his pipe did play with such skill,
That those who heard him could never keep still;
Whenever they heard they began for to dance,
Even pigs on their hind legs would after him
    prance.

46
Sing a song of sixpence,
    A pocket full of rye;
Four and twenty blackbirds
    Baked in a pie.

When the pie was opened,
    The birds began to sing;
Wasn't that a dainty dish
    To set before the king?

The king was in his countinghouse
    Counting out his money;
The queen was in the parlor
    Eating bread and honey;

The maid was in the garden
    Hanging out the clothes,
When along came a blackbird
    And pecked off her nose.

47
The Queen of Hearts,
She made some tarts,
    All on a summer's day;

The Knave of Hearts
He stole those tarts
    And took them clean away.

The King of Hearts
Called for the tarts,
    And beat the knave full sore;
The Knave of Hearts
Brought back the tarts,
    And vowed he'd steal no more.

48
Old Mother Hubbard
Went to the cupboard
To get her poor dog a bone;
But when she came there
The cupboard was bare,
And so the poor dog had none.

She went to the baker's
To buy him some bread;
But when she came back
The poor dog was dead.

She went to the joiner's
To buy him a coffin;
But when she came back
The poor dog was laughing.

She took a clean dish
To get him some tripe;
But when she came back
He was smoking a pipe.

She went to the tavern
For white wine and red;
But when she came back
The dog stood on his head.

She went to the hatter's
To buy him a hat;
But when she came back
He was feeding the cat.

She went to the barber's
To buy him a wig;
But when she came back
He was dancing a jig.

She went to the fruiterer's
To buy him some fruit;
But when she came back
He was playing the flute.

She went to the tailor's
To buy him a coat;
But when she came back
He was riding a goat.

She went to the cobbler's
To buy him some shoes;
But when she came back
He was reading the news.

She went to the seamstress
To buy him some linen;
But when she came back
The dog was spinning.

She went to the hosier's
To buy him some hose;
But when she came back
He was dressed in his clothes.

The dame made a courtesy,
The dog made a bow;
The dame said, "Your servant,"
The dog said, "Bow, wow!"

49

Tom, Tom, the piper's son,
Stole a pig and away he run;
The pig was eat,
And Tom was beat,
And Tom went howling down the street.

50

There was an old man who lived in a wood,
As you may plainly see;
He said he could do as much work in a day,
As his wife could do in three.
"With all my heart," the old woman said,
"If that you will allow,
Tomorrow you'll stay home in my stead,
And I'll go drive the plow.

"But you must milk the Tidy cow,
For fear that she go dry;
And you must feed the little pigs
That are within the sty;
And you must mind the speckled hen,
For fear she lay away;
And you must reel the spool of yarn,
That I spun yesterday."

The old woman took a staff in her hand,
And went to drive the plow.
The old man took a pail in his hand,
And went to milk the cow;
But Tidy hinched, and Tidy flinched,
And Tidy broke his nose,
And Tidy gave him such a blow,
That the blood ran down to his toes.

"High, Tidy! Ho, Tidy! High!
Tidy, do stand still
If ever I milk you, Tidy, again,
'Twill be sore against my will"

He went to feed the little pigs
    That were within the sty;
He hit his head against the beam,
    And he made the blood to fly.
He went to mind the speckled hen,
    For fear she'd lay astray,
And he forgot the spool of yarn
    His wife spun yesterday.

So he swore by the sun, the moon, and the stars,
    And the green leaves on the tree,
"If my wife doesn't do a day's work in her life,
    She shall ne'er be ruled by me."

51

This is the house that Jack built.

This is the malt
That lay in the house that Jack built.

This is the rat,
That ate the malt
That lay in the house that Jack built.

This is the cat,
That killed the rat,
That ate the malt
That lay in the house that Jack built.

This is the dog,
That worried the cat,
That killed the rat,
That ate the malt
That lay in the house that Jack built.

This is the cow with the crumpled horn,
That tossed the dog,
That worried the cat,
That killed the rat,
That ate the malt
That lay in the house that Jack built.

This is the maiden all forlorn,
That milked the cow with the crumpled horn,
That tossed the dog,
That worried the cat,
That killed the rat,
That ate the malt
That lay in the house that Jack built.

This is the man all tattered and torn,
That kissed the maiden all forlorn,
That milked the cow with the crumpled horn,
That tossed the dog,
That worried the cat,
That killed the rat,
That ate the malt
That lay in the house that Jack built.

This is the priest all shaven and shorn,
That married the man all tattered and torn,
That kissed the maiden all forlorn,
That milked the cow with the crumpled horn,
That tossed the dog,
That worried the cat,
That killed the rat,
That ate the malt
That lay in the house that Jack built.

This is the cock that crowed in the morn,
That waked the priest all shaven and shorn,
That married the man all tattered and torn,
That kissed the maiden all forlorn,
That milked the cow with the crumpled horn,
That tossed the dog,
That worried the cat,
That killed the rat,
That ate the malt
That lay in the house that Jack built.

52

Jenny Wren fell sick
    Upon a merry time,
In came Robin Redbreast
    And brought her sops and wine.

Eat well of the sop, Jenny,
    Drink well of the wine.
Thank you, Robin, kindly,
    You shall be mine.

Jenny Wren got well,
    And stood upon her feet;
And told Robin plainly,
    She loved him not a bit.

Robin he got angry,
    And hopped upon a twig,
Saying, Out upon you, fie upon you!
    Bold faced jig!

53

Who killed Cock Robin?
  "I," said the Sparrow,
    "With my bow and arrow,
I killed Cock Robin."

Who saw him die?
  "I," said the Fly,
    "With my little eye,
And I saw him die."

Who caught his blood?
  "I," said the Fish,
    "With my little dish,
And I caught his blood."

Who made his shroud?
  "I," said the Beadle,
    "With my little needle,
And I made his shroud."

Who shall dig his grave?
  "I," said the Owl,
    "With my spade and showl,
And I'll dig his grave."

Who'll be the parson?
  "I," said the Rook,
    "With my little book,
And I'll be the parson."

Who'll be the clerk?
  "I," said the Lark,
    "If it's not in the dark,
And I'll be the clerk."

Who'll carry him to the grave?
  "I," said the Kite,
    "If 'tis not in the night,
And I'll carry him to his grave."

Who'll carry the link?
  "I," said the Linnet,
    "I'll fetch it in a minute,
And I'll carry the link."

Who'll be the chief mourner?
  "I," said the Dove,
    "I mourn for my love,
And I'll be chief mourner."

Who'll bear the pall?
  "We," said the Wren,
    Both the cock and the hen,
"And we'll bear the pall."

Who'll sing a psalm?
  "I," said the Thrush,
    As she sat in a bush,
"And I'll sing a psalm."

And who'll toll the bell?
  "I," said the Bull,
    "Because I can pull";
And so, Cock Robin, farewell.

All the birds in the air
  Fell to sighing and sobbing,
    When they heard the bell toll
For poor Cock Robin.

SHEER NONSENSE

54

A man in the wilderness asked me,
How many strawberries grow in the sea.
I answered him, as I thought good,
As many red herrings as swim in the wood.

55

A bear went over the mountain,
A bear went over the mountain,
A bear went over the mountain,
To see what he could see.

The other side of the mountain,
The other side of the mountain,
The other side of the mountain,
Was all that he could see.

56

Goosey, goosey gander,
  Whither shall I wander?
Upstairs and downstairs
  And in my lady's chamber.
There I met an old man
  Who would not say his prayers,
I took him by the left leg
  And threw him down the stairs.

"A bear went over the mountain," from *The Rooster Crows,* by Maude and Miska Petersham. Published by The Macmillan Company.

57
What are little boys made of, made of?
What are little boys made of?
  Frogs and snails
  And puppy-dogs' tails,
That's what little boys are made of.

What are little girls made of, made of?
What are littles girls made of?
  Sugar and spice
  And all things nice,
That's what little girls are made of.

58
  HUSKY HI/Norwegian

Husky hi, husky hi,
Here comes Keery galloping by.
She carries her husband tied in a sack,
She carries him home on her horse's back.
Husky hi, husky hi,
Here comes Keery galloping by!

59
JONATHAN/Dutch

  Jonathan Gee
  Went out with his cow;
  He climbed up a tree
  And sat on a bough.

  He sat on a bough
  And it broke in half,
  And John's old cow
  Did nothing but laugh.

60
Simple Simon met a pieman
  Going to the fair;
Says Simple Simon to the pieman,
  "Let me taste your ware."

Says the pieman to Simple Simon,
  "Show me first your penny."

"Husky Hi" and "Jonathan Gee" from the book *Picture Rhymes from Foreign Lands* by Rose Fyleman. Copyright 1935, 1963 by Rose Fyleman. Reprinted by permission of J. B. Lippincott Company.

Says Simple Simon to the pieman,
  "Indeed, I have not any."

Simple Simon went a-fishing
  For to catch a whale;
All the water he had got
  Was in his mother's pail!

61
The grand old Duke of York,
He had ten thousand men;
He marched them up to the top of the hill
And he marched them down again!

And when they were up, they were up,
And when they were down, they were down,
And when they were only half-way up
They were neither up nor down.

62
Pease porridge hot,
  Pease porridge cold,
Pease porridge in the pot,
  Nine days old.
Some like it hot,
  Some like it cold,
Some like it in the pot,
  Nine days old.

63
The man in the moon
Came down too soon,
And asked his way to Norwich;
He went by the south,
And burnt his mouth,
With supping cold plum porridge.

64
Outside my door, I heard some one say,
A man bit a dog in a vicious way!
Such news I ne'er for a moment could stand,
So I lifted my door to open my hand;
I snatched up the dog with a slow double-quick
And tossed him with force at a very soft brick.
The brick—I'm afraid you will not understand—
I found in a moment had bitten my hand.
So I mounted a chair, on a horse I was borne,
While I blew on a drum and beat on a horn!

65

The heaven is bright,
The earth is bright,
I have a baby who cries all night.

66

Little Miss Muffet
Sat on a tuffet,
Eating of curds and whey;
There came a big spider,
And sat down beside her,
And frightened Miss Muffet away.

67

TRADJA OF NORWAY/Norwegian

Little Tradja of Norway,
She sat in the doorway,
Eating her reindeer-broth;
There came a big badger
And little Miss Tradja
Soon carried her meal farther north.

68

GRETCHEN/Dutch

Little Dutch Gretchen sat in the kitchen,
Eating some nice sauerkraut,
When the little dog Schneider
Came and sat down beside her,
And little Dutch Gretchen went out.

69

There was an old woman who lived in a shoe;
She had so many children, she didn't know what
    to do;
She gave them some broth without any bread;
She whipped them all well and put them to bed.

70

Diddle, diddle, dumpling, my son John,
Went to bed with his stockings on;

"Outside my door, I heard someone say" and "The heaven
is bright" reprinted by permission of The World Publishing Company from *Chinese Mother Goose Rhymes*,
selected and edited by Robert Wyndham. Special contents
of this edition copyright © 1968 Robert Wyndham.
"Tradja of Norway" and "Gretchen" from the book *The
Land of Nursery Rhyme*, edited by Ernest Rhys and Alice
Daglish. Published by E. P. Dutton & Co., Inc. Reprinted
by permission of E. P. Dutton & Co., Inc., and J. M.
Dent & Sons Ltd.

One shoe off, the other shoe on,
Diddle, diddle, dumpling, my son John.

71

There was a crooked man, and he went a crooked
    mile
And found a crooked sixpence against a crooked
    stile;
He bought a crooked cat that caught a crooked
    mouse,
And they all lived together in a little crooked
    house.

72

POP GOES THE WEASEL

Up and down the City Road,
    In and out the Eagle,
That's the way the money goes,
    Pop goes the weasel!

Half a pound of tuppenny rice,
    Half a pound of treacle,
Mix it up and make it nice,
    Pop goes the weasel!

Every night when I go out
    The monkey's on the table;
Take a stick and knock it off,
    Pop goes the weasel!

73

Adam and Eve and Pinch-me
Went down to the river to bathe.
Adam and Eve got drown'ded,
Which one of the three was saved?

74

It's raining, it's pouring,
The little old man is snoring;
He went to bed with a bump on his head,
And didn't get up in the morning.

75

Mary went down to Grandpa's farm;
The billy goat chased her round the barn,
Chased her up the sycamore tree,
And this is the song she sang to me:
"I like coffee, I like tea,
I like the boys and the boys like me."

76

Way down South where bananas grow,
A grasshopper stepped on an elephant's toe.
The elephant said, with tears in his eyes,
"Pick on somebody your own size."

RIDDLES

77

Humpty Dumpty sat on a wall,
Humpty Dumpty had a great fall;
Threescore men and threescore more
Cannot place Humpty Dumpty as he was before.

(An *egg*)

78

Little Nancy Etticoat,
In a white petticoat,
And a red nose;
The longer she stands,
The shorter she grows.

(A *candle*)

79

Thirty white horses upon a red hill,
Now they tramp, now they champ,
    Now they stand still.

(*Teeth and gums*)

80

Lives in winter,
    Dies in summer,
And grows with its roots upward!

(An *icicle*)

81

A hill full, a hole full,
Yet you cannot catch a bowl full.

(*The mist*)

82

Higher than a house,
Higher than a tree,
Oh! whatever can that be?

(A *star*)

"Adam and Eve and Pinch-me," "It's raining," "Mary
went down to Grandpa's farm," and "Way down South"
from *A Rocket in My Pocket*, compiled by Carl Withers.
Copyright 1948 by Carl Withers. Reprinted by permission
of Holt, Rinehart and Winston, Inc.

83

As round as an apple, as deep as a cup,
And all the king's horses can't fill it up.

(A *well*)

84

Hick-a-more, Hack-a-more,
On the King's kitchen door;
All the King's horses,
And all the King's men,
Couldn't drive Hick-a-more, Hack-a-more,
Off the King's kitchen door.

(*Sunshine*)

85

A riddle, a riddle, as I suppose,
A hundred eyes and never a nose!

(A *sieve*)

86

As I was going to St. Ives,
I met a man with seven wives;
Every wife had seven sacks,
Every sack had seven cats,
Every cat had seven kits;
Kits, cats, sacks, and wives,
How many were there going to St. Ives?

(*One*)

87

Black within and red without;
Four corners round about.

(A *chimney*)

88

Old Mother Twitchett had but one eye,
And a long tail which she let fly;
And every time she went through a gap,
A bit of her tail she left in a trap.

(*Needle and thread*)

89

In marble walls as white as milk,
Lined with a skin as soft as silk,
Within a fountain crystal clear,
A golden apple doth appear;
No doors there are to this stronghold,
Yet thieves break in and steal the gold.

(An *egg*)

90

Two legs sat on three legs,
With one leg in his lap;
In comes four legs,
And runs away with one leg,
Up jumps two legs,
Catches up three legs,
Throws it after four legs
And makes him bring back one leg.

(Two legs = a man)
(Three legs = a stool)
(One leg = leg of meat)
(Four legs = a dog)

91

Old man Chang, I've oft heard it said,
You wear a basket upon your head;
You've two pairs of scissors to cut your meat,
And two pairs of chopsticks with which you eat.

(A crab)

92

It has a head like a cat, feet like a cat,
A tail like a cat, but it isn't a cat.

(A kitten)

93

House full, yard full,
You can't catch a spoonful.

(Smoke)

94

Riddle me! riddle me! What is that:
Over your head and under your hat?

(Hair)

95

A milk-white bird
Floats down through the air.
And never a tree
But he lights there.

(Snow)

96

I washed my hands in water
That never rained nor run;
I dried them with a towel
That was never wove nor spun.

(Dew and Sun)

97

Two-legs sat on Three-legs by Four-legs.
One leg knocked Two-legs off Three-legs;
Two-legs hit Four-legs with Three-legs.

(An old man sat down on a three-legged stool to milk his cow. When the cow kicked him, he hit her with the stool.)

TONGUE-TWISTERS

98

How much wood would a woodchuck chuck
If a woodchuck could chuck wood?
A woodchuck would chuck as much as he would
    chuck
If a woodchuck could chuck wood.

99

Peter Piper picked a peck of pickled peppers;
A peck of pickled peppers Peter Piper picked;
If Peter Piper picked a peck of pickled peppers,
Where's the peck of pickled peppers Peter Piper
    picked?

100

Robert Rowley rolled a round roll 'round;
A round roll Robert Rowley rolled 'round;
If Robert Rowley rolled a round roll 'round,
Where rolled the round roll Robert Rowley rolled
    'round?

101

Theophilus, the thistle sifter, while sifting a sifter
full of thistles, thrust three thousand thistles
through the thickness of his thumb.

102

Betty Botter bought some butter,
But, she said, the butter's bitter;
If I put it in my batter
It will make my batter bitter,
But a bit of better butter
Will make my batter better.
So she bought a bit of butter
Better than her bitter butter,
And she put it in her batter
And the batter was not bitter.
So 'twas better Betty Botter bought a bit of better
    butter.

103

ONE LINE TWISTERS

A big baby buggy with rubber buggy bumpers.

Toy boat, toy boat, toy boat.

If he slipped should she slip?

Black bug's blood, black bug's blood.

Does your shirt shop stock short socks with spots?

Double bubble gum bubbles double.

Each sixth chick sat on a stick.

Eat fresh fried fish at the fish fry.

Three gray geese in the green grass grazing.

Six slim slick sycamore saplings.

Round and round the rugged rock the ragged
    rascal ran.

An old scold sold a cold coal shovel.

Pardon me, madam, may I show you to a seat?

The cat ran over the roof with a lump of raw liver.

I bought a box of biscuits, a box of mixed biscuits,
    and a biscuit-mixer.

She sells sea shells by the seashore.

"One line twisters" from *A Rocket in My Pocket* compiled
by Carl Withers. Copyright 1948 by Carl Withers. Reprinted by permission of Holt, Rinehart and Winston, Inc.

ACTION RHYMES

104

This is the way the ladies ride,
    Tri, tre, tre, tree,
    Tri, tre, tre, tree!
This is the way the ladies ride,
    Tri, tre, tre, tre, tri-tre-tre-tree!

This is the way the gentlemen ride,
    Gallop-a-trot,
    Gallop-a-trot!
This is the way the gentlemen ride,
    Gallop-a-gallop-a-trot!

This is the way the farmers ride,
    Hobbledy-hoy,
    Hobbledy-hoy!
This is the way the farmers ride,
    Hobbledy-hobbledy-hoy!

105

To market, to market, to buy a fat pig,
Home again, home again, dancing a jig;
To market, to market, to buy a fat hog,
Home again, home again, jiggety-jog;
To market, to market, to buy a plum bun,
Home again, home again, market is done.

106

This little cow eats grass,
This little cow eats hay,
This little cow drinks water,
This little cow runs away,
This little cow does nothing,
But just lie down all day;
    We'll whip her.
            (The five toes)

107

FISHING/Danish

Row to the fishing-ground, row away,
How many fish have you caught to-day?

"This little cow" from *Chinese Mother Goose Rhymes* by
Isaac Taylor Headland. Reprinted by permission of Fleming H. Revell Company.

"Fishing" from the book *Picture Rhymes from Foreign
Lands* by Rose Fyleman. Copyright, 1935, 1963 by Rose Fyleman. Reprinted by permission of J. B. Lippincott Company.

One for my father and one for my mother
One for my sister and one for my brother;
One for you and another for me
And one for the fisher who went to sea.

108

This little pig went to market,
This little pig stayed at home,
This little pig had roast beef,
This little pig had none,
This little pig cried, "Wee, wee, wee, I want
    some!"

                (The five toes)

109

This is the church,
This is the steeple;
Open the door
And see all the people.
      (Ten fingers)

110

Brow-brinker,
Eye-winker,
Nose-nopper,
Mouth-eater,
Chin-chopper,
Chin-chopper,
Chin.
    (The face)

111

London Bridge is broken down,
    Dance o'er my Lady Lee;
London Bridge is broken down,
    With a gay lady.

How shall we build it up again?
    Dance o'er my Lady Lee;
How shall we build it up again?
    With a gay lady.

Build it up with silver and gold,
    Dance o'er my Lady Lee;
Build it up with silver and gold,
    With a gay lady.

Silver and gold will be stole away,
    Dance o'er my Lady Lee;
Silver and gold will be stole away,
    With a gay lady.

Build it up with iron and steel,
    Dance o'er my Lady Lee;
Build it up with iron and steel,
    With a gay lady.

Iron and steel will bend and bow,
    Dance o'er my Lady Lee;
Iron and steel will bend and bow,
    With a gay lady.

Build it up with wood and clay,
    Dance o'er my Lady Lee;
Build it up with wood and clay,
    With a gay lady.

Wood and clay will wash away,
    Dance o'er my Lady Lee;
Wood and clay will wash away,
    With a gay lady.

Build it up with stone so strong,
    Dance o'er my Lady Lee;
Huzza! 'twill last for ages long,
    With a gay lady.

RHYMES FOR JUMPING ROPE

112

Charlie Chaplin went to France
To teach the ladies how to dance.
Heel, toe, and around we go;
Salute to the captain,
Bow to the queen,
Turn your back
On the old submarine.

113

Lady bird, lady bird, turn around,
Lady bird, lady bird, touch the ground.
Lady bird, lady bird, fly away home,
Lady bird, lady bird, you have gone.

Lady bird, lady bird, go upstairs,
Lady bird, lady bird, say your prayers.
Lady bird, lady bird, turn out the light,
Lady bird, lady bird, say Good night.
Teddy bear, teddy bear, point to the sky,
Teddy bear, teddy bear, show your glass eye.
Teddy bear, teddy bear, pull off your wig,
Teddy bear, teddy bear, dance a jig.

COUNTING RHYMES

114
One, two,
Buckle my shoe;
Three, four,
Shut the door;
Five, six,
Pick up sticks;
Seven, eight,
Lay them straight;
Nine, ten,
A good fat hen;
Eleven, twelve,
Who will delve?
Thirteen, fourteen,
Maids a-courting;
Fifteen, sixteen,
Maids a-kissing;
Seventeen, eighteen,
Maids a-waiting;
Nineteen, twenty,
My stomach's empty.

115
One for the money,
Two for the show,
Three to make ready,
And four to go.

116
One potato, two potato,
Three potato, four;
Five potato, six potato,
Seven potato, MORE.

"One for the money" and "One potato, two potato," revisions of "Mary had a little lamb" and "Humpty Dumpty" from *A Rocket in My Pocket* compiled by Carl Withers. Reprinted by permission of Holt, Rinehart and Winston, Inc.

REVISED NURSERY RHYMES

117
Mary had a little lamb,
She set it on the shelf;
And every time it wagged its tail,
It spanked its little self.

118
Mary had a little lamb,
Its coat was black as tar;
And everywhere that Mary went,
They thought it was a b'ar.

119
Mary had a little lamb,
Its coat was white as cotton;
And everywhere that Mary went,
That lamb came a-trottin'.

120
Mary had a little lamb,
Its fleece as white as snow;
And everywhere that Mary went
—She took a bus.

121
Humpty Dumpty sat on a wall,
Humpty Dumpty had a great fall.
All the king's horses and all the king's men
Had scrambled eggs.

122
Little Miss Muffet
Sits on her tuffet
In a nonchalant sort of a way.
With her force field around her
The spider, the bounder,
Is not in the picture today.

123
Solomon Grundy
Walked on Monday

"Little Miss Muffet" and "Solomon Grundy" from *The Space Child's Mother Goose*. Copyright © 1956, 1957, 1958 by Frederick Winsor and Marion Parry. Reprinted by permission of Simon & Schuster, Inc.

Rode on Tuesday
Motored Wednesday
Planed on Thursday
Rocketed Friday

Spaceship Saturday
Time Machine Sunday
Where is the end for
Solomon Grundy?

Related Reading

References for Adults

Arbuthnot, May Hill. *Children and Books*, 3d ed. Glenview, Ill.: Scott, Foresman, 1964.

Baring-Gould, William S. and Cecil. *The Annotated Mother Goose* with introduction and notes by William Baring-Gould and Cecil Baring-Gould; the complete text and illustrations in a full annotated edition; illus. by Caldecott, Crane, Greenaway, Rackham, Parrish, and historical woodcuts. Chapter decorations by E. M. Simon. Clarkson Potter, 1962.

Brett, Henry. *Nursery Rhymes and Tales: Their History and Origin*. New York: Holt, Rinehart and Winston, 1924. A brief history of nursery rhymes and folk-tales.

Eckenstein, Lina. *Comparative Studies in Nursery Rhymes*. London: Duckworth, 1906. Reissued by Singing Tree Press. A discussion of the folk origins of nursery rhymes.

Huck, Charlotte S., and Doris Young Kuhn. *Children's Literature in the Elementary School*, 2d ed. New York: Holt, Rinehart and Winston, 1968.

Opie, Iona, ed. *Ditties for the Nursery*. Illustrated by Monica Walker. Oxford University Press, 1954. "Rhymes which delighted children in the reign of George III . . . published about 1805 under the title *Original Ditties for the Nursery, So Wonderfully Contrived that They May Be Either Sung or Said by Nurse or Baby*." Unfamiliar rhymes from the early nineteenth century.

Opie, Iona and Peter. *The Oxford Dictionary of Nursery Rhymes*. Oxford University Press, 1951. A scholarly work of more than 500 traditional rhymes, whose variations, histories, literary associations, and parallels in other languages are discussed.

———, eds. *The Oxford Nursery Rhyme Book*. Oxford University Press, 1955. Over 800 rhymes. The 400 illustrations are reproductions of wood-cuts from eighteenth- and nineteenth-century children's books and chapbooks.

Sackville-West, Virginia. *Nursery Rhymes: An Essay*. Illustrated by Philippe Julian. London: Michael Joseph, 1950.

Smith, Lillian H. *The Unreluctant Years: A Critical Approach to Children's Literature*. Chicago: American Library Association, 1953.

Books for Children

Briggs, Raymond, editor-illustrator. *The Mother Goose Treasury*. New York: Coward-McCann, 1966. This large book contains 897 illustrations, black and white as well as color, and 408 rhymes. A delightful and comprehensive collection. While the book is too large for most children to hold, it is one they will enjoy looking at with an adult. (Preschool–grade 3)

———. *The White Land*. New York: Coward-McCann, 1963. Twenty-three rhymes, both the familiar and the lesser known. (Grades K–2)

Brooke, Leslie, *Ring O'Roses*. New York: Warne, 1923. The lovely illustrations make this a charming book. (Preschool–grade 3)

Cooney, Barbara, illustrator. *The Courtship, Merry Marriage, and Feast of Cock Robin and Jenny Wren, to which is added the Doleful Death of Cock Robin*. New York: Scribner, 1965. These illustrations so excellently interpret this old nursery rhyme it is a book all children should read. (Grades 1–3)

De Angeli, Marguerite. *Marguerite de Angeli's Book of Nursery and Mother Goose Rhymes*. New York: Doubleday, 1954. Almost four hundred rhymes and over 250 illustrations. (Grades K–3)

———. *A Pocket Full of Posies: A Merry Mother Goose*. New York: Doubleday, 1961. Seventy-seven of the most familiar verses from the illustrator's larger collection. (Preschool–Grade 2)

Emrich, Duncan, compiler. *The Nonsense Book of Riddles, Rhymes, Tongue Twisters, Puzzles and Jokes from American Folklore.* Illustrated by Ib Ohlsson. New York: Four Winds, 1970. The former chief of the Folklore Section of the Library of Congress has compiled a collection of nonsense chants and rhymes that will be enjoyed by everyone with a sense of humor. Excellent for the storyteller and teacher. (Grades 4–6)

Fowke, Edith, collector-editor. *Sally Go Round the Sun: Three Hundred Children's Songs, Rhymes and Games.* Musical arrangements by Keith Macmillan. Illustrated by Carlos Marchiori. New York: Doubleday, 1970. A collection of many of the songs and chants current in Canada; many will be familiar to American children. Awarded the 1970 Book of the Year for Children Medal by the Canadian Association of Children's Librarians. (Grades K–4)

Frasconi, Antonio, illustrator. *The House That Jack Bulit.* New York: Harcourt, 1958. Picture book treatment of a popular nursery rhyme. (Grades K–2)

Galdone, Paul. *The History of Simple Simon.* New York: McGraw-Hill, 1966. Other picture-book treatments by Mr. Galdone of individual nursery rhymes are: *The House That Jack Built,* 1961; *Old Mother Hubbard and Her Dog,* 1960; *The Old Woman and Her Pig,* 1960; *Tom, Tom, the Piper's Son,* 1964. (Preschool–grade 2)

Greenaway, Kate. *Mother Goose: or, the Old Nursery Rhymes.* New York: Warne, n.d. A small book done in the traditional Greenaway style. (Grades K–2)

Lines, Kathleen. *Lavender's Blue.* Illustrated by Harold Jones. New York: F. Watts, 1964. A beautifully illustrated book of nursery rhymes. (Preschool–grade 2)

Nic Leodhas, Sorche. *All in the Morning Early.* Illustrated by Evaline Ness. New York: Holt, Rinehart and Winston, 1963. A picture book of an old Scottish nursery tale. (Grades K–3)

Reed, Philip, compiler-illustrator. *Mother Goose and Nursery Rhymes.* New York: Atheneum, 1963. A delightful collection of old rhymes and a few proverbs beautifully illustrated in six-color wood engravings. A great deal of quaint humor that will be enjoyed by both children and adults. (Preschool–grade 2)

Reeves, James, compiler. *One's None: Old Rhymes for New Tongues.* Illustrated by Bernadette Watts. New York: Watts, 1969. Although these are tra-

ditional rhymes, this is not a collection of the usual and familiar. Readers of any age will be delighted with the book. (Preschool–grade 2)

Rojankovsky, Feodor. *The Tall Book of Mother Goose.* New York: Harper & Row, 1942. A tall narrow book with almost one hundred rhymes, over one hundred black and white illustrations, and more than fifty in color. (Grades K–2)

Tudor, Tasha. *Mother Goose.* New York: Walck, 1944. Seventy-seven verses, many seldom found except in comprehensive editions. Quaint, charming illustrations. (Preschool–grade 2)

Wildsmith, Brian. *Brian Wildsmith's Mother Goose.* New York: F. Watts, 1965. Lush, sophisticated illustrations. (Grades K–2)

Withers, Carl. *A Rocket in My Pocket: The Rhymes and Chants of Young Americans.* Illustrated by Susanne Suba. New York: Holt, Rinehart and Winston, 1948. (Grades 1–4)

_____. *I Saw a Rocket Walk a Mile.* Illustrated by John E. Johnson. Holt, Rinehart and Winston, 1966. Includes chants and songs from many countries. (Grades 1–6)

Wood, Ray, compiler. *The American Mother Goose.* Illustrated by Ed Hargis. Philadelphia: Lippincott, 1940. American variants of traditional European nursery rhymes as well as rhymes unique to this country. (Grades K–3)

_____. *Fun in American Folk Rhyme.* Illustrated by Ed Hargis. Philadelphia: Lippincott, 1952. (Grades 1–3)

Wright, Blanche Fisher. *The Real Mother Goose.* Skokie, Ill.: Rand McNally, 1965. Over three hundred rhymes with color pictures on each page. A very popular collection. (Preschool–grade 2)

Nursery Rhymes in Translation

Alexander, Frances, et al. *Mother Goose on the Rio Grande.* Dallas, Tex.: Banks Upshaw, 1944. Mexican nursery rhymes translated into English. (Grades K–3)

Dalgliesh, Alice, and Ernest Rhys. *The Land of Nursery Rhyme.* New York: Dutton, 1932. Nursery rhymes from different lands translated into English. (Grades K–3)

DeForest, Charlotte B., adapter. *The Prancing Pony, Nursery Rhymes from Japan.* Illustrated by Keiko Hida. New York: Walker, 1968. The verses, most very old, are adaptions of folk poetry, lullabies, and children's songs. The kusa-e illustrations are quite effective.

Fyleman, Rose. *Picture Rhymes from Foreign Lands.*

Philadelphia: Lippincott, 1935. Nursery rhymes translated into English; many parallel traditional verses. (Grades K–3)

Headland, I. T. *Chinese Mother Goose Rhymes*. Old Tappan, N.J.: Revell, 1901. (Grades K–4)

Mother Goose in Spanish. Translated by Alastair Reid and Anthony Kerrigan. Illustrated by Barbara Cooney. New York: Crowell, 1968. What a delightful way to learn Spanish! Familiar rhymes, printed in Spanish, are illustrated with paintings of Spain. This book will be enjoyed by students of the language as well as by Spanish-speaking children. For those learning to speak French, Miss Cooney has also illustrated Mother Goose rhymes in that language: *Mother Goose in French*. Translated by Hugh Latham. New York: Crowell, 1964. (Grades K–3)

Petersham, Maud and Miska, compilers-illustrators. *The Rooster Crows: A Book of American Rhymes and Jingles*. New York: Macmillan, 1945. Awarded the 1946 Caldecott Medal. (Grades K–4)

Ross, Patricia Fent. *The Hungry Moon: Mexican Nursery Tales*. Illustrated by Carlas Merida. New York: Knopf, 1946. (Grades K–3)

Wyndham, Robert, compiler-editor. *Chinese Mother Goose Rhymes*. Illustrated by Ed Young. Cleveland: World, 1968. Traditional Chinese rhymes are printed in English script and Chinese characters. Several are quite similar to those known by English-speaking children, others are quite unique.

Chapter 15

Selected Poems

From A *Child's Calendar*, by John Updike, illustrated by Nancy Burkert. Copyright © 1965 by John Updike and Nancy Burkert. Reprinted by permission of Alfred A. Knopf, Inc.

ood poetry does not become boring, for true poems are fresh no matter how often they are re-read. In this section well-written and poorly written poems will be examined to reveal the differences between poetic excellence and mediocrity. For clarification, the following discussion will apply the term poetry only to works of artistic merit. The trite, superficial, or patronizing pieces that awkwardly adopt a few poetic devices will be identified by the term verse. This is not an arbitrary separation, for as Babette Deutsch, an American poet, says in *Poetry Handbook:*

> the distinction between poetry and verse is at least as old as Sidney . . . Eliot, without defining the difference, implies that verse is merely a matter of structure, while poetry is marked by intensity of feeling and gravity of import, which find expression in a musicianly concern for resonance in both the sounds and the associations of the words chosen. The distinguishing feature of verse is its formal aspect, that of poetry is its imaginative power.[1]

Following, the elements of poetry are discussed to reveal how the poet's careful use of language differs from the versifier's.

Because poetry attempts to evoke rather than inform, its language is more concentrated than prose. The poet shares his experience, vision, or narrative through figurative language, imagery, connotation, symbolism, rhythm, and rhyme. Lyric poetry attempts to recreate for the reader the poet's experience, insight, or emotion. Narrative poetry uses the above poetic devices to tell a story.

While poetry does contain some verifiable statements, it more often says things indirectly. "Poetic indirection . . . is a method of putting into words, with exact fidelity, ideas and emotions and moods that might otherwise elude the capacities of language."[2]

IMAGERY

Images, the concrete details meant to involve the reader in the poem, are not simply visual; many appeal to the reader's senses of touch, sound, taste, and smell. Images enable the reader to better understand what the poet is saying. Some verses are little more than rhymed lists of images, as in the following unimaginative verse by Christina Georgina Rossetti.

> What is pink? A rose is pink
> By the fountain's brink.
> What is red? A poppy's red
> In its barley bed.
> What is blue? The sky is blue
> Where the clouds float thro'.
> What is white? A swan is white
> Sailing in the light.
> What is yellow? Pears are yellow,
> Rich and ripe and mellow.
> What is green? The grass is green,
> With small flowers between.
> What is violet? Clouds are violet
> In the summer twilight.
> What is orange? Why, an orange,
> Just an orange![3]

Compare this list with the more interesting use of imagery in the excerpt from "Swimmers" by Louis Untermeyer (page 930). "Swimmers," un-

[2] Chad Walsh, *Doors into Poetry.* Englewood Cliffs, N.J.: Prentice-Hall, Inc., © 1962, p. 61.
[3] "What Is Pink?" by Christina Georgina Rosettti.

like the above verse, includes tactile and auditory images to give the reader the feel and sound of the sea.

FIGURATIVE LANGUAGE

The most common figures of speech are the simile, the metaphor, and personification. When appropriate to the experience, subject, and mood of the poem, figurative language brings preciseness to what is being expressed. Only the poet knows the experience he wishes to share. Through comparisons to objects and experiences the reader will recognize, the poet clarifies his personal feelings and knowledge.

Both the simile and the metaphor compare two basically unlike entities, but the simile uses the words like, as, or than.

> O my Luve's like a red, red rose
> That's newly spring in June:
> O my Luve's like the melodie
> That's sweetly played in tune.[4]

The metaphor dispenses with the words like, as, and than and says one thing *is* another. Hilda Conkling's metaphor compares a dandelion and a soldier.

> O Little Soldier with the golden helmet,
> What are you guarding on my lawn?
> You with your green gun
> And your yellow beard,
> Why do you stand so stiff?
> There is only the grass to fight!

A simile or a metaphor can be only a word or phrase, or the comparison may be extended through the poem—as is the metaphor in "Dandelion" and simile in the following poem, "Lincoln."

> Like a gaunt, scraggly pine
> Which lifts its head above the mournful sand-
> hills;
> And patiently, through dull years of bitter
> silence,
> Untended and uncared for, starts to grow.
> Ungainly, laboring, huge,

The wind of the north has twisted and
  gnarled its branches;
Yet in the heat of mid-summer days, when
  thunder clouds ring the horizon,
A nation of men shall rest beneath its shade.
And it shall protect them all,
Hold everyone safe there, watching aloof in
  silence;
Until at last, one mad stray bolt from the
  zenith
Shall strike it in an instant down to earth.[6]

Personification attributes human characteristics to nonhuman creatures and inanimate objects. When willows weep, clouds cry, the sun smiles, or flowers dance they have been personified. Another form of personification gives inanimate objects characteristics of animals. This occurs in Carl Sandburg's "Fog."

> The fog comes
> on little cat feet.
>
> It sits looking
> over harbor and city
> on silent haunches
> and then, moves on.[7]

Figurative comparisons are not used only by poets to clarify and express feelings and insights. Most people use them every day until many comparisons become cliches: "it's right as rain," "fresh as a daisy," "pretty as a picture."

Readers should be aware of the quality of the imagery and figures of speech in poems because most versifiers use cliches and generalizations. Images and figures of speech are used to give clarity to the poem and bring new insights to the reader. Overworked expressions and vague terms can not do this. Compare the following poems in which two poets who feel the same joy use imagery and language with different degrees of accuracy and skill. Edna St. Vincent Millay's poem is effective because her images are more precise, controlled, and concrete.

4 "My Luve's Like a Red, Red Rose" by Robert Burns.
5 "Dandelion" (written at the age of eight) from *Poems by a Little Girl* by Hilda Conkling. Copyright, 1920 by J. B. Lippincott Company. Renewal, 1948 by Hilda Conkling. Reprinted by permission of the author.

6 "Lincoln" from *Selected Poems* by John Gould Fletcher. Copyright 1938 by John Gould Fletcher. Copyright © 1966 by Charlie May Fletcher. Reprinted by permission of Holt, Rinehart and Winston, Inc.
7 From *Chicago Poems* by Carl Sandburg. Copyright 1916 by Holt, Rinehart and Winston, Inc. Copyright 1944 by Carl Sandburg. Reprinted by permission of Holt, Rinehart and Winston, Inc.

O World, I cannot hold thee close enough!
    Thy winds, thy wide grey skies!
    Thy mists that roll and rise!
Thy woods, this autumn day, that ache and
    sag
And all but cry with colour! That gaunt
    crag
To crush! To lift the lean of that black
    bluff!
World, World, I cannot get thee close
    enough!

Long have I known a glory in it all,
    But never knew I this;
    Here such a passion is
As stretcheth me apart. Lord, I do fear
Thou'st made the world too beautiful this
    year.
My soul is all but out of me — let fall
No burning leaf; prithee, let no bird call.[8]

William Brighty Rands' poem is superficial, diffusive, repetitive, and vague.

Great, wide, beautiful, wonderful world,
With the wonderful water round you curled,
    And the wonderful grass upon your breast,—
    World, you are beautifully drest!

The wonderful air is over me,
And the wonderful wind is shaking the tree;
    It walks on the water, and whirls the mills,
    And talks to itself on the tops of the hills.

You friendly earth! how far do you go
With the wheat fields that nod, and the rivers
    that flow?
    With cities and gardens, and cliffs, and isles,
    And people upon you for thousands of miles?

Ah, you are so great, and I am so small,
I tremble to think of you, World, at all;
    And yet, when I said my prayers today,
    A whisper inside me seemed to say,—
"You are more than the earth, though you are
    such a dot:
You can *love* and *think*, and the earth can not."[9]

Good poets choose their words with great care, because poetry uses the conventions of compression and allusion and each word has greater significance than it would have in prose. It is, then,

extremely important that each word be understood by the reader. This includes the connotations of words as well as their denotations. A word's denotation is its lexical meaning, the meaning found in the dictionary. The connotations are those subtle associations that surround the word. Some words such as love, mother, home, and war have many connotations, while other words have little connotation when used out of context. In poetry a word's connotation may be more important than its denotation because of the overtones and meaning they add to the poem. This can be seen in the deceptively simple poem "Dust of Snow" by Robert Frost.

The way a crow
Shook down on me
The dust of snow
From a hemlock tree

Has given my heart
A change of mood
And saved some part
Of a day I had rued.[10]

The persona, the person speaking in this poem —and it must not be assumed that the poet himself is always the speaker—tells the reader that an experience he has had has lightened his mood for a time. The reader senses that the persona's first mood was somber and that he has suffered some loss. Frost implies this through his images. As a master poet he did not use the word "crow" because it rhymes with "snow" but because it has connotations of blackness and somberness that help develop the mood he wanted to express. That the tree is a hemlock, a tree associated with poison and Socrates' death, suggests the connotation of death. To these overtones Frost carefully adds the word dust with its connotation of the biblical "from dust to dust." When the entire poem is read with careful attention to each word it reveals a deeply moving mood and experience.

Children as well as adults need to be aware that good poems are the result of many deliberate, conscious choices; poems do not occur by chance

---

[8] "God's World" from *Collected Poems* by Edna St. Vincent Millay, Harper & Row, Publishers. Copyright 1913, 1940 by Edna St. Vincent Millay.
[9] "The Wonderful World" from *Lilliput Lectures* by William Brighty Rands. Published by Strahan & Co., 1871.

[10] From *The Poetry of Robert Frost* edited by Edward Connery Latham. Copyright 1916, 1923, 1928, 1930, 1939, © 1967, 1969 by Holt, Rinehart and Winston, Inc. Copyright 1944, 1951, © 1956, 1958 by Robert Frost. Copyright © 1967 by Lesley Frost Ballantine. Reprinted by permission of Holt, Rinehart and Winston, Inc.

and rarely write themselves. Since the poet spends much thought to select the precise words to best convey his meaning, readers must ask themselves, why was this word used? Why that comparison? How do the images and figures of speech reveal the poem's meaning? The language of poetry is not meant to be deceptive. Most poets want their readers to understand what is being expressed, but reading poetry does demand attention and thought.

SYMBOLISM

When the imagery or figures of speech contain a meaning beyond the poem's statement, that image or figure becomes symbolic. Symbolism is not as important or obvious to children as it is to adults. Yet there are some poems children like because they sense the depth symbolism gives. Frost's "The Road Not Taken" is such a poem.

Two roads diverged in a yellow wood,
And sorry I could not travel both
And be one traveler, long I stood
And looked down one as far as I could
To where it bent in the undergrowth;

Then took the other, as just as fair,
And having perhaps the better claim,
Because it was grassy and wanted wear;
Though as for that the passing there
Had worn them really about the same,

And both that morning equally lay
In leaves no step had trodden black.
Oh, I kept the first for another day!
Yet knowing how way leads on to way,
I doubted if I should ever come back.

I shall be telling this with a sigh
Somewhere ages and ages hence:
Two roads diverged in a wood, and I—
I took the one less traveled by,
And that has made all the difference.[11]

Even grade school students are aware that this poem has several levels. They all see the physical images: a wood, two roads, and a man. But many children also sense the roads are more than physical roads and that the poem is not simply a description of an afternoon's walk. Some fifth and six graders and many junior high students realize

[11] From *The Poetry of Robert Frost.*

the roads represent two choices and that the poem is about a decision. Children do not know the literary terms but they sense the symbolic element in this poem.

Children should never be forced to search for symbols, but when one is as obvious and important as in "The Road Not Taken" it should be briefly and nontechnically discussed. The great danger for the inexperienced reader is in over-personalizing symbols. Some older students insist this poem is about Frost's decision to become a poet, others claim it is about the choice between good and evil. Both of these are too specific and do not come from the poem itself. It is natural for the reader's knowledge of Frost's life to influence his interpretations of Frost's poems, but this restricts and often distorts meaning.

Some people believe each reader can find a personal meaning in a poem; that a poem can mean something different to each reader and that any interpretation is correct simply because it was thought of by someone. This is little more than an excuse for lazy and thoughtless reading. While it would be an oversimplification to claim each poem has only one meaning, every abstraction made about a poem must come from a careful reading of the poem itself. When personal biases, lack of knowledge, or language weakness control interpretation, the poem's insights are lost.

SOUNDS OF POETRY

Rhyme

The most familiar of the sounds of poetry is rhyme. It adds to a poem's pleasure by giving a sense of order and pattern. In strict rhyme the vowel and consonant sounds at the ends of the word are repeated. While these words sound alike they may not look alike: go, sew, row, hoe. English, however, has relatively few rhyming words because it has borrowed so many words from other languages. For this reason and for greater flexibility in their patterns, English and American poets use near rhyme. Consonance or slant rhyme is one near rhyme. Instead of having the final vowel and consonant sounds identical, as in strict rhyme, only the final consonants must be the same: boat, hat, cricket. When the words end in stressed vowels they too are considered consonate: he, boy, glue, now.

Another type of near rhyme is bracket rhyme. Again the stressed vowels of the rhyming words are different but everything before and after them must be identical: wives, waves; shop, shape; admitted, muted; done, down; chest, chaste.

Still another type of near rhyme is sight rhyme which, in contrast to strict rhyme, is a visual rather than vocal rhyme—the eye is aware of the pattern but the ear is not: home, come, dew, sew; do, so; food, good.

In some poems the rhyme scheme is the most obvious feature. This occurs when the poet is unable to handle the demands of his pattern and so sacrifices the experience or the narrative for his rhyme. Consider the next poem, "My Dog."

> I have no dog, but it must be
> Somewhere there's one belongs to me—
> A little chap with wagging tail,
> And dark brown eyes that never quail,
> But look you through, and through, and
>   through
> With love unspeakable, but true.
>
> Somewhere my doggie pulls and tugs
> The fringes of rebellious rugs,
> Or with the michief of the pup
> Chews all my shoes and slippers up,
> And when he's done it to the core,
> With eyes all eager pleads for more.
>
> Somewhere a little dog doth wait,
> It may be by some garden gate,
> With eyes alert and tail attent—
> You know the kind of tail that's meant—
> With stores of yelps of glad delight
> To bid me welcome home at night.
>
> Somewhere a little dog is seen,
> His nose two shaggy paws between,
> Flat on his stomach, one eye shut,
> Held fast in dreamy slumber, but
> The other open, ready for
> His master coming through the door.[12]

Mr. Bangs has used several words unusually, not to add greater meaning or precision, but because he needed rhyming words. He has also used inverted word order, a standard poetic device that adds beauty when done well. Mr. Bangs' concern,

however, was not to have a more pleasing sound but to make certain a rhyming word ended the line.

Rhyme must be handled with great skill and control if it is to add to the poem. Too few people who write "children's poetry" have the strength to control their rhyme pattern and instead are driven by it.

Robert Frost was a master of rhyme. He evidently enjoyed the challenge of writing with strong rhyme schemes, but they seldom intrude and make the reader wonder if certain words were used only because they suited the rhyme pattern. "Stopping by Woods on a Snowy Evening" is one of Frost's most famous poems, but too few of its admirers are aware that he used a very demanding rhyme scheme: the first, second, and fourth lines of each stanza rhyme—a difficult pattern in English. But he also repeats the unrhymed last word in the third line of each stanza by using it as the basis of the three-line rhyme in the next stanza. The only change in this rhyme chain is in the last stanza. If the first rhyme is noted by "a," the second rhyme by "b," the third by "c," and the fourth by "d," the rhyme scheme of "Stopping by Woods on a Snowy Evening" is aaba, bbcb, ccdc, dddd. Even with this involved rhyme pattern, no word seems forced or out of place.

> Whose woods these are I think I know.
> His house is in the village though;
> He will not see me stopping here
> To watch his woods fill up with snow.
>
> My little horse must think it queer
> To stop without a farmhouse near
> Between the woods and frozen lake
> The darkest evening of the year.
>
> He gives his harness bells a shake
> To ask if there is some mistake.
> The only other sound's the sweep
> Of easy wind and downy flake.
>
> The woods are lovely, dark and deep,
> But I have promises to keep,
> And miles to go before I sleep,
> And miles to go before I sleep.[13]

Children are aware, sometimes more clearly than adults, that this poem is about a man's response to beauty, and in most fifth and sixth

[12] "My Dog" by John Kendrick Bangs from *The Foothills of Parnassus.*

[13] From *The Poetry of Robert Frost.*

grade classrooms there are students who wonder why Frost repeated the second from the last line. There is usually a child who feels this repetition of sleep implies death and adds meaning to the poem. Is this a correct interpretation of the repetition? It is a common one and one that can grow out of the poem. It should not be used to explain the "meaning" of the poem, but if children discover this symbol, it certainly should be accepted, but not expanded at length or forced.

Here is another Frost poem with a demanding rhyme scheme. Compare this poem with the verse written by John Kendrick Bangs. Where his rhymes are uninteresting and forced, Frost's adds humor to the poem.

> As I went out a Crow
> In a low voice said, "Oh,
> I was looking for you.
> How do you do?
> I just came to tell you
> To tell Lesley (will you?)
> That her little Bluebird
> Wanted me to bring word
> That the north wind last night
> That made the stars bright
> And made ice on the trough
> Almost made him cough
> His tail feathers off.
> He just had to fly!
> But he sent her Good-by,
> And said to be good,
> And wear her red hood,
> And look for skunk tracks
> In the snow with an ax—
> And do everything!
> And perhaps in the spring
> He would come back and sing."[14]

Alliteration and Assonance

Two other sounds of poetry are alliteration and assonance. Alliteration is the repetition in several words of the same consonant sound at the beginning of the stressed syllables. Spelling does not control alliteration since it is a vocal device: the alliteration of cycle and scissors, phone and flower can be heard but not seen. When alliteration is overused it can be monotonous and hinder meaning. However, it can be successfully used to create a humorous effect. When used in this way it brings children great delight. The next poem

is an example of alliteration being successfully used in this way.

> The pickety fence
> The pickety fence
> Give it a lick it's
> The pickety fence
> Give it a lick it's
> A clickety fence
> Give it a lick it's
> A lickety fence
> Give it a lick
> Give it a lick
> Give it a lick
> With a rickety stick
> Pickety
> Pickety
> Pickety
> Pick[15]

Assonance is the repetition of the same vowel sound in the stressed syllables: lady, baby; sit, sing, thin; fine, climb.

John Ciardi's use of alliteration, assonance, and rhyme in the following poem is as important as what he says.

> One day, a fine day, a high-flying-sky day,
> A cat-bird, a fatbird, a fine cat-bird
> Was napping, cat-napping on a stump by the
>   highway.
> Just sitting. And singing. Just that. But a cat
>   heard.
> A thin cat, a grin-cat, a long thin grin-cat
> Came creeping the sly way by the highway to
>   the stump.
> "O cat-bird, the cat heard! O cat-bird scat!
> The grin-cat is creeping! He's going to jump!"
>
> —One day, a fine day, a high-flying-sky day,
> A fat cat, yes, that cat we met as a thin cat
> Was napping, cat-napping on a stump by the
>   highway.
> And even in his sleep you could see he was a
>   grin-cat.
> Why was he grinning?—He must have had a
>   dream.
> What made him fat?—A pan full of cream.
> What about the cat-bird?—What bird, dear?
> I don't see any cat-bird here.[16]

[14] "The Last Word of a Bluebird: As Told to a Child" from *The Poetry of Robert Frost.*

[15] "The Pickety Fence" from *Far and Few* by David McCord, by permission of Little, Brown and Co. Copyright 1952, by David McCord.

[16] "The Cat Heard the Cat-Bird" by John Ciardi from *I Met a Man.* Copyright © 1961 by John Ciardi. Reprinted by permission of the publishers, Houghton Mifflin Company.

Alliteration and assonance are important in the next examples by John Masefield. Both poems express the same longing, but the first is more pleasing to the ear because of the sounds of his language. The primary functions of the sounds of poetry are to please the ear and evoke the mood and tone.

I must go down to the seas again, to the
    lonely sea and the sky,
And all I ask is a tall ship and a star to steer
    her by,
And the wheel's kick and the wind's song and
    the white sail's shaking,
And a gray mist on the sea's face and a gray
    dawn breaking.

I must go down to the seas again, for the call
    of the running tide
Is a wild call and a clear call that may not
    be denied;
And all I ask is a windy day with the white
    clouds flying,
And the flung spray and the blown spume,
    and the sea-gulls crying.

I must go down to the seas again to the
    vagrant gypsy life,
To the gull's way and the whale's way where
    the wind's like a whetted knife;
And all I ask is a merry yarn from a laughing
    fellow-rover,
And quiet sleep and a sweet dream when the
    long trick's over.[17]

Compare the sounds of "Sea-Fever," above, with the following, "A Wanderer's Song."

A wind's in the heart of me, a fire's in my
    heels,
I am tired of brick and stone and rumbling
    wagon-wheels;
I hunger for the sea's edge, the limits of the
    land,
Where the wild old Atlantic is shouting on
    the sand.

Oh I'll be going, leaving the noises of the
    street,
To where a lifting foresail-foot is yanking
    at the sheet;
To a windy, tossing anchorage where yawls
    and ketches ride,
Oh I'll be going, going, until I meet the tide.

And first I'll hear the sea-wind, the mewing
    of the gulls,
The clucking, sucking of the sea about the
    rusty hulls,
The songs at the capstan in the hooker warping
    out,
And then the heart of me'll know I'm there
    or thereabout.

Oh I am tired of brick and stone, the heart of
    me is sick,
For windy green, unquiet sea, the realm of
    Moby Dick;
And I'll be going, going, from the roaring of
    the wheels,
For a wind's in the heart of me, a fire's in
    my heels.[18]

Meter

Rhythm is one of the most important sounds and, like rhyme, it is one of the most abused poetic elements. If well handled, meter can add a great deal because when appropriate to the subject it reinforces the poem's tone, as in "Hoppity" by A. A. Milne.

Christopher Robin goes
Hoppity, hoppity,
Hoppity, hoppity, hop.
Whenever I ask him
Politely to stop it, he
Says he can't possibly stop.

If he stopped hopping, he couldn't go anywhere,
Poor little Christopher
Couldn't go anywhere . . .
That's why he always goes
Hoppity, hoppity,
  Hoppity,
    Hoppity,
      Hop.[19]

However, when meter does not complement the subject, it detracts from the mood. A jogging meter, for example, distorts the author's intent in a serious poem. This happens in "Trees" by Joyce Kilmer and "All Things Bright and Beautiful" by Cecil Frances Alexander (page 932).

[17] "Sea-Fever" by John Masefield. Reprinted with permission of The Macmillan Company from *Poems* by John Masefield. Copyright 1912 by The Macmillan Company, renewed 1940 by John Masefield.

[18] "A Wanderer's Song" by John Masefield. Reprinted with permission of The Macmillan Company from *Poems* by John Masefield. Copyright 1916 by John Masefield, renewed 1944 by John Masefield.

[19] From *When We Were Very Young* by A. A. Milne. Illustrated by E. H. Shepard. Copyright 1924 by E. P. Dutton & Co., Inc. Renewal copyright 1952 by A. A. Milne. Published by E. P. Dutton & Co., Inc., and reprinted with their permission.

Too many versifiers who write for children use a sing-song pattern. They seem to feel tight rhymes and meters are the most important poetic elements. Unfortunately, this rigidity can be successfully handled only by master poets who can avoid monotony. When rhyme and rhythm dominate a verse, as in "My Dog" by John Kendrick Bangs (page 927), they not only oppose the author's mood but also reveal his lack of skill.

In the following excerpt from "Swimmers" by Louis Untermeyer, rhythm is effective in evoking within the reader the persona's vitality and excitement as well as the ocean's power. Notice how the author varies his metric pattern to recreate the rhythms of both the surf and the swimmer.

> Then, the swift plunge into the cool, green
>   dark—
> The windy waters rushing past me, through me;
> Filled with a sense of some heroic lark,
> Exulting in a vigor clean and roomy.
> Swiftly I rose to meet the cat-like sea
> That sprang upon me with a hundred claws,
> And grappled, pulled me down and played with
>   me.
> Then, held suspended in the tightening pause
> When one wave grows into a toppling acre,
> I dived headlong into the foremost breaker;
> Pitting against a cold and turbulent strife
> The feverish intensity of life.
> Out of the foam I lurched and rode the wave,
> Swimming, hand over hand, against the
>   wind. . . .[20]

CHILDREN AND POETRY

Young children respond to poetry with enthusiasm because the rhythms of poetry are like the rhythms of life: heart beating, eyes blinking, walking, breathing. The sounds of poetry appeal to children's linguistic explorations. Young children are forced to be language explorers as they learn their language patterns. They enjoy the interesting sounds and words of poetry. As they jump, skip, and play games they chant. Rhymes are used to tease or taunt peers. Youngsters listen joyfully to nursery rhymes and often repeat phrases that delight them.

Why, then, do older children turn from poetry?

Why is poetry sometimes considered too "sissy" for ten-year-old boys? Why are volumes of poetry in most libraries the least read books, not only by children, but also by adults? To those who love both children and poetry, these are disturbing questions. But when examples of what is traditionally called "children's poetry" are read, the answers are easily seen. Unfortunately much "children's poetry" is wishy-washy, trivial, and trite. It often talks down to children and embarrasses them. Too often it is unimportant and uninteresting. Compare the following verses with poetry by Frost, Ciardi, and Untermeyer.

> Some one came knocking
>   At my wee, small door;
> Some one came knocking,
>   I'm sure—sure—sure;
> I listened, I opened,
>   I looked to left and right,
> But nought there was a-stirring
>   In the still dark night;
>
> Only the busy beetle
>   Tap-tapping in the wall,
> Only from the forest
>   The screech owl's call,
> Only the cricket whistling
>   While the dewdrops fall,
> So I know not who came knocking,
>   At all, at all, at all.[21]

The above poem is patronizing; it contains a condescending whimsey that some adults assume will appeal to children, as do the following verses.

> There are fairies at the bottom of our garden!
>   It's not so very, very far away;
> You pass the gardener's shed and you just keep
>   straight ahead —
>   I do so hope they've really come to stay.
> There's a little wood, with moss in it and beetles,
>   And a little stream that quietly runs through;
> You wouldn't think they'd dare to come merry-
>   making there —
>   Well, they do.
>
> There are fairies at the bottom of our garden!
>   They often have a dance on summer nights;
> The butterflies and bees make a lovely little
>   breeze,

---

[20] Excerpt from "Swimmers" by Louis Untermeyer. Copyright, 1917, 1945, by Louis Untermeyer. Reprinted from his volume, *Long Feud*, by permission of Harcourt Brace Jovanovich, Inc.

[21] "Some One" by Walter de la Mare. From *Collected Poems*, published by Holt, Rinehart and Winston, Inc. Reprinted by permission of The Literary Trustees of Walter de la Mare, and The Society of Authors as their representative.

And the rabbits stand about and hold the
lights.
Did you know that they could sit upon the
moonbeams
And pick a little star to make a fan,
And dance away up there in the middle of the
air?

Well, they can.

There are fairies at the bottom of our garden!
You cannot think how beautiful they are;
They all stand up and sing when the Fairy
Queen and King
Come gently floating down upon their car.
The King is very proud and *very* handsome;
The Queen — now can you guess who that
could be?
(She's a little girl all day, but at night she steals
away)

Well — it's *me*![22]

It's not that children today do not believe in
fairies; children have always and will always fan-
tasize just as they will always make plans for
when they are adults. But the tone of "The
Fairies" and the next verse is not honest; it is
"cute" and "sweet."

I keep three wishes ready,
Lest I should chance to meet
Any day a fairy
Coming down the street.

I'd hate to have to stammer,
Or have to think them out,
For it's very hard to think things up
When a fairy is about.

And I'd hate to lose my wishes,
For fairies fly away,
And perhaps I'd never have a chance
On any other day.

So I keep three wishes ready,
Lest I should chance to meet
Any day a fairy
Coming down the street.[23]

[22] "The Fairies" by Rose Fyleman. From *Fairies and
Chimneys* by Rose Fyleman. Copyright 1918, 1920 by
George H. Doran Company. Reprinted by permission of
Doubleday & Company, Inc., and The Society of Authors
as the literary representative of the Estate of Rose Fyleman.
[23] "I Keep Three Wishes Ready" by Annette Wayne.
From the book *All Through the Year* by Annette Wynne.
Copyright, 1932, renewal, ©, 1960 by Annette Wayne.
Reprinted by permission of J. B. Lippincott Company.

These poems do not represent true poetry; they
are, rather, verse—the type of verse that has turned
too many children away from poetry. Verses such
as these give the impression that poetry is unimportant and false.

POETRY BY ASSOCIATION

Many people respond to "The Wonderful
World," (page 925) because it is about nature.
Most people are conditioned to respond to God,
love, patriotism, nature, etc. This type of conditioned response is what allows so much verse to
be called poetry when it is only poetry by association—verse that uses the outward forms of poetry
plus "poetic" subjects. These fail to become
poetry when they are shallow, sentimental and
cliche-ridden.

Joyce Kilmer's "Trees" is such a verse. References to nature, God, prayer, the sweet earth, combined with a strong rhythm and rhyme, have made
many people believe it to be a good poem.[24]

Any one who reads "Trees" with thought is
struck by the monotony of the meter which gives
the poem a jerky quality that detracts from the
seriousness of Kilmer's feeling. Very little attention is necessary to discover that the basic comparison of a tree to a female person is confused.
As Cleanth Brooks and Robert Penn Warren
showed in the 1938 edition of *Understanding
Poetry*[25] the comparison in lines 3 and 4 is a
standard image of a young babe, but in lines 5
and 6 the tree is compared with a girl suddenly
old enough and religious enough to raise her arms
in prayer—all day. If it is not physically impossible to raise both arms in the air while the mouth
is on the ground it is at least uncomfortable. Such
criticism is not "nit-picking"; visual imagery is
meant to be seen, to actually be visualized by
the reader, for when the image is appropriate,
visualization adds meaning and depth to the
poem. Kilmer next compares the tree to a woman
who wears decorations in her hair and then with
a woman who is alone with nature. Not only are
the images confused and confusing, they have no

[24] Permission was refused to reprint "Trees" in this text,
but the poem unfortunately is still to be found in school
books and children's poetry anthologies.
[25] The third edition was published by Holt, Rinehart and
Winston in 1960 and a fourth edition is in preparation.

depth nor uniqueness for they have been used many times before and since Kilmer wrote his verse.

Another trite verse is "All Things Bright and Beautiful" by Cecil Frances Alexander.

> All things bright and beautiful,
>   All creatures great and small,
> All things wise and wonderful
>   The Lord God made them all.
>
> Each little flower that opens,
>   Each little bird that sings,
> He made their glowing colors,
>   He made their tiny wings.
>
> The purple-headed mountain,
>   The river running by,
> The sunset and the morning,
>   That brighten up the sky:
>
> The cold wind in the winter,
>   The pleasant summer sun,
> The ripe fruit in the garden,
>   He made them every one.
>
> The tall trees in the greenwood,
>   The meadows where we play,
> The rushes by the water
>   We gather every day:
>
> He gave us eyes to see them,
>   And lips that we may tell
> How great is God Almighty,
>   Who has made all things well.[26]

This verse is still anthologized for children. Again, the references to God and nature and the man's appreciation of beauty may make this accepted as a poem. But what is its poetic merit? The images are commonplace, the words vague. Both Kilmer and Alexander rely more on sentimentality, the exploitation of basic and deep feelings, than upon insight. No matter how sincere the sentimental poet may be, the cliches, stock responses, and lack of originality make his poem seem shallow and false.

Poetry can be the most truthful literature a child reads because the best poets have a greater depth of perception than most people. They also possess the language skills that enable them to share their insights. Good poets see more deeply,

express more precisely, use words more carefully than other people. They do not limit poetry to the "pretty" or profound, for it may be written about any experience, feeling, insight, or narrative. It can be serious or nonsensical, but if it is to be good it must be valid. It must go beyond abstraction and generalization and appeal to the reader's senses so that the poet's experience, feeling, insight, or story will be real to his audience.

Children need poetry but will only continue to read it if they are given poems that interest them. If adults hope to instill a love of poetry, they must be able to distinguish between the artificial and the honest, between the versifier and the poet.

The previous discussion briefly covers only the most basic elements of poetry. It is included primarily to help teachers and librarians approach poetry with an understanding of how it operates. It does not, then, follow that children need to formally study the poetic elements. Hearing, reading, and enjoying good poetry is the best introduction and background they can have. Children need opportunities to discover how poems can clarify, expand, and deepen their insights and enjoyment of life.

POEMS FOR COMPARISON

The three groups of poems following have been chosen to facilitate comparisons under the subject categories of Trees, Snow, and The Moon and Night. Each group contains examples of successful and unsuccessful attempts to write poetry. Discussing the quality of imagery, figures of speech, and rhyme schemes will help develop an understanding of the difference between poetry and verse.

The following points can be considered: What rhyme and rhythm patterns are used? Do they naturally grow out of and complement the subject or mood or do they seem artificially imposed?

Are figures of speech used? If so, do they clarify or add depth to the author's insight? Are they obvious comparisons or do they reveal the poet's view of the world?

What is the quality of the imagery? Does the writer rely on commonplace descriptive words that touch only obvious surface appearance? Is the verse only a list of descriptive words?

[26] "All Things Bright and Beautiful" from *Hymns for Little Children* by Cecil Frances Alexander. Published by Gorham, 1850.

What of the words? Are the nouns and verbs carefully chosen to evoke within the reader the poet's emotions or vision? Are the connotations of the words as important as the denotations? Remember that the poet does not have to write down or simplify his language to compensate for his reader's limited vocabulary. While Emily Dickinson's poetry is beyond young children, fifth grade and older students can learn a great deal about specific description and comparisons by studying "It Sifts from Leaden Sieves," as exact a description of a cold, country winter as has ever been written. The true poets choose the most exact words that will reveal to the reader what they have seen and felt.

What sounds of poetry have been used? Do they suit the tone and so add to the reader's understanding?

Is the poem a straight description with no symbolism? If so, is the poem original and fresh or does it rely primarily on cliches or on the reader's associations toward "poetic" subjects?

GROUP A/Trees

TREES

Harry Behn

Trees are the kindest things I know,
They do no harm, they simply grow

And spread a shade for sleepy cows,
And gather birds among their boughs.

They give us fruit in leaves above,
And wood to make our houses of,

And leaves to burn on Hallowe'en,
And in the Spring new buds of green.

They are the first when day's begun
To touch the beams of morning sun,

They are the last to hold the light
When evening changes into night,

And when a moon floats on the sky
They hum a drowsy lullaby

Of sleepy children long ago . . .
Trees are the kindest things I know.

A SALUTE TO TREES

Henry van Dyke

Many a tree is found in the wood,
And every tree for its use is good.
Some for the strength of the gnarled root,
Some for the sweetness of flower or fruit,
Some for shelter against the storm,
And some to keep the hearthstone warm,
Some for the roof, and some for the beam,
And some for a boat to breast the storm.
In the wealth of the wood since the world began,
The trees have offered their gifts to man.

I have camped in the whispering forest of pines,
I have slept in the shadow of olives and vines;
In the knees of an oak, at the foot of a palm,
I have found good rest and slumber's balm.
And now, when the morning gilds the boughs
Of the vaulted elm at the door of my house,
I open the window and make a salute:
"God bless thy branches and feed thy root!
Thou hast lived before, live after me,
Thou ancient, friendly, faithful tree!"

TREES

Sara Coleridge

The Oak is called the King of Trees,
The Aspen quivers in the breeze,
The Poplar grows up straight and tall,
The Pear Tree spreads along the wall,
The Sycamore gives pleasant shade,
The Willow droops in watery glade,
The Fir Tree useful timber gives,
The Beech amid the forest lives.

THE POPLARS

Theodosia Garrison

My poplars are like ladies trim,
Each conscious of her own estate;
In costume somewhat over prim,
In manner cordially sedate,
Like two old neighbors met to chat
Beside my garden gate.

My stately old aristocrats—
I fancy still their talk must be
Of rose conserves and Persian cats,
And lavender and India tea;
I wonder sometimes as I pass
If they approve of me.

I give them greeting night and morn,
I like to think they answer, too,
With that benign assurance born
When youth gives age the reverence due,
And bend their wise heads as I go,
As courteous ladies do.

Long may you stand before my door,
O kindly neighbors garbed in green,
And bend with rustling welcome o'er
The many friends who pass between;
And where the little children play
Look down with gracious mien.

LOVELIEST OF TREES

A. E. Housman

Loveliest of trees, the cherry now
Is hung with bloom along the bough,
And stands about the woodland ride
Wearing white for Eastertide.

Now, of my threescore years and ten,
Twenty will not come again,
And take from seventy springs a score,
It only leaves me fifty more.
And since to look at things in bloom
Fifty springs are little room,
About the woodland I will go
To see the cherry hung with snow.

GROUP B/Snow

VELVET SHOES

Elinor Wylie

Let us walk in the white snow
    In a soundless space;
With footsteps quiet and slow,
    At a tranquil pace,
    Under veils of white lace.

I shall go shod in silk,
    And you in wool,
White as a white cow's milk,
    More beautiful
    Than the breast of a gull.

"Loveliest of Trees" by A. E. Housman. From "A Shropshire Lad"—Authorized Edition—from *The Collected Poems of A. E. Housman.* Copyright 1939, 1940, © 1959 by Holt, Rinehart and Winston, Inc. Copyright © 1967, 1968 by Robert E. Symons. Reprinted by permission of Holt, Rinehart and Winston, Inc., and The Society of Authors as the literary representative of the Estate of A. E. Housman, and Jonathan Cape Ltd., publishers of A. E. Housman's *Collected Poems.*

"The Poplars" from *Dreamers and Other Poems* by Theodosia Garrison. Published by Doubleday & Company, Inc.

We shall walk through the still town
    In a windless peace;
We shall step upon white down,
    Upon silver fleece,
    Upon softer than these.

We shall walk in velvet shoes:
    Wherever we go
Silence will fall like dews
    On white silence below.
    We shall walk in the snow.

FALLING SNOW

Anonymous

See the pretty snowflakes
    Falling from the sky;
On the walk and housetop
    Soft and thick they lie.

On the window-ledges,
    On the branches bare;
Now how fast they gather,
    Filling all the air.

Look into the garden,
    Where the grass was green;
Covered by the snowflakes,
    Not a blade is seen.

Now the bare black bushes
    All look soft and white,
Every twig is laden,—
    What a pretty sight!

IT SIFTS FROM LEADEN SIEVES

Emily Dickinson

It sifts from leaden sieves,
It powders all the wood
It fills with alabaster wool
The wrinkles of the road.

It makes an even face
Of mountain and of plain, —
Unbroken forehead from the east
Unto the east again.

It reaches to the fence,
It wraps it, rail by rail,
Till it is lost in fleeces;
It flings a crystal veil

On stump and stack and stem, —
The summer's empty room,
Acres of seams where harvests were,
Recordless, but for them.

It ruffles wrists of posts,
As ankles of a queen, —
Then stills its artisans like ghosts,
Denying they have been.

SNOW

Dorothy Aldis

The fenceposts wear marshmallow hats
On a snowy day;
Bushes in their night gowns,
Are kneeling down to pray—
And all the trees have silver skirts
And want to dance away.

GROUP C/The Moon and Night

THE MOON

Emily Dickinson

The moon was but a chin of gold
    A night or two ago
And now she turns her perfect face
    Upon the world below.

Her forehead is of amplest blond;
    Her cheeks like beryl stone;
Her eye unto the summer dew
    That likest I have known.

Her lips of amber never part;
    But what must be the smile
Upon her friend she could bestow
    Were such her silver will!

And what a privilege to be
    But the remotest star!
For certainly her way might pass
    Beside your twinkling door.

Her bonnet is the firmament,
    The universe her shoe,
The stars the trinkets at her belt,
    Her dimities of blue.

THE MOON'S THE NORTH
WIND'S COOKY
(*What the little girl said*)

Vachel Lindsay

The Moon's the North Wind's cooky.
He bites it, day by day,
Until there's but a rim of scraps
That crumble all away.

"The Moon" by Emily Dickinson From *Collected Poems
of Emily Dickinson*, edited by Thomas H. Johnson. Published by Little, Brown and Co.

The South Wind is a baker.
He kneads clouds in his den,
And bakes a crisp new moon *that . . . greedy
North . . . Wind . . . eats . . . again!*

MOONLIGHT

Maud E. Uschold

Like a white cat
Moonlight peers through windows,
Listening, watching.
Like a white cat it moves
Across the threshold
And stretches itself on the floor;
It sits on a chair
And puts white paws on the table.
Moonlight crouches among shadows,
Watching, waiting
The slow passing of night.

CHECK

James Stephens

The Night was creeping on the ground.
She crept and did not make a sound,

Until she reached the tree; and then
She covered it, and stole again

Along the grass beside the wall.
I heard the rustling of her shawl

"The Moon's the North Wind's Cooky" by Vachel Lindsay. Reprinted with permission of The Macmillan Company from *Collected Poems* by Vachel Lindsay. Copyright
1916 by The Macmillan Company, renewed 1942 by Elizabeth C. Lindsay.
"Moonlight" by Maud E. Uschold. © 1951 by The New
York Times Company. Reprinted by permission.

As she threw blackness everywhere,
Along the sky, the ground, the air,

And in the room where I was hid.
But, no matter what she did

To everything that was without,
She could not put my candle out!

So I stared at the Night! And she
Stared solemnly back at me!

FROM ANOTHER TIME

Two forces helped create children's literature: the need for laughter and pleasure and the desire to teach children to live wisely. Much early European poetry for youngsters was serious and moralistic because adults in the eighteenth and nineteenth centuries used it to instruct children in proper social and religious beliefs. Through literature they were taught to fear God, obey their superiors, and to know their social position and responsibilities. Many of these early poems are bluntly admonitory and include a moral precept. Sometimes, as in "Old Sarah," they can seem rather heartless today. Poetic didacticism was not limited to the first children's poetry; it retained a significant role even into the 1890s, as can be seen in "Dreams," the last example in this section.

Didacticism, however, was not the only trend in the eighteenth and nineteenth centuries. Blake's Songs of Innocence is in direct contrast with the harshness of many of his contemporaries. Some of Ann and Jane Taylor's poetry is gentle and quietly amusing. And for children who were allowed to read them, there were even a number of riotous and at times bawdy poems. A few of these and the more serious poems are anthologized in Leonard de Vries' collection of early children's literature, Flowers of Delight, and in Andrew W. Tuer's Old-Fashioned Children's Books.

The following selections have been chosen to reflect these two important trends in children's literature and also to allow comparisons of early children's poetry with that written in this century.

A CRADLE SONG

Isaac Watts

(From *Divine and Moral Songs* by Isaac Watts, also entitled *Divine Songs Attempted in Easy Language for the Use of Children,* 1715.)

Hush! my dear, lie still and slumber;
   Holy angels guard thy bed!
Heavenly blessings without number
   Gently falling on thy head.

Sleep, my babe; thy food and raiment,
   House and home, thy friends provide;
All without thy care or payment
   All thy wants are well supplied.

How much better thou'rt attended
   Than the Son of God could be,
When from Heaven He descended,
   And became a child like thee!

Soft and easy is thy cradle:
   Coarse and hard thy Saviour lay;

When His birth-place was a stable,
    And His softest bed was hay.

See the kindly shepherds round Him,
    Telling wonders from the sky!
When they sought Him, there they found Him,
    With His Virgin-mother by.

See the lovely Babe a-dressing:
    Lovely Infant, how He smiled!
When He wept, the mother's blessing
    Soothed and hushed the Holy Child.

Lo, He slumbers in His manger,
    Where the hornéd oxen fed;—
Peace, my darling! here's no danger!
    Here's no ox a-near thy bed!—

Mayst thou live to know and fear Him,
    Trust and love Him all thy days:
Then go and dwell forever near Him;
    See His face, and sing His praise.

I could give thee thousand kisses,
    Hoping what I most desire;
Not a mother's fondest wishes
    Can to greater joys aspire.

TOMMY TRIP'S HISTORY . . .

(From *A Pretty Book of Pictures for Little Masters and Misses: or, Tommy Trip's History of Beasts and Birds. With a Familiar Description of Each in Verse and Prose. . . . Ninth Edition.* London: Printed for J. Newbery, in St. Paul's Churchyard, 1767.)

OF THE FOX

So artful, so serious he looks and so sly
    At the goose when he casteth his eye on't,
That he seems like a gamester intent on his die,
    Or a lawyer surveying his client.

OF THE LEOPARD

Few beasts can with the Leopard vie
    His beauteous skin allures the eye,
His form, like Vice, serves to decoy
    Those whom his nature would destroy.

OF THE RHINOCEROS

Should some fine lady view this beast
    His beauties ne'er could charm her,
Oh, how unlike Sir Foplin dressed
    Appears this hog in armour.

INTRODUCTION

William Blake

Piping down the valleys wild,
    Piping songs of pleasant glee,
On a cloud I saw a child,
    And he laughing said to me:

"Pipe a song about a lamb!"
    So I piped with merry cheer.
"Piper, pipe that song again";
    So I piped: he wept to hear.

"Drop thy pipe, thy happy pipe;
    Sing thy songs of happy cheer!"
So I sang the same again,
    While he wept with joy to hear.

"Piper, sit thee down and write
    In a book that all may read."
So he vanished from my sight;
    And I plucked a hollow reed,

And I made a rural pen,
    And I stained the water clear,
And I wrote my happy songs
    Every child may joy to hear.

LAUGHING SONG

William Blake

When the green woods laugh with the voice of
    joy,
And the dimpling stream runs laughing by;

"Of the Fox," "Of the Leopard," and "Of the Rhinoceros" from *Tommy Trip's History of Beasts and Birds.* Reprinted in *Stories from Old-Fashioned Children's Books,* compiled by Andrew W. Tuer. The Leadenhall Press, 1899–1900, London. Reissued by Singing Tree Press. "Introduction" and "Laughing Song" from *Songs of Innocence* by William Blake, 1789.

When the air does laugh with our merry wit,
And the green hill laughs with the noise of it;

When the meadows laugh with lively green,
And the grasshopper laughs in the merry scene;
When Mary and Susan and Emily
With their sweet round mouths sing, "Ha ha he!"

When the painted birds laugh in the shade,
When our table with cherries and nuts is spread;
Come live, and be merry, and join with me,
To sing the sweet chorus of "Ha ha he!"

NURSE'S SONG

William Blake

When the voices of children are heard on the
    green
    And laughing is heard on the hill,
My heart is at rest within my breast,
    And everything else is still.

"Then come home, my children, the sun is gone
    down.
    And the dews of night arise;
Come, come, leave off play, and let us away
    Till the morning appears in the skies."

"No, no, let us play, for it is yet day,
    And we cannot go to sleep;
Besides in the sky little birds fly,
    And the hills are covered with sheep."

"Well, well, go and play till the light fades away,
    And then go home to bed."
The little ones leaped and shouted and laughed;
    And all the hills echoed.

ORIGINAL POEMS FOR INFANT MINDS

WASHING AND DRESSING

Ann Taylor

(From *Original Poems for Infant Minds. By several Young Persons.* 2 vols. First Edition 1804, Twentieth Edition 1821. Harvy & Darton, No. 55 Gracechurch Street, London.)

Ah! why will my dear little girl be so cross,
    And cry, and look sulky, and pout?
To lose her sweet smile is a terrible loss,
    I can't even kiss her without.
You say you don't like to be wash'd and be drest,
    But would you be dirty and foul?
Come, drive that long sob from your dear little
        breast,
    And clear your sweet face from its scowl.
If the water is cold, and the comb hurts your
        head,
    And the soap has got into your eye;
Will the water grow warmer for all that you've
        said?
    And what good will it do you to cry?
It is not to tease you and hurt you, my sweet,
    But only for kindness and care,
That I wash you, and dress you, and make you
        look neat,
    And comb out your tanglesome hair.
I don't mind the trouble, if you would not cry,
    But pay me for all with a kiss;
That's right—take the towel and wipe your wet
        eye,
    I thought you'd be good after this.

THE STAR

Jane Taylor

Twinkle, twinkle, little star,
How I wonder what you are,
Up above the world so high,
Like a diamond in the sky.

When the blazing sun is set,
And the grass with dew is wet,
Then you show your little light,
Twinkle, twinkle, all the night.

Then the traveler in the dark
Thanks you for your tiny spark,
He could not see where to go
If you did not twinkle so.

"Washing and Dressing" by Ann Taylor and "The Star" by Jane Taylor. Reprinted in *Stories from Old-Fashioned Childrens Books*, compiled by Andrew W. Tuer. Published by The Leadenhall Press, 1899–1900, London. Reissued by Singing Tree Press.

In the dark blue sky you keep,
And often through my curtains peep,
For you never shut your eye
Till the sun is in the sky.

As your bright and tiny spark
Lights the traveler in the dark,
Though I know not what you are,
Twinkle, twinkle, little star.

CHILD AND MAMMA

Jane Taylor

(From *Jane Taylor's Hymns for Infant Minds.*)

CHILD

Tell me, mamma, if I must die
    One day as little baby died;
And look so very pale, and lie
    Down in the pit-hole by his side?

Shall I leave dear papa and you,
    And never see you any more?
Tell me, mamma, if this is true;
    I did not know it was before.

MAMMA

'Tis true, my love, that you must die;
    The God who made you says you must;
And every one of us shall lie,
    Like the dear baby, in the dust.

These hands, and feet, and busy head,
Shall waste and crumble right away;
But though your body shall be dead,
    There is a part which can't decay.

"Child and Mamma" by Jane Taylor. Reprinted by permission of The World Publishing Company and Arthur Barker Ltd. from *Little Wide Awake, An Anthology from Victorian Children's Books and Periodicals in the Collection of Anne and Fernand G. Renier*, copyright © 1967 by Leonard de Vries for this selection.

THE KITTEN AT PLAY

William Wordsworth

See the kitten on the wall,
Sporting with the leaves that fall,
Withered leaves, one, two, and three
Falling from the elder-tree,
Through the calm and frosty air
Of the morning bright and fair.

See the kitten, how she starts,
Crouches, stretches, paws and darts;
With a tiger-leap half way
Now she meets her coming prey.
Lets it go fast and then
Has it in her power again.

THE LILY

(The following four poems are from *The Lily, a Book for Children Containing Twenty-two Trifles in Verse*. Adorned with cuts. London. Printed for J. Harris, St. Paul's Church-Yard, 1808).

THE ROD

Little George would not be dress'd,
    He pouted, scream'd and cried;
Repulsed the maid, if she caress'd
    And all her threats defied.

He gave her many a fruitless blow,
    To keep off soap and water;
But, at last was made to know
    'Twas wrong that he had fought her.

For when the rod appear'd in sight,
    His passion soon was cool'd,
His face was wash'd, and all was right;
    And George was quickly rul'd.

THE SCHOOL

There was a little girl so proud,
She talked so fast and laughed so loud,

"The Rod," "The School," "The Contrast," and "The Remedy" reprinted in *Stories from Old Fashioned Children's Books*, compiled by Andrew W. Tuer. Published by The Leadenhall Press, 1899–1900, London. Reissued by Singing Tree Press.

That those who came with her to play
Were always glad to go away,
In bracelets, necklace she did shine;
Her clothes were always very fine.
Her frocks through carelessness were soiled,
In truth she was already spoiled.
Her mother died; she went to school,
And there obliged to live by rule.
Though oft before the time for bed,
A cap with bells disgraced her head.
Tickets—for *idleness* she had,
And these sometimes would make her sad.
So when she'd been at school a year,
And Christmas holidays were drawing near,
Her greatest faults were all amended
And to her learning she attended.
When false indulgence warps the mind,
The discipline of school we find
Most efficacious to correct
The ills arising from neglect.

THE CONTRAST

On the cold stones a boy was laid;
    Whilst tears bedewed his pallid cheek,
"Oh pity me!" was all he said,
    From weakness he could hardly speak.

A bigger boy was passing by,
    Whose garb bespoke abundant wealth;
He saw the tear, he heard the sigh,
    And the pale cheek devoid of health.

Unmov'd he heard—*"Oh pity me!"*
    Pity ne'er touched his callous heart;
He bade the child that moment flee,
    Or he would force him to depart.

"Away young rascal, instant go,
    "Or I will make you feel my stick;
" 'Tis all a lie—your tale of woe:
    "And I am sure you are not sick.

"You look so young, you ought to work,
    "And not sit idling here all day;
"But in this place you shall not lurk,
    "Thus filling up the common way."

Then on his head he laid the cane,
    The little boy soon felt the smart;

And growing bolder from the pain,
    Told him *he would not then depart*.

Just now, advancing came a youth
    His satchell hung with careless grace;
And innocence and heav'n-born truth
    Both shone resplendent in his face.

The unequal contest soon he heard;
    He pulled th' opponent by the nose
Called him a coward, most absurd,
    For ridiculing infant woes.

The coward slunk in fear away;
    The champion hooted as he ran;
Now tell me readers—tell me pray,
    Which will make the braver man?

THE REMEDY

Louisa was a pretty child
Her temper flexible and mild.
She learnt her lessons all with ease,
And very seldom failed to please.
But still Louisa had a fault:
So fond of tasting sugar, salt,
Or anything, in short, to eat,
Puddings, pies, or wine or meat;
And as she was so often sick,
Mamma soon guessed the foolish trick
And, planning for her little daughter,
By stratagem she fairly caught her.
Unseen, Louisa would remain,
And all the dirty glasses drain;
Or carefully some closet shut,
Until a slice of cake she cut.
The dinner done, one winter's day,
And guests removed, their cards to play,
Louisa stole where they'd deserted,
And by her usual pranks diverted,
Here see this foolish, greedy lass
Draining the bottom of each glass,
Eating the parings of the fruit,
And scraping a pine-apple root;
When, lo, a tumbler caught her sight,
Which gave Louisa new delight,
For it appeared half full of wine,
So sparkling, and so clear and fine,
She drank it quick, and hardly tasted,
Nor one drop of the liquor wasted.

Had you at that moment seen her face,
So much distorted by grimace,
How she stamped and cried and spluttered
Complained, grew sick, and faintly muttered,
Then sought the nursery and her bed;
And glad thereon to lay her head,
You soon, I think, had understood
The wine Louisa thought so good,
Was mixed with physic by her mother
And slyly placed there by her brother.

And from the sickness she endured
Her love of tasting soon was cured.

THE EVIL OF GOING
TOO NEAR THE FIRE

(From *Familiar Representations with Suitable
Descriptions and Useful Observations in Prose
and Verse. Beautified with various Engravings.*
London: Printed for John Chappell, Hayden
Square, Minories, n.d.)

Julia did as she had done
    On many days before;
And from her eldest brother's books
    The printed pages tore.

But as she o'er the fender reach'd
    The lighted coals below;
The paper burnt her muslin frock
    And burnt her person too!

Such blisters on her arms appear'd
    Such scars upon her face!
As neither doctor can remove
    Nor time itself erase.

And what excruciating pain
    She suffered for her play;
Which made her promise not to do
    The same another day.

GAMMER GURTON'S GARLAND

(From *Gammer Gurton's Garland: or the Nursery
Parnassus. A Choice Collection of Pretty Songs
and Verses, for the amusement of all little good
children who can neither read nor run.* London:

Printed for R. Triphook, 37, St. James's Street, by
Harding and Wright, St. John's Square, 1810.)

THE OLD WOMAN
THAT WAS TOSS'D
IN A BLANKET

There was an old woman toss'd in a blanket
    Seventeen times as high as the moon;
But where she was going no mortal could tell,
    For under her arm she carried a broom.

Old woman, old woman, old woman, said I,
    Whither, ah whither, ah whither so high?
To sweep the cobwebs from the sky,
    And I'll be with you by and by.

THE SONG OF THE THREE
WISE MEN OF GOTHAM,
WHO WENT TO SEA
IN A BOWL

Three wise men of Gotham
Went to sea in a bowl,
And if the bowl had been stronger
My song had been longer.

THE SURPRIZING
OLD WOMAN

There was an old woman, and what do you think
She lived upon nothing but victuals and drink;
And tho' victuals and drink were the chief of her
    diet,
This plaguy old woman could never be quiet.

She went to the baker to buy her some bread,
And when she came home, her old husband was
    dead;
She went to the clerk to toll the bell,
And when she came back her old husband was
    well.

"The Old Woman That Was Toss'd in a Blanket," "The
Song of the Three Wise Men," and "The Surprizing Old
Woman" reprinted in *Stories from Old-Fashioned Children's Books*, compiled by Andrew W. Tuer. Published
by The Leadenhall Press, 1899–1900, London. Reissued
by Singing Tree Press.

BOOK OF TRADES

(From *Book of Trades*. March's Penny Library. London: Printed by J. March. Circa 1850.)

THE ENGINEER

Come along Master Gray, let's be off for the day,
    The steam it is up, and is puffing away;
Our cares we can lighten at Windsor or Brighton,
    The distance is great, and there's little to pay.

So rapid the pace, no horse in a race
    Could equal the speed of our train;
How frightfully fast the other trains past.
    I wish we were safe out again.

Thus on railways we fly (or at least very nigh),
    Few birds on the wing can go faster;
With a staunch Engineer there is nothing to fear
    Except now and then a disaster.

THE BLACK-SMITH

The bellows roar, the fire burns,
    The Smiths their hammers raise in turns;
The Iron then begins to show
    A different shape at every blow.
Useful in every form it takes,
    Horses shoes, ploughs, spades, or rakes;
In short, for *use* we are truely told
    That Iron far surpasses gold.

THE FIREWORKS

(From *The Misfortunes of Toby Ticklepitcher*. March's Penny Library. London: Printed by J. March. Circa 1850.)

Hal, Jerry, and Toby were all lazy boys,
    Neglecting their lessons, and breaking their toys;
Not heeding a word that their parents might say,
    But wasting their time in the streets all the day:
Till one fatal eve, they had cause to remember
    Hal's wicked mishap ('twas the fifth of November),

When Jerry bought fireworks—filled both his pockets
    With crackers & blue-lights, squibs, serpents, & rockets.

Hal call'd out to Toby, 'come let's have a lark,'
    Then lighted a paper, and planted a spark
In poor Jerry's pocket, which blazed away
    With such fatal effect, that he died the next day.

TIT BITS FOR TINY WITS

(*Tit Bits for Tiny Wits* from *Birdie's Book*. London: Published by George Routledge and Sons. 1880.)

GOOD NATURE

Two good little children, named Mary and Ann,
Both happily live, as good girls always can;
And though they are not either sullen or mute,
They seldom or never are heard to dispute.

If one wants a thing that the other would like—
Well, what do they do? Must they quarrel and strike?
No: each is so willing to give up her own,
That such disagreements are there never known.

THE VULGAR LITTLE LADY

'But, mamma, now,' said Charlotte, 'pray don't you believe
    That I'm better than Jenny, my nurse?
    Only see my red shoes, and the lace on my sleeve;
    Her clothes are a thousand times worse.'

'Gentility, Charlotte,' her mother replied,
    'Belongs to no station or place;
And nothing's so vulgar as folly and pride,
    Though dress'd in red slippers and lace.'

"The Engineer," "The Black-Smith," "The Fireworks," "Good Nature," "The Vulgar Little Lady," "Old Sarah," "The Little Cripple," and "Morning" reprinted by permission of The World Publishing Company and Arthur Barker Ltd. from *Little Wide Awake, an Anthology from Victorian Children's Books and Periodicals in the Collection of Anne and Fernand G. Renier.* Copyright © by Leonard de Vries for these selections.

OLD SARAH

Old Sarah everybody knows,
Nor is she pitied as she goes—
    A melancholy sight.
For people do not like to give
Relief to those who idle live,
    And work not when they might.

LITTLE MITES FOR TINY SPRITES

(*Little Mites for Tiny Sprites* from *Birdie's Book*.
London: Published by George Routledge and
Sons. 1880.)

THE LITTLE CRIPPLE

I'm a helpless cripple child,
    Gentle Christians, pity me;
Once in rosy health I smiled,
    Blithe and gay as you can be,
And upon the village green
First in every sport was seen.

Let not then the scoffing eye
    Laugh, my twisted leg to see:
Gentle Christians, passing by,
    Stop awhile, and pity me;
And for you I'll breathe a prayer;
Leaning in my easy chair.

MORNING

Awake, little girl, it is time to arise,
    Come, shake drowsy sleep from your eye;
The lark is now warbling his notes to the skies,
    And the sun is far mounted on high.

Oh, come, for the fields with gay flowers abound,
    The dewdrop is quivering still,
The lowing herds graze in the pastures around,
    And the sheep-bell is heard from the hill.

RING-A-RING

Kate Greenaway

Ring-a-ring of little boys,
    Ring-a-ring of girls;
All around — all around,
    Twists and twirls.

You are merry children.
    "Yes, we are."
Where do you come from?
    "Not very far.

"We live in the mountain,
    We live in the tree;
And I live in the river bed
    And you won't catch me!"

DREAMS

(From *The Child World*. London: Published by
John Lane. The third edition, 1896.)

If children have been good all day,
    And kept their tongues and lips quite clean,
They dream of flowers that nod and play,
    And fairies dancing on the green.

But if they've spoken naughty words,
    Or told a lie, they dream of rats:
Of crawling snakes, and ugly birds;
    Of centipedes, and vampire bats.

"Ring-a-Ring" from *Marigold Garden* by Kate Greenaway.
London: Published by Frederick Warne and Company,
1885.

"Dreams" reprinted by permission of The World Publishing Company and Arthur Barker Ltd. from *Little Wide
Awake, an Anthology from Victorian Children's Books
and Periodicals in the Collection of Anne and Fernand
G. Renier,* copyright © 1967 by Leonard de Vries for this
selection.

THROUGH THE SEASONS

JANUARY BRINGS THE SNOW

Mother Goose

January brings the snow,
    Makes our feet and fingers glow.
February brings the rain,
    Thaws the frozen lake again.
March brings breezes loud and shrill,
    Stirs the dancing daffodil.

April brings the primrose sweet,
    Scatters daisies at our feet.
May brings flocks of pretty lambs,
    Skipping by their fleecy dams.
June brings tulips, lilies, roses,
    Fills the children's hands with posies.

Hot July brings cooling showers,
    Apricots and gillyflowers.
August brings the sheaves of corn,
    Then the harvest home is borne.
Warm September brings the fruit,
    Sportsmen then begin to shoot.

Fresh October brings the pheasant,
    Then to gather nuts is pleasant.
Dull November brings the blast,
    Then the leaves are whirling fast.
Chill December brings the sleet,
    Blazing fire and Christmas treat.

A PATCH OF OLD SNOW

Robert Frost

There's a patch of old snow in a corner,
    That I should have guessed
Was a blow-away paper the rain
    Had brought to rest.

It is speckled with grime as if
    Small print overspread it,
The news of a day I've forgotten—
    If I ever read it.

MARCH

William Wordsworth

The cock is crowing,
The stream is flowing,
The small birds twitter,
The lake doth glitter,
The green field sleeps in the sun;
The oldest and youngest
Are at work with the strongest;
The cattle are grazing,
Their heads never raising;
There are forty feeding like one!

Like an army defeated
The snow hath retreated,
And now doth fare ill
On the top of the bare hill;
The Plowboy is whooping — anon — anon:
There's joy in the mountains;
There's life in the fountains;
Small clouds are sailing,
Blue sky prevailing;
The rain is over and gone!

BLUE-BUTTERFLY DAY

Robert Frost

It is blue-butterfly day here in spring,
And with these sky-flakes down in flurry on flurry
There is more unmixed color on the wing
Than flowers will show for days unless they hurry.

"A Patch of Old Snow" from *The Poetry of Robert Frost* edited by Edward Connery Lathem.

But these are flowers that fly and all but sing:
And now from having ridden out desire
They lie closed over in the wind and cling
Where wheels have freshly sliced the April mire.

THE FLOWER-FED BUFFALOES

Vachel Lindsay

The flower-fed buffaloes of the spring
In the days of long ago,
Ranged where the locomotives sing
And the prairie flowers lie low:—
The tossing, blooming, perfumed grass
Is swept away by the wheat,
Wheels and wheels and wheels spin by
In the spring that still is sweet.
But the flower-fed buffaloes of the spring
Left us, long ago.
They gore no more, they bellow no more,
They trundle around the hills no more:—
With the Blackfeet, lying low.
With the Pawnees, lying low,
Lying low.

FOUR LITTLE FOXES

Lew Sarett

Speak gently, Spring, and make no sudden sound;
For in my windy valley, yesterday I found
New-born foxes squirming on the ground—
            Speak gently.

Walk softly, March, forbear the bitter blow;
Her feet within a trap, her blood upon the snow,
The four little foxes saw their mother go—
            Walk softly.

Go lightly, Spring, oh, give them no alarm;
When I covered them with boughs to shelter
            them from harm,
The thin blue foxes suckled at my arm—
            Go lightly.

Step softly, March, with your rampant hurricane;
Nuzzling one another, and whimpering with pain,
The new little foxes are shivering in the rain—
            Step softly.

IN JUST-SPRING

E. E. Cummings

in Just-
spring   when the world is mud-
luscious the little
lame balloonman

whistles   far   and wee

and eddieandbill come
running from marbles and
piracies and it's
spring

when the world is puddle-wonderful

the queer
old balloonman whistles
far   and   wee
and bettyandisbel come dancing

from hop-scotch and jump-rope and

it's
spring
and
        the
                goat-footed

balloonMan   whistles
far
and
wee

"Blue-Butterfly Day" from *The Poetry of Robert Frost* edited by Edward Connery Lathem.
"The Flower-Fed Buffaloes" from *Going to the Stars* by Vachel Lindsay. Copyright © 1926 by Vachel Lindsay. Published by D. Appleton and Co.

"Four Little Foxes" from *Covenant with Earth* by Lew Sarett. Edited and copyrighted, 1956, by Alma Johnson Sarett, and published by University of Florida Press, 1956. Reprinted by permission of Mrs. Sarett.
"In Just-spring" by E. E. Cummings, reprinted from his volume, *Poems 1923–1954* by permission of Harcourt Brace Jovanovich, Inc. Copyright 1923, 1951, by E. E. Cummings.

AUTUMN WOODS

James S. Tippett

I like the woods
    In autumn
When dry leaves hide the ground,
When the trees are bare
And the wind sweeps by
With a lonesome rushing sound.

I can rustle the leaves
    In autumn
And I can make a bed
In the thick dry leaves
That have fallen
From the bare trees
Overhead.

DOWN! DOWN!

Eleanor Farjeon

Down, down!
Yellow and brown
The leaves are falling over the town.

GLIMPSE IN AUTUMN

Jean Starr Untermeyer

Ladies at a ball
    Are not so fine as these
    Richly brocaded trees
That decorate the fall.

They stand against a wall
    Of crisp October sky,
    Their plumèd heads held high,
Like ladies at a ball.

SOMETHING TOLD THE WILD GEESE

Rachel Field

Something told the wild geese
    It was time to go.
Though the fields lay golden
    Something whispered, "Snow."
Leaves were green and stirring,
    Berries, luster-glossed,
But beneath warm feathers
    Something cautioned, "Frost."
All the sagging orchards
    Steamed with amber spice,
But each wild breast stiffened
    At remembered ice.
Something told the wild geese
    It was time to fly—
Summer sun was on their wings,
    Winter in their cry.

THEME IN YELLOW

Carl Sandburg

I spot the hills
With yellow balls in autumn.
I light the prairie cornfields
Orange and tawny gold clusters
And I am called pumpkins.
On the last of October
When dusk is fallen
Children join hands
And circle round me
Singing ghost songs
And love to the harvest moon;
I am a jack-o'-lantern
With terrible teeth
And the children know
I am fooling.

HERE IN PUGET SOUND NOVEMBER

H. A. S. Nelson

The gold storm is over;
The maple leaves are thawing
On the skirts of the fir tree,
And on the wet path.
The rain forest is musty with odor,
Breath of slow winter sleep;
Ferns reach green hands through the mulch;
Mushrooms pop up with tiny bright heads,
Like chicks out of hens' wings.

THE MORNS ARE MEEKER THAN THEY WERE

Emily Dickinson

The morns are meeker than they were,
The nuts are getting brown;
The berry's cheek is plumper,
The rose is out of town.

The maple wears a gayer scarf,
The field a scarlet gown.
Lest I should be old-fashioned,
I'll put a trinket on.

SPLINTER

Carl Sandburg

The voice of the last cricket
across the first frost
is one kind of good-by.
It is so thin a splinter of singing.

EVENING HYMN

Elizabeth Madox Roberts

The day is done;
The lamps are lit;
Woods-ward the birds are flown.
Shadows draw close,—
Peace be unto this house.

The cloth is fair;
The food is set.
God's night draw near.
Quiet and love and peace
Be to this, our rest, our place.

THE NORTH WIND DOTH BLOW

Anonymous

The north wind doth blow,
And we shall have snow,
And what will the robin do then, poor thing?
    He'll sit in a barn,
    And keep himself warm,
And hide his head under his wing, poor thing!

The north wind doth blow,
And we shall have snow,
And what will the swallow do then, poor thing!
    Oh, do you not know
    That he's off long ago,
To a country where he will find spring, poor thing!

The north wind doth blow,
And we shall have snow,
And what will the dormouse do then, poor thing?
    Roll'd up like a ball,
    In his nest snug and small,
He'll sleep till warm weather comes in, poor thing!

The north wind doth blow,
And we shall have snow,
And what will the honey-bee do then, poor thing?
    In his hive he will stay

Till the cold is away,
And then he'll come out in the spring, poor thing!

The north wind doth blow,
And we shall have snow,
And what will the children do then, poor things?
When lessons are done,
They must skip, jump and run,
Until they have made themselves warm, poor
things!

WEATHER

LOST

Carl Sandburg

Desolate and lone
All night on the lake
Where fog trails and mist creeps,
The whistle of a boat
Calls and cries unendingly,
Like some lost child
In tears and trouble
Hunting the harbor's breast
And the harbor's eyes.

MORNING ON PUGET SOUND

H. A. S. Nelson

The fog is sleeping late this morning.
Lost on the bay a groping ship
Shouts irritably.
A siren shrieks from the ferry landing;
And from the blinded lighthouse
Bells struggle out to grapple with the weather
Which smothers my window too,
Making me unsure
As I peer out from my safe shore,
Knowing I can't stay home today,
Not being rich enough to sleep late.

A DEVONSHIRE RHYME

Anonymous

Walk fast in snow,
In frost walk slow,
And still as you go,
Tread on your toe.
When frost and snow are both together
Sit by the fire and spare shoe leather.

THE RAIN

Anonymous

Rain on the green grass,
And rain on the tree,
And rain on the house-top,
But not upon me!

THE RAIN

Robert Louis Stevenson

The rain is raining all around,
It falls on field and tree,
It rains on the umbrellas here,
And on the ships at sea.

RUBBER BOOTS

Rowena Bastin Bennett

Little boots and big boots,
Traveling together
On the shiny sidewalks,
In the rainy weather,
Little boots and big boots,
Oh, it must be fun
To splash the silver raindrops
About you as you run,
Or scatter bits of rainbow
Beneath the April sun!

Big boots and little boots,
    You know how it feels
To have the white clouds drifting
    Far below your heels;
And it is dizzy pleasure,
    Along the way to school,
To walk the lacy tree tops
    That lie in every pool.

Little boots and big boots,
    How you like to putter
In every slender streamlet
    That scampers down the gutter!

RAIN SIZES

John Ciardi

Rain comes in various sizes.
Some rain is as small as a mist.
It tickles your face with surprises,
And tingles as if you'd been kissed.

Some rain is the size of a sprinkle
And doesn't put out all the sun.
You can see the drops sparkle and twinkle,
And a rainbow comes out when it's done.

Some rain is as big as a nickle
And comes with a crash and a hiss.
It comes down too heavy to tickle.
It's more like a splash than a kiss.

When it rains the right size and you're wrapped in
Your rainclothes, it's fun out of doors.
But run home before you get trapped in
The big rain that rattles and roars.

AFTER RAIN

Eleanor Farjeon

The rain is clinging to the round rose-cheek,
And the sweet clustered larkspur heads are wet,

Like dark blue crumpled butterflies grown weak
Beneath their watery load; a silver fret
Of dew is sprinkled on the lupin-leaf,
And its green star is at the center lit
By one bright diamond-drop, to shine a brief
Life out until the sun recaptures it.

PLOUGHING ON SUNDAY

Wallace Stevens

The white cock's tail
Tosses in the wind.
The turkey-cock's tail
Glitters in the sun.

Water in the fields.
The wind pours down.
The feathers flare
And bluster in the wind.

Remus, blow your horn!
I'm ploughing on Sunday,
Ploughing North America.
Blow your horn!

Tum-ti-tum,
ti-tum-tum-tum!
The turkey-cock's tail
Spreads to the sun.

The white cock's tail
Streams to the moon.
Water in the fields.
The wind pours down.

I SAW THE WIND TODAY

Padraic Colum

I saw the wind to-day:
I saw it in the pane

Of glass upon the wall:
A moving thing,—'twas like
No bird with widening wing,
No mouse that runs along
The meal bag under the beam.

I think it like a horse,
All black, with frightening mane,
That springs out of the earth,
And tramples on his way.
I saw it in the glass,
The shaking of a mane:
A horse that no one rides!

THE OLD TREE

Andrew Young

The wood shakes in the breeze
  Lifting its antlered heads;
Green leaf nor brown one sees
  But the rain's glassy beads.

One tree-trunk in the wood
  No tangled head uprears,
A stump of soft touchwood
  Dead to all hopes and fears.

Even the round-faced owl
  That shakes out his long hooting
With the moon cheek-a-jowl
  Could claw there no safe footing.

Riddled by worms' small shot,
  Empty of all desire,
It smoulders in its rot,
  A pillar of damp fire.

WINDY NIGHTS

Robert Louis Stevenson

Whenever the moon and stars are set,
  Whenever the wind is high,
All night long in the dark and wet,
  A man goes riding by.
Late in the night when the fires are out,
  Why does he gallop and gallop about?

Whenever the trees are crying aloud,
  And ships are tossed at sea,
By, on the highway, low and loud,
  By at the gallop goes he.
By at the gallop he goes, and then
  By he comes back at the gallop again.

DO YOU FEAR THE WIND?

Hamlin Garland

Do you fear the force of the wind,
  The slash of the rain?
Go face them and fight them,
  Be savage again.

HAIKU

Snow melts,
  and the village is overflowing—
    with children.
                    —*Issa*

Not even a hat—
  and cold rain falling on me?
    Tut-tut! think of that!
                    —*Bashō*

"The Old Tree" from *The Collected Poems of Andrew Young* by Andrew Young. Reprinted by permission of Granada Publishing Limited.
"Windy Nights" from *A Child's Garden of Verses* by Robert Louis Stevenson.
"Do You Fear the Wind?" from *Prairie Song and Western Story* by Hamlin Garland. Copyright 1928 by Allyn and Bacon, Inc. Reprinted by permission of Allyn and Bacon, Inc.

"Snow melts," "Not even a hat," "Out comes the bee," "Summer night," "A garden butterfly," "Up the barley rows," "The falling leaves," "In all this cool," "Get out of my road," "The lost child cries," "Above the veil," and "In my old home" from *An Introduction to Haiku* by Harold G. Henderson. Copyright © 1958 by Harold G. Henderson. Reprinted by permission of Doubleday & Company, Inc.

The sunrise tints the dew;
The yellow crocuses are out,
And I must pick a few.
—*Jōsa*

In spite of cold and chills
That usher in the early spring
We have the daffodils.
—*Kikuriō*

Out comes the bee
from deep among peony pistils—
oh, so reluctantly!
—*Matsuo Bashō*

Up the barley rows,
stitching, stitching them together,
a butterfly goes.
—*Sora*

A garden butterfly;
the baby crawls, it flies . . .
she crawls, it flies. . . .
—*Issa*

Summer night:
from cloud to cloud the moon
is swift in flight.
—*Rankō*

The falling leaves
fall and pile up; the rain
beats on the rain.
—*Gyōdai*

In all this cool
is the moon also sleeping?
There, in the pool?
—*Ryusui*

Get out of my road
and allow me to plant these
bamboos, Mr. Toad!
—*Chora*

The lost child cries,
and as he cries, he clutches
at the fireflies.
—*Ryusui*

Above the veil
of mist, from time to time
there lifts a sail.
—*Gakoku*

In my old home, still
my parents live.—The insect-cries
are shrill. . . .
—*Anonymous*

Don't swat it!
the fly is wringing his hands . . .
he's wringing his feet.
—*Issa*

On the weathered shelf
a self-cleaned cat in autumn
curls around itself.
—*Thomas Roundtree*

On a leaf, a leaf
is casting a green shadow—
and the tree-frog sings!
—*O. M. B. Southard*

Wild geese! I know
that they did eat the barley;
but when they go. . . .
—*Yasui*

A family—all
leaning on staves and white-haired—
visiting the graves.
—*Bashō*

On a withered branch
a crow has settled . . .
autumn nightfall.
—*Bashō*

Behind me the moon
brushes a shadow of pines
on the floor lightly.
—*Kikaku*

Little bird flitting,
twittering, trying to fly . . .
my, aren't you busy!
—*Bashō*

Turning from watching
the moon, my comfortable old
shadow led me home.
—*Shiki*

In spring the chirping
frogs sing like birds . . . in summer
they bark like old dogs.
—*Onitsura*

When my canary
flew away, that was the end
of spring in my house.
—*Shiki*

Leaf falling on leaf,
on mounds of leaves, rain splashing
in pools of rain . . .
—*Gyodai*

POEMS FOR HOLIDAYS

There are hundreds of holiday poems, and each season more are printed. Few of them, however, are well written; most are jingles or poetry only by association.

The following selections can be supplemented by poems from other sections. Appropriate poems for Lincoln's and Washington's birthdays and Columbus Day can be found in the next section, "Famous Men."

HOLIDAYS

Henry W. Longfellow

The holiest of all holidays are those
   Kept by ourselves in silence and apart;
   The secret anniversaries of the heart,
   When the full river of feeling overflows;
The happy days unclouded to their close;
   The sudden joys that out of darkness start
   As flames from ashes; swift desires that dart
   Like swallows singing down each wind that
      blows!

"Behind me the moon," "Little bird flitting," "Turning from watching," "In spring the chirping," "When my canary," and "Leaf falling on leaf," from *Cricket Songs: Japanese Haiku*, translated and © 1964, by Harry Behn. Reprinted by permission of Harcourt Brace Jovanovich, Inc.

White as the gleam of a receding sail,
   White as a cloud that floats and fades in air,
   White as the whitest lily on a stream,
These tender memories are — a fairy tale
   Of some enchanted land we know not where,
   But lovely as a landscape in a dream.

LINCOLN MONUMENT: WASHINGTON

Langston Hughes

Let's go see old Abe
Sitting in the marble and the moonlight,
Sitting lonely in the marble and the moonlight,
Quiet for ten thousand centuries, old Abe.
Quiet for a million, million years.

Quiet—

And yet a voice forever
Against the
Timeless walls
Of time—
Old Abe.

MY VALENTINE

Robert Louis Stevenson

I will make you brooches and toys for your delight
Of bird song at morning and starshine at night.
I will make a palace fit for you and me,
　　Of green days in forests
　　And blue days at sea.

SONG FROM HAMLET

William Shakespeare

　　Tomorrow is Saint Valentine's day,
　　　　All in the morning betime,
　　And I a maid at your window,
　　　　To be your Valentine.

RING OUT, WILD BELLS

Alfred Tennyson

Ring out, wild bells, to the wild sky,
　　The flying cloud, the frosty light;
　　The year is dying in the night;
Ring out, wild bells, and let him die.

Ring out the old, ring in the new,
　　Ring, happy bells, across the snow;
　　The year is going, let him go;
Ring out the false, ring in the true.

Ring out the grief that saps the mind,
　　For those that here we see no more;
　　Ring out the feud of rich and poor,
Ring in redress to all mankind.

Ring out a slowly dying cause,
　　And ancient forms of party strife;
　　Ring in the nobler modes of life,
With sweeter manners, purer laws.

Ring out the want, the care, the sin,
　　The faithless coldness of the times;
　　Ring out, ring out my mournful rhymes,
But ring the fuller minstrel in.

Ring out false pride in place and blood,
　　The civic slander and the spite;
　　Ring in the love of truth and right,
Ring in the common love of good.

Ring out old shapes of foul disease,
　　Ring out the narrowing lust of gold;
　　Ring out the thousand wars of old,
Ring in the thousand years of peace.

Ring in the valliant men and free,
　　The larger heart, the kindlier hand;
　　Ring out the darkness of the land,
Ring in the Christ that is to be.

AN EASTER CAROL

Christina Georgina Rossetti

　　Spring bursts today,
For Christ is risen and all the earth's at play.
　　Flash forth, thou Sun.
The rain is over and gone, its work is done.

　　Winter is past,
Sweet spring is come at last, is come at last.
　　Bud, fig, and vine,
Bud, olive, fat with fruit and oil and wine.

　　Break forth this morn
In roses, thou but yesterday a thorn.
　　Uplift thy head,
O pure white lily through the winter dead.

　　Beside your dams
Leap and rejoice, you merrymaking lambs.
　　All herds and flocks

Rejoice, all beasts of thickets and of rocks.
   Sing, creatures, sing,
Angels and men and birds and everything.

IN FLANDERS FIELDS

John McCrae

In Flanders fields the poppies blow
Between the crosses, row on row,
   That mark our place, and in the sky
   The larks, still bravely singing, fly,
Scarce heard amid the guns below.

We are the dead; short days ago
We lived, felt dawn, saw sunset glow,
   Loved and were loved, and now we lie
   In Flanders fields.

Take up our quarrel with the foe!
To you from failing hands we throw
   The torch; be yours to hold it high!
   If ye break faith with us who die,
We shall not sleep, though poppies grow
   In Flanders fields.

FOURTH OF JULY NIGHT

Carl Sandburg

The little boat at anchor
in black water sat murmuring
to the tall black sky.

     ***

A white sky bomb fizzed on a black line.
A rocket hissed its red signature into the west.
Now a shower of Chinese fire alphabets,
a cry of flower pots broken in flames,
a long curve to a purple spray,
three violet balloons—
   Drips of seaweed tangled in gold,
   shimmering symbols of mixed numbers,
   tremulous arrangements of cream gold folds
   of a bride's wedding gown—

     ***

A few sky bombs spoke their pieces,
then velvet dark.

The little boat at anchor
in black water sat murmuring
to the tall black sky.

THE HAG

Robert Herrick

   The Hag is astride,
   This night for to ride;
The Devil and she together;
   Through thick and through thin,
   Now out and then in,
Though ne'er so foul be the weather.

   A thorn or a burr
   She takes for a spur,
With a lash of a bramble she rides now;
   Through brakes and through briars,
   O'er ditches and mires,
She follows the Spirit that guides now.

   No beast, for his food
   Dares now range the wood,
But hushed in his lair he lies lurking;
   While mischiefs, by these,
   On land and on seas,
At noon of night are a-working.

   The storm will arise
   And trouble the skies;
This night, and more for the wonder,
   The ghost from the tomb
   Affrighted shall come,
Called out by the clap of the thunder.

WHAT AM I?

Dorothy Aldis

They chose me from my brothers: "That's the
Nicest one," they said,
And they carved me out a face and put a
Candle in my head;

And they sat me on the doorstep. Oh, the
Night was dark and wild;
But when they lit the candle, then I
Smiled!

WHAT NIGHT WOULD IT BE?

John Ciardi

If the moon shines
On the black pines
And an owl flies
And a ghost cries
And the hairs rise
On the back
   on the back
      on the back of your neck—

If you look quick
At the moon-slick
On the black air
And what goes there
Rides a broom-stick
And if things pick
At the back,
   at the back,
      at the back of your neck—

Would you know then
By the small men
With the lit grins
And with no chins,
By the owl's *hoo*,
And the ghost's *boo*,

By the Tom Cat,
And the Black Bat
On the night air,
And the thing there,
By the thing,
   by the thing,
      by the dark thing there

(Yes, you do,
   yes, you do
      know the thing I mean)

That it's now,
   that it's now,
      that it's—Halloween!

HALLOWE'EN

Harry Behn

Tonight is the night
When dead leaves fly
Like witches on switches
Across the sky,
When elf and sprite
Flit through the night
On a moony sheen.

Tonight is the night
When leaves make a sound
Like a gnome in his home
Under the ground,
When spooks and trolls
Creep out of holes
Mossy and green.

Tonight is the night
When pumpkins stare
Through sheaves and leaves
Everywhere,
When ghoul and ghost
And goblin host
Dance round their queen.
It's Hallowe'en!

THE BOUGHS DO SHAKE

Mother Goose

The boughs do shake and the bells do ring,
So merrily comes our harvest in,
Our harvest in, our harvest in,
So merrily comes our harvest in.

We've ploughed, we've sowed,
We've reaped, we've mowed,
We've got our harvest in.

FIRST THANKSGIVING OF ALL

Nancy Byrd Turner

Peace and Mercy and Jonathan,
And Patience (very small),
Stood by the table giving thanks
The first Thanksgiving of all.
There was very little for them to eat,
Nothing special and nothing sweet;
Only bread and a little broth,
And a bit of fruit
   (and no tablecloth);
But Peace and Mercy and Jonathan
And Patience, in a row.
Stood up and asked a blessing on
Thanksgiving, long ago.
Thankful they were their ship had come
Safely across the sea;
Thankful they were for hearth and home,
And kin and company;
They were glad of broth to go with their bread,
Glad their apples were round and red,
Glad of mayflowers they would bring
Out of the woods again next spring.
So Peace and Mercy and Jonathan,
And Patience (very small),
Stood up gratefully giving thanks
The first Thanksgiving of all.

DREIDEL SONG

Efraim Rosenzweig

Twirl about, dance about,
  Spin, spin, spin!
Turn, Dreidel, turn—
  Time to begin!

Soon it is Hanukkah—
  Fast Dreidel, fast!
For you will lie still
  When Hanukkah's past.

"First Thanksgiving of All" by Nancy Byrd Turner, reprinted from *Child Life*. © 1937 by Rand McNally, © 1962 by Nancy Byrd Turner, author, by permission of the author.
"Dreidel Song," from *Now We Begin* by Marian J. and Efraim M. Rosenzweig. Published by Union of American Hebrew Congregations.

BLESSINGS FOR CHANUKAH

Jessie E. Sampter

Blessed art Thou, O God our Lord,
Who made us holy with his word,
And told us on this feast of light
To light one candle more each night.

(Because when foes about us pressed
  To crush us all with death or shame,
The Lord his priests with courage blest
To strike and give his people rest
And in the House that he loved best
  Relight our everlasting flame.)

Blest are Thou, the whole world's King,
Who did so wonderful a thing
For our own fathers true and gold
At this same time in days of old!

HEAP ON MORE WOOD

Sir Walter Scott

Heap on more wood!—the wind is chill;
But let it whistle as it will,
We'll keep our Christmas merry still.

A VISIT FROM ST. NICHOLAS

Clement C. Moore

"Twas the night before Christmas, when all
  through the house
Not a creature was stirring, not even a mouse;
The stockings were hung by the chimney with
  care,
In hopes that St. Nicholas soon would be there;
The children were nestled all snug in their beds
While visions of sugarplums danced in their
  heads;
And Mamma in her 'kerchief, and I in my cap,
Had just settled our brains for a long winter's nap,
When out on the lawn there arose such a clatter,
I sprang from my bed to see what was the matter.

"Blessings For Chanukah" by Jessie E. Sampter, from *Around the Year in Rhymes for the Jewish Child*. Reprinted by permission of Bloch Publishing Co.

Away to the window I flew like a flash,
Tore open the shutters and threw up the sash.
The moon on the breast of the new-fallen snow
Gave a lustre of midday to objects below,
When, what to my wondering eyes did appear,
But a miniature sleigh and eight tiny reindeer,
With a little old driver, so lively and quick,
I knew in a moment it must be St. Nick.
More rapid than eagles his coursers they came,
And he whistled, and shouted, and called them
      by name:
"Now, Dasher! now, Dancer! now, Prancer and
      Vixen!
On, Comet on, Cupid! on, Donder and Blitzen!
To the top of the porch! to the top of the wall!
Now dash away! dash away! dash away, all!"
As dry leaves that before the wild hurricane fly,
When they meet with an obstacle, mount to the
      sky,
So up to the housetop the coursers they flew,
With the sleigh full of toys, and St. Nicholas too.
And then, in a twinkling, I heard on the roof
The prancing and pawing of each little hoof.
As I drew in my head, and was turning around,
Down the chimney St. Nicholas came with a
      bound.
He was dressed all in fur, from his head to his
      foot,
And his clothes were all tarnished with ashes and
      soot;
A bundle of toys he had flung on his back,
And he looked like a peddler just opening his
      pack.
His eyes—how they twinkled! his dimples, how
      merry!
His cheeks were like roses, his nose like a cherry!
His droll little mouth was drawn up like a bow,
And the beard on his chin was as white as the
      snow;
The stump of a pipe he held tight in his teeth,
And the smoke, it encircled his head like a
      wreath;
He had a broad face and a little round belly
That shook, when he laughed, like a bowlful of
      jelly.
He was chubby and plump, a right jolly old elf,
And I laughed when I saw him, in spite of myself;
A wink of his eye and a twist of his head,
Soon gave me to know I had nothing to dread;

He spoke not a word, but went straight to his
      work,
And filled all the stockings; then turned with a
      jerk,
And laying his finger aside of his nose,
And giving a nod, up the chimney he rose.
He sprang to his sleigh, to his team gave a
      whistle,
And away they all flew like the down of a thistle.
But I heard him exclaim, ere he drove out of
      sight,
"HAPPY CHRISTMAS TO ALL,
AND TO ALL A GOOD-NIGHT!"

CHRISTMAS CAROL

Anonymous

God bless the master of this house,
    The mistress also,
And all the little children,
    That round the table go,
And all your kin and kinsmen
    That dwell both far and near;
I wish you a Merry Christmas
    And a Happy New Year.

AN OLD CHRISTMAS GREETING

Anonymous

Sing hey! Sing hey!
For Christmas Day
Twine mistletoe and holly
For friendship glows
In winter snows,
And so let's all be jolly.

BUT GIVE ME HOLLY

Christina Georgina Rossetti

But give me holly, bold and jolly,
Honest, prickly, shining holly;
Pluck me holly leaf and berry
For the day when I make merry.

"A Visit from St. Nicholas" by Clement C. Moore, from
the *Sentinel*, a Troy, New York, newspaper, 1823.
"But Give Me Holly, Bold and Jolly" from *Sing-Song* by
Christina Georgina Rossetti, 1872.

CHRISTMAS

Mother Goose

Christmas is coming, the geese are getting fat,
Please to put a penny in an old man's hat;
If you haven't got a penny a ha'penny will do,
If you haven't got a ha'penny, God bless you.

IN THE WEEK WHEN
CHRISTMAS COMES

Eleanor Farjeon

This is the week when Christmas comes.

Let every pudding burst with plums,
And every tree bear dolls and drums,
   In the week when Christmas comes.

Let every hall have boughs of green,
With berries glowing in between,
   In the week when Christmas comes.

Let every doorstep have a song
Sounding the dark street along,
   In the week when Christmas comes.

Let every steeple ring a bell
With a joyful tale to tell,
   In the week when Christmas comes.

Let every night put forth a star
To show us where the heavens are,
   In the week when Christmas comes.

Let every stable have a lamb
Sleeping warm beside its dam,
   In the week when Christmas comes.

This is the week when Christmas comes.

CAROL, BROTHERS, CAROL

William Muhlenberg

Carol, brothers, carol,
Carol joyfully,

Carol the good tidings,
Carol merrily!
And pray a gladsome Christmas
For all good Christian men,
Carol, brothers, carol,
Christmas comes again.

CHANSON INNOCENTE II

E. E. Cummings

little tree
little silent Christmas tree
you are so little
you are more like a flower

who found you in the green forest
and were you sorry to come away?
see   i will comfort you
because you smell so sweetly

i will kiss your cool bark
and hug you safe and tight
just as your mother would,
only don't be afraid

look   the spangles
that sleep all the year in a dark box
dreaming of being taken out and allowed to shine,
the balls the chains red and gold the fluffy threads,

put up your little arms
and i'll give them all to you to hold
every finger shall have its ring
and there won't be a single place dark or unhappy

then when you're quite dressed
you'll stand in the window for everyone to see
and how they'll stare!
oh but you'll be very proud

and my little sister and i will take hands
and looking up at our beautiful tree
we'll dance and sing
"Noel Noel"

FAMOUS PEOPLE

*While there are hundreds of poems written about our past heroes and leaders,
unfortunately few are good examples of poetry.*

CHRISTOPHER COLUMBUS

Stephen Vincent Benét

There are lots of queer things that discoverers do
But his was the queerest, I swear.
He discovered our country in One Four Nine Two
By thinking it couldn't be there.

It wasn't his folly, it wasn't his fault,
For the very best maps of the day
Showed nothing but water, extensive and salt,
On the West, between Spain and Bombay.

There were monsters, of course, every watery mile,
Great krakens with blubbery lips
And sea-serpents smiling a crocodile-smile
As they waited for poor little ships.

There were whirlpools and maelstroms, without
        any doubt
And tornadoes of lava and ink.
(Which, as nobody yet had been there to find out,
Seems a little bit odd, don't you think?)

But Columbus was bold and Columbus set sail
(Thanks to Queen Isabella, her pelf),
For he said "Though there may be both monster
        and gale,
I'd like to find out for myself."

And he sailed and he sailed and he *sailed* and he
        SAILED,
Though his crew would have gladly turned round
And, morning and evening, distressfully wailed
"This is running things into the ground!"

But he paid no attention to protest or squall,
This obstinate son of the mast,
And so, in the end, he discovered us all,
Remarking, "Here's India, at last!"

He didn't intend it, he meant to heave to
At Calcutta, Rangoon or Shanghai,
There are many queer things that discoverers do,
But his was the queerest. Oh my!

COLUMBUS

Joaquin Miller

Behind him lay the gray Azores,
    Behind the Gates of Hercules;
Before him not the ghost of shores,
    Before him only shoreless seas.
The good mate said: "Now must we pray,
    For lo! the very stars are gone.
Brave Admiral, speak, what shall I say?"
    "Why, say 'Sail on! sail on! and on!'"

"My men grow mutinous day by day;
    My men grow ghastly wan and weak."
The stout mate thought of home; a spray
    Or salt wave washed his swarthy cheek.
"What shall I say, brave Admiral, say,
    If we sight naught but seas at dawn?"
"Why, you shall say at break of day,
    'Sail on! sail on! sail on! and on!'"

They sailed and sailed, as winds might blow,
    Until at last the blanched mate said,
"Why, now not even God would know
    Should I and all my men fall dead.
These very winds forget their way,
    For God from these dread seas is gone.
Now speak, brave Admiral, speak and say"—
    He said: "Sail on! sail on! and on!"

"Christopher Columbus" from *A Book of Americans* by
Rosemary and Stephen Vincent Benét, published by Holt,
Rinehart and Winston, Inc. Copyright, 1933, by Rose-
mary and Stephen Vincent Benét. Copyright renewed ©
1961, by Rosemary Carr Benét. Reprinted by permission of
Brandt & Brandt.

They sailed. They sailed. Then spake the mate:
  "This mad sea shows his teeth tonight.
He curls his lip, he lies in wait,
  With lifted teeth, as if to bite!
Brave Admiral, say but one good word:
  What shall we do when hope is gone?"
The words leapt like a leaping sword:
  "Sail on! sail on! sail on! and on!"

Then, pale and worn, he kept his deck,
  And peered through darkness. Ah, that night
Of all dark nights! And then a speck—
  A light! a light! a light! a light!

BENJAMIN FRANKLIN 1706–1790

Rosemary and Stephen Vincent Benét

Ben Franklin munched a loaf of bread while
  walking down the street
And all the Philadelphia girls tee-heed to see him
  eat,
A country boy come up to town with eyes as big
  as saucers
At the ladies in their furbelows, the gempmum
  on their horses.

Ben Franklin wrote an almanac, a smile upon his
  lip,
It told you when to plant your corn and how to
  cure the pip,
But he salted it and seasoned it with proverbs sly
  and sage,
And people read "Poor Richard" till Poor Richard
  was the rage.

Ben Franklin made a pretty kite and flew it in
  the air
To call upon a thunderstorm that happened to
  be there,
—And all our humming dynamos and our electric
  light
Go back to what Ben Franklin found the day he
  flew his kite.

Ben Franklin was the sort of man that people like
  to see,
For he was very clever but as human as could be.
He had an eye for pretty girls, a palate for good
  wine,

And all the court of France were glad to ask him
  in to dine.

But it didn't make him stuffy and he wasn't
  spoiled by fame
But stayed Ben Franklin to the end, as Yankee as
  his name.

"He wrenched their might from tyrants and its
  lightning from the sky."
And oh, when he saw pretty girls, he had a taking
  eye!

LEWIS AND CLARK

Rosemary and Stephen Vincent Benét

Lewis and Clark
Said, "Come on, let's embark
For a boating trip up the Missouri!
It's the President's wish,
And we might catch some fish,
Though the river is muddy as fury."

So they started away
On a breezy May day,
Full of courage and lore scientific,
And, before they came back,
They had blazed out a track
From St. Louis straight to the Pacific

Now, if *you* want to go
From St. Louis (in Mo.)
To Portland (the Ore. not the Me. one),
You can fly there in planes
Or board limited trains
Or the family car, if there be one.

It may take you two weeks,
If your car's full of squeaks
And you stop for the sights and the strangers,
But it took them (don't laugh!)
Just one year and a half,
Full of buffalo, Indians, and dangers.

They ate prairie-dog soup
When they suffered from croup,
For the weather was often quite drizzly.
They learned "How do you do?"
In Shoshone and Sioux,
And how to be chased by a grizzly.

They crossed mountain and river
With never a quiver,
And the Rockies themselves weren't too big for
       them,
For they scrambled across
With their teeth full of moss,
But their fiddler still playing a jig for them.

Missouri's Great Falls,
And the Yellowstone's walls
And the mighty Columbia's billows,
They viewed or traversed,
Of all white men the first
To make the whole Northwest their pillows.
And, when they returned,
It was glory well-earned
That they gave to the national chorus.
They were ragged and lean
But they'd seen what they'd seen,
And it spread out an Empire before us.

NANCY HANKS

Rosemary and Stephen Vincent Benét

If Nancy Hanks
Came back as a ghost,

Seeking news
Of what she loved most,
She'd ask first
"Where's my son?
What's happened to Abe?
What's he done?

"Poor little Abe,
Left all alone
Except for Tom,
Who's a rolling stone;
He was only nine
The year I died.
I remember still
How hard he cried.

"Scraping along
In a little shack,
With hardly a shirt
To cover his back,
And a prairie wind
To blow him down,
Or pinching times
If he went to town.

"You wouldn't know
About my son?
Did he grow tall?
Did he have fun?
Did he learn to read?
Did he get to town?
Do you know his name?
Did he get on?"

ABOUT ANIMALS

CAT

Eleanor Farjeon

    Cat!
    Scat!
After her, after her,
    Sleeky flatterer,

Spitfire chatterer,
Scatter her, scatter her
    Off her mat!
    Wuff!
    Wuff!
    Treat her rough!
Git her, git her,
Whiskery spitter!

Catch her, catch her,
Green-eyed scratcher!
  Slathery
  Slithery
  Hisser,
  Don't miss her!
Run till you're dithery,
  Hithery
  Thithery
  Pfitts! Pfitts!
How she spits!
  Spitch! Spatch!
Can't she scratch!
Scritching the bark
Of the sycamore-tree,
She's reached her ark
And's hissing at me
  Pfitts! Pfitts!
  Wuff! Wuff!
    Scat,
    Cat!
    That's
    That!

CAT

Mary Britton Miller

The black cat yawns,
Opens her jaws,
Stretches her legs,
And shows her claws.

Then she gets up
And stands on four
Long stiff legs
And yawns some more.

She shows her sharp teeth,
She stretches her lip,
Her slice of a tongue
Turns up at the tip.

Lifting herself
On her delicate toes,
She arches her back
As high as it goes.

She lets herself down
With particular care,
And pads away
With her tail in the air.

MACAVITY: THE MYSTERY CAT

T. S. Eliot

Macavity's a Mystery Cat: he's called the Hidden
  Paw—
For he's the master criminal who can defy the
  Law.
He's the bafflement of Scotland Yard, the Flying
  Squad's despair:
For when they reach the scene of crime—*Macav-
ity's not there!*

Macavity, Macavity, there's no one like Macavity,
He's broken every human law, he breaks the law
  of gravity.
His powers of levitation would make a fakir stare,
And when you reach the scene of crime—*Macav-
ity's not there!*
You may seek him in the basement, you may look
  up in the air—
But I tell you once and once again, *Macavity's
not there!*

Macavity's a ginger cat, he's very tall and thin;
You would know him if you saw him, for his eyes
  are sunken in.
His brow is deeply lined with thought, his head
  is highly domed;
His coat is dusty from neglect, his whiskers are
  uncombed.
He sways his head from side to side, with movements like a snake;

And when you think he's half asleep, he's always
    wide awake.
Macavity, Macavity, there's no one like Macavity,
For he's a fiend in feline shape, a monster of
    depravity.
You may meet him in a by-street, you may see him
    in the square—
But when a crime's discovered, then *Macavity's
    not there!*

He's outwardly respectable. (They say he cheats
    at cards.)
And his footprints are not found in any file of
    Scotland Yard's.
And when the larder's looted, or the jewel-case is
    rifled,
Or when the milk is missing, or another Peke's
    been stifled,
Or the greenhouse glass is broken, and the trellis
    past repair—
Ay, there's the wonder of the thing! *Macavity's
    not there!*

And when the Foreign Office find a Treaty's gone
    astray,
Or the Admiralty lose some plans and drawings
    by the way,
There may be a scrap of paper in the hall or on
    the stair—
But it's useless to investigate—*Macavity's not
    there!*
And when the loss has been disclosed, the Secret
    Service say:
"It *must* have been Macavity!"—but he's a mile
    away.
You'll be sure to find him resting, or a-licking of
    his thumbs,
Or engaged in doing complicated long division
    sums.

Macavity, Macavity, there's no one like Macavity,
There never was a Cat of such deceitfulness and
    suavity.
He always has an alibi, and one or two to spare:
At whatever time the deed took place—MACAV-
    ITY WASN'T THERE!
And they say that all the Cats whose wicked deeds
    are widely known,

(I might mention Mungojerrie, I might mention
    Griddlebone)
Are nothing more than agents for the Cat who
    all the time
Just controls their operations: the Napoleon of
    Crime!

THE NAMING OF CATS

T. S. Eliot

The Naming of Cats is a difficult matter,
    It isn't just one of your holiday games;
You may think at first I'm as mad as a hatter
    When I tell you, a cat must have THREE
        DIFFERENT NAMES,
First of all, there's the name that the family use
    daily,
    Such as Peter, Augustus, Alonzo or James,
Such as Victor or Jonathan, George or Bill
    Bailey—
    All of them sensible everyday names.
There are fancier names if you think they sound
    sweeter,
    Some for the gentlemen, some for the dames:
Such as Plato, Admetus, Electra, Demeter—
    But all of them sensible everyday names.
But I tell you, a cat needs a name that's particular,
    A name that's peculiar, and more dignified,
Else how can he keep up his tail perpendicular,
    Or spread out his whiskers, or cherish his pride?
Of names of this kind, I can give you a quorum,
    Such as Munkustrap, Quaxo, or Coricopat,
Such as Bombalurina, or else Jellylorum—
    Names that never belong to more than one cat.
But above and beyond there's still one name left
    over,
    And that is the name that you never will guess;
The name that no human research can discover—
    But THE CAT HIMSELF KNOWS, and will
        never confess.

DIAMOND CUT DIAMOND

Ewart Milne

Two cats
One up a tree
One under the tree
The cat up a tree is he
The cat under the tree is she
The tree is witch elm, just incidentally.
He takes no notice of she, she takes no notice of he.
He stares at the woolly clouds passing, she stares at the tree.
There's been a lot written about cats, by Old Possum, Yeats and Company
But not Alfred de Musset or Lord Tennyson or Poe or anybody
Wrote about one cat under, and one cat up, a tree.
God knows why this should be left for me
Except I like cats as cats be
Especially one cat up
And one cat under
A witch elm
Tree.

MICE

Rose Fyleman

I think mice
Are rather nice.

Their tales are long,
Their faces small,
They haven't any
Chins at all.
Their ears are pink,
Their teeth are white,
They run about
The house at night.
They nibble things
They shouldn't touch
And no one seems
To like them much.

But *I* think mice
Are nice.

DUCK'S DITTY

Kenneth Grahame

All along the backwater,
Through the rushes tall,
Ducks are a-dabbling,
Up tails all!

Ducks' tails, drakes' tails,
Yellow feet a-quiver,
Yellow bills all out of sight
Busy in the river!

Slushy green undergrowth
Where the roach swim—
Here we keep our larder,
Cool and full and dim!

Every one for what he likes!
We like to be
Heads down, tails up,
Dabbling free!

High in the blue above
Swifts whirl and call—
We are down a-dabbling
Up tails all!

THE BLACKBIRD

Humbert Wolfe

In the far corner
Close by the swings,
Every morning
A blackbird sings.

His bill's so yellow,
His coat's so black,
That he makes a fellow
Whistle back.

Ann, my daughter,
Thinks that he
Sings for us two
Especially.

FIREFLIES IN THE GARDEN

Robert Frost

Here come real stars to fill the upper skies,
And here on earth come emulating flies,
That, though they never equal stars in size
(And they were never really stars at heart),
Achieve at times a very starlike start.
Only, of course, they can't sustain the part.

TO A SQUIRREL AT KYLE-NA-NO

W. B. Yeats

Come play with me;
Why should you run
Through the shaking tree

As though I'd a gun
To strike you dead?
When all I would do
Is to scratch your head
And let you go.

THE HENS

Elizabeth Madox Roberts

The night was coming very fast;
It reached the gate as I ran past.

The pigeons had gone to the tower of the church
And all the hens were on their perch,

Up in the barn, and I thought I heard
A piece of a little purring word.

I stopped inside, waiting and staying,
To try to hear what the hens were saying.

They were asking something, that was plain,
Asking it over and over again.

One of them moved and turned around,
Her feathers made a ruffled sound,

A ruffled sound, like a bushful of birds,
And she said her little asking words.

She pushed her head close into her wing,
But nothing answered anything.

THE SNARE

James Stephens

I hear a sudden cry of pain!
There is a rabbit in a snare:
Now I hear the cry again,
But I cannot tell from where.

But I cannot tell from where
He is calling out for aid!
Crying on the frightened air,
Making everything afraid!

Making everything afraid!
Wrinkling up his little face!
As he cries again for aid;
—And I cannot find the place!

And I cannot find the place
Where his paw is in the snare!
Little one! Oh, Little One!
I am searching everywhere!

THE SANDHILL CRANE

Mary Austin

Whenever the days are cool and clear
The sandhill crane goes walking
Across the field by the flashing weir
Slowly, solemnly stalking.
The little frogs in the tules hear
And jump for their lives when he comes near,
The minnows scuttle away in fear,
When the sandhill crane goes walking.
The field folk know if he comes that way,
Slowly, solemnly stalking,
There is danger and death in the least delay
When the sandhill crane goes walking.
The chipmunks stop in the midst of their play,
The gophers hide in their holes away
And hush, oh, hush! the field mice say,
When the sandhill crane goes walking.

THE STORY OF THE BABY SQUIRREL

Dorothy Aldis

He ran right out of the woods to me,
Little and furry and panting with fright;

I offered a finger just to see—
And both of his paws held on to it tight.

Was it dogs that had scared him? A crashing limb?
I waited a while but there wasn't a sign
Of his mother coming to rescue him.
So then I decided he was mine.

I lifted him up and he wasn't afraid
To ride along in the crook of my arm.
"A very fine place," he thought, "just made
For keeping me comfortable, safe and warm."

At home he seemed happy to guzzle his milk
Out of an eye dropper six times a day.
We gave him a pillow of damask silk
On which he very royally lay.

He frisked on the carpets, he whisked up the stairs
(Where he played with some soap till it made him
    sneeze).

He loved it exploring the tables and chairs,
And he climbed up the curtains exactly like trees.

He watched his fuzzy gray stomach swell.
He grew until he could leave a dent
In the pillow on which he'd slept so well—
And then . . . Oh, then one morning he went.

Perhaps a squirrel around the place
Adopted him: oh, we're certain it's true
For once a little looking down face
Seemed to be saying: "How do you do?"

THE RUNAWAY

Robert Frost

Once when the snow of the year was beginning to
    fall,
We stopped by a mountain pasture to say,
    "Whose colt?"
A little Morgan had one forefoot on the wall,
The other curled at his breast. He dipped his
    head

And snorted at us. And then he had to bolt.
We heard the miniature thunder where he fled,
And we saw him, or thought we saw him, dim and
　　　　gray,
Like a shadow against the curtain of falling flakes.
"I think the little fellow's afraid of the snow.
He isn't winter-broken. It isn't play
With the little fellow at all. He's running away.
I doubt if even his mother could tell him, 'Sakes,
It's only weather.' He'd think she didn't know!
Where is his mother? He can't be out alone."
And now he comes again with clatter of stone,
And mounts the wall again with whited eyes
And all his tail that isn't hair up straight.
He shudders his coat as if to throw off flies.
"Whoever it is that leaves him out so late.
When other creatures have gone to stall and bin,
Ought to be told to come and take him in."

THE EAGLE

Alfred, Lord Tennyson

He clasps the crag with crooked hands;
Close to the sun in lonely lands,
Ringed with the azure world, he stands.

The wrinkled sea beneath him crawls;
He watches from his mountain walls,
And like a thunderbolt he falls.

SNAKE

D. H. Lawrence

A snake came to my water-trough
On a hot, hot day, and I in pyjamas for the heat,
To drink there.

In the deep, strange-scented shade of the great
　　　　dark carob-tree
I came down the steps with my pitcher
And must wait, must stand and wait, for there he
　　　　was at the trough before me.

He reached down from a fissure in the earth-wall
　　　　in the gloom

"The Runaway" from *The Poetry of Robert Frost* edited
by Edward Connery Lathem.

And trailed his yellow-brown slackness soft-bellied
　　　　down, over the edge of the stone trough
And rested his throat upon the stone bottom,
And where the water had dripped from the tap,
　　　　in a small clearness,
He sipped with his straight mouth,
Softly drank through his straight gums, into his
　　　　slack long body,
Silently.

Someone was before me at my water-trough,
And I, like a second comer, waiting.

He lifted his head from this drinking, as cattle do,
And looked at me vaguely, as drinking cattle do,
And flickered his two-forked tongue from his lips,
　　　　and mused a moment,
And stooped and drank a little more,
Being earth brown, earth golden from the burning
　　　　burning bowels of the earth
On the day of Sicilian July, with Etna smoking.

The voice of my education said to me
He must be killed,
For in Sicily the black, black snakes are innocent,
　　　　the gold are venomous.
And voices in me said, If you were a man
You would take a stick and break him now, and
　　　　finish him off.

But I must confess how I liked him,
How glad I was he had come like a guest in quiet,
　　　　to drink at my water-trough
And depart peaceful, pacified, and thankless,
Into the burning bowels of this earth.

Was it cowardice, that I dared not kill him?
Was it perversity, that I longed to talk to him?
Was it humility, to feel so honoured?
I felt so honoured.

And yet those voices:
If you were not afraid, you would kill him!

And truly I was afraid, I was most afraid,
But even so, honoured still more
That he should seek my hospitality
From out the dark door of the secret earth.

He drank enough
And lifted his head, dreamily, as one who has
    drunken,
And flickered his tongue like a forked night on
    the air, so black,
Seeming to lick his lips,
And looked around like a god, unseeing, into
    the air,
And slowly turned his head,
And slowly, very slowly, as if thrice adream,
Proceeded to draw his slow length curving round
And climb again the broken bank of my wall-face.

And as he put his head into that dreadful hole,
And as he slowly drew up, snake-easing his
    shoulders, and entered farther,
A sort of horror, a sort of protest against his
    withdrawing into that horrid black hole,
Deliberately going into the blackness, and slowly
    drawing himself after,
Overcame me now his back was turned.

I looked around, I put down my pitcher,
I picked up a clumsy log
And threw it at the water-trough with a clatter.

I think it did not hit him,
But suddenly that part of him that was left behind
    convulsed in undignified haste,
Writhed like lightning, and was gone
Into the black hole, the earth-lipped fissure in
    the wall-front,
At which, in the intense still noon, I stared with
    fascination.

And immediately I regretted it.
I thought how paltry, how vulgar, what a mean
    act!
I despised myself and the voices of my accursed
    human education.

And I thought of the albatross,
And I wished he would come back, my snake.

For he seemed to me again like a king,
Like a king in exile, uncrowned in the underworld,
Now due to be crowned again.
And so, I missed my chance with one of the lords
Of life.

And I have something to expiate;
A pettiness.

WHITE SEASON
Frances M. Frost

In the winter the rabbits match their pelts to the
    earth.
With ears laid back, they go
Blown through the silver hollow, the silver thicket,
Like puffs of snow.

A BIRD CAME DOWN THE WALK
Emily Dickinson

A bird came down the walk:
He did not know I saw;
He bit an angle-worm in halves
And ate the fellow, raw.

And then he drank a dew
From a convenient grass,
And then hopped sidewise to the wall
To let a beetle pass.

LONE DOG
Irene Rutherford McLeod

I'm a lean dog, a keen dog, a wild dog, and lone;
I'm a rough dog, a tough dog, hunting on my own!
I'm a bad dog, a mad dog, teasing silly sheep;
I love to sit and bay the moon, to keep fat souls
    from sleep.

I'll never be a lap dog, licking dirty feet,
A sleek dog, a meek dog, cringing for my meat,

Not for me the fireside, the well-filled plate,
But shut door, and sharp stone, and cuff and kick
    and hate.

Not for me the other dogs, running by my side,

Some have run a short while, but none of them
    would bide.

O mine is still the one trail, the hard trail, the best
Wide wind, and wild stars, and hunger of the
    quest!

A CERTAIN MOOD

FIRST SONG

Galway Kinnell

Then it was dusk in Illinois, the small boy
After an afternoon of carting dung
Hung on the rail fence, a sapped thing
Weary to crying. Dark was growing tall
And he began to hear the pond frogs all
Calling upon his ear with what seemed their joy.

Soon their sound was pleasant for a boy
Listening in the smoky dusk and the nightfall
Of Illinois, and then from the field two small
Boys came bearing cornstalk violins
And rubbed three cornstalk bows with resins,
And they set fiddling with them as with joy.

It was now fine music the frogs and the boys
Did in the towering Illinois twilight make
And into dark in spite of a right arm's ache
A boy's hunched body loved out of a stalk
The first song of his happiness, and the song woke
His heart to the darkness and into the sadness of
    joy.

EVENING AT SALMON BEACH

H. A. S. Nelson

    A fisherman returning
    With the tide's run,
    Silhouetted
    Against the sun,

Dips in his oars,
And he pulls straight back;
He drips them out,
And he dips them back,

Till the mountain horizon
Buries the light,
And seagulls on a log
Drift into night,

As he dips in his oars,
And he pulls straight back;
He drips them out,
And he dips them back,

And motors of a tug,
Hauling out-bay,
Yearn for the morning,
Miles and miles away.

But his cabin on the beach,
Listening to sea roll,
Lights at the windows:
His compass pole,

As he dips in his oars,
And pulls straight back;
He drips them out,
And he dips them back;

Then stores them inboard,
His dory crunching sand;
Helloes to the windows,
Home from his land.

THE BLACK FINGER

Angeline W. Grimke

I have just seen a beautiful thing
  Slim and still,
Against a gold, gold sky,
  A straight cypress,
  Sensitive,
  Exquisite,
A black finger
Pointing upwards.
Why, beautiful, still finger are you black?
And why are you pointing upwards?

STARS

Sara Teasdale

  Alone in the night
   On a dark hill
  With pines around me
   Spicy and still,

  And a heaven full of stars
   Over my head,
  White and topaz
   And misty red;

  Myriads with beating
   Hearts of fire
  That aeons
   Cannot vex or tire;

  Up the dome of heaven
   Like a great hill,
  I watch them marching
   Stately and still,

  And I know that I
   Am honored to be
  Witness
   Of so much majesty.

SEA SHELL

Amy Lowell

Sea Shell, Sea Shell,
  Sing me a song, O please!
A song of ships, and sailormen,
  And parrots, and tropical trees,

Of islands lost in the Spanish Main
Which no man ever may find again,
Of fishes and corals under the waves,
And sea horses stabled in great green caves.

Sea Shell, Sea Shell,
Sing of the things you know so well.

A PASSING GLIMPSE

Robert Frost

I often see flowers from a passing car
That are gone before I can tell what they are.

I want to get out of the train and go back
To see what they were beside the track.

I name all the flowers I am sure they weren't:
Not fireweed loving where woods have burnt—

Not bluebells gracing a tunnel mouth—
Not lupine living on sand and drouth.

Was something brushed across my mind
That no one on earth will ever find?

Heaven gives its glimpses only to those
Not in position to look too close.

ROADS GO EVER EVER ON

J. R. R. Tolkien

Roads go ever ever on,
  Over rock and under tree,

By caves where never sun has shone,
  By streams that never find the sea;
Over snow by winter sown,
  And through the merry flowers of June,
Over grass and over stone,
  And under mountains in the moon.

THE COROMANDEL FISHERS

Sarojini Naidu

Rise, brothers, rise; the waking skies pray to the
    morning light,
The wind lies asleep in the arms of the dawn like
    a child that has cried all night;
Come, let us gather our nets from the shore and
    set our catamarans free
To capture the leaping wealth of the tide, for we
    are the kings of the sea!

No longer delay, let us hasten away in the track
    of the sea-gull's call,
The sea is our mother, the cloud is our brother,
    the waves are our comrades all,
What though we toss at the fall of the sun where
    the hand of the sea-god drives?
He who holds the storm by the hair will hide in
    his breast our lives.

Sweet is the shade of the coconut glade and the
    scent of the mango grove,
And sweet are the sands at the fall of the moon
    with the sound of the voices we love;
But sweeter, O brothers, the kiss of the spray, and
    the dance of the wild foam's glee;
Row, brothers, row, to the blue of the verge, where
    the low sky mates with the sea.

THE PASTURE

Robert Frost

I'm going out to clean the pasture spring;
I'll only stop to rake the leaves away

(And wait to watch the water clear, I may):
I sha'n't be gone long.—You come too.

I'm going out to fetch the little calf
That's standing by the mother. It's so young
It totters when she licks it with her tongue.
I sha'n't be gone long.—You come too.

BLUEBELLS

Walter de la Mare

Where the bluebells and the wind are,
  Fairies in a ring I spied,
And I heard a little linnet
  Singing near beside.

Where the primrose and the dew are—
  Soon were sped the fairies all:
Only now the green turf freshens,
  And the linnets call.

THIS IS JUST TO SAY

William Carlos Williams

I have eaten
the plums
that were in
the icebox

and which
you were probably
saving
for breakfast

Forgive me
they were delicious
so sweet
and so cold

PERSONAL RESPONSES

I MEANT TO DO MY WORK TODAY

Richard Le Gallienne

I meant to do my work today,
But a brown bird sang in the apple-tree,
And a butterfly flitted across the field,
And all the leaves were calling me.

And the wind went sighing over the land,
Tossing the grasses to and fro,
And a rainbow held out its shining hand—
So what could I do but laugh and go?

I'M NOBODY! WHO ARE YOU?

Emily Dickinson

I'm nobody! Who are you?
Are you nobody too?
Then there's a pair of us—don't tell!
They'd banish us, you know.

How dreary to be somebody!
How public, like a frog
To tell your name the livelong day
To an admiring bog.

I NEVER SAW A MOOR

Emily Dickinson

I never saw a moor,
I never saw the sea;
Yet know I how the heather looks,
And what a wave must be.

I never spoke with God,
Nor visited in heaven;
Yet certain am I of the spot
As if the chart were given.

A SONG OF GREATNESS
(A Chippewa Indian Song)

Transcribed by Mary Austin

When I hear the old men
Telling of heroes,
Telling of great deeds
Of ancient days,
When I hear them telling,
Then I think within me
I too am one of these.

When I hear the people
Praising great ones,
Then I know that I too
Shall be esteemed,
I too when my time comes
Shall do mightily.

THE FIDDLER OF DOONEY

William Butler Yeats

When I play on my fiddle in Dooney,
Folk dance like a wave of the sea;
My cousin is priest in Kilvarnet,
My brother in Moharabuiee.

I passed my brother and cousin:
They read in their books of prayer;
I read in my book of songs
I bought at the Sligo fair.

When we come at the end of time
To Peter sitting in state,
He will smile on the three old spirits,
But call me first through the gate;

For the good are always the merry,
Save by an evil chance,
And the merry love the fiddle
And the merry love to dance:

And when the folk there spy me,
They will all come up to me,
With 'Here is the fiddler of Dooney!'
And dance like a wave of the sea.

THIS IS MY ROCK

David McCord

This is my rock,
And here I run
To steal the secret of the sun;

This is my rock,
And here come I
Before the night has swept the sky;

This is my rock,
This is the place
I meet the evening face to face.

POTOMAC TOWN IN FEBRUARY

Carl Sandburg

The bridge says: Come across; try me; see how
    good I am.
The big rock in the river says: Look at me; learn
    how to stand up.
The white water says: I go on; around, under,
    over, I go on.

A kneeling, scraggly pine says: I am here yet; they
    nearly got me last year.
A sliver of moon slides by on a high wind calling:
    I know why; I'll see you tomorrow; I'll
    tell you everything tomorrow.

A TIME TO TALK

Robert Frost

When a friend calls to me from the road
And slows his horse to a meaning walk,
I don't stand still and look around
On all the hills I haven't hoed,
And shout from where I am, "What is it?"
No, not as there is a time to talk.
I thrust my hoe in the mellow ground,
Blade-end up and five feet tall,
And plod: I go up to the stone wall
For a friendly visit.

MENDING WALL

Robert Frost

Something there is that doesn't love a wall,
That sends the frozen-ground-swell under it
And spills the upper boulders in the sun,
And makes gaps even two can pass abreast.
The work of hunters is another thing:
I have come after them and made repair
Where they have left not one stone on a stone,
But they would have the rabbit out of hiding,
To please the yelping dogs. The gaps I mean,
No one has seen them made or heard them made,
But at spring mending-time we find them there.
I let my neighbor know beyond the hill;
And on a day we meet to walk the line
And set the wall between us once again.
We keep the wall between us as we go.
To each the boulders that have fallen to each.
And some are loaves and some so nearly balls
We have to use a spell to make them balance:
"Stay where you are until our backs are turned!"
We wear our fingers rough with handling them.

Oh, just another kind of outdoor game,
One on a side. It comes to little more:
There where it is we do not need the wall:
He is all pine and I am apple orchard.
My apple trees will never get across
And eat the cones under his pines, I tell him.
He only says, "Good fences make good neighbors."
Spring is the mischief in me, and I wonder
If I could put a notion in his head:
"*Why* do they make good neighbors? Isn't it
Where there are cows? But here there are no cows.
Before I built a wall I'd ask to know
What I was walling in or walling out,
And to whom I was like to give offense.
Something there is that doesn't love a wall,
That wants it down." I could say "Elves" to him,
But it's not elves exactly, and I'd rather
He said it for himself. I see him there
Bringing a stone grasped firmly by the top
In each hand, like an old-stone savage armed.
He moves in darkness as it seems to me,
Not of woods only and the shade of trees.
He will not go behind his father's saying,
And he likes having thought of it so well
He says again, "Good fences make good
    neighbors."

THE DREAM KEEPER

Langston Hughes

    I loved my friend.
    He went away from me.
    There's nothing more to say.
    The poem ends,
    Soft as it began—
    I loved my friend.

THE LAKE ISLE OF INNISFREE

William Butler Yeats

I will arise and go now, and go to Innisfree,
And a small cabin build there, of clay and wattles
    made;

Nine bean rows will I have there, a hive for the
    honey bee,
    And live alone in the bee-loud glade.

And I shall have some peace there, for peace
    comes dropping slow,
Dropping from the veils of the morning to where
    the cricket sings;
There midnight's all a glimmer, and noon a purple
    glow,
    And evening full of the linnet's wings.

I will arise and go now, for always night and day
I hear lake water lapping with low sounds by the
    shore;
While I stand on the roadway, or on the
    pavements gray,
    I hear it in the deep heart's core.

DREAM VARIATION

Langston Hughes

    To fling my arms wide
    In some place of the sun,
    To whirl and to dance
    Till the white day is done.
    Then rest at cool evening
    Beneath a tall tree
    While nights comes on gently,
        Dark like me—
    That is my dream!

    To fling my arms wide
    In the face of the sun,
    Dance! Whirl! Whirl!
    Till the quick day is done.
    Rest at pale evening . . .
    A tall, slim tree . . .
    Night coming tenderly
        Black like me.

"Mending Wall" from *The Poetry of Robert Frost* edited by Edward Connery Lathem.
"The Dream Keeper" from *The Dream Keeper and Other Poems*, by Langston Hughes. Copyright 1932 and renewed 1960 by Langston Hughes. Reprinted by permission of Alfred A. Knopf, Inc.

"The Lake Isle of Innisfree," reprinted with permission of The Macmillan Company, Mr. M. B. Yeats, and The Macmillan Co. of Canada from *Collected Poems* by William Butler Yeats. Copyright 1906 by The Macmillan Company, renewed 1934 by William Butler Yeats.
"Dream Variation," reprinted from *Selected Poems*, by Langston Hughes, by permission of the publisher. Copyright 1926 by Alfred A. Knopf, Inc. and renewed 1954 by Langston Hughes.

FIRE AND ICE

Robert Frost

Some say the world will end in fire,
Some say in ice.
From what I've tasted of desire
I hold with those who favor fire.
But if it had to perish twice,
I think I know enough of hate
To say that for destruction ice
Is also great
And would suffice.

HOLD FAST YOUR DREAMS

Louise Driscoll

Hold fast your dreams!
Within your heart
Keep one still, secret spot
Where dreams may go,
And sheltered so,
May thrive and grow—
Where doubt and fear are not.
Oh, keep a place apart
Within your heart,
For little dreams to go.

BARTER

Sara Teasdale

Life has loveliness to sell,
    All beautiful and splendid things,
Blue waves whitened on a cliff,
    Soaring fire that sways and sings,
And children's faces looking up
Holding wonder like a cup.

Life has loveliness to sell,
    Music like a curve of gold,
Scent of pine trees in the rain,
    Eyes that love you, arms that hold,
And for your spirit's still delight,
Holy thoughts that star the night.

Spend all you have for loveliness,
    Buy it and never count the cost;
For one white singing hour of peace
    Count many a year of strife well lost,
And for a breath of ecstasy
Give all you have been, or could be.

DREAMS

Langston Hughes

Hold fast to dreams
For if dreams die
Life is a broken-winged bird
That cannot fly.

Hold fast to dreams
For when dreams go
Life is a barren field
Frozen with snow.

TRIFLE

Georgia Douglas Johnson

Against the day of sorrow
Lay by some trifling thing
A smile, a kiss, a flower
For sweet remembering.

Then when the day is darkest
Without one rift of blue
Take out your little trifle
And dream your dream anew.

A WORD

Emily Dickinson

A word is dead
When it is said,
Some say.

"Fire and Ice" from *The Poetry of Robert Frost* edited by Edward Connery Lathem.
"Hold Fast Your Dreams," © 1916 by The New York Times Company. Reprinted by permission.

"Barter," reprinted with permission of The Macmillan Company from *Collected Poems* by Sara Teasdale. Copyright 1917 by The Macmillan Company, renewed 1945 by Mamie T. Wheless.
"Dreams" by Langston Hughes. From *The Dream Keeper and Other Poems* by Langston Hughes. Copyright 1932 and renewed 1960 by Langston Hughes. Reprinted by permission of Alfred A. Knopf, Inc.

I say it just
Begins to live
That day.

PRIMER LESSON

Carl Sandburg

Look out how you use proud words.
When you let proud words go, it is not easy to
      call them back.
They wear long boots, hard boots; they walk off
      proud; they can't hear you calling—
Look out how you use proud words.

INCIDENT

Countee Cullen

Once riding in Old Baltimore,
Heart filled, head filled with glee,
I saw a Baltimorean
Staring straight at me.

Now I was eight and very small,
And he was no whit bigger
And so I smiled, but he
Stuck out his tongue and called me nigger.

I saw the whole of Baltimore
From May until November.
Of all the things that happened there—
That's all that I remember.

LITTLE GIRL, BE CAREFUL WHAT YOU SAY

Carl Sandburg

Little girl, be careful what you say
when you make talk with words, words—
for words are made of syllables
and syllables, child, are made of air—
and air is so thin—air is the breath of God—
air is finer than fire or mist,
finer than water or moonlight,
finer than spider-webs in the moon,
finer than water-flowers in the morning:
    and words are strong, too,
      stronger than rocks or steel
stronger than potatoes, corn, fish, cattle,
and soft, too, soft as little pigeon-eggs,
soft as the music of hummingbird wings.
    So, little girl, when you speak greetings,
when you tell jokes, make wishes or prayers,
    be careful, be careless, be careful,
    be what you wish to be.

BALLADS AND SONGS

SIR PATRICK SPENCE

The king sits in Dumferling town,
    Drinking the blood-red wine:
"O where will I get a good sailor,
    To sail this ship of mine?"

Up and spoke an elderly knight,
    (Sat at the king's right knee),
"Sir Patrick Spence is the best sailor
    That sails upon the sea."

The king has written a broad letter,
    And signed it with his hand,

And sent it to Sir Patrick Spence,
   Was walking on the sand.

The first line that Sir Patrick read,
   A loud laugh laughed he;
The next line that Sir Patrick read,
   A tear blinded his eye.

"O who is this has done this deed,
   This ill deed done to me,
To send me out this time of year,
   To sail upon the sea!

"Make haste, make haste, my merry men all,
   Our good ship sails the morn:"
"O say not so, my master dear,
   For I fear a deadly storm.

"Late late yestereven I saw the new moon
   With the old moon in her arm,
And I fear, I fear, my master dear,
   That we will come to harm."

O our Scotch nobles were right loathe
   To wet their cork-heeled shoes;
But long after the play was played
   Their hats floated into view.

O long, long may their ladies sit,
   With their fans within their hand,
Or ever they see Sir Patrick Spence
   Come sailing to the land.

O long, long may their ladies stand,
   With their gold combs in their hair,
Waiting for their own dear lords,
   For they'll see them never more.

Half o'er, half o'er to Aberdour,
   It's fifty fathoms deep,
And there lies good Sir Patrick Spence,
   With the Scotch lords at his feet.

ROBIN HOOD RESCUING THE WIDOW'S THREE SONS

There are twelve months in all the year,
   As I hear many say,
But the merriest month in all the year
   Is the merry month of May.

Now Robin Hood is to Nottingham gone,
   With a link and a down, and a day,
And there he met a silly old woman,
   Was weeping on the way.

"What news? what news? thou silly old woman,
   What news hast thou for me?"
Said she, "There's my three sons in Nottingham town
   Today condemned to die."

"O, have they parishes burnt?" he said,
   "Or have they ministers slain?
Or have they robbèd any virgin?
   Or other men's wives have ta'en?"

"They have no parishes burnt, good sir,
   Nor yet have ministers slain,
Nor have they robbèd any virgin,
   Nor other men's wives have ta'en."

"O, what have they done?" said Robin Hood,
   "I pray thee tell to me."
"It's for slaying of the king's fallow deer,
   Bearing their long bows with thee."

"Dost thou not mind, old woman," he said,
   "How thou madest me sup and dine?
By the truth of my body," quoth Robin Hood,
   "You could not tell it in better time."

Now Robin Hood is to Nottingham gone,
   With a link and a down, and a day,
And there he met with a silly old palmer,
   Was walking along the highway.

"What news? what news? thou silly old man,
   What news, I do thee pray?"
Said he, "Three squires in Nottingham town
   Are condemned to die this day."

"Come change thy apparel with me, old man,
   Come change thy apparel for mine;
Here is ten shillings in good silver,
   Go drink it in beer or wine."

"O, thine apparel is good," he said,
   "And mine is ragged and torn;
Wherever you go, wherever you ride,
   Laugh not an old man to scorn."

"Come change thy apparel with me, old churl,
　Come change thy apparel with mine;
Here is a piece of good broad gold,
　Go feast thy brethren with wine."

Then he put on the old man's hat,
　It stood full high in the crown:
"The first good bargain that I come at,
　It shall make thee come down."

Then he put on the old man's cloak,
　Was patch'd black, blue and red;
He thought it no shame all the day long,
　To wear the bags of bread.

Then he put on the old man's breeks,
　Was patch'd from leg to side;
"By the truth of my body," bold Robin gan say,
　"This man loved little pride."

Then he put on the old man's hose,
　Were patched from knee to wrist;
"By the truth of my body," said bold Robin Hood,
　"I'd laugh if I had any list."

Then he put on the old man's shoes,
　Were patch'd both beneath and aboon;
Then Robin Hood swore a solemn oath,
　"It's good habit that makes a man."

Now Robin Hood is to Nottingham gone,
　With a link a down, and a down,
And there he met with the proud sheriff,
　Was walking along the town.

"Save you, save you, sheriff!" he said,
　"Now heaven you save and see!
And what will you give to a silly old man
　Today will your hangman be?"

"Some suits, some suits," the sheriff he said,
　"Some suits I'll give to thee;
Some suits, some suits, and pence thirteen,
　Today's a hangman's fee."

Then Robin Hood he turns him round about,
　And jumps from stock to stone;
"By the truth of my body," the sheriff he said,
　"That's well jumpt, thou nimble old man."

" I was ne'er a hangman in all my life,
　Nor yet intends to trade;
But curst be he," said bold Robin,
　"That first a hangman was made."

"I've a bag for meal, and a bag for malt,
　And a bag for barley and corn;
A bag for bread, and a bag for beef,
　And a bag for my little small horn."

"I have a horn in my pocket,
　I got it from Robin Hood,
And still when I set it in my mouth,
　For thee it blows little good."

"O, wind thy horn, thou proud fellow!
　Of thee I have no doubt.
I wish that thou give such a blast,
　Till both thy eyes fall out."

The first loud blast that he did blow,
　He blew both loud and shrill;
A hundred and fifty of Robin Hood's men
　Came riding over the hill.

The next loud blast that he did give,
　He blew both loud and amain,
And quickly sixty of Robin Hood's men
　Came shining over the plain.

"O, who are those," the sheriff he said,
　"Come tripping over the lee?"
"They're my attendants," brave Robin did say;
　"They pay a visit to thee."

They took the gallows from the slack,
　They set it in the glen,
They hanged the proud sheriff on that,
　Released their own three men.

THE RAGGLE, TAGGLE GYPSIES

An Old Folk Song

There were three gypsies a-come to my door,
　And downstairs ran this lady, O.
One sang high and another sang low,
　And the other sang "Bonnie, Bonnie Bis-
　kay, O."

Then she pulled off her silken gown,
    And put on hose of leather, O.
With the ragged rags about her door
    She's off with the Raggle, Taggle Gypsies, O.

'Twas late last night when my lord came home,
    Inquiring for his lady, O.
The servants said on every hand,
    "She's gone with the Raggle, Taggle Gyp-
        sies, O."

"Oh, saddle for me my milk-white steed,
    Oh, saddle for me my pony, O,
That I may ride and seek my bride
    Who's gone with the Raggle, Taggle Gyp-
        sies, O."

Oh, he rode high and he rode low,
    He rode through woods and copses, O,
Until he came to an open field,
    And there he espied his lady, O.

"What makes you leave your house and lands?
    What makes you leave your money, O?
What makes you leave your new-wedded lord
    To go with the Raggle, Taggle Gypsies, O?"

"What care I for my house and lands?
    What care I for my money, O?
What care I for my new-wedded lord?
    I'm off with the Raggle, Taggle Gypsies, O."

"Last night you slept on a goose-feather bed,
    With the sheet turned down so bravely, O.
Tonight you will sleep in the cold, open field,
    Along with the Raggle, Taggle Gypsies, O."

"What care I for your goose-feather bed,
    With the sheet turned down so bravely, O?
For tonight I shall sleep in a cold, open field,
    Along with the Raggle, Taggle Gypsies, O."

THE WIFE OF USHER'S WELL

There lived a wife at Usher's well,
    And a wealthy wife was she;
She had three stout and stalwart sons,
    And sent them o'er the sea.

They had not been a week from her,
    A week but barely one,
When word came to the carline wife
    That her three sons were gone.

They had not been a week from her,
    A week but barely three,
When word came to the carline wife
    That her sons she'd never see.

"I wish the wind may never cease,
    Nor fishes in the flood,
Till my three sons come home to me
    In earthly flesh and blood!"

It fell about the Martinmas,
    When nights are long and dark,
The carline wife's three sons came home,
    And their hats were of birch bark.

It neither grew in trench nor ditch,
    Nor yet in any furrow;
But at the gates of Paradise
    That birch grew fair enough.

"Blow up the fire, my maidens!
    Bring water from the well!
For all my house shall feast this night,
    Since my three sons are well."

And she has made for them a bed,
    She's made it large and wide;
And she's put her mantle about her,
    And sat at their bedside.

Up then crowed the red, red cock,
    And up and crowed the gray;
The eldest son to the youngest said,
    " 'Tis time we were away."

The cock he had not crowed but once,
    And clapped his wings at all,
When the youngest to the eldest said,
    "Brother, we must awa'."

"The cock doth crow, the day doth dawn,
    The fretting worm doth chide;
When we are out of our place,
    A sore pain we must bide."

"Lie still, lie still but a little wee while,
  Lie still but if we may;
When my mother misses us when she wakes
  She'll go mad before it's day."

"Fare ye well, my mother dear!
  Farewell to barn and byre!
And fare ye well, the bonny lass
  That kindles my mother's fire."

GET UP AND BAR THE DOOR

It fell about the Martinmas time,
  And a gay time it was then,
When our goodwife got puddings to make,
  And she's boild them in the pan.

The wind sae cauld blew south and north,
  And blew into the floor;
Quoth our goodman to our goodwife,
  "Gae out and bar the door."

"My hand is in my hussyfskap,
  Goodman, as ye may see:
An it should nae be barrd this hundred year,
  It's no be barrd for me."

They made a paction tween them twa,
  They made it firm and sure,
That the first word whaeer shoud speak,
  Shoud rise and bar the door.

Then by there came two gentlemen,
  At twelve o'clock at night,
And they could neither see house nor hall,
  Nor coal nor candle-light.

"Now whether is this a rich man's house,
  Or whether is it a poor?"
But neer a word wad ane o them speak,
  For barring of the door.

And first they ate the white puddings,
  And then they ate the black;
Tho muckle thought the goodwife to hersel,
  Yet neer a word she spake.

Then said the one unto the other,
  "Here, man, tak ye my knife;

Do ye tak aff the auld man's beard,
  And I'll kiss the goodwife."
"But there's nae water in the house,
  And what shall we do than?"
"What ails ye at the pudding-broo,
  That boils into the pan?"

O up then started our goodman,
  An angry man was he:
"Will ye kiss my wife before my een,
  And scad me wi pudding-bree?"

Then up and started our goodwife,
  Gied three skips on the floor:
"Goodman, you've spoken the foremost word,
  Get up and bar the door."

GREEN BROOM

There was an old man lived out in the wood,
His trade was a-cutting of Broom, green Broom;
He had but one son without thrift, without good,
Who lay in his bed till 'twas noon, bright noon.

The old man awoke one morning and spoke,
He swore he would fire the room, that room,
If his John would not rise and open his eyes,
And away to the wood to cut Broom, green
      Broom;

So Johnny arose, and slipped on his clothes,
And away to the wood to cut Broom, green
      Broom;
He sharpened his knives, for once he contrives
To cut a great bundle of Broom, green Broom.

When Johnny passed under a lady's fine house,
Passed under a lady's fine room, fine room,
She called to her maid, "Go fetch me," she said,
"Go fetch me the boy that sells Broom, green
      Broom."

When Johnny came in to the lady's fine house,
And stood in the lady's fine room, fine room;
"Young Johnny," she said, "will you give up your
      trade,
And marry a lady in bloom, full bloom?"

Johnny gave his consent, and to church they both
      went,

And he wedded the lady in bloom, full bloom.
At market and fair, all folks do declare,
There is none like the boy that sold Broom, green
    Broom.

THE FORSAKEN MERMAN

Matthew Arnold

Come, dear children, let us away;
Down and away below.
Now my brothers call from the bay;
Now the great winds shorewards blow;
Now the salt tides seawards flow;
Now the wild white horses play,
Champ and chafe and toss in the spray.
Children dear, let us away.
This way, this way.
Call her once before you go.
Call once yet.
In a voice that she will know:
"Margaret! Margaret!"
Children's voices should be dear
(Call once more) to a mother's ear
Children's voices, wild with pain.
Surely she will come again.
Call her once and come away.
This way, this way.
"Mother dear, we cannot stay."
The wild white horses foam and fret.
Margaret! Margaret!
Come, dear children, come away down.
Call no more.
One last look at the white-wall'd town,
And the little grey church on the windy shore.
Then come down.
She will not come though you call all day.
Come away, come away.

Children dear, was it yesterday
We heard the sweet bells over the bay?
In the caverns where we lay,
Through the surf and through the swell,
The far-off sound of a silver bell?
Sand-strewn caverns, cool and deep,
Where the winds are all asleep;
Where the spent lights quiver and gleam;

Where the salt weed sways in the stream;
Where the sea-beasts rang'd all round

Feed in the ooze of their pasture-ground;
Where the sea-snakes coil and twine,
Dry their mail and bask in the brine;
Where great whales come sailing by,
Sail and sail, with unshut eye,
Round the world for every and aye?
When did music come this way?
Children dear, was it yesterday?
Children dear, was it yesterday
(Call yet once) that she went away?
Once she sate with you and me,
On a red gold throne in the heart of the sea,
And the youngest sate on her knee.
She comb'd its bright hair, and she tended it well,
When down swung the sound of the far-off bell.
She sigh'd, she look'd up through the clear green
    sea.
She said: "I must go, for my kinsfolk pray
In the little grey church on the shore to-day.
'Twill be Easter-time in the world—ah me!
And I lose my poor soul, Merman, here with
    thee."
I said: "Go up, dear heart, through the waves;
Say thy prayer, and come back to the kind sea-
    caves."
She smil'd, she went up through the surf in the
    bay.
Children dear, was it yesterday?
Children dear, were we long alone?
"The sea grows stormy, the little ones moan.
Long prayers," I said, "in the world they say.
Come," I said, and we rose through the surf in
    the bay.
We went up the beach, by the sandy down
Where the sea-stocks bloom, to the white-wall'd
    town.
Through the narrow pav'd streets, where all was
    still,
To the little grey church on the windy hill.
From the church came a murmur of folk at their
    prayers,
But we stood without in the cold blowing airs.
We climb'd on the graves, on the stones, worn
    with rains,
And we gaz'd up the aisle through the small
    leaded panes.
She sate by the pillar; we saw her clear;
"Dear heart," I said, "we are long alone.
The sea grows stormy, the little ones moan."
But, ah, she gave me never a look,

For her eyes were seal'd to the holy book.
Loud prays the priest; shut stands the door.
Come away, children, call no more.
Come away, come down, call no more.
Down, down, down.
Down to the depths of the sea.

She sits at her wheel in the humming town,
Singing most joyfully.
Hark, what she sings; "O joy, O joy,
For the humming street, and the child with its
       toy.
For the priest, and the bell, and the holy well.
For the wheel where I spun,
And the blessed light of the sun."
And so she sings her fill,
Singing most joyfully,
Till the shuttle falls from her hand,
And the whizzing wheel stands still.
She steals to the window, and looks at the sand;
And over the sand at the sea;
And her eyes are set in a stare;
And anon there breaks a sigh,
And anon there drops a tear,
From a sorrow-clouded eye,
And a heart sorrow-laden,
A long, long sigh,
For the cold strange eyes of a little Mermaiden,
And the gleam of her golden hair.

Come away, away, children.
Come children, come down.
The hoarse wind blows colder;
Lights shine in the town.
She will start from her slumber
When gusts shake the door;
She will hear the winds howling,
Will hear the waves roar.
We shall see, while above us
The waves roar and whirl,
A ceiling of amber,
A pavement of pearl.
Singing, "Here came a mortal,
But faithless was she.
And alone dwell for ever
The kings of the sea."
But, children, at midnight,
When soft the winds blow;
When clear falls the moonlight;
When spring-tides are low:

When sweet airs come seaward
From heaths starr'd with broom;
And high rocks throw mildly
On the blanch'd sands a gloom;
Up the still, glistening beaches,
Up the creeks we will hie;
Over banks of bright seaweed
The ebb-tide leaves dry.
We will gaze, from the sand-hills,
At the white, sleeping town;
At the church on the hill-side—
And then come back down.
Singing, "There dwells a lov'd one,
But cruel is she.
She left lonely for ever
The kings of the sea.

THE BOSTON TEAPARTY[1]

There was an old woman lived over the sea
And she was an island queen
Her daughter lived off in a lone coun-tree
With an ocean of water between.

The old lady's pockets were filled with gold
But never contented was she
So she called on her daughter to pay her a tax
Of three pence a pound on her tea.

"Oh Mother, dear Mother!" the daughter replied,
"I can't do the thing you ask.
I'm willing to pay a fair price for the tea
But *never* a three penny tax."

"You *shall*!" Quoth the mother and reddened with
       rage
"For you're my own daughter, you see.
And surely 'tis proper the daughter should pay
Her mother a tax on her tea!"

And so the old lady her servants called out
And packed off a budget of tea
And eager for three pence a pound she put in
Enough for a large family.

The tea was conveyed to the daughter's door
All down by the ocean's side.

---

[1] The ballad tradition is still alive in America. This old ballad was often sung by the compiler's grandfather, Alfred Gilley Stanley, who was born on Baker Island, Maine.

And the bouncy girl poured out every ounce
On the dark and lonely tide.
And then she called out to the island queen
"Ah Mother, dear Mother," quoth she
"Your tea you may have when 'tis steeped enough
But never a tax from me."

CASEY JONES

Anonymous

Come all you rounders if you want to hear
The story of a brave engineer;
Casey Jones was the hogger's name,
On a big eight-wheeler, boys, he won his fame.
Caller called Casey at half-past four,
He kissed his wife at the station door,
Mounted to the cabin with orders in his hand,
And took his farewell trip to the promised land.

　　Casey Jones, he mounted to the cabin,
　　Casey Jones, with his orders in his hand!
　　Casey Jones, he mounted to the cabin,
　　Took his farewell trip into the promised land.

"Put in your water and shovel in your coal,
Put your head out the window, watch the drivers
　　　roll,
I'll run her till she leaves the rail,
'Cause we're eight hours late with the Western
　　　Mail!"
He looked at his watch and his watch was slow,
Looked at the water and the water was low,
Turned to his fireboy and said,
"We'll get to 'Frisco, but we'll all be dead!"

　　Casey Jones, he mounted to the cabin,
　　Casey Jones, with his orders in his hand!
　　Casey Jones, he mounted to the cabin,
　　Took his farewell trip into the promised land.

Casey pulled up Reno Hill,
Tooted for the crossing with an awful shrill,
Snakes all knew by the engine's moans
That the hogger at the throttle was Casey Jones.
He pulled up short two miles from the place,
Number Four stared him right in the face,
Turned to his fireboy, said, "You'd better jump,

'Cause there's two locomotives that's going to
　　bump."

　　Casey Jones, he mounted to the cabin,
　　Casey Jones, with his orders in his hand!
　　Casey Jones, he mounted to the cabin,
　　Took his farewell trip into the promised land.

Casey said, just before he died,
"There's two more roads I'd like to ride."
Fireboy said, "What can they be?"
"The Rio Grande and the Old S.P."
Mrs. Jones sat on her bed a-sighing,
Got a pink that Casey was dying.
Said, "Go to bed, children; hush your crying,
'Cause you'll get another papa on the Salt Lake
　　line."

　　Casey Jones! Got another papa!
　　Casey Jones, on the Salt Lake Line!
　　Casey Jones! Got another papa!
　　Got another papa on the Salt Lake Line!

PAUL REVERE'S RIDE

Henry Wadsworth Longfellow

Listen, my children, and you shall hear
Of the midnight ride of Paul Revere,
On the eighteenth of April, in Seventy-five;
Hardly a man is now alive
Who remembers that famous day and year.

He said to his friend, "If the British march
By land or sea from the town tonight,
Hang a lantern aloft in the belfry arch
Of the North Church tower as a signal light—
One, if by land, and two, if by sea;
And I on the opposite shore will be,
Ready to ride and spread the alarm
Through every Middlesex village and farm,
For the country folk to be up and to arm."

Then he said, "Good night!" and with muffled
　　oar
Silently rowed to the Charlestown shore,
Just as the moon rose over the bay,
Where swinging wide at her moorings lay
The Somerset, British man-of-war;

A phantom ship, with each mast and spar
Across the moon like a prison bar,
And a huge black hulk, that was magnified
By its own reflection in the tide.

Meanwhile, his friend, through alley and street,
Wanders and watches with eager ears,
Till in the silence around him he hears
The muster of men at the barrack door,
The sound of arms, and the tramp of feet,
And the measured tread of the grenadiers,
Marching down to their boats on the shore.

Then he climbed the tower of the Old North
    Church,
By the wooden stairs, with stealthy tread,
To the belfry-chamber overhead,
And startled the pigeons from their perch
On the somber rafters, that round him made
Masses and moving shapes of shade—
By the trembling ladder, steep and tall,
To the highest window in the wall,
Where he paused to listen and look down
A moment on the roofs of the town,
And the moonlight flowing over all.

Beneath, in the churchyard, lay the dead,
In their night-encampment on the hill,
Wrapped in silence so deep and still
That he could hear, like a sentinel's tread,
The watchful night-wind, as it went
Creeping along from tent to tent,
And seeming to whisper, "All is well!"
A moment only he feels the spell
Of the place and the hour, and the secret dread
Of the lonely belfry and the dead;
For suddenly all his thoughts are bent
On a shadowy something far away,
Where the river widens to meet the bay—
A line of black that bends and floats
On the rising tide, like a bridge of boats.

Meanwhile, impatient to mount and ride,
Booted and spurred, with a heavy stride
On the opposite shore walked Paul Revere.
Now he patted his horse's side,
Now gazed at the landscape far and near,
Then, impetuous, stamped the earth,
And turned and tightened his saddle-girth;
But mostly he watched with eager search

The belfry-tower of the Old North Church,
As it rose above the graves on the hill,
Lonely and spectral and somber and still.
And lo! as he looks, on the belfry's height
A glimmer, and then a gleam of light!
He springs to the saddle, the bridle he turns,
But lingers and gazes, till full on his sight
A second lamp in the belfry burns!

The hurry of hoofs in a village street,
A shape in the moonlight, a bulk in the dark,
And beneath from the pebbles, in passing, a spark
Struck out by a steed flying fearless and fleet—
That was all! And yet through the gloom and the
    light,
The fate of a nation was riding that night;
And the spark struck out by that steed, in his
    flight,
Kindled the land into flame with its heat.

He has left the village and mounted the steep,
And beneath him, tranquil and broad and deep,
Is the Mystic, meeting the ocean tides;
And under the alders, that skirt its edge,
Now soft on the sand, now loud on the ledge,
Is heard the tramp of the steed as he rides.

It was twelve by the village clock
When he crossed the bridge into Medford town.
He heard the crowing of the cock,
And the barking of the farmer's dog,
And felt the damp of the river-fog
That rises after the sun goes down.

It was one by the village clock
When he galloped into Lexington.
He saw the gilded weathercock
Swim in the moonlight as he passed,
And the meeting-house windows, blank and bare,
Gaze at him with a spectral glare,
As if they already stood aghast
At the bloody work they would look upon.

It was two by the village clock
When he came to the bridge in Concord town.
He heard the bleating of the flock,
And the twitter of birds among the trees
And felt the breath of the morning breeze
Blowing over the meadows brown.
And one was safe and asleep in his bed

Who at the bridge would be first to fall,
Who that day would be lying dead,
Pierced by a British musket-ball.

You know the rest. In the books you have read
How the British Regulars fired and fled—
How the farmers gave them ball for ball,
From behind each fence and farm-yard wall,
Chasing the red-coats down the lane,
Then crossing the fields to emerge again
Under the trees at the turn of the road,
And only pausing to fire and load.

So through the night rode Paul Revere;
And so through the night went his cry of alarm
To every Middlesex village and farm—
A cry of defiance and not of fear,
A voice in the darkness, a knock at the door,
And a word that shall echo forevermore!

For, borne on the night-wind of the Past,
Through all our history, to the last,
In the hour of darkness and peril and need,
The people will waken and listen to hear
The hurrying hoof-beats of that steed,
And the midnight message of Paul Revere.

LITTLE ORPHANT ANNIE

James Whitcomb Riley

Little Orphant Annie's come to our house to stay,
An' wash the cups and saucers up, an' brush the
    crumbs away,
An' shoo the chickens off the porch, an' dust the
    hearth, an' sweep,
An' make the fire, an' bake the bread, an' earn
    her board-an'-keep;
An' all us other children, when the supper things
    is done,
We set around the kitchen fire an' has the mostest
    fun
A-list'nin' to the witch tales 'at Annie tells about,
An' the Gobble-uns 'at gits you
        Ef you
           Don't
               Watch
                  Out!

Onc't they was a little boy wouldn't say his
    prayers,—
So when he went to bed at night, away upstairs,
His Mammy heered him holler, an' his Daddy
    heerd him bawl,
An' when they turn't the kivvers down, he wasn't
    there at all!
An' they seeked him in the rafter room, an'
    cubbyhole, an' press,
An' seeked him up the chimbly flue, an'
    ever'wheres, I guess;
But all they ever found was thist his pants an'
    roundabout:—
An' the Gobble-uns 'll git you
        Ef you
           Don't
               Watch
                  Out!

An' one time a little girl 'ud allus laugh an' grin,
An' make fun of ever'one, an' all her blood an'
    kin;
An' onc't, when they was "company," an' ole folks
    was there,
She mocked 'em an' shocked 'em, an' said she
    didn't care!
An 'thist as she kicked her heels, an' turn't to run
    an' hide,
They was two great big Black Things a-standin'
    by her side,
An' they snatched her through the ceilin' 'fore
    she knowed what she's about!
An' the Gobble-uns 'll git you
        Ef you
           Don't
               Watch
                  Out!

An' little Orphant Annie says, when the blaze is
    blue,
An' the lamp-wick sputters, an' the wind goes
    woo-oo!
An' you hear the crickets quit, an' the moon is
    gray,
An' the lightnin' bugs in dew is all squenched
    away,—
You better mind yer parents, and yer teachers
    fond an' dear,
An' churish them 'at loves you, an' dry the
    orphant's tear,

An' he'p the pore an' needy ones 'at clusters all
about,
Er the Gobble-uns 'll get you
Ef you
Don't
Watch
Out!

MIDSUMMER MAGIC

Ivy O. Eastwick

Midsummer Eve, a year ago, my mother she
commanded,
"Now don't you go a'running down to Ragwort
Meadow!
And don't you go a'plucking of the bracken-seed
or nightshade;
Stay out of the moonlight, mind! and keep out of
the shadow,
For they say that the Ragtag,
Bobtail,
Merry-derry
Fairy-men
Tonight will go a'dancing down in Ragwort
Meadow!"

Midsummer Eve, a year ago, my mother she
commanded,
"Now don't you go a'playing down in Ragwort
Meadow!
Keep away from thorn-tree, from adders' tongue
and henbane!
Keep away from moonlight and don't venture in
the shadow,
For they say that the Ragtag,
Bobtail,
Merry-derry
Fairy-men
Are out a'snaring mortals down in Ragwort
Meadow."

I wouldn't heed my mother's words! I wouldn't
heed her warning!
I ran through the moonlight, through the starlight
and the shadow!
And I never stopped a'running though my breath
came quick and gasping,
Till I reached the very middle of Ragwort
Meadow,
And there I heard the Ragtag,
Bobtail,
Merry-derry
Fairy-men
A'laughing fit to kill themselves in Ragwort
Meadow.

I heard 'em! But I couldn't see, no! not a little
sight of 'em!
I pulled a curly bracken-leaf a'growing in the
meadow,
I scratched out all the bracken-seeds and rubbed
them on my eyelids—
The moon gave brilliant sunlight! There wasn't
any shadow!
And there I saw the Ragtag,
Bobtail,
Merry-derry
Fairy-men
A'dancing round me in a ring in Ragwort
Meadow.

Half-a-hundred fairy-men and half-a-score of
rabbits;
Half-a-dozen squirrels down in Ragwort Meadow,
Dancing round me in a ring—you never saw the
like of it!—
Underneath the daylight which the bright moon
shed! Oh!
A blessing on the Ragtag,
Bobtail,
Merry-derry
Fairy-men
Who showed themselves to me down in Ragwort
Meadow.

"Little Orphant Annie" from *Afterwhiles* by James Whitcomb Riley. Published by The Bobbs-Merrill Company, Inc., 1891.

"Midsummer Magic" from *Fairies and Such Like* by Ivy O. Eastwick. Copyright 1946 by E. P. Dutton & Co., Inc. and reprinted with their permission.

NONSENSE POETRY

In the past when children had only serious, didactic poetry written for them, they were able to escape into a world of humor and nonsense through nursery rhymes. In the mid-1800s, while most poets were writing moralizing poetry, a few writers began to return to the fun and freedom of the Mother Goose rhymes. Edward Lear and Lewis Carroll are noted for their efforts to revive nonsense poetry for children. Many of Carroll's poems in his Alice books were parodies of serious, popular poems. While Lear did not develop the limerick form, he did popularize it, in addition to writing many other amusing poems.

A poem may be funny because it deals with a nonsensical situation, as in "The Fox Rhyme" where a fox runs away with Aunt or in "The Owl and the Pussy Cat" where two animals go to sea in a pea-green boat. Or a surprise ending may make a poem amusing, as in "How doth the little crocodile" and "About the Teeth of Sharks." Many poems, however, play with words and sounds to create a light mood and the feeling of nonsense. John Ciardi's "The Cat Heard the Cat-Bird" is delightful because of his abundant use of assonance and alliteration. So is Carroll's uninhibited, creative experimentation with words in " 'Twas brillig and the slithy toves." Some nonsense poetry, perhaps the best, combines all of these elements.

For those many children who claim to "hate" poetry, the best way to erase their negative memories of boring poems is to give them many experiences with nonsense poetry. But care must be taken not to use the coy, "cute," and patronizing verse that sometimes passes for true nonsense.

Nonsense poetry is an excellent introduction to more serious poetry, for it contains the same poetic elements of rhyme and other sound patterns, imagery, figures of speech, and rhythm. Children who learn through nonsense verse that poems can offer valuable experiences will turn to and accept other forms of poetry. They will unconsciously learn about the tunes of their language and, perhaps, learn to use it more imaginatively and effectively. There is no more enjoyable approach to poetry than nonsense verse.

WHY NOBODY PETS THE LION AT THE ZOO

John Ciardi

The morning that the world began
The Lion growled a growl at Man.

And I suspect the Lion might
(If he'd been closer) have tried a bite.

I think that's as it ought to be
And not as it was taught to me.

I think the Lion has a right
To growl a growl and bite a bite.

And if the Lion bothered Adam,
He should have growled right back at 'im.

The way to treat a Lion right
Is growl for growl and bite for bite.

True, the Lion is better fit
For biting than for being bit.

But if you look him in the eye
You'll find the Lion's rather shy.

He really wants someone to pet him.
The trouble is: his teeth won't let him.

He has a heart of gold beneath
But the Lion just can't trust his teeth.

SOMETIMES I FEEL THIS WAY

John Ciardi

I have one head that wants to be good,
    And one that wants to be bad.
And always, as soon as I get up,
    One of my heads is sad.

"Be bad," says one head. "Don't you know
    It's fun to be bad. Be as bad as you like.
Put sand in your brother's shoe—that's fun.
    Put gum on the seat of your sister's bike."

"What fun is that?" says my other head.
    "Why not go down before the rest
And set things out for breakfast? My,
    That would please Mother. Be good—that's
        best."

"What! Better than putting frogs in the sink?
    Or salt in the tea-pot? Have some fun.
Be bad, be bad, be good and bad.
    You know it is good to be bad," says One.

"Is it good to make Sister and Brother sad?
    And Mother and Daddy? And when you do,
Is it good to get spanked? Is it good to cry?
    No, no. Be good—that's best," says Two.

So one by one they say what they say,
    And what they say is "Be Good—Be Bad."
And if One is happy that makes Two cry.
    And if Two is happy that makes One sad.

Someday maybe, when I grow up,
    I shall wake and find I have just one—
The happy head. But which will it be?
    I wish I knew. They are both *some* fun.

WHAT DO *YOU* THINK HIS DADDY DID?

John Ciardi

Not in all of time, I think
Has there been such a do, such a do, do do,
As there was the day I spilled the ink,
The red ink, into my daddy's shoe.

The shoe was white, the ink was red.
But not as red as my daddy got
When he looked at me. And what he said
Was a little loud and a little hot.

No, not as loud and not as hot
As a gun going off with a boom, boom, boom.
But all the same he said a lot
Before he sent me up to my room.

. . . I am here in my room and I can't forget
What Daddy said. Not a word of it.
Forget? My goodness, no! Not yet.
So far I still can't sit.

WHAT DID YOU LEARN AT THE ZOO?

John Ciardi

What did I learn at the zoo?
Monkeys look like you.

Some are bald and some have curls,
But monkeys look like boys and girls.

Some are quiet and some make noise,
But all of them look like girls and boys.

What did *you* learn at the zoo?
Oh, much the same as you:

Gorillas are good, gorillas are bad,
But all of them look a lot like Dad.

Some do one thing, some another,
But all of them scream a lot like Mother.

What did *we* learn at the zoo?
Just what we wanted to:

That it's fun to tease if you make it rhyme
(Though you mustn't do it all the time),
That kangaroos hop and monkey's climb,
And that a bottle of lemon-and-lime
Is a very good way to spend a dime.

(And so is a bag of peanuts.)

THE OCTOPUS

Ogden Nash

Tell me, O Octopus, I begs,
Is those things arms, or is they legs?
I marvel at thee, Octopus;
If I were thou, I'd call me Us.

THE PANTHER

Ogden Nash

The panther is like a leopard,
Except it hasn't been peppered.
Should you behold a panther crouch,
Prepare to say Ouch.
Better yet, if called by a panther,
Don't anther.

THE GUPPY

Ogden Nash

Whales have calves,
Cats have kittens,
Bears have cubs,
Bats have bittens,
Swans have cygnets,
Seals have puppies,
But guppies just have little guppies.

THE PURIST

Ogden Nash

I give you now Professor Twist,
A conscientious scientist.

"The Octopus," "The Panther," and "The Purist" from
Verses from 1929 On by Ogden Nash, by permission of
Little, Brown and Co. Copyright, 1942, by Ogden Nash.
"The Guppy" from *Versus*, 1949. Reprinted by permission
of Curtis Brown, Ltd. Copyright © 1944, The Curtis
Publishing Co.

Trustees exclaimed, "He never bungles!"
And sent him off to distant jungles.
Camped on a tropic riverside,
One day he missed his loving bride.
She had, the guide informed him later,
Been eaten by an alligator.
Professor Twist could not but smile.
"You mean," he said, "a crocodile."

THE FOX RHYME

Ian Serraillier

Aunt was on the garden seat
    Enjoying a wee nap and
Along came a fox! teeth
    Closed with a snap and
He's running to the woods with her
    A-dangle and a-flap and—
Run, uncle run
    And see what has happened.

A CENTIPEDE

Anonymous

A centipede was happy quite,
Until a frog in fun
Said, "Pray, which leg comes after which?"
This raised her mind to such a pitch,
She lay distracted in a ditch,
Considering how to run.

SOME FISHY NONSENSE

Laura E. Richards

Timothy Tiggs and Tomothy Toggs,
They both went a-fishing for pollothywogs;
    They both went a-fishing
    Because they were wishing
To see how the creatures would turn into frogs.

Timothy Tiggs and Tomothy Toggs,
They both got stuck in the bogothybogs;
    They caught a small minnow,
    And said 't was a sin oh!
That things with no legs should pretend to be
    frogs.

"The Fox Rhyme" from *The Tale of the Monster Horse*
by Ian Serraillier, published by Oxford University Press. Reprinted by permission of the author.

THE OLD WOMAN

Beatrix Potter

You know the old woman
    Who lived in a shoe?
And had so many children
    She didn't know what to do?

I think if she lived in
    A little shoe-house—
That little old woman was
    Surely a mouse!

GALOSHES

Rhoda W. Bacmeister

Susie's galoshes
Makes splishes and sploshes
And slooshes and sloshes,
As Susie steps slowly
Along in the slush.

They stamp and they tramp
On the ice and concrete,
They get stuck in the muck and the mud;
But Susie likes much best to hear

The slippery slush
As it slooshes and sloshes,
And splishes and sploshes,
All round her galoshes!

THE LITTLE ELF

John Kendrick Bangs

I met a little Elf man, once,
    Down where the lilies blow.
I asked him why he was so small,
    And why he didn't grow.

He slightly frowned, and with his eye
    He looked me through and through.
"I'm quite as big for me," said he,
    "As you are big for you."

MISS JAMES

A. A. Milne

Diana Fitzpatrick Mauleverer James
Was lucky to have the most beautiful names.
How awful for fathers and mothers to call
Their children Jemima!—or nothing at all!
But *hers* were much wiser and kinder and cleverer,
They called her Diana Fitzpatrick Mauleverer
    James.

THE COMMON CORMORANT

Anonymous

The common cormorant or shag
Lays eggs inside a paper bag.
The reason you will see no doubt
It is to keep the lightning out.
But what these unobservant birds
Have never noticed is that herds
Of wandering bears may come with buns
And steal the bags to hold the crumbs.

THE FROG

Hilaire Belloc

Be kind and tender to the Frog
    And do not call him names,
As "Slimy skin," or "Polly-wog,"
    Or likewise "Ugly James,"
Or "Gap-a-grin," or "Toad-gone-wrong,"
    Or "Bill Bandy-knees":
The Frog is justly sensitive
    To epithets like these.
No animal will more repay
    A treatment kind and fair

"Some Fishy Nonsense" from *Tirra Lirra* by Laura E. Richards. Published by Little, Brown and Co.
"The Old Woman" reprinted by permission of Frederick Warne & Co., Ltd.
"Galoshes" from *Stories To Begin on* by Rhoda W. Bacmeister. Copyright 1940 by E. P. Dutton & Co., Inc. Renewal, ©, 1968 by Rhoda W. Bacmeister. Published by E. P. Dutton & Co., Inc. and reprinted with their permission.

"The Little Elf" from *St. Nicholas Book of Verse* by John Kendrick Bangs. Published by D. Appleton Company.
"Miss James" from *A Gallery of Children* by A. A. Milne. Copyright 1925 by David McKay Company and reprinted by permission of the publishers.

At least so lonely people say
Who keep a frog (and, by the way,
They are extremely rare).

THE OSTRICH IS A SILLY BIRD

Mary E. Wilkins Freeman

The ostrich is a silly bird,
    With scarcely any mind.
He often runs so very fast,
    He leaves himself behind.

And when he gets there, has to stand
    And hang about till night,
Without a blessed thing to do
    Until he comes in sight.

HE WAS A RAT

Anonymous

He was a rat, and she was a rat,
    And down in one hole they did dwell,
And both were as black as a witch's cat,
    And they loved one another well.

He had a tail, and she had a tail,
    Both long and curling and fine;
And each said, "Yours is the finest tail
    In the world, excepting mine."

He smelt the cheese, and she smelt the cheese,
    And they both pronounced it good;
And both remarked it would greatly add
    To the charms of their daily food.

So he ventured out, and she ventured out,
    And I saw them go with pain,
But what befell them I never can tell,
    For they never came back again.

ONLY MY OPINION

Monica Shannon

Is a caterpillar ticklish?
    Well, it's always my belief
That he giggles, as he wiggles
    Across a hairy leaf.

PURPLE COW

Gelett Burgess

I never saw a Purple Cow,
    I never hope to see one;
But I can tell you, anyhow,
    I'd rather see than be one.

THERE *ONCE* WAS A PUFFIN

Florence Page Jaques

Oh, there once was a Puffin
Just the shape of a muffin,
And he lived on an island
In the
        bright
            blue
                sea!

He ate little fishes,
That were most delicious,
And he had them for supper
And he
        had
            them
                for tea.

But this poor little Puffin,
He couldn't play nothin',
For he hadn't anybody
To
    play
        with
            at all.

"The Frog" from *Cautionary Verses*, by Hilaire Belloc. Published 1941 by Alfred A. Knopf, Inc. Reprinted by permission of Alfred A. Knopf, Inc., and Gerald Duckworth & Co. Ltd.
"The Ostrich Is a Silly Bird" reprinted from *Harpers Magazine*, August 1905.

"Only My Opinion" from *Goose Grass Rhymes* by Monica Shannon. Copyright 1930 by Doubleday & Company, Inc. Reprinted by permission of Doubleday & Company, Inc.
"Purple Cow" from *The Burgess Nonsense Book* by Gelett Burgess. Copyright, 1929, by Gelett Burgess. Reprinted by permission of J. B. Lippincott Company.

So he sat on his island,
And he cried for awhile, and
He felt very lonely,
And he
    felt
       very
          small.

Then along came the fishes,
And they said, "If you wishes,
You can have us for playmates,
Instead
    of
       for
         tea!"

So they now play together,
In all sorts of weather,
And the puffin eats pancakes,
Like you
    and
       like
         me.

JOHN COOK

Anonymous

John Cook he had a little grey mare,
    Hee, haw, hum;
Her legs were long and her back was bare,
    Hee, haw, hum;
John Cook was riding up Shooter's Bank,
    Hee, haw, hum;
The mare she began to kick and to prank,
    Hee, haw, hum;
John Cook was riding up Shooter's Hill,
    Hee, haw, hum;
His mare fell down and made her will,
    Hee, haw, hum;
The bridle and saddle were laid on the shelf,
    Hee, haw, hum;
If you want any more you may sing it yourself,
    Hee, haw, hum.

"There ONCE Was a Puffin" from *Child Life Magazine.* Copyright 1930, 1958 by Rand McNally & Company. Reprinted by permission of the publisher and author.

THE POBBLE

Edward Lear

The Pobble who has no toes
    Had once as many as we;
When they said, "Some day you may lose them
      all,"
    He replied, "Fish fiddle-de-dee!"
And his Aunt Jobiska made him drink
Lavender water tinged with pink,
For she said, "The World in general knows
There's nothing so good for a Pobble's toes!"

The Pobble who has no toes
    Swam across the Bristol Channel;
But before he set out he wrapped his nose
    In a piece of scarlet flannel,
For his Aunt Jobiska said, "No harm
Can come to his toes if his nose is warm;
And it's perfectly known that a Pobble's toes
Are safe—provided he minds his nose!"

The Pobble swam fast and well,
    And when boats or ships came near him,
He tinkledy-binkledy-winkled a bell,
    So that all the world could hear him,
And all the Sailors and Admirals cried,
When they saw him nearing the further side,
"He has gone to fish for his Aunt Jobiska's
Runcible Cat with crimson whiskers!"

But before he touched the shore,
    The shore of the Bristol Channel,
A sea-green Porpoise carried away
    His wrapper of scarlet flannel,
And when he came to observe his feet,
Formerly garnished with toes so neat,
His face at once became forlorn
On perceiving that all his toes were gone.

And nobody ever knows,
    From that dark day to the present,
Whoso had taken the Pobble's toes,
    In a manner so far from pleasant.
Whether the shrimps or crawfish grey,
Or crafty mermaids stole them away—
Nobody knew; and nobody knows
How the Pobble was robbed of his twice five toes.

The Pobble who has no toes
    Was placed in a friendly Bark,
And they rowed him back, and they carried him
      up
    To his Aunt Jobiska's Park.
And she made him a feast at his earnest wish
Of eggs and buttercups fried with fish:—
And she said, "It's a fact the whole world knows
That Pobbles are happier without their toes."

THE LADY AND THE BEAR

Theodore Roethke

A Lady came to a Bear by a Stream.
"O why are you fishing that way?
Tell me, dear Bear there by the Stream,
Why are you fishing that way?"

"I am what is known as a Biddly Bear,—
That's why I'm fishing this way.
We Biddly's are Pee-culiar Bears.
And so,—I'm fishing this way.

And besides, it seems there's a Law:
A most, most exactious Law
Says a Bear
Doesn't dare
Doesn't dare
Doesn't DARE
Use a Hook or a Line,
Or an old piece of Twine,
Not even the end of his Claw, Claw, Claw,
Not even the end of his claw.
Yes, a Bear has to fish with his Paw, Paw.
A Bear has to fish with his Paw."

"O it's wonderful how with a flick of your Wrist,
You can fish out a fish, out a fish, out a fish,
If I were a fish I just couldn't resist
You, when you are fishing that way, that way,
When you are fishing that way."

And at that the Lady slipped from the Bank
And fell in the stream still clutching a Plank,
But the Bear just sat there until she Sank;

As he went on fishing his way, his way,
As he went on fishing his way.

JOHNNIE CRACK AND FLOSSIE SNAIL

Dylan Thomas

Johnnie Crack and Flossie Snail
Kept their baby in a milking pail
Flossie Snail and Johnnie Crack
One would pull it out and one would put it back

O it's my turn now said Flossie Snail
To take the baby from the milking pail
And it's my turn now said Johnnie Crack
To smack it on the head and put it back

Johnnie Crack and Flossie Snail
Kept their baby in a milking pail
One would put it back and one would pull it out
And all it had to drink was ale and stout
For Johnnie Crack and Flossie Snail
Always used to say that stout and ale
Was *good* for a baby in a milking pail.

MY MOTHER SAID I NEVER SHOULD

Anonymous

My mother said I never should
Play with the gipsies in the wood;
If I did, she would say,
Naughty girl to disobey.
Your hair shan't curl
And your shoes shan't shine
You gipsy girl,
You shan't be mine.
And my father said that if I did
He'd rap my head with the tea-pot lid.
The wood was dark; the grass was green;
In came Sally with a tambourine.
I went to the sea—no ship to get across;
I paid ten shillings for a blind white horse;
I up on his back and was off in a crack,
Sally tell my mother I shall never come back.

JEMIMA

Anonymous

There was a little girl, and she wore a little curl
  Right down the middle of her forehead.
When she was good, she was very, very good,
  But when she was bad, she was horrid!

One day she went upstairs, while her parents,
    unawares,
  In the kitchen down below were occupied with
    meals,
And she stood upon her head, on her little
    truckle bed,
  And she then began hurraying with her heels.

Her mother heard the noise, and thought it was
    the boys
  A-playing at a combat in the attic,
But when she climbed the stair and saw Jemima
    there,
  She took and she did whip her most emphatic.

GRANDMOTHER'S VISIT

William Wise

This morning I was bad,
But it really didn't matter:
I came down the stairs
With a terrible clatter;
I jumped and I shouted,
I tried to pinch sister,
I called father "Pop"
and the garbage man "Mister";
I pretended I was deaf
And I said I liked beer.
But it really won't matter
'Cause Grandmother's here.

When Grandmother's here,
Then everything's fine:
She says a boy shouts
To strengthen his spine;
She says a boy jumps
To make him grow tall;
And when I pretend
She doesn't mind at all.
This morning I was bad,

But there's nothing to fear;
My troubles are over
When Grandmother's here!

DON'T-CARE DIDN'T CARE

Anonymous

Don't-care didn't care;
  Don't-care was wild.
Don't-care stole plum and pear
  Like any beggar's child.
Don't-care was made to care,
  Don't-care was hung;
Don't-care was put in the pot
  And boiled till he was done.

MATILDA
Who told Lies, and was Burned to Death

Hilaire Belloc

Matilda told such Dreadful Lies,
It made one Gasp and Stretch one's Eyes;
Her Aunt, who, from her Earliest Youth,
Had kept a Strict Regard for Truth,
Attempted to Believe Matilda:
The effort very nearly killed her,
And would have done so, had not She
Discovered this Infirmity.
For once, towards the Close of Day,
Matilda, growing tired of play,
And finding she was left alone,
Went tiptoe to the Telephone
And summoned the Immediate Aid
Of London's Noble Fire-Brigade.
Within an hour the Gallant Band
Were pouring in on every hand,
From Putney, Hackney Downs and Bow,
With Courage high and Hearts a-glow
They galloped, roaring through the Town,
"Matilda's House is Burning Down!"
Inspired by British Cheers and Loud
Proceeding from the Frenzied Crowd,
They ran their ladders through a score
Of windows on the Ball Room Floor;

"Grandmother's Visit," reprinted by permission of Brandt
& Brandt from *Jonathan Blake, The Life and Times of a
Very Young Man.* Copyright 1956 by William Wise.

And took Peculiar Pains to Souse
The Pictures up and down the House,
Until Matilda's Aunt succeeded
In showing them they were not needed,
And even then she had to pay
To get the Men to go away!
It happened that a few Weeks later
Her Aunt was off to the Theatre
To see that Interesting Play
The Second Mrs. Tanqueray.
She had refused to take her Niece
To hear this Entertaining Piece:
A Deprivation Just and Wise
To punish her for Telling Lies.
That Night a Fire *did* break out—
You should have heard Matilda Shout!
You should have heard her Scream and Bawl,
And throw the window up and call
To People passing in the Street—
(The rapidly increasing Heat
Encouraging her to obtain
Their confidence)—but all in vain!
For every time she shouted "Fire!"
They only answered "Little Liar!"
And therefore when her Aunt returned,
Matilda, and the House, were Burned.

I WOKE UP THIS MORNING

Karla Kuskin

I woke up this morning
At quarter past seven.
I kicked up the covers
And stuck out my toe.
And ever since then
(That's a quarter past seven)
They haven't said anything
Other than "no."

They haven't said anything
Other than "Please, dear,
Don't do what you're doing,"
Or "Lower your voice."
Whatever I've done

And however I've chosen,
I've done the wrong thing
And I've made the wrong choice.

I didn't wash well
And I didn't say thank you.
I didn't shake hands
And I didn't say please.
I didn't say sorry
When, passing the candy,
I banged the box into
Miss Witelson's knees.
I didn't say sorry.
I didn't stand straighter.
I didn't speak louder
When asked what I'd said.
Well, I said
That tomorrow
At quarter past seven,
They can
come in and get me
I'M STAYING IN BED.

A MORTIFYING MISTAKE

Anna Maria Pratt

I studied my tables over and over, and backward
    and forward, too;
But I couldn't remember six times nine, and I
    didn't know what to do,
'Til sister told me to play with my doll, and not
    to bother my head.
"If you call her 'Fifty-four' for a while, you'll
    learn it by heart," she said.

So I took my favorite, Mary Ann (though I
    thought 'twas a dreadful shame
To give such a perfectly lovely child such a
    perfectly horrible name),
And I called her my dear little 'Fifty-four' a
    hundred times, till I knew
The answer of six times nine as well as the answer
    of two times two.

Next day Elizabeth Wigglesworth, who always
    acts so proud,

Said "Six times nine is fifty-two," and I nearly
    laughed aloud!
But I wished I hadn't when teacher said, "Now,
    Dorothy, tell if you can."
For I thought of my doll and—sakes alive!—I
    answered, "Mary Ann!"

ARITHMETIC

Carl Sandburg

Arithmetic is where numbers fly like pigeons in
    and out of your head.
Arithmetic tells you how many you lose or win if
    you know how many you had before you lost
    or won.
Arithmetic is seven eleven all good children go
    to heaven—or five six bundles of sticks.
Arithmetic is numbers you squeeze from your head
    to your hand to your pencil to your paper till
    you get the answer.
Arithmetic is where the answer is right and
    everything is nice and you can look out of the
    window and see the blue sky—or the answer is
    wrong and you have to start all over and try
    again and see how it comes out this time.
If you take a number and double it and double
    it again and then double it a few more times,
    the number gets bigger and bigger and goes
    higher and higher and only arithmetic can tell
    you what the number is when you decide to
    quit doubling.
Arithmetic is where you have to multiply—and
    you carry the multiplication table in your head
    and hope you won't lose it.
If you have two animal crackers, one good and
    one bad, and you eat one and a striped zebra
    with streaks all over him eats the other, how
    many animal crackers will you have if some-
    body offers you five six seven and you say No
    no no and you say Nay nay nay and you say
    Nix nix nix?
If you ask your mother for one fried egg for break-
    fast and she gives you two fried eggs and you
    eat both of them, who is better in arithmetic,
    you or your mother?

MANUAL SYSTEM

Carl Sandburg

Mary has a thingamajig clamped on her ears
And sits all day taking plugs out and sticking
    plugs in.
Flashes and flashes—voices and voices calling for
    ears to pour words in
Faces at the ends of wires asking for other faces
    at the ends of other wires:
All day taking plugs out and sticking plugs in,
Mary has a thingamajig clamped on her ears.

A TRAGIC STORY

William Makepeace Thackeray

There lived a sage in days of yore,
And he a handsome pigtail wore;
But wondered much and sorrowed more,
    Because it hung behind him.

He mused upon this curious case,
And swore he'd change the pigtail's place,
And have it hanging at his face,
    Not dangling there behind him.

Said he, "The mystery I've found—
I'll turn me round"—he turned him round,
    But still it hung behind him.

Then round and round, and out and in,
All day the puzzled sage did spin;
In vain—it mattered not a pin—
    The pigtail hung behind him.

And right and left, and roundabout,
And up and down and in and out
He turned; but still the pigtail stout
    Hung steadily behind him.

And though his efforts never slack,
And though he twist, and twirl, and tack,
Alas! still faithful to his back,
    The pigtail hangs behind him.

BROWN'S DESCENT OR THE WILLY-NILLY SLIDE

Robert Frost

Brown lived at such a lofty farm
    That everyone for miles could see
His lantern when he did his chores
    In winter after half-past three.

And many must have seen him make
    His wild descent from there one night,
'Cross lots, 'cross walls, 'cross everything,
    Describing rings of lantern-light.

Between the house and barn the gale
    Got him by something he had on
And blew him out on the icy crust
    That cased the world, and he was gone!

Walls were all buried, trees were few:
    He saw no stay unless he stove
A hole in somewhere with his heel.
    But though repeatedly he strove

And stamped and said things to himself,
    And sometimes something seemed to yield,
He gained no foothold, but pursued
    His journey down from field to field.

Sometimes he came with arms outspread
    Like wings, revolving in the scene
Upon his longer axis, and
    With no small dignity of mien.

Faster or slower as he chanced,
    Sitting or standing as he chose,
According as he feared to risk
    His neck, or thought to spare his clothes.

He never let the lantern drop.
    And some exclaimed who saw afar
The figures he described with it,
    "I wonder what those signals are

"Brown makes at such an hour of night!
    He's celebrating something strange.
I wonder if he's sold his farm,
    Or been made Master of the Grange."

He reeled, he lurched, he bobbed, he checked;
    He fell and made the lantern rattle
(But saved the light from going out.)
    So halfway down he fought the battle,

Incredulous of his own bad luck.
    And then becoming reconciled
To everything, he gave it up
    And came down like a coasting child.

"Well—I—be—" that was all he said,
    As standing in the river road
He looked back up the slippery slope
    (Two miles it was) to his abode.

*   *   *

But now he snapped his eyes three times;
    Then shook his lantern, saying, "Ile's
'Bout out!" and took the long way home
    By road, a matter of several miles.

THE PIRATE DON DURK OF DOWDEE

Mildred Plew Meigs

Ho, for the Pirate Don Durk of Dowdee!
He was as wicked as wicked could be,
But oh, he was perfectly gorgeous to see!
    The Pirate Don Durk of Dowdee.

His conscience, of course, was as black as a bat,
But he had a floppety plume on his hat
And when he went walking it jiggled—like that!
    The plume of the Pirate Dowdee.

His coat it was crimson and cut with a slash,
And often as ever he twirled his mustache
Deep down in the ocean the mermaids went
    splash,
    Because of Don Durk of Dowdee.

Moreover, Dowdee had a purple tattoo,
And stuck in his belt where he buckled it through
Were a dagger, a dirk and a squizzamaroo,
    For fierce was the Pirate Dowdee.

So fearful he was he would shoot at a puff,
And always at seat when the weather grew rough
He drank from a bottle and wrote on his cuff,
   Did Pirate Don Durk of Dowdee.

Oh, he had a cutlass that swung at his thigh
And he had a parrot called Pepperkin Pye,
And a zigzaggy scar at the end of his eye
   Had Pirate Don Durk of Dowdee.

He kept in a cavern, this buccaneer bold,
A curious chest that was covered with mould,
And all of his pockets were jingly with gold!
   Oh jing! went the gold of Dowdee.

His conscience, of course, it was crook'd like a
   squash,
But both of his boots made a slickery slosh,
And he went through the world with a wonderful
   swash,
   Did Pirate Don Durk of Dowdee.

It's true he was wicked as wicked could be,
His sins they outnumbered a hundred and three,
But oh, he was perfectly gorgeous to see,
   The Pirate Don Durk of Dowdee.

THE WORLD HAS HELD GREAT HEROES

Kenneth Grahame

The world has held great Heroes,
   As history-books have showed;
But never a name to go down to fame
   Compared with that of Toad!

The clever men at Oxford
   Know all that there is to be knowed.
But they none of them know one half as much
   As intelligent Mr. Toad!

The animals sat in the Ark and cried,
   Their tears in torrents flowed.
Who was it said, "There's land ahead?"
   Encouraging Mr. Toad!

The army all saluted
   As they marched along the road.
Was it the King? Or Kitchener?
   No. It was Mr. Toad!

The Queen and her Ladies-in-waiting
   Sat at the window and sewed.
She cried, "Look! who's that *handsome* man?"
   They answered, "Mr. Toad."

HOW DOTH THE LITTLE CROCODILE

Lewis Carroll

How doth the little crocodile
   Improve his shining tail,
And pour the waters of the Nile
   On every golden scale!

How cheerfully he seems to grin,
   How neatly spreads his claws,
And welcomes little fishes in,
   With gently smiling jaws!

SPEAK ROUGHLY TO YOUR LITTLE BOY

Lewis Carroll

Speak roughly to your little boy,
   And beat him when he sneezes;
He only does it to annoy,
   Because he knows it teases.
     Wow! Wow! Wow!

I speak severely to my boy,
   I beat him when he sneezes;
For he can thoroughly enjoy
   The pepper when he pleases!
     Wow! Wow! Wow!

JABBERWOCKY

Lewis Carroll

'Twas brillig, and the slithy toves
   Did gyre and gimble in the wabe:

All mimsy were the borogoves,
  And the mome raths outgrabe.

"Beware the Jabberwock, my son!
  The jaws that bite, the claws that catch!
Beware the Jubjub bird, and shun
  The frumious Bandersnatch!"

He took his vorpal sword in hand:
  Long time the manxome foe he sought—
So rested he by the Tumtum tree,
  And stood awhile in thought.

And, as in uffish thought he stood,
  The Jabberwock, with eyes of flame,
Came whiffling through the tulgey wood,
  And burbled as it came!

One, two! One, two! And through and through
  The vorpal blade went snicker-snack!
He left it dead, and with its head
  He went galumphing back.

"And hast thou slain the Jabberwock?
  Come to my arms, my beamish boy!
O frabjous day! Callooh! Callay!"
  He chortled in his joy.

'Twas brillig, and the slithy toves
  Did gyre and gimble in the wabe:
All mimsy were the borogoves,
  And the mome raths outgrabe.

YOU ARE OLD, FATHER WILLIAM

Lewis Carroll

"You are old, Father William," the young man
    said,
  "And your hair has become very white;
And yet you incessantly stand on your head—
  Do you think, at your age, it is right?"

"In my youth," Father William replied to his
    son,
  "I feared it might injure the brain;
But, now that I'm perfectly sure I have none,
  Why, I do it again and again."

"You are old," said the youth, "as I mentioned
    before.
  And have grown most uncommonly fat;
Yet you turned a back-somersault in at the door—
  Pray, what is the reason for that?"

"In my youth," said the sage, as he shook his grey
    locks,
  "I kept all my limbs very supple
By the use of this ointment—one shilling the
    box—
  Allow me to sell you a couple?"

"You are old," said the youth, "and your jaws are
    too weak
  For anything tougher than suet;
Yet you finshed the goose, with the bones and
    the beak—
  Pray, how did you manage to do it?"

"In my youth," said his father, "I took to the law,
  And argued each case with my wife;
And the muscular strength, which it gave to my
    jaw
  Has lasted the rest of my life."

"You are old," said the youth, "one would hardly
    suppose
  That your eye was as steady as ever;
Yet you balanced an eel on the end of your nose—
  What made you so awfully clever?"

"I have answered three questions, and that is
    enough,"
  Said his father. "Don't give yourself airs!
Do you think I can listen all day to such stuff?
  Be off, or I'll kick you down-stairs!"

BEAUTIFUL SOUP

Lewis Carroll

Beautiful Soup, so rich and green,
  Waiting in a hot tureen!
Who for such dainties would not stoop?
Soup of the evening, beautiful Soup!
Soup of the evening, beautiful Soup!
  Beau-ootiful Soo-oop!
  Beau-ootiful Soo-oop!

Soo-oop of the e-e-evening,
    Beautiful, beautiful Soup!

Beautiful Soup! Who cares for fish,
    Game, or any other dish?
Who would not give all else for two
Pennyworth only of beautiful Soup?
Pennyworth only of beautiful Soup?
    Beau-ootiful Soo-oop!
    Beau-ootiful Soo-oop!
Soo-oop of the e-e-evening,
    Beautiful, beauti-FUL SOUP!

THE WALRUS AND THE CARPENTER

Lewis Carroll

The sun was shining on the sea,
    Shining with all his might;
He did his very best to make
    The billows smooth and bright—
And this was odd, because it was
    The middle of the night.

The moon was shining sulkily,
    Because she thought the sun
Had got no business to be there
    After the day was done—
"It's very rude of him," she said,
    "To come and spoil the fun!"

The sea was wet as wet could be,
    The sands were dry as dry.
You could not see a cloud, because
    No cloud was in the sky;
No birds were flying overhead—
    There were no birds to fly.

The Walrus and the Carpenter
    Were walking close at hand;
They wept like anything to see
    Such quantities of sand—
"If this were only cleared away,"
    They said, "it would be grand!"

"If seven maids with seven mops
    Swept it for half a year,
Do you suppose," the Walrus said,
    "That they could get it clear?"

"I doubt it," said the Carpenter,
    And shed a bitter tear.

"O Oysters, come and walk with us!"
    The Walrus did beseech.
"A pleasant walk, a pleasant talk,
    Along the briny beach;
We cannot do with more than four,
    To give a hand to each."

The eldest Oyster looked at him,
    But never a word he said;
The eldest Oyster winked his eye,
    And shook his heavy head—
Meaning to say he did not choose
    To leave the oyster-bed.

But four young Oysters hurried up,
    All eager for the treat;
Their coats were brushed, their faces washed,
    Their shoes were clean and neat—
And this was odd, because, you know,
    They hadn't any feet.

Four other Oysters followed them,
    And yet another four;
And thick and fast they came at last,
    And more, and more, and more—
All hopping through the frothy waves,
    And scrambling to the shore.

The Walrus and the Carpenter
    Walked on a mile or so,
And then they rested on a rock
    Conveniently low—
And all the little Oysters stood
    And waited in a row.

"The time has come," the Walrus said,
    "To talk of many things:
Of shoes—and ships—and sealing-wax—
    Of cabbages—and kings—
And why the sea is boiling hot—
    And whether pigs have wings."

"But wait a bit," the Oysters cried,
    "Before we have our chat;
For some of us are out of breath,
    And all of us are fat!"

"No hurry!" said the Carpenter.
   They thanked him much for that.

"A loaf of bread," the Walrus said,
   'Is what we chiefly need;
Pepper and vinegar besides
   Are very good indeed—
Now, if you're ready, Oysters dear,
   We can begin to feed."

"But not on us!" the Oysters cried,
   Turning a little blue.
"After such kindness, that would be
   A dismal thing to do!"
"The night is fine," the Walrus said.
   "Do you admire the view?

"It was so kind of you to come!
   And you are very nice!"
The Carpenter said nothing but,
   "Cut us another slice.
I wish you were not quite so deaf—
   I've had to ask you twice!"

"It seems a shame," the Walrus said,
   "To play them such a trick.
After we've brought them out so far,
   And made them trot so quick!"
The Carpenter said nothing but,
   "The butter's spread too thick!"

"I weep for you," the Walrus said;
   "I deeply sympathize."
With sobs and tears he sorted out
   Those of the largest size,
Holding his pocket-hankerchief
   Before his streaming eyes.

"O Oysters," said the Carpenter,
   "You've had a pleasant run!
Shall we be trotting home again?"
   But answer came there none—
And this was scarcely odd, because
   They'd eaten every one.

THE OWL AND THE PUSSY-CAT

Edward Lear

The Owl and the Pussy-Cat went to sea
   In a beautiful pea-green boat;

They took some honey, and plenty of money
   Wrapped up in a five-pound note.
The Owl looked up to the stars above,
   And sang to a small guitar,
"O Lovely Pussy, O Pussy, my love,
   What a beautiful Pussy you are,
      You are!
      You are!
   What a beautiful Pussy you are!"

Pussy said to the Owl, "You elegant fowl,
   How charmingly sweet you sing!
Oh! Let us be married; too long we have tarried:
   But what shall we do for a ring?"
They sailed away, for a year and a day,
   To the land where the bong-tree grows;
And there in a wood a Piggy-wig stood,
   With a ring at the end of his nose,
      His nose,
      His nose,
   With a ring at the end of his nose.

"Dear Pig, are you willing to sell for a shilling
   Your ring?" Said the Piggy, "I will."
So they took it away, and were married next day
   By the Turkey who lives on the hill.
They dined on mince and slices of quince,
   Which they ate with a runcible spoon;
And hand in hand, on the edge of the sand,
   They danced in the light of the moon,
      The moon,
      The moon,
   They danced in the light of the moon.

THE JUMBLIES

Edward Lear

They went to sea in a sieve, they did;
   In a sieve they went to sea:
In spite of all their friends could say,
On a winter's morn, on a stormy day,
   In a sieve they went to sea.
And when the sieve turned round and round,
And every one cried, "You'll all be drowned!"
They called aloud, "Our sieve ain't big;
But we don't care a button, we don't care a fig:
   In a sieve we'll go to sea!"
    Far and few, far and few,
     Are the lands where the Jumblies live:

Their heads are green, and their hands are
    blue;
    And they went to sea in a sieve.

They sailed away in a sieve, they did,
    In a sieve they sailed so fast,
With only a beautiful pea-green veil
Tied with a ribbon, by way of a sail,
    To a small tobacco-pipe mast.
And every one said who saw them go,
"Oh! won't they be soon upset, you know?
For the sky is dark, and the voyage is long;
And, happen what may, it's extremely wrong
    In a sieve to sail so fast."
      Far and few, far and few,
        Are the lands where the Jumblies live:
      Their heads are green, and their hands are
        blue;
        And they went to sea in a sieve.

The water it soon came in, it did;
    The water it soon came in:
So, to keep them dry, they wrapped their feet
In a pinky paper all folded neat;
    And they fastened it down with a pin.
And they passed the night in a crockery-jar;
And each of them said, "How wise we are!
Though the sky be dark, and the voyage be long,
Yet we never can think we were rash or wrong,
    While round in our sieve we spin."
      Far and few, far and few,
        Are the lands where the Jumblies live:
      Their heads are green, and their hands are
        blue;
        And they went to sea in a sieve.

And all night long they sailed away;
    And when the sun went down,
They whistled and warbled a moony song,
To the echoing sound of a coppery gong,
    In the shade of the mountains brown.
"O Timballoo! How happy we are

When we live in a sieve and a crockery-jar!
And all night long, in the moonlight pale,
We sail away with a pea-green sail
    In the shade of the mountains brown."
      Far and few, far and few,
        Are the lands where the Jumblies live:
      Their heads are green, and their hands are
        blue;
        And they went to sea in a sieve.

They sailed to the Western Sea, they did,—
    To a land all covered with trees:
And they bought an owl, and a useful cart,
And a pound of rice, and a cranberry-tart,
    And a hive of silvery bees;
And they bought a pig, and some green jackdaws,
And a lovely monkey with lollipop paws,
And forty bottles of ring-bo-ree,
    And no end of Stilton cheese.
      Far and few, far and few,
        Are the lands where the Jumblies live:
      Their heads are green, and their hands are
        blue;
        And they went to sea in a sieve.

And in twenty years they all came back,—
    In twenty years or more;
And every one said, "How tall they've grown!
For they've been to the Lakes, and the Torrible
    Zone,
    And the hills of the Chankly Bore."
And they drank their health, and gave them a
    feast
Of dumplings made of beautiful yeast;
And every one said, "If we only live,
We, too, will go to sea in a sieve,
    To the hills of the Chankly Bore."
      Far and few, far and few,
        Are the lands where the Jumblies live:
      Their heads are green, and their hands are
        blue;
        And they went to sea in a sieve.

LIMERICKS

LIMERICKS BY EDWARD LEAR

There was an old man of Boulak,
Who sat on a crocodile's back;
    But they said, "Tow'rds the night
    He may probably bite,
Which might vex you, old man of Boulak!"

There was an old person of Dean
Who dined on one pea, and one bean;
    For he said, "More than that
    Would make me too fat,"
That cautious old person of Dean.

There was an Old Man in a tree,
Who was horribly bored by a Bee;
    When they said, "Does it buzz?"
      he replied, "Yes, it does.
    It's a regular brute of a Bee."

There was an Old Man with a beard,
Who said, "It is just as I feared!—
Two Owls and a Hen, four Larks and a Wren,
Have all built their nests in my beard."

There was an Old Man who said, "How
Shall I flee from this horrible cow?
    I will sit on this stile,
    And continue to smile,
Which may soften the heart of that cow."

There was an old man in a barge,
Whose nose was exceedingly large;
    But in fishing by night,
    It supported a light,
Which helped that old man in a barge.

There was a Young Lady whose chin
Resembled the point of a pin;
So she had it made sharp, and purchased a harp,
And played several tunes with her chin.

There was an old lady of Chertsey,
Who made a remarkable curtsey;
    She twirled round and round,
    Till she sunk underground,
Which distressed all the people of Chertsey.

There was a Young Lady of Norway,
Who casually sat in a doorway;
    When the door squeezed her flat,
      she exclaimed, "What of that?"
This courageous Young Lady of Norway.

OTHER LIMERICKS

There was a young man of Bengal,
Who went to a fancy dress ball;
    He went, just for fun,
    Dressed up as a bun,
And a dog ate him up in the hall.

There was a young lady from Woosester
Who ussessed to crow like a roosester.
    She ussessed to climb
    Seven trees at a time—
But her sisester ussessed to boosester.

A diner while dining at Crewe,
Found a quite large mouse in his stew.
    Said the waiter, "Don't shout,
    And wave it about,
Or the rest will be wanting one, too."

There was an old man of Blackheath,
Who sat on his set of false teeth;
    Said he, with a start,
    "O Lord, bless my heart!
I've bitten myself underneath!"

For beauty I am not a star,
There are others more handsome by far;
    But my face I don't mind it,
    For I am behind it,
It's the people in front that I jar.
                —Anthony Euwer

There was a young farmer of Leeds,
Who swallowed six packets of seeds.
    It soon came to pass
    He was covered with grass,
And he couldn't sit down for the weeds.

There once was a boy of Bagdad,
An inquisitive sort of a lad.
    He said, "I will see
    If a sting has a bee."
And he very soon found that it had!

There was a young lady of Kent,
Whose nose was most awfully bent.
    One day, I suppose,
    She followed her nose,
For no one knew which way she went.

A flea and a fly in a flue
Were caught, so what could they do?
    Said the fly, "Let us flee."
    "Let us fly," said the flea.
So they flew through a flaw in the flue.

There was a young man of Herne Bay,
Who was making explosives one day;

    But he dropped his cigar
    In the gunpowder jar.
There *was* a young man of Herne Bay.

One day I went out to the zoo,
For I wanted to see the old gnu,
    But the old gnu was dead.
    They had a new gnu instead,
And that gnu, well, he knew he was new.
                                —*G. T. Johnson*

I said to a bug in the sink,
"Are you taking a swim or a drink?"
    "I," said the bug,
    "Am a sea-going tug.
Am I headed for land, do you think?"

"What a silly!" I said. "That's no sea—
It's a sink!"—"A sink it may be.
    But I'd sooner I think
    Be at sea in the sink
Than sink in the sea, sir," said he.
                                —*John Ciardi*

WRITTEN BY CHILDREN

BUTTERFLY

Hilda Conkling

As I walked through my garden
I saw a butterfly light on a flower.
His wings were pink and purple:
He spoke a small word . . .
It was *Follow!*
"I cannot follow"
I told him,
"I have to go the opposite way."

THE OLD BRIDGE

Hilda Conkling

The old bridge has a wrinkled face.
He bends his back
For us to go over.
He moans and weeps
But we do not hear.
Sorrow stands in his face
For the heavy weight and worry
Of people passing.
The trees drop their leaves into the water;
The sky nods to him.
The leaves float down like small ships
On the blue surface
Which is the sky.

He is not always sad;
He smiles to see the ships go down
And the little children
Playing on the river banks.

RED ROOSTER

Hilda Conkling
(*Written at the age of seven*)

Red rooster in your gray coop,
O stately creature with tail-feathers red and blue,
Yellow and black,
You have a comb gay as a parade
On your head:
You have pearl trinkets
On your feet:
The short feathers smooth along your back
Are the dark color of wet rocks,
Or the rippled green of ships
When I look at their sides through water.
I don't know how you happened to be made
So proud, so foolish,
Wearing your coat of many colors,
Shouting all day long your crooked words,
Loud . . . sharp . . . not beautiful!

LITTLE SNAIL

Hilda Conkling

I saw a little snail
Come down the garden walk.
He wagged his head this way . . . that way . . .
Like a clown in a circus.
He looked from side to side
As though he were from a different country.
I have always said he carries his house on his
        back . . .
Today in the rain
I saw that it was his umbrella!

SUNSET ON THE SEA

Lori Ubell (age 11, United States)

We sat there and watched as Pen, the sun god
In his fiery wrath drove his chariot behind a cloud
To give his horses water.
And waving purple and pink banners behind him
        were his servants in yellow cloaks
        and his wives in stunning scarlet.
He, in a cloak of glittering diamonds and gold,
        his pale blue horses, his wives, his servants,
Reflected their souls upon the sea.

Pen, the sun god, looked over his kingdom:
The coal-black sea; the fishes, purple, white and
        silver;
        the crabs; the eels, and me in my boat.
He smiled; a purple banner rippled and amidst
        waving banners
        pink dimples showed,
And he went from his chariot to his people
        beneath.

TREES

Nelda Dishman (age 12, United States)

The trees share their shade with
        all who pass by,
But their leaves whisper secrets
        only to the wind.

I LOVE THE WORLD

Paul Wollner (age 7, United States)

I love you, Big World.
I wish I could call you
And tell you a secret:
That I love you, World.

SPLISH SPLOSH

Stefan Martul (age 7, New Zealand)

I feel
        drops of rain,
And it goes;
SPLISH! SPLOSH!

on my head.
And sometimes it goes;
SPLASH! BANG! CRASH!
on my coconut.

MY FEELINGS

Paul Thompson (age 6, New Zealand)

I am fainty,
I am fizzy,
I am floppy.

MY UNCLE JACK

Bill O'Shea (age 10, Australia)

My Uncle Jack collects door knobs;
Door knobs here, door knobs there
Door knobs simply everywhere;
Six on the window, twelve on the door
There's hardly room for any more;
Door knobs on the light switch and on the wall,
My Uncle Jack has got them all;
Blue ones, green ones, yellow ones and red
And a row of gray ones on the bottom of his bed.

THE WITCH

Patricia Thornton (age 7, England)

A witch went into the forest
    Down
        Down
            Down
Into the deep deep forest.
Picking lots of mushrooms in the
    Deep
        Deep
            Forest.
And the wood is very still
And the witch flew into the forest
To make many spells.
Now she's making them
Nasty wicked spells

Making all the people
    Turn
To lots of pigs.
In the
    Deep
        Deep
            Forest.
Now she goes home
To make quite sure
They have
            Worked.

TWO MILLION TWO HUNDRED THOUSAND FISHES

Danny Marcus (age 8, United States)

One cold, winter morning
I got out of bed
And went downstairs
And went outside
And went fishing.

I put in my line
And started to pull
And I pulled and pulled
And, after a while,
I pulled out:
Two million two hundred thousand fishes!

Then I remembered
To get them all home
I needed to have
Two million two hundred thousand wagons!

When I got home
I went to my mother
And my mother said,
"What shall we do with
Two million two hundred thousand fishes!"

My mother sat down
And she thought and she thought
And, after a while she got up.
She opened the window
And threw out:
Two million two hundred thousand fishes!

A BOY

Benny Graves (age 6, United States)

A boy tried to get killed
He ran up and down the road
Until a taxi ran over him.
Why?
Because his mother fussed at him.

SOMEONE

Lee Jaffe (age 12, United States)

And she looked at me,
Saying with her eyes
A lie like she always
said a lie.
And I would listen

for truths when I
listened to her,
which was rare,
but when I did,
I would try to

hear truths but,
I would never
hear them,
I would hear
only lies . . .

I DON'T MIND

Carolyn Jackson (age 11, United States)

I Carolyn Jackson am a pure-blooded Negro in
    soul and mind.
My mother's from North Carolina and my father's
    from Florida.
I know when I go to that old wooden bed,
Somewhere on the other side of town, there is a
    child being put to bed in a soft cuddly
    nest.
But being a Negro isn't so bad (if you know what's
    going on)
Down South my cousin is being beat up—
And Look There . . . My aunt got put in jail for
    drinking from a white fountain.
But here I feel better because I have more free-
    dom.
When I ride the train and sit next to a person of
    the opposite race
I feel like a crow in a robin's nest
And I feel dirty.
I'm not prejudiced or anything . . .
If we go on a trip and they call me names,
I Don't Mind.

Related Reading

References for Adults

Arnstein, Flora J. *Poetry in the Elementary Class-room*. Appleton, 1962.

Behn, Harry. *Chrysalis: Concerning Children and Poetry*. Harcourt, 1968.

Brewton, John E. and Sara W., compilers. *Index to Children's Poetry*. H. W. Wilson, 1942. First Supplement, 1954; Second Supplement, 1965.

Brooks, Cleanth, and Robert Penn Warren. *Understanding Poetry*, 3d ed. Holt, Rinehart and Winston, 1960.

Ciardi, John. *How Does a Poem Mean?* Houghton Mifflin, 1959.

Deutsch, Babette. *Poetry Handbook: A Dictionary of Terms*, new rev. ed. Funk & Wagnalls, 1962.

Huck, Charlotte S. and Doris Young Kuhn. *Children's Literature in the Elementary School*, 2d ed. New York: Holt, Rinehart and Winston, 1968.

Haviland, Virginia, and William Jay Smith, compilers. *Children & Poetry, a Selective, Annotated Bibliography*. Washington, D.C.: Library of Congress, 1969.

MacLeish, Archibald. *Poetry and Experience*. Houghton Mifflin, 1961.

Books for Children

GENERAL COLLECTIONS

Although all of the following anthologies contain some verse and can be recommended only with reservations, they are some of the better collections for children.

Adoff, Arnold, compiler. *I Am the Darker Brother: An Anthology of Modern Poems by Negro Americans*. Illustrated by Benny Andrews. Foreword by Charlemae Rollins. New York: Macmillan, 1968. The compiler explains that his purpose was to "present good, interesting, and evocative poems" that are "outstanding in their ethnic vision." (Grades 6–12)

Austin, Mary C., and Queenie B. Mills, compilers. *The Sound of Poetry*. Boston: Allyn and Bacon, 1963. A useful collection for the classroom. (Grades 1–3)

Blishen, Edward, compiler. *Oxford Book of Poetry for Children*. Illustrated by Brian Wildsmith. New York: F. Watts, 1963. Especially good nonsense poetry. The rest of the book relies on the traditional and has too much verse. (Grades 3–7)

Bontemps, Arna W., compiler. *Golden Slippers, an Anthology of Negro Poetry for Young Readers*. Illustrated by Henrietta Bruce Sharon. New York: Harper & Row, 1941. Selections from Countee Cullen, Claude McKay, Langston Hughes, Arna Bontemps, and others. (Grades 5–12)

Causley, Charles, compiler. *Modern Ballads and Story Poems*. Illustrated by Anne Netherwood. New York: Watts, 1965. Dramatic narrative poems are often effective in reviving flagging interest in poetry. This is a good introduction to the genre. (Grade 5–up)

Cole, William, compiler. *I Went to the Animal Fair*. Illustrated by Colette Rosselli. Cleveland: World Publishing, 1958. A collection of animal poems for younger children. (Grades K–3)

————. *Poems of Magic and Spells*. Illustrated by Peggy Bacon. Cleveland: World Publishing, 1960. (Grades 1–6)

————. *Poems for Seasons and Celebrations*. Illustrated by Johannes Troyer. Cleveland: World Publishing, 1961. (Grades 1–6)

————. *The Sea, Ships and Sailors: Poems, Songs and Shanties*. Illustrated by Robin Jacques. New York: Viking, 1967. (Grades 4–7)

————. *Story Poems, New and Old*. Illustrated by Walter Buehr. Cleveland: World Publishing, 1957. (Grades 4–9)

Doob, Leonard W., ed. *A Crocodile Has Me by the Leg: African Poems*. Illustrated by Solomon Irein Wangboje. New York: Walker, 1967. A collection of poems unknown in North America, some humorous, some prayers, some insults to be taunted; all interesting. (Grade 4–up)

Dunning, Stephen, Edward Leuders, and Hugh Smith, compilers. *Reflections on a Gift of Watermelon Pickle. . . .* Glenview, Ill.: Scott, Foresman, 1966. A fine collection of modern poetry for junior high schoolers. (Grades 7–9)

Forberg, Ati, compiler-illustrator. *On a Grass–Green Horn: Old Scotch and English Ballads*. New York: Atheneum, 1965. A collection of eighteen ballads about love and treachery appropriate for fourth graders and older children. (Grade 4–up)

Hannum, Sara, and Gwendolyn E. Reed, compilers. *Lean out the Window*. Illustrated by Ragna Tischler. New York: Atheneum, 1965. A collection of twentieth-century poetry that children will like, although few of the selections were written specifically for them. Robert Frost, Robert Graves, A. E. Housman, William Carlos Williams, Dylan Thomas, Richard Wilber, Wallace Stevens, T. S. Eliot, Edith Sitwell, Gertrude Stein, and e. e. cummings are among those represented. (Grade 4–up)

Larrick, Nancy, ed. *On City Streets: An Anthology of Poetry*. Illustrated with photographs by David Sagarin. New York: Evans, 1968. With the help of many children, Miss Larrick chose poems about city life. Many children will respond to these poems about experiences familiar to them. (Grades 3–7)

Lewis, Richard, ed. *Out of the Earth I Sing: Poetry and Songs of Primitive Peoples of the World*. Illustrated with photographs of primitive art. New York: Norton, 1968. These poems reveal the closeness primitive peoples feel to nature. Some are old poems, some still a part of the oral folk tradition. (Grade 4–up)

McGovern, Ann. *Arrow Book of Poetry*. Illustrated by Grisha Dotzenka. New York: Scholastic, 1965. An inexpensive paperback collection with relatively little verse. Very useful in the classroom and a book children enjoy owning. (Grades 3–6)

Parker, Elinor M., compiler. *The Singing and the Gold: Poems Translated from World Literature*. Illustrated by Clare Leighton. New York: Crowell, 1962. Many of the translations from thirty-four languages are by well-known English and American poets. The selections range from medieval Latin to North American Indian poetry. (Grades 6–12)

Reed, Gwendolyn E., compiler. *Out of the Ark: An Anthology of Animal Verse*. Illustrated by Gabriele Margules. New York: Atheneum, 1968. Poems from many countries, China, France, Greece, Germany, etc. and from the past as well as the present make this an interesting anthology. (Grades 6–8)

Sheldon, William, Nellie Lyons, and Polly Rouault, compilers. *The Reading of Poetry*. Boston: Allyn and Bacon, 1963. A useful book for the classroom. (Grades 3–6)

INDIVIDUAL POETS

Austin, Mary H. *The Children Sing in the Far West*. Illustrated by Gerald Cassidy. Boston: Houghton Mifflin, 1928. Some of these poems about the west, its flora and fauna, are still enjoyed by contemporary children; some, however, seem old-fashioned. The Indians songs are very valuable. (Grades 3–6)

Behn, Harry. *All Kinds of Time*. New York: Harcourt, 1950. Mr. Behn has written many poems for the young child. Other collections (Grades 3–6) are:

————. *The Golden Hive*. New York: Harcourt, 1966.

————. *The House beyond the Meadow*. New York: Pantheon, 1955.

————. *The Little Hill*. New York: Harcourt, 1949.

————. *Windy Morning*. New York: Harcourt, 1953.

————. *The Wizard in the Well*. New York: Harcourt, 1956.

Belting, Natalia. *Calendar Moon*. Illustrated by Bernarda Bryson. New York: Holt, Rinehart and Winston, 1964. Folk beliefs for each month have been collected from many parts of the world. (Grade 4–up)

————. *Winter's Eve*. Illustrated by Alan E. Cober. New York: Holt, Rinehart and Winston, 1969. A long poem for older children that explores the English traditions and folk practices of holidays from Winter's Eve, September 28, to Halloween, October 31. (Grades 6–9)

Benét, Rosemary C., and Stephen Vincent Benét. *A Book of Americans*. Illustrated by Charles Child. New York: Rinehart, 1933. Fifty-six poems about famous Americans. Children enjoy them. (Grades 4–7)

Blake, William. *William Blake: An Introduction*. Edited by Anne Malcolmson. Illustrations from Blake's paintings and engravings. New York: Harcourt, 1967. A fine introduction to a great poet's works. Selections are from *Songs of Innocence*, *Songs of Experience*, and other books. (Grade 6–up)

————. *Songs of Innocence*. Music and illustrations by Ellen Raskin. New York: Doubleday, 1966. A selection of Blake's poems for children. The woodcut illustrations do not always appropriately reflect the mood. (Grade 6–up)

Brooks, Gwendolyn. *Bronzeville Boys and Girls*. Illustrated by Ronni Solbert. New York: Harper & Row, 1965. Poignant poems about Negro children in the inner city. (Grades 3–5)

Browning, Robert. *The Pied Piper of Hamelin*. Illustrated by Harold Jones. New York: F. Watts, 1962. A picture book treatment of a popular narrative poem. (Grades 4–7)

Coleridge, Samuel T. *Poems*. Selected by Babette Deutsch. Illustrated by Jacques Hnizdovsky. New York: Crowell, 1967. A well-designed introduction to a poet who conveys a sense of wonder. (Grade 5–up)

Davis, Katherine, Henry Onorati, and Harry Simeone. *The Little Drummer Boy*. Illustrated by Ezra Jack Keats. New York: Macmillan, 1968. The Nativity poem by Katherine Davis has been beautifully illustrated by Keats. (Grades 1–3)

Frost, Robert. *In the Clearing*. New York: Holt, Rinehart and Winston, 1962. A selection of poems by an excellent poet that will interest children. (Grade 4–up)

————. *You Come Too*. Illustrated by Thomas W. Nason. New York: Holt, Rinehart and Winston, 1959. (Grade 4–up)

Gasztold, Carmen Bernos de. *Prayers from the Ark*. Translated from the French by Rumer Godden.

Illustrated by Jean Primrose. New York: Viking, 1962. Twenty-seven brief, fervent prayers that reveal the animals' natures. (Grade 4–up)

Graves, Robert. *The Penny Fiddle: Poems for Children*. Illustrated by Edward Ardizzone. New York: Doubleday, 1961. Interesting selections by a fine poet. (Grades 4–7)

Hughes, Langston. *The Dream Keeper and Other Poems*. Illustrated by Helen Sewell. New York: Knopf, 1945. Many moving poems, some rollicking songs, and Negro blues. (Grade 5–up)

Lawrence, David H. *D. H. Lawrence: Poems Selected for Young People*. Edited by William Cole. Illustrated by Ellen Raskin. New York: Viking, 1967. The poems are divided into four sections: Animals; Man, Woman, Child; Celebrations and Condemnations; Love. An interesting introduction to this writer's poetry. (Grade 6–up)

Longfellow, Henry Wadsworth. *Paul Revere's Ride*. Illustrated by Paul Galdone. New York: Crowell, 1963. A picture book of Longfellow's dramatic narrative poem. (Grade 4–up)

————. *The Skeleton in Armor*. Illustrated by Paul Kennedy. Englewood Cliffs, N.J.: Prentice-Hall, 1963. Another picture book from one of Longfellow's narratives. (Grade 4–up)

Milne, A. A. *Now We Are Six*. Illustrated by E. H. Shepard. New York: Dutton, 1927. Although some of Milne's poems laugh at children or are nostalgic, many of his works still amuse youngsters. Other Milne favorites are: *When We Were Very Young*, 1924; *The World of Christopher Robin*, 1958. (Grades K–3)

Roethke, Theodore. *I Am! Says the Lamb*. Illustrated by Robert Leydenfrost. New York: Doubleday, 1961. A collection for children arranged by the author, a fine modern American poet. Both nonsense and serious poems. (Grade 4–up)

Sandburg, Carl, compiler. *The American Songbag*. New York: Harcourt, 1927. A selection of American folk songs and ballads. (Grade 4–up) Two collections of Sandburg's poetry for young students are:

————. *Early Moon*. Illustrated by James Daugherty. New York: Harcourt, 1930 (Grades 4–8)

————. *Wind Song*. Illustrated by William A. Smith. New York: Harcourt, 1960. (Grades 4–8)

Shakespeare, William. *Poems of William Shakespeare*. Compiled by Lloyd Frankenberg. Illustrated by Nonny Hogrogian. New York: Crowell, 1966. Many songs and poems from Shakespeare's plays as well as fifty-eight sonnets were selected to provide an introduction to Shakespeare's works. (Grade 5–up)

Yeats, William B. *Running to Paradise*. Introduction by Kevin Crossley-Holland. Illustrated by Judith Valpy. New York: Macmillan, 1967. A wide selection of Yeats' poems; the first made for children. (Grade 4–up)

JAPANESE AND CHINESE POEMS

Baron, Virginia O., compiler. *The Seasons of Time: Tanka Poetry of Ancient Japan*. Illustrated by Yasuhide Kobashi. New York: Dial Press, 1968. The tanka, a five-line poem with 5-7-5-7-7 syllable pattern, is still the most popular form of Japanese poetry. (Grade 4–up)

Behn, Harry, compiler. *Cricket Songs*. New York: Harcourt, 1964. A collection of haiku poems in translation. (Grade 3–up)

Beilenson, Peter, translator. *Japanese Haiku*. New York: Peter Pauper, 1955–1956. (Grade 4–up)

Cassedy, Sylvia, and Kunihiro Suetake, translators. *Birds, Frogs, and Moonlight*. Calligraphy by Koson Okamura. Illustrated by Vo-Dinh. New York: Doubleday, 1967. Twenty-one Japanese haiku are presented in English characters and Japanese calligraphy, each illustrated with a brush drawing in ink and water color. This is excellent for introducing children to writing haiku, for the editors have included information about the form and suggestions for the beginning writer. (Grade 4–up)

Lewis, Richard, compiler. *In a Spring Garden*. Illustrated by Ezra Jack Keats. New York: Dial Press, 1965. Twenty-three haiku, each illustrated by Keats, make a beautiful picture book introduction to this Japanese poetry form. (Grade 1–up)

Lewis, Richard, ed. *The Moment of Wonder: A Collection of Chinese and Japanese Poetry*. New York: Dial, 1964. The book includes poems from the ninth century to the twentieth and is illustrated with reproductions of painting by Japanese and Chinese masters. This will be appreciated by adults and children, especially those who want more than the haiku in Harry Behn's excellent *Cricket Songs*. (Grade 4–up)

NONSENSE POETRY

Belloc, Hillaire. *The Bad Child's Book of Beasts*. Illustrated by Basil T. Blackwood. New York: Knopf, 1965. First published 1896. Humorous poems that will delight children. (Grade K–3)

————. *More Beasts for Worse Children*. Illustrated by Basil T. Blackwood. New York: Knopf, 1966.

A companion collection of nonsense poetry to *The Bad Child's Book of Beasts*. (Grades 1–3)

Brewton, Sara and John E., compilers. *Laughable Limericks*. Illustrated by Ingrid Fetz. New York: Crowell, 1965. (Grades 3–6)

Ciardi, John. *I Met a Man*. Illustrated by Robert Osborn. Boston: Houghton Mifflin, 1961. Nonsense poems by a master of the genre. Ciardi's books are very effective in developing an interest in poetry for those children who think it is boring. (Grades 1–4) Other works by this poet are:

————. *The Man Who Sang the Sillies*. Illustrated by Edward Gorey. Philadelphia: Lippincott, 1961. (Grades 1–6)

————. *The Monster Den or Look What Happened at My House— and to It*. Illustrated by Edward Gorey. Philadelphia: Lippincott, 1966. Ostensibly a book of poetry for children, Ciardi's nonsense poems about his youngsters, the monsters of the title, will bring more enjoyment to adults than to children. A fun book to give harried mothers. (Adults)

————. *The Reason for the Pelican*. Illustrated by Madeleine Gekiere. Philadelphia: Lippincott, 1959. (Grades 1–6)

————. *You Know Who*. Illustrated by Edward Gorey. Philadelphia: Lippincott, 1964. (Grades 1–4)

————. *You Read to Me and I'll Read to You*. Illustrated by Edward Gorey. Philadelphia: Lippincott, 1962. (Grades 1–6)

Cole, William, compiler. *Beastly Boys and Ghastly Girls*. Illustrated by Tomi Ungerer. Cleveland: World Publishing, 1964. An amusing collection of nonsense poetry. (Grade K–up)

————. *The Birds and Beasts Were There*. Illustrated by Helen Siegl. Cleveland: World Publishing, 1963. (Grade K–up)

————. *Humorous Poetry for Children*. Illustrated by Ervine Metzl. Cleveland: World Publishing, 1955. (Grade K–up)

————. *Oh What Nonsense!* Illustrated by Tomi Ungerer. New York: Viking, 1966. (Grade K–up)

Dodgson, Charles L. *The Humorous Verse of Lewis Carroll, the Rev. Charles Lutwidge Dodgson*. Illustrated by Sir John Tenniel, et al. New York: Dover, 1960. All the humorous poems from Lewis Carroll's books. Published in 1933 under the title *The Collected Verse of Lewis Carroll*. (Grade 4–up)

Eliot, Thomas S. *Old Possum's Book of Practical Cats*. New York: Harcourt, 1939. Delightful nonsense poems about cats; enjoyed by children and adults (Grade 4–up)

Holmes, Oliver Wendell. *The Deacon's Masterpiece or the Wonderful One-Hoss Shay*. Illustrated by Paul Galdone. New York: McGraw-Hill, 1965. A picture book treatment of an amusing poem. (Grades 4–7)

Hopkinson, Francis. *The Battle of the Kegs*. Illustrated by Paul Galdone. New York: Crowell, 1964. An old Revolutionary War ballad about a group of colonists who plan to blow up English ships with kegs of gunpowder. (Grades 3–7)

Langstaff, John, reteller. *Frog Went a-Courtin'*. Illustrated by Feodor Rojankovsky. New York: Harcourt, 1955. Excellent picture book treatment of a nonsensical old Scottish ballad. Awarded the 1956 Caldecott Medal. (Grades K–2)

Lear, Edward. *The Complete Nonsense Book, Containing All the Original Pictures and Verses Together with New Material*. Edited by Lady Strachey. Introduction by the Earl of Cromer. New York: Dodd, Mead, 1948. (Grade 4–up)

————. *The Dong with the Luminous Nose*. Illustrated by Edward Gorey. New York: Young Scott Books, 1969. A picture book of one of Lear's longer nonsense poems. The illustrations are especially suitable for the wild humor. (Grade 3–up) Some other picture books of Lear's poems are:

————. *The Jumblies*. Illustrated by Edward Gorey. New York: Young Scott Books, 1968. (Grades K–3)

————. *The Scroobious Pip*. Completed by Ogden Nash. Illustrated by Nancy Ekholm Burkert. New York: Harper & Row, 1968. Nash added two lines and two missing words. The pictures seem too pretty for the narrative. (Grade 3–up)

————, author-illustrator. *Lear Alphabet: A B C*. New York: McGraw-Hill, 1965. The text, reproduced from a recently discovered manuscript, is in Lear's handwriting and with his original illustrations. (Grade 1–up)

————. *Teapots and Quails, and Other Nonsenses*. Edited and introduced by Angus Davidson and Philip Hofer. London: J. Murray, 1953. (Grade 4–up)

————. *The Two Old Bachelors*. Illustrated by Paul Galdone. New York: Whittlesey, 1962. A picture book treatment of one of Lear's narrative poems. (Grade 3–up)

Morgenstern, Christian. *The Three Sparrows, and Other Nursery Poems*. Translated from the German by Max Knight. Illustrated by Nonny Hogrogian. New York: Scribner, 1968. Humorous poems long popular with German-speaking children. (Preschool–grade 4)

Nash, Ogden. *Custard the Dragon*. Illustrated by

Linell. Boston: Little, Brown, 1959. A picture book treatment of Nash's narrative about a cowardly dragon. (Grades K–3)

Nash, Ogden, compiler. *Everybody Ought to Know.* Illustrated by Rose Shirvanian. Philadelphia: Lippincott, 1961. An anthology of nonsense poetry and verse compiled by a writer of the genre. (Grades 2–8)

————. *The Moon Is Shining Bright as Day.* Philadelphia: Lippincott, 1953. Subtitled *An Anthology of Good-Humored Verse.* A collection of the compiler's favorites. (Grades 2–8)

Rees, Ennis. *Riddles, Riddles Everywhere.* Illustrated by Quentin Blake. New York: Abelard, 1964. Riddles in verse from all over the world. (Grade 2–up)

Richards, Laura E. H. *Tirra Lirra, Rhymes Old and New.* Foreword by May Hill Arbuthnot. Illustrations by Marguerite Davis. Boston: Little, Brown, 1955. Narrative nonsense poems. (Grades 1–6)

Smith, William Jay. *Laughing Time.* Illustrated by Juliet Kepes. Boston: Little, Brown, 1955. Nonsense poems for the very young. (Preschool–grade 2)

Withers, Carl, compiler. *A Rocket in My Pocket.* Illustrated by Susanne Suba. New York: Holt, Rinehart and Winston, 1948. A fine collection of American children's chants and nonsense rhymes. (Grades 1–4)

WRITTEN BY CHILDREN

Conkling, Hilda. *Poems by a Little Girl.* Philadelphia: Stokes, 1920. These poems were dictated to her mother when the author was quite young. (Grades 2–6)

Hughes, Langston, ed. *I Never Saw Another Butterfly. Children's Drawings and Poems from Theresienstadt Concentration Camp 1942–1944.* New York: McGraw-Hill, 1964. A moving collection of poems. (Grade 4–up)

Lewis, Richard, compiler. *Miracles: Poems by Children of the English-Speaking World.* New York: Simon, 1966. Sponsored by the U.S. National Commission for UNESCO. Mr. Lewis toured the English-speaking countries to gather poems written by children. Each poet is identified by name, age, and country. Children find this one of the most fascinating books of poetry; they love to read what others their age have written and then want to try to write their own. *Miracles* is not a collection of amateurish trivia, but contains poetry of real merit. (Grades 1–7)

————, ed. *The Wind and the Rain: Children's Poems.* Illustrated with photographs by Helen Buttfield. New York: Simon, 1968. This collection of poems by children about the weather, a few of which were in the editor's *Miracles*, makes a welcome companion to the earlier book. (Grades 3–7)

Book Awards

Book award lists can be very helpful in the selection of books to read or suggest to children, but it is important to remember that not all prizes are awarded for high *literary* quality. The Caldecott Award is given for the best illustrations; while the text is considered, the award may be given even if the text is not of high quality. The Newbery Award has been bestowed on books that do not meet the highest literary standards. Very few of the Newbery winners have been as well written as *Johnny Tremain*, the 1944 selection. A number of the Newbery winners in the 1950s and 1960s are books more of interest to adults than to children. This is not to deny the importance and value of the Newbery Award, for it is a coveted prize and does encourage the publishing of children's literature. Award lists can guide teachers and librarians in selecting books for children but do not release them from the responsibility of a careful evaluation of each book's literary merits.

AMERICAN AWARDS

RANDOLPH J. CALDECOTT MEDAL

Each year a medal is given "the artist of the most distinguished American picture book for children." Named for the famous nineteenth-century English illustrator, the award is donated by the Frederic G. Melcher family. A committee appointed by the American Library Association Children's Services Division chooses both the Caldecott Award and the Newbery Award winners.

1938
ANIMALS OF THE BIBLE by Helen Dean Fish, ill. by Dorothy P. Lathrop (Lippincott)
Runners-up
SEVEN SIMEONS by Boris Artzybasheff (Viking)
FOUR AND TWENTY BLACKBIRDS by Helen Dean Fish, ill. by Robert Lawson (Stokes)

1939
MEI LI by Thomas Handforth (Doubleday)
Runners-up
THE FOREST POOL by Laura Adams Armer (Longmans)
WEE GILLIS by Munroe Leaf, ill. by Robert Lawson (Viking)
SNOW WHITE AND THE SEVEN DWARFS by Wanda Gág (Coward-McCann)
BARKIS by Clare Newberry (Harper & Row)
ANDY AND THE LION by James Daugherty (Viking)

1940
ABRAHAM LINCOLN by Ingri and Edgar d'Aulaire (Doubleday)
Runners-up
COCK-A-DOODLE DOO . . . by Berta and Elmer Hader (Macmillan)
MADELINE by Ludwig Bemelmans (Viking)
THE AGELESS STORY ill. by Lauren Ford (Dodd, Mead)

1941
THEY WERE STRONG AND GOOD by Robert Lawson (Viking)
Runner-up
APRIL'S KITTENS by Clare Newberry (Harper & Row)

1942
MAKE WAY FOR DUCKLINGS by Robert McCloskey (Viking)

Runners-up

AN AMERICAN ABC by Maud and Miska Petersham (Macmillan)
IN MY MOTHER'S HOUSE by Ann Nolan Clark, ill. by Velino Herrera (Viking)
PADDLE-TO-THE-SEA by Holling C. Holling (Houghton Mifflin)
NOTHING AT ALL by Wanda Gág (Coward-McCann)

1943

THE LITTLE HOUSE by Virginia Lee Burton (Houghton Mifflin)

Runners-up

DASH AND DART by Mary and Conrad Buff (Viking)
MARSHMALLOW by Clare Newberry (Harper & Row)

1944

MANY MOONS by James Thurber, ill. by Louis Slobodkin (Harcourt)

Runners-up

SMALL RAIN: VERSES FROM THE BIBLE selected by Jessie Orton Jones, ill. by Elizabeth Orton Jones (Viking)
PIERRE PIDGEON by Lee Kingman, ill. by Arnold E. Bare (Houghton Mifflin)
THE MIGHTY HUNTER by Berta and Elmer Hader (Macmillan)
A CHILD'S GOOD NIGHT BOOK by Margaret Wise Brown, ill. by Jean Charlot (Scott, Foresman)
GOOD-LUCK HORSE by Chih-Yi Chan, ill. by Plao Chan (Whittlesey)

1945

PRAYER FOR A CHILD by Rachel Field, ill. by Elizabeth Orton Jones (Macmillan)

Runners-up

MOTHER GOOSE ill. by Tasha Tudor (Walck)
IN THE FOREST by Marie Hall Ets (Viking)
YONIE WONDERNOSE by Marguerite de Angeli (Doubleday)
THE CHRISTMAS ANNA ANGEL by Ruth Sawyer, ill. by Kate Seredy (Viking)

1946

THE ROOSTER CROWS . . . (Mother Goose) ill. by Maud and Mishka Petersham (Macmillan)

Runners-up

LITTLE LOST LAMB by Golden MacDonald, ill. by Leonard Weisgard (Doubleday)
SING MOTHER GOOSE by Opal Wheeler, ill. by Marjorie Torrey (Dutton)
MY MOTHER IS THE MOST BEAUTIFUL WOMAN IN THE WORLD by Becky Reyher, ill. by Ruth Gannett (Lothrop)
YOU CAN WRITE CHINESE by Kurt Wiese (Viking)

1947

THE LITTLE ISLAND by Golden MacDonald, ill. by Leonard Weisgard (Doubleday)

Runners-up

RAIN DROPS SPLASH by Alvin Tresselt, ill. by Leonard Weisgard (Lothrop)
BOATS ON THE RIVER by Marjorie Flack, ill. by Jay Hyde Barnum (Viking)
TIMOTHY TURTLE by Al Graham, ill. by Tony Palazzo (Welch)
PEDRO, THE ANGEL OF OLVERA STREET by Leo Politi (Scribner)
SING IN PRAISE: A COLLECTION OF THE BEST LOVED HYMNS by Opal Wheeler, ill. by Marjorie Torrey (Dutton)

1948

WHITE SNOW, BRIGHT SNOW by Alvin Tresselt, ill. by Roger Duvoisin (Lothrop)

Runners-up

STONE SOUP by Marcia Brown (Scribner)
McELLIGOT'S POOL by Dr. Seuss (Random House)
BAMBINO THE CLOWN by George Schreiber (Viking)
ROGER AND THE FOX by Lavinia Davis, ill. by Hildegard Woodward (Doubleday)
SONG OF ROBIN HOOD ed. by Anne Malcolmson, ill. by Virginia Lee Burton (Houghton Mifflin)

1949

THE BIG SNOW by Berta and Elmer Hader (Macmillan)

Runners-up

BLUEBERRIES FOR SAL by Robert McCloskey (Viking)
ALL AROUND THE TOWN by Phyllis McGinley, ill. by Helen Stone (Lippincott)
JUANITA by Leo Politi (Scribner)
FISH IN THE AIR by Kurt Wiese (Viking)

1950

SONG OF THE SWALLOWS by Leo Politi (Scribner)

Runners-up

AMERICA'S ETHAN ALLEN by Stewart Holbrook, ill. by Lynd Ward (Houghton Mifflin)
THE WILD BIRTHDAY CAKE by Lavinia Davis, ill. by Hildegard Woodward (Doubleday)
THE HAPPY DAY by Ruth Krauss, ill. by Marc Simont (Harper & Row)
BARTHOLOMEW AND THE OOBLECK by Dr. Seuss (Random House)
HENRY FISHERMAN by Marcia Brown (Scribner)

1951

THE EGG TREE by Katherine Milhous (Scribner)

Runners-up

DICK WHITTINGTON AND HIS CAT by Marcia Brown (Scribner)

THE TWO REDS by Will [William Lipkind], ill. by Nicolas [Mordvinoff] (Harcourt)
IF I RAN THE ZOO by Dr. Seuss (Random House)
THE MOST WONDERFUL DOLL IN THE WORLD by Phyllis McGinley, ill. by Helen Stone (Lippincott)
T-BONE, THE BABY SITTER by Clare Newberry (Harper & Row)

1952
FINDERS KEEPERS by Will [William Lipkind], ill. by Nicolas [Mordvinoff] (Harcourt)
Runners-up
MR. T. W. ANTHONY WOO by Marie Hall Ets (Viking)
SKIPPER JOHN'S COOK by Marcia Brown (Scribner)
ALL FALLING DOWN by Gene Zion, ill. by Margaret Bloy Graham (Harper & Row)
BEAR PARTY by William Pène du Bois (Viking)
FEATHER MOUNTAIN by Elizabeth Olds (Houghton Mifflin)

1953
THE BIGGEST BEAR by Lynd Ward (Houghton Mifflin)
Runners-up
PUSS IN BOOTS by Charles Perrault, ill. and trans. by Marcia Brown (Scribner)
ONE MORNING IN MAINE by Robert McCloskey (Viking)
APE IN A CAPE by Fritz Eichenberg (Harcourt)
THE STORM BOOK by Charlotte Zolotow, ill. by Margaret Bloy Graham (Harper & Row)
FIVE LITTLE MONKEYS by Juliet Kepes (Houghton Mifflin)

1954
MADELINE'S RESCUE by Ludwig Bemelmans (Viking)
Runners-up
JOURNEY CAKE, HO! by Ruth Sawyer, ill. by Robert McCloskey (Viking)
WHEN WILL THE WORLD BE MINE? by Miriam Schlein, ill. by Jean Charlot (Scott, Foresman)
THE STEADFAST TIN SOLDIER by Hans Christian Andersen, ill. by Marcia Brown (Scribner)
A VERY SPECIAL HOUSE by Ruth Krauss, ill. by Maurice Sendak (Harper & Row)
GREEN EYES by A. Birnbaum (Capitol)

1955
CINDERELLA, OR THE LITTLE GLASS SLIPPER by Charles Perrault, trans and ill. by Marcia Brown (Scribner)
Runners-up
BOOK OF NURSERY AND MOTHER GOOSE RHYMES ill. by Marguerite de Angeli (Doubleday)
WHEEL ON THE CHIMNEY by Margaret Wise Brown, ill. by Tibor Gergely (Lippincott)
THE THANKSGIVING STORY by Alice Dalgliesh, ill. by Helen Sewell (Scribner)

1956
FROG WENT A-COURTIN' ed. by John Langstaff, ill. by Feodor Rojankovsky (Harcourt)
Runners-up
PLAY WITH ME by Marie Hall Ets (Viking)
CROW BOY by Taro Yashima (Viking)

1957
A TREE IS NICE by Janice May Udry, ill. by Marc Simont (Harper & Row)
Runners-up
MR. PENNY'S RACE HORSE by Marie Hall Ets (Viking)
1 IS ONE by Tasha Tudor (Walck)
ANATOLE by Eve Titus, ill. by Paul Galdone (McGraw-Hill)
GILLESPIE AND THE GUARDS by Benjamin Elkin, ill. by James Daugherty (Viking)
LION by William Pène du Bois (Viking)

1958
TIME OF WONDER by Robert McCloskey (Viking)
Runners-up
FLY HIGH, FLY LOW by Don Freeman (Viking)
ANATOLE AND THE CAT by Eve Titus, ill. by Paul Galdone (McGraw-Hill)

1959
CHANTICLEER AND THE FOX adapted from Chaucer and ill. by Barbara Cooney (Crowell)
Runners-up
THE HOUSE THAT JACK BUILT: LA MAISON QUE JACQUES A BATIE by Antonio Frasconi (Harcourt)
WHAT DO YOU SAY, DEAR? by Sesyle Joslin, ill. by Maurice Sendak (Scott, Foresman)
UMBRELLA by Taro Yashima (Viking)

1960
NINE DAYS TO CHRISTMAS by Marie Hall Ets and Aurora Labastida, ill. by Marie Hall Ets (Viking)
Runners-up
HOUSES FROM THE SEA by Alice E. Goudey, ill. by Adrienne Adams (Scribner)
THE MOON JUMPERS by Janice May Udry, ill. by Maurice Sendak (Harper & Row)

1961
BABOUSHKA AND THE THREE KINGS by Ruth Robbins, ill. by Nicholas Sidjakov (Parnassus)
Runner-up
INCH BY INCH by Leo Lionni (Obolensky)

1962
ONCE A MOUSE . . . by Marcia Brown (Scribner)

Runners-up
THE FOX WENT OUT ON A CHILLY NIGHT
ill. by Peter Spier (Doubleday)
LITTLE BEAR'S VISIT by Else Holmelund
Minarik, ill. by Maurice Sendak (Harper & Row)
THE DAY WE SAW THE SUN COME UP by
Alice E. Goudey, ill. by Adrienne Adams (Scribner)

1963
THE SNOWY DAY by Ezra Jack Keats (Viking)

Runners-up
THE SUN IS A GOLDEN EARRING by Natalia
M. Belting, ill. by Bernarda Bryson (Holt, Rinehart
and Winston)
MR. RABBIT AND THE LOVELY PRESENT
by Charlotte Zolotow, ill. by Maurice Sendak
(Harper & Row)

1964
WHERE THE WILD THINGS ARE by Maurice
Sendak (Harper & Row)

Runners-up
SWIMMY by Leo Lionni (Pantheon)
ALL IN THE MORNING EARLY by Sorche Nic
Leodhas, ill. by Evaline Ness (Holt, Rinehart and
Winston)
MOTHER GOOSE AND NURSERY RHYMES
ill. by Philip Reed (Atheneum)

1965
MAY I BRING A FRIEND? by Beatrice Schenk de
Regniers, ill. by Beni Montresor (Atheneum)

Runners-up
RAIN MAKES APPLESAUCE by Julian Scheer,
ill. by Marvin Bileck (Holiday)
THE WAVE by Margaret Hodges, ill. by Blair
Lent (Houghton Mifflin)
A POCKETFUL OF CRICKET by Rebecca
Caudill, ill. by Evaline Ness (Holt, Rinehart and
Winston)

1966
ALWAYS ROOM FOR ONE MORE by Sorche
Nic Leodhas, ill. by Nonny Hogrogian (Holt,
Rinehart and Winston)

Runners-up
HIDE AND SEEK FOG by Alvin Tresselt, ill. by
Roger Duvoisin (Lothrop)
JUST ME by Marie Hall Ets (Viking)
TOM TIT TOT by Evaline Ness (Scribner)

1967
SAM, BANGS AND MOONSHINE by Evaline
Ness (Holt, Rinehart and Winston)

Runner-up
ONE WIDE RIVER TO CROSS by Barbara
Emberly, ill. by Ed Emberly (Prentice-Hall)

1968
DRUMMER HOFF by Barbara Emberly, ill. by
Ed Emberly (Prentice-Hall)

Runners-up
FREDERICK by Leo Lionni (Pantheon)
SEASHORE STORY by Taro Yashima (Viking)
THE EMPEROR AND THE KITE by Jane Yolen,
ill. by Ed Young (World Publishing)

1969
THE FOOL OF THE WORLD AND THE
FLYING SHIP by Arthur Ransome, ill. by Uri
Shulevitz (Farrar, Straus)

Runner-up
WHY THE SUN AND THE MOON LIVE IN
THE SKY by Elphinstone Dayrell, ill. by Blair Lent
(Houghton Mifflin)

1970
SYLVESTER AND THE MAGIC PEBBLE by
William Steig (Windmill Books/Simon and
Schuster)

Runners-up
GOGGLES by Ezra Jack Keats (Macmillan)
ALEXANDER AND THE WIND-UP MOUSE
by Leo Lionni (Pantheon)
POP CORN & MA GOODNESS by Edna Mitchell
Preston, ill. by Robert Andrew Parker (Viking)
THY FRIEND, OBADIAH by Brinton Turkle
(Viking Press)
THE JUDGE by Harve Zemach, ill. by Margot
Zemach (Farrar, Straus)

1971
A STORY—A STORY by Gail E. Haley
(Atheneum)

Runners-up
THE ANGRY MOON by William Sleator, ill.
Blair Lent (Little, Brown)
FROG AND TOAD ARE FRIENDS by Arnold
Lobel (Harper & Row)
IN THE NIGHT KITCHEN by Maurice Sendak
(Harper & Row)

THE NEW YORK TIMES CHOICE OF BEST ILLUSTRATED CHILDREN'S BOOKS OF THE YEAR

An annual list of the best children's illustrated
books has been published by *The New York Times*
since 1952. Chosen by three judges, the list varies
in length from year to year.

1952
THE MAGIC CURRANT BUN by John Symonds,
ill. by André François (Lippincott)

BEASTS AND NONSENSE by Marie Hall Ets
(Viking)

FIVE LITTLE MONKEYS by Juliet Kepes
(Houghton Mifflin)
THE DOGCATCHER'S DOG by Andre Dugo
(Holt, Rinehart and Winston)
THE ANIMAL FAIR by Alice and Martin
Provensen (Golden Press)
THE HAPPY PLACE by Ludwig Bemelmans
(Little, Brown)
A HOLE IS TO DIG by Ruth Krauss, ill. by
Maurice Sendak (Harper & Row)

1953
GREEN EYES by A. Birnbaum (Golden Press)
MADELINE'S RESCUE by Ludwig Bemelmans
(Viking)
MOTHER GOOSE RIDDLE RHYMES by Joseph
Low (Harcourt)
A HERO BY MISTAKE by Anita Brenner, ill. by
Jean Charlot (Scott, Foresman)
PITSCHI by Hans Fischer (Harcourt)
LUCKY BLACKY by Eunice Lackey, ill. by
Winifred Greene (Watts)
THE GOLDEN BIBLE FOR CHILDREN:
THE NEW TESTAMENT ed. by Elsa Jane
Werner, ill. by Alice and Martin Provensen (Golden
Press)
WHO GAVE US? by Madeleine Gekiere
(Pantheon)
FAST IS NOT A LADYBUG by Miriam Schlein,
ill. by Leonard Kessler (Scott, Foresman)
FLORINA AND THE WILD BIRD by Selina
Chonz, ill. by Alois Carigiet (Walck)

1954
HEAVY IS A HIPPOPOTAMUS by Miriam
Schlein, ill. by Leonard Kessler (Scott, Foresman)
I'LL BE YOU AND YOU BE ME by Ruth Krauss,
ill. by Maurice Sendak (Harper & Row)
THE ANIMAL FROLIC by 12th century Japanese
artist, probably Toba Sojo (Putnam)
ANDY SAYS BONJOUR by Pat Diska, ill. by
Chris Jenkyns (Vanguard)
THE SUN LOOKS DOWN by Miriam Schlein,
ill. by Abner Graboff (Abelard)
A KISS IS ROUND by Blossom Budney, ill. by
Vladimir Bobri (Lothrop)
THE HAPPY LION by Louise Fatio, ill. by Roger
Duvoisin (Whittlesey)
JENNY'S BIRTHDAY BOOK by Esther Averill
(Harper & Row)
THE WET WORLD by Norma Simon, ill. by
Jane Miller (Lippincott)
CIRCUS RUCKUS by Will, ill. by Nicolas
(Harcourt)

1955
SEE AND SAY by Antonio Frasconi (Harcourt)
BEASTS FROM A BRUSH by Juliet Kepes
(Pantheon)
SWITCH ON THE NIGHT by Ray Bradbury, ill.
by Madeleine Gekiere (Pantheon)

PARSLEY by Ludwig Bemelmans (Harper & Row)
CHAGA by Will, ill. by Nicolas (Harcourt)
THE HAPPY LION IN AFRICA by Louise Fatio,
ill. by Roger Duvoisin (McGraw-Hill)
UNCLE BEN'S WHALE by Walter Edmonds,
ill. by William Gropper (Dodd, Mead)
A LITTLE HOUSE OF YOUR OWN by Beatrice
Schenk de Regniers, ill. by Irene Haas (Harcourt)
RUMPELSTILTSKIN by Jan B. Balet (Rand
McNally)
THE THREE KINGS OF SABA by Alf Evers, ill. by
Helen Sewell (Lippincott)

1956
CROCODILE TEARS by André François
(Universe)
JONAH THE FISHERMAN by Reiner Zimnik
(Pantheon)
I KNOW A LOT OF THINGS by Ann Rand, ill. by
Paul Rand (Harcourt)
I WANT TO PAINT MY BATHROOM BLUE
by Ruth Krauss, ill. by Maurice Sendak (Harper &
Row)
THE LITTLE ELEPHANT by Ylla (Harper &
Row)
BABAR'S FAIR by Laurent de Brunhoff (Random
House)
WAS IT A GOOD TRADE? by Beatrice Schenk
de Regniers, ill. by Irene Haas (Harcourt)
LITTLE BIG-FEATHER by Joseph Longstreth,
ill. by Helen Borten (Abelard)
I WILL TELL YOU OF A TOWN by Alistair Reid,
ill. by Walter Lorraine (Houghton Mifflin)
REALLY SPRING by Gene Zion, ill. by Margaret
Bloy Graham (Harper & Row)

1957
THE FISHERMAN AND HIS WIFE by the
Brothers Grimm, ill. by Madeleine Gekiere
(Pantheon)
FAINT GEORGE by Robert E. Barry (Houghton
Mifflin)
THE UNHAPPY HIPPOPOTAMUS by Nancy
Moore, ill. by Edward Leight (Vanguard)
THE BIRTHDAY PARTY by Ruth Krauss, ill. by
Maurice Sendak (Harper & Row)
SPARKLE AND SPIN by Ann Rand, ill. by
Paul Rand (Harcourt)
THE FRIENDLY BEASTS by Laura Baker, ill. by
Nicolas Sidjakov (Parnassus)
DEAR GARBAGE MAN by Gene Zion, ill. by
Margaret Bloy Graham (Harper & Row)
BIG RED BUS by Ethel Kessler, ill. by Leonard
Kessler (Doubleday)
THE RED BALLOON by Albert Lamorisse
(Doubleday)
CURIOUS GEORGE GETS A MEDAL by H. A.
Rey (Houghton Mifflin)

1958
THE HOUSE THAT JACK BUILT by Antonio Frasconi (Harcourt)
ROLAND by Nelly Stephane, ill. by André François (Harcourt)
WHAT DO YOU SAY, DEAR? by Sesyle Joslin, ill. by Maurice Sendak (Scott, Foresman)
THE GOLDEN BOOK OF ANIMALS by W. Suschitzky (Golden Press)
THE DADDY DAYS by Norma Simon, ill. by Abner Graboff (Abelard)
CHOUCHOU by Françoise (Scribner)
ALL ABOARD by Mary Britton Miller, ill. by Bill Sokol (Pantheon)
A FRIEND IS SOMEONE WHO LIKES YOU by Joan Walsh Anglund (Harcourt)
HOW TO HIDE A HIPPOPOTAMUS by Volney Croswell (Dodd, Mead)
THE MAGIC FEATHER DUSTER by Will, ill. by Nicolas [Mordvinoff] (Harcourt)

1959
THE REASON FOR THE PELICAN by John Ciardi, ill. by Madeleine Gekiere (Lippincott)
LITTLE BLUE AND LITTLE YELLOW by Leo Lionni (Obolensky)
PABLO PAINTS A PICTURE by Warren Miller, ill. by Edward Sorel (Little, Brown)
FULL OF WONDER by Ann Kim (World Publishing)
THIS IS LONDON by Miroslav Sasek (Macmillan)
THE GIRL IN THE WHITE HAT by W. T. Cummings (McGraw-Hill)
KASIMIR'S JOURNEY by Monroe Stearns, ill. by Marlene Reidel (Lippincott)
ANIMAL BABIES by Arthur Gregor, ill. by Ylla (Harper & Row)
THE FIRST NOEL by Alice and Martin Provensen (Golden Press)
FATHER BEAR COMES HOME by Else Holmelund Minarik, ill. by Maurice Sendak (Harper & Row)

1960
THIS IS NEW YORK by Miroslav Sasek (Macmillan)
BABOUSHKA AND THE THREE KINGS by Ruth Robbins, ill. by Nicolas Sidjakov (Parnassus)
TWO LITTLE BIRDS AND THREE by Juliet Kepes (Houghton Mifflin)
SCRAPPY THE PUP by John Ciardi, ill. by Jane Miller (Lippincott)
A B C by Bruno Munari (World Publishing)
26 WAYS TO BE SOMEBODY ELSE by Devorah Boxer (Pantheon)
THE ADVENTURES OF ULYSSES by Jacques le Marchand, ill. by André François (Criterion)
THE SHADOW BOOK by Beatrice Schenk de Regniers, ill. by Isabel Gordon (Harcourt)
OPEN HOUSE FOR BUTTERFLIES by Ruth Krauss, ill. by Maurice Sendak (Harper & Row)
INCH BY INCH by Leo Lionni (Obolensky)

1961
THE SNOW AND THE SUN by Antonio Frasconi (Harcourt)
SANDPIPERS by Edith Hurd, ill. by Lucienne Block (Crowell)
THE BIG BOOK OF ANIMAL STORIES ed. by Margaret Green, ill. by Janusz Grabianski (Watts)
DEAR RAT by Julia Cunningham, ill. by Walter Lorraine (Houghton Mifflin)
LISTEN—THE BIRDS by Mary Miller, ill. by Evaline Ness (Pantheon)
ONCE A MOUSE . . . ed. and ill. by Marcia Brown (Scribner)
THE HAPPY HUNTER by Roger Duvoisin (Lothrop)
UMBRELLAS, HATS, AND WHEELS by Ann Rand, ill. by Jerome Snyder (Harcourt)
MY TIME OF YEAR by Katherine Dow, ill. by Walter Erhard (Walck)
THE WING ON A FLEA by Ed Emberly (Little, Brown)

1962
GENNARINO by Nicola Simbari (Lippincott)
BOOKS! by Murray McCain, ill. by John Alcorn (Simon & Schuster)
THE SINGING HILL by Meindert DeJong, ill. by Maurice Sendak (Harper & Row)
KAY-KAY COMES HOME by Nicholas Samstag, ill. by Ben Shahn (Obolensky)
THE TALE OF THE WOOD by Henry B. Kane (Knopf)
THE ISLAND OF FISH IN THE TREES by Eva-Lis Wuorio, ill. by Edward Ardizzone (World Publishing)
THE PRINCESSES by Sally P. Johnson, ill. by Beni Montresor (Harper & Row)
LITTLE OWL by Reiner Zimnik, ill. by Hanne Axmann (Atheneum)
THE EMPEROR AND THE DRUMMER BOY by Ruth Robbins, ill. by Nicolas Sidjakov (Parnassus)
THE THREE ROBBERS by Tomi Ungerer (Atheneum)

1963
WHERE THE WILD THINGS ARE by Maurice Sendak (Harper & Row)
KAREN'S CURIOSITY by Alice and Martin Provensen (Golden Press)
GWENDOLYN AND THE WEATHERCOCK by Nancy Sherman, ill. by Edward Sorel (Golden Press)
SWIMMY by Leo Lionni (Pantheon)
THE GREAT PICTURE ROBBERY by Leon Harris, ill. by Joseph Schindelman (Atheneum)
HURLY BURLY AND THE KNIGHTS by Milton Rugoff, ill. by Emanuele Luzzata (Platt & Munk)

A HOLIDAY FOR MISTER MUSTER by Arnold Lobel (Harper & Row)
JOHN J. PLENTY AND FIDDLER DAN by John Ciardi, ill. by Madeleine Gekiere (Lippincott)
PLUNKETY PLUNK by Peter J. Lippman (Farrar, Straus)
ONCE UPON A TOTEM by C. Harris, ill. by John Frazer Mills (Atheneum)

1964
THE CHARGE OF THE LIGHT BRIGADE by Alfred Lord Tennyson, ill. by Alice and Martin Provensen (Golden Press)
RAIN MAKES APPLESAUCE by J. Scheer, ill. by Marvin Bileck (Holiday)
THE GIRAFFE OF KING CHARLES X by Miche Wynants (McGraw-Hill)
CASEY AT THE BAT by E. L. Thayer, ill. by Leonard Everett Fisher (Watts)
THE HAPPY OWLS by Celestino Piatti (Atheneum)
THE WAVE by Margaret Hodges, ill. by Blair Lent (Houghton Mifflin)
EXACTLY ALIKE by Evaline Ness (Scribner)
THE LIFE OF A QUEEN by Colette Portal (Braziller)
THE BAT POET by Randall Jarrell, ill. by Maurice Sendak (Macmillan)
I'LL SHOW YOU CATS by C. N. Bonsall, ill. by Ylla (Harper & Row)

1965
PLEASE SHARE THAT PEANUT by Sesyle Joslin, ill. by Simms Taback (Harcourt)
THE ANIMAL FAMILY by Randall Jarrell, ill. by Maurice Sendak (Pantheon)
ALBERIC THE WISE AND OTHER JOURNEYS by N. Juster, ill. by Domenico Gnoli (Pantheon)
KANGAROO & KANGAROO by K. Braun, ill. by Jim McMullan (Doubleday)
SVEN'S BRIDGE by Anita Lobel (Harper & Row)
PUNCH & JUDY by Ed Emberly (Little, Brown)
HIDE AND SEEK FOG by Alvin Tresselt, ill. by Roger Duvoisin (Lothrop)
A DOUBLE DISCOVERY by Evaline Ness (Scribner)

1966
ZLATEH THE GOAT AND OTHER STORIES by Isaac Bashevis Singer, ill. by Maurice Sendak (Harper & Row)
WONDERFUL TIME by Phyllis McGinley, ill. by John Alcorn (Lippincott)
THE MONSTER DEN by John Ciardi, ill. by Edward Gorey (Lippincott)
THE MAGIC FLUTE by Stephen Spender, ill. by Beni Montresor (Putnam)
SHAW'S FORTUNE by Edwin Tunis (World Publishing)
ANIMAL ABC by Celestino Piatti (Atheneum)

THE JAZZ MAN by Mary H. Weik, ill. by Ann Grifalconi (Atheneum)
NOTHING EVER HAPPENS ON MY BLOCK by Ellen Raskin (Atheneum)
A BOY WENT OUT TO GATHER PEARS by Felix Hoffman (Harcourt)
ANANSE THE SPIDER by Peggy Appiah, ill. by Peggy Wilson (Pantheon)

1967
FABLES OF AESOP by Sir Roger L'Estrange, ill. by Alexander Calder (Dover)
THE HONEYBEES by Franklin Russell, ill. by Colette Portal (Knopf)
FREDERICK by Leo Lionni (Pantheon)
HUBERT by Wendy Stang and Susan Richards, ill. by Robert L. Anderson (Quist)
ANIMALS OF MANY LANDS ed. and ill. by Hanns Reich (Hill & Wang)
SEASHORE STORY by Taro Yashima (Viking)
KNEE-DEEP IN THUNDER by Sheila Moon, ill. by Peter Parnall (Atheneum)
A DOG'S BOOK OF BUGS by Elizabeth Griffin, ill. by Peter Parnall (Atheneum)
BRIAN WILDSMITH'S BIRDS by Brian Wildsmith (Watts)

1968
THE SECRET JOURNEY OF HUGO THE BRAT by Francois Ruy-Vidal, ill. by Nicole Claveloux (Quist)
SPECTACLES by Ellen Raskin (Atheneum)
HARRIET AND THE PROMISED LAND by Jacob Lawrence (Windmill)
MISTER CORBETT'S GHOST by Leon Garfield, ill. by Alan E. Cober (Pantheon)
STORY NUMBER 1 by Eugene Ionesco, ill. by Etienne Delessert (Quist)
TALKING WITHOUT WORDS by Marie Hall Ets (Viking)
THE REAL TIN FLOWER by Aliki Barnstone, ill. by Paul Giovanopoulos (Macmillan)
THE VERY OBLIGING FLOWERS by Claude Roy, ill. by Alain LeFoll (Grove)
MALACHI MUDGE by Edward Cecil, ill. by Peter Parnall (McGraw-Hill)
A KISS FOR LITTLE BEAR by Else Holmelund Minarik, ill. by Maurice Sendak (Harper & Row)

1969
ARM IN ARM by Remy Charlip (Parents')
CIRCUS IN THE MIST by Bruno Munari (World Publishing)
SARA'S GRANNY AND THE GROODLE by Gill, ill. by Seymour Chast (Doubleday)
WINTER'S EVE by Natalia Belting, ill. by Allen E. Cober (Holt, Rinehart and Winston)
BANG BANG YOU'RE DEAD by Louise Fitzhugh and Sandra Scoppetone, ill. by Louise Fitzhugh (Harper & Row)

FREE AS A FROG by Elizabeth Hodges, ill. by Giovanopoulos (Addison-Wesley)
THE DONG WITH A LUMINOUS NOSE by Edward Lear, ill. by Edward Gorey (W. R. Scott)
WHAT IS IT FOR by Henry Humphrey (Simon and Schuster)
BIRDS by Juliet Kepes (Walker)
THE BIRDS OF BASEL by Marian Parry (Knopf)
THE LIGHT PRINCESS by George MacDonald, ill. by Maurice Sendak (Farrar, Straus)

1970
IN THE NIGHT KITCHEN by Maurice Sendak (Harper & Row)
HELP, HELP, THE GLOBOLINKS by Gian-Carlo Menotti, adapted by Leigh Dean, ill. by Milton Glaser (McGraw-Hill)
TIMOTHY'S HORSE by Vladimir Mayakovsky,
adapted by Guy Daniels, ill. by Flavio Constantini (Pantheon)
MATILDA WHO TOLD LIES AND WAS BURNED TO DEATH by Hillaire Belloc, ill. by Steven Kellogg (Dial)
TOPSY-TURVIES: PICTURES TO STRETCH THE IMAGINATION by Mitsumasa Anno (Walker)
FINDING A POEM by Eve Merriam, ill. by Seymour Chwast (Atheneum)
ALALA by Guy Monreal, ill. by Nicole Claveloux (Quist)
YOU ARE RIDICULOUS by André François (Pantheon)
LIFT EVERY VOICE AND SING by James Weldon Johnson and James Rosamond Johnson, ill. by Mozelle Thompson (Hawthorn)
THE GNU AND THE GURU GO BEHIND THE BEYOND by Peggy Clifford, ill. by Eric von Schmidt (Houghton Mifflin)

The Book World Children's Spring Book Festival Awards

From 1937 to 1967 these awards were sponsored by *The New York Herald Tribune*; from 1968 they have been sponsored by *Book World*, published by the *Washington Post* and the *Chicago Tribune*. "Y" designates books for Younger Children; this was changed to "P" for Picture Books in 1960. "O" designates books for Older Children and "M" those for Middle Ages. Only two awards were given for each of the first four years.

1937
Y SEVEN SIMEONS by Boris Artzybasheff (Viking)
O THE SMUGGLER'S SLOOP by Robb White (Doubleday)

1938
Y THE HOBBIT by J. R. R. Tolkien (Houghton Mifflin)
O THE IRON DUKE by John R. Tunis (Harcourt)

1939
Y THE STORY OF HORACE by Alice M. Coats (Coward-McCann)
O THE HIRED MAN'S ELEPHANT by Phil Stong (Dodd, Mead)

1940
Y THAT MARIO by Lucy Herndon Crockett (Holt, Rinehart and Winston)
O CAP'N EZRA, PRIVATEER by James D. Adams (Harcourt)

1941
Y IN MY MOTHER'S HOUSE by Ann Nolan Clark (Viking)
M PETE by Tom Robinson (Viking)
O CLARA BARTON by M. M. Pace (Scribner)

1942
Y MR. TOOTWHISTLE'S INVENTION by Peter Wells (Holt, Rinehart and Winston)
M I HAVE JUST BEGUN TO FIGHT by Cmdr. Edward Ellsberg (Dodd, Mead)
O NONE BUT THE BRAVE by Rosamund Van der Zee Marshall (Houghton Mifflin)

1943
Y FIVE GOLDEN WRENS by Hugh Troy (Oxford)
M THOSE HAPPY GOLDEN YEARS by Laura Ingalls Wilder (Harper & Row)
O PATTERNS ON THE WALL by Elizabeth Yates (Knopf)

1944
Y A RING AND A RIDDLE by M. Ilin and F. Segal (Lippincott)
M THEY PUT OUT TO SEA by Roger Duvoisin (Knopf)
O STORM CANVAS by Armstrong Sperry (Holt, Rinehart and Winston)

1945
Y LITTLE PEOPLE IN A BIG COUNTRY by Norma Cohn (Oxford)
M GULF STREAM by Ruth Brendze (Vanguard)
O SANDY by Elizabeth Janet Gray (Viking)

1946
Y FARM STORIES. Award divided between Gustaf Tenggren, illustrator, and Katherine and Buron Jackson, authors (Simon and Schuster)
M THE THIRTEENTH STONE by Jean Bothwell (Harcourt)
O THE QUEST OF THE GOLDEN CONDOR by Clayton Knight (Knopf)

1947
Y OLEY: THE SEA MONSTER by Marie Hall Ets (Viking)
M PANCAKES–PARIS by Claire H. Bishop (Viking)
O THE TWENTY-ONE BALLOONS by William Pène du Bois (Viking)

1948
Y MY FATHER'S DRAGON. Award divided between Ruth S. Gannett, author, and Ruth H. Gannett, illustrator (Random House)
M DAUGHTER OF THE MOUNTAINS by Louise Rankin (Viking)
O THE CRIMSON ANCHOR by Felix Riesenberg, Jr. (Dodd, Mead)

1949
Y BONNIE BESS: THE WEATHERVANE HORSE by Tresselt and Hafner (Lothrop)
M BUSH HOLIDAY by Stephen Fennimore (Doubleday)
O START OF THE TRAIL by Louise D. Rich (Lippincott)

1950
Y SUNSHINE: A STORY ABOUT NEW YORK by Ludwig Bemelmans (Simon & Schuster)
M WINDFALL FIDDLE by Carl Carmer (Knopf)
O AMOS FORTUNE, FREE MAN by Elizabeth Yates (Dutton)

1951
Y JEANNE-MARIE COUNTS HER SHEEP by Francoise (Scribner)
M GINGER PYE by Eleanor Estes (Harcourt)
O AMERICANS BEFORE COLUMBUS by Elizabeth C. Baity (Viking)

1952
Y LOOKING-FOR-SOMETHING by Ann Nolan Clark (Viking)
M THE TALKING CAT by Natalie S. Carlson (Harper & Row)
O BIG MUTT by John Reese (Westminster)

1953
Y PET OF THE MET by Lydia and Don Freeman (Viking)
M CAPTAIN RAMSEY'S DAUGHTER by Elizabeth F. Torjeseon (Lothrop)
O THE ARK by Margot Benary-Isbert (Harcourt)

1954
Y ALPHONSE, THAT BEARDED ONE. Award divided between Natalie S. Carlson, author, and Nicolas, illustrator (Harcourt)
M WINTER DANGER by William O. Steele (Harcourt)
O ENGINEERS' DREAMS by Willy Ley (Viking)

1955
Y FROG WENT A-COURTIN' by Feodor Rojankovsky and John Langstaff (Harcourt)
M CRYSTAL MOUNTAIN by Belle Dorman Rugh (Houghton Mifflin)
O THE BUFFALO TRACE by Virginia S. Eifert (Dodd, Mead)

1956
Y LION by William Pène du Bois (Viking)
M BEAVER WATER by Rutherford G. Montgomery (World Publishing)
O COLD HAZARD by Richard Armstrong (Houghton Mifflin)

1957
Y MADELINE AND THE BAD HAT by Ludwig Bemelmans (Viking)
M GONE-AWAY LAKE by Elizabeth Enright (Harcourt)
O BECAUSE OF MADELINE by Mary Stolz (Harper & Row)

1958
Y CRICTOR by Tomi Ungerer (Harper & Row)
M CHUCARO: WILD PONY OF THE PAMPA by Francis Kalnay (Harcourt)
O SONS OF THE STEPPE by Hans Baumann (Walck)

1959
Y SIA LIVES ON KILIMANJARO by Astrid Lindgren (Macmillan)
M THE LONG NOSED PRINCESS by Priscilla Hallowell (Viking)
O AN EDGE OF THE FOREST by Agnes Smith (Viking)

1960
P THE SECRET HIDING PLACE by Rainey Bennett (World Publishing)
M THE TROUBLE WITH JENNY'S EAR by Oliver Butterworth (Little, Brown)
O THE WALLS OF WINDY TROY by Marjorie Braymer (Harcourt)

1961
P GWENDOLYN, THE MIRACLE HEN by Edward Sorel, ill. by Nancy Sherman (Golden Press)
M ADVENTURE IN THE DESERT by Herbert Kaufmann (Obolensky)
O NORWEGIAN FOLK TALES by Peter Christen Asbjörnsen and Jorgen Moe (Viking)

1962
P ADAM'S BOOK OF ODD CREATURES by Joseph Low (Atheneum)
M THE ORPHANS OF SIMITRA by Paul Jacques Bonzon (Criterion)
O DAWN WIND by Rosemary Sutcliff (Walck)

1963
P THE SEVEN RAVENS by the Brothers Grimm, ill. by Felix Hoffman (Harcourt)
M A DOG SO SMALL by Philippa Pearce (Lippincott)
O THE COSSACKS by B. Bartos-Hoppner (Walck)

1964
P THE COCONUT THIEVES adapted by Catherine Fournier, ill. by Janina Domanska (Scribner)
M THE FAMILY CONSPIRACY by Joan Phipson (Harcourt)
O THE STORY OF DESIGN by Marion Downer (Lothrop)

1965
P SALT adapted by Harve Zemach, ill. by Margot Zemach (Follett)
M DORP DEAD by Julia Cunningham (Pantheon)
O JAZZ COUNTRY by Nat Hentoff (Harper & Row)

1966
P NOTHING EVER HAPPENS ON MY BLOCK by Ellen Raskin (Atheneum)
M BOY ALONE by Reginald Ottley (Harcourt)
O THIS IS YOUR CENTURY by Geoffrey Trease (Harcourt)

1967
P MOON MAN by Tomi Ungerer (Harper & Row)
M THE EGYPT GAME by Zilpha Keatley Snyder (Atheneum)
O THE LITTLE FISHES by Erik Christian Haugaard (Houghton Mifflin)

1968
P WHY THE SUN AND THE MOON LIVE IN THE SKY by Elphinstone Dayrell, ill. by Blair Lent (Houghton Mifflin)
M A RACE COURSE FOR ANDY by Patricia Wrightson (Harcourt)
O YOUNG MARK by E. M. Almedingen (Farrar, Straus)

1969
P THY FRIEND, OBADIAH by Brinton Turkle (Viking)
M WHOSE TOWN? by Lorenz Graham (Crowell)
O MY ENEMY, MY BROTHER by James Forman (Meredith Press)

1970
P TELL ME A MITZI by Lorre Segal, ill. by Harriet Pincus (Farrar, Straus)
M SUNDIATA: THE EPIC OF THE LION KING retold by Roland Bertol, ill. by Gregorio Prestopino (Crowell)
O FIREWEED by Jill Paton Walsh (Farrar, Straus)

1971
P ALL UPON A STONE by Jean George, ill. by Don Bolognese (Crowell)
M None; the judges were unable to decide.
O REGGIE AND NILMA by Louise Tanner (Farrar, Straus)

JOHN NEWBERY MEDAL

Like the Caldecott Award, the Newbery is donated by the Frederic G. Melcher family. It is awarded annually to "the author of the most distinguished contribution to American literature for children" of the preceding year. The winner of both the Newbery and Caldecott Awards must be a citizen or permanent resident of the United States. A twenty-three member committee of the Children's Services Division of the American Library Association selects the winner and the runners-up.

The medal is named for one of England's early printers of children's books.

1922
THE STORY OF MANKIND by Hendrik Willem van Loon (Liveright)
Runners-up
THE GREAT QUEST by Charles Hawes (Little, Brown)
CEDRIC THE FORESTER by Bernard Marshall (Appleton)
THE OLD TOBACCO SHOP by William Bowen (Macmillan)
THE GOLDEN FLEECE AND THE HEROES WHO LIVED BEFORE ACHILLES by Padraic Colum (Macmillan)
WINDY HILL by Cornelia Meigs (Macmillan)

1923
THE VOYAGES OF DOCTOR DOLITTLE by Hugh Lofting (Lippincott)
Runner-up: No record

1924
THE DARK FRIGATE by Charles Hawes (Little,
Brown)
Runner-up: No record

1925
TALES FROM SILVER LANDS by Charles Finger
(Doubleday)
Runners-up
NICHOLAS by Anne Carroll Moore (Putnam)
DREAM COACH by Anne Parrish (Macmillan)

1926
SHEN OF THE SEA by Arthur Bowie Chrisman
(Dutton)
Runner-up
VOYAGERS by Padraic Colum (Macmillan)

1927
SMOKY, THE COWHORSE by Will James
(Scribner)
Runner-up: No record

1928
GAYNECK, THE STORY OF A PIGEON
by Dhan Gopal Mukerji (Dutton)
Runners-up
THE WONDER SMITH AND HIS SON by Ella
Young (Longmans)
DOWNRIGHT DENCEY by Caroline Snedeker
(Doubleday)

1929
THE TRUMPETER OF KRAKOW by Eric P.
Kelly (Macmillan)
Runners-up
PIGTAIL OF AH LEE BEN LOO by John Bennett
(Longmans)
MILLIONS OF CATS by Wanda Gág (Coward-
McCann)
THE BOY WHO WAS by Grace Hallock (Dutton)
CLEARING WEATHER by Cornelia Meigs (Little,
Brown)
RUNAWAY PAPOOSE by Grace Moon
(Doubleday)
TOD OF THE FENS by Elinor Whitney
(Macmillan)

1930
HITTY, HER FIRST HUNDRED YEARS by
Rachel Field (Macmillan)
Runners-up
DAUGHTER OF THE SEINE by Jeannette Eaton
(Harper & Row)
PRAN OF ALBANIA by Elizabeth Miller
(Doubleday)
JUMPING-OFF PLACE by Marian Hurd McNeely
(Longmans)
TANGLE-COATED HORSE AND OTHER
TALES by Ella Young (Longmans)
VAINO by Julia Davis Adams (Dutton)

LITTLE BLACKNOSE by Hildegarde Swift
(Harcourt)

1931
THE CAT WHO WENT TO HEAVEN by
Elizabeth Coatsworth (Macmillan)
Runners-up
FLOATING ISLAND by Anne Parrish (Harper
& Row)
THE DARK STAR OF ITZA by Alida Malkus
(Harcourt)
QUEER PERSON by Ralph Hubbard (Doubleday)
MOUNTAINS ARE FREE by Julia Davis Adams
(Dutton)
SPICE AND THE DEVIL'S CAVE by Agnes
Hewes (Knopf)
MEGGY MACINTOSH by Elizabeth Janet Gray
(Doubleday)
GARRAM THE HUNTER by Herbert Best
(Doubleday)
OOD-LE-UK THE WANDERER by Alice Lide
and Margaret Johansen (Little, Brown)

1932
WATERLESS MOUNTAIN by Laura Adams
Armer (Longmans)
Runners-up
THE FAIRY CIRCUS by Dorothy Lathrop
(Macmillan)
CALICO BUSH by Rachel Field (Macmillan)
BOY OF THE SOUTH SEAS by Eunice Tietjens
(Coward-McCann)
OUT OF THE FLAME by Eloise Lownsbery
(Longmans)
JANE'S ISLAND by Marjorie Allee (Houghton
Mifflin)
TRUCE OF THE WOLF AND OTHER TALES
OF OLD ITALY by Mary Gould Davis (Harcourt)

1933
YOUNG FU OF THE UPPER YANGTZE
by Elizabeth Lewis (Holt, Rinehart and Winston)
Runners-up
SWIFT RIVERS by Cornelia Meigs (Little, Brown)
THE RAILROAD TO FREEDOM by Hildegarde
Swift (Harcourt)
CHILDREN OF THE SOIL by Nora Burglon
(Doubleday)

1934
INVINCIBLE LOUISA by Cornelia Meigs (Little,
Brown)
Runners-up
THE FORGOTTEN DAUGHTER by Caroline
Snedeker (Doubleday)
SWORDS OF STEEL by Elsie Singmaster
(Houghton Mifflin)
ABC BUNNY by Wanda Gág (Coward-McCann)
WINGED GIRL OF KNOSSOS by Erik Berry
(Appleton)

NEW LAND by Sarah Schmidt (McBride)
BIG TREE OF BUNLAHY by Padraic Colum
(Macmillan)
GLORY OF THE SEAS by Agnes Hewes (Knopf)
APPRENTICE OF FLORENCE by Anne Kyle
(Houghton)

1935
DOBRY by Monica Shannon (Viking)
Runners-up
PAGEANT OF CHINESE HISTORY by Elizabeth
Seeger (Longmans)
DAVY CROCKETT by Constance Rourke
(Harcourt)
DAY ON SKATES by Hilda Van Stockum
(Harper & Row)

1936
CADDIE WOODLAWN by Carol Brink
(Macmillan)
Runners-up
HONK, THE MOOSE by Phil Stong (Dodd, Mead)
THE GOOD MASTER by Kate Seredy (Viking)
YOUNG WALTER SCOTT by Elizabeth Janet
Gray (Viking)
ALL SAIL SET by Armstrong Sperry (Holt,
Rinehart and Winston)

1937
ROLLER SKATES by Ruth Sawyer (Viking)
Runners-up
PHEBE FAIRCHILD: HER BOOK by Lois Lenski
(Frederick A. Stokes)
WHISTLERS' VAN by Idwal Jones (Viking)
GOLDEN BASKET by Ludwig Bemelmans
(Viking)
WINTERBOUND by Margery Bianco (Viking)
AUDUBON by Constance Rourke (Harcourt)
THE CODFISH MUSKET by Agnes Hewes
(Doubleday)

1938
THE WHITE STAG by Kate Seredy (Viking)
Runners-up
PECOS BILL by James Cloyd Bowman (Little,
Brown)
BRIGHT ISLAND by Mabel Robinson (Random
House)
ON THE BANKS OF PLUM CREEK by Laura
Ingalls Wilder (Harper & Row)

1939
THIMBLE SUMMER by Elizabeth Enright
(Holt, Rinehart and Winston)
Runners-up
NINO by Valenti Angelo (Viking)
MR. POPPER'S PENGUINS by Richard and
Florence Atwater (Little, Brown)
"HELLO THE BOAT!" by Phyllis Crawford (Holt,
Rinehart and Winston)
LEADER BY DESTINY: GEORGE

WASHINGTON, MAN AND PATRIOT by
Jeanette Eaton (Harcourt)
PENN by Elizabeth Janet Gray (Viking)

1940
DANIEL BOONE by James Daugherty (Viking)
Runners-up
THE SINGING TREE by Kate Seredy (Viking)
RUNNER OF THE MOUNTAIN TOPS by
Mabel Robinson (Random House)
BY THE SHORES OF SILVER LAKE by Laura
Ingalls Wilder (Harper & Row)
BOY WITH A PACK by Stephen W. Meader
(Harcourt)

1941
CALL IT COURAGE by Armstrong Sperry
(Macmillan)
Runners-up
BLUE WILLOW by Doris Gates (Viking)
YOUNG MAC OF FORT VANCOUVER by
Mary Jane Carr (Crowell)
THE LONG WINTER by Laura Ingalls Wilder
(Harper & Row)
NANSEN by Anna Gertrude Hall (Viking)

1942
THE MATCHLOCK GUN by Walter D. Edmonds
(Dodd, Mead)
Runners-up
LITTLE TOWN ON THE PRAIRIE by Laura
Ingalls Wilder (Harper & Row)
GEORGE WASHINGTON'S WORLD by
Genevieve Foster (Scribner)
INDIAN CAPTIVE: THE STORY OF MARY
JEMISON by Lois Lenski (Lippincott)
DOWN RYTON WATER by Eva Roe Gaggin
(Viking)

1943
ADAM OF THE ROAD by Elizabeth Janet Gray
(Viking)
Runners-up
THE MIDDLE MOFFAT by Eleanor Estes
(Harcourt)
"HAVE YOU SEEN TOM THUMB?" by Mabel
Leigh Hunt (Lippincott)

1944
JOHNNY TREMAIN by Esther Forbes
(Houghton Mifflin)
Runners-up
THESE HAPPY GOLDEN YEARS by Laura
Ingalls Wilder (Harper & Row)
FOG MAGIC by Julia Sauer (Viking)
RUFUS M. by Eleanor Estes (Harcourt)
MOUNTAIN BORN by Elizabeth Yates (Coward-
McCann)

1945
RABBIT HILL by Robert Lawson (Viking)

Runners-up
THE HUNDRED DRESSES by Eleanor Estes
(Harcourt)
THE SILVER PENCIL by Alice Dalgleish
(Scribner)
ABRAHAM LINCOLN'S WORLD by Genevieve
Foster (Scribner)
LONE JOURNEY: THE LIFE OF ROGER
WILLIAMS by Jeanette Eaton (Harcourt)

1946
STRAWBERRY GIRL by Lois Lenski (Lippincott)
Runners-up
JUSTIN MORGAN HAD A HORSE by Marguerite
Henry (Rand McNally)
THE MOVED-OUTERS by Florence Crannell
Means (Houghton Mifflin)
BHIMSA, THE DANCING BEAR by Christine
Weston (Scribner)
NEW FOUND WORLD by Katherine Shippen
(Viking)

1947
MISS HICKORY by Carolyn Sherwin Bailey
(Viking)
Runners-up
WONDERFUL YEAR by Nancy Barnes (Messner)
BIG TREE by Mary and Conrad Buff (Viking)
THE HEAVENLY TENANTS by William Maxwell
(Harper & Row)
THE AVION MY UNCLE FLEW by Cyrus Fisher
(Appleton)
THE HIDDEN TREASURE OF GLASTON
by Eleanore Jewett (Viking)

1948
THE TWENTY-ONE BALLOONS by William
Pène du Bois (Viking)
Runners-up
PANCAKES–PARIS by Claire Huchet Bishop
(Viking)
LI LUN, LAD OF COURAGE by Carolyn
Treffinger (Abingdon)
THE QUAINT AND CURIOUS QUEST OF
JOHNNY LONGFOOT by Catherine Besterman
(Bobbs-Merrill)
THE COW-TAIL SWITCH, AND OTHER
WEST AFRICAN STORIES by Harold Courlander
(Holt, Rinehart and Winston)
MISTY OF CHINCOTEAGUE by Marguerite
Henry (Rand McNally)

1949
KING OF THE WIND by Marguerite Henry
(Rand McNally)
Runners-up
SEABIRD by Holling C. Holling (Houghton
Mifflin)
DAUGHTER OF THE MOUNTAIN by Louise
Rankin (Viking)

MY FATHER'S DRAGON by Ruth Gannett
(Random House)
STORY OF THE NEGRO by Arna Bontemps
(Knopf)

1950
THE DOOR IN THE WALL by Marguerite de
Angeli (Doubleday)
Runners-up
TREE OF FREEDOM by Rebecca Caudill
(Viking)
THE BLUE CAT OF CASTLE TOWN by
Catherine Coblentz (Longmans)
KILDEE HOUSE by Rutherford Montgomery
(Doubleday)
GEORGE WASHINGTON by Genevieve Foster
(Scribner)
SONG OF THE PINES by Walter and Marion
Havighurst (Holt, Rinehart and Winston)

1951
AMOS FORTUNE, FREE MAN by Elizabeth
Yates (Dutton)
Runners-up
BETTER KNOWN AS JOHNNY APPLESEED
by Mabel Leigh Hunt (Lippincott)
GANDHI, FIGHTER WITHOUT A SWORD
by Jeanette Eaton (Morrow)
ABRAHAM LINCOLN, FRIEND OF THE
PEOPLE by Clara Ingram Judson (Follett)
THE STORY OF APPLEBY CAPPLE by Anne
Parrish (Harper & Row)

1952
GINGER PYE by Eleanor Estes (Harcourt)
Runners-up
AMERICANS BEFORE COLUMBUS by Elizabeth
Baity (Viking)
MINN OF THE MISSISSIPPI by Holling C.
Holling (Houghton Mifflin)
THE DEFENDER by Nicholas Kalashnikoff
(Scribner)
THE LIGHT AT TERN ROCKS by Julia Sauer
(Viking)
THE APPLE AND THE ARROW by Mary and
Conrad Buff (Houghton Mifflin)

1953
SECRET OF THE ANDES by Ann Nolan Clark
(Viking)
Runners-up
CHARLOTTE'S WEB by E. B. White (Harper &
Row)
MOCCASIN TRAIL by Eloise McGraw
(Coward-McCann)
RED SAILS TO CAPRI by Ann Weil (Viking)
THE BEARS ON HEMLOCK MOUNTAIN by
Alice Dalgliesh (Scribner)
BIRTHDAYS OF FREEDOM, vol. 1, by
Genevieve Foster (Scribner)

1954
. . . AND NOW MIGUEL by Joseph Krumgold
(Crowell)

Runners-up
ALL ALONE by Claire Huchet Bishop (Viking)
SHADRACH by Meindert DeJong (Harper & Row)
HURRY HOME CANDY by Meindert DeJong
(Harper & Row)
THEODORE ROOSEVELT, FIGHTING
PATRIOT by Clara Ingram Judson (Follett)
MAGIC MAIZE by Mary and Conrad Buff
(Houghton Mifflin)

1955
THE WHEEL ON THE SCHOOL by Meindert
DeJong (Harper & Row)

Runners-up
THE COURAGE OF SARAH NOBLE by Alice
Dalgliesh (Scribner)
BANNER IN THE SKY by James Ullman
(Lippincott)

1956
CARRY ON, MR. BOWDITCH by Jean Lee
Latham (Houghton Mifflin)

Runners-up
THE SECRET RIVER by Marjorie Kinnan
Rawlings (Scribner)
THE GOLDEN NAME DAY by Jennie Lindquist
(Harper & Row)
MEN, MICROSCOPES, AND LIVING THINGS
by Katherine Shippen (Viking)

1957
MIRACLES ON MAPLE HILL by Virginia
Sorensen (Harcourt)

Runners-up
OLD YELLER by Fred Gipson (Harper & Row)
THE HOUSE OF SIXTY FATHERS by Meindert
DeJong (Harper & Row)
MR. JUSTICE HOLMES by Clara Ingram Judson
(Follett)
THE CORN GROWS RIPE by Dorothy Rhoads
(Viking)
BLACK FOX OF LORNE by Marguerite de Angeli
(Doubleday)

1958
RIFLES FOR WATIE by Harold Keith (Crowell)

Runners-up
THE HORSECATCHER by Mari Sandoz
(Westminster)
GONE-AWAY LAKE by Elizabeth Enright
(Harcourt)
THE GREAT WHEEL by Robert Lawson (Viking)
TOM PAINE, FREEDOM'S APOSTLE by Leo
Gurko (Crowell)

1959
THE WITCH OF BLACKBIRD POND by
Elizabeth George Speare (Houghton Mifflin)

Runners-up
THE FAMILY UNDER THE BRIDGE by Natalie
S. Carlson (Harper & Row)
ALONG CAME A DOG by Meindert DeJong
(Harper & Row)
CHUCARO: WILD PONY OF THE PAMPA
by Francis Kalnay (Harcourt)
THE PERILOUS ROAD by William O. Steele
(Harcourt)

1960
ONION JOHN by Joseph Krumgold (Crowell)

Runners-up
MY SIDE OF THE MOUNTAIN by Jean George
(Dutton)
AMERICA IS BORN by Gerald W. Johnson
(Morrow)
THE GAMMAGE CUP by Carol Kendall
(Harcourt)

1961
ISLAND OF THE BLUE DOLPHINS by Scott
O'Dell (Houghton Mifflin)

Runners-up
AMERICA MOVES FORWARD by Gerald W.
Johnson (Morrow)
OLD RAMON by Jack Schaeffer (Houghton
Mifflin)
CRICKET IN TIMES SQUARE by George Seldon
(Farrar, Straus)

1962
THE BRONZE BOW by Elizabeth George Speare
(Houghton Mifflin)

Runners-up
FRONTIER LIVING by Edwin Tunis (World
Publishing)
THE GOLDEN GOBLET by Eloise Jarvis McGraw
(Coward-McCann)
BELLING THE TIGER by Mary Stolz (Harper
& Row)

1963
A WRINKLE IN TIME by Madeleine L'Engle
(Farrar, Straus)

Runners-up
THISTLE AND THYME: TALES AND
LEGENDS FROM SCOTLAND by Sorche Nic
Leodhas (Holt, Rinehart and Winston)
MEN OF ATHENS by Olivia Coolidge (Houghton
Mifflin)

1964
IT'S LIKE THIS, CAT by Emily Neville (Harper
& Row)

Runners-up
RASCAL by Sterling North (Dutton)
THE LONER by Ester Wier (McKay)

1965
SHADOW OF A BULL by Maia Wojciechowska
(Atheneum)

Runner-up
ACROSS FIVE APRILS by Irene Hunt (Follett)

1966
I, JUAN DE PAREJA by Elizabeth Borten de Treviño (Farrar, Straus)
Runners-up
THE BLACK CAULDRON by Lloyd Alexander (Holt, Rinehart and Winston)
THE ANIMAL FAMILY by Randall Jarrell (Pantheon)
THE NOONDAY FRIENDS by Mary Stolz (Harper & Row)

1967
UP A ROAD SLOWLY by Irene Hunt (Follett)
Runners-up
THE KING'S FIFTH by Scott O'Dell (Houghton Mifflin)
ZLATEH THE GOAT by Isaac Bashevis Singer (Harper & Row)
THE JAZZ MAN by Mary Hays Weik (Atheneum)

1968
FROM THE MIXED-UP FILES OF MRS. BASIL E. FRANKWEILER by E. L. Konigsburg (Atheneum)
Runners-up
JENNIFER, HECATE, MACBETH, WILLIAM McKINLEY, AND ME, ELIZABETH by E. L. Konigsburg (Atheneum)
THE BLACK PEARL by Scott O'Dell (Houghton Mifflin)

THE FEARSOME INN by Isaac Bashevis Singer (Scribner)
THE EGYPT GAME by Zilpha Keatley Snyder (Atheneum)

1969
THE HIGH KING by Lloyd Alexander (Holt, Rinehart and Winston)
Runners-up
TO BE A SLAVE by Julius Lester (Dial)
WHEN SHLEMIEL WENT TO WARSAW & OTHER STORIES by Isaac Bashevis Singer (Farrar, Straus)

1970
SOUNDER by William Armstrong (Harper & Row)
Runners-up
OUR EDDIE by Sulamith Ish-Kishor (Pantheon)
THE MANY WAYS OF SEEING: AN INTRODUCTION TO THE PLEASURES OF ART by Janet Gaylord Moore (World Publishing)
JOURNEY OUTSIDE by Mary Q. Steele (Viking)

1971
SUMMER OF THE SWANS by Betsy Byars (Viking)
Runners-up
KNEEKNOCK RISE by Natalie Babbitt (Farrar, Straus)
ENCHANTRESS FROM THE STARS by Sylvia Louise Engdahl (Atheneum)
SING DOWN THE MOON by Scott O'Dell (Houghton Mifflin)

NATIONAL BOOK AWARDS

This award began to recognize excellence in children's literature in 1969. The National Book Committee administers the awards which are contributed by the Children's Book Council. Only books written by Americans and published in the United States are eligible for the $1,000 prize.

1969
JOURNEY FROM PEPPERMINT STREET by Meindert DeJong (Harper & Row)
Leading Contenders
THE HIGH KING by Lloyd Alexander (Holt, Rinehart and Winston)
CONSTANCE by Patricia Clapp (Lothrop)
THE ENDLESS STEPPE by Esther Hautzig (Crowell)
LANGSTON HUGHES by Milton Meltzer (Crowell)

1970
A DAY OF PLEASURE: STORIES OF A BOY GROWING UP IN WARSAW by Isaac Bashevis Singer (Farrar, Straus)
Leading Contenders
WHERE THE LILIES BLOOM by Vera and Bill Cleaver (Lippincott)
POP CORN & MA GOODNESS by Edna Mitchell Preston (Viking)
SYLVESTER AND THE MAGIC PEBBLE by William Steig (Simon and Schuster)
THE YOUNG UNITED STATES 1783 TO 1830 by Edwin Tunis (World Publishing)

SPECIAL INTEREST AWARDS

George G. Stone Center for Children's Books Recognition of Merit Awards

The Claremont (California) Reading Conference in 1965 began giving a scroll to the author or artist of a children's book that helped children become aware of the beauty of their universe.

1965
CRICKET SONGS translated by Harry Behn (Harcourt)
1966
CALENDAR MOON by Natalia Belting (Holt, Rinehart and Winston)
1967
DURANGO STREET by Frank Bonham (Dutton)
1968
WHITE BIRD by Clyde Robert Bulla (Crowell)

1969
MY SIDE OF THE MOUNTAIN by Jean George (Dutton)
1970
CHARLOTTE'S WEB by E. B. White (Harper & Row)
1971
THE PHANTOM TOLLBOOTH by Norton Juster (Random House)

Jane Addams Book Award

Each fall the Jane Addams Peace Association and the Women's International League for Peace and Freedom present a certificate to the author of the best book with artistic and literary merit that deals with the theme of brotherhood and understanding.

1953
PEOPLE ARE IMPORTANT by Eva Knox Evans (Golden Press)
1954
STICK-IN-THE-MUD by Jean Ketchum (Scott, Foresman)
1955
RAINBOW ROUND THE WORLD by Elizabeth Yates (Bobbs-Merrill)
1956
STORY OF THE NEGRO by Arna Bontemps (Knopf)
1957
BLUE MYSTERY by Margot Benary-Isbert (Harcourt)
1958
PERILOUS ROAD by William O. Steele (Harcourt)
1959
No Award
1960
CHAMPIONS OF PEACE by Edith Patterson Meyer (Little, Brown)
1961
"WHAT THEN, RAMAN?" by Shirley L. Arora (Follett)

1962
THE ROAD TO AGRA by Aimee Sommerfelt (Criterion)
1963
THE MONKEY AND THE WILD, WILD WIND by Ryerson Johnson (Abelard)
1964
PROFILES IN COURAGE by John F. Kennedy (Harper & Row)
1965
MEETING WITH A STRANGER by Duane Bradley (Lippincott)
1966
BERRIES GOODMAN by Emily Cheney Neville (Harper & Row)
1967
QUEENIE PEAVY by Robert Burch (Viking)
1968
THE LITTLE FISHES by Erik Christian Haugaard (Houghton Mifflin)
1969
THE ENDLESS STEPPE by Esther Hautzig (Crowell)

Thomas Alva Edison Foundation National Mass Media Awards

Four prizes of $250 and award scrolls were presented each year for the following categories:

For Special Excellence in Contributing to
the Character Development of Children
The Best Children's Science Book

The Best Science Book for Youth
For Special Excellence in Portraying
America's Past

In 1967 the Foundation halted its presentation of the Mass Media Awards.

*For Special Excellence in Contributing to
Character Development of Children*

1955
HIS INDIAN BROTHER by Hazel Wilson
(Abingdon)

1956
MR. JUSTICE HOLMES by Clara Ingram
Judson (Follett)

1957
ARMED WITH COURAGE by May McNeer
and Lynd Ward (Abingdon)

1958
THAT DUNBAR BOY by Jean Gould (Dodd,
Mead)

1959
WILLIE JOE AND HIS SMALL CHANGE
by Marguerite Vance (Dutton)

1960
TOUCHED WITH FIRE: ALASKA'S
GEORGE WILLIAM SELLER by Margaret
E. Bell (Morrow)

1961
THOMAS JEFFERSON: HIS MANY
TALENTS by Johanna Johnston (Dodd, Mead)

1962
SEEING FINGERS: THE STORY OF LOUIS
BRAILLE by Etta DeGering (McKay)

1963
THE PEACEABLE REVOLUTION by Betty
Schechter (Houghton Mifflin)

1964
THE WHITE BUNGALOW by Aimee
Sommerfelt (Criterion)

1965
THE SUMMER I WAS LOST by Phillip
Viereck (John Day)

1966
BOY ALONE by Reginald Ottley (Harcourt)

The Best Children's Science Book

1955
THE BOY SCIENTIST by John Lewellen
(Simon & Schuster)

1956
EXPLORING THE UNIVERSE by Roy A.
Gallant and Lowell Hess (Garden City Books)

1957
THE WONDERFUL WORLD OF ENERGY
by Lancelot Hogben (Garden City Books)

1958
SCIENCE IN YOUR OWN BACK YARD
by Elizabeth K. Cooper (Harcourt)

1959
EXPERIMENTS IN SKY WATCHING
by Franklin M. Branley (Crowell)

1960
ANIMAL CLOCKS AND COMPASSES
by Margaret Hyde (Whittlesey)

1961
EXPERIMENTS IN SOUND by Nelson C.
Beeler (Crowell)

1962
STARS, MEN AND ATOMS by Heinz Haber
(Golden Press)

1963
THE GLOBE FOR THE SPACE by S. Carl
Hirsch (Viking)

1964
THE UNIVERSE OF GALILEO AND
NEWTON by William Bixby (American Heritage)

1965
BIOGRAPHY OF AN ATOM by J. Bronowski
and Millicent E. Selsam (Harper & Row)

1966
THE LIVING COMMUNITY by S. Carl Hirsch
(Viking)

Best Science Book for Youth

1957
BUILDING BLOCKS OF THE UNIVERSE
by Isaac Asimov (Abelard)

1958
ELEMENTS OF THE UNIVERSE by Glenn
T. Seaborg and Evans G. Valens (Dutton)

1959
IGY: YEAR OF DISCOVERY by Sidney
Chapman (University of Michigan Press)

1960
SATURDAY SCIENCE by Scientists of the
Westinghouse Research Laboratories (Dutton)
1961
THE ATOMS WITHIN US by Ernest Borek
(Columbia University Press)
1962
KNOWLEDGE AND WONDER by Victor F.
Weisskopf (Doubleday)
1963
YOU AND YOUR BRAIN by Judith Groch
(Harper & Row)
1964
THE EARTH BENEATH US by Kirtley F.
Mather (Random House)
1965
EXPLORATIONS IN CHEMISTRY
by Charles A. Gray (Dutton)
1966
THE LANGUAGE OF LIFE by George and
Muriel Beadle (Doubleday)

For Special Excellence in Portraying America's Past
1955
THE BUFFALO TRACE by Virginia S. Eifert
(Dodd, Mead)
1956
THE STORY OF THE "OLD COLONY" OF
NEW PLYMOUTH by Samuel Eliot Morison
(Knopf)

1957
COLONIAL LIVING by Edwin Tunis
(World Publishing)
1958
THE AMERICANS by Harold Coy (Little, Brown)
1959
THE GREAT DISSENTERS by Fred
Reinfeld (Crowell)
1960
PETER TREEGATE'S WAR by Leonard
Wibberley (Farrar, Straus)
1961
THE FIGHT FOR UNION by Margaret L.
Coit (Houghton Mifflin)
1962
WESTWARD ADVENTURE by William O.
Steele (Harcourt)
1963
VOICES FROM AMERICA'S PAST
by Richard B. Morris and James Woodress
(Dutton)
1964
YANKEE DOODLE BOY ed. George F. Scheer
(Scott, Foresman)
1965
IN THEIR OWN WORDS: A HISTORY OF
THE AMERICAN NEGRO, 1865–1916
ed. by Milton Meltzer (Crowell)
1966
INTRODUCTION TO TOMORROW by
Robert G. Abernathy (Harcourt)

Jewish Council of America, Isaac Siegel Memorial Award

This award, a citation and $400, is given annually to the author of the best children's book about a Jewish subject or to an author for "cumulative contributions to Jewish juvenile literature."

1952
ALL-OF-A-KIND FAMILY by Sydney Taylor
(Follett)
1953
STAR LIGHT STORIES: STORIES OF KING
DAVID by Lillian S. Freehof (Bloch)
1954
THE JEWISH PEOPLE: BOOK THREE
by Deborah Pessin (United Synagogue
of America)
1955
KING SOLOMON'S NAVY by Nora Benjamin
Kubie (Harper & Row)
1956
Sadie Rose Weilerstein—"For her cumulative
contributions to Jewish juvenile literature."

1957
Elma E. Levinger—"For her cumulative
contributions to Jewish juvenile literature."
1958
JEWISH JUNIOR ENCYCLOPEDIA
by Naomi Ben-Asher and Hayim Leaf
(Shengold)
1959
BORDER HAWK by Lloyd Alexander
(Farrar, Straus)
1960
KEYS TO A MAGIC DOOR by Sylvia
Rothchild (Farrar, Straus)
1961
DISCOVERING ISRAEL by Regina Tor
(Random House)

1962
TEN AND A KID by Sadie Rose Weilerstein
(Doubleday)
1963
RETURN TO FREEDOM by Josephine Kamm
(Abelard)
1964
A BOY OF OLD PRAGUE by Sulamith
Ish-Kishor (Pantheon)
1965
WORLDS LOST AND FOUND by Dov Peretz
Elkins and Azriel Eisenberg (Abelard)
1966
THE DREYFUS AFFAIR by Betty Schechter
(Houghton Mifflin)

1967
THE STORY OF ISRAEL by Meyer Levin
(Putnam)
1968
No Award
1969
No Award
1970
MARTIN BUBER: WISDOM IN OUR TIME by
Charlie May Simon (Dutton)
THE STORY OF MASADA by Yigael Yidin, retold
by Gerald Gottlieb (Random House)

Nancy Bloch Memorial Award

Since 1955 this award has been given by New York City's Downtown Community School for the year's best book dealing with intergroup relations.

1955
SUSAN CORNISH by Rebecca Caudill
(Viking)
1956
KNOCK AT THE DOOR, EMMY by Florence
C. Means (Houghton Mifflin)
1957
THE SWIMMING POOL by Alice Cobb
(Friendship)
1958
CAPTAIN OF THE PLANTER by Dorothy
Sterling (Doubleday)
1959
MARY JANE by Dorothy Sterling
(Doubleday)
1960
No Award
1961
ANTELOPE SINGER by Ruth M. Underhill
(Coward-McCann)

1962
No Award
1963
ROOSEVELT GRADY by Louisa Shotwell
(World Publishing)
1964
No Award
1965
THE JAZZ COUNTRY by Nat Hentoff
(Harper & Row)
1966
LIONS IN THE WAY by Bella Rodman
(Follett)
1967
ZEELY by Virginia Hamilton (Macmillan)
1968
TO BE A SLAVE by Julius Lester (Dial)
1969
THE OTHER CITY by Ray Vogel (David White)

Child Study Association, Children's Book Award

Begun in 1943, this award honors books for young people which deal realistically with contemporary problems. The selection committee is appointed by the Child Study Association of America.

1943
KEYSTONE KIDS by John R. Tunis
(Harcourt)
1944
THE HOUSE by Marjorie Hill Allee
(Houghton Mifflin)

1945
THE MOVED-OUTERS by Florence Crannell
Means (Houghton Mifflin)
1946
HEART OF DANGER by Howard Pease
(Doubleday)

1947
JUDY'S JOURNEY by Lois Lenski
(Lippincott)
1948
THE BIG WAVE by Pearl Buck (John Day)
1949
PAUL TIBER by Maria Gleit (Scribner)
1950
THE UNITED NATIONS AND YOUTH
by Eleanor Roosevelt and Helen Ferris
(Doubleday)
1951
No Award
1952
TWENTY AND TEN by Claire Huchet Bishop
(Viking)
JAREB by Miriam Powell (Crowell)
1953
IN A MIRROR by Mary Stolz (Harper & Row)
1954
HIGH ROAD HOME by William Corbin
(Coward-McCann)
THE ORDEAL OF THE YOUNG HUNTER
by Jonreed Lauritzen (Little, Brown)
1955
CROW BOY by Taro Yashima (Viking)
PLAIN GIRL by Virginia Sorensen
(Harcourt)
1956
THE HOUSE OF SIXTY FATHERS
by Meindert DeJong (Harper & Row)
1957
SHADOW ACROSS THE CAMPUS by Helen
R. Sattley (Dodd, Mead)
1958
SOUTH TOWN by Lorenz Graham (Follett)
1959
JENNIFER by Zoa Sherburne (Morrow)

1960
JANINE by Robin McKown (Messner)
1961
THE ROAD TO AGRA by Aimee Sommerfelt
(Criterion)
THE GIRL FROM PUERTO RICO by Hila
Colman (Morrow)
1962
THE TROUBLE WITH TERRY by Joan
Lexau (Dial)
1963
THE ROCK AND THE WILLOW by Mildred
Lee (Lothrop)
THE PEACEABLE REVOLUTION by Betty
Schechter (Houghton Mifflin)
1964
THE HIGH PASTURES by Ruth Harnden
(Houghton Mifflin)
1965
THE EMPTY SCHOOLHOUSE by Natalie
Savage Carlson (Harper & Row)
1966
QUEENIE PEAVY by Robert Burch
(Viking)

Special Award

CURIOUS GEORGE GOES TO THE
HOSPITAL by Margaret and H. A. Rey
(Houghton Mifflin)
1967
THE CONTENDER by Robert Lipsyte
(Harper & Row)
1968
WHAT IT'S ALL ABOUT by Vadim Frolov
(Doubleday)
1969
THE EMPTY MOAT by Margaretha Shemin
(Coward-McCann)

Edgar Allan Poe Award

The Mystery Writers of America each year present an "Edgar," a ceramic bust of the award's namesake, to the author of the previous year's best children's mystery.

1960
THE MYSTERY OF THE HAUNTED POOL
by Phyllis A. Whitney (Westminster)
1961
THE PHANTOM OF WALKAWAY HILL
by Edward Fenton (Doubleday)
1962
CUTLASS ISLAND by Scott Corbett (Little,
Brown)

1963
THE MYSTERY OF THE HIDDEN HAND
by Phyllis A. Whitney (Westminster)
1964
THE MYSTERY AT CRANE'S LANDING
by Marcella Thum (Dodd, Mead)
1965
THE MYSTERY OF 22 EAST by Leon Ware
(Westminster)

1966
SINBAD AND ME by Kin Platt (Chilton)
1967
SIGNPOST TO TERROR by Gretchen
Sprague (Dodd, Mead)

1968
THE HOUSE OF DIES DREAR by Virginia
Hamilton (Macmillan)

Western Writers of America Spur Awards

Each June a plaque is awarded to the best Western written for children the previous year.

Separate awards were given to fiction and nonfiction beginning in 1966.

1953
SAGEBRUSH SORRELL by Frank C.
Robertson (Nelson)

1954
YOUNG HERO OF THE RANGE by Stephen
Payne (Lantern)

1955
No Award

1956
TRAPPING THE SILVER BEAVER
by Charles Niehuis (Dodd, Mead)

1957
WOLF BROTHER by James Kjelgaard
(Holiday)

1958
STEAMBOAT UP THE MISSOURI by Dale
White (Viking)

1959
HOLD BACK THE HUNTER by Dale White
(John Day)

1960
THEIR SHINING HOUR by Ramona Maher
(John Day)

1961
THE HORSE-TALKER by J. R. Williams
(Prentice-Hall)

1962
THE WESTERN HORSE by Natlee Kenoyer
(Meredith)

1963
BY THE GREAT HORN SPOON by Sid
Fleischman (Little, Brown)
THE STORY CATCHER by Mari Sandoz
(Westminster)

1964
RIDE A NORTHBOUND HORSE by Richard
Wormser (Morrow)

1965
THE STUBBORN ONE by Rutherford
Montgomery (Duell)

1966
Fiction
THE BURNING GLASS by Annabel and
Edgar Johnson (Harper & Row)
Nonfiction
VALLEY OF THE SMALLEST
by Aileen Fisher (Crowell)

1967
Fiction
THE DUNDERHEAD WAR by Betty
Baker (Harper & Row)
HALF BREED by Evelyn Lampman
(Doubleday)
Nonfiction
TO THE PACIFIC WITH LEWIS AND CLARK
by Ralph Andrist (Heritage)

1968
Fiction
MIDDL'UN by Elizabeth Burleson (Follett)
Nonfiction
RIFLES AND WARBONNETS by Marian T. Place
(Washburn)

1969
Fiction
THE MEEKER MASSACRE by Lewis D. Patten
and Wayne D. Overholser (Cowles)
Nonfiction
CONQUISTADORS AND PUEBLOS: THE
STORY OF THE AMERICAN SOUTHWEST
1540–1848 by Olga Hall-Quest (Dutton)

AWARDS FROM OTHER COUNTRIES

Canadian Library Awards, Book-of-the-Year-for-Children

Beginning in 1954, the Canadian Library Association each June has presented two Bronze Medals: one for the best children's book written in English and one for the best written in French. The authors must be Canadian to be eligible.

1947
STARBUCK VALLEY WINTER by Roderick Haig-Brown (Collins)

1948
KRISTLI'S TREES by Mabel Dunham (McClelland & Stewart)

1949
No Award

1950
FRANKLIN OF THE ARCTIC by Richard S. Lambert (McClelland & Stewart)

1951
No Award

1952
THE SUN HORSE by Catherine Anthony Clark (Macmillan)

1953
No Award

1954
No English Award
MGR DE LAVAL by Emile S. J. Gervais (Comité des Fondateurs de l'Eglise Canadienne)

1955
No Awards

1956
TRAIN FOR TIGER LILY by Louise Riley (Macmillan)
No French Award

1957
GLOOSKAP'S COUNTRY by Cyrus Macmillan (Oxford)
No French Award

1958
LOST IN THE BARRENS by Farley Mowat (Little, Brown)
LE CHEVALIER DU ROI by Béatrice Clément (Les Editions de l'Atelier)

1959
THE DANGEROUS COVE by John F. Hayes (Copp Clark)
UN DROLE DE PETIT CHEVAL by Hélène Flamme (Editions Léméac)

1960
THE GOLDEN PHOENIX by Marius Barbeau and Michael Hornyansky (Oxford)
L'ETE ENCHANTE by Paule Daveluy (Les Editions de l'Atelier)

1961
THE ST. LAWRENCE by William Toye (Oxford)
PLANTES VAGABONDES by Marcelle Gauvreau (Centre de Psychologie et de Pedagogie)

1962
No English Award
LES ILES DU ROI MAHA MAHA II by Claude Aubry (Editions du Pélican)

1963
THE INCREDIBLE JOURNEY by Sheila Burnford (Little, Brown)
DROLE D'AUTOMNE by Paule Daveluy (Les Editions du Pélican)

1964
THE WHALE PEOPLE by Roderick Haig-Brown (Collins)
FEERIE by Cécile Chabot (Librairie Beauchemin Ltée.)

1965
TALES OF NANABOZHO by Dorothy Reid (Oxford)
LE LOUP DE NOEL by Claude Aubry (Centre Psychologie de Montréal)

1966
TIKTA'LIKTAK by James Houston (Longmans)
LE CHENE DES TEMPTES by Andrée Maillet-Hobden (Fides)
THE DOUBLE KNIGHTS by James McNeill (Oxford)
LE WAPITI by Monique Corriveau (Jeunesse)

1967
RAVEN'S CRY by Christie Harris (McClelland & Stewart)
No French Award

1968
THE WHITE ARCHER by James Houston (Longmans)

LEGENDES INDIENNES DU CANADA
by Claude Mélançon (Editions du Jour)
1969
AND TOMORROW THE STARS: THE STORY
OF JOHN CABOT by Kay Hill (Dodd, Mead)
No French Award

1970
SALLY GO ROUND THE SUN by Edith Fowke,
ill. by Carlos Marchiori (McClelland & Stewart)
LA MERVEILLEUSE HISTORIE DE LA
NAISSANCE by Lionel Gendron, ill. by Jack
Tremblay (Les Éditions de l'Homme)

Kate Greenaway Medal

The British Library Association presents an award to the most distinguished illustrated book published in the United Kingdom. When the book has subsequently been published by an American firm, that company is indicated after the English publisher in the following list.

1955
No Award
1956
TIM ALL ALONE by Edward Ardizzone
(Oxford; Walck)
1957
MRS. EASTER AND THE STORKS by V. H.
Drummond (Faber; Barnes)
1958
No Award
1959
KASHTANKA AND A BUNDLE OF BALLADS
by William Stobbs (Oxford; Walck)
A BUNDLE OF BALLADS edited by Ruth
Manning-Sanders, ill. by William Stobbs
(Oxford; Lippincott)
1960
OLD WINKLE AND THE SEAGULLS
by Elizabeth Rose, ill. by Gerald Rose
(Faber; Barnes)
1961
MRS. COCKLE'S CAT by Philippa Pearce,
ill. by Antony Maitland (Constable; Lippincott)
1962
BRIAN WILDSMITH'S A B C by Brian
Wildsmith (Oxford; F. Watts)

1963
BORKA by John Burningham (Cape; Random
House)

1964
SHAKESPEARE'S THEATRE by C. W.
Hodges (Oxford; Coward-McCann)

1965
THREE POOR TAILORS by Victor Ambrus
(Oxford; Harcourt)

1966
MOTHER GOOSE TREASURY by Raymond
Briggs (Hamish Hamilton; Coward-McCann)

1967
CHARLIE, CHARLOTTE & THE GOLDEN
CANARY by Charles Keeping (Oxford)

1968
DICTIONARY OF CHIVALRY by Grant Uden,
ill. by Pauline Baynes (Longmans)

1969
QUANGLE-WANGLE'S HAT by Edward Lear,
ill. by Helen Oxenbury (Watts)
DRAGON OF AN ORDINARY FAMILY by
Margaret Mahy, ill. by Helen Oxenbury (Watts)

Carnegie Medal

The British Library Association presents a medal each year to the outstanding children's book written by a British subject and published in England. For two years during World War II the award was not presented.

For those books that have also been printed in America, the name of the American publisher follows that of the English in the following list.

1936
PIGEON POST by Arthur Ransome (J. Cape)

1937
THE FAMILY FROM ONE END STREET
by Eve Garnett (Muller; Vanguard)

1938
THE CIRCUS IS COMING by Noel
Streatfield (Dent)
1939
RADIUM WOMAN by Eleanor Doorly
(Heinemann)

1940
VISITORS FROM LONDON by Kitty Barne
(Dodd, Mead)
1941
WE COULDN'T LEAVE DINAH by Mary
Treadgold (J. Cape)
1942
THE LITTLE GREY MEN by B. B. (Eyre
& Spottiswoode)
1943
No Award
1944
THE WIND ON THE MOON by Eric
Linklater (Macmillan)
1945
No Award
1946
THE LITTLE WHITE HORSE by Elizabeth
Goudge (Brockhampton; Coward-McCann)
1947
COLLECTED STORIES FOR CHILDREN
by Walter de la Mare (Faber)
1948
SEA CHANGE by Richard Armstrong
(Dent)
1949
THE STORY OF YOUR HOME by Agnes
Allen (Faber; Transatlantic)
1950
THE LARK ON THE WING by Elfrida
Vipont Foulds (Oxford)
1951
THE WOOL-PACK by Cynthia Harnett
(Methuen)
1952
THE BORROWERS by Mary Norton (Dent;
Harcourt)
1953
A VALLEY GROWS UP by Edward Osmond
(Oxford)
1954
KNIGHT CRUSADER by Ronald Welch
(Oxford; Walck)

1955
THE LITTLE BOOKROOM by Eleanor
Farjeon (Oxford; Walck)
1956
THE LAST BATTLE by C. S. Lewis (Bodley
Head; Macmillan)
1957
A GRASS ROPE by William Mayne (Oxford;
Dutton)
1958
TOM'S MIDNIGHT GARDEN by Philippa
Pearce (Oxford; Lippincott)
1959
THE LANTERN BEARERS by Rosemary
Sutcliff (Oxford; Walck)
1960
THE MAKING OF MAN by I. W. Cornwall
(Phoenix House; Dutton)
1961
A STRANGER AT GREEN KNOWE by Lucy
Boston (Faber; Harcourt)
1962
THE TWELVE AND THE GENII by Pauline
Clarke (Faber; Coward-McCann, titled RETURN
OF THE TWELVES)
1963
TIME OF TRIAL by Hester Burton
(Oxford; World Publishing)
1964
NORDY BANK by Sheena Porter (Oxford)
1965
THE GRANGE AT HIGH FORCE by Philip
Turner (Oxford)
1966
No Award
1967
THE OWL SERVICE by Alan Garner
(Collins)
1968
THE MOON IN THE CLOUD by Rosemary
Harris (Faber)
1969
FLAMBARDS IN SUMMER by K. M. Peyton
(World Publishing)

AN INTERNATIONAL CHILDREN'S BOOK AWARD

Hans Christian Andersen Award

Every two years the International Board on Books for Young People give awards to an author and, since 1966, to an illustrator for their total contributions to children's literature. No national restrictions are placed on this first international award. The recipients are chosen by five judges, each from a different country, from recommendations of national boards or library associations.

1956
Eleanor Farjeon for THE LITTLE BOOKROOM
ill. by Edward Ardizzone (Oxford;
Walck): Great Britain

1958
Astrid Lindgren for RASMUS PA LUFFEN
ill. by Eric Palmquist (Rabén and Sjögren; Viking,
titled RASMUS AND THE VAGABOND):
Sweden

1960
Erich Kästner "for his complete work for
children and young people": Germany

1962
Meindert DeJong: United States

1964
René Guillot: France

1966
Author's Medal
Tove Jansson: Finland

Illustrator's Medal
Alois Carigiet: Switzerland

1968
Author's Medal
For the first time in the award's history there was a
tie vote for the Author's Medal.
James Kruss: Germany
Jose Maria Sanchez-Silva: Spain
Runners-up
Elizabeth Coatsworth: U.S.A.
Gino Rodari: Italy

Illustrator's Medal
Jiri Trnka: Czechoslovakia
Runners-up
Roger Duvoisin: U.S.A.
Ib Spang Olsen: Denmark
Brian Wildsmith: Great Britain

1970
Author's Medal
Gianni Rodari: Italy
Runners-up
E. B. White: U.S.A.
Ela Peroci: Yugoslavia

Illustrator's Medal
Maurice Sendak: U.S.A.
Runners-up
Ib Spang Olsen: Denmark
Daihachi Ota: Japan
Lidija Osterc: Yugoslavia

Index

Page numbers in italics refer to comments and discussions by the editor; other page numbers refer to selections and illustrations.